P9-AOB-217

# ENCYCLOPEDIA *of* Recreation *and* Leisure *in* AMERICA

# Editorial Board

# ENCYCLOPEDIA *of*
# Recreation *and* Leisure
## *in* AMERICA

**Gary S. Cross**

EDITOR IN CHIEF

*Volume*

1

Adapted – Little

**CHARLES SCRIBNER'S SONS**

*An imprint of Thomson Gale, a part of The Thomson Corporation*

Detroit • New York • San Francisco • San Diego • New Haven, Conn. • Waterville, Maine • London • Munich

**Encyclopedia of Recreation and Leisure in America**

Gary S. Cross, Editor in Chief

© 2004 by Charles Scribner's Sons

Charles Scribner's Sons is an imprint of The Gale Group Inc., a division of Thomson Learning, Inc.

Charles Scribner's Sons® and Thomson Learning ™ are trademarks used herein under license.

*For more information, contact*
Charles Scribner's Sons
An imprint of the Gale Group
12 Lunar Dr.
Woodbridge, CT 06525

*Permissions Department*
The Gale Group, Inc.
27500 Drake Rd.
Farmington Hills, MI  48331-3535
Permissions Hotline:
248-699-8006 or 800-877-4253, ext. 8006
Fax: 248-699-8074 or 800-762-4058

**Library of Congress Cataloging-in-Publication Data**

Encyclopedia of recreation and leisure in America / Gary S. Cross, editor in chief.
   v. cm. — (The Scribner American civilization series)
   Includes bibliographical references and index.
   ISBN 0-684-31265-4 (set hardcover : alk. paper) — ISBN 0-684-31266-2 (v. 1) — ISBN 0-684-31267-0 (v. 2)
   1. Leisure—United States—Encyclopedias. 2. Recreation—United States—Encyclopedias. I. Cross, Gary S. II. Series.
   GV53.E53 2004
   790'.0973'03—dc22

                                                              2004004617

This title is also available as an e-book.
ISBN 0-684-31450-9

Contact your Gale sales representative for ordering information

Printed in the United States of America
10 9 8 7 6 5 4 3 2

# Editorial and Production Staff

**Project Editors**
Brad Morgan
Ken Wachsberger

**Manuscript Editors**
Andrew C. Claps, Jason M. Everett, Nancy Matuszak, Noah Schusterbauer

**Additional Editing**
Lisa C. DeShantz-Cook
John Krol
Richard Rothschild, Print Matters, Inc.

**Proofreader**
Tracy Siddall

**Indexing**
Janet Perlman, Southwest Indexing

**Design**
Kate Scheible, Art Director

**Imaging**
Tory Cariappa
Dean Dauphinais
Randy Bassett
Lezlie Light

**Permissions**
Margaret A. Chamberlain

**Compositor**
GGS Information Services
York, Pennsylvania

**Manufacturing**
Wendy Blurton

**Senior Editor**
Nathalie Duval

**Publisher**
Frank Menchaca

# Contents

# Preface

Pursuit of leisure is one of the primary goals of Americans, for many the purpose of work and wealth. Yet, until recently, this longing has not won the attention of many social scientists or humanists. Among the ironies of contemporary life is the ambiguity many feel about leisure. Modern Americans congratulate themselves for creating an economy that has eliminated the drudgery of endless hours of work, are proud of the varied choices that leisure time has brought, and take delight in the economic opportunities that tourism, sports, hobbies, and other leisure activities bring. Yet leisure and recreation have long seemed to be a threat to the work ethic and unimportant compared to the serious activities of war, politics, religion, and business. However, not only has increased affluence and the liberation of time from work made leisure far more central to daily life in contemporary America, but scholars have discovered the many ways that leisure has shaped American history and culture.

It is the guiding proposition of this encyclopedia that the diverse activities of leisure and recreation in many ways define American life and identity, both in 2004 and in the past, and the understanding of these activities explains much about American culture and society. The range of free-time pursuits, in their variety and particularity, is itself fascinating, but leisure cannot be isolated from other aspects of American life and history. It is both the cause and consequence of economic, technological, and social change.

The *Encyclopedia of Recreation and Leisure in America* (*ERLA*) joins other titles in Scribner's acclaimed American Civilization series, including *Violence in America* and *Encyclopedia of American Social History*. Written to be read by a diverse audience, the encyclopedia is designed for use by high school, college, and graduate students, as well as for general and scholarly readers. Our goal is to make these topics accessible to young readers and nonspecialists, but also to provide sufficient bibliography and analysis to satisfy the needs of researchers. Although essays are generally presented from an historical perspective, the encyclopedia is multidisciplinary and contributions also offer the perspectives of scholars from the fields of American studies; cultural studies; sociology; recreation, sport, and leisure studies; as well as history and other disciplines. Detailed, factual entries cover all facets of American leisure, from the barn raising and frolics of colonial times to the computer gaming and NASCAR racing of the early twenty-first century. At the same time, the essays strive to place these recreation and leisure activities within the contexts of broader social, economic, political, and cultural change.

This encyclopedia, like all reference works, depends upon the existence of a community of scholars sufficient to produce a comprehensive treatment of the subject. Only by the early 2000s had we reached that point for this topic. Before the late 1970s, few American historians considered leisure activities an appropriate topic of study. History remained primarily the chronicle and analysis of the public acts of elites in the realms of politics, war, business, technology, and intellectual life. The scope of people's free time was "private" and not subject to serious historical inquiry. As a result, historians had neglected the story of the modern emergence of free time, the changing meaning of leisure as an activity of intrinsic value, and the ways that leisure had shaped economic, social, and political trends. Until recently, Foster Rhea Dulles's *America Learns to Play* (1940) was the only serious historical treatment of the subject of leisure.

The rise of the new social history in the 1960s and 1970s helped to change that attitude: This scholarly movement (which extended from the United States to Western Europe) insisted that the past could be fully understood only by exploring the aspirations, attitudes, and behaviors of Americans in their daily lives and by examining the diversity of those experiences across the lines of class, ethnicity, region, and race, and slightly later, gender and generation. While much of the research focused on work and dissident social movements, inevitably historians (including Roy Rosenzweig, Kathy Peiss, and Paula Fass) began to look seriously at how American social groups were defined through their leisure activities. These studies used research into leisure-time pursuits to explore questions about class, gender, and generational change in critical periods of American history. Others looked to leisure sites to understand broad changes in American culture. A good example is John Kasson's *Amusing the Million: Coney Island at the Turn of the Century* (1978), a study of the way that New Yorkers, especially immigrants, used Coney Island to break from older genteel and ethnic attitudes and behaviors. Most of these studies saw leisure as a means of furthering the understanding of other questions: the fate of the labor movement, the rise of feminism or youth consciousness, and changes in social interactions and sensibilities. In the 1980s, still others (including Benjamin Kline Hunnicutt, David Roediger, and Gary Cross) explored how and why leisure time increased and changed due to economic, social, and political pressures (especially the latter two) to reduce work time. A somewhat distinct, but still parallel, stream of scholarship was the social and cultural history of sport. Although these historians were sometimes housed in recreation and physical education departments of American colleges and universities, they shared with the broad social history movement an interest in explaining the evolution of sports from the perspective of social diversity (race, gender, ethnicity, and class). They also explored how urbanization, technology, business, and national identity shaped the development of American sports.

By the start of the twenty-first century, scholarly interest in the subject of leisure and sports no longer served primarily to explain questions raised in the fields of labor, urban, gender, and family history. Although leisure had not become a clear research subdiscipline in American history, with its own journals and professional organizations, the study of how Americans used their free time had become a major theme of historians within their specialties.

Scholars from other humanities subjects have also joined the study of leisure, especially in the exploration of audiences and readers. This interest reflects a shift from the analysis of high art and literature to the exploration of the reception of the arts (as leisure). In turn, that trend parallels the shift from the traditional history of elites to a new history of the experiences of ordinary people in their free time. This group of scholars, ably represented in this volume by academics such as Richard Butsch and Heather S. Nathans, studies the audiences of theater, music, popular reading, and other arts, asking questions such as: What brings these audiences to a particular entertainment? How do they interact with each other and with performers? Why and how do these audiences change?

Although the historical approach is a major component of this encyclopedia, much of the research into specific leisure activities—especially those that are recent or are predominate at the start of the new century—is done by scholars who primarily employ sociological and related social science methods. These researchers, often housed in departments of leisure studies or recreation, have explored the social and cultural issues of leisure in general and often have surveyed the sociological dimensions of contemporary leisure and recreational activity.

Since the emergence of the American playground and recreation movement in the first decade of the twentieth century, practitioners and their scholarly allies have explored the developmental and administrative aspects of recreational activities in schools, parks, camps, and other mostly noncommercial settings. With the development and professionalization of the hospitality and tourist industries, schools for training managers and developers of commercial leisure have emerged and, with them, research on the economics and management of hotels, restaurants, resorts, and other tourist or entertainment facilities. Aware of the need for broader, more theoretical understandings of the contemporary leisure phenomenon, these schools and departments have gradually included scholars committed to studying a wide variety of contemporary leisure activities from sociological and anthropological perspectives. They have also contributed to the theoretical study of play. All of these issues are amply represented in these volumes. Because of the significance of sport in modern leisure activities, we have also drawn on the well-developed literature of the sociology of sports participation.

The encyclopedia's editors reflect the diversity of these emerging aspects of leisure studies. Gary S. Cross, the editor in chief, is a historian, very much in the tradition of the social history of leisure. Meanwhile. the two associate editors, Garry Chick and John W. Loy, represent the social science of leisure and sport.

Working together, the board members ensured that the table of contents reflected the full range of topics that have emerged over the past generation. For a further analysis of the book's contents, turn to the Systematic Outline of Contents that appears on page 451 of Volume 2. That outline shows the conceptual framework of the *Encyclopedia of Recreation and Leisure in America* and directs readers to entries associated with broad areas of interest. Entries are grouped under seven major categories and then further separated into twenty-six subcategories.

*Gary S. Cross*
**State College, Pennsylvania, May 2004**

# ADAPTED LEISURE FORMATS

Adapted recreation and leisure refers to the provision of recreation and leisure services that have been modified or adapted in such a way as to permit the participation of people with disabilities.

## Origins

One of the oft-cited origins of organized recreation in the United States is the social concern for the plight of urban immigrants at the turn of the twentieth century. Many early community-based providers of recreation viewed the provision of wholesome recreation activities as a way to improve the welfare of the underprivileged. Although the origins of organized recreation in the United States were focused on the development of the underprivileged, it was not until much later in the century that such opportunities were afforded to individuals with disabilities.

Janet Pomeroy noted in an early work on recreation and people with disabilities, entitled *Recreation for the Physically Handicapped*, that there were a number of movements that led to the provision of recreation and leisure opportunities for this segment of the population. One of the first movements was the development of special education programs. During the 1920s, special attention was focused on the educational needs of children with severe disabilities through the development of state commissions. This emphasis was to provide day schools, as opposed to residential schools, to meet the educational needs of children with developmental disabilities. How-

ever, Pomeroy observed that while some communities did provide such services in the 1920s, for most communities special classes, or day schools, were not provided until the 1950s. Although many of these programs did not specifically provide recreation activities, they did increase the presence and visibility of children with disabilities in their communities.

Another influence was the organization of parents of children with disabilities. Pomeroy noted that such organizations were particularly common among parents of children with cerebral palsy and mental retardation. One of the first such organizations was the National Society for Crippled Children (now the Easter Seals), begun in 1919. Although the original intent of the Easter Seals was to provide medical rehabilitation services to children with disabilities, its services quickly expanded to include a variety of activities, including camping and recreation. Similarly, the Arc of the United States (ARC)—begun as the National Association for Retarded Children and then renamed the Association for Retarded Children before adapting its current name—traced its origins to parents' groups that were independently formed in the 1930s and 1940s. Although the national association did not officially form until 1951, these parents' organizations formed to assist children who were excluded from public schools. In addition, part of the impetus for the formation of such parent support organizations was the lack of community services available to their children with disabilities.

A final influence on the provision of leisure and recreation opportunities for people with disabilities was the return of veterans with disabling injuries following World

War II. Pomeroy noted that men who acquired disabilities during the war were accepted back into their communities following their return. In addition, during the war the U.S. Civil Service Commission reported that people with disabilities were an untapped resource in terms of the needed workforce for war production. Thus, even as early as the 1940s, there was official recognition of the value of people with disabilities as contributing citizens.

The experiences in the early to middle parts of the twentieth century increased the visibility of people with disabilities in their communities. Through actions by parents' groups, early educational reform, and expanding services for war veterans with disabilities, society began to recognize that people with disabilities should be considered, and included as, participants in their own communities. Much of the impetus for early services was to provide rehabilitation and educational opportunities, yet over time most voluntary organizations expanded to include the provision of recreation and leisure activities.

These developments, however, were not without problems. Peter A. Witt characterized the approach to services for people with disabilities during this period as paternalistic. This was because most of the decisions about the needs and desires of people with disabilities were made by parents, social service providers, and voluntary associations, rather than by the people with the disabilities. In addition, much of the early influence was the result of parents' organizations that were acting on behalf of their children. As services were expanded to serve the needs of adults, the same paternalistic orientation to making decisions was included. As a result of this desire to shelter people with disabilities, segregated services provided outside of society's mainstream tended to develop.

Witt stated that it was not until the 1960s and 1970s that the organizations and people with disabilities began to be concerned with the practices of segregation and exclusion in community recreation services. By the end of the 1970s, Witt estimated that that fewer than 50 percent, and generally less than 30 percent, of municipal recreation departments reported services for people with disabilities. In addition, most agencies that did offer services provided them only for children. Finally, volunteer associations began to evolve in their missions from one of protection to one of advocacy. In this new role, people with disabilities began to advocate for their rights to full access to society.

Adapted recreation programs developed in a number of areas. Programs of adapted recreation developed historically in the areas of camping, sports, and general recreation.

## Adapted Camping and Outdoor Recreation

One of the earliest areas of recreational activities adapted for people with disabilities was organized camping. Among the first providers of adapted camping was the Easter Seals. The oldest Easter Seals camp for children with disabilities was established in 1938, at Camp Wawbeek in Wisconsin Dells, Wisconsin. As of 2004, Easter Seals provided more than one hundred camping facilities across the United States for children and adults, and programs included summer camps, weekend camps, and day camps.

Other free-standing camps for people with disabilities also developed. One example of an early camping program for children with disabilities began at Indiana University's Bradford Woods in 1952. The Bradford Woods camping program served children with a variety of disabilities through a partnership with the Riley Children's Foundation. These programs continue to provide adapted camping programs for children with disabilities, including children with severe and multiple disabilities.

In addition to camping programs, a number of adapted outdoor recreation programs were developed, largely in the 1970s and 1980s. Such programs as the National Sports Center for the Disabled (1970) in Winter Park, Colorado; Wilderness Inquiry (1978) in Minneapolis, Minnesota; the National Ability Center (1985) in Park City, Utah; and Northeast Passage (1990) in Durham, New Hampshire; all focused on adapting outdoor recreation activities to facilitate the participation of people with disabilities. Adapted outdoor recreation programs provide year-round activities such as skiing, canoeing, backpacking, and rafting.

## Adapted Sports

One of the more widely recognized programs for adapted sports is the Special Olympics. The Special Olympics credits its origins to a summer day camp begun by Eunice Kennedy Shriver in Washington, D.C., in June 1963, to serve people with mental retardation. From these origins, the first International Special Olympics competition was held in Chicago, Illinois, in July 1968. Although the Special Olympics competitions had always been named the "International Special Olympics," it was not until the summer of 2003 in Dublin, Ireland, that the summer games were held outside of the United States. The Special Olympics has focused on encouraging participation in sports activities for people with mental retardation as a means for development and social integration. In contrast, some adapted sports for people with physical disabilities have evolved to focus on the competitive, as opposed to participative, aspects of adapted sport.

Sports for people with physical disabilities developed largely as a result of the influence of World War II veterans. These sports began with the organization of wheelchair sports, the first of which was wheelchair basketball. The first noted wheelchair basketball game was played in 1945, at the Corona Naval station in California. Due to the fact that there were so few wheelchair basketball teams, many of the early teams played teams of players without disabilities, who would use wheelchairs. From 1946 to 1949, a number of wheelchair basketball teams emerged. By 1949, there were enough teams in the United States for a national wheelchair basketball tournament to be held. As a result of the organization of this tournament, the National Wheelchair Basketball Association was created.

Similarly, developments in adapted sports were occurring in Europe that eventually gave rise to the Paralympics movement. In July 1948, under the guidance of Sir Ludwig Guttman, a neurosurgeon at the Stoke Mandeville Spinal Injuries Unit in Aylesbury, England, the first Stoke Mandeville Games for the Paralysed was held. It included sixteen participants. These games were held annually and gradually grew in size. By 1960, there were 600 competitors from twenty-three countries who took part in the Rome Paralympic Games. The first Paralympic Games of the twenty-first century, held in Sydney, Australia, in 2000, included 3,824 athletes from 122 countries. In addition, Winter Games competitions were begun in 1976, and have grown to include 416 athletes from thirty-six countries at the 2002 games in Salt Lake City, Utah.

## Adapted Recreation

A recognized leader in the development of adapted recreation programs was Janet Pomeroy. Pomeroy was the founder of the Recreation Center for the Handicapped (RCH) in San Francisco, which began providing programs in 1952 to six young adults with physical disabilities. RCH was able to offer year-round programs in the 1960s, at its own facilities funded through grants from both foundations and federal sources. In the early twenty-first century, RCH provided services to more than 2,000 individuals of all ages per week in programs such as aquatics, sports, theatre, gardening, and day camps.

Another somewhat unique development in adapted recreation was the formation of Special Recreation Associations (SRA) in the state of Illinois. State legislation passed in 1969 provided the authorization for the formation of "special recreation" cooperatives. These cooperatives were a partnership of local park districts and community recreation departments that were formed to provide community-based recreation programs for people with disabilities. The first SRA was the North Suburban SRA in Northbrook, Illinois, which began services in 1970. In the early 2000s, there were twenty SRAs in the state of Illinois that provided a variety of recreation activities such as camping and outdoor recreation, athletics and fitness activities including Special Olympics training, cultural travel, and arts and music programs.

## Current Perspectives

As noted by Witt, one of the challenges raised in the 1970s to adapted recreation programs was their segregated and exclusionary nature. It was during the later 1970s and 1980s that recreation for people with disabilities was influenced by ideas of mainstreaming and inclusion. Mainstreaming implied that people with disabilities were best served in the "mainstream" of society, and that segregated programs perpetuated negative stereotypes. The concept of inclusion assumes that people with and without disabilities have the most satisfactory lives when they are fully integrated into their communities. The challenges of mainstreaming and inclusion mandated that public recreation and leisure service providers in all communities acknowledge and provide in their programs for the needs of their constituents with disabilities. In addition, even voluntary associations such as the Easter Seals and ARC, which continue to provide adapted recreation, have recognized the need for providing inclusive services to aid their constituents in participating to their fullest capacity in their communities.

*See also:* Disability and Leisure Lifestyles, Leisure and Civil Society

## BIBLIOGRAPHY

Adams, Ronald C., and Jeffrey A. McCubbin. *Games, Sports and Exercises for the Physically Disabled.* 4th ed. Malvern, Pa.: Lea and Febiger, 1995.

The Arc of the United States. "A History of the National Association for Retarded Children, Inc." Available from http://www.thearc.org/.

Dattilo, John D. *Inclusive Leisure Services.* State College, Penn.: Venture Publishing, 1994.

Easter Seals. "Camp Without Barriers For Children And Adults With Disabilities." Available from http://nh.easterseals.com/.

———. "The Story of Easter Seals." Available from http://www.easterseals.com/.

Indiana University School of Health, Physical Education, and Recreation. "History of Bradford Woods." Available from http://www.bradwoods.org/history.html.

International Paralympic Committee. "Paralympic Sydney Games 2000." Available from http://www.paralympic.org/.

————. "Paralympic Winter Games." Available from http://www.paralympic.org/.

Pomeroy, Janet. *Recreation for the Physically Handicapped.* New York: Macmillan, 1964.

————. "The Handicapped Are Out of Hiding: Implications for Community Recreation." *Therapeutic Recreation Journal* 8, no. 3 (1974): 120–128.

Recreation Center for the Handicapped, Inc. "History." Available from http://www.rchinc.org/.

Smith, Ralph W., David R. Austin, and Dan W. Kennedy. *Inclusive and Special Recreation: Opportunities for Persons with Disabilities.* 4th ed. Boston: McGraw-Hill, 2001.

Special Olympics. "History." Available from http://www.specialolympics.org/.

Special Recreation Associations of Northern Illinois. "What's SRANI?" Available from http://www.fvsra.org/srani/.

Steadman, R. D., and Cynthia Peterson. *Paralympics.* Edmonton, Calif.: One Shot Holdings, 1997.

Wisconsin Easter Seals. "Easter Seals Camp Wawbeek." Available from http://www.wi-easterseals.org/Camping/.

Witt, Peter A. *Community Leisure Services and Disabled Individuals.* Washington, D.C: Hawkins and Associates, 1997.

*Bryan P. McCormick*

# ADULT EDUCATION (EARLIER)

The term "adult education" was coined in England in 1810 in reference to promotion of adult literacy. Across the Atlantic, adult education emerged in the nineteenth century as a means to enculturate recently arrived immigrants in the United States and Canada. During the early twentieth century, adult education primarily referred to vocational training for the labor force and academic programs for adults who had not completed primary or secondary school. The term lifelong learning, when used to refer to an organized program, often is used synonymously with adult education. The idea of lifelong learning as a means of ensuring personal and community development for all adults throughout adulthood emerged in the early twentieth century. Development of government policy and funding for lifelong learning programs began in the post World War II years and expanded through the 1960s and 1970s.

The Third International Conference on Adult Education held in Tokyo from 25 July to 7 August 1972 provided a new impetus for the growth of adult education and lifelong learning programs in North America and around the globe during the latter part of the twentieth century. As a result of work accomplished during the international conference, a recommendation on the development of adult education was adopted by UNESCO in 1976 that set forth the first international standards regarding adult education.

The UNESCO recommendation defined adult education as: the entire body of organized educational processes, whatever the content, level, and method, whether formal or otherwise, whether they prolong or replace initial education in schools, colleges, and universities as well as in apprenticeship, whereby persons regarded as adult by the society to which they belong develop their abilities, enrich their knowledge, improve their technical or professional qualifications or turn them in a new direction, and bring about changes in their attitudes or behavior in the twofold perspective of full personal development and participation in balanced and independent social, economic, and cultural development.

The recommendation also called for the recognition of adult education as an integral component of lifelong learning that extends through the individual's lifespan, restructuring of current educational systems to incorporate adult education, and development of opportunities for learning external to the current educational system. In contemporary America, adult education is used to refer to adult basic education, vocational-technical education, and community-based continuing education or lifelong learning programs. In this article, adult education refers to the latter.

The pairing of community recreation services and adult education began in Milwaukee, Wisconsin, in the early twentieth century. In 1911, Wisconsin became the first state to pass legislation providing for public support of adult education and community recreation programs. Dorothy Enderis, a pioneer in community recreation and adult education, used this legislation in Milwaukee to bring to fruition her vision of adult education and productive community recreation extending from the school system into the community. Milwaukee, the "City of the Lighted Schoolhouse," became a model for communities throughout the nation as an expansive adult education and community recreation program developed with the Milwaukee Public School system. During the latter half of the twentieth century, municipal parks and recreation departments around the country followed the lead of Milwaukee and developed adult education programs. In

4

the early 2000s, adult education was a mainstay of municipal recreation services.

## The Chautaugua Movement

The Chautauqua Institution, located on a 750-acre site beside Chautauqua Lake in southwestern New York, was founded in 1874 by Lewis Miller and John Heyl. Although at first organized to train Methodist Sunday School teachers, the leadership and audience quickly included many Protestant denominations and became a center for adult education in a summer vacation setting. From almost the beginning, it offered short courses in music, art, religion, and physical training. By 1880, the Chautauqua Institution also presented prominent lecturers and discussions of current affairs and international issues as well as science and literature. Music grew in importance, with a symphony orchestra program offered regularly from 1920 and opera from 1929. From the 1920s, various New York universities have conducted summer courses at the Chautauqua Institution. Although in decline since the 1930s, in the early twenty-first century about 7,500 persons participated daily during the nine-week summer school. Some 100 lecturers spoke each year at Chautauqua Institution summer gatherings and special programs continued for youth and children, combining adult education with a family vacation in a camp-like setting.

In addition, inspired by the original Chautauqua Institute, were traveling chautauquas that appeared first in Iowa in 1904 under the leadership of Keith Vawter. Growing out of the city-based lyceum movement of popular lecturers and dramatic presentations, the traveling or tent chautauqua introduced mostly small town Americans to a variety of preachers, politicians, poets, and actors who were booked in regional circuits. Local chautauqua organizers, often educators and professional people, guaranteed ticket sales and publicized the five- to seven-day event. Farmers as well as townspeople gathered, often under tents, to hear dramatic readings of Shakespeare or inspirational speakers such as the politician William Jennings Bryan or preacher Billy Sunday. Music groups, especially concert bands, also were prominent on the programs.

Although many speakers were entertaining, and crowds eagerly anticipated Chautauqua Week as a release from the boring routine of farm and small town life, organizers saw their mission as educational by providing up-to-date information about world affairs, science, and art as well as platforms for reformers—especially prohibition and woman's suffrage. Themes of patriotism and moral uplift appealed to the mostly white middle class audiences.

The traveling chautauquas declined in the 1920s with the advent of radio that offered more assessable means of obtaining entertaining education. The moralistic and self-improving ethos of the movement also appealed less to audiences. Despite efforts to make programs more entertaining (for example, with more humor and music), the Great Depression ended the movement's traveling shows.

## Modern Adult Education

In 1999, approximately 45 percent of adults 17 years of age and older participated in some type of adult education program. More than one-third of participants were involved in basic or vocational education. The remaining participants sought a multiplicity of personally motivated outcomes from their experiences, including outcomes related to leisure. Adult education is directly linked to leisure as individuals utilize education programs to learn about leisure and also enjoy educational programs as leisure experiences. Leisure interests of individuals may reflect innate characteristics, but those interests and related skills are developed through learning. For many individuals, a primary motivation for leisure is personal development—a significant outcome of learning. Individuals are driven to seek experiences that increase their understanding of themselves and the world around them, enhance personal skills, and provide novelty. Community-based adult education programs are an excellent tool for meeting these needs.

Community-based adult education programs are offered through a variety of providers, including municipal parks and recreation departments, college and university continuing education programs, vocational and technical school programs, nonprofit organizations, local governments through adult education and community centers, hospitals and health centers, cooperative extension, libraries, museums, and Internet services. Financial support generally originates from one or a combination of the following sources: subsidies from sponsoring organizations, participant fees, auxiliary enterprises and sales or other fundraising activities, private grants, corporate sponsorships, and government funds. Adult education programs also serve as a revenue stream for the day-to-day operation of community-based organizations. Adult education programs usually are offered in the evening and vary in duration from two-hour workshops to semester-long courses. The subject matter of adult education programs usually falls into one of two categories:

- Responsibilities and Tasks of Adult Life—This topical area includes an array of issues related to day to day living, including: family roles, career development, personal development, leisure, travel, hobbies, spiritual development, and living in a community.

5

• Society—The focus of programs in this category range from issues specific to the local community to matters of international concern. Politics, innovations in technology, health-care advances, and a wide range of social concerns are popular subjects in contemporary adult education programs.

The scope of community-based adult education programs has expanded since the 1960s to reflect the diverse interest and lifestyles of the population of the United States.

An area of significant growth in adult education is programming designed for older adults. Senior centers and recreation programs offer an assortment of courses and workshops. Popular topics include technology, health, genealogy, arts and crafts, personal development, literature, and current events. Elderhostel is an international travel education organization that offers a remarkably diverse program of one to two week intensive, learning experiences at locations around the world. The Elderhostel Institute Network is a voluntary association of more than 220 Institutes for Learning in Retirement. Each of the institutes is affiliated with a college or university and directed by a group of older adults. On-line learning programs are offered by AARP and other providers. The number and variety of education programs for older adults will expand with the growth of the older population over the next several decades.

*See also:* Church Socials, Leisure Education, Rational Recreation and Self-Improvement

## BIBLIOGRAPHY

Butler, George D. *Pioneers in Public Recreation.* Minneapolis, Minn.: Burgess Publishing Company, 1965.

Caffarella, Rosemary. *Planning Programs for Adult Learners: A Practical Guide for Educators, Trainers, and Staff Developers.* San Francisco: Jossey-Bass, 2002.

Camenson, Blythe. *Opportunities in Adult Education Careers.* Lincolnwood, Ill.: VGM Career Horizons, 2000.

Cookson, Peter, ed. *Program Planning for the Training and Continuing Education of Adults: North American Perspectives.* Malabar, Fla.: Krieger Publishing Company, 1998.

Edginton, Christopher, Debra Jordan, Donald DeGraaf, and Susan Edginton. *Leisure and Life Satisfaction.* Boston: McGraw Hill, 2002.

Godbey, Geoffrey. *Leisure in Your Life: An Exploration.* State College, Pa.: Venture Publishing, 2003.

Hooyman, Nancy, and H. Asuman Kiyak. *Social Gerontology: A Multidisciplinary Perspective.* Boston: Allyn and Bacon, 2002.

*Nancy Brattain Rogers*

# AEROBIC EXERCISE

Aerobics is a popular fitness activity worldwide. The name itself is a derivate of "aerobic," which means "with oxygen." However, since the early 1970s, aerobics has assumed a particular meaning as a group exercise form that is primarily developed and practiced by women. Aerobics now is an integral part of the fitness industry with its own professional body, IDEA, the Health and Fitness Association, which was founded in 1982 in the United States by Kathy and Peter Davis. When IDEA polled its business members in 2002 as part of its Fitness Programs and Equipment Survey, 72 percent of fitness facilities offered aerobics classes. In addition to being a popular exercise form, aerobics is a sport practice with national- and international-level competitions.

## Aerobics and Physical Fitness

A typical aerobics class is designed as an effective package to improve four components of health-related physical fitness: cardiovascular fitness, body composition, flexibility, and muscle strength and endurance. A sixty-minute class consists of four segments: warm-up, aerobics routine, toning, and cooldown. The warm-up, which lasts about five to ten minutes, is designed to gradually prepare the participants' cardiovascular system (the heart and lungs) for the increased workload to follow. The choreographed aerobics routine focuses on further improving cardiovascular fitness and contains a minimum of twenty minutes of continuous exercise at 40 to 80 percent of individuals' maximum heart rate. The aerobics routine should end in a cooldown that gradually lowers the heart rate and prepares the participants for the toning exercise segment. The toning exercises—such as abdominal exercises, leg lifts, and upper body exercises—are designed to improve muscle strength and endurance. Lastly, the cooldown lowers the heart rate to the level of normal activity and includes stretching exercises to improve flexibility.

## History of Aerobics

The word "aerobics" first appeared on the fitness scene in 1968 when Kenneth Cooper, a medical doctor for the U.S. Air Force, published his book *Aerobics.* Cooper was concerned about Americans' increased heart disease rates and decreased physical activity rates. In response, he developed a training system called "Aerobics" that referred to a variety of exercises—such as running or swimming—that stimulated heart and lung activity for a time period sufficiently long to produce beneficial training changes in

**Jane Fonda.** In 1981 Jane Fonda released her best-selling aerobics book *Jane Fonda's Workout Book.* In December 1983 she exercises for the press in Beverly Hills, California, to contradict rumors that she had suffered a heart attack. © *Bettmann/Corbis*

the body. Although millions took up Cooper's "aerobic challenge," this movement was mostly associated with running. In 1969, however, Jacki Sorensen took the principles of Cooper's training program, combined it with popular ballroom and folk dance movements and music, and created aerobic dancing. Simultaneously, Judy Sheppard Missett, a former dance teacher, simplified jazz dance movement into a nontechnical "Jazzercise" class. While these exercise forms gained popularity among American women in the following years, aerobics became a mass movement when actress Jane Fonda published her first exercise videotape and *Jane Fonda's Workout Book* (1981). Fonda was important to the development of aerobics in two senses: She provided a widely distributed image for the "perfect aerobics body" and, because of her image, she pioneered the celebrity "self-help" exercise books and videos that remain popular. When aerobics became a means to achieve the perfect body, it also became increasingly commercialized, specialized, institutionalized, and professionalized.

Aerobics' first specialties were high-impact and low-impact forms; the latter was introduced in the first IDEA annual conference in 1985. To reduce lower-limb injuries resulting from the high impact of jumping and hopping, low-impact aerobics has one foot always kept on the ground. The next important development in aerobics occurred in 1989 when Gin Miller, as a rehabilitation device for her own knee injury, created step aerobics. This form, which involves stepping up and down on a platform with different, choreographed patterns, became immensely popular. By 2002, step classes had passed "hi-lo" aerobics classes in popularity. In its 2002 survey, 82 percent of health clubs queried by IDEA offered step aerobics, while 74 percent offered mixed-impact classes. Because of the specialization and a continuous search for new, commercially viable exercise classes, the meaning of aerobics has become increasingly blurred.

## Future Directions

Since the late 1990s, fitness professionals prefer the term "group exercise" or "studio classes" to aerobics. Instructor-led exercise-to-music classes have diversified to include equipment-based exercise (such as circuit training and a specialized indoor cycling commonly referred to as spinning) and water fitness. While aerobics continues to be a popular women's group exercise form, it continually evolves due to the changing market. In 2002, women comprised the largest group of health club members (52 percent) in the United States, thus providing a steady market for aerobics. However, the age composition of exercisers has changed since the 1990s; in 2002, the largest group of health club members in America (37 percent) was thirty-five- to fifty-three-year-olds (12.4. million), and an additional 17 percent were over fifty-five years old. The fitness industry recognized the changing market, with 61 percent of health clubs offering programs specifically for seniors. Fitness professionals, however, need to consider how aerobics can appeal to more mature consumers. Developments that make a concession toward this older demographic are "mindful fitness forms"—such as yoga, Pilates, and tai chi—and numerous incorporated mind-body exercise forms that combine elements of mindfulness with other exercise forms. Examples of such forms include yogaerobics, yogalates, yoga sculpt, mind-body step, and any physical exercise executed with a profound, inwardly directed awareness or focus. These forms can shift the emphasis away from creating a perfect, youthful body to a more holistic sense of self, proper breathing, body alignment, and the use of intrinsic energy.

This trend might reflect the increasing popularity of "softer" mindful fitness activities over traditional group exercise forms such as aerobics. Based on its 2002 survey, IDEA predicted that group exercise forms such as core conditioning (functional muscle conditioning for the core of the body, for example, abdominals and lower back), yoga, Pilates, and water fitness would appeal to people of many ages and fitness levels and would grow at the expense of high- and low-impact aerobics. Those early aerobic forms, which for many still conjure up the image of a class filled with Lycra-clad, hollering, thin, "perfect" women, have become less appealing to the majority of health club clients.

*See also:* Commercialization of Leisure; Dance Classes

**BIBLIOGRAPHY**

Cooper, Kenneth H. *Aerobics.* New York: Simon & Schuster, 1968.

Fonda, Jane. *Jane Fonda's Workout Book.* New York: Simon & Schuster, 1981.

International Health, Racquet and Sportsclub Association. Home page at http://www.ihrsa.org.

Markula, Pirkko. "Total-Body-Tone-Up: Paradox and Women's Realities in Aerobics." Ph.D. diss., University of Illinois at Champaign-Urbana, 1993.

———. "Firm but Shapely, Fit but Sexy, Strong but Thin: The Postmodern Aerobicizing Female Bodies." *Sociology of Sport Journal* 12 (1995): 424–452.

Ryan, Patricia. "5 Trends for 2002." *IDEA Fitness Manager* (October 2002).

Sorensen, Jacki. *Aerobic Dancing.* New York: Rawson, Wade Publishers, 1979.

*Pirkko Markula*

# AFRICAN AMERICAN LEISURE LIFESTYLES

Ralph Ellison was once quoted by David W. Stone in *Lingua France* on the influence of African American cultural customs on American life by saying, "Without the presence of Negro American style our jokes, our tall tales, even our sports would be lacking in the sudden turns, the shocks, the swift changes of pace (all jazz-shaped) that serve to remind us that the world is ever unexplored, and that while a complete mastery of life is mere illusion, the real secret of the game is to make life swing" (p. 71). Indeed, Ellison pointed out what many would consider the essence of leisure life in America: joking, storytelling, participating in sports, playing jazz and other music forms, and making life swing and having fun. Ellison notes that the specific cultural way African Americans perform their leisure and life has added to the mix of what makes Americans unique in so many ways.

The leisure practices of African Americans have evolved over the years in very divergent ways from white leisure practices. The advent of the slave trade and forced migration from Africa meant that cultural ties to the homeland were very different for those with black, rather than white, ancestors. Whereas many leisure practices by whites could be easily expected to transfer via families and friends to the New World, Africans were pulled out of Africa and pushed into plantation life often with people they did not know and languages and customs they did not practice. What is more, the key component of leisure life is *time*—and slaves had little to bargain with.

William Leonard's definition of leisure in *A Sociological Perspective of Sport* is "free time from obligations, time to choose or not to choose to do certain things" (p. 400). The sociological concept of leisure, especially terms such as "work," "obligations," and "choice," seems more appropriately linked to a people who are "free," rather than the severely restricted African American lifestyle during slavery and the post–Civil War Jim Crow segregation era. It is nonetheless instructive to review what freedoms and leisure activities African American slaves engaged in given their peculiar situation.

## The Impact of Slavery on Black Leisure and Play Customs

Given the average slave's daily lifestyle of sunup to sundown work, preparing evening meals, and conducting household chores six days per week (Sunday was the "off" day), one suspects that little time was had for leisure pursuits. Combine the scarcity of time with the restrictions placed on slave mobility and there remain very limited options for leisure activity.

Adult slaves used evenings, Sundays, and the occasional holiday to explore leisure activities. Children, as David K. Wiggins notes in *Glory Bound: Black Athletes in a White America*, had the most time to pursue leisure both inside of and outside the plantation, as they were often exempt from hard field labor until the age of fourteen or fifteen. When not lugging water to friends and family in the fields or doing odd chores around the estate, slave children's leisure time was spent exploring the world around them. Activities included, as one former slave Acie Thomas notes, "Roaming over 'broad acres' of his master's plantation with other slave children . . . [we] waded in the streams, fished, chased rabbits and always knew where the choicest wild berries and nuts grew" (Wiggins, p. 5). In addition, boys and sometimes girls would contribute to family welfare by hunting and fishing with their fathers at night; this was also time exempt from field labor. Families often engaged in trapping small game or fishing in streams. One might consider this "work" of sorts as it was to provide food and sustenance, but Wiggins notes that families (most often, it would appear, the boys and men) would "realize a much needed feeling of self-worth by adding delicacies to the family table" (pp. 5–6). Further, "There were not many activities in the plantation community where slave fathers and their children could share in the excitement of common pursuits. They both enjoyed the camaraderie and spirit that characterized these occasions" (p. 6). More typical of the leisure pursuits of children in the early 2000s, slave children also engaged in games. "Skeeting" (running and sliding on ice), cards (with grains of corn), racing, horseshoes, stilt walking, pole jumping, jump rope, and marbles were prevalent games around the South. Some were traditional games learned and passed down over genera-

tions, and other games were concocted on the spot and adjusted to fit the situation, adhering to Ellison's earlier hypothesis about black style and improvisation. According to authors Lawrence Levine, Shane White and Graham White, and Lerone Bennett, Jr., black men, women, and children on plantations around the South enjoyed other common leisurely pleasures such as humor, laughter and storytelling, constructing and singing songs of all sorts, the making of colorful garments for annual festivals and enjoying the celebration surrounding weddings. Black slaves were making the best of a bad situation by making life, such as it was, liveable in what spare time was available.

## Emancipation

Resulting from the brutal Civil War that the American North and South engaged in between 1861 and 1865, black "freedmen" would be able to pursue gainful employment, their own housing, families not torn by the master's whip, and movement not restricted to the master's property. The Reconstruction Era (1865–1877) was the Union's answer to the challenge of 4 million penniless slaves, and though this period is known as a time when blacks gained many institutional advantages, it was a time also marred by governmental contradictions, restrictive black codes (a complex system of social, economic, and political controls on black behavior enacted by whites) and social confusion; the upshot, though, is that African Americans gained their freedom.

Though many ex-slaves, according to the *Ebony Pictorial History of Black America*, suffered the malaise of the time and "wandered from place to place, disillusioned, hungry, and ill. Others staked out small farms and began new lives. Still others, sensing their plight and deeply concerned, held conventions in various cities to discuss problems and map strategy" (p. 8). Leisure life, such as it was, was limited, but much less constraining than before. But the sheer joy of not *having* to work sixteen-hour days in the summer months must have begat an incredible lightness of being among the former bondsmen and women, and one must guess that despite scarce jobs and food, blacks engaged in all manner of leisurely pursuits, from hunting and fishing for sustenance to various games, dancing, and singing activities. Two institutions—education and the black church—greatly aided the black pursuit of freedom and liberty and were havens for leisurely pursuits.

## Religion, Education, and Leisure

Educational institutions were set up by the U.S. government's "Freedman's Bureau" and numbered more than

4,000 by 1870. These schools included "day schools, night schools, industrial schools, colleges—even Sunday schools. . . . Among the schools founded during the period were Howard University, Hampton Institute, Fisk University, Atlanta University" and many others, according to the *Ebony Pictorial History of Black America* (p. 17). These schools allowed for the pursuit of the leisurely activities of reading, conversing, laughter, dating, and various other small bits of taken-for-granted social interactions that combine to make life pleasant and uplifting. Thus, this baseline social leisure, while not elaborate as fox hunting or attending the opera as others did at the time, was new and different and, one has to guess, not much tarnished by the lack of gainful employment and wealth.

An aid to education—and one of the breakthroughs for black culture at the time—was that the black church came into formal existence and became the center of black life and leisure, in addition to fellowship. The church was the first black social institution controlled entirely by African Americans. Prior to emancipation, most blacks who were Christian had to sit in "crow's nests" in the back of white churches and allowed only limited leadership roles. After emancipation, black preachers were free to evangelize and form larger institutions, such as the African Methodist Episcopal Church, which grew from 20,000 scattered members in 1856 to more than 200,000 by 1876.

This increase in size meant more money for the church, which in turn led to facilities for cooking, picnics, weddings, funerals, and other cultural events that are part and parcel of collective group leisure and key to individual esteem and self-identity. The church was thus much more central to black life than other social institutions, as James Horton and Lois Horton note in *A History of the African American People*. The church provided an "anchor for black communities. One of the few institutions that African Americans could completely control, the church provided an arena for mobilization, education and collective expression" (p. 106). Some churches provided leisure outlets for congregants, such as classes in sewing and cooking, concerts, lectures, and a gymnasium. Some even provided child-care facilities, freeing up time for these leisure activities.

While other centers of leisurely conversation and gathering places were important, such as pool halls and barbershops, these were primarily the domain of men. Horton and Horton note that "The church provided women with an opening to public life, often leading them into the women's club movement and . . . the political arena . . . women were the activists, representing two-thirds of the membership of the National Baptist Convention, the largest organization of black Americans" (p. 107). Leisure, recreation, and sporting activity would grow over the next 100 years as blacks moved north and west and gained a foothold in employment, property ownership, educational institutions, and politics—all aided, in some way, by the assistance of the black church and its members.

## Northern and Western Migration

Slowly, blacks began to realize that the economic pursuits that preceded leisurely lifestyles could be had by leaving the South. Inspired by reading in periodicals such as the *Chicago Defender* that jobs and safe living awaited them across the infamous Mason-Dixon line (demarking the North from the South), many chose to migrate north from 1900 to 1920 to cities such as New York, Chicago, Philadelphia, Detroit, and Cleveland, in addition to many other smaller cities. African Americans were thus both "pushed" out of the South by racial hatred and "pulled" to the North by the promise of jobs, safety, and a much more leisurely lifestyle.

Though migration north was problematic—violence awaited blacks who were seen both as wage reducers and strikebreakers by white unions—these problems were small in comparison to the bigger problems if blacks stayed in the South. As it turns out, migration north opened up multiple social opportunities for advancement, aided by organizations such as the Urban League, the YMCA, the NAACP, and, as noted above, the black church and its many denominations. The move west to cities such as Richmond, Oakland, San Francisco, Seattle, and Los Angeles happened primarily post–World War II and added to both the fabric of these communities and the fabric of black social and economic life in shipyards across the west coast.

Gainful employment meant money for more leisurely pursuits in the evenings and weekends, and thus taverns opened up in west coast cities such as Oakland and Richmond. These places provided respite for blacks to relax, listen to black music, and fraternize with the opposite sex. Employers such as Kaiser Shipyards in Richmond sponsored baseball programs and other organized leisurely pursuits for employees, who often participated, but more often, according to Shirley Ann Moore in "Getting There, Being There: African American Migration to Richmond, California, 1910–1945," African Americans "chose their own recreational pursuits." Many of these "round-the-clock" shipyards insisted on Sunday work, which severely cut into the leisure pursuits of many black workers intent on a better life. Thus, absenteeism was high on Sundays, and many blacks, like "European immigrants of the turn of the century . . . viewed their unauthorized absences as a way of reaffirming their cultural value system which placed great emphasis on kinship, friendship, and religious ties"—all part of the greater framework of leisure and cultural belonging which was becoming vital to black life (Moore, p. 122).

World War II was also the first time that black and white truly functioned side by side in any organized fashion. This came about during service in all branches of the military, it and was a humbling experience for whites as, according to Arthur Ashe in *A Hard Road to Glory,* "It was a difficult adjustment to make since blacks dominated sports contests in all branches of the armed forces. It put to rest notions of the natural superiority of whites over blacks . . ." (p. 6). The postwar period led to a boom both in black economics and in black participation in sports and other entertainment avenues. William Leonard notes, in *A Sociological Perspective of Sport,* that more and more people pursue leisurely activities such as sport and entertainment—products of popular culture—due to the increasing rise in discretionary time over the past 150 years. This trend certainly is true for black culture, and sport and entertainment are also significant as they are channels of opportunity in which African Americans have been allowed to advance socially and economically.

## City Life's Impact on Black Leisure and Play Customs

City life in the twentieth century had many advantages and disadvantages for the black population of the United States. The advantages of having a critical mass meant small businesses, churches, and social life thrived for a time in large communities such as Harlem, Chicago, and Oakland. Recreation facilities were swamped with black kids seeking shelter from the heat and often tough conditions. As Arthur Ashe notes in *A Hard Road to Glory,* "Factories, churches, Urban League Chapters, Travelers Aid societies, fraternal organizations, YMCA's, and YWCA's struggle to make life more pleasant for new arrivals" (p. 4). These new arrivals sought shelter in these community organizations and sought leisure activities.

More and more, though, as Ashe noticed, the recreational and leisure activities of black urban youth more and more were geared toward the "big five: baseball, basketball, football, boxing and track" (p. 5). These were sports stressed in the public school system and were thus free of charge to poor youth. These sports formed the nu-

cleus of future black sports participation and of leisurely viewing by black fans of sport.

Indeed, the movie *Hoop Dreams* plays on the very notion that sports was a way for black youth to escape harsh postindustrial conditions in urban America. The documentary film, released in 1994, was premised, notes Liam Kennedy in *Race and Urban Space in Contemporary American Culture,* "on the dream of upward mobility, the movement from margin to mainstream . . . which traditionally features narratives of impoverished athletes triumphing over great odds in pursuit of the American Dream" (pp. 100–101). This pursuit of the American dream—and sport as a vehicle—has been fed by the commercialization of American culture in general, and the targeted urban black young male consumer culture, specifically. But leisure/recreation activity as career option is predominantly the domain of black youth.

African American adults in cities have engaged over the years in a variety of leisurely pursuits, from fishing and gardening to singing and dancing; summer barbeques and picnics; games such as chess, cards, and dominoes; attendance at theaters, concerts, and sports events; membership in civic and fraternal organizations, and meeting at social centers such as bars, pool halls, and barbershops for neighbourly or political conversations. In these activities, black Americans have converged with the larger society, while retaining, as Ellison noted earlier, a specific, deliberate "style" that moves toward improvisation, spontaneity, and individuality. Many black family and civic celebrations happen in and around local urban parks. And though blacks use local parks much more than they use National Parks, urban facilities are often fraught with problems, as Dorceta E. Taylor notes in *Identity in Ethnic Leisure Pursuits.* Those problems extend beyond unwatered grass or poor baseball diamonds into such security hazards as gang hangouts, local dens of drug abuse, homelessness, and parks as places of violence.

## African American Diversity and Other Recent Trends

With the advent of other avenues of mobility in post–civil rights America, African Americans began to expand both their leisure options and career options. The diversification of African American culture—as a result of the end of Jim Crow segregation, the civil rights movement, voting rights, expanded education options, affirmative action, and other legislation—led to more blacks entering the working- and middle-class ranks. With more money and more time come more African American options for leisure, including a wider variety of entertainment, recreation, leisurely travel and vacations, and expensive hobbies such as skiing and golf. Both of these latter activities—which cross the boundaries of sport and leisure—have large numbers of African American participants, and many are members of either local or national clubs and organizations.

With the diversification of school systems and increased black entry into university ranks, youth are finding that leisure need not be tied to sport/career options. Hiking, camping, and urban gardening can go side by side with break-dancing, surfing the Internet, and riding dirt bikes as options for urban/suburban and rural leisure. The elderly are finding "mall walking" and travel to be enjoyable forms of leisure later in life, and families are finding leisurely enjoyment in packing up the minivan with local soccer or softball players after the game and heading to the local pizza parlor. Leisure pursuits of African Americans are as diverse in the new century as employment options, locales for living, university affiliations, fraternal and sorority allegiances, parochial sports team fanaticism, and degrees of religiosity. If nothing else, one can be assured that those leisure choices will grow as black style and creativity produce black success in American social institutions in the future.

*See also:* Expansion of Leisure, Rap Music Audiences, Slave Singing/Music Making, Southern America Leisure Lifestyles

**BIBLIOGRAPHY**

Abercrombie, Nicholas, Stephen Hill, and Bryan S. Turner. *The Penguin Dictionary of Sociology.* Middlesex, U.K.: Penguin Books, 1994.

Andrews, Vernon L. "Black Bodies—White Control: Race, Celebratory Expression and the Contested Terrain of Sportsmanlike Conduct. *Journal of African American Men* 2, no. 1 (1996): 33–59.

Ashe, Arthur R., Jr. *A Hard Road to Glory: A History of the African American Athlete, 1919–1945.* Volume 2. New York: Warner Books, 1988.

*Ebony,* Editors of. *Ebony Pictorial History of Black America.* Volume 2. Nashville, Tenn.: Southwestern Company, 1971.

Horton, James, and Lois Horton. *A History of the African American People.* London: Salamander Books Limited, 1995.

Kennedy, Liam. *Race and Urban Space in Contemporary American Culture.* Edinburgh: Edinburgh University Press, 2000.

Leonard, William M., Jr. *A Sociological Perspective of Sport.* Needham Heights, Mass.: Allyn and Bacon, 1998.

Levin, Lawrence W. *Black Culture and Black Consciousness: Afro-American Folk Thought from Slavery to Freedom.* Oxford: Oxford University Press, 1977.

Moore, Shirley A. "Getting There, Being There: African American Migration to Richmond, California, 1910–1945." In *The Great Migration in Historical Perspective.* Edited by Joe W. Trotter, Jr. Bloomington: Indiana University Press, 1991.

Morris, William, ed. *American Heritage Dictionary of the English Language.* Boston: Houghton Mifflin Company, 1981.

Stone, David W. "Uncolored People." *Lingua Franca* 6 (September–October 1996): 71.

Taylor, Dorceta E. *Identity in Ethnic Leisure Pursuits.* San Francisco: Mellen Research University Press, 1992.

White, Shane, and Graham White. *Stylin': African American Expressive Culture from its Beginnings to the Zoot Suit.* Ithaca, N.Y.: Cornell University Press, 1998.

Wiggins, David K. *Glory Bound: Black Athletes in a White America.* Syracuse, N.Y.: Syracuse University Press, 1997.

*Vernon Lee Andrews*

# AGRICULTURAL FAIRS

To effectively understand contemporary American agricultural fairs, one must examine the historical context from which these fairs originated. Following the American Revolution, the relative alienation from Europe forced American farmers to develop independently their own technologies and methods for agricultural production. Efforts to improve agricultural efficiency also fostered the development of agricultural societies and associations whose mission served to disseminate and display agricultural technologies and practices. In particular, these associations afforded farmers who operated small holdings opportunities to exhibit and view displays of livestock and produce in which theory had been transformed into practice. Farmers could win premiums in competitions in the areas that interested them. Organizers gave prizes for sheep shearing and plowing trials. Sheepshearing contests were especially important because of nationalistic and commercial implications. The raising of fine wool for cloth implied domestic self-sufficiency and the beginnings of a competitive trade base for agriculturalists. While all of these early efforts petered out, they functioned as forerunners to the present-day county fairs.

Agricultural societies eventually began to spread from New England to the South and Midwest by the 1820s. Even though the agricultural societies attempted to serve the interests of all social levels for their constituents, it was still a small group of gentlemen farmers who organized and benefited most from the events. Few travelers' accounts or journals of this period name agricultural shows as rural amusement or as significant agricultural endeavors. Many farmers with small holdings still lacked markets and were concerned with breaking ground and surviving the next several seasons rather than with improving production and the quality of goods. Consequently, agricultural organization declined to some extent between 1825 and 1840 as European settlement expanded. Public money that had been allotted to aid the formation of the agricultural societies was often withdrawn for lack of interest.

The scarcity of labor following the Civil War and the expanding industrial sector of the economy conferred more importance on agricultural fairs than they had enjoyed in the 1840s. Leslie Prosterman noted that at the fairs, farmers could find labor-saving devices and means by which they could improve the quality and yield of their products to feed the increasing numbers of factory workers and city dwellers. With the development of a larger population and a more complex agricultural-industrial economy, the need also grew for institutionalized social organization. W. J. Gates argued that the agricultural fairs of the turn of the century, "which reached a dispersed rural population whose isolation was ordinarily difficult to penetrate, provided a unique opportunity to apprise the farmers and their wives of current social concerns and efforts to accomplish change. . . . Socialization in consequence of a shared experience, annually renewed, offset rural isolation and contributed to a sense of community," (p. 277). The agricultural fairs supplied information and examples illustrating new agricultural practices while they presented an arena for social gatherings and interaction. Thus, the establishment of social and economic codes of judgment and behavior was assured to those who lived on isolated farms.

## The Development of the Modern Fair

The type of farming practiced during different periods also affected the look of the county fair. Through the late nineteenth century and until the latter half of the 1930s, farming from the Mid-Atlantic region to the Midwest was very diversified. From the 1940s on, farms in those regions became much more specialized. This change in farming was also reflected in changes to county fairs. From the 1940s to the 1970s, county fairs suffered a decline in participation. Fair organizers cited the rise in specialization, laziness, lack of community spirit, television, and the automobile's dominance in society as the main reasons. Prosterman suggested that this specialization diminished the number of potential exhibits because the soybean farmer bought milk and vegetables and meat at the grocery store; tilled and harvested with machines, not horses and oxen; and bought household items at the shopping center. She also felt that laziness and lack of community spirit were often attributed to the popularity of television and the resultant ability to be entertained in one's own armchair at home. She suggested, however, that the automobile has had the opposite effect, conveying people farther away to urban centers, where they saw more crowds, ingested a greater volume of information, and viewed more sophisticated entertainment than the county fairs could present.

During that same three-decade time period (1940s to 1970s), a final factor affecting county fairs was the shrinking population of rural America, as changes in agribusiness allowed for fewer farmers running larger farms. This meant that fewer rural participants were available to work in fairs.

Since the 1970s, fairs have experienced a renaissance and become a major social and economic event for rural communities of all sizes, typically lasting between seven to ten days. With the growing use of the fair as a local central gathering place, entertainment played a larger role in the fair's avowed purpose, acting as a draw and a moneymaker. In response, exhibits grew more numerous, and so did casual visitors. Fair managers formed cooperative associations with other fairs to establish policies concerning carnivals, date setting, sharing certain traveling exhibits, common problems, and standardized rules of conduct.

It used be that agriculturalists would come to the fair and make a whole day of it. At modern fairs, they came for shorter periods to fulfill many specific objectives, leaving once those objectives were fulfilled. Fairs also became increasingly oriented toward youth. Urban groups became more involved in fairs after the 1960s, mirroring the shift from agriculture to entertainment. Prosterman noted that periods of recession also appeared to help fairs—there was less money available to spend on expensive vacations, making a day at the fair seem more attractive, while neighbors seemed to care more about cementing community relations. W. J. Gates suggested the back-to-the-land movement and nostalgia, allied with economic constraints, led people to grow more vegetables, can more produce, make their own clothes, raise their prized animals, and present the results of their efforts at the fair.

The social-world configuration of contemporary fairs also helps to define the nature of leisure experiences enjoyed by the populations associated with the fair. For the most part, the various regions of the fair also spatially define these social worlds, which can be broken down into

**Future Farmers of America.** As part of their learning experience with the Future Farmers of America (FFA), these students from the local chapter do field work by evaluating sheep during the Umatilla County Fair in Hermiston, Oregon, on 5 August 2003. The FFA brings students, teachers, and agribusiness together for agricultural education and is active at county and state fairs. © *Don Ryan for AP/Wide World Photos*

three distinct populations: agriculturists, casual visitors, and carnival and fair employees. Agricultural arenas and livestock halls typically lie on the fairground perimeter. As one ventures toward the center of the fairground, exhibit halls for both agriculture and other private industry become more populous. Finally, from the center of the fairground and often extending toward the outer perimeter opposite the agricultural arenas, a multitude of vendors, amusements, and carnival rides occupy the remaining areas of the fairground.

## Fair Attendance: Who and Why

The occupants of these spatial contexts that define the social worlds consist primarily of three broadly defined groups. First and perhaps foremost, agriculture remains the focus of most fairs. As in years past, many attend the fair to view the latest trends in farming equipment, exhibit livestock and produce, and socialize with others whose living is or was intimately connected with the land. These people also often hold some administrative position within the fair association and volunteer their time to help stage the event. While agriculturalists will inevitably take in the variety of amusements, rides, games of chance, and

food vendors, their primary motivation for attending lies in the camaraderie associated with their vocation and the desire to explore more efficient methods of agriculture. These preferences and behaviors are passed from generation to generation with the assistance of organizations such as 4-H. Many exhibitors have also become very specialized in their interests, and their passion for their exhibits could be considered a form of serious leisure; they have spent their lives refining their skills to produce the exhibit, be it craft, livestock, or produce.

Alternately, casual visitors are drawn to fairs for more hedonic reasons. These visitors typically have no commercial association with the fair. While agriculturalists are inclined to pass by "side shows" that have begun to encroach upon their agricultural interests, casual visitors are drawn to such shows; in fact, the shows often constitute the fair's major attraction to that group. In addition to the social interaction with other family and friends attending with them, casual visitors gain a full day of entertainment from the thrills of amusements, rides, and vendors offering sweet and rich treats.

The last social world is composed of the carnival operators and vendors (often referred to as "carnies"), whose attendance is driven by the prospect of economic gain. Members of this social world travel the nation from fair to fair, providing the amusements that sustain casual visitors.

*See also:* Carnivals, Hobbies and Crafts

**BIBLIOGRAPHY**

Adams, J. H. "The Decoupling of Farm and Household: Differential Consequences of Capitalist Development on Southern Illinois and Third World Family Farms." *Society for the Comparative Study of Society and History* 30 (1988): 453–482.

Farnham, Eliza W. *Life in Prairie Land.* New York: Harper and Brothers, 1946.

Gates, W. J. "Modernization as a Function of an Agricultural Fair: The Great Granger's Picnic Exhibition at Williams Grove, Pennsylvania, 1873–1916." *Agricultural History* 58 (1984): 277.

Kyle, G. T. "An Examination of Enduring Leisure Involvement." Ph.D. dissertation, Pennsylvania State University, 2001.

Prosterman, Leslie. *Ordinary Life, Festival Days: Aesthetics in the Midwestern County Fair.* Washington, D.C.: Smithsonian Institution Press, 1995.

Stebbins, Robert A. *The Organizational Basis of Leisure Participation: A Motivational Exploration.* State College, Pa.: Venture Publishing, 2002.

Tocqueville, Alexis de. *Democracy in America.* New York: Harper and Row, 1966.

*Gerard Kyle*

# AIR TRAVEL AND LEISURE

Twenty-first-century Americans, long blasé about constant technological innovations, accept flying as a necessary fact of life, despite the persisting small percentage who still refuse to board a plane. A century ago there was no airline industry, even though the military made use of aircraft in its operations by 1910. Beginning with the 1920s, with the ranks of trained pilots swelled by aviator veterans of World War I, flying was increasingly used to deliver the U.S. mail, to manage crops, and to provide thrill seekers with excitement at state fairs. When a particularly plucky midwestern postal pilot named Charles Lindbergh flew his *Spirit of St. Louis* across the Atlantic Ocean in 1927, a veritable craze began for organized passenger flights.

## The Demand for Flying Increases

From these small beginnings, plane repair, airport, and cargo facilities were constructed as the necessary infrastructure for the global corporate industry that existed at the beginning of the twenty-first century. Yet, it was not until the 1960s that a mass market for passenger travel emerged. Among the confluence of factors at the critical juncture that created the ubiquitous and heavily used industry were the introduction in 1963 of the Boeing 727 jet passenger plane—the veritable workhorse of the industry that remains in service on some flights even today; the accelerating growth of personal income and general prosperity after the 1950s recession that created a mass consumer and leisure industry market; advances in computers, such as the IBM 360, that revolutionized booking, scheduling, and accounting; and the rise of a mass tourist industry aimed at specialized domestic destinations, such as Las Vegas and Miami, along with foreign locations in the Caribbean and Europe.

By the year 2000, a mature air travel industry consisting of numerous carriers and almost infinite destinations carried over 700,000 passenger trips domestically. To be sure, frequent business travel comprises a significant percentage of total journeys. However, the bulk of passenger flights take place because of the increasing use of flying for vacations, family purposes, and short-duration leisure activities such as ski, gambling, and golf excursions to specialized destinations.

From that peak, the events of 11 September 2001 made cutbacks in travel inevitable. Passenger trips, after dropping off drastically immediately after the terror attacks, rose again, but in 2003 they were still at only about 80 percent of their peak levels. Hardest hit was the international tourist industry. Recreation, tourism, and leisure activities that once involved flights to foreign destinations began to exploit opportunities close to home. In the summer of 2003, for example, tourist visits to Alaska and Hawaii were more popular than trips outside U.S. boundaries.

The mass market for leisure and recreation depends greatly on the ability of consumers to access particular locations by air. Gamblers cycle in and out of McCarren International Airport in Las Vegas, for example, at a level of more than 20 million arrivals a year, and spend an average of three to four days in town. Ski resorts in Utah, New Mexico, and Colorado cater to short-term visitors who jet in and out when both snow and flying conditions are attractive. Even avid golfers and fishermen or hunters take advantage of low fares to squeeze in a few days of recreation in places such as the Southwest or Alaska, locations known for their attractiveness. Added to these specialized recreational activities are the many packaged junkets put together by the airline and tourist industries to attract short-term vacationers with a week or less of leisure time for fully organized getaways at resorts. In short, highly efficient jet travel on planes that carry large numbers of passengers to various specialized destinations has helped to create a mass consumer industry of recreation and leisure that combines vacations with sport activities for all seasons. Even after the effects of 11 September, the basic pattern of frequent air travel trips to pursue tourism, recreation, and leisure activities remains in place.

## Changes in the Air Travel Industry

Until the 1960s, travel by air was occasional for most Americans. Flights in propeller-driven planes were long, dull, and uncomfortable. The planes were especially prone to the effects of bad weather. A stormy trip experience could make even the most willing air passenger leery of flying again. The introduction of jetliners in the 1960s changed commercial aviation into a mass industry. Effects were not limited to the success of the Boeing 727. During the 1970s, a further technological and engineering innovation occurred. Huge-capacity, wide-bodied passenger jets were introduced, including the Boeing 747, the Lockheed L-1011, and the McDonnell Douglas DC-10. These planes could carry many more passengers per trip in even greater comfort, and they made travel by air cheaper and more convenient. Wide-bodied jets also transformed airports, enabling them to add to the flying experience. They required greater parking space at the gates of terminals and more taxiing space out on the runways. To accommodate the wide-bodies, terminals were stretched and reshaped through renovation and the building of new facilities. Terminals now had room between the expansive corridors of gates for shops and restaurants. Airports became malls, destination places for dining and shopping.

The change in airport design created a new experience for international travelers. Duty-free shopping at the terminals became almost as important as the trips to foreign destinations themselves. Airports such as Frankfurt International in Germany and Schiphol International outside of Amsterdam, Holland, turned into consumer destinations in their own right. Schiphol, for example, has over forty different outlet stores, hundreds of shops, a movie theater, and even a gambling casino. Although the European Union consolidation and the introduction of free trade zones within Europe eliminated the appeal of duty-free shopping for domestic residents, the activity has remained a strong draw for citizens of the United States,

Japan, and other countries with consumers known for their frequent trips abroad.

An infrastructure for mass and frequent flying that existed in the early 2000s also provided people with another change in the way they experienced travel from the period before 1970. People who flew considerable distances encountered the phenomenon of "space-time compression." To cite one example, a person enmeshed in the mundane tasks of everyday life in New York City could, at noontime, leave work with a set of golf clubs, take a taxi to the airport, and fly down to a resort in Florida in time to complete nine holes of golf that same day. With an earlier start, this same person could play nine holes in southern California instead. As these examples show, leisure and tourist destinations became simply an extension of people's lived space. They joined the locations of work and home in the experiential world as places where people could visit almost as easily as the more mundane sites of their daily lives. Obsessive theatergoers, for example, often take advantage of quick trips to London in order to see a play or two without any other goal in mind. In the most extreme case of space-time compression, individuals may fly from one city, where they maintain a home, to another, where they work during the same day. A small percentage of professionals are "bicoastal," that is, they maintain homes in cities on both coasts, usually Manhattan and Los Angeles.

The mass industry of air travel also has its downside, as all flyers can attest. Flight delays, overcrowding, overbooking, and cancellations are but some of the incidents that traumatize passengers. Perhaps the worst experience for people seeking leisure activities involves the cancellation of flights en route, thereby causing the disruption of vacation plans. Consumers on ski, gambling, fishing, or golf excursions who become stranded in out-of-town airports may discover that all their leisure time will be lost in transit. Often it is the unpredictability with which airlines switch and/or cancel flights that is the most disturbing aspect of this ordeal.

Other difficulties emerged following the events of 11 September 2001. Increased security at airports meant considerably longer check-in times and increased scrutiny of baggage, a change especially aggravating for golfers and skiers carrying their equipment. Once a relatively quick although stressful activity, by late 2001, checking in required a major allocation of time that invariably cut into the period devoted to vacation and leisure travel. Despite these and other negatives, however, tourism, recreation, and leisure activities require frequent air service, and flying remains the best way to schedule vacation breaks from the entanglements of everyday life.

By the end of the twentieth century, the domestic air travel industry handled 27 million takeoffs. That figure was expected to increase by almost one-third in the first decade of the twenty-first century. Although dampened by the acts of terrorism, passenger trips may reach the 1 billion mark by the year 2012. Mass travel of this magnitude will severely strain the already stressed infrastructure of the industry. When trips reached their peak in the year 2000, Congress was mobilized to address the crush of consumer complaints against the system. As peak flying declined due to terrorism, some of the measures that were contemplated were pushed to the back burner of legislative action. Yet, the system was still grossly overtaxed; when mass flying expands, which it is sure to do in the future, the same problems of overcrowding, cancellations, and general system failures will exist.

## Passenger Rights Gain in Popularity

In 1999, Senators Ron Wyden (D-Oregon) and John McCain (R-Arizona) introduced legislation aimed at codifying the rights of commercial passengers on domestic trips. Later that year, Congressman Bud Shuster (R-Pennsylvania), the powerful chairman of the House Transportation Committee, drafted passenger rights legislation of his own. By the summer of 2003, neither of these bills had moved through the Congress. Should predictions of further increases in the frequency and volume of air passenger trips turn out to be true, air travelers will no doubt renew their pressure on government officials to revisit this legislation. At the same time, commercial airlines have released voluntary reforms of their own to address some of the more serious passenger concerns. Congressman Shuster's bill called for compensation to passengers whenever airline companies held people in planes for more than two hours. Absent approved legislation of this kind, airlines have no obligations to passengers who are delayed in this fashion, but they have announced policies that express concern for travelers trapped in these circumstances, and they have publicly stated that every effort will be made to make passengers comfortable in the future. Compensation for such inconveniences seems unlikely. Airlines have begun to follow policies aimed at being more honest with passengers, at providing them with more information whenever problems arise, and at assisting passengers who are caught in a system breakdown affecting one airline with suitable and timely accommodations on other airlines that are still operating. Because our domestic air travel infrastructure has not been stressed in the way it was before 11 September, it is difficult to assess how voluntary policies enacted by carriers have improved the air travel experience. However, the problems with mass air transportation have not disappeared. Along with the many benefits of rapid and convenient travel, its many nuisances will also mark this experience for years to come.

*See also:* Automobiles and Leisure; Tourism

**BIBLIOGRAPHY**

Davies, R. *Airlines of the United States Since 1914.* London: Putnam, 1972.

Fairechild, Diana. *JetSmart.* Berkeley, Calif.: Celestial Arts Publishing, 1992.

Gottdiener, M. *Life in the Air: Surviving the New Culture of Air Travel.* Lanham, Md.: Rowman and Littlefield, 2001.

Hart, W. *The Airport Passenger Terminal.* N.Y.: J. Wiley and Sons, 1985.

Langewiesche, N. *Inside the Sky.* N.Y.: Pantheon Books, 1998.

Morris, S., and C. Wilson. *The Evolution of the Airlines Industry.* Washington, D.C.: Brookings Institution, 1995.

*Mark Gottdiener*

# AIRPLANES

**See** *Air Travel and Leisure, Modeling (Airplanes, Trains, Etc.)*

# ALCOHOL

**See** *Drinking, Drinking Games, Home Brewing, Prohibition and Temperance, Spring Break, Wine Tasting*

# AMATEUR RADIO

Given our familiarity with digitally tuned radios, we easily overlook the technical skills once required to enjoy radio. Through the 1920s, radio listening demanded technical skills for tuning, tinkering with, and constructing rudimentary receivers. The clear reception of a radio signal testified to the abilities of both radio operator and equipment. Enthusiastic listeners kept logs to document the conditions under which they received broadcasts. Into the late 1930s, radio stations sent "verified reception stamps" or postcards to listeners who wrote in reporting that they had heard a particular broadcast.

Many radio listeners chose to build their own receivers, either to save money or to control the design. Even those who bought ready-made radio receivers faced tasks such as wiring in a battery and assembling an antenna from parts sold separately before they could spend evenings searching the dial for new stations. Radio handbooks of the 1910s and 1920s commonly referred to listeners as one type of radio amateurs.

The other kind of radio amateurs listened to and additionally sent out their own radio signals. From the beginning of the twentieth century, "transmitting amateurs" or "hams" experimented with two-way radio. Hobbyists in home workshops made technical improvements to radio communication that rivaled those made by the U.S. military. Bickering over access to the radio spectrum strained the relationship between these groups of radio innovators. Hams eavesdropped on and sent false messages to sailors and also inadvertently interfered with naval communications. Antagonism between amateurs and the navy precipitated the first federal radio regulation, the Radio Act of 1912. In the process of playing tricks on the military, however, hobbyists showed off their skills and the capabilities of their equipment. The U.S. Navy put aside past grievances and turned to the self-trained amateurs to fill communications posts when World War I broke out. Targeted campaigns by the navy and the Army Signal Corps recruited amateur radio operators and asked hobbyists to donate homemade radio stations.

Much as the leisure tinkering of amateur radio operators contributed to military communications, so did it shape the broadcasting industry. Hams sent messages mostly from one person to another and often by Morse code, a system associating combinations of long and short electrical pulses to letters of the alphabet. In the 1910s, some amateurs shifted to talking over the airwaves using everyday speech. These personal conversations attracted an audience of eager listeners in the days before commercial radio stations. When amateurs acknowledged the wider audience by offering "concerts" of recorded music, they crossed the line into broadcasting. Development of broadcast radio as a business in the 1920s, including the greater commercial availability of receivers, split the general hobby of amateur radio into two forms of leisure. Since the 1930s, broadcast listening has required no skill and little effort; listeners can absorb radio entertainment passively. The sending and receiving of radio signals between individuals, on the other hand, demands the kind of activity and specialized knowledge typical of hobbies. Only the two-way hobby of radio communication retained the name "amateur radio" after the 1920s.

## Hobby Participants and Activities

From the point at which the transmitting hams separated from broadcast listeners until the 1980s, the practice of amateur radio remained remarkably stable. The Federal Communications Commission (FCC) regulates amateur activities and licenses operators in the United States. To obtain a license, a hobbyist has to pass a written examination of radio theory and rules. A second component of the test (dropped in 1991) required demonstrating the ability to understand Morse code and send it using a telegraph key. In the early 1990s, the number of Americans with ham radio licenses exceeded half a million and continued to grow, but the hobby began to change subtly as many amateurs incorporated personal computers and the Internet into their radio pastime. Though there were fewer ham radio participants in the third quarter of the twentieth century—with around 100,000 amateur license holders in the United States in the early 1950s, twice that many by 1960, and 375,000 in 1979—that period is generally considered the heyday of amateur radio. Hams' global communications during the politically tense Cold War and the interference of ham radio operators' signals with neighbors' television reception contributed to the hobby's public prominence.

To communicate "on the air," an amateur needed specialized devices such as a transmitter, a receiver tunable over the frequency range reserved for hobbyists, and an array of accessories and tools. An active ham might pass several hours after work seemingly alone in his "shack," the space that held his radio gear. Typically the shack was located in a basement, attic, or garage, but amateurs prized this unrefined space because it was totally dedicated to the hobby. Postcards confirming individual radio contacts decorated the walls, along with awards from ham contests and the hobbyist's license. The amateur often set up his home station atop or around a desk; ideally he would have enough space nearby for a workbench, where he could complete construction and repair projects. Hams saved an assortment of manuals and magazines (such as *CQ, Ham Radio Magazine, QST, The Radio Amateur's Handbook*, and *73 Magazine*) that composed their technical reference libraries. Depending on his personal style, the hobbyist left assorted spare parts strewn about or kept them stored neatly in bins. During periods of tinkering with equipment that could stretch on for weeks, the ham resembled the stereotypical lone inventor. Then the flip of a switch and the spin of a dial brought the many voices of amateur radio rushing into the shack.

Layers of conversations, in different languages, competed with staccato strings of Morse code across the ham frequencies. Only with precise tuning and some luck

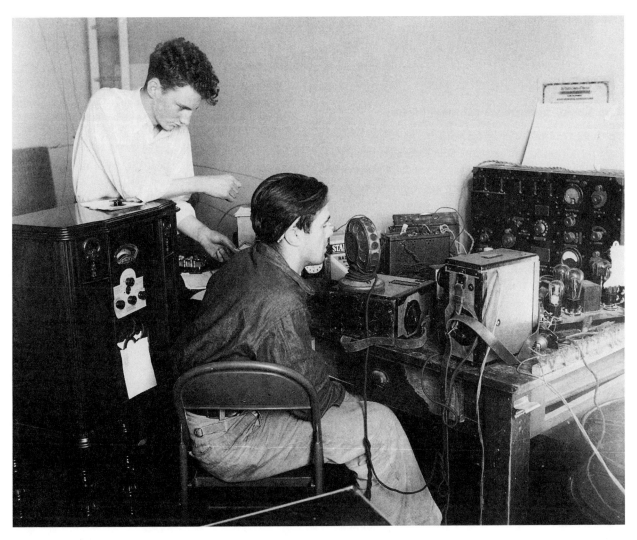

**Long Beach earthquake.** Amateur radio operators Tom Morrissey and Al Freeman sent messages via their amateur radio equipment during the Long Beach, California, earthquake on 10 March 1933. © *Bettmann/Corbis*

could a clear signal be isolated. When two amateurs successfully exchanged messages, the social side of this technical hobby began. During the rush of a contest or when conditions were poor, an "on-air" conversation might be limited to swapping data about station location and reception strength. Under other circumstances, two hams meeting for the first time might speak at length about their lives and hobby experiences. Random meetings over the airwaves occasionally grew into friendships that continued via letters and further wireless discussions. Hobbyists who lived near one another gathered in clubs and met informally for "eyeball contacts" with people they knew through radio only as disembodied voices. Drawn together by their technical interests and skills, hams referred to the group of hobbyists as a fraternity.

Members of the amateur radio community had far more than an unusual pastime in common. Though this brief profile should not be taken as invariable, it is helpful to have in mind a description of the typical radio hobbyist. An estimated 95 to 99 percent of the group were male. On average, the ham completed more years of schooling—and after World War II, his education usually included some college—than the nonhobbyist, and he was far more likely to hold a job in a technical field. These factors contributed to the fact that ham radio operators generally belonged to middle and upper socioeconomic classes. In a proportion probably equal to the gender disparity, hams were white and not inclined to identify ethnically. The hobby community discouraged all internal divisions except geographic ones, deriding religious and ethnic clubs as "political." Amateurs vehemently opposed the use of the airwaves or hobby publications for any political purpose not related to radio regulation, an attempt to avoid ideological battles with the FCC. Though the potential for international communication created a great deal of excitement and anxiety about ham radio, Americans dominated the hobby.

## The Social Side of a Technical Hobby

The hobby culture of amateur radio produced a technical fraternity. That is, the amateur radio community existed as a separate, almost exclusively male social group with barriers to entry—radio know-how and equipment—that were grounded in technology. The social dimension of ham radio appeared equally important as the technical dimension after World War II. Before the war, a period sometimes called the "radio age," wireless communicators had stood at the forefront of technical developments. The FCC even banned hobby radio transmissions during the war for security reasons. Yet with the postwar emergence of a new technical culture, the "age of electronics," interest in amateur radio grew instead of turning to the latest cutting-edge technology. Hams continued to enjoy social benefits from identifying as radio hobbyists even when they no longer contributed to technical innovation.

In adopting a technology that their neighbors considered strange, amateurs cordoned off a community with distinct values. Hams passed judgments about outsiders' technical practices and skills in order to establish a technical hierarchy in which radio hobbyists were an elite minority. When defending airspace allocation, hams invoked their close interaction with technology. This characteristic, so went a typical claim, made amateurs more entitled to airwave access than were the "button-pushing" citizens' band radio operators. Similarly, hobbyists who stood accused of interfering with television reception patronized viewers as not understanding the causes of electrical interference and dismissed television as a frivolous form of entertainment. Along with these social boundaries, amateur radio drew physical boundaries within the home. The noise and clutter of a station helped a ham gain isolated quarters for his shack, clarifying his personal identity apart from the family. In these private, masculine havens, hobbyists could temporarily escape job and household responsibilities and spend hours talking with like-minded men around the world.

*See also:* Hobbies and Crafts; Radio Listening, Car and Home; Television's Impact on Youth and Children's Leisure

## BIBLIOGRAPHY

Douglas, Susan J. *Inventing American Broadcasting, 1899–1922.* Baltimore: Johns Hopkins University Press, 1987.

Haring, Kristen. "Technical Identity in the Age of Electronics." Ph.D. diss., Harvard University, 2002.

Hilmes, Michele. *Radio Voices: American Broadcasting, 1922–1952.* Minneapolis: University of Minnesota Press, 1997.

United States Federal Communications Commission. Annual Report. Washington, D.C.: United States Government Printing Office, 1935–present.

*Kristen Haring*

# AMATEUR THEATRICS

American amateur theatrics is characterized by the variety and scope of its forms and its makers. The first known theatrical entertainment in America occurred in 1567: two comedies were performed for the governor's visit to the Spanish mission at Tequesta in Florida. The conquistadors, following royal Spanish policies of 1526, used theatrical entertainment to convert the indigenous people to Catholicism as they marched through what became Mexico and the southern United States. In addition, the conquistadors re-enacted their military successes to keep morale high, as in 1598, when Captain Farfán devised a play to celebrate Don Juan de Oñate's conquest of New Mexico.

While these Spanish-speaking performances served a particular ideological function, the intent behind the first amateur performances in English was vastly different. As English-speaking settlements thrived along the Atlantic coast and colonists embraced life beyond survival mode, their desire for leisure activities grew. The first recorded amateur theater in English was in 1665, when Virginia landholder William Darby performed his play, *Ye Bare and Ye Cubb*, causing him to face complaints that he had broken colonial laws against theater.

Laws like these, influenced by the religions of colonial founders, kept professional theater companies from establishing until the mid-1700s, and also made amateur theatrics sporadic events. While strolling players and mountebanks found taverns and greens with sympathetic audiences, the dominant Quaker and Puritan influences challenged itinerant performers. Yet the expanding elite class wanted diversions during their newfound leisure time. Amateur theatrics sprung up in Charleston, Williamsburg, Philadelphia, and New York with varying controversy and success. These events were devised by members of the communities: students at the College of William and Mary publicly performed dialogues as early as 1702, and in 1718, a play was produced in Williamsburg by the owner of the dancing school to honor King George I's birthday. Local gentry were likely cast in *The Orphan*, in Charleston in 1735.

The relative success of amateur performers often hinged on geography and politics. Amateur theatrics struggled more in the North, where the Puritan and Quaker ethics still had measurable influence, but began to make inroads nonetheless. A troupe of strolling players featuring rope-dancers clashed with the Quaker mayor of Philadelphia over performances in 1723, yet was able to perform in a "booth theatre" outside the city limits because the governor of Pennsylvania refused to reinforce the entertainment ban. In anti-theatrically inclined Boston, dancing schools and assembly halls opened by the 1730s, defying Puritan beliefs to cater to the mercantile class.

The antitheatrical prejudice seemed to wane by the mid-eighteenth century, but it rekindled as the colonies moved toward independence. While some amateur theatrics were still performed in taverns, in 1774 the Continental Congress enforced an injunction on entertainments as anti-British sentiment and antitheatrical sentiment united. Yet during the Revolutionary War, both the British and the colonial military embraced theatrical entertainments to boost morale and marshal support. When the British army occupied Boston and New York in 1775 and 1776, the commanders encouraged theatrical entertainments as diversions for their troops. One such entertainment was the *Meschianza*, a lavish extravaganza created in honor of General William Howe's resignation as commander of the British forces in April, 1778. The *Meschianza* was an event that included boating parades, bands, fifty costumed young Philadelphian women escorted in procession, mock battles, dancing, and impressive fireworks displays. The colonial military also embraced morale-boosting theatrics: two weeks before the *Meschianza*, George Washington approved the plays as diversions for winter-weary soldiers at Valley Forge. At the end of the war, Washington attended the *Dauphinade*, a pageant reminiscent of the *Meschianza*.

As Americans gained more affluence and leisure time, and demanded more forms of entertainment, what had traditionally been the amateur theatrics of showmen—itinerant performers of medicine shows, freak shows, animal acts, acrobats, and rope-dancers—became professional touring circuses at the beginning of the nineteenth century. This, coupled with the ease of travel that arose with railroad expansion, reshaped the nature of public entertainment into "high" and "low" (or popular) art, and brought amateur theatrics into the parlor. Popular forms of parlor entertainments ranged from private musical concerts to tableaux vivants (or living pictures) and included pantomimes, charades, short plays, and adaptations of minstrel shows. These entertainments, given for family, friends and neighbors, developed the concept of the "real amateur," who excelled in skills honed expressly to amuse and entertain family and friends, leaving public entertainment to the professionals.

The foundational moral concepts of parlor entertainments were also the underpinnings of pageant dramas popular at the turn of the twentieth century. Percy Mackaye, a "dramatic engineer" with a theatrical heritage, was in large part responsible for the revival of pageant drama similar to the *Meschianza*. Mackaye viewed pageants and masques as expressive democratic art, and developed mass participatory spectacles celebrating the history of specific American communities on an enormous scale. His 1914 *Masque of St. Louis* used 7,500 citizen-players and was attended by almost 500,000 people in a five-day span.

As pageants became popular, another amateur theatrical movement came to the United States in the early twentieth century: the Little Theatre movement. Based on the European Art Movement that nurtured the drama of artists like André Antoine, Vsevolod Meyerhold, and others who pursued solely artistic rather than commercial goals, this movement also had roots in the parlors, where women's clubs met to pursue intellectual endeavors. While this movement gained momentum as an amateur venue in the 1910s, many Little Theaters did not have amateurism as their aim. These theaters slowly developed into professional regional theaters. A wealth of amateur community theaters continued to arise in more remote areas without professional theaters, serving as social centers and creative outlets for Americans who still saw amateur theatrics as a worthwhile leisure activity. By the 1960s, these theaters, often associated with social or educational groups, included collectives developed to explore issues of race, ethnicity, and gender theatrically.

In the early 2000s, as the concept of performance continued to expand, amateur theatrics embraced players as various as the costumed "playtrons" attending Renaissance festivals, participants in live-action roleplaying interacting at organized events, and "How to Host a Murder" costumed parties that echo nineteenth century parlor entertainments. These diverse performances characterize rich diversity and complex roots of amateur theatrics in the United States.

*See also:* Art Exhibit Audiences; Historical Reenactment Societies; Home Movies; Performing Arts Audiences; Theater, Live

## BIBLIOGRAPHY

Bellew, Frank. *The art of amusing. Being a collection of collection of graceful arts, merry games, odd tricks, curious puzzles, and new charades; together with suggestions for private theatricals, tableaux, and all sorts of parlor and family amusements.* New York: S. Low, Son and Company, 1866. (Reprint edition 1974 by Arno Press, Inc.)

Kasson, John F. *Rudeness and Civility: Manners in Nineteenth-Century Urban America.* New York: Hill and Wang, 1990.

Kuftinec, Sonja. *Staging America: Cornerstone and Community-Based Theater.* Carbondale: Southern Illinois University Press, 2003.

McNamara, Brooks. *The New York Concert Saloon: The Devil's Own Nights.* Cambridge: Cambridge University Press, 2002.

Nathans, Heather S. *Early American Theatre from the Revolution to Thomas Jefferson: Into the Hands of the People.* Cambridge: Cambridge University Press, 2003.

Perry, Clarence Arthur. *The Work of the Little Theatres: The Groups They Include, the Plays They Produce, Their Tournaments, and the Handbooks They Use.* New York: Russell Sage Foundation, 1933.

Quinn, Arthur Hobson. *A History of the American Drama: From the Beginning to the Civil War.* 2 Vols. New York: Appleton-Century-Crofts, Inc., 1930.

Rankin, Hugh F. *The Theater in Colonial America.* Chapel Hill: The University of North Carolina Press, 1965.

*Carrie J. Cole*

# AMUSEMENT PARKS

**See** *Coney Island, Disneyland, Sea World, Theme and Amusement Parks, Walt Disney World*

# ANIMALS

**See** *Bird Watching, Circuses, Pet Care, Zoos*

# ANTIQUES

Antiquing, or collecting antiques, combines the thrill of the hunt with the joy of having desired items. Antiquing is gambling, intrigue, and adventure rolled into one leisure pursuit. People often collect antiques to re-create their childhoods, or the childhoods of their parents or grandparents. The connection to the past and to history is fascinating. It is also fun to find treasures in the midst of what others might consider junk. Ron Zoglin and Deborah Shouse personalized antiquing, and said: "Collecting antiques is like falling in love: You are constantly discovering new and interesting aspects of the antiques. The more you know, the more you want to know. You never get bored with your explorations, and you want the relationship to last forever" (p.1).

For centuries, people were fascinated with and collected old items. The interest in antiquing increased after the end of World War II. Baby boomers with disposable income and a sense of nostalgia are currently at the head of the interest in collecting antiques. Since antiquing is such a broad topic, it is difficult to determine the number of people who collect antiques. In 2003 it was estimated more than 20 million Americans collected something, although it was not clear how many of these people solely collected antiques. It was also difficult to determine overall sales in the antique industry. There were approximately 1.5 billion visits a year to places like flea markets or antique malls, with flea markets alone generating more than $30 billion in annual sales. Antiquing clearly was a leisure activity many people invested time and money in pursuing.

## Antique? Collectible?

In general, most people think anything old is an antique. Others subscribe to the "Grandmother theory" that notes items as old as your grandmother are antiques (Jenkins, p. 6). The legal definition of an antique, however, is any object that is 100 years or older. This definition evolved from the 1930s when antiques were considered artwork, and could be brought into the United States duty-free. Customs agents began to question what should actually be considered an antique. They determined objects that predated mass production of the 1830s, and thus were 100 years old, should be considered antiques. The 100-year threshold became the benchmark for an item to be legally considered an antique, or to be duty-free when brought into the United States.

The legal definition of antique is not accepted without question. Antique connoisseurs feel that an antique is an object that predated the Industrial Revolution, and was handmade. Connoisseurs believe true antiques ceased to be made when machines took over from individual craftspeople. For these connoisseurs, the benchmark years for something to be considered an antique are before 1820 to 1840. Those who collect toys also question the 100-year benchmark of the legal definition. They consider toys made before World War II to be antique.

Other terms such as antiquities, antiques-in-waiting, and collectibles are inaccurately interchanged with the term antique. Each of these terms has unique definitions. Antiquities are items that are unearthed and represent ancient cultures like Greek, Roman, and Egyptian. These items are extremely old, rare, and valuable. Art Nouveau, Art Deco, and Art Moderne period articles are pieces that are highly valued and often collected. Using the 100-year benchmark, these pieces are not old enough to be antique, but are antiques-in-waiting; items that will eventually become high-quality antiques. Collectible items are fun to collect, but they are also too young to be antiques. Collectibles are defined as items that were mass-produced, are less than 100 years old, and were relatively inexpensive when made. Items such as Hummel figures, Harley Davidson tree ornaments, Jim Beam bottles, Mickey Mouse watches, Beanie Babies, or baseball cards are examples of collectibles.

## Antique Collectors

Palmer and Forsyth conducted a qualitative research study to observe shoppers in antique malls. These researchers identified six types of customers or shoppers. There are people who are "just looking." These customers come into the mall for entertainment, as if they were going to a museum. They really have no intention to buy, but they may want to determine the value of old or antique items that were handed down to them by family members. "Casual shoppers" buy items they can afford and happen to catch their attention. "Knowledgeable buyers" are often more informed collectors. They have an idea of what they want and the general worth of the item. "Repeat customers" are collectors who have specific antique items or categories of antiques they prefer, and who have previously bought items from a dealer. "Dealer customers" are dealers who buy items to resell or to add to their own collections. Many dealers are true collectors who travel thousands of miles looking for special items. Finally, "value customers" are not really antique collectors or interested in antiques, but they look for functional items, such as wrought-iron bed headboards or wicker swings, because they are disappointed in the cost and quality of items that can be purchased in today's marketplace. At varying levels of involvement, the first five of these groups could be considered antique collectors.

People who go antiquing might also be called "collectors" or "accumulators". Collectors look for the finest items to complement their collection. They purchase only select pieces. Accumulators, however, buy what attracts them or anything they find, regardless of quality, in a chosen area. In reality, most antique collectors are somewhere along a continuum from true collector to accumulator, with many in between the two extremes. For example, a person may accumulate every piece of vintage jewelry they see, but be selective of Queen Anne furniture by only purchasing a piece that took years to locate. Regardless of whether they are accumulators or collectors, true lovers of antiques are very knowledgeable of the objects they collect. True lovers' involvement in antiquing could be considered serious leisure, leisure that requires specific skills and knowledge.

## Antiquing Skills and Knowledge

Antique collectors tend to focus their collections on specific categories of antiques. There are, however, as many categories of antiques as there are authors who write antique books and articles. For example, Milan Vesely indicated there were major categories of antiques that are divided into subcategories, including numerous specialty areas. In his book, Vesely identified fourteen major categories: porcelain; furniture; glassware; silverware; jewelry; commemorative antiques; toys; oriental; clocks, barometers, and instruments; memorabilia; militaria; collectibles; architectural antiques; miscellaneous antiques. Carol Prisant listed eleven categories, many of which are similar to the categories noted by Vesely (for example, furniture, silver, and toys). Prisant added categories (such as paintings; metal work; rugs, quilts, and samplers; books and manuscripts), and deleted categories (such as commemorative antiques, memorabilia, militaria, architectural antiques) to form her list. Other authors also categorize antiques, but most lists differ slightly from one another.

As the various categories demonstrate, antiquing can be fascinating, confusing, and very complicated. Preparation for hunting antiques requires conducting thorough research. Collectors learn about products, periods, markings, signatures, construction, prices, etc. Antiquing also has its own language and rituals, including when and how to negotiate prices. Numerous books, price guides, and magazines are published to help with the research. Some collectors build their own reference libraries, while others rely on public libraries. The Internet has made a wide range of information readily available to collectors. Two of the best ways to learn about antiques, however, are through firsthand experience in antique shops and talking to dealers.

There are also numerous places to hunt for antiques. The freestanding antique and specialty shops are the backbone of the antiquing business. In these shops one can find people who are walking encyclopedias of history and antiques. The dealers are like scholars who spend their entire lives studying antiques, and just listening to them can be fun. In addition to talking with the dealers, another excitement of antiquing is heading down a road looking for an elusive treasure. Stops might be made at flea markets, yard sales, antique malls, estate sales, thrift shops, galleries, antique shows, and so forth. Auctions are also locations where one can find antiques. Auctions might be sophisticated national auctions, like Sotheby's and Christie's, or local auctions with their own unique settings and rituals. The literature on antiquing advises collectors to buy expensive items from reputable dealers, but sometimes a great buy is found in an out-of-the-way flea market or some other place off the beaten track. The knowledgeable collector knows what to look for, where to go to find antiques, and how much the items should realistically cost.

## Antiquing and the Internet

The Internet has certainly impacted antiquing. It has added new dimensions and new headaches. The Internet changed the nature of antiquing from ventures into dusty antique malls and quaint shops to international competition that can be accessed twenty-four hours a day, seven days a week from a person's family room. The success of the Internet caused traditional auction houses and dealers to have online auctions or shops. Some antique dealers have traditional brick–and-mortar shops, as well as a presence online. Others moved to having only "virtual shops," while some dealers sell a few of their items on Web sites like eBay or Yahoo! With the explosion of antique selling online, dealers fear freestanding shops may become a thing of the past. Others fear novices who shop online, but who are not educated on quality or value of items, may artificially inflate the cost of antiques.

The good news is that some dealers discover increased business due to Internet exposure. The dealers now have access to more potential buyers than to just those people who might physically wander into their store or mall booth. The other good news is that collectors can buy without travel, sell items they no longer want, chat with others interested in antiques, find informational and educational materials about antiques, locate addresses of antique shops, auction houses, museums, and so forth. They can also conduct comparison-shopping and research on prices, access appraisal services, and shop anywhere in the world. It is too early to know if the Internet's influence on antiquing will be primarily positive or negative.

## Antiquing and Television

No discussion of antiquing is complete without a look at antiquing and television. *The Antiques Roadshow,* which had its television debut in 1996, grew from a few hundred viewers to over 14 million viewers per week and approximately 7,000 people at each taping stop during the summer of its fourth season (Prisant, p. xi). *The Antiques Roadshow* was the most-watched prime-time series on public television in 2003, and was one of the leading television shows connected to antiquing. This pop-culture phenomenon is similar to standing in line to buy a lottery ticket, playing a game show, attending a revival meeting, or going to a rock concert. Bishop noted "the function of the *Roadshow* is to acquaint and reacquaint us with the joys of collecting, and to sustain an ongoing dialogue about searching for and acquiring items for our collections" (2001, p. 196). Thus, the purpose of the television shows is to get a wide range of people excited about collecting antiques and learning about history.

People travel hundreds of miles to bring their items to the *Roadshow* so that well-known antique dealers or people from auction houses, like Sotheby's or Christie's, can appraise the items. Thousands of people talk to the appraisers, but few actually appear on the television show. Those selected to be on the show give a brief history of their item and an idea of its worth. The appraiser expands the history, and ultimately announces a dollar value of the item. Watchers of the show identify with the everyday people they see on the television screen, and feel they too could have valuable items in their basements or attics. The watchers may also believe their items are worth as much as those seen on television, when in reality they most likely are not.

As the show progresses from the appraisal segments, the camera scans the location and televises pictures of people walking with their items, appraisers giving advice, and large crowds of people at the show. Other segments of the show will include topics like how to recognize and care for antiques. At times the producers show historical locations in the city where the show is taped. All scenes are shown for a purpose, namely to educate viewers about the joys of hunting for and having antiques. The picture sends the message that collecting antiques is an incredibly popular activity. Between the actual show and the show's Web site, with games, membership, shopping, and opportunities to relive memorable shows, antiquing as a leisure interest becomes accessible and inviting to a wide

**Antiques Roadshow on PBS.** In 1996 the first season of Chubb's *Antiques Roadshow* debuted, and in the years that followed, it became PBS's most-watched primetime series. The show features antiques appraisers informing people as to the value of the items they bring to the show, which are staged at large convention centers and filmed for later airplay. Here, at the final stop of the 1999 season at the Rhode Island Convention Center in Providence, Lark E. Mason Jr., an appraiser at Sotheby's in New York estimates that the 1920s Edward Farmer Jade and 18K gold jewelry box he is appraising is worth approximately $125,000. © *Susan E. Bouchard for AP/Wide World Photos*

range of potential collectors. The show attempts to get people hooked, or to keep people hooked, on antiquing. Like the unknown overall impact of the Internet on antiquing, it is not clear how television shows like *The Antiques Roadshow* will ultimately effect antiquing.

*See also:* Auctions, Auto Shows, Clocks and Watches, Coin Collecting, Collecting, Internet, Sporting Memorabilia

**BIBLIOGRAPHY**

*Antiques Roadshow.* Available from http://www.pbs.org.

Bishop, Ronald. "What Price History? Functions of Narrative in Television Collectibles Shows." *Journal of Popular Culture* 33, no. 3 (Winter 1999): 1–28.

———. "Dreams in the Line: A Day at the *Antiques Roadshow.*" *Journal of Popular Culture* 35, no. 1 (2001): 195–209.

Edwards, Simon, Phil Ellis, and Joyce Hanes. *Miller's Antiques, Art & Collectables on the Web.* London: Octopus Publishing Group, 2000.

Hirshey, Gerri. "Together, They Collect Memories." *Parade Magazine* (11 May 2003): 4–5.

Jenkins, Emyl. *The Complete Idiot's Guide to Buying and Selling Antiques.* Indianapolis, Ind.: Alpha Books, 2000.

Palmer, C. Eddie, and Craig J. Forsyth. "Dealers and Dealing in an Antique Mall." *Sociological Spectrum* 22 (2002): 171–190.

Prisant, Carol. *Antiques Roadshow Primer.* New York: Workman Publishing, 1999.

Vesely, Milan. *Antiques for Amateurs: Secrets to Successful Antiquing.* Iola, Wisc.: Krause Publications, 1999.

Zoglin, Ron, and Deborah Shouse. *Antiquing for Dummies.* Foster City, Calif.: IDG Books Worldwide, 1999.

*Sandra Wolf Klitzing*

# ARCHERY

The sport of archery has been around since the days of King Henry VII of England, and in the early twenty-first century it was enjoyed by millions of people all over the world, including more than 2.5 million Americans. The popularity of archery is due to its limitless capacity to be performed by people of both sexes, all ages, and differing physical conditions. Archery is adaptable to individual physical needs, because of flexibility in types of equipment used, distances shot, types of archery practiced, and the year-round nature of the sport. The action of deliberately, and with total control, aiming at and hitting an object gives the individual a sense of pride in accomplishment, and builds self-esteem and confidence.

Archery is individualistic by nature, as it requires the archer to draw the bow, physically hold back the weight, aim the arrow, and release with accuracy on a consistent basis. However, the sport does offer opportunity for social interaction with family and other enthusiasts. In contrast to the social opportunities offered by participating in archery, no partner or team is necessary, and the individual can practice and compete without contact with other people, if so desired.

## Benefits

Benefits associated with participation in archery are both physical and emotional. The physical requirement of drawing the bow and holding the anchor position helps to build strength and endurance in shoulder and upper back muscles, and requires the contraction of abdominal muscles, which is necessary for maintenance of erect posture. Additionally, shooting a bow on a regular basis helps to counteract the atypical muscular actions and fatigue caused by prolonged sitting. Emotionally, archery requires deep, quiet concentration, and in this state the individual is able to find release from the tensions and pressures caused by daily life. The sense of accomplishment in handling a bow and arrow competently is personally gratifying and requires control in disciplining the mind and body, and in this context allows the individual to truly experience themselves.

## History

The use of archery as a military weapon and hunting tool declined with the development of gunpowder and firearms. By the nineteenth century, archery was a recreational activity participated in by the "leisure class." The

first organized archery club in America was formed in Philadelphia in 1828. Its early members were interested more in exercise and social camaraderie than in promoting the sport. However, it wasn't until after the Civil War that there was a renewed interest in archery in the United States. After the war, former Confederate soldiers were prohibited from using firearms, and two brothers, Will and Maurice Thompson, lived, for the most part, on game they killed with the bow and arrow. In 1878, a collection of articles written by the brothers was published. Although most of the articles concerned hunting with the bow, the last was on target archery, which led to the first period of archery as a popular sport in the United States. By 1879, the interest generated by the book led to the founding of the National Archery Association.

This popularity was short lived, and by 1883 archery began to decline. Reasons for this loss in popularity include the cost of equipment and the difficulty of its importation, along with the emergence of alternatives such as lawn tennis, baseball, football, and golf. A reemergence of interest in archery occurred in 1904 at the St. Louis World's Fair, which included in the athletic program the Third Olympic Games. Archery was then included in the 1908 and 1920 Olympics, sparking a brief growth of interest. This sporadic inclusion in the Olympics was due to the fact that if archery was not popular in the host country, the event was not held.

World War I interrupted the resurging popularity of archery, and its revival did not occur until after the war, with the motion picture industry being recognized as a contributing factor. In 1923, the silent classic *Robin Hood* was released. As a promotional campaign for the movie, the pastime was spotlighted, and this attention had the effect of popularizing archery as a sport once again.

Another contributing factor to the slow but growing interest in archery in the United States after World War I was the Boy Scout movement, which encouraged the revival of archery as not only a sport but also for developing young men's moral qualities. Two events during this time period added to the growing interest in the sport. In 1934, Wisconsin became the first state to grant a special deer season for archers, and when word spread that it was possible for a modern bowman to bag a deer, other states began adding an archery season. The second event was the founding of the Federation International de Tir A L'Arc (FITA) as an international governing body. The FITA established universal rules for international competition, and as international competition grew and gained momentum, archery was readopted for the 1972 Olympics. The growing interest in bowhunting and tar-

**Bow and arrow lessons.** Accomplished archer Donna McMillion assists Zach Schwartz, nine, during an archery demonstration at Camp Craig in Milford, Ohio, on 18 October 2003. She took up the sport in 1995 after twenty-four years of her husband leaving her behind on weekends to bow hunt and later went on to win a world championship. © *Tom Uhlman for AP/Wide World Photos*

get archery was instrumental in developing the popularity of archery as a recreational activity and sport in contemporary society.

## Technology and Archery

Technical advances in materials and design of bows and arrows have increased shooting accuracy and, consequently, interest in archery. The progression in bow construction moved from wood (traditional bows) to fiberglass (straight limb bows) to laminations of wood and fiberglass (recurve and compound bows). The most significant advance in bow design was the development of the compound bow, patented in 1966. The compound bow uses off-center pulleys, or cams, mounted on each limb tip. The result is that the energy required to pull back the bowstring is greatest at mid-draw and smallest at full draw, when the archer is holding to aim, resulting in increased accuracy. Similarly, advances in materials used for arrows have progressed from wood to fiberglass to aluminum to carbon. The advances in materials used

to manufacture arrows have resulted in lighter and, therefore, faster arrows.

*See also:* Hunting, Olympics, Target Shooting

### BIBLIOGRAPHY

Barrett, Jean A. *Archery.* Santa Monica, Calif.: Goodyear Publishing, 1980.

Gillelan, Howard G. *The Complete Book of the Bow and Arrow.* Harrisburg, Pa.: Stackpole Books, 1971.

Haywood, Kathleen M., and Catherine F. Lewis. *Archery: Steps to Success.* Champaign, Ill.: Human Kinetics, 1997.

Heath, Ernest G. *A History of Target Archery.* Cranbury, N.J.: A.S. Barnes and Company, 1974.

McKinney, Wayne C., and Mike W. McKinney. *Archery.* Dubuque, Iowa: William C. Brown Publishers, 1985.

Pszczola, Lorraine, and Lois J. Mussett. *Archery.* New York: Saunders College Publishing, 1984.

*John J. Weber*

# ART

**See** *Graphic Arts, Museum Movements, Performing Arts Audiences*

# ART EXHIBIT AUDIENCES

**See** *Museum Movements*

# ASIAN AMERICAN LEISURE LIFESTYLES

Presenting a broad overview of the leisure lifestyles of Asian Americans can lead to deceptive stereotypes in our understanding of a population that is extremely heterogeneous. The term "Asian American" originated as an outcome of the post–civil rights movement of the 1960s. A consensus among U.S.-born Asian American civil rights activists to dismantle the then-commonly held stereotype of "Orientals," led to their initiation of the term "Asian American" as a political tool for recognition and empowerment (Kibria). The U.S. Census Bureau identifies "Asian Americans" as those individuals having ancestral origins in countries in the Far East, Southeast Asia, or the Indian subcontinent, such as China, Japan, Korea, the Philippines, Thailand, Vietnam, Laos, Cambodia, Malaysia, India, and Pakistan (Humes and McKinnon).

An effort to collectively understand the leisure lifestyles of people from a wide array of nationalities and cultural backgrounds, consolidated under an umbrella denomination or group, such as Asian American (as determined by the U.S. Bureau of Census) would not yield many meaningful results. The Asian American population in the early twentieth century was largely composed of individuals from Chinese and Japanese backgrounds. Asian Americans in the early 2000s were diverse in their originating nationalities and thus represented a mosaic of ancestral and cultural traits, languages, religions, and lengths of residence in the United States (Kibria). The identification of distinctive Asian American leisure patterns would require a full-scale analysis of the lifestyles of all U.S. cultural groups originating in Asia, the world's largest continent, which includes more than forty-five countries and various islands and archipelagos. Leisure behaviors and patterns of Asian Americans encompass all special activities and characteristics of a multitude of dis-

tinct subethnic groups, because each Asian group has its own unique set of distinctive culturally oriented leisure preferences and lifestyles. Hence, it is difficult if not impossible to generalize anything about Asian Americans. The following discussion highlights some of the demographic, social, and economic characteristics of Asian Americans and corresponding implications for the leisure lifestyles of this population.

## Immigration and Acculturation

An overarching factor that dynamically influences the construction of Asian American leisure lifestyles is the role of immigration. Although Asian Americans composed only 4 percent of the total U.S. population, they were the fastest increasing group with annual growth rates that could exceed 2 percent until 2030 (Day). Factors that contributed to that high rate of growth included increasing immigration and dramatic increases in the number of births. Most Asian Americans were recent immigrants (as of 2004), and that trend was expected to increase in the future. According to the U.S. Census Bureau, approximately one-fourth of the 32.5 million foreign-born U.S. residents were of Asian origin (Schmidley). Further, approximately 88 percent of the 12.5 million Asian Americans were foreign-born (Schmidley). During the process of establishing their roots in U.S. society, it was commonly assumed that new Asian immigrants would experience acculturation and begin to gradually replace traditional culturally oriented leisure lifestyles with American leisure practices. Since the majority of Asian Americans were recent immigrants, the diasporic communities of Asians residing in the United States were likely to resist cultural assimilation with the dominant society. Rather than gradually acculturating and adopting dominant leisure lifestyles, Asian Americans were likely to maintain their native qualities as a combined consequence of the continuing influx of new Asian immigrants and strong cultural and homeland ties of new immigrants.

One of the significant findings of Ping Yu and Doris Berryman's 1996 study was that recreation participation among Chinese individuals generally matched immigrant lifestyles. Since acculturation takes place at the individual level and changes take place at varying rates, new immigrants may continue to reinforce and retain native cultural leisure lifestyles in order to maintain high cultural loyalty and identity. Within the context of leisure, while some native cultural characteristics are rapidly replaced by host traits, others happen gradually. Further, improved global communication technologies that allow virtual networking with ethnic peer groups may facilitate ongoing strong linkages between the high proportions of Asian immi-

**Chinese Opera company.** Members of Qi Shu Fang's Peking Opera Company perform. They are based in New York City where they formed in 1988. © *Jack Vartoogian*

grants in the United States and their origin countries. Thus, continued homeland connections will allow foreign-born Asian Americans to maintain and strengthen their culturally oriented leisure lifestyles. For example, Kenneth Thompson notes that Asian immigrants from the Indian subcontinent use old and new technologies (and media outlets) such as cable and satellite TV, video, radio, telephone, and the Internet as means to stay connected with ethnic-group lifestyles. Such technologies are major components of the leisure lifestyles of this group and play a central role in maintaining pronounced resistance among South Asian immigrants (such as Indians, Pakistanis, Afghans, and Bangladeshis), particularly those of middle-class status, toward cultural assimilation with the dominant U.S. society.

## Urban Concentration and Socioeconomic Conditions

Asian Americans are predominantly urban, with almost 96 percent living in metropolitan areas (Humes and McKinnon). Asian Americans are more likely to reside along the western seaboard of the United States than in any other region of the nation. They are particularly concentrated in gateway metropolitan areas that already have an existing Asian presence, and much of this concentration is a result of chain migration, where friends and family members follow those who have already immigrated and established residence in the United States. Accessibility to Asian American social networks in gateway communities provides group-based resources that aid new Asian immigrants in making advancement in the host society (Sanders, Nee, and Sernau). The high urban concentration of Asian Americans has several implications for their leisure lifestyles. Since the majority of households within an Asian enclave tend to consist of people from the same ethnic background, ethnic-based social networks and cultural preferences tremendously influence the leisure activities of Asian Americans living in such areas. Further, most Asian groups in the United States see religion as a tool for identity formation. As a result, it is traditional for Asian American groups to regularly congregate with others from the same religio-ethnic backgrounds at religious institutions such as churches, temples, and mosques. Such religious venues play a dominant role in the formation and strengthening of ethnic-based social networks, thus further reinforcing the propensity among Asian Americans to follow culturally oriented leisure lifestyles.

With increasing affluence and education, Asian Americans tend to move away from the tenements of ethnic enclaves and choose prosperous residential neighborhoods with fewer Asian households. Asian American households residing in non-ethnic neighborhoods are more likely to engage in Western leisure practices than those living in ethnic enclaves. According to Yu and Berryman, social and economic situations determine the leisure lifestyles of Asian Americans. Their study of the Chinese community in New York City indicated that highly acculturated Chinese Americans with high levels of education and income were greatly influenced by Western culture and exhibited patterns of leisure participation that were closely similar to those of mainstream U.S. society. Further, Chinese Americans with high levels of acculturation were less likely to participate in leisure activities involving other Chinese individuals. But increased acculturation combined with longer work hours among Chinese Americans resulted in sedentary lifestyles involving lack of participation in leisure and recreation activities.

## Asian Concepts of Leisure and Recreation

Asian Americans, in general, exhibit low frequencies of participation in leisure activities that are physical in nature. Low involvement in physically challenging leisure activities is particularly evident among new Asian immigrant women. Long hours of family-oriented household work, language barriers, and lack of transportation greatly reduce the availability of and access to leisure opportunities for these women. Their sedentary leisure lifestyles pose severe health consequences. In fact, according to the U.S. Census Bureau, the percentage of deaths occurring to the Asian American group is expected to more than quadruple by the middle of the next century, as this group both ages and increases its share of the population (Day).

An examination of physical activity participation among college students reveals that lack of physical activity is most widespread among male and female Asian American college students. One reason for their lack of physical leisure activities could be the cultural orientation of Asian leisure. Yu and Berryman confirm that the leisure activities of the Chinese are characterized by passive, spectator-like involvement as opposed to vigorous physical exertion. Additionally, Chinese individuals tend to favor games that are oriented toward the individual over pastimes that require group interaction, such as outdoor recreation and sporting as well as activities involving team work or group play. Thus, leisure activity

preferences of Asian Americans, especially among new Asian immigrants, might vary significantly from traditional U.S. leisure and recreation practices. Yu and Berryman noted that new Chinese immigrants in New York City's Chinatown were more likely to participate in leisure, often indoor activities that were readily available, requiring minimal organization and physical skills and less financial commitment. These activities included watching Chinese programs (television and video), listening to Chinese music, talking on the telephone, and reading Chinese newspapers, magazines, books, and comics. While girls preferred arts and crafts activities such as singing, ballet and modern dance, letter writing, paper cutting and folding, and needlework and sewing, boys preferred woodworking and sports such as baseball, basketball, soccer, billiards and pool, swimming, weight lifting, and karate.

A study investigating differences in urban park visitation by ethnic groups, conducted by Vinod Sasidharan found that Asian Americans with lower acculturation levels visit parks, forests, and recreational areas in large groups consisting of members from the same ethnic/racial groups. This characteristic may be attributed to the collectivistic orientation of Asian cultural groups and the profound emphasis given to a closely integrated social framework. While collectivist cultures stress the importance of the "rights and needs of the group," individualistic cultures emphasize "individual achievement and rights of the individual" (Rosenthal and Feldman, pp. 495–514). Thus, visitation to parks in larger groups with members from the same ethnic/racial background may be an indication of the significance of "group efforts" among the lower acculturated Asian American groups. The higher acculturated groups may have somewhat weaker collectivistic orientations (coupled with varying degrees of individualistic orientations) compared to the lower acculturated groups, thus exhibiting a lower propensity to visit parks in groups with members from the same ethnic/racial background. While the higher acculturated Asian American groups are more likely to establish leisure networks with individuals from other ethnic/racial backgrounds, lower acculturated groups generally tend to take recreation with relatives and friends of the same ethnicity.

## Centrality of Family, Kinship, and Community

Family and kinship are central to most Asian Americans and fulfillment of filial obligations is considered a fundamental responsibility in Asian society. Asian household members are expected to maintain cultural traditions and subordinate their individual needs and

**New Year Festival.** Moua Vang participates in a New Year festival in Fresno, California, in 1996. In the Hmong community, as in many other Asian American communities, New Year's is an important and festive holiday © *AP/Wide World Photos*

wants to accommodate overall family interests. The core importance of family and kinship ties among Asian American households and the ascribed responsibility of Asian children to take care of their parents and siblings have a profound influence on family size. Among married-couple Asian American families, almost 23 percent consisted of five or more household members (Humes and McKinnon) while 21 percent of foreign-born Asian Americans live in households that have five or more family members. Strong collectivistic values among Asian American households and the roles played by individual members of the family greatly determine the types of leisure and recreation activities pursued. According to Sasidharan, Asian Americans tend to visit urban parks and recreational areas in groups (of families and friends) that are larger than the traditional Anglo recreation groups. Paul Gobster and Antonio Delgado reported that, while Anglos visit parks on their own or as couples with an average group size of 1.6, Asians usually visit parks with families with an average group size of 5.0. Gobster reports that almost 47 percent of the Asian American users of Chicago's Lincoln Park visited the park with extended families, consisting of the immediate family along with close relatives (2002). These findings suggest that families and organized groups are the most important social units of leisure participation for Asian Americans.

Community (group) orientation plays a significant role in Asian American leisure. Sasidharan's study indicates that Korean and Chinese Americans usually visit urban parks with others from their own racial/ethnic group. Korean and Chinese Americans frequently participate in group-oriented, weekend activities such as social activities (playing with children, talking with friends, playing board games), team activities (soccer, basketball, softball and baseball, Frisbee), community activities (festivals, parties), and food-related activities (picnicking, eating, barbecuing), usually requiring longer durations of time. Tingwei Zhang and Paul Gobster's study of Chicago's Chinatown residents found that "socially relaxing" (including people watching, sitting, and chatting) along with team sports such as basketball, baseball, volleyball, and tennis were among the top outdoor activities of Chinese American respondents. Hutchison found team sports such as soccer and volleyball, and community events and festivals to be major outdoor activities among the Hmong population residing in Green Bay, Minnesota.

The predominance of social activities, team activities, community activities, and food-related activities during the recreation and leisure pastimes of Asian Americans may be attributed to the cultural importance of social gatherings to this group. Once again, the argument of the centrality of family and friends in leisure settings may be a compelling factor for the central focus of picnicking, playing, and relaxing with family members within Asian American recreation practices. The importance of family life and family cohesion to the Asian cultures and the heightened dependence on the family among Asian individuals may cause an aversion to solitary activities within Asian American households, especially among lower acculturated groups. For most Asian American groups, especially among those with low levels of acculturation, frequency of participation in food-related activities is significantly higher compared to Anglos (Sasidharan). The symbolic significance of food as a means of reinforcing ethnic identity in traditional Asian cultures, especially during ethnic gatherings, may explain the high incidence of food-related activities as part of their leisure lifestyles.

Leisure activities that are culturally oriented are highly prevalent among Asian Americans (Sasidharan). This pattern might suggest the possibility of using cultural activities as part of the ethnic identity reinforcement process among Asian American groups, whereby closer social networks (or ties) are established between subethnic members through group recreation and leisure activities.

*See also:* Urbanization of Leisure

## BIBLIOGRAPHY

Day, Jennifer C. "Population Projections of the United States by Age, Race, and Hispanic Origin: 1995 to 2050." In *Current Population Reports Series P25-1130.* U.S. Census Bureau. Washington, D.C.: U.S. Government Printing Office, 1996.

Eyler, Amy E., Sara Wilcox, Dyann Matson-Koffman, Kelly R. Evenson, Bonnie Sanderson, Janice Thompson, JoEllen Wilbur, and Deborah Rohm-Young. "Correlates of Physical Activity Among Women from Diverse Racial/Ethnic Groups." *Journal of Women's Health and Gender-Based Medicine* 11 (2002): 239–253.

Gobster, Paul H. "Managing Urban Parks for a Racially and Ethnically Diverse Clientele." *Leisure Sciences* 24 (2002): 143–159.

Gobster, Paul H., and Antonio Delgado. "Ethnicity and Recreational Use in Chicago's Lincoln Park: In-Park User Survey Findings." In *Managing Urban and High-Use Recreation Settings.* Edited by Paul H. Gobster. St. Paul, Minn.: U.S. Department of Agriculture, 1993.

Humes, Karen, and Jesse McKinnon. "The Asian and Pacific Islander Population in the United States: March 1999." In *Current Population Reports Series P20-529.* U.S. Census Bureau. Washington, D.C.: U.S. Government Printing Office, 2000.

Hutchison, Ray "Hmong Leisure and Recreation Activity." In *Managing Urban and High-Use Recreation Settings.* Edited by Paul H. Gobster. St. Paul, Minn.: U.S. Department of Agriculture, 1993.

Kibria, Nazil. "The Contested Meanings of 'Asian American': Racial Dilemmas in the Contemporary United States." *Ethnic and Racial Studies* 21 (1998): 939–958.

Rosenthal, Doreen A., and S. Shirley Feldman. "The Acculturation of Chinese Immigrants: Perceived Effects on Family Functioning of Length of Residence in Two Cultural Contexts." *Journal of Genetic Psychology* 151 (1990): 495–514.

Sanders, Jimy, Victor Nee, and Scott Sernau. "Asian Immigrants' Reliance on Social Ties in a Multiethnic Labor Market." *Social Forces* 81 (2002): 281–314.

Sasidharan, Vinod. "The Urban Recreation Experience: An Examination of Multicultural Differences in Park and Forest Visitation Characteristics." Ph.D. dissertation, Pennsylvania State University, 2001.

Schmidley, Dianne. "Profile of the Foreign-Born Population in the United States: 2000." In *Current Population Reports Series P23-206.* U.S. Census Bureau. Washington, D.C.: U.S. Government Printing Office, 2001.

———. "The Foreign-Born Population in the United States: March 2002." In *Current Population Reports Series P20-539.* U.S. Census Bureau. Washington, D.C.: U.S. Government Printing Office, 2003.

Shaull, Sandra L., and James H. Gramann. "The Effect of Cultural Assimilation on the Importance of Family-Related and Nature-Related Recreation Among Hispanic Americans." *Journal of Leisure Research* 30 (1998): 47–63.

Suminski, Richard R., Rick Petosa, Alan C. Uter, and James J. Zhang. "Physical Activity Among Ethnically Diverse College Students." *Journal of American College Health* 51 (2002): 75–80.

Tae-Ock, Kauh. "Intergenerational Relations: Older Korean-Americans' Experiences." *Journal of Cross-Cultural Gerontology* 12 (1997): 245–271.

Thompson, Kenneth. "Border Crossings and Diasporic Identities: Media Use and Leisure Practices of an Ethnic Minority." *Qualitative Sociology* 25 (2002): 409–418.

Yu, Ping, and Doris L. Berryman. "The Relationship Among Self-esteem, Acculturation, and Recreation Participation of Recently Arrived Chinese Immigrant Adolescents." *Journal of Leisure Research* 28 (1996): 251–273.

Zhang, Tingwei, and Paul H. Gobster. "Leisure Preferences and Open Space Needs in an Urban Chinese American Community." *Journal of Architectural and Planning Research* 15 (1998): 338–355.

*Vinod Sasidharan*

# ATLANTIC CITY

Atlantic City, located in southeastern New Jersey on the Atlantic Ocean, was founded in 1854 by a local doctor, Jonathan Pitney, and a Philadelphia civil engineer, Richard Osborne, who saw the site as an opportunity to provide health-giving cool sea breezes to city people in the summer. They built the Camden and Atlantic Railroad, the shortest railroad line connecting Philadelphia (sixty miles away) to the wide beaches of the Jersey shore. In 1870, in order to reduce the tramping of sand into stores and hotels, an eight-foot wide wooden walk was built, linking the beach with the town. Ten years later, a much longer boardwalk was constructed along the shore. Eventually, the wooden walkway extended six miles and was sixty feet wide. This innovation attracted genteel crowds who strolled along its smooth and sand-free walkway, delighting in the vistas of ocean and displaying themselves to other usually well-dressed walkers.

The new influx of customers led to the building of luxury hotels such as Surf House and United State Hotel, along with rooming houses and smaller, less commodious hotels for the middle class. Atlantic City became famous for its well-ordered beaches (controlled by a patrol established in 1881) and Sunday restrictions on drinking and popular music. Modern technology came early too, such as an electric trolley in 1893. Genteel standards were assured by the presence of substantial and large summer cottages used by the families of business and professional elites from Philadelphia.

Nevertheless, more plebeian crowds were attracted to the piers that sprang up along the boardwalk. These piers featured new mechanical rides in the 1890s, as well as freak shows and shooting galleries. While the town attempted to preserve a respectable middle-class social tone, pressure from the down-market day trippers with cheap train tickets from Philadelphia and New Jersey towns gradually eroded these standards.

By 1900, Atlantic City was drawing more than 100,000 visitors on peak summer weekends. In the twentieth century, attractions ranged from vaudeville and jazz bands to the Miss America pageant, which has been held in Atlantic City every September since 1921. Productions headed for Broadway often first tried out their shows in Atlantic City in the 1920s and 1930s.

These and other attractions failed to draw patrons after World War II, when the more affluent deserted the ocean-front hotels to rent or purchase beach houses on Long Beach Island, New Jersey; the Hamptons on Long Island, New York; or farther afield. Low-income vacationers also left the rooming houses for newer motels and flashier boardwalks elsewhere along the Jersey shore. The availability of cars freed vacationers from the old haunts of their train-dependent parents, and by the 1970s cheap and fast air travel, especially to the Caribbean and Florida (especially Disney World, established in 1971) further contributed to the decline of Atlantic City. The town had not only failed to invest in improvements, but its dependence on customers during the relatively short summer season made it impossible to compete with new southern resorts.

In 1976, New Jersey voters approved a referendum allowing casino gambling in Atlantic City. Promoters hoped to reverse the town's fortunes by introducing gamblers from the East Coast to legal and local games. By 1995, the city's casino industry employed 30,000 people directly and 40,000 in related industries; in 1993, 30 million visitors to the city wagered more than $3 billion in the city's thirteen major hotel-casinos. Once the nation's premier beach resort, Atlantic City (population 40,517 in 2000) became the East Coast's gambling mecca, with a daily pilgrimage made by many people of relatively modest means, often retirees traveling by bus, to its casinos.

The 1976 gambling referendum was intended to restore the city to prosperity and to yield revenue for the state's programs for education, senior citizens, and the disabled. Gambling revenues certainly aided these groups, but Atlantic City remained divided in the 1990s between the glitz of the beachfront casinos and the poverty of the rest of the city. Moreover, its future as a gambling center became uncertain as other states legalized casino and riverboat gambling or permitted Native Americans to operate casinos on their own territory.

Casino gambling brought prosperity back to the boardwalk, but hopes that gambling would restore prosperity to the entire city had not been met by the early 2000s. Most visitors to the city continued to be daytrippers, who went directly to the casinos and avoided the rest of the city. Additionally, casino jobs were held predominantly by commuters from outside the city. Decaying tenement buildings and empty lots still stood in the shadow of the casinos in the early twenty-first century,

**Trump casino.** One of entrepreneur Donald Trump's casinos towers over pedestrians on the Atlantic City boardwalk in New Jersey. Casinos brought an influx of cash to the famous New Jersey resort city, but critics say most of that money stays in the casinos and does little to develop the city's businesses or neighborhoods. © *PhotoEdit*

despite attempts by developers to diversify the city's economy with a convention center and shopping malls. Atlantic City has not suffered the fate of its New York counterpart, Coney Island, with the demolition of almost all of its early twentieth century attractions. However, as a representative of an earlier commercial leisure site built around a mix of genteel hotels, boardwalks, and shows on the one hand, and plebeian pleasures of amusement parks and sideshows on the other, it has only partially been able to shift to a new mode of commercialized leisure, modern casino gambling.

*See also:* Beaches, Gambling, Las Vegas, Senior Leisure Lifestyles

**BIBLIOGRAPHY**

Funnell, Charles. *By the Beautiful Sea: The Rise and High Times of That Great American Resort, Atlantic City.* New York: Random House, 1975.

Levi, Vicki Gold, and Lee Eisenberg. *Atlantic City: 125 Years of Ocean Madness.* New York, 1979.

Paulsson, Martin. *The Social Anxieties of Progressive Reform: Atlantic City, 1854–1920.* New York, 1994.

Riverol, Armando. *Live from Atlantic City: The History of the Miss America Pageant Before, After, and in Spite of Television.* Bowling Green, Ohio: Bowling Green State University Popular Press, 1992.

Sternlieb, George, and James W. Hughes. *The Atlantic City Gamble.* Cambridge, Mass.: Harvard University Press, 1983.

*Gary Cross*

# AUCTIONS

Among the most elementary forms of buyer-seller exchange, auctions are a public transaction of goods where items are sold to the highest bidder. As a means for conducting business, the flexibility of auctions allows them to take on a range of forms and serve a variety of social and commercial functions. Economists theorize that auctions are most useful when there is uncertainty about the right price or the real value of an object. In practice, however, auctions are just as valuable for the enjoyable interactions that take place between participants as they are for the exchange of goods and services.

## American Auctions from the Early Years to the Early Twenty-First Century

The history of auctions in the United States mirrors the lifestyles and values of the American people. Among colonial merchants, fish and fur were common auction wares. In agrarian communities, auctions were a prominent method for trading livestock and farm equipment. Prior to the abolition of slavery, auctions were the preferred method for buying and selling slaves in the American South. In urban locales, swap meets and penny markets turned up as an underground economy when there was a need for cheap used goods.

The history of what was sold at auction, from stamps to Beanie Babies, coins to autographs, weapons and firearms to jewelry, gives insight into what Americans collected during different time periods. In the early 2000s, auctions flourished in the Unites States as community organizations and charities held silent auctions to raise funds at their annual dinners. Individuals sold collectibles on Internet auction platforms. Members of the social A-list bid on fine art, celebrity paraphernalia, and culturally historical artifacts. Auctions can be light hearted and relaxing events, with an enjoyable atmosphere where people peruse the goods at open air flea markets, acquiring pieces of Americana. They can also be serious business ventures, as seen by the fact that nearly 7 percent of all real estate transactions in the United States in 2001 were conducted at auction.

## The Dynamics of Buyers and Sellers

The most common type of auction practiced in the United States in the early twenty-first century was the English auction. True to the entomology of the word auction (from the Latin, *auctio,* meaning to increase), this auction style starts bids at a low price and increases them as competing bidders better one another. The bidding continues until one bidder, the winner, remains.

Sellers in this type of auction tend to be less educated than bidders when it comes to knowing the price the goods could command at market. While sellers are sometimes simply looking to turn a part of their estate into

cash, bidders are often hobbyists, collectors, professional dealers, or representatives for institutional collections, who are well versed in what signifies value or rarity in an item. Because of this disparity in market knowledge, bidders are often drawn to auctions with hopes of being able to acquire items at less than their true value. Lesser-educated bidders will often try to take cues from industry insiders to acquire choice pieces. For this reason, bidders may choose not to reveal their expertise in a field. Bidding, however, is not an exact science, and bidding skill is not always commensurate with market knowledge. Emotion can often play a role in driving up the price of merchandise. When bidders become more motivated by emotion than by their understanding of the market, they can fall victim to the "winner's curse"—the realization that one has just bid more than the actual value of the item. In this case the winner has won the goods, but has lost more money than the goods are worth.

To improve their chances of getting a good price, sellers often employ a third party agent, an auctioneer or an auction house, to publicize the event, lure potential buyers, and conduct the sale. Auction houses will work with the seller to determine the opening bid amount and, if necessary, set a reserve price below which the seller is not willing to part with his or her goods. A reserve is also used as a preventative measure against collusive bidding, where dealers agree not to bid against each other to keep the price low, and later divide the goods among themselves. If the reserve is not met, the goods are "bought in" by the house and returned to the owner. After the sale, bidders who are still interested in items that went unsold can make an offer directly to the owner. For their services, the auction house charges the seller a percentage of the sale price that is returned to the auction house in the form of a buyer's premium. Traditionally, the buyer's premium is 15 percent of the winning bid for a sale $50,000 and less, 10 percent for sales in excess of $50,000.

## Participants in the Auction Event

An auction's appeal is frequently attributed to the thrilling experience and spectacle of the event. Auction houses call on the services of a wide variety of support staff to make the event successful, from transportation experts who make sure delicate products make it to the block unscathed to catalog production teams who photograph and market the goods. Auction houses employ industry specialists to research and determine the authenticity of goods, and keep these people on hand to counsel buyers and sellers on auction day. At large auctions, hundreds of hands are needed to register bidders, distribute bidding paddles, and serve concessions.

**Kennedy Onassis auction.** In New York City, Sotheby's CEO Diana Brooks takes bids during the estate sale of Jacqueline Kennedy Onassis (1929–1994) in April 1996. The event earned a total of $34 million, with proceeds going to Onassis's estate. © *AP/Wide World Photos*

The most important figure supplied by the auction house is the auctioneer. A skilled auctioneer can play a large role in an auction's success through his or her ability to relate to the bidders, build up the pageantry of the sale, and encourage a jovial and sociable setting. Whether they are selling high- or low-dollar goods, auctioneers do their best to evoke quintessential American sentiments: competition, freedom, control of one's destiny, and an entrepreneurial spirit. By perpetuating the myths of the market, buyers are encouraged to follow their dreams, and the audience participates more readily in the bidding.

Much like the conductor of a symphony, an auctioneer must balance the excitement of performance with technical control. Commanding the rostrum entails managing the emotions of bidders, setting the proper pace so that prices increase quickly, yet not so fast that control is compromised. Some say that one either has the talents of a good auctioneer or one doesn't, but this is not deterring would-be auctioneers from applying to auctioning schools. The success rate from Christie's auctioneering

schools in London and New York, however, speaks to the difficulty of mastering the auctioneer's skills and flare. Only one in three makes it to the rostrum.

The introduction of new technologies has opened the door to ever-wider audiences at auctions. Controlling the auction, however, now means that auctioneers must also monitor bids from those participating via telephone or computer. When these participants are solicited from countries that use a different currency, that introduces the challenge of converting bid into the currency used for the sale. To top it off, auctioneers are still expected to protect the anonymity of some bidders in the live audience. To remain anonymous, some people who prefer to use secret signs, like a subtle gesture or the lifting of one's glasses, rather than traditional bid indicators like colored numbered paddles provided by the auction house.

## Implications of the Auction House: Sotheby's, Christie's, and eBay

Two auction houses emerged in eighteenth-century England that persisted as the preeminent auction houses op-

**Carail Museum.** Richard Kughn's private Carail Museum in Detroit, Michigan, auctioned off its trains, vintage toys, artwork, and classic cars in a two-day event that was held by RM Auction beginning on 20 September 2003. Sales from the auction totaled $4.6 million and were highlighted by a world record price of $218,000 for this custom-built 1,500–square foot model train display. Shown here by museum employee Chris Pace, left, to Karl Fava and his eleven-year-old daughter Emily, the display includes eleven trains on five levels and featured hundreds of extremely rare Lionel period pieces. © *Paul Warner for AP/Wide World Photos*

erating in the early twenty-first century. Initially specializing in the auctioning of books and literary goods, Sotheby's was founded in 1744, and in 1766 Christie's opened its doors and started auctioning paintings and decorative arts. In the early 2000s, both houses auctioned goods from fine wines to photography to entire estates. As the range of goods sold at these auction houses expanded, and as they opened auctions on the Internet, their sales dollars increased. In its inaugural year, Sotheby's sold 826 sterling pounds of literary material. By 1999, Sotheby's auctions topped $2.25 billion, and in its inaugural year Sotheby's online drew in $53 million in sales.

In 1995, the emergence of eBay, the world's largest web auction house in the early twenty-first century, opened a new marketplace for the anonymous exchange of second-hand wares. The lucrative appeal of online auctions drew in 3.8 million participants to eBay alone in 1999. By 2003, eBay was predicting net revenues up to $1.55 billion. The lucrative appeal of such a high traffic online web site has prompted some to quit their jobs in

brick and mortar retail stores and set up shop exclusively on the cyber auction block.

Bidders at both online and live auctions are cautioned to beware the dangers of price fixing, collusion, fraudulent goods, and underhanded bidding practices. Between 1997 and 1999, incidents of reported online auction fraud increased hundred-fold from roughly 100 to 10,700, and in 2000, online auction fraud represented more than 50 percent of the consumer complaints on the Internet. In one publicized case, eBay invalidated the sale of a $135,000 painting when it was revealed that the seller had bid on his own work. Online auctions have had their share of success stories too, including the sale of an original copy of the Declaration of Independence that had been found inside a painting frame bought for $4 at a garage sale. When the document was sold for $8.14 million, it became the most expensive item ever auctioned online.

*See also:* Antiques, Computer's Impact on Leisure, Garage and Yard Sales, Internet

## BIBLIOGRAPHY

Belk, Russell W., John F. Sherry Jr., and Melanie Wallendorf. "A Naturalistic Inquiry into Buyer and Seller Behavior at a Swap Meet." *Journal of Consumer Research.* 14 (1988): 449–468.

Berman, Anne E., and Philip Herrera. "The Art of the Auctioneer." *Town and Country* 153 (1999): 109ff.

Cassady, Ralph, Jr. *Auctions and Auctioneering.* Berkeley: University of California Press, 1967.

Eisinger, Jane. "The Word on Silent Auctions . . . and When a Live or Combination Event Is a Better Option." *Association Management* 52 (2000): 67ff.

Goldberg, Robert J. "Going, Going, Gone!" *New Orleans Magazine* 36 (2002): 48+.

"Gregg Manning Discusses the Market for Collectibles and the Changing Art of Auctioneering." *Business News New Jersey* 10 (1997): 11.

Harden, Leland, and Bob Heyman. *The Auction-App: How Companies Tap the Power of Online Auctions to Maximize Growth.* New York: McGraw-Hill, 2002.

"The Heyday of the Auction." *Economist* 352 (1999): 67ff.

Hildesley, Hugh C. *The Complete Guide to Buying and Selling at Auction.* New York: W.W. Norton & Company, Inc., 1997.

Lacey, Robert. *Sotheby's—Bidding for Class.* Boston: Little, Brown and Company, 1998.

Maisel, Robert. "The Fleamarket as an Action Scene." *Urban Life and Culture* 2 (1974): 488–505.

Masciere, Christina. "New Orleans' Thriving, Auction Industry." *New Orleans Magazine* 30 (1996): 34ff.

O'Loughlin, Luanne, and Mary Millhollon. *Online Auctions: the Internet Guide for Bargain Hunters and Collectors.* Edited by Jaclyn Easton. New York: McGraw-Hill, 2000.

Reynolds, Kate. "Going . . . Going . . . Gone!" *Agorics Inc.* Available from http://www.agorics.com/.

Rothfeder, Jeffrey. "Going, Going, Gone!" *This Old House.* 8 (2003): 66ff.

Schuyler, Nina, and Gregg Keizer. "Going . . . Going . . . Gotcha!" *PC World* 18 (2000): 181ff.

Sotheby's Holdings, Inc. Annual Report 2000. Available from http://www.jumpmedia.net/.

Steiner, Ina. "eBay Releases 2nd Quarter Financials." *Auctionbytes-NewsFlash,* 362 (19 July 2002). Available from http://www.auctionbytes.com/.

Weilheimer, Neil. "Buying by Paddle." *Commercial Property News* 17 (2003): 14

*Caitlin W. Haskell*

# AUTO RACING

In auto racing, drivers compete amid breakdowns and crashes in order to reach the finish line first. They race on drag strips, deserts, city streets, road courses, and closed-circuit tracks made of asphalt or dirt. The cars they race are as diverse as the races in which they compete. Stock cars resemble ordinary passenger cars, while some dragsters have long slender frames with large wide back tires and small narrow front tires, plus a parachute for stopping. Open-wheel racers are characterized by a bullet shape with a single seat and exposed wheels.

## Automobile Development and Auto Racing: A Parallel Progression

The concomitant development of the automobile and rise of auto racing began in the United States during the late 1800s. The first recorded automobile race, however, wasn't really a race at all, and it didn't occur in the United States. The Paris to Rouen race in France in 1894 was more of a reliability test with the purpose of motivating European inventors to work the kinks out of their self-propelled vehicles so that they could travel farther and faster in a dependable fashion.

Meanwhile, Americans hoping to strike it rich worked to transform a nation of horses and buggies into one of automobiles. Would-be inventors designed vehicles that were powered by everything from steam and electricity to gasoline. It was not until 21 September 1893, however, when brothers Frank and Charles Duryea affixed a one-cylinder gasoline engine to a carriage that the U.S. automobile era was born.

As news of early European auto races crossed the ocean, a *Chicago Times Herald* newspaper correspondent convinced his boss, H. H. Kohlsaat, to organize the first race on U.S. soil. Intrigued by the circulation possibilities for his paper, Kohlsaat set the date of 2 November 1895 for a race from Chicago to Evanston and back. Nearly 100 eager auto builders signed up, but only two cars arrived to race that day.

Kohlsaat, hoping to garner more entrants, postponed the race to Thanksgiving Day. This time five cars showed up for the fifty-four-mile-long race: an electric, three Benz, and a Duryea. A major snowstorm hampered a sixth driver's efforts to get to the starting line. After more than eight hours, Frank Duryea won $2,000 when his gasoline-powered car crossed the finish line traveling an average of 7.5 miles per hour. More than an hour later the second and last car, Oscar Mueller's Benz, crossed the line. The facts remain dubious about who actually crossed the line with Mueller's car, as some reports indicate that Mueller had collapsed from the cold. Other cars either crashed or quit working. Still, the race proved successful for the *Chicago Times Herald* as eager readers sought to

**Barney Oldfield.** Known as the first to drive a car a mile a minute in 1903, Barney Oldfield (1878–1946) was an auto racing pioneer who enjoyed driving fast cars such as his "Lightning" Blitzen Benz. © *AP/Wide World Photos*

learn everything about the race, the automobiles, and their drivers.

The next race in the United States occurred in 1896 and was 104 miles long. *Cosmopolitan* magazine organized the race from Manhattan to Irvington-on-Hudson, New York, and back, with a grand prize of $3,000. Only three of the six race entrants made it out of Manhattan. Those three cars, unable to ascend Ardsley Hill in Westchester, had to be pushed to the top by spectators. Frank Duryea eventually won that race as well.

## Impact of Early Auto Racing

Early auto racing had both a social and technological impact on American society. Prior to the Rhode Island State Fair in 1896, auto races were run on road courses. That year the fair organizers planned the first race on a closed-circuit dirt track previously used for harness (horse) rac-

ing. This approach proved lucrative for the organizers because the estimated 50,000 spectators could be charged admission. Meanwhile, contented fans were able to watch the entire race from one location. By 2003, U.S. racing venues were predominated by closed-circuit tracks with elaborate spectator stands.

Advancing the development of the automobile was K. K. Vanderbilt's primary objective when he organized a series of road races on Long Island in 1904. The Vanderbilt Cup, the first race in the series, was won by A. L. Campbell in a Mercedes that averaged about thirty miles per hour. Eighteen cars entered the race, with only five having been made in America. Controlling the spectators was a difficult task; some were nearly killed as they ran out into the road to see the cars pass. Although the Vanderbilt races were recognized for the publicity they gave to auto racing, especially through newspaper reporting, they eventually were discontinued when foreign cars kept winning the races and too many accidents affected both drivers and onlookers. Still, the Vanderbilt races were so influential to society that a Broadway musical—*Vanderbilt Cup*—was named after them. As middle-class fans followed the races, automaker Henry Ford began to see increases in passenger-car sales.

Three transcontinental auto races during the early 1900s underscored the need for reliable cars, as well as a reliable road system complete with signs and maps. Newspapers reporting on the coast-to-coast racing events influenced the public to buy autos. It took only ten years to move auto racing in the United States and Europe into a highly popular and exciting sport characterized by the juxtaposition of humans and mechanical technology.

## Geographic Division of Racing Types

Some of the most common types of automobiles raced in the United States include, but are not limited to, stock cars, dragsters, Formula 1 cars, and Indy-style cars. Many of these racing types share the same racing venues today; however, each originated in different geographic regions.

**Stock Car Origins** The genesis of stock cars occurred in the South during the Prohibition era between the 1920s and 1930s. Southern bootleggers in the business of transporting illegal alcohol used passenger cars that had been modified to travel faster and handle better in order to flee the police. They continued to transport moonshine after Prohibition because it was less expensive and had a higher alcohol content than the legal brands, resulting in the development of even faster cars. Soon interest arose in finding out which bootlegger's car was the fastest. Illegal races were organized in cow pastures on tracks made of dirt. Onlookers tipped bottles of moonshine as they watched drivers who donned old football helmets for protection.

During the mid-1930s, city officials in Daytona, Florida, organized a series of beach races for the so-called stock cars. In 1937, William France began promoting the races until they were interrupted by World War II. After the war, dirt-track races continued to grow in popularity at places like Pennsboro Motor Speedway in West Virginia, which was originally converted from a horse track.

Bill France's creation of the National Association for Stock Car Automobile Racing (NASCAR) in 1947 promoted stock car racing throughout the South. More tracks were quickly constructed around the region as the sport grew in popularity. The most famous track for stock car racing, the Daytona Speedway, was completed in 1959. Lee Petty won the first Daytona 500, with an average speed of 135.521 miles per hour.

The popularity of stock car racing has evolved from its southern origins to become a sport with national appeal. A key event that brought stock car racing into national prominence was when the NASCAR Winston Cup series (stock car racing's top level, which was renamed the Nextel Cup starting in 2004) introduced the Brickyard 400 race at the Indianapolis Motor Speedway (IMS) in 1994. The race was significant because the speedway—which for years had hosted only Indy car races—was considered to be the mecca of U.S. auto racing. By racing at Indianapolis, NASCAR proved it had national—not just regional—appeal. In 2004, racetracks were located all over the United States, offering both professional- and amateur-level stock car events.

**Indy Car Origins** Unlike stock cars, the Indy car has its roots in the northern region of the United States. The name "Indy" car originated from the Indianapolis 500 race held at the Indianapolis Motor Speedway. The 2.5-mile-long rectangular speedway, constructed in 1909, held its first Indy 500 in 1911.

The American Automobile Association (AAA), through the races it sanctioned across the country, was instrumental in promoting Indy car racing. During World War II, however, racing in all forms was sparse. In 1955, after more than eighty people were killed at a race in Le Mans, France, the AAA quit sanctioning auto races and the U.S. Auto Club (USAC) took over as the American sanctioning body in racing.

During the 1970s, several Indy car drivers felt USAC was no longer meeting their needs, so they broke away from USAC and formed Championship Auto Racing Teams (CART) in 1978. CART sanctioned races in the United States, Canada, and Australia each year on four distinct types of tracks: large ovals, short ovals, permanent road courses, and temporary road courses. Large ovals are generally between 2 and 2.5 miles long and are characterized by speedways, such as those at Indianapolis and the Michigan International Speedway in Brooklyn, Michigan. The Pennsylvania International Raceway epitomizes the second type of track, which is a short, mile-long oval. The Mid-Ohio Sports Car Course characterizes the third type, a 2.4-mile-long permanent road course with fifteen turns. The last type is a temporary road course that may be completed on city streets as well as highways.

Since 1996 there have been two top levels of open-wheel racing in the United States: CART, and the Indy Racing League (IRL). The IRL was founded by IMS president Tony George, who wanted to make it easier for American drivers to race in a top-level Indy car circuit. He developed a separate race series with its own racing schedule, which of course included the famous Indy 500. To complicate matters, the IRL restricted the number of CART cars that could compete in the Indy 500. CART, in retaliation, created a competing event called the U.S. 500, to be held on the same date as the Indy 500. This created a dilemma: the Indy 500 was the best race, but CART had all the top drivers, meaning that fans would ultimately have to decide which event they would attend: the Indy 500, with virtually unknown race drivers, or the new, unknown event (the U.S. 500) with all the top-level drivers.

The split between the two organizing bodies remained contentious until 2000. That year, a CART driver raced in the Indy 500 for the first time since the breakup. In fact, not only did a CART driver run in the race—he won it. Juan Montoya, racing for the Chip Gannasi team, stunned IRL drivers when he raced to victory. Another CART driver, Helio Castroneves, won the race in 2001. Castroneves won again in 2002, but by then he was once again an IRL driver—earlier that year, his team owner, Roger Penske, became the first major owner to switch from CART to IRL.

Despite these moves toward reconciliation, as of 2003, many differences still existed between the two groups. CART allowed their cars to be turbocharged and raced on both oval courses and road courses in North America, Europe, and Australia. The IRL did not allow turbochargers and raced on ovals, D-ovals, and tri-ovals in North America only. Open-wheel racing aficionados were optimistic that CART and IRL would eventually be able to resolve their differences and reunite, as the division between the two led to lower attendance and fan support, less media attention, and the impression that an inferior product was being put on the track because the best drivers were not facing each other every week.

**Formula I** Compared to Indy cars, Formula 1 (F1) cars have a unique history due to strong European origins. Another distinguishing feature of F1 is the international race series that they compete in called the Grand Prix. F1 drivers are the highest paid and most elite racers in the world, having established their skills in lower echelons of racing, such as Formula 3.

**Al Unser Sr.** The 62nd Indianapolis 500 (1978) was won by Al Unser Sr. (1939– ). He won the race again in 1987, making him a four-time champion of the event. © *AP/Wide World Photos*

The first Grand Prix race organized by the Automobile Club of France occurred in 1906 in Le Mans, France. Francois Szisz, driving a Renault, won the two-day-long competition, which involved racing twelve laps around a 103-kilometer closed track. A key factor in his win was the quick tire changes made with his detachable Michelin rims. Everyday drivers eventually benefitted from such innovations when automakers and tire manufacturers passed the improvements on to their consumer divisions. The first American Grand Prix was held in Savannah, Georgia, in 1908 and was followed by eight years of races until 1916 when the open-wheel Indianapolis 500 race captured the allure of fans with its speedway and spectator stands.

Race cars had no weight or engine restrictions until 1904 when the Federation Internationale de l'Automobile (FIA) introduced the first "formula." When Formula 1 began in 1948, the FIA invoked specifications largely for engine capacity, car design, and weight, with the formulae changing every few years.

The World Driver's Championship and the manufacturer's championship were created in 1950 and 1958, respectively. According to FIA regulations, there must be at least eight and no more than sixteen races held annually in order to award the World Championship Driver and World Championship Constructor titles. Although the races take place around the world, most occur in Europe, and only one takes place in the United States (Indianapolis Motor Speedway).

**Drag Racing Origins** Much like stock car racing, drag racing also had illegal beginnings. In the 1930s, young drivers in southern California began racing side by side on city streets, back roads, lonely stretches of highway, and even on dry lake beds to see whose car was the fastest. It is said that the term "drag racing" refers to the powerful acceleration of the engine that forces the front wheels up into the air, thus sometimes dragging the rear of the car on the pavement. Dragsters are also called "hot rods." The basic objective of drag racing is to see which of two drivers can cross the finish line first in a quarter-mile-long race.

Finding places to race was a problem due to the illegal nature of the sport. Still, California became an early leader in drag racing history when, in 1950, the state highway patrol permitted the use of the tarmacs on a closed-down naval air base for racing. A year later the National Hot Rod Association (NHRA) was formed. Strict rules for participation ensured the sport's safety. In less than ten years the sport had strong national appeal as rivalries developed between the two coasts. In 2003, twenty-three national events were scheduled to be held at twenty drag strips throughout the nation.

## Diversification of Types of Autos Raced

Race cars can be compared according to general appearance (stock versus open wheel) and by comparing the races in which they participate. Based solely on appearance, most stock cars look like modified versions of ordinary sedans that are used on streets and highways. Open-wheel racers have single seats, are low to the ground, and exist for the sole purpose of racing (see Figure 1 for a comparison of stock to open wheel cars).

**FIGURE 1**

Race car comparisons: stock car vs. open wheel

|  | Stock car | Open wheel | | |
|---|---|---|---|---|
|  | Winston Cup | Indy Car | Champ Car | Formula 1 |
| Shape | Passenger car | Bullet shaped | Bullet shaped | Wedge shaped |
| Driver's position | Left front side | Centered low | Centered low | Centered low |
| Open wheels | No | Yes | Yes | Yes |
| Height | 51″ | 37″ | 37″ | 38″ |
| Weight | 3400 lbs. without driver | 1550 lbs. without driver | 1550 lbs. without driver | 1322 lbs. without driver |
| Length | N/A | 193.74″ | 195″ | 173″ |
| Width | N/A | 79.55″ | 79″ | 71″ |
| Fuel | Octane gasoline | Methanol | Methanol | High Octane gasoline |
| Transmission | Manual (4 gears) | Manual (6 gears) | Manual (4–6 gears) | Semiautomatic (4–7 gears) |
| Horsepower | 700+ | 650+ | 830+ | 800+ |
| Roll bar | Yes | Yes | Yes | Yes |
| Windshield, rearview mirror, fenders, front/rear bumpers | Yes | No | No | No |
| Wheel base | 110″ | 110″ minimum | 120–126″ | 106–120″ |
| Tires | 15″ | 15″ | 15″ | 14″ |
| Traction control | Not allowed | Not allowed | Allowed | Allowed |
| Engine location | Under front hood | Rear | Rear | Rear |
| Engine | 358 cubic inches V8 | 3.5 L V8 | 2.65 L V8 Turbo | 3.0 L V10 |
| Top speed | Approx. 200 m.p.h. | Approx. 230 m.p.h. | Approx. 240 m.p.h. | Approx. 225 m.p.h. |

SOURCE: CART Car comparisons, 2002.

**FIGURE 2**

**Comparison of top-level auto races**

| | Nextel Cup (NASCAR) | Indy Cars (IRL) | Champ Cars (CART) | Formula 1 (FIA) |
|---|---|---|---|---|
| Start of race | At race speed using pace car | At race speed using pace car | At race speed using pace car | Stopped position |
| Number of races annually | 39 | 16–17 | 20 | 16 |
| Race locations | Only U.S. | Mostly U.S., plus one in Japan (2003) | International | International |
| Racing circuit | Ovals | Ovals | Ovals and Road courses | Road course |
| Number of cars raced | 33 | | | |
| Race duration | Unlimited | Unlimited | Unlimited | 2 hours |
| Drivers accessible to fans? | Yes | Yes | Yes | No |
| Rain during race | Race is delayed | Race is delayed | Race is delayed | Race continues with grooved tires |

SOURCE: Vielhaber, Dan. Dan s Indianapolis Motor Speedway Homepage. Available from http://www.indymotorspeedway.com/. 2002.

Another way to illustrate the differences among race cars is to compare selected aspects of the races such as the overall objective, shape of the track, location of races, and so forth. Compared to other top-level race series, Formula 1 is the only race with a time limit of two hours. The other races (Nextel Cup, IRL, and CART) complete a designated number of miles within the shortest amount of time. Formula 1 has another distinguishing feature in that the race is not delayed by rain—grooved tires are put on the cars and the race is continued (see Figure 2).

Dragsters are vehicles that participate in a unique kind of race unlike the other top-level racing cars. Top Fuel cars belong to the highest and fastest level of drag racing in the National Hot Rod Association. They are characterized by large wide back wheels and small thin front wheels that sit on a long chassis with the driver sitting down low and in the center.

The 6,000-horsepower cars are raced two at a time over a quarter-mile strip, reaching speeds of over 300 miles per hour in less than six seconds. A parachute is released at the finish line to aid in deceleration. Top Fuel cars must weigh at least 2,150 pounds (including the driver) and have a wheelbase of 180 to 300 inches. In addition to the Top Fuel class, the NHRA also offers the Funny Car class, which features a wide variety of cars that started out as everyday sedans or coupes that were then wildly modified for racing, and the Pro Stock class, in which the cars must be a two-door sedan or two-door coupe with stock headlights and parking lights that is no more than five years old (National Hot Rod Association). Although there are many other types of racing cars, those described in this section are perhaps the most recognizable to Americans due to television broadcasts, marketing, and advertising.

## Participation of Auto Manufacturers in Racing

In addition to designing street vehicles, automakers design cars and car parts for Nextel Cup, IRL, CART, and Formula 1 cars, as well as for lower levels of racing. In the early 2000s, open-wheel cars were built by a combination of foreign and domestic automakers. For years, Nextel Cup stock cars were made entirely by domestic manufacturers Chevrolet, Pontiac, Ford, and Dodge, but in 2004, Toyota began racing that circuit for the first time.

Indy cars were originally made in the United States; however, in the early 2000s, the chassis used in the IRL were either Italian (Dallara) or British (G-Force). American manufactures still dominated IRL car engines (Chevrolet and Infiniti) and tires (Firestone).

CART car chassis were also made in Britain (Lola and Reynard) and were noted for their lightweight, yet strong composite materials. Engines were either Japanese (Toyota and Honda) or American (Ford). Firestone made the tires for all CART cars.

All Formula 1 chassis, engines, and tires were foreign made. Some manufacturers built both the engine and chassis for the same car. Hybrid cars obtained parts from several makers. Participating auto manufacturers in Formula 1 included, but were not limited to, Ferrari, Mercedes, Renault, BMW, Porsche, and Honda. Several manufacturers who specialized in race cars were Benetton, Williams, and McLaren. F1 cars used tires made by Michelin (France) or Bridgestone (United States).

## Track Development

Early auto racing took place on road courses, converted harness tracks, and dirt tracks. When Carl Fisher built the closed-circuit track known as the Indianapolis Speedway in 1909, he envisioned its use for testing new automobiles as well as for competition. The original track surface, made of crushed stones and tar, was not very durable and resulted in potholes and serious accidents, so it was repaved entirely with bricks. Asphalting of portions of the track began between 1936 and 1937; by 1939, only one yard of bricks remained at both the start and finish lines, and it remained that way into the 2000s. The famous nickname for the track—"the Brickyard"—came from the more than 3 million bricks used to replace the original stone and tar surface.

Tracks in the United States continue to expand in size (track length) and seating capacity. Condominiums, luxury boxes, and suites are fast becoming standard features at racetracks. At some tracks, lighting has increased the number of night races. Traffic flow to, from, and around racetracks has been under constant improvement especially due to the growing popularity of NASCAR racing. Other attractions at or near racetracks include museums, gift shops, and even driving schools for those interested in driving a race car.

Race ovals range in length from less than 1 mile to 2.5 miles and have three general shapes: oval, tri-oval, or D-shaped. The degree of banking in the turns and length of the straightaways varies widely from track to track. Bristol Motor Speedway has the highest banks in Nextel Cup racing at 36 degrees, compared to the turns at Indianapolis, which are banked at only 12 degrees (Buchanan). As a rule, stock cars are associated with higher banked turns than open wheel cars. Wide tracks or "grooves" allow for side-by-side racing by as many as three cars. Narrow, or single-groove tracks, offer less side-by-side racing. Road courses like the one at Watkins Glen, New York, have many turns, producing slower racing speeds as drivers maneuver the curves.

According to the NHRA, there are twenty official drag strips in the United States. The strips are a quarter-mile in length and are located as separate venues or within other auto racing venues, such as super speedways. Near the drag strip is the pit area, where final car adjustments are made before the race. From the pit area, drivers move to a staging area, where they await the start of their race.

Within this area and near the starting line is the box where drivers warm up their tires (also known as "slicks") just prior to the race.

At the drag-strip starting gate, in the middle of the strip, is the Chrondek Timer, which is more commonly known as the "Christmas tree" because of the series of colored lights that adorn each side of the timer. The lights signify a countdown to the start of the race, beginning with red lights at the top, then amber in the middle, and, finally, the green light at the bottom. Once the two cars race over the quarter-mile strip, they enter a half-mile-long shutdown strip to decelerate after the race. The fastest cars use parachutes that deploy out of the back of the car for deceleration. The dragster leaves the strip via a turnout road near the end of the drag strip.

## Technological Developments

"Race on Sunday, Sell on Monday" has been a common slogan for auto manufacturers, suggesting that first-place finishers help promote sales the next business day. Automakers use the racetrack as an automotive proving ground before innovations are incorporated into passenger models. Ford, for example, in collaboration with CART and Sensor Technologies, has designed a crash sensor box that evaluates crashes, much like a black box in airliners. Eventually the data will be used create safer cars through the use of computer simulations of crash impacts.

Computers inside race cars send chassis and engine information to pit crews. Also, instrument panels display information to the driver, such as water temperature, laps times, and engine speed. NASCAR fans could purchase scanners and heavy-duty earphones to follow all the conversations between their favorite driver and pit crew for a complete, uncensored race perspective (For fans who prefered to watch races on television, such in-car commentary was also made available on some satellite and digital cable television systems on a pay-per-view basis.)

The concern for safety has been the impetus for many technological developments in auto racing. Starting with the driver, protective fire suits and helmets are standard in all forms of professional racing. Drag racing drivers also must wear full-face breather masks. A special head and neck protection unit called the HANS device is used by NASCAR and CART drivers to reduce serious injuries associated with the violent head and helmet movements that happen during auto racing accidents. The device, made of Kevlar and carbon fiber, is connected to the helmet in a manner that restricts extreme head and neck movements.

## Amateur and Professional Racing Organizations

Generally, within each racing sanctioning body are several levels of racing, culminating in a top level that features the best, most well-known drivers. NASCAR's top series is the Nextel Cup, while the IRL offers the IndyCar Series, CART has the FedEx Championship Series, the FIA (Formula 1) has the Grand Prix, and the NHRA offers the POWERade Drag Racing Series. Below those top-level circuits are lower-levels that offer drivers and owners a means of breaking into their sport, although some teams are content to remain at the lower levels and have no desire to move up to the highest tier. Others enter the lower levels with the expressed intent of one day racing at their sport's highest level. Figure 3 shows the names of each of the racing circuits offered by the sports' major sanctioning bodies.

It used to be that race car drivers aspired to be Indy car drivers and win the Indy 500; however, in the late 1990s, Nextel Cup and Formula 1 attracted many promising drivers. Part of the allure to race on the Nextel Cup circuit is that it could be a lucrative option for stock car drivers due to its increased popularity and the number of races in a season (thirty-nine compared to sixteen in the IRL in 2003).

A plethora of racing opportunities around the country awaits amateur motor sports enthusiasts in all racing forms and skill levels. Central to the mission of both professional and amateur racing organizations is a commitment to safety. Many top-level professional drivers begin their racing careers by moving up from amateur racing to the professional ranks.

The Sports Car Club of America (SCCA) has membership levels for professionals and amateurs. The professional-level Trans-Am Series of the SCCA is the oldest road-racing series in North America that is open to sedans and sports cars. Many top-level drivers in the IRL, Formula 1, or NASCAR get their start in places like the Trans-Am Series. The amateur section of SCCA has every kind of racing, from open-wheel to modified street cars and sports cars.

The FIA supports the organization of both amateur and professional motor sport events through member clubs in participating countries. FIA is most noted for the establishment of racing regulations covering a wide range of racing series including Formula 1, Formula 3, European Touring Car, Sports Car, and World Rally, to name a few.

The National Auto Sport Association (NASA) also provides racing opportunities for aspiring as well as accomplished racers. NASA establishes rules and regulations for series such as the American Stock Car Challenge, the

**FIGURE 3**

Racing series by sanctioning bodies

| NASCAR | IRL | CART | Formula 1 | NHRA |
|---|---|---|---|---|
| Nextel Cup | Infiniti Pro Series | FedEx | Grand Prix | PowerAde Series |
| Busch Series | | Toyota Atlantic | | Lucas Oil Series |
| Craftsman Truck | | Barber Dodge Pro | | Summit Sport Compact Series |
| | | Formula Dodge | | Pro Bonus Series |

Camaro/Mustang Challenge, and the Classic Roadster. The Race Car Club of America is for beginning Formula-style drivers and races on both ovals and road courses. Located mostly in the Northeast, the group's of providing race opportunities at a "reasonable cost" is popular among members.

## Increasing Numbers of Spectators

Auto racing is a popular spectator sport in the United States. U.S. Census figures from 1999 indicated that auto racing events had the second highest monthly attendance by adults, 9,272,000, which was surpassed only by baseball, with 20,022,000. Research by Simmons Market Research Bureau, Inc. and Performance Research (in Champion Marketing) reported that motor sports were the fastest-growing spectator sport in the United States. Spectatorship continued to rise due to television coverage, suitability of auto racing as a spectator sport, and brand loyalty of fans. As a result, Champion Marketing claimed that hundreds of major corporations were using motor sports in their marketing tactics.

Goodyear Tire and Rubber Company estimated that 17,079,004 people attended twelve North American racing series in 1998. This figure was up 21 percent from 13,123,706 estimated attendees in 1992 (Goodyear Racing). Goodyear's general manager of worldwide racing, Stu Grant, indicated that the annual attendance reports would no longer be published after 1998 because it was felt that individual sanctioning bodies were better prepared to monitor racing attendance. The Goodyear race attendance figures from 1998 indicated that the most popular racing series was NASCAR with 37 percent of the total attendance. Attendance at CART Champ cars and NHRA events followed in second and third place with 15 percent and 13 percent, respectively.

## NASCAR's Popularity

As of 1999, between 15 and 17 million people watched NASCAR every year (Weissman). Bell South, 3M, and Lycos joined the sponsorship ranks, along with the more traditional tobacco, alcohol, and car parts companies; and they were experiencing tremendous success in doing so. Half of NASCAR fans were shown to have annual incomes over $50,000, and 64 percent were married. Women made up almost 40 percent of NASCAR fans. Twenty-two percent had college degrees, and another 24 percent had some college.

Fan loyalty in NASCAR was largely responsible for the financial success of sponsorship, as fans supported their sponsor's products. Another reason for NASCAR's growing popularity was the Entertainment and Sports Programming Network (ESPN). ESPN brought NASCAR racing to the forefront by using well-designed graphics, erudite announcers, and camera technology in the cars (Buchanan). While ESPN no longer carried NASCAR (as of 2003, NASCAR had moved to Fox and NBC, as well as other cable networks) Buchanan argued that ESPN built the foundation.

## Conclusion

From the early races with just six entrants to 2004's plethora of high-tech racing cars, series, and venues, auto racing has become a part of the American psyche. Race car drivers range from the weekend amateur stock car drivers at local dirt tracks to highly paid professionals. Auto manufacturers use racing to test technological innovations that result in passenger cars that are safer, more efficient, and of higher quality. Americans' love affair with racing is growing and parallels its love affair with the automobile. As long as one does well, so will the other. Perhaps it is just a matter of time before auto racing becomes the number one spectator sport in the United States.

*See also:* Auto Shows, Automobiles and Leisure, Drag Racing, Hot Rodding, Open Wheel Racing, Sports Car Racing, Stock Car Racing

### BIBLIOGRAPHY

Accipiter, A. "A Field Guide to Open Wheel Race Cars." Available from http://www.fortunecity.com/silverstone.

Buchanan, Keith. *Complete Guide to Stock Car Racing.* Charlottesville, Va.: Howell Press, 2001.

Champion Marketing. "Motorsports Demographics." Available from http://www.championmarketingteam.com/.

Chick, Garry. "Formula 1 Auto Racing." In *Encyclopedia of World Sport: From Ancient Times to the Present.* Edited by D. Levinson and K. Christensen, Santa Barbara, Calif.: ABC-CLIO, 1996.

Ford Racing. "Racing Technology: Safety." Available from http://www.fordracing.com/.

Formula 1 Database. "Frequently Asked Questions." Available from http://www.f1db.com/formula1/.

Goodyear Racing. "1998 Goodyear Racing Attendance Report." Available from http://www.racegoodyear.com/98attend.html.

Indy Racing On-line. "2002 Indy Racing League Tracks." Available from http://www.indyracing.com/.

Jenkins, Chris. "Indy Racing Eats NASCAR's Dust." *USA Today.* (10 May 2000): p. 1C.

McConnell, Curt. *Coast-to-Coast Auto Races of the Early 1900s: Three Contests That Changed the World.* Warrendale, Pa.: Society of Automobile Engineers, 2000.

National Association of Stock Car Auto Racing (NASCAR). "Manufacturers." Available from http://www.nascar.com/.

National Hot Rod Association. "About National Hot Rod Association." Available from http://www.nhra.com.

North American Sports Pages. "Oval Track Racing." Available from http://www.na-motorsports.com/.

Sports History. "Auto Racing Early History." Available from http://www.hickoksports.com/.

Stewart, Mark. *Auto Racing: A History of Fast Cars and Fearless Drivers.* New York: Franklin Watts, 1998.

Toyota Racing Development. "About Us." Available from http://www.trdusa.com.

U.S. Bureau of the Census. *Adult Attendance at Sports Events: 1999.* Bureau of the Census: Washington, D.C., 2001.

Motor Sports. *USA Today.* Available from http://www.usatoday.com/.

Vielhaber, Dan. Dan's Indianapolis Motor Speedway Available from http://www.indymotorspeedway.com/.

Weissman, Rachel. "The Green Flag Is Up." *American Demographics* 21, no. 4 (April 1999): 33–36.

Wukovits, John. *The Composite Guide to Auto Racing.* Philadelphia: Chelsea House Publications, 1998.

Young, Jesse. *Indy Cars.* Minneapolis, Minn.: Capstone Press, 1995.

*Barbara Elwood Schlatter*

# AUTO SHOWS

Almost immediately after the invention of the automobile, manufacturers and designers eagerly sought a venue to promote their inventions, discuss the future of this growing industry, and prove the worthiness of the automobile as a form of transportation. They soon discovered that automotive shows were an effective platform to share their inventions and new product developments to a fascinated public. Automotive shows are entertainment events open to the public for the purpose of bringing consumers together with automotive manufacturers and their products. These events frequently mix automotive technology with an entertaining atmosphere in order to provide information on new products, a place to dream about owning exotic cars, and an opportunity to relive past automotive eras.

## Fledging Events for a Fledgling Industry

The first major auto show was held in Chicago on 23 March 1901. Dozens of other auto shows quickly appeared as this new invention brought out spectators, curiosity seekers, and doubters. Many of the earliest auto show participants were more likely to be attracted to the novelty of automobiles and the spectacle of the show rather than out of a sincere interest in purchasing a new car. For example, in 1907, the first auto show in Atlanta attracted 150,000 spectators over a seven-day period, yet only 1,300 motorcars were actually owned by its citizens at that time (Metro Atlanta Automobile Dealers Association). Compared to later auto shows, these early events were modest affairs, taking place under a single carnival tent or fairground. The Los Angeles Auto Show was originally held under a large circus-style tent. The now famous North American International Auto Show was first held at a Detroit beer garden in 1907, where seventeen exhibitors showcased thirty-three vehicles.

The earliest auto shows focused on automobile displays and demonstrations. However, given that the ordinary family attended these events for recreational purposes, show planners experimented with many other forms of entertainment as a way to entice widespread participation and acceptance from the public. Similar to circuses, fairs, and other expositions of that era, spectator-oriented recreational activities such as contests, races, live musical performances, and food were ubiquitous at these early auto shows. For example, the Chicago Auto Show included a test track for manufacturers and inventors to prove to a skeptical public that their automobiles actually could run. However, despite the obvious recreational quality of auto shows, shows during this era focused primarily on promoting automobiles as a viable transportation alternative.

## From Automotive Curiosity to Obsession

In a span of just twenty years, the growing popularity of the automobile had moved auto shows into the mainstream of American culture. With this transformation also came a change in the characteristics and motivations of auto show attendees. That maintaining the public's thirst for new product designs and innovations would be essential to the growth of this fledgling industry was quickly apparent. In the mid-1920s, the adoption of planned product obsolescence allowed manufacturers to keep the public interested in purchasing new vehicles (and new designs) more frequently. This policy helped to ensure that public interest in new automotives would be sustainable. As competition intensified among the automotive Big Three ( Ford Motor Company, General Motors, and Chrysler), auto shows were used to stimulate buying behavior and brand loyalty, rather than to merely prove the worthiness of the automobile. Automotive dealers partnered with the manufacturers to produce auto shows to showcase the newest innovations and styles that the different brands had to offer. Auto shows often provided the public's first chance of seeing new vehicles and style changes, comparing new models, and fantasizing about the latest automotive inventions/designs. The American public was no longer a passive onlooker, but rather an active participant in learning about and purchasing automotive innovations, and in defining how automobiles fit into both their work and recreational lifestyles. The growth in auto shows during this time period was remarkable. For example, attendance at the Chicago Auto Show grew from 4,000 in 1901 to more than 200,000 by 1941.

## The Modern Auto Show

During the 1930s and 1940s, public interest in automobiles and attendance at auto shows was tempered by the hardships of the Great Depression and the manufacturing demands of World War II. However, in 1949, automotive supply and demand began to favor the industry. Auto shows made a comeback during this era and, in the early 2000s, remained a mainstay of American and international automotive culture. The addition of more extravagant displays and entertainment added to the excitement of the new automobiles and broadened the appeal of auto shows to an even wider family audience. It was during this modern era that the concept car became an important part of the auto show. Concept cars were futuristic designs that were used to spark public imagination and test new technologies or styles before they went into production. Concept cars were used not only to create excitement at the shows, but also to gauge market feasibility for new innovations on existing models. Public reaction to concept cars helped the manufacturers to determine which concepts were marketable and from which segment of the public they were desired.

**Chicago Auto Show.** Saab vehicles were among the automobiles on exhibit during the eighty-ninth annual Chicago Auto Show as final preparations were made. The Chicago show, first held in 1901, was the first auto show in the United States. © *AP/Wide World Photos*

As the automotive industry matured, different types of automotive shows came into existence. Antique and classic car shows allowed car enthusiasts to display restored vehicles, swap rare or discontinued parts, and judge the restoration efforts of fellow enthusiasts. Antique shows also offered its attendees a window into the history and development of the automobile and to reminisce about its impact on various time periods in American and world history. Demand in specialized automotive restoration and after-market customization also spawned the creation of after-market parts and accessory shows (such as the Specialty Equipment Manufacturers Association Show) as well as collector and historic car sales (such as the Barrett Jackson Automobile Auction).

In the early twenty-first century, the proliferation of specialized auto shows, product demonstrations, and an increased emphasis on entertainment continued to make auto shows appealing recreation opportunities. Throughout the last century, auto shows have reflected changes in American society, trends, and values. Car shows in the early 2000s were quite different from those of the earlier time periods. In the beginning years, spectators watched

new cars being unveiled in a single stage show with glamour models and other entertainments. Current auto show attendees were more likely to browse massive event complexes, moving from exhibit to exhibit, while participating in interactive, computerized simulations and product testing. For example, the 2002 North American International Auto Show (NAIAS) comprised 60 automotive exhibits, 54 new vehicle introductions, 614 automotive analysts, 257 television networks, and was viewed by 759,907 attendees (North American International Auto Show). Despite their recreational value, automotive manufacturers maintained that their reasons behind supporting auto shows were essentially the same as they were in earlier eras: to connect buyers with the products and stimulate continued purchase of new vehicles. America's love affair and obsession with the automobile remained as intense as it was in its early years. The widespread popularity and attendance at auto shows continued to reflect this fascination.

*See also:* Automobiles and Leisure, Auto Racing, Drag Racing, Hot Rodding, Open Wheel Racing, Sports Car Racing, Stock Car Racing

## BIBLIOGRAPHY

Bermingham, Walter. "1941 History of the Chicago Auto Show." Chicago Auto Show. Available from http://www.chicagoautoshow.com.

Los Angeles Auto Show. "Nearly a Century of Los Angeles Auto Show Tradition." Available from http://www.laautoshow.com/history.

Metro Atlanta Automobile Dealers Association. "The Metro Atlanta Automobile Dealers Association Will Celebrate Atlanta's Long Auto Show History!" Available from http://www.maada.com/autohistory.

National Association of Consumer Shows. "About NACS." Available from http://www.publicshows.com.

North American International Auto Show. "Auto Show History." Available from http://www.naias.com.

———. "NAIAS 2002 Statistics." Available from http://www.naias.com.

Shoenfein, Liza. "Looking into the Rear-View Mirror." Available from http://www.chicagoautoshow.com.

*Andrew J. Mowen*

# AUTOMOBILES AND LEISURE

Although cars have been primarily used for commuting, shopping, and running errands, much of their appeal has resided in the opportunities for fun and adventure that they promise. In 2004, the recreational uses of private vehicles accounted for a significant portion of the mileage they covered. According to the U.S. Federal Highway Administration, in 1995 the "social and recreational" uses of privately owned vehicles accounted for more than 18 percent of annual vehicle trips per household and nearly 23 percent of annual mileage.

When the automobile industry emerged and began to take shape in the late nineteenth and early twentieth centuries, recreational uses of the automobile were paramount. Few bought cars with the intention of using them only for quotidian tasks. Automobiles represented effortless speed, coupled with privacy and the ability to travel without being limited to the routes and schedules of public conveyances. Although much has changed in the design and performance of automobiles since then, the same qualities are an important source of the automobile's appeal today

## Automotive Travel and Touring

In a fundamental sense, all early automobiles were recreational vehicles (RVs). That is, their main purpose was to provide enjoyment, exhilaration, adventure, and a feeling of control. Despite the many faults of early automobiles, people eagerly seized upon the new invention as a source of recreation. Early motorists embarked on ambitious tours. In the summer of 1903, barely a decade after the emergence of the first American-built automobile, H. Nelson Jackson and his codriver, Sewall K. Crocker, set out from San Francisco with the East Coast as their destination. Sixty-three days later their Winton arrived in New York City. Numerous other crossings soon followed, and between 1905 and 1913 long-distance automobile travel received an institutional backing through the establishment of the Glidden reliability runs. These tours were used to good advantage by early automobile manufacturers to demonstrate the reliability of their products and thereby to boost sales.

While automobile travel offered an escape from everyday existence, motorists' adventures were not always of the sort that they had sought. Carburetors got out of adjustment, valves burned, gears stripped, clutches fried, and electrical systems succumbed to mysterious ailments. Successful trips often hinged on the ability of drivers and passengers to do roadside repairs. Most problematic of all were tires, which had a useful life of only a couple thousand miles and were prone to go flat at the most inopportune times. Fixing a flat tire entailed wrestling it off the rim, patching the tube, remounting the tire on the rim, and energetically working a hand pump to reinflate the tire. These difficulties were alleviated during the first decade of the twentieth century when cars began to be fitted with demountable rims or wheels, allowing the replacement of a flat or blown-out tire with a spare that had been carried onboard. Even so, changing a tire was a dirty, disagreeable task.

For all their mechanical shortcomings, early automobiles were usually better than the roads on which they traveled.. Towns and cities had some paved roads, but the dirt roads between population centers were dusty when it was dry and muddy when it was wet, sometimes to the point of being impassable. Efforts to improve roads originated with bicyclists' organizations toward the end of the nineteenth century, and motorists eagerly joined the movement. Growing numbers of automobiles created a new opportunity for financing road improvements: fuel taxes. In the United States, gasoline taxes were used exclusively for road construction and maintenance; hence, they could be viewed as users' fees rather than taxes, and as such they met with little opposition.

Fortified with growing tax revenues, federal, state, and local authorities took up the cause of road improve-

**Chrysler advertisement.** A 1939 advertisement urges consumers to "Be Modern, Buy Chrysler!" The automobile company was founded in 1924 by Walter Chrysler (1875–1940) and merged with Mercedes-Benz in 1998 to form DaimlerChrysler. © *Corbis*

ment, and by the 1920s the Lincoln Highway—which stretched from New York City to San Francisco—and its successors allowed motorists to journey from the Atlantic Ocean to the Pacific Ocean with relative ease. With better roads on which to drive, growing numbers of people eagerly embarked on motoring vacations, making long-distance automobile trips commonplace. According to one reckoning, no fewer than 20,000 cars traveled from coast to coast in 1921 (Belasco, p. 72).

## Auto Camping

While improvements in cars and roads made long-distance travel more reliable, rapid, and comfortable, there still remained the problem of where to stay at the end of the day. Major hotels were located either close to railroad stations or in downtown areas, so many were not readily accessible to motorists, and most lacked parking facilities. Moreover, the hotel culture of the time emphasized formal decorum, including dress codes. These rules were inimical to the spirit of early automobile touring, which valued informality, spontaneity, and

the egalitarianism that came from sharing the adventure of automobile touring.

With hotels unavailable or lacking in appeal, camping was a natural complement to traveling by automobile. As automotive touring gained in popularity during the first decade of the twentieth century, some enterprising motorists equipped their cars with dishes, utensils, and cooking gear for on-the-road dining and altered the seats so they could be folded into makeshift beds for on-the-road sleeping. Motorists could avail themselves of collapsible cots especially manufactured for automobile-based camping. From about 1910 onward, manufacturers offered vehicles equipped at the factory for car-based camping, although few were sold. Motorists could also avail themselves of tent trailers, which provided temporary quarters to set up as well as a place to store additional gear.

Even with better equipment the problem remained of finding a suitable campsite. At first, motorists set up camp at any opportune spot, but as more people embarked on road trips, permanent sites began to spring up, many of them established by local governments who saw automobile tourists as a source of revenue for local businesses. By 1922, more than a thousand camps were in operation throughout the United States. It was not long, however, before local authorities began to express concern that perpetual transients, migratory workers, and criminal elements were descending upon public camping grounds. A common means of discouraging "the wrong sort of people" from using public campgrounds was to set time limits and to charge fees for the use of these facilities. These policies in turn paved the way for private operators to go into the campground business, a development that many local officials were happy to see.

While campground operators attempted to weed out "undesirables," middle- and upper-class motorists often viewed themselves as spiritual kin to gypsies and other vagabonds, taking to the open road in order to leave behind the schedules, responsibilities, and worries of their everyday existence. Yet for these "motor hoboes" or "tin-can tourists," as they called themselves, the days or weeks spent motoring and camping marked only a temporary change of lifestyle. Automobile touring did not signal a rejection of the dominant culture; for most, an automobile vacation was a way to refresh and reinvigorate oneself, and to solidify family bonds.

## From Tourist Cabin to Motel Chain

Although auto camping promised a carefree life on the road, in reality it could be an onerous enterprise. Travelers had to stow a fair amount of paraphernalia in and on their cars, and then set up a tent and cooking facilities at the end of a long and often exhausting day on the road. In response to the evident needs of travelers, in the mid-1920s some auto camp entrepreneurs began to offer permanent shelter for travelers. The structures were simple in the extreme, little more than shacks or even converted chicken coops. But before long these spartan facilities began to give way to more luxurious accommodations, as entrepreneurs provided cabins with kitchenettes, inner-spring mattresses, fresh linen, refrigerators, and even attached garages. In 1925, James Vail gave the English language a new word when he opened his Motel Inn in San Luis Obispo, California. Motel Inn was really a conventional hotel with facilities for automobiles, but the term "motel" soon had wide currency as lodgings for motorists sprang up along the nation's highways.

Although the United States was gripped by economic depression throughout the 1930s, automobile travel continued to flourish. While hard economic times resulted in modest increases in the size of the automobile population, gasoline consumption had increased by 25 percent by the end of the decade. But legions of automobile travelers were not always well served by existing motels, many of which left a great deal to be desired as far as amenities, cleanliness, and even safety were concerned. Finding good accommodations was a hit-and-miss affair, as motorists venturing into unfamiliar territory usually had no way of knowing what awaited them at the end of the day.

In the years following World War II a number of entrepreneurs began to fill the need for better roadside lodgings as postwar prosperity allowed unprecedented numbers of people to take to the highways. One of them was Kemmons Wilson, a resident of Memphis, Tennessee, who had been displeased with the motels where his family had stayed during a road trip to Washington, D.C., in 1951. His response was to join with a builder of prefabricated homes to create the first Holiday Inn. Within a few years, a chain of Holiday Inns had spread throughout the country, offering travelers accommodations that, while not luxurious, were always predictable. Other firms followed suit, sometimes through the direct ownership of individual motels, but more often by franchising arrangements that provided nationwide marketing and other services while requiring franchisees to meet strict quality standards.

From their thrown-together origins in the 1920s, motels have become a significant part of the consumer economy. In the early 1990s, the U.S. Census Bureau counted more than 25,000 "motels, motor hotels, and tourist courts" that employed nearly 300,000 people and ac-

counted for more than $11.7 billion in revenues. In addition to their economic significance, automobile-oriented lodgings have exercised a major influence on the landscape, as motels and the massive signs advertising their location dominated significant portions of the roadside environment.

## Roadside Business

While the auto camp and then the motel offered a place of repose for automobile travelers, other enterprises sprung up to meet the needs of the motoring public. Some of these establishments were conventional restaurants and cafés built along the highway, but the growth of automobile travel was paralleled by the emergence of new kinds of enterprises. On the East Coast and in the Midwest especially, eating establishments known as diners enjoyed considerable popularity. Streamlined in form and constructed from stainless steel, diners offered simple fare at affordable prices. For many of them, the key to the success was a location on the fringes of metropolitan areas, where they could be easily accessed by car.

While diners were the epitome of machine-age functional architecture, other roadside establishments went in the opposite direction as they attempted to lure motorists with large signs calling attention to the products and services they offered. Even more striking efforts to snare passing motorists entailed having the entire building serve as a sign. The result was architecture that might best be described as outlandish, even bizarre. These eye-catching designs were intended to attract the attention of the occupants of fast-moving cars, who had only a few seconds to discern a roadside establishment before deciding to stop and patronize it. The result was a wild cacophony of roadside images: hamburger stands shaped like enormous dogs, doughnut shops with gigantic concrete doughnuts on their roofs, cafés built inside permanently grounded stucco airplanes, and motel rooms that mimicked tepees. On a more restrained level, the patronage of automobile travelers was solicited by roadside businesses made to look like English Tudor cottages, log cabins, and other historical reconstructions. More innovative architectural styles also were used to encourage patronage. During the 1930s, the streamline moderne look that featured curved corners and glass-block windows found favor among some motel builders, while the highway architecture of the 1950s often exhibited the soaring roof overhangs and kidney-shaped signs that defined the style of that era.

Still, some entrepreneurs were not content with luring travelers out of their cars to shop or eat; rather, they

**Holiday Inn.** At the New York Stock Exchange on 30 September 1963, Chairman Kemmons Wilson (left) and President Wallace E. Johnson (right) are present as Holiday Inn becomes the first hotel company to be publicly traded. © *Corbis*

hoped to enhance the appeal of their establishments by serving drivers and passengers right in their cars. Although the basic idea dates back to horse-and-buggy days, credit for being the first drive-in restaurant usually goes to J. G. Kirby's Pig Stand, which opened in 1921 on the Dallas–Fort Worth highway. Drive-in restaurants expanded rapidly during the 1950s, but most of them were relatively short-lived. The noise, litter, and traffic associated with drive-ins were a nuisance, and many drive-ins failed to generate sufficient revenues because teenagers and other hangers-on would place small orders and then remain parked for long periods of time, sharply limiting the influx of paying customers. Most drive-in restaurants had faded into history by the 1970s.

Much more successful in the long run were standardized restaurant chains, which, like many motels, were often run as franchised operations. One of the most enduring automobile-oriented dining establishments emerged in the mid-1930s, when a Boston restaurant

owner named Howard Johnson began to build a series of roadside restaurants along the Massachusetts coast. By the late 1950s, there were 500 of them coast to coast Even more prominent have been fast-food establishments, led by the McDonald's chain. With more than 22,000 restaurants worldwide, and nearly 12,000 in the United States, McDonald's has defined the fast-food industry. Its business success has been built around a limited menu, low prices, decent quality, and fast service. But McDonald's and its competitors would not have been such smashing successes in the absence of the cars and highways that provided easy access to them, while at the same time encouraging travel and a consequent desire for familiar products available far from home.

**Drive-In Movies**

Paralleling the drive-in restaurant was the drive-in movie theater. Although drive-in movies are often associated with amorous encounters, not all patrons have used them for that purpose. At the height of their popularity, drive-ins appealed to anyone who wanted to see a movie without getting dressed, parking, standing in line to buy a ticket, and then finding a seat in a dark theater. They were especially suited to the needs of families with young children, and their heyday coincided with the early years of the post–World War II baby boom.

The drive-in movie theater was the invention of Richard M. Hollingshed, who in 1933 received a patent on it, and in the same year opened his first theater in Camden, New Jersey. This theater set the pattern that endured for decades: Cars were parked in rows on a gently sloped plot of land so their occupants had a good view of the large screen in front of them. In early drive-ins a movie's soundtrack emanated from speakers located in the building that housed the projectors, creating an annoyance for neighboring homes and businesses. It also posed a problem for the patrons—because the sound took a moment to reach the viewers, sight and sound were not always in synchronization. By the late 1930s, individual in-car speakers had overcome these problems.

Hollingshed's patent was overturned in 1938 in a case that went all the way to the Supreme Court, but not many entrepreneurs seized the opportunity to go into the drive-in movie business; only a few dozen were in operation in 1941. The drive-in's great era of expansion took place in the years immediately following World War II. By 1950, 1,700 were serving the American moviegoing public, and four years later there were 4,200 of them.

This era was the high water mark. Television competed for patrons' leisure time, and a relative decline in the number of children and teenagers eroded a major component of the drive-in's clientele. Even more damaging was suburban expansion and rising land values, as drive-ins could not produce the revenue offered by other uses for valuable real estate. By the beginning of the twenty-first century, the number of drive-ins had dwindled to 433, many of which survive by using their facilities for swap meets and other such purposes.

The topic of drive-in movies inevitably leads to a discussion of the automobile's role in encouraging and facilitating sexual encounters. Although the opportunities afforded by a car's backseat fill a major chapter in our popular culture, there is little solid evidence of the extent of car-based romance. Still, the role of the automobile in fostering romance has been thoroughly played out in popular music. One of the biggest hits of the early twentieth century was "My Merry Oldsmobile," which concludes with this risqué promise: "You can go as far as you like with me, Lucille, in my merry Oldsmobile." Since then, more than 1,000 songs on automotive themes have graced the musical scene.

Automobiles also have been prominently featured in movies; one of the first films viewed by the public was *Automobiles on Parade*, a 1900 Edison production. "Road movies" like *Vanishing Point* and *Easy Rider*, which often play on the interrelated themes of rebellion and the search for personal freedom, have been film staples. Even when cars and driving have not been the primary subjects, some of the most memorable cinematic scenes have been car chases that range from the buffoonery of the Keystone Kops to the deadly serious pursuits featured in *Bullitt* and *The French Connection*.

## Trailers and Motor Homes

Despite the widespread availability of motels, fast-food restaurants, and other roadside amenities, a substantial portion of the traveling public still seeks a self-contained experience, a trend that began in earnest with the "trailer craze" of the 1930s. Although the depression had cut severely into discretionary income, substantial numbers of people were able to acquire trailers, many of them homemade, and put them on the road. Trailer manufacture came to be one of the few economic bright spots of the depression; in 1937, nearly 400 companies were manufacturing and marketing upward of 100,000 trailers a year. The vast majority of those trailers were used for travel rather than permanent living, but the population shifts and consequent housing shortages that were brought on by World War II reversed the ratio, and as many as 90 percent of trailers owned or purchased during that period were used as permanent housing. The years following World War II saw a return to the recreational uses of trailers, but at the same time the use of trailers—or "mobile homes" as they came to be known—as fixed residences increased substantially.

For all their utility, trailers had a number of disadvantages. They taxed the engines, brakes, and suspensions of the cars towing them, and driving with a trailer could be tricky, especially when backing up or parking was involved. Many states forbade passengers to ride in trailers, so everyone had to find a place in the tow car. Numerous states also mandated lower speed limits for car-and-trailer combinations. Some of these drawbacks could be remedied by combining a car and a living space in one vehicle, a "house car," as it was originally called. Some early house cars were built on automobile chassis, while others started as buses or delivery trucks. As with trailers, many early house cars were home-built jobs. Often following plans that appeared in do-it-yourself magazines, amateur builders used wood, metal, canvas, and fiberboard to create homes on wheels. At the other end of the house-car spectrum were professionally built vehicles sold to the wealthy. With varnished woodwork, silk curtains, and even rear observation platforms in some cases, they approached private railroad cars in comfort and elegance.

House cars went into relative decline in the 1930s as trailers became the preferred means of keeping the comforts of home while on the road. House cars—or "motor homes—enjoyed a revival in the years following World War II, when aircraft construction techniques were used to build light, streamlined vehicles. Their cost still kept them out of the reach of most people, but many vacationers found an acceptable substitute in station wagons that could hold a fair amount of camping equipment while providing a modicum of space for sleeping. Offering considerably more elbow room were camper shells that could be mounted in the beds of pickup trucks, as well as vans that had been converted into modest-sized traveling homes. Both types became popular from the 1950s onward, even though they suffered from significant shortcomings as far as space and amenities were concerned.

Sales of motor homes surged in the 1960s as incomes rose and the industry learned how to cut production costs. Major automobile manufacturers benefited from this trend by supplying their chassis to outside constructors, who outfitted them as motor homes complete with furniture and fixtures. Further expanding the sales of motor homes was the success of Winnebago Industries in using true mass-production techniques to drive down costs. Echoing the vertically integrated manufacturing philosophy pioneered by Henry Ford, Winnebago made virtually everything that went into its products, even the wooden furniture and window drapes. Also like Ford, Winnebago built its vehicles on moving assembly lines, lowering costs even more. Sales of motor homes soared to more than 65,000 in 1973 as other firms followed suit. Further encouraging the growth of motor homes, travel trailers, campers, and other vacation-oriented vehicles was the expansion of the interstate highway system; its long, straight stretches, sweeping curves, and gentle gradients were ideal for vehicles that were anything but nimble. But affordable prices and smooth roads were of little importance when service stations ran out of gasoline in the wake of politically induced supply disruptions in 1973 to 1974 and in 1979. Dealers' lots filled with unsold trailers, campers, and motor homes, and numerous firms went out of business, a situation that was exacerbated by a severe economic recession during the late 1970s and early 1980s.

Sales rebounded in the years that followed, stimulated by a buoyant economy and cheap fuel. At the be-

ginning of the twenty-first century, the recreational vehicle industry was enjoying some of its best years, as 311,000 motor homes, travel trailers, camping trailers, and truck campers, along with 67,700 van and pickup truck conversions, were delivered to dealers in 2002. By this time, a total of 7.2 million RVs (not including van and pickup truck conversions) were on the road.

## Car Shows

From its inception, the automobile industry has been eager to put its wares on display. The most significant locales are international car shows in cities like Geneva, London, Detroit, and Tokyo, where manufacturers draw attention to their latest models, along with "concept cars" that indicate future directions in automobile engineering and design. While manufacturers and dealers use shows as a means of selling cars and increasing profits, the typical car show is an amateur event where people can put on display special-interest vehicles, many of which have been restored or modified by their owners. Automobile shows are hugely popular; according to the U.S. Bureau of the Census, in 1998, nearly 14 million people, 7.1 percent of the population, attended an auto show at least once in the preceding twelve months.

Events put on by and for car collectors are not necessarily modest affairs. At the summit of the car show pyramid are the exhibitions of classic cars known as *concours d'elegance*. Held in fashionable places like Pebble Beach, California, these shows feature cars that may be valued at several million dollars, and are rarely, if ever, driven on the road. More typical are local car shows featuring Ford Model As, 1950s vintage Chevrolets, and mass-produced British sports cars instead of Duesenbergs, Ferraris, and Pierce-Arrows. Many shows are organized by clubs catering to the owners of a single make of automobile. Participants have ample opportunities to share technical tips and discuss the relative merits of different model years of a particular make of car. These shows are often accompanied by swap meets where enthusiasts can find everything from complete cars to out-of-print shop manuals.

## Hot Rods and Customs

Car shows are an essential component of two important examples of the recreational use of the automobile: hot rods and custom cars. The origins of hot-rodding can be traced to southern California in the late 1920s, when modified Ford Model Ts and other cars began to compete in speed trials staged on dry lake beds. In order to improve their cars' performance and appearance, early

**Henry Ford.** In 1896 automobile inventor Henry Ford (1863-1947) sits atop the "Quadricycle" in Detroit. The vehicle represents his first gasoline-powered car; it ran on four bicycle tires (thus the name). Its success eventually led to the founding of Ford Motor Company in 1903. © *Bettmann/Corbis*

hot-rodders modified engines, chassis, and bodywork, often on low budgets. By the late 1930s, speed trials on dry lakes and illegal street racing had become fixtures of the southern California car culture, but World War II put an end to them. With the war's end, veterans brought new skills back home and found relatively high-paying jobs. When combined with a love of cars, money and mechanical skills produced hot rods in infinite varieties: Model Ts modified beyond recognition, roadsters from the 1930s with modern overhead valve V-8 engines, and souped-up versions of more recent models.

Customizing (or Kustomizing, the spelling often used by practitioners of the craft) began with a similar desire to improve on mass-produced and often unimaginative designs. The heyday of car customization was the

1950s and early 1960s, when Detroit products like the 1949 to 1951 Mercury were prime candidates for customization. The repertoire of customizers included lowering the car by modifying the springs, chopping (lowering the roofline), sectioning (removing a fore-and-aft section of the body to make the car lower and sleeker), and "frenching" (enclosing the taillights and other protuberances in a kind of cowl), as well as changing grilles, bumpers, and other body parts. Interiors also came in for special treatment through the use of innovative upholstery materials and the installation of elaborate accessories.

At the far fringe of the contemporary customization scene are "art cars"—cars, vans, and trucks modified and decorated in an innovative, many would say absurdly weird, manner. Examples of art cars include vehicles shaped like high-heel shoes or telephones, as well as vans with their bodywork covered with cameras or decorative objects, and cars that make rococo buildings look like the epitome of functionalist restraint. Where traditional custom cars represent an attempt to extend and amplify the aesthetic appeal of the automobile, the creators of art cars often obliterate the shape of a vehicle to the point of making them into parodies of cars in particular and the consumer society in general. Art cars have a devoted following; the largest gathering of art cars, the Houston Art Car parade, draws more than 200 vehicles and 125,000 viewers.

Today, the legacy of traditional car customizers continues with the construction and display of low riders. Originally created by Mexican Americans in California and the Southwest, low riders now have an international following. Essential to a low rider are hydraulically mounted wheels that can vary a car's height, allowing it to ride a fraction of an inch from the road when on display, and then lifting it up to provide ground clearance for normal driving. Hydraulics also enable cars to vigorously hop up and down, which, of course, has led to car high-jump contests. Some hydraulic-equipped cars and small trucks have been designed to perform elaborate dances.

## Automobile Racing

Low riders are not about speed and acceleration; "low and slow" has been the motto of their creators. In contrast, hot-rodding began as an effort to extract more top-end performance from available cars. After World War II, attention shifted from speed trials on dry lakes to drag racing—getting down a quarter-mile track as quickly as possible. As the 2000s begin, drag racing is an important spectator sport, with major events drawing tens of thousands of spectators. Although drag racing has become a big business with substantial corporate sponsorship, it continues to attract a large numbers of amateur competitors. The National Hot Rod Association is the world's largest motor sports organization, boasting more than 85,000 members and 32,000 licensed competitors competing in nearly 4,000 events on 144 tracks. Although 6,000-horsepower dragsters capable of exceeding 320 miles per hour in a standing-start quarter mile draw the crowds, many drag races feature far more modest vehicles, including cars that take their owners to work during the rest of the week.

Drag racing is one of the few motor sports with substantial amateur participation. Other forms of racing are primarily spectator sports. The largest in terms of audience size is NASCAR, the sanctioning body for racing cars that vaguely resemble Chevrolets, Dodges, Fords, and Pontiacs. In fact, they share virtually no parts with ordinary passenger cars, but the willingness of spectators to identify racing cars with the cars in their own garages is an important source of NASCAR's appeal. In recent years NASCAR has gained a substantial following outside its southern heartland, and televised races often pull higher ratings than all other televised sports with the exception of pro football.

While NASCAR racers maintain a visual kinship with ordinary passenger cars, open-wheel cars hark back to an earlier time when race cars were stripped of nonessential items like fenders. The most prestigious (and vastly expensive) series is Formula One, which stages races in Europe, Asia, and the United States. Similar in appearance to Formula One cars but slightly less expensive to build and operate are the open-wheel racers of Championship Automobile Racing Teams (CART) and the Indy Racing League (IRL). Large numbers of fans also follow races that take place on dirt or paved ovals of one mile or less. Several kinds of cars compete on these tracks, including stock cars, sprint cars, and midgets. The racing scene also includes sports car races that have events for stock vehicles as well as cars built solely for racing. All in all, automobile racing is a major spectator sport. More than 11 million fans attended some sort of auto race in 1998, about the same number as attended professional football games. Motorcycle racing, which includes a variety of events ranging from flat track to road racing to stadium motocross, drew 3 million fans in 1998.

Whether it has been through attendance at a motor race or car show, restoring an old car, or hitching up a trailer and taking to the open road, the automobile has been closely associated with a multitude of recreational activities. Given the massive personal and societal costs that it has engendered, the automobile would never have emerged as the most significant technology of the last century were it not for the amusement, adventure, and recreation that it has offered.

*See also:* Auto Shows, Drag Racing, Fast Food, Open Wheel Racing, Shopping, Shopping Malls, Sports Car Racing, Stock Car Racing, Tourism

**BIBLIOGRAPHY**

Belasco, Warren James. *Americans on the Road: From Autocamp to Motel, 1910-1945.* Cambridge, Mass., and London: MIT Press, 1979.

Flink, James J. *The Automobile Age.* Cambridge, Mass., and London: MIT Press, 1988.

Jennings, Jan, ed. *Roadside America: The Automobile in Design and Culture.* Ames: Iowa State University Press, 1990.

Liebs, Chester H. *Main Street to Miracle Mile: American Roadside Architecture.* Boston: Little, Brown and Company, 1985.

Rae, John B. *The American Automobile: A Brief History.* Chicago: University of Chicago Press, 1965.

U.S. Census Bureau. *Statistical Abstract of the United States.* Washington, D.C.: U.S. Government Printing Office, annual.

Wallis, Allan D. *Wheel Estate: The Rise and Decline of Mobile Homes.* New York: Oxford University Press, 1991.

White, Roger B. *Home on the Road: The Motor Home in America.* Washington, D.C.: Smithsonian Institution Press, 2000.

*Rudi Volti*

# BACKPACKING AND HIKING

"I think that I cannot preserve my health and spirits unless I spend four hours a day at least—and it is commonly more than that—sauntering through the woods and over the hills and fields absolutely free from all worldly engagements" (Sattelmeyer, p. 99). Henry David Thoreau's words, first spoken in 1851, still capture for many Americans the meaning and significance of walking into one world and, temporarily at least, leaving behind another. Although Thoreau's woods of New England may have largely succumbed to the forces of industrialization and economic expansion, there still exist today many natural areas where hikers and backpackers continue to restore their health and spirits.

By many accounts, the backpacker of today would have difficulty recognizing his or her counterpart of a hundred, or even fifty, years ago. In the early twentieth century, America was experiencing a physical and social transformation characterized by increased urbanization, industrialization, and mechanization that caused many people to seek respite from the ills of urban life by getting back to nature. From these circumstances emerged a popular recreation movement, known as "woodcraft," that "celebrated a working knowledge of nature" and was "preoccupied with an independent masculine ideal rooted in the frontier" (Turner, p. 464). The woodsman possessed an intimate knowledge of his surroundings and was capable of living off the land by utilizing the resources at hand. Hunting, building fires, identifying edible plants, and constructing shelter were some of the outdoor skills

a woodsman needed in order to tame the wildness of nature and re-create the comforts of home. Many books were published with titles such as *The Way of the Woods* and *Camping and Woodcraft* extolling the rewards and virtues of the self-sufficient woodsman. The Boy Scouts of America also formally adopted this utilitarian wilderness ethic early in the twentieth century.

While the woodsman movement was a direct reaction against the encroaching mechanization of society, this same industrial force provided a network of new railways and highways for the average citizen to access public lands. Cars permitted people to drive to rivers, mountains, and open spaces for the purposes of camping, fishing, and hiking. In a short period of time, the nation's public lands became a legitimate and significant tourist destination for both individuals and families.

As more and more people demanded automobile access to the nation's public lands and national parks, the government responded by building an extensive network of roads that cut ever deeper into the wilderness. In order to protect some of the remaining untouched lands, several outspoken environmental visionaries, including Aldo Leopold and Bob Marshall, ushered in a new wilderness ethic that celebrated the aesthetic and spiritual qualities of nature. These appeals were specifically directed at mobilizing the increasing ranks of hikers and backpackers who used public lands for recreation. The growing number of wilderness advocates, such as the Sierra Club and Appalachian Mountain Club, believed in protecting and preserving some of the remaining public land in its pristine state and were largely responsible for securing ad-

**Appalachian Trail.** Hikers Phillip Zappone of Shrewsbury, Massachusetts (left), and Brodie Trickey of Greenville, Tennessee, stand at the summit of Mount Katahdin in September 2001 after a five-month, 2,155-mile trip. Located in Maine's Baxter State Park, the land was purchased by former governor, Percival Baxter (1876–1969), and donated to the state to ensure that it stayed "forever wild." Besides the more than 200,000 acres of land, he also left a trust fund of $7 million for maintenance purposes. © *Robert F. Bukaty for AP/Wide World Photos*

ministrative support for wilderness protection. The most significant legislative document to come out of this movement was the Wilderness Act in 1964. In it, wilderness is defined as "an area where the earth and its community of life are untrammeled by man, where man himself is a visitor who does not remain."

By setting aside vast tracts of land that would forever remain unspoiled by man, Congress essentially provided hikers and backpackers with their own exclusive province. As the number of hikers and backpackers visiting the nation's wilderness and backcountry areas increased during the 1970s and 1980s, concerns regarding the impact these numbers would have on the land and its inhabitants influenced yet another wilderness ethic. The Leave No Trace (LNT) mantra of "take only pictures, leave only footprints" was uniformly adopted by many organizations and companies, including Outward Bound, the North Face, and, recently, the Boy Scouts of America. The hiker and backpacker in America's wilderness was now not only a visitor who did not remain, but also one who traveled lightly on the land, both literally and figuratively.

One of the unexpected consequences of the LNT movement was the marketing of outdoor clothing and equipment that was technologically advanced, more efficient, and, most important, lighter. Suddenly compact gas stoves replaced campfires, nylon tents fitted with aluminum poles replaced lean-tos, and a working knowledge of how to operate these devices replaced a working knowledge of the land. Two of the more controversial technological gadgets that have altered the once self-sufficient posture of most backpackers and hikers are the use of mobile phones and global positioning system (GPS) devices in the backcountry. Proponents of these technologies appreciate the ease with which the phone can keep them in touch with the outside world whenever necessary (especially if lost or injured), as well as the GPS's accuracy in locating one's exact position in the woods. Opponents argue that these devices provide a false sense of security that encourages reliance on technology at the expense of navigational skills and common sense.

This trend in applying the latest technologies to the equipment and tools of backpacking and hiking has created a multibillion-dollar market that leads the outdoor sporting goods industry in overall sales (May). Consumerism, though not often associated with an image of the lone backpacker walking off into the wilderness, has become an essential element in today's minimal-impact hiking and backpacking ethic.

The commercialization of hiking and backpacking encourages and permits increasing numbers of people to walk comfortably and safely in the wilderness and backcountry areas of America's public lands. Fortunately, the United States has nearly 200,000 miles of existing trails on public land for people of all abilities to explore. These range from short, interpretive trails posted with information about the local flora and fauna to National Scenic Trails like the Pacific Crest Trail and the Appalachian Trail that extend continuously for thousands of miles, providing hikers and backpackers seemingly endless opportunities to get back to nature.

*See also:* Camping, National Parks, Orienteering, Park Movements, State Parks

**BIBLIOGRAPHY**

May, Mike. "The Outdoors: America's Playground." Sporting Goods Manufacturers Association Press Release. Available from http://www.sgma.com/press/.

Meier, Joel F. *Backpacking.* 2d edition. Champaign, Ill: Sagamore Publishing, 1993.

Sattelmeyer, Robert, ed. *The Natural History Essays.* Salt Lake City, Utah: Peregrine Smith, 1980.

Turner, James M. "From Woodcraft to 'Leave No Trace': Wilderness, Consumerism, and Environmentalism in Twentieth-Century America." *Environmental History* 7, no. 3 (2002): 462–484.

*John R. Persing*

# BALLET

**See** *Performing Arts Audiences*

# BAND PLAYING

During the eighteenth century, the term "band" was used in several European languages to describe military and civic ensembles that featured oboes, bassoons, and clarinets. Horns and trumpets were employed less frequently. Ensembles usually ranged from six to eight members.

As Europeans settled in the colonies, they brought band instruments with them. The first documented performance of a military band was in 1714, when oboes and trumpets were used to celebrate the crowning of George I. The first documented civic concert of instrumental music took place in Boston in 1729. Moravian immigrants, well known for the importance they placed upon music, formed some of the first civilian bands in North Carolina and Pennsylvania.

## From Nationhood Through the Civil War

During the Revolutionary War, several American military bands were founded. The Third and Fourth Continental Artillery units had bands of exceptional renown. When state militia groups replaced the Continental Army in 1783, many of the militias formed small bands. They performed for ceremonial purposes and also at town dances and parades. In 1800, the U.S. Marine Corps established a permanent band that performed public concerts; this original band included two oboes, two clarinets, two horns, one bassoon, and one drum.

During the second decade of the nineteenth century, instrument makers developed valved brass instruments that were easier to play and more versatile. The keyed bugle was introduced in America in 1815 and enjoyed several decades of popularity. The bass drum and cymbal (which made their way into European and American ensembles through an enthusiasm for Turkish military, or "anissary" music) were gradually popularized. As a result, brass instruments quickly replaced woodwinds as the bands' basic element.

The Civil War saw the proliferation of many brass bands. Many militia bands enlisted as a group. The Union is estimated to have had 500 bands with 9,000 players. These bands consisted of anywhere from eight to twenty-four musicians.

## The Rise of Amateur Band Playing

After the Civil War there was a dramatic rise in amateur band playing. Instruments became more affordable as American manufacturing replaced the importation of instruments from Europe; in addition, instrument quality increased. Both brass and woodwind instruments were sold in high quantities, reversing the previous trend toward the exclusive use of brass instruments. Local manufacturers implemented massive advertising campaigns

**Civil War band.** In 1862 during the Civil War, the Third New Hampshire Infantry Military Band stands with their instruments in Hilton Head, South Carolina. Military bands served several purposes, including attracting new recruits, serving as a morale booster by playing lively marches, and sometimes even working as medics. © *Corbis*

that emphasized the positive effects of playing in a band: the health benefits of marching, the fact that women found bandsmen more attractive, and the ability of a band to draw a crowd for political or commercial reasons.

Amateur bands were funded and organized by a number of institutions. Many town governments funded bands, arguing that the presence of a town band reflected the town's high level of taste and civilization. Fraternal and sororital organizations formed bands, pointing to the positive moral influence of band playing. Bands were also formed around industrial ties (such as factory bands and railroad bands), by the Salvation Army (in 1878), and (after World War I) by American Legion posts and veterans' organizations. Bands were conducted by local music "professors" and rehearsed once or twice a week. Membership was generally restricted to adult males, though a small number of women's bands were formed around

1900. The standard size of a band rose steadily, peaking at about twenty members.

## Role of Bands in Town Life

From 1850 to World War I (often called "the golden age of bands"), bands could be found in almost every town in America. In most communities, bands provided the main source of music outside the home. Bands performed a wide repertoire of music, from marches and dance music to arrangements of everything from the latest opera aria to Stephen Foster songs to European symphonic literature. They performed at paid political rallies, fairs, parades, picnics, and excursions. During the summer months, bands would perform at unpaid summer evening concerts once a week at the town bandstand. These events in the center of town drew large crowds.

During this period, rivalry between bands was high. Community bands fought to recruit the best players, and bands worked hard to have the most appealing repertoire, the best instruments, and the most exotic costumes. During the 1870s and 1880s, instrument manufacturers and chambers of commerce often staged competitions. Several of these competitions reached mammoth proportions, lasting three to four days and drawing crowds from great distances.

## The Origins and Development of Band Playing in Schools

While the number of civic bands has sharply declined since World War I, bands can now be found in most educational institutions across America. The University of Notre Dame Band, formed in 1842, claims to be the oldest band in continuous existence. After the Civil War, bands were formed at the Officer's Training Corps, which could be found at most colleges and universities. The combination of military training and music making converged in the marching band, which, in the early 2000s, remained the most prominent type of school band. By 1900, it was common to have bands performing at halftime shows of sporting events.

The end of World War I saw many military bandleaders return to their communities and form bands in public high schools. These bands benefited from the increasing tendency toward publicly funded music instruction. Their popularity was also fueled by intense competition. In 1923, in a bid to increase sales, musical instrument manufacturers sponsored the first national school band contest. Organizations for the promotion of school bands were founded: the National School Band Association in 1926, the College Band Directors National Association in 1941.

Recent years have seen the rise of "wind ensembles" in many universities and colleges. This trend began in 1952 with the foundation of the Eastman School of Music Symphonic Wind Ensemble by Frederic Fennell. Wind ensembles generally have fewer members than bands, and their instrumentation is modeled on the symphony orchestra. These ensembles attempt to rival the symphony orchestra in terms of virtuosity, sophistication, and versatility.

*See also:* Choral Singing, Performing Arts Audiences, Piano Playing, Traditional Folk Music Festivals

### BIBLIOGRAPHY

Bryant, Carolyn. *And the Band Played On: 1776–1976.* Washington, D.C.: Smithsonian Institution Press, 1975.

Hazen, Margaret Hindle, and Robert M. Hazen. *The Music Men: An Illustrated History of Brass Bands in America.* Washington, D.C.: Smithsonian Institution Press, 1987.

Kreitner, Kenneth. *Discoursing Sweet Music: Town Bands and Community Life in Turn-of-the-Century Pennsylvania.* Urbana-Champaign: University of Illinois Press, 1990.

Schwartz, Harry Wayne. *Bands of America.* New York: Da Capo Press, 1975.

*Alexander Kahn*

# BARBERSHOP QUARTETS

In the mid-1900s, the barbershop quartet most often was made up of four white males, dressed in matching attire, singing unaccompanied songs that were well known between 1860 and 1920. "Aura Lee," "Hello My Baby," "Wait Till the Sun Shines, Nellie," and "Moonlight Bay" were typical favorites of those who liked this close-harmony style. The melody line was somewhat simple, the harmony progressions followed what is known as the circle of fifths, and the tenor part (often performed in a falsetto or head tone) was sung above the melody or lead line. The barbershop seventh, or dominant seventh chord, was the hallmark of the style.

Though many barbershop quartets still perform and dress as they did several decades ago, entering the second millennium it is not uncommon to hear some different sounds. Intricate harmony progressions and an expanded chord selection provide a more modern sound with altered chords, non-chord melody notes, and sometimes rather complicated jazz-type rhythms.

## Early Influences

People were singing long before barbershop quartets were identified, and many vocal music concepts impacted what is now known as the barbershop style. In the eleventh century, it is reported that most singing was done in unison and octaves. In the era of the Gregorian chant, the perfect fifth was introduced, hundreds of years before physicists were able to document the overtone production created by this interval. As early as the fourteenth century, church musicians introduced major and minor triads, providing more harmonic opportunity. But it was the seventh chord (made up of the root, third, fifth, and seventh positions in a scale), developed by classical music composers in the sixteenth and seventeenth centuries, that would have the greatest impact on barbershop

**Gas House Gang performs.** This quartet from St. Louis won the 1993 International Championship of the Society for the Preservation and Encouragement of BarberShop Quartets Singing in America (SPEBSQSA) and is one of the most popular quartets in the United States. *Courtesy of Miller Photography*

music. With four voices, each singer produced a different pitch, and the potential overtone patterns allowed for a truly expanded sound. The rich harmonics of the properly tuned and balanced seventh chord are the hallmark of the barbershop sound.

Though indeed men often sang while loitering in barbershops, sometimes with a guitar or other instruments for support, the concept of barber's music originated in Elizabethan England. It referred to spontaneous, or idle music, whereby an individual might begin to sing and others would harmonize, never having heard the melody before and without the privilege of looking at notes written on a musical staff. This type of music was transplanted to America in the late 1700s and became very popular in the South, especially among Negro slaves. Though it is a relatively lost art form, there are barbershop singers who still enjoy woodshedding, a type of barber's music.

After 1850, numerous musical influences affected the soon-to-be-identified barbershop style. Stephen Foster wrote many simple songs that were easily harmonized. Groups such as the Hutchinson Family Singers began performing in New England, Negro quartets arose in the South, and minstrel, vaudeville, and Chautauqua shows became popular opportunities for barbershop style singing.

Recently, historians have suggested that African American musicians may have had the greatest influence on barbershop quartet singing. At the turn of the twentieth century, phonograph recordings became a venue for an increasing number of quartets to be heard. Scott Joplin and Irving Berlin, ragtimer and composer respectively, represented a new influence in music style, and, by 1900,

amateur quartets were being heard all across America, often sponsored by clubs, churches, businesses, and even baseball teams. Jack Benny, Eddie Cantor, Bing Crosby, Al Jolson, Groucho Marx, and Abbot and Costello are but a few of many famous entertainers reported to have had barbershop singing experiences. The big band sound of the 1930s also influenced songwriters and performers.

## Early Barbershop Singing Society History

A chance meeting between Tulsa businessmen Owen C. Cash and Rupert Hall turned out to be the beginnings of what is now known as the Society for the Preservation and Encouragement of Barbershop Quartet Singing in America (SPEBSQSA). Agreeing that radio and recorded music were replacing a valued men's a cappella close harmony singing influence, they invited several friends and acquaintances to join them for some vocal musical fellowship. Twenty-six men appeared at the Roof Garden of the Tulsa Club on 11 April 1938. A third such gathering of 150 men occurred on 31 May and created a traffic jam in downtown Tulsa. Wire services reported the event throughout the country, and, perhaps as a spoof to the acronym naming of governmental projects of the day—CCC, WPA, etc.—the initials SPEBSQSA were eventually adopted. Much to the chagrin of those who were concerned with the image of this new organization, the Bartlesville Bar Flies won the first SPEBSQSA contest in 1939.

Because only four men could sing in a quartet, it became common to find small ensembles being formed. In central Illinois, a man named John Hansen traveled among various towns, teaching unwritten melodies and harmonies to small groups that at some later time would join as a mass chorus to sing barbershop-style music; this Corn Belt Chorus once placed nearly 300 men on stage to perform barbershop harmony.

## The Barbershop Singing Society After Sixty-five Years

Though it is the desired goal that all members gain some quartet experience, the vast majority of men never sing in organized quartets, but rather experience barbershop singing in chapters whose choruses range in size from a dozen to nearly 200 members. Nonetheless, there are some 1,800 registered quartets in the society, which currently has its headquarters in Kenosha, Wisconsin.

In 2003, the society boasted some 31,000 members (down from a peak of 38,000 in 1983); however, the number of chapters/choruses in this country increased from 750 to 835 during that twenty-year time period. There

**Vocal Majority Chorus.** Since 1874, this 125-man-plus chorus has won the International Chorus Contest 10 times, most recently in 2000. Though the group is banned from winning the title for three years when it does win, it continues to perform during that period, entertaining crowds at the Charles W. Eisemann Center, it's home theater in Richardson, Texas. *Courtesy of Miller Photography*

were seven foreign affiliate organizations from Australia, England, Germany, The Netherlands, South Africa, Sweden, and New Zealand. Barbershop quartets from China and Russia have also toured the United States.

Sixteen geographically defined districts, some including as many as seven states while others are comprised of just one or two, provide the infrastructure for the organization. The society has nearly fifty paid staff members who provide a variety of services, from field representatives who visit chapters around the country to music librarians. The annual budget for 2003 was $6.3 million. The largest source of income is the International Convention and Quartet/Chorus competition, held in preselected sites annually and drawing an average audience of 10,000 listeners. Other income results from membership dues, philanthropic contributions, and the revenue earned through sales of sheet music, recordings, clothing, and other related items.

The contest and judging system is thought to be the most thorough in all of vocal music. Whereas early competitors were judged by community dignitaries—former New York governor Al Smith judged the 1940 competition—quartets and choruses are now judged by highly trained panels of certified judges in the categories of music, presentation, and singing.

As early as 1971, society leaders expressed the desire to involve young men in this close harmony singing fellowship. As older members died, it became evident that the society would die with them unless vigorous efforts were made to attract a new, younger breed of singers. The Young Men in Harmony (YMIH) program soon began publishing appropriate arrangements of songs written more recently—songs with which the younger generation could identify. In 2003, more than 400 society members acknowledged their initial exposure was through YMIH programs. SPEBSQSA leaders are also playing a major

role in coalition with national music teacher groups to keep viable vocal music programs alive in the public schools.

Though not structured as musical organizations, many social, fraternal, and public service clubs continue to sing some type of theme song at their periodic gatherings. The vast majority of men's barbershop chapters open and close their weekly meetings with "The Old Songs" and "Keep the Whole World Singing," two standards that still summarize two major objectives of the organization.

## Associated Items of Interest

Sweet Adelines—the national women's organization—was formed in 1945. There are 30,000 members found in some 600 chapters that represent twenty-nine regions across the country. Harmony Incorporated, another female singing organization, was formed in 1958 and has a membership of approximately 3,000 members. Both organizations promote the barbershop style, and, in addition to community performances, they sponsor international competitions for choruses and quartets.

The image of the barbershop quartet has also been enhanced in other venues. In addition to records, tapes, and CDs, barbershop quartets have provided interesting performances in the theater and in film. One of the most famous quartets, The Buffalo Bills, helped create interest in the barbershop singing as they portrayed the school board in the 1957 Broadway musical *The Music Man*. It played for nearly 1,400 performances and received numerous awards; since that time, both film and video productions of the play have helped maintain the wholesome image of the barbershop quartet. The films *Babe* and *Hoosiers* depicted the role that barbershop singing played in early-twentieth-century sporting activities. It was not uncommon for quartets to sing songs between innings of professional baseball games, and, just as in the famous *Hoosiers* film, quartets continue to sing the national anthem prior to basketball and football games.

*See also:* Choral Singing; Men's Leisure Lifestyles

**BIBLIOGRAPHY**

Averill, Gage. *Four Parts, No Waiting: A Social History of American Barbershop Harmony.* New York: Oxford University Press, 2003.

Henry, Jim. "The Historical Roots of Barbershop Harmony." *The Harmonizer* (July–August 2001): 13–17.

Hicks, Val. *Heritage of Harmony.* Friendship, Wis.: New Past Press, 1988.

———. *The Six Roots of Barbershop Harmony.* Ivins, Utah: Val Hicks Publications, 2003.

*M. Thomas Woodall*

# BARN RAISING

Barns throughout nineteenth-century America grew in size, as well as importance for the farm, and a common tradition to meet the challenge of building the barn was to turn the task of construction into a community event. The vernacular term "raising" referred to the task of lifting into place erect "bents" or large vertical frames that formed the skeleton of the barn and connecting them with cross-girts (horizontal framing members connecting end posts below the roof plate). The task of raising, the visually exciting highlight of barn building, required many men to work cooperatively and use ropes and poles (or "pikes") to erect the heavy wooden bents. The expectation arose that the community would create a festive family atmosphere around this laborious event. The barn raisings featured large communal dinners, sometimes liquor and cider, and play opportunities for children. Sources for this kind of festival

**Building a barn.** In Pulaski, Pennsylvania Amish farmers raise a barn in 1971. With 100 workers it takes only a single day to complete the large structure. © *Bettmann/Corbis*

can be found in medieval England and continental Europe, but evidence suggests it is associated with pre-industrial America because of the increased frequency of barn building on individual farms. Although the image of the rugged, independent pioneer building his home by himself was common in American popular iconography, the visual culture of the barn emphasized the spirit of community offering mutual aid and generosity in expanding America.

Despite the communal image, a hierarchy in organizing the raising was usually evident. A master carpenter or foreman was hired to direct the construction and supervise the crew. The typical procedure was to connect tie beams (horizontal pieces of wood between the feet of a pair of rafters in a roof structure) to end posts below the roof plate. In addition to building the bents on the ground before they were lifted into place, the crew constructed temporary scaffolding made from boards around the site. The men laid the boards across the horizontal beams to provide platforms from which they could work. In Pennsylvania, an alternative to raising completely assembled H-bents was to join the tie beam over the roof plate and end post. Workers laid long planks against the uppermost girts at the rear of the frame to serve as ramps or skids on which upper-frame members could be slid to their proper height. They rotated the tie beams after moving them up the skids and secured the barn frame. They then erected the roof framework and rafters and completed the barn with roofing and siding. By most accounts, the raising process usually took a day. Women prepared an abundance of food for the event, and often served it in a large communal dinner. It was common to have a dance at the house after the raising, and many accounts recall the prevalence of drunkenness at these parties.

The growth of agribusiness, introduction of mechanical devices for raising bents, use of lighter presawn timbers, and professionalization of farm construction in the twentieth century resulted in the decline of barn raisings as festive communal events. However, among agrarian groups holding on to communal values, such as the Amish and Old Order Mennonites, barn raisings continued and, indeed, became tourist attractions for modern viewers seeking a nostalgic reminder of pre-industrial communal ways of life. In popular culture, they also became associated with the Amish because of the inclusion in the movie *Witness* of the barn-raising scene as a significant symbol of wholesome communal values. Ethnographies of Amish societies showed that the barn was important not only because of its function for farming activity, but also as space for religious services (the Amish do not have churches; instead, they use members' barns).

The raising became part of a system of insurance. After a fire, the community pitched in by restoring the barn or raising a new one. Sociologist Don Kraybill calls the barn raising the most dramatic example of "social capital" among the Amish, which includes face-to-face relationships, extended family, and long-standing traditions and rituals that support them. Continuing features of a communal meal, visual excitement for spectators, and festive atmosphere, the Amish barn raising is a productive integration of pleasure and labor serving the needs, and underscoring the importance, of the community.

*See also:* Colonial-Era Leisure and Recreation; Early National Leisure and Recreation; Frolics

**BIBLIOGRAPHY**

Ensminger, Robert F. *The Pennsylvania Barn: Its Origin, Evolution, and Distribution in North America.* Baltimore: Johns Hopkins University Press, 1992.

Glassie, Henry. "The Variation of Concepts Within Tradition: Barn Building in Otsego County, New York." *Geoscience and Man* 5 (1974): 177–235.

Hostetler, John A. *Amish Society.* Baltimore: Johns Hopkins University Press, 1963.

Kraybill, Don, *The Riddle of Amish Culture*, Revised Edition. Baltimore: Johns Hopkins University Press, 2001.

Walbert, David. *Garden Spot: Lancaster County, the Old Order Amish, and the Selling of Rural America.* New York: Oxford University Press, 2002.

*Simon J. Bronner*

# BARS

Fundamentally, a bar is a commercial establishment selling alcohol by the drink. Yet this minimal definition hardly captures the essence of an institution that has served as the chief leisure headquarters for millions of Americans for nearly four centuries. More than a mere drink dispensary, a bar also serves as a social club, a place where regular customers gather to tell stories, play games, enjoy music, and share meals in addition to "hoisting a few." Certainly alcohol is a powerful draw, but sociability is the principal goal of bar life.

Drinking establishments have been known by many names from the colonial era to the present day. In the seventeenth and eighteenth centuries, the most common term was "tavern." By 1797, citizens of the newly formed United States were using "barroom," later shortened to

**Schlitz Hotel.** Opened on 3 July 1886 the bar at the old Schlitz Hotel in Milwaukee, Wisconsin, is now the site of The Grand Avenue shopping mall. *Courtesy of The Library of Congress*

"bar." In the 1840s, "saloon" began to catch the public fancy, becoming the favorite term from the 1870s until the advent of nationwide prohibition in 1920. Then, after a brief period of illegal "speakeasies," the modern era of drinking establishments dawned in 1933. Bar owners at first eschewed the now besmirched term "saloon," which was even outlawed in some areas. Instead, they employed "bar," "tavern," "lounge," or the euphemistic "grill." In the late twentieth century, "saloon" began to make a comeback, ironically due in part to its nostalgic charm. By the early twenty-first century, then, "bar," "tavern," "lounge," and "saloon" had emerged as the favored terms, with "bar" probably the most common. But all of these terms (and many others not mentioned) mean essentially the same thing: a commercial enterprise offering drink and companionship in a semipublic space.

Even the straight-laced Puritans acknowledged the social benefits of taverns and alcohol, as long as enjoyed in moderation. Indeed, they valued drink not only as a social lubricant, but also as a food, as an item of barter, and as medicine in cases of fever, fatigue, and injury. Cotton Mather, the venerable seventeenth-century preacher, called alcohol the "good creature of God" and agreed with his contemporaries that well-regulated taverns were a community necessity for both townsfolk and travelers.

Colonial drinking establishments were generally called "taverns," but they were also known as "inns," "public houses," and "ordinaries," the latter named for the regular meal or "ordinary" offered midday at a fixed price. Tavern meals with alcoholic refreshments were often occasions for conviviality, with locals and transients swapping political news, regional gossip, and travel stories while eating at long tables or relaxing afterward by the fireplace. Both men and some women partook of these pleasures, the latter often being travelers seeking overnight shelter. Drinks of choice in the colonial period included rum (the favorite), hard cider, brandy, ale, beer, and wine.

Though colonial drinking establishments did cater to both male and female patrons, local men were the backbone of the tavern trade. Forming into friendship circles or "companies," they often drank communally by dipping their cups into a shared bowl of spiked punch or by passing around a container of beer or wine to become what one contemporary observer called "pot companions." When properly lubricated, some customers spontaneously sang traditional folksongs or popular broadsides, while others brought out fiddles and pipes to accompany a bit of dancing. Tavern groups played games of dice and cards, or they ventured outside to engage in bowling and handball contests or to witness the occasional turkey shoot, cockfight, or horse race. Customers often made small wagers on such contests, though colonial leaders frowned on gambling except for official revenue-raising lotteries. On special occasions such as militia musters, elections, and court days, taverns became important community focal points where the townsfolk met and mingled, and some indulged in days-long communal binges.

Tavern playfulness sometimes got out of hand in the waterfront grogshops of colonial seaport towns such as Boston, New York, and Charleston. As court records show, government officials tried but frequently failed to prevent proprietors from serving slaves, servants, minors, known drunkards, and prostitutes. Instead, these lowly folk as well as sailors and other laborers shamelessly caroused together regardless of gender, race, or social status. They drank excessively, danced wildly, gambled extravagantly, brawled frequently, arranged sexual encounters openly, and even plotted occasionally to stage a mob uprising or slave revolt. Apart from waterfront dives, however, taverns in the colonies were generally respectable gathering places for small, mostly male groups of artisans, shopkeepers, and local farmers who engaged in casual drinking and socializing.

The American Revolution brought a measure of revolution to tavern society as well. Political talk, long a popular pastime in urban bars, became more widespread and more urgent as customers swapped war news and partisan views. Revolutionary leaders sometimes held strategy meetings in taverns. But not all drinking establishments in the revolutionary era became hotbeds of political action; many merely percolated along as best they could in wartime. One thing did change in most taverns, however: rum, once the colonial favorite, now began to fall from favor (along with tea) as a symbol of British domination. Instead, freshly independent Americans who drank hard liquor increasingly turned to whiskey, which had the advantage of being both patriotic and cheap.

In the early nineteenth century, profit-minded businessmen of the rising market economy demanded a sober workforce and a sharp division between work and leisure hours. Gone were the days of "dram drinking," when colonials sipped small doses of alcohol throughout the day. Instead, many workers pursued a pattern of abstinence at work and intoxication at play, usually in taverns. In the same years, whiskey emerged as the drink of choice, and Americans drank more of it per capita than ever before or since. As a result, the communal binge, once an occasional community-wide celebration, now became a regular ritual of working-class tavern life. Meanwhile, middle- and upper-class people withdrew to their elegant hotel bars, private clubs, or homes to consume diluted drinks (called "cocktails" since at least 1806) or to not drink at all.

Antebellum workmen, often trapped in low-paying, dead-end jobs, were turning to the realm of leisure to cultivate a sense of social identity and self-worth as men. Taverns hosted a wide variety of such male peer groups. These ranged from informal barroom cliques to more organized entities, including volunteer fire companies, fledgling unions, political clubs, and ethnic neighborhood gangs. Women sometimes joined in their revelries, but the barroom was becoming an increasingly masculine preserve.

Leisure activities varied according to tavern location and customer inclination. In smaller towns, most bars still had access to open space. Customers there participated in outdoor sporting events inherited from colonial times, such as handball or cockfights. In growing urban centers, indoor recreation became increasingly important. Billiards and cards, especially poker, were favorite pastimes by the late antebellum period. Also popular were lotteries, though they were notoriously corrupt. Perhaps the most controversial barroom sport was boxing, in which bare-fisted fighters pummeled each other in endless rounds until one man finally collapsed. Though offensive to bourgeois sensibilities, such contests were rituals of manhood for working-class bar patrons more interested in earthy camaraderie than polite respectability.

Singing and storytelling were also favorite pastimes in antebellum taverns. Touring minstrelsy shows and the beginnings of vaudeville provided new material for drinkers to try out in their midnight choirs. In the rougher frontier areas, bargoers swapped humorous tall tales and boasted of wilderness adventures. Urban tavern customers were more likely to discuss workplace woes, local political rivalries, or the supposed superiority of one ethnic group over another. When sectional conflicts eventually erupted into the Civil War, bar talk turned to the latest war news. And as happens after every war, the old soldiers told and retold their battle stories to a new generation of patrons who would soon face a world-shaking upheaval of their own: the Industrial Revolution.

Factories, tenements, saloons—these were the ubiquitous symbols of the stupendous industrial expansion that engulfed American society from 1870 to 1920. Ripples of the revolution reached even the most remote frontier towns. In the bar business, for example, large breweries refined their production and distribution methods and soon placed beer alongside whiskey as America's favorite drinks. Similarly, sizable manufacturing concerns like the Brunswick Company began to ship standardized barroom equipment throughout America, giving bars from Cheyenne to Charleston the same general appearance. In consequence, bars were better stocked and far more comfortable than their humbler antebellum counterparts. This might explain the long-lived popularity of the fanciful name "saloon," apparently derived from the French "salon," meaning an elegant social hall.

A central feature of saloon culture after 1870 was the treating ritual. Though inherited from taverns past, the practice became universally popular during the saloon period. The idea was simple: one person bought a drink for another, who was then honor-bound to reciprocate with a drink purchase or other equivalent favor. The gesture symbolized camaraderie and mutual respect, whether the participants were a drinker and his comrades, a saloonkeeper and his regulars, a sports celebrity and his fans, or a politician and his supporters. Antisaloon reformers bemoaned the overindulgence that the practice often entailed, with the politician's treat being deemed particularly odious because the recipients were expected to reciprocate in votes. For saloon goers, however, the treat, often accompanied by a friendly toast, was both a pleasurable party starter and an affirmation of brotherhood.

Another distinctive feature of the saloon was its legendary free lunch. Made possible by brewery subsidies, the lunch was "free" with the purchase of at least one five-cent beer. The fare might include ethnic and regional specialties such as German blood sausage in New York, a cowboy's repast of beef and greens in Colorado, or a plate of Mexican beans in California. Served buffet-style, the free lunch introduced customers to the cuisines of various native and immigrant cultures and permitted even the poorest men to eat heartily and well. By the 1890s, some poor women were also partaking of this attractive bargain, shocking everyone by merrily consuming their hot plates and cold beers in the back room.

Saloons were the scene of much spontaneous barside singing. The regulars embraced a broad repertoire, including indigenous folksongs such as "Frankie and Johnny," immigrant airs such as the Irish "Wearin' of the Green," labor anthems such as "Pie in the Sky When You Die," or Tin Pan Alley hits such as "Sweet Adeline." Many of these songs were first popularized in the era's ubiquitous vaudeville theaters and dance halls and then brought back to neighborhood saloons. Some contemporaries reported that sprightly band music emanated from the saloon's back room when unions, lodges, and political clubs held their seasonal parties. Other observers claimed, however, that bargoers generally preferred melancholy melodies praising beloved mothers and lost lovers, a revealing commentary on the lonely lives that many immigrants and rural migrants led in the cities of industrializing America.

Regarding barroom talk and storytelling, most customers preferred to engage in casual banter with their drinking comrades, often turning to the saloonkeeper to provide points of fact on sporting events, news stories, or neighborhood gossip.

Games and gambling also occupied much of the saloon goers' leisure time. Though wagering was common, the stakes were usually low, amounting to a few nickels, some cigars, or a round of drinks. Workers had little cash to spare, and their main aim was sociability, not profit. Several games of chance were popular, including craps and poker dice, roulette, and slot machines. Lotteries had been outlawed everywhere but a few southern states like Louisiana and Kentucky. Nevertheless, bargoers still clandestinely participated in the side game called "numbers" or "policy," in which a bettor "insured" a partial interest in his chosen lottery number.

Games of competition were also popular. Pocket billiards, now widely called "pool," was a barroom favorite, as were chess, checkers, and other board games. Card games of many kinds were popular, including poker, faro, euchre, casino, fan tan, and pinochle. A few sizable saloons offered indoor handball courts, bowling alleys, and exercise rooms. Some very large establishments with stages, known as "concert saloons," featured boxing matches.

The saloon period of 1870 to 1920, which H. L. Mencken dubbed "the Golden Age of American drinking" (Mencken, p. 164), was a wild and wide-open time for bars. Indeed, anti-drink crusaders so deplored the central role that saloons had come to play in workers' leisure time that they eventually succeeded in outlawing both bars and alcohol through a constitutional amendment. Many of the reformers' criticisms of the saloon were justified, but the lore of the barroom was never richer.

Officially, bars were forbidden while the Eighteenth Amendment held sway from 1920 to 1933. Actually, bars simply went underground, though they underwent a drastic change for the worse in the process. These illegal establishments were generally known as "speakeasies" or "blind pigs." The better speakeasies, supplied and sometimes owned by bootleggers with mafia connections, attracted mostly middle-class couples who could afford the exorbitant prices charged for a shot of awful and undetermined liquor in a decoy coffee cup. For working-class people, underground bars were smaller, simpler operations, often undecorated and sometimes in fact just somebody's kitchen with the curtains pulled down. These modest enterprises offered alcohol obtained from bootleggers or made on the premises. Such "hooch" was usually of poor quality and sometimes downright dangerous. Most working-class customers did not linger long, but rather simply drank and departed, sometimes with a package of take-home alcohol in hand. Thus, bars did persist during the supposedly "dry decade," though they were hardly the popular centers of leisure that saloons had been.

When the Eighteenth Amendment was repealed in 1933, bars quickly resurfaced, but much had changed since the old saloon days. During prohibition, respectable women had begun drinking openly while entertaining at home, and many now wished to expand their drinking horizons. To accommodate the increased presence of women, proprietors added bar stools and tables and generally spruced up the joint. Prohibition had also affected drinking practices. Thirteen years of bootleg liquor had prompted many to use mixers to disguise the taste. Men who once had drunk their liquor straight were now calling for cocktails, which were popular with the women as well. Some bars shunned all such innovations, but many others rushed to capitalize on the new trends, calling themselves "cocktail lounges" and catering to women in "cocktail dresses" who sat and sipped alongside the men.

Following prohibition's repeal, barroom pastimes such as singing, gaming, and storytelling were profoundly affected by technological advancements. Regarding music, bar customers now only rarely did any singing themselves. Instead, most came to prefer professional renderings of popular tunes delivered to barrooms through radio programs since the 1930s, jukeboxes since the 1940s, and television broadcasts since the 1950s (from Ed Sullivan to MTV). In the typical neighborhood bar, drinkers might still spontaneously dance to such "canned" music, and some proprietors might provide live music on occasion. With the advent of recorded music, however, the long-standing tradition of barroom singing steadily faded from the scene.

Gaming technology is a different matter. Devices such as pinball, slot machines, and video poker invite bargoers' active participation, with small crowds sometimes gathering to monitor the players' progress. Radio and television broadcasts of sporting events such as ballgames, horse races, and boxing matches also provoke lively reactions from bargoers, especially if accompanied by friendly wagers. Indeed, when television newscasters want to capture public reaction to major contests such as the Super Bowl, they invariably show film of bar crowds shouting madly at television screens and each other. Some customers still prefer to play "low-tech" games, including cards, dice, and pool. When modern gaming technology is in play, however, customers are generally actively engaged, in contrast to the impact of music technology, which has transformed most bargoers into listeners rather than performers.

Modern media have affected the oral traditions of taverns as well. On the one hand, barrooms have faced stiff competition from the storytelling power of movies, radio, and television. On the other, bars equipped with radio and television do brisk business when major news stories break, for many people prefer witnessing such events in good drinking company. Whether during the Kennedy assassination in 1963 or the World Trade Center terrorist attack in 2001, barrooms have served as centers of communication and commiseration for their news-hungry clienteles.

The bar is the chameleon of American institutions. It appears in many incarnations over the centuries, whether as the colonial tavern, the antebellum grogshop, the industrial age saloon, the prohibition speakeasy, or the modern bar and lounge. And it is as variable as the customers who patronize it. This has been the key to its enduring success despite efforts of more sober citizens to curb it, reform it, or even destroy it down through the years. It is indeed one of America's most remarkable leisure institutions: the infinitely adaptable bar.

*See also:* Colonial-Era Leisure and Recreation, Dance Halls, Drinking

## BIBLIOGRAPHY

Conroy, David W. *In Public Houses: Drink and the Revolution of Authority in Colonial Massachusetts.* Chapel Hill: University of North Carolina Press, 1995.

Duis, Perry R. *The Saloon: Public Drinking in Chicago and Boston, 1880–1920.* Urbana: University of Illinois Press, 1983.

Mencken, H. L. *The American Language.* 4th edition, abridged. New York: Alfred A. Knopf, 1980.

Murdock, Catherine Gilbert. *Domesticating Drink: Women, Men, and Alcohol in America, 1870–1940*. Baltimore: Johns Hopkins University Press, 1998.

Powers, Madelon. *Faces along the Bar: Lore and Order in the Workingman's Saloon, 1870–1920*. Chicago: University of Chicago Press, 1998.

Rorabaugh, W. J. *The Alcoholic Republic: An American Tradition*. New York: Oxford University Press, 1979.

Rosenzweig, Roy. *Eight Hours for What We Will: Workers and Leisure in an Industrial City, 1870–1920*. New York: Cambridge University Press, 1983.

Rotskoff, Lori. *Love on the Rocks: Men, Women, and Alcohol in Post–World War II America*. Chapel Hill: University of North Carolina Press, 2002.

Salinger, Sharon V. *Taverns and Drinking in Early America*. Baltimore: Johns Hopkins University Press, 2002.

Sinclair, Andrew. *Era of Excess: A Social History of the Prohibition Movement*. New York: Harper and Row, 1962.

Thompson, Peter. *Rum Punch and Revolution: Taverngoing and Public Life in Eighteenth-Century Philadelphia*. Philadelphia: University of Pennsylvania Press, 1999.

West, Elliott. *The Saloon on the Rocky Mountain Mining Frontier*. Lincoln: University of Nebraska Press, 1979.

*Madelon Powers*

# BASEBALL, AMATEUR

Since the 1870s, amateur baseball has existed in various forms as a reaction to the professionalism of the game. Generally referring to players over seventeen years old who have never been paid to play, amateur baseball has been managed nationally within the context of college athletics, various baseball organizations, and summer baseball leagues, and internationally with the goal of becoming part of the Olympic movement.

Amateurism has been positioned as "pure sport," as athletes do not receive payment for playing, and the concept has been associated with notions of fair play and character building. However, despite claims that the amateur ethos was a legacy of ancient Greek sport, it was a tradition invented in England by members of the upper class in the early nineteenth century as a manner to reinforce their social superiority. According to Steven Pope, amateurism in the United States was a reaction to an already-established professional tradition, against which members of the middle and upper classes developed sporting institutions and ideologies designed to strengthen class boundaries.

## Baseball's Early Years: Amateurism vs. Professionalism

Players during baseball's formative years of the 1840s and 1850s did not necessarily consider themselves amateurs because playing baseball was a social activity, not a commercial enterprise. As such, many early baseball players were members of the middle class, or tradesmen who had disposable free time; they joined clubs to play for health or camaraderie. However, as the game became increasingly popular as a spectator sport and grew more competitive, clubs began to induct and pay expert players for their skill rather than social standing. In 1858, the National Association of Base Ball Players (NABBP) was formed to govern the game, and, shortly thereafter, the organization banned the practice of paying players for their services. However, the rule had little effect at curbing professionalism; it was frequently disregarded and rarely enforced, and increasing numbers of working-class players were paid.

Following the successful tour of the 1869 Cincinnati Red Stockings, the first openly all-professional team, the rift was irresolvable between amateurs who sought to play the game for fun, social interaction, and physical improvement, and professionals for whom baseball was a career. As Warren Goldstein discusses in *Playing for Keeps*, the leading professional and amateur clubs formed their own leagues by 1871, with the National Association of Amateur Base Ball Players (NAABBP) seeking to return the game to its previous status as a pastime. Mirroring the terms used to denote status in English cricket, newspapers distinguished professional "players" from amateur "gentlemen." However, the NAABBP lasted only until 1874, when it dissolved for lack of fan interest and poor governance.

## College Baseball

As amateur baseball failed as a commercial enterprise, attention of those who rejected professionalism within the game moved toward college athletics. However, the college game was not immune from frequent controversies surrounding amateurism and professionalism and the issue of "summer baseball." Starting in the 1880s, many collegiate players were paid by elite eastern summer resorts to provide baseball as entertainment for guests. The issue remained unresolved for several decades, even following the 1906 establishment of the National Collegiate Athletic Association (NCAA), which could not reach agreement among its members to ban the practice. Despite the NCAA Committee on Summer Baseball determining that "the playing of baseball in summer for gain is distinctly opposed to the principles of amateurism,"

**College World Series.** On 8 June 1996 Louisiana State defeats Miami to win the national championship at the College World Series in Omaha, Nebraska. Brad Wilson (10) came in to score off of Warren Morris's decisive two-run homer in the bottom of the ninth inning. © *John Gaps III for AP/Wide World Photos*

dissent among university faculty and staff and popular opinion supported baseball as reasonable summer employment. The controversy was resolved during the 1950s when the NCAA developed more rigorous mechanisms to enforce amateurism.

With effective control of college baseball players, the NCAA began to sanction summer baseball leagues during the 1960s. Reviewed annually by the NCAA and partially subsidized by Major League Baseball, ten sanctioned summer leagues played in 2003, with the Cape Cod League (established in 1885), Central Illinois Collegiate League (1963), and Valley League Baseball (1962) among the oldest.

## Other Amateur Organizations

The NCAA has not been the only organization governing amateur baseball throughout the twentieth and twenty-first centuries, as other groups have organized amateur competition and championships on a national basis. The National Baseball Federation (NBF—now the National Baseball Amateur Federation) was founded in 1915 and included semipro teams for several years while maintaining a classification for amateur teams. The American Baseball Congress (ABC—now American Amateur Baseball Congress, or AABC) was started as an explicitly amateur organization in 1935, in part with

dissatisfied NBF members. By 1937, the ABC had grown larger than the NBF, with more than 25,000 teams taking part in 350 tournaments to qualify for its national championship. The AABC remains the largest amateur baseball association in the United States, sponsoring competition in seven divisions, ranging from subteens to adults. The National Baseball Congress also formed during the 1930s as a semipro alternative to the AABC but, with the resurgence of the minor leagues during the 1980s, now organizes a wholly amateur tournament.

## International Amateur Baseball

Efforts to organize amateur baseball were not limited to the United States. In 1938, an international governing body was established following the first "Baseball World Cup." The International Baseball Federation (FIBA) resulted from the efforts of Leslie Mann, and was supported by groups such as the NCAA and ABC. As of 2004. FIBA includes 112 countries as members and sponsored international competitions ranging from junior baseball to the Olympics. USA Baseball, which was created in 1978 under the Amateur Sports Act, represents the United States in FIBA and organizes national teams for international competitions.

One of FIBA's main efforts has been in establishing baseball as a competitive sport within the Olympic movement. Baseball first appeared as an exhibition sport at the 1912 Olympics in Stockholm, a status it would repeat five times through 1964. Full competition as a demonstration sport occurred in 1984 in Los Angeles and 1988 in Seoul, with baseball becoming an official medal sport in the 1992 Barcelona Games. Amateur players, mostly collegians, represented the United States in Olympic competition through the 1996 Atlanta Games, with professional minor leaguers playing in 2000 in Sydney

*See also:* Baseball, Crowds; Little League; Softball

**BIBLIOGRAPHY**

Goldstein, Warren J. *Playing the Field: A History of Early Baseball.* Ithaca, N.Y.: Cornell University Press, 1989.

International Baseball Federation. Home page at http://www.baseball.ch.

Pope, Steven W. "Amateurism and American Sports Culture: The Invention of an Athletic Tradition in the United States, 1870–1900." *International Journal of the History of Sport* 13 (1996): 290–309.

Seymour, Harold. *Baseball: The People's Game.* New York: Oxford University Press, 1990.

Smith, Ronald A. "History of Amateurism in Men's Intercollegiate Athletics: The Continuance of a 19th-Century Anachronism in America." *Quest* 45 (1993): 430–447.

*Michael Friedman*

# BASEBALL CROWDS

It was long held that baseball was created on a lazy summer afternoon in Cooperstown, New York, in 1839 by Abner Doubleday, a young, resourceful player, who made up the rules for the game and then called it baseball. This tale was promoted by a patriotic sporting goods entrepreneur named Albert Spalding and others, who were eager to prove that baseball was a uniquely American invention. Research has since shown the Doubleday story to be myth. Baseball actually evolved slowly out of several bat-and-ball games, such as rounders and its offshoots "town ball" and "old cat," which were played in England and the American colonies (Rossi).

The Industrial Revolution was a major influence on the development of baseball as a spectator sport in the West. As workers left the countryside to take jobs in the new industrial cities, they needed new forms of recreation. By the 1830s, ball-and-bat games had become popular in the United States. Virtually every region had a different version. In New England "town ball" was played on a square field with no distinction for foul territory. A player made an out by "plunking" the base runner with a thrown ball. One out retired the side, and a set number of runs, often 100, won the game. The Knickerbocker Base Ball Club of New York, the first organized baseball team about which much is known, viewed a ball game as genteel amateur recreation and polite social intercourse rather than a hard-fought contest for victory. Until about 1855, play was largely informal; although there were organized clubs, they mostly played intramural games. New York City had about a dozen clubs, and the city's newspapers began to refer to baseball as the "national game." In 1856, the *New York Mercury* coined the phrase "the national pastime"(Tygiel, p. 6).

The British sport of cricket also enjoyed wide popularity in the United States and vied with baseball for supremacy. Many American cities and towns had cricket clubs, and matches often attracted larger crowds and received more attention in the press than did baseball. In 1859, over 24,000 spectators attended a cricket match in Hoboken, New Jersey, between an all-star American team and a touring professional English club (Rader, 1990). Unlike baseball, however, cricket was mostly an immigrant game, played mainly by white-collar and skilled British expatriates. Cricket was hailed for its capacity to instill "manly virtues" in its players.

One of the first newspapers devoted to covering sporting events, *Porter's Spirit of the Times,* called for a game "peculiar to the citizens of the United States, one distinctive from the games of the British like cricket" (Tygiel, p. 6). America had a national flag, national anthem, national government, and national symbols, but no national game. The desire for a "national game," a sport separate from the foreign games of cricket and soccer, was fulfilled in baseball after 1865. The Civil War (1861–1865) did much to popularize the game in all areas of the country since soldiers in both armies played the game in camps and prison compounds. By the late 1860s, popular opinion held that cricket was boring while baseball was exciting. Cricket, which had been the preeminent American bat-and-ball game of the first half of the nineteenth century, gradually faded and was irrelevant by 1900.

## Origins of the Baseball Crowd

The National Baseball Association was established in 1871, effectively marking the birth of professional baseball in America. Baseball soon became a mass spectator sport, with the construction of urban ballparks and the professionalization of teams and leagues. Baseball was also a great social leveler. Whereas early in the century baseball was primarily the domain of upper-middle-class men, by the end of the century its appeal had broadened to encompass the middle and working classes, who mingled together on equal terms. "The spectator at a ball game," noted one observer, "is no longer a statesman, lawyer . . . or doctor, but just plain everyday man, with a heart full of fraternity and good will to all his fellow men. . . The oftener he sits in grandstand . . . the kindlier, better man and citizen he must tend to become" (Kimmel, p. 293).

Baseball as a spectator sport was well suited to industrial capitalism, providing a leisure-time diversion for working-class men. Ballparks were located in the city and admission fees were affordable, resulting in attendance at baseball games being more broadly based than other spectator sports, such as boxing. Watching baseball was regarded as a catharsis. City dwellers who worked long and arduous hours at boring, repetitive jobs needed an opportunity to relax and relieve themselves of their built-up "aggressions," which they might otherwise direct at their families or employers. They would do this at the ballpark. It was believed that young men learned to become better people not just by playing baseball but also by watching it. The values and benefits that were thought to come from playing baseball had made the imaginative leap to being instilled merely by watching baseball.

While sports entrepreneurs had been charging admission to horse races, cricket matches, and prizefights for some time, no admission was charged to attend baseball games until the early 1860s. In 1862, fans were charged a 10-cent fee to watch clubs play at Brooklyn's new Union Grounds. Soon prominent clubs began playing for a share of the gate money, breaching the amateurism of early baseball. Officials refined the rules of the game to make it more interesting to spectators. As fans demonstrated a willingness to pay to see a ball game, admission fees rose so that by 1880, 50 cents was the standard charge (Rader, 2002). A seat at a popular theater of the time cost 25 to 75 cents, so baseball tickets were not out of line. For a time the National League sought middle-class fans while the rival American Association (1882–1891) appealed mostly to working-class fans. Compared to men, women rarely patronized professional baseball, despite the scheduling of special "ladies" days and special sections of the stands being reserved for women. Early photographs of baseball crowds reveal an overwhelming preponderance of males.

As the popularity of baseball increased, more improvements were made—the baseball diamond was standardized, teams and leagues were organized, rules were refined, game schedules were instituted, and soon grand tours were undertaken by professional baseball teams. By 1910, there were an estimated 2,000 organized baseball clubs across the nation. Professional baseball reached its highest development in the rapidly growing urban centers. There the baseball park was one of the new important locations for social life, especially for white, native-born men. The prestige and reputation of cities was affected by the status of their professional clubs. Owners and sports writers insisted that baseball was an excellent source of community pride. Feelings about one's city could depend on how the team performed. By 1900, baseball was firmly embedded in American culture as a popular pastime for boys and men, as a spectator sport, as a subject of national and local news reporting, and as an increasing source of national pride. It would grow even stronger in the new millennium.

## Radio

After the first baseball game was broadcast in 1921, many team owners questioned whether regular radio broadcasting would keep ticket buyers away from the actual game. Fearing a decline in attendance, the American League initially prohibited broadcasts from their ballparks. *The Sporting News*, the sport's premier publication, warned that baseball was a game better seen than heard, that fans would stay home and listen to the games for free (Rossi). But the excitement generated by the broadcast of the 1926 World Series changed opinions. Radio broadcasts of the World Series became an annual rite, until upstaged by television in the 1950s.

In 1925 the Cubs let any Chicago station broadcast their games free of charge and over the next six years they saw their home attendance increase 117 percent. Their league rivals who did not broadcast their games saw their attendance increase only 27 percent. By 1935, only the three New York teams—Dodgers, Giants, and Yankees—had no regular radio broadcasts of their games. Soon, New York's resistance weakened, however, as radio stations discovered they could sell commercials during the broadcast and thus pay clubs for broadcast privileges. With new income from radio, club owners were less concerned about the loss of some of their gate receipts.

After World War II, the number of big-league games aired on radio ballooned astronomically when the number of local AM radio stations in the country doubled. Baseball had become a staple of radio programming on the local, regional, and national levels. By the time radio was eclipsed by television in the 1950s, radio broadcasts had created many new fans and spread the popularity of the game far beyond major league cities.

## Television

The first televised major league game, the Cincinnati Reds playing the Brooklyn Dodgers at Ebbets Field in Brooklyn, was on 26 August 1939. Few fans would have seen it though, as only 400 sets were in existence in the United States, and most of them were not in homes but in companies interested in the new technology. It wouldn't have made any difference because, while the players were clearly distinguishable, it was not possible to see the ball. The New York Yankees, who were the last club to allow radio broadcast, were the first team to sell television rights, in 1946 for $75,000 per year. Major league games were not regularly televised until a few years later. As with the beginning of radio, most baseball executives did not understand the new medium and rejected the early television deals, thinking they would negatively impact attendance. Branch Rickey, usually an innovator, feared television, saying, "Radio stimulates interest. Television satisfies it"(Rossi, p. 159). "TV Must Go—Or Baseball Will" was the cautionary title of one news article (Tygiel, p. 155).

Families who did not yet own TV sets could watch the game with neighbors, or in other venues such as bars and restaurants, which had recently discovered that televising sports attracted patrons. Some even watched in small crowds around TVs in windows of appliance stores. ABC aired the first regular weekly network telecast in 1953; its *Game of the Week* became a fixture lasting until 1992. Still unsure whether telecasts would keep fans at home, most teams nonetheless signed lucrative television deals in the 1950s. Most teams contracted for broadcasts of every game, the cautious few broadcast only road games. By 1955, only four teams were without television deals.

Television's impact on attendance was mixed. Allowing telecasts of nearly all their home games, the Boston Braves saw their attendance decline nearly 81 percent between 1948 and 1952 (Rader, 1990). Attendance at other ballparks, however, seemed to be unaffected by television. It was also difficult to separate out the effect of television from new competing leisure-time activities that were also hurting attendance.

But unlimited major league telecasts were a disaster for minor league baseball. Fans in minor league towns across the country, who could now see big leaguers play on television for free, had less interest in going out to the ballpark. Minor league attendance fell from 42 million in 1949, before the advent of televised major league games, to 15 million in 1957, and to just 10 million in 1969. The new interstate highway system, which gave fans access to big league baseball, also contributed to the decline; and a

few of the more profitable minor league cities, such as Los Angeles and Seattle, were overtaken by major league baseball.

## Baseball's New Geography

Until 1953, major league baseball could be found only in the Northeast and Midwest, the two areas of the country where the game had been founded at the turn of the century. St. Louis was the westernmost and southernmost outpost of the "national" pastime. Yet the fastest growing areas in the nation were the West and the South. In 1953, the Boston Braves, a weak franchise and less popular than the same town Red Sox, moved to Milwaukee. It was the first franchise shift in more than fifty years; no team had moved since the 1903 transfer of the Baltimore Orioles to New York City, where they ultimately became the Yankees. Following the Braves' success in their new home, nine other teams uprooted themselves over the next two decades, including the St. Louis Browns moving to Baltimore (and becoming the Orioles), the Philadelphia Athletics to Kansas City, the Brooklyn Dodgers to Los Angeles, the New York Giants to San Francisco, and the Washington Senators to Minnesota (becoming the Twins). Understandably, many fans, most famously in Brooklyn, deeply resented the loss of their team. The Dodgers' owner, Walter O'Malley, became one of the most maligned figures in modern sport. As Brooklyn fans saw it, O'Malley's greed had cost them their beloved Bums. His fat face, sleek hair, and perpetual cigar made him an easy villain. The Dodgers, like the Giants who had departed New York at the same time, had merely acted the way baseball teams had historically behaved—searching for greater profits. Besides, defenders of the relocation said, baseball's move west was long overdue, as California had become the nation's most populous state. The expansion of major league baseball in the West and South broadened the game's national appeal and created droves of new fans. Cities that acquired the relocated franchises took great pride in becoming part of the elite fraternity of big-league cities. Becoming "big league" gave them a new identity.

## Free Agency

Free agency, which enables players to switch teams, selling their services to the highest bidder, has affected the loyalty of fans toward their teams. Until 1975, all major and minor league ballplayers were tied to the teams that signed them by a "reserve clause." In the late 1960s, the Major League Baseball Player's Association (MLBPA), led by Marvin Miller, began to chip away at baseball's

**San Diego Chicken.** Voted by *The Sporting News* as one of the "Top 100 Most Powerful People in Sports for the 20th Century" Ted Giannoulas' San Diego Chicken performs for the crowd during the San Diego Padres–Colorado Rockies game on Friday, 26 September 2003 at the final homestand of Qualcomm Stadium (moved to Petco Park in 2004). The Chicken began entertaining at sporting and other events in the 1970s. © *Lenny Ignelzi for AP/Wide World Photos*

venerable reserve clause. In 1975, a federal arbitrator effectively abolished the clause in ruling that players could be reserved for only one year at the end of their contracts, after which they would become "free agents." In response, players' salaries jumped from an average of $45,000 in 1975 to $144,000 in 1980 and to over $2 million in 2000. After the 1975 decision, a compromise was reached in 1976 as part of the collective bargaining agreement between the players' union and club owners in which players were now tied to their teams for six years, after which they could become free agents. The new freedoms enjoyed by the players and their escalating salaries resulted in more conflict between team owners and the players' union. Fans grew increasingly alienated by labor-management warfare and what was perceived as greed on the part of both sides.

For fans, the largest impact of free agency has been that their favorite team loses veteran players every year and has to reinvent itself before each new season. Old-timers, who grew up watching nearly the same lineup year after year, are bewildered by all the new faces. A few defenders of the new status quo say that it's exciting to ponder how the new collection of talent will perform. Will the new crowd finally bring the Cubs or the Red Sox a championship?

Not only do team rosters change more today; so do owners. In the old days, family dynasties were common—Tom Yawkey, William Wrigley, Walter O'Malley, Horace Stoneham, Calvin Griffith—and they held their teams for decades. Today, few owners have been in the baseball business more than ten years. Many fans don't even know their names; indeed, powerful media conglomerates like the Tribune Company (Cubs) and Turner Broadcasting (Braves) own a few teams.

## Ballparks

The earliest ballparks, built in the 1850s, were for more than just baseball, and they were not enclosed. Efforts to enclose them, known as the "enclosure movement," allowed owners to charge admission and brought order at games. Fans could no longer simply sit wherever they pleased, sometimes encroaching on the field. The earliest parks accommodated only a few thousand fans on wooden benches. Most parks were rectangular to fit into the setup of long city blocks. Often the result was a short right field that favored left-handers. Fans were close to the action; they could see their sports heroes sweat, they could witness their emotions, and they cared about them because they knew them. Constructed of wood, the parks were often in need of repair, and sometimes burned to the ground. One, Redland Park in Cincinnati, collapsed in 1892, killing one spectator.

The first concrete and steel park, Shibe Park in Philadelphia, wasn't built until 1909. It seated 20,000. The first triple-decked ballpark, Yankee Stadium, was finished in 1923 and could seat 57,545. Twelve years later, the first major league park with lights was built—County Stadium in Milwaukee in 1935.

By the 1950s many major league ballparks were handicapped by a shortage of parking and by their location in decaying neighborhoods. Americans had abandoned public transportation in favor of automobiles, thereby requiring large parking lots at their ballparks. Built in residential neighborhoods, many of the old parks could not find space to accommodate parking. Hence, in the 1960s baseball left the city, and clubs replaced the old ballparks with new, concrete multisport ovals, some of which had artificial turf as well. Their design and uniform dimensions made them impersonal and soulless, with no suggestion of history and no sense of place. They were so similar to one another that they came to be referred to as "cookie-cutter ballparks." As one player said, they looked like they had been built more for bullfights than for baseball. They blighted the baseball landscape for over two decades. In the 1990s, baseball began to tear down the cookie-cutter coliseums and replace them with new "old" ballparks with a retro feel. Oriole Park at Camden Yards began the trend, and by the early 2000s had spawned the construction of ten other postmodern ballparks with frills and loads of character. Indoor stadiums are also on their way out, as is artificial turf, which has proved hard on players, shortening their careers. At its peak, ten teams played on artificial turf; in 2004, only three were left.

Baseball fans have a closer attachment to their ballparks than in any other sport. Ballparks are "magical places," with the sweep of their grandstands, the rainbow of color in the different sections of seating, the emerald green fields crisply outlined in chalk. Fans speak with reverence about Fenway Park, Yankee Stadium, and Wrigley Field, and with admiration of a different sort for the new retro ballparks such as Pac Bell in San Francisco, Safeco in Seattle, and Camden Yards in Baltimore. Phillip Lowry called his book on ballparks *Green Cathedrals* because the more he studied ballparks the more he thought they resembled mosques, synagogues, churches, and similar places of worship. He believes many Americans have a "spiritual reverence for ballparks, because they hold treasured memories and serve as a sanctuary for the spirit" (Lowry, p. 52). In no other sport do fans plan vacations around visiting ballparks. "When was the last time you heard a football fan making a pilgrimage to all the NFL stadiums or a basketball fan bragging about which NBA arenas he's been to?" asked Craig Wright and Tom House in *The Diamond Appraised* (p. 299).

Besides the game itself, there are other activities at the ballpark that entertain its spectators, such as the antics of mascots, games and video played on the scoreboard, and between-inning competitions and races involving children. Fans sometimes create their own diversions such as the "wave," in which thousands of spectators join together in rising to their feet in proper sequence to produce a human ripple across the stadium. Or fans bat beach balls around the stands, directing them from one section of the seats to another. In one of the venerable rituals of the game, all fans stand to stretch in the seventh inning and often sing a chorus or two of "Take Me Out to the Ball Game," the most popular song ever associated with a particular sport. Throughout the game, fans follow developments elsewhere in the major leagues on the scoreboard, noting how division rivals are faring.

## Ebb and Flow of Ballpark Crowds

Despite baseball's popularity, crowds at ballparks in the nineteenth century were small compared to the early 2000s. During the 1871 to 1875 National Association seasons, for example, teams averaged less than 3,000 per game. The Boston Red Stockings drew only 1,750 per game in 1875 when they finished first. In the 1890s, National League teams averaged about 2,500 per game.

Attendance increased in the first decade of the twentieth century due to high interest in the World Series, a decline in ballpark rowdyism, and close pennant races. But in the following decade (1909–1919), attendance dropped off due to a slumping economy, World War I, and competition from new leisure activities such as motion pictures.

Spectators came in droves again after the end of the war and through the 1920s as prosperity returned to the country and the home run became common with the arrival of larger-than-life Babe Ruth. In 1920, the Yankees drew over 1 million fans, the first team ever to do so. Attendance then suffered heavily from the Great Depression through World War II. At its low point in 1934, the National League averaged just 5,200 per game. Even the Cardinals, who won the pennant that year, could attract only 4,200 per game.

Attendance didn't recover until after the war; the 1946 season saw 15,000 per game, a 70 percent increase over the 1945 season. Crowds grew larger in the 1950s, and then slipped in the 1960s when major league baseball expanded. The new unwieldy ten-team leagues, with no divisional play, saw too many teams eliminated early in the season. Attendance was also hurt by the dominance of the New York Yankees, who won every pennant from 1960 through 1964, causing fans in other cities to lose interest early in the season. Attendance and interest continued to decline through 1974 (the period from 1966 to 1974 is sometimes referred to as the "Dark Ages of Baseball") in part due to the growing popularity of football. An exciting 1975 World Series between the Boston Red Sox and the Cincinnati Reds, however, reignited interest. (Game 6 of that World Series is considered by many to be the most exciting baseball game ever played.)

In an effort to broaden its appeal, especially to younger fans, the 1970s and 1980s saw most teams adopt mascots. Many were trying to emulate the hugely successful San Diego Chicken. The new mascots wore oversized animal costumes, such as the Cardinals' Fred Bird, the Pirate Parrot, the Mariner Moose, and the Phillie Fanatic. Curiously, in 1984 the San Francisco Giants fans voted overwhelmingly against having a mascot. The Giants persisted, and when their new Crazy Crab arrived in the middle of the fifth inning, fans booed and threw trash at it. It was discontinued after a few games. As the new millennium begins, the Giants have a new mascot in Lou the Seal. Early in the last century, it was not uncommon for teams to use dwarves, hunchbacks, or mentally disabled adults as mascots.

Crowds increased steadily from 1975 until 1991, and then labor strife between the club owners and the players' union alienated many fans. A strike ended the 1994 season in August, canceling the World Series. The following season, after a new contract was finally agreed upon, attendance declined by 29 percent. Many unhappy fans turned to minor league baseball, which enjoyed a re-naissance and record attendance all across the country after the 1994 strike. Many Americans had first become aware of the lure of minor league baseball in the 1988 movie *Bull Durham*. In minor league ballparks fans found a sense of community and a charm that is often absent in major league stadiums.

## The Minor Leagues

The minor leagues, as the name suggests, is the level of professional baseball below that of the major leagues. There are sixteen minor leagues today, about the same number as in the 1960s—far fewer, however, than the fifty-nine leagues that existed in 1949, the all-time high. The minor leagues are categorized into six levels: AAA (the highest), AA, high A, low A, short season A, and rookie (the lowest). Each major league team has six minor league teams whose primary purpose is to develop talent. Commonly known as the "farm system," the minor leagues were the creation of Branch Rickey, one of the most influential baseball executives of all time. While general manager of the St. Louis Cardinals, Rickey began in 1917 purchasing minor league clubs. By producing their own players, the poverty-stricken Cardinals, Rickey hoped, could avoid expensive player purchases and also offset some of the advantages enjoyed by clubs in the large market areas, such as the New York Yankees. The owners of the other major league clubs resisted acquiring their own minor league teams, believing that the cost outweighed the benefits. But the success of Rickey's system eventually forced all owners to follow his example. Between 1926 and 1946, the Cardinals won nine league championships, finished second six times, and had greater profits than any other league club—most of their profits came not from attendance but from players' sales. In one year alone, sixty-five players who were products of the Cardinal farm system were on the rosters of other big-league clubs.

The new popularity of the minor leagues in the 1990s led to a building boom in new, top-rated ballparks. Over half of all minor league teams in the early 2000s play in ballparks that were built in the previous decade. Where most major league stadiums are separated from communities by freeways and enormous parking lots, minor league ballparks often exist in neighborhoods. Their smaller size (seating capacities are just one-eighth to one-quarter that of major league ballparks) means fans are closer to the field—they not only see the action better but they can hear the umpire's voice and see the players' emotions. Fans easily obtain autographs and can even chat with players along the sidelines before the game. Parking is never a problem, tickets are cheap, and the quality of

**Piedmont Boll Weevils.** The crowd at Fieldcrest Cannon Stadium near Kannapolis, North Carolina watches "Bo the Weevil" during the game on 8 April 1996. A member of the South Atlantic League, the Class A minor league team started up in 1995 and was originally named the Phillies for just its rookie season. © *Chuck Burton for AP/Wide World Photos*

baseball is high. The downside for fans is that the development of talent is more important than winning and the top-performing players don't stay in one place long enough to generate an identity for their team.

## Fans

The word "fan" first appeared in 1682, short for "fanatic," referring to a person with an extreme or unreasonable enthusiasm or zeal. Most fans are socialized into a sport role at a young age. Parents purchase their children sports paraphernalia as gifts—toy baseballs and bats, and T-shirts and caps bearing the logo of their favorite teams. Fathers and mothers introduce and teach them the game. Soon they begin paying attention to sporting events on television on their own, and gradually they learn the rules

of the game. Those who have the requisite skills participate in their sports as athletes, but participation is not necessary to become a fan.

Scholars like Arnold Beisser, author of *The Madness in Sports*, have tried to explain the motivations of fans—why they give so much of their energy and interest to following professional sports when in strictly utilitarian terms sporting contests serve no tangible purpose. They assert that sports provide fans a sense of belonging and identification with a social group beyond the immediate family. Rooting for a team enhances ties with other people who support the same team. This is an important benefit in our socially atomized, highly urbanized American society in which family ties have become attenuated, where geographical mobility has scattered relatives, and where people often have few roots or ties to the places in which they live. Scholars also talk about the "normative social influence" of fandom (Edwards). Simply, people become fans because sports are popular; young people see others enjoy cheering for a favorite team and following sports figures and want to do the same. Put differently, people become fans because of the snowballing effects of sport's initial popularity.

Sport can have another meaning as well. For many fans, team identification represents an extension of the self, and enhances their self-esteem. But such an identification can be double-edged. When your team wins, your self-esteem is enhanced, but when it loses, it can be strained. The effects of team identification have been referred to as "BIRGing" (basking in reflected glory). Conversely, CORFing (cutting off reflected failure) is an effort to distance oneself from a losing team and is induced by the desire to maintain a positive self-identity.

Baseball fans are said to have an especially strong connection to their sport. Most fans first developed a relationship to baseball in childhood. Most boys in America play the game at some point, or at least have worn a glove and tossed a ball; an increasing numbers of young girls play softball. As youngsters, many collected baseball cards and autographs, idolized and memorized the statistical histories of their favorite players. Many boys are taught the game by fathers, an act long memorialized as one of the most significant in father-son relationships. At the ballpark the fans enjoy unusual freedom to voice their feelings about the performance of the players and managers on the field. They cheer and boo perhaps more than fans in any other sport. To speak their minds is a presumed right that goes with having paid the price of admission. They do so because they care, because they emotionally identify with their team, and because sloppy play and losing leave them in despair. In no other sport are fans given the opportunity to vote on most of the players who appear in the mid-season all-star game.

Baseball fandom has been enhanced by a number of baseball novels that have woven romanticism out of folklore and nostalgia. Several, such as Bernard Malamud's *The Natural* (1952) and W. P. Kinsella's *Shoeless Joe* (1982), became popular movies, the latter as *Field of Dreams*. The film's most memorable incantation, "If you build it, he will come," has entered the nation's cultural language. Baseball fans also celebrated the Public Broadcasting Service's (PBS) eighteen-hour documentary *Baseball: A Film by Ken Burns* (1994), which integrated captivating historical footage with lyrical ruminations of celebrity fans about the meaning of the national pastime to them and its role in American life.

While an increasing number of people are watching baseball, others have become disillusioned with it or with professional sports in general. Competition has been diluted by expansion, by too many playoff games, by free agency, by high turnover in team rosters, and by greed. The avarice of players and owners, which fans blame for ongoing labor strife, has caused many Americans to view major league baseball as no different from other areas of institutional life in America, whether it be business, politics, or religion. In becoming part of the corporate landscape, baseball may be losing the capacity to inspire Americans as it once did.

Fans no longer worship baseball superstars the way they once did. Boys growing up in the 1950s read player-hero biographies, such as Yogi Berra, Mickey Mantle, and Joe DiMaggio. These were tall tales of splendid performers who won fame through hard work, clean living, and battling obstacles. In the 1960s, several books, but notably Jim Bouton's *Ball Four*, began to demythologize baseball stars. Most fans no longer view ballplayers as desirable role models for their children. Although major league games draw nearly twice what they did in the 1960s, about 25,000 versus 14,000 per game, many observers say there are fewer diehard fans in attendance. Few spectators keep score on a scorecard. Many love baseball not so much for what it is, but for what it used to be—when the faces didn't change every year, when pitchers went nine innings, when players weren't multimillionaires, and when all games were played outdoors and on grass. A Gallup poll in the early 2000s reported that baseball was a favorite sport of only 12 percent of Americans. In 1964, that figure was 48 percent. Many fans complain that the game is slow, even leaden. Major league baseball is responding to the complaints in various ways, notably by trying to speed up the game by reducing the dead time.

Concerned that the game is no longer sufficiently entertaining for many of today's spectators, both major and minor league baseball have turned to mascots and zany stunts and contests—water balloon tosses, girls dancing on dugout roofs, kids racing the mascot around the bases—to inject fun and amusement. Huge electronic scoreboards now entertain with quizzes and video displays. Fans can picnic at the ballpark. Other tactics to entice fans include the giveaway—key chains, miniature bats, seat cushions, and bobble-head dolls—distributed at the gate, and air guns shooting T-shirts into the crowd between innings. One cost of all this new activity is that ballparks have been less a place for conversation between friends or between fathers (or mothers) and sons (or daughters) than they once were.

Some fans have traded sunshine and the roar of the crowd for keeping track of baseball statistics on their own home computers. In the mid-1980s, the widespread availability of the personal computer made possible a new type of fandom in the form of fantasy baseball and Rotisserie leagues. Fantasy leagues, based on the day-to-day statistics of major league players, give fans the opportunity to "manage" their own teams and to win or lose based on their player's daily performances. "Owners" draft big-league talent onto their teams and then follow their key statistics (e.g., batting averages, home runs, RBIs) daily. The total of all these categories for all the players on one's "team" determines the standings in each fantasy league.

Ultimately, the fans are the ones who determine baseball's popularity and its financial success. Spectators are as much a part of the sport as the players. If people don't buy tickets, owners can't meet their payrolls. If fans don't watch televised games, the networks won't spend billions for the rights to air games. The fans make professional sports possible.

*See also:* Baseball, Amateur; Little League; Fans and Fan Clubs; Fantasy Sports; Softball; Stadiums

**BIBLIOGRAPHY**

Beisser, Arnold. *The Madness in Sports.* New York: Appleton-Century-Crofts, 1967.

Edwards, Harry. *Sociology of Sport.* Homewood, Ill.: Dorsey Press, 1973.

Gmelch, George. *In the Ballpark: The Working Lives of Baseball People.* Washington, D.C.: Smithsonian Institution Press. 1998.

Kimmel, Michael. "Baseball and the Reconstitution of American Masculinity, 1880–1920." In *Cooperstown Symposium on Baseball in American Culture.* Edited by Alvin Hall. Westport, Conn.: Meckler Publishing, 1989.

Koppett, Leonard. *Koppett's Concise History of Major League Baseball.* Philadelphia: Temple University Press, 1998.

Leonard, Wilbert Marcellus, II. *A Sociological Perspective of Sport.* New York: Macmillan Publishing Company, 1993.

Light, Jonathan Fraser. *The Cultural Encyclopedia of Baseball.* Jefferson, N.C., and London: McFarland and Company, 1997.

Nixon, Howard, and James Frey. *A Sociology of Sport.* Wadsworth Publishing Company, 1996.

Rader, Benjamin G. *American Sports.* Englewood Cliffs, N.J.: Prentice-Hall, 1990.

———. *Baseball: A History of America's Game.* Urbana and Chicago: University of Illinois Press, 2002.

Rossi, John P. *The National Game.* Chicago: Ivan R. Dee, 2000.

Seymour, Harold. *Baseball: The Early Years.* New York: Oxford University Press, 1960.

Skolnik, Richard. *Baseball and the Pursuit of Innocence.* College Station: Texas A&M University Press, 1994.

Smith, Curt. *Storied Stadiums.* New York: Carroll & Graf Publishers, 2001.

Tygiel, Jules. *Past Time.* New York: Oxford University Press, 2000.

*George Gmelch and Kaitlyn Richards*

# BASKETBALL

Basketball can be clearly identified with a date and place of origin—December 1891, in Springfield, Massachusetts. James Naismith, a physical education instructor at the International YMCA Training School was asked to help solve a problem that had arisen: finding an indoor activity—other than calisthenics or marching—that the young men could do during cold New England winters. Naismith, after trying to modify outdoor games unsuccessfully, developed a new game that utilized a large ball being thrown into elevated boxes. He worked out a series of rules, and then proposed trying the new game out with one of his classes. Unfortunately the custodian charged with finding and mounting the boxes could only come up with peach baskets and he mounted these from the base of the running track that surrounded the gymnasium. Rather than "box ball" came "basketball". The basket height, of approximately ten feet, was coincidental with the height of the overhead track, but that height seemed appropriate and has been maintained in the more than 100 years since the game was invented.

Naismith proposed a set of thirteen rules, which were written and published in the school paper in January 1892. Because the students were training to be instructors at YMCAs throughout the country and Canada, the game of basketball spread rapidly as these students traveled about the country. The first rules designated things that have continued to endure in the playing of the game. These included a prohibition from carrying the ball, but rather batting or throwing it (a rule that later was interpreted to include dribbling); use of the hands only for controlling the ball; a foul call for pushing, tripping, or striking an opponent; a goal being scored for throwing the ball in the basket; the ball being awarded to the opposite team from the one touching it before it went out of bounds; the use of two officials (since changed to three plus scorers and timekeepers).

In 1892, Naismith took his players on an exhibition tour of upstate New York and Rhode Island, which helped spread knowledge of the new game. In that same year a game was played between two teams of girls, and the game spread slowly among that gender, fostered mostly by the efforts of Senda Berenson, who befriended Naismith shortly after reading about the game in 1892. Berenson divided the court into three sections that girls could not leave, believing that girls did not have the stamina to run up and down the entire court for a full game. This division later evolved into the six-person game with the three defenders not allowed to cross half court and play offense and the three offensive players facing a similar restriction at their end of the court. This stayed in effect until the women's game was totally "converted" to the more popular "male" rules of basketball in the 1970s.

Basketball's invention and development coincided with the great influx of immigrants to the United State in the late nineteenth and early twentieth centuries. It was quickly adopted by the youth of many of these groups because of the wide exposure the game received in urban settlement houses throughout the northeastern United States. Teams comprised of particular ethnic groups or representing particular crafts formed at this time, and spectators of the same groups, often were the main spectators. Thus teams such as the Celtics (Irish), South Philadelphia Hebrew Association/SPHAs (Jewish), Pulaskis (Polish), Original Italian Club, Chinese Athletic Club, Reading (PA) Transit and Light Shop, and the Bell Telephone Equipment team were typical of the squads that were popular in this era. During the early 1900s, Irish and Jews were viewed as ethnic groups with "natural" talents for the game.

The game itself, during its development, was much different than its more modern form. The floor was not a standard size and could range from sixty to ninety feet in length. Games were played on stages, dance floors, and in armories. Sometimes pillars impeded the flow of the game. There was no rule on length of time that the ball could be held before a shot was taken, so early basketball was more a ball-control game with fewer shots taken, almost soccerlike in style and movement. The baskets protruded farther from the backboard than today, and, in some instances, the basket hung from a metal pole suspended from the ceiling, with no backboard at all. After each basket, a jump ball was held so teams eventually sought good "tappers," even if they could not run or shoot. The game was played on the floor; players did not leave their feet to shoot or rebound. A much rougher game than today was the norm, with players often being knocked unconscious in the course of a contest.

The collegiate game in the 1920s was seen as cleaner and had a set foul limit that led to elimination, while

**James A. Naismith.** Canadian-born inventor of the game of basketball, Dr. James A. Naismith (1861–1939) developed a set of "13 rules" in 1891 in Springfield, Massachusetts, that established the principles behind the modern-day game. © *Corbis*

the professional game saw players disqualified only if the referee deemed their play too rough. During this time, three professional teams arose and dominated the sport in the 1920s and 1930s. First was the Original Celtics of New York City, comprised of players who were Irish Catholic, German Catholic, Jewish, and Czech. The South Philadelphia Hebrew Association squad lasted in some form until the 1950s; they were most outstanding in the 1930s and 1940s, winning a number of Eastern and American League titles. The New York Renaissance team, begun and managed by Bob Douglas, was the first and greatest African American squad, playing almost exclusively on the road and winning unofficial and "official" world championship tournaments. Basketball, particularly professional basketball, was often played in a cage until the late 1920s when the cage was abandoned. The cage was metal wire and kept the ball in play almost continuously. Players could play the ball off the cage or use the cage to push off of it for greater elevation. ""

College leagues formed during this same period of time and professional leagues were located throughout areas of the East. In 1925, the first truly national professional league, the American Basketball League, was formed, with teams stretching from Boston to Chicago. This league dropped the use of the cage, standardized to some degree the court specifications, employed regular referees, and led to a more popular game. Meanwhile, in the Midwest, the game became popular as early as the early 1900s; the small team size allowed rural communities to field squads and compete with much larger communities. The game was played both indoors and outdoors and became extremely popular in rural Indiana, Kentucky, and Illinois, where baskets were often hung on trees and various objects were substituted for basketballs.

The basketball was originally a leather ball stitched together, inside of which was a bladder that was pumped up through a prominent valve where a needle was inserted. The ball was hardly ever round, did not bounce well, and was bigger than today's, so it was harder to grip and very "lumpy." This, combined with lack of real practice facilities or standard playing facilities, made shooting success problematic. Nevertheless, the game became exceedingly popular in the middle of the twentieth century because of the small number of players needed to field a team, the relative simplicity of the game, and the flexibility of playing venues needed. A number of states—including Indiana, Illinois, Kentucky, and North Carolina—became "hotbeds" of high school basketball, with large community support and playing facilities often seating more than the population of the community itself. In the latter part of that century, Florida, Georgia, and California also had successful and popular high school programs, a reflection of increasing populations in those states.

A number of colleges took to basketball early in the century, most notably in the Northeast and Midwest. By the late 1930s, there was interest in having some sort of tournament to determine basketball superiority; in 1938, the National Invitation Tournament (NIT) was held in New York City, with six top teams competing for the title won by Temple University. The next year the National Collegiate Athletic Association (NCAA) sponsored a postseason tournament, which included eight teams and was won by the University of Oregon. Until the mid or late 1950s, the NIT was seen as a "better" tournament than the NCAA, and, at that time, they were held during different weeks so a team could possibly compete and win both. This happened only in 1950, when the City College of New York, coached by Nat Holman, a former Original Celtic player, led his team to both titles. By the 1960s, the NCAA was viewed as the top tournament, though restricting its participants solely to league champions left a

number of outstanding teams for the NIT. The NCAA expanded gradually from eight, to sixteen, then thirty-two teams. In the early 2000s, there were sixty-five teams invited to this tournament, and they participated in March, leading to the sobriquet "March Madness."

Through the 1940s, many of the major college conferences had few, if any, African American players, but the victories of Loyola University of Chicago in 1963 with four African American starters, and Texas Western (now the University of Texas at El Paso) in 1966 with an all–African American starting five changed the segregation policies of many schools. The Texas Western triumph was even more meaningful because it came against the University of Kentucky, with its fabled coach, Adolph Rupp.

The change in the composition of the college game was later reflected in that of the professional game, where more than 75 percent of the players of the National Basketball Association (NBA) are African American. The NBA had been formed in 1949 through a merger of two other professional basketball leagues, the National Basketball League (which operated since 1937, largely in the Midwest) and the Basketball Association of America (which had begun in 1946 and played mostly in large venues in the Northeast). The NBA struggled for many years financially, but the increased television coverage helped the league and the game to "take off" in the 1980s.

At one time basketball was seen as an activity exclusively for children and young adults, almost all male, but over the past forty years, leagues have continued to form and prosper for adult males and females. There are now many adult leagues only for women, mostly run by local Parks and Recreation Departments. Men's leagues have continued to expand even more, and many now are age-bracketed, with some being for those over thirty-five or over forty. National and regional tournaments for men now are age grouped in five-year brackets up to the sixty to sixty-five group, and an over-sixty-five category.

Children's leagues are often no longer gender-based until adolescent years, and most of these leagues are also conducted by local parks programs. There are also leagues sponsored by churches or synagogues for both children and adults. Some of these leagues have existed for more than seventy years. Children's leagues now extend downward to as low as first graders; portable and adjustable baskets make the game accessible to these youngsters.

Over the past seventy-five years, a number of significant rule changes have been implemented that have altered and improved basketball. In the 1920s, the three-second rule was initiated. This prevented any offensive player from maintaining a position in the free-throw lane for more than three consecutive seconds without exiting that area. In the

1950s, that lane was widened. In the late 1930s, the alternate possession after a basket or free throw was inaugurated. This replaced a center tap after each score and sped up the game and increased scoring. In 1954, the NBA adopted a twenty-four second rule, whereby teams had twenty-four seconds to shoot after gaining possession of the ball. Later in the 1990s, a shot clock was begun in college basketball. The dunk was outlawed in high school and college from 1967 to 1976. The three-point shot was begun at various levels from the late 1970s. Before being adopted by high schools, colleges, and the NBA, it had been utilized in the American Basketball League as early as 1961 and the Olympics from the late 1960s.

Though basketball has become "big business" with the NBA and the NCAA tournament, it remains a simple game played at playgrounds and schoolyards by young and old alike.

*See also:* African American Leisure Lifestyles, "Muscular Christianity" and the YM(W)CA Movements, Urbanization of Leisure

**BIBLIOGRAPHY**

Bjarkman, Peter. *Hoopla: A Century of College Basketball.* Indianapolis, Ind.: Masters Press, 1996.

Hollander, Zander, ed. *The Modern Encyclopedia of Basketball.* Garden City, N.Y.: Doubleday and Company, 1979.

Isaacs, Neil. *All the Moves: A History of College Basketball.* Philadelphia: Lippincott, 1975.

Neft, David, and Richard Cohen. *The Sports Encyclopedia: Pro Basketball.* 2d edition. New York: St. Martin's Press, 1989.

Nelson, Murry. *The Originals: The New York Celtics Invent Modern Basketball.* Bowling Green, Ohio: Bowling Green University Popular Press, 1999.

Peterson, Robert. *Cages to Jump Shots: Pro Basketball's Early Years.* New York: Oxford University Press, 1990.

Savage, Jim. *The Encyclopedia of the NCAA Basketball Tournament: The Complete Independent Guide to College Basketball's Championship Event.* New York: Dell Publishing, 1990.

Telander, Rick. *Heaven Is a Playground.* New York: St. Martin's Press, 1976.

*Murry R. Nelson*

# BEACHES

Not counting Alaska, the mainland United States has more than 88,000 miles of tidal shoreline, much of it marked by the concave arcs of "wave-deposited sediment" that geologists define as beaches. Yet since the early nineteenth century, Americans have treated beaches as more than dynamic geological formations subject to the shifting patterns of wind, wave, and tide. Beaches have become the most cherished and coveted feature of the nation's natural geography. Although making up only 17 percent of the nation's land mass, the narrow coastal fringe is home to more Americans (153 million in 1998) than the rest of the United States combined. In the early nineteenth century, only the richest and most leisured elite had any interest in spending time at the shore; today, a quarter of the American population—and two-thirds of California's—visits a beach one or more times every year. The "beach" has become the nation's universal playground and a primary symbol of what constitutes the "good life" in the United States.

In the most important sense, going to the beach specifically has meant not going to work. Beaches seemed to be a part of nature; thus, they seemed to encourage communion with elemental forces lurking beneath the veneer of civilized life, or acting outside the bounds and rules that confined ordinary life. Yet Americans have continuously worried that the pleasures of sun and surf could become dissipations that compromise individual integrity and undermine social morality. Does a beach outing refresh the vacationer to be more productive at work, or make her or him wish never to work again? Does swimwear free the body to enjoy nature's goodness, or turn women into sexual objects? Such vexed questions and ambivalent attitudes, which have been part of the larger history of work and leisure in the modern period, suggest how beaches and beachgoing in particular have paralleled important social, cultural, and economic changes of the last two centuries.

## Attitudes Toward Beaches in Eighteenth- and Nineteenth-Century America

Until the mid-eighteenth century, most Western Europeans and Euro-Americans who did not make their livings at the seaside avoided it. Instructed by local lore as well as Judeo-Christian accounts of the flood, most people fearfully beheld the ocean as the "great abyss" of disorder, incomprehensible mysteries, and ferocious sea creatures. But after 1750, Westerners began reimagining the sea and seaside as resources for revitalization. Physicians and former invalids led the way, hailing the curative powers of inhaling salty air and submerging the naked body into the icy wintertime ocean. Romantic artists and growing numbers of ordinary urban dwellers sought similar coastal therapies. If they felt confused about who they

**Florida state park.** In 2003 a New Hampshire family enjoys part of the ten miles of white sand beach that St. Joseph Peninsula State Park offers. Located off the shore of the Gulf of Mexico in Port St. Joe, Florida, it was named the best U.S. beach in 2002 by Stephen Leatherman, author of *America's Best Beaches* and is known for its beautiful dunes. © *David Langford for AP/Wide World Photos*

really were or believed city life had alienated them from nature, wandering the beach and contemplating the clash of the elements on the shoreline, the historian Alain Corbin has observed, was a way "to discover—or better yet, perhaps, to rediscover—who they were" (p. 164). American writers and painters searching for such self-knowledge led the way to the seashore. The poet Walt Whitman, for example, recalled haunting beaches near New York City in the 1830s, watching "the ocean perpetually, grandly, rolling in" and pondering how to make "this liquid, mystic theme" into poetry (p. 67).

Aside from artists, the earliest seaside tourists usually belonged to the northern mercantile and southern planter elite. These people not only could afford days or even months of leisure at a time; they also believed they needed to recuperate in this manner. In the 1820s and 1830s, a commercial leisure economy emerged in the Northeast to serve such desires. Regular steamboat service carried Boston's leading citizens to the rocky shoreline of Nahant, a peninsula jutting into Massachusetts Bay north of the city. Wealthy Philadelphians amused themselves on the New Jersey shore at Cape May. Newport,

Rhode Island, was the era's premier seaside resort. Located near the southern tip of Aquidneck Island in Narragansett Bay, Newport had been a leading Atlantic port and manufacturing center in the 1770s, but rapidly went into decline in the postrevolutionary period. In the 1820s and 1830s, though, as the nation's growing commercial aristocracy sought places for relaxation and recreation, Newport rebounded as a stylish getaway within proximity of Boston, Philadelphia, and New York. By 1860, America's "fashionable resort for rank, fashion, and beauty" featured eleven hotels and twenty-nine boardinghouses. Yet all of these facilities and kindred amusements were positioned out of sight of the dramatic coastline. The resort population avoided the beach except during the fashionable morning bathing hours. Socializing was the preeminent occupation, which prompted Henry David Thoreau to observe that Newport's leisured set much preferred "wine" to "brine."

Newport's high life offended the modest purses and sensibilities of many middle-class Americans, but the seaside camp-meeting grounds spawned by the great religious revivals of the era did not. Wesleyan Grove on the

Massachusetts island of Martha's Vineyard, which held its first outdoor revival in 1835, was typical of such "Christian retreats." By the late 1850s, Wesleyan Grove's original communal accommodations had been replaced by hundreds of private tent residences spread over almost fifteen acres near the shore. In the late 1860s, small cottages were replacing the tents, and the Methodists consolidated their camp with the speculative shoreline development of Oak Bluffs. The two areas together blossomed into a resort offering beach recreation with a clear conscience: no gambling or drinking, but plenty of bathing, except on Sunday. For the rest of the century, other "Christian" (that is, Protestant) retreats—Ocean Grove, New Jersey; Rehoboth Beach, Delaware; Lake Bluff, north of Chicago on Lake Michigan—followed a similar pattern of accommodating "innocent" or hygienic beach recreations with Christian self-improvement.

The transformation of revival campgrounds into recreational beach resorts at mid-century prefigured what historian Cindy Aron calls "the democratization of vacationing" in the United States between 1850 and 1950. Once considered the luxury of a privileged few, vacations came to be regarded as a national necessity and entitlement, first for the growing urban population of middle-income corporate and professional workers, then, in the decades before World War II, for working-class families, too. The emergence of the vacationing American reflected important developments in the nineteenth century: first, the new medical and popular consensus that time away from work, especially in the salubrious environment of clean sea or mountain air, was essential to a man's vigor; second, the growing agreement among leading Protestant religious authorities that pleasure was not an evil in itself, especially if it served, as one minister put it, to "send us back to our daily duties invigorated in body and spirit;" third, the growth of what historian Orvar Löfgren calls a "new mode of consumption . . . based on the idea of leaving home and work in search of new experiences, pleasures, and leisure" (p. 5).

By the 1870s and 1880s modestly priced summer resorts and cottage communities were proliferating at the nation's lakefronts and mountain passes, but seashores were the preferred getaway, especially for the weary breadwinning man. "There is nothing so restful to the restless American," a businessman observed in 1896, "as the sight and sound of the unresting sea" (Lencek, p. 154). In the late century New Jersey's 100 miles of Atlantic shoreline had fifty-four seaside resort cities, foremost of which was Atlantic City, which featured 400 hotels by 1900. Sojourners to Put-in-Bay Island, Ohio, an inland shore resort in the western basin of Lake Erie, reported hotels "full to overflowing" with refugees from Detroit,

Cleveland, Toledo, and other points west. Even further west, white-collar families from Portland flocked to Clatsop Beach, "the great watering place of Oregon"; those from San Francisco crossed the mountains to Santa Cruz, the "Naples of the Pacific Coast." Middle-class African Americans frequented resorts friendly to them at Oak Bluffs on Martha's Vineyard or Highland Beach on Chesapeake Bay.

Vacations were refreshing, but they were not a waste of time; taking time off signaled middle-class respectability. Vacationers usually bathed in the morning to avoid the intense sun, and they devoted their afternoons and evenings to strolling on boardwalks, napping (the hammock became a fixture of beach cottage life in this period), dining, and pursuing commercial amusements. Victorians counseled restraint and modesty, but beach behavior and use proved difficult to regulate. While Europeans bathed at gender-segregated beaches, American women and men usually swam "happily" together, as a newspaper reported in 1885, "without reference to age [or] sex." Middle-class women donned cumbersome bathing suits of light flannel or muslin, plus caps, stockings, and even gloves; men's suits covered their upper legs and torsos. But a lively surf tossed women's and men's bodies together and destabilized self-control. Moreover, wet bathing suits revealed more than was respectable. Just being at the beach encouraged men and, especially, women to feel less restrained by convention. Like other new leisure practices at the turn of the century, beachgoing contributed to a new middle-class style of living by undermining Victorian restraints and encouraging a more heterosocial culture in which women pursued pleasure in public, sometimes with men and sometimes not.

## Popularity of Beaches in the Twentieth Century

Throughout the twentieth century, Americans have continued to look to beaches as refreshing resorts where living the "simple life" enabled introspection, self-awareness, and revitalization. Yet the ways in which they used and understood beaches underwent dramatic changes in the interwar years. For one, beaches were more popular and crowded. Inexpensive mass transit systems linked urban working-class neighborhoods to nearby shorelines, like New York's Coney Island. The rapid growth of automobile ownership and construction of roadways made it easy for urban and suburban working people to make a day's excursion or longer to the shoreline. The Dixie Highway, completed in 1927, snaked from Chicago and the Great Lakes region to Miami, the new Mecca for wintertime "snowbirds." By the end of the 1930s, too, most full-time American workers received week-long paid summer vacations. Persons of limited means not only could afford, but also desired extended stays at Atlantic City's inexpensive hotels, or a week at oceanside campgrounds, where they enjoyed the same views, if not accommodations, as rich folks. As many as 10,000 vacationed each summer at Tent City on Coronado Beach near San Diego, where $4.50 rented a furnished canvas tent for a week next door to the grand Hotel del Coronado, a favored resort for celebrities.

White Americans also went to the beach to frolic in the sun. Victorians had prized fair skin, which not only marked a person's inner virtue but also reinforced the racial and class boundaries between white and non-white and non-manual and manual laborers. But in the 1920s Americans, who were still concerned that urban life weakened them, became sun worshipers. A tan suggested the physical power and athleticism valued in men and, increasingly, in women. Many whites also coveted a tan because of the stereotype that dark-skinned races possessed a savage and sexual vigor. At Cape May in 1925, an African American newspaper noted that black people were confined to an undesirable corner of the beach, but white "life-guards, burnt so dark that they were eligible for the jim-crow car, were the envy, particularly of the [white] women." Lifeguards aside, a suntan broadcast the bearer's position of privilege, rather than lack of it; she or he had the leisure to sunbathe.

The suntan craze in the 1920s suggested how the beach had become a setting for staging and celebrating the well-groomed body. In the 1910s, the Portland (Oregon) Knitting Company introduced the affordable Jantzen line of swimsuits for women. Made of colorful form-fitting jersey knit, Jantzen suits symbolized the "new woman" of the 1920s who loved "to dive into clear, cool water and feel every muscle active—stroke after stroke as [she swam]!" Meanwhile, ads for the muscleman Charles Atlas promised weakling men that beach bullies would never kick sand in their faces again—if they purchased his fitness program. Glistening in leopard-skin briefs, Atlas also modeled the bare-chested look that American men would adopt for the beach by the end of the 1930s.

After 1945, getting away to the beach became an American pastime, and the laid-back and sun-filled beach "lifestyle" a well-advertised expression of postwar consumerism, although the nation's rapidly growing population of affluent suburbanites were no longer trying to escape the frenzy of city life. America's new premier beach escape was Hawaii. A year after the U.S.

Congress made the islands an American territory in 1900, the first modern resort opened in Honolulu. Hawaii remained an exclusive destination for the rich and famous until World War II brought working- and middle-class sailors and GIs to the bases there. Many would return in the mid-1950s once affordable jet travel moved the beaches of Waikiki within reach of the mainland middle-class masses. A one-time family vacation or honeymoon seemed the height of luxury, glamour, and the exotic, which was why, through the 1960s and 1970s, a week in Hawaii was the luxurious grand prize on TV game shows like *Let's Make a Deal*.

An alternative, but related, hedonistic counterculture of sun, sea, and heterosexual sensuality developed in California in the postwar decades. Southern California surfers were an obscure subcultural tribe until the early 1960s, when beach movies and "surfing music" popularized the "Endless Summer" lifestyle: baggie shorts, huarache sandals, bushy blond hair, and, as the duo Jan and Dean explained in their song "Surf City," "two girls for every boy." Later, hippies, seeking to live in harmony with untouched nature, set up camps on the Baja Peninsula south of the Mexican border. Movie stars and celebrities settled the magnificent Malibu beach as their private preserve. The teenage surfing set's bonfire parties, soirees at Malibu, and makeshift settlements at Baja consciously rejected the packaged paradise of volcano tours and luaus that drew middle-class adults to Hawaii, but all of these uses of the beach exploited fictions about communing with nature, retreating from civilization, and playing instead of working at the seaside—motivations that had drawn Americans to beaches since the early nineteenth century.

Since the early 1980s, new concerns that the beach may be bad for health have arisen. Warnings of ozone layer depletion heightened fears that cancer-causing ultraviolet rays were shooting down unfiltered onto the bodies of sunbathers. At the end of the decade, New York and New Jersey beaches closed when used needles and other medical waste washed onshore. Outbreaks of fecal coliform bacteria, usually attributable to sewage runoff in areas of dense residential development, continually shut down freshwater and saltwater beaches to swimmers. Residential developments on the Gulf of Mexico from Florida through Texas—one of the fastest-growing regions in the country—have devastated coastal fishing and shellfish populations. Hurricanes and the severe beach erosion attributed to global warming make buying beach property a risky venture. Yet even if the beach seems more and more a dimension of modern industrial, urban, and consumer culture than a haven from it, Americans still go there to discover or announce who they are, although the journeys often follow a multiplicity of routes reflecting interest group preferences. The very wealthy fight for property in expensive coastal areas in Santa Barbara, California. Gay men claim Provincetown in Massachusetts and Fire Island in New York as their particular playgrounds. Retirees bake in the sunshine of Florida's "Gold Coast," from Palm Beach to Miami Beach, while each spring, more than 100,000 students from historically black colleges descend on Daytona Beach, 250 miles to the north, for Black College Reunion. Much as a coastal vacation announced that Americans had "arrived" in the late nineteenth century, a day or longer at the shore remains an important way in which Americans define themselves through the pleasures and liberties the beach affords.

*See also:* Atlantic City; Boating, Power; Coney Island; Spas

**BIBLIOGRAPHY**

Aron, Cindy S. *Working at Play: A History of Vacations in the United States.* New York: Oxford University Press, 1999.

Corbin, Alain. *The Lure of the Sea: The Discovery of the Seaside in the Western World.* Translated by Jocelyn Phelps. Berkeley: University of California Press, 1994.

Culliton, Thomas J. "Population: Distribution, Density and Growth." National Oceanic and Atmospheric Administration's (NOAA) State of the Coast Report. Silver Spring, Md.: NOAA, February 1998.

Immerso, Michael. *Coney Island: The People's Playground.* New Brunswick, N.J.: Rutgers University Press, 2002.

Lencek, Lena, and Gideon Bosker. *The Beach: The History of Paradise on Earth.* New York: Viking, 1998.

Löfgren, Orvar. *On Holiday: A History of Vacationing.* Berkeley: University of California Press, 1999.

Nasaw, David. *Going Out: The Rise and Fall of Public Amusements.* New York: Basic Books, 1993.

Peiss, Kathy. *Cheap Amusements: Working Women and Leisure in Turn-of-the-Century New York.* Philadelphia: Temple University Press, 1987.

———. *Hope in a Jar: The Making of America's Beauty Culture.* New York: Metropolitan Books, 1998.

Sterngass, Jon. *First Resorts: Pursuing Pleasure at Saratoga Springs, Newport & Coney Island.* Baltimore: Johns Hopkins University Press, 2001.

Stilgoe, John R. *Alongshore.* New Haven, Conn.: Yale University Press, 1994.

Whitman, Walt. *Specimen Days.* Boston: David R. Godine, 1971.

Woodroffe, Colin D. *Coasts: Form, Process and Evolution.* Cambridge, England: Cambridge University Press, 2003.

*Woody Register*

# BEAUTY CULTURE

Personal beauty, and the cultivation thereof, have played an important part in defining the self in western culture. Religious and popular beliefs have long conferred to beauty the ability to witness the personal qualities of an individual, linking beauty with inner goodness, and ugliness with vice. But coupled with these beliefs is the Cartesian notion of the plasticity of the body and the supremacy of the soul. Put more simply, a strong self can conquer the inadequate body, and through disciplined practices, can cultivate an appearance that reflects the true nature of the inner self.

## Beauty and Goodness

Associating goodness with beauty is not a new practice. The Greek New Testament uses the word beautiful to describe the Christian life, with God describing his devoted subjects as "beautiful" people. Thus, good works in Matthew 5:16 are literally "beautiful" works. In the fifth century, St Augustine wrote in his sermons that appearance was the litmus of character. He explained that a strong person would see beauty reflected in the mirror no matter how truly ugly or beautiful he was. "Don't blame the mirror," if you see yourself as ugly he said. "Go back to yourself. The mirror isn't deceiving you, take care you don't deceive yourself." (p. 336)

These beliefs are also contained in a range of nonreligious texts. Baldessar Castiglione, a sixteenth century Italian courtier and author of courtesy books, instructed his readers that a beautiful soul and a beautiful body seemed to go hand in hand and that a person's outward beauty would spread to their inner being "and in bodies this comeliness is imprinted more and lesse (as it were) for a marke of the soule." (p. 309)

Renaissance portraiture embodied a relationship between appearance and the true self, conveying a complex system of social and moral signifiers through the artistic representation of individuals, notably along gendered lines. Portraits of women were often used to arrange marriages, and as such, were required to express as much information as possible about the portrait subject. Female beauty signified morality and virtue as well as elite social class. Closely linked in Renaissance thought and art, the relationship between beauty and virtue was further highlighted by mottoes and emblems on the reverse of female portraits, punctuating the meaning portrayed by the primary image. The back of Leonardo da Vinci's portrait of *Ginevra de' Benci,* for example, is inscribed with the words: "Beauty Adorns Virtue."

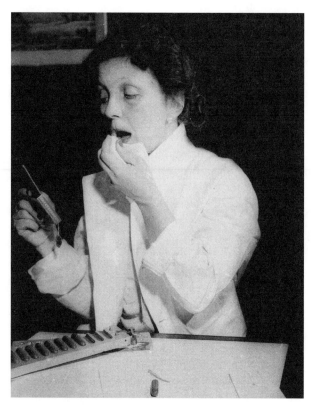

**Hazel Bishop.** Research chemist and cosmetics creator Hazel Bishop (1906–1998) began her own business by developing the first "kissable" long-lasting lipstick. Lipstick and other makeup helped women attain beauty, which some social critics viewed as their "job" in the 1800s. © *AP/Wide World Photos*

## Cultivating Beauty—Demonstrating Virtue

While the link between virtue and goodness is immutable, the formula nonetheless contains some flexibility. Beauty culture is based on the belief that the absence of beauty is not insurmountable. Through disciplined activities of self-improvement, a virtuous individual can achieve the look that reflects his or her inner character. St. Augustine had already, at least metaphorically, suggested that when confronted with ugliness, one could, and should, make an attempt to alter the image. "Pass judgment on yourself," he wrote, "be sorry about your ugliness, and so as you turn away and go off sorry and ugly, you may be able to correct yourself and come back beautiful" (p. 336). Later-eighteenth- and nineteenth-century commentators generally agreed that while beauty emanated from internal goodness, they conceded the need for some degree of artificial beautification. They recognized that women, in particular, should look after their appearance. In line with the discourse on virtue and beauty, the need for the woman to look after her body was couched in terms of morality, implying not only that she must be prepared to

be seen, but that her appearance was of greater importance than that of a man's; she had a duty to beauty.

## Women's Duty to Beauty

The notion of beauty as a social contract and a woman's moral responsibility was implied in texts that refer to beauty as a woman's "business." "Man's face is bound to be clean, and may be allowed to be picturesque; but it is a woman's *business* to be beautiful," declared an anonymous columnist for *Godey's Lady's Book* in 1852, emphasizing that beauty is a woman's job (p. 105). Considering beauty a job incorporates two important tenets: beauty is simultaneously an obligation and realistically attainable. Annie Starr, in *Demorest's Monthly Magazine*, reminded readers of this feminine responsibility in 1880, "any harmless method that you can adopt to make your visible selves attractive is perfectly proper—even your duty." (p. 502) Echoing this, Warne's *Bouquet Series—Etiquette for Ladies and Gentlemen* also discussed beauty in terms of obligation and responsibility, reminding ladies that, "to please is one of the minor morals of life, which it is our duty not to neglect," and that, as a result, "we should endeavor to understand what good dress is, and to practice what we have learnt with regard to it" (p. 11).

The business of beauty was more than just an obligation to women to look beautiful. It resulted in, according to Kathy Peiss, an industry built both by and for women. While women were restricted in access to many other forms of industry, beauty culture offered career opportunities for women otherwise denied access to business. They availed themselves of these chances by establishing beauty schools, developing and delivering courses, and promoting and distributing mail-order cosmetic products. While standards of beauty varied along ethnic, class and cultural lines, successful entrepreneurs emerged from all categories.

The cultivation of a socially pleasing appearance is also an important motivating principle in the contemporary women's fitness movement. Vigorous aerobic exercise drives many women to achieve what Carol Spitzack refers to as an aesthetic of health. This aesthetic defines health in visual terms of body size, proportion, muscularity, skin color and tone. A conviction that the disciplined and committed self can craft a body in line with this aesthetic reinforces the link between character and appearance; a virtuous body "shows" and its virtue is illustrated by its athletic form. Achieving the aesthetic of health may result in approving gazes from others, but speaks, as Spitzack writes, to an equation of health and culturally-defined attractiveness that can be tyrannical.

The act of beautification is denounced by many as oppressive to women. Naomi Wolf's seminal *The Beauty*

*Myth* reveals the ways in which female beauty imperatives result in the political, physical, and psychological oppression of women. Sandra Bartky echoes that for women, the standards of body size and shape and the nature of body ornamentation are mandated, controlled, and regulated. As a result of this, the female becomes hesitant, dependent, constrained, modest, and deferent. Woman's becomes a practiced and subjected body, with an inferior status. This inferiority is reinforced by the elaborate aesthetic preparation of the body that implies the deficiency of the woman's body. According to Bartky, "The disciplinary project of femininity is a 'setup': it requires such radical and extensive measures of bodily transformation that virtually every woman who gives herself to it is destined in some degree to fail."(p. 34).

However, the culture of beauty is also viewed as a potentially empowering practice for women, and indeed, even Wolf maintains that her critique of the beauty myth is not anti-beauty: pleasure and adornment are legitimate choices, she argues. bell hooks provides an example, recalling the rituals and relationships created by, and associated with, getting her hair pressed with her sisters. Far from being a constraint, it constituted, she said, a coming of age.

> For each of us getting our hair pressed is an important ritual. It is not a sign of our longing to be white. It is not a sign of our quest to be beautiful. We are girls. It is a sign of our desire to be women. It is a gesture that says we are approaching womanhood—a rite of passage. Before we reach the appropriate age we wear braids and plaits that are symbols of our innocence, our youth, our childhood. Then we are comforted by the parting hands that comb and braid, comforted by the intimacy and bliss. There is a deeper intimacy in the kitchen on Saturday when hair is pressed, when fish is fried, when sodas are passed around, when soul music drifts over the talk. We are women together. This is our ritual and our time. (p. 92)

Similarly, Wendy Chapkis writes that "playing with the way we look, creating a personally or sexually provocative image has pleasures of its own. Denying ourselves those pleasures because they have been used against us in the past is understandable but hardly the final word in liberation" (p. 146).

## Men and Beauty Culture

In contrast, attitudes towards men's personal beauty and its cultivation are quite different. Late nineteenth century recommendations to men focused on posture and cleanliness, rather than on beauty and its cultivation. The gentlemanly attribute of rectitude was evidenced by upright carriage and bearing. In contrast to texts for women, there is no moral obligation to please. Excessive preoccupation with beauty or with fashion is denounced as foppish, considered a sign of weakness, or lack of masculine individuality. Being well groomed, on the other hand, is imperative for the gentleman. "The first point which marks the gentleman in appearance," explains Warne's *Etiquette Book for Ladies and Gentlemen,* "is rigid cleanliness" (p. 74). And Maurice Egan wrote in 1893 that "to be clean outside and in gives [a man] a solid respect for himself that makes others respect him" (p. 66). Acknowledging that all men cannot be "six-footer Apollos," William Stevens advises men to make the most of their physical equipment by reflecting on their looks. "Make your appearance an asset not a liability," he advises. (p.5) But, as in many early twentieth century handbooks for young man, his emphasis is on bearing, posture and again, cleanliness. The correct posture is one where shoulders are back, diaphragm in, and carriage erect.

The postural requirements mandated for men reflect, in many ways, the virtuous beauty expected of women. Virtue is witnessed in appearance that suggests masculinity, with physical conditioning and its external manifestations lauded as a means to achieve self-esteem, moral rectitude, and virility. "Do honour to your bodies. Reverence your physical natures, not simply for themselves. Only as ends they are worthy of it, but because in health and strength lies the true basis of noble thought and glorious devotion, " writes Phillips Brooks in 1909 (p. 114).

However, this does not suggest that beauty culture has no bearing upon men and their self-identity. Twentieth-century physical culture texts laud the improvements in men's appearance that can be gained through disciplined exercise and dietary regulation. The shaping and strengthening of the body was seen as a duty to country and to race, a remedy to the increasing sedentary nature of city life. Twentieth-century physical culturists such as Bernarr Macfadden firmly believed that people could enhance their lives and their longevity through physical culture—exercise, dietary regimens, enemas, and a number of ascetic practices including sleeping on the floor, walking barefoot, fasting and doing handstands (to name a very few). He published the magazine *Physical Culture*, which was aimed at solving the medical problems of Americans through healthy living, and through careful attention to, and care of, the body.

While strongmen traveled with carnivals and fairs, weight lifting and bodybuilding was promoted for

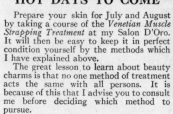

**Elizabeth Arden ad.** Beautician and business executive Elizabeth Arden (1878–1966) ran an international cosmetics company that started with her first salon opening in 1907; an advertisement for her products and salon appeared in the July 1916 *Vanity Fair* magazine. © *New York Public Library*

American men as an antidote to the perception of their flailing strength. In this vein, much later, President John Kennedy established the standardized President's Physical Fitness Tests as part of youth education in the United States in response to what he called growing softness and lack of physical fitness, which he perceived as a menace to American security.

The popularity of the display of the muscular male body, and the gym culture that spawns it, has been strongly nurtured in the late-twentieth and early-twenty-first centuries by the increased visibility of homosexual culture and homoerotic images. A hypermasculine aesthetic within homosexual circles—a response, believe many, to homophobic attitudes—featuring revealing clothes to emphasize the intentional development of the hard male body has infused into general male attitudes towards appearance and self-culture.

Hypermasculinity is the exaggeration of those traits thought to be associated with masculine identity, such as determination, energy, and independence. The pursuit of the hypermasculine body is, according to Alan Klein, often associated with an insecurity about sex role identity.

But contemporary consumer capitalism is also driving the new preoccupation with male appearance, according to Susan Bordo. The late twentieth century saw a blossoming of men's fitness and beauty culture, of fashion magazines and representations of the eroticized male body. Images of the male body are skillfully used for consumer appeal, and are featured in a range of advertisements, from underwear to sound systems, cologne to beer, normally highlighting the muscular male body as a strong and challenging individual. In contrast to previous traditional representations of the male body, men are also cast in subservient or acquiescent postures in advertising images, suggesting a sexual availability previously typical of the use of women in advertising.

Seeing the male body cast in the same light as one is accustomed to seeing its female counterpart, objectified and subjected to standards of normative beauty, results in many similar pressures as described by Wolf and Bartky above. Male insecurity about appearance is a new gold mine for the diet, exercise, cosmetic surgery, and drug industries, previously targeting an entirely female clientele.

However, beauty culture is not, as described above, simply about oppression and constraint. The uneasy and contradictory beliefs that on the one hand the body can betray the inner self, revealing deeply grounded deficiencies, and on the other, the self can control the body and bring it to conform to an appearance that fairly represents the self, make awkward bedfellows. But other meanings can be associated with the focus on appearance. As third-wave feminists point out, understanding is empowering. It is not the image of, and search for beautification that are innately oppressive; rather, it is the power relations embodied within these images that have the potential to subjugate. Beauty culture and its discourses do not have one unique, fixed, and essential meaning that cannot be manipulated. As a result, beauty practices can focus on choice and enjoyment rather than on fine-tuning of inner virtue with appearance, and contain simultaneously the potential to be fulfilling, fun, and liberating.

*See also:* Beauty Pageants, Body Culture and Physical Culture, Bodybuilding, Gay Men's Leisure Lifestyles, Women's Leisure Lifestyles

## BIBLIOGRAPHY

Bartky, Sandra Lee. "Foucault, Femininity and the Modernization of Patriarchal Power." In *The Social Politics of Women's Bodies: Sexuality, Appearance and Behavior.* Edited by Rose Weitz. New York: Oxford, 1998.

Bordo, Susan. "Beauty (Re)Discovers the Male Body." In *Beauty Matters.* Edited by Peg Zeglin Brand. Bloomington: Indiana University Press, 2000.

*Bouquet Series—Etiquette for Ladies and Gentlemen.* London: Frederick Warne and Co., n.d.

Brooks, Philip. In King, Elisha Alonzo, and F. B. Meyer, *Clean and Strong: A Book for Young Men.* Boston and Chicago: United Society of Christian Endeavor, 1909.

Castiglione, Baldessar. *The Book of the Courtier.* Translated by Sir Thomas Hoby. London: J.M. Dent and Sons, 1948. The original edition was published in 1561.

Chapkis, Wendy. *Beauty Secrets.* Boston: South End Press, 1986.

Egan, Maurice. *A Gentleman.* New York: Benziger Brothers, 1893.

*Godey's Lady's Book.* "The Business of Being Beautiful." July 1852.

hooks, bell. *Bone Black: Memories of Girlhood.* New York: Henry Holt, 1996.

Klein, Alan. *Little Big Men: Bodybuilding Subculture and Gender Construction.* Albany: State University of New York Press, 1993.

Peiss, Kathy. *Hope in a Jar: The Making of America's Beauty Culture.* New York: Metropolitan Books, 1998.

Saint Augustine. *Sermons II,* trans. Edmund Hill. Brooklyn, N.Y.: New City Press, 1990.

Spitzack, Carole. *Confessing Excess: Women and the Politics of Body Reduction.* Albany: State University of New York Press, 1990.

Starr, Annie. "To The Homely—Greeting." *Demorest's Monthly Magazine* (September 1880).

Stevens, William. *The Correct Thing.* New York: Dodd, Mead and Company, 1934.

Walker, Alexander. *Beauty; Illustrated Chiefly by and Analysis and Classification of Beauty in Woman.* Hartford, Conn: S. Andrus and Son, 1848.

Wolf, Naomi. *The Beauty Myth.* New York: Anchor Books, 1992.

*Annemarie Jutel*

# BEAUTY PAGEANTS

Beauty pageants are popular events that are staged and sometimes seen on television in most countries around the world. Their many forms range from very local pageants that are staged by schools and small towns, up to global-scale pageants such as Miss Universe Inc., which is owned by Donald Trump and NBC (and includes Miss USA and Miss Teen USA), and Miss World Inc. which is owned by Rupert Murdoch and his News Corporation (and includes Miss America). Global pageants reach a media audience of over 2 billion, and have franchise holders in more than 150 countries, where choosing a national representative is a popular (and lucrative) annual event. In between these extremes there are pageants that celebrate ethnic identity, sports, commercial shows and trade fairs, and a host of civic and religious events. They may be single events, or part of a hierarchical structure in which winners of lower-level pageants go on to compete at higher levels. In the United States there is a commercial beauty pageant industry that organizes thousands of local and regional events for all ages for profit, supporting magazines like *Pageantry* and *Pride of Pageantry*, the online epiczine.com, Pageant News Bureau, and *The Crown Magazine*, and a host of retailers of everything from tiaras to cosmetic surgery. In the United States, at least, pageantry is increasingly like a competitive sport, with a hall of fame, professional contestants and coaches, and a movement toward standardized formats and judging. Contestants are often enticed to pay hefty entrance fees by the (often illusory) prospect of modeling contracts that are awarded to the winners.

The common structure of pageantry includes a live audience, a group of contestants in a specified age range,

**Miss America 2003.** Erika Harold of Urbana, Illinois is crowned Miss America at the eighty-second annual pageant held on 21 September 2002 in Atlantic City's New Jersey Convention Center. The University of Illinois graduate's prize included more than $80,000 in scholarship money that she planned to use to attend Harvard Law School. © *Brian Branch-Price for AP/Wide World Photos*

and a series of public performances that are judged and ranked. Within this structure there is an enormous range of variation in contestants and content. Contestants are most often judged on their physical appearance, their dress and comportment, and some kind of performance demonstrating talent or skill. Pageants can call attention to unique characteristics of the contestants—they may be distinguished by region; by ethnic group or skin color; by size (Miss Petite, Miss Big and Beautiful); by gender identity (Miss Gay America, various lesbian and transgendered pageants); and by age (from newborn babies on up to those over age sixty, who have the Ms. American Classic Woman event). Pageants for heterosexual men are rare, though bodybuilding competitions can be seen as a partial mirror of pageants.

Because pageantry often reflects conflicting ideas about such important issues as proper gender roles, reli-

gious morality, ethnic identity, and globalization, they are often the focus of controversy and even violence. Protests at the 1968 Miss America pageant signaled an important point in the feminist movement, and gave rise to the persistent myth of "bra-burning" demonstrations. The controversy over spending money to hold the Miss Universe pageant in El Salvador in 1975 was instrumental in starting a civil war. Recent global pageants have led to violent demonstrations over the way the events violate local standards of religion and morality in India (1996) and Nigeria (2002), where over 200 died. In addition, controversy and scandal are common in the beauty pageant world.

## History

Choosing symbolic kings and queens for May Day and other festivities is an ancient custom in Europe, where beautiful young women also symbolized the nation, virtue, or other abstract ideals. The first modern pageant was staged by P. T. Barnum in 1854, but his beauty contest was closed down by public protest (he had previously held dog, baby, and bird beauty contests). He substituted daguerreotypes for judging, a practice quickly adopted by newspapers, which held photo beauty contests for many decades. The first "bathing beauty" pageant took place as part of a summer festival to promote business in Rehoboth Beach, Delaware, in 1880. Contests became a regular part of summer beach life, with the most elaborate at Atlantic City, where the "Fall Frolic" attracted contestants from many cities and towns in competition for the title of Miss America. They eventually added preliminary eliminations, an evening gown competition, musical variety shows, and panel judging. Still, the contest was hardly considered respectable entertainment and was shunned by middle-class society. Pageants did not become respectable until World War II, when beauty queens were recruited to sell bonds and entertain troops; scholarships and talent competitions accompanied closer scrutiny of contestants' morals and background. Modern pageants have gained increased respectability by raising money for charities; Miss America is the largest private scholarship fund in the world.

With the worldwide distribution of American films and newsreels in the 1920s and 1930s, other countries began to adopt and adapt beauty pageants. For countries like Thailand and Venezuela, pageants represented modernity and international recognition. With this history, pageants became firmly emplaced local traditions in South America and Southeast Asia. Pageants caught on in most of Europe, the Caribbean, and South Asia after World War II. In each place, pageants find different audiences and emphasize different aspects of femininity, culture, and performance. The fall of the Soviet Union was marked by a revival of beauty pageants, as was the fall of the Taliban in Afghanistan, the end of apartheid in South Africa, and the rise of capitalism in China.

## Critique and the Future

For many years pageants excluded minority groups and offered conservative notions of femininity. American pageants generally opened to African Americans in the 1960s and 1970s (the first in the Miss America system was Miss Indiana University in 1959), and pageants became symbolic of inclusion and ethnic success. Some still see pageants as creating conformity, pushing American middle-class values on the rest of the world, and reducing women to sex objects, all while enriching large media conglomerates. Defenders say pageants offer positive role models and provide another avenue for women to enter public careers.

In the early twenty-first century, after a number of years of declining audiences, pageants again grew in number and popularity. They diversified, and in many countries they no longer resembled the original model from which they were born. In the future, pageantry will further adapt to media globalization; many are already web broadcast, and there are virtual pageants, pageants with international web voting, and thousands of Web sites devoted to pageantry and fandom.

*See also:* Beauty Culture; Women's Leisure Lifestyles

### BIBLIOGRAPHY

Cohen, Colleen, Richard Wilk, and Beverley Stoeltje, eds. *Beauty on the Global Stage: Pageants and Power.* New York: Routledge, 1995.

Deford, Frank. *There She Is.* New York: Viking Press, 1971.

Dworkin, Susan. *Miss America, 1945: Bess Myerson's Own Story.* New York: Newmarket Press, 1987.

Riverol, A. R. *Live from Atlantic City: The History of Miss America Before, After and in Spite of Television.* Bowling Green, Ohio: Bowling Green State University Popular Press, 1992.

*Richard R. Wilk*

# BEER-MAKING

**See** *Home Brewing*

# BICYCLING

The German agriculturist Karl von Drais is generally acknowledged as the "father of the bicycle." His idea for a wooden, two-wheeled, running machine, which he patented in 1818, was soon copied by inventors in America. In 1819, "hobbyhorses" made their appearance on the streets of Boston and New York, and laws were quickly promulgated to prohibit their use on sidewalks. The novelty of these cumbersome forms of locomotion soon wore off, until the inventive spirit of the Industrial Revolution sparked new ideas in transport, leading to three major boom periods for cycling in America.

**John Boyd Dunlop.** Credited with the invention of the first usable pneumatic tire in 1888, Scottish inventor John Boyd Dunlop (1840–1921) is the founder of the modern-day Dunlop Tire Corp. © *Corbis*

The initial craze for cycling began in the 1860s with the invention of the velocipede, a cast-iron machine with pedal cranks attached to the front wheel. The development of this "boneshaker" created a new mode of transport and industry, fostering different forms of sporting and recreational activities. Although velocipedes were originally popularized in France, transatlantic trade ensured intense competition in its manufacture and marketing. The velocipede craze peaked in America around 1869, when nearly every major city built at least one rink for the machine. However, new patents and fierce rivalries for profits continued to drive improvements to the velocipede.

## The Cycling "Craze"

The next boom period—the late 1870s, and early 1880s—saw the advent of the high-wheeler, also known as the "ordinary" or "penny farthing." The first ordinary appeared at the 1876 Centennial Exhibition in Pennsylva-

nia. Entrepreneur colonel Albert Pope of Boston soon began manufacturing these novel machines and, with control of patents and aggressive marketing, he became known as the "father of American bicycling." Advertising posters for the Pope Manufacturing Company show that the sleek, superior, and relatively cheap high-wheeler quickly superseded the heavy and expensive velocipede. Many of the basic elements present in the modern bicycle, including ball bearings, tangent-spoked wheels, and hollow steel tubing, were introduced at this time. In 1878, the Boston Bicycle Club signaled the beginning of cycling clubs, introducing some people to a whole new way of life. Young males in particular enjoyed not only the inherent camaraderie of the group, but also the collective protection from unprovoked harassment aimed at lone cyclists.

The League of American Wheelmen (LAW), formed in 1880 with just forty-four members at Newport, Rhode Island, reflected this upsurge in popularity. Membership grew from almost 12,000 in 1894 to more than 141,000 cyclists in 1898. This group promoted numerous cycling activities, including touring and racing, and was a strong advocate for better roads and legislation. Most cycling enthusiasts were located in the eastern states, particularly Massachusetts and Connecticut.

Competitive cycling became highly popular and usually occurred in connection with other athletic sports. Considerable prize money was offered, generating a much-publicized and fierce quest for speed by "scorchers," growth in professionalism, and the consequent involvement of bookmakers. Racing became increasingly formalized, and, in 1886, the American Cyclists Union was created to help regulate the sport. A number of American track stars achieved notable success overseas, including Arthur Zimmerman, nicknamed "The Flying Yankee," and Major Taylor, an African American whose remarkable and controversial career was "marked by his speed, his skin color [in what was then a white-dominated sport], and his religious convictions" (Perry, p. 364).

Bicycle touring also became popular, with numerous trans-American trips and world tours undertaken by groups of cyclists as well as individuals. Noteworthy was American Thomas Stevens, who achieved the first overland circuit of the globe on a high-wheeler between 1884 and 1887. Women also rode remarkably long distances. For example, in July 1894, Mrs. E. Witchie became the first woman in the Midwest to cover a hundred miles in one day.

Cyclists met with considerable opposition, particularly by people using horse-drawn transport. Newspapers commented that it seemed as if all America were divided into two classes—those who rode bicycles and those who did not. The more individualistic activity of cycling diverted many young males from more established team sports and recreations. This new leisure pursuit, accompanied by a proliferation of bicycle-riding schools, marketing of cycling accessories, and publication of numerous books and magazines, thus presented a challenge to the popularity of customary recreational activities.

The breakthrough that ensured the continued popularity of the bicycle was the pneumatic tire. While the concept of an air-filled tire had its beginnings in Scotland in 1845, it was 1888 before Scotsman John Dunlop designed a tire suitable for use on the "safety" bicycle, developed in the mid-1880s. The pneumatic tire was introduced into America in 1890, and the burgeoning cycling industry received a noticeable boost as buyers clamored for the mechanically superior and safer machines. Consequently, long-standing objections to women cycling were swept aside. The widespread popularity and availability of the safety bicycle thus created the third, and biggest, boom for cycling throughout the industrialized world. Initially more expensive than the solid-tired high-wheeler, sales of safety bicycles quickly overtook those of the "ordinary" and bicycle production increased markedly.

## Women's Cycling in the Nineteenth Century

In the late nineteenth century, the bicycle gave middle-class women independence and social freedom, but not without controversy. Compared to a horse and carriage, the machines were more economical to maintain and run and easier to manage, and they required no special clothing, equipment, accommodation, or staff. With her own bicycle, a woman was able to determine where and when she would ride. Social criticism, however, focused on the masculinity of the new activity—it was unfeminine to ride and to wear cycling clothes, and it made respectable women conspicuous in public.

Logistically, shopping and visiting became more straightforward, but the bicycle also opened up new recreational and sporting opportunities. Group rides and activities were a regular feature of the cycling season, and the club environment enhanced women's knowledge of bicycles and cycling techniques. Clubs also introduced young females to a wider social network, affording favorable occasions for meeting and mixing with young men, sometimes on tandems, without the expected chaperone. Excursions were a major attraction of cycling. In addition to day or weekend trips, major cycle tours appealed to the more adventurous woman, who explored not only her city or state, but also nationally and inter-

### Popular Culture and Bicycling

During the 1890s, the bicycle, including the tandem, became a feature in songs, poems, jokes, pictures, and literature, many of which often had a romantic theme. In 1892, Henry Dacre published the now-famous song, "Daisy Bell."

Daisy, Daisy,
Give me your answer do,
I'm half crazy
All for the love for you!
It won't be a stylish marriage,
I can't afford a carriage
But you'll look sweet upon the seat
Of a bicycle built for two.

nationally. Cycle racing offered a new sporting opportunity for competitive women, and American riders won international acclaim. Both track and road racing were highly popular with audiences throughout the 1890s, partly because of the spectacle of women in scant clothing. Women's racing was rarely taken seriously, however, and declined until a gradual revival in the 1930s.

For some women, cycling symbolized the principles of self-determination and social equality and offered the perfect opportunity to promote issues such as dress reform, female suffrage, and temperance, as well as the more general idea of women's social progress. Riding a bicycle necessitated changes in attitudes toward fashion, for dangerous clothing, as well as comfort and convenience, were mutual concerns of cyclists and dress reformers alike. Bloomers, named after Amelia Bloomer, an ardent supporter of dress reform, were promoted in earlier decades, but with limited success. It was not until the bicycle boom of the 1890s that dress reform cyclists readily adopted bloomers.

## Early to Mid-Twentieth Century

Prices of new cycles continued to fall from 1895 onward. With the ever-increasing secondhand market, and the easily available installment purchase schemes, cycling remained a popular pursuit, despite competition from the automobile. But, unlike in Britain and Europe, in America the period spanning World War I was characterized by a steady decline in cycling. Colonel Pope had turned to automobile manufacture. Cycling generally came in a poor second to the attraction of the motorcar and,

## Frances Willard

Frances Willard (1839–1898) was well-known in the United States and abroad for her social reform efforts. She served as president of the Women's Christian Temperance Union (WCTU) from 1879 until her death in 1898, building it into the largest women's organization of its time, and founded the World WCTU. She learned to ride a bicycle when aged 53 years. She called her bicycle "Gladys" on account of the "exhilarating motion of the machine, and the gladdening effect of its acquaintance and use."

according to McGurn, also suffered competition from new electric mass transportation systems. Children's cycles continued to appeal, but it was only the gasoline shortages of the 1940s that caused another brief, but significant, demand for bicycles. After World War II, Americans, like the British and Europeans, sought relief from wartime austerity by enthusiastically engaging in recreation activities. Sports stadiums, cinemas, holiday camps, and seaside resorts were immensely popular, but the pursuit of leisure increasingly involved the acquisition of consumer goods and use of the motorcar, all to the apparent detriment of cycling.

### Revival of Bicycling

In the latter decades of the twentieth century there was a marked revival of cycling, stimulated both by market differentiation and environmental and health concerns. During the 1960s, American manufacturers were developing lighter-weight models with the adolescent market in mind. The twenty-six-inch wheel size distinguished these bicycles from the smaller-wheeled children's models and sold well. For the younger set, the Raleigh "chopper," or "high-rise" cycle, with its ape-hanger handlebars, curved "banana" seat, and raised frame behind the seat, was launched in 1969, marking the first of the action bicycles that subsequently evolved. Over time, the "high-rise" design incorporated derailleur gears (used to shift the chain from sprocket to sprocket to change gears, especially in multigeared bicycles, where very low gearing enabled easy hill climbing) and hand brakes and then led to the more sophisticated ten-speed models that dominated the 1970s. This was a highly profitable period for the cycle industry, signified by what cycle historian Frank Berto calls the "Great American Bike Boom of

1971–1974." Conventional wisdom states that this American boom was caused by the oil shortage and recession that followed the Arab-Israeli war, but Berto disagrees, pointing out that the war began in late 1973 and, by the end of that year, the shortage was over. The bicycle boom, nearing its end at this stage, was extended mainly because of public perceptions of the energy crisis. Notwithstanding, bicycling grew steadily into the 1980s and beyond.

Market differentiation gave potential riders a vast array of options, playing on the desire for novelty, adventure, and identity. Image became a key feature of new designs, which were aimed at teenagers. The increasing sophistication of the ten-speed, with its inverted curved handlebars and sleek appearance, appealed to the now-adult post-chopper riders, bolstered by the strong popular interest in health and fitness that marked the late 1970s. The BMX (bicycle motorcross) machine, which enabled riders to negotiate offroad dirt tracks, and to perform stunts, soon replaced the chopper. In the mid-1970s, the mountain bike began its evolution. The first widely available models were the "Specialized Stump Jumper," by San Jose company Specialized Bicycle Imports, and the Univega Alpina Pro, by Long Beach company Univega. Both models were manufactured in Japan. Throughout the 1980s, mountain bike designs were highly popular, and by the mid-1980s, sales of these machines had exceeded road bikes. Mountain bikes differed from road bikes in several key ways: They had wide, knobby tires instead of skinny smooth tires; handlebars were usually upright instead of the inverted curved handlebars; and the frame, seat, and wheels were designed to handle rough terrain comfortably.

Aggressive tourism marketing in the 1990s helped to swell the number of riders who explored their local environs and farther afield. In the early 2000s, a network of creative designers continued to develop new and innovative designs to cater to all cycling needs, including riders with disabilities. A small group of designers produced various recumbent (more horizontal, with the rider sitting low to the ground with legs extended to the front) designs for comfort and energy efficiency, as well as folding cycles for carriage on public transport. Even more enterprising individuals designed bicycles equipped with computers and global positioning systems for long-distance touring.

### Networks of Enthusiasts

A number of key American organizations actively promote cycling. The League of American Bicyclists (LAB) encourages bicycling for fun, fitness, and transportation, and works through advocacy and education for a bicycle-

"**Keating Bicycle.**" A poster advertises Keating Wheel Company's bicycle. Located in Holyoke, Massachusetts, the business ran from 1892 to 1898. © *Corbis*

friendly society. Originally the League of American Wheelmen, it was responsible for improving terrible road surfaces and helping to establish the current national highway system through its Good Roads movement. Another important organization is the Bicycle Federation of America (BFA), a national, nonprofit corporation established in 1977 to create bicycle-friendly and walkable communities. Now operating as the National Center for Bicycling and Walking (NCBW), its major focus is greater involvement of the public health sector in transportation policy and land-use planning to help create more physically active communities. The passage of the Intermodal Surface Transportation Efficiency Act (ISTEA) in 1991 has provided tangible support for numerous bicycle projects that has resulted in significant increases in cycling numbers and, concurrently, decreases in cycle-related fatalities. The 1997 report "Share the Road" stressed the importance of continued cash flow from ISTEA's funding framework and planning provisions.

A conference in 2000 brought together for the first time a diverse group of bicycle advocates, injury prevention specialists, and government representatives. The resulting "National Strategies for Advancing Bicycle Safety" was the first step in changing the cycling environment in significant ways. The National Bicycle Safety Network (NBSN)—a public-private coalition of federal and state agencies, professional and nonprofit safety groups, and bicycling advocacy organizations—volunteered to facilitate implementation of activities for selected portions of the strategy. Similarly, Probicycle, a key advocacy group that promotes education and safety and the skills of effective advocacy, has the motto "Same Roads, Same Rights, Same Rules." Children's participation in cycling was also a key concern of cycle advocacy. Parents and teachers were encouraged to teach sound cycling skills, road rules, and the wisdom of wearing a helmet.

In the early 2000s, cycling was integral to community health policies and programs. Physical activity, com-

bined with overeating, steadily increased the incidence of overweight or obese adults from 47 percent in 1976, to 56 percent in 1994, and 61 percent in 1999. For children and adolescents, the prevalence doubled during the same period (Wilkinson et al., p. 2). The 2001 Surgeon General's report stressed the importance of physical activity in reducing these and other lifestyle diseases and ailments,

## Bloomers

These loose fitting trousers were adapted from harem pants and first worn by members of the New York Oneida Community in 1848. Bloomers were worn in public around 1851, and popularized by Elizabeth Smith Miller, but named for her friend Amelia Bloomer, editor of the reform journal, *Lily*. Bloomer supported their use in order to free women from the cumbersome long skirts of the day. Short-lived in popularity, their use was revived during the bicycle boom of the 1890s.

and, in response, the National Center for Bicycling and Walking published a guide for public health practitioners in which it advanced the argument that more people would bicycle more often if they had safer places to ride.

A wide array of cycling organizations in America cater to specific interest groups, aside from traditional racing. Cyclo-cross, for example, is the cycling equivalent of cross-country running. The sport originated in Europe around seventy-five years ago as an off-season training option as well as to develop advanced riding skills. Cyclists ride on forest trails, parks, and fields, carrying their bikes over unridable sections such as streams and fallen trees. The sport is well developed in the United States, with numerous clubs staging local events.

The American Bicycle Association (ABA) was created in the late 1970s to administer what is now known as BMX, an activity with an enormous following. Similarly, in response to the immense interest in mountain biking in the 1980s, the International Mountain Bike Association (IMBA) was formed. Since 1988, IMBA has encouraged environmentally sound and socially responsible low-impact riding, volunteer trail building, cooperation among different trail-user groups, and more.

## Cycle Routes and Trails

Cycle routes and trails are popular with riders, not only because of their high safety record but also because of their aesthetic appeal. Although dedicated routes are a safe alternative to sharing roads or pathways, many communities lack paths that are separate from road traffic. Trails are also popular. Some examples of the hundreds of successful trails that now exist include the Burke-Gilman Trail in Seattle, Washington; the Eliza Furnace Trail in Pittsburgh, Pennsylvania; and the Riverfront Trail in Missoula, Montana. For longer rides, cyclists can ac-

cess trails fostered by the Rails-to-Trails Conservancy, which aims to enrich America's communities by creating a nationwide network of public trails out of former rail lines and connecting corridors. Besides riding rail trails, cycle tourists can take advantage of the hundreds of groups now organizing extensive tours within America. The NCBW calls for more trails to be built, not only because they are safer for cyclists but also because they encourage more people to take up cycling, thereby increasing community fitness and health.

## Conclusion

While precursors of the bicycle can be traced back to the Renaissance, it was only during the nineteenth century that advances in technology and design throughout Europe and the United States resulted in the modern form of the machine. Cycling rapidly gained popularity not only as a means of transport, but also as a leisure pursuit and sporting activity for both men and women. The bicycle became the fastest mode of self-propelled locomotion, and the sensation of speed, a completely novel feeling, became one of the pleasures of cycling. Cycling remains an immensely popular leisure activity for Americans of all ages, and the bicycle remains the epitome of an urban machine. While the bicycle has represented the benefits of technological progress and typified the refinements of civilized existence, according to Richard Harmond and others, it has also been the means of escape from a tension-prone industrialized society. On this basis, the activity of cycling will continue to be an emotional palliative for many of today's urban problems.

*See also:* Automobiles and Leisure, Commercialization of Leisure, Progressive-Era Leisure and Recreation, Tourism, Urbanization of Leisure

### BIBLIOGRAPHY

Beeley, Serena. *A History of Bicycles.* London: Studio Editions, 1992.

Berto, Frank J. "The Great American Bike Boom." *Rivendell Reader* no. 19 (Spring 2002): 12–17.

Cohen, Brian, Richard Wiles, Chistopher Campbell, Bill Wilkinson, and James Corless. *Share the Road: Let's Make America Bicycle Friendly.* Washington D.C.: Environmental Working Group/The Tides Center, 1997.

Dunham, Norman L. "The Bicycle Era in American History." Ph.D. diss., Harvard University, 1956.

Harmond, Richard. "Progress and Flight: An Interpretation of the American Cycle Craze of the 1890s." *Journal of Social History* 5, no. 2 (1971–1972): 235–257.

Herilihy, David V. "The Velocipede Craze in Maine." In *Cycle History: Proceedings of the 8th International Cycle History Conference.* Edited by Nicholas Oddy and Rob van der Plas. San Francisco: Van der Plas Publications, 1998.

McGurn, Jim. *On Your Bicycle: The Illustrated Story of Cycling,* 2d ed. New York: Open Road Publishers, 1999.

Norcliffe, Glen. *The Ride to Modernity: The Bicycle in Canada, 1869.–1900.* Toronto: University of Toronto Press, 2001.

Perry, David B. *Bike Cult: The Ultimate Guide to Human-Powered Vehicles.* New York: Four Walls Eight Windows, 1995.

Smith, Robert A. *A Social History of the Bicycle.* New York: American Heritage Press, 1972.

Wilkinson, W. C., N. Eddy, G. MacFadden, and B. Burgess. *Increasing Physical Activity Through Community Design.* Washington: National Center for Bicycling and Walking, 2002.

Willard, Frances E. *How I Learned to Ride the Bicycle: Reflections of an Influential 19th Century Woman.* Edited by Carol O'Hare, with an introduction by Edith Mayo. Sunnyvale, Calif.: Fair Oaks Publishing, 1991.

*Clare Simpson and Rob Hess*

# BILLIARDS/POOL

Billiards refers to a category of games played with hard balls, between 2-$\frac{1}{16}$ and 2-$\frac{27}{64}$ inches in diameter, on a raised, rectangular, cloth-covered table surrounded by padded walls, or "rails," that prevent the balls from leaving the table. There are two general forms of billiards. In one, players score points by propelling one of the balls (the "cue ball") into others, thus scoring a "carom." In the second type, scoring is accomplished when the cue ball is propelled into "object balls" causing the latter to fall into one of six pockets on the table, one in each corner and one on either side of the long sides of the table. Hence, there are two principal types of tables, those without pockets and those with pockets. Tables are half as wide as long and range between 6 and 12 feet in length. Most "standard" tables in the United States are 8 feet long and 4 feet wide. The bed, or playing surface of the table, should be between 29-$\frac{1}{4}$ and 30-$\frac{1}{4}$ inches from the floor. The best table beds are made of slate—between $\frac{1}{2}$- and 2-inches thick—resting on wooden supports.

Players propel the cue ball using a "cue stick," a tapered cylindrical rod approximately 57 inches long and weighing between 14 and 22 ounces. The tip of the cue is affixed with a rounded leather tip and is approximately $\frac{1}{2}$-inch in diameter. Most cue sticks are made of wood, but other materials, such as aluminum or graphite, are sometimes used as well. The handle end of the cue stick is often covered with a material to provide a pleasant grip and may be decorated with inlays.

## Origins of Billiards

The earliest known reference to billiards as an indoor game is in a 1470 inventory of the accounts of King Louis XI of France, who reigned from 1461 to 1483. The game most likely developed from outdoor games similar to croquet, wherein balls were propelled at various sorts of targets, such as hoops, sticks, or other balls, by cudgels, maces, hammers, or similar devices.

"Billiards" probably derives from the medieval Latin word "billa," which comes, in turn, from the Latin "pila," meaning "ball." "Cue," is from the French "queue," meaning "tail," and may refer to the handle of the billiard mace, the device that preceded the modern cue stick. The mace, which had a wide, flat-faced head attached to a shaft, was used to shove the cue ball into contact with the other balls on the table. The cue stick first appeared in the late 1600s but did not completely supplant the mace until the early twentieth century.

## Billiards in America

While knowledge of billiards may have arrived in Florida in the 1580s with the Spanish, it is certain that British and Dutch colonists brought the game to America by the 1600s. American cabinetmakers were producing small numbers of tables in the early 1700s, and the game spread rapidly through the colonies and to the west. A billiard parlor, built in 1764, was one of the first buildings to be erected by the French in St. Louis. Billiard tables had reached Bent's Fort, a trading post on the Santa Fe train route in present-day southeastern Colorado, by the 1830s. The billiard industry, producing tables, balls, and cues, was well established in America by the 1850s.

Despite its popularity, billiards has not always enjoyed a positive reputation in America. "Blue laws" enacted in New England in the 1600s severely restricted recreational activities on the Sabbath and were directed, in particular, at taverns, which frequently had billiards tables. The Commonwealth of Massachusetts Act of 1830 was an effort to control both players and the play of billiards by sanctioning tables. Owners of unauthorized tables could be arrested and their billiard equipment seized and destroyed. Because of its association with gambling, billiards was outlawed in other areas of the country from time to time, as well.

While the term "billiards" technically includes both carom and pocket games, pocket billiards games have come to be known as "pool." In the nineteenth century,

**World Pool Championships.** In July 2003 Earl "The Pearl" Strickland (1961– ) waits in the background en route to his defeat of Mark Williams (1975– ) at the World Pool Championships at the Cardiff International Arena in Cardiff, United Kingdom. His second consecutive victory brought him a prize of $65,000. © *Lawrence Lustig for EPA, PA/Lustig Photography*

however, a "pool" was a bet or ante, such as in poker, and betting parlors for horse racing were called "poolrooms." Billiards tables were often installed in poolrooms so that patrons could play between races. Over the years, the game became associated with the betting parlors. Billiards became "pool" and billiard halls became "pool halls." The games also came to be associated with the hustlers, thugs, and other unsavory characters who presumably frequented betting parlors. In the late twentieth century, however, with increased popularity of home pool tables, the establishment of family oriented pool parlors, and, especially, the frequent television coverage on ESPN and ESPN2 of both men's and women's tournaments, the reputation of billiards was substantially rehabilitated.

Early billiard games varied greatly in terms of the design of the tables, the number of balls, and how the balls were propelled on the table. Four-Ball was the most popular billiards game in America during the first half of the nineteenth century. It was played on a four-pocket table with a white cue ball, one white object ball and two red object balls. Scoring was accomplished in several ways, including pocketing balls, making caroms, and combina-

tions of both. In the 1870s, Four-Ball was largely replaced by Straight Rail, a carom game played with three balls on a pocketless table and American Fifteen Ball, played on a six-pocket table with a cue ball and fifteen object balls. These games were the forerunners of modern carom and pocket games, although others have now surpassed them in popularity. Eight-Ball, invented around the turn of the twentieth century, and Nine-Ball, which first appeared around 1920, are the most common billiard games in America in the early 2000s. Nine-Ball is frequently seen in televised tournaments because it requires exquisite shotmaking and games are of short duration when played by skilled professionals. These features make it ideal for television viewing.

*See also:* Colonial-Era Leisure and Recreation, Gambling

**BIBLIOGRAPHY**

Billiard Congress of America. *Billiards: The Official Rules and Records Book.* Iowa City, Iowa: Billiard Congress of America, 1995.

Hendricks, William. *William Hendricks' History of Billiards.* Roxana, Ill: William Hendricks, 1974.

Mizerak, Steve, with Michael E. Panozzo. *Steve Mizerak's Complete Book of Pool.* Chicago: Contemporary Books, 1990.

Shamos, Mike. "A Brief History of the Noble Game of Billiards," In *Billiards: The Official Rules & Records Book.* Iowa City, Iowa: Billiard Congress of America, 1995, pp. 1-5.

Stein, Victor, and Paul Rubino. *The Billiard Encyclopedia: An Illustrated History of the Sport.* Minneapolis, Minn.: Blue Book Publications, 1996.

*Garry Chick*

# BIRD WATCHING

Bird watching (or simply birding) involves observing and listening to birds in their natural habitats. Birding is aided by the use of binoculars, a spotting scope, and a field guide. Until the late 1800s, bird watching was synonymous with collecting. Ornithologists and bird watchers would routinely shoot birds and collect eggs and nests for scientific study and the pleasures associated with developing collections. In 1874, Elliot Coues, an imminent American ornithologist, provided advice to would-be bird watchers of his day: "The double barreled shotgun is your main reliance. Get the best one you can afford for your particular purpose which is the destruction of small birds with the least possible damage to their plumage. Begin by shooting every bird you can" (Kastner, p. 51).

Collecting gave way to modern bird watching with the introduction of improved optics and a growing concern about the decline of birds. The introduction of prisms in modern binoculars made it easier to identify birds in the field without shooting them. Simultaneously, rising concern about the killing of birds shrouded collecting with controversy. Millions of birds were shot (some to extinction) for commercial purposes—for example, their feathers were used to adorn women's hats. Early conservationists lobbied successfully for laws that would protect birds from commercial and noncommercial shooting and collecting.

A 2002 survey estimated that 46 million American adults participate in bird watching; but only 40 percent do so away from home and only 8 percent could identify more than forty birds by sight or sound (*U.S. Bureau*). However, many birders are highly serious, if not fanatical, about their avocation. Many enjoy counting bird species and keep "life lists" of all the birds they have identified in their home states, in the United States and Canada, and throughout the world. Some of these birders have world lists in the thousands and are highly driven to add new species.

In the early 2000s, a variety of venues existed for bird watchers. Organized tours took clients to all corners of the globe and to well-known birding "hot spots." A handful of states (for example, Texas and Arizona) developed "birding trails." In some areas, bed-and-breakfasts popped up near birding hot spots. Nearly 200 bird-watching and wildlife-watching festivals were held throughout the United States and Canada. There were also bird censuses, such as the Annual Christmas Bird Count, and birding competitions. At these events, which birders referred to as Bird-a-Thons or "Big Days," the goal was to list as many bird species as possible within a twenty-four-hour period. These competitions were typically organized by local Audubon societies to raise money for habitat conservation.

***See also:*** Backpacking and Hiking, Camping

**BIBLIOGRAPHY**

Kastner, Joseph. *A World of Watchers.* New York: Alfred A. Knopf, 1986.

U.S. Bureau of the Census. *National Survey of Fishing, Hunting, and Wildlife-Associated Recreation 2001–2002.* Prepared by the U.S. Department of Interior, Fish and Wildlife Service and U.S. Department of Commerce. Washington, D.C.: U.S. Government Printing Office, 2002.

*David Scott*

# BIRTHDAYS

Birthday celebrations honor individuals, reflect the cultural construction of cyclical time, and reinforce a universal emphasis on human maturation. In the United States, a birthday party is a public occasion during which the social status of a person changes. Children specifically value birthdays because these occasions are public declarations of a movement toward adulthood. Because birthday celebrations are not typically restricted by nations or religions, these annual events are anticipated and cherished around the world. In fact, birthdays are the most celebrated of all modern holidays.

**Party time!** Children celebrate at a birthday party with presents and party favors. © *Richard Hutchings/Corbis*

## Origins of the Birthday Party

Birthday celebrations in North America in the early 2000s reflect worldwide influences and the popularization of certain rituals and elements. Some rituals date from the ancient Mesopotamians and Egyptians, who first recognized patterns in time and developed calendars. In those societies, only members of the nobility were honored with birthday parties; nevertheless, the nobility often invited townspeople to participate, reinforcing the social order in the process. Some historians believe the custom of wearing crowns on birthdays originated at these early birthday festivals. Parham observes that early Christians celebrated "death days" because they did not believe in celebrating birthdays, as induction into heaven was viewed as more important than birth. However, in the fourth century, the Catholic Church decreed there should be a day to celebrate Jesus' birth; afterward, celebrating birthdays for common folk became widespread.

Around the same time, the custom of having birthday parties for children began in Germany with the "Kinderfeste," which translates into "children's party."

During this event, family members woke the child and presented him or her with gifts and a cake topped with candles matching the child's age, with an additional candle to symbolize the "light of life" or good luck (Rinkoff, p. 62).

## The Birthday Party in America

After the decline of the Puritan influence, which restricted celebrations in America, wealthy Protestants began hosting children's parties in the nineteenth century. By the twentieth century, people of all religions practiced this custom. In the late 1800s, children's parties were organized by parents and featured many guests. In the early 1900s, parties more influenced by peer culture began to dominate, especially among older children, where the guest of honor had more control over the guest list and entertainment. With the introduction of party-planning books in the 1920s, new norms surrounding birthday parties emerged, such as that of inviting one guest for every year of the celebrant's age. Moreover, by the 1920s, children had come to associate birthday parties with cakes, gifts, and party decorations.

## Birthday Traditions

Americans imported the idea of a birthday cake directly from the German Kinderfeste. In 1859, a Kentucky schoolteacher named Mildred Hill composed a musical melody to sing to her students and titled it "Good Morning to You/All." Her sister, Patty Hill, penned the lyrics and in 1893 added a verse that began "Happy Birthday to You." The song was published in 1935 and has been translated into countless languages worldwide. At birthday celebrations, upon presentation of the cake and after the guests complete the song, the honoree is supposed to make a private wish and then try to blow out the candles on the cake. If all the candles are extinguished with the first breath, tradition has it the wish will come true.

The use of the piñata, a tradition imported from Mexico, is now a standard feature at many children's birthday parties in North America. Piñatas are hollow figures in the shape of animals, flowers, automobiles, or other objects. They are filled with candy and small toys and are hung from a tree or ceiling. Blindfolded children take turns hitting the piñata with a stick. The child responsible for breaking open the piñata is believed to have good luck in the future. After the piñata is broken, the children rush to collect as much of its contents as possible.

In England, the practice of sending birthday cards started about 100 years ago; now worldwide millions of cards are sent each year to wish loved ones a happy birthday. Birthday gifts were first offered by the ancient Romans, who believed that the celebrant was vulnerable to evil spirits. Thus, surrounding the honoree with gifts and loved ones was a way of offering protection. In America, the burgeoning retail industry quickly recognized the value of reinforcing the tradition of birthday gifts. Stores often publicized children's birthdays and sent letters to celebrants, informing them that "we have a little present . . . waiting at the store" (Pleck, p. 152).

Game playing has long been a tradition at both American and foreign birthday parties, with hide-and-seek, pin the tail on the donkey, tag, and relay races commonly played at children's birthday parties. Other games enjoyed in the nineteenth century included horseshoe pitching, ninepins (bowling), and wood-chopping contests (Rinkoff, p. 16).

Pleck observes that some women have chosen to "outsource" the work associated with the birthday party since as early as the 1920s. As more women have entered the work force, birthday parties have increasingly moved out of the home and into commercial venues such as McDonald's, miniature golf courses, movie theaters, pizza parlors, and swimming pools. These venues have contributed to a recent escalation in the elaborate nature of the birthday party, and have also meant that guest lists may be longer to reflect the size of these facilities. Moreover, extended families and the increase in divorce mean children often have multiple parties. Thus, increases in both expenses and the quantity of parties mean birthday celebrations for children have increased in social status and visibility.

## BIBLIOGRAPHY

Klavir, Rama. "When Astronomy, Biology, and Culture Converge: Children's Conceptions about Birthdays." *Journal of Genetic Psychology* 163 (2002): 239–253.

Linton, Ralph, and Adelin Linton. *The Lore of Birthdays.* New York: Henry Schuman, 1998.

Parham, Betty. "A Little Birthday History." *Atlanta Journal and Constitution* (28 June 2001): 14F.

Pleck, Elizabeth, H. *Celebrating the Family: Ethnicity, Consumer Culture, and Family Rituals.* Cambridge, Mass.: Harvard University Press, 2000.

Rinkoff, Barbara. *Birthday Parties Around the World.* New York: M. Barrows, 1967.

*Cele Otnes*

# BLOOD SPORTS.

Although the term "blood sports" is no longer in popular usage, the words are sufficiently descriptive to suggest a workable definition. Violent sporting activities that inflicted serious injuries, pain, or death—not as ancillary or accidental dangers but as direct goals—constituted blood sports as they were understood by early modern English people and by colonial Americans. Also called the "butcherly sports," these activities commonly pitted animals against animals, humans against animals, or humans against humans. Few sporting activities in the twentieth- or twenty-first-century United States would qualify as blood sports in the truest sense of the phrase. Boxing and ice hockey do frequently spill blood, but theoretically the rules of each sport are designed to prevent excessive injuries, not encourage them. Bullfighting—illegal and not practiced in the United States—would qualify as a blood sport, as would dogfighting, which is also illegal throughout the United States. So, too, would cockfighting, which

**"The Cockpit" by William Hogarth.** Mocking his home country's passion for cockfighting in "The Cockpit" (print, 1759) British painter William Hogarth (1697–1764) was best known for his "moral" works that satirized their subjects. © *Burstein Collection/Corbis*

is illegal in forty-seven states, but wildly popular in several geographic areas.

Probably most people think immediately of imperial Rome and the gladiatorial contests staged in the Roman coliseum when they think of blood sports. No sport has exceeded them for sheer horror in Europe or the Americas in the fifteen hundred years since. Bears, lions, rhinoceroses, and elephants fought one another or more commonly were pitted against men who were usually slaves, criminals, or prisoners of war. Men often, of course, competed against one another, and the popular culture has attached a patina of romance to many of these contests or famed combatants. Medieval England and Europe created another romantic blood sport, the jousting tournaments of the High Middle Ages, which perhaps rivals Rome for notoriety in the popular imagination. People do not always associate jousting with blood sports, but often these mock battles spilled blood and produced death as if they were real.

Early modern Europe had no grand spectacles such as gladiator contests in large arenas or knights jousting to the cheers of scarf-waving partisans, but, nevertheless, England on the eve of colonization embraced a harsh range of sport, which often had bloody outcomes. Dogfights and cockfights to the death were common. So, too, was bearbaiting, in which participants ritually tortured a bear—as modern bullfighters torture a bull—and then inevitably slaughtered the subject animal to the cheers of bloodthirsty spectators. Falconry also might qualify as a blood sport, but if so, we may have to consider adding modern hunting, which many present Americans would reject on the grounds that causing pain is never a primary goal of a hunter. He or she would prefer a clean shot that delivered a minimum of pain instead of a slow, lingering, ritual death. Although no one referred to public executions as blood sports, in a sense they were: huge crowds in England and the English colonies gathered to watch criminals be hanged sometimes in groups of more than five. Other activities in England on the eve of colonization such as boxing and football were sufficiently intended to cause pain to qualify. Cudgel fighting may have been the most extreme Elizabethan human blood sport and the closest parallel to the cruel gladiator games of Rome. Two men—invariably of low social class, who would be paid for their pain—were tied together by a short rope and would bludgeon each other with cudgels until one could no longer continue. Onlookers bet heavily on the outcome. On the eve of colonization, foxhunting, which may be twenty-first-century England's last "respectable" blood sport, had already established itself as the preserve of the most exclusive members of the gentry and the nobility.

Thus, as they set about creating versions of English culture up and down the Atlantic seaboard in the seventeenth century, the transplanted English Americans had a rich heritage of blood sports to choose to replicate if they wished. In general, they transplanted far fewer than they left behind, but this, of course, varied according to region. Puritan New England imported virtually no blood sports. Puritans, long regarded by posterity as being antisport, were, in reality, not hostile to sport and leisure, but they had many tests they applied to separate acceptable from unacceptable recreational activities. Many of the tests were drawn from scriptural prohibitions, but sociology and empiricism also played a dominant role in assessment. Puritans forbade sports that tended to injure either individuals or the commonweal. Thus, they prohibited boxing since it almost always inflicted pain but allowed wrestling because it did not. The Puritans condemned ball sports, which might seem surprising to modern sensibilities, but makes sense if one considers that English football games usually produced dozens of serious injuries and even death on occasion. Typically played by landless peasants, football pitted village against village. The men of each village—perhaps hundreds of them—would try to carry a ball several miles to the center of the opposing village. The contest could take a day or more and leave casualties all along the way.

The middle colonies of New York, New Jersey, Pennsylvania, and Delaware were less abstemious than Puritan New England in many matters, but they, too, generally avoided most organized blood sports. The rough-and-tumble world of the colonial south was a different story. Virginia set the standards in most ways for southern mores and morals and the aggressive, entrepreneurial culture that emerged in the Chesapeake region was unrestrained by Puritan piety, village quietude, or Quaker pacifism. Virginian men competed at virtually everything in their lives and deliberately spilled plenty of blood doing so.

Violence simmered just beneath the surface of the alehouse culture that swathed the ubiquitous Chesapeake tavern and it took little provocation to bring forth an eruption. Gentlemen and laborers alike indulged in an extravagant ritual of repartee that was meant to be charmingly combative but not insultingly contemptuous. Too often an extra beer or two goaded a respondent into crossing the line, and a challenge would be forthcoming for either an apology or a physical defense. Neither a gentlemen nor a roughneck could back down without losing face in this highly status-conscious male society. Fights, therefore, were epidemic in taverns, and they were bloody as a general matter of course, beyond almost anything we could imagine in similar circumstances in the twentieth or twenty-first centuries. Gouging eyes, tearing genitals, and biting ears were commonplace. Curiously enough, however, fighters often made arrangements about what was to be and what was not to be tolerated before the fighting began: thus, in a strange way, rules did apply to these battles, and an honor code dictated adherence to them. But these bloody contests were epidemic.

The same spirit of competitiveness and face-saving at all costs frequently turned horse racing in the colonial south into a blood sport. The quarter horse and the quarter-mile race—a slam, bam, twenty-five-second or so duel between two rivals—became the norm of southern racing. But planters often arranged the races to take place in congested physical circumstances, and riders commonly attacked each other during the race. Always a risky business, horse racing in modern times tries to minimize injuries to man and beast, but, in the colonial south, the win-at-any-cost culture promoted injuries to both. Well-praised was the rider who unseated his opponent and left him to be trampled. And, of course, arguments over horse races after they were finished often spilled over into bloody fights between partisans.

More than anything else, the cockfight captured the violent essence of the South. Today, cockfighting is closely associated with less than savory elements of modern society. Not so in the colonial Chesapeake. Cockfights may have originated with the common folk, but before many generations had passed, they came under the shaping guidance of Virginia's well-placed planters. The Chesapeake gentry itself had rough origins. Early emigrants who were sufficiently tough to survive the challenging health and economic rigors of tobacco culture built up large estates by the second half of the seventeenth century and took on many of the airs of the English gentry. Much of the roughness and coarseness of their character remained, however, and was manifested in many cultural activities such as cockfighting.

Planters viewed their best cocks as extensions of their own manliness and competed against their fellow gentlemen with an ungentlemanly ferocity. They hired trainers or trained slaves to be cock handlers, arranged all-day or sometimes two-day battles involving scores of cocks from a large surrounding geographic radius, bet heavily on their own birds, and crowed in bloody triumph when they won. The birds wore sharpened spurs and fought to the death. Males of all ages and stations in life—children, poor farmers, and slaves—all formed the outer rings around the gentlemen who crowded the cockpits. Some particularly successful cocks were known throughout a county and remembered by name for years after they suffered the inevitable defeat.

The cockfight captures the essence of the relationship between blood sports and colonial American society. Absent in New England and the middle colonies where religious impulses sought to reform the world, cockfighting flowered as both reality and metaphor for the excessively masculine and rough south in the seventeenth century. Then in mid-eighteenth century, cockfighting went underground in the Chesapeake, where it became the preserve of the less-than-desirable elements at the bottom of society. Virginia cleaned up the worst of its blood-sporting traditions in the late colonial years and in the early national period exported some of them across the Appalachians. In the early nineteenth century, Kentucky and Tennessee became famed for the bare-knuckled, eye-gouging, anything-goes bar fights that had previously characterized the Chesapeake. Cockfighting also crossed the mountains.

In the colonies and post-revolutionary Atlantic states, a new graciousness characterized sport, and, as the few old blood sports disappeared, the only new one to emerge was the foxhunt. Never as popular in America as in England, the new-world gentry did begin having ritual foxhunts in the Chesapeake, the Carolinas, and even in the Narragansett country of Rhode Island, where warm-weather sojourners imported several southern traditions. In general, however, and with the above-noted exceptions, the early American world escaped the worst of the excesses that bloodied early modern England's sporting traditions.

*See also:* Boxing, Gambling, Horse Racing, Hunting, Recreational Fighting

## BIBLIOGRAPHY

Bailey, Peter. *Leisure and Class in Victorian England: Rational Recreation and the Contest for Control.* London: Taylor and Francis Books, 1978.

Brailsford, Dennis. "Religion and Sports in Eighteenth-Century England: For the Encouragement of Piety and Virtue." *British Journal of Sports History* 1 (1984): 141–148.

Carson, Jane. *Colonial Virginians at Play.* Williamsburg, Va.: Colonial Williamsburg Foundation, 1989.

Daniels, Bruce C. *Puritans at Play: Leisure and Recreation in Colonial New England.* New York: St. Martin's Press, 1995.

Guttmann, Allen. "English Sports Spectators: The Restoration to the Early Nineteenth Century." *Journal of Sport History* 12: (1985): 103–110.

Henrichs, Thomas. "Sports and Social Hierarchy in Medieval England." *Journal of Sport History* 9 (1982): 21–32.

Isaac, Rhys. *The Transformation of Virginia, 1740–1790.* Chapel Hill, N.C.: University of North Carolina Press, 1982.

Powell, R. E. "Sport, Social Relations and Animal Husbandry: Early Cock-Fighting in North America." *International Journal of Sport History* 5 (1993), 361–381.

Struna, Nancy. S. *People of Prowess: Sport, Leisure, and Labor in Early Anglo-America.* Urbana, Ill.: University of Illinois Press, 1996.

Wagner, Peter. "Puritan Attitudes Towards Physical Recreation in Seventeenth-Century New England." *Journal of Sport History* 3 (1976), 135–142.

*Bruce C. Daniels*

# BOARD GAMES

Board games have been in existence for centuries, with the first board game being recorded in 4000 B.C. Although many of the classics, such as mancala, draughts (checkers), chess, and backgammon have survived through time, we have seen significant changes, adaptations, and additions of others. The themes of board games have changed just as much as the games played. The first board games were developed for religious and moral teachings as well as general education purposes. By the nineteenth century, games were as likely to be educational as they were to be fun. Games were, and still are, a symbol of our culture. They reflect current events, history, and our traditions. Exploring the history of games illustrates some of the changes in society that are reflected in games as we know them today.

## The Classics

David Partlett suggested that games have four categories: classics, specialist games, family games, and pulp games. Games considered classics are played by a very broad audience and have grown beyond mere board games to in-

**Alfred Butts.** SCRABBLE inventor Alfred Butts at a Milton Bradley plant surrounded by tens of thousands of letter tiles from SCRABBLE. Butts worked with James Brunot to manufacture the game that was trademarked in 1948. © *AP/Wide World Photos*

clude clubs and national and international tournaments, and have emerged into computer formats. The classics include such games as mancala, backgammon, chess, checkers, Scrabble, and Monopoly.

Thought to evolve in Egypt, mancala is often considered one of the oldest games in the world. The traditional wooden board with cups was once played on the ground with holes dug in the dirt, using pebbles as playing pieces. Mancala, while many think is a game itself, is really a generic name for several variations of games such as Ayo and Wari. The object of the game is to move pieces strategically so they ultimately land in the last bin, or *kalaha*. The prominent differences in mancala games is the number of rows on the board and whether it is a single lap, multiple lap, or "Indian-style" lap game.

Backgammon was developed in Egypt and dates as far back as the early part of the first century. Although the origin of backgammon is much disputed, historians do know that the Romans played a game called Duodecim, which was modified and renamed Tabula, or Tables, and then later called backgammon. Researchers have suggested but not confirmed that the originator of the game designed the board with twenty-four points to represent the twenty-four hours in a day, twelve points on each half the board to correspond with the twelve months a year, thirty pieces equating the thirty days in the month, and the two dice representing day and night.

Created to test intellect and courage, train for military strategies, and raise the I.Q. of youth, chess was thought to originate in Ancient India in the sixth century. The game originated from Chaturanga, and the pieces represented the four branches of the Indian army—chariots, cavalry, elephants, and the infantry as well as the king and his chief counselor. It was not until the fifteenth century that chess began to transform into the modern version of the game by changing the names of the pieces to reflect the culture at the time as well as increasing the power and movement of the queen and bishop. These changes made the game faster and required more strategy from the onset of play.

Considered a derivative from other games, checkers originated in Europe around 1100 A.D. The original game modeled its pieces after backgammon pieces, its board after a chessboard, and the movement of its pieces after those of a game called Alquerque. Known by the British as draughts, only North Americans refer to the game by the configuration of its board. The rules for checkers were formally established in 1852 and have changed very little since that time, however, there are roughly twelve different documented versions of the game.

The 1920s and 1930s saw the emergence of crossword puzzles. Capitalizing on a favorite pastime, Alfred Butts put puzzles in board game form in 1931. He analyzed the use of letters in words and came up with the number of each letter for the game called Criss Cross Words. This letter distribution still stands today. Big game companies rejected the game for having no commercial possibilities until it was trademarked as SCRABBLE in 1948.

Arguably, Monopoly is one of the most popular games ever made. Many thought that Monopoly was a result of the Great Depression, when in actuality it was a game that was first developed and patented in 1904 by Lizzie J. Magie and called The Landlord's Game. Magie liked the idea of Henry George's single-tax theory where only land was taxed and developed a game around this idea. In 1924, Parker Brothers rejected Magie's game because it was deemed too political. The game was then adapted by several different people until Charles Darrow copyrighted the rules and the board in 1933. Initially, Parker Brothers rejected the game because of fifty-two errors in the rules, and it was not until 1935 that they purchased the rights to the game. By 1935, Monopoly had become America's best-selling game, and, in 1999, a sack of money was added as the newest Monopoly token.

## Specialist Games

David Partlett defined specialist games as those that required thought, skill, and strategy to play. Players were typically adults, and, although similar to the classics, specialist games appealed to a smaller market segment. Specialist games include Life, Clue, and Parcheesi, and began to emerge in the early 1800s.

Traveller's Tour Through the United States, developed in 1822, was the first game to originate in the United States, and it was the only game being manufactured until 1843 when Mansion of Happiness was introduced. However, Mansion of Happiness was a copy of an English version originally developed in 1800.

Many Victorian parlor games were considered specialist games. Although during this era some of the old favorites were chess, checkers, and backgammon, many new ones were introduced and focused on education and morality. For example, the Errand Boy game was developed in the 1800s to teach about good deeds and hard

work. In addition to board games, the Victorian era saw the rise of dominoes, marbles, cribbage, bridge, and other card games.

The golden age of games was sparked in 1860 when Milton Bradley produced the Checkered Game of Life. The company's fortune came when they made this game in travel size for soldiers during the Civil War. The goal of the game was to strive for happy old age. The game was revamped in 1960 and changed to the Game of Life. Given the changes in society over the ensuing 100 years, the goal was altered so players attempted to become millionaires. Also, in the later 1870s, the rights to Parcheesi were purchased by Selchow and Righter, and the game was trademarked in 1874, making it one of the earliest trademarks for an American game. Parcheesi is an adaptation of Pachisi, the National Game of India and the English version of Ludo. Parcheesi is the third best-selling board game of all time in the United States, behind Monopoly and Scrabble.

To emulate society in the early 1900s, games reflecting World War I, such as Soldiers of the Advance Guard and the Great War emerged. Charles Lindbergh's 1927 solo flight across the Atlantic Ocean sparked development of Lindy, The Flight to Paris, and Ski-Hi.

The 1930s also brought about the Great Depression. The game industry, however, did not feel the impact of the depression until 1933 because games were an inexpensive way to entertain the family. During this time jigsaw puzzles and money games such as Values and The Money Management Game also became popular.

Even with the country in strife due to World War II, a worldwide popular game emerged at the end of the 1940s. The game known as Cluedo (in Europe, China, and Australia), Clue (in North America), and Mystery Game (in Japan), was a "who done it" game invented by Anthony Pratt in 1949. Although the names of the players have changed somewhat from the original version, the weapons have seen a dramatic transformation. The original ten weapons included the lead pipe, candlestick, rope, revolver, dagger, spanner (wrench), hypodermic syringe, axe, poison, and bomb. This mystery game also has the distinction of being the first game to be made into a movie.

The 1980s megahit was Trivial Pursuit. Trivial Pursuit revived a declining board game industry that was being impacted by electronic games. The game officially debuted in 1982, and over forty-five variations of the game have been developed since. The game is one of the best-selling adult board games in history, with over 70 million units purchased.

## Family Games

David Partlett defined the third category, family games, as being designed primarily for children, but playable by adults. These games have a tendency to focus on the throw of a dice, racing to a winning destination, or accumulating resources such as money or points.

Uncle Wiggily, a popular family game created in 1916, was based on Howard R. Garis's book called *Uncle Wiggily Bedtime Stories*. The game is played by drawing cards, following the rhymes on the cards, and moving the playing pieces to Dr. Possum's house on space 100.

During the 1930s and 1940s several long-standing games were introduced. Sorry, derived from the English version of Parcheesi, was released in 1934. Battleship also became a popular game created in the 1930s. In the 1940s, Milton Bradley manufactured Chutes and Ladders. This game was derived from second-century Indian and Hindu games called Snakes and Ladders. These versions of the game were based on morality, with the shorter paths to the end characterized by good deeds and the longer paths by evil, vice, and human sin. The current version also emphasizes good and bad behavior by rewarding good behaviors—such as helping to sweep a mess—while allowing the player to move forward, and punishing bad behaviors—such as eating too much candy—with having the player move back spaces on the board. The 1940s also saw the manufacturing of Candyland (1949) by Milton Bradley. In this race game, players draw cards indicating the number of spaces to move.

Yahtzee was invented in 1956 by a wealthy Canadian couple who played the dice game on their yacht, thus leading to the name Yahtzee. Soon after Yahtzee was first manufactured, Risk was offered to the public. This game of global domination was created in 1959.

The 1990s was the decade of the children's versions of many popular games. Games such as Monopoly Junior, Clue Junior, Boggle Junior, and Trivial Pursuit Junior were put on the market.

## Pulp Games

Pulp games follow trends, fads, fashions, television programs, and characters. Following the creation of television, there was an onslaught of pulp games manufactured. Many games were modeled after the popular shows such as *Route 66*, *Groucho's*, and *You Bet Your Life*. This trend continued through the 1970s with such games as The Love Boat and As the World Turns. Game-show board games also emerged, such as Hollywood Squares (1974) and Concentration (1958), as well as games about cartoon characters like Scooby Doo (1983) and the Flintstones (1961).

## Board Game Manufacturers

Although there are a number of companies that have produced board games through the years, a select few have made the biggest impact on the industry. W. and S. B. Ives was the first major game manufacturer in the United States when they began making games in 1843. In 1858, McLoughlin Brothers began producing games that were known for their beautifully hand illustrated wooden boards and boxes. Their games reflected pop culture and are some of the most sought-after board games by collectors today. McLoughlin Brothers was eventually sold in 1920 to Milton Bradley.

Milton Bradley began when it produced the Checkered Game of Life. This company had the ability to use lithography and became the first manufacturer to mass-produce games. Today, Milton Bradley is probably most known for producing The Game of Life, Chutes and Ladders, and Candyland.

Selchow and Righter began producing games for other companies in 1867, and their own games in the 1920s. They are most known for owning the rights to Parcheesi, Scrabble, and Trivial Pursuit.

Parker Brothers began in 1883 when George Parker, then sixteen, took $40 from his savings account to publish and market his own game called Banking. As the company grew George continued to write the rules himself and play all of the games produced by the company with employees and friends before releasing them to the public. Some of the best-known games produced by Parker Brothers include Monopoly, Clue, Sorry, and Risk.

Hasbro entered the market in 1923 as a children's leisure time and entertainment company. The company focused more on toys with such brand names as Playskool, Tonka, and Mr. Potato Head. One of Hasbro's only games at the time was Monopoly (1935). Hasbro became the leader in game production when they acquired Milton Bradley in 1984 and Parker Brothers in 1991. Even though Hasbro owns these companies, they have continued to produce their own original lines of games.

## Board Games Today and Tomorrow

As society has changed, so has the face of board games. They have become more diversified. For those who like technology, handheld versions of a number of games have been produced from Battleship and Boggle to Yahtzee and

Scrabble. Interactive electronic games also entered the market with Merlin, Simon, and Bop It.

Keeping in mind that games are not just for children, party games emerged in the 1990s. The focus was on entertaining adults and promoting social interactions. Such games as Catch Phrase, Guesstures, Jenga, Outburst, and Pictionary hit the store shelves.

People remember spending hours playing Monopoly, Clue, Sorry, Battleship, and many others. The face of board games has changed and evolved from those games drawn in the dirt to what they are today. They have entertained generations, demonstrated what was happening in society at the time, and endured a depression, wars, and the computer age. Given the strength and longevity of this popular pastime, board games will most likely remain a mainstay during years to come.

*See also:* Card Games

**BIBLIOGRAPHY**

Bell, Robert C. *The Boardgame Book.*. Los Angeles: Knapp Press, 1979.

Botermans, Jack, Tony Burrett, Pieter van Delft, and Carla van Splunteren. *The World of Games: Their Origins and History, How to Play Them, and How to Make Them.* New York: Facts on File, 1989.

Cluedo Fan. "The History of Cluedo and Clue." Available from http://www.cluedofan.com.

Costello, Matthew J. *The Greatest Games of All Times.* New York: John Wiley and Sons, 1991.

Games of the Victorian Era. Available from http://www.geocities.com/victorianlace12/games.html.

Grunfeld, F. V. *Games of the World: How to Make Them, How to Play Them, How They Came to Be.* New York: Holt, Rinehart and Winston, 1975.

Hasbro. "Hasbro Company History." Available from http://www.hasbro.com.

Mohr, M. S. *The Game Treasury: More Than 300 Indoor and Outdoor Favorites with Strategies, Rules, and Traditions.* Shelburne, Vt.: Chapters Publishing, 1993.

Online Guide to Traditional Games: "Mancala." Available from http://www.tradgames.org.

Partlett, Davis S. *The Oxford History of Board Games.* New York: Oxford University Press, 1999.

University of Waterloo. "Elliott Avedon Museum and Archive of Games." Available from http://www.gamesmuseum.uwaterloo.ca.

Whitehill, Bruce. *Games: American Boxed Games and Their Makers 1822–1992.* Radnor, Pa.: Wallace-Homestead Book Company, 1992.

*Amy R. Hurd*

# BOATING, POWER

While the earliest dugout tree trunks used as boats 20,000 years ago no doubt offered exhilaration, their primary role was transporting goods and people for reasons of surviving, discovering, conquering, and waging battle. It was not until the boat was coupled with another invention—the portable gas engine—in the early twentieth century that pleasure was added to boating's purposes. In the early 2000s, millions of people owned boats just for fun. In fact, boats are often called "pleasure craft."

The earliest powerboat was steam-powered. After steam, electrical power was harnessed in 1881 when Gustave Trouve of France successfully propelled a boat using bichromate-potash batteries. This provided a clean and quiet motorized boat, but this first outboard motor (that is, a motor attached to the back of the boat) was in constant need of recharging, making its operation cumbersome. In the 1890s several mechanics were tinkering with a portable outboard gasoline engine for boats, and the German engineer Gottlieb Daimler was the first to produce one for the personal "autoboat." It wasn't until the commercial success of Ole Evinrude's outboard motor and Johnson Motors' inboard motor (located near the center of the boat's hull) in the United States in the early 1920s, however, that recreational power boating really caught on.

Since that time, the excitement of using powerboats for fishing, waterskiing, cruising, sunbathing, swimming, scuba diving, racing, partying, and even full-time living, has spawned a large world of specialty magazines, clubs and associations, retailers, marinas, and annual shows. Ambitions and curiosities about powerboating have also led to a wide array of different crafts—from motor yachts, cruisers, and houseboats to pontoons, runabouts, jet skis, and bass boats. As more lakes, rivers, bays, and inlets host faster, both larger and smaller, and more agile powerboat craft, the more nonprofit associations and governmental agencies have joined in efforts to keep powerboating safe and nonpolluting. Such organizations as the United States Power Squadrons, the United States Coast Guard, and state departments of natural resources provide boat handling and navigation instruction, registration programs, and safety regulations. Motorized recreational watercraft must abide by numerous and wide-ranging law-enforced rules covering speed, sound, lights, passengers, sanitation, ventilation, communication, anchoring, towing, signaling, distress, alcohol consumption, and weather. This is because powerboating, readily accessible to anyone who can start an ignition and steer, requires extended practice and knowledge to perform responsibly.

In situations where power-driven boats are not enjoyed responsibly, problems and controversies have resulted. For example, rooted vegetation in waterways does not develop in the pathways of outboard engines, disturbances to the nesting areas of waterfowl by boaters results in the birds' significant decline, and wave action by high-speed boats erodes the shoreline.

*See also:* Fishing, Freshwater; Fishing, Saltwater/Deep Sea; Sailing and Yachting; Water Skiing

**BIBLIOGRAPHY**

Armstrong, Bob. *Getting Started in Powerboating.* Ragged Mountain Press, 1995.

Beebe, Robert P., and James F. Leishman, eds. *Voyaging Under Power.* Ragged Mountain Press, 1994.

Lindsey, Sandy, and Molly M. Gross, eds. *Power Boating: A Woman's Guide.* Ragged Mountain Press, 2000.

*Ruth Russell*

# BODY CULTURE AND PHYSICAL CULTURE

Physical fitness movements can be defined as those efforts to maintain bodily health and increase physical strength and stamina. The ideal of the physically fit man or woman has ancient roots, as evidenced by the depictions of muscular heroic figures engaged in warfare or sporting competition in the sculpture of the Mediterranean classical era or of ancient India and Southeast Asia. Epic poetry, sagas, and other chronicles of the origins and history of peoples, such as the Norse *Edda* or Virgil's *Aenead,* carefully described the physical characteristics of their larger-than-life warrior heroes, whose stature and stamina were out of reach of the ordinary mortal.

The men and women of these tales, paintings, and sculpture were not the only human forms depicted as ideal types in the ancient and premodern world. Figures of great religious devotion, such as Christian saints, were often thin and ethereal, suggesting that the spiritual life was the antithesis of the physical. Renditions of the *Buddha,* on the other hand, were usually round in form and placid in expression, perhaps reflecting a closer connection between physicality and spirituality, even as the faith itself stressed transcendence over the physical.

## Warfare, Sport, Competition, and Prowess

Common practices of and beliefs about sport and recreation, military preparedness, domestic animal breeding, and medicine in England in 1600 were the foundation of nineteenth-century Americans' discovery of physical fitness. Americans blended new ideas and folk practices from these seemingly disparate roots to produce an evolving—though often contested—ideal of the healthy body and, by extension, the healthy society.

The nearly constant state of war between the major European powers in the seventeenth and eighteenth centuries—England, Spain, France, the Netherlands, Denmark, Sweden, and Russia—demanded much from their citizens, not only to pay for war but also to provide men for fighting. Thus, in 1617, when King James I of England encountered a small-scale uprising of the Lancashire peasantry over a clerical ban on sporting activities on the Sabbath, he concluded that allowing sport and games was in his military as well as political interest, no matter how potent the church was. As historian Nancy Struna demonstrates in *People of Prowess,* sports and exhibitions of physical skills in the British colonies of North America were hotly contested, both as individual events and as policy issues. James's "Declaration of Sport" (subsequently referred to as the "Book of Sports") gave royal sanction to morning church attendance on the Sabbath, but specifically protected the tradition of sport during the remainder of the day. Hurling, wrestling, football, and blood sports such as bull and bear baiting were long-established diversions that James reckoned necessary for developing effective warriors. These were the proletarian or peasant counterparts to the aristocratic activities more closely associated with battle, such as fencing, archery, jousting (horsemen try to unseat each other), and tilting (horsemen trying to spear a target object while riding at full "tilt").

Horse racing was both an opportunity to gamble and show off one's ability to recognize superior mounts; and a diversion that enriched the gentry's and Crown's military arsenal. The foundation for what in the late nineteenth century would become the eugenics movement was laid in the control and recording of animal breeding practices in horses well before the American Revolution. Scrutiny of human genealogy among the aristocracy in both Europe and the United States was likewise a precursor to eugenics, but not for purposes of breeding for physical prowess or strength.

By the late eighteenth century, horse racing and gambling had gone well beyond the status of friendly competition in the southern colonies of British North America. In villages, towns, and the countryside men and women

**"Digestit."** W.L. Brown offers a stomach relief product named "Digestit" at his store in April 1915. Patent medicines such as this one were a common "cure" in the late nineteenth and early twentieth centuries. *Courtesy of The Library of Congress*

gathered to pursue their passion for the fast horse, provoking some of the same chiding from clerics that had occasioned James's "Book of Sports." Critics of these "horse-shed Christians" lambasted them for their perfunctory church attendance, and for their enthusiasm for what historian Elliot Gorn in *The Manly Art* described as "stomp and gouge" fighting. But, like King James, squires and ordinary farmers valued the military potential of fighting and racing, given the nearly constant frontier skirmishes and outright warfare not only between Europeans and Native Americans, but also between the European powers fighting wars on American soil. Military readiness also assuaged fears engendered by slave insurrection.

The evolution of medical theory also contributed to the genesis of fitness movements. Dissection of cadavers had allowed physicians to gain greater knowledge of the structure of the body, but exploration of the dead did little to reveal the dynamics of the living organism. Thus, while

anatomy was relatively well known among physicians, the interrelationships of the blood, flesh, and bones was speculative, often based on a priori principles of equilibrium modeled after the workings of machines—especially clocks.

Traditional medical theory held that the healthy individual had in balance four "humours"—blood, phlegm, black bile, and yellow bile. Illness and death were a result of tangible or spiritual incursions that caused disruption in the humoural balance. Human intervention might right the difficulty. Bleeding relieved "pressure"; purgation of the digestive system with calomel (mercuric chloride) or some other substance worked on "bile" disaffections; prayer was more appropriate for those dis-eased by spiritual causes. Often a combination of treatments was employed. Some patients even survived.

In the United States, public advocacy of physical fitness and its goals began around 1830. The first number of the monthly magazine *The Journal of Health* appeared in September 1829; Dr. Edward Hitchcock's compendium of observations on the health and fitness of Americans, *Dyspepsy Forestalled and Resisted, or Lectures on Diet, Regimen and Employment,* was published in 1831. Both works traded upon the pervasive enthusiasm for reform and regeneration in the United States in this era, and heralded an impetus and obsession that has abated little since. Published in Philadelphia by four physicians, *The Journal of Health* argued that individual health depended on temperance in diet and drink, rest and moderate exercise, and linked personal fitness to the health of the body politic.

*The American Turf Register,* which also first appeared in September 1829, was for the most part a magazine for the hunter, fisherman, and especially the aficionado of the racetrack. Published in Baltimore, it was filled with records of races and accounts of hunting and fishing, with hints for the most effective methods of tracking and bagging game and luring and catching fish. But the magazine also included articles on the bloodlines of famous horses and (less commonly) hunting dogs, and the best means of keeping them healthy and productive in the field or on the track. Early issues contained large foldout charts of champion horses' lineage, with written descriptions of the benefits and drawbacks of certain unions. Diseases of the animals were discussed at length.

The sporting magazine brought its readers—and reveals to historians—an empirical approach to medicine and fitness that had been in common practice for generations. Years of painstakingly recording equine lineage, racing performance, and careful study of the anatomy and diseases of horses laid the groundwork for empirical approaches to human fitness and health. Religious linkages of ill health to sinful behavior, and the abrupt and wide chasm the human species had established between itself and the rest of the living world, compromised traditional medical practice for humans. Training the scientist and the physician's eye on the beasts and plants, however, was acceptable; such inquiry into the nature of human beings could be—or was—a much more treacherous endeavor.

## Reform of Spirit and Body

By 1830, however, the religious and cultural context of the United States had become receptive to considerations of human health and fitness. It was not that the horsemen and the huntsmen had convinced the rest of the populace to employ their methods of caring for their animals to the health of humans. Instead, the religious pressures against the scientific examination and treatment of human diseases had eased, opening up the practice of medicine and the pursuits of fitness and health to the scientific inquiry for which the sportsmen had created a model.

The alteration was grounded in both the Second Great Awakening and the political climate of the United States. The pursuit of health and fitness was both a scientific revolution and a religious refocusing of the populace. Beginning in the waning years of the eighteenth century, emotionally powerful religious revivals brought tens of thousands of newly "awakened" Protestants to their faith. Some of the newly regenerate believed that the prophecies contained in the New Testament indicated that the Second Coming of Christ was imminent. Others believed that a more gradualist approach, in which human agency was critical in the preparation of the Earth for the return of Christ, was mandated by the Bible. Whatever their differences in interpretation, these newly committed adherents were steadily growing in number in the early nineteenth century, and all believed that sin had to be eradicated. The sins were many—ill treatment of the insane and those unable to see, hear, or speak; drunkenness; an apparent rise in criminal behavior; and, for some, slavery. The solutions devised included "asylums" for the insane, special modes of education and treatment for those with physical limitations, temperance, "penitentiaries" to reform the criminal, and abolitionism or colonization of African Americans.

Physical fitness and health reforms were an integral part of this broad movement. "Perfectionists" sought to eliminate ill health as a necessary precursor to the Second Coming. Some groups formed model societies apart from the "world"; others sought reform through socially connected channels such as medicine, dietary reform, temperance; and physical education and exercise.

Medical theory and practice was multifaceted and often contradictory. "Regular" physicians favored strong, "heroic" intervention, provoking the "crisis" they thought necessary for cures with purgatives, plasters, and bleeding. They were challenged by a coterie of "alternative" physicians whose patient practices grew as licensing restrictions eased throughout most of the United States by the 1830s.

The prick of the lancet and the pain of the purge provided the gentler ministrations of the homeopathic and botanic physicians and the water curists with an environment literally aching for them. Homeopathy's stress on the collection of personal medical history and the infinitesimally dilute solutions of natural materials that produced symptoms similar to the disease to be treated sat well with patients. Botanic physicians' avoidance of bleeding and reliance on plant materials likewise found favor, as did the water curists' use of cold and hot water to relieve ailments.

In the context of religious and secular reform activities, treating disease was less important than avoiding it. By taking steps to prevent disease and debility (defined as a general weakness), one was taking part in the great social and ultimately religious experience that would bring on the millennium. Many of the most important advocates of health reform in this era were in some way connected with the ministry, whether as churchmen or as close relatives of them.

Americans were criticized from the pulpit, the news desk, and the book for their drinking and eating habits. In 1856, Catherine Beecher—the sister of minister Henry Ward Beecher and Harriet Beecher Stowe, and the daughter of minister Lyman Beecher—published *Physiology and Calisthenics for Schools and Families*. She criticized Americans' drinking and eating habits, alcohol consumption, penchant for fatty and greasy foods, tobacco consumption, clothing styles, and lack of exercise. She outlined a series of calisthenic exercises for boys, girls, men, and women, and provided hints on the sorts of clothing women ought to wear.

Other health reformers such as William Alcott, Sylvester Graham, Ellen White, Joel Shew, and R. T. Trall pushed vegetarianism and hydrotherapy as the pathway to health. In their critique of Americans' physical condition, each linked the body and the mind with the condition of the nation as a whole. All worried about a vaguely described and even more ill-defined condition termed "nerves," or "nervousness." In 1830, Edward Hitchcock argued that "nervous maladies [are] already a formidable national evil." Four years later Dr. Charles Caldwell, in *Thoughts on Physical Education*, worried about the "drain on the nervous fountain" that strong drink caused. He argued that the "inordinate sum of insanity, which prevails in the United States, is too plain to be held in doubt . . . a result of the cankered and fierce religious and political passions which are constantly goading the American brain" (p. 93).

The mobile and seemingly wide-open nature of American society provided room for more outré solutions to the problems of ill health and weakness. Early experimentation with direct-current electricity from wet-cell batteries seemed to indicate that the nervous system was in some way electrical. Looking for a panacea to the variety of ailments plaguing Americans or just looking for a quick buck, enterprising individuals figured that they might reinstate some of the "lost" supply of the patient's "nervous energy" or "vital force" by connecting the debilitated to the new source of power. Others reasoned that since electricity could enable electroplating base metals with precious metals, reversing the process of elec-

trolysis would remove the body's metallic "impurities." Fortunately the power source was too weak in most of these "electric baths" to electrocute the unfortunates.

## An "Athletic Revival"

In 1860, the national magazine *Harper's Weekly* noted that there was an "athletic revival" afoot in the United States. Similar movements were present in England, Sweden, Germany, and the Austro-Hungarian Empire. The 1860 boxing match between the American John C. Heenan and the Briton Thomas Sayers, according to historian Elliot Gorn's *The Manly Art*, garnered more attention than any other athletic event in midcentury America and linked boxing—and by extension the boxer's body form—with manliness and fitness.

Soon after the big fight, Bostonian Diocletian Lewis began his campaign to improve the fitness of Americans, in much the same way Beecher had done five years earlier. After two failed magazines on the subject, Lewis, an advocate of women's rights, homeopathy, and temperance, and a calisthenics instructor, published *New Gymnastics for Men, Women, and Children* in 1862. The book was a great success, and Lewis toured the country for years afterward preaching his gospel of exercise, moderation in diet, and opposition to "regular" medicine.

Like many of the advocates of physical fitness in the latter half of the nineteenth century, Lewis was a committed Protestant and a "muscular Christian." Seeking to jettison the image of Christ as weak and effeminate, muscular Christians imbued Christianity with the masculine vigor of elite sportsmen and the working class. Based on the early nineteenth-century "Tom Brown" novels of English author Thomas Hughes, muscular Christianity provided middle-class and wealthy Americans with a socially acceptable linkage between religion, sport, and fitness activities and in turn altered popular conceptions about the ideal body types for men and women.

Late eighteenth-century paintings and engravings of European and American elite males depicted them as refined and at "ease" by means of a gentle S-curve of the body. Women of similar station were usually shown in a similarly relaxed position, with rounded but not overly fleshy bodies. Academic painters seldom painted men and women of ordinary means, and the itinerant artists who painted them were often unable or unwilling to render their subjects in poses that were not angular and stiff. But the physical demands of everyday life on farms and in the trades suggest that the actual body form—and the ideal type—of men and women was somewhat heavyset and muscular. Poorer women cooked with iron pots and skillets that were heavy when empty. When filled and lugged into hearth fires, they were of formidable weight and required muscular backs, legs, shoulders, and arms. Hauling water and fuel to the hearth and the tasks of the kitchen garden gradually built female bodily bulk. Workingmen were much the same size; the demands of field, factory, and workshop were inconsistent with diminutive musculature.

The boxers and the athletes changed the elite ideal, at least for younger people, after the Civil War. While the robber barons might be enormous about the middle (and were lampooned for that in the press), many high school and college athletes on rowing, baseball, and football teams were lean and sinewy. Some coaches went to extremes: Charles Courtney, the rowing coach at Cornell, starved his teams of food and water until he provoked a rebellion in 1904. Contact sports such as football attracted large—but not fat—"bruisers," as did the wrestling and boxing rings. Weight lifters such as George Windship ("the Boston Hercules"), wrestlers such as George Hackenschmidt, and showmen such as Eugene Sandow brought another physical role model to the masses. Sandow's singular muscle definition—in particular his rippling stomach and abdominal muscles—indicated that humans could indeed make themselves look like Greek statuary. In his exhibition in the Ziegfeld Follies he simply struck poses on a cleverly lit stage, often wearing only sandals and a form of loincloth. In popular "cabinet" photographs he sometimes wore only an oak leaf. His understudy and successor in the Follies, Bernarr MacFadden, traded upon health concerns and sensationalism for decades afterward, publishing, among other products, *Physical Culture* and *True Story* magazines.

Photographs of normal people from the turn of the century indicate that the ordinary adolescents and young adults were not much different in musculature than their modern analogs. The most popular model for young adult women was the "New Woman" and the "Gibson Girl" (modeled after the popular illustrations of Charles Dana Gibson). These women were buxom, but lacked the fleshy lower bodies found in romantic paintings of the era, resembling instead the dreamy beauties of Pre-Raphaelite painters such as the Briton Sir Lawrence Alma-Tadema.

## Xenophobia and Neurasthenia

Athletes and slender young adults were alluring ideals in the late nineteenth century. They were the antithesis of what earlier generations had termed the "nervous" American. Some Americans had seen only decline as the price of the largesse of the Industrial Revolution—more goods, more money, and less physical activity for the middle class and the wealthy. When the *Report of the Federal Census of 1880* revealed that white, Anglo-Saxon, and northern European families were having fewer children than they had had in the early nineteenth century, social and medical critics concluded that the "Anglo-Saxon race" was committing "suicide." Debilitated by their white-collar desk jobs and their excessive book work, these "brain workers" were losing ground to the sturdier and more fertile working-class Catholic and Jewish "new immigrants" from southern and eastern Europe. This explanation was perhaps most clearly stated in Madison Grant's xenophobic polemic of 1899, *The Passing of the Great Race.*

More than any other single factor, neurasthenia propelled the fitness activities of the turn of the century and the genesis of the physical education movement. Greasy foods and food preparation brought Americans a life-long case of indigestion. Tuberculosis and other diseases regularly swept thousands to an early grave. But dyspepsia could be easily treated and prevented, if people had the will. By 1900, healthier foods—especially breakfast cereals—were marketed as easy-to-prepare antidotes to the rest of the normal daily diet. Patent medicine hucksters offered their cures. Contagious diseases were frightening, but after the discovery of the connection between microbes, filth, and disease in 1883 (when the germ theory of disease was first revealed to the professional and lay public), it seemed that human agency could conquer these maladies through cleanliness crusades and (eventually) inoculation.

Neurasthenia was different. In his treatise of 1881, *American Nervousness, Its Causes and Consequences, a Supplement to Nervous Exhaustion (Neurasthenia)*, physician George Beard linked the condition to a white-collar economy and society. Adrift from their often-romanticized moorings in a "golden age" of handwork and productive labor, the new middle class and wealthy suffered for their success. (The working class had no such troubles; life in the factory and city was judged no challenge to one's mental well-being.) The price of "civilization" was ennui, lack of energy, and a host of other ill-defined and unquantifiable maladies, some of which were sexual in nature. Impotence, "lack of vital force," apparent low fertility in men and women, and other discomfitures modern analysts might call "stress" seemed to be plaguing Americans.

Sexual functions were a special concern. Men were urged to limit ejaculation to the act of procreation to maintain their "life force" and energy, practicing what the medical community and their cultural counterparts called the "spermatic economy." Masturbation was strictly forbidden, considered both a sin and a threat to physical and mental health. Young women were warned about certain bicycle seats lest they accidentally (and then purposefully) practice the "solitary vice" while taking part in the "bicycle craze" of the turn of the century. Self-control, social control of the working class, control of alcoholic spirits, even control of the elements of the economy that threatened free enterprise provided the foundation for the political movement of the Progressives, temperance advocates, and suffragists in the early twentieth century. Long before Sigmund Freud wrote about sublimation, health and fitness advocates had spotted a useful concept for their cause.

Numerous remedies for neurasthenia were offered. Camping and adventuring in the outdoors as a "tonic" to the desk-drained and parlor-weary became broadly popular, especially after guidebooks such as William H. H. Murray's *Adventures in the Wilderness* was published in 1869. Entrepreneurs built resorts and spas for those in need of vacation. A few spas, such as the Greenbrier in White Sulfur Springs, West Virginia, and the Catskill Mountain House and "Our Home on the Hillside" in New York State had catered to the unwell for decades before "Murray's Rush," but they had a limited clientele. By 1900, private and public "camps" for young, old, tired, ill, and the merely bored opened all over the United States, offering water treatments and an array of dietary and exercise regimens to cleanse, feed, and strengthen visitors for the rigors of white-collar struggle in the Darwinian world of the office. From Hot Springs in the South to cold air in the Minnesota winter, there was a cure for anyone who needed it.

The active sporting man and woman had no need for such cures and treatments. A life of strenuous activity, in the outdoors if possible, was the best preventive. The exemplar of this position was Theodore Roosevelt. On his ranch or in the woods hunting with his dogs and guides, the "Rough Rider" made the case for action. His conquest of childhood asthma and seemingly boundless energy propelled him to fame as a politician, writer, and soldier and to the presidency in 1901. But as Roosevelt was achieving mythic status in the Spanish-American War, nearly one-third of the enlistees were failing their physical examinations for military service. Concern over this and other evidence of physical decline helped physical education gain a stronger foothold in American schools. Teachers colleges expanded their curricula to include training physical educators, and regular classes and sports became integral parts of the grade and high school experience.

Fitness and self-control were a harder "sell" after World War I, in the giddy expansiveness of the postwar economy and the new freedoms enjoyed by the young. Brothers John H. and William K. Kellogg, C. W. Post, and other cereal barons, in business since the late nineteenth century, still found a ready market for their goods, often pitching grains and bran as a way to combat the "sluggishness" and "auto-intoxication" wrought by constipation. Advertising agencies devised clever strategies that traded on the insecurities of white-collar jobs, in which quantifying the successes and capabilities of employees was difficult. Failure to "get ahead" might be due to lack of energy or even worse, qualities about which one's "best friends" would remain silent.

These afflictions seemed irrelevant in the Great Depression and in World War II. Sporting figures such as Joe Louis, "Red" Grange, "Babe" Zaharias, and Bill Tilden kept the athlete and athletic body in the public eye, but after 1941, the armed forces promised fitness would come to all who served. The masculine ideal body form remained the same through the 1930s and 1940s, though the female film stars and pinups of the period regained some of the curves of the Gibson Girl that the 1920s "flappers" had rejected.

## Cold War and Counterculture

The Cold War and the stalemate in Korea helped raise the question of Americans' physical condition and preparedness in the late 1950s. John Kennedy, who conveyed an aura of youthful vigor and athleticism even as he suffered from Addison's disease and a severely damaged back, defeated Richard Nixon in part because the latter seemed less fit and because Kennedy used his physical presence as a backdrop for his charge that the United States had lost "prestige" in the world. The successful launch of *Sputnik* in 1957 made Kennedy's task easier. Soon after his narrow election to the presidency, he established the President's Council on Youth Fitness, headed by the University of Oklahoma's legendary football coach, "Bud" Wilkinson. Decrying the state of American children's health and fitness, the "new frontiersmen" emphasized physical education as well as mathematics and science. The Royal Canadian Air Force exercise manuals became bestsellers in the early 1960s.

Like other bestsellers, the guides eventually declined in popularity. Students went off to college, where some of them turned on their parents' generation and to drugs and new music. Physical education and swimming requirements gradually were abandoned in American colleges and universities while big-time athletic programs serving fewer undergraduates grew larger and professional sports assumed a greater public role in American life. The "counterculture" found fault with their elders for the tacit and overt support of racial discrimination in the United States, and of the war in Vietnam. Some turned their backs on sport and fitness as well, linking these activities with the older generation, conservatism, and the war.

The "counterculture" did not, however, simply drop acid, smoke grass, listen to music their parents hated, and oppose the war. The organic foods movement—now a vibrant and important part of the agricultural economy—has some of its strongest roots in the "sixties" generation. Many of these now middle-aged "baby boomers" have connected with physical fitness activities, whether to try to slow the effects of aging or because it makes them feel better. Their children and (increasingly) their grandchildren are in many cases dedicated to "working out" in ways and in frequency that make the manufacturers of home and institutional fitness machines sing with joy. College and university administrators who once thought a gymnasium, playing fields, and a pool were sufficient now find they must lure the young with "fitness centers" that resemble the spas and resorts of the wealthy more than they do the lockers, showers, and gymnasia of their youth.

In spite of this surge in health-related activities and the mushrooming sales of bottled drinking water, U.S. health and medical agencies point to a growing national health risk—obesity. The United States government's Centers for Disease Control (CDC) notes that since 1985 "there has been a dramatic increase in obesity in the United States. Today, 20 states have obesity prevalence rates of 15-19 percent; 29 states have rates of 20-24 percent; and one state reports a rate over 25 percent." Under the new definition of "overweight" that the Centers for Disease Control introduced in the mid-1990s, five states—Michigan, Indiana, Kentucky, West Virginia, and Mississippi—counted 35-36% of their populations in that category. The rest of the states reported levels of overweight populations of at least 25% (Centers for Disease Control).

Part of the response to this national crisis in public health was the CDC's "Guidelines for School Health Programs to Promote Lifelong Healthy Eating." The initiative identified fat-laden foods in the marketplace, children and adults who are physically inactive, and less emphasis on the ordinary child in a school's physical education program as major causes of this problem. The CDC embarked on an ad campaign promoting healthy lifestyles for young people, and there are nationwide leg-

**John Harvey Kellogg.** Surgeon and nutritional expert Dr. John Harvey Kellogg (1852–1943) is well-known for assisting his brother William K. Kellogg in the creation of corn flakes. He was the director of health sanitariums in Battle Creek, Michigan, and Miami, Florida, that were popular with the rich and famous as health improvement retreats. He wrote nearly fifty books and medical treatises that focussed on his beliefs that good health could be attained through proper diet, exercise, posture, fresh air, and sleep. © *Bettmann/Corbis*

islative efforts to attack the obesity and overweight problems, modeled after the antismoking campaigns of the 1960s. Following successful efforts in Arkansas and Texas, twenty-five states were considering restrictions on the sale of soda and candy in schools by the year 2000.

The U.S. government–recommended food "pyramid" stresses grains, fresh fruits and vegetables, and minimal consumption of animal and hydrogenated fats. Ordinary folk wanting to have the muscular look of film stars and athletes feverishly work out and desperately try alternative diets that promise weight loss. Some take more dangerous routes, consuming drugs to curb their appetite. Anorexia and bulimia have become national plagues for women seeking to have slender fashion models' bodies. Three-hundred-and-fifty-pound linemen are no longer freaks in the National Football League; body builders have shown that they can add seemingly limitless muscle mass to their bodies. The use of anabolic steroids and other "enhancing" drugs is rampant as manufacturers and users race to keep ahead of detecting squads. The Internet is full of offers to lose weight, grow larger breasts, or increase penis size. None of this is particularly new. Similar advertisements and enticements graced the pages of health and fitness magazines throughout the twentieth century, albeit with more subtlety. New, unregulated electronic communications systems reveal both the pervasive nature of the business and the frailties of the vendors' customers.

The bright side of this situation is the growth of knowledge about a healthy lifestyle for those who wish it and the expansion of athletics for women that have occurred in the United States since the passage of Title IX of the National Defense Education Act. In spite of the protests of those who see athletics as a zero-sum game, women's sports will not go away. The message of more exercise and better foods may be spreading, however haltingly, through the American public.

*See also:* Aerobic Exercise, Bodybuilding, Horse Racing, Hunting, "Muscular Christianity" and the YM(W)CA Movements

## BIBLIOGRAPHY

Budd, Michael Anton. *The Sculpture Machine: Physical Culture and Body Politics in the Age of Empire.* New York: New York University Press, 1997.

Caldwell, Charles. *Thought on Physical Education.* Boston: Marsh, Capen & Lyon, 1834.

Centers for Disease Control. "Nutrition and Physical Activity: U.S. Obesity Trends 1985 to 2001." Available from http://www.cdc.gov/.

Ernst, Robert. *Weakness Is a Crime: The Life of Bernarr Macfadden.* Syracuse, N.Y.: Syracuse University Press, 1991.

Gorn, Elliott J. *The Manly Art: Bare-Knuckle Prize Fighting in America.* Ithaca, N.Y.: Cornell University Press, 1986.

Green, Harvey. *Fit for America: Health, Fitness, Sport and American Society, 1830–1940.* New York: Pantheon Books, 1986.

"Guidelines for School Health Programs to Promote Lifelong Healthy Eating." Morbidity and Mortality Weekly Report: Recommendations and Reports (14 June 1996). Available from http://www.cdc.gov/mmwr/.

Haley, Bruce. *The Healthy Body and Victorian Culture.* Cambridge, Mass.: Harvard University Press, 1978.

Leavitt, Judith Walzer, and Ronald Numbers, eds. *Sickness and Health in America: Readings in the History of Medicine and Public Health.* Madison: University of Wisconsin Press, 1985.

Levenstein, Harvey. *Revolution at the Table: The Transformation of the American Diet.* New York: Oxford University Press, 1988.

———. *Paradox of Plenty: A Social History of Eating in America.* New York: Oxford University Press, 1993.

Lindeman, Janet Moore, and Michele Lise Tartar, eds. *A Center of Wonder: The Body in Early America.* Ithaca, N.Y.: Cornell University Press, 2001.

Mrozek, Donald J. *Sport and American Mentality, 1880–1910.* Knoxville: University of Tennessee Press, 1983.

Nissenbaum, Steven. *Sex, Diet and Debility in Jacksonian America: Sylvester Graham and Health Reform.* Westport, Conn.: Greenwood Press, 1980.

Struna, Nancy. *People of Prowess: Sport, Labor and Leisure in Early Anglo-America.* Urbana: University of Illinois Press, 1996.

Whorton, James C. *Crusaders for Fitness.* Princeton, N.J.: Princeton University Press, 1982.

———. *Inner Hygiene: Constipation and the Pursuit of Health in Modern Society.* New York: Oxford University Press, 2000.

*Harvey Green*

# BODYBUILDING

Bodybuilding is an amateur and professional performance sport that is defined by its competitive element as well as its rich complexity as a sporting subculture and social identity. The competitive element of bodybuilding requires that participants display their physiques onstage through a series of mandatory poses and choreographed routines. Status as a bodybuilder includes a competitive past or present and/or the motive to compete at some point in the future. The muscular physiques of both women and men are judged by several criterion: muscular density, symmetrical proportions, and somatic conditioning, including visible striations and definition (subculturally referred to as "being cut"), vascularity (visibility of the veins), thinness of the skin, and skin tone. Posing is the apex for judging bodybuilding. Because of this emphasis on display of the physique, some sports researchers and others have challenged whether bodybuilding is a "real" sport. To the uninitiated spectator, bodybuilding competition "appears" to be missing an essential element of sports competition—physical exertion. But an analysis from an embodied position argues otherwise. Although posing is strenuous and hard work, the competitor's face and physique should never give this away. A bodybuilder must be able to hold the muscular pose without shaking and showing signs of tiredness (achieved by practice).

Bodybuilding competition, while only occupying a small part of the bodybuilders' total training, serves to create seasons of training related to different phases in which the bodybuilder's focus may change from an emphasis on muscular growth to a pre-contest phase in which preparation for competition occurs. The pre-contest phase is typically a period of twelve to sixteen weeks before the date of the competition. During this phase a dietary regimen is followed along with an added or increased component of cardiovascular exercise. The emphasis during this period is on losing body fat while maintaining muscles. Paradoxically, the bodybuilder becomes "smaller" by losing adipose tissue, although they may actually appear larger on the stage. Few sports, other than perhaps gymnastics and wrestling, have such an emphasis on diet. In addition, unlike many other sports, bodybuilders do not usually participate in numerous competitions. It is not unusual at the amateur level to compete in only one or two contests in a year, while professional bodybuilders may compete more often as part of commercial contracts and career opportunities.

## History

### 1860s–1920s: Sandow, MacFadden, Atlas

In its infancy, bodybuilding was built on mid-nineteenth-century movements that included health reform with linkages between athletics and religion with a cult of manliness co-evolving with turn-of-the-century American intersections of exercise and the moral order. Euro-American physical culture was expressed in strength acts in music halls and theaters in Europe and America and associated with a developing industry of resistance-training machines, weights, and exercise/training programs. American bodybuilding claims as its lineage elder Eugene Sandow, who first displayed his beautiful physique at the Chicago Word's Fair in 1893, after training with former strongman Professor Attila in Brussels. Sandow can be credited with promoting women's exercise as well as stimulating the industry of American physical culture through his own entrepreneurship. He promoted the first major bodybuilding show in 1901 in Britain, which was followed in 1903 by the first major American bodybuilding show, sponsored by Bernarr MacFadden.

These two physique competitions were unique because prior to these shows, strength acts, not physiques, were the focus of the exhibitions. Sandow and MacFad-

**Body builders.** Lou Ferrigno (1951– ), shown kneeling, and Arnold Schwarzenegger (1947– ) assume typical bodybuilder poses. The two men were frequent adversaries in competitions including Mr. Universe and Mr. Olympia during the 1970s. © *Corbis*

den were dedicated to displaying men's physical perfection and showcasing the muscular physique. They rode the waves of an emerging American middle class, urbanization, and concern over increasing sedentarism. Their criteria for judging were remarkably contemporary, emphasizing balanced muscular development. MacFadden subsequently made his physique competitions into an annual event. He also gained notoriety for also hosting the first women's bodybuilding contests from 1903 to 1905.

Despite these efforts, the dominant trends for physique competitions through the 1920s and 1930s emphasized displays of strength in tandem with muscular physiques. The most prominent person during this era of bodybuilding was Angelo Siciliano, also known as Charles Atlas, who, after winning McFadden's 1921 contest, founded a successful exercise mail-order business based on an American industrial discourse of the "self-made man." The 1930s marked separation and individuation of bodybuilding from weightlifting.

**1930s–1960s: Bob Hoffman vs. Joe and Ben Weider**
Bodybuilding entered the modern era of sports through the Amateur Athletic Union (AAU), which hosted its first Mr. America bodybuilding contest in 1939. At this time, the AAU was the sole organization in America, and the AAU Mr. America Crown was the apex of bodybuilding titles. Initially, physique contests were staged with weightlifting competitions, but in 1966, the first independent AAU physique contest was held.

Bob Hoffman was an important figure in the development of American bodybuilding through his York Barbell Company, weightlifting/bodybuilding club, and influence on the AAU. He published *Strength and Health* magazine, representing the official voice of the AAU. His athletes dominated bodybuilding and weightlifting through the 1940s and 1950s. For example, John Grimek, associated with York Barbell, was regarded as the King of Bodybuilders during this era.

However, Hoffman's control over bodybuilding was not unchallenged. Joe and Ben Weider launched their efforts to claim hegemony over the sport of bodybuilding in the 1940s. In 1940, they established a successful magazine, *Your Physique,* which evolved into *Muscle Builder* in 1953. In 1947, Joe and Ben Weider established the International Federation of Bodybuilders (IFBB) to unify, coordinate, and control bodybuilding throughout the world. They also began to wrest control of bodybuilding from the AAU, in part by offering their own rival Mr. Universe and Mr. America contests. For nearly two decades Hoffman and the Weiders "vied for control of muscledom" through their respective commercial and organizational efforts (Fair, *Muscletown USA,* p. 5).

The Weiders developed an immensely successful business that grew rapidly as a result of the 1970s health and fitness movement in America. By this time York Barbell's proprietary influence had begun to wane in bodybuilding. According to Joe Roark, IFBB men's historian, the IFBB came of age in 1960s, although it took about ten years for the Weiders really to monopolize the sport. In 1965 the IFBB Mr. Olympia title was created, and by the 1990s, it was firmly established as the penultimate title of men's bodybuilding. By the 1990s, the IFBB had come to dominate the sport of bodybuilding in America and on the international scene, although its hegemony is not absolute and other organizations continue to hold competitions. The AAU eventually dropped the physique competitions from their venue at the end of 1999.

In contrast to the 1940s and 1950s, which continued to be influenced by the concerns of physical culture, the 1960s saw the growth of a new kind of bodybuilder less concerned with the ideals of the physical culture movement. Bodybuilding was influenced by general trends toward the professionalization of sports and by the sociocultural upheavals of that era, which included a youth culture with liberal attitudes toward politics, sexuality, and recreational drug usage. These trends were coupled with the availability of anabolic steroids for enhancing athletic performance. Athletes from the Olympic level to the amateur level rapidly incorporated anabolic steroids, created in the 1930s but developed in the late 1950s for sporting competitions. A new generation of bodybuilders was born of this era.

**1970s–1990s: Gold's Gym and Arnold Schwarzenegger**
The 1960s and 1970s may be regarded as the adolescence of bodybuilding. Gold's Gym of Venice Beach, California, became its mecca. The 1960s and 1970s hardcore "cult" era of bodybuilding had its subcultural ethos captured in George Butler's 1978 docudrama *Pumping Iron,* featuring Mike Katz, Lou Ferrigno, Arnold Schwarzenegger, Franco Columbo, Ed Corney, Ken Waller, and others, as they prepared for and competed in the 1975 Mr. Olympia staged in South Africa. This, too, was the era of Arnold Schwarzenegger, who can still claim cultural cache in the bodybuilding community in the early 2000s. Other than Steve Reeves, Arnold Schwarzenegger was one of the few bodybuilders to parlay his bodybuilding into a Hollywood career, although the division between bodybuilding as sport and spectacle has always been blurred from its inception.

The growth of bodybuilding can be associated with the growth of capitalism in the late twentieth century and the expansion of the fitness industry as baby boomers began to age. Arthur Jones first manufactured his Nautilus equipment in the 1970s. And Gold's Gym morphed into a huge franchise along with World Gym. By the end of the 1980s, elite fitness training facilities and health spas replaced the hardcore gyms of the previous decade. Bodybuilding was transformed by wider trends in American society, including the women's rights movement and Title IX, resulting in the emergence of women's bodybuilding as a sport.

## Women's Bodybuilding

Women's bodybuilding has antecedents in physical culture and strength exhibitions and was included in the entrepreneurial efforts of both Sandow and MacFadden. In fact, from 1903 to 1905, MacFadden hosted physique competitions for women's bodily perfection, until he encountered Anthony Comstock, of the Society for the Suppression of Vice, who had MacFadden arrested for the dissemination of pornography related to pictures of both female and male competitors dressed in form-fitting or scanty clothing, respectively. Women's bodybuilding remained as part of strength feats until the 1970s. Bob Hoffman supported and promoted women's weightlifting as part of York Barbell Company and physical culture. However, it was not until 1975 that the competitive beginnings of women's bodybuilding began to occur. The first Miss (now Ms.) Olympia was held in 1980. Women bodybuilders have moved with the men from the hardcore dungeons of the 1980s into the contemporary arenas of bodybuilding. It was not until the 1980s that women's bodybuilding began to claim its own identity, beyond functioning as a sideshow for men's competitions. However, unlike men's bodybuilding, women's bodybuilding has been plagued by a femininity/muscularity debate. At various points in its history, the IFBB and the National Physique Committee (the NPC: the American national organization for bodybuilding at the national level) have critiqued women bodybuilders for excessive muscularity. While steroid use has undoubtedly inflamed this debate, this discourse existed prior to the reported use of steroids among women bodybuilders in its early days in 1980.

The sport of women's bodybuilding continues to grow despite challenges from fitness and figure competitions whose contestants embody a more conventional and compliant femininity. Numbers of women competitors continue to rise, despite various claims by editors and other voices that women's bodybuilding is dead. The USA show, a competitive show for women seeking professional status is indicative: in 1999, there were thirty-six women; 2000 saw an increase to fifty-three; and in 2004 there were fifty-six. The 2003 Women's National Bodybuilding Championships with its eighty-two women competitors had its largest slate in the twenty-three year history of that contest.

## "Natural" Bodybuilding

In the years following *Pumping Iron*, bodybuilding expanded exponentially. As of the early 2000s the IFBB was the seventh-largest sports organization in the world, with 171 affiliated member nations. The Mr. Olympia has grown from an average of three contestants in its early years from 1965 to 1973 to twenty-plus competitors two decades later, testimony to the increasing professionalization of the sport. In 1994, the Master's Olympia was created as a venue for more mature competitors who didn't want to age out of their sport. From 1965 to 1983, the IFBB averaged about two and a half professional events a year to an increase of ten events a year.

Until the late twentieth century, the IFBB and its national organizations were, for the most part, the only game in town. However, since the latter part of the 1980s a growing number of "natural" organizations have been emerging and hosting their own banned substance tested competitions employing polygraph and/or urine testing and barring not only the use of anabolic steroids, but also over-the-counter products that mimic steroids. The growth of these organizations is a result of increased public awareness of the problems of anabolic steroid use among athletes in general. There are more than twenty natural organizations including the World Natural Bodybuilding Federation, the National Gym Association, and the Organization of Competitive Bodybuilding, and special drug-tested competitions sponsored by the IFBB and the NPC, among others. Currently there is no overarching organization for these numerous sanctioning agents, although this may occur in the future.

*See also:* Body Culture and Physical Culture, "Muscular Christianity" and the YM(W)CA Movements, Olympics, Professionalization of Sport

**BIBLIOGRAPHY**

Bolin, Anne. "Flex Appeal, Food and Fat: Competitive Bodybuilding, Gender and Diet. In *Building Bodies*. Edited by Pamela L. Moore. New Brunswick, N.J.: Rutgers University Press, 1997.

———. "Muscularity and Femininity: Women Bodybuilders and Women's Bodies in Culturo-Historical Context." In *Fitness as Cultural Phenomenon*. Edited by Karin A. Volkwein. New York, NY: Waxmann Munster, 1998.

———. "Beauty or the Beast: The Subversive Soma." In *Athletic Intruders: Ethnographic Research on Women, Culture and Exercise*. Edited by Anne Bolin and Jane Granskog. Albany, N.Y.: State University of New York Press, 2003.

———. "Vandalized Vanity: Feminine Physiques Betrayed and Portrayed." In *Tattoo, Torture, Mutilation, and Adornment: The Denaturalization of the Body in Culture and Text*. Edited by Frances E. Mascia-Lees and Patricia Sharpe. Albany: State University of New York Press, 1992.

Chapman, David. *Sandow the Magnificent: Eugene Sandow and the Beginnings of Bodybuilding*. Urbana: University of Illinois Press, 1994.

Fair, John. "The Iron Game and Capitalist Culture: A Century of American Weightlifting in the Olympics. 1986–1996." *The International Journal of the History of Sport* 15, no. 3 (December 1998): 18–35.

———. "America's Mecca for Muscle Builders." *Pennsylvania Heritage* 25, no 2 (1999): 24–31.

———. *Muscletown USA: Bob Hoffman and the Manly Culture of York Barbell*. University Park: Pennsylvania State University Press, 1999.

Gains, Charles, and George Butler. *Pumping Iron*. New York: Simon and Schuster, 1974.

Klein, Alan. *Little Big Men: Gender Construction and Body-building Subculture.* Albany: State University of New York Press, 1993.

———. "Factoids." *Flex* 18, no. 10 (2000): 252–253.

Todd, Jan. "Bernarr MacFadden: Reformer of Feminine Form." *Iron Game History* 1 (April/May 1991): 3–8.

*Anne Bolin*

# BOOKS AND MANUSCRIPTS

From the earliest colonial days, Americans have enjoyed and valued books and manuscripts as beautiful and significant objects themselves, beyond the pleasures of reading them. Whether inspired by the centrality of books to Western civilization or the intimacy of rare and even unique materials associated with a favorite subject or author, many Americans enjoy gathering, organizing, and displaying personal collections of books and manuscripts.

Colonial book collectors rarely considered their activities recreational; before the advent of institutional libraries, literate Americans who wished or needed to consult printed works had to purchase their own. Until nearly the end of the eighteenth century, this meant buying them from Europe, either directly or through one of the few booksellers centered in Philadelphia or Boston. These early collectors were typically wealthy, educated, professional men—usually lawyers, physicians, or clergymen. While they often made discerning judgments about books' material forms—well-printed pages, carefully edited editions, handsomely bound volumes—these early collectors were more concerned with forming functional libraries than with gathering distinctive collections in the more modern sense. When American publishing and bookselling industries took root in the early nineteenth century, however, making books generally more accessible, "collecting" books emerged as a pleasurable activity distinct from simply owning them.

As Donald C. Dickinson explains in his 1986 *Dictionary of American Book Collectors*, the stature of a collection depends upon its quality and depth more than its sheer quantity of materials. Such qualitative stature depends upon evidence of a discriminating coherence and unity, as well as at least one piece considered rare. Such rarity might result from sheer scarcity, but often it involves other factors as well. While opinions vary about what features bestow such distinction, most collectors to-day value materials whose condition is unblemished by time or wear, ideally as close to its original state as possible; signatures or inscriptions by those associated with its making, such as the author, printer, or illustrator; and inscriptions or other evidence of a noteworthy provenance, or past ownership or associations.

Beyond these general aspects, the nature of the books and manuscripts that Americans have most eagerly sought has changed over time. Throughout the first half of the nineteenth century, most Americans shared the tastes of their European counterparts by building collections that emphasized traditional Western history, literature, and culture, sometimes focusing on works produced by the great printers of Europe's past. While few collectors were fortunate enough to own work from Gutenberg's presses, several acquired prized work by the fabled Venetian printer Aldus Manutius, early English printer William Caxton, the Dutch House of Elziver, and other notable printing establishments. By the end of the Civil War, however, influential collectors' interests shifted to Americana, reflecting emerging national sensibilities. Notably, John Carter Brown and James Lenox built impressive collections of materials pertaining to colonial and early national American history, exploration, geography, and so on.

The 1880s marked the beginning of a great "golden age" of collecting as a burgeoning number of newly wealthy industrialists and businessmen discovered the personal and cultural satisfactions of book collecting. Many of them focused on collecting materials pertaining to current or recent figures or events. This focus helped spur the new (and controversial) practice of extra-illustration, in which a collector embellished an original printed book with myriad associated material, much of it original—portraits, maps, manuscripts. The original book would then be taken apart and rebound to include the supplementary material, creating a unique copy. Excessively zealous instances of this practice are legendary; one leading New York collector, for example, extra-illustrated thirty copies of Izaac Walton's *Compleat Angler*, one of which grew from two volumes to ten when he added over 1,300 illustrations to it.

A more enduring legacy from this exuberant era is the prestigious book-collecting clubs founded in major cities between 1880 and 1900. These clubs offered eminent camaraderie to their members, cultural luster to their communities, and a variety of public programs to promote knowledge and appreciation of the American and Western bibliographic heritage as well as the "arts of the book"—especially beautiful bookbinding and printing. One of the first such clubs remains among the most active, New York's Grolier Club, founded in 1884. Similar clubs soon flourished in Boston (The Club of Odd Volumes), Cleveland (The Rowfant Club), Chicago (The Caxton Club), and Philadelphia (The Philobiblon Society), as well as in other cities on a less ambitious scale. In 1912, the Book Club of California was formed, completing the ranks of the most influential American book clubs still active in 2004. Unlike the others, it allowed women to be members; most of these elite book clubs eventually admitted women by the 1970s.

In the 1920s and early 1930s, collecting interests shifted again as many Americans avidly sought first editions of living authors. Shrewd writers and publishers responded by issuing a profusion of explicit "firsts," editions nearly always limited and sometimes featuring numbered copies, distinctive bindings or papers, and author signatures. In the heady economic climate of the late 1920s, prices for both these new collectors' editions and older collected materials spiraled to dizzying heights on collectors' confidence that such books were lucrative investments as well as desirable objects in their own right. The now-fabled auction of Jerome Kern's collection in 1929 garnered more than $1.7 million—a fabulous figure not surpassed for many years.

The Depression and World War II subdued the mania for book collecting, but since the 1950s a new generation of skilled and dedicated collectors has emerged. They tend to emphasize extensive bibliographic and historical knowledge of their materials, foregrounding the intellectual and scholarly pleasures of developing important, and increasingly eclectic and diverse, cultural collections. While modern collectors, like their predecessors, undoubtedly enjoy both hunting for and owning choice materials, no small part of their satisfaction comes in the personal and civic prowess that a major collection entails. In fact, a strong collection often yields a kind of cultural immortality when it eventually endows a library. Beginning in 1638 with the Reverend John Harvard's bequest of books to the new college that soon bore his name, private book collectors have endowed public institutions with substantial, sometimes nearly priceless, collections of books and manuscripts. As the names of many of the nation's most important research and academic libraries—including Henry E. Huntington, J. Pierpont Morgan, and Henry Clay Folger—testify, book collectors have played an integral role in shaping and preserving the material record of American cultural development.

*See also:* Collecting, Literary Societies and Middle Brow Reading

**BIBLIOGRAPHY**

Basbanes, Nicholas A. *A Gentle Madness: Bibliophiles, Bibliomanes, and the Eternal Passion for Books.* New York: Henry Holt and Company, 1995.

Carter, John. *A B C for Book Collectors.* 7th edition. New Castle, Del.: Oak Knoll Books, 1995.

Dickinson, Donald C. *Dictionary of American Book Collectors.* New York: Greenwood Press, 1986.

*The Grolier Club, 1884–1984: Its Library, Exhibitions, and Publications.* New York: The Grolier Club, 1984.

*Megan L. Benton*

# BOTANICAL GARDENS

There are many botanical gardens in the United States, most of which were created to provide both a natural environment for people to enjoy and a laboratory for scholars to study plant diversity. They generally contain various botanical species along with libraries, herbaria, museums, and research and educational facilities. Traditionally distinguished by their use of some kind of classification system, botanical gardens use the science of taxonomy to arrange and compare the plants and herbarium material collected by them. This practice has enabled botanical gardens to serve as acclimatization stations through which plants native to one part of the world can be established and introduced to the public in other parts of the world. Recent developments such as the emphasis on horticulture and the inclusion of greenhouses and conservatories have broadened the scientific and recreational appeal of botanical gardens across the nation.

## Origins and Development

Although there are records of a botanical garden in Cambridge, Massachusetts, as early as 1672, the Missouri Botanical Garden, founded in 1859, was the first in the United States to follow the European model that developed in the seventeenth and eighteenth centuries. The founding occurred at exactly the time that the parks movement was beginning in the United States; botanical gardens were soon established in New York and Philadelphia in 1891, and in Brooklyn in 1910, in concert with the parks designed by men such as Frederick Law Olmstead and Calvert Vaux. Most of these new American botanical gardens combined scientific endeavors with a more civic purpose that encouraged the use and enjoyment of the gardens by the public. They also tended to

**New York Botanical Garden.** Located in the Bronx in New York City is the New York Botanical Garden, founded in 1891 by botanist Nathaniel Lord Britton (1857–1934). Covering some 250 acres, this national landmark boasts waterfalls, rocks, hills, and rivers along with trees and flowers. © *Lee Snider/Corbis*

have a horticultural rather than purely scientific emphasis that involved the collection and maintenance of various plants and the exchange of seeds with other botanical gardens around the world, using the global Index Seminum system. During the twentieth century, several private botanical gardens were created that did not fit into the mainstream international tradition. Such gardens often do not participate in seed exchange or other global networks, preferring to focus on educational and recreational programs with strong support from their local community.

## Major Botanical Gardens

**Missouri** The Missouri Botanical Garden in St. Louis has led the scientific study of plants in the United States since it was established in 1859. It was founded by Henry Shaw, a wealthy Englishman who settled in St. Louis in 1819 and subsequently decided to turn the garden he was building at his country home, Tower Grove, into a scientific one that would be bequeathed to the people of Missouri. Shaw received assistance in the development of

the garden from two well-qualified friends: Sir Joseph Hooker, who was the director of the world-renowned Royal Botanic Gardens at Kew in England, and Shaw's physician, Dr. George Engelmann, who was also a trained botanist. In 2004 Shaw's garden consisted of an urban garden of approximately seventy acres (thirty hectares), as well as an arboretum of about 1,500 acres (607 hectares) outside the city with various tree and shrub species, and a tropical station in Panama. Key figures who worked on the garden include directors Dr. William Trelease and Dr. George Moore, as well as landscape architect Frederick Law Olmsted, who was also responsible for the architecture of New York's Central Park and the Arnold Arboretum at Harvard. The garden's scientific reputation is based largely on its herbarium, which houses 2.5 million specimens, and its extensive library containing 80,000 volumes. Its most famous feature, built in 1960 by Director Fritz Went, is the Climatron, one of the garden's six public greenhouses. The world's first conservatory built on the Buckminster Fuller geodesic principle, the Climatron is a suspended dome that is 175 feet (53 meters) in diameter and 80 feet (24 meters) high, with a skeleton of aluminium, Plexiglas glazing, and no internal supports. This design enables the creation of several different climates within the dome through the mechanical control of hot and cold air and humidity. The Climatron was planted with a variety of tropical species from both arid and rain-forest habitats, making it a unique and appealing tropical jungle. More recently, a large Japanese garden has been added to the diverse styles that draw both experts and novices to the Missouri Botanical Gardens.

**New York** Established in 1891, the New York Botanical Garden followed the scientific example of its Missouri predecessor, with its current influence often compared to the Royal Botanic Gardens at Kew. The Torrey Botanical Club, a group of wealthy men and women who shared an interest in plants, conducted an energetic public campaign that convinced the city's Department of Parks to set aside 250 acres in Bronx Park for a New York Botanical Garden alongside additional land that had been earmarked for the Bronx Zoo. While the city agreed to provide up to $500,000 for the necessary developments, it stipulated that the garden's backers must provide an additional $250,000 in private funds to demonstrate their commitment to the public the garden was intended to serve. The corporation that was set up to raise such a significant amount of money enlisted the support of some of the nation's most influential and wealthy citizens, including Cornelius Vanderbilt II, Andrew Carnegie, J. Pierpont Morgan, and John D. Rockefeller. Their involvement began a tradition of active service at the gardens from civic leaders that continues today.

The original site of the New York Botanical Garden incorporated a dramatically varied landscape that included rolling fields, water features, rock outcroppings, and native trees. These natural features were gradually enhanced with an extensive network of roads and paths as well as various outdoor growing areas, a conservatory, and a museum, making it a botanical garden that served both scientific and recreational purposes. Its features now include a herbarium of over 4 million specimens, a library of 170,000 volumes, research laboratories, publishing facilities, and a greenhouse complex called the Great Conservatory that was restored in 1997. It is considered a world leader in the fields of horticulture, science, and education, and continues its original purpose of combining the scientific endeavors of botany with the provision of an appealing natural space for the citizens of New York City.

**Other** The Missouri and New York Botanical Gardens are among the oldest and most internationally acclaimed of the more than 100 botanical gardens listed in the United

States. Several other botanical gardens that specialize in particular areas also deserve mention. The Arnold Arboretum of Harvard University, landscaped between 1872 and 1898 on 250 acres (101 hectares) of land just outside of Boston, concentrates on trees and shrubs with a current collection of approximately 6,200 arborescent species. The smaller Brooklyn Botanical Garden (1910) and the Strybing Arboretum in San Francisco (1937) emphasize the educational purpose of their diverse collections. The Huntington Garden in San Marino, Los Angeles (1907), is famous for its unusual combination of ornamental and desert gardens, while Miami's Fairchild Tropical Garden (1935) is an important collection of tropical species. Finally, the U.S. National Arboretum, established on 415 acres (168 hectares) of land in Washington, D.C., in 1927, has an extensive collection with particular emphasis on cultivated material. These represent a small selection of the botanical gardens that have flourished in the United States throughout the twentieth century.

## Attractions

While purists insist that botanical gardens should serve only scientific purposes, most of the botanical gardens in the United States have a decidedly community-oriented focus that distinguishes them from the mainstream international tradition. They each combine various degrees of scientific endeavor with a strong educational and public purpose. Since the early 2000s, it has become increasingly apparent that promoting recreational activities within botanical gardens is essential to attract the public and subsequent public funding. Various forms of passive recreation have been incorporated into the botanical garden setting, including botanical art exhibitions, tearooms or restaurants, gift shops, and musical performances. Their museums and libraries also provide a source of interest, along with the many educational programs that increasingly tend to emphasize conservation and the environmental issues facing the United States. These recreational activities are designed to complement the scientific projects engaged in at the gardens and the overriding appeal of a communal property that provides a source of natural beauty and inspiration to the people.

*See also:* Central Park, City Parks, National Parks, Parks Movement, State Parks, Zoos

### BIBLIOGRAPHY

Bramwell, D., O. Hamann, V. Heywood, and H. Synge, eds. *Botanic Gardens and the World Conservation Strategy.* London: Academic Press, 1987.

Houk, Walter. *Botanical Gardens at the Huntington.* New York: Abrams, 1996.

Hyams, Edward, and William MacQuitty. *Great Botanical Gardens of the World.* London: Bloomsbury Books, 1985.

Solit, Karen. *The History of the United States Botanic Garden, 1816–1991.* Washington, D.C.: Congressional Sales Office, 1993.

Sonderstrom, Mary. *Re-creating Eden: A Natural History of Botanical Gardens.* Montreal: Vehicule Press, 2001.

Tanner, Ogden, and Adele Auchincloss. *The New York Botanical Garden: An Illustrated Chronicle of Plants and People.* New York: Walker and Company, 1991.

*Glenn Moore and Jessica Freame*

# BOW HUNTING

**See** *Archery; Hunting*

# BOWLING

Knocking down objects by rolling a ball is an activity that has attracted players in many countries all over the world throughout the years. The tombs of the ancient Egyptians contained equipment for a bowling-type game, demonstrating that its popularity dates back at least 7,000 years. There are also records of a centuries-old bowling game in the Polynesian Islands.

The modern sport of bowling, as it is known in the United States, probably evolved from a third-century A.D. religious ceremony in Germany. At that time, all peasants carried a "Kegel," a club used for protection. Many churches challenged their parishioners to test their faith by rolling a stone at their Kegel in an attempt to knock it down. If they hit the target, they were considered chaste and free from sin.

Over time, the game became secularized and moved away from the churches. By the thirteenth century, balls replaced the stones, and multiple pins replaced the single Kegel. These modifications to "kegel" may have been influenced by a northern Italian game called "bowls." The new game called "ninepins" spread to the Netherlands and England in the 1300s. As the sport's popularity grew, people started placing bets on the outcomes of matches. In fact, Berlin and Cologne established a maximum limit on bets in 1325. It became so popular by the Middle Ages that indoor bowling centers called Kegelbahns in Germany were often built adjacent to local gathering places like inns and taverns.

As bowling spread to other European cities, laws and edicts were enacted to control participation in the activities surrounding bowling. While most of the laws were enacted to control gambling, there were exceptions. One of England's kings banned the activity because it distracted the troops from their archery training. Around 1555, bowling centers, as well as inns and taverns, were sometimes used as meeting places for revolutionaries. Because of their role related to the civil unrest and rebellion in Western Europe, they were considered places of "unlawful assembly" and were sometimes shut down.

The "problems" associated with bowling extended across the Atlantic Ocean to North America as European settlers moved to the New World. In 1611, in the Jamestown, Virginia, colony, it was reported that, even though food was scarce and people were starving, the colonists were enjoying bowling. A law was quickly passed that condemned anyone caught bowling to three weeks in the stockade.

The form of bowling that is believed to be the forerunner of modern ten-pin bowling was the Dutch game of nine-pins. In the early 1600s, Dutch colonists set up nine pins in a diamond shape, 1-2-3-2-1, at the end of an alley. This alley was a plank, ninety feet (twenty-seven meters) long and about eighteen inches (forty-six centimeters) wide. In the mid-1800s, nine-pin bowling was banned in Connecticut because of the gambling that accompanied its practice. It has been speculated that ten-pin bowling was invented to "get around the law." In addition to the extra pin, the shape of the pins changed from tall and slender to the heavier, bottle-shaped pins used today.

By 1850, the number of bowling alleys in New York City had grown to more than 400. After that time, bowling's popularity decreased for a few years. Blame for the decrease in popularity was attributed to the prevalence of gambling and the new, larger pins that made bowling too easy.

In order to create profits, early bowling alleys in the 1880s and 1890s, primarily in New York City, organized bowling leagues that took place after many "blue-collar" employees got out of work. Many of these league teams were comprised of coworkers who were sponsored by their employers. This pattern of league participation was assisted by long-term stable employment and fixed work schedules. At the same time German immigrants moving to midwestern cities like Chicago, Cincinnati, Detroit, St. Louis, and Milwaukee were also establishing leagues and clubs.

**Floretta D. McCutcheon.** The first woman to gain national attention as a bowler (shown here in 1932), Floretta D. McCutcheon (1889–1967) competed in tournaments and provided many exhibitions in addition to running bowling schools. © *Corbis-Bettman*

## Bowling Organizations

The National Bowling Association (NBA) was established in 1875. While it standardized the rules of bowling, it failed in its attempt to eliminate gambling among its members and folded several years later. In 1895, the American Bowling Congress (ABC) was founded. Under this organization's leadership bowling became popular and respectable. As prize money, supplied by member leagues and the ABC, began to be awarded at local, regional, and national levels for outstanding scores, gambling became less prevalent.

In the early 1900s, women began bowling in large numbers. The Women's National Bowling Association (WNBA) held its first national championship in 1917, only a year after it was founded. In 1971, it changed its name to the Women's International Bowling Congress (WIBC).

During the 1960s and 1970s, bowling's popularity soared partially because large bowling events like the Professional Bowling Association (PBA) Tour were televised. In the early 2000s, major bowling membership organizations included the ABC and WIBC, as well as the Young American Bowling Alliance (YABA) and USA Bowling. Representatives from the four organizations met 1–2 November 2003 to discuss the details of a merger. The representatives came to a consensus on the plan. Two of the organizations (ABC and WIBC) voted to approve the revised plan. The other two organizations (YABA and USA Bowling) were to vote on the merger by May 2004.

## Technology

Technological advances in the 1950s provided for physical and demographic changes in the sport of bowling. The invention of the automatic pin-setting machine allowed for quicker reset time between bowls, which appealed to larger numbers of participants. Shoe manufacturers like Capezio introduced lines of bowling shoes, and television and print marketing campaigns depicted "society ladies" bowling. The public relations campaigns helped make bowling popular to a wide variety of socioeconomic classes.

The invention of computers also helped revolutionize the way people bowled. Previously, people tallied and added their scores by hand. With computers, the scores are automatically entered and calculated, so people who do not know the rules for scoring can still play without advance preparation.

## Trends

In 1976, over 25 percent of the U.S. population participated in bowling; over the next fifteen years that participation rate dropped to 14.5 percent because of the larger number of activities that competed for people's time and entertainment budgets. League play was too demanding for most people's schedules. During the five years from 1991 to 1996, there was a resurgence in popularity, with participation rates moving back toward 20 percent. This resurgence may have been due to increases in bowling technology (computer-generated scores), availability of bowling centers for special events (birthday parties, corporate celebrations), and marketing to young people (gutter blockers for young children, glow in the dark bowling and laser light shows). It is interesting to note, however, that the number of "regular bowlers" dropped from 31 to 21 percent, while the number of "occasional bowlers" increased from 56 to 69 percent (Kelly and Warnick; Simmons). This shift reflects the impact of more irregular weekly schedules and a decline in the number of leagues. Bowling centers have tried to improve league participation numbers by shortening league play (sixteen weeks) or making the games every other week instead of every week. They also have changed the times to earlier in the evening so that people can get home sooner.

By the early 2000s, fewer and fewer people worked a "typical" eight-hour workday. This change in work schedules along with other societal shifts changed the patterns of participation in modern-day bowling. The activity that once consisted primarily of weekly league competitions shifted to small groups of occasional drop-in bowlers, "couple bowling," and special events. One impact of this shift is the increased emphasis on bowling as a social activity rather than as a sport.

*See also:* Professionalization of Sport

**BIBLIOGRAPHY**

Burgin, Sandy. "Bowling, Once a Mainstay, Competes More for Its Players. But the Numbers Are Still Strong." 24 May 2000. Available from http://www.active.com/.

"History—Bowling." Available from http://www.hickoksports.com.

Kelly, John R., and Rodney B. Warnick. *Recreation Trends and Markets: The 21st Century.* Champaign, Ill.: Sagamore Publishing, 1999.

Mood, Dale P., Frank F. Musker, and Judith E. Rink. *Sports and Recreational Activities.* 13th edition. Boston, Mass.: McGraw Hill, 2003.

"News from the Fast Lane." Available from http://www.bowl.com.

Simmons Market Research Bureau. "Study of Media and Markets." New York, 1995.

*Tammie L. Stenger and Sarah E. Hardin*

# BOXING

Fighting of one sort of another appears so "natural" a part of the history of the United States that it would be hard to quarrel with eminent boxing writer A. J. Leibling, who once observed that "the Sweet Science [of boxing] is joined onto the past like a man's arm to his shoulder" (Rotella, p. 597). While it is generally perceived as one of the more "traditional" and taken-for-granted of masculine pursuits, boxing, like other sports, did not assume its generally recognizable form until well after the first settlers washed ashore during the colonial era. Nor, despite its popularity throughout the twentieth century, is there any guarantee that it will continue to thrive in the twenty-first.

Boxing in the current century has changed so much that some people may have trouble recognizing the sport. For instance, it may be difficult for some of those people to imagine a time when African Americans did not command a strong presence at the top of the boxing world (while serving as icons of the country's societal troubles or national ascendance, no less). Others may find it equally curious that boxing clubs were once a visible part of the urban landscape, or that radio and television (of the pre-cable variety) regularly featured boxing matches as part of their broadcasts. For still others, it may be hard to conceive of a time when women did not participate in aerobic boxing or take part in sanctioned amateur or professional bouts. All of these statements speak to the historicity of boxing as well as to the ideas, issues, and relationships it speaks both to and for.

Though occasional boxing matches did occur in the eighteenth century, such fistic engagements were rare. Even the championship bout between Briton Thomas Cribb and the free black American Tom Molineaux, held in England in 1810, drew little attention from the American press. More common forms of fighting at this time included cockfights and honorific gouging matches in the southern backcountry. The difference between gouging and boxing hinged on the inclusion of referees, and seconds to monitor the action in the ring. Ring codes adopted at this time attempted to define and refine the etiquette of fighters and spectators alike, ranging from prohibitions on eye gouging, hair pulling, head-butting, making offensive remarks, and hitting below the belt, to guidelines for creating the ring itself. But while bare-knuckle prizefighting by the 1840s was beginning to emerge out of the everyday textures and enmities of male working- and lower-class urban culture, historians Elliott Gorn and Steven Riess suggest that it remained a local, sporadic affair most evident in cities with larger ethnic communities such as New York, Philadelphia, Boston, Baltimore, and New Orleans. Although patterns were developing, the lines demarcating everyday grievances from battles fought in the ring, or from the combatants and their audiences, remained permeable.

The intensification of certain trends in the 1850s—the growth of cities and immigrant populations, expanding consumer markets and leisure time, and developments in transportation and communications, especially—allowed for matches to be arranged through newspapers and information about these bouts to circulate in advance, thus creating a more regular menu of bouts and a paying audience to witness these burgeoning spectacles. John Morrisey's victory over Yankee Sullivan for the American championship in 1853, for instance, elevated Morrissey to the status of Irish folk hero and reflected many of these transformations. The Civil War, which gathered men of a similar class standing and shared male culture from across the country, widened the spread of boxing and deepened the bonds of toughness through a regimen of sparring and regulated matches that contained the internal conflicts that flared up in the midst of real combat.

Yet while these more structured exhibitions helped to channel the tensions of wartime and seemed to put the sport on firmer footing, prizefighting remained illegal in many states well into the early twentieth century. Bouts were frequently held in saloons or dance halls in order to avoid police interference. Though contests of particular interest were often announced in the *National Police Gazette,* by this time the most important source for sports information, news of upcoming bouts usually spread by word of mouth so that participants and spectators alike gathered hastily at a designated location.

By the late nineteenth century, however, a confluence of forces altered the course of pugilism and elevated both the sport and its practitioners to a prominence that would last for nearly half a century. The social, economic, and technological forces that gave rise to factory produc-

tion, transformed the nature of work and working-class life, provided opportunities for immigrants, and reshaped relations of class, gender, and race crested at the turn of the twentieth century. Specifically, more efficient and streamlined methods of production reconfigured the meaning of work, increased leisure time, and recast notions of masculinity for men of both the managerial and laboring classes. For those who worked primarily with their minds (the new managerial class) or their hands (who were losing control over the work process), new outlets and mediums had to be found for exercising, asserting, or imagining a new relationship to one's body; one's masculinity.

Alongside, then, the newer amusements appearing near the century's end—whether dance halls, movies, fairs, or attractions such as Coney Island—boxing assumed a starring role in the commercial entertainments that would dominate the urban-industrial landscape. The Marquis de Queensbury rules adopted in 1892 mirrored many of the rationalizing tendencies and rhythms of the industrial age. The new codes dictated an end to bare-knuckle fighting, as combatants would now wear thinly padded gloves in the ring; created rounds of three minutes with intervals of rest lasting one minute; dispensed with holding or wrestling moves; created a new knockdown rule of ten seconds; continued the tradition of fighting to the finish by refusing to set a limit on the number of rounds in a match. These rules also smoothed some of the sport's rougher edges, thus making it somewhat palatable and comprehensible to a broader, more "respectable" audience.

Perhaps more than anyone, the mighty John L. Sullivan ushered in the age of boxing celebrity. His career bridged the end of the bare-knuckle era and the beginnings of the Marquis de Queensbury generation. His magnetic physique, Irish American working-class background, and forceful ring prowess translated into a persona that appealed to people within and beyond the working class. The increasing circulation of newspapers, in addition to new promotional techniques within the sport of boxing, nourished and cultivated this appeal with a broader audience. Sullivan's loss at the hands of a more slender, technically proficient James Corbett in 1892 marked, for many, the beginning of the "modern" generation—in boxing and U.S. history. In their differing styles and roles as "fighter" and "boxer," Sullivan and Corbett also embodied a contrast that would continue to mark the most riveting championships of the twentieth century.

Fighting styles were not the only differences that made for a compelling match: race had become a factor as well. While Steven Riess has noted that five African

**Ali vs. Liston.** Muhammad Ali (1942– ) defeats Sonny Liston for a second time in a rematch in Lewiston, Maine, on 25 May 1965 that lasted a mere 105 seconds. Ali taunts Liston to "get up and fight, sucker!" © *Corbis*

Americans held championships between 1890 and 1908, none of these men were as famous or infamous as Jack Johnson, the first black man to win the heavyweight title. Johnson's proficiency within the ring and his seemingly brash, confident demeanor outside it offended the sensibilities of many who were particularly troubled by his relationships with white women. Johnson's championship match with Jim Jeffries in 1910 drew intense media scrutiny both before and after his victory, which touched off racial skirmishes in as many as fifty cities. Johnson's reign—which lasted until 1915—also initiated a pattern whereby African American heavyweights throughout the twentieth century—including Joe Louis, Muhammad Ali, Sonny Liston, and Mike Tyson—would alternately serve as princes of the nation's loftiest ideals or emblems of its most worrisome disorders.

In a broader sense, Johnson's title run intersected with and was embedded within a host of social transformations that would dramatically reshape the significance of boxing generally and of individual fighters specifically. The exploits and personalities of heavyweight champions during the first half of the twentieth century were pack-

aged and marketed in such a way as to make them celebrities on the order of movie stars. Indeed, boxing and film grew up together, as clips from boxing matches were some of the first and most popular moving images displayed on screen. Both were part of the same constellation of forces—an emerging visual (film), sonic (radio), and more standardized print culture—that reshaped the production and consumption of images.

It is because of these changes, in part, that Jack Dempsey's title run (1919–1926) drew some of the largest crowds to ever witness live sporting events, including the estimated 150,000 who packed Soldier Field in Chicago to "see" Dempsey fight Gene Tunney in 1927—a fight that was also heard by millions on radio. The sophisticated use and circulation of such images helped to raise Joe Louis's fighting prowess and personal qualities into the embodiment of national virtue during the 1930s and World War II era. In addition to these iconic figures, local boxing clubs flourished during the industrial era and provided an alternative form of labor, recreation, or bodywork for many young men, whether Irish, Jewish, Italian, or African American.

By the end of Louis's career in the late 1940s, television was already beginning to supplant radio as the primary medium for gaining access to national and local fights. While televised fights proved immensely popular initially, they eventually led to the diminished attendance at, and demise of, local boxing clubs.

Television also became intertwined with growing evidence of, and concerns about, the role of organized crime in fixing the outcomes of particular matches. While such activity had always existed, sustained efforts to regulate the sport were launched in the post–World War II era in an effort to curtail such practices. Well-known fighters such as Rocky Graziano, Sugar Ray Robinson, Jake LaMotta, and others, were asked to provide information about racketeering and the Kefauver Commission held hearings in 1960 to investigate these and related problems. Though several bills were proposed in response to the findings of this commission, no legislative action was taken until an amendment to Title XVIII of the U.S. Code was adopted in 1964 during President Lyndon Johnson's administration.

The timing of that amendment coincided with Cassius Clay's/Muhammad Ali's ascendance during one of the most tumultuous periods in U.S. history. If there is any one thread that can be woven through Ali's remarkable twenty-year career, it is Gerald Early's insistence that "like all great heroes," Ali embodied the "incendiary poetics of actual self-determination" (Early, p. 14). Able to glide among and between various constituencies without being captured by any of them, Ali remained true to his religious principles in refusing to serve in Vietnam, losing three and a half years of a luminous career and remaking himself upon his return. In reclaiming the championship he lost, Ali also absorbed a great deal of punishment and later developed Parkinson's disease, rekindling concerns about the brutal effects of such a nakedly violent sport.

As contrasted with more recent developments in the heavyweight division—which has always buoyed the sport generally—Ali was pushed throughout his career by other African American heavyweights, including Joe Frazier and George Foreman. Though many expected the young and ferocious Mike Tyson to continue this tradition when he won the title at the age of twenty in 1986, his career was derailed by violent episodes outside and within the ring, incidents that effectively rewrote the narrative of greatness predicted of him.

While the heavyweight division was nearly dormant by 2004 and waiting for the "next" great heavyweight to appear—if he will appear—good boxers could still be found in the lighter-weight divisions, where a host of Latino and African American fighters, among others, kept interest in the professional side of the sport afloat. Those who make it to the top can expect paydays in the millions, their fights viewed on cable television channels such as HBO.

Equally interesting—if not more compelling, in fact—is a quieter, more recent development among women who are taking up the sport at the amateur and professional levels in the postindustrial era, honing their craft in boxing clubs nestled imperceptibly in the urban landscape. Well-known fighters such as Christy Martin and Laila "She-Bee Stingin'" Ali represent only the most visible side of this general movement. They, and other men and women who practice the sport as a way of reclaiming the body and physical labor in a society radically different from the one that nurtured boxing early in the twentieth century, may be reshaping the manly art while still drawing on its finer traditions of craft, skill, and bodywork. As Carlo Rotella has observed, reflecting on the masculine heritage of boxing, "The sweet science, still joined to the past like a man's arm to his shoulder, can only sustain itself if it remains joined to its traditions and accumulated lore. But boxing may also find itself joined to the present, and the future, like a woman's arm to her shoulder" (Rotella, p. 598).

*See also:* Blood Sports, Colonial-Era Leisure and Recreation, Crowds and Leisure, Gambling, Men's Leisure Lifestyles

**BIBLIOGRAPHY**

Early, Gerald, ed. *The Muhammad Ali Reader.* New York: Ecco Press, 1998.

Gorn, Elliott. *The Manly Art: Bare-Knuckle Prizefighting in America.* Ithaca, N.Y.: Cornell University Press, 1986.

———, ed. *Muhammad Ali: The People's Champion.* Urbana: University of Illinois Press, 1995.

Mead, Chris. *Champion Joe Louis: Black Hero in White America.* New York: Charles Scribner's Sons, 1985.

O' Connor, Daniel, ed. *Iron Mike: A Mike Tyson Reader.* New York: Thunder's Mouth Press, 2002.

Riess, Steven. *City Games: The Evolution of American Urban Society and the Rise of Sports.* Urbana: University of Illinois Press, 1989.

Roberts, Randy. *Jack Dempsey: The Manassa Mauler.* Baton Rouge: Louisiana State University Press, 1983.

———. *Papa Jack: Jack Johnson and the Era of White Hopes.* New York: Free Press, 1983.

Rotella, Carlo. "Good with Her Hands: Women, Boxing, and Work." *Critical Inquiry* 25, no. 3 (Spring 1999): 566–598.

Sammons, Jeffrey. *Beyond the Ring: The Role of Boxing in American Society.* Urbana: University of Illinois Press, 1988.

*Jill Dupont*

# BOY SCOUTS

**See** *Scouting Movement*

# BRIDGE

**See** *Card Games*

# BROTHELS

A brothel, or bordello, is a management tool used to coordinate the presentation of sexually associated and closely related commercial goods and services between consumer and provider. Although a brothel's nature will reflect its particular environment, it will always involve provider and consumer in a traditional "exchange of value for value" relationship.

The perceived appropriateness, or inappropriateness, of a brothel varies with class, religious belief, point in the life course, political setting, economic circumstances, racial dynamic, and related features. Nonetheless, the essential mechanics of bordellos or brothels—houses of ill repute—remain the same across time and over geographic space, even while the perception of the bordello's social place and function varies greatly.

## Western Emergence

In the Greco-Roman world, viewed by many as the roots of Western civilization, the vision of appropriate sexuality among the elite (the only class for which records exist) was based on a triad: wife, concubine, and courtesan. But by the Great Age of Exploration, roughly in the time frame of the Italian renaissance, Western values, now colored both by commercial vigor and nascent capitalism and by a Paulist, repressive view of human sexuality, were generally exported and widely distributed. Paulist doctrine included teaching that sexual passion was by its nature damning (only slightly ameliorated by holy matrimony), and that capitalism was a mechanism for the accumulation of wealth. Passion could safely be focused into the accumulation of wealth without censure, especially if one was a patron of the Church. Great feats of commerce and great acts of art were accomplished.

Brothels are always similar: once the basic model of provision of human sexuality via exchange of value was

**Mustang Ranch.** Nevada's first legal brothel closed its doors in August 1999 after the owners were convicted of tax fraud. Brian Maine takes some items out of the 104-room bordello that was established in 1955 by Joe Conforte. © *David Hunter for Associated Press (AP)*

developed centuries ago, local area provision is mere variation. There are a number of ways to describe bordello environments. For example, the United States may be said to have three styles: the fully "Europeanized" houses that eventually grew on each coast as cities developed and all urban infrastructure matured; the "boomtown" echelon of commercial sex worker setting, which was a typically rapid response to a spike in local area wealth; and the "provincial" or "frontier" brothels that existed as an immediate answer to demographic dynamics.

## Commercial Sexuality: Commodification of Adult Leisure

Various social or religious belief systems attempt to explain, and by extension, control, human behavior. Thus some interpret human sexuality as a dangerous power. From this perspective, simple participation, including mere watching, as in the case of pornographic renderings, has a debilitating moral effect on men and women. Because of this belief, leaders have often sought to control or regulate sexual participation, especially commercialization of human sexuality. In the early 2000s, most North

## Bordellos and Sex Slavery

Claiming that technology and globalization have created new opportunities for organized crime, the United Nations, and other activist organizations, have responded to continued claims of sex slavery by consistently renouncing it as fait acompli. The UN has over time signed several treaties intended to fight this real or imagined vast activity in international sex slavery. The claims, notoriously difficult to corroborate and within a setting weak on critical distance, involve estimations of trafficking in human beings for sexual purposes near those of trafficking in human beings for other cheap or forced labor. Criminal gangs are alleged to organize and participate in this sexual slavery, said to be second only to running drugs in profitability, moving many thousands of human beings about the globe for the purpose. "Women and children destined for (usually unpaid) work in brothels constitute the second main category of human cargo," one report said. Social services are often overwhelmed. And little infrastructure and funding exist to intervene in the trafficking of human beings if such practice exists in large scale.

However, the uncontested figures are often generated solely by self-proclaimed and unregulated "human rights" activists who may claim, for example, that "some 75,000 women from Brazil, a leading exporter of sex slaves, work in European brothels against their will." Indeed, a UN conference in Thailand in March 2000 estimated that thousands of children were forced to work in Asia's flourishing sex industry, although no mechanism exists to carry out such a survey. Nonetheless, seventy-two nations signed a second protocol against trafficking in persons for the sex trade, while sixty-nine countries have signed a treaty against the smuggling of migrants, taking a very reasonable "better safe than sorry" approach. Because activists have virtually usurped the role of disinterested investigators entirely, it is impossible to determine any of the dimensions or magnitudes of the real or imagined social problem of international trafficking in sex slaves.

Jo Doezema, Institute of Development Studies, University of Sussex, Brighton, UK at the International Studies Convention in Washington, D.C. in 1999, pointed out that a common misconception exists that development policies in the 1980s lead to trafficking in women. These sex industry workers, assumed to be under forced transport, may be called "sex slaves." Because women are often thought of as bearing the brunt of economic change, by extension they are seen as prey for illegal activity. Development policy or change is often blamed for the impoverishment of women, which in turn provides cause for selling children into prostitution. A third suggested feature claims that economic growth is tied to "sex tourism." In this theory, bordellos are filled, as are red light districts, with sex professionals who are essentially forced to offer themselves to wealthy, western, male tourists who develop a taste for the exotic.

The popular notion that sex slavery is widespread is contested by significant research. The mythical nature of this paradigm—that economic refugees or economic opportunists are necessarily acting under coercion—has been demonstrated by historians. Indeed, the stereotypical idea of women as victim seems contrary to indications of women migrating for work in the sex industry. Policy based on fear or concern for "white slavery" or sexual slavery and depredation is based on a misconception involving innocent women which are unwilling victims. As is often the case, prostitutes working in bordellos or independently become doubly jeopardized, caught between the jaws of regulatory punishment and underworld, illegal privation.

---

American towns and cities forbade or strongly regulated both bordellos and nonsexual but sexually-related activity, such as striptease dancing or pornography.

The Enlightenment allowed both method and opportunity for a great increase of information. As a result, the United States was emerging at a historic moment marked by inquiry into the role of brothels in society. Brothels, depending on socially constructed view, can be seen as specialized businesses designed to provide a useful and desired service, offered by willing employees, to a motivated audience. Or, contrarily, bordellos may be seen as predatory sites of labor exploitation, flourishing in various forms, essentially wherever conditions allowed.

When the Industrial Revolution also revolutionized the brothel, so-called "moralists" set about on a program of social "improvement." Management of prostitutes moved from *craft* to *industrial* in model form. Because little observable damage flows from recreational human sexuality, in order to regulate brothels in a law-based environment, the brothel was necessarily viewed as a unique public health danger. Although human sexuality varies little, bordellos lost community support and gained censure over time.

In the meantime, as the warrens of factory workers expanded during the Industrial Revolution, the myth of a "white slave trade" proved useful to both the yellow press and to activists, especially those associated with the so-called "muscular Christianity" movement. Proponents of muscular Christianity proselytized sport participation as a way to avoid what is now seen as normal human sexual desire. Because the Industrial Revolution also stimulated the phenomena of economic migration (or labor market opportunism), it was convenient to claim movement of women toward fruitful roles in successful bordellos was slavery. Because it is the ease of access, and the immediate cash income that was attractive to many sex professionals, appropriate narratives were invented and promulgated. In reality, cash often lets women in traditional settings resist and reject their repressive, imposed roles. Thus, as a rule, sex work was not viewed as legitimate labor.

## Brothels in a Day-to-Day Setting

Brothels were part of the urban fabric of city life in the 1800s. One example was Washington, D.C., with its unusually high population of soldiers, government workers, and other nonresidents. Generally, prostitution was not officially a crime or, if an infraction, it was very selectively prosecuted. Thus, houses of prostitution, while perhaps regulated, were not typically suppressed. Records suggest that during the Civil War, there were about 500 registered brothel houses and perhaps more than 5,000 prostitutes in the nation's capital. Following the Civil War, brothels continued to operate on a smaller scale until 1914, when, after steady lobbying by special interest groups, and a mania based on tales of "white slavery," Congress passed legislation banning them.

Archaeological investigation of a Washington, D.C., site allowed a careful comparison of the material from Mary Ann Hall's brothel with Civil War–era brothels associated with General Hooker's Union Army Division. This work revealed a number of differences within the constraints of providing similar services. The household goods, including ceramics, of Hall's brothel were generally more upscale than those used in the other brothels. On the other hand, consumables from Hooker's Division brothels (designed to help control soldier's behavior) may have been as good, or even better. And the employees may have donated "hooker" to the language as a colloquial for prostitute. Interestingly, this comparison did not reveal what was called "a simple artifact signature of a brothel." Regardless of popular culture folklore about brothels or whorehouses, evidence here uncovered no coercion or restraint. Both the archaeological record and historical documents indicate these examples were meaningfully different from the households of their working-class comparisons, especially that the food was better. Indeed, according to the report ordered by the Smithsonian Institution, Hall's house was a big, well-appointed one, a prosperous household offering material comforts to both inmates and guests. Hall was made a wealthy woman.

Social activists fired with religious zeal, following the mandates of their faith, felt compelled to control and regulate actions and activity of their fellow citizens. At the same time, the letter and the philosophy of the founding documents of the United States seem designed to shield, or appear as though they should have shielded, these people from such activist's repressive enthusiasm. The U.S. government was constituted in a way to guarantee maximum liberty, to support the pursuit of happiness, not to provide a "moral" atmosphere." The Mann Act was established in 1910 to fill a particular need in regulating illegal prostitution, but by 1986, any man who traveled with a woman other than his wife across the state line in America could be found guilty of a federal felony. The act, created in the hysteria of white slave trade propaganda, was to be a weapon against forced prostitution. However, the Supreme Court soon extended its coverage to include any man who crossed state lines with the intention to perform an "immoral act." The bizarre history of the Mann Act is instrumental as an illustration of the legislation of morality associated with bordellos and other sites of commercial sex in the industrialized West.

## Brothels and Cultural Performance

Brothels have been important sites of socializing, especially allowing male bonding and participation of male-oriented pastimes— drinking, eating, gaming, smoking, and whoring. Thus, they were seen as potential sites of conflict with feminized domesticity. The factory system demanded reservoirs of workmen. But this volatile population tended to prefer recreation motifs common to their rural experience. Pacification of the workforce demanded positioning male behavior as a public "harm." The rowdiest of the pastimes were suppressed first, for example, folk football, blood sport, and brawling. As a result, bordellos have been especially vital tidal pools of creative activity, representing commercial settings that replicate informal social gatherings.

While it is always difficult to establish the roots of a hybridized product of cultural confluence, it seems likely that the origins of the tango dance were partly in the brothel or bordello. This now sophisticated performance form, which was originally a street dance, and a dance of the bars and brothels of Buenos Aires, emerged in the last third of the 1800s. African slaves in Argentina brought with them memories of the rhythmic patterns of the *candombe*; black Cubans added the *habanera*. With the addition of the polka and the mazurka, the dynamic dance became known as the *milonga*. Before long, European immigrants and Creoles were performing the new dance style. The tango then evolved. African elements admixed with European walks and turns within the framework of the characteristic close embrace, perhaps rooted in the brothel experience, and created the basic tango vocabulary. Tango immigrated to the United States and was immediately absorbed.

Jazz may also be seen as a brothel art form, although the association is again largely happenstance. Brothels were typical and normal social settings of the time, being only occasionally targets of citizen action. The music, which accepts New Orleans as its nominal birthplace, combines elements of African and Western European music. Black Creoles, many originally from the West Indies, lived under Spanish and French rule in Louisiana. With the Louisiana Purchase in1803, these black Creole folk became citizens. Changing economic circumstances, especially the repression of black populations during the Jim Crow period, brought Creoles (with knowledge of the Western tradition) into contact with other African American and similar ethnic groups performing in New Orleans.

Preexisting music included simple melodies as well as complex cross rhythms. These qualities were mixed with verbal slurs, use of vibrato, and syncopated rhythms. It was also common to play so-called "blues notes." However, by the end of the century, segregation laws brought upper-class black Creoles into contact with other African Americans, traditionally living on New Olean's West Side. Cultures collided.

## Brothels in the Early 2000s

There is no reason to imagine that human biology or emotion has altered since antiquity. Brothels probably exist in all American urban centers, though only Nevada allows legal ones to do business.

"It's sure been a wild ride," Douglas Cruickshank, with *Salon*, reported a former working girl saying in 1999 when federal authorities shut down America's most famous legal brothel. The move came after the brothel owners were convicted of fraud. "It's the end of the road for the Mustang Ranch," she sighed. The Mustang, the world-famous bordello, with more than 100 rooms, was established on a 440-acre spread near Reno, Nevada, by former cabdriver Joe Conforte in 1955. A decade and a half later, Conforte won a court case that paved the way

for the legalization of prostitution in Nevada. A dozen of Nevada's seventeen counties now permit the operation of bordellos. Estimates are that about forty or so bordellos operated in Nevada in 2004. When the Mustang closed because of non-sex-related infractions, the Moonlight Bunny Ranch nearby announced plans to approximately double the staff of working girls, and to follow regulations absolutely faithfully.

In the past, such undertakings were either tolerated (with occasional repression) or ghettoized into a special area. The so-called Barbary Coast in San Francisco was one such informal setting, while Storyville, in New Orleans, established from 1898 until November 1917, roughly correlated with the entry of the United States into the war, is a fine example of a formal bordello or "red light" neighborhood. First, in the late 1800's, during the Recreation Reform Movement, the warrens of working class entertainments were ransacked. Many of the predominantly male pastimes began a process of "demonization" that continues, with the possible exception of football, to be in force in the early twenty-first century. Prostitution was increasingly criminalized, supported by a wealth of literature about white slavery and yellow, red, or black peril in the yellow journalism of the day. The red light neighborhoods were destroyed, the sex workers shunned and dispersed.

Individual prostitutes are often left with little or no protection under color of law. When predation predictably comes, it may come from activists zealous to prosecute their beliefs; it may come from management, understanding the worker has little recourse to remedy; it may come from client, comprehending that legal protection of person and commerce often fails to embrace the sex professional. Otherwise, law-abiding people are caught up in politically, socially, or strategically motivated "sweeps," or broad enforcement actions. In part as a response, the sex industry has often reconstituted the traditional bordello or brothel form into a telecommunications-based tool, still maintaining its organizational function. The brothel, as a management tool to coordinate the provision of desired goods and services, seems destined to survive.

*See also:* Las Vegas, "Muscular Christianity" and the YM(W)CA Movements, Prostitution, Regulation and Social Control of Leisure

### BIBLIOGRAPHY
Bourdin, Ruth. *Women and Temperance: The Quest for Power and Liberty, 1873–1900.* New Brunswick, N.J.: Rutgers University Press, 1990.

Cooper, M., and J. Hanson. "Where There Are No Tourists. . . Yet: A Visit to the Slum Brothels in Ho Chi Minh City, Vietnam." In *Sex Tourism and Prostitution: Aspects of Leisure, Recreation, and Work.* Edited by Martin Oppermann. Elmsford, N.Y.: Cognizant Communication Corporation, 1998.

Doezema, Jo. "Loose Women or Lost Women—The Reemergence of the Myth of 'White Slavery' in Contemporary Discourse of 'Trafficking in Women.'" *Gender Issues* 18 (2000): 23–50.

Donlon, Jon G. "A Travel Model in the Runway Setting: Strip-Tease as Exotic Destination." In *Sex Tourism and Prostitution: Aspects of Leisure, Recreation, and Work.* Edited by Martin Oppermann. Elmsford, N.Y.: Cognizant Communication Corporation, 1998.

Gay, Peter. *Pleasure Wars: The Bourgeois Experience—Victoria to Freud.* New York: W. W. Norton and Company, 1998.

Hobson, Barbara Meil. *Uneasy Virtue: The Politics of Prostitution and the American Reform Tradition.* New York: Basic Books, 1987.

MacLeod, David I. *Building Character in the American Boy: The Boy Scouts, YMCA, and Their Forerunners 1870–1920.* Madison: University of Wisconsin Press, 1983.

Macy, Marianne. *Working Sex.* New York: Carroll and Graf Publishers, 1996.

Odzer, Cleo. *Patpong Sisters.* New York: Blue Moon Publishers, 1994.

Stansell, Christine. *American Moderns.* New York: Henry Holt and Company, 2000.

Sweetman, David. *Explosive Acts: Toulouse-Lautrec, Oscar Wilde, Felix Feneon and the Art and Anarchy of the Fin de Siècle.* New York: Simon and Schuster, 1999.

Tyrrell, Ian. *Woman's World/Woman's Empire: The Woman's Christian Temperance Union in International Perspective, 1880–930.* Chapel Hill: University of North Carolina Press, 1991.

Wiltz, Christine. *The Last Madam: A Life in the New Orleans Underworld.* Cambridge, Mass.: Da Capo Press, 2000.

*Jon Griffin Donlon*

# CAFÉ SOCIETY

**See** *Coffee Houses and Café Society*

# CAMPING

The history of organized camping in the United States is, paradoxically, also a history of the industrialization and urbanization of the nation. For many centuries, Native Americans traveled to traditional hunting and fishing grounds on a seasonal basis, living in temporary accommodations. White settlers, as they made claims on the land and pushed progressively farther west, often camped out on their travels. But the development of camping as a recreational activity, from the nineteenth century onward, was a much more self-conscious enterprise. Camping gained momentum in the nineteenth century, when increasing numbers of better-off Americans grew concerned that both the natural world and American traditions were being eroded by modernity. Anxious about a growing and increasingly heterogeneous population, the development of cities, and the impact of new technologies, the first proponents of camping saw in it a potential antidote to these modern ills. Thus, the camping impulse was at its inception sentimental, romantic, and nostalgic. Through a temporary return to nature, camping proponents claimed, Americans would rediscover physical vigor and find spiritual contentment.

From its inception, the practice of camping attempted to balance the glories of nature with various creature comforts. Proponents of camping did not necessarily expect to "rough it." While Americans were receptive to the idea of wilderness, few were actually prepared to tough it out in the woods. In 1869, Boston clergyman William H. H. "Adirondack" Murray's portrayal of his camping trips, *Adventures in the Wilderness; or, Camp-Life in the Adirondacks,* achieved wide popularity. A sudden rush of visitors to this upstate New York region followed, claiming to have been inspired by the book's glowing descriptions of the area's natural beauty and Murray's testament to its positive effects upon his own vigor and health. But so many tourists came, so quickly, to a region unequipped to provide them with adequate guides and hotels, that they were soon dubbed "Murray's Fools."

## The Growth of a Camping Economy

Within a decade, however, the local economy had caught up to its vacationers' desires. Visitors could choose among a fair number of lodges and fancy resorts, complete with eight-course menus. Some of the wealthiest Americans purchased lavish country places, called "Great Camps," that combined luxury and privacy. For more strenuous hunting and fishing trips through the woods, urbanites could hire local guides who knew the terrain, carried the provisions, set up camp, and made dinner each night.

A new body of camping literature offered advice for those traveling into the woods without a guide: how to

**Mount Rainier campgrounds.** Established in 1899 Mount Rainier National Park in Washington state was declared a National Landmark Historic District in 1997. The popular destination had a bustling motor campground in 1926; in modern times travelers can choose to stay in RVs or resort-style accommodations. © *E.O. Hoppé/Corbis*

choose a site, pitch a tent, select provisions and equipment, start a camp fire, fish with bait, and travel by canoe. By the end of the nineteenth century, specialized magazines for sportsmen, such as *Forest and Stream* (1873), *Outing* (1885), and *Outdoor Life* (1897), further attested to the increasing popularity of camping trips. For those who could not afford a guide, at a cost of several dollars per day, camping literature filled the gap; as one 1911 camping guide pointed out, "many campers are emphatically 'tenderfeet.'" This literature assumed their readers' class position; only middle- and upper-class Americans could afford the time away from work, the expense of outfitting their expeditions, and the cost of travel.

The movement to create national parks and other protected spaces outside the reach of industrial and agricultural sprawl further improved American camping opportunities. George Perkins Marsh's *Man and Nature,* published in 1864, argued that the physical environment would decline without reform. At a time when the government was transferring more and more land from Native Americans, there was support in Congress for the preservation of at least some areas of particular scenic beauty from development or private ownership. The first American national park was founded in 1872 when Yellowstone National Park, the site of many unusual geysers, was created in Wyoming for the use and enjoyment of Americans. Other early National Parks included Mackinac National Park in Michigan (1875), and Yosemite National Park and the Sequoia National Park (both 1890) in California. These areas were successful as tourist centers, drawing some who stayed in resortlike facilities and others who camped out in the woods. Campers were attracted not only by the opportunity to pitch a tent, but also by hiking, hunting, and fishing in these protected wilderness areas.

## The Camping World Expands: Men, Women, and Children

A good number of the nineteenth-century Americans who first celebrated the idea of camping out saw the wilderness lifestyle of an earlier era as exactly the kind of rugged, primal experience that would enhance manhood in the modern age. For late-nineteenth-century and early-twentieth-century proponents of muscular Christianity, who aimed to build a stronger, more virile church through manly physicality, camping was at once a celebration of God's creation and a means to express strength and vigor. However, from the late nineteenth century onward, increasing numbers of women, many of them college graduates with expanded social horizons, also ventured out in

the woods. By the turn of the century, family groups were not uncommon, and camping trips were sometimes domestic affairs, with several families camping together, sharing meals and one another's company.

From the late nineteenth century onward, many thousands of children had their first camping experiences at summer camps. These child-centered leisure institutions were first organized on behalf of elite white Christian boys. For "muscular Christians," camping vacations for boys were antidotes to the seeming softness of modern life and family vacations at resort hotels. Further, as turn-of-the-century psychologist G. Stanley Hall contended, a "primitive" sojourn into savagery was particularly critical to the development of white boys, providing, amid the safety of select peers and adult supervision, a kind of inoculation against the effeminizing effects of civilized culture. By the turn of the twentieth century, adults were establishing camps for girls of similar backgrounds; later, as the industry extended and diversified its reach, they established camps for an increasingly wide spectrum of children.

In the early twentieth century, the summer camp industry expanded rapidly, propelled in part by the growth of new youth organizations of the 1910s, such as the Boy Scouts, Girl Scouts, and Camp Fire Girls, as well as camps founded by private owners and charitable organizations. By the 1920s, thousands of camps taught children about campfires, swimming, canoeing, and fishing, while usually providing comfortable accommodations and cafeteria-style food. Because these camps responded so directly to anxieties about urbanization, they achieved their greatest popularity near the cities of the densely settled Northeast, in New England, New York, and Pennsylvania. Here they served increasingly diverse populations. In the first half of the twentieth century, an era marked by exclusionary Christian-only vacation spaces, Jewish camps were particularly successful, serving both religiously observant and acculturated families. But only in the late 1930s and early 1940s would northeastern organizational camps begin to move toward racial integration of white and black campers, and only from the 1950s onward would organizational camps in southern states begin to integrate campers of both races.

## Twentieth-Century Camping Vacations

Modern transportation advances have been critical to the growth of recreational camping. In the second half of the nineteenth century, as railroad lines expanded, travel to remote regions became easier and more comfortable. In the twentieth century, the development of automobiles had an even more striking effect. Camping out became a vacation option for working-class car owners because it was less expensive than hotel tourism. After World War I, Americans camped out in increasing numbers, both for pleasure and to save money on the road. Some packed their cars with tents and beds. Others converted their cars into the first trailers and campers, precursors to recreational vehicles (RVs). One national organization of car campers, the Tin Can Tourists (1919–1977), was named for the practice of soldering a tin can (from cans used in cooking) to their cars' radiator caps as a means of identification among members. Such travelers stayed at campgrounds that ranged from the primitive to the fairly luxurious; in the 1930s, when commercial RVs came onto the market, new organized campgrounds with electricity and water hookups arose to serve them. In more recent years, RV campers have battled with tent campers over their respective places at state and national parks. Many tradition-minded campers continue to praise backcountry camping, away from modern conveniences and other campers, as preferable to fixed campsites. An industry devoted to camping equipment has, over the last decades, produced tents, cookstoves, and food supplies that are lighter, smaller, and more portable than ever, to serve the needs of those who wish to camp farther in the woods.

The question of what constitutes "true" camping has been contested since the origins of recreational camping. But the movement has clearly shifted from its elite origins to become an activity enjoyed by all classes of Americans. In the early 2000s more than 8 million children and adolescents between the ages of five and seventeen attend a wide variety of camps; some focus on "traditional" camping skills, while others offer instruction in everything from music to computers. Meanwhile, camping out remains a fairly affordable means of vacationing for many more adults and families.

*See also:* Automobiles and Leisure, Backpacking and Hiking, "Muscular Christianity" and the YMC(W)A Movements, National Parks, Recreational Vehicles, Scouting Movements, State Parks

## BIBLIOGRAPHY

Aron, Cindy. *Working at Play: A History of Vacations in the United States.* New York: Oxford University Press, 1999.

Bederman, Gail. *Manliness and Civilization: A Cultural History of Gender and Race in the United States, 1880–1917.* Chicago: University of Chicago, 1995.

Deloria, Philip J. *Playing Indian.* New Haven, Conn.: Yale University Press, 1998.

Eells, Eleanor. *Eleanor Eells' History of Organized Camping: The First 100 Years.* Martinsville, Ind.: American Camping Association, 1986.

Joselit, Jenna Weissman, ed. *A Worthy Use of Summer: Jewish Summer Camping in America.* Philadelphia: National Museum of American Jewish History, 1993.

Nash, Roderick. *Wilderness and the American Mind.* New Haven, Conn.: Yale University Press, 1967.

Paris, Leslie. "Children's Nature: Summer Camps in New York State, 1919–1941." Ph.D. dissertation, University of Michigan, 2000.

Schmitt, Peter J. *Back to Nature: The Arcadian Myth in Urban America.* New York: Oxford University Press, 1969.

Sears, John F. *Sacred Places: American Tourist Attractions in the Nineteenth Century.* New York: Oxford University Press, 1989.

*Leslie Paris*

# CARD GAMES

Playing cards are used around the world in games that range from simple children's activities, to high-stakes gambling in casino games, and world championships in forms such as bridge. Playing cards can be regarded as randomization devices, similar to dice or roulette wheels, in that they are shuffled (randomized) prior to their distribution to players. A few simple card games involve pure chance, with winning and losing depending on who gets the "best" and "worst" collection of cards at distribution, while most card games involve strategy in that players can choose to add cards to their hands, discard some and add others, or make some other wise attempt to improve their odds of winning through decision making.

## The Modern Deck

It is surprising to many that what is considered the "standard" deck of playing cards varies around the world. The standard deck in use in the United States, and the most commonly used deck worldwide, consists of fifty-two cards in four suits of thirteen cards each. Card values in each suit include numbered cards of two through ten, an ace, and three "face" or "court" cards consisting of a jack, queen, and king. The appearance of the face cards has become fairly standardized since cards have been mass-produced. Decks also often include two "joker" cards that are sometimes included for game variations. Many games also make use of "stripped" decks in which certain cards are removed for play.

**Union playing cards.** Printed during the American Civil War, Union playing cards displayed military leaders and emblems. *Courtesy Henry Ford Museum and Greenfield Village*

Suits are identified by symbols or "pips," which on an English deck consist of the familiar spades, clubs, diamonds, and hearts. In decks from other countries, suits are often represented by different pips. For example, hearts, leaves, bells, and acorns are found on German cards; shields, "roses," bells, and acorns on Swiss cards; and coins, cups, swords, and cudgels on Spanish cards. Generally, there is no ranking system for the various suits in a deck of cards, however, ranks are assigned to suits in certain games.

There is no standard back or card reverse, so these designs vary widely. At one time, blank card backs were common. Card reverses have also been used to advertise a wide array of products, including soft drinks, airlines, beer, sports teams, soup, motorcycles, and more. There are a variety of card decks available today, from miniatures less than an inch in height, to oversized cards sometimes used as shooting targets. One can find rectangular decks, round decks, and even "crooked" decks. There are often specialty or commemorative decks created with face cards that depict actual people (the John F. Kennedy deck issued in 1963) or fictional characters (The Simpsons, Spider-Man), instructional decks (the Red Cross deck with safety and first-aid procedures or instructions), informational decks (depicting plants, animals, or other items), and cards marked in Braille. Also available are decks depicting artwork held in European museums and packs with scenic views of a state or city. Many popular card games can also be found as computer programs, complete with illustrated faces and backs.

## History and Evolution of Playing Cards

It is generally believed that playing cards first developed in either the Middle East or East Asia, but beyond this there is no consensus on how modern-day decks of playing cards developed. It is unlikely that playing cards have one discrete point of origin, and, like many other pastimes, playing cards experienced a long evolution into the modern decks. There are, however, many stories, some rather improbable, that attempt to describe the origins of playing cards. One popular legend is that playing cards were invented by the irritable wife of an Indian maharaja who became increasingly annoyed by her husband's habit of pulling at his beard. The wife devised cards as a means of occupying both her husband's hands and his mind, thereby lessening the causes for her irritability. A second story of Chinese origins contends that playing cards were invented by members of the Imperial harem in 1120 A.D. as a cure for the perpetual boredom associated with palace living. At this time, there were an estimated 3,000 members (the empress, spouses, consorts, and concubines) of the inner chamber of the Chinese Imperial Palace; thus, a means of passing the time was necessary.

Other, less fanciful theories include the possibility of Chinese playing cards originating from the adaptation of Korean divinatory arrows. In support of this theory individuals have cited the long, narrow shape of early Chinese playing cards in conjunction with apparent feather marks on the ends of the cards as evidence of this connection. A case can also be made for Indian cards giving rise to European cards because of similarities in early suits—cups, coins, swords, and batons—and the inclusion of face cards that were absent from the Chinese decks. Historians have often suggested that knights on the Crusades brought packets of cards to Western Europe upon their return home, although this theory has been largely disregarded.

Whatever their origins, playing cards appeared in European countries in approximately 1370. There was no mention of cards in gaming ordinances in the 1360s, and cards were included in ordinances issued in the 1370s. Decks of cards in the 1370s are described as having four kings in a deck of fifty-two cards.

Decks of playing cards were first brought to the Americas by Spanish explorers, and playing cards were undoubtedly used in the early American colonies. There are numerous examples of laws pertaining to or forbidding the use of playing cards. The joker cards found in today's English decks originated in the United States around 1863. American euchre players introduced the "Best Bower," as it was originally called, as an extra trump card. The card was renamed the "Jolly Joker" before being shortened to the "Joker" of today. Contrary to popular legend, the court cards of modern English decks are not named and do not represent any particular nobility.

## Playing for Fun

While playing cards themselves are not a game, they have been described as one of the most convenient and portable props for instant game playing. Their widespread availability combined with the variety of games that appeal to different ages and skill levels makes playing cards one of the most popular forms of leisure throughout the world.

It is often difficult to find the definitive rules for any particular card game. Even though there are many books that purport to share the rules of a particular card game, there are many regional differences in game rules, and they continue to adapt and evolve over time. Some games—such as bridge—have an official governing body that has a standard set of rules for tournaments. However, many card games do not have such a governing body and so the rules in social play are those that everyone has agreed upon at the start of play. These are generally referred to as "house rules."

Card games may be classified into one of several game types according to the general objective of play. The first category is that of solitaire or patience games, which are played by a single player, although many can be adapted for play by more than one person. There are over 150 varieties of solitaire games documented, and doubtless many more that have not been recorded. The largest classification of card games is that of trick-taking games, which include euchre, spades, bridge, hearts, and other variations. A "trick" is a set of cards where each player has contributed one card. In trick-taking games there is often a group of cards identified as "trump" that will win against any other card.

Rummy games include gin rummy, canasta, straight rummy, and many lesser-known variations. Interestingly, rummy games take their names from the fact that at one time they were played primarily for drinks. The primary object of rummy-type games is to create matched sets or sequences. The most popular class of card games is the poker family. More money exchanges hands and more individuals play poker in its many forms than any other class of card game. In poker, players attempt to win the "pot" by causing the other players to drop out of the competition or by having the highest ranked hand. Card games that do not fit into the previously mentioned categories or that have categories of their own include stop games, cribbage, skarney, and children's games.

A popular trend among game manufacturers is to create special decks of cards that can be used for traditional card games. These specialized decks are typically useful only to play the game for which they were created, and cannot be used for other games. Originally, many examples could be seen in children's card games, such as special decks for Old Maid or Crazy Eights. This trend has expanded to "adult" card games where traditional games are given an update or twist when packaged for sale. Examples include Canasta Caliente, Rummy 21, and SeaNochle (a pinochle variation).

## Playing Cards and Gambling

Long before the establishment of Las Vegas, playing cards were used for gambling. The earliest references to playing cards in Western Europe are, in fact, found in gambling ordinances of the time. Both church and civil authorities issued prohibitions against playing cards, and cards were considered to be the devil's tools to entice men to lives of sin and sloth.

In some American colonies, cards and gambling were strictly prohibited. In other colonies, card playing and gambling with cards were accepted pastimes. For example, a 1624 Virginia law forbade ministers to play cards, and, as recently as 1832, one could be fined $50 in Ohio for selling a pack of playing cards.

Gambling in the United States has experienced several periods of growth and decline over the years. During the 1800s, New Orleans became the hub of gambling in the United States. Rooms and tables for gambling were initially available in area taverns. Gambling was legalized in New Orleans in 1823, at which time a gambling license was available for the hefty sum of $5,000. On 19 March 1931, gambling was institutionalized in the United States when it was legalized in the state of Nevada. One month later, the city of Las Vegas issued six gambling licenses. In addition to Las Vegas, Nevada, and Atlantic City, New Jersey, the modern card player can gamble on riverboat casinos or in reservation casinos hosted by Native American tribes. Today gambling with cards, both commercial and private, results in a substantial exchange of money in the United States and worldwide.

Card games found in North American casinos are typically limited to blackjack (twenty-one), variations of poker, and baccarat. Casino games can be played in homes, though modifications to the rules are sometimes necessary. Card games where the primary objective is to gamble rather than to facilitate social interaction are completed more quickly and require little player interchange.

## Collectible Card Games

A recent phenomenon, collectible card games (CCGs) have created a unique place in the world of playing cards. CCGs typically focus on a particular world or theme, and players acquire cards to build decks for play against decks built by other players. The rules governing play vary from game to game, but a common goal is to reduce your opponent's points (or life points) to zero through a combination of attacks with the cards. There is a wide selection of collectible card games designed to appeal to a variety of audiences. Popular examples of collectible card games include Magic: The Gathering, Pokémon, Star Wars, Harry Potter, Buffy the Vampire Slayer, Lord of the Rings, Star Trek, and Yu-Gi-Oh!

Collectible card games are played both in social settings and competitively. Most CCGs have sanctioned tournament programs associated with the games, many of which culminate in a "world championship" tournament. Some individuals focus not on play, but rather on the collectible aspect of the cards. Cards are typically assigned a rating, such as "rare," "uncommon," and "common," that influences the value of cards to potential collectors and players. New expansions and additions to the various collectible card games are another frequent occurrence, with older editions becoming excluded from some tournament play.

***See also:*** Atlantic City, Gambling, Las Vegas

### BIBLIOGRAPHY

Beal, George. *Playing Cards and Their Story.* New York: Arco Publishing Company, 1975.

Hargrave, Catherine Perry. *A History of Playing Cards.* New York: Dover Publications, 1966.

Tilley, Roger. *Playing Cards: Pleasures and Treasures.* New York: G. P. Putnam's Sons, 1967.

———. *A History of Playing Cards.* New York: Clarkson N. Potter, 1973.

*Rachelle Toupence and Louis Hodges*

# CARNIVALS

Carnival in the United States has very different connotations to that of European or Caribbean traditions of carnival. Intimately connected to and partially developing out of nineteenth-century American circus culture, American variants of carnival were posited primarily on a financial, not a cultural, basis. Rather than a festival or annual celebration (the "time out of time" of European carnival modes, for instance, in which normal duties, routines of work, and social hierarchies are suspended), U.S. carnival was centered in the fantastical through the display of "freaks," the construction of vast rides and technological wonders, and the development of fantasy worlds of entertainment. The lure of making profits by way of exhibitions of the perceived abnormal in sideshows and freak shows, for example, grounds American carnival forms within particular fields of contrived and manipulated

**Maryland State Fair.** When it was established in 1879 the Maryland State Fair originally operated on 37 acres. The 11-day event now resides on 100 acres providing plenty of space for rides, games, and food stands for its half-million annual visitors. © *Kevin Fleming/Corbis*

vision. The world of the traveling carnival, its development in the nineteenth century masterminded by men like P. T. Barnum (1810–1891), showman and proprietor of the New York–based Museum of America, insists by its very nature upon a culture of continuous carnival as opposed to the weeklong festivals that were tied to religious observances or fertility rituals in other parts of the world. A staple American entertainment form from the 1860s—Barnum took his museum of oddities on the road after a fire destroyed his New York base on 2 March 1868—to the middle decades of the twentieth century, when its hold on the American public's imagination was challenged by the rise of television, the traveling carnival brought the fantastical and the spectacular to Americans across the nation. By the end of the twentieth century the ritual exhibition of "freaks" for amusement and financial profit had almost completely vanished, with only a handful of such shows left in the United States.

## World's Fairs Culture

Circuses, carnivals, dime museums, or world's fairs in the nineteenth and early twentieth centuries were closely interlinked events and entertainment arenas, despite their nuanced differences of presentation and content. While the American world's fairs (particularly the Columbian Exposition in Chicago in 1893) displayed technological or imperial gains within the tradition of the great exhibitions begun at London's Crystal Palace in 1851, the carnivals manipulated the world of the spectacular and of the unknown in their production of novelty shows. Developing in tandem with American world's fairs of the period, the carnivals produced versions of reality that perpetrated some of the most deceptive illusions of the day. Alongside those exhibits deemed to be "born freaks" (e.g., Siamese twins, or the boy with flippers for arms) were placed contrived shows of human "monstrosity" and deformity for the titillation of the paying audience. One of the main features of the sideshow worlds of the carnivals was the midway, a section dedicated entirely to the housing of the "exotic" or the "monstrous." The first midway appeared at the 1893 Columbian Exposition: the "White City" of this fair was a space of technological and cultural innovation where the first Ferris wheel battled for visual primacy with the carnival midway exhibits of alleged cannibalistic African tribes and similar exhibits of nonwhite, non-American identities that owed their presentation and their construction to the racialized methods of seeing and display culture of the period. This fair also collected together a range of traveling showmen whose renown and reputation were spreading throughout the nation (e.g., Buffalo Bill's Wild West show).

## Circus

Although the golden age of the traveling carnival can be dated roughly between 1870 and 1920, the first circus that was self-promoted as a traveling circus or carnival was that of Waring, Raymond and Company in 1837. Carnival circus culture grew exponentially between 1850 and 1900, but declined by the 1920s with the development of resorts and amusement parks in major cities, such as Luna Park (created by Frederic Thompson and Elmer "Skip" Dundy in 1903) and William H. Reynolds's Dreamland of 1904. The various elements that had made up the traditional circus—jugglers, clown shows, trained animals, high-wire performers—were joined in the traveling carnival, and eventually superceded by the display of human oddities; what had stood originally as the sideshow attraction to the main circus event began to take center stage. More famous circus companies such as Ringling Brothers also included minstrel shows, in which mostly white (but on occasion black) performers "blacked-up" to perform song-and-dance routines to entertain the audience during interludes at their attractions from the 1880s. In essence, this was a variation on the freak show form in that they capitalized on the display and exaggeration of "Otherness" within American culture through the burlesquing of black identity. Elsewhere, a freak show or museum of human oddities accompanied the traveling Ringling Bros., Barnum, and Bailey Circus until 1956.

Carnival, then, was an alternative to, but was clearly intertwined with, American circus culture. That it now holds a rather tawdry reputation is due mainly to its use of freak shows.

## Traveling Carnival

Developed as the upshot of other amusement cultures in the late nineteenth century, traveling carnivals provided smaller American towns with their own miniature amusement parks, an annual incursion of the outside or urban world into the American heartlands. As a collection of games of chance, waxworks, museums of oddities, and rudimentary mechanically operated rides (smaller variations on the Ferris wheel for instance, or miniature versions of New York's Steeplechase Park's

horseracing attraction), it shared a modicum of the ethos of more famous carnival events such as Mardi Gras. Usually, such carnivals were not owned by one person, but were organized by a group of individuals and proprietors; indeed, it was not until the early 1890s that an amusement-company culture came to the fore. Barnum brought out on the road the formula that had been successful at his Museum of America in New York: the Siamese twins, Chang and Eng, had been housed there in 1860; Charles Stratton, more famously known as Tom Thumb, was another major attraction; among other displays, Barnum staged reenactments of Native American ceremonials, and constructed a waxworks that reflected the growing temperance ethos within society depicting the individual's inevitable death resulting from one sip of alcohol. Following the 1868 fire, Barnum toured his museum of oddities, continuing to add various attractions to his exhibitions.

The advent of the railroad connected these traveling shows with a wider range of American towns; carnivals could then appear at times coordinated with local festivals and fairs. In the new century's first decade, the attraction of guaranteed audiences nationwide persuaded certain showmen and promoters (prime among them Otto Schmidt) to develop the idea of what would become the twentieth-century traveling carnival, which kept to a tour itinerary that traversed the United States. Indeed, agricultural fairs, begun in the early nineteenth century, provided ideal occasions and locations for a visiting carnival show, with most states and local counties having their own fair at a designated time in the year, depending on seasonal conditions and regional preference. Financial considerations were negotiated locally, with some carnivals paying a fee for their inclusion at a fair while others handed over a percentage of their takings. In 1902, seventeen carnivals were on tour; by 1905, this number had risen to forty-six, and by 1937, there were an estimated 300 traveling carnivals in the United States. This rising success of the carnival can be directly related to a decline in circus culture; simultaneously, there was a transfer of particular exhibits from the circuses, replacing lesser-freak exhibits, such as the geek show (an abject spectacle in which a caged man was reduced to the dismemberment of chickens and even rats on occasion—for which purpose he was equipped with razor blades concealed in his palm). It was inevitable that sideshow elements from the circus would leak into carnival culture, finding a new home within a slightly altered realm of visual entertainment. Before their popularity waned by 1940, the central feature of any good carnival was its freak show.

## From Circus to Freak Show

Where clown shows perform a comic transgression (e.g., a spoof robbery, or a ludicrous attempt at some physical feat) that is ultimately denied, American freak shows were forged around the presentation of racially transgressive identities. As Robert Bogdan points out in *Freak Show,* such exhibitions were "the formally organized exhibition of people with alleged and real, physical, mental, or behavioral anomalies for amusement and profit" (p. 110). Barnum was the innovative and creative force behind the early forms of both American circuses and freak shows, but was later rivaled by the success of the Ringling Brothers. Barnum was also the creator of the three-ring circus, a design principle central to the development of Disney's theme parks in the twentieth century. His "Greatest Show on Earth" was the most elaborate and renowned of the traveling carnival shows, collecting together aspects of the carnivals throughout the United States: from human oddities such as the Bearded Lady and purported midgets or giants to exhibits more in keeping with circus culture, such as performing animals or exotic creatures not indigenous to America. Amid the falsifications on display, such as the woman purported to be a mermaid, were placed individuals who suffered from either physical or mental disabilities. One of the longest serving was the performer known as "Zip, the What-Is-It?" and doubts remain as to his exact identity: he was either an intelligent black man (William Henry Jackson) born with a physical deformity, or he was William Henry Johnson, born in 1840, suffering from microcephaly and exhibited by the Barnum circuses and at Coney Island between 1860 and 1926. This individual was placed in a variety of manipulated and, later, farcical situations including boxing matches and musical performances. Displayed as "the missing link" between humans and apes, the racial dimension to his exhibition status should not be overlooked. Indeed, it was the black coloring of this man that facilitated such carnivalized renditions of his identity.

## Amusement Resorts

With increasing immigration and the exponential growth of America's cities, particularly on the eastern seaboard, in the closing decades of the nineteenth century, town planners and America's carnival and circus proprietors turned to the development of amusement resorts. Designed to entertain the urban masses, locations such as Coney Island in New York or Asbury Park and Atlantic City in New Jersey appeared, fitted out with the latest technological and mechanical amusement innovations, twinned with the more traditional elements of the American carnival. Roller coasters sprang up in the 1880s, the first at Coney Island in 1884 built by LaMarcus Adna Thompson, soon followed by the dedicated theme parks of Thompson, Dundy, and Reynolds. The ability of these fixed locations to develop and enhance their rides and attractions over time counteracted the traveling carnivals' success: unable to keep up with the changing times and technologies and limited in the amount of equipment and staff that they could move about the country, the traveling carnival entered the period after World War II with a diminishing horizon of possibility ahead of it. With the majority of the American population now living in urban areas, and with increasingly easier access through the automobile and other transportation methods to the growing number of amusement resorts dotted across the United States, the old carnival forms entered an irreversible decline.

*See also:* Coney Island; Impresarios of Leisure, Rise of; Mardi Gras; Urbanization of Leisure

### BIBLIOGRAPHY

Bogdan, Robert. *Freak Show: Presenting Human Oddities for Amusement and Profit.* Chicago: University of Chicago Press, 1988.

Brown, Bill. *The Material Unconscious: American Amusement, Stephen Crane, and the Economies of Play.* Cambridge, Mass.: Harvard University Press, 1996.

Culhane, John. *The American Circus: An Illustrated History.* New York: Henry Holt and Company, 1990.

Gresham, William Lindsay. *Monster Midway: An Uninhibited Look at the Glittering World of the Carny.* London: Gollancz, 1954.

Gresham, William Lindsay. *Nightmare Alley.* 1946. In *Crime Novels: American Noir of the 1930s and 40s.* New York: Library of America, 1997.

Kasson, John. *Amusing the Million: Coney Island at the Turn of the Century.* New York: Hill and Wang, 1978.

McGowan, Philip. *American Carnival: Seeing and Reading American Culture.* Westport, Conn.: Greenwood Press, 2001.

*Philip McGowan*

# CARS

**See** *Auto Racing, Auto Shows, Automobiles and Leisure, Cruising, Drag Racing, Hot Rodding, Open Wheel Racing, Sports Car Racing, Stock Car Racing*

# CAVING

Exploring caves and caverns, or caving, is the recreational companion of speleology, which is the scientific study of natural caves. Caving enthusiasts call themselves cavers rather than "spelunkers," which is a term often used by noncavers.

The word "spelunkers" was used during 1950s as a general term for those who explored caves. Later in the 1960s, the term spelunking began to convey the idea of amateurs who were untrained in caving. In general, caving is the recreational sport of exploring caves. Back in the history of mankind, caves were first used as protected places and served for shelter of early family groups and tribes. For this reason, a number of archaeologists are solely interested in exploring caves as places of historical settlements, and conducting excavations to enlighten certain pages of history. Since caves stay at the same temperature during the whole year, they were favorite places of shelter for humans as well as animals.

Caving has become a hobby for many different reasons. Some cavers are interested in gathering hard data about caves. Geologists explore caves for the purpose of studying rock formations and sedimentation. Some cavers are interested in plant and animal life in caves, and study bats, fish, salamanders, small lizards, insects, and mammals. Finally, some cavers are interested in conservation of this kind of nonrenewable natural resource. But most people who visit are interested in them for recreational purposes.

Each cave is a unique experience and provides excellent opportunity for learning and having fun. Visitors feel a thrill of excitement as they follow underground pathways through a cave or cavern. Some caves are entered by walking, others by boat or elevator, and at one cave, the visitors ride through in a tram. Because trails follow the natural contours of the cave, visitors with disabilities should inquire about the accessibility of the caves they plan to visit. Those with serious medical problems such as high blood pressure, heart conditions, and breathing difficulties are cautioned about the risks of being underground. Comfortable walking shoes and light sweaters are recommended during the guided tours. In the United States (including Puerto Rico and Bermuda) there are ninety-one caves that are called show caves because they provide guided tours and other visitor services. These caves are registered members of the National Caves Association (NCA), which was founded in 1965 as a nonprofit organization of publicly and privately owned show caves and caverns developed for public visitation. All are nat-

ural caves and caverns. Members of the association stress the preservation and conservation of these natural resources. Cooperation and exchange of information between member caves is promoted as owners and operators work together for the betterment of all aspects of the show cave industry and to better serve the traveling public. Many NCA show caves have received special recognition as Historical Sites or as Registered Natural Landmarks. The NCA is a member of the Travel Industry Association of America. On the international level there is the International Show Caves Association, which has members in nineteen countries. The organization has objectives similar to those of the NCA: to preserve these natural resources; to promote cooperation and the exchange of information between member caves as owners and operators work together for the betterment of all aspects of the show cave industry; to better serve the traveling public.

It is interesting to note that about 90 percent of caves in the United States are on private property, and that some of them are managed as show caves and others remain closed for the public viewing for various reasons like protection of underground water, accessibility, and legislation. Those caves that are located in public lands like national parks, national forests, Bureau of Land Management lands, and other lands administered by various federal departments are subject to the provisions of the Federal Cave Resources Act of 1989. This legislation was designed to prevent destruction of caves on federal lands. Protection of caves is especially important because it takes thousands of years to repair damages to cave formations. Several states have enacted cave protection laws. It should also be noted that endangered species protection legislation also covers caves. One important point deals with karst areas above caves, which are not covered by legislation. The pollution above the caves can easily seep through and reach to the water source in the caves and may create health problems due to contamination. For this reason preservation of the surface area is as important as the cave in protecting water resources.

Since the majority of caves are located on private lands, especially in rural areas, several problems must be addressed for those interested in exploration as well as the landowners. Another important issue deals with multiple alternatives for owners like quarrying, mining, farming, and raising livestock. In these cases protection becomes a delicate matter among the interested parties. Damage caused by excessive visitation, vandalism, and souvenir collection is one of the problems that cave owners face.

Another important problem deals with left-over carbide on grazing areas that may poison grass and water.

**Guadalupe Mountains National Park.** In 1978 a man explores part of the 2,000-foot limestone walls and caves that are among the popular attributes of Guadalupe Mountains National Park, located near El Paso, Texas. © *Buddy Mays/Corbis*

In order to alleviate the problems, various caving organizations recommend good education as a remedy. First of all, the National Speleological Society (NSS) recommends that visitors to caves take nothing but pictures; leave nothing but footprints; kill nothing but time ("A Guide to Responsible Caving").

Most of the show caves operate like theme parks, with regular tours and educational programs. Some of the caves, in addition to their regular tours, offer adventure tours for those who are interested in exploration. Show caves operate almost year-round because they are protected from inclement weather. Most of the show caves have gift shops, craft shops, trading posts, or country stores, in which to browse, and select gifts and souvenirs related to caves. At some caves it is possible to find historic, pioneer or Indian villages; museums; rock and mineral displays; wildlife parks; and boats and canoes. At other places there are theme parks. One show cave also provides prospecting facilities for gold and other precious metals and gems enthusiasts. Some caves also provide rock-climbing facilities and rental equipment. There are often picnic areas, playgrounds, and nature trails. Special

seasonal festivals and events are held throughout the year. Many caves operate snack bars, restaurants, cabins, and motels that are located on their property or nearby.

Safety is the most important issue in caving. Hazards can include light failure, falls, rock instability, floods, getting lost, getting stuck, exhaustion, and hypothermia. Depending on the level of difficulty and the length of the cave visited, caving can be a strenuous activity requiring reasonably good fitness and health. For all of these reasons, especially for those participating in exploration as adventure, certain safety precautions—such as never caving alone, carrying multiple lights, leaving notice where you will be caving—should always be taken before any attempt.

The NSS has a long list of other recommendations for safe caving practice, as well as suggested reading, that can be found on their Web site, http://www.caves.org. Visitors should have in place a plan for rescue for each cave in case of unexpected accidents and mishaps.

The NSS also states that visitors to caves and caverns should follow this conservation policy:

Caves have unique scientific, recreational, and scenic values.

These values are endangered by both carelessness and intentional vandalism.

These values, once gone, cannot be recovered.

The responsibility for protecting caves must be formed by those who study and enjoy them.

In line with their stated policy, the NSS encourages projects such as:

Establishing cave preserves

Placing entrance gates where appropriate

Opposing the sale of speleothems (cave formations)

Supporting effective protective measures

Cleaning and restoring over-used caves

Cooperating with private cave owners by providing them knowledge about their cave and assisting them in protecting their cave and property from damage during cave visits

Encouraging commercial cave owners to make use of their opportunity to aid the public in understanding caves and the importance of their conservation ("A Guide to Responsible Caving")

It seems that there is excellent cooperation between cavers and cave owners in protecting this nonrenewable resource. The NSS recently established a reward for protection of caves from vandalism and visitor abuses.

Restoration of damaged caves is very difficult because of the possibility of contamination during cleaning processes. In general, volunteer groups under scientific supervision perform restoration work. If not done properly, restoration may cause more harm than benefit.

In conclusion, caving is a growing outdoor activity for those who are interested in exploration and adventure. Caving also represents a leisure activity similar to visiting theme parks and museums. Caves are nonrenewable resources and must be protected through legislation and proper education.

*See also:* Backpacking and Hiking, Mountain Climbing, National Parks, State Parks

**BIBLIOGRAPHY**

"A Guide to Responsible Caving." National Speleological Society (NSS). Available from http://www.caves.org.

"Caves and Caverns Directory." National Caves Association (NCA). Available from http://www.cavern.com.

McKenzie, Ian. "What Is Caving?" Canadian Speleological Society. Available from http://www.cancaver.ca.

*Turgut Var*

# CD COLLECTING AND LISTENING

**See** *Record, CD, and Tape Collecting and Listening*

# CENTRAL PARK

Situated in the heart of New York City, Central Park was the first landscaped public park in the United States. Conceived as a democratic park, which all people could enjoy regardless of class or station in life, it occupies an 843-acre rectangle of land approximately two and a half miles long and a half-mile wide. Central Park creates the impression of a natural oasis preserved against an encroaching city. It is, however, almost entirely constructed—the result of a carefully designed and engineered plan of landscape architecture.

## Origins of the Park: The Greensward Plan

As New York City became increasingly urbanized in the 1840s, prominent citizens, merchants, and landowners were prompted to advocate for a public park. While it is uncertain who originated the idea for Central Park, historical records show that several noteworthy citizens championed the initiative. In 1844, William Cullen Bryant, poet and editor of the *New York Evening Post*, published an editorial proposing a city park. Later, in 1849 and 1850, Andrew Jackson Downing, the nation's foremost landscape gardener, also urged that a park be built. Upon returning from a tour of Europe in 1849, an affluent couple, Robert Minturn and Anna Mary Wendell, publicized that, in comparison to the grand parks abroad, their city sorely lacked a large public park. As interest in a park grew, a circle of elite New Yorkers was gathered with the objective of identifying and purchasing land for the creation of a park in the center of the city.

In 1856, following three years of dispute over the site and cost of the park, the state legislature appropriated roughly $5 million to buy nearly all the land upon which the park stands in the early twenty-first century. Controversially, the purchase of the land evicted approximately 1,600 poor inhabitants from their homes, including the residents of Seneca Village, a long-standing African American settlement, as well as Irish and German residents, who were primarily gardeners and keepers of goats and hogs.

On 13 October 1857, the Board of Commissioners of the Central Park announced a competition for the design of the park. Of the thirty-three entries, the first place prize of $2,000 was awarded to Frederick Law Olmsted (1822–1903), who had been the superintendent of the park since September of 1857, and Calvert Vaux (1824–1895), an English architect who had emigrated to the United States in 1850. Their proposal, called the Greensward Plan, was guided by an aesthetic impulse to create a unified and democratic work of landscape art that would insulate New Yorkers from the surrounding city and offer them the respite of a pastoral landscape. Olmsted was designated architect in chief, responsible for the overall aesthetic design and management of the park, and Vaux was responsible for overseeing the design and construction of the park structures including pavilions, bridges, and boathouses.

## Constructing the Park

The Greensward Plan drew its inspiration from the naturally rugged topography of the existing land. A particularly swampy area became a lake. An area of rocky

**Central Park.** This aeriel view captures the beauty of autumn in New York City's Central Park, the first landscaped public park in the United States. ***Courtesy of Photo Researchers Inc.***

outcroppings was retained so those who would never visit the Catskills or the Adirondacks could experience a mountainous environment. While the natural features inspired the overall plan, dramatic changes to the land were made to construct the park. Dynamiting, excavating, leveling, grading, and hauling of soil occurred to the extent that, altogether, the entire surface of the park was changed by four feet.

Amid the atmosphere of an informal park, there was one formal area, the Mall, which was reminiscent of the public promenades and gathering places of European cities. One hundred and fifty American elms were planted to border the Mall. These majestic trees, along with two and a half miles of elms that line Fifth Avenue, remain as the two largest stands in North America to survive the infestation of Dutch elm disease in the 1930s.

Another unique feature of the park, and a precursor of modern highway systems, was the construction of four transverse roads (stipulated in the competition rules), which ran the width of the park, from east to west, to accommodate cross-town traffic. Of all the contestants, Olmsted and Vaux were the only ones to submerge the roads so visitors could pass through countryside, uninterrupted by traffic, for the entire length of the park. The Greensward Plan also called for multiple gates to allow the visitor to enter the park from many directions and immediately become enveloped in nature, insulated from the surrounding city. The visitor could then travel the many footpaths and drives to ramble among the park's lawns, lakes, hills, glens, woods, rocky ravines, and scenic vistas.

Most of the park was built during the first five years of construction, from 1858 to 1863. Olmsted served as foreman to thousands of German, Irish, and New England laborers who exerted tremendous human effort to transform the land into a park. By 1866, 20,000 men had toiled to build the park, and $5 million had been spent on labor and materials. Central Park officially opened in 1876, a masterpiece of landscape architecture.

## A Park for All People

Olmsted and Vaux envisioned Central Park as a public pastoral setting open to all urban dwellers, rich and poor alike. For the first decade, however, largely only the elite used the park. Gatekeepers' accounts recorded that most people arrived by horse or carriage, which only the wealthy could afford. Guidebooks allotted more space to directions by horseback than by public transportation. Most working people lived south of the park—too far to walk—and train fare was more than most laborers could afford, even with a six-day workweek

Gradually, the park evolved to serve the larger needs of a growing population. Ball clubs were allowed to play games in the park, "Keep Off the Grass" signs were removed, and events such as band concerts were held on Sunday, the only day of rest for the working class. With the installation of the first playground in 1920, increasing numbers of middle- and working-class families began to use the park regularly. The playground was such a success that, by the 1940s, more than twenty playgrounds had been built.

## Contemporary Role of the Park

By the late 1970s, the park fell to overuse, disrepair, and vandalism. The grounds became a site of frequent muggings and more violent crimes. To rebuild the park and regain its safety, civic leaders came together in 1980 to found the Central Park Conservancy, a private nonprofit organization designed to manage, restore, and preserve the park—a project that culminated in the 150th anniversary of the park in 2003.

It is estimated that, in the early 2000s, 25 million people visit Central Park each year. Much loved by New Yorkers, the park means many things to many people and serves a wide range of recreational and cultural needs. While most people come to the park to stroll, others jog, rollerblade, ice skate, cross-country ski, rock climb, or bicycle for exercise. Nature lovers bird watch and identify plants, flowers, and trees. Visitors picnic, sunbathe, canoe, or meditate to relax and rejuvenate themselves. Many cultural activities such as concerts and plays are held in the park, and two museums, including the Metropolitan Museum of Art, are within the park boundaries. Central Park has served as the backdrop for dozens of movies, and many historical and cultural figures are remembered with statues, monuments, and memorials. The vision of Olmsted and Vaux to create a public pastoral landscape to enhance the recreation, health, and pleasure of all people has surely been realized in the contemporary use of Central Park.

*See also:* Botanical Parks, City Parks, National Parks, State Parks, Theme and Amusement Parks, Urbanization of Leisure

**BIBLIOGRAPHY**

Cedar Miller, Sara. *Central Park, An American Masterpiece.* New York: Harry N. Abrams, 2003.

Central Park. Home page at http://www.centralparknyc.org.

Gittelman, Philip. *Olmsted and Central Park* (videorecording). New York: ABC Video Enterprises, 1983.

Olmsted, Frederick Law, and Calvert Vaux. "A Review of Recent Changes, Letter II. 'Examination of the Design of the Park and of Recent Changes Therein.'" *Forty Years* (February 1872): 268.

Reed, Henry H., and Sophia Duckworth. *Central Park: A History and a Guide.* New York: Clarkson N. Potter, 1972.

Rosenzweig, Roy, and Elizabeth Blackmar. *The Park and the People: A History of Central Park.* Ithaca, N.Y.: Cornell University Press, 1992.

*Linda A. Heyne*

# CHARITABLE WORK

**See** *Civic Groups, Men; Civic Groups, Women; Leisure and Civil Society; Philanthropy*

# CHAUTAUQUA MOVEMENT

**See** *Adult Education (Earlier)*

# CHILDHOOD AND PLAY

A substantial body of literature regarding children and play exists in the fields of child psychology, child psychotherapy, human geography, anthropology, and studies of children's folklore. The research presents a range of benefits for children and their development. Traditional studies have focused on benefits of play to the individual child; more recently, the focus shifted to the positive impact of play on society as a whole. Previous research has indicated not only a strong belief in the value of play for children but also concern about some of the trends identified in the following review. Examples of research topics include restrictions on children's access to their local environments; the loss of free time; children with disabilities or from ethnic minority groups; and shortages of appropriate play provision. In general, researchers have found that children's play influences their development of social competence, language, and cognition, though findings concerning the impact of play on creativity are mixed. Social, linguistic, and cognitive meaning is the significant center of children's play as well as their education.

This summary of research about children and play is categorized in five broad yet interrelated sections: (1) History of children and play. A brief history of children development is introduced; (2) Theories of children and play. The general theories and principles of children and play are summarized; (3) Themes of children's play. An overview of various themes of play (e.g., toys and games) and play settings for children are illustrated; (4) Cognitive development of children and play. The impact of play on children's cognitive development, such as culture, literary, language, and creativity, are outlined; and (5) The commercialization of children's play. This section focuses on the impact of commodified play on children development in which problems are addressed.

## History of Children and Play

One of the first Western philosophers to discuss the childhood and play was Heraclitus (c. 535–470 B.C.) of Ephesus. David Miller quotes an aphorism attributed to Heraclitus, "Time is a child playing, moving counters on a game board" (p. 102). In attempting to unravel this bit of wordplay, Miller recalls a story told by Diogenes Laërtius about Heraclitus. When asked to accept a position of responsibility in his city-state's government, Heraclitus replied that it would be better for him to play knucklebones with the children of Ephesus. The context of this story was that Heraclitus considered the act of playing to be more virtuous than the act of governing. Friedrich Ni-

etzsche, who was interested in Heraclitus's enigma, recalled that the followers of Dionysus, active in sixth century B.C. Ephesus, usually pictured their god as a child playing. If Heraclitus's use of the word time meant "eternity," Heraclitus could be viewed as suggesting play should be an ideal for the proper life. As the gods play, so should man. A basic point in Heraclitus's view was that there was no necessary dichotomy between play and the serious aspects of life.

The play movement in North America began in response to child labor and crowded urban conditions. Early efforts at providing play environments for children drew inspiration from examples of Germans, who valued play and had systematized it as a part of their approach to education. Henry Curtis, writing in *The Play Movement and Its Significance,* outlined five distinct and independent play movements in the United States: (1) Play spaces. Campaigns for play movement sought to provide a place where children could spend their leisure time and be off the street away from the evil influences they might encounter. Play spaces offered constructive leadership of trained directors as well. (2) Play and child development. The second play movement was built on the assumption that play was essential to the development of children and it must be furnished to every child every day. The focus of this type of play program was in the schools. (3) Outdoor play for young children. This phase of the play movement desired an adequate opportunity for outdoor life and play to children below school age. It came through the facilities and yards of houses, in the interior courts of tenements, and by leaving an open park and playground in the center of all congested blocks. (4) Public recreation. The movement for public recreation asserted that the development of recreation would mean the providing of social centers in the schools with public gymnasiums, dance halls, and swimming pools, either there or elsewhere, the municipalizing of the moving picture and the subsidizing of drama and the opera, and the development of parks and amusement resorts. (5) Spirit of play. The fifth element was not a movement for the rebirth of play, but the spirit of play. The essential values in life and the joy of the work have become more important.

Early studies on children and play focused upon playgrounds, which offer a combination of large playthings in one location, usually outdoors. The first American playground, the Boston Sand Garden, was established in 1885. The original purpose was to provide city children a substitute for a natural setting, and climbing apparatuses took the place of trees. The National Recreation Association, founded in 1930, developed guidelines for certain equipment for playgrounds like providing a sand box, swings, a small slide, and a climber,

**Belle Isle, Detroit.** In 1905 on a playground on Belle Isle in Detroit, Michigan, children play on a teeter-totter. Early playgrounds were designed to provide urban youth with a substitute for natural rural settings. *Courtesy of The Library of Congress*

known as the traditional components of playground. To arouse children's interest, a playground emphasizes exploration, investigation, and manipulation, provides opportunities for play and exercise that go beyond gross motor activity, and provides both sun and shade. Playground games provide two avenues for children's development: unstructured and structured learning. Most of the child's development is from unstructured activities that most do not comprehend.

In recent decades, the construction of playgrounds catered to children with a safer and varied play environment. Modern playgrounds provide places for quiet play and social interaction and large areas for motor play. Equipment is safe, reliable, easy to install, and manufactured in an array of colors and shapes. Studies show that children particularly value play structures that have the following characteristics: complexity and variety; mystery and suspense; perceived risk and challenge; linkage and creative opportunities; lookouts and private hideaways;

refuges for social and dramatic play; potential for adult interaction. The passage of the Americans with Disabilities Act of 1990 regulated the design of playground games to make facilities accessible to children with disabilities.

In 1990, the United Nations Convention on the Rights of the Children set out fifty-four articles that identify a range of principles and standards for the treatment of children. A number of the convention's articles are specifically relevant to children's experiences in their local environment and their access to play. The United Nation Declaration of the Rights of the Child suggests that children should have the full opportunity for play and recreation. Play opportunities and playthings stimulate children's development—physical, mental, emotional, and social. These implications highlight three main areas that need to be addressed in terms of a child's right to play: (1) The provision of space, which is a basic resource that children need in order to play. It is by this measure to judge how seriously a community is attending to the needs of its children. (2) Consultation with young people: an explicit requirement underpinning the United Nation Convention; however, in order for this to happen, children and young people need help in making their views known and structures need to be put in place to promote their participation in the planning process. (3) Integration of all children—in particular, those with disabilities—is highlighted by "play is the right of all children" (Article 23), which thus requires the provision of play settings and provide "comfortable and equitable opportunities for integration of children with and without disabilities" (Adams and Ingham, p. 38).

## Theories of Children and Play

Most of the research about childhood play provides models and conceptualizations on the issue of goodness for play. In recent decades, research shifts from "Is play good for child development?" to "Why is play good for childhood?" A dozen or more separate theories have been proposed to explain what play is good for. Gene Bammel and Lei Lane Burrus-Bammel group the earliest explanations as "biological theories." It includes the pre-exercise theory that play prepares children for adult roles, and the recapitulation theory that children's play represents the inheritance of physical skills we received from our animal ancestors, for example, tree climbing from monkeys. These theories were eventually replaced by a set that Bammel and Burrus-Bammel label "environmental theories." The emphasis is on the role of external causes in shaping the desire to play, rather than on instinctual or biological causes. Two main theories from this set are Clark Hull's stimulus-response hypothesis and Sigmund Freud's psychoanalytic model. Hull believed that children were taught to play through a complex series of rewards given for participation in play: attention, praise, recognition, status, and so on. Freud, on the other hand, felt that children naturally turned to play to relieve emotional problems and to release frustration resulting from pent-up, immature sexual urges.

Bammel and Burrus-Bammel categorize a third set of theories about children and play as cognitive theories. The common theme for these theories is that play is seen as a function of information processing. Jean Piaget developed an influential theory of play as a part of this larger model of childhood development. The child begins at birth in the "sensory-motor stage," and then progresses through three other stages of development. Each stage has a distinctive set of play forms that helps the child's cognitive growth. Based on Piaget's theories of cognitive development, children begin to role-play as early as two years of age; they begin to use mental representation of

what they have seen and heard to create an all-new experience in their mind. In more literal terms, they imagine what could happen if thoughts were rearranged, and this process can quickly become a game. This mental exploration is essential to life, as it prepares children to think logically and reason through events and emotions. Studies done on the effects of imagination in childhood have produced a belief that fantasy play has a strong role in the development of a child's mind, but on exactly what that role is, psychologists differ. Furthermore, the research findings are often correlational, and psychologists can consider them to be theories only (because of the roles that a multitude of other factors could play); in addition, these findings do not address the potential dangers in role-play, such as fake violence and discrimination.

Play and games have a major role in the main forms of leisure activity during the period from birth to adolescence. Play does not have to be taught or justified during this period of life because it is a self-motivated behavior; one cannot force a child to play. However, for the children, play is often serious business. Children's sociodramatic play, in which their meanings predominate and in which they employ their personal power, serves as a particularly significant force in integrating their development. For example, children feel power when they play. Their sense of personal power grows out of the dynamic cultural context in which they acquire experiences. Ultimately, children feel competent within the "predictable unpredictability" of play.

In his research, Johan Huizinga identified the following characteristics of play: voluntary, steps outside of ordinary life, limited in time and space, not serious but consuming for participants, bounded by rules, and promotes cultural values and as such is an important means of learning for younger children. Children have much to teach adults about play. Tim Hansel refers to young children as midget gurus of play in that gurus teach people profound truth. He has identified that infants and young children can teach us some of the following principles: (1) Total immersion. No matter what children do, they do it completely and do not worry about any inhibitions. They have the ability to let life embrace them. (2) Total concentration. Children concentrate on one thing and one thing only. Watch children and you will notice how free they are from the problems that plagues our society. (3) Ability to bounce back. The spirit of children is indomitable, as they are able to bounce back from failure to try again and again. (4) Total honesty and expression. Children, according to Hansel, have a wonderful sense of spontaneity, and they tend to be completely open and honest with their feelings.

## Themes of Children's Play

Children's play themes grow out of their experiences. Before the growth of television and film culture, children already imitated the behavior of teenagers. For example, children act out adolescent or adult sexual styles or behaviors. Street games, such as stickball and handball, provide an opportunity for children to play with adolescents. Gender themes are always popular for children's play. Beginning early, girls' and boys' play interests and toy choices tend to be gender-oriented. Most girls engage in more sedentary, small-muscle activities, homemaking and fashion themes, while boys engage in more rough-and-tumble, construction, and outdoor-activity themes. Preschool children often play with toilet talk as part of their sense of humor and power. Children are naturally curious about their own bodies, other people, and the world. Their curiosity can be playful, spontaneous, occasional, and voluntary. The sexual exploration differs from anxiety-based, obsessive, or aggressive behavior that involves contextually or personally inappropriate sexual behavior.

Another phenomenon suggests that children's play encompasses various themes—for example, games end with a single winner. In games of two or more children, there are necessarily several (or many) losers, and for the victor, winning itself is the reward. In team-based games, team members who lose together may feel some compensation in the experience of collective effort and camaraderie. Therefore, an emphasis on the fun of playing the game, the exercise of improved skills in completing increasingly difficult games, and the celebration of completion might provide children with some balance when they lose a game. Some researchers recommend that noncompetitive games provide one way to reduce or eliminate teasing and bullying. In addition, many commercial games offer more variables than children may be able to juggle. A child will quite probably approach a game much in the same manner that they approach life: willingness to compete or standout, willing to take a risk to win or lose, desires to be in control, refusal to engage in the game, demonstration of foresight and planning, responses to loss or victory. Games can either be a simple way to break the ice, make introductions, or serve as a tool to gain some limited insight into the thoughts and feelings of the child.

Discussion revolving the impacts of toys on children's play is common. Toys inspire the imagination and help children learn new skills. As children express their thoughts and feelings through play, toys assist in the process. When organizing play situations, an objective basis for the selection of toys and materials is important.

Items must be intentionally selected rather than just accumulated. The list of toys that have been found most likely to generate interaction and conversation are dishes, blocks, dolls and dollhouses, puppets, wagons, telephones, blocks, colored cubes, balls, crayons, and clay or play dough. Other items commonly found in therapeutic playrooms include cars, trains, balls, paper and scissors, baby bottles, chalkboards and chalk, playing cards and games, and a sink or tub for water play. The rationale for selecting these toys is that they allow, in their own way, the child to create or reconstruct reality from their own perspective. Another suggestion is to include props that specifically pertain to the situation with which the child is currently dealing. For example, if the child were facing an illness, he or she would include a doctor kit in the playroom.

Children who have access to a wide variety of playthings designed for both sexes appear to have the advantage over those whose choices are restricted. Although research suggests that boys tend to play more aggressively with dolls than girls do, dolls provide better outlets for working through problems than do trucks or cars. Michael Ellis, in his book *Why People Play,* suggested that children have access to toys that enhance the development of a wide variety of skills: imagination, cooperation, turn taking, organizing, physical coordination, and spatial relationships. Well-designed playthings provoke exploration, investigation, manipulation, and contemplation. If an object is sufficiently complex and responsive, the child will investigate its physical properties and seek answers to questions that arise during the investigation, thus developing problem-solving skills. With due consideration for issues of safety, children should be allowed to use toys as they wish, not necessarily as a parent, teacher, or manufacturer thinks they should be used. Studies suggest that using toys may help reduce differences in verbal and other skills between children from middle-income and low-income families.

On the other hand, Gary Cross, in his book *Kids' Stuff: Toys and the Changing World of American Childhood,* relates a joyless world of useless plastic objects and manipulative advertising aimed at children. It begins with a discussion of how the concept of toys has changed since the nineteenth century, positing that toys are a prime example of a consumer economy run amok. What started out as the manufacture of toys meant to function as educational tools (e.g., building blocks, Legos, etc.) has metamorphosed into Barbies, Power Ranger action figures, and the latest knockoffs from Disney-animated films. The worst thing is that parents have virtually been removed from the equation as toy manufacturers first decide what kind of toys to make and then market them directly to children via Saturday-morning cartoons and the

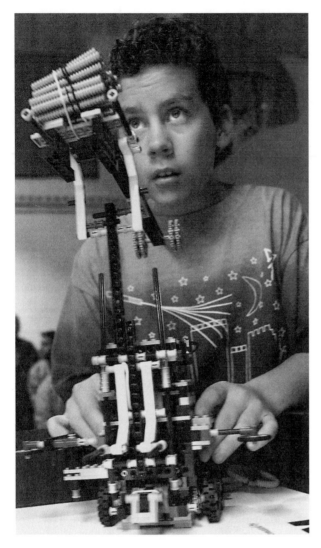

**LEGO League.** In Janesville, Wisconsin, Garrett Bennett operates a LEGO robot vehicle that his team, the Urban Wizards of St. Williams School, designed. The FIRST LEGO League holds tournaments internationally that begin with an annual "challenge" announced in the fall. © *Dan Lassiter AP/Wide World Photos*

backs of cereal boxes. The world of childhood was controlled by the manufactured fantasies that fuel it. Miriam Formanek-Brunell's *Made to Play House: Dolls and the Commercialization of American Girlhood, 1830–1930,* addresses a significant issue in the history of childhood through the examination of the links between material objects designed for children, the societal construction of childhood, and children's participation as agents of their own socialization. It explores the dynamic interaction between patterns of production and consumption in the emerging twentieth-century consumer culture, and it proposes that the history of dolls in America (their creation, marketing, and use) documents the struggle of

women and girls to gain cultural control of representations of their gender identity. Another book, *Purchasing Power: Black Kids and American Consumer Culture,* by Elizabeth Chin, studies a group of young African American children in Newhallville, Connecticut, in order to develop and explain a new brand of consumer culture that many previous anthropologists fail to recognize. Chin's research contradicts the stereotypical images in society and those portrayed by the media of African American children. She defines a new image of African American children's culture that goes against commodity fetishism and the need for brand-name goods. She discovers one that deals with the harsh world of being poor and black, where opportunity and survival are major factors of consumer culture. Chin demonstrates the complexity of this issue by displaying how play is woven in with and affected by society. In this way, children's play, as part of consumerism, relates to social injustices, race relations, class diversity, gender differences, cultural baggage, and social relationships.

## Cognitive Development of Children and Play

The cultural context of children's play varies depending on the perspectives of play expressed by different scholars. Some investigators generally contend that what may be play in one time and place may be ritualistic or religious, frivolous, or technical behavior elsewhere. The cultural context also determines who may, or is likely to, engage in various kinds of play. The culture teaches what to expect and how to categorize reality and pretend play. Gregory Bateson identifies the concept of a play frame that functions as a territory or context for play. He suggests that children demonstrate by their verbal or nonverbal behavior that they are able to categorize play and not-play as they enter into and step outside the framework of play situations. By planning their parts and actions together, children communicate about their communication (metacommunication). The process of metacommunication takes place outside the play frame. In this way, play is progress in the child's "evolution of communication" and "metacommunication" (Bateson, pp. 121, 125). The metacommunication that takes place in social play makes it possible for children to pretend together because without this type of communication, they would be playing by themselves. When children use an object to bridge the gap between real and make believe, such as using a block as a telephone, or when they interact with others to define a play territory together, they are engaging in symbolic representation, a process that seems to advance youngsters' development. Therefore, play serves as a kind of lymphatic function in childhood education.

Play formats include solitary or social play with objects and others. Sociodramatic play is a particularly powerful form in which children use both imagery and communication about their imagery in seamless ways. Although their imagery grows out of particular personal and cultural contexts, their capacity to engage in metacommunication seems to exist across cultures. Children move comfortably inside and outside the play framework.

Children who play with one another learn that others have views that may differ from their own. They also learn that others have feelings that are similar to their own. They are "decentering" from themselves (Fromberg, p. 26). Therefore, in their social interaction, they are building their "theory of mind," the sense that others have their own ideas and feelings. This insight constitutes an influential aspect of multicultural education. Children's play with others as well as with objects influences their cognitive development. In both cases, the key to competence is flexibility in dealing with ongoing object construction or social construction. Developmental progress can take place more easily when a child uses alternative approaches and perspectives. Further, when children play with others, they get opportunities to expand their knowledge as well as refine their language skills. During play, children engage in activities that expand their imaginations. They work together on problems, create their own games, and take on different roles.

When literacy is included in these types of play, there is no limit to what children can learn. Children who play together in a literate environment are frequently seen to put together the "pieces" of their individual mental work and building up their knowledge in the discourse process. They help each other in figuring out what words, signs, and symbols signify. Children share with one another all the information they know, and together, by brainstorming, they are able to reach a conclusion as to what the sign or symbol may represent or what the word means. Allowing children to play together helps them to take the risks that are involved in thinking aloud. The thinking and sharing atmosphere make it easy for children to sort out their knowledge and bring their implicit understandings to a conscious level. Children engage in more literacy activities and increase their literacy skills when play-area props include literacy materials such as writing tools, signs, posters, banners, books, labels, receipt and appointment books, price lists, and magazines. Other research showed children using more varied and extensive language when play props suggested varied themes. As a haven for controlled risk taking and an attempt to see what is possible, play is a creative process. Researchers have found a relationship between direct tutoring and encouragement to use thematic play with chil-

dren's later creative use of unstructured props. Greta Fein saw "pretense as an orientation in which the immediate environment is deliberately treated in a divergent manner" (p. 21). However, there is ongoing debate about these findings concerning the connection between play and children's creativity. Some researchers have questioned the impartiality of particular researchers, their definition of children's behavior as play, and the validity of research procedures.

## The Commercialization of Children's Play

There is an increasing worry that children have become sedentary and have solitary lifestyles. A number of studies from the field of urban studies raise concerns that children have been conceptualized as problems and the result has been their marginalization and increasing exclusion from a hostile urban environment. What some researchers have termed commercialization of play space and the "commodification" of childhood includes, among other things, issues about access and about whether certain forms of play provision can actually sustain exclusion. Interest in the growing commercialization of play provision and in the considerable expansion of out-of-school provision, is evident in a number of areas of the literature. Both developments have implications for children's opportunities for free play—in particular, because such provision usually involves parental choice and often has a cost implication that also requires adult agreement. According to John McKendrick, Michael Bradford, and Anna Fielder, the growth of commercial playgrounds is adult-led and can be attributed to the conjunction of a number of discrete trends that rendered their development viable. These include the proliferation of the service and leisure industries, the availability of land and buildings, and the growing recognition of children as consumers.

The lives of children today are much more structured and supervised, with limited opportunities for free play. Parents are paranoid of their children being abducted, kidnapped, or physically harmed in the outdoors and public places. In turn, the children's physical boundaries have been limited. A number of factors have led to this: parents are afraid for their children's safety when they leave the house alone; many children are no longer free to roam their neighborhoods or even their own yards unless accompanied by adults; some working families can't supervise their children after school, giving rise to latchkey children who stay indoors or attend supervised after-school activities; children's lives have become scheduled by adults, who hold the biased belief that this sport or that lesson will make their children more successful as adults.

There are also concerns that within the education system, children are under mounting pressure to achieve success in academics. As a result, the opportunities for free play are being increasingly squeezed out or downgraded in learning value. These phenomena suggest a greater control over children's play activities, driven in part by parents' concerns for safety and concerns about the quality of facilities within the local environment.

Another important influence has been a major change in family life that has taken place over the last few decades, which is leisure as a shared family experience. For example, commercial playgrounds, largely based on pay-for-play, raise the possibility that they will not cater to all groups and could therefore potentially be a cause of exclusion. With regard to the trend toward increasingly supervised leisure and recreational activities in out-of-school hours, a number of studies have highlighted the significant expansion of out-of-school clubs, often to provide child care for working parents or to promote study support.

Therefore, the definitions used for children's play are often imprecise and the boundaries between play, game, sport, learning, and education remain poorly defined. Furthermore, there are unresolved disputes as to whether positive outcomes are necessarily related to play-specific processes or more generic processes, such as social interaction.

The commodification of play involves looking at play as a something to be bought and sold. With this in mind, people have worked to develop games and toys around this idea of play as a commodity. For example, online team play can be viewed as a form of commercialization in which children can communicate with one another through their PlayStations, or through media such as message boards and text messaging. While the manufacturers have created many commercial toys that can interact with children, the video game technology made a huge contribution to children's play in recent years. Technology and the video game industry continue to change and improve, which will make games better and more interactive for children. The better the gaming experience, the more children will play and talk about the game.

Due to all of the new technologies being designed and put into production, there are many different outcomes for play. Young children play at being television superheroes and superheroines, enact teenage behavior, and explore violent themes or behavior. Across the industry, children are generally the first to decide what is fashionable, and consumer electronics and software are no different. Children influence functionality as well as style and have already driven trends like online messaging and gaming in various fields. On the other hand, it is important to remember that technological advancements can produce both threats and potentialities for children's development. The findings by Stephen Kline, Nick Dyer-Witherford, and Greig Peuter, show that children's play, such as video games are worthy of serious study because they represent the "ideal-type" postmodern commodity. So whereas the automobile is closely associated with the "industrial capitalism" of the Fordist era, the video game embodies the "information capitalism" of today's "perpetual innovation" society for children's development.

In sum, play is to a child what work is to an adult: it depends upon what they do. Children learn about their world and the things in it through play, which allows children the chance to explore their environment, to learn how it works and how they relate to it. This summary presents that a child can express feelings and emotions through various types of play activities far earlier than they can express them in words. Play serves the outlet through which children convey emotions that they are either unwilling to share verbally or do not have the sufficient vocabulary to express. Through play, professionals as well as the general public can identify children's feelings, confusions, and questions. The technology advancement has influenced the types of play for children, in which play has become a commodity. Children interact through online video games and create online messaging. A new form of play is emerged and evolved to be an integral part of children's development. Therefore, play provides a wide variety of choices for children, who can be anyone, at any place, at anytime.

*See also:* Children's Reading, Commercialization of Children's Play; Computer/Video Games; Playgrounds; Teenage Leisure Trends

**BIBLIOGRAPHY**

Adams, Eileen, and Sue Ingham. *Changing Places—Children's Participation in Environmental Planning.* London: Children's Society, 1998.

Bammel, Gene, and Lei Lane Burrus-Bammel. *Leisure and Human Behavior.* Dubuque, Iowa: William C. Brown, 1992.

Bateson, Gregory. "A Theory of Play and Fantasy." In *Play: Its Role in Development and Evolution.* Edited by Jerome Bruner, Alison Jolly, and Kathy Sylva. New York: Basic Books, 1976.

Chin, Elizabeth. *Purchasing Power: Black Kids and American Consumer Culture.* Minneapolis: University of Minnesota Press, 2001.

Cross, Gary. *Kids' Stuff: Toys and the Changing World of American Childhood.* Cambridge, Mass.: Harvard University Press, 1997.

Curtis, Henry. *The Play Movement and Its Significance.* New York: Macmillan, 1917.

Ellis, Michael. *Why People Play*. Upper Saddle River, N.J.: Prentice-Hall, 1973.

Fein, Greta. "The Affective Psychology of Play". In *Play Inter-actions: The Role of Toys and Parental Involvement in Children's Development*. Edited by Catherine Brown and Allen Gottfried. Skillman, N.J.: Johnson and Johnson, 1985.

Formanek-Brunell, Miriam. *Made to Play House: Dolls and the Commercialization of American Girlhood, 1830–1930*. New Haven, Conn.: Yale University Press, 1993.

Freud, Sigmund. "Beyond the Pleasure Principle." In *The Standard Edition of the Complete Psychological Works of S. Freud, 1920–1922*. Volume 18. Edited and translated by James Strachey. London: Hogarth and the Institute of Psychoanalysis, 1955.

Fromberg, Doris Pronin. *Play and Meaning in Early Childhood Education*. Boston: Allyn and Bacon, 2002.

Hansel, Tim. *When I Relax I Feel Guilty*. Elgin, Ill.: David Cook Publishing, 1979.

Huizinga, Johan. *Homo Ludens—A Study of the Play Element in Culture*. Boston: Beacon Press, 1962.

Hull, Clark. "S-R Analysis of Cognitive Processes." In *Mechanisms of Adaptive Behavior: Clark Hull's Theoretical Papers*. Edited by Abram Amsel and Michael Rashotte. New York: Columbia University Press, 1984.

Kline, Stephen, Nick Dyer-Witherford, and Greig Peuter. *Digital Play: The Interaction of Technology, Culture, and Marketing*. Toronto: McGill-Queens University Press, 2003.

McKendrick, John, Michael Bradford, and Anna Fielder. "Kid Customer? Commercialization of Playspace and the Commodification of Childhood." *Childhood* 7 (2000): 295–314.

Miller, David. *Gods and Games: Toward a Theology of Play*. New York: Harper Colophon, 1973.

Morris, Charles G., and Albert A. Maisto. *Understanding Psychology*. Upper Saddle River, N.J.: Prentice-Hall, 2001.

Nietzsche, Friedrich. "Ecce Homo." In *The Philosophy of Nietzsche*. Volume 10. Edited by Geoffrey Clive. New York: New American Library, 1965.

Piaget, Jean. *Play, Dreams, and Imitation in Childhood*. Translated by C. Gattegno and F. N. Hodgson. New York: Norton, 1962.

Smith, Peter. *Play in Animals and Humans*. New York: Basil Blackwell, 1984.

———. "Play and Associative Fluency: Experimenter Effect May Be Responsible for Previous Positive Findings." *Developmental Psychology* 23, no. 1 (1987): 49–53.

*Philip F. Xie*

# CHILDREN'S MUSEUMS

Children's museums are places that encourage learning, exploration, and discovery through playful interactive ex-

**Interior Atrium Space, Children's Museum of Indianapolis.** Currently the world's largest, The Children's Museum of Indianapolis was founded in 1925 by Mary Stewart Carey, a long-time resident of Indianapolis. The museum, which works cooperatively with local schools, attracts millions of visitors annually to its 300,000-square foot building. *Courtesy of Jawaid Haider*

hibits. There are subtle differences among all children's museums as each embodies the social and cultural values of the local context or community. Children's museums differ from other museums in a number of ways: they are specifically planned for children, place a high priority on interdisciplinary education, and use their collections as teaching tools—not as an end in themselves, but as a means to an end. In contrast to the subject-centered approach of many regular museums, children's museums have embraced a client-centered philosophy.

In the United States alone there are already more than 300 children's museums, a development that implies a greater role for this institution in the life of a community. Museums were once regarded as sanctuaries of high culture remote from the interests of children at large. Traditional museums served a select group of people through their collections, but contemporary museums are now changing as some curators and exhibition developers, trained in design or education, attempt to reach the general public, especially children. Children's museums—along with discovery, nature, and science centers—are partially responsible for these changes. Arguably, as contemporary museums take on a new look, the boundaries are minimized among children's museums, science centers, and other museums that cater to families. It is essential to point out that the emphasis in children's museums on hands-on experience is often confused with exclusively entertainment places that may have little educational value.

The first facility of its kind in the world, the Brooklyn Children's Museum was established in 1899. The most

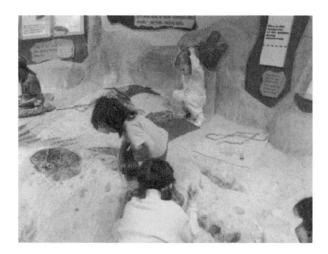

**Dinosaur dig area, Children's Museum of Indianapolis.** This realistic simulation of an actual dinosaur excavation site encourages children to dig through the dirt and help uncover the dinosaur skeleton that is buried there. The exhibit is an excellent example of how children's museums are using multisensory exhibits to enhance the learning experience. *Courtesy of Juwaid Haider*

evocative feature of this building today is the metal "people tube," which is lit by neon lights and connects exhibit spaces at different levels. The Brooklyn Children's Museum was one of the first to house exhibits specifically designed for children when it began its operation in a house. These exhibits were conceived for helping the presentation of nature work in elementary schools with content based on a number of fields: botany, zoology, geology, human anatomy, history, and so forth. In 1904, Anna B. Gallop, as the curator of the museum, was instrumental in transforming the mission of the museum into an educational institution with children's needs in mind. The Brooklyn Children's Museum became synonymous with a place where learning was fun.

The Children's Museum in Boston was established in 1913 through the efforts of a group of enlightened science teachers who wanted to enrich the materials offered in a classroom. During the next few decades, the Children's Museum in Boston became a model in the country and abroad. The 1960s, however, were the turning point in the history of this museum when the young Michael Spock was appointed the director of the museum. Spock, son of the famous pediatrician Benjamin Spock, substantially redefined the children's museum. He is credited with developing interactive or participatory exhibits. Today, these hands-on exhibits are popular attractions in children's museums throughout the world.

The next historically significant museum, the Children's Museum in Detroit, began in 1917. The underlying philosophy of this museum was based on making objects available to visitors rather than keeping them in storage. Through the years, this museum has endeavored to meet the historical, artistic, scientific, and cultural needs of children.

Currently the world's largest, the Children's Museum of Indianapolis was founded in 1925 by Mary Stewart Carey, a long-time and civic-minded resident of Indianapolis. It has moved to a large new building with an area of approximately 300,000 square feet. This institution is the most successful children's museum and attracts more than a million visitors annually. It has close ties with schools and other learning organizations, and offers exciting nontraditional learning opportunities for children of all ages.

## Concept of Play and Learning

The notion of child's play constitutes an indispensable core value for children's museums. Psychologists and educators have argued most cogently that children instinctively seek to play because it motivates them to learn about concepts essential to an understanding of the world around them. Child's play is metaphorically work. The emphasis on "hands-on" learning in museums becomes the catalyst for a "minds-on" approach, which views play and learning as an integrated endeavor. Music, science, art, dance, role-playing, and simply playing in special spaces with creative participatory exhibits become the means to stimulate and educate. Exhibits respect the child's spontaneous drive to learn through touch and the adult's desire to share and encourage the inquisitiveness of the young mind. Successful interactive exhibits are generally "experience-based" and embody a concept such as water, environment, or nature that manifests the qualities and functions of the concept as it relates to our lives.

The Children's Museum of Indianapolis houses many fascinating exhibits that integrate a didactic agenda with imaginative learning. For instance, a walk-through replica of an Indiana limestone cave engages the child's sense of sight, touch, smell, and sound, while the children learn about stalagmites and stalactites and experience the dampness of an actual cave. The educational intent of this exhibit is to introduce to children the processes of geological formation.

The enormously popular climbing sculpture at the Children's Museum in Boston is a maze of platforms and cutouts in midair that heightens children's awareness of their bodies in space. It is a mathematics exhibit that enables children to estimate how their bodies work through space—as they intuitively learn about scale and proportion.

The Treehouse at the Philadelphia Zoo provides a sense of enchantment through a variation of scale or size. The exhibits encourage kids to understand and experience animal habitats, which are scaled so that the child is the size of the insect that occupies the space. Children can pretend they are bees at the beehive exhibit because that bee is about the same size as the child.

Exhibits at children's museums attempt to demystify complex technological inventions or objects by giving children an idea about how they work and by making them fun and imaginative, such as a huge model of a submarine at the Children's Museum of Indianapolis.

The majority of children's museums serve kids from the ages of birth through twelve years. Many museums make special efforts to attract teenagers. Some of these institutions, such as the Children's Museum of Indianapolis, involve child volunteers, including teenagers, who are trained to participate in the teaching process.

## Objectives of Children's Museums

Children's museums have common universal goals, which include emphasis on creating a child-centered environment for learning, encouragement to broaden children's horizons and to challenge themselves, and the interaction of adults and children. Although it can be argued that the phrase "children's museum" is a misnomer, these places definitely draw their roots from the museum field and house exhibits that provide learning experiences for children—very distinct from pure entertainment. Children's museums encourage imagination, critical thinking, and creativity through participatory exhibits.

Children's museums promote nontraditional learning in the spirit of exploration and discovery—even for adults. Through creative programs and engaging exhibit design, museums have the ability to create an environment conducive to intergenerational socialization. These institutions produce numerous exhibits and programs to help children relate to the world in which they live through play and hands-on experience. Bonnie Pitman-Gelles argues that understanding how things work and what they are made of helps children become more comfortable with their environment.

## Outreach Programs and Partnerships

All established children's museums are organized and permanent nonprofit institutions that have elaborate outreach programs with other institutions, including schools. Many schools in cities and towns that have children's museums arrange for their students' regular visits to these places as an integral part of their curricula.

Based on a 2002 survey of 200 members of the Association of Children's Museums (ACM), more than 31 million children and families visited children's museums in 2001, and outreach programs involved more than 6.6 million people in the same year. Increasing numbers of children's museum programs are designed to complement and extend the activities and curricula of the formal classroom. This development has significant implications for schools, early education, and other children's institutions such as child-care centers. Because children's museums stress multisensory experiences, learning is more effective.

As a dynamic institution that collaborates with other civic organizations, children's museums are likely to play a larger role in the future where children and their families have fun and learn together. It is not a coincidence that the goals of children's museums symbolize the idea of learning through play and instill a passion for lifelong learning. Theories of learning and their relationship with museums, particularly children's museums, are becoming a focus of study as people face the challenge of designing new and hybrid institutions to meet the complex demands of the twenty-first century. The concept of "Museums Uniting with Schools in Education" (MUSE) is rapidly gaining momentum as a timely innovative idea. Conceivably, the current successes of traditional school partnerships with youth and science museums will be replicated extensively in the near future. The Henry Ford Academy, a public charter high school in Dearborn, Michigan, housed in the Henry Ford Museum, is an inspiring model. Likewise, the museum-school partnership in Acton, Massachusetts, between the Discovery Museums and Uxbridge Public School, is an innovative concept in inquiry-based learning. The imaginative possibilities that children's museums offer in this regard are endless.

Many children's museums are cognizant of the fact that the paramount "hands-on" or interactive philosophy is still useful, but it is imperative to go beyond. Thus, the idea of the narrative museum is gaining currency. Lisa Roberts points out that learning is an interpretive activity, which involves a constant negotiation between the stories given by museums and those brought by visitors. These visitors include children and their families from all walks of life and various strata of society.

## The Future of Children's Museums

With the current concern about the plight of children, there is growing awareness of the importance of institutions such as children's museums. These places have the potential to enhance the lives of disadvantaged children.

Although many museums have genuinely intensified their efforts to reach out to less fortunate groups of our society, more needs to be done.

Janet Rice Elman argues that social problems such as poverty, crime, and violence have had a corrosive effect on families and communities, and communities have responded to these challenges by creating new institutions, which include children's museums. In this context, these places have become safe gathering spaces and function as contemporary "town squares." The impetus that results from community involvement in the creation of children's museums affords a deeper appreciation for children's issues in the contemporary world. The last two decades have witnessed an emphasis on the concept of children's recreation and leisure activity, particularly in urban areas. As our cities and suburban areas become more and more inimical to the young, children's museums make significant contributions by providing alternative activities that have cultural value for children—an aspect mostly ignored by commercial enterprises that cater to children. It would not be an exaggeration to predict that the role of children's museums in the twenty-first century will become even more consequential.

*See also:* Childhood and Play, Museum Movements

**BIBLIOGRAPHY**

Association of Children's Museums. *2002–2003 ACM Membership Directory.* Washington D.C.: Association of Children's Museums (ACM), 2002.

Cleaver, Joanne. *Doing Children's Museums: A Guide to 265 Hands-On Museums.* Charlotte, Vt.: Williamson Publishing Company, 1992.

Din, Herminia Weihsin. "A History of Children's Museums in the United States, 1899–1997: Implications for Art Education and Museums Education in Museums." Ph.D. dissertation, Ohio State University, 1998.

Elman, Janet Rice. "The Role of Children's Museums in the Twenty-first Century." Association of Children's Museums (ACM). Home page at http://www.childrensmuseums.org.

Haider, Jawaid. "The Invisible Child and the City: Fostering Play and Interplay in the Design of Public Space." First European Congress and Trade Show Proceedings, Child in the City Foundation. The Netherlands, September 2002, pp. 1–7.

Moore, Robin. *Childhood's Domain: Play and Place in Child Development.* Berkeley, Calif.: MIG Communications, 1990.

Pitman-Gelles, Bonnie. *Museums, Magic, and Children: Youth Education in Museums.* Washington, D.C.: Association of Science-Technology Centers, 1981.

Platten, Marvin Roger. "The Effects of a Museum Esthetic Education Program on Self-Concept: Selected Attitudes and School Absences of Elementary School Children." Ph.D. dissertation, Texas Tech University, 1976.

Roberts, Lisa C. *From Knowledge to Narrative: Educators and the Changing Museum.* Washington, D.C.: Smithsonian Institution Press, 1997.

UNICEF. Partnerships to Create Child-Friendly Cities: Programming for Child Rights with Local Authorities. UNICEF Brochure, 2001, pp. 1–8.

Zervos, Cassandra. "Children's Museums: A Case History of the Foundations of Model Institutions in the United States." Master's thesis, Pennsylvania State University, 1990.

*Jawaid Haider*

# CHILDREN'S READING

Learning to read is a primary task of childhood; reading for pleasure is often regarded as a form of play. Over the past 200 years, children's recreational reading in America has thrived in two different ways: The provision of adult-approved literature has flourished and expanded through a variety of institutions, and the success of direct marketing of less literary texts straight to children has raised adult questions of whether any and all reading is good for a child.

## Early Days

This duality between approved and popular reading became apparent early. John Newbery, a London bookseller, was the world's first children's publisher, and he packaged books and toys together. His first book specifically for children, *A Little Pretty Pocket Book* (1744), sold for sixpence, or eightpence if packaged with a ball for boys or a pincushion for girls. The marketing of books and commodities together and the strong gender bias of the sales pitch are familiar elements to today's book-buying public and clearly have strong historical roots.

Newbery operated out of London but exported books to the American colonies, where his books were also widely pirated. He also produced an early children's magazine, inaugurating a format that would increase in importance over subsequent centuries.

In the first half of the nineteenth century, adults emphasized the provision of useful knowledge, and all children's reading was designed to be "good" for children, to make them better people because of what they read (Avery, pp. 78–81). The Sunday school library was often the only reliable source of books for children. Public schools, where they existed, were not open year-round. By 1850, there were nearly 2,000 Sunday school libraries in the United States (Lerner, p. 155). The American Sunday School Union set up preselected libraries of 100 volumes in many isolated communities. Sunday school books purveyed images of diligence and spiritual grace; temperance and antigambling tracts were also popular.

The second half of the nineteenth century marked the start of a recognizably more modern scene. Public libraries became significant players in the book universe Serious services to children began in the last decade of the century, and public and school librarians began their long reign as gatekeepers of quality, vetting titles for literary virtues and introducing countless children to the joys of reading.

## Marketing Directly to Children

During this same half-century, however, dime novels also attracted the attention of many children. These cheap paperback novels told sensational Western and detective stories written by hack writers, using numerous pseudonyms. Indeed, one persuasive argument for the establishment of children's public libraries was the need to provide an uplifting alternative to the lurid offerings of the dime novel series.

In 1900, the publication of one single novel presaged many developments that distinguish current reading developments. *The Wizard of Oz* was a huge success and led its creator, L. Frank Baum, and several successors to produce endless sequels. Baum organized publicity tours, created a marketing film for the book as early as 1908, and, in 1913, produced a full-length feature movie based on the characters (*The Patchwork Girl of Oz*). The huge success of the 1939 MGM musical film version was an important but relatively late stage in the transmogrification of the *Oz* fiction from print to other media. Baum also indefatigably marketed spin-off souvenirs and toys from *Oz*.

Librarians disliked the *Oz* books. They also decried another publishing phenomenon of the early twentieth century: the success of the Stratemeyer Syndicate and its endless proliferation of series books. Edward Stratemeyer, originally a dime novelist, established a workshop of writers who pseudonymously produced series novels from plot outlines. Many much-loved series were produced in this way: Nancy Drew, the Bobbsey Twins, the Hardy Boys, Tom Swift, the Rover Boys. Some of these series continue to be published but often are written in simpler language and tell more violent stories. By the early 2000s, series books were still often highly gender-specific in their appeal.

During the early twentieth century, such books were regarded with something of the same horror that today greets violent video games. The chief librarian of the Boy Scouts of America complained vigorously about the Stratemeyer series in 1914:

> The fact is . . . that the harm done [by sensational cheap novels] is incalculable. I wish I could label each one of these books: "Explosives! Guaranteed to Blow Your Boy's Brains Out." . . . [A]s some boys read such books, their imaginations are literally "blown out," and they go into life as terribly crippled as though by some material explosion they had lost a hand or foot (Mathiews, p. 653).

As late as 1991, series books remained the subject of harsh, though slightly less apocalyptic criticism in *Harper's Magazine*. Tom Engelhardt slammed current series books as a form of bland and heavily marketed product with no literary qualities. He charged that publishers encourage children's dependency on series labels, in hopes that it will lead to adult commitment to equally simplistic brands of series titles.

## Promoting Literature

Meanwhile, through the early twentieth century, public librarians in particular were championing higher-quality reading, and doing all they could to promote the publication and purchase of good literature for children. Many of the most prestigious annual awards for children's books date from this era; the Newbery Medal for best children's book was first awarded by the American Library Association in 1922, the Caldecott Medal for best picture book in 1938.

Picture books have been an important part of children's literature from the very beginning. The combination of improved production technologies and increased access to relatively expensive books through public libraries meant that the early twentieth century saw a remarkable growth in the number of wonderful picture books for children of all ages. When the development of the paperback democratized access to books of all kinds in midcentury, the picture book became much more widely available. Over the latter half of the twentieth century, access to a reasonable range of picture books and novels began to be considered part of every American child's intellectual birthright. Good books could also be cheap books.

By mid-twentieth century, another development altered the shape of young people's reading: the creation of a market for literature directed at young adults, or teenagers. Not everyone agrees on what title qualifies as the first young adult novel, but the demarcation of the young people's reading into children's and young adult became more pronounced as the century moved to its end.

## Issues of Representation

As access to books became more broadly democratic, other questions became more urgent. White, middle-class publishers and librarians had not really registered how much the world of children's literature was exclusively white, nor how examples of overt racism slid into many stories, but in the 1960s and 1970s, the question of racism in children's books began to draw significant attention. For example, the first edition of *The Bobbsey Twins*, which would have been considered wholesome fare by many, tells us how Flossie ensured that the "colored" doll given her by the family servants would not contaminate her other dolls: "Flossie always took pains to separate Jujube from the rest by placing the cover of a pasteboard box between them" (Hope, p. 57). Changes in general social attitudes played a role in the diminution of such appalling observations, but a broader book-buying public also had a role to play. By the early 2000s, children's literature often valorized multicultural tolerance, but antiracist campaigners and librarians still sometimes clashed over such values as what is legitimate freedom of speech, and what is hateful and harmful to minority children. Some children's books play it safe by presenting one or two token "multicultural" characters, or by addressing only the "exotic" aspects of different cultures (sometimes known as the "fun, food, and festivals" approach). There are also serious questions about how children's books tackle the issue of racism, and how historical fiction in particular deals with the kind of derogatory language that was common in the past. The temptation to sanitize what children are told about the world is still strong.

## New Media

Radio and film arrived more or less together in American cultural life in the early twentieth century, and both challenged the role of novels as the prime source of fiction for young people (outside the ongoing role of oral storytelling, of course). Adaptation and cross-marketing moved in both directions: The new media adapted novels into movies and radio plays, and books told stories about media plots and characters.

The second half of the twentieth century saw the domestic triumph of television and then videos, the latter of which, like books, could be replayed at will. Toward the end of the century, computers entered the mix of entertainment options available to many children in their homes. Research in the early 2000s suggests that reading is one option among many for today's young people. A 1999 report from the Kaiser Family Foundation, based on a national survey, found that more than eight out of ten children read or are read to on a typical day, and that children on average spend about three-quarters of an hour on pleasure reading every day (Rideout et al., 1999, p. 30). However, there is little doubt that screen media of various kinds are very important even to the youngest children. A more recent report indicates that children aged from six months to six years are exposed to a wide variety of media in their homes (Rideout et al., 2003, p. 2). However, the reading percentages remain constant. Eight out of ten of these small children spend an average of nearly fifty minutes with books on a typical day and nearly all parents consider books "very important" to their children's development (Rideout et al., 2003, p. 9).

Conventional wisdom is that television and computer games are driving out reading, but much contemporary evidence suggests that the proportion of committed readers has not changed greatly over the century. What children read and whether the adults in their lives perceive it as a valuable use of their time are different questions. Today's marketing priorities often inculcate an obsessive approach to texts, so children feel they must read (and often own) everything available on a particular topic—the books, the videos, the trading cards, the computer games. Reading is often only one part of an intensely cross-media fictional experience.

Although funding for school libraries diminished over the last quarter of the twentieth century in the face of heavy spending on computers, at the start of the twenty-first century, First Lady Laura Bush, a librarian herself, sponsored new initiatives to support school libraries. The dynamic of the gatekeeper and the free market will continue to influence children's reading for the foreseeable future.

*See also:* Childhood and Play, Comic Book Reading, Comic Magazines, Commercialization of Children's Play, Television's Impact on Youth and Children's Leisure

## BIBLIOGRAPHY

Association for Library Service to Children. *The Newbery and Caldecott Awards: A Guide to the Medal and Honor Books.* Chicago: American Library Association, 2002.

Avery, Gillian. *Behold the Child: American Children and Their Books 1621–1922.* Baltimore: Johns Hopkins University Press, 1994.

Billman, Carol. *The Secret of the Stratemeyer Syndicate: Nancy Drew, the Hardy Boys, and the Million-Dollar Fiction Factory.* New York: Ungar, 1986.

Cart, Michael. *From Romance to Realism: 50 Years of Growth and Change in Young Adult Literature.* New York: HarperCollins, 1996.

Engelhardt, Tom. "Reading May Be Harmful to Your Kids." *Harper's Magazine* (June 1991): 55–62.

Greenfield, Eloise. "Writing for Children—A Joy and a Responsibility." In *The Black American in Books for Children: Readings in Racism.* 2d edition. Edited by Donnarae MacCann and Gloria Woodard. Metuchen, N.J.: Scarecrow Press, 1985.

Hearn, Michael Patrick. "Introduction." In *The Annotated Wizard of Oz.* Centennial edition. Edited by Michael Patrick Hearn. New York: W. W. Norton and Company, 2000.

Hope, Laura Lee. *The Bobbsey Twins.* New York: Grosset and Dunlap, 1904.

Johnson, Deidre. *Edward Stratemeyer and the Stratemeyer Syndicate.* New York: Twayne Publishers, 1993.

Lerner, Fred. *The Story of Libraries: From the Invention of Printing to the Computer Age.* New York: Continuum, 1998.

Long, Harriet G. *Public Library Service to Children: Foundation and Development.* Metuchen, N.J.: Scarecrow Press, 1969.

McQuillan, Jeff. "Seven Myths about Literacy in the United States." *Practical Assessment, Research & Evaluation* 6, no. 1 (1998). Available from http://ericae.net/pare.

Mathiews, Franklin K. "Blowing Out the Boy's Brains." *The Outlook* 108, no. 12 (November 18, 1914): 652–654.

Rideout, Victoria J., Ulla G. Foehr, Donald F. Roberts, and Mollyann Brodie. *Kids & Media @ the New Millennium: A Comprehensive National Analysis of Children's Media Use.* Menlo Park, Calif.: Kaiser Family Foundation Report, 1999.

Rideout, Victoria J., Elizabeth A. Vandewater, and Ellen A. Wartella. *Zero to Six: Electronic Media in the Lives of Infants, Toddlers and Preschoolers.* Menlo Park, Calif.: Kaiser Family Foundation Report, 2003.

*Margaret Mackey*

# CHORAL SINGING

Choral singing can refer to either a choir or a chorus. Church singing groups are usually called choirs, as are small, professionally trained groups. Large secular groups are referred to as choruses. Choral groups can be all-male, all-female, or mixed-voice, for which a common model is SATB: soprano, alto, tenor, and bass. This article discusses the history and development of choral singing in the United States, opportunities for choral singing, and the social, religious, and community functions of choral singing.

Choral singing in the United States has a history as old as the country itself. Some early religious groups of settlers in the seventeenth and eighteenth centuries maintained choirs. In the eighteenth century, traveling "Yankee tunesmiths" sold simple songbooks and formed choruses. In the East, those who valued orthodox musical learning looked instead to Europe's more sophisticated musical traditions for inspiration. This imitation of Europe contributed to the proliferation of choral groups in the nineteenth century, including the Handel and Haydn Society of Boston (1815), the Sacred Music Society of New York (1823), and choruses founded by émigrés from Germany and England. Black Americans developed a choral style combining African and European elements with vigor and expressiveness. In the early twentieth century, the United States saw a decline in choral singing except for church and college/university ensembles such as the St. Olaf Choir in Minnesota, and the Westminster Choir in Princeton, New Jersey. These choruses were often involved with the "a cappella choir movement," emphasizing unaccompanied singing. The renaissance of American choral music may have been in 1938, when Robert Shaw came to New York to add choral music to Fred Waring's popular radio program. Shaw, who died in 1999, set the global standard for choral music in the twentieth century with his various world-class choruses and meticulous directing techniques, and helped elevate choral singing to its current popularity.

Choral performance was the most popular form of public arts activity in the nation in 2004. Almost 29 million American adults and children performed regularly in one or more of approximately 250,000 choruses. Opportunities abounded for choral singing in the United States. Growing especially fast were children's choirs and affiliation choirs organized around ethnicity or lifestyle such as Jewish, Hispanic, Korean, black, and gay and lesbian choirs. Other opportunities included church and community choirs, barbershop quartets (and the women's Sweet Adelines), choruses associated with symphony orchestras, and university choruses, glee clubs, and small a cappella groups.

Choral singing's popularity may be attributed to its importance in social, community, and religious life. Not everyone can play an instrument, but almost everyone can participate in the communal experience of choral singing. Singing in church can create a sense of spiritual as well as literal harmony; community choirs such as the intentionally interethnic Berkeley Community Chorus help foster America's democratic culture. Singing in a choir can be a joyous, thrilling experience, using the most basic instrument—the voice—to create harmony, togetherness, and a sense of contributing to a whole greater than the self.

*See also:* Amateur Theatrics, Barbershop Quartets, Performing Arts Audiences, Slave Singing/Music Making, Traditional Folk Music Festivals

## BIBLIOGRAPHY

Keillor, Garrison. "The Power of Choral Singing." *Choral Journal* 41, no. 5 (December 2000): 43–45.

Smith, James G. "Chorus (i)." Grove Music Online. Available from http://www.grovemusic.com.

Sparks, John D. "Americans Rank Choruses as #1 Form of Arts Participation." *The Voice of Chorus America* 26, no. 3 (Spring 2003): 12–14.

Tobias, Sheila, and Shelah Leader. "Vox Populi to Music." *Journal of American Culture* 22, no. 4 (Winter 1999): 91–101.

*Rebecca E. Barry*

# CHRISTMAS

The history of Christmas in America is rich and diverse. Beginning as an occasion that was prohibited by the Puritans, it has become what is arguably the most elaborate and socially visible holiday in American culture. On the way to achieving this status, the "traditional" American Christmas has incorporated a variety of myths and traditions with both religious and nonreligious origins.

## Christmas and the Puritans

The Puritan movement against the holiday began in England in the seventeenth century, when they labeled the celebration of Christmas as "pagan" and an "Antichrist's Mass" (Whitaker, 2000, p. 72). In an effort to rid England of the holiday, Puritan soldiers went so far as to invade private homes on Christmas Day and put a stop to any feasting or celebrating they encountered. When the Puritans arrived in Massachusetts in 1620, they treated December 25 as an ordinary day. However, as immigrants began to import Christmas customs to the New World, the Puritans outlawed the celebration of Christmas, along with any "such ffestivalls as were superstitiously kept in other countrys, to the great dishonnor of God & offence of others" (Woodward, 1997, p. 32). Anyone feasting or

celebrating on Christmas Day, or choosing to take the day off from labor, was fined five shillings.

Stephen Nissenbaum observes the Puritans believed they had good reasons to outlaw Christmas, for at the time its celebration was characterized by a ritualistic inversion of the social order. During the holiday, the poor believed it was their right not only to call upon the wealthier members of society and demand gifts and money, but to celebrate these new acquisitions by drinking heavily and engaging in riotous behavior in the streets of the young New England cities. As Elizabeth Pleck observes, the colonial celebration of Christmas "was often celebrated as a drunken festival of carousing, begging, overeating, and masquerading" (p. 45). The Puritan law banning public celebrations of Christmas remained in place until 1681, when Charles II of England demanded its repeal.

## Emergence of Christmas as a National American Holiday

Although Christmas was reinstated, Americans did not regard it as a national holiday until the early nineteenth century. Penne Restad asserts, in fact, that until that time, most Americans, regardless of geographic location or religious beliefs, did not celebrate Christmas. Those who chose to celebrate the holiday did so by keeping their own personal or subcultural traditions. For example, planters in Virginia celebrated by feasting, gambling, dancing, and hunting, emulating what they believed to be the Christmas customs characteristic of the manor-born in England. In short, across the regions of the United States, there was no nationally recognized holiday or even similarity of traditions.

The national regard for Christmas changed in the nineteenth century when the many variants of the holiday began to converge into a "more singular and widely celebrated home holiday" (Restad, p. 13). During this time, Americans began to take old traditions and combine them with new symbols and traditions, to help create the Christmas Americans know today. The strongest reemergence of the holiday began in the Northeast. The industrialized, urbanized nature of that region meant its residents began to long for the intimacy they had felt in their towns or villages prior to the proliferation of large cities. As they began looking for something to unite them with a common past, they hit upon celebrating Christmas as the solution.

By the 1850s, the newfound tradition of Christmas was making its way to the South via the railroads and increased cross-country communication. These innovations helped disseminate ideas and customs to previously

*It's a Wonderful Life.* Actors James Stewart and Donna Reed take center stage as George and Mary Bailey in the 1946 holiday movie classic *It's a Wonderful Life.* The film, which was directed by Frank Capra, received a lukewarm response when it was first released but has since become one of the most beloved Christmas films. © *The Kobal Collection*

isolated areas of the country. Just a decade later, the Civil War further helped solidify the status of Christmas as a national holiday. Restad attributes this popularity to an increased desire for celebrations of the family in the wake of soldiers who had left home. The holiday also brought the message of peace and goodwill, which "spoke to the most immediate prayers of all Americans" (Restad, p. 13). While the war helped to promote the celebration of Christmas, much of the actual shaping of the modern holiday can be attributed to the Northern victory. Since the North gained control of the publishing trade and became the most powerful region of the country, myths and traditions that had begun in the immigrant-rich North became integral aspects of the American Christmas.

Around the end of the Civil War, Christmas also began to reemerge as a religious holiday. The first indication of this reappearance occurred in Sunday Schools during the 1860s and 1870s. During this time, the American Sunday School Society began integrating Christmas programs into their Sunday School lessons. According to Cynthia Hart, John Grossman, and Priscilla Dunhill, the

clergy had mixed feelings about these curricular materials, but became convinced that the teaching of the Nativity was a great learning tool for the children, as well as a way to boost attendance in churches.

## Elements of the Victorian Christmas

Although religion began to play an important part in the Christmas celebration, the establishment of what became known as the Victorian Christmas is attributed to Charles Dickens. Beginning in 1867 and 1868, Dickens began reading his popular work *A Christmas Carol* in sold-out theaters, with audiences of up to 35,000, painting the picture of "a glowing warmth of the family circle" (Hart, Grossman, and Dunhill, p. 75). The popularity of Dickens's tale contributed to the strong emergence of Christmas as a family holiday in Victorian times. This new emphasis on the family was supported by the widespread adoption of the Christmas feast, which typically required several weeks of preparation, and resulted in dinners of three or four hours in length with up to eight courses

**Christmas celebration.** A family gathers together in its living room to celebrate Christmas by singing carols. Suppressed in Puritan times, carols first became popular during the Victorian era. © *Corbis*

(Hart, Grossman, and Dunhill, p. 75). A family Christmas program, in which celebrants would contribute tableaux, recitals, and music for entertainment, and would participate in group sing-alongs and parlor games, followed the family dinner. Such games included snap dragon, a game where players tried to retrieve raisins out of a dish after the rim was set on fire, as well as blind man's bluff, drop the handkerchief, musical chairs, charades, and reenactments of historical events.

## Christmas Symbolism

During the nineteenth century, many myths and rituals definitive of the modern Christmas celebration began to emerge. One of the most prolific and enduring symbols of the American Christmas is the image of Santa Claus. Joe Woodward argues that the original character of Santa Claus is largely based on the Catholic Saint Nicholas. He asserts that a combination of Saint Nicholas's alleged generosity toward children, combined with the fact that his death fell just nineteen days before Christmas, makes him the most likely model for this figure. Although the Puritans had attempted to suppress interest in Saint Nicholas

(as well as all other saints), the character reemerged under the names of "Father Christmas" and "Kris Kringle" in England and Germany, respectively.

Woodward dates the broad dissemination of the Santa Claus figure to the American public to 1809, when Washington Irving included the character in a collection of Dutch-American tales entitled *The Knickerboeker History* (1995). Publication of this book seemed to greatly enhance the popularity of Santa Claus, because shortly after, a children's book entitled *The Children's Friend* featured a character called "Santeclaus" driving a sleigh pulled by reindeer. While these pieces of literature helped to introduce Santa Claus, Woodward maintains the Santa Claus myth we know today really captured the attention of the American public in 1822, when Clement C. Moore wrote the poem "The Night Before Christmas." The article states that this poem introduced the "eight tiny reindeer" concept along with the description of Santa Claus that was fashioned after Moore's childhood memories of white-bearded Dutch merchants who carried leather bells and wore red coats. While the concept of Santa Claus was now firmly entrenched in the minds of Americans, the final step in the visualization of the Santa Claus image occurred forty years later during the Civil War, when the cartoonist Thomas Nast drew the jolly, portly, costumed version of Santa Claus that became the standard for future journalistic and commercial depictions.

A second major symbol of the American Christmas is the Christmas tree. While this artifact was already in existence as far back as the 1300s, Hart, Grossman, and Dunhill attribute its inclusion in the American celebration to a custom imported by German settlers in Pennsylvania. Pleck observes that by the 1830s, neighbors were invited to see the trees decorated by German families. By 1848, the Christmas tree was a commodity in Pennsylvania markets. However, the success of the tradition is attributed to a New York merchant, Mark Carr, who began selling Christmas trees on the New York City docks in 1851. Hart, Grossman, and Dunhill report that less than thirty years later, there were as many as 400 tree merchants in New York City alone, with tree sales amounting to up to 200,000 a year.

Soon to follow the popularity of Christmas trees was Christmas tree decoration. Penne Restad states that the early Christmas tree decorations were homemade items, consisting of strings of nuts, popcorn, and beads. However, it was not long before an entire industry devoted to Christmas ornaments emerged in the United States. In 1870, merchants began to import large quantities of German ornaments and sell them in the marketplaces. Such items as wax angels and metal and glass-based decorations, which were vastly different from the original homemade food-based ornaments, began to dominate the Christmas trees of Americans. Most ornaments were based on popular styles and materials of the time, but some aspects of the Christmas tree decoration also have religious origins. Woodward attributes the custom of lighting the Christmas tree to Martin Luther, who fixed candles onto his fir tree to "remind children of heaven" (1997, p. 34). He adds that the tradition of placing a star atop the tree was meant to symbolize the Bethlehem star that the Magi followed on Christmas Eve.

Another Christmas tradition that emerged in the mid-nineteenth century was that of exchanging Christmas cards. A New York storeowner named R. H. Pease created the first American-made Christmas card in the 1850s (Restad). However, the expansion of the Christmas card custom was largely due to the entrepreneurial efforts of Louis Prang, a German immigrant. In 1870, Prang owned approximately two-thirds of the printing presses in America and first distributed the cards at the 1873 International Exhibition. After this event, he added a Christmas greeting to the cards and introduced them to America

in 1875. Restad observes that the increased mobility and urbanization of America meant people viewed Christmas cards as adequate substitutes for the more time-consuming traditions of Christmas letters and visits.

The 1870s and 1880s similarly saw the rise of the American gift-giving tradition at Christmas. Prior to these decades, gifts had played only a small role in family Christmas celebrations. Personal gifts became regarded as a way to sort out and maintain personal relationships; likewise, gifts were used as a means of offering charity to the less fortunate. The blossoming of gift popularity led to a divide between store-bought and homemade gifts, and this discrepancy ultimately led to the introduction of another tradition: gift wrapping. In short, the wrapping of presents heightened the experience of receiving a "special something," and also helped to transform the gift from an ordinary commodity that anyone could buy to an item that would be properly regarded as a gift.

Another popular holiday tradition is the singing of Christmas carols. Ian Bradley states that Christmas carols were suppressed by the Puritan regime, only to be rediscovered in Victorian times. Moreover, a voluminous amount of new carols were written during this era. Many of these carols were written with more than religious themes in mind. For example, a popular theme of Victorian carols was moralizing, through such lyrics as "Christian children all must be, mild, obedient, good as He" from Cecil Frances Alexander's carol "Once in Royal David's City" (Bradley, p. 42). It was during the Victorian era that the sentiment for a "white Christmas" became popular, through Christina Rosetti's "In the Bleak Mid-Winter," which added snow to the Nativity story.

Other Christmas myths that remain somewhat popular include hanging mistletoe and holly wreaths. Woodward observes that the hanging of mistletoe began as a Dutch fertility symbol; subsequently, the English borrowed both the tradition and the meaning and brought it to America. The holly wreath is derived from religious origins, which according to Woodward symbolized Christ's blood, placed into a wreath to symbolize Gods' eternity.

## Christmas Shopping

Despite the growing popularity of Christmas, gifts, cards and wrappings, the creation of the holiday shopping season is attributed to something else entirely besides the Christmas Spirit. Richard Henderson observes that, while there was a large surplus of mass-manufactured goods at the beginning of the nineteenth century, sluggish economic times meant there was essentially no market for them. Thus, leaders of the Industrial Revolution felt compelled to devise ways to boost sales that would permeate the consciousness of Americans who were just beginning to embrace the tenets of consumer culture. Henderson credits Philadelphia merchant John Wanamaker, founder of one of the first department stores in the United States, as being the driving force for the proliferation of commercial Christmas gifts, through the invention of new advertising media as well as innovative retailing techniques. Prior to Wanamaker's efforts, holiday gifts had been given more commonly at New Year's, but there was no real organized effort by retailers to encourage people to exchange gifts.

Other innovations in technology also helped to encourage people to purchase items beyond the traditional gifts of Bibles and decorative books that had dominated the early decades of the 1800s. Henderson credits the inventions of lightbulbs and plate glass, which were used to create window displays, with the development of the pastime of window shopping. This activity, he argues, helped lure shoppers into the stores, increasing their desire for mass-marketed goods. Moreover, the advent of cast iron as a building material allowed retailers to create much larger retail establishments than ever before, with more room for displays. All of these factors combined to help encourage consumers to embrace the concept of Christmas shopping as real and important ritual work.

## Controversies Surrounding Christmas

As Christmas became reconfigured as more of a commercial holiday, two objections to this transition arose. The first was from religious conservatives, who argued it was important to "put the Christ back in Christmas" (Pleck, p. 44), and to focus on making the celebration one that focused on heavenly virtues such as charity and sacrifice, rather than more earthly desires. The second controversy emerged as the nation began to engage in a dialogue around the issue of what it means to live in an increasingly multicultural, multiethnic society. John Leo argues that the underlying Christian theme of Christmas means those who embrace other religions such as Judaism and Islam—as well as those who do not share a European heritage—feel excluded from such a culturally pervasive celebration. Elizabeth Pleck asserts that Jews have responded by elevating Hanukkah, a relatively minor holiday that occurs around the same time as Christmas, to a more elaborate holiday. Leo asserts that, rather than trying to include these new religions, civic authorities have taken steps to eliminate any religious theme or allusion to Christmas. Such measures include the banning of Christmas trees, Nativity scenes, and poinsettias in public places, and banning religious themes in workplaces. Moreover, the pervasiveness of Christmas has led to a reemergence of the debate on religion in schools, and even the banning of holiday celebrations from the curriculum by some educators.

Even as the commercial and religious aspects of Christmas and the holiday season are rescinded in schools and workplaces, those same themes seem to have become more entrenched in the media. Both Elizabeth Pleck and Jeremy Lott contend that portrayals of Christmas in films have become "a normal part of the holiday hustle and bustle" (Lott, p. 45). Christmas movies now encompass all film genres, from children's movies to comedy to religion to drama. Moreover, producers in both the television and film industry have even satirized the commercialism that drives their own business. Lott offers the film *Jingle All the Way*, which jokes about parents fighting over the "hot toy" of the Christmas season, as an example of this phenomenon.

In summary, Christmas in America has had a long and often controversial history. No doubt the Puritans would be dismayed at the way Christmas has captured the American consciousness—and checkbook—with a vengeance. The celebration of Christmas has affected many segments of American society, including religion, tourism, shopping, entertaining, and media offerings. Moreover, many of its traditions—such as decoration of trees and gift wrapping—have contributed to the growth of other holidays. Finally, Christmas has become one of the central engines driving American consumer culture today.

*See also:* Easter

## BIBLIOGRAPHY

Bradley, Ian. "Sing Choirs of Angels." *History Today* 28 (December 1998): 42–47.

Carrier, James. *Gifts and Commodities: Exchange and Western Capitalism Since 1700.* London: Routledge, 1995.

Hart, Cynthia, John Grossman, and Priscilla Dunhill. *Joy to the World.* New York: Workman Publishing, 1990.

Henderson, Richard. "Christmas Shopping." *Billboard* 113, no. 22 (September 2001): 63.

Leo, John. "Undecking the Halls." *U.S. News and World Report* 24 (December 2001): 47.

Lott, Jeremy. "It's a Wonderful Movie." *Newsmagazine* 131 (16 December 2002): 45.

Nissenbaum, Stephen. *The Battle for Christmas.* New York: Alfred A. Knopf, 1997.

Pleck, Elizabeth H. *Celebrating the Family: Ethnicity, Consumer Culture, and Family Rituals.* Cambridge, Mass.: Harvard University Press, 2000.

Restad, Penne. "Christmas in Nineteenth-Century America." *History Today* 45 (December 1995): 13–19.

Whitaker, Mark. "When Christmas Was Illegal." *New States-man* 129 (25 December 2000): 72.

Woodward, Joe. "The Enduring Power of Saint Nicholas." *Alberta Report* 23 (18 December 1995): 24.

———. "A Ffestivall Superstitiously Kept." *Alberta Report* 25 (22 December 1997): 32.

*Cele C. Otnes*

# CHURCH SOCIALS

Social events are an important part of the religious lives of many Americans. Religious congregations organize a wide variety of socials, including coffee hours or receptions before or after services, formal dinners, less formal "potlucks" (with the food brought by participants), and events for children and youth. These events play important religious and social roles for congregations and their members.

While colonial Americans no doubt met informally before or after services, organized church socials first became common in the mid- to late nineteenth century. These events—such as picnics and excursions—were important on the frontier and in the growing cities but for different reasons. On the frontier families were widely scattered; churches may have been the only social organization available. In the city, on the other hand, there were too many temptations, particularly for young men and women. There churches had lots of competition for people's attention and time—including amusement parks, restaurants, pool halls, and the dreaded saloon. In this competition, church social events provided morally safe entertainment.

Soon church social events became more organized and elaborate. By the early twentieth century, gender-segregated formal meals for men and women mimicked the grand banquets of the larger culture. National organizations, such as the Epworth League, brought young people together for food, games, and sports. The league offered local chapters suggested party themes, including "literary salad," "illustrated nursery rhymes," and a "rose lawn party." These events provided Christian youths with a place to meet and court within a controlled environment. After World War II the church followed its members into the rapidly growing suburbs; many congregations built well-equipped social halls, complete with kitchens and bowling alleys. These facilities were a social island on the suburban frontier, and gave baby boom families a welcome outlet. By the end of the twentieth century some larger congregations had food services with professional cooks and food courts.

To an outsider these social events don't seem "religious." They rarely have explicit theological or ritual meanings, and they usually mimic more secular events. But they play important roles in participants' religious lives, both theologically and socially. Church socials create community among members of a congregation, building what Christian theology calls "the body of Christ." They echo the Eucharist—also known as communion—Christianity's food-centered ritual. In these formal and informal meals Christians believe they are offering God's hospitality to one another.

Church socials also have social functions. They provide entertainment in a "safe" environment, especially for children. They keep youth and young adults coming to the church, and they provide a place for courtship within the Christian community. They often reinforce traditional gender roles, with women doing most of the cooking and men doing the preaching, although that began to change in the 1970s.

Social events for a religious congregation are not exclusively Christian; other religious traditions have discovered the social value of such events. They do seem, however, to be uniquely American, responding to particular characteristics of American culture, including the social needs of a mobile population and the competition for the time and attention of church members.

*See also:* Traditional Folk Music Festivals

**BIBLIOGRAPHY**

Humphrey, Theodore C., and Lin T. Humphrey. *We Gather Together: Food and Festival in American Life.* Logan: Utah State University Press, 1991.

Sack, Daniel. *Whitebread Protestants: Food and Religion in American Culture.* New York: St. Martin's Press, 2000.

*Daniel Sack*

# CIRCUSES

The American circus represents a synthesis of various international entertainment traditions. The traveling menagerie, clowning, acrobatics, trick riding, wire walking, juggling, and sleight of hand all coalesced inside a circular arena surrounded by an outer ring of spectators

**Circus poster.** A poster announces Barnum & Bailey's "Greatest Show on Earth"—formed by P. T. Barnum (1810–1891) and James Bailey (1847–1906) in 1881. In the foreground are the railroad cars that made it easy to move the huge circus around the country. © *Corbis*

that came to define this unique form of entertainment. The birth of the American circus roughly correlated with the birth of the nation; the circus's growth and development—from the relative intimacy of the early one-ring show, to a gargantuan Gilded Age aggregation—paralleled the nation's transformation from a pastoral society to an industrial powerhouse.

### The Early American Circus: 1792–1865

An English trick rider, John Bill Ricketts, brought the circus to the United States in 1792 when he opened a riding school in Philadelphia, the new nation's most populous city. Ricketts was a pupil of the English horseman Philip Astley, who started a school for trick riders in London in 1768. Opening his inaugural show in April 1793, Ricketts's program included rope walking, clowning, and acrobatic riding. His respectable audience of

Philadelphia society (including President George Washington) was suitably impressed. Ricketts and subsequent competitors performed in ungainly, expensive wooden arenas in profitable urban centers like New York City and Boston, where they stationed themselves for months at a time before moving to the next city. However, these wooden arenas were tinderboxes. Although many showmen forbade smoking at the circus, devastating fires were common and forced several proprietors out of business. Ricketts journeyed into Maine and the Canadian wilderness in 1797, but other showmen stayed in the lucrative urban market. Competition became so fierce by 1800 that Ricketts departed the U.S. mainland, sailed for the West Indies, and vanished at sea.

The horse was the primary animal star at these early shows. Although the elephant and tiger have achieved iconic status in defining "circus" in the contemporary cultural imagination, neither animal was part of the first

American circuses. All were exhibited in a then separate entertainment, the traveling animal menagerie. Showing at tavern yards, town squares, and theaters since the seventeenth century, scraggly menageries roamed under cover of darkness so that residents would not get a free "peek" at the animals. A lion first arrived in 1716; a tiger initially came in 1806; and the eventual marquee animal feature of the circus, the elephant, first landed in 1796. The ship captain Jacob Crowninshield, a native of Salem, Massachusetts, purchased the youthful female elephant for $450 in Bengal, India, but promptly sold her for a reported $10,000 shortly after reaching New York City on 13 April 1796. Exhibited from Providence, Rhode Island, to New Orleans, Louisiana, over the next nine years, "Rajah" dazzled thousands of people, including President John Adams, wherever she was shown. Indeed, the experience of "seeing the elephant" was so profound that this phrase soon became a metaphor for experiencing battle. Other profitable menagerie elephants followed "Rajah," including "Old Bet," an African female pachyderm, who toured the eastern seaboard from 1804 to 1816, and "Little Bet," another female, who was exhibited from 1817 to 1826. Both elephants were shot and killed by provincial northeastern spectators for reasons unknown.

Old Bet and Little Bet were owned by a businessman named Hachaliah Bailey (1775–1845), based in Somers, New York, who became a powerhouse in the traveling menagerie business in the 1830s. As legend has it, Bailey and his partners declared that they would "put [their] foot down flat" to play the state of New York exclusively as a monopoly operation. Critics subsequently referred to this combination as the "Flatfoots." Another Somers showman named Joshua Purdy Brown (1802?–1834) adopted the canvas tent in 1825. Able to set up and tear down with relative speed and little capital, Brown moved his circus into isolated rural areas and instituted the daily show stops that quickly came to define the American circus. In 1828, Brown was the first to merge the traveling animal menagerie with the circus, thus giving the circus its recognizably modern form. Brown's ability to move his nomadic tent show into the southern Mississippi River Valley and the old Northwest Territories was made possible by internal improvements such as roads and canals, and by new technologies like the steam ship. After the Erie Canal was finished in 1825, circus showmen had ready access to the Midwest, a burgeoning and profitable population center.

Giant steamship circuses containing upward of a thousand spectators glided down the Mississippi and the Ohio Rivers in antebellum America. These "river palaces," as they were known, treated audiences to tradi-tional circus acrobatics and animal acts, in addition to contemporary temperance dramas like *Ten Nights in a Bar Room*. A key circus figure in antebellum America was the clown; show proprietor Dan Rice (1823–1900) gained national visibility while performing this role on Gilbert "Doc" Spalding's (1812–1880) floating North American Circus in 1844. Endowed with an enormous voice, astonishing memory, and keen political wit, Rice dazzled audiences with his quick repartee and his menagerie of trained animals such as his blind, stair-climbing horse Excelsior Jr. Although Rice found his greatest fame on his own show, "Dan Rice's Great Show," a tent circus in the 1850s and 1860s, his rise to national prominence was launched on the river palaces. During the Civil War, the nation's riverine topography became a critical site for military sieges and the transport of troops and supplies, which consequently put an end to the age of the great river palaces. The Civil War also damaged the national profile of Dan Rice, who denounced abolitionism from the circus ring in New Orleans on the same night that Louisiana seceded from the Union.

## The Gilded Age Railroad Circus

Although the majority of circuses remained horse-drawn wagon shows until the expansion of the automobile in the 1920s, the largest outfits grew rapidly once they perfected the use of the railroad after the Civil War. A handful of circuses traveled by railroad in the 1830s, but they bore little resemblance to the giant railroad outfits of the 1880s and beyond. Smaller than their wagon show competitors, these early railroad shows contained no menagerie, sideshow, or street parade. They were barebones operations composed of a canvas big top, assembly equipment, a sparse collection of performers, and a few animals. Audiences felt cheated by these stripped down railroad shows and savvy wagon showmen responded accordingly in their advertising campaigns: "This is no railroad show!" Rail travel was cumbersome because track gauge was not yet nationally standardized, nor had circus proprietors created an effective system for loading and unloading their stock, tents, and supplies. Until the post–Civil War years, many so-called "railroad" circuses were also "gilley" shows because they carried all supplies from the railroad depot to the show grounds by hand, a dangerous and time-consuming procedure. Moreover, railroad travel was financially risky: Showmen had to pay all railroad-related costs up front, whereas wagon proprietors had only to purchase the lot rental and the license in advance. However, railroad travel afforded circus workers a sound rest between stops; in addition, a newly standardized transcontinental railroad from 1869 onward meant that circus showmen could now travel coast to coast. Indeed, just weeks after the completion of the first transcontinental railroad in 1869, Dan Castello's Circus and Menagerie, traveling overland part of the time, became the first American circus to make a transcontinental tour, thus effectively nationalizing the circus's marketplace.

In 1871, the museum proprietor, best-selling author, and former politician P. T. Barnum (1811–1891) entered the circus business with two seasoned circus partners from Wisconsin, W. C. Coup (1836–1895) and Dan Castello (1832?–1909). When their circus moved to the rails in 1872, Coup helped design special railroad cars that expedited the loading and unloading of the wagons. Railroad companies offered the largest railroad shows discounted rates, which allowed the circus to grow in terms of its scale and content. In 1880, Barnum merged his operations with those of the veteran proprietor James A. Bailey (1846–1906), and the following year, their three-ring circus was born. Thereafter, the biggest railroad circuses soon contained multiple rings, two stages, an outer hippodrome track, a sideshow, parade, grand entry, spectacle, menagerie, and after-show concert.

In the competitive Gilded Age marketplace, the biggest circuses became virtual monopolies and tried to run their competitors out of business with charges of fraud and by sheer physical intimidation. After the Ringling Bros. circus rose quickly from a small, midwestern wagon outfit in 1884 to a railroad show with a national market in 1890, the five Ringling brothers faced intense opposition from better-established shows like Barnum and Bailey, the Adam Forepaugh circus, and the Sells Brothers circus. The Ringling brothers constantly faced "sticker wars" as competing shows tore down their posters at future show stops and brawled with the Ringlings' advance advertising team.

Gilded Age showmen were pioneers in the nascent field of market research and advertising. In determining where to perform most profitably, circus proprietors analyzed complex variables such as an area's incidence of drought and rain, bank clearings, crop reports, factory conditions, and the number of resorts. Once they chose their route, they sent teams of "advance men" to blanket future show stops across the country with some 5,000 colorful posters per locality. In advance of "Circus Day," railroad companies offered audiences discounted "excursion fares" from distant hamlets to town for the day of the show. On Circus Day itself, towns became temporary cities as thousands of people from all walks of life flocked to the show. The elaborate set-up and tear-down of a ten-acre "tented city" was even part of the show as audiences

rose before dawn and stayed past dark to watch the workingmen's efficient, assembly line–style performance of labor. The scene was much the same in large urban centers. During the free morning parade, schools closed. Shops offered Circus Day bargains to keep folks in a spending mood—which the circus itself encouraged mightily as audiences parted with their money on concessions, an extra dime for the sideshow, or after-show concert.

## Circus Audiences

During the Gilded Age, P. T. Barnum and the Ringling brothers recognized women and children as an important audience base. In contrast to the rough-and-tumble adult male crowds, grifters, and gamblers who dominated the antebellum wagon shows, Gilded Age railroad showmen promoted their circuses as safe, respectable, educational family fare. Like Dan Rice had done during the 1850s, these proprietors targeted the growing middle class as their ideal audience. Well versed in the art of attracting middle-class customers when he owned the American Museum in New York City (1841–1868), P. T. Barnum emphasized propriety and wholesome entertainment, perhaps his biggest contribution to the American circus. He beckoned children to the show with half-price tickets (rationalizing that kids would be accompanied by full-paying adults). A vehement temperance advocate, Barnum stipulated that all of his employees remain sober.

In 1891, the Ringling brothers similarly began calling themselves a "New School of American Showmen" because they prohibited graft, alcohol, and gambling on the show grounds. By 1894, they were widely known as a "Sunday School" show that hired Pinkerton railroad detectives to ensure a crime-free environment. Both Barnum and Bailey's "Greatest Show on Earth" and the Ringling Bros. circus emphasized the high moral standards of their performers as well. In particular, showmen were eager to offset the potentially lurid implications of their female acrobats and riders who—by necessity of their athletic labor—wore tight leotards and brief skirts (which made them appear virtually nude according to the standards of the day). Proprietors crafted elaborate publicity stories of circus women's high moral standards, their modesty, superior physical stamina, their impending marriages, and their close relationships with their families in press releases that mirrored a nascent culture of celebrity.

Despite showmen's emphasis on wholesome propriety, they ultimately had little control over the some 20,000 people who flocked into town on Circus Day. Fights erupted, horse thieves and pickpockets prowled the grounds, men drank, idle teenagers set fires, and voyeurs peeked into the women's dressing tent. Some local residents, itching for travel and opportunity, even "ran away" with the circus once it rumbled to the next show stop. Given the racially diverse audiences that flocked to the show, Circus Day also served as an occasion for racial violence.

## The Changing Place of the Circus in American Culture

By 1900, the largest railroad circuses offered their audiences a dizzying window into the wider world, including a menagerie of exotic animals stationed alongside an ethnological congress of so-called "strange and savage tribes" from around the world, and a reenactment of historical or contemporary events such as key scenes from the American Revolution, Indian Wars, or the recent Spanish-American War (1898). But during the 1920s, the vast railroad circus began its gradual retreat. Fewer independent circuses existed because gigantic new combinations like the Ringling Bros. and Barnum and Bailey circus and the American Circus Corporation bought out competing shows. The largest showmen largely abandoned the free pre-show circus parade and the historical spectacle in an era when film and radio were offering audiences even more exacting facsimile representations of the world.

The circus faced other setbacks as well. During World War II, the circus traveled under the auspices of the Office of Defense Transportation, and attendance figures were solid; however, a tragic big-top fire at Hartford, Connecticut, in July 1944 killed 168 people. The tent had been waterproofed with a volatile mixture of paraffin and gasoline and consequently burst into flames by a lighted cigarette or match. The show's management vehemently declared that the federal government had denied the circus access to wartime priority fireproofing materials. But this claim was dubious; consequently, lawsuits and indictments followed, and the nation's largest circus nearly unraveled in the fire's aftermath.

Restive laborers provided yet another challenge to the American railroad circus: Faced with wage cuts, unionized circus workers engaged in a bitter, protracted strike in 1938, as part of the broader industrial labor movement during the Great Depression; and from 1955 to 1956, the Teamsters Union, under the leadership of Jimmy Hoffa, engaged in an unsuccessful but brutal union drive that prompted the showman John Ringling North to abandon the canvas big top in favor of indoor arenas—a move that dramatically reduced the workforce of the Ringling Bros. and Barnum and Bailey circus in 1956.

During the Cold War, the biggest circuses lost money, owing to rising railroad costs and falling attendance figures as consumers and capital moved to the suburban periphery. Moreover, popular tastes were changing. In the jet age, many audiences now considered the circus to be old fashioned. Recent transportation technologies—taken in conjunction with a burgeoning tourist industry—enabled Americans to visit faraway lands. Furthermore, new media like television and movie documentaries largely supplanted the circus as a site of education and amusement. Yet the circus's live (and thus unpredictable) presence has allowed it to endure, although in a truncated form. In the late twentieth century, this venerable American entertainment institution began to enjoy a renaissance. Nurtured in the vibrant, countercultural street theater scene of the 1960s, a new generation of circus performers and impresarios such as Hovey Burgess and Paul Binder created thriving new shows such as Circus Flora and the Big Apple Circus, whose one-ring intimacy echoed that of the antebellum circus. Furthermore, the American circus has been enlivened by the arrival of foreign circuses, most notably Cirque du Soleil ("circus of the sun"). Founded in Quebec by a French Canadian street performer named Guy Laliberté in 1984, this circus has become a global, multimillion-dollar enterprise. The show is animal free, which makes it a favorite among animal rights activists. It is also tremendously expensive: Ticket prices range from $45 to well over $150. Consequently, this "boutique circus" targets a mostly middle- and upper-class audience base, a shadow of a more democratic form of entertainment a hundred years ago that shut entire towns down across the nation on Circus Day.

*See also:* Carnivals; Gilded Age of Leisure and Recreation; Impresarios of Leisure, Rise of; Zoos

**BIBLIOGRAPHY**

Albrecht, Ernest. *The New American Circus.* Gainesville: University Press of Florida, 1995.

Carlyon, David. *Dan Rice: The Most Famous Man You've Never Heard Of.* New York: Public Affairs, 2001.

Dahlinger, Fred, and Stuart Thayer. *Badger State Showmen: A History of Wisconsin's Circus Heritage.* Baraboo, Wis.: Circus World Museum, 1998.

Davis, Janet M. *The Circus Age: Culture and Society Under the American Big Top.* Chapel Hill: University of North Carolina Press, 2002.

Hammarstrom, John Lewis. *Big Top Boss: John Ringling North and the Circus.* Urbana: University of Illinois Press, 1992.

Slout, William L. *Olympians of the Sawdust Circle: A Biographical Dictionary of the Nineteenth-Century American Circus.* San Bernardino, Calif.: Borgo Press, 1998.

Thayer, Stuart. *Traveling Showmen: The American Circus Before the Civil War.* Detroit, Mich.: Astley and Ricketts, 1997.

*Janet M. Davis*

# CITY PARKS

City parks can be defined as naturalistic areas in urban environments. Public markets, shared-use areas for keeping and grazing domestic animals, and places for religious, governmental, and other celebrations all contributed to the concept of open spaces for public use. These areas, however, were not the same as modern city parks. They were simply areas open to public use.

Areas that would more closely fit the idea of parks as areas of natural types of settings for passive and active enjoyment were originally the domain of nobility and the very rich. The Hanging Gardens of Babylon, very likely a terraced pyramid, complete with irrigation, are the best known from the ancient world. But park-like settings existed in almost all early cities as part of palaces or royal grounds.

The evolution of parks remained the purview of the rich for centuries. People of lesser means would not have had access to extensive green spaces in urban areas. Nor would they have had the means to escape to the countryside to catch a respite from urban life. Areas set aside for public exhibitions, fairs, festivals, and so on would have been the limits for most individuals.

## Early American City Parks

In America, the Boston Commons stands as an early example of shared space that evolved into a cherished city park. Originally set aside as pasturage and as a military parade ground, the Boston Commons evolved into an area used for more recreational pursuits. A public green space in the heart of a rapidly growing city became a "right" of all Bostonians over time. The exact moment that the Boston Commons became a park is unknowable. It is very likely that the idea took time to evolve and occurred at different times for people in Boston. Similar evolutions of open space in urban areas occurred throughout the United States.

The most famous example of park construction in the United States is, of course, Central Park in New York City. Initially, such a park was subject to tremendous heated debate among the citizens of New York City. De-velopers and park supporters were heavily at odds with one another in a manner remarkably similar to fights for city parks in the early 2000s.

A design competition for Central Park took place in 1857, and the ultimate winners were Calvert Vaux and Frederick Law Olmsted. Vaux, being an Englishman, was heavily influenced by the naturalistic design of rich country estates in England, while Frederick Law Olmsted was an American, though also heavily influenced by the naturalistic style of English manors. Olmsted's influence on American design through his own efforts and through his firm, which continued on well into the 1900s, is difficult to overestimate. Communities on both coasts and numerous places in between have parks designed by Olmsted and his firm. The deliberate placing of plant material and taking advantage of natural rolls of the land to open up and create view scapes is a trademark seen nationwide in city parks designed or influenced by Olmsted.

## Olmsted's Influence on City Parks

The popularity of such designs has led to fierce protection of Olmsted-designed parks to keep them from being altered in any manner by newer developments. Interestingly, this has led to strong advocates of city parks battling one another over design concepts, creating conflict that parallels that of preservationists and conservationists on the use of larger-scale lands. The point of conflict is whether parks should be preserved for activities that are primarily passive in nature or for pursuits that are more active in nature and require green space more as a backdrop.

The concept of "showcase" parks caught on quickly, and cities throughout the United States competed to create parks of a compellingly beautiful nature, each city trying to create something unique and different that would "balance" the ills of living in urban environments.

Variations on parks occurred quite frequently over time. Initially parks were very much in the Olmsted tradition—places to enjoy naturalistic scenes. Visitors to these parks were to enjoy them passively, meaning that they were to enjoy them at a leisurely and stately pace. Peaceful walks, picnics, enjoyment of nature, fishing, or rowing on ponds were typical pursuits. The point of the parks was to escape the hustle and bustle of the city, not to create more noisy and active areas.

## City Parks Evolve

The Boston Sand Gardens of the late 1800s created a different concept of city parks. The Boston Sand Gardens were to be a park where children could escape the dangers of the street to play in safety and to pursue wholesome activities. These parks were designed for activities where the landscape was secondary to the activity. And these parks were extremely successful. Children were no longer being a nuisance, bother, or hazard on the streets. Instead, they were drawn to parks that promised activities that were fun and enjoyable. The concept quickly spread to other cities throughout the United States.

Cook County, in Illinois, created forest preserves in the early 1900s. These areas were not landscaped as Olmsted-type parks were. Rather, these areas were supposed to be kept more or less in their natural state. Development was limited to appropriate activities that did not take away too greatly from the natural forest landscape. Trails, picnic areas, and open playfields were, and are, common features of such forest preserves. Similar types of such preserves are commonly found throughout the United States in the early twenty-first century.

Parks designed to accommodate sport activities also have a long history. The Olympic Games in ancient Greece, the Coliseums of the Roman Empire, and early horse-race tracks are common examples. More frequently thought of as playfields, sport areas are part of many parks. Activities such as organized baseball, soccer, softball, field hockey, lacrosse, and so on, can be found on such fields. Sport fields are the most activity-intensive areas of parks. Conflicts over the inclusion of sport fields in a park design are common. Managers of parks with mixed active and passive use make use of landscape design principles to separate active and passive users from each area for their own protection.

Linear parks are parks that are transportation corridors that preserve natural features along their length. The Emerald Necklace that Frederick Law Olmsted originally designed to connect the parks he designed in Boston is an example. The Emerald Necklace is still awaiting completion, but there has been a great deal of effort to move it along in the late 1990s and early 2000s. Such parks may be greenways that allow automobile use such as parkways in many eastern states. Or a linear park may make use of abandoned railroad beds as in the Rails-to-Trails program common across the United States.

The Rails-to-Trails Program emerged in the Midwest in the mid-1960s. This program converts railroad beds into hiking and biking trails. Such trails are also used by a host of others, some of whom are welcome, some not. Conflicts occur on such trails between those using the trails for passive enjoyment by walking or biking slowly and those who use the trails to practice sport activities such as running, race biking, skateboarding, and so on.

**Olmsted park.** This quiet, naturally landscaped pond in Seneca Park (Monroe County Park, Rochester, NY) is a perfect example of a park designed by Frederick Law Olmsted. Heavily influenced by the naturalistic style of English manors, American designer Olmsted was known for using the natural rolls of the land to open up and create viewscapes and for his deliberate placement of plants. *Courtesy of Edward Udd.*

Resolving these conflicts is a necessary task for many parks departments across the country.

## Benefits and Costs of City Parks

City parks help connect urban dwellers with their environment, and may even preserve or restore natural areas to close to pristine conditions. Contact with nature, even in urban environments, allows educators and nature interpreters a forum for allowing urban dwellers to understand their dependence on nature for their survival. And this connection can be made even in the middle of the concrete jungle that otherwise surrounds them.

To be sure, city parks also have their negative attributes. They can be perceived as, and sometimes are, dangerous places. Muggings are not unknown in some city parks, even during daylight hours. Some parks are home to drug dealers and to the mentally disabled turned loose to fend for themselves, and parks can act as gathering places for youth with no other place to gather late at night. Changes in design, increased patrolling by police, neighborhood cooperation and activism, and renewed interest in parks as a community asset are combating social problems that spill over into parks.

## City Parks Are Solidly in America's Future

City governments no longer need to sell the public on the need for parks as they once did. People in cities see parks as an amenity they do not wish to live without. City governments instead struggle with managing various demands put on parks. They struggle to find areas for new parks; they work to minimize inappropriate uses of parks; and they have to find creative ways to fund parks even when budgets may be very tight. The benefits of parks to cities have become very clear: the billions of dollars invested in park structures and real estate is evidence in and of itself. The political will of people to protect, maintain, and operate their parks continues without question across the country.

City parks continue to evolve. In many places, skateboard parks are appearing as areas to accommodate youth who otherwise would be out on the streets participating in their favorite activities. While skateboarders still persist in using inappropriate places for practice of their sport, the popularization of skateboarding via television coverage of extreme sports has served to legitimize both the sport and the appropriateness of skateboard parks, which emulate the venues used in competition. Cities, much like Boston with its Sand Gardens, would prefer children to play in environments safer than the streets. Increasing sensitivity to diverse users of parks is forcing park designers and managers to rethink how parks are designed and to what purpose. There is little doubt that conflicts will continue to occur about city parks. But what once was a radical, forward-thinking idea is now safely in the American mainstream. The social experiment of parks for people is a success.

*See also:* Botanical Gardens, Central Park, Park Movements

**BIBLIOGRAPHY**

Cross, Gary. *A Social History of Leisure: Since 1600.* State College, Pa.: Venture Publishing, 1990.

Ewert, Alan W., Rodney B. Eiser, and Alison Voight. "Conflict and the Recreational Experience." In *Leisure Studies: Prospects for the Twenty-First Century.* Edited by Edgar L. Jackson and Thomas L. Burton. State College, Pa.: Venture Publishing, 1999.

Frye, Mary V. *The Historical Development of Municipal Parks in the United States: Concepts and Their Application.* Ph.D. dissertation, University of Michigan, 1964.

Gobster, Paul H. "Urban Parks as Green Walls or Green Magnets?: Interracial Relations in Neighborhood Boundary Parks." *Landscape and Urban Planning* 41 (1998): 43–55.

———. "Visions of Nature: Conflict and Compatibility in Urban Park Restoration. " *Landscape and Urban Planning* 56 (2001): 35–51.

Goodale, Thomas, and Geoffrey Godbey. *The Evolution of Leisure.* State College, Pa.: 1995.

Hargett, Terra. "Restoring Urban Parks: New Life in Old Spaces." *American City and County* 116 (2001): 38–44.

Kelly, John R. "Sociological Perspectives on Recreation Benefits." In *Benefits of Leisure.* Edited by B. L. Driver, Perry J. Brown, and George L. Peterson. State College, Pa.: Venture Publishing, 1991.

Knudson, Douglas M., Ted T. Cable, and Larry Beck. *Interpretation of Cultural and Natural Resources.* State College, Pa.: Venture Publishing, 1995.

Merchant, Carolyn. *Major Problems in American Environmental History.* Lexington, Mass.: D. C. Heath, 1993.

Molnar, Donald J., and Albert J. Rutledge. *Anatomy of a Park.* New York: McGraw-Hill Book Company, 1986.

Nash, Roderick. *Wilderness and the American Mind.* New Haven, Conn.: Yale University Press, 2001.

Rosenzweig, Roy, and Elizabeth Blackmar. *The Park and the People: A History of Central Park.* Ithaca, N.Y.: Cornell University Press, 1992.

Rybczynski, Witold. *A Clearing in the Distance: Frederick Law Olmsted and America in the Nineteenth Century.* New York: Scribner, 1999.

Taylor, Dorceta E. "Central Park as a Model for Social Control: Urban Parks, Social Class and Leisure Behavior in Nineteenth-Century America." *Journal of Leisure Research* 31 (1999): 420–456.

Young, Terrence. "Modern Urban Parks." *The Geographical Review* 85 (1995): 535–546.

*Edward Udd*

# CIVIC CLUBS, MEN

Fraternal organizations—voluntary societies built about secret rituals, the encouragement of morality and close ties among members, and the practice of mutual aid—played a central role in nineteenth- and early twentieth-century American society. Developing out of eighteenth-century Freemasonry, fraternal orders became widespread in the 1840s. By 1910, perhaps one out of every three men (and a smaller, but significant, number of women) belonged to at least one. Although these organizations have become much less widespread since the 1930s, they still attract millions of Americans and provide hundreds of million dollars in charity.

## The First Fraternity

Freemasonry was the earliest and most influential fraternal society. Although it claimed ancient origins, the modern fraternity, with its ideal of brotherhood among men of different religious, political, and ethnic affiliations, emerged out of London trade organizations in the early eighteenth century. Lodges first met in England's Amer-

**Freemasons celebrate anniversary.** Thousands of freemasons attend the 275th anniversary of the formation of Grand Lodge in June 1992 at the Earls Court Convention Center in London, England. The Grand Lodge was formed when four separate London lodges merged creating the first Grand Lodge worldwide. © *Corbis*

ican colonies around 1730, by which time the fraternity had already spread through much of Great Britain and the European continent. Colonial Masonry was small, and limited to a select group of urban elites.

Although the Revolution disrupted lodges, it helped prepare the ground for further expansion. The Masonic membership of such leading patriots as Benjamin Franklin and George Washington helped to identify the order with a new nation also based on Enlightenment ideals of religion, learning, and self-sacrificing virtue. In a 1793 ceremony led by President Washington himself, Masons laid the cornerstone of the United States Capitol. Many other public buildings received a similar dedication. By the 1820s, lodges met in nearly every locality in the United States. A Masonic organization in 1823 estimated national membership (conservatively) at 80,000. This expansion, however, also created religious and social tensions. After 1826, when a group of Masons (acting without official approval) kidnapped and possibly killed William Morgan, an upstate New York brother who planned to publish the fraternity's rituals, a substantial anti-Masonic movement emerged attacking the fraternity

as undemocratic and anti-Christian. Masonic membership declined dramatically, especially in the North.

## The Golden Age

Although Freemasonry revived in the 1840s, its temporary decline (as well as a new familiarity with its rituals made possible by hostile exposés) allowed a range of other fraternal orders to emerge. Odd Fellowship, another English import, grew dramatically after the 1830s. By the turn of the century, it had surpassed Masonry as the nation's most popular fraternal society. A host of new national orders developed after the middle of the century, including the Benevolent and Protective Order of Elks and the Improved Order of the Red Men.

During what W. S. Harwood in 1897 called "the Golden Age of Fraternity," the fraternal model pioneered by Masonry became a primary means of organizing groups for a wide range of purposes (Beito, p. 1). Fraternal societies could encourage ethnic solidarity (the Jewish B'nai Brith and the Irish Ancient Order of Hibernians), affect politics (the Grand Army of the Republic and the Ku Klux

Klan), and organize both labor (the Knights of Labor and the Granger Movement) and college life (Greek letter fraternities). The Knights of Columbus, established in 1882, provided fraternal fellowship for Roman Catholic men. African Americans, excluded by almost universal racial discrimination from white orders, formed their own groups. Prince Hall Freemasonry, rooted in the activities of ex-slaves in Revolutionary Boston, helped members (who have included Duke Ellington, Thurgood Marshall, and Jesse Jackson) claim the dignity and social acceptance often denied them by American society.

Although both the specific purpose and the metaphoric foundations of fraternal orders varied widely, they typically included a number of common elements. Each sought to create close ties (usually defined as familial) among members drawn from different families, neighborhoods, and even regions. Each was superintended by state and national organizations that established broader policies and larger projects. But the center of fraternal activities was the local group, generally referred to (using the Masonic term) as the "lodge." A small town might have only one body; a larger locality several. Each served as a center not only for the convivial eating and drinking that were part of most meetings, but also the order's secret rituals. Used both to initiate members and to mark progress in mastering the moral ideals and lore of the group, these ceremonies, based on the group's origin myth, formed the largest element in most lodge meetings.

## Mutual Aid

Lodge membership was particularly valuable for young men seeking to negotiate the difficult transition to manhood. Members of fraternities typically joined while they were in their twenties, using their affiliation to help establish their reputation and to build business and political ties within the community and with other leaders. Fraternal orders encouraged members to provide particular assistance to one another.

Despite the masculine derivation of the term, fraternal orders were not solely male. They often included women, although primarily as part of the ladies' auxiliaries of national orders. The Knights of the Macabees established the Ladies of the Macabees in the 1890s. But the group quickly became the separate Women's Benefit Association, with local "hives" providing life insurance for a female membership that numbered more than 200,000 in 1920. Although limited to female relatives of Masons, the Order of the Eastern Star, established in the mid-nineteenth century, numbered more than 200,000 women members in 1900 and more than 2 million in

1950. Twentieth-century Freemasonry established organizations for children as well.

The broad appeal of fraternalism also rested on the range of social services provided by societies. Although Masonry, as the most elite fraternal society, refused to establish a set of defined benefits, other orders were more explicit. The Modern Woodmen of the World and other societies helped pioneer life insurance in America. In 1895, fraternities accounted for half the value of the nation's policies. Medical aid became another common benefit. Organizations sometimes moved beyond cash payments to contract with doctors for what was called "lodge practice." Fraternal orders also sponsored hospitals, orphanages, retirement homes, and even colleges. Such charity was primarily limited to members and their families, but most groups made some effort to provide aid beyond the membership; the Shriners, a Masonic group, created a national network of hospitals in the twentieth century that provided free orthopedic and burn care for all children.

## The Decline of the Fraternal Form

The enormous growth of fraternalism that began in the middle of the nineteenth century came to an end in the early twentieth century. By then, perhaps one-third of all American men (and a large number of women) belonged to at least one fraternal order. But the societies began to grow more slowly in the 1920s and actually decline in the 1930s, a trend that has continued ever since. The reasons for this shift are complex. The Great Depression clearly created some difficulties. But continuing membership losses suggest that other causes were also involved. New government programs such as Social Security and workman's compensation, and new employer-sponsored benefits such as pensions and insurance made the mutual aid of fraternal societies less essential. Sports, commercial entertainment, and mass media all helped crowd out fraternal activities—and often included women—making the fraternities' single-sex environment more unusual.

Alone among the fraternal orders, Freemasonry was able to revive and even expand markedly in the 1940s and 1950s. But even Freemasonry began to lose members in the 1960s. By then, most societies had either ceased altogether or weakened dramatically. Despite this widespread membership loss, fraternal societies continue to be important to many men and women. The Loyal Order of the Moose had about 1 million male and 500,000 female members, mostly in the United States, at the end of the twentieth century. American Freemasonry had some 1.8 million brothers. Even for these orders, the future of fraternalism is unclear. It seems unlikely, however, that fraternal organizations will ever regain the extraordinary importance they had in American society in the century after 1840.

*See also:* Civic Clubs, Women; Leisure and Civil Society; Men's Leisure Lifestyles

## BIBLIOGRAPHY

Beito, David T. *From Mutual Aid to the Welfare State: Fraternal Societies and Social Services, 1890–1967.* Chapel Hill: University of North Carolina Press, 2000.

Bullock, Steven C. *Revolutionary Brotherhood: Freemasonry and the Transformation of the American Social Order, 1730–1840.* Chapel Hill: University of North Carolina Press, 1996.

Carnes, Mark C. *Secret Ritual and Manhood in Victorian America.* New Haven, Conn.: Yale University Press, 1989.

Clawson, Mary Ann. *Constructing Brotherhood: Class, Gender, and Fraternalism.* Princeton, N.J.: Princeton University Press, 1989.

Dumenil, Lynn. *Freemasonry and American Culture, 1880–1930.* Princeton, N.J.: Princeton University Press, 1984.

Muraskin, William A. *Middle-Class Blacks in a White Society: Prince Hall Freemasonry in America.* Berkeley: University of California Press, 1975.

*Steven C. Bullock*

# CIVIC CLUBS, WOMEN

The impetus for the women's club movement, usually periodized as 1890 to 1920, originated in female benevolent and church societies, maternal associations, and sewing and reading circles in the early-to-mid 1800s. Through their charitable outreach, these groups learned organizational and fund-raising skills, as well as engaged in discussion of moral and social reform, such as "fallen women," indigent children, and common schools. However, as early as the 1810s, northern African American women had organized literary societies that established libraries, night schools, and other educational institutions for African American youth and adults. Most members of these organizations were middle or upper class, but during the 1850s some young working-class women formed their own clubs. Lucy Larcom and other Lowell female mill workers organized the Improvement Circle, wherein they shared and published their writing.

The first formal female city clubs were Sorosis of New York City and the New England Women's Clubs of Boston, both founded in 1868. When the Press Club of New York denied women admission to a speech by Charles Dickens, they founded Sorosis so that women could engage in their own study of literature and the arts. Many Sorosis members likewise supported female artists by buying paintings and creating scholarship funds for female students. Although not a philanthropic club per se, members were concerned with reform, especially of female labor, schools, and suffrage. Conversely, the New England Women's Club focused less on culture and more on reform. Many of its members, for example, also joined suffrage associations. Additionally, the club established the Friendly Evening Association, a place for working women to meet. However, the association was discontinued one year later because so few working women had the time or interest.

Thereafter, women throughout the country founded study clubs, thereby promoting a separate female culture where members could study and discuss literature, history, art, and social issues such as temperance and suffrage. Because many members were not college-educated, clubs also were a means of education and self-cultivation. For example, many clubs read classical writers, wrote and presented interpretive papers, and critiqued one another's content and delivery. In some cases, clubs brought in lecturers to guide them in their study; the Chicago Woman's Club, for example, hired Professor James Angell from the University of Chicago.

For native-born white club women, the study of arts, literature, history, and psychology was not frivolous. Rather, during the early twentieth century, club women used this knowledge to further their understanding of social problems and recommend reforms. As a matter of course, club women expanded their maternalistic sphere of influence beyond their homes to municipalities, arguing that they should be concerned with all matters pertaining to children's welfare. As "municipal housekeepers," they advocated for civic improvements, demanded that city ordinances be enforced, and engaged in community-building enterprises. To illustrate, they helped to create playgrounds, parks, social settlements, and kindergartens. They insisted that city officials enforce sanitation codes and that police protect children and youth from the "dangers" of saloons, roadhouses, and movie theaters. Some female clubs' advocacy was critical in the passage of legislation that regulated child labor, created mother's pensions, and established the first juvenile court in the United States. These reforms were not unique to urban clubs: rural clubs, too, focused on community improvements. The

**"Sorosis" by Charles Bush.** Bush's illustration appeared in *Harper's Weekly* on 15 May 1869. It depicts a meeting of the women's group that was created in 1868 by New York journalist Jane Croly (1829–1901) so women could study literature and the arts. © *Corbis*

resulting achievements gave further momentum to their demands for suffrage.

By 1890, Sorosis and other native-born white women's clubs organized nationally into the General Federation of Women's Clubs (GFWC). That year alone, the GFWC had a membership of 40,000; six years later, its membership increased more than twofold to 100,000. However, that membership was exclusionary in terms of social class and race. One African American club, the Woman's Era Club of Boston, was refused membership. This and other events led to the formation of a national organization of African American women's clubs. In 1895, Josephine St. Pierre Ruffin, president of the Woman's Era Club, published a copy of a southern journalist's letter that castigated African American women's moral character. In response, African American club women convened and organized the National Association of Colored Women's Clubs (NACWC) in 1896.

African American women realized their tremendous responsibility in "social uplift," particularly as it pertained to children, women, and the elderly. They established day nurseries, kindergartens, and homes for working girls, or-

phans, dependent and delinquent children, and the sick and elderly. Through a constellation of club networks, they sustained these organizations as teachers, staff, and fund-raisers. Although African American women, like native-born white women, drew from a maternalistic ideology, one critical difference was that African American women had been historically denied the opportunity to express motherhood in culturally veritable ways. Motherhood, then, was the NACWC's central concern, expressed in community-building activities, as well as in the establishment of mothers' clubs for poorer African American women.

Historian Linda Gordon, in her comparisons of African American and white women's club, has discussed their similarities. First, like white club women, their African American counterparts were members of the middle class, although some African American clubs did include working-class women. Secondly, both groups of women were usually married, often to professionals. As such, they frequently demonstrated class distinctions, for example, in their study of literature. Similarly, they drew class lines in their fund-raising events of charity balls, promenades, and teas. As such, they upheld the two-tiered motto of the NACWC, "lifting as we climb."

However, Gordon has also emphasized significant differences between the two groups of club women. Although African American club women may have held more privilege than most of their community members, they still experienced discrimination and racism. They knew that despite their exemplary respectable behavior, they were subject to derogatory remarks. They, too, like poorer African American women, faced discrimination in employment, transportation, and access to public facilities. For this reason, they protested such forms of discrimination, as well as advocated for antilynching legislation. Given the NACWC's large membership—50,000 women in more than 1,000 clubs and twenty-eight state federations as of 1914—the organization wielded a great deal of influence, especially in African American communities.

Immigrant women, too, formed their own clubs and associations. German American women joined church and secular clubs to retain German traditions and language. Not unlike African American women, they and other northern European immigrant women founded and sustained community homes for orphans, working-women, and the elderly. In the upper Midwest, Finnish women formed their own sewing circles and cooperative guilds, of which the latter organized youth camps, fairs, and homemaking projects. German-Jewish women founded their own national organization, the National Council of Jewish Women, in 1893. One Jewish women's club, the Chicago Hebrew Literary Society, sponsored lectures on the Hebrew language, Jewish literature, and history. Clearly, religion played a significant role in the establishment of many ethnic women's societies and auxiliaries.

Social settlement workers also created clubs for immigrant women in their neighborhoods, especially mother's clubs. For example, the Chicago Commons had both an Italian mother's club and a Polish mother's club, among others. These clubs provided lessons in housekeeping, cooking of American foods, sewing, child care, and sanitation. Immigrant women found some of these lessons useful, such as those on health and nutrition. More often than not, though, more immigrant women attended club meetings if there was a celebration or recreation. As such, settlement workers often recruited immigrant women as club members by sponsoring such activities.

Working-class women also organized their own organization, the National League of Women Workers (later the Association of Working Girls' Clubs). By the early 1900s, however, the group's focus had shifted from labor reform, in large part because club sponsors emphasized wholesome recreation. Accordingly, club leaders organized middle-class and respectable forms of entertainments, such as masquerade parties, teas, musicals, dances, and travel lectures. Clearly, these activities were popular: membership in the association mushroomed from 7,000 in 1900 to 30,000 in 1920.

After the 1920s, membership in women's clubs generally declined for four reasons. First, suffrage, the major political reform advocated by club women, had been achieved. Second, college-educated women turned to sororities and professional organizations instead of clubs. Third, organizations such as the Young Women's Christian Association created clubs for their own working-class members, including interracial clubs during World War II. Fourth, women became increasingly involved in other social reform organizations. For example, during the 1950s, women participated in the more traditional organizations of Parent-Teacher Associations and the League of Women Voters. But by the 1960s, more politically liberal women joined the National Organization of Women to advocate for further improvements in the status of American women.

Despite new women's organizations, some ethnic women have continued their involvement in women's clubs. The NACWC, for example, has remained active in the passage of the Equal Rights Amendment and the preservation of the Frederick Douglass Home in Anacostia, Washington, D.C. Some of the African American women's clubs formed in the early twentieth century in Chicago existed through the 1980s. There may well be other groups that have continued the tradition of women's clubs, although the dearth of scholarship indicates otherwise.

*See also:* Civic Clubs, Men; Leisure and Civil Society; Women's Leisure Lifestyles

## BIBLIOGRAPHY

Blair, Karen J. *The Clubwoman as Feminist: True Womanhood Redefined, 1868–1914.* New York: Homes and Meier Publishers, 1980.

Gere, Anne Ruggles. *Intimate Practices: Literacy and Cultural Work in U.S. Women's Clubs, 1880–1920.* Urbana: University of Illinois Press, 1997.

Gordon, Linda. "Black and White Visions of Welfare: Women's Welfare Activism, 1890–1945." *Journal of American History* 18 (February 1991): 559–590.

Haarsager, Sandra. *Organized Womanhood: Cultural Politics in the Pacific Northwest, 1840–1920.* Norman: University of Oklahoma Press, 1997.

Knupfer, Anne-Meis. *Toward a Tenderer Humanity and a Nobler Womanhood: African American Women's Clubs in Turn-of-the-Century Chicago.* New York: New York University Press, 1996.

———. *In Defense of Culture: Women's Activism and the Chicago Black Renaissance.* Urbana: University of Illinois Press, 2004.

Martin, Theodora Penny. *The Sound of Our Own Voices: Women's Study Clubs, 1860–1910.* Boston: Beacon Press, 1987.

Murolo, Priscilla. *The Common Ground of Womanhood. Class, Gender, and Working Girls' Clubs, 1884–1929.* Urbana: University of Illinois Press, 1997.

Wesley, Charles Harris. *The History of the National Association of Colored Women's Clubs: A Legacy of Service.* Washington, D.C.: National Association of Colored Women's Clubs, 1984.

*Anne Meis Knupfer*

# CLIMBING

**See** *Mountain Climbing; Rock Climbing*

# CLOCKS AND WATCHES

Clock and watch collecting has both blossomed and evolved over the past several decades. Ancient Greek and Chinese cultures were knowledgeable about the mechanics of timekeeping as early as the fourth century B.C., and European clock making began in monasteries around 1270. By 1550, the first domestic clocks and watches had appeared. Early collectors valued handmade or batch-produced seventeenth- and eighteenth-century French and English pieces, but the average contemporary collector probably focuses on American factory-produced timekeepers from the nineteenth and early twentieth centuries.

## Why Collect?

The modern collector varies in his or her motivations, although the main indicators of a timepiece's value—appearance and period of origin—remain constant. While some enthusiasts are fascinated by the technical expertise of long-dead crafters, others celebrate the artistry of the casings that house the gears. Historians also value clocks and watches for the historical narrative they pro-

vide, although the history of horology (the art of making instruments for recording time) is still largely unexplored and often complicated by the enduring and problematic presence of fakes. Other collectors like to acquire broken pieces that they can challenge themselves to repair. Even if the collector does not wish to undertake the intricate, painstaking work of repairing or even cleaning their prizes, clocks and watches need not be functional to be valuable. Many people collect them for aesthetic or decorative purposes, and in these cases, the silence of the timepiece may enhance its appeal as a relic of an earlier time.

## Types of Collectible Clocks

Of notable value are American wall and shelf clocks from the mid-nineteenth century, when clocks appeared in styles as diverse as the beehive, acorn, and banjo, particularly when accompanied by a manufacturer's card. Double-decker clocks featured a calendar face below the timekeeping face, telling the day of the month and sometimes the day of the week as well. The grandfather clock, the first mass-produced item in the world, is quite popular. Cuckoo clocks from Germany's Black Forest, manufactured before World War II, are also a favorite collectible. Features such as the movable beaks and wings of the wooden cuckoo birds enhance their value. Unique styling, such as reverse-painted or etched-glass panels, stenciling, or patriotic decorations, increases any clock's value. For collectors focused on watches and alarm clocks, each decade has its particular trends and desirable manufacturers. Additionally, collectors often value pocket watches for their detailed cases, especially enameled ones. The nature of the scene adorning the case can add to or lessen the value of the watch.

## Resources for the Collector

The American Clock and Watch Museum, the first of its kind, was established in the clock-making town of Bristol, Connecticut, in 1954. It houses more than 1,500 clocks and watches, both American and international in origin, and provides enthusiasts with resources such as a research library and seminars. The American Watchmakers-Clockmakers Institute, a not-for-profit trade association, publishes *Horological Times* and offers courses in clock repair. Many European organizations also exist.

## Conclusion

Collecting clocks and watches provides an invaluable exploration of how technology, design, and taste have changed over the years. A collector combines scientific curiosity with an appreciation of art. Additionally, and most fundamentally, historical timepieces document the human fascination with marking the passage of time.

*See also:* Coin Collecting, Collecting, Stamp Collecting

**BIBLIOGRAPHY**

Cumhaill, P. W. *Investing in Clocks and Watches.* New York: Clarkson N. Potter, 1967.

Palmer, Brooks. *A Treasury of American Clocks.* New York: Macmillan Publishing Company, 1967.

Smith, Alan. *Clocks and Watches.* London: Connoisseur, 1975.

*Elissa L. David*

# CLOTHING
**See** *Fashions*

# COCK FIGHTING
**See** *Blood Sports*

# COFFEE HOUSES AND CAFÉ SOCIETY

Unlike American bars and taverns, the cafés or "coffee houses" of America have not yet found their historian. Best defined as public spaces where coffee is the prominent—but not necessarily the only—drink served, the American prototype tends to take a more leisurely attitude toward socializing without the necessity for buying a lot of food and drink. Across a wide variety of cultures and eras, moreover, these cafés tend to be places where upper classes, artists, and intellectuals congregate. The term "café society," associated since the 1960s with coffee house talk and sociability, originally referred to nightclubs and nightlife in New York City during the 1920s. Although coffee came to America as early as John Smith, and although the United States is the largest consumer in the world, the institution of the coffee house, has not, until more recently, been as central to American life as it is to European life.

American coffee consumption has an English origin. Seventeenth- and eighteenth-century England developed a flourishing coffee house culture. Indeed, coffee houses opened in England and cafés appeared in Paris or Vienna. By the early eighteenth century, Joseph Addison and Richard Steele were writing some of the first newspapers based on the "talk of the town" they heard in London cafés, and Lloyd's coffee house was the spatial catalyst that would produce the notable insurance company. English coffee houses remained a vital literary, commercial, and political institution until the early nineteenth century when, with changing mores, most coffee houses became transformed into middle-class clubs.

Coffee houses in the colonies emerged not long after they appeared in England. As in London, the greatest concentration occurred around stock exchanges and marketplaces. Indeed, Charleston, South Carolina; New York, New York; Boston, Massachusetts; Annapolis, Maryland; and Norfolk, Virginia, all had coffee houses connoting economic life "exchange." The London Coffee House in Philadelphia was the venue of much of the area's commercial life. New York City's Tontine Coffee House, built between 1792 and 1794, had on its first floor a primary "coffee room" that was the original site of the New York Stock Exchange. Coffee houses in America, as in England, generally became sites where business was conducted and mail was dropped off and picked up. David Shields talks about a "transatlantic network of coffee houses" for ships' captains. Indeed, these cafés often developed the same atmosphere as many English coffee houses, serving as "penny universities" where men from the artisanal classes and above could read newspapers and discuss current events with merchants and businessmen.

Perhaps spurred on also by such actions as the Boston Tea Party, national coffee consumption increased dramatically and by the 1830s had overtaken tea drinking. This rise in coffee consumption coincided significantly with the development of the temperance movement. One might even hypothesize that the temperance movement would have been far less successful without an alternative beverage, given the dubious health benefits of most water supplies. However the temperance movement, with only a few exceptions, did not accept the European-style café as an antidote to the saloon. Instead, for most of the nineteenth century, coffee drinking remained connected to domestic consumption, or was tied to restaurants or workplaces rather than having its own distinctive sites.

The only exceptions were immigrant groups, largely those of southern Europe, especially Italians, Slovenes, and Greeks. Some elegant restaurants in nineteenth-

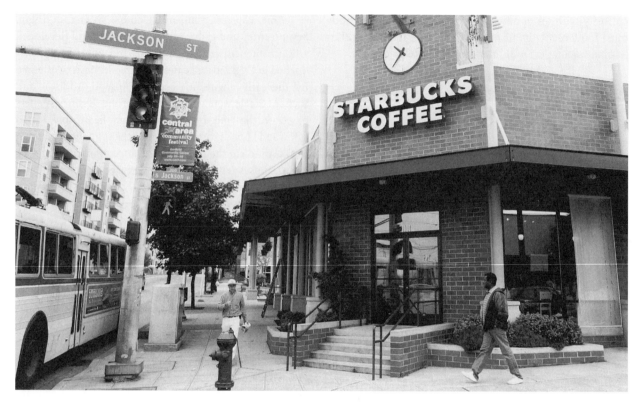

**Starbucks boycott.** Starbucks, which is perhaps the modern extension of early coffee houses in the United States. The popular Seattle-based company—shown here is one of its first Seattle stores—has spread across the United States and now offers customers more than 19,000 different combinations of its custom-made coffee blends and mix-ins. © *AP/Wide World Photos*

century New York City continued the genteel sociable tradition. The Waldorf-Astoria Hotel, for example, in its public corridors near the luxurious Palm Garden restaurant, maintained the Men's Café, "a place for stock brokers and men of affairs to pick up stock tips, deliver financial advice, drink, and keep their eye on business, all within view of one of the main social dining rooms in all of New York and the nation." (Erenberg, p. 35) But for the most part the immigrant establishments remained ethnic enclaves and did not attract working-class Americans or even the artist groups of the Greenwich Village neighborhood. Late nineteenth- and early twentieth-century bohemians around the country primarily frequented bars and saloons rather then coffee houses. Even in Prohibition years, speakeasies rather than cafés became the preferred haunt.

Coffee consumption did increase through the 1920s, and coffee houses and cafeterias did grow in numbers. One of the most famous owners, Alice Foot MacDougall, opened a series of shops in New York City. But the Prohibitionist hope—that coffee would become the accepted social drink and coffee houses would take the place of the saloon—did not materialize. What did emerge was the notion of café society, tied to the rise of such nightclubs

as the Stork Club and linked more to European-style cabarets than to coffee houses. One of the most important of these establishments, actually called Cafe Society, strove consciously to break the color barrier. Under its spotlights Billie Holiday introduced what some consider the greatest song of the twentieth century, the antilynching protest "Strange Fruit."

Only after World War II did true European-style coffee houses emerge outside of immigrant enclaves. New York's Greenwich Village and San Francisco's North Beach, centers of the rising Beat generation, led the way. Important establishments included the Bitter End Cafe, Café Whoa?, the Cino, David's, Figaro's, the Riezi, the Bizarre, the Epitome, and the Caravan. The most popular places for Beat readings were the Gaslight, the Bizarre, and the Epitome. Nightclub owners pressed the police to shut down the cabaret owners or at least force them to get cabaret licenses. In the North Beach section of San Francisco, the Beat generation also had cafés: the Coffee Gallery, the Cellar, Vesuvio's, the Anxious Asp, the hungry i, Six Gallery, and the Black Cat Cafe. Here the Beat generation pioneered much of the literary, artistic, sexual, and interracial experimentation that would become even more prominent during the 1960s.

The 1960s produced a bevy of trends in coffee consumption. On the one hand, American coffee consumption peaked in1962 and then began a steady decline that would not be arrested until the 1990s. On the other hand, immigrants and countercultural entrepreneurs would reverse a decline in coffee quality (due to a steady growth in instant and lower-quality blends) with the introduction of specialty coffees. In 1966, Alfred Peet, an immigrant of Dutch descent, opened his premium coffee shop in Berkeley, and, in 1971, three young college students—Jerry Baldwin, Gordon Bowker and Zev Siegal—opened up the first Starbucks in Seattle. The rich and diverse blends these entrepreneurs sold were a far cry from the homogenized, mass-production coffees such as Folgers or Maxwell House. At the same time, the cultural and political movements of the 1960s broadened the appeal of the café as a site of conversation, education, and organization like that first developed with the Beats. Student protest germinated in the cafés surrounding the University of California at Berkeley campus, for example. A G.I. coffee house movement emerged around military bases providing space "for hippies who couldn't avoid military service." The women's liberation movement also utilized cafés in New York and around college campuses.

By the late 1980s, as the computer and telecommunications revolution exploded, a hybrid between the café and the emerging Internet developed in Silicon Valley: the cyber café. These shops, wired by both caffeine and electronics, have proliferated around the world, but they have become increasingly rare in the United States as computer connectivity moves into the home.

During the 1980s and 1990s, America began to develop its first true nationwide coffee house culture. The small-scale, countercultural coffee houses of the 1960s and 1970s transformed into chains. The most important one, obviously, was Starbucks. Much as Ray Kroc, an immigrant's grandson, bought out the McDonald brothers and turned a small local chain into an international brand, so Howard Schultz, a product of New York's projects, did the same for Starbucks. In 1982, after working for a Swedish plastics company that sold thermoses to Starbucks, Schultz became the company's head of marketing. In the spring of 1983, as Schultz remembers, "it was like an epiphany" when he discovered the espresso bars of Milan. With a vision of re-creating this "barista" culture in the United States in 1987, he bought the company. By end of 2003, Starbucks had opened 4,200 coffee shops across the United States, with an additional 1,500 coffee houses in cities worldwide, including that cradle of café life, Paris.

The dawn of the twenty-first century sees ordinary Americans in unprecedented numbers drinking specialty coffee in public settings. Although Americans then consumed only 20 percent of the world's coffee (as opposed to 50 percent after World War II), the quality of the brew had improved. Coffeehouses became an integral part of liberal-middle and upper-middle-class culture, what David Brooks calls "Bobo," for bourgeois-bohemian. He also classifies as "latte towns" such cities as Burlington, Vermont; Madison, Wisconsin; Missoula, Montana; and Berkeley and San Francisco, California. The rise of the coffee house, often as a site of neighborhood and civic discussion and activity, Robert D. Putnam notes in his influential *Bowling Alone,* helped to offset the decline in the number of eating and drinking establishments in the United States and helped reinvigorate American civic culture. In an age of increasingly media-activated communication, cafés may become a privileged site of face-to-face interaction, which, in turn, is no longer banal, but an increasingly exotic form of human communication.

*See also:* Bars, Diners, Dining Out

## BIBLIOGRAPHY

Blumenthal, Ralph. *Stork Club: America's Most Famous Nightspot and the Lost World of Café Society.* Boston: Little, Brown and Company, 2000.

Erenberg, Lewis A. *Steppin' Out: New York Nightlife and the Transformation of American Culture, 1890–1930.* Chicago: University of Chicago Press, 1981.

Klinger-Vartabedian, Laurel, and Robert A. Vartabedian. "Media and Discourse in the Twentieth-Century Coffeehouse Movement." *Journal of Popular Culture* 26 (Winter 1992): 211–218.

McDarrah, Fred W., and Gloria S. McDarrah. *Beat Generation: Glory Days in Greenwich Village.* New York: Schirmer Books, 1996.

Margolick, David. *Strange Fruit: The Biography of a Song.* New York: Ecco Press, 2003.

Patterson, George James. *The Unassimilated Greeks of Denver (Immigrant Communities and Ethnic Minorities in the United States and Canada).* New York: AMS Press, 1989.

Pendergrast, Mark. *Uncommon Grounds: The History of Coffee and How It Transformed Our World.* New York: Basic Books, 1999.

Putnam, Robert D. *Bowling Alone: The Collapse and Revival of American Community.* New York: Simon and Schuster, 2000.

Shields, David S. *Civil Tongues & Polite Letters in British America.* Chapel Hill: University of North Carolina Press, 1997.

*W. Scott Haine*

# COIN COLLECTING

Sometimes called the "Hobby of Kings," coin collecting is a branch of the science of numismatics—the study or collecting of coins, tokens, medals, orders and decorations, paper money, stock certificates, checks, and notes of financial obligations. When one learns that a 1933 Saint-Gaudens twenty-dollar gold coin issued by the U.S. Mint sold for over $7.5 million on 30 July 2002, one might indeed be led to think that coin collecting is a rich man's hobby, particularly since this coin was once owned by King Farouk of Egypt. Practitioners of this hobby, however, range from children to adults from every economic level of society.

## A Short History of Coin Collecting

Coin collecting began over 2,000 years ago soon after the advent of coinage, with some of the earliest collections probably being hoards. Without banks, people tended to hold on to the coins of greater value—those having higher silver or gold content—while spending those that were plated or of debased content. Some, because of their artistic beauty, were doubtlessly retained longest. During the Renaissance period, Europeans developed an intense interest in classical arts and ancient Roman coins came into such high demand that forgeries made expressly for this market began to appear in the sixteenth century. These Paduan forgeries, primarily the work of Giovanni da Cavino, are today also considered valuable and collectible. Through the end of the Victorian period, an educated and refined gentleman of culture had a collection of antiquities, including a coin cabinet.

U.S. presidents, including John Adams and Thomas Jefferson, were coin collectors as well as students of antiquity, but the earliest collections of U.S. coins were actually assembled in Britain, where collectors developed an interest in the coinage of the former colony. Coin collecting in the United States developed slowly through the nineteenth century, but two major collector organizations—the American Numismatic Society (ANS) and the American Numismatic Association (ANA)—were formed in 1858 and 1891, respectively.

The World's Columbian Exposition of 1893 impacted the popularity of coin collecting through the minting of the first U.S. commemorative coins—a half dollar depicting Columbus on the obverse and the Santa Maria on the reverse, and a quarter dollar that depicted Queen Isabella of Spain on the obverse only. Both were sold at above face value in order to assist in financing the fair, but many remained unsold and numerous half dollars

were subsequently placed into circulation. By the end of the nineteenth century, there were over twenty full- and part-time coin dealers in business in the United States.

The past century, especially the last three decades, saw an explosion of interest in the collecting of U.S. coins. By the mid-1960s, the number of coin dealers had increased to an estimated 8,000 to 10,000. In the early 2000s, with many part-time dealers operating over the Internet, the number was approximately 50,000. The creation of a circulating commemorative series with the Bicentennial coinage of 1976 and the introduction in 1999 of the state quarter series created a public awareness of and interest in the hobby. Of the nearly 1.7 billion Bicentennial quarters minted for circulation, few were found in change by 2003, and the half dollars and dollars were hardly ever encountered. An additional 21 million coins of each denomination were minted for collectors as proof and uncirculated sets. The U.S. Mint generated a similar interest with the state quarters series, and Congress authorized an expansion of commemorative coinage—half dollars, dollars, and gold pieces—issued to honor people and events in our history. In 2003, collectors were excited to learn that the Mint would be issuing a newly designed nickel coin for the first time in more than 60 years. Two new nickels were announced that year—one featuring the Lewis and Clark expedition and another the Louisiana Purchase.

## Collectors and Collections

While many hobbyists will collect whatever they chance to find in circulation or purchase from the U.S. Mint, others are more selective, concentrating their efforts in particular areas of interest. For some, their involvement with the hobby may be no more sophisticated than dropping coins into a box or jar, a behavior often classified as hoarding behavior; these individuals are probably only marginally aware of their role in the hobby. Other participants in the hobby include novices, advanced collectors, dealers, and investors.

The novices include those who notice such aspects as dates and mint marks as well as foreign coins that they find in change. Novices often purchase coin albums to organize their growing collections and may expand into different denominations as their interest grows.

The advanced collector often specializes in a particular area of collecting, investing time as well as money in coins, publications, and travel to conventions and organizational meetings. While there is no complete listing of collecting specializations, they may be broadly classified as based on

- Time period (ancient, medieval, modern)
- Country (foreign, U.S.)
- Composition (gold, silver, copper/bronze)

Within those major categories coin-collecting specializations can be further classified—as in the case of U.S. coins—as:

- Series (each date and/or mint mark from a series, such as Lincoln cents)
- Type (a coin of each major design within a denomination—Shield, Liberty Head, Buffalo, and Jefferson nickels, for example)
- Commemoratives (special issues honoring events or people)
- Colonials (Pine Tree shilling, Fugio cent)
- Patterns (trial strikes of new coin designs or different metals)
- Pioneer (gold and private issues)
- Errors and or die varieties (off-center strikes, brockages [when a struck coin "sticks" to a die, the next coin struck will have a mirror image of the design from one side impressed on the opposite side, known as a First Strike Mirror Brockage])
- Unusual money (engraved coins, elongated cents, magicians' coins, coin jewelry)
- Exonumia (coinlike objects), including Medals (U.S. presidents, National Parks, World's Fair); Tokens (Hard Times, Merchant, and state sales tax tokens; Civil War "cents;" ration coupons; wooden nickels); Encased postage stamps; and Currency (fractional currency, large notes, military currency)

Examples of specialized collections include portraits of the Roman emperors and empresses; coins minted by the Crusaders; coins of the Napoleonic era; Condor tokens of England; obsolete U.S. coins (half cents, silver and nickel three-cent pieces, half dimes, twenty-cent pieces); Liberty Seated design coins of the United States (nineteenth century); modern U.S. commemorative coins; and mis-struck coins (there are nine types of errors: off-center strikes, wrong planchet or metal, blank planchet, brockages, clipped planchet, double or multiple strikes, broadstrikes, overstrikes, and die errors).

Two other groups of numismatists include the dealer and the investor, both of whom have a primary interest in the profit-making potential of the hobby. Just as some individuals invest funds in the stock market, others invest in high-grade, rare coins with the expectation that the rising market will provide a good return. The dealer, like the stockbroker, makes money by doing business with either the investor or the collector. While many collectors are not pleased with the activities of investors (which may drive up prices), many also expect to eventually sell their collections at a profit. Beginning collectors are often advised to collect items they enjoy without expecting to make profits, because investing does require both knowledge and capital. Investors purchase coins based on their condition (proof and uncirculated coins generally being preferred), scarcity (low mintages), or both.

## Terminology Used

Like most specialized fields, numismatics has a vocabulary of terms that, while understood by advanced collectors, can be perplexing to a novice or noncollector. Two excellent listings can be found on the Internet at the following addresses:

http://www.coinworld.com/NewCollector/
Glossary.asp

http://www.coinfacts.com/Administrative/glossary
.htm

At these sites one can find definitions for condition grades from poor to proof, numerical grading codes, error terminology, knife and lettered edges, Fugio cents and other colonial issues, and other terms that one is likely to encounter in the numismatic literature.

## Organizations and Collections

For each collecting interest there is probably one or more organizations devoted to the subject as well as several larger organizations, most of which can be located on the Internet. Some of these include

- the American Numismatic Association (ANA) (http://www.money.org/index.shtml)
- the American Numismatic Society (ANS) (http://www.amnumsoc.org)
- the Professional Numismatists Guild (PNG) (http://www.pngdealers.com/Public)

There are nearly fifty active specialty organizations in the United States involved with coin collecting, as well as numerous local or community organizations devoted to numismatics. These organizations include diverse groups such as the Associated Collectors of Encased Coins, the Civil War Token Society, the Elongated Collectors, Liberty Seated Collectors Club, Love Token Society, and the Token and Medal Society (for a more complete listing, see http://www.money.org/clubnatl .html).

Several major collections of U.S. coins have been assembled for viewing by the public or study by serious collectors. Most notable among these are the National Collection in the Smithsonian Institution and the collection of the American Numismatic Society. Other collections are held by universities (such as the Garrett Collection, housed at Johns Hopkins University) and museums; or may be displayed at annual numismatic conventions.

## Publications

Numerous periodicals and books are available to inform the coin collector. Periodicals include *Coin World*, *Numismatic News*, and *The Numismatist* as well as other weekly or monthly magazines. Bookstores, especially those with major Internet sites such as Amazon and Barnes & Noble, generally offer 250 or more publications, both current and out-of-print. Specialized Web sites devoted to coin collecting offer extensive listings of current publications.

## Developments and Trends

The Internet had a major impact on coin collecting by making dealers more accessible to the collector market. Many dealers who formerly advertised in hobby publications began including web addresses where collectors could view the actual coins and purchase them electronically. Additionally, Internet auction sites facilitated direct transactions between collectors, resulting in higher profit for the seller and lower cost for the buyer than if transacting business through a dealer. The auction sites also benefited the dealers, many of whom sold surplus or slow-moving items while also advertising their web addresses as a means of increasing their clientele. As of 2003, it was not unusual to find 75,000 or more different items listed on eBay and other online auctions under the category of "U.S. coins."

A second major influence on the hobby of coin collecting was the advent of professional grading and the "slabbing" of coins. Although grading does not provide absolute uniformity between particular service providers, it does provide the collector with a professional opinion. Combined with slabbing, where the coin is placed within a protective holder, grading serves as a near guarantee that the coin is genuine and as described. This assurance is of particular value to individuals who seek high-grade investments. A difference of a few points in grade (between MS60 and MS64, both signifying uncirculated coins) can mean a difference of a few hundred to thousands of dollars in value. While slabbing was initially limited to U.S. coins, it has expanded to include ancient and foreign coins as well. For high-value coins, this trend will probably continue.

*See also:* Clocks and Watches, Collecting, Stamp Collecting

**BIBLIOGRAPHY**

Bowers, Q. David. *Coins and Collectors*. New York: Bonanza Books, 1971.

Deisher, Beth. "New Specialty Clubs Emerging." Coin World Online Edition. Available from http://www.coinworld .com/

Gilkes, Paul. "1933 #20 Attracts Egyptian Attention." *Coin World* 43, no. 2211 (26 August 2002): 1.

Yeoman, R. S. *A Guidebook of United States Coins*. New York: St. Martin's Press, 2001.

*Louis Hodges and Rachelle Toupence*

# COLLECTING

It has been estimated that one of every three Americans collects something (Schiffer, Downing, and McCarthy). Just how common collecting is depends on how it is defined. If the definition encompasses acquiring and possessing a clothing wardrobe, family photographs, and music, then few people in the more affluent world are not collectors. are not collectors.However, that definition is not widely held and can generally be ignored. Rather, collecting is the process of actively, selectively, and passionately acquiring and possessing things removed from ordinary use and perceived as part of a set of nonidentical objects or experiences (Belk 1995b, p. 67).

By this definition, individuals who seek, acquire, and keep different music CDs, records, or tapes and who listen to these recordings (ordinary use) would not be collectors, even if they are passionate in their music consumption experiences. But those who acquire and keep music in order to treasure it as part of a set of music would be collectors. The same is true of clothing. Individuals who collect and treasure hats but do not normally wear them are collectors, while those with closets full of shoes that they wear are not collectors. Individuals who take photos of family and vacations in order to recall these people and events are not collectors, even if they maintain photo albums or digital archives with thousands of such photos. But those who ardently build

**Beanie Babies.** "Beanie World" in Framington, Massachusetts, is the home base for Ty, Inc.'s famous Beanie Babies bears and other stuffed toys. © *AP/Wide World Photos*

sets of photos of particular types (e.g., photos of old barns, daguerreotypes, photos by Robert Mapplethorpe) because of their rarity, beauty, or interest are collectors.

This definition also distinguishes collecting from curating, hoarding, and accumulating. People who have collections can be curators without being collectors if they do not actively add to or modify their collections. Although they may have once been collectors while they assembled the objects, if they no longer make new acquisitions, they are no longer collectors. Hoarders fail to be collectors on two counts: They quite likely have multiple identical objects (e.g., rolls of toilet paper), and they plan to put these objects to their ordinary use. Likewise, packrats who cannot bear to part with objects are not collectors because they are neither selective nor passionate about the objects they retain. They also may envision a possible future use for these objects.

Each year auction houses like Sotheby's sell billions of dollars of collectibles. At the lower end of the market, baseball cards alone have sales of over $500 million in the U.S. market (Rogoli). The $250 million in annual sales by the Bradford Exchange suggests the size of the collectible plate market (Berman and Sullivan). While until recently the vast majority of collectors could not hope to recoup

their investments in their collections, much less profit from their collections, the Internet and online auctions like eBay are rapidly changing the potential to find ready buyers and establish market prices for virtually any collectible object. But these observations falsely suggest that collecting is an investment activity. This is seldom the case, and investing may be the antithesis of collecting.

## Collecting as Consuming

A collection is a special set of objects pursued and cherished by the collector for reasons other than the use value of these objects. A collection of interesting pebbles in an 80,000-year-old cave habitat in France suggests that collecting is not a new human passion. Nevertheless, it appears that the incidence and magnitude of collecting increases with the growth of societal affluence and during periods when contact between cultures introduces new and novel objects into circulation.

In the United States, the earliest collections were likely of Indian arrowheads and hunting trophies. Except for a small number of the elite, few early Americans had the time or money to devote to collecting purchased objects such as books or art. Among the less elite, some of the earliest U.S. collectors were artists and clergymen. Charles Wilson Peale was a prominent collector-artist who collected and eventually exhibited portraits, fossils, insects, minerals, stuffed birds, and busts of heroes of the American Revolution. Ministers with noted collections included Cotton Mather and his son Samuel, who collected books; William Sprague, who collected autographs; and William Bentley, who collected portraits, prints, books, manuscripts, furniture, coins, and various specimens of natural history, ethnology, and archaeology. By the late nineteenth century collecting had become more of a mass phenomenon in the United States; popular areas of collecting included postage stamps, cigarette cards and other chromolithographs, pressed flowers, cigar bands, coins, and antiques.

Since the Industrial Revolution, the increase in collecting in the United States has been aided by decreasing work hours, increased affluence, and greater alienation in the workplace. Organizations like the Campfire Girls, Girl Scouts, Cub Scouts, and Boy Scouts have also played a part in legitimizing collecting as an activity among children. As collecting became more popular, advertisers like cigarette companies provided collectible objects to win loyal patrons, and other companies began to market products specifically intended to be purchased and collected, like model airplanes or Christmas plates.

Inasmuch as collecting can be thought of as a perpetual quest for inessential luxury objects, it is easy to infer that collecting is an exaggerated expression of consumer culture. Certain aspects of collecting do seem to be related to consumerism, especially in an era like the new millennium, when the majority of collectible objects are purchased (rather than found or made by the collector) and when many objects are produced and marketed with the express intent of inspiring people to collect them. For most collectors desire is born and reborn as they hunt or save for the objects of their dreams. Evidence from the early 2000s suggests that such object desires may be prompted by an underlying desire for the state of unfulfilled but hopeful desire itself.

But to summarize collector motives as an expression of materialism and consumerism and to conclude that the phenomenon of collecting is simply a socially sanctioned manifestation of living in a consumer society is to overlook other factors that help to account for our fascination with this particular leisure activity. At an individual psychological level, explanations of collecting emphasize possible benefits of this activity to the collector: being able to control a small world of collectible objects, feeling accomplishment, achieving success in competition with other collectors, gaining status within a narrow avoca-

tional realm, deriving interpersonal pleasures from interacting with other collectors, seeking economic gain, enjoying the "thrill of the hunt" in seeking rare objects and bargain-priced treasures, developing expertise and connoisseurship, pursuing self-definition and self-extension in the collection, kindling nostalgia and recapturing childhood joys, feeling a sense of contribution to society by "rescuing" treasures overlooked by others, and even gaining immortality through the postmortem preservation of a collection. At a more psychoanalytic level, collecting has been characterized as a striving to earn parental love denied or frustrated in childhood. With so many people collecting such a wide array of objects, no single motive can fully account for all of this activity.

## Collecting and Society

A more sociological set of factors also needs to be taken into consideration in trying to understand why we collect. Collecting requires that the collector perceive value in the set of objects collected, and this valuation depends on the judgments of others. Whether these others are fellow collectors competing for the same objects or those who learn of the collector's activities and collection, social appraisal of collecting activity is hard to avoid. This appraisal likely starts in childhood when parents sanction collecting and subtly or overtly suggest rules of order, pattern, and selectivity that distinguish a "good" collection from a "bad" one. In a broader sense the activity or hobby of collecting has been characterized as "serious leisure" (Stebbins; Gelber, 1999). That is, collecting can be approached as a purposeful and productive activity that is more worklike than playlike. This orientation likely appeals to those steeped in puritanical guilt that their leisure activity might otherwise be characterized as frivolous, playful, self-indulgent, or childlike. As Steven Gelber explains, because the objects of most collections are luxury products from a consumer society, social approval is more likely to be forthcoming if collecting can be framed as an act of production (of a meaningful, purposeful collection) rather than an act of consumption (of the baubles of a consumer society).

That a worklike orientation and justification for collecting is adopted by some collectors is not surprising considering the opprobrium often directed toward collecting. In most fiction about collectors, including John Fowles's *The Collector*, Honoré de Balzac's *Cousin Pons*, Gustave Flaubert's *Bouvard et Pécuchet*, and Bruce Chatwin's *Utz*, collecting is portrayed as a strange obsession and collectors are characterized as silly, asocial, and narrowly focused isolates who have chosen the world of things over the world of people. While such views of col-

**Star Wars action figures.** Displayed at the 2002 American International Toy Fair in New York City (held in February 2002) were Hasbro's Star Wars action figures that included a mix of characters from the original trilogy and the two prequels (from left to right): Han Solo, Padmé Amidala, Jar Jar Binks, R2D2, Yoda, and Count Dooku. © *Stephen Chernin for Associated Press (AP)*

lectors are most prevalent in fiction, they are found in behavioral analyses as well. For example, Jean Baudrillard describes collectors as infantile and deficient personalities; Werner Muensterberger suggests that there is a parallel between the activities of collectors and the "fetishes of preliterate human kind" (p. 9).

Besides taking a worklike approach, a further escape from social critiques of collecting can be found in the romantic notion of the collectors' passion. Passionate collectors yearn to add adored objects to their collections and can be carried away by these emotions. Collecting transcends the here and now and transports collectors to a special realm filled with myth, ritual, and sacred objects that are revered and seen as sublime. Within this discourse collectors are saviors who risk all to rescue treasures that are inadequately appreciated by noncollectors. Unlike those who see empty beer cans or used postage stamps as trash, collectors find these objects to be sources of intense desire for the blissful delight their possession is imagined to bring.

Passionate collectors also potentially escape the critique that collecting is the epitome of materialism. Rather than striving for status or economic gain, romantic col-

lectors place the collection above nearly everything else, including the money and labor that are sacrificed in the noble pursuit of these objects. Dealers in collectible objects are accordingly seen as noncollectors who instead pursue the base motives of profit and gain. By elevating the collection and its objects to the extreme where passion overwhelms reason, collectors behave in a way that can be seen as antithetical to the charge of materialism. At the same time, others have charged that this is merely a sublimation of sexual desire and that, like romantic love, collectors overesteem and idolize the beloved, which in this case is a collectible object.

While collecting passion is a romantic ethos to which many may aspire, for many collectors collecting is not an all-embracing enterprise. One example includes collectors who would not be collecting were it not for the frequent receipt of collectible gifts in a certain category (e.g., nutcrackers, souvenir spoons, representations of frogs, owls, elephants, or pigs). Others may simply stop collecting and become curators of "dead" collections or dispose of former collections. Collecting is common in childhood, but often as children approach puberty they abandon their collections. Increased sexual interests and the association of former collections with an earlier period of childhood are likely responsible for this decline in interest. Thus, Beanie Babies, Pokéman characters, stickers, baseball cards, Barbies, and other once-revered objects may find themselves unceremoniously dispatched to a box, closet, or drawer.

Occasionally, marketer-inspired fads make temporary collectors of those who normally express little or no interest in collecting. For instance, in 1998, McDonald's introduced in its 147 Hong Kong restaurants three-inch-tall plastic Snoopy dolls. The restaurants featured Snoopy dressed in a different national costume each day. People began queuing up early to buy the dolls; when fights broke out over queue jumping, police had to be called in to restore order. Although the dolls cost less than U.S.$1 with the purchase of an Extra Value Meal, some people paid more than U.S.$100 per doll to complete their collections. While most commercial promotions are not as successful as this one, the mania found among these temporary Hong Kong collectors demonstrates how collecting something can become fashionable and intensely competitive, simply because others are doing it.

At a political and institutional level, it is easy to see the links between collecting and the capitalist system of commodity relations. Indeed, Gelber characterizes stamp collecting as a metaphor for the free market system; it teaches competition, accumulation, buying, trading, and profit making. Daniel Cook characterizes 1990s fads of collecting sports "chase" cards, Beanie Babies, and Pokémon trading cards as teaching children to value acquisition for acquisition's sake. Brenda Danet and Tamar Katriel report that not even religion is exempt from collecting commodification, as children in Israel collect rabbi trading cards. Stamp collecting was prevalent in the former Soviet Union and contemporary China. A similar phenomenon was observed in Romania from 1991 to 1992. Romanians, who were barred from leaving the country during the years of communism, collected stamps and maps that allowed them to travel vicariously.

## The Collector

Not all childhood collections are abandoned; adults, especially middle-age men, also start new collections. Sigmund Freud, for example, began collecting antiquities upon the death of his father. Women also collect, but men dominate most areas of collecting. This dominance may be a reflection of economic power, competitiveness, or desire for mastery, but collecting also involves stereotypically feminine traits such as creating, preserving, and nurturing the collection. However, the gender bias in collecting may be diminishing or disappearing. Susan Pearce

finds that in the United Kingdom at least as many women as men are collectors.

There are, nevertheless, gender differences in the types of objects collected. Gender role stereotypes help account for the predominance of men as collectors of military objects, weapons, machines (including cars, model trains, and tractors), sports memorabilia, and beer cans, and the predominance of women as collectors of dolls, jewelry, housewares, and animal replicas. In analyzing a pair of husband and wife collectors in which he collected antique fire engines and African hunting trophies and she collected mouse replicas, Belk, Wallendorf, Sherry, and Holbrook detected the following Female to Male differences in symbolism:

| Female | Male |
| --- | --- |
| Tiny | Gigantic |
| Weak | Strong |
| Home | World |
| Nature | Machine |
| Nurturing | Extinguishing |
| Art | Science |
| Playfulness | Seriousness |
| Decorative | Functional |
| Inconspicuous | Conspicuous |
| Animate | Inanimate |

Pearce expands upon this list in a similar vein. As these contrasts suggest, the woman's collection not only exhibits stereotypical female traits, but also is likely to be esteemed as less important than the man's. There are exceptions to such patterns, however, and there are women who have been prominent in many areas of collecting.

The collector can be disparaged on two opposing grounds. One criticism, especially likely to be directed at women, is that collecting is a trivial and wasteful consumption activity. The gendered and class-related nature of this criticism is evident in Rémy Saisselin's observation that in nineteenth-century France women who collected were seen as "mere buyers of bibelots," while male collectors were seen to be seriously enacting purposeful and meaningful vision.

A historical grain of truth that may underlie this characterization of female collectors is that women have historically commanded fewer economic resources, and therefore, like poorer classes, have found it more difficult to assemble the "best" collections in the highest status areas of collecting such as fine art.

The other criticism of collectors is that they are obsessive-compulsive personalities who are addicted to an unhealthy acquisitive and possessive habit. As Thatcher Freund observes of one antique collector:

His love for objects consumed him in a way that it consumes many collectors and dealers. Those who called him "obsessive". . . generally admitted . . . that "We're all neurotic. We're bugged. People involved with objects are compulsive. They care more about objects than they do about people sometimes. Their relationships with people are difficult" (pp. 183–184).

While a small portion of collectors may be clinically obsessive-compulsive (including historical examples of those who steal, kill, and impoverish themselves for the sake of their collections), this characterization does not apply to the vast majority of collectors. Nevertheless, a number of collectors themselves describe their collecting activity as an addiction, refer to their "habit," and speak of needing to get their "fix." This self-characterization is partly a humorous tongue-in-cheek effort to justify their unusual dedication to the pursuit of their collecting hobbies through hyperbole, and partly a semiserious attempt to excuse their behavior by invoking a recognizable medical model. Furthermore, by invoking the label of obsession, collectors may attempt to participate in the romantic model of passionate artists giving everything to their creations, which in this case are their collections.

But the romantic notion of passionate collectors differs from the romantic notion of passionate artists in that collectors are more consumers than they are artists. The notion of a perpetual desire to desire brings to mind Colin Campbell's contention that the essence of contemporary consumer culture is Romanticism and an endless cycle of desire and purchase. So too with collectors who simultaneously long for completion of the collection and fear this final end to collecting. When collectors see the end in sight with completion of a collection, they often either increase the standard they had previously set for their collections or switch to other collecting areas entirely. Thus, desire is renewed, and collecting continues.

The idea of completing a collection is applicable to the sort of collection exemplified by stamp collecting, where any given category contains a fixed set of stamps. This type of taxonomic box-filling collecting is called Type A collecting by Danet and Katriel. By contrast, Type B collectors follow aesthetic criteria and thus can never definitively complete a collection. Here art collectors are exemplary, although Type A approaches might also be possible with art if, for instance, someone sought to have an example of every artist in a given genre. Thus, when Gelber says, "Completing a set is so closely identified with collecting that it stands as a virtual definition of the hobby" (1999, p. 74), he is describing only Type A collectors. It seems reasonable to assume that Type A collectors are more prone to the excesses of obsessiveness, while Type B collectors are more prone to the excesses of Romanticism.

## Conclusion: Collecting as a Response to Existential Angst

What then should we make of collecting as an individual practice and a societal institution? Besides the composite of individual collectors and the sanctions for or criticisms of their behavior, society jointly collects in its museums, galleries, zoos, libraries, and other "legitimate" collecting institutions that are less commonly subject to criticism than are individual collections of matchbooks, baseball cards, comic books, or salt and pepper shakers. It is likely that collecting at both personal and institutional levels is an attempt to make a statement to ourselves and others about who we are. Often the collection signifies roots, stability, golden days of the past, and pathways to the future.

As Ernest Becker has suggested, we do not fear death as much as we fear a life without meaning. If so, one effort to create meaning is to make a collection that can stand as a "monument to the self" (Belk et al., 1991, p. 180). In reflecting on his book collection, Walter Benjamin was prompted by his treasures into a Proustian reverie, not about his life as perhaps the last of the great intellectuals, but about his life as a book collector. In an increasingly commodified world, collecting offers a way to singularize objects by taking them out of their functional circulation and ritually enshrining them within the collection. Collecting fights against the sterility of appraising objects according to their use value and in so doing offers an approach to the sacred. Just as a gift from a loved one is a singular treasure not readily exchangeable for its marketplace equivalent, so too is an object within a collection set apart and revered for its extraordinary contextual meaning. Thus, while collecting may superficially appear to be the most materialistic manifestation of consumer culture, to the collector it is just the opposite. It is the antidote to the impersonal marketplace, the disposable society, and the alienation of fungible commodities.

*See also:* Antiques; Books and Manuscripts; Clocks and Watches; Coin Collecting; Comic Magazines; Crafts and Hobbies; Record, CD, Tape Collecting and Listening; Stamp Collecting

## BIBLIOGRAPHY

Abraham, Karl. *Selected Papers on Psychoanalysis.* London: Hogarth, 1927.

Ackerman, Paul H. "On Collecting: A Psychoanalytic View." *Maine Antique Digest* (May 1990): 22A–24A.

Appadurai, Arjun. "Introduction: Commodities and the Politics of Value." In *The Social Life of Things: Commodities in Cultural Perspective.* Edited by Arjun Appadurai. Cambridge: Cambridge University Press, 1986.

Baekeland, Frederick. "Psychological Aspects of Art Collecting." *Psychiatry* 44 (February 1981): 45–49.

Balzac, Honoré de. *Cousin Pons.* Translated by Herman J. Hunt. Harmondsworth, Middlesex: Penguin, 1968 (original 1847).

Barker, Stephen, ed. *Excavations and Their Objects: Freud's Collection of Antiquity,* Albany: State University of New York Press, 1996.

Baudrillard, Jean. "The System of Collecting." In *The Cultures of Collecting.* Edited by John Elsner and Roger Cardinal. Cambridge, Mass.: Harvard University Press, 1994.

Bazin, Germain. *The Museum Age.* Translated by Jane van Nuis Cahil. New York: Universe Books, 1967.

Becker, Ernest. *Escape from Evil.* New York: Free Press, 1975.

Belk, Russell W. "Collecting as Luxury Consumption: Effects on Individuals and Households." *Journal of Economic Society* 16 (February 1995a): 477–490.

———. *Collecting in a Consumer Society.* London: Routledge, 1995b.

———. "The Double Nature of Collecting: Materialism and Antimaterialism." *Etnofoor* 11, no. 1 (1998): 7–20.

Belk, Russell W., Güliz Ger, and Søren Askegaard. "The Fire of Desire: A Multi-Sited Inquiry into Consumer Passion." *Journal of Consumer Research* 30 (December 2003).

Belk, Russell W., and Melanie Wallendorf. "Of Mice and Men: Gender, Identity, and Collecting." In *The Material Culture of Gender; the Gender of Material Culture.* Edited by Kenneth Ames and Katherine Martinez. Ann Arbor: University of Michigan Press, 1997.

Belk, Russell W., Melanie Wallendorf, John F. Sherry, Jr., and Morris B. Holbrook. "Collecting in a Consumer Culture." In *Highways and Buyways: Naturalistic Research from the Consumer Behavior Odyssey.* Edited by Russell W. Belk. Provo, Utah: Association for Consumer Research, 1991.

Berman, Phyllis, and R. Lee Sullivan. "Limousine Liberal." *Forbes* 150 (October 26, 1992): 168+.

Bosco, Joseph. "The McDonald's Snoopy Craze in Hong Kong." In *Consuming Hong Kong.* Edited by Gordon Mathews and Tai-lok Lui. Hong Kong: Hong Kong University Press, 2001.

Campbell, Colin. *The Romantic Ethic and the Spirit of Modern Consumerism.* Oxford: B. Blackwell, 1987.

Chatwin, Bruce. *Utz.* New York: Penguin Books, 1989.

Clifford, James. "Objects and Selves—An Afterword." In *Objects and Others: Essays on Museums and Material Culture,* Edited by George W. Stocking, Jr. Madison: University of Wisconsin Press, 1985.

Cook, Daniel Thomas. "Exchange Value as Pedagogy in Children's Leisure: Moral Panics in Children's Culture at Century's End." *Leisure Sciences* 23 (2000): 81–98.

Danet, Brenda, and Tamar Katriel. "Stamps, Erasers, Table Napkins, 'Rebbe Cards': Childhood Collecting in Israel." Paper presented at the Eighteenth Annual Meeting of the Popular Culture Association. New Orleans, La., March 1988.

———. "No Two Alike: The Aesthetics of Collecting." *Play and Culture* 2, no. 3 (1989): 253–277.

———. "Glorious Obsessions, Passionate Lovers, and Hidden Treasures: Collecting, Metaphor, and the Romantic Ethic." In *The Socialness of Things.* Edited by Stephen H. Riggen. New York: Mouton de Gruyter, 1994.

Dutton, Michael, ed. *Streetlife China.* Cambridge: Cambridge University Press, 1998.

Flaubert, Gustave. *Bouvard et Pécuchet.* Translated by T. W. Earp and G. W. Stonier. New York: New Directions, 1954 (original 1881).

Fowles, John. *The Collector.* Boston: Little, Brown and Company, 1963.

Freund, Thatcher. *Objects of Desire: The Lives of Antiques and Those Who Pursue Them.* New York: Penguin Books, 1993.

Gamwell, Lynn, and Richard Wells, eds. *Sigmund Freud and Art: His Personal Collection of Antiquities.* Binghamton: State University of New York, 1989.

Gelber, Steven M. "A Job You Can't Lose: Work and Hobbies in the Great Depression." *Journal of Social History* 24 (Summer 1993): 741–766.

———. *Hobbies: Leisure and the Culture of Work in America.* New York: Columbia University Press, 1999.

Gere, Charlotte, and Marina Vaizey. *Great Women Collectors.* London: Philip Wilson, 1999.

Grant, Jonathan. "The Socialist Construction of Philately in the Early Soviet Era." *Comparative Studies in Society and History* 37 (1995): 476–493.

Mechling, Jay. "The Collecting Self and American Youth Movements." In *Consuming Visions: Accumulation and Display of Goods in America, 1880–1920.* Edited by Simon J. Bronner. New York: W. W. Norton and Company, 1989.

Muensterberger, Werner. *Collecting: An Unruly Passion.* Princeton, N.J.: Princeton University Press, 1994.

Neal, Arminta. "Collecting for History Museums: Remembering Our Splintered Existence." *Museum News* 58 (May/June 1980): 24–29.

Pearce, Susan M. *On Collecting: An Investigation into Collecting in the European Tradition.* London: Routledge, 1995.

———. *Collecting in Contemporary Practice.* London: Sage Publications, 1998.

Rigby, Douglas, and Elizabeth Rigby. *Lock, Stock, and Barrel: The Story of Collecting.* Philadelphia: J. B. Lippincott, 1944.

Rogoli, Bob. "Racism in Baseball Card Collecting: Fact or Fiction?" *Human Relations* 44 (March 1991): 255–264.

Saisselin, Rémy G. *Bricobracomania: The Bourgeois and the Bebelot,* New Brunswick, N.J.: Rutgers University Press, 1984.

Schiffer, Michael, Theodore Downing, and Michael McCarthy. "Waste Not, Want Not: An Ethnoarchaeological Study of Refuse in Tucson." In *Modern Material Culture: The Archaeology of Us.* Edited by Michael Gould and Michael Schiffer. New York: Academic Press, 1981.

Stebbins, Robert A. *Amateurs: On the Margins Between Work and Leisure.* Beverly Hills, Calif.: Sage Publications, 1979.

Stewart, Susan. "Death and Life, in That Order, in the Works of Charles Wilson Peale." In *Visual Display: Culture Beyond Appearances.* Edited by Lynne Cooke and Peter Wollen. Seattle, Wash.: Bay Press, 1995.

Stillinger, Elizabeth. *The Antiquers.* New York: Alfred A. Knopf, 1980.

*Russell Belk*

# COLLEGE SPORTS

**See** *Basketball; Football, Collegiate; Ice Hockey*

# COLONIAL-ERA LEISURE AND RECREATION

In his copious diaries from the early years of the eighteenth century, Virginian William Byrd II, one of the colonies' most prominent landed citizens, kept a daily chronicle of the events that he attended, the activities in which he partook, and the recreations that he observed. His diary catalogs the most popular entertainments that the colonists enjoyed prior to the Revolution, including gaming, dancing, and cock fighting. So prevalent were these activities throughout the colonies that when the Continental Congress met in 1774 to pass resolutions for the governance of the new nation, they expressly forbade the practice of gaming, cock fighting, horse racing, theatergoing, and all other diversions calculated to distract the minds of the colonists from the seriousness of the impending war with Great Britain. Yet up until the Revolution, the colonists continued to enjoy a wide variety of entertainments. Many had roots in Europe, but their form underwent a sea change in the movement across the Atlantic.

Though many colonists enjoyed seemingly similar forms of entertainment—whether it was music, dancing, or sport—significant regional distinctions reflected the varying settlement patterns. Religious and ethnic differ-

ences also played an important role in shaping the popular culture of each colony, as the Scots-Irish Presbyterians or the staunch Quakers of Pennsylvania banned certain entertainments in which their Anglican brothers to the South felt free to indulge. Beyond regional, religious, and ethnic differences, gender and community relationships necessarily guided the way in which leisure activities would be enjoyed and understood in specific cultures. For example, women in rural Virginia or North Carolina favored horseback riding, an activity not considered unwomanly in a culture where hunting and outdoor sports were common. Their northern counterparts seem to have preferred tea parties or other more sedate pastimes. The recreational activities and leisure entertainments of the colonists, from the earliest settlement of the country up to the age of the Revolution, reveal a great deal about how Americans understood their local cultural identity, and how they shaped that identity into a broader American character.

## Dancing Instruction

Dancing was one of the first forms of entertainment to be publicly condemned in the northern colonies, in Increase Mather's 1684 *An Arrow Against Profane and Promiscuous Dancing Drawn Out of the Quiver of the Scriptures.* Yet social dancing formed an important part of the colonists' repertoire of diversions. Almost before there was sufficient population to sustain them, dancing schools sprang up throughout the colonies in cities as varied as Boston, Newport, Philadelphia, Charleston, Williamsburg, Annapolis, and Savannah. These schools trained their pupils in the latest dances from both France and England, including the minuet, the cotillion, and the allemande. Lessons in English and Scottish country-dances became increasingly popular throughout the eighteenth century. The craze for dancing schools was fed by the passion for private and public balls—described extensively in the diaries of the period. For example, Philip Fithian (New Jersey–born tutor at Nomini Hall, the home of the Carters, a prominent Virginia family) recorded plantation entertainments centering around formal balls that lasted for several days—in one case from a Monday through the following Saturday. In the Virginia capital of Williamsburg, William Byrd attended two separate balls within two days, including both a public fete hosted by Charles Stagg (a former actor at the failed Williamsburg Theatre who subsequently opened a dancing school) and a private dance hosted by the governor of Virginia .

Traditionally the minuet (a French formal dance characterized by its slow stateliness) opened the festivities, with the highest-ranking couple present leading the

**Tea party.** Pen and ink drawing by Howard Pyle (1853–1911) portrays an outdoor tea party in eighteenth-century colonial New England. © *The Granger Collection Ltd.*

dance. The evening would then be rounded out by a host of other popular dances, including French quadrilles and Scottish reels. The steps for these intricate dances could be found in John Playford's *The English Dancing Master,* first published in England in 1651, and reprinted at least seventeen times in both England and the United States over the next seventy-five years. Playford's guide, along with *The Art of Dancing* (based on numerous translations from the French text of Raoul A. Feuillet), and John Weaver's *Orcheseography of the Art of Dancing by Characters* (1716), helped lay the foundation for the development of American dance. Colonial dancing masters relied on these sources to teach their pupils, and the books themselves allowed those individuals without access to a dancing master to assimilate and practice the steps on their own.

## Assemblies

Though many of the colonies' most well-to-do citizens enjoyed the luxury of private balls, their passion for dancing demanded a more organized venue in which to display their carefully cultivated skills. Evenings at the Philadelphia Dancing Assembly (founded in 1749) followed a spe-

cific format, beginning with a minuet, followed by popular country-dances and gigues, the French court version of the Irish jig, popular among the upper classes in England and America. Among those dances known to have been enjoyed at Philadelphia's Dancing Assembly were "Sweet Richard," "Munster Lass," "Ahi Caira," "The Prince's Favorite," "Egham Races," "Virginia," and "The Duke of Clarence's Fancy" (Brooks, p. 4). These dances gradually supplanted the older "box" style, in which groups of couples formed separate squares, joining hands and exchanging partners. As assemblies grew increasingly formal, the emphasis shifted to dances that consisted of lines of couples arranged up and down the room. Socializing was a critical element of the assembly. According to dance historian Lynn Matluck Brooks, the managers of the Philadelphia Dancing Assembly took pains to ensure that there was an even number of couples on the dance floor and that all those present were members of the assembly, or had been expressly invited.

In Philadelphia, Savannah, and elsewhere, the dancing assemblies offered a ritualized way of establishing who was or was not an accepted member of the cities' elite cultures. None of the mechanic or small merchant class was offered admittance to these elite activities. Other wealthy colonists followed similar patterns of excluding the poor from their lavish entertainments, whether it was the 1744 ball given by "most of the Ladies of note" in Annapolis, or the 1752 King's birthday ball held in Williamsburg and attended by a "brilliant appearance of Ladies and Gentlemen" (Spruill, pp. 90–94). For the colonies' elite citizens, dancing was a means of establishing social status and demonstrating gentility.

## Dancing at Weddings, at Fairs, and at Home

For those colonists unable to afford either dancing lessons or assembly dues, what were the options for enjoying social dancing? Weddings, court days, log rollings, house raisings, corn shuckings, harvestings, and fairs provided festive occasions when any citizen could join in a host of popular entertainments—including dancing. As Julia Spruill has noted, "The dances on these occasions were not the minuets and country dances enjoyed by more polite society but three- and four-handed reels and jigs" (pp. 110–111). While guests at an elite assembly often danced to music provided by a small orchestra, or at least a French horn, harpsichord, and violins, the informal gatherings of the colonies' less wealthy citizens were more likely to rely on a bagpipe or a group of fiddles (or even a single one) to provide musical accompaniment.

Not surprisingly, the steps at these less formal gatherings rarely conformed exactly to those outlined in Playford's or Weaver's guides. Historian Bruce Daniels has observed that most New England colonists drew their folk dancing traditions from English rural dances, and suggests that these country-dances (or "contra dances," as they came to be known by the end of the century) were the most prevalent form in prewar Massachusetts and Connecticut. Northerners found the country-dance more respectable, disdaining the French minuet as symptomatic of French (i.e., Popish) degeneracy. New Englanders also objected to Irish jigs (which, it should be noted, were different from the French adaptation of gigue mentioned above). They derided the native Irish jigs as wild and uncontrolled, and associated them with lewd or aggressive behavior. Although most jigs had their roots in Irish or sailors' folk culture, some eighteenth-century observers described jigs as having the appearance of "Negro dances."

## Cock fighting

As an entertainment that flourished under the Stuart monarchs and among the nobility of seventeenth-century England, cock fighting ranked among the most popular sports in the colonies in the years before the American Revolution, one that helped colonists to sustain their sense of connection to the mother country. Far from "home," transplanted Englishmen in the colonies could enjoy accounts of English cock fights (reprinted in local newspapers) and imagine that their own sports, staged in a variety of locations from tavern rooms to city squares, were emulating the entertainments of their brethren across the Atlantic. They could even purchase English training manuals, including Gervase Markham's *The Pleasure of Princes* (1614) or Charles Cotton's *The Compleat Gamester* (1674), for advice on preparing their animals. Trainers who followed Markham's and Cotton's regimens fed their animals a special diet, gave them sweat baths, and trained them to fight with "spurs" made of silver, steel, or bone attached to their legs. Fights were traditionally to the death. In the colonies, a series of fights might last a day, rather than an entire week (as in England), for it was a rare trainer with forty or fifty fighting cocks at his disposal.

Cock fighting was enjoyed both on southern plantations and in larger cities such as New York, Williamsburg, and Charleston. The sport appears to have been less prevalent in New England, though there are scattered records of fights, including one held at the "Town House" in Salem, Massachusetts, in 1744. In fact, northern and foreign visitors frequently criticized their southern counterparts for engaging such a bloody pastime. As one commented, "I soon sickened of this barbarous sport" (Dulles, p. 35).

Cock fighting was also an activity that crossed all classes of society, as the diaries and letters of the period attest. The cock fights advertised in newspapers like the *Virginia Gazette* in 1752, 1755, and 1770 drew spectators who could afford to wager large sums, and the fights were often coupled with dancing assemblies after the day's sport. Some of the wealthiest and most prominent men in the colonies are known to have been cock fighting enthusiasts, including William Byrd II, Robert Carter (of Virginia), and George Washington.

Those who castigated southerners for participating in cock fights did so partly on the grounds that it encouraged a "promiscuous" mingling of "genteel people . . . with the vulgar and debased." The public cock fights held at fairs and court days offered too many opportunities for the poorer classes to associate with the wealthy, and in the days before the Revolution, the nation was still a class-based society that depended on a system of social deference. Of even greater concern to some observers was the fact that the sport fostered interracial interaction as well, since both blacks and whites attended the fights and wagered on the outcome (Dulles, pp. 34–35).

Apart from its entertainment value, cock fighting was associated with long-standing English folk traditions. The practice appears something akin to the European traditions of mumming or charivari, with participants making noise in the streets and acting out episodes of mock violence. Evidence of American "cock-skailing" appears as early as 1687 in the diary of New Englander Samuel Sewall, who complained of a fellow citizen, walking the streets while ringing a bell and carrying a rooster in a bag as others followed him, striking at the bag with "cart-whips" (Wright, p. 189).

Cock fighting was a male-dominated form of entertainment; there are few mentions of women's involvement in the sport. However, the *South Carolina Gazette* of 1732 advertised a fight at a tavern described as "the House of Mrs. Eldridge on the Green" (Spruill, p. 296). Cock fights were often held in assembly rooms at taverns, and it is interesting to note that, even while women may not have been active participants in the fights, they were certainly not unwilling to sponsor them in their places of business.

By the mid-eighteenth century, cock fighting had become such a popular pastime in the southern and mid-Atlantic colonies that local officials periodically passed laws for its regulation. However, these were largely ineffective, and it was not until the Continental Congress ban of 1774 that the new nation took its first unified stance against the sport. Many colonists came to associate the cruelty of cock fighting with the tension and self-destructiveness plaguing the colonies on the eve of war. Thus, to renounce cock fighting meant to renounce not only the luxury and wastefulness of the sport, but its brutality as well. Though cock fighting did not die out in the wake of the Revolution, it did diminish in popularity, becoming much less prevalent than its pre-Revolutionary rival, horseracing.

## Horse racing

One of the most widespread and widely enjoyed forms of entertainment in the colonies, horse racing crossed class, geographic, racial, and gender boundaries. Some participants claimed that horse racing benefited both the animals and their owners, since it allowed the owners to gauge a horse's stamina and suitability for breeding. Others viewed it as a natural outgrowth of the colonists' fascination with horses and horseback riding. From the 1680s up until the Revolution, both men and women were regular riders—especially in those areas with the least-developed roads, where trail or cross-country riding was the best option for traveling from place to place.

Although New England Puritans feared the potential taint of English sporting habits and tried to suppress other forms of English spectator sports, horseback racing was the one temptation to which they succumbed. By the 1730s, Newport, Boston, Narragansett, and South Kingsport had instituted organized horseracing, and in the years before the Revolution the custom spread throughout Massachusetts and Connecticut. Yet the sport enjoyed its greatest popularity in the mid-Atlantic and southern colonies, where at times it verged on an obsession.

The most widespread style of horse racing throughout the colonies was the "Quarter" race, run along a quarter-mile straight, flat track. Generally, the owners rode their horses themselves (rather than hiring riders). Jane Carson describes a typical eighteenth-century racetrack as ten or twelve feet wide, with poles to mark the finish line, and space at either end of the track to steer the horses at the end of the race. Although races were often held at fairs or on court days in conjunction with other celebrations and diversions, by the middle of the eighteenth century, horse racing had spread to the extent that some areas (including cities in Rhode Island and Virginia) held weekly races, separate from any other kinds of entertainment.

## Racing and the Revolution

Ann Fairfax Withington has suggested that racehorses became symbols of both luxury and decadence by the time of the American Revolution. In the troubled years before the war, anti-British sentiment targeted southern planters, who by training horses to race, rather than to work, "spoiled" good animals.

In the *South Carolina Gazette* of 1758, one critic observed, "If Horse-Racing and other expensive Diversions are encouraged, the Descendants of many of them, may have little else left in time, but their [winner's] Plates to show" (Withington, p. 214). A planter's willingness to forgo horse racing was seen as a sign of solidarity with the American cause. Nor were the planters alone in their efforts to curb horse racing. By 1774, "Jockey Clubs" in cities including Annapolis and New York canceled their events out of respect for the Continental Congress's warning against horse racing. Only ten years earlier, more than a thousand people had attended races at Hempstead Heath, Long Island, where members of New York's foppish "Macaroni Club" wagered hundreds of pounds on the winners.

Unlike cock fighting, horse racing successfully reestablished itself as an elite entertainment in the post-Revolutionary period. New Yorkers reversed the ban on the sport in 1802 and established what would be one of the most famous racetracks in the country, the Union Course in Queens County, Long Island. Southerners, too, reclaimed the pastime, even as they developed their taste for racing's natural outgrowth, the hunt.

## Music

Of all the leisure entertainments that the colonists enjoyed, music was perhaps the most common, the most accessible, and the most accepted. The first book published in America, *The Bay Psalm Book* (Boston, 1640), suggests the significant role music played in the life of the colonists.

The English Civil War and the Interregnum interrupted the development of both court and church music forms in seventeenth-century England. Perhaps in keeping with the Puritan austerity of Cromwell's regime, the nation's music lost much of its operatic flavor (a legacy from the Italians), relying instead on rhythmic vocal blending—a form that was thought to foster both community within the congregation and humility (in music shorn of elaborate trills).

The Restoration of the monarchy in 1660 had a profound impact on the development of both the English and the colonial musical tradition. Though he had passed his exile in the most extravagant European courts, exposed to many of the greatest artists of the age, Charles II had little patience for complicated music, and, according to one of his contemporaries, "He was a lover of slight songs" (Ford, p. 212). Thus, the music of the Restoration emphasized both simple themes and a direct musical structure. As the king was inordinately fond of the theater, popular music began to intersect with court entertainments. The trend of incorporating popular song into performance reached its apotheosis in 1728 with the debut of John Gay's *The Beggar's Opera*, a ballad-opera that interpolated sixty-nine well-known English songs (with some new lyrics) into the drama.

Though political controversy over *The Beggar's Opera* ultimately produced the Licensing Act of 1737 and effectively ended the genre in England, in its heyday authors produced almost fifty ballad operas that became standards in the English and colonial repertoires. *Flora, or Hob in the Well*, performed in Williamsburg in 1735, was the first ballad opera staged in America, and data collected from the Tuesday Club of Annapolis records the club's performance of at least 161 ballad opera songs in 1752 alone (Talley, p. 123). Theatrical advertisements in both England and the colonies featured notices of which favorite songs would be sung in the playhouse—a signal that the audience attended in part to hear music with which they were already familiar.

After the Licensing Act, pastiche opera moved into the forefront as another English musical form that combined music by well-known composers with new story lines. For example, Thomas Arne's score for *Love in a Village* (1762) borrowed tunes from Handel, Henry Carey, and William Boyce, among others. Again, these pastiche operas rapidly made their way across the Atlantic into the colonial playhouse, and, perhaps more important, into the hands of colonial printers, where they became the source for colonists looking for ways to entertain themselves at home. For example, Philip Fithian's diary records an informal evening concert in 1773 at Nomini Hall when his employer offered a selection on the harmonica from one of Arne's operas, *Artaxerxes*, a performance Fithian described as "charming" (Farish, p. 49).

## Musical Teachers and Training

Fithian's praise of his employer's performance testifies to how highly many colonists prized musical training. Well-to-do young women often received instruction in the forte-piano, the harpsichord, or the spinet, while gentlemen were more likely to play the horn, flute, or violin. Again, Fithian's diary offers a glimpse into the musical education that his pupils received in the 1770s. The children on the Carter plantation were taught by an itinerant German music master named Mr. Stadley, who traveled up and down the East Coast from New York to Virginia, staying in the homes of his patrons while he instructed their children. In other cities, music teachers offered lessons in their homes or in assembly or tavern rooms.

Though many members of the colonial elite were passionate music lovers, there was simply not enough demand for ongoing instruction in America's urban centers to sustain permanent music schools. What evolved instead were concert groups of gifted amateurs, who, while they may have worked on an individual basis with a music instructor, for the most part learned their music out of the myriad books and guides available at their local printers. Newspapers ran advertisements for collections of "marches, duets, minuets, and country dances" (Byrnside, p. 26). There were special handbooks for playing a wide variety of instruments, from the bagpipe to the harmonica to the guitar. Both popular music and formal music were readily available from the score of *The Beggar's Opera* to Handel to a *Collection of Scotch and English Songs*.

## Regional, Religious, and Gender Differences in Amateur Performance

The colonists brought a diverse musical heritage to the new nation, ranging from Scots-Irish to German to English to French to Spanish, and many of these regional differences appeared in the private, amateur performances that they enjoyed in the years before the Revolution. Yet changing tastes in musical styles and practices as well as shifting gender roles throughout the eighteenth century also colored colonists' musical experience.

In the early decades of the eighteenth century, composers like George Friedrich Handel had begun creating increasingly complex church music, much of it for the organ. By the 1730s, American churches from Boston to Williamsburg to Charleston had begun installing their own organs to keep pace with the trend in English ecclesiastical music; as historian Carl Bridenbaugh has noted, by the 1750s most American churches (not including the Quakers and Congregationalists) had incorporated organ music and even horns and strings into their services. This improvement of their church music encouraged citizens of Boston, New York, Philadelphia, and other cities and towns throughout the colonies to undertake formal musical training. Peter Muhlenberg observed that New York Lutherans sang "very beautifully and acceptably" because "they have a very fine organ in their church and have been taught how to sing" (Bridenbaugh, p. 194).

As Bridenbaugh has also noted, this movement toward more formal choral training among church choirs spawned a spate of instruction books, each of which offered hints and tips for the amateur. Thus, by the 1750s, the "five hundred different tunes [that] roared out at the same time" (Daniels, p. 64) had become polished and unified.

Secular performance in the home and among amateur music clubs began to gain popularity during the mid-1740s and 1750s. Up until the early eighteenth century, amateur music training, especially among gentlemen of the upper classes, had been viewed as unmanly or effeminate. As John Brewer notes in his *Pleasures of the Imagination,* John Locke had criticized musical teaching because "it wastes so much of a young Man's time" (Brewer, p. 532). Others impugned it as a pastime fit only for professionals, since it involved manual labor (of a sort). A gentleman should have an appreciation of music, but not the skill to make it himself. The stigma attached to the "gentleman-fiddler" persisted in England through the middle of the eighteenth century (Brewer, p. 533). In the colonies, however, musical training became, if not an essential component of a young man's education, at least a desirable accomplishment that would allow him to sing duets with fashionable young ladies or to entertain guests in his home.

While the gentleman amateur in his home might play a selection from *The American Mock-Bird: A Collection of the Most Familiar Songs Now in Vogue* (Philadelphia, 1760), music clubs would be more likely to offer selections from Handel or Arne. Concerts held at taverns in New York, Boston, Philadelphia, Annapolis, Williamsburg, and Charleston showcased the talents of colonists on organ, base violin, and flute. Women were seldom featured in these public performances (unless they were members of an acting company giving a concert benefit). Women's musical activities remained largely in the home, where their performances were imagined to have a gentling effect on their families and guests. As Cynthia Kierner has argued, in the last half of the eighteenth century, women played a significant role in establishing genteel cultural practices within the domestic sphere, while men's performance of gentility occupied a more prominent and public realm.

## Regional Differences

Throughout the eighteenth century, the colonial gentry made every effort to keep pace with development in British musical taste, and, thus, similar patterns of development can be seen in American musical culture from Savannah to Boston. The greatest differences among the colonies appear both along the frontiers and in those areas of least wealth and privilege, regions less successfully assimilated into the consumer culture of the Atlantic world. While some folk songs appear to have been shared throughout the colonies, including "Barbara Allan," "Lord Thomas and Fair Lady Eleanor," "Lord Randall," and "The Outlandish Knight," according to music historian Ron Byrnside, these songs evolved differently in each colony over the course of the eighteenth century (p. 10). Thus, he argues, it is possible to distinguish a Georgia version of "Barbara Allan" from a New England version, both by subtle alterations in the lyrics and by changes in the instrumentation. For example, a Georgia version of "Barbara Allan" might call for banjo (or, as it was sometimes known, "banjar") accompaniment. The banjo was a slave adaptation of an African instrument, and consequently enjoyed much greater popularity in the South than the North (though it later became an important component of the nineteenth-century minstrel show).

The southern colonies were home to communities of transplanted Scots, like the ones who settled in New Inverness, Georgia, in 1735, and to the Moravians, who had fled their native Austria and gone first to Germany, then to Pennsylvania and North Carolina in 1736. The Scots brought both their folk songs and their bagpipe music to the New World where they quickly reestablished their transplanted cultural forms. The Moravians brought a tradition of complex choral music, which they disseminated through the churches and schools that they established in their new communities.

Florida, which did not become a British colony until 1763 at the end of the Seven Years' War, has one of the colonies' most complicated musical histories. In Florida, Spanish, French, and Indian influences fought for sway with more recent English additions. From the Choctaw tribes in the region came "doleful songs" accompanied by a "tambour and rattle," according to Quaker William Bartram who traveled to Florida in 1765 to chronicle his observations on the colony's culture and landscape (Housewright, p. 10). From the Spanish priests who had settled there in the sixteenth and seventeenth centuries came a heritage of liturgical music, which used the harp and the *vihuela de arco* —a plucked instrument that evolved into the modern-day guitar. From the French, who had established their first permanent settlement in Florida in 1562, came both French courtly music as well as French lullabies such as "Frère Jaques."

Eighteenth-century Pennsylvanians saw an influx of Ulster Irish, who occupied the frontier regions of the colony and brought with them a tradition of folk songs played on the *fidel* (fiddle) and *bodhran* (drum). As Patrick Griffin has noted, churches were few and far between in the frontier territories, but taverns clustered in abundance, and thus they became the focus for much of the Irish immigrant cultural life in eighteenth-century rural Pennsylvania.

Yet even though American folk music and songs may have developed differently according to regional tastes and influences, Rhys Isaac argues that one central theme tended to emerge no matter what the location. Isaac notes that the pre-Revolutionary folk song emphasized traditions of deference and "property-based patriarchal systems" (p. 206). Recurring stories of impetuous young lovers who defy parental authority with tragic consequences underscored the colonists' dependence on the guidance of the "mother" country. As Jay Fliegelman has suggested in *Prodigals and Pilgrims: The American Revolution Against Patriarchal Authority,* it was not until the Revolution that the colonists severed the psychological bond of parent/child relationship that had held them to England, and it might be argued that it was not until after the Revolution that American folk music could

emerge as a language of defiance, rather than submission (p. 160).

By 1775, "camp songs" had become fashionable among American troops and patriots. Although they were often sung to familiar British folk or drinking tunes (much like the "Star Spangled Banner"), the rebellious spirit of these songs reinvented them as something uniquely American. Of course the most famous camp song to emerge from the American Revolution was the 1776 "Yankee Doodle," a name that came to symbolize both the American cause and character. As Kenneth Silverman has noted, "At the same time the enduring text of the song appeared [1776], the tune received a new genealogy. Americans began to think of it . . . as an American tune originally"—rather than the British song it actually was (p. 290). In the wake of the Revolution, Americans would continue their quest for a music that reflected their new national identity.

## Other Entertainments

While dancing, horse racing, cock fighting, and music were among the most popular entertainments that the colonists enjoyed, and ones that could be found throughout the New World, from the meanest tavern on the Pennsylvania frontier to the wealthiest homes in Boston, a host of other diversions sustained early American life. Chief among them were the physical sports featured at fairs, weddings, and court days throughout the eighteenth century. A fair or court day that ended in a ball or assembly would most likely have begun with footraces, wrestling, jumping contests, bowling, and even foot-ball (a version of modern soccer). These contests were not for the wealthy, though the elite often served as spectators, perhaps watching from the tents set up on the town green, where they took their leisure during the day's events. Physical sports were generally the province of the poorer citizens of the colonies, with prizes ranging from a purse of money to a bottle of liquor awarded to the winner.

Country weddings often featured similar physical competitions, including one Virginia and Pennsylvania horse racing tradition known as "running for the bottle." On the morning of a wedding, the groom's friends would ride toward his house, waiting to hear an "Indian yell" from the woods. At that signal, they would begin racing to the bride's house, where the winner received a bottle of liquor.

In colonies with strict religious laws like Massachusetts and Pennsylvania, these kinds of diversions were among the only lawful ones permitted. Manly and productive pastimes, in which citizens could engage without fear of being led astray by the corrupting influences of secular music, dancing, or theatricals, included swimming, boating, skating, fishing, and hunting. Women's quilting bees and sewing circles likewise provided innocent and productive amusement.

In the evenings or during the colder months, many colonists moved indoors for entertainment, both to their own homes and to public taverns, which, as Bridenbaugh notes, had become the center for middle- and lower-class activities by the mid-eighteenth century. In taverns, colonists could enjoy a range of games, including whist, backgammon, chess, checkers (one of Samuel Sewall's favorites), dice, dominoes, cribbage, lotto, billiards, and piquet. Some critics condemned these games for their tendency to encourage gaming (gambling), and indeed, by the 1750s, gambling had become such an epidemic among the middle and upper classes in both England and America that many British plays, including Edward Moore's popular 1756 tragedy, *The Gamester*, addressed the addictive nature of the pastime. Women's gambling was seen as especially destructive, since it rendered them unfit wives and mothers. Again, many British plays took up the problem of women's gaming, urging women to submit to their husbands' better judgment and relinquish their spendthrift and unwomanly habit. These plays were widely enjoyed in the colonies, though whether their audiences appreciated their moral lesson is less certain. Certainly by the time of the Continental Congress's 1774 resolution against gaming, many Americans had recognized the need to separate these diversions from their publicly competitive context and return them to entertainments enjoyed within the private sphere of the home.

By the coming of the Revolution, Republican virtue had become the byword for gauging the suitability of all of the colonists' entertainments and leisure activities. Those pastimes with obvious connections to British traditions of luxury and extravagance, such as horse racing and cock fighting, were suspended for the duration of the war. Those entertainments with more tenuous, but still visible connections, such as singing and dancing, were reinvented as "American." Words to songs could be altered, formal dance steps transformed into something more egalitarian. In short, the citizens of the new nation discovered that their inherited cultural traditions could be modified to reflect the colonists' rejection of British political tyranny, while still sustaining links to the cultural tradition from which they had evolved.

*See also:* Blood Sports, Early National Leisure and Recreation, Frolics, Mumming, Parades, Plantation Entertaining, Puritan Leisure

## BIBLIOGRAPHY

Brewer, John. *Pleasures of the Imagination: English Culture in the Eighteenth Century*. New York: Farrar, Straus and Giroux, 1997.

Bridenbaugh, Carl. *Cities in Revolt: Urban Life in America, 1743–1776*. New York: Alfred A. Knopf, 1955.

Brooks, Lynn Matluck. "The Philadelphia Dancing Assembly in the Eighteenth Century." *Dance Research Journal* 21, no. 1 (Spring 1998): 1–6.

Broyles, Michael. *Music of the Highest Class: Elitism and Populism in Antebellum Boston*. New Haven, Conn.: Yale University Press, 1992.

Burrows, Edward, and Mike Wallace. *Gotham: A History of New York City to 1898*. Oxford: Oxford University Press, 1999.

Byrnside, Ron. *Music in Eighteenth-Century Georgia*. Athens: University of Georgia Press, 1997.

Carson, Jane. *Colonial Virginians at Play*. Williamsburg, Va.: Colonial Williamsburg Foundation, 1989.

Daniels, Bruce C. *Puritans at Play: Leisure and Recreation in Colonial New England*. New York: St. Martin's Press, 1995.

Dulles, Foster Rhea. *America Learns to Play: A History of Popular Recreation, 1607–1940*. Gloucester, Mass.: Peter Smith, 1963.

Farish, Hunter Dickinson, ed. *Journal and Letters of Philip Vickers Fithian, 1773–1774: A Plantation Tutor of the Old Dominion*. Williamsburg, Va.: Colonial Williamsburg Inc., 1943.

Fliegelman, Jay. *Prodigals and Pilgrims: The American Revolution Against Patriarchal Authority, 1750–1800*. Cambridge, U.K.: Cambridge University Press, 1982.

Griffin, Patrick. "The People with No Name: Ulster's Immigrants and Identity Formation in Eighteenth-Century Pennsylvania." *William and Mary Quarterly* 58, no. 3 (July 2001): 587–614.

Isaac, Rhys. "Stories and Constructions of Identity: Folk Tellings and Diary Inscriptions in Revolutionary Virginia." In *Through a Glass Darkly: Reflections on Personal Identity in Early America*. Edited by Ron Hoffman, Mechal Sobel, and Fredrika Teute. Chapel Hill: University of North Carolina Press, 1997.

Kierner, Cynthia. "Hospitality, Sociability, and Gender in the Southern Colonies." *Journal of Southern History* 57, no. 3 (August 1996): 449–481.

Porter, Susan L. *With an Air Debonair: Musical Theatre in America, 1785–1815*. Washington, D.C.: Smithsonian Institution Press, 1991.

Silverman, Kenneth. *A Cultural History of the American Revolution: Painting, Music, Literature, and the Theatre in the Colonies from the Treaty of Paris to the Inauguration of George Washington, 1763–1789*. New York: Thomas E. Crowell Company, 1976.

Spruill, Julia Cherry. *Women's Life and Work in the Southern Colonies*. New York: W. W. Norton and Company, 1972.

Stoutamire, Albert. *Music of the Old South: Colony to Confederacy*. Rutherford, N.J.: Fairleigh Dickinson University Press, 1972.

Talley, John Barry. *Secular Music in Colonial Annapolis: The Tuesday Club, 1745–56.* Chicago: University of Illinois Press, 1988.

Withington, Ann Fairfax. *Toward a More Perfect Union: Virtue and the Formation of American Republics.* New York: Oxford University Press, 1991.

Wright, Louis B. *The Cultural Life of the American Colonies, 1607–1763.* New York: Harper and Row Publishers, 1957.

Wright, Louis B., and Marion Tinling, eds. *William Byrd of Virginia: The London Diary (1717–1721) and Other Writings.* New York: Oxford University Press, 1958.

*Heather S. Nathans*

# COMIC BOOK READING

Children were the first readers of comic books. This young audience enjoyed titles like *Famous Funnies* that reprinted funny, familiar newspaper comic strips. Mickey Mouse and other famous characters also had popular comic books during the mid-1930s. This audience would shift slightly with the publication of *Detective Comics #1* (dated March 1937). With its mystery stories, it attracted a young adult audience familiar with the genre from movies, radio serials, and pulp magazines. The pulps were inexpensive periodicals that featured short genre fiction. Thanks to the cheapness of the paper on which they were published, their relative lack of literary value, and the frequently lurid cover illustrations, critics disparaged the pulps. Nevertheless, they reached a substantial audience interested in detective, science fiction, and adventure stories. As the publishers of pulp magazines saw the success of comic books, many of them expanded in that direction. Pulp heroes like Doc Savage and the Shadow would appear in the comics themselves and influence the creation of characters like Superman (1938) and Batman (1939).

## Readers in the 1940s and 1950s

At the beginning of the 1940s, Superman and other super-powered adventurers dominated the industry. They were also establishing the profitability of the comic book industry, attracting a huge percentage of the youth market. A survey commissioned in 1943 showed that 95 percent of children ages eight to eleven were regular comic book readers. In addition, 84 percent of those from twelve to seventeen and even 35 percent of people ages eighteen to thirty were regular readers. To encourage young readers' sense of identification, some heroes were given adolescent sidekicks (like Batman's Robin), but most readers still focused their fantasies on the more powerful adult counterparts.

World War II played an important role in the growth of the industry, as heroes like Captain America appealed to Americans' patriotism. Publishers made sure to give their young readers a vicarious role to play in fighting the Nazis and Japanese. Groups like the Young Allies and the Boy Commandos, made up of pre-adolescent boys who joined together to protect America's home front, frequently engaged the enemy while virtually every superhero of the era found himself or herself battling spies, saboteurs, and sometimes even Hitler himself.

As the war came to an end, superheroes became much less popular. For example, *Captain Marvel Adventures,* the top-selling comic book of the early part of the 1940s, lost half of its circulation by 1949. Despite this change in readers' tastes, sales for the industry peaked in the early part of the 1950s. Some of this growth was driven by an increase in the adult audience for comic books. During the later part of the 1940s, adult-oriented genres like romance and crime stories became more popular. In 1948, the crime genre made up 15 percent of all comic sales. A 1950 survey of an Ohio town showed that 54 percent of all comic book readers were over twenty years of age.

The youth audience for comics was still certainly important. Although many younger readers were still enjoying the adventures of superheroes, others were turning to genres like science fiction and horror. EC Comics was especially important during this period for its establishment of a distinctive community of fans. Letters pages and editorial features in titles like *Weird Science* and *Vault of Horror* provided readers with a sense of participation in the production of the comics, while the company's formulaic stories of sometimes gruesome retribution appealed to both the readers' morality and their sense of humor.

## Opposition to Comic Books

With more Americans reading comic books, critics and educators became increasingly worried about their influence. Some of the earliest criticism focused on how comic books were threatening the quality of the nation's culture. Comics, some argued, required no thought and hence would rob people of their ability to read and think intelligently. Some educators claimed that reading too many comic books would cause reading disabilities. Other critics, like Gershon Legman, writing in *Love and Death: A Study in Censorship* (1949), were concerned

**Superman's first comic book.** Jerome Siegel (1914–1996) and Joel Shuster (1914–1992) co-created the comic book action hero Superman. The premiere copy was published in June 1938. © *DC Comics Inc. Reproduced with permission.*

about the political implications of superheroes, arguing that Superman, Captain Marvel, and others encouraged fascism.

The most prominent comic book critic was Fredric Wertham, a psychiatrist who believed that psychological disorders and criminal behavior could be best understood by looking at the social environment of patients. Working with disturbed juveniles, he found that comic books were a common part of their backgrounds. This realization led him to the conclusion that these stories were one cause of their destructive and criminal behavior. Beginning in 1948, Wertham began writing and speaking about this issue, blaming comic books for the outbreak of "juvenile delinquency" throughout the United States.

His theories about comic books' influence on young readers were encapsulated in *Seduction of the Innocent,* published in 1954. Although many scientists were doubtful about his methods, the book struck a nerve with the American public. Wertham even testified about comic books at a 1954 session of the Senate Subcommittee on Juvenile Delinquency. He was generally opposed to censorship, though, and had come out of a liberal intellectual tradition of critiquing mass culture. Nonetheless, Wertham's book motivated many people opposed to comic books to work harder for their control, either by limiting children's access or by censoring the industry as a whole.

To deflect charges that comic books were harmful to children, publishers formed the Comics Magazine Association of America to create a body of standards that would define what would and would not be acceptable in the pages of their publications. Passed in 1954, the Comics Code restricted story content, visual images, and even words that could be used in titles. Among other limitations, the code mandated that police never be shown in a disrespectful way, that respect for parents be fostered at all times, and that romantic stories should emphasize the value of marriage and the home. To enforce the code, publishers were required to submit their original pages before they had been printed. In the case of objectionable material, reviewers would then either suggest changes or reject material outright.

## Reaction to the Comics Code

As a result of all this controversy (as well as the rise of television and movement of families away from cities into suburbs), the sales of comic books dropped precipitously after 1954. From 1952 to 1956, the number of different comic book titles published in the United States fell from 630 to 250. Monthly sales dropped from 60 million to 34.6 million over the same period. As a result, many pub-

lishers went out of business, while others changed the content of their comics. EC Comics, for example, dropped its crime and horror comics for safer titles about doctors and journalists. After continued objections from the Comics Code, publisher William Gaines decided that the industry was no longer worth the frustration. He converted his successful humor title *Mad* into a magazine and ended his association with comic books.

Another result of the passage of the code was the loss of an adult market for comic books. The standards in the code essentially mandated that the products of the entire industry be safe for children. Adult fans of romance and crime comics found little of interest in comic books now aimed at a much younger audience. Characters like Archie and the Disney stable became more popular, as did superheroes. Beginning with the introduction of a new Flash in *Showcase #4* (September–October 1956), DC Comics spearheaded what would come to be called the Silver Age of Comics by updating many of its characters that had thrived during the first half of the 1940s.

## Transformations in the 1960s

This young audience for comic books grew older in the 1960s, first thanks to the growth of Marvel Comics. With the introduction of the Fantastic Four (November 1961) and Spider-Man (August 1962), the company joined DC as one of the major publishers of superheroes. Marvel demonstrated that these characters were different from DC's heroes by emphasizing the everyday problems they experienced. Its stories were infused with melodramatic elements that attracted a slightly older, adolescent audience. Teenaged heroes like Spider-Man and the Human Torch helped to give these readers strong sources for identification. Similar to EC's fan community, Marvel "true believers" were invited to participate in letters pages where debates about the nature of various characters and the meanings of stories were common. This, in turn, helped to encourage the growth of comics' fandom that was becoming increasingly significant during this period.

The late 1960s also saw the birth and growth of underground "comix" that were clearly aimed at an adult audience. Sex, drugs, and politics were common themes as creators like Robert Crumb, Spain Rodriguez, and Gilbert Shelton tapped into the concerns of the social and cultural radicals on college campuses. As part of the counterculture, underground comix were sold through head shops alongside drug paraphernalia. When laws were passed in the early 1970s to crack down on these shops, underground comix went into a decline. Despite a relatively brief period of prominence, these radical comic books helped to establish genres like autobiography, to show that the medium could address serious issues, and to demonstrate that adults would read comic books when the subject matter appealed to them.

## Development of Specialized Cultures

Underground comix also pointed to possibilities of new outlets for comic books. Through the 1970s, most comic books were sold at drugstores and newsstands. Devoted fans were often frustrated by this arrangement since distribution companies would occasionally fail to deliver every issue to their neighborhood stores. This situation changed in the late 1970s when a handful of comic book fans started a system in which comic books would be distributed directly to shops that specialized in them. This "direct market" meant that collectors would be guaranteed never to miss an issue. As these shops became increasingly common during the 1980s, newsstand sales continued to drop. As a result, the comic book audience became more insular, with less gender diversity and fewer young readers than ever before. Without comics at mass-market outlets, it was harder for new or casual readers to be exposed to them.

The rise of specialty shops, though, helped to create a boom in comics published by small companies or even individuals. These "independent" comics, often in black and white, appealed to an older audience interested in a broader variety of stories. Traditional superhero comics began courting an older audience as well. Frank Miller's *Batman: The Dark Knight Returns* (1986) and Alan Moore's *Watchmen* (1986) gave their characters new levels of psychological depth and put them into increasingly violent situations while telling politically and philosophically meaningful stories. DC Comics also attempted to broaden its audience through its Vertigo imprint by featuring dark, literary stories that appealed to a more educated audience that included a significant number of women.

Transforming the audience even more dramatically were the so-called alternative comics. Inspired by underground comix, they helped the form attract critical and academic interest. Art Spiegelman's *Maus: A Survivor's Tale* (1987)—a biographical tale of the Holocaust, told with the Jews as mice and the Nazis as cats—won a Pulitzer Prize and has been taught in countless college courses. Like their underground precursors, many alternative comics are filled with political commentary and sexual imagery. Many alternative comics particularly appeal to young, college-educated adults, members of the so-called Generation X.

Publishers continue trying to expand the audience for comic books. The appearances of characters like Spider-Man, the X-Men, and the Hulk in major Hollywood films renewed the interest of some readers who had given up on comics. DC has courted children with its "all-ages" comics that mimic the style of animated television programs starring Batman and the Justice League. The audience is expanding in other ways as well. Manga—Japanese comics translated into English—is becoming increasingly popular, thanks to the success of anime and video games. Older readers can still turn to alternative comics, but even superhero comics are telling more complex, even self-aware stories.

*See also:* Children's Reading, Collecting, Comic Magazines, Genre Reading, Men's Magazines, Women's Magazines

**BIBLIOGRAPHY**

Daniels, Les. *Marvel: Five Fabulous Decades of the World's Greatest Comics.* New York: Harry N. Abrams, 1991.

Estren, Mark James. *A History of Underground Comics.* Berkeley: Ronin, 1993.

Feiffer, Jules. *The Great Comic Book Heroes.* New York: Bonanza Books, 1965.

Nyberg, Amy Kiste. *Seal of Approval: The History of the Comics Code.* Jackson: University Press of Mississippi, 1998.

Pustz, Matthew J. *Comic Book Culture: Fanboys and True Believers.* Jackson: University Press of Mississippi, 1999.

Sabin, Roger. *Adult Comics: An Introduction.* New York: Routledge, 1993.

Witek, Joseph. *Comic Books as History: The Narrative Art of Jack Jackson, Art Spiegelman, and Harvey Pekar.* Jackson: University Press of Mississippi, 1989.

Wright, Bradford W. *Comic Book Nation: The Transformation of Youth Culture in America.* Baltimore: Johns Hopkins University Press, 2001.

*Matthew J. Pustz*

# COMIC MAGAZINES

Rodolphe Topffer created the first newspaper comic strip in 1827. Soon after, Topffer began reprinting his strips in book form in Europe, though the exact date is still unknown. The first American comic book was Topffer's *The Adventures of Mr. Obadiah Oldbuck,* a reprint of a comic book first published widely in Europe. It appeared as a supplement to *Brother Jonathan,* a newspaper, on 14 September 1842.

The 196-page *The Yellow Kid in McFadden's Flats,* published in 1897 by Dillingham Company, featured reprints of the popular Yellow Kid newspaper comics, and began what comic book historians call the "Platinum Age" of comic books, which continued until 1932.

In 1933 came the publication of *Detective Dan* (Humor Publications Company), the first comic book that contained original art rather than reprints from newspaper comics. This began the pre-Golden Age of comics, which ran from 1933 to 1938.

## The Different "Ages" of Comic Books

**The Golden Age** National Periodical Publications (better known as DC Comics) published *Action Comics #1* in June 1938, kicking off comics' Golden Age. *Action #1* featured the first appearance of the character Superman, created by writer Jerry Siegel and artist Joe Shuster. Superman was immediately popular with readers, and other costumed superheroes featured in comic books soon followed, including Batman (*Detective #27,* May 1939, DC), Captain Marvel (*Whiz Comics #2,* February 1940, Fawcett), the Sub Mariner and the Human Torch (*Marvel Comics #1,* October 1939, Timely), and Captain America (*Captain America Comics #1,* March 1941, Timely).

**The Atom Age** The end of World War II saw a waning of interest in powerful superheroes, and the circulation of many comic books began to drop. Some comic companies went out of business; others adapted by adjusting the content in comic books to include romance, western, science fiction, and horror. Historians refer to this period as the Atom Age, beginning in 1946 with the dropping of the first atom bomb and ending in 1956.

One way that publishers beefed up comic sales was to make comic books graphic and shocking. EC Comics led the way, publishing macabre and highly successful comics like *Tales from the Crypt* and *Vault of Horror.* In 1954, Dr. Fredric Wertham published *Seduction of the Innocent,* which asserted that sex and violence in comic books was corrupting American children. When the U.S. Senate Subcommittee on Juvenile Delinquency began an inquiry into comic book content, the comic industry chose to police itself, creating the Comics Code Authority, which acts to censor material deemed objectionable.

**The Silver Age** In 1956, DC Comics published *Showcase #4,* featuring the Flash, which led to a resurgence in the popularity of superheroes and ushered in the Silver Age of comic books. The Silver Age gained momentum with the founding of Marvel Comics, which published the *Fan-*

*tastic Four #1* in November 1961, followed by the introduction of a host of new, contemporary-styled superheroes, including Spider-Man (*Amazing Fantasy #15,* August 1962), Thor (*Journey into Mystery #83,* August 1962), and X-Men (*X-Men #1,* September 1963).

**The Bronze Age** The period from 1970 to 1979 is referred to by comic book historians and collectors as the Bronze Age of comic books. During this period comic collecting evolved from a loose, informal activity into a profitable industry. Comic values skyrocketed, as did public awareness of comic books.

**The Modern Age** The Modern Age of comic books began in 1980 with changes in the system by which comic books were distributed. These changes opened the door for small independent publishers to create comic books. Soon the market was swamped with new and original material, including Mirage Studio's surprisingly successful Teenage Mutant Ninja Turtles, created by Kevin Eastman and Peter Laird and published in 1984.

In the early 2000s, many popular comic characters were altered dramatically to beef up interest and sales. Meanwhile, comic book–based movies raised the visibility of characters such as Spider-Man, Batman, and X-Men.

## Comic Books as Collectibles

Most comic book collectors and readers are young (ten- to twenty-one-years-old) males and are motivated by a number of psychological and economic forces. Most comic collectors are active participants in the comic culture, frequenting comic shops and conventions to interact with other collectors, usually displaying an extensive knowledge of comic books, and using a jargon peculiar to comic book collectors. In this way comic book collecting fosters a sense of belonging and identity.

Other comic collectors are more concerned with profit. These speculators buy comics they think will increase in value and seal them in bags without reading them.

Of course, pleasure and escape—the joy of reading—motivate collectors as well. Comic book stories tend to be formulaic (though this was truer in earlier times than it is today), and readers enjoy comics because they provide enjoyment that comes from having their expectations fulfilled.

Comic book collecting developed as an offshoot of "comic fandom," the gathering of fans to share their love of comics, which began during the Silver Age. Jerry Bails and Roy Thomas, two long-time comic fans, developed the first comic "fanzine" (an amateur magazine for comic fans), *Alter Ego*, in March 1961. As fans found one another they began to buy, sell, and trade comics. The first comic book conventions began in the mid-1960s.

Robert Overstreet published the first edition of *The Comic Book Price Guide* in 1970, providing normative data on comic values as well as historical data. An updated edition of *The Comic Book Price Guide* has been published every year since.

Before the 1980s comic books were not manufactured for longevity. They were produced from cheap paper, and most were thrown away soon after they were read. This practice has resulted in a scarcity of comic books from the Silver Age and earlier, especially in nice condition.

As comic book collecting became more advanced, the condition of a comic became more crucial in determining its value. In the early 1970s, a comic in mint (perfect, newsstand-fresh) condition was worth approximately twice as much as the same comic in good (well worn but complete) condition. Today a comic in mint condition is worth eight to twelve times that of a comic in good condition.

Because of the importance of condition, comic book restoration services developed in the 1970s and still existed in 2004. While these services can make dramatic improvements in the appearance of a comic book, collectors place a high premium on comics that are unrestored.

Following the lead of coins and baseball cards, professional third-party grading and slabbing (sealing in a clear plastic holder) of comics began in the late 1990s by CGC (Comics Guaranty Corporation) and has become the driving force in the market. Condition has become more crucial than ever, and a high premium is placed on top grades.

Beyond condition, comic book values are influenced by factors such as genre (superhero comics are the most valuable; romance and humor comics the least), the artist who drew the comic's art, important or historic content (such as retelling a character's origin, the first appearance of a new character, a character's death), and perceived scarcity of the issue.

Most comic books have increased dramatically in value over the years, and are mentioned as serious investments by financial advisers. As an example, the most valuable comic book, *Action Comics #1*, was worth $2,000 in near mint condition in 1973. Thirty years later, in 2003, it is worth $300,000 or more. The appreciation of most pre-1970 comic books has been comparable.

## Comic Books as Modern Mythology and Real-World Reflection

Comic books have produced cultural icons recognizable across the world. They are the domain of young people, and help them define their sense of self. Although comics have been frowned upon by generations of adults, their message is typically far from subversive. Instead, comics typically reflect and support the culture's worldview, while also helping to define it.

It is with superheroes that comics made their most indelible mark on Western culture. The birth of the superhero took place during the Great Depression, and consequently superheroes were depicted as powerful crusaders for social justice. Like the classic American western frontier hero, superheroes were individualistic and depicted as a balance of invincible god and common man. Superman, for example, was also Clark Kent, mild-mannered reporter.

With the onset of World War II, superheroes were even more clearly defined as reflecting core American values, fighting for "truth, justice, and the American way." Good and evil were clearly demarcated, and good always triumphed over evil by legitimate use of force. Rarely did comic books question the integrity of legitimate authority.

After World War II, as superhero comic sales dropped, plots became less serious. Superman became a godlike figure, above political and social concerns, now possessing an array of powers such as X-ray vision and supercold breath, while Batman went from a dark, brooding vigilante to a father figure working beside Commissioner Gordon, well within the law.

With the onset of the Silver Age in the 1960s, Marvel Comics led the way with a new breed of superhero typified by Spider-Man, who was uncertain, neurotic, sometimes making blunders and looking foolish. Exhibiting all-too-human foibles (including being attracted to members of the opposite sex—something glaringly absent from earlier superheroes), Marvel superheroes spoke to youth in a personal and introspective manner during a time of upheaval, uncertainty, and social revolution.

The power of technology emerged as an important theme during the Silver Age. Heroes no longer came from other planets (Superman), or mythical islands (Wonder Woman), or acquired their powers through magic (Captain Marvel). Instead, scientists developed their own heroic powers (Iron Man, Mr. Fantastic of the Fantastic Four, the Atom), or the powers resulted from a technological mishap (Spider-Man, Daredevil, the Hulk, the Human Torch, the Thing, Flash).

By 2004, comic books had become edgier, more violent, and more complex, perhaps reflecting those changes in society at large. But they still typically maintained the classic formula of the virtuous superhero defeating evil and defending American values.

It has been noted by comic book historians that comics, and the characters they depict, are commodities, and comic book content has consistently depicted America's consumer culture positively. Sometimes through anticommunist themes, sometimes by extolling the virtues of technology, always by depicting primarily well-off, upper-middle-class and wealthy people, comic books have been proponents of consumer culture.

Comic book heroes have also spread successfully to other media, extending their mythology even more broadly into Western culture. The first successful forays were radio shows, followed by a Superman TV program in the 1950s, then TV programs of Batman, the Hulk, an army of superhero cartoons, and finally big-budget Hollywood films, beginning with Superman in 1978, followed by Batman, X-Men, Spider-Man, Daredevil, the Hulk, and likely many more to come.

*See also:* Children's Reading, Collecting, Comic Book Reading, Genre Reading, Men's Magazines, Women's Magazines

## BIBLIOGRAPHY

Benton, Mike. *The Comic Book in America: An Illustrated History.* Cutten, Calif.: Taylor Publishing, 1989.

Goulart, Ron. *Comic Book Culture: An Illustrated History.* Portland, Oreg.: Collector's Press, 2000.

Inge, M. Thomas. "A Chronology of the Development of the American Comic Book." In *The Overstreet Comic Book Price Guide.* Volume 31. Edited by Robert M. Overstreet. Timonium, Md.: Gemstone Publishing, 2001.

McAllister, Matthew P. *Comics & Ideology.* New York: Peter Lang, 2001.

Nyberg, Amy Kiste. *Seal of Approval: The History of the Comics Code.* Jackson: University of Mississippi Press, 1998.

Overstreet, Robert M. *The Overstreet Comic Book Price Guide.* Timonium, Md.: Gemstone Publishing, 2002.

Pustz, Matthew J. *Comic Book Culture.* Jackson: University of Mississippi Press, 1999.

Steranko, James. *The Steranko History of Comics.* Volume 1. Reading, Pa.: Supergraphics Publications, 1970.

———. *The Steranko History of Comics.* Volume 2. Reading, Pa.: Supergraphics Publications, 1972.

Thompson, Don, and Dick Lupoff. *The Comic-Book Book.* Iola, Wis.: Krause Publications, 1998.

Thompson, Don, Richard Lupoff, and Dick Lupoff. *All in Color for a Dime.* Iola, Wis.: Krause Publications, 1997.

Weist, Jerry. "A Short History of Comic Book Fandom and Comic Book Collecting in America." In *The Overstreet Comic Book Price Guide.* Volume 26. Edited by Robert M. Overstreet. Timonium, Md.: Gemstone Publishing, 1996.

Wertham, Fredric. *Seduction of the Innocent.* New York: Rinehart and Company, 1954.

Wright, Bradford W. *Comic Book Nation.* Baltimore: Johns Hopkins University Press, 2001.

*William D. McIntosh*

# COMMERCIALIZATION OF CHILDREN'S PLAY

The term "commercialization of play" is very contentious, referring simultaneously to the transformation of children's playthings industries, and the critique of those industries as alienating children from authentic play. At its root, commercialization refers to the inclusion of playthings into the marketplace. Yet the growth of toy and game production, from a local craft enterprise to a multibillion dollar global marketing powerhouse over the last century, means that this term hardly does justice to the complex web of play merchandising that linked toy and game production with films, TV, advertising, fast food, theme parks, and toy stores. Nor does it explain why the commodification of play activities, rather than the products themselves, has acquired such a degree of disdain among culture critics who are apprehensive about this destructive force eroding children's natural innocence and free play.

This discussion of commercialization therefore focuses on the history of American children's toy and game marketing emphasizing the promotional strategies that have been developed by children's entertainment marketers over the last century. Among these innovations in commercial expansion are techniques for display and pricing of goods, for undertaking the study and tracking of child consumers, and for distribution deals with other children's merchandisers. Synergistic corporate public relations, media promotion and advertising, and the use of media including television programming, product placements, theme parks, and web-marketing have been part of this transformation of children's play industries. In the process, children's play has expanded dramatically as commercialization of play has given new scope and accelerated pace to the global promotion of toys and games.

As this historical overview will suggest, toy and game marketing has been at the heart of the progressive commercialization of children's culture. This major "'restructuring'" of children's global cultural industries has been so pervasive that it is linked to the strangulation of funds for state educational broadcasters, to the deregulation of commercial media, to the growing funding of films through product placements, the preponderance of new thirty-minute toy commercials on TV, and even the rental of advertising space within educational web sites such as NeoPets. American children have become so accustomed to commercial marketing that 30,000 schools receive television broadcasts from satellite as part of the daily curriculum (under the aegis of media education) while the digital media industries collude to produce a video game curriculum for media-savvy children who have grown tired of reading and watching the news on TV. It can already be seen, in the concern about violent video games, that debates about the commercialization of play are growing more intense.

## From Play to Toys

Throughout the nineteenth century, while children were increasingly barred from the sphere of industrial work and production, modernizing nations underwent significant transformation in public conceptions of childhood that gave new force and legitimacy to both children's leisure and learning. Indeed, turn-of-the-century conceptions of play were not intimately bound up with toys, nor were toys considered the preferred means for children's socialization. Nineteenth century play became intertwined with children's natural exuberance associated with learning and with release from the tensions of everyday life.

Friedrich Froebel popularized this romantic view of play, and the kindergartens he proposed in 1837 were intended as "spielraum" to help nourish children's natural instincts for imaginative play. The kindergarten was intended to loosen the social and moral control typical of restrictive pedagogies by imbuing education with the freedom of the garden world of childhood innocence. Rudolph Stiener recommended, for the young, only those play activities that explicitly avoided the association of play with the restrictive world of manufactured toys (exploring, gardening, tag, hide and seek, drawing, simple manipulation and crafts):

> Small children can be very pleased with simple things, and they sense the caring that goes into creating something for themselves. They can bring a wonderful imaginative world of their own to surround a simple toy.

Celebrated in children's literature too, this romantic sensibility of childhood innocence expressed an absolute faith in free play that needed few toys.

Although very young children were sometimes given rattles and similar toys as much for the benefit of parents as children (they were sometimes called "child quieters"), throughout most of the nineteenth century few toys were available for older children. While most children seldom had time away from the work imposed by adults for play, because child labor was often intermittent, the young found opportunities to play traditional games and to test their physical and mental stamina. Early American children also made their own playthings with whittled sticks, castaway bits of cloth, and wood. They taught each other to make dolls of rags stuffed with straw or out of cornhusks. Animal wastes provided materials for balls and knucklebones and corncobs served as miniature log cabins or forts. Traditional toys such as hoops (from discarded wheels) pushed along the street with a stick survived until the end of the nineteenth century. And, of course, much play required no manufactured props. Children played without toys or board or card games in a wide variety of chasing, racing, hiding, and role playing activities in unsupervised groups. Their games came in many variations that were passed on from one brief generation to the next for many years. Toys, games, and other commercial playthings were rare, offered to children only on rare festive occasions or restricted to the homes of the rich. In children's books too, is encountered this gold-tinged image of the imaginative child happily occupied in their leisure pursuits without toys, besides those things they "discovered," made themselves (such as bows and arrows, skipping ropes, hand made balls, and fishing rods), or sometimes received as a treasured special gift.

Yet lest "idle hands" get up to the devil's work, children's play was also increasingly extolled as an important means of social control and character development integral to socialization in an "enlightened and progressive era." Wellington's edict that the "battle of Waterloo was won on the playing fields of Eton" had long provided a social justification that made sports, wrestling, and structured games of action and strategy part of the preparation for the rigors of life. The idea of controlling youth and guiding their character formation through play was enthusiastically taken up by the playground movement of the 1900s when organized and specialized sports and playgrounds began to dot the urban landscape. Throughout the twentieth century, toys, playgrounds and sports equipment increasingly became visible within the child-oriented spaces and environments. Anywhere that children were socialized or educated—in the school rooms, playgrounds, parks and bedrooms of the modernizing world—play was being linked with the socialization of the vulnerable child in the confusing and rapidly changing modern world.

Toy manufacture in the United States circa 1900 was a quite limited craft industry, and until World War I 90 percent of the toys sold were imported from Germany. Even middle-class children might have only two or three manufactured playthings; for example, a doll that could be clothed and repaired at home, a Noah's Ark play set (often to be used only on Sundays), a set of wooden circus figures, or a cast iron horse and buggy. Wooden puzzles and board games became fairly common in the 1880s and the more affluent might possess "educational toys" (such as the "moving picture" zoetrope, miniature steam engines, or puppet theatres). Many toys, especially expensive breakable dolls, were kept on shelves, admired by adults, but seldom played with.

As the nineteenth century interest in children's socialization and maturation grew, so did a broad reconsideration of the role of play in early education. Play was proposed as the primary work of childhood, and toys or playthings, more generally, the necessary tools of their training and happiness. The acceptance of toys as an educational technology was particularly pronounced among North American educators. The alphabet blocks devised by John Locke for his children were among the first educational toys that were experimented with in some U.S. nursery schools. The ability to learn through performative doing was the central motif in the growing theorization of the maturational benefits of developmental toys that encouraged childrens' eye-hand coordination, problem solving, language skills, or conceptual development. While Milton Bradley manufactured blocks and other educational playthings for kindergartens from the 1870s, Playskool emerged in the 1920s as a leader in this type of toy with their hammer and peg game that became a common artifact found in many U.S. nurseries. In the 1920s and 1930s, the toy makers began working with educators, aligning their claims about the benefits of the perception toys, pull toys, skill toys, and puzzle games with the new theories of play's educational value.

The acceptance of educational toys, playgrounds, and sports as beneficial to children's maturation provided the first impetus for the commercialization of play. The American Toy Manufacturers Association (TMA) was formed in 1916 to help mobilize and lobby on behalf of the toy makers. Because many were small scale craft industries, the TMA was crucial in leading U.S. toy makers to gradually realize that convincing the public that toys were developmentally useful could contribute to the expansion of their industry. Fisher-Price's corporate "creed" developed during this period reflected perhaps the whole industries modernist belief that children's interest in play was sustained by the quality of their toys, which must possess intrinsic play value, ingenuity, strong construction, value for money and action.

The mass market potential for playthings was dramatically demonstrated to toy makers in the late 1920s by the popularity of the yo-yo, the first toy fad to catch the worlds imagination. The yo-yo, a toy found in Egyptian tombs, is a classic toy: it requires practice, patience, and the mastering of basic body motions. Simple and relatively cheap to produce, the yo-yo was a perfect mass toy. The yo-yo makers quickly learned to promote these toys with travelling shows, demonstrations, contests, and star turns, which fueled the growing public fascination with the performance of these simple tricks. The yo-yo's widespread popularity confirmed for some toy makers the need to learn about the mass production and marketing of toys. They began to innovate product lines as they developed new understanding of children's play which motivated purchase.

Yet as they applied the modern mass production techniques, manufacturers found toys could be made more cheaply, with less labor at lower prices. Moreover, these more industrial toy makers realized that if kids didn't play with their toys, then parents and teachers wouldn't buy them. Fisher-Price, a company that started as a maker of wooden pull toys that moved and made noise, discovered that developmental toys also had to have what they began to call "play value." Fisher of Fisher-Price articulated this changing notion of play:

> Children love best the cheerful, friendly toys with amusing action, toys that appeal to their imagination, toys that DO something new and surprising and funny. This ideas is so simple it is sometimes overlooked — but if you have forgotten your own younger days, test it out on the nearest children.

They had realized the central concept of mass production that focused on "play values" as the key to the mass-market. So they began to design cuter pull and manipulation toys with unusual movements and surprise actions more for the kids than the adults. Fisher-Price and Marx were among those early wooden toy makers who began diversifying by using metal and later plastic in their products.

These changes in production resulted in an expanding array of toys: novel construction toys (such as Albert Gilbert's Erector sets first appearing in 1913, Lego arriving in the U.S. in 1964), moving model cars, and soft playable dolls and plush animals (manufactured first about 1906) were made possible by the changing materials and techniques of production adopted in the toy industries. The electric train (manufactured first in 1903 by Joshua Lionel Cowen) is perhaps the exemplar of this industrialization of toys. Yet Lionel was also one of the first toy makers to successfully use mass advertising in their marketing plans, especially in boys' magazines. So too, as cultural historians have noted, did the Daisy air rifle (or BB gun) have a special place within American boyhood, not only as the precursor to hunting and rights of individual self defense, but also as the essential sign of maturation. Ads in boys' magazines encouraged children to pester their parents to buy Daisy guns. The task facing these early mass playthings advertisers was to give verbal expression to the values of play in their advertising.

## Commercialization of Play in the Age of Television

Roland Barthes' famous critique of "plastic" and other manufactured toys therefore fails to note that the transformed appearance of toys is only the surface symptom of the underlying commercial dynamics of the transformation of craft into industrial mass marketed toys that have accelerated since World War II. Two concepts are central to understanding this new meaning of commercialization. First, the toy merchandisers must come to see children as a viable market in its own right: the notion implies the expanding discourses on children as consumers in their own right. Secondly, they must come to see television advertising as a viable channel for marketing their goods directly to kids. These changes took place first in the 1950s, as U.S. children's toy and game manufacturers turn to commercial television to expand the market for their products.

Some 1950s toy merchandisers did not at first see children as their market: they continued to sell toys to parents. Many were not yet convinced that children watched enough television, or that they were capable of remembering the brands and their attributes shown so briefly in TV commercials. In the United States, then, the growth of toy marketing rested on the incorporation of television into the patterns of family life. The decisive precondition for commercialization was the toy industry's belief in viability of children's television through which they could target children's preferences and saturate children's culture. Indeed with few commercial print channels (a few magazines and comic books), toy marketing to children was rather limited. So the progressive commercialization of the American media must be considered a major contributor to the expansion of toy merchandising.

Few other companies were in as good a position to realize the importance of these changes as that of Walt Disney, who had already cashed in on toy and clothing spin-offs from his animated films since the 1930s (with the licensing of Disney cartoon images on many toys and games). Disney built on that earlier success in attracting children by embracing TV, as was evident in his popular frontier adventure, *Davy Crockett*. Soon kids everywhere in the United States were demanding coon-skin hats and plastic Bowie knifes. The daily TV show "Mickey Mouse Club" of 1955 that featured a revue of children with which kids of different ages could identify, became the first children's television program to enjoy sufficient audience to attract major advertising support ($20 million for the season). Not surprisingly, the upstart toy producer Mattel was among the first advertisers whose innovative saturation campaigns for the Burp gun proved the fad-creating efficacy of children's television marketing—selling one million units within a month (Schneider, 1987). With the growing reach of television, direct-to-children advertising expenditures on campaigns that targeted and addressed children therefore grew steadily in the United States, from a few million in 1954 to almost $7 billion by the end of the millenium—enough to fund the films, books, magazines, websites, educational and cartoon programming that provide the foundation of children's media culture.

## Marketing in a Mass Mediated Culture

From the early 1960s onward, most major toy marketers realized the importance of marketing research for providing insights into children's motivations and preferences for toys. Fisher-Price sponsored a nursery school's tracking of favorite programs on television, monitored children's requests in shops, and assessed their allowances and influence within the family. Children, they discovered, knew a lot about their products, and how to get the things they wanted. Not only were children demonstrating their influence within the post-war family, but many had discretionary spending, which made their own product preferences and life-long brand loyalties an issue for marketers. Given the rapid increase in children's allowances, influence in the family, and television viewing to about 3.5 hours per day, it is easy to see why during the 1960s and 1970s American children's merchandisers began to intensify their advertising to the young.

It doesn't take advertising to make children desire toys, as the makers of yo-yos and Lego (who advertise little) know; but advertising and point of purchase display can increase the popularity and recognition of particular toy lines, significantly increasing sales. Susan Small-Weil notes that advertising builds relationships "between toy manufacturers and consumers which create an immediate demand for a specific product." (*Playthings*, 1990). It was during this period that children's peer advertising formats were tested and the power of television proven in the United States. Since children did have some trouble remembering the attributes of branded products and brand names, advertisers began to employ recognizable characters or brand persona (Tony the Tiger; Snap, Crackle, and Pop) for maintaining the child's interest in products and increasing brand recognition and requests. Marketers also learned that children's consumption was rooted in a logic of desire and judgment, highly influenced by peer processes and oriented by media.

It was during the 1960s and 1970s that toy (and food) merchandisers really learned to use TV advertising to generate excitement and brand awareness of their products. Television was an excellent storyteller, with the ability to not only to make people aware of the product but also locate it within a symbolic field. Introduced in 1959 by Mattel with a high profile advertising campaign, Barbie's immediate success showed that understanding this dimension of symbolic design was fast becoming the crucial tool of children's toy marketing. Although Barbie was fabricated in Japan, her style was clearly American in spirit and design. The television ad was not only intended to furnish Barbie's "backstory" as a fashion model but also to stimulate little girls' fantasies about teen life that research had revealed grounded the fashion play activity. Barbie, Mattel learned, was not just a faddish toy such as hoola hoops and yo-yos, but a new way of thinking about the meanings and fantasy processes that motivated girls to play with symbolic toys.

Projected through saturation advertising, Mattel's ability to gain acceptance of Barbie's novel fashion doll pretext among young girls crystallized an emerging commercial dynamic of kids toy marketing. Mattel learned to build on its initial product concept to maintain Barbie's fashion-doll stature in children's culture by constant symbolic makeovers. Fine-tuning fantasies to fight off her rivals, Mattel has been able to parlay their original advertising investment, achieving both continuity and saturation in the U.S. market, where between 90 to 95 percent of young girls have at least one Barbie doll and many have two or three. At the same time, Barbie has been transformed from a unique fashion doll into a lifestyle concept at the vortex of an expanding the range of accoutrements and accessories that include couturier clothing, lifestyle clothes, home furnishings and cars, bedding, and curtains on a global scale. Comprehensive marketing of toys, Mattel found, promoted symbolic universes or ensembles of playthings rather than specific toys or personalities, establishing a new promotional efficiency in children's marketing.

When Mattel introduced Barbie in the 1960s to Europe and Asia, it was not successful. Symbolic toys proved more culturally sensitive sells than faddish hoola hoops or universal Lego. To Britain of the sixties, Barbie's American style proved brash and unattractive. Yet after the opening up of European and Asian commercial television (through cable, satellite, and deregulation) Mattel has expanded its global merchandising efforts, spearheaded by Barbie. The company has learned that to market a world product similarly around the globe is not easy. So Cindy, as she was re-dubbed, required a slightly different back-story, and a much different hair and wardrobe array to achieve moderate success in England. But in the process Mattel learned to re-position Barbie in a more culturally diverse world with explicit internationalized themes. In the United States, the Barbie line has been expanded to include a UNICEF Barbie doll, and Mattel sponsored a "children's Barbie Summit" in 1990, which flew forty children from twenty-eight countries to the Waldorf Astoria hotel in New York to discuss world peace. Barbie is so well established now around the world that Mattel is negotiating with global retailers for Barbie Boutiques.

## Into the Merchandising Stratosphere

This is where the commercialized media become important not only for advertising the products but for the promotional saturation of children's culture with media characters and narratives. Certainly, many in the U.S. toy industry didn't fully appreciate the scope that media-generated promotion offered in until Lucas Film's 1977 *Star Wars,* and the eventual *Star Wars* trilogy, met enthusiastic children's audiences around the world. The $1 billion world wide sales of Tai Fighters, Darth Vadar dolls, and R2D2 robots were a timely eye opener for many children's marketers especially in the United States and Japan, stimulating a new interest among merchandisers in licensing spin-offs from highly popular children's fantasy world films and cartoons. Because conditions that allowed for promotional marketing on television emerged first in the Japanese and U.S. markets, the major makers of toy and game majors in these countries got a head start in developing the new marketing techniques and infrastructure.

As the demographic echo created by the baby-boomers reached their child-bearing years, significant renovations were undertaken in the major toy marketing practices. With the 1980s deregulation of television, toy merchandisers began to co-produce or affiliate with each new animated television serials (the thirty-minute commercial) or in some cases to produce films or TV specials featuring the back-stories of a host of licensed characters. The "tie-in" marketing of animated characters required a comprehensive promotional plan forged around licensing agreements that created affiliations between media and product producers. It also required a new breed of children's culture impresarios who could design hit properties and manage the cross-marketing and distribution deals. The new entrance barrier to the children's toy market became the cost of producing a successful animated film or syndicated television series ($20 million to $40 million).

In the 1980s TV cartoons featuring the Transformers, Go-Bots, G.I. Joe, He-Man, Sun-tots, Ghostbusters, Ninja Turtles, Jem, Barbie and the Rockers, Care Bears, My Little Pony, Power Rangers, and Kermit populated the children's mediascape with a succession of promotional persona who won the hearts and minds of children. The cross-marketing and licensing arrangements had a profound impact on the American toy industries as toymakers concentrated on these promotional toys " to realize massive volume sales of products with little intrinsic appeal, but with a strong marketing and fashion content." (*Playthings*, 1987). In fact, many of these cartoons were developed for the toy companies to promote their product lines of action figures and other sets of playthings, and thus they were called "program-length commercials." Between 1982 and 1986 American toy sales swelled from 4.6 to 12.3 billion dollars, but it was licensed toy sales (action figures, plush and fashion dolls based on TV shows) that rose most quickly from 20% of total sales in 1977 to about 70% of the 18 billion dollar US toy and game market in 1992 (*Playthings*, 1992).

### Toward the Global Playground

Although films were only fully commercialized in the United States recently, they have long been vehicles for character marketing too. Disney's pre-eminence in the children's entertainment market is similarly based a succession of movie hits from *Snow White* to *Pocahontas*. The 1992 *Aladdin*, for example, illustrated the new scope and pattern of global marketing through media promotion. This mega-hit took a traditional folkloric tale and charmingly animated it for about $25 million. Brought to the cinema with about $20 million of promotional hype, *Aladdin* achieved ticket sales of $200 million in the first twenty-two weeks of its North American release, and has since generated another $250 million from videocassette, DVD, and product licensing spin-offs (dolls, pyjamas, Nintendo video games), not to mention becoming a popular new exhibit at Disneyland. The subsequent global

launch netted an additional $250 million worldwide in seat, admission, and product sales. *The Lion King*, which cost $50 million to produce, garnered $780 million in box office receipts and another 1 billion in global merchandise sales in 1994. Theme parks now account for 45 percent of Disney income while merchandising adds another 20 percent. The new Disney merchandising chain is therefore just another step along this path to realizing the merchandising and spin-off potential of popular media megahits. Indeed it was the growing profitability of Disneyland Enterprises that revealed the downwind benefits of careful management of the global merchandising spin-offs of Disney's global media exposure.

### Troubles in Toyland

Clearly one of the important consequences of this promotional restructuring of the children's cultural industries is the growing concentration of ownership and increasing reliance on a very few innovative promotional characters for profitability. The accelerated fashion cycle of promotional marketing, however, meant that not all new character lines could succeed in the competitive, cultural, and faddish children's market. By 1987, the saturation of the U.S. toy market, flooded with competing Japanese promotional toys, resulted in new uncertainties for toy merchandisers. At its peak in 1986, the U.S. toy market accounted for 70 percent of total global toy sales although only 3 percent of the world's children between three and ten years of age participated in this market. Yet as commercial media spread through Europe and Asia, the toy industries expanded. By 1990, global trade in toys had grown to $30 billion as the European toy market increased by 12% between 1985 and 1989, with the Netherlands growing by 41% and Sweden by 30% (*Playthings*, 1991). Per-child expenditures on toys in Germany even exceeded those of U.S. families at $429 (compared to $383 in the U.S.). For this reason, the years since 1999 have seen a dramatic shift to the international marketing of children's products by the world's six leading toy makers.

But perhaps more important, the playthings market was being transformed by the rapid development of the video game medium. As early as 1972, Nolan Bushnell was using new microprocessor technology to introduce his Atari. Originally an arcade game machine, in 1975 it was adapted to the home TV with a minicomputer console. When Atari and others introduced the arcade machines, entrepreneurs were quick to follow. Tico Bonomo placed his Time Out game parlors in malls in the Northeast and made them parent-friendly by using orange lighting that created mystery for kids, but did not produce the dark and dirty look of bars and lounges. By 1981,

$5 billion in quarters were being spent in video arcades. While some health experts and more parents believed that Pac Man and other video games were addictive, the video game industry was surprised to find that, in 1977 and again in 1983, bored kids passed by arcades and overflowing bins of home game cartridges, leading major companies such as Mattel and Magnavox to abandon the video game industry, and for major makers, especially Atari, to go under. While this craze died in the early 1980s, the much-improved graphics and action of Nintendo brought the video game back.

In 1986 Nintendo had become the leading survivor in this novel playthings market by spending $30 million on its marketing. By the early 1990s, video game consoles were found in more than one-quarter of U.S. households, and the rapid development of this play technology led to intensified TV marketing battles between Sega and Nintendo, who relied on TV advertising to merchandise their play systems. The game makers were spending $100 million on advertising annually as the cost of doing business in the market. Both Sega's Sonic the Hedgehog and Nintendo's Mario Bros. became stars in their own promotional film and TV series. *Nintendo Power* also became the leading commercial magazine in the children's market, and Internet sites featuring tips and gamer deals were proliferating. The Pokemon brand, launched in Japan in 1997, has been sold around the world through saturation advertising campaigns and two promotional films, and is the most successful playthings brand ever, grossing more than $3 billion for the company. With competition from the computer gaming industry, along with Sony's Playstation and Microsoft's X-box, which invested $500 million in launching the product line, the video game sector has become the fastest-growing and most-commercialized sector in the entertainment market, with gross global sales approaching $30 billion.

## Conclusion

Starting with modest advertising of toys in a few magazines in the 1900s, playthings have become intimately bound to the expanding global reach of children's promotional industries. The progressive transformation of children's commercial media into promotional outlets for the merchants of playthings appears to be an unstoppable global trend embedding common regimes of symbolic play in leisure around the world: kids in the early 2000s are fascinated by the same characters in movies, repeat the same stories from TV, and play the same games. Children have more opportunities to play and learn than ever before; yet an estimated 80 percent of children's play is designed, produced, and sold by only twelve leading

multinational corporations, mostly Japanese and American. Some will celebrate this impact of progressive commodification of play as helping to establish a globalized digitally connected culture where children play in "perfect harmony"; others will lament the passing of traditional pastimes and local folkways seemingly eroded by the markets expansionary pressure to cultural convergence. But no one can deny that the commodification of play over the twentieth century marks a profound transformation of American play cultures.

*See also:* Board Games, Childhood and Play, Children's Museums, Commercialization of Leisure, Computer/Video Games, Disneyland, Fads, Television's Impact on Youth and Children's Leisure, Walt Disney World

## BIBLIOGRAPHY

Aries, Phillipe. *Centuries of Childhood.* Translated by Robert Baldick. New York: Alfred A. Knopf, 1962.

Buckingham, David. *After the Death of Childhood: Growing Up in the Age of Electronic Media.* London: Polity Press, 2000.

Caillois, Roland. *Man, Play and Games.* Translated by Meyer Barash. New York: Free Press of Glencoe, 1962.

Carpenter, Humphrey. *Secret Gardens: A Study of the Golden Age of Children's Literature.* Boston: Houghton Mifflin, 1985.

Cross, Gary. *Kids? Stuff: Toys and the Changing World of American Childhood.* Cambridge, Mass.: Harvard University Press, 1997.

Jenkins, Henry. *Children's Culture Reader.* New York: New York University Press, 1998.

Kinder, Marsha. *Playing with Power in Movies, Television and Video Games: From Muppet Babies to Teenage Mutant Ninja Turtles.* Berkeley: University of California Press, 1991.

Kline, Stephen. *Out of the Garden: Toys, TV and the Children's Culture in the Age of Marketing.* New York and London: Verso, 1993.

McNeal, James. *The Kids Market: Myths and Realities.* Ithaca, N.Y.: Paramount Market, 1999.

Schneider, Cy. *Children's Television: The Art, The Business, and How it Works.* Chicago: NTC Business Books, 1987.

Seiter, Ellen. *Sold Separately: Children and Parents in Consumer Culture.* New Brunswick, N.J.: Rutgers University Press, 1993.

Stern, Sydney, and Ted Schoenhaaus. *Toyland: The High-Stakes Game of the Toy Industry.* Chicago: Contemporary Books, 1990.

Sutton-Smith, Brian. *Toys as Culture.* New York: Gardner Press, 1986.

*Stephen Kline*

# THE COMMERCIALIZATION OF LEISURE

The ongoing commercialization of leisure in American culture continues to inform the character and reach of American culture. Implying a change over time, the notion of commercialization indicates a process whereby market-oriented business interests, practices, and institutions come to direct, rather than respond to, the character, trajectory, and shape of leisure pursuits.

Historically speaking, commercial leisure not only has provided new content for recreation—i.e., objects, places, and activities. Commercialization has also been involved in the creation of new contexts through which emerging social relationships could be played out on the changing cultural-economic landscape during the early period of industrialization in and on the streets of the industrial city. These contexts and relationships have themselves become the basis for new markets and new forms of leisure into the twenty-first century. In contemporary, postindustrial, postmodern social relations, leisure and consumer culture now feed upon and inform each other in a progressive, reciprocal fashion.

The tight, practical relationship between leisure and commerce should not be mistaken for political, conceptual, or philosophical harmony, historically or presently. Lingering tensions and contradictory tendencies arise whenever the pursuit of fun and pleasure is coupled with the realization of profit and pecuniary interest. There remains a tension between the privatizing thrust of business interests, on the one hand, and a concern that leisure and recreation provide social benefits, on the other. As well, concerns about the "polluting" effects of money on the "purity" of leisure and recreation have taken many forms since the nineteenth century and continue to structure contemporary discourses about, for instance, how the market has affected professional and amateur athletics. These "effects" or consequences of the marriage of commerce and leisure have not been uniform, unidirectional, or inevitable. A gradual and uneven process, commercialization must be understood with regard to specific historical periods and in particular social contexts, rather than thought of as a single, overarching process.

## Early Industrialization and the Loss of Traditional Rhythms

The Industrial Revolution began around 1790 in England and was at its height in the United States from about 1810 to 1850. Characterized by the substitution of mechanical power for human or animal power and the replacement of hand tools by machines, industrialization necessarily affected the nature and organization of work and, concomitantly, the larger social structure, including the nature and use of time in general, gender roles, and the family. These changes were felt most fundamentally in disruptions of everyday rhythms and, more generally, in the realm of ritual celebrations that were often religious in nature.

Changes in the nature and structure of work went hand in hand with industrialized production. Increased mechanization made for ever-finer divisions of labor requiring workers to engage in smaller and smaller tasks, making work tedious and repetitive for the laborer and profitable for the owner. In addition to requiring anywhere from ten- to fourteen-hour workdays six, sometimes seven, days a week, the new mode of industrial organization allowed business owners to bring all or most of production under one roof in the form of the factory. In this setting, worker time use could be measured and managed in the service of extending the reach of capital.

The new industrial order set in motion fundamental changes in relationship between time and work. Traditional rhythms based on "task orientation"—whereby the nature of the task would determine the time involved—were gradually, but not completely, coming to be dominated by a "time discipline" orientation. Farmwork necessarily followed the dictates of the seasons and of the weather, which made for alternating periods of busyness and idleness. Under conditions of wage labor, tasks conformed to the needs of capital expansion, and sometimes to the whims of supervisors and foremen. Henry Ford's use of the assembly line and Frederick Taylor's time-motion studies of worker productivity in the early twentieth century represent something of a culmination of industrialists' penchant for time orientation and time discipline.

Time, in a sense, came to serve money, the ramifications of which crescendoed well beyond the workplace to radically transform many elements of social structure and many aspects of daily life. Religious feast days, festivals, and traditional absenteeism from work, in preindustrial Europe as well as those practices brought to the New World, were gradually whittled down to fit the emerging patterns of work and rest. Except for the Sabbath, as a traditional day of nonlabor, and a few other important holidays, the industrial workweek and work year became the standard template for the distinction between work and free time.

Industrialization also ushered in and made possible other changes in social structure, in particular in relation to the household and the domestic division of labor. The home or farm, in agricultural society, often employed the integration of men's, women's, and children's work. Under preindustrial conditions, most work was house- or farmwork; it was accomplished by a division of labor based on gender and age, which interlaced various tasks into an interdependent, usually localized, system of women's, men's, and children's work. As new technologies (e.g., steam power, the spinning jenny) both centralized and increased production in the form of the factory, an expanding cash-based market drew increasing numbers of men, women, and children out of the home to labor for wages. Those women who did not seek employment were faced with an ever-larger share of household work once performed by men.

The split of home from work entailed a number of consequences. It often increased women's work in the home, where new labor-saving devices did not offset the new burdens of taking on what had once been men's and children's chores. Men's daily experiences outside the home involved participating in market economy and contrasted with the experiences of married women who remained in the relatively circumscribed domestic sphere. The nineteenth-century doctrine of separate spheres—i.e., that women's "natural" place was in the home—helped solidify an emergent sentiment that the home should serve as "haven" from what was often thought of as the moral pollution of the workaday world. Part of a woman's "duty" was to serve as the caretaker of this haven. By the mid-1800s, the heartless world, represented by the money economy and market values generally, was seen as threatening to an emergent white, American middle-class sense of sentimental domesticity. In this context, many religious celebrations such as Christmas and Easter, which had been public events involving the surrounding community and church, increasingly turned inward toward private celebration and toward the celebration of the family itself. The task of creating and re-creating "the family" as a buttress against the incursion of the market and market values became definitive of the emotional labor expected of women.

Even as family sentiment turned inward toward itself, the institution of the family and the larger economy became increasingly enmeshed with each other. Less able to make goods for themselves or to barter for needed goods, the family could not avoid contact with the new industrial order in the form of a money economy. Money that flowed into the household in the form of wages flowed out in the form of purchases. The household, rather than serving as a site for the material production of goods as it did on the preindustrial farm and cottage industries, came to function primarily as a unit of con-

sumption. In this context, commercialized leisure and recreation found fertile ground on which to flourish—the industrial city.

## Democratization, Commercialized Leisure, and the Industrial City

Large, crowded, and vibrant cities grew from towns at exponential rates throughout the 1800s. Propelled by the social changes wrought by industrialization and fed with surging immigrant populations from first Western then Eastern and Southern Europe over the period from 1880 to 1924, a historically unique public culture arose on the streets of the new industrial cities. In the latter decades of the nineteenth century and extending into the early part of the twentieth, cheap, public amusements became increasingly available to a growing number of city dwellers. Spurred on by technological advances in lighting and electricity, evening performances on the Vaudeville circuit, nickel movie houses known as nickelodeons, amusement parks like those found at Coney Island in New York City, sports arenas, dance halls, and large, extravagant department stores became some of the most popular and visible of entertainments.

The new public culture increasingly was experienced as a consumer culture of shopping places, entertainment, and amusements outside the home. Often understood as having had a "democratizing" influence on social arrangements, the urban cultures of consumption and amusement offered places and activities whereby different people and different kinds of people could come into contact with one another. In these contexts, different ways of life brought from different national traditions could be on display for and mix with one another. On the other hand, the new forms of public, urban leisure gave expression to the many social cleavages and social distinctions—such as race, ethnicity, class, and gender—already existing in American life.

The public world of fun and amusement represented a different "culture" than what could be found in the immigrant neighborhoods of working people. In the neighborhoods, old-world sensibilities dominated, particularly regarding the proper arrangement between the sexes. For unmarried women of European descent, the home was often the site of traditional authority, where restrictive social and sexual mores were enforced by immigrant parents. The public world was heterosocial—mixing males and females—and, by its nature, most often took place outside the surveillance of family and community. Moralists publicly decried the mixing of sexes in the dark movie theaters. The numerous dance halls, spurred by liquor industry interests, were places where "unescorted" women were welcome and where meeting an unknown man would not automatically call the women's "virtue" into question.

"Going out" meant to leave, physically and socially, one world behind and to enter a new one that was characterized by a sense of freedom. For the heterosexual woman, conflicts with her parents were often over how much of her pay she could keep, and thus over her independence and privacy. Women's dress was also often an issue. Evidence from diaries and subsequent testimonials indicate that some women would hide their "American" clothes somewhere outside their residence to be put on in secret for an evening out. The "freedom" women experienced in the anonymity of the city and the public nature of amusements also allowed a gay, male world to exist in the interstices of straight culture. In New York in the 1920s and 1930s, for instance, commercialized leisure spaces such as ballrooms, saloons, and cafeterias existed where forms of dress, code words, and other coded signals marked out a discontinuous, half-secret, and half-known geography of homosexual association.

Married or unmarried, men or women, gay or straight, those of the working classes spent what meager money they had outside their small, often crowded rooms mixing with others on city streets. Weekend excursions to amusement places like New York's Coney Island in the early twentieth century gave single women another opportunity to be away from parents and to go on "dates." Coney Island was also a family destination, accessible by inexpensive streetcars. Its several parks, most notably Luna Park and Dreamland, respectively accommodated working-class and middle-class consumers. Sunday, the Christian Sabbath and the only day off work for many, often became less a day of worship and more a day of nonwork and active leisure.

The new leisure landscape also divided genders, classes, sexualities, and races even as it appeared to have united them. African Americans remained virtually absent from urban public culture, particularly in the industrial cities of the North. Saloons, the haven of workingmen, were not welcoming to women. People brought their ethnicities with them into movie houses and dancing halls, and those establishments located adjacent to or within particular ethnic enclaves surely imprinted their character and culture on those spaces. The well-to-do created their own exclusive sport clubs in the suburban areas of cities so as to ensure and promote race and class solidarity. These forms of commercialized leisure are inseparable from the industrial American city, giving cities and neighborhoods a character related to yet distinct from that associated with the labor performed by its inhabitants.

In many quarters, commercialism was seen as having deleterious effects on social life. For moralists, the sense of freedom and choice fostered in the dance halls and amusement parks was itself the problem. The mixing of different ethnicities, the licentious behavior exhibited in the dance halls and at the gay pageants and saloons, the "low," base content of dime novels and films all signaled a debasing of "culture." Concerns about the lowering of culture have been voiced since the nineteenth century, but they became acute when the "masses" (a code work often for ethnic, working-class people) rose in prominence on the streets of the industrial city. Reformers felt responsible to provide moral "uplift" to audiences by exposing the working classes to high culture in the form of ballets, opera, and literary plays. The Chicago social reformer Jane Addams made literary education part of her program to assist delinquent juveniles at her Hull House. As well, many of those in the advertising industry, particularly in the 1920s and 1930s, took it as their mission and duty to depict scenes of "good living" as morally worthy of emulation.

## The Rise of Consumer Culture

In this same context, a new institution took root—the department store—that similarly bespoke a democratic ethos of goods and that was a morally palatable activity for the rising middle classes. With the increased efficiency and high productivity of mechanized factory production, large varieties and quantities of goods were made available at low prices. When Henry Ford, automobile manufacturer, uniformly raised the wages of his workers to $5 a day and limited them to eight-hour workdays in 1914, he was giving concrete recognition that his workers were also consumers who were in need of time and money to participate in the new world of commercial goods and leisure activities. Concomitantly, in the early twentieth century, professional occupations emerged that were needed to service and coordinate the new economy —secretaries, accountants, lawyers, copywriters, editors, among others—thereby giving rise to a new middle class with a growing disposable income. As increasing numbers of working people found more and more goods within their reach, new goods, styles, and fashions arose to meet the demands of those better off who sought to maintain their social distinction.

The lavish display of varieties of goods in department stores, such as Marshall Field's store in Chicago or John Wanamaker's in Philadelphia, recalled that of great palaces or cathedrals. They welcomed women to indulge in shopping as a personal pleasure rather than as the mere exercise of domestic labor. Many of the goods on display—silks, perfumes, jewelry—were, in previous times, available only to royalty and the well-to-do. Now they were within the physical, monetary, and social research of the middle-class woman shopper. Shopping in these stores and among the goods, being able to touch and handle them, evoked images and feelings of abundance and luxury and encouraged fantasy. Many working-class and immigrant women were relegated to another kind of fantasy—window shopping—by viewing the goods separated by the new, large windows that faced the street.

Working or not, a woman's first "duty" remained that of domestic caretaker and, in the 1910s and beyond, a wife or mother increasingly fulfilled this duty by physically and socially leaving the domestic sphere of the home and entering the public world of ready-made goods to purchase needed and wanted goods for the family. Catered to by managers and deferred to by sales clerks, the middle-class woman shopper often experienced the department store as a place more fully hers in some ways than her own home, where she was often seen as a servant.

Shopping for pleasure would not remain limited to middle-class women or to department stores. An emergent ethos of consumption, which connected the expression of personal identity with the ownership and display of consumer goods, extended beyond the confines of the department store to inform virtually every aspect of life.

## The Pressures of Standardization

The push and pull of commercialized leisure on social relations witnessed in the early twentieth century combined an egalitarian ideology with the pursuit of profit. Public amusements in the industrial city revealed that the impact of commercialization was not uniform across social life. On the one hand, it made a wide variety of goods and activities available to increasing numbers of people, and yet, on the other hand, these goods and activities also provided the basis for maintaining social divisions.

The "democratization" of leisure through commercial means had a noticeable but limited range of impact because successful capital enterprise requires continual expansion of existing markets as well as the creation of new ones. Commercial capital in this way puts a premium on what distinguishes people and groups from one another and less emphasis on what unites them. Commercialized leisure took forms other than those encountered in public amusements and, as well, embodied other tendencies that continue to inform and shape leisure and recreation into the twenty-first century.

In a gradual, uneven manner, commercialization has often meant a consolidation of ownership within industries producing leisure goods and services. Concentrated ownership often had direct effects upon the activities, often standardizing rules and practices to fit the needs of mass production. The Spalding Company and others in the late 1800s, for instance, worked to standardize rules for baseball equipment across disparate localities by distributing rule books, forming leagues and clubs, and seeking celebrity endorsements, all in an effort to secure a market for their goods. The Theatre Syndicate and the United Booking Office eventually wrested control of theater and vaudeville circuits, thereby putting themselves in a position to determine which acts would play and in which localities. Boxing, bicycling, and building model airplanes are among those leisure activities, once specific to locality and social class, that came under the auspices of business influence resulting in a change in the locus of control from the group or locality to the business operation. Government action furthermore often assisted the movement toward concentration of ownership through patent and copyright laws, curfews, and selective enforcement of vice crimes.

Changes in the rules of sports and games were not the exclusive product of business concentration. Players and practitioners in various localities around the county continue to exhibit their own particular styles of play. In many cases, a degree of standardization is needed to have competition and communication across space and time. Nevertheless, the rise of industries devoted to delivering leisure goods and services inevitably changed the nature of the equation from local origins and practices to standards suitable for market distribution, for instance, in the concentration of ownership of goods and services.

## Tourism and Authenticity

Perhaps the most pernicious social tension to accompany commercialization is that surrounding the idea of authenticity. The ever-present influence of the interests of profit-maximizing enterprises on the pursuit of pleasure and recreation continually calls into question the motives of the owners or promoters of the leisure and the experiences of the users or patrons. Questions of and concerns about authenticity tend to arise in reaction to a felt loss of something deemed to be "real." Since industrialization, many social theorists have lamented the ways in which modern, capitalist society has put asunder traditional practices, places, and experiences. Under the leveling power of the money economy, so this thinking goes, that which is local, specific, and unique dissipates into a bland similarity—e.g., food becomes standardized, experiences become mass-produced, sport stadiums begin to look and feel identical to one another. Counter to this view is the charge that the pureness implied in the idea of "authenticity" never existed and that worries about its loss reflect a romanticized version of history, community, and nature.

Tourism is the exemplary site where issues of authenticity and commercialization have played out at least since the 1920s and continue to do so into the twenty-first century. Prior to the nineteenth century, few people traveled to have experiences or to see objects for reasons other than business purposes. With the growth of industry, the rise of cities, and, eventually, the increase in time away from work and rising incomes, Americans increasingly sought to spend time away from their home communities. Train travel and, later, automobile travel made day, weekend, and extended stays increasingly within the reach of many. Roadside attractions, motels, and diners grew to service a growing tourist culture of travelers who sought to see and often photograph "sights." The sights and destinations were often designated as such in brochures and booklets often published by various local chambers of commerce seeking to draw the tourist business to or through their particular locales.

Natural phenomena, like Niagara Falls and Yosemite and Yellowstone National Parks, offer one kind of destination. As early as 1913, the U.S. Forest Service and National Park Service sought to connect park visitation and services with commercial interests in an effort to "popularize" the natural areas. Making the parks automobile-accessible, with the inspiration and consultation from the Ford Motor Company, became a priority. In the ensuing decades, particularly after World War II, such developments as lodges and ski slopes, concessions within parks, along with marketing and media campaigns, have become routine elements of the "park experience." In a paradox of contemporary wilderness tourism, it takes a great amount of human effort in wildlife and forest management to make it appear as if humans are not involved.

Tourism also turned the cultures and life ways of people into "sights" and "experiences" for the traveling market, often with the effect of reducing complex, multilayered cultures into a type or a single set of images. The ethnic postcard of the 1900–1970 period, for instance, made use of stereotyped poses and situations—some of which were erroneous—to depict Native Americans and Mexicans/Mexican Americans as part of the "natural" scenery of the American West and Southwest. Inhabitants of many of these destinations made use of the tourist expectation and stereotypes of ethnic authenticity and began to produce trinkets, hold performances, give tours, and dress specifically for the tourists. Their authenticity, often a purposely staged performance, was a reaction to

having been put on stage themselves. The idea of "staging authenticity" captures well the paradox of tourism, whereby people, things, places, and sights are pursued for their "real," or untouched quality, and yet the very act of engaging in the pursuit guarantees that they will be "touched" or transformed, often by commercial means. Historical villages like Sturbridge Village in Massachusetts and Colonial Williamsburg in Virginia take their relationship to authenticity seriously with actors who, playing people of the historical period replicated, give demonstrations of lost arts like house building and smithing.

## Postmodern Leisure in Postindustrial Society

There is no widespread agreement as to what exactly constitutes the postmodern era, but postmodern society often refers to social changes that occurred with the decline of industrial mass production in the 1970s. In the place of mass production, flexible forms of production that respond to increasingly specific markets and market fragments have arisen. Part-time labor, the rise of the service sector and loss of manufacturing jobs, the growth of cable and satellite television, and the availability of the Internet and World Wide Web are among the key developments that have made for the transition to a postindustrial economy. Generally, the term "postindustrial" refers to the time period after the mid-1970s when the dominant form of production began to change, while "postmodern" describes the cultural changes often thought to accompany the change in production.

Television, although becoming popular in the 1950s, both makes possible and embodies a kind of postmodern, commercialized leisure. Until the late 1970s, there were only about three to six stations in any given market. Viewers nationwide watched the same shows and commercials. Since that time, "narrowcasting"—as opposed to broadcasting—has been made possible by the spread of cable and satellite delivery systems, which leave hundreds of television channels at one's disposal. The programs and commercials on these numerous channels together offer a glimpse at the lifestyle landscape that is populated with narrowly targeted groupings specific to interest and leisure activity as well as age, race, and gender. Not only does television serve as a medium for the depiction of leisure lifestyles and identities, but watching television is a leisure activity unto itself. In the United States, it is the most common and most time-consuming form of leisure.

In postmodern society, personal identity and social processes become increasingly fragmented due, in part, to a loss in the faith that a stable, identifiable "reality" can be unambiguously identified underneath the advertising imagery and media representations that saturate daily life. As a result, simulated realities abound to such an extent that the line separating simulation and the "reality" to which it supposedly refers is ambiguous and often irrelevant to the participation in, or enjoyment of, the activity. The relation between historical authenticity and its staged performance no longer matters. It is performance for entertainment's sake—to escape from one's everyday experience.

The Disney theme parks in California and Florida, though opened in 1955 and 1971 respectively, represent prototypes for hypersimulated, postmodern entertainment. The various "worlds" and "lands" one can visit, the reproductions of streets and buildings of France, China, and Mexico, the animatronic robots of presidents of the United States at the EPCOT Center in Florida, the live, costumed Disney cartoon characters (who are never out of character in public) do not gesture toward a reality they supposedly represent as much as invite the consumer to engage in fantasy. The California Adventure, which is an amalgam of California tourist "sights" miniaturized at the Anaheim park, renders seeing the rest of the "real California" somewhat superfluous. Film studios, such as Universal and MGM, have made their own theme parks, where much of the entertainment centers on either thrilling the visitors with rides that scare or shock, or demonstrating how film works its "magic" by showing backstage tricks of the trade. The city of Las Vegas has rebuilt itself since the 1980s into a metropolis of simulations, whereby hotel-casinos replicate the pyramids at Giza, an Italian piazza, and the sights of New York City, and erupting volcanoes line the strip.

Theming has taken root in numerous contexts beyond the theme park and Las Vegas. Many restaurants offer themed decors, often combining historical periods or cultures in ways that could not have been encountered without commercial intervention and organization. In some, the waitstaff becomes part of the theme, dressing and acting out the corporate-designed motifs; in others, live performances draw the patrons into participating in the staging of the scene. Beyond "eatertainment," as it is known, contemporary cities have developed and marketed entire areas as themed, commercial shopping spaces. As the cities generally have moved from being sites of industrial production to postindustrial places of entertainment and consumption, developers have sought to turn historically working areas into themed, consumer environments, like the former fish market of South Street Seaport in lower Manhattan, which is now restored and sanitized into shops and restaurants for tourists.

Marketing and simulation are part of leisure and recreational activities and part of the access to those activities. Leisure in contemporary, postmodern times—from Internet-based games and memberships to the nearly complete sponsorship of sports events and venues, to children's television shows that serve as program-length commercials for action figures and other products—can no longer be separated from commercial enterprise. The enjoyment and experience of leisure, moreover, are not strictly tied to their authenticity or the extent to which they are felt to have commercial origins. Tie-ins and cross promotions between children's products and fast-food restaurants, the blurring of sports figure, celebrity and product endorser and the complicated relationship between music stars, music videos, and clothing styles for various segments of youth all point to the impossibility of making convincing distinctions between leisure, lifestyle, and the consumption.

Not everything has changed in postindustrial society. The leveling effects of the money economy continue to exert pressure on every new activity or sport that arises, such as the new "gravity games" like snowboarding and skateboarding, both of which originated in a culture that positioned itself in opposition to the commercialization of sport but that now relies upon corporate sponsorship for its widespread exposure and success. For women, although in the workforce in greater numbers than ever, the responsibilities of mothering and being caretaker of the household have diminished little. A woman's leisure time often remains restricted to the spaces in between working a "double shift" of laboring for wages outside the home and caring for the family when she returns. African Americans, Latinos, and other minorities remain virtually absent from large sports venues and national parks due in part to lack of financial resources but also to a felt sense that these places still belong culturally to the diminishing white majority of the country. Yet, the democratization of leisure first encountered in the industrial city of the late 1800s remains an ideal and sometimes is found in practice as social relations continue to transform and, in the process, remold the social landscape of leisure.

Commerce has emerged as the key context for the creation and exercise of leisure. More than offering only new content, marketing and the money economy have increasingly forged the very arenas where entertainment, recreation, and leisure take place. In the movement from traditional to modern and then to postmodern social arrangements, the interplay between the interests and thrust of capital and the desires of people to find fun and enjoyment away from the world of work and obligations have also allowed for the testing and performing of new identities. The issues facing those of the present center around determining what, if anything, has been lost with the transformation of leisure into consumption, what to keep that is new, and how to take control of the processes informing the production of leisure now and in the future.

*See also:* Commercialization of Children's Play; Impresarios of Leisure, Rise of; Media, Technology, and Leisure; Urbanization and Leisure

## BIBLIOGRAPHY

Albers, Patricia C., and William R. James. "Travel Photography: A Methodological Approach." *Annals of Tourism Research* 15 (1988): 134–158.

Benson, Susan Porter. *Counter Cultures.* Bloomington: Indiana University Press, 1986.

Butsch, Richard, ed. *For Fun and Profit.* Philadelphia: Temple University Press, 1990.

Chauncey, George. *Gay New York.* Chicago: University of Chicago Press, 1994.

Cowan, Ruth Schartz. *More Work for Mother.* New York: Basic Books, 1983.

Cross, Gary. *A Social History of Leisure.* State College, Pa.: Venture Publishing, 1990.

———. *Time and Money.* London: Routledge, 1993.

Gottdiener, Mark. *The Theming of America.* Boulder, Colo.: Westview Press, 1997.

Hannigan, John. *Fantasy City.* London: Routledge, 1998.

Harvey, David. *The Condition of Postmodernity.* Cambridge, Mass.: Blackwell, 1989.

Kinder, Marsha. *Kids' Media Culture.* Durham, N.C.: Duke University Press, 1998.

Leach, William. *Land of Desire.* New York: Pantheon Books, 1993.

McCannell, Dean. *The Tourist.* New York: Schocken Books, 1976.

Marchand, Roland. *Advertising the American Dream.* Berkeley: University of California Press, 1985.

Nasaw, David. *Going Out: The Rise and Fall of Public Amusements.* New York: Basic Books, 1993.

Peiss, Kathy. *Cheap Amusements.* Philadelphia: Temple University Press, 1986.

Pleck, Elizabeth. *Celebrating the Family.* Cambridge, Mass.: Harvard University Press, 2000.

Reiss, Steven. *City Games: The Evolution of American Urban Society and the Rise of Sports.* Urbana: University of Illinois Press, 1991.

Rojek, Chris. *Decentring Leisure.* London: Sage Publications, 1995.

Thompson, E. P. "Time, Work-Discipline and Capitalism." *Past and Present* 38 (1967).

Urry, John. *The Tourist Gaze.* London: Sage Publications, 2002.

*Daniel Thomas Cook*

# COMMODIFICATION OF LEISURE GOODS

See *Commercialization of Leisure Goods*

# COMPACT DISC COLLECTING AND LISTENING

See *Record, CD, and Tape Collecting and Listening*

# COMPUTER/VIDEO GAMES

Play is universal, yet our current fascination for matching wits with machines is quintessentially modern. Building on the traditions of play established by the one-arm bandit, pachinko, and pinball machines, video games went through a remarkable transformation in their over fifty years of development, lurching from laboratory curiosity to $20 billion global entertainment industry. Many historians of computing prefer the terms "interactive play" or "digital entertainment" to refer to this fortuitous conjuncture of the computer and mass entertainment industries. "Video gaming" refers generically to the synergy of technological invention, computer entrepreneurialism, and cultural creativity emerging from related technological innovations—on mainframes, on PCs, in arcades, on purpose-built consoles, on handhelds, and in Internet computing. Thanks to key technological advancements, the competing corporations, and foundational genres (that is sports games, first-person shooter games, puzzle games, and others), video games have become the fastest-growing sector in the entertainment economy.

Early in the 1950s mathematicians conceived of programming computers to play chess—an idea that culminated in Gary Kasparov's humiliating defeat at the hands of Deep Blue in May 1997. But the first operational video game was a tennis-simulation game demonstrated in 1958 as an instrumentation curiosity by the physicist William Higinbotham at the U.S. Department of Nuclear Energy's Brookhaven National Laboratory to visiting scientists. Higinbotham wrote a program for an analog computer he called Tennis for Two played on a five-inch black-and-white oscilloscope screen from two control boxes—each with direction knob and serve button. He never bothered to patent the game.

**ATARI video games.** One of ATARI Video Computer System's most popular games in the 1980s was "Asteroids." The game led to the International Asteroids Tournament, which was first held in November 1981. © *AP/Wide World Photos*

As legend would have it, the "ur" video game Space Wars was programmed on a multimillion dollar, closet-sized PDP-1 computer lodged in the basement of MIT (Massachusetts Institute of Technology). The inspiration for this first space "shooter" genre is attributed to Steve Russel, who, aided by a group of geeky fellow students, created a computerized "pinball machine" to amuse themselves in off hours. By today's standards Space Wars was not a sophisticated game. The program consisted mainly of a proto "game engine"—in the form of interactive software that linked the "controls" on the computer to a "display" on an oscilloscope screen. The two players interacted through the computer attempting to maneuver two navigable "space ship blips" against a backdrop of moving stars. Toggles on the computer console controlled the space ships by altering each ship's trajectory. The game had no sound track, no color, no levels, and no back story, and the only goal was to outmaneuver your opponent and shoot a missile that hit the enemy ship. Yet Space War marks a historically important juncture in our cultural history, notes Allucquere Stone, because, long before mainframes were networked by DARPA (Defense Advanced Research Projects Agency), serious computer engineers began to "make space for play in the very belly of the monster that is the communication industry" (Stone, pp. 12–13). Soon games like Space Wars, Star Trek, Adventure, Asteroids, and NetHack were being shared among an underground network of mainframe engineering students and played usually in the off-peak evening hours. Entrepreneurs among them began to imagine the profitable possibilities of fun in the computer industry.

## The Making of an Interactive Medium

In 1966, Ralph Baer, an engineer at Sanders Associates, a military electronics consulting firm, approached video gaming from a different direction—as a novel use for surplus television screens. Baer, who had seen Tennis for Two, later stated, "You should be able to do something else with television besides just watch it." By linking a TV screen display to electronic input controls Baer realized that video gaming involved eye-hand coordination. He developed Tennis as a prototype military training device. By 1967, Baer's interactive television gadget had taken shape as a primitive version of the Pong system—consisting of two knobs that can control the movement of two paddles on the screen. More microelectronics than computerized, this demo was shown to a Pentagon review board.

The Pentagon couldn't see any future in video games as training simulators. So by the end of the 1960s, as microprocessor components were becoming available, Baer decided to upgrade the training system in ways that made it more enjoyable to play: Now two players could twist knobs on the console to control the movement of the rackets on the screen. Precise movements of the knobs produced immediately visualized effects on the TV screen, giving the game the excitement of "body English" and variable acceleration of the ball. Baer sold this game design to Magnavox, and Magnavox developed it as Odyssey, which was placed in bars and arcades as a welcome alternative to pinball. The game was later licensed to Atari, which distributed it more widely as Pong; its familiar sound began to resonate in road side cafés and airports, competing with Nolan Bushnell's Computer Space.

Bushnell was an engineering graduate student at the University of Utah, where he first played Space Wars on PDP mainframes. But his ambition went beyond designing and playing new games to selling them. A shrewd businessman with feet planted in the world of technological innovation and eyes fixed on the mass entertainment marketplace, Bushnell cobbled together a company called Syzgy in 1972 to build and market a cabinet-sized version of Space Wars, which he dubbed Computer Space. His prototype, by all accounts, was more a cobbled together bit of microelectronics rather than a proper computerized game. It could perform only one task: play Computer Space. He sold this prototype to Nutting Associates, the first company whose main ambition was to make video gaming into a popular entertainment. Nutting, which later evolved into Atari, tested the market for Pong by taking the machine to the Dutch Goose Tavern near Stanford, California. It proved an immediate hit. Atari's savvy way of popularizing Pong and Computer Space is regarded by historians as a turning point in gaming. Once video games acquired "fad" status, the medium's future lay beyond the grasp of any single game developer or corporation. For the next thirty years, the trajectory of video-gaming design and development was in the hands of the marketplace—and the complex negotiation between corporate developers, consumers, and regulators that is transacted therein.

In the wake of the first *Star Wars* film, arcade entertainment stalwarts Nintendo, Namco, Sega, Midway, Bally, and Capcom decided to invest in high-tech game design. The late 1970s saw a great ferment in the entertainment industries, as the excitement generated by Space Invaders, Astroids, Lunar Lander, and Tank brought a flood of young players into the arcades looking for friendly rivalry. Improving rapidly on the "space and sport" formats by developing maze and puzzle games like Pac Man, Frogger, and Break Out, these games proved that video games based on strategic thinking or problem solving could be as popular as "twitch" games. The arcade sector's revenues soared to more than $5 billion in 1981, inducing Atari to launch a lab devoted to gaming. Shortly after, the first books began to appear on video game design principles and programming techniques. The crowds of enthusiastic young men crowding into these "halls of iniquity," however, also gained arcades growing notoriety in the press. Several municipalities set out to clean up the perceived threat to public order by regulating arcade gaming.

## Into the Home

Although mainframe computers were the original playground of the playfully curious hacker generation (as opposed to the more malicious hacker of the early 2000s), their limited graphics and sound capacities long hampered their development as gaming sites. Games like Adventure and Find the Wumpus did gain hacker notoriety, but computers were still principally designed to meet the military and business computing needs of the industrial world. Although the potential of home computers capable of crunching words and numbers was loudly proclaimed in the early 1980s, Apple's and IBM's first PCs proved poorly suited for gaming. With no sound and with limited graphics memory and data processing, few customers bought these pricey home computers for gaming alone. But as software design became more and more important to gaming, many young hackers got their first exposure to "Basic" programming (the first simplified programming language), trying their hand at simple games. Soon some primitive games like Chess, Lunar Lander, and Adventure were available for the PC.

Building on the growing popularity of their arcade games, in 1975 Atari also set out to build a domestic model gaming device that they called Home Pong and marketed through Sears Roebuck. It was remarkably successful. The arcade entertainment sector led by Nintendo, Bally, and Sega conceived of dedicated multigame consoles that could build on television's established place as the hub of home entertainment. As microprocessor chips improved, dedicated home-gaming consoles with faster graphic processors and greater memory needed to bring the "arcade experiences into the home" were developed. Although they lacked the full sound and graphics of the arcades, they were capable of playing several different games that could be distributed as "code" on tapes or cartridges. Worried that this popular new medium would impact their toy sales, Coleco (Coleco-vision) and Mattel (Intellivision) also developed chip-based video-game consoles connected to the television. Hit games from the arcades like Frogger, Space Invaders, and Pac Man, albeit without the full range of colors or sounds, were now available at home. As competition grew fierce, the whole industry experienced a period of profitable ferment in technology and game design. By the early 1980s, hardware and software sales soared into the billions as home-gaming profits rivaled that of the arcades.

Foreseeing gaming's market threatened by the growing popularity of Apple user-friendly GUI (graphics user interface) computers, some in the microelectronics sector developed user-programmable "family computers," such as the Commodore 64 and the Atari Adam, that could be sold more cheaply than other PCs because they plugged into TV sets. These were followed by prototype multimedia PCs like the Atari 500 and the Commodore Amiga. Not only were these systems full-function computers (with the Motorola 68000 series CPU), but, equipped with specialized sound and graphics chips, they were also capable of arcade-style game genres, including racing games like Monaco, adventure games like Duke Nukem and Final Fantasy, and RPGs (role-play games) like Myst, Leisure Suite Larry, and Ultima. With the growing educational interest in computing, some of the first strategy, simulation, and puzzle games, like Tetris, Math Blaster, Sim City, and Carmen Sandiego, were all first programmed for this generation of family computers.

Yet by 1985, the gaming fad seemed to have run its course. Most kids were not interested in programming their own primitive "Basic" games on their Adam, Apple, or Amiga. Many grew bored with the console game systems whose primitive chips failed to deliver the ever more dynamic graphics, sound, and speed of the arcades. Moreover, games cobbled together by novice programmers might intrigue at first, but they had little sustaining play value. In addition, many of the systems cost too much to be left on the shelf. The market crashed, financially crippling most of these early gaming companies, including Atari and Commodore, and leading Coleco eventually to file for bankruptcy. Yet by the late 1980s, the genres of gaming had all been prototyped.

## Console Wars

Nintendo entered the U.S. home-gaming market in 1986 with its 8-bit Famicom machine, which had proved popular in Japan. Nintendo's console had a faster-loading cartridge system, good sound, and better graphics chips, which enabled the company to bundle them with popular side-scrolling arcade-style games like Mario Bros. and Donkey Kong. Nintendo's gaming machine sparked renewed interest in home entertainment during the late 1980s. Sega followed Nintendo into the U.S. market with its Sega Master System, and Atari launched an improved programmable console design called 7800. By 1990, Nintendo consoles could be found in over 25 percent of American households, buoying video-game sales in the United States over the $2.3 billion high-water mark. Mario was so popular that his character was featured in films and a TV show.

Believing that video gaming would displace TV viewing, Japanese arcade rival Sega launched its 16-bit Mega Drive. In 1989, Nintendo responded, launching its first Game Boy handheld system, and then its upgraded 16-bit Super NES system in 1991. Both these systems had excellent sound and color graphics, were far more powerful than home PCs, and cost one-tenth the price. Since hit games had multiple levels, each with lavish graphics, more storage and quicker loading time were crucial. Sega's next system, the Genesis, possessed a CD-ROM device and featured the popular character Sonic the Hedgehog. Launched in 1992 with what can only be described as an "in yer face" marketing campaign, Sega targeted those adolescent gamers who were tired of playing Mario Bros. on their Game Boys. The adolescent male market expected more mature action, sports, racing, and adventure games, and it got it when Sega released a version of Mortal Kombat, a fighting game that had blood and gore programmed into its "fatality moves." The game won immediate notoriety, becoming the focus of congressional hearings on video-game violence. To avoid regulation, Sega suggested self-regulating video games, helping to establish the first ratings board, which has evolved into the ESRB (Electronic Software Ratings Board).

Three technological requirements emerged as the gaming market matured: processing capacity, graphic display, and memory. During the 1990s, the console makers played a game of technological leapfrog: Sega released the 32-bit Saturn in 1995, followed by the Sony

Playstation, and then the Nintendo 64 in 1996. These systems were purpose-built high-end gaming systems. All possessed fast CPUs for the game engine, rapid loading and storage memory, high-resolution graphics, multiple-player controllers, and stereo sound, which all together gave console games their immersive feel. Each also offered a long list of the most popular fighting, role-play, sports, racing, and adventure game genres. In the combat games, the characters were given detailed back stories, specific weapons, and special moves or powers that had to be learned through trial and error. In the racing games, cars acquired a different "look and feel," responding realistically with skids and motor roars to conditions on the elaborately replicated tracks. In adventure games, the imaginary dungeons were lavished with fantastical dangers that presented seemingly impenetrable barriers. From the first roar of the crowd in sports games to the last crack of the bat, the uniforms, moves, and statistics were faithfully sampled from real athletes and played in faithfully drawn three-dimensional arenas, providing a televisual quality to their look and feel (including advertising). Games not only adapted formats and genres from popular films and television shows (*Star Wars, Jurassic Park, The Simpsons* ), but popular games like Mortal Kombat, Tomb Raider, and Final Fantasy also inspired hit Hollywood movies.

### The Computer Empire Fights Back

Equipped with color, video-graphics chips, stereo sound, and the CD-ROM drive, the upgraded home PC was busy competing from the back of the pack. In the early 1990s, rebranded as a multipurpose family computer capable of business, entertainment, and education applications, the multimedia computer set out to compete with the game system. Bundled now with sound cards, joystick ports, and CD-ROM drives, the multimedia PC could play some of the most popular games that fueled the second boom.

But computers also had one unique advantage that was realized when ID software updated its popular shooting game called Doom. Doom was not only a well-designed, classic, first-person POV (point-of-view) dungeon shooter, but it also could be played by two individuals connected via modems over the Internet. Although multiplayer games had existed on university mainframes and been accessed by modem, Doom pioneered a new kind of online multiplayer gaming on PCs, which has grown with the spread of the Internet. Now referred to as MMRPGs (massively mulitplayer role-play games), games like Quake, Everquest, and Counterstrike illustrate the popularity of this unique mode of interac-

tivity: Everquest has over 300,000 subscribers who pay around $10 per month to explore, trade, and fight other players in this online fantasy world. Although it remains an overpriced gaming console in the early 2000s, the multimedia computer is an attractive entertainment system because it can also play music, surf the Internet, and do banking.

### The Age of Synergy

The success of the Internet as an entertainment environment inspired console makers to rethink the future of digital entertainment. In 2000, led by the Sega Dreamcast, and soon followed by the Sony Playstation II, the Microsoft Xbox, and then the Nintendo Gamecube, console systems went through another generation of technological upgrading. Adding Internet options adapted from the home PC, all possessed three-dimensional graphics and promised online options. Some doubled as DVD players or digital music boxes as well.

Over the years, video gaming has become integrated into the entertainment economy. Games now take two years to bring to the market and costs of development are often similar to Hollywood films. Since Mario Bros., the video-game industry has become gradually integrated into the entertainment marketplace, and games like Mortal Kombat, Die Hard, Enter the Dragon, Star Wars IV, and the Matrix are often developed in tandem with movies. For example, Nintendo's Pokémon games, launched first in Japan in 1997, spearheaded over $3 billion in world sales by masterfully linking video games, films, and television.

As of 2004, many games were published for different platforms. Game designers like to combine all elements necessary to produce a blockbuster on every platform, including dynamic music, complex sound effects, multiple points of view, multiplayer options, complex characters, fantastical environments, and Internet connectivity. As a result, the established genres are blurring: Sports games like NHL hockey are programmed with bloody stickwork and fighting sequences; fighting games have cinematic introductions, rich back stories, and speech options; racing cars are equipped with laser-guided missiles and are driven through faithfully reproduced real cities; and role-play games involve elaborate strategy and teamwork. Taken together, the video-game sector accounts for over $10 billion a year in North American sales.

***See also:*** Commercialization of Children's Play, Computer's Impact on Leisure, Internet, Men's Leisure Lifestyles, Teenage Leisure Trends

**BIBLIOGRAPHY**

Herz, J. C. *Joystick Nation: How Videogames Ate Our Quarters, Won Our Hearts and Rewired Our Minds.* Boston: Little, Brown and Company, 1997.

Kent, Steven L. *The Ultimate History of Video Games: From Pong to Pokémon and Beyond—The Story Behind the Craze That Touched Our Lives and Changed the World.* Roseville, Calif.: Prima Publishing, 2001.

Kline, Stephen, Nick Dyer Witherford, and Greig de Peuter. *Digital Play: On the Interaction of Technology, Culture and Marketing.* Montreal: McGill-Queens University Press, 2003.

Poole, Steven. *Trigger Happy: Videogames and the Entertainment Revolution.* New York: Arcade Publishing, 2000.

Sheff, David. *Game Over. How Nintendo Zapped an American Industry, Captured Your Dollars and Enslaved Your Children.* New York: Random House, 1993.

Stone, Allucquere. *The War of Desire and Technology at the Close of the Mechanical Age.* Cambridge, Mass.: MIT Press, 1996.

*Stephen Kline*

# COMPUTER'S IMPACT ON LEISURE

Children and teenagers today were born into a world of technology. They experience a leisure lifestyle very different from generations who grew up before the technology boom. In 2002, it was estimated that 70 percent of U.S. households with children under the age of nineteen used computers, compared with 55 percent in 2000 and 43 percent in 1995. In 1953, there were only about 100 computers in existence worldwide. Computers are now commonplace in schools, with 95 percent of schools having at least one Internet connection as of 1999.

Computers provide the benefit of easy access to information and have expanded communication capabilities. Favorable or unfavorable, technology has become an unavoidable part of life for most Americans. Computers play a vital role in the areas of education, business, and leisure. Development of personal computers, the Internet, the World Wide Web (WWW), and other computer-related technologies such as video games and virtual reality have dramatically influenced the leisure lifestyles of people in modern society.

Technology continues to influence the nature and diversity of economic, social, interpersonal, and leisure patterns of people. Both benefits and negative ramifications can be identified in our new technological world. Technology has the capacity for creating changes in our concepts of organization as well as redefining the leisure experiences of contemporary Americans.

## History and Development of the Computer

Broadly speaking, a computer is any mechanical device that can perform numerical calculations. According to this definition, even a simple adding machine, an abacus, or slide rule can be regarded as a computer. However, *Merriam-Webster's Collegiate Dictionary* defines the term "computer" as "a programmable electronic device that can store, retrieve, and process data."

The abacus, a system of strings and moving beads, is regarded as the first mechanical calculator. It was devised in Babylonia about 2,500 years ago (500 B.C.). The abacus was the fastest and most powerful calculator until the French scientist Blaise Pascal invented a mechanical calculator made of wheels and cogs in 1642. Both the abacus and Pascal's wheels and cogs were simple adding machine.

The British mathematician Charles Babbage invented one of the first versions of the modern computer in 1833. His computer contained all of the basic elements of a modern computer: input devices, a memory unit, a computing unit, a control unit, and output devices. During the 1880s, Herman Hollerith, an American inventor, developed a calculating machine called a "tabulator" that counted, collated, and sorted information stored on punched cards. The tabulator was used to sort statistical information for the United States census in 1890. It took only six weeks for the tabulator to count simple statistics for the census. In 1896, Hollerith founded the Tabulating Machine Company, which became the IBM (International Business Machines) Corporation in 1924. Until the late 1960s, IBM produced punch-card machinery for the business world.

World War II accelerated the development of modern computers. An operational computer (the Z3 and Z4) was first used in German military systems in 1941. In the United States, an electronic computer (the Harvard-IBM Automatic Sequence Controlled Calculator, named the Mark I) using electromechanical relays as on-off switches was invented to create ballistics tables to make navy artillery more accurate. In Great Britain, in 1943, the Colossus, the first fully functioning electronic computer that used vacuum tubes, was developed to break secret German military codes. However, the ENIAC (Electronic Numerical Integrator And Calculator), which was designed by two American engineers in 1946, is regarded as the first modern general-purpose electronic computer.

A revolution in computer development was brought forth by the invention of the transistor in 1947. Later,

**Reader Rabbit.** A kindergartener uses Reader Rabbit® software to help build his reading skills. Educational software is popular in both the home and in school curriculums. © *Corbis*

small germanium transistors were designed, which led to the miniaturization of computers, as we know them today. In 1958, an American engineer named Jack Kilby designed the first integrated circuit (IC), which helped rapidly develop the use of silicon microchip technology. The personal computer (PC) revolution occurred in the 1970s after an American engineer Marcian E. Hoff invented the microprocessor in 1971. The emergence of the microprocessor contributed to the cost reduction of electronic components required for a computer. The first major manufacturer of personal computers was the Tandy Corporation in 1977. IBM began to produce its personal computer in 1981. Since the early 1980s, the prices for personal computers have declined drastically, while the productivity and speed have increased.

Computers became more versatile in the 1990s, and this versatility opened the multimedia age. The term "multimedia" encompasses the computer's ability to combine text, charts, maps, animations and video, along with music and audio sounds, into interactive presentations. In order to store the enormous amounts of information that audio and video clips require, manufacturers

began producing CD-ROMs (Compact Disc-Read-Only Memory). The enormous storage potential of CD-ROMs prompted the development of various types of video games and virtual reality programs. CD-R and CD-RW are more advanced forms of CD-ROM. CD-R is short for "CD-Recordable." Recordable CDs are WORM (Write Once, Read Multiple) media that work just like standard CD-ROMs. The advantage of CD-R over other types of optical media is that you can use the discs with a standard CD player. The disadvantage is that you can't rewrite a disc. On the contrary, CD-RW (CD-Rewritable) allows you to erase discs and reuse them, but the CD-RW media doesn't work in all players. CD-Rewritable drives are able to write both CD-R and CD-RW discs. In the late 1990s, a more advanced technology called DVD-ROM (Digital Video Disc-Read Only Memory) was invented. This technology can store greater amounts of data such as an entire feature-length motion picture on one disc.

## The Internet and the World Wide Web

The era of information was brought forth by the advent of the Internet and the World Wide Web (WWW). The

232

Internet is a system of networked computers. The first computer link began in the 1960s by the U.S. Department of Defense, and the project began by connecting four computers. Nowadays, the system of networks and computers spans the globe, and it is difficult to know just how big the Internet is. However, it is estimated that the global online population has grown to over 600 million as of 1 November 2002 (NUA Internet Surveys). Research indicates that Europe currently has the biggest online population in the world with 190.91 million Internet users. In September 2002, the North American Internet population reached 182.67 million and accounted for 30.1 percent of global Internet users.

The World Wide Web, on the other hand, which is an information retrieval system, was created only over a decade ago (1990). The WWW can transport documents (that is, Web sites or Web pages) containing text, graphics, audio, and video, while the Internet is the vehicle that allows users to access to the information. In other words, the WWW distributes information on the Internet. The WWW uses hypertext, a document type that contains information and links to other links. Thus, users can find information or Web sites by using a page's URL (universal resource locator). The WWW is a huge multimedia information resource and a convenient and efficient way to distribute information. It is growing at an exponential rate each year. By the early twenty-first century, the availability of Web-site development software allowed users to create their own Web sites such as personal home pages, marketing and business Web sites, and organizational advocacy pages.

Electronic mail (e-mail) is another tremendously convenient communication tool via the Internet, and it is becoming a more and more important way of communicating among people. E-mail enables people with e-mail accounts to create and send information to any other individual or group of individuals who also have e-mail access. Therefore, e-mail provides convenient and speedy communication. E-mail allows people to keep in touch with others at their convenience. Many people think that returning e-mails is easier than returning phone calls, and less intrusive as well. Some find that keeping in touch with friends and family out of state through the use of e-mail is more affordable than long-distance phone calls. With current advances in technology, it is now even possible to view the person you are instant messaging through the use of digital cameras.

## Video Games

Playing video games is a preferred leisure time activity for many people. Playing video games at home or in a video arcade setting became popular in the 1970s and tapered off during the late 1980s. Ralph Baer is credited as the inventor of the video game, with his design of a television set that incorporated an interactive game. A prototype was created in 1968, known as Brown Box, which played ball-and-paddle games and shooting games. Upon seeing a demonstration, Magnavox signed an agreement in 1971 resulting in the release of the first video game system, Odyssey, in 1972. It was also in 1972 when the first successful arcade video game, Pong, was released. Designed by Nolan Bushnell and Alan Alcorn, this simplistic game ignited the video arcade industry. Several home versions were created as well. Bushnell is responsible for creating Atari Inc., which introduced games such as Pong, Tank, Gunfight, Breakout, and Space Invaders. The incredible popularity of Space Invaders is credited with bringing video games into the public consciousness, with games showing up in restaurants, malls, and bars. The public's growing interest in playing video games created an environment of competition for game makers. Striving to create the most exciting game playing experience, home video game companies continue to engage in constant innovation and improvement. Although video arcades could still be found in the early 2000s, their popularity decreased significantly since the 1980s.

Computer-based home video games are the fasted growing type of entertainment except for Internet usage. According to a recent study, an average American spends seventy-five hours per year playing video games (Lewis). More than half of American households have some kind of game machine. Sony PlayStation and Microsoft Xbox are examples of dedicated game computers that can be connected to regular television screens. People also use their own personal computers to play games, with numerous CD-ROMs for computer games currently available. Internet gaming is another way of enjoying computer games. People visit Internet game parlors and enjoy interactive computer games with other Internet users. For example, numerous people (i.e., over 30,000 in 2003) have played pool online at Yahoo Games, and thousands more play card games on AOL Games, MSN Games, or Gamespot. Currently, handheld gaming computers and personal digital assistants (PDA) such as portable Nintendo Game Boys, Palm Pilots, and Pocket PCs are gaining significant amounts of attention. More recently, playing games on cellular phones became available.

The popularity of home game systems, however, has decreased the social element of video games that existed in the arcade atmosphere. Although more than one individual can play home game systems, they are more often played solitarily.

Youth between the ages of eight and eighteen spend more than forty hours per week using some type of media, not counting school or homework assignments. Although television is still the most frequently used medium, electronic video games are rapidly growing. More specifically, among the age group of eight- to thirteen-year-old boys, the average is more than seven and a half hours per week. And 14.8 percent of high school senior students played at least six hours per week in 1999 (Anderson and Bushmen).

## Virtual Reality

Virtual Reality (VR) is a new human-computer interaction in which users are no longer simply external observers of images on a computer screen, but are active participants within a computer-generated three-dimensional virtual world. VR environments differ from traditional displays in that computer graphics and various display and input technologies are integrated to give the user a sense of presence or immersion in the virtual environment. The most common approach to the creation of a virtual environment is to outfit the user with a head-mounted display. Head-mounted displays consist of separate display screens for each eye along with some type of display optics and a head-tracking device. The head-tracking device provides head location and orientation information to a computer graphics workstation that computes visual images on the display screen consistent with the direction in which the user is looking within the virtual environment. In short, VR integrates real-time computer graphics, body-tracking devices, visual displays, and other sensory input devices to immerse a participant in a computer-generated virtual environment.

## Technology for Everyone

The appeal of technology is obvious for young people who grew up with technology, as well as for adults who were somewhat forced to incorporate it into their working lives. The use of technology, however, is not limited to young people and adults. Interestingly, seniors are the largest growing group of Internet users. With 13 percent of Americans age sixty-five and older having Internet access, it is obvious that older adults appreciate the benefits of technology. Although this percentage is relatively low, studies show that those seniors who do have access to the Internet are among the most avid users with 63 percent going online daily, compared with 54 percent of people under thirty. Web sites such as senior.com, seniornet.com, and computersforseniors.org are only a few examples of the multitudes of sites designed to interest

seniors. These sites offer information on health, travel, news, and computer tips specifically geared toward the retired population. E-mailing is one of the most popular online activities engaged in by seniors, with half of the online senior population sending and receiving e-mails on any given day. Many senior community centers offer computer classes, and even nursing homes are building computer labs within their facilities. The use of technology in leisure shows great promise in this faction of the population.

Technology and computers have also widened the doors of leisure opportunity for people with disabilities. Communication devices and specialized personal computers allow people with mobility or communication impairments to communicate their needs to others effectively. Screen readers and voice output technology allow individuals with visual impairments to surf the Web and to e-mail. Advances in assistive technology are growing constantly, allowing individuals with disabilities to enjoy the benefits of the Internet.

## Increase in Popularity

Certainly one of the most convincing reasons for the increase in popularity of computer technology is the convenience with which one can obtain any type of information. With very little instruction, one is prepared to surf the Internet and obtain knowledge on nearly any subject of interest. E-mailing and instant messaging are uncomplicated tasks and allow for ease in communication with others. The appeal of Web surfing and e-mailing from the privacy of one's own home, without even having to change out of one's pajamas is undeniable. Becoming informed has never been easier, and the face of communicating with others has changed forever.

The use of computers and technology in leisure has become increasingly popular in part due to decreased costs of computers. Whereas in the 1980s a home computer was an expensive luxury, by the turn of the century it was considered to be affordable by many families. Computers are available for personal use at libraries and community centers, often at no cost. Children become familiar with computers at school, and often teach their own families how to use them. Becoming adept at computer use is a practically unavoidable part of life for many people. Even those who are hesitant to learn and intimidated by the computer often are required to learn simple computer tasks in their workplace. Once it becomes evident that using a computer does not require tremendous knowledge and skill, people become more comfortable with exploring the various uses of their computers.

Economically, the WWW has opened up new and exciting opportunities for the business world (that is, e-commerce or e-business). Companies began to sell their products online, with great success, and home shopping by the Internet is becoming very popular, especially among young generations. People can purchase nearly any item online, from airline tickets to a baby pacifier. Although online sales are not dominant revenue streams yet in most industry sectors, e-business transactions from 1993 to 2003 sharply increased. By the early 2000s, companies in the United States generated an average of 15 to 18 percent of their revenues from e-business (InformationWeek Research's E-business Agenda Study).

Factors addressed above do not entirely explain the surge in popularity of computerized and technological leisure activities. Computers may provide some psychosocial benefits, as well. Computers may allow people to compensate for their own perceived lack of power. In today's huge corporate, educational, and government bureaucracies, individuals easily feel lost. However, people can feel a sense of control when they sit in front of computers. A computer operates only as the control of people, and it never judges or rejects them. If someone knows how to use a computer, it does only what that person wants it to do.

Surfing the Internet, playing games, and visiting chat rooms provide individuals with a sense of escape from their everyday life. The appeal of computer games, fantasy sports, and virtual reality is the convincing realism that is experienced while playing. The graphics and sound effects draw the player deep into the activity, eliciting a feeling of real participation on the player's part. Investing oneself in a virtual reality permits a temporary and partial relief from one's own reality. Many people enjoy visiting chat rooms because of the anonymity associated with the process. A sense of freedom and adventure can be experienced due to the decreased inhibitions associated with being anonymous. Some people even visit chat rooms under an assumed identity, an identity that does not resemble their own life. Escapism is part of the appeal of technology in leisure.

Many argue that our dependence on computers results in a lack of socialization with others. It can be argued, however, that computers have created rather than eliminated ways of communicating with people through the use of e-mail, instant messaging, chat rooms, and message boards. Face-to-face communication may indeed be decreasing, but a new kind of communication may not necessarily be viewed as negative.

The psychosocial impact of computer use has been a topic of interest to researchers. John Robinson and Meyer Kestnbaum published a study in which they compared cultural and other free-time activities of heavy users, light users, and nonusers of personal computers, based on a 1997 survey of more than 6,000 respondents. According to the study results, heavy computer use was associated with significantly greater participation in cultural and other free-time activities than light users and nonusers of computer. In particular, computer users tend to be more active in activities such as arts, going to movies, playing sports, and engaging in outdoor activities. These results may indicate that new technology users are more likely to engage in other cultural and leisure activities as well.

Another interesting study, done by Matthew S. Kerner, Michael Kalinski, Anthony B. Kurrant, Eric Small, Eugene Spatz, and Stacy Gropack, followed 295 adolescent African American girls and revealed that leisure-time Internet use was not correlated with a lack of physical activity or a decreased physical fitness level. These results are also somewhat contradictory to the traditional beliefs that computer users may neglect the importance of physical activities and experience physical inactivity.

As illustrated above, computers and the Internet have become an integral and essential part of education, business, leisure, and everyday life. However, technology not only provides us with positive benefits, but also with negative ramifications.

## Negative Ramifications of Technology

The onset of computer technology, especially the Internet, has occurred so quickly that most could not predict the potential dangers. Because the Internet is so vast, managing and monitoring its contents is difficult. Although steps are taken to monitor illegal activity on the Internet, it is possible for things to slip through the cracks. Criminals can enter the Internet just like regular people. Fraud and money scams are pervasive problems online, as well as identity theft. Chat rooms can become dangerous places for young people when child predators enter and persuade them to meet in person. Online dating poses similar risks when people present themselves under false pretenses.

For example, although e-mail is a tremendously convenient communication tool, there are some concerns regarding the its use. One of the concerns is an issue of its security. While an e-mail message travels from one computer to another computer, a third party such as marketing companies and hackers can retrieve it. Spamming occurs when a company sends numerous e-mails to an intended audience. That is why e-mail users receive numerous commercial e-mails from unexpected senders. Users' names and personal information can spread widely throughout the Internet.

As contradictory to the results discussed in the previous section, some researchers found that excessive Internet use leads to the inherent lack of socialization due to the solitary nature of the activity. That is, Internet users spend less time with people, often resulting in strain in personal relationships. Users may be avoiding social interactions, thereby deterring the development of social skills. They also reported that many heavy users of computers experience academic problems, dysfunctional personal relationships, financial problems, work-related problems, and physical risk factors such as sleep deprivation and lack of exercise.

Information overload and the threat to reliable information are other problematic areas that resulted from the availability of numerous Web-site development tools and the explosive growth in Web sites. Countless Web sites can be found for one keyword. However, it is not always easy for users to obtain information that is relevant and reliable. Not every Web site provides accurate, complete, dated, and reliable information. That is, the integrity of information on the Internet is threatened by numerous inaccurate, incomplete, outdated, and unreliable data. In order to use information on Web sites wisely, users should examine the accuracy of the information by checking citations, an author's credibility, the existence of copyright protection, and when a site was updated. Users also need to examine whether the information on the Web is a commercial advertisement or factual information. Therefore, importance should be placed on the reliability of information rather than the availability.

Advanced technology exacerbated another significant societal problem: media violence. Although numerous educational, nonviolent strategic, and sporting games are available to players of all ages, the most heavily marketed and consumed games are violent in nature. Mortal Kombat and Street Fighter are examples of the violent video games, both of which were best-selling games in the video game market in 1990s. The main goal of the games is to wound and kill opponents. By the end of the twentieth century, even more graphically violent and audibly vivid violent games became available.

There are some arguments regarding the positive aspects of violent video games. Some espouse the belief that playing violent games teaches youth how to deal with pent-up feelings of aggression and hostility. Others justify the violent games as pro-social by seeing violence as an acceptable method for defending good from evil. However, the majority of the numerous studies on media violence and aggression claim that playing violent video games increases aggressive behavioral tendencies both in children and adults. Playing violent video games also increases physiological arousal and aggressive-related thoughts and feelings, as well as decreases pro-social behavior.

Properly selected, age appropriate video games have the potential to foster creativity and promote pro-social behavior. Playing video games may be used both for educational and clinical purposes. Video game play can enhance hand-eye coordination and fine motor skills, and can increase an individual's ability to pay attention to detail. Therefore, careful game selection (such as examination of game description and rating code) should be made based on a player's developmental level, personality, and his or her purpose for the involvement. Placing limits on playing time is recommended as well.

## Computer Pornography

Pornography has been a controversial topic since the Internet and WWW became popular. Pornography can be defined as any sexually explicit representation to arouse its audience. Traditional forms of pornography such as soft-core magazines (such as *Playboy*) and hard-core films depicting explicit sexual acts are now available on the Internet in different formats. There are thousands of sex-related Usenet groups (Internet news groups) and numerous WWW pages showing pornographic images, video clips, and sounds. Text-based Internet chat can also be used for sexual conversations. Video conferencing programs are now being used for sexual interaction among Internet users and for users to view and direct real-time online sex shows.

Pornography is one of the most profitable ventures on the Internet, and accessing pornography Web sites is one of the Internet's most common uses. Although no official figures are available, industry executives estimate that the worth of the Internet pornography market increased from $1 billion in 1997 to $1.75 billion by 2001.

While adult pornography is legal and has become more accepted in society as a legitimate leisure activity, it is also true that the cyber pornography can pose potential problems. Repeated Internet pornography use may become an addiction when the user becomes obsessed with the behavior. For example, a study in 2000 projected that at least 200,000 Web porn users are "cybersex compulsives," spending more than eleven hours viewing Web porn each week. Internet pornography is also a threat to many parents. According to a statistics, one in four children online sees sexually explicit images and one in five children are aggressively solicited online for sex (Garcia). More than 725,000 children were asked online to meet someone face-to-face for a sexual encounter. Protecting children from Internet pornography and exploitation has continued to be an issue, as the Internet creates a loosely monitored space for child predators to roam. Creating and maintaining legal boundaries for Internet pornography continues to pose legal and social conflicts for Internet users.

## Technology and Leisure: Changes in Leisure Pursuits and Patterns

It is generally well accepted that the primary characteristics of leisure are enjoyment, freedom of choice, feelings of control, and intrinsic personal satisfaction. From this perspective, playing through the use of a computer can be regarded as a new type of leisure time activity because it is usually a self-directed activity and it appears to provide enjoyable and satisfying experience to the voluntary users.

According to a survey conducted by Price Waterhouse Coopers Consumer Technology, the two top reasons people visit the Internet are research (90 percent of the respondents) and e-mail (89 percent). Shopping was next at 42 percent, while interactive entertainment like gaming was listed by 37 percent of the users.

The leisure lifestyles of contemporary Americans can be enhanced by computer technology. Having access to the Internet eliminates some of the hassles inherent in preparing for a leisure activity. The convenience of using the Internet to plan vacations, for example, has allowed people to make all the preparations from the comfort of their homes. One can book a cruise or a flight for a vacation, make hotel arrangements, get advanced knowledge of all the attractions near their destination, make restaurant reservations, and even see the menu for dining selections. All of this is possible without having to make phone calls or visit a travel agency. Practically any recreation activity outside the home can be explored via the Internet before an individual actually goes. Internet users can view movie listings, show times, and even buy a ticket. People can obtain maps ahead of time for backpacking, canoeing, and camping trips. They can purchase sporting goods online, or buy tickets to sporting events, gallery openings, Broadway shows, and concerts from the privacy of their home. The convenience of technology also allows people to save time and frustration when planning an outing, although it also eliminates the opportunity to make connections with real people. Although the leisure activities themselves may not be different, the way people prepare for an experience has changed with the technological advances.

Computer technology has created new spaces for leisure participation. The increasing use of the Internet

and computer-related technologies during and/or for leisure time have prompted a transformation in the leisure activities of people today. Jo Bryce coined the term "virtual leisure spaces" to describe this new computer-related space. While traditional leisure activities occurred within the home, bars, restaurants, parks, and outdoor spaces, today's leisure can also be experienced through the computer and virtual spaces.

Traditional notions of leisure have been transformed by technology and the use of virtual spaces. For instance, computer games can reproduce board games, sporting activities, shopping, and social interaction with others. These technological leisure activities can also provide relaxation, stimulation, escape, and the development of self-identity and lifestyle. For the purposes of socializing and information exchange, people can form discussion groups to discuss a range of topics. Chat rooms allow for online conversation with people from all over the world. Players who are geographically distant can play competitive games over the Internet. Thus, the traditional concept of spatial organization of leisure is now being challenged by the advent of virtual leisure spaces, resulting in the boundaries between domestic, virtual, and commercial leisure spaces becoming blurred.

## Legal and Moral Challenges of the Technological World

The virtual leisure space also plays a role in testing the limits of moral and legal acceptability. Victor Turner used the term "liminal leisure" to describe the phenomenon. According to Chris Rojek, leisure activities are often significant causal factors in explaining deviant behaviors, including violence and murder. Liminal leisure sites are those that are organized around deviant leisure activities, such as fetishism and pedophilia, suicide, racism, and satanic worship. People wishing to test the limits of acceptable moral standards may explore these types of sites.

The Internet has the capacity for posing great dangers to people of all ages, especially those who are impressionable (such as young people). First Amendment laws of free speech apply to the online community, permitting hate groups, cults, and other negative affiliations to vie for members. Access to these Web sites is as simple as any other site, allowing people to view ideas to which they may not have previously had access. Instructional Web sites are available to teach things such as how to make bombs or drugs. Parents must understand the magnitude of the availability of all kinds of information and carefully supervise their children online.

Online activities need not be illegal to pose risks to computer users. Online casinos are legal, yet they become addictive and problematic for some users. Easy access to pornography can exacerbate sexual disorders. Some Internet users spend excessive amounts of time on the computer, leading to problems with their families, their jobs, and their social lives in general. The term "Internet addiction" has been coined to describe people preoccupied with the Internet and unable to control their Internet use. Many problematic Internet users report symptoms of depression, anxiety, low self-esteem, and loneliness. This may explain why nearly 80 percent of participants in a study on Internet abuse reported using the Internet for two-way communication such as interactive multiplayer character games, e-mail, and chat rooms.

## Technology in Our Everyday Lives

Research results on the relationship between technology-based leisure activities and health are controversial and debatable. However, in general, the use of computer or technology as a major focus for leisure activity appears to reduce participation in active and health-enhancing leisure activities, thereby influencing the individuals' physical health. A sedentary lifestyle and the lack of regular physical exercise are known to be detrimental to health. On the contrary, it is possible that technology-based leisure activities such as Internet use may improve mental health when used properly. The opportunities for communication, social support, and interaction may provide interpersonal resources in times of crisis and contribute to satisfying social experiences. The proliferation of online self-help groups and numerous Web sites providing information about illnesses and heath issues can be valuable resources. Online participation may enable people with psychosocial difficulties (such as depression, stress, helplessness, lack of social support, etc.) to overcome their difficulties by providing greater control, anonymity, and social support. The same principle can be applied to people with disabilities and illnesses who may have limited accessibility to traditional leisure spaces. It should be noted that research on the influence of computer-based technology on health is still inconsistent and incomplete. Further research considering a variety of behavioral, psychological, and health outcomes will be required for clearer conclusions.

Whether new technologies are truly effective tools to make our lives more convenient and our leisure more productive is another debatable issue. Although it was expected that computers would streamline our workload, make life easier, and give us more free time for leisure activities, this may not necessarily be the case. Many people are spending as much, or even more, time at their desks toiling away on their computers. Just answering e-

mail can take hours. Computers can be serious time wasters in the workplace, as well. Writing and receiving personal e-mail, paying bills online, shopping, and surfing the Internet are activities that many perform while they are at work. In the long run, this may be keeping us at work longer.

Using technology for leisure at work doesn't necessarily constitute a negative situation. Being able to communicate with your loved ones while at work is soothing to many. Performing menial tasks and errands on coffee breaks gets those tasks out of the way and off individuals' minds. Some parents view their children at day care via a digital camera placed in the day-care center and posted on the Web. This may provide some reassurance for many parents throughout the workday. Companies that allow for this type of "play" during work hours find that their employees are happier and thus more productive. Companies with strict rules on leisure at work may find that employees are going elsewhere, where their needs can be accommodated. The future may hold a workplace that incorporates leisure into the everyday job.

## The Future Outlook for Technology and Leisure

Computer-related technologies are transforming the contemporary experience and the organization of many important aspects of people's lives such as education, business, and leisure. Specifically in leisure, the interactional, spatial, and temporal experiences of leisure are transformed by a variety of leisure experiences provided by the computer-based virtual spaces.

Both benefits and dangers are inherent in the technological world. For some, the novelty of new technology has already worn off. Online businesses are closing at an alarming rate, and many people are heading back to the stores to do their shopping. However, regardless of people's whims, technology is here to stay. It has become a necessity for the way people conduct business, educate their children, and entertain themselves in today's world.

Whether people like them or not, the new technologies have opened up new worlds of opportunity for more efficient and productive life. The next step will be to embrace the technologies for the ways they can help people. When used wisely, the new technologies promise to open new doors of opportunity for more efficient and productive lifestyles in the future.

*See also:* Computer/Video Games; Fantasy Sports; Internet; Media, Technology, and Leisure

**BIBLIOGRAPHY**

Anderson, Craig A., and Brad J. Bushmen. "Effects of Violent Video Games on Aggressive Behavior, Aggressive Cognition, Aggressive Affect, Physiological Arousal, and Pro-Social Behavior: A Meta-Analytic Review of the Scientific Literature." *Psychological Science* 12, no. 5 (2001): 353–359.

Barrett, Randy. "Scorned Porn." *Interactive Week* 8, no. 32 (2001): 37–40.

Bryce, Jo. "The Technological Transformation of Leisure." *Social Science Computer Review* 19 (2001): 7–16.

Hunter, William. "Classic Video Game History." EmuUnlim. Available from http://www.emuunlim.com/doteaters.

InformationWeek Research's E-Business Agenda Study. "Behind the Numbers: Sun Hasn't Set on E-business. On-Line" Available from http://www.informationresearch .com.

Kerner, Matthew S., Michael Kalinski, Anthony B. Kurrant, Eric Small, Eugene Spatz, and Stacy Gropack. "Leisure-Time Internet Use Does Not Correlate with Physical Activity or Physical Fitness Level of Ninth Grade African-American Girls." *Pediatric Exercise Science* 13 (2001): 402—412.

Kuittinen, Petri. History of Video Games. Available from http://www.hut.fi/&thksim;eye/videogames.

Lewis, Peter. "The Biggest Game in Town." *Fortune* 148 (2003): 132–139.

NUA Internet Survey On-Line. "The Global Online Population." Available from http://www.nua.ie/surveys.

Robinson, John P., and Kestnbaum, Meyer. "The Personal Computer, Culture, and Other Uses of Free Time." *Social Science Computer Review* 17 (1999): 209–216.

Rojek, Chris. *Leisure and Culture.* London: Macmillan, 2000.

Rothbaum, B. O., and L. F. Hodges. "The Use of Virtual Reality Exposure in the Treatment of Anxiety Disorders." *Behavior Modification* 23, no. 4 (1999): 507–526.

Scherer, Kathleen. "College Life On-Line: Healthy and Unhealthy Internet Use." *Journal of College Student Development* 38 (1997): 655–665.

Turner, Victor. *Blazing the Trail.* Tucson: University of Arizona Press, 1992.

Winter, David. "Pong-Story." Available from http://www .pong-story.com.

Young, Kimberly S. "Internet Addiction: the Emergence of a New Clinical Disorder." *Cyber Psychology Behavior* 1 (1998): 237–244.

*Heewon Yang and Kelly Chandler*

# CONEY ISLAND

Coney Island is a five-mile stretch of Atlantic coastline located ten miles southeast of lower Manhattan on the edge of New York City's borough of Brooklyn. From the mid-seventeenth century, when Dutch colonists acquired it from Native Americans, until the mid-nineteenth century, the area was a remote and largely uninhabited slip of sandbars and marshland separated from the mainland by a tidal creek. Although the poet Walt Whitman relished escaping there in the 1830s to run barefoot on the unpopulated shoreline, Coney Island was out of sight and mind for most New Yorkers. But in the half-century after the Civil War, the lonely beaches treasured by artists were absorbed by greater New York City's expanding economy, the vanguard of the urban, industrial, and consumer revolutions then shaping the nation. Coney lost its true island status during this period as developers filled in the tidal creek and transit systems, thoroughly linking the beaches to Brooklyn and New York City.

But even as the resort was physically integrated into the metropolitan region's burgeoning economy, Coney's renown as a metaphorical, rather than actual, island intensified. Generations of ambitious and often creative amusement entrepreneurs have marketed Coney as an island getaway of pleasure and play surrounded by the hostile everyday world of vexatious cares and responsibilities. From the 1880s until the mid-1950s, Coney Island continuously lured the masses with its promise of a rollicking summertime "Carnival of Plenty," where the sensational and bizarre ruled. For most of this time, amusement proponents touted Coney's diversions as part of a broadly American "playground," where all could join in the common pursuit of fun. This essential ingredient of its mass appeal placed it at the center of the development of twentieth-century America's consumer economy.

Much of the island's history has been shaped by the transportation technologies that have abridged its geographical inaccessibility. By the end of the 1840s, several small hotels had been ventured at the island, and they were attracting day tourists and excursionists. Coney Island was difficult and expensive to reach for most New Yorkers, who were mostly uninterested in what was still the eccentric aristocratic practice of taking saltwater baths. These geographical and cultural impediments gradually gave way between 1850 and 1890, Coney's first period as a resort for the masses. A plank road completed in 1850 launched regular, though time-consuming, transit service from central Brooklyn. Steamboat lines from Manhattan, begun in 1847, cut the trip to two hours. Construction of hotels and boardinghouses, restaurants, saloons, and bathhouses boomed in this period as the taste for the "luxury" of a dip in the surf, the wish to escape the city heat, and the excitement of being part of the crowd spread among middle- and working-class city dwellers. The era's celebrities—the showman P. T. Barnum, the writer Edgar Allan Poe—gathered there along

**Coney Island beach.** With the amusement park as its backdrop, the beach at Coney Island in Brooklyn, New York, was a popular attraction, as shown here in 1928. Located at the mouth of New York Harbor, it featured roller coasters, carousels, and Ferris wheels, along with many sideshow acts. © *Bettmann/Corbis*

with less-celebrated folk. By the end of the 1870s, nine steamboats and five rail lines made Manhattan to Coney a half-hour journey. The hordes grew exponentially, cementing Coney's identity with the hallmark feature of modernity—"the crowd." Investments in amusements expanded simultaneously, to about $10 million in 1880.

By the early 1890s, the island had split into three amusement areas. The wealthy bourgeoisie stayed in fancy hotels at Manhattan Beach on the far eastern end of the island, while less moneyed middle-class patrons gathered in hostelries and bathhouses at neighboring Brighton Beach to the west. Norton's Point, at the island's far western end, attracted the sporting male crowd with horse racing, gambling, saloons, and prostitutes. Located between these extremes was West Brighton, which featured the "Bowery"—a street several blocks long and lined with beer gardens, gargantuan restaurants, arcades, and belly-dancer sideshows. West Brighton's cheap amusements and public bathhouses were the island's focal point, attracting a half million working people on hot summer Sundays. Its noisy entertainments catered to the

"cultural style" of working-class New Yorkers, rather than to the polite tastes of the Manhattan Beach set.

But the island's economy made such cultural and social boundaries unenforceable in practice. The enormous capital investments had to be offset by economies of mass scale, which meant that such businesses had to manufacture demand rather than just respond to it. Steamboat lines invested in "iron piers," which, in addition to docks, featured saloons, oyster houses, restaurants, and covered promenades, both luring and capitalizing on the 2 million individuals traveling to Coney by water in the 1880s. Railways owning beachside properties near their terminals leased lots to amusement entrepreneurs. On the eastern end of Coney, the tony Manhattan Beach (1877) and Oriental (1880) hotels were built by the railroad company whose own lines tied the resorts to the city. Though advertised as exclusive retreats, the hotels also profited from a short-line rail connection to West Brighton, which funneled the multitudes into their beehive of bathhouses and massive restaurants, able to manufacture thousands of meals at a time. All regions of the island—whether the high-end Oriental Hotel or the Bowery's dance halls—sold "fun" to the masses who were looking for diversion from life's conventions and confinements.

Coney Island's reputation as a footloose consumer playground entered a new era in the mid-1890s with the construction of several large amusement parks enclosed within fences. Sea Lion Park (1896) was the first, but the more important was Steeplechase Park, opened the following year by George C. Tilyou, one of the era's great showmen. Its name came from the mechanical racetrack that circled its perimeter. In 1903, Fred Thompson and Elmer "Skip" Dundy leased the Sea Lion property, razed most of its structures, and built in its place the orientalist fantasy Luna Park. Mobbed its first summer, Luna Park immediately inspired an imitator, Dreamland, even larger in size and grander in scope.

The Coney Island parks, while unusual in many ways, were a spectacular dimension of the new urban-industrial economy that underwrote the explosive growth of mass consumer enterprises after 1890. Dense urban populations and mass transit systems to transport them made possible the enormous fixed-capital investments (land, buildings, equipment) in entertainment businesses, from low-priced theaters and vaudeville houses to opera companies, ballparks, and amusement parks. The markets for commercial leisure also expanded as working people's hours on the job gradually declined, especially as the Saturday half-holiday was extended to growing numbers of urban workers at the end of the century. New audiences, too, had emerged, notably young, single women and men employed in the rapidly expanding corporate and retail workplace. Coney Island targeted such people and, in doing so, undermined Victorian rules against the sexes mixing outside the home. The amusements fostered instead the modern expectation that women and men, although strangers to each other, could and should "go out" together for fun in their off hours. At Coney they could escape the surveillance of family and neighborhood and join the crowd in purchasing entertainment.

For more than a decade, Steeplechase, Luna, and Dreamland gave the island its striking identity as a respectable playground for the city's growing population of middle-class consumers. The enclosures were supposed to ensure standards of propriety by preventing rowdies and prostitutes from gaining entrance; gates enabled management to charge admission (usually a dime). Fences also lent each park a specific identity that was greater than the sum of its parts. Steeplechase's Pavilion of Fun (1901) was an antic warehouse of pranks and illusions—a disorderly inversion of the everyday world that jostled people out of their familiar composure.

Fred Thompson, on the other hand, staged Luna Park as a luxurious oasis of pleasure and fun in a pedestrian world. Luna was, in one sense, little more than a transient stage set made of inexpensive plaster and lath. But its impermanence did not diminish the splendor of its twenty-two (and later more) acres of white palaces, onion domes, towers, minarets, and spraying fountains. At night, the glittering spectacle of its fantastic buildings outlined by hundreds of thousands of small incandescent lights dazzled onlookers. Patrons could watch outdoor circus performances, float serenely on Venetian-style canals, or parade the streets on the backs of camels and elephants. "Scenic illusions" transported them undersea to the North Pole or through space to the moon. Rejecting conventional middle-class expectations that leisure should incorporate wise and constructive use of spare time, Thompson framed Luna's exotic, festive otherworldliness to sell frivolousness to adult consumers. He believed that contemporary Americans, especially middle-class men, longed to escape the burdens of modern life, that they wanted to return to a time when "play was everything; when responsibility had never been dreamed of" (Register, p. 87). Luna, which inspired hundreds of imitators around the nation and world, was such a playground, littered with toys for grown-ups. Rather than marketing themselves to children or families, Coney's amusement parks sold childhood play to adult consumers.

The heyday of these parks lasted about twenty years. Dreamland burned to the ground in 1911. Luna Park passed into the hands of new and less inventive owners in 1912. Amusement parks, dazzlingly original in the early 1900s, seemed tired and tawdry as moving pictures generated more exciting fantasies for American consumers. The suburbanization of middle-class populations and their increasing use of automobiles for pleasure affected those parks that were dependent on cities and mass transit systems. Park owners sought to expand their markets, incorporating more attractions for children and pitching themselves as destinations for families, but they closed by the hundreds in the 1920s. Developers who revived amusement parks after 1945 targeted car-driving, vacationing families and built their facilities out of longer-lasting materials. They also deliberately rejected the tawdry image of Coney Island as it had become by 1945. But the most influential, such as Disneyland (1955) near Los Angeles, modeled themselves according to the original premise of Coney's Dreamland and Luna Park, where respectable play was everything.

As middle-class New Yorkers tired of Coney, the summertime crowds of day-trippers swelled to unprecedented numbers, most of them from the city's immigrant-based working-class neighborhoods. When the public subway system came to Coney in 1920, the cheap nickel fare transformed the island into the playground of the city's proletariat. The Bowery and parks remained, but massive new private and public projects shaped the island's amusement topography. The skyline featured new mechanical marvels—the Wonder Wheel (1920), a mammoth double Ferris wheel, and the Cyclone Racer (1927), a mile-a-minute roller coaster. After a 1915 court decision declared the island's shoreline public property, the city rebuilt the badly eroded beaches and sank $4 million into a public boardwalk (1923), eighty feet wide and almost two miles long. Coney still played to the swell set, but they mattered little compared to the million people arriving by subway on a summer Saturday. A foreign observer described Coney as the "city of cheap pleasure for cheap people." No business more aptly represented 1920s Coney than Nathan's Famous, the home of the nickel hot dog, 75,000 of which were sold on a typical weekend.

The unrestrained appetite for cheap pleasures revealed the changing economy of Coney Island. The parks, sideshows, and roller coasters continued to do big business in the 1920s and 1930s, but revenues declined when they lowered prices to attract small-spenders. The vast numbers of people came to Coney for the cheapest pleasures of all—the surf and beaches and the sensual spectacle of hot, unclad bodies in the sun. Depression-era crowds grew even larger, but working-class families and couples on the "Poor Man's Riviera" practiced penny-pinching economies, such as bringing their own food or using the underside of the boardwalk instead of a bathhouse to undress. The Amusement Zone's bottom line still suffered even after wartime revitalized the island's economy (46 million went to Coney in 1943 alone).

On 4 July 1955, a record 1.5 million people packed the beaches, but such numbers were the exception to the postwar Coney Island. Though Luna had closed during the war, hundreds of amusements, including Steeplechase Park, still worked the island; but hostile public officials and urban planners increasingly treated such businesses as unwelcome anachronisms. The city's parks commission tried to rein in beachgoers with rules against such rambunctious behavior as building human pyramids. "Urban renewal" in the late 1950s built the New York City Aquarium (1957) on the former Dreamland site, and Luna Park Houses, a Stalinesque-style public housing project (1961). Steeplechase's last season was 1964. Coney Island's resident population has since grown enormously, most recently with the influx of Russian and Eastern European immigrants. Amusements and sideshows still operate, including the Wonder Wheel and Cyclone Racer, now in their ninth decade of business. The city's multicultural populace still promenades on the boardwalk, while a more upscale set crowds KeySpan Park (2001) to watch the Brooklyn Cyclones, a minor-league baseball outfit. Since 1983, the Mermaid Parade of costumed and cross-dressed sea life has annually conjured up some of the island's transgressive and otherworldly past, drawing 750,000 spectators at least once since the turn of the millennium. In other words, Coney Island still offers plenty of fun attractions, but it no longer functions or thrives as either the nation's or the city's unfettered playground of plenty.

*See also:* Atlantic City, Beaches, Park Movements, Theme and Amusement Parks, Urbanization of Leisure

**BIBLIOGRAPHY**

Adams, Judith A. *The American Amusement Park Industry: A History of Technology and Thrills.* Boston: Twayne Publishers, 1991.

Immerso, Michael. *Coney Island: The People's Playground.* New Brunswick, N.J.: Rutgers University Press, 2002.

Kasson, John F. *Amusing the Million: Coney Island at the Turn of the Century.* New York: Hill and Wang, 1978.

McCullough, Edo. *Good Old Coney Island: A Sentimental Journey into the Past: The Most Rambunctious, Scandalous, Rapscallion, Splendiferous, Pugnacious, Spectacular, Illustrious, Prodigious, Frolicsome Island on Earth.* 1957. Reprint, New York: Fordham University Press, 2000.

Nasaw, David. *Going Out: The Rise and Fall of Public Amusements.* New York: Basic Books, 1993.

Peiss, Kathy. *Cheap Amusements: Working Women and Leisure in Turn-of-the-Century New York.* Philadelphia: Temple University Press, 1987.

Pilat, Oliver, and Jo Ranson. *Sodom by the Sea: An Affectionate History of Coney Island.* Garden City, N.Y.: Doubleday, 1941.

Register, Woody. *The Kid of Coney Island: Fred Thompson and the Rise of American Amusements.* New York: Oxford University Press, 2001.

Sterngass, Jon. *First Resorts: Pursuing Pleasure at Saratoga Springs, Newport & Coney Island.* Baltimore, Md.: Johns Hopkins University Press, 2001.

*Woody Register*

# CONTEMPORARY LEISURE PATTERNS

It is paradoxical that people in modern societies have more free time compared to 100 years ago but also feel more time constraints. Additionally, work is taking a smaller and smaller fraction of the hours of one's life. An analysis of British citizens, for instance, found that:

Although the average career length has remained around 40 years, the total life hours worked shrank from 124,000 hours in 1856 to 69,000 in 1983. The fraction of disposable lifetime hours spent working declined from 50 percent to 20 percent. (Ausubel and Grubler, p. 195)

The portion of people's lives devoted to both paid work and housework is decreasing, and it appears that such declines are predicted by rising economic standards of living within a country. Jonathan Gershuny, after a meta-analysis of time use in fifteen countries, drew this conclusion and added: "There is no basis, theoretical or empirical, for thinking that we are 'running out of time.'" (p. 18)

The dilemma Americans face, however, is similar to that of a water flea.

The wish to live as intensely as possible has subjected humans to the same dilemma as the waterflea, which lives 108 days at 8 degrees Centigrade, but only twenty-six days at 28 degrees, when its heartbeat is almost four times faster, though in either case its heart beats 15 million times in all. Technology has been a rapid heartbeat, compressing housework, travel, entertainment, squeezing more and more into the allotted span. Nobody expected that it would create the feeling that life moves too fast. (Zeldin, p. 127)

When people are asked about constraints to leisure in survey research, "lack of time" is often the number one answer given to explain why one hasn't participated in some activity. Such an answer, unfortunately, has a number of meanings, none of which the researcher can be sure.

If all time constraints disappeared, the world would descend into chaos. Parks would overflow with people, museums would be jammed, the meaningfulness of much activity that springs directly from its limitedness would disappear. The millionth beer party or softball game would lack meaning. If time constraints were somewhat minimized, however, the world might be a better place. This writer has simplistically suggested that people might do this by owning less, doing less, and saying "no" more often. While many Americans and others in modern nations are in a position to follow this suggestion, in general, it appears they don't want to. Americans, in particular, still want to own even bigger cars and houses, do more things and consume, experience and achieve more.

There is, however, some evidence to the contrary. In the early 2000s there are 50 million "Cultural Creatives," providing the potential for a cultural revolution—one that is already under way (Ray and Anderson).

The "Moderns," who are currently dominant, accept the commercialized urban-industrial world and the goal of economic growth without looking for alternatives. "Cultural Creatives" are different. Their values are such that they love nature and are deeply concerned about its destruction; give a lot of importance to developing and maintaining relationships and helping other people; care intensely about psychological or spiritual development; see spirituality and religion as important in their own lives but are also concerned about the role of the "religious Right" in politics; have their finances and spending under control; and dislike the modern emphasis on "making it" and on wealth and luxury goods.

If time constraints to leisure are going to be minimized, it is likely this segment of society that will do so. For the dominant "Moderns," time constraints, to both work and leisure, will remain a way of life and a penalty willingly, if grudgingly, paid.

Its interpretation is highly political. Are rushed people who sometimes work long hours slaves to a rationalized economy and right-wing capitalism, or are they greedy individuals who want money and possessions more than tranquility and simplicity? The fact that higher income and education individuals are more likely to report feeling rushed than those with lower ones is also subject to multiple interpretations.

What does seem clear is that the distinctions between work and "free time" have been minimized for many. The industrial separation of fast, long work time and slow, short free time has come apart. Postmodernity has produced a way of life in which time is perceived as the most valuable commodity and efficient as the most prevalent value.

## More Customized Leisure Behavior

While it would appear that leisure in everyday life is characterized more by mass behavior, such as eating at MacDonald's, shopping in look-alike malls, and watching network TV, a number of factors have begun to customize leisure in terms of when it takes place, what is done, the style of the activity, and the meanings and satisfactions such activity holds. Following are some reasons for more customized leisure behavior.

**Explosive Population Growth** About half the population increase in developed countries is coming from international migration. In the early 2000s, 15 percent of Canadians and of French were born in another country, as were one out of nine of those in the United States. These immigrants are not melting in a pot but rather customizing the culture to produce differing mosaics within each city, region, and country. What people think, eat, or do for fun will become more diverse—and so will when they do it.

**Increasing Urbanization and Population Density** For the first time in history, more than half the world's population will be living in urban areas by 2010, and by 2030, the United Nations projects, 60 percent of the population will be urbanized (McGee). Increased urbanization will customize leisure behavior not only by social class, income, and ethnicity as it always has, but due to the increasing cultural differences of urban residents and visitors, such differences will be magnified.

As higher population densities occur, the sequencing of daily life's routines will need to be customized. Centralized periods of vacations, holidays, and other forms of mass leisure will be less likely to occur. For instance, as the number of cars on the beltways around Washington, D.C., increases, producing permanent gridlock, there will be mass customization of travel patterns. When people go to work (if they go at all), when they shop, vote, or visit the beach, will need to be spread out. Most models of "mass" transit will also require customization since there is increasingly no "center" of work for people to be transported to. "Rush hour" may take place across most of the hours of the day and night. Those who manage leisure and tourism services will do more to "guide" visitors to their sites, and such guidance will become customized for any inquiring visitor. Such customized guidance will be increasingly valuable to the potential visitor, as the logistics of visitation become more complex due to higher volumes of traffic, whether such traffic is automobiles, motor scooters or bicycles, or other people movers. "In sum, most forms of mass activity, including leisure, will be customized to the extent the population increases and becomes more dense and urban. If the whole world flushed the toilet at once . . . .." (Godbey, De-Jong, Sasidharan, and Yarnal)

**A Revolution in the Life Course and the Family** Modernity is reshaping the life course and family structure. Many developmental psychologists no longer speak of "life stages," since the comparatively common stages of life that individuals went through in an industrial economy no longer occur or don't occur at common ages. Modern nations are also "de-familied," with more than one-fifth or more of households having only one person

in them and the average household having less than three occupants. In the United States, almost half of the adult population is not married. Where there is a family, it is likely to be more diverse in form, often the result of divorce and remarriage, or it may be a gay or lesbian family, a multiethnic or multiracial family, or a "family" of unrelated individuals. All these trends encourage more customization of leisure behavior.

**Rapid Aging of the World Population** People are also becoming more different because they are living longer. The average life expectancy in the world in the early 2000s is about sixty-five years and more than ten years higher than average in modern nations. Germany, together with other Western European nations and Japan, are the advance guard of the historic demographic changes accompanying the rise of technological societies. If the global economy continues to raise living standards, developing countries will most likely follow the European model to eventual low fertility and large elderly populations. In 2025, those sixty and older will account for 25 percent of the U.S. population, compared with 31 percent in Western Europe.

**From Specialists to Generalists** People are in the process of moving from being "specialists" in regard to time use, such as taking care of children and a household or working at a given occupation or pursuing a single form of leisure expression, to becoming generalists. Since the mid-twentieth century, in most modern societies the percentage of people who undertake both paid work and housework is increasing. So, too, is the percentage of people doing activities previously limited to the elite, such as going to museums. "Task combination and the combination of cultural with leisure activities are on the rise. In their respective domains, both combinations imply a time squeeze. . . .." (van den Broek, p. 21)

**Increasing Levels of Education** Higher levels of education, particularly for women, are occurring in many regions of the world. People with higher levels of education are more likely to become "specialized" in a given form of leisure behavior, moving from the general to the specific within the activity form and, often, from catharsis to pleasure to meaning in terms of benefits sought. Those with higher education are more likely to participate in most forms of outdoor recreation, sports, high culture, continuing education, reading, tourism, and volunteer activities.

More highly educated people will become more individually distinct in their participation in leisure activity, seeking more information and complexity in the experience. The increasingly diverse mix of education levels of people residing in close proximity will mean that providing mass leisure activities, such as local festivals, will need to be undertaken with multiple strategies.

**Revolutionary Changes in the Roles of Women and Men** What it means to be female (and consequently, to be male) is in the middle or beginning of a revolution in every country in the world. One reason for this is simply massive declines in birth rates and increases in longevity. While women in eighteenth-century Europe, for example, gave birth to an average of eight children, in the early twenty-first century birth rates are well below two, and life expectancy exceeds seventy years. While industrialism was built on specialization of work and other obligated activity, the postindustrial society is producing generalists, who undertake a broader range of activities and roles. Males are already beginning to emerge as the educationally disadvantaged group, compared to females. In knowledge economies, this will change numerous forms of relationships.

There is cultural lag in Americans' perception of the educational attainment and achievements of girls and boys. While the feeling persists that girls are ignored in public school, remain passive, have low self-esteem, and so forth, girls are far higher achievers in public schools than boys, and they are more likely to go to college. According to the U.S. Department of Education, girls get better grades in public schools, are slightly more likely to enroll in higher-level math and science courses, and outnumber boys in student government, honor societies, school newspapers, and debating teams. Girls read more books than boys, outperform them on tests for artistic and musical ability, and are more likely to study abroad. Boys are more likely to be suspended from school, held back, drop out, or be involved in crime, alcohol, or drugs. Boys are more than three times more likely to receive a diagnosis of attention deficit hyperactivity disorder. While girls are more likely to attempt suicide, boys are more likely to succeed in killing themselves by a ratio of more than five to one. In 1996, there were 8.4 million women but only 6.7 million men enrolled in college, and the projections are that by 2007, women will outnumber men in college even more substantially—9.2 million women and 6.9 million men. (Sommers, p. 29)

The comparative power of women with high levels of education will increase, the wage gap will close or favor women, more joint career decisions will be made that consider women's job prospects first, and the centrality of women as decision makers will increase in regard to use of free time within families and couples.

Such changes may mean that women's leisure patterns will diversify and their leisure desires will be addressed to a greater extent. When they are not, women will make increasing demands for differentiation of leisure sites and services to meet their interests, and they will exert more power in shaping them.

**A Revolution in Work** Changes in technology have revolutionized work in ways that are revolutionizing the rest of life, customizing every individual's life in the process. When the factory system standardized work in Europe and North America, which was done outside the home in big ugly buildings, public education followed suit. The factory approach to public education resulted in standardized buildings, standardized curricula, standardized textbooks and teacher qualifications, and standardized notions of the truth.

Leisure became more standardized, too, from bowling alleys to shopping malls to TV shows, which more than half the households in the country watched. The scientific management of factory work, including time and motion studies undertaken by Fredrick Taylor, carried over into leisure activity such as sport; coaches began to use the same time and motion analysis of athletes and specialization of tasks that Taylor used for workers (Kanigel). Standardized retirement assistance, social security, produced a standardization of the age of retirement—sixty-five—in Germany first and later in many countries.

Work is undergoing a revolution. The notion that a "job" is a fixed bundle of tasks is disappearing. "Jobs" are moving targets, demanding continuous learning and change on the part of the worker. More people work part-time, work at home, have no designated place to work, or combine work with college, raising children, or retirement. Workers who work during daylight hours on weekdays may become the minority.

Work will intrude into every aspect of life, including leisure, and leisure will intrude into work. "The barrier that since the 1800s has separated work and the rest of life is being shattered" (Boyett, p. 5). The "home" will often be where work is done, as it was prior to the Industrial Revolution. Leisure behavior will be customized to reflect such changes. Among some of the major impacts will be less distinction between weekday and weekend in terms of leisure activity. Already, the majority of hours of "free time" occur during weekdays, and this trend may intensify (Robinson and Godbey).

As more workers telecommute or use satellite offices, cities no longer will be the center of commerce. Cities in developed nations will atrophy or re-create themselves at centers of leisure, culture, tourism, and entertainment.

Simultaneously, cities in developing nations will become more critical, and the migration from rural to urban to suburban to small town will continue and intensify.

**A Revolution in the Bases of Modern Economies—Postcapitalist Economies of Knowledge and Experience** In most countries and even within individual cities, a mosaic of economies exists alongside one another: from hunter-gatherer to agriculture to mercantilism and trade to industrialism to services to a knowledge and experience economy. The most modern economies are "postcapitalist." That is, the ultimate basis of wealth is not capital but rather knowledge and the application of knowledge to produce profit (Drucker).

While part of the new economy may be described as a "knowledge" economy, another increasingly important part of the new economy is the offering of memorable experiences:

> When a person buys a service, he purchases a set of intangible activities carried out on his behalf. But when he buys an experience, he pays to spend time enjoying a series of memorable events that a company stages—as in a theatrical play—to engage him in a personal way (Pine and Gilmore, p. 2).

Such experiences are as distinct from services as services are from products. The emergence of an experience economy may progress as follows: in the emerging experience economy, the experiential component of a product or service is increasingly the basis of profit. "Just as people have cut back on goods to spend more money on services, now they also scrutinize the time and money they spend on services to make way for the more memorable—and more highly valued—experiences" (Pine and Gilmore, p. 12).

Experiences are not synonymous with entertainment but rather with engaging the guest. While many experiences are entertainment, experiences may also be educational, escapist, or aesthetic in nature.

As the experience economy grows, many managers of leisure and tourism sites will find that the issue will be less of managing people and natural resources than of managing "meaning." What does this site mean? What is worth doing, seeing, hearing, tasting, touching, smelling, feeling, and ultimately remembering? Those who seek to consume "experiences" in their leisure will exist side by side with those who seek to consume material goods. The desire for memorable experience will both make diversity of environment and culture more valuable while simultaneously threatening it, as those seeking memorable ex-

perience want to swim with dolphins, visit the South Pole, or spend the night in a bamboo forest.

**A Revolution of Networked Economies and Globalization** As every nation moves toward an economy that is networked by computers and globalized, the provision of leisure and tourism services will change how they operate in numerous ways, customizing services based on increasing levels of information about customers. The characteristics of a networked economy, as described by Kevin Kelly, include numerous implications for the delivery of leisure and tourism services. Such an economy requires operating in real time, mass customization of products and services, and company boundaries that stretch across borders. A networked economy reshapes not only when leisure takes place but also how organizations that provide leisure and tourism services function to customize experience.

**The Impact of Globalization** Globalization of commerce has brought with it increasingly differentiated conditions both among countries and within countries. It is also an engine that drives immigration at a startling rate. The top fifth of the world's people in the early 2000s have 86 percent of the gross domestic product and the bottom fifth about 1 percent (UN Development Report, cited by Mitchell). As northern nations have increasingly pressured southern nations to open their economies to foreign trade and investment, about 20 percent of southern residents have increased their wealth but 80 percent have become poorer. Overall, southern nations have become poorer. "That gives southern nations less and less incentive to manage legal and illegal immigration" (Sassen, p. 2).

This process also makes it certain that "terrorism" and low-intensity wars will become the ways of fighting for the "have-nots" against the "haves." The line between crime and war is disappearing, and, as that happens, low-intensity conflicts of attrition will largely replace wars fought from traditional strategies. Terrorism as a long-term condition of life will make leisure and especially tourism behavior more deliberate and more subject to sudden change. It may also mean that assurances of safety, predictability, and isolation from the increasing conflict between haves and have-nots will be more appealing.

While globalization will bring sameness to some parts of life—"McDonaldization"—in many other ways it will further customize life. While federal governments may seek to "harmonize" currencies, policies, and procedures, leisure behavior becomes more diverse. Even the celebration of holidays becomes customized as political or religious-based holidays become factionalized. Ramadan, Cinco de Mayo, or "Chinese" New Year celebrations may occur in San Diego, London, or Jakarta.

## Multipolar and Multicivilizational Politics and Power

Globalization takes place in a post–Cold War era in which "power is shifting from the long predominant West to non-Western civilizations" (Huntington, p. 29). Global politics have become multipolar and multicivilizational. In the early twenty-first century, the most important countries in the world come from civilizations that are vastly different civilizations, and "modernization" of such countries does not mean that they will "Westernize." While, during the last 400 years, relations among civilizations "consisted of the subordination of other societies to Western civilization" (Huntington, p. 51), this pattern has been broken.

> The West won the world not by the superiority of its ideas or values or religion (to which few members of other civilizations are converted), but rather by its superiority in applying organized violence. Westerns often forget this fact; non-Westerners do not. (Huntington, p. 51)

Christianity accounts for slightly less than 30 percent of the world's people. Islam, which accounts for a bit less than 20 percent of the world's population, will continue to increase in numbers since ". . . Christianity spreads primarily by conversion, Islam by conversion and reproduction." (Huntington, p. 65) The ways in which various religions react to globalization will be diverse and unpredictable.

All these trends mean that the power to shape leisure, popular culture, sport, tourism, hobbies, crafts, mass media, outdoor recreation, and a variety of other behavioral forms related to leisure will be diversified.

**Revolutionary Changes in Environment** Perhaps the most important revolution that is taking place is the transformation of the environment of the planet in ways that have no historical precedent. Such change includes the mass extinction of animal life and plant life at a rate and magnitude unknown in human history. Additionally, "we have driven atmospheric carbon dioxide to the highest levels in at least two hundred thousand years, unbalanced the nitrogen cycle, and contributed to a global warming that will ultimately be bad news everywhere." (Wilson, p. 23)

A combination of exponentially rising consumption and increasing population means that: "In short, earth has lost its ability to regenerate—unless global consumption is reduced, or global production is increased, or both." (Wilson, p. 27) Since poverty and the second-class status of women are largely responsible for the plague of human population growth, the chances for human survival are linked to the elimination of poverty and changes in the rights, education, and life chances of women in most nations.

Environmentally, the human race is entering an unprecedented era. The cost of natural disasters in 1998 alone, for instance, exceeds the cost for the entire previous decade. Although the causes remain disputed, the fact is that sea level rise in the twentieth century was double the rate of the nineteenth century. Much of the shoreline of the world will be changed, sweeping many island nations under water in the process. Bangladesh, for example, may suffer a catastrophe. "There is complete certainty that stratospheric ozone depletion will increase the amount of harmful ultraviolet radiation reaching the surface, while there is high certainty that global warming will increase average temperature and raise sea level. It is less certain, but still likely, that extreme weather and climate events (e.g., intense rain and snowstorms, floods, and droughts) will increase." (Fisher et al., 2000)

Environmental change will customize leisure behavior everywhere. Many beaches will disappear, "tourist seasons" change and customize, extreme weather events cancel or interfere with more planned events, attitudes toward exposure to sunlight become dialectic, and environmental degradation will render some leisure environments uninhabitable or more highly regulated.

**A Revolution in Urban Areas** Nucleated cities emerged in the nineteenth century where industrialization occurred. They had a well-defined commercial area, known as downtown; industry was lined up along the railroad tracks; and residential areas were arrayed around the edges and segregated along lines of income, ethnicity, and race.

These cities were replaced by emerging "galactic" cities, as the automobile became the primary means of transport. Rather than think of this as urban sprawl, Peirce Lewis contends this is a new kind of city. Galactic cities, which take lots of space and have no real center, help ensure that travel by automobile dominates. Walking is often useless to get anywhere. Public transportation is sometimes ineffective because the city has no center.

Such urban patterns ensure customization of daily life, transportation, work arrangement, and leisure. The automobile is the ultimate customizer of travel and, therefore, of daily life. It can carry one person on a customized travel pattern. Innovation in urban "mass" transportation will seek to mimic the automobile in terms of allowing the individual to undertake customized travel patterns

**A Revolution in the Mass Customization of Products and Services** In the early twenty-first century, technological change is being organized around biological models, and biology operates on the principle that difference is better. The revolution in how work is done is producing a revolution in what work provides: mass customized services based on greatly expanded information about the client or customer. Medicine, for instance, is beginning to be custom-made, taking the patient's medical history and physical condition into account.

While every living thing has its own unique sense of time, the ideal of the industrial society was to treat people *equally* and regiment them to common time patterns. The ideal will now become be to treat people *appropriately*—and that means having sufficient information about them to recognize their unique needs with regard to time. Daily life will be reorganized with time patterns and schedules that vary for every single person. Treating people equally makes no sense in a decentralized society since people are not interchangeable parts. Treating people appropriately will make more sense, as diversity becomes even more prevalent. Leisure and its use will be reshaped by this fundamental shift in human relations.

*See also:* Leisure Education; Leisure, Theory of; Urbanization of Leisure; Work and Leisure Ethics

## BIBLIOGRAPHY

Anderson, David, with an introduction by B. Joseph Pine II. *Agile Product Development for Mass Customization, Niche Markets, JIT, Build-to-Order, and Flexible Manufacturing.* Chicago and New York: McGraw-Hill, 1997.

Ashford, Lori S. "New Perspectives on Population: Lessons from Cairo." *Population Bulletin* 1, no. 50. Washington, D.C.: Population Reference Bureau, 1995.

Attali, Jacques. *Millennium—Winners and Losers in the New World Order.* New York: Random House, 1991.

Ausubel, Joseph, and A. Grubler. "Working Less and Living Longer: Long-Term Trends in Working Time and Time Budgets." Working Paper 94-99. Laxenburg, Austria: International Institute for Applied Systems Analysis, 1994.

Boyett, Joseph. *21st-Century Workplace Trends and Their Implications.* Alpharetta, Ga.: Boyett and Associates, 1996.

Bridges, William. *Jobshift—How to Prosper in a Workplace Without Jobs.* Reading, Mass.: Addison-Wesley, 1994.

Drucker, Peter. *Post-Capitalist Society.* New York: Harper-Collins, 1993.

Gershuny, Jonathan. "Are We Running Out of Time?" *Futures* (January/February 1992): 1–18.

Godbey, Geoffrey. *Leisure and Leisure Services in the 21st Century.* State College, Pa.: Venture Publishing, 1998.

———. "After the Anthill Was Stomped: The Future of Leisure and Tourism." Conference on Leisure Futures. Center for Tourism and Service Economics at the University of Innsbruck, Austria. Keynote speech, 23 May 2002.

Godbey, Geoffrey and Alan Graefe. "Rapid Growth in Rushin' Americans." *American Demographics* (April 1993): 5–7.

Godbey, Geoffrey, Gordon DeJong, Vinod Sasidharan, and Careen Yarnal. *The Northeastern United States in the Next Two Decades—Implications for the Northeast Region of the National Park Service.* Philadelphia, Pa: NPS, Northeast Region, 2001.

Goldman, Steven, Roger Nagel, and Kenneth Preiss. *Agile Competitors and Virtual Organizations.* New York: Van Nostrand Reinhold, 1995.

Huntington, Samuel. *The Clash of Civilizations and the Remaking of World Order.* New York: Simon and Schuster, 1996.

Kanigel, Robert. *The One Best Way: Fredrick Winslow Taylor and the Enigma of Efficiency.* New York: Viking Press, 1997.

Kelly, Kevin. *Out of Control: The New Biology of Machines, Social Systems and the Economic World.* Reading, Mass.: Addison-Wesley, 1996.

Lewis, Peirce. "The Urban Invasion of Rural America: The Emergence of the Galactic City." In *The Changing American Countryside: Rural People and Places.* Edited by Emery Castle. Lawrence: University of Kansas Press, 1995.

Pine, B. Joseph, II, and James Gilmore. *The Experience Economy.* Boston: Harvard Business School Press, 1999.

Robinson, John, and Geoffrey Godbey. *Time for Life: The Surprising Ways Americans Use Time.* Revised Edition. University Park: Pennsylvania State University Press, 1999.

Sassen, Saskia. "Globalization After September 11." *The Chronicle for Higher Education,* 18 January 2002.

Sommers, Christina Hoff. "The War Against Boys." *Atlantic Monthly* (May 2000): 60.

Van Crevald, Martin. *The Transformation of War.* New York: Free Press, 1991.

Van den Broek, A. "From Specialists to Generalists? Despecialization in Daily Life in the Netherlands, 1975-1995. Paper presented at the International Sociological Association Conference. Montreal, Canada, 1 August 1998.

Wilson, Edward O. *The Future of Life.* New York: Alfred A. Knopf, 2002.

Zeldin, T. *An Intimate History of Humanity.* New York: Harper Perennial, 1994.

*Geoffrey Godbey*

# COOKING FOR FUN

Cooking for fun is a relatively new concept in the American kitchen. Since the beginning of the twentieth century, attitudes about food and its preparation have changed drastically.

## Early Attitudes about Cooking

Recipes and cookbooks have been around for hundreds of years, yet during colonial times, cooking was a necessity, and not meant to be fun. The housewife had endless chores, and cooking had to remain simple. This was still true into the twentieth century. A 1905 cookbook had a page of "instructions to be read carefully" that gave all the rules of cooking, including keeping one's hands and the kitchen very clean, wiping the grease off of dishes, and not throwing cabbage water down the sink.

During the twentieth century, food manufacturers began to print recipe booklets telling Americans all the ways their products could be baked, fried, and boiled into appetizers, main dishes, and desserts. Making their products fun to cook with was to the advantage of the manufacturer, and would lead to the consumer buying more. Each product that offered a recipe made sure that product was the key ingredient in the recipe, such as a recipe for cucumber cream salad in a booklet from a gelatin manufacturer that, of course, featured gelatin, and a recipe for hamburger loaf that came in a recipe booklet for Bond White Bread —hence the loaf in hamburger loaf.

Another innovation was the writing of *Joy of Cooking* by Irma S. Rombauer, privately printed in 1931 and distributed from her home. This was the first real cookbook to speak to the home cook as something more than a housewife or home economist, treating them instead as food lovers who were ready for more adventurous recipes. The book included recipes, illustrations, and cooking techniques, and has been revised numerous times since then to reflect the changing tastes of the public.

## New Technology

The advent of the refrigerator during the early twentieth century, first mass produced during the 1930s, resulted in a dramatic change in methods of food storage. It allowed perishable items to be kept longer and foods to be frozen on a long-term basis, providing cooks with greater flexibility. The refrigerator also introduced a new type of dessert, the "refrigerator cake," which did not require baking. Various ingredients were assembled and then solidified in the refrigerator for twenty-four hours. As a 1949 Westinghouse refrigerator manual explained: "The food your family eats is going to be better and easier to prepare... Proper chilling or freezing of ingredients is vital to many of today's favorite foods." Pamphlets instructed consumers on how to properly freeze foods.

New, affordable cooking tools of the early and mid-twentieth century were designed to give the public greater enjoyment in the kitchen. Products such as electric blenders, beaters, choppers, and food processors enabled cooks to save significant time: for example, the beating of egg whites or heavy cream by hand was no longer necessary. These electronic devices enticed people who might not ordinarily cook.

Meanwhile, the new technology of television brought the first cooking show to NBC in 1946, featuring the chef James Beard, who went on to found a cooking school in 1955 and write more than twenty cookbooks.

## Fun Cooking

With suburban sprawl becoming prevalent during the 1950s, corner grocery stores and butcher shops gave way to the one-stop shopping of the supermarket. Housewives now had more choices to make interesting dishes for their husbands and families. A 1950 cookbook proclaimed that the kitchen is a laboratory to be used for experimentation. Cooking was also touted as a way for a woman to get to a man's heart. A prize-winning recipe submitted by a sixteen-year-old girl was called "blueberry boy-bait." Many recipes were titled "Dad's favorite" or listed under a category of "men's favorites."

The "fun" cooking of the decades immediately following World War II was often filled with fat and calories. These recipes included "fried potato logs," "creamed vegetable patties," and "burger-onion shortcake." Besides high fat content, cooking of the 1940s and 1950s also involved making colorful dishes such as "Pink Enchantment Cake," a three-tiered "Party Cake" with red yellow and green shredded coconut, a "Christmas Tree Cake" with green shredded coconut and red candles and candies, and a green pimiento cheese spread-covered "Party Sandwich Cake" that featured colorful layers of ham spread, relish-butter, egg salad, and tuna.

Recipe contests in newspapers (for a $5 prize) and others such as the Pillsbury Bake-Off (begun in 1949) helped reinforce the image of cooking as a fun and rewarding pastime. Books started to appear focusing on just one key ingredient or type of ingredient; cooking with beer, wine, apples, or spices, for example.

**Naked Chef.** British chef Jamie Oliver hosts *The Naked Chef* on cable television's Food Network channel. "Star" chefs such as Oliver and Emeril Lagasse have made the network a popular destination for food fans. © *AP/Wide World Photos*

### New Foods and Cooking Styles

As the population of the United States became more diverse, so did the variety of ethnic food available. With the arrival of Chinese workers who helped build the transcontinental railroad during the nineteenth century, Chinese cuisine was introduced to the American taste. At first limited to a few main dishes, such as chop suey, Chinese cooking expanded with the introduction of the regional cooking of different provinces, including Hunan and Szechuan. Italian cooking for the American public used to consist of a few main dishes, relying heavily upon red sauce (spaghetti and meatballs, for example), but during the late twentieth century, Americans were introduced to the wider variety of flavorful Italian dishes that were truer to the actual cuisine of the different regions of Italy.

The influx of Latin cultures during the latter half of the twentieth century popularized cooking Mexican-style with hot spices. During this time, second-generation Americans rediscovered their ethnic roots and helped popularize many Old World recipes. Regional American cooking styles also broke out of their local areas during the mid-twentieth century, bringing Texas-style barbecue

to Massachusetts, and southern soul food to New York. Sometimes, ethnic or regional restaurants were the catalyst that piqued the public interest in that cooking style. In 1954, for example, the Pink Teacup café opened in New York City, serving southern-style soul food. Over the years, their recipe for sweet potato pie has become a classic, reprinted in Liz Smith's newspaper column annually.

### Diet and Health Cooking

In the early years of the of the twentieth century, the amount of processed food available increased dramatically. Canned, processed, and preserved foods were being turned out in massive amounts by factories. There was little concern over the amount of fat in a diet. Most of America enjoyed high fat, high calorie diets, and the recipes of the time reflected this trend. Butter, eggs, and cooking oil were common. When nutrition was mentioned in old cookbooks, it was to promote the values of fatty foods such as butter.

Diet recipes and books existed, but did not focus so much on cooking, but rather on which foods were safe to eat and which foods could be harmful. As time passed, diet values began to change, but there were still mixed messages in the recipes. Wheat germ was praised as useful for women who wanted to give their families good food and good nutrition, yet published recipes using wheat germ included bacon waffles and pork and liver loaf.

By the end of the twentieth century, eating smart had become the leading priority in cooking. Cookbooks of the early 2000s cover every possible type of healthy cooking: vegetarian, organic, low fat, low carbohydrate, low salt, and low sugar, to name a few. Specific diet plans have their own cookbooks too. For example, the Weight Watchers support program began during the 1960s and evolved into a dieting and cooking subculture. Other popular diet plans include The Zone Diet and the Atkins Diet. With the mandatory inclusion of nutrition facts on all packaged foods during the 1990s, Americans have become more aware of the amount of calories, sodium, and fat they eat.

### Julia Child

When the well-to-do Julia McWilliams met Paul Child during World War II, she knew a great deal about entertaining but little about cooking. When they married, the thirty-three-year-old Julia Child decided to learn how to cook for her gourmand husband. When his government job landed them in France, he gave her a tour of French food. Falling in love with the cuisine, Child enrolled at the famous Cordon Bleu cooking school.

Child began to teach French cooking in her own kitchen in Paris, then set out on a decade-long venture to write a complete cookbook of French recipes adapted for American taste and ingredient availability, where the home cook was increasingly using boxed, canned, and frozen foods. Years of recipe testing and revision, along with consultations with French chefs and cookbooks, culminated in a precedent-setting cookbook, *Mastering the Art of French Cooking* published in 1961 by Knopf.

The book earned her rave reviews and TV spots, as well as a tour of cooking demonstrations. Viewers of Boston public television loved watching her cook, and the station manager and program director convinced Child to film three pilot episodes, leading to a public TV show in 1963. Child's sense of humor and ability to improvise through mistakes were a hit with viewers. Eventually, they made 119 shows.

Child helped bring about a great change in the way Americans looked at food and cooking, bringing joy and enthusiasm to the process and encouraging people not to fret over mistakes. She also did a special for the Public Broadcasting System (PBS) with chef Jacques Pepin in 1994, "Julia Child and Jacques Pepin: Cooking in Concert." The wildly popular show brought together the home chef and the professional chef and led to a series.

In addition to shows with Child, Pepin has hosted his own shows and written his own books. Focusing on teaching skills in the kitchen, his 1976 book *La Technique: An Illustrated Guide to the Fundamental Techniques of Cooking* is a step-by-step guide to such basic things as separating eggs and carving meat. Pepin believes that while creativity is key to successful cooking, that cannot be accomplished without mastering basic skills with knives and other equipment and understanding how food cooks.

## Chef/Superstar

The lines between chef, cookbook author, TV contributor, entrepreneur, and celebrity have been blurred. Emeril Lagasse, chef and owner of a number of popular New Orleans restaurants, was given his own TV show teaching the basics. *How to Boil Water* was followed by *Emeril and Friends*. When cable television formed the first network devoted to cooking, The Food Network, in 1993, Emeril hosted one of its first shows, *Essence of Emeril* and later *Emeril Live*. He has authored a number of cookbooks and appeared as food correspondent on *Good Morning America*. He also markets his own line of food products, including his famous "Essence" spice mix.

Lagasse followed in the footsteps of Paul Prudhomme, another popular New Orleans chef, who has hosted television shows, written for magazines, authored cookbooks, and sells a line of food products. Yet another celebrity restaurant chef who has crossed over into television and cookbooks is Wolfgang Puck. Many Food Network chefs, such as the Naked Chef, have attracted a large following. Many of these celebrity chefs also have their own line of cooking products such as pots or utensils, or, as in the case of Wolfgang Puck, they endorse them. Jacques Pepin designed his own line of kitchen textiles.

Sometimes even without a TV series, chefs will publish a cookbook based on the popularity of their restaurant or bakery. The Magnolia Bakery in New York enjoys considerable popularity; its chef owners Jennifer Appel and Allysa Torey published *The Magnolia Bakery Cookbook: Old-Fashioned Recipes from New York's Sweetest Bakery* in 1999, replete with recipes for muffins, cookies, layer cakes, pies, cheesecakes, icings, and fillings. Theme cooking books cover a wide variety of topics, such as the Beatles and the Civil War. Cooking dishes with silly Beatles-esque names or concocting the food eaten by confederate soldiers can turn music and history buffs into cooking buffs.

## Contemporary Cooking for Fun

The main goal of all of these shows and books is to make cooking more accessible to those who cannot or do not like to cook, and more fun and interesting for those who do. One effect of the explosion of cooking shows and cookbooks has been the opening of the kitchen to men. With the average marriage age several years later than in the mid-twentieth century, and more men living on their own before marrying, they have more time to learn how to cook.

As more fast food restaurants and ready-made foods flood the market, cooking from scratch has become a hobby, no longer a necessity. With more women entering the work force toward the mid- and late-twentieth century, cooking for fun was relegated to weekends. Many people who cook regularly in the early 2000s make time for it because they enjoy it so much.

*See also:* Coffee Houses and Café Society, Diners, Dining Out, Fast Food

**BIBLIOGRAPHY**

Bastianich, Lidia M. *Lidia's Italian-American Kitchen.* New York: Alfred A. Knopf, 2001.

Ferrone, John, ed. *The Armchair James Beard.* New York: The Lyons Press, 1999.

Fitch, Noel Riley. *Appetite for Life: The Biography of Julia Child.* New York: Doubleday, 1997.

Lagasse, Emeril. *Emeril's TV Dinners: Kickin' It Up a Notch with Recipes from* Emeril Live *and* Essence of Emeril *as Seen on the Food Network.* New York: William Morrow and Co. Inc., 1998.

Pepin, Jacques. *La Technique: An Illustrated Guide to the Fundamental Techniques of Cooking.* New York: Quadrangle/ New York Times Books, 1976.

Perl, Lila. *Slumps, Grunts, and Snickerdoodles: What Colonial America Ate and Why.* New York: The Seabury Press, 1975.

Torres, Jacques. *Dessert Circus: Extraordinary Desserts You Can Make at Home, Companion to the National Public TV Series.* New York: William Morrow and Co. Inc., 1998.

Appel, Jennifer, and Alyssa Torrey. *The Magnolia Bakery Cookbook: Old-Fashioned Recipes from New York's Sweetest Bakery.* New York: Simon and Schuster, 1999.

Spignesi, Stephen J. *She Came in Through the Kitchen Window: Recipes Inspired by the Beatles and Their Music.* New York: Citadel Press, 2000.

Rombauer, Irma S., and Marion Rombauer Becker. *The Joy of Cooking.* Indianapolis, Ind.: Bobbs-Merrill Co. Inc., 1964.

———., *The Joy of Cooking.* New York: Scribner, 1997.

*Richard Panchyk and Caren Prommersberger*

# COUNTRY MUSIC AUDIENCES

Hillbilly music, as country music was more often called in its early days, emerged as a form of mass entertainment with the rise of radio broadcasting in the 1920s. Using a variety show format featuring folk, popular, and ethnic music, the producers of the first radio "barn dances" hoped to appeal to audiences composed mainly of middle- and working-class white listeners in rural areas and small towns. Different styles predominated in different regions, as stations tailored their shows to local talent and preferences. The available anecdotal evidence and the listener mail received by the most popular barn dances suggest that the initial audience for hillbilly music was sizable and socioeconomically diverse.

In the absence of systematic demographic information, observers constructed a fanciful image of the country music audience. As soon as commercial hillbilly music appeared, critics began to indulge in the worst kind of stereotyping. *Variety* 's oft-quoted 1926 description of hillbilly listeners as "illiterate and ignorant, with the intelligence of morons" was a particularly vitriolic expression of the popular hick image that was applied to the country audience.

Despite such negative stereotypes, however, fans embraced country music to establish social identities, build communities, and negotiate change and tradition. In the 1920s, many listeners viewed hillbilly music as a way of preserving rural culture against encroaching urbanism. Listening patterns, which often assimilated the new medium into older social occasions such as dances and group work, helped to create a sense of continuity and allowed listeners to imagine a rural community on a national scale. Barn dance radio also helped ease the transition to modernity and city life for rural-to-urban migrants by offering images of family, home, and tradition that allowed them to remain connected to their personal pasts.

Hillbilly fans were not only consumers. They also played a pivotal role in the economy of the nascent industry, which relied heavily on personal appearances at local community and church events. Women usually organized these events; their importance in the early hillbilly business likely provided a foundation for later fan club activity.

## Urban Migration

Shortly before the start of World War II, millions of rural Americans began moving to urban centers in search of industrial jobs. They took their music with them, exposing new audiences to the sounds of fiddles and steel guitars. Honky-tonks—nightclubs featuring live and jukebox hillbilly music—sprang up throughout the urban North and West and created a new, somewhat unsavory context for listening to country music. At the same time, the regional diversity that characterized the barn dance era began to give way to a more homogenous sound dominated by southern styles and produced primarily in Nashville.

The rise of the honky-tonk and the distinctive southern sound created popular stereotypes about class and country music that narrowed the genre's potential audience. The family-friendly, middle-class appeal of barn dance radio receded, and country music became firmly identified with the urban working class. Lewis Killian, a sociologist observing post–World War II migrants to Chicago, noted that honky-tonks were perhaps the most important social institution in the migrant community, offering a public space to meet and create a common culture. Indeed, he speculated that the derogatory term "hillbilly" was applied to all southern white migrants, regardless of origin, because of the recognized popularity of hillbilly music among them.

Fan clubs appeared in the 1940s and multiplied in the 1950s, even as the music's general popularity waned.

Fans were encouraged to understand and participate in the business of country music. Club participation offered members an alternative to mainstream commercial media, provided an opportunity to develop friendships with other fans, and affirmed the value of a genre that was often portrayed as trashy. Club officers fulfilled many public relations, management, and concert promotion duties that would later be assumed by professionals. Many promoted the genre as a whole by working for several stars or for club-monitoring organizations.

## Mass Appeal

In spite of its rough honky-tonk image, the country industry aspired to mainstream popularity for most of the 1950s. But the advent of television as the primary mass appeal medium and the subsequent fragmentation of the radio audience rewarded specialization over general programming. In the 1960s, Nashville embraced the genre's working-class image, capturing radio's blue-collar advertising market, even though the statistical correlation between social class and a preference for country was low by decade's end. In its effort to sell its working-class audience to advertising sponsors, the industry worked to revise popular understandings of southern migrants, emphasizing their economic success and consumer power in contrast to prevailing hillbilly stereotypes.

During the early 1970s, the country audience became an emblem of working-class conservatism. Observers of all political stripes identified country as the music of the Silent Majority, an assessment that persists in the historical debate about country's role in the "southernization" of American culture. Proponents of the southernization theory argue that country music became popular among northern, white, ethnic workers during these years because its traditionalism expressed their rising disaffection with liberalism in the civil rights era. Opponents counter that beneath their "superficial conservatism," country lyrics frequently celebrated notions of individualism and rebellion more in keeping with countercultural values than reactionary politics.

Ironically, just over a decade after the industry's decision to narrow its demographic focus, country music became popular with a mass audience. By the mid-1990s, country was the most popular radio format in America, dominating more than half of the hundred largest urban markets and attracting the best-educated, wealthiest audience of any genre. Even country's traditional racial imbalance diminished. Although the industry remained segregated, one survey found that about 25 percent of African American listeners over eighteen listened to country radio in 1997.

## Country Music Audiences

During the 1960s, the country industry used its audience's working-class image to attract advertising sponsors, as in this ad for San Francisco radio station KSAY. Sponsor, 8 August 1966.

"It would be interesting to know how many people there are in this class [hillbilly listeners]. The writer, as one might suspect, is a dealer in sound-reproducing machines. He sells these records daily to farmers, laborers and mechanics, to young and old, rich and poor——yes, even to bankers, contractors, salesmen and merchants."

**Smith, Arthur. "'Hill Billy' Folk Music: A Little-Known American Type,"** *Etude Magazine* 51 (March 1933): 154, 208.

Professionalization and centralization in Nashville ultimately minimized opportunities for fan involvement in the industry, but the rituals of country music continue to celebrate fans. At Fan Fair, Nashville's annual tribute to its fans, country's biggest stars host tens of thousands of devotees for free barbecues, concerts, and autograph sessions. The event traces its origins to a fan convention, originally held in conjunction with the industry's annual business meeting, organized by club members so they could network and share information. In the early 2000s, although its business functions have long since dissipated, Fan Fair remains an important pilgrimage for many aficionados and demonstrates the unique audience culture of country music.

*See also:* Rap Music Audiences, Rock Concert Audiences, Southern Leisure Lifestyles, Traditional Folk Music Festivals

### BIBLIOGRAPHY

Berry, Chad. *Southern Migrants, Northern Exiles.* Urbana: University of Illinois Press, 2000.

Ellison, Curtis W. *Country Music Culture: From Hard Times to Heaven.* Jackson: University Press of Mississippi, 1995.

Feiler, Bruce. "Gone Country." *New Republic* 214, no. 6 (February 5, 1996): 19–26.

Gregory, James N. "Southernizing the American Working Class: Post-War Episodes of Regional and Class Transformation." *Labor History* 39, no. 2 (1998): 135–154.

Grundy, Pamela. "'We Always Tried to Be Good People': Respectability, Crazy Water Crystals, and Hillbilly Music on the Air, 1933–1935." *Journal of American History* 81 (1995): 1591–1620.

Killian, Lewis. M. "Southern White Laborers in Chicago's Local Communities." Ph.D. diss., University of Chicago, 1949.

McCusker, Kristine M. "'Dear Radio Friend': Listener Mail and the National Barn Dance, 1931–1941." *American Studies* 39, no. 2 (Summer 1998): 173–195.

Newman, Kathleen Michelle. "Critical Mass: Advertising, Audiences, and Consumer Activism in the Age of Radio." Ph.D. diss., Yale University, 1997.

Pecknold, Diane. "The Selling Sound of Country Music: Class, Culture, and the Early Radio Marketing Strategy of the Country Music Association." In *Country Music Annual 2002*. Edited by Charles K. Wolfe and James E. Akenson. Lexington: University Press of Kentucky, 2002.

Peterson, Richard A. *Creating Country Music: Fabricating Authenticity*. Chicago: University of Chicago Press, 1997.

Peterson, Richard A., and Paul DiMaggio. "From Region to Class, the Changing Locus of Country Music: A Test of the Massification Hypothesis." *Social Forces* 53, no. 3 (March 1975): 497–506.

Sugrue, Thomas. "The Incredible Disappearing Southerner?" *Labor History* 39, no. 2 (1998): 161–166.

*Diane Pecknold*

# CROSSWORD PUZZLES.

The crossword puzzle is a game in which a number of clues, divided in groups titled Across and Down, lead the solver to answers that are placed accordingly in a grid, one letter per square. The most important precursor to the crossword puzzle was the word square, created in England. In 1859, the earliest-known example of a word square used the words shown in Figure 1.

Published in the same year in the United States, it inspired the creation of many other puzzles with words crossing based on geometrical forms, from the late 1860s onward. On 21 December 1913, the editor of *The New York World*'s Sunday "Fun" supplement, Arthur Wynne (1862–1945), published another of these forms, resembling a hollow diamond and containing sixteen across and sixteen down answers—with two major innovations: the words were to be placed inside a grid, one letter per square, and, in ten of the lines and columns, two words were defined instead of just the usual one. First titled Word-Cross Puzzle, Wynne's creation became Cross-Word Puzzle from 11 January 1914 on.

**FIGURE 1**

Soon, the *World* readers began sending their own puzzles to Wynne, who published the first of them on 8 February 1914. Despite the popularity of these puzzles, until 1924, only a small but growing number of U.S. newspapers (around twenty) offered crosswords in their Sunday editions. On 10 April 1924, Simon and Schuster began its business with *The Cross Word Puzzle Book*, the first book ever published containing only crossword puzzles

At this point, the crossword craze took over the United States. The three Simon and Schuster *Cross Word Puzzle Books* published in 1924 became best-sellers; sales of dictionaries increased tenfold; newspapers and magazines offered up to $30,000 in contests; dresses, bracelets, watches, hats, and fabrics with crossword themes were produced; tournaments attracted hundreds of enthusiasts; libraries limited the reading time of dictionaries, avidly sought by contestants. Even the radio, through aired programs, explored the novelty, and the puzzle became a regular feature in many newspapers and magazines.

In 1925, the crossword turned into an international fad. Then, a slow technical evolution began, in which the rules of the modern American game were established: symmetry in the overall disposition of the black squares; all-over interlocking of words; no words with fewer than three letters; short and precise clues; a minimum of obscure or archaic answers. The 1960s saw the inclusion of themes and wordplay, and, in the 1980s, popular culture increasingly found its place in the puzzle.

In England, the cryptic style was created in the 1930s. Its clues contain two parts, the first one being a synonym of the answer, which is also indicated enigmatically by the second part, by means of a pun, anagram, reversal, dropped letter, and so forth.

By 2003, thousands of daily newspapers and monthly magazines published crosswords in the United States and throughout the rest of the world. Didactic books used the puzzle to fix their lessons, and doctors recommended it to strengthen the memory, for both the young and the old. On the Web, interactive puzzles abounded, showing why the crossword is the most popular word game in history.

*See also:* Board Games, Hobbies and Crafts

**BIBLIOGRAPHY**

Arnot, Michelle. *What's Gnu? A History of the Crossword Puzzle.* New York: Vintage Books, 1981.

Hovanec, Helene. *The Puzzlers' Paradise. From the Garden of Eden to the Computer Age.* London: Paddington Press, 1978.

Millington, Roger. *The Strange World of the Crossword.* London: Book Club Associates, 1975.

*Sérgio Barcellos Ximenes*

# CROWDS AND LEISURE

A crowd is a large number of people engaged in non-routine activities. Because such behavior is not planned and supervised, participants are able to decide collectively and spontaneously how they wish to behave. A crowd then is not controlled by an outside authority who defines what behavior is expected, but rather is able to define its own behavior. At work, bosses or the task itself determines activities. Activities within most organizational settings, such as school or church, home or hospital, are similarly determined. Even playing organized games, as contrasted to watching, structures the activity of a group and thus removes it from the non-routine category of crowd. Groups not engaged in such organized activity are crowds whose behavior may be unpredictable. Spectators more than participants are likely to be such crowds. Gatherings of hobbyists, for example, are unlikely to be called crowds.

A crowd, therefore, is a group that presents a problem of social control, especially when the group gathered together for leisure is composed of people of subordinate status. Crowds may easily slip from control by authority and become a mob, as elites from Edmund Burke to Gustave LeBon used to characterize crowds. Similarly, modern historians and social scientists have conceived crowd actions as the lower class means to exercise power.

The perennial elite concern about leisure in public places has been about control of crowds. Parades, festivals, even indoor entertainment created crowds that periodically rioted. Carnivalesque events were especially dangerous because authority over subordinate groups traditionally loosened. Such concerns about sports spectators and rock concert crowds continue into the new millennium.

Authorities of all sorts wished to alleviate these concerns by imposing a regimen of discipline for most activities. Employers excluded free time for workers during work hours and disciplined the workday using the clock. Hospitals, prisons, and schools regiment their inmates' movements minute to minute. Social historians have documented a wide range of social control efforts by public and private authorities over the activities of subordinate groups in public spaces, the only place where such people could usually gather.

In the nineteenth century, elites as either reformers or repressors attempted to control the leisure of working people. The Progressive parks and playground movements hoped to supervise the free time of lower-class children and adults, and to cultivate and "Americanize" them. Frederick Law Olmsted believed his physical landscapes would not only offer relaxation, but also channel behavior and shape minds.

The state joined in these efforts, deploying police, social services, and public recreational and park facilities. Metropolitan police were organized to maintain order, that is, control street crowds, and to enforce a whole range of laws about behavior in public places. These laws, which were often posted in parks and other civic spaces, defined "order" and provided legal grounds for police to enforce this order.

Restriction on use of open land in rural areas and on behavior in urban public spaces by police drove lower classes onto private property, where owners could control and charge admission to lower classes seeking to pursue leisure not allowed in public, and to upper classes seeking to withdraw from such crowds. At first, leisure entrepreneurs found subordinate groups ready customers who had few alternatives where they could "be themselves" rather than conform to norms of higher classes. They provided what reformers denied lower classes. But gradually some owners and managers of commercial amusements sought greater profits and lower costs by reining in crowd behavior, and they gained the legal power to police behavior within their own establishments.

In the twentieth century, as working people became a significant consumer market and leisure was increasingly commercialized, social control became less overt. Advertising and a culture of consumption replaced police as the means to manage people's behavior. The recent rising concern about consumption is in part a concern about the social control of leisure through commercial products and services. Essentially, advertising is an attempt to persuade people to buy goods and services that presume specific scripted enactments. Dress and equipment, among other purchases, imply their use for specific performances and specific situations. In other words, they provide a script and rules of behavior that suit the goods purchased. A. G. Spaulding sold not only sports equipment, but also literally the rules of the games. Unregulated "sandlot" play was organized by rules and equipment from manufacturers and transformed crowds of kids into teams and leagues.

The recent scripting of spectators' time has done the same, changing unorganized crowds into regulated groups. Professional sports arenas provide not only a game but music, half-time entertainment, videos on big screen scoreboards, and even TV monitors at concession stands and in hallways. Such orchestration of activities specifically for crowd participation throughout the game reduces the likelihood of rowdiness or riot by spectators.

By the same token, crowds have not always succumbed to such discipline. Efforts to transform crowds into disciplined groups have not been ipso facto successful. Crowds rebelled, rioted, or moved to places where their rowdy behavior was acceptable. Even as some entrepreneurs sought higher-class clientele and broader markets, others continued to find profit serving lower classes by accepting and tailoring amusements to their culture. This autonomy, however, created a dilemma, greater probability that patrons might "get out of control," refuse to pay, demand refunds, or, worse, damage or destroy the property and even attack the entertainers, managers, or owners.

More subtle forms of imposing control were also common. The strain between autonomy and control was played out in many leisure settings. Lower-class blood sports such as bull and bear baiting, cock fights, and prize fights (but not fox hunting) were banned or restricted in the nineteenth century. Yet they thrived in illegitimate settings. The parks and playground movements were unsuccessful in removing lower-class kids and adults from the streets and saloons and placing them in locations where middle-class professionals could better supervise their leisure. Commercial amusements like Coney Island succeeded where reformers failed, attracting crowd from streets and saloons. They allowed lower-class patrons to talk, move about, eat, and flirt as well as enjoy the purchased entertainments.

Despite mechanisms of control, sports spectators still are unruly, and rock concert fans still sometimes riot, demonstrating the continued existence of uncontrolled, autonomous leisure crowds. Media critics typically abhor such behavior and call for police control of such lower-class displays—in contrast to newspapers' tolerance of Ivy League football fan rowdiness at the turn of the twentieth century. Privatized leisure in the home, such as radio and television, solved the problem of uncontrolled crowds by dispersing them to their homes, where danger would be contained by their families and small numbers. Such private leisure inspired different worries, most notably of a too-passive audience.

The history of theater audiences illustrates the perennial strain between control of gatherings in public and their autonomy or resistance. From the beginnings of European and American commercial theater in the early modern era, it was customary for audiences to "manage" performances by calling for tunes and encores as well as calling performers and managers before the curtain for criticism, and even to riot when their "rights" were not recognized. This custom has been called audience sovereignty. These rights had their roots in street performances, where performers played to crowds whose entry and behavior they did not control. *Commedia dell'arte* performances in Italy incorporated audience participation through asides to and repartee with the audience. Performers stepped down from improvised stages to mingle in and accost the crowd as part of the performance. Similar outdoor performers were typical at fairs and market days in England and France also. These circumstances gave the crowd significant control over the performance. As performances moved indoors, the lower classes in the pit or gallery continued to assert control over performances.

The history of American theater audiences has been one of gradual erosion of audience sovereignty, resulting in subdued audiences disciplined by their reduced legal prerogatives, managerially established rules of conduct, and norms of middle-class decorum. Before 1850, Amer-

**Lollapalooza.** A woman crowd-surfs in the mosh pit during the Lollapalooza tour at Green Mountain Fairgrounds on 9 July 1996 in Pownal, Vermont. The stop featured a variety of rock bands including Metallica, the Ramones, and Soundgarden. © *AP/Wide World Photos*

ican theater audiences, particularly the lower classes in the pit and gallery, exhibited typical crowd behavior of rowdiness. Theater riots were not uncommon. These riots typically involved mostly lower-class participants objecting to some incursion on their right or politics. By the 1850s, however, with cities becoming sufficiently large to demand regular amusements, and the middle class growing sufficiently large to support and sufficiently accept such amusements, theater managers began to tame such rowdy audiences through a number of measures: replacing benches with individual seats, bolting these seats to the floor, and issuing reserved seat tickets; introducing rules of conduct and hiring ushers to enforce these rules in cheaper sections; excluding prostitutes, restricting alcohol and cigars, and changing the entertainment to appeal to women and middle-class more than male and working-class clientele.

Nevertheless, other theaters continued to service lower classes where rules of conduct were less stringent. The crowds in these theaters were freer to converse, move about, hiss, and behave in ways akin to the era of audience sovereignty. Immigrant theaters were particularly

noted for this atmosphere. Riots were rarer, but they still occurred occasionally.

Nickelodeon movie audiences continued this same tradition. Some observers referred to these storefront theaters, especially in working-class neighborhoods, as social clubs because so much socializing occurred while movies were being shown. As movies moved into buildings built for that purpose and capital investment increased, theater owners sought a higher-class clientele and eschewed the "social club" atmosphere. The epitome of this trend was the movie palace. By the 1930s neighborhood theaters had lively audiences, but mostly during Saturday matinees for children.

With the rise of rock and roll and teenager culture in the 1950s, teenage crowds became feared as sources of trouble. At such music venues raucous audiences were more prone to acting as a crowd than the more mature audiences in adult theaters. Gatherings of working-class teenagers anywhere—dances, drag races, drive-in movies, and restaurants—were seen as a problem. Police were encouraged to disperse them. Teen dances and clubs were organized to supervise and control their behavior. Today, such rowdiness among young audiences continues and appears periodically in news reports.

*See also:* Coney Island, Country Music Audiences, Rap Music Audiences, Raves/Raving, Regulation and Social Control of Leisure, Rock Concert Audiences, Urbanization and Leisure

**BIBLIOGRAPHY**

Boyer, Paul. *Urban Masses and Moral Order in America, 1829–1920.* Cambridge, Mass.: Harvard University Press, 1978.

Butsch, Richard, ed. *For Fun and Profit: The Transformation of Leisure into Consumption.* Philadelphia: Temple University Press, 1990.

———. *Making of American Audiences from Stage to Television, 1750–1990.* Cambridge: Cambridge University Press, 2000.

Cook, Daniel, ed. *Leisure Sciences* 23, no. 2 (April 2001). Special issue on commodification.

Davis, Susan G. *Parades and Power: Street Theater in Nineteenth-Century Philadelphia.* Philadelphia: Temple University Press, 1986.

Edwards, Richard. *Contested Terrain: The Transformation of the Workplace in the Twentieth Century.* New York: Basic Books, 1979.

Gilbert, James. *A Cycle of Outrage: America's Reaction to the Juvenile Delinquent in the 1950s.* New York: Oxford University Press, 1986.

Gilje, Paul. *Rioting in America.* Bloomington: Indiana University Press, 1996.

Goffman, Erving. *Asylums: Essays on the Social Situation of Mental Patients and Other Inmates.* Garden City, N.Y.: Anchor Books, 1961.

Kasson, John. *Amusing the Million: Coney Island at the Turn of the Century.* New York: Hill and Wang, 1978.

Katz, Michael. *The Irony of Early School Reform: Educational Innovation in Mid-Nineteenth Massachusetts.* Cambridge, Mass.: Harvard University Press 1968.

Lane, Roger. *Policing the City: Boston, 1822–1885.* Cambridge, Mass.: Harvard University Press, 1967.

Newman, Simon. *Parades and Politics of the Street: Festive Culture in the Early Republic.* Philadelphia: University of Pennsylvania Press, 1997.

Oriard, Michael. *Reading Football: How the Popular Press Created an American Spectacle.* Chapel Hill: University of North Carolina Press, 1993.

Palladino, Grace. *Teenagers: An American History.* New York: Basic Books, 1996.

Peiss, Kathy. *Cheap Amusements: Working Woman and Leisure in Turn-of-the-Century New York.* Philadelphia: Temple University Press, 1985.

Pencak, William, Matthew Dennis, and Simon Newman, eds. *Riot and Revelry in Early America.* State College: Pennsylvania State University Press, 2002.

Ritzer, George. *The McDonaldization of Society.* Thousand Oaks, Calif.: Pine Forge Press, 2000.

Rosenzweig, Roy, and Betsy Blackmar. *The Park and the People: A History of Central Park.* Ithaca, N.Y.: Cornell University Press, 1992.

Rudé, George. *The Crowd in History: A Study of Popular Disturbances in France and England, 1730–1848.* New York: John Wiley and Sons, 1964.

Taylor, Dorceta, "Central Park as a Model for Social Control." *Journal of Leisure Research* 31, no. 4 (1999): 420–477.

Tilly, Charles. *From Mobilization to Revolution.* Reading, Mass.: Addison-Wesley Publishing Company, 1978.

Turner, Ralph, and Lewis Killian. *Collective Behavior.* Englewood Cliffs, N.J.: Prentice Hall, 1972.

Wilmer, Steve. "Partisan Theatre in the Early Years of the United States." *Theatre Survey: The Journal of the American Society for Theatre Research* 40, no. 2 (1999): 1–26.

*Richard Butsch*

# CRUISING

I'm gettin' bugged driving up and down this same
    old strip
I gotta find a new place where the kids are hip
    —"I Get Around," *The Beach Boys*

Take one automobile, one full tank of gas, as many teenagers as will fit into the car, and a strip of pavement frequented by all other teens and the mix is a recipe for cruising. The latter years of the 1950s through the 1960s were the heyday of this most emancipating of teenage leisure pursuits. As a form of teenage expression, cruising afforded a generation of young Americans a sense of liberation never before realized. It's no wonder then that the car has been referred to as the "machine of freedom" (Goodale and Godbey).

When cruising, the motivation is neither to get somewhere nor even necessarily to be somewhere. Rather, cruisers are motivated by the expectation of seeing, meeting, and being with other teens, particularly beyond the gaze of parents. Cruising is simply the means by which these expectations are realized. Another motivation of cruising is the desire to be on the move, even if there is no end destination. Despite this intent, cruising can be a misnomer particularly in heavily congested areas where the sheer number of cruisers can bring traffic to a crawl. Because cruising affords teens a freedom away from par-

**Dream Cruise.** According to organizers the Dream Cruise, held in the northern suburbs of Detroit, Michigan, has over 1 million people attend the annual event that began in 1994. Held on the third Saturday in August, classic car owners come to cruise down historic Woodward Avenue while spectators line the sidewalks. © *Paul Warner for AP/Wide World Photos*

ents and their homes, cruising teens are largely left to interact with other teens unsupervised. This is a particularly appealing option when hoping to meet members of the opposite sex, since cruising vehicles are often segregated according to gender.

A number of social, economic, and geographic influences conspired to give rise to cruising during its early years. The first wave of Baby Boomers reached legal driving age in the late 1950s. This large influx of teenagers stretched private and public resources and as a result teens took it upon themselves to carve out their own unique form of recreation. Leisure choices then were facilitated by a rapidly expanding economy and the attendant affordability of automobiles. Vance Packard documents the automotive industry's strategy of "planned obsolescence" in which new models continually replaced older models thereby making used cars relatively inexpensive, thus affordable even to teenagers. For the first time in history, teens had the means, both financial and vehicular, to gather away from home on their own terms and under their own prescriptions, as opposed to attending scheduled athletic contests or school dances. Finally, the spread of suburbia resulted in towns built for the automobile owner. Not surprisingly then, cruisers too would have access to the edges of town and beyond. Drive-in restaurants and theaters in

particular became popular during the 1950s and early 1960s. In 1950 there were 450 A&W Drive-Ins across the country; just ten years later there were more than 2,000.

## In Popular Culture

As an illustration of the prevalence of cruising during the late 1950s and mid-1960s consider the pervasiveness of this activity in popular culture. It appears the first use of the term "cruisin" in print was by Max Shulman in his 1957 novel, *Rally Round the Flag, Boys*. Although primarily identified with surfing, the Beach Boys released a number of songs, and even whole albums (e.g., *Little Deuce Coupe* ), devoted to cars and cruising. Most obvious might be their song "I Get Around," which describes the essence of driving around on a Saturday night with a car full of friends. Other musical artists of this time who sang the praises of cars and cruising include Jan and Dean, Chuck Berry, and Gene Vincent and His Blue Caps. Tom Wolfe's 1965 essay on the "Kandy-Kolored Tangerine Streamline" addressed the lure of having a custom car when cruising. In 1979 George Lucas's movie *American Graffiti* told the story of teenage hopes and dreams against the backdrop of cruising during one summer night in 1962. Following *American Graffiti*, the spin-off television series, *Happy Days*, took the theme of teens and their cars and transported them from southern California to Milwaukee, Wisconsin. In this series, the principal characters would often use Arnold's Drive-In as a hub of their nightly cruising.

## The Demise of Cruising

With cruising identified as one of the most popular teen leisure options in the 1950s and 1960s, one might ask if the activity has since faded away. Cruising continues to be a mainstay leisure option for a number of teenagers in the early 2000s. However, as a widespread, teenage phenomenon it has been replaced by a number of other leisure pursuits: playing video games, surfing the net, and going to the mall. The last of these, going to the mall, carries a number of parallels to cruising, especially the opportunity to find and meet other teens. And just as a mixture of social, economic, and geographic influences combined to contribute to the rise of cruising, a similar mix has abetted in its dwindling popularity. Where once the town's main street or boulevard defined the boundaries of the cruising area, now four-lane highways connect once-sovereign towns and urban and suburban sprawl have created decentralized commercial zones. As a result, the malt shop or drive-in has given way to the strip mall along the four-lane highway or to the mega-mall with its multicultural food court.

Additionally, anti-cruising legislation has been adopted by a number of towns in an effort to alleviate the traffic and other social problems associated with cruising. For example, between the hours of 2:00 p.m. and 4:00 a.m. from April through September in Virginia Beach, Virginia, it is illegal to drive a motor vehicle past a traffic control point two times in the same direction within any three-hour period (Cardon).

A booming economy in the 1990s continued to make automobile ownership affordable, yet not as affordable as it was half a century ago. Still, having access to a vehicle does not appear to be a limiting factor in the popularity of cruising in the early years of the twenty-first century. Rather, teens now have greater options to escape from parents and their homes. The mall has become the preeminent gathering place for teens; malls are ubiquitous and serve the teens' needs in any weather and any time of day. Of course, malls do not satisfy the motivation of being on the move or just going anywhere and nowhere. It is with this goal in mind that cruising may well continue in some form, as the desire to be mobile is best and most conveniently served while sitting in a car watching people and places pass by.

*See also:* Automobiles and Leisure, Drag Racing, Hot Rodding, Shopping Malls, Teenage Leisure Trends

**BIBLIOGRAPHY**

Cardon, David A. "You Cruise, You Lose at the Oceanfront." Available from http://www.cardonlaw.com/cruising.

Goodale, Thomas, and Geoffrey Godbey. *The Evolution of Leisure: Historical and Philosophical Perspectives.* State College, PA: Venture Publishing, 1988.

Jackson, Kenneth T. *Crabgrass Frontier: The Suburbanization of the United States.* New York: Oxford University Press, 1985.

Kunstler, James Howard. *The Geography of Nowhere: The Rise and Decline of America's Man-Made Landscape.* New York: Simon and Schuster, 1993.

Packard, Vance. *The Status Seekers.* New York: David McKay Co., 1959.

*James Harding*

# CYBER DATING

Cyber dating has grown in popularity and respectability since the advent of online personals in the mid-1990s. Computer dating began in the 1960s, when scientists used mainframe computers to match people based on interests and appearances. Journalist Andrea Orr, however, suggests that cyber dating puts a technological spin on a much older trend: matrimonial services, which matched couples in the 1800s.

More than 40 million Americans visited online dating sites each month in 2003. Americans spent $302 million on cyber dating that year, making it the most profitable market on the Web. This interest is fueled by growing numbers of singles—a record 40 percent of American adults are single, and half of them visited online dating sites in 2003. Cyber dating also signals significant changes in dating and marriage trends: Americans are marrying later in life, which makes them less likely to meet partners in high school or college. Workplace romances are dwindling, partly due to the rise in sexual harassment suits. As singles become more mobile and attend religious services less frequently, community organizations such as clubs and churches have decreased in importance. Cyber dating provides an appealing alternative to singles bars, and new technologies such as broadband and digital cameras have made browsing profiles and uploading photos easier than ever.

Millions gravitate to sites such as Match.com, where users can post a free personal profile but must pay a monthly subscription fee to e-mail other users. Online daters scan hundreds of profiles per visit, limiting searches based on categories such as region, age, ethnicity, height, weight, politics and religion. Although half of Match.com subscribers are under 30, older singles who may be divorced or widowed are increasingly using online services. Specialized dating sites have grown in recent years: Blacksingles.com caters to African Americans, while RightStuffDating.com enables Ivy League graduates to meet others of their intellectual ilk. Gays and lesbians, while represented on mainstream dating sites, also connect on sites such as PlanetOut.com.

Once connected, cyber daters often exchange e-mail messages for weeks or months before talking on the phone or meeting in person: a pace that mirrors traditional courtship. The anonymity of online personals provides safety, but may also encourage fabrication, as users often present themselves as younger, thinner, taller or more successful than they actually are. Up to 30 percent of cyber daters are married—some openly seeking affairs, others posing as single. Cautious cyber daters may search public records to verify the identity and marital status of people they meet online.

Two of the newest dating sites in the early 2000s—Friendster.com and eHarmony.com—made online dating more familiar and precise. After posting a profile and photo on Friendster.com, users invite their friends to join and help create a searchable network of social contacts. Couples who connect through the site can honestly say they were introduced by mutual acquaintances. Founded by a psychologist, eHarmony.com gives users a 500-question survey covering subconscious desires and personality traits, then strategically matches couples for online dates. The questionnaire identifies users who might be liars or otherwise undesirable—16 percent of those who take the survey are asked to leave the site (Mulrine).

Some singles have successful online dating experiences: eHarmony.com reports that more than 1,500 couples met and married through the site in its first three years, and Match.com boasts 90,000 successful matches each year. Others, however, grow weary of endless profile searches and disappointing dates, and opt for a lower-technology, less commercialized way of finding prospective partners.

*See also:* Computer's Impact on Leisure, Dating, Hook-Ups, Internet, Men's Leisure Lifestyles, Teenage Leisure Trends, Women's Leisure Lifestyles

**BIBLIOGRAPHY**

Brooks, David. "Love, Internet Style." *The New York Times* (8 November 2003): A15.

Duryee, Tricia. "Be Your Own Detective in the Murky World of Online Dating." *Seattle Times* (13 May 2002).

Egan, Jennifer. "Love in the Time of No Time." *The New York Times* (23 November 2003): 6:66.

Harmon, Amy. "Online Dating Sheds its Stigma as Losers .com." *The New York Times* (29 June 2003): A1.

Kim, Gina. "Online Dating Industry Offers Something for Everyone." *Seattle Times* (14 Feb. 2003).

Mulrine, Anna. "Love.com." *U.S. News and World Report* (29 September 2003): 52–56.

Orr, Andrea. *Meeting, Mating and Cheating: How the Internet is Revolutionizing Romance* . Upper Saddle River, N.J.: FT Prentice Hall, 2004.

Potts, Leanne. "Won't You Be My Friendster?" *The Albuquerque Journal* (15 February 2004): E8.

Starling, Kelly. "The Joys and Dangers of Love on the Internet." *Ebony* (February 2000): 46.

*Katherine Lehman*

# DANCE CLASSES

Since colonial times, there have been dancing masters in America, often itinerant, to teach the art of social dancing. John Playford's *The English Dancing Master* (1651) is a landmark guide for social dance classes that eventually took root in the United States. William B. DeGarmo wrote *The Dance of Society* in 1875. Instruction in dancing included instilling the moral and physically corrective aspects of dance. The 1820s Jacksonian era generated rudeness, and, in response, eighteen dance/etiquette manuals came into circulation in the 1830s.

Social dancing classes were offered in the European waltz and contra (country) dance in the nineteenth century. Then came lessons in the dances of the jazz era with its "tough" dances. From about 1910 on, as part of a dance craze that swept the United States, social dance fads have cascaded in and out of popularity. Numerous dance academies mushroomed during the commercial culture of dance halls from 1880 to 1920 to accommodate neophytes. Dance classes helped people keep up with the latest steps. In 1911, New York City alone listed 100 dancing academies serving 100,000 paying pupils, 90 percent under age twenty-one. Dance halls also offered classes in fashion. The New York Society of Teachers of Dancing formed to counter new vulgar dances and customs, such as "cutting in" from the ballroom.

Although most people of the world learn to dance by watching and being coached, at the beginning of the twenty-first century, there were about 18,000 dance stu-dios offering classes in the dance art forms that people learn for recreation. The age of students taking dance classes for leisure ranges from preschool to seniors. Recreational dance classes that are open to all comers differ from preprofessional dance classes that admit students who are selected through an audition process. Sometimes a recreational dance student becomes smitten with a dance form and wants to become a professional. A teacher might direct the student elsewhere for more serious training among like peers. Either type of student may participate in dance recitals or competitions to demonstrate proficiency. There are also schools and workshops for teachers of different dance genres and degrees of certification related to training completed.

Dance classes are commonly offered in ballet, modern, jazz, street jam, funk or hip-hop (music video dancing), jazz, contact improvisation, African dance, Balinese dance, Latin salsa and tango, ballroom, Spanish flamenco, Middle Eastern dance, swing/jitterbug (Charleston, lindy hop, hand dancing), clogging, Brazilian *capoeira*, and Irish step. In the early 2000s, striptease aerobics made its debut.

Dance classes are usually for groups of children, teens, or adults at different levels of dance skill, including dance fundamentals classes for pre-beginners. Teachers may also offer private lessons to individuals. Dance instruction involves verbal explanation and modeling by the teacher. Typically, a class begins with warm-ups, exercises that prepare the student's body to learn movements of a dance genre without injury. Teachers break down parts of a dance for students to learn. These parts

**Ballet lessons.** Young girls attend ballet class in Little Silver, New Jersey in 1990. Ballet is one of the most common dance classes taken by students. © *Corbis*

are eventually put together so students can perform the entire routine.

The amount of dedication and discipline required in dance classes varies, ballet being one of the more demanding. It has sequential, standardized curriculum teaching methods, as well as examination procedures within each of several traditions for the progressive education of dancers, including the Cecchetti Method of classical ballet training, the Royal Academy of Dancing, the August Bournonville School, the Vaganova Ballet Academy, and the School of American Ballet. Modern dance, too, has its pedagogies (for example, the technique taught at the Martha Graham Conservatory of Contemporary Dance or at the studios of Erik Hawkins, Merce Cunningham, and Alvin Ailey).

In addition to dance academies and studios, dance classes are offered in recreation departments, community centers, senior centers, churches, schools, summer camps, hospitals, and prisons. Individuals can take "dance classes" with an instructor in their own home via videos. Lots of how-to books that codify rules of a dance form and explain dance floor etiquette are available.

Over time, books have provided increasingly detailed information about how to perform individual steps, their combinations in dance phrases, and phrases in the complete dance.

Classes in modern dance at the kindergarten through university levels often focus on creative choreography. In these classes, students are taught the elements of dance (time, space, and effort in gesture and locomotion) and ways of putting them together to make an artistic dance. Then students are given problems, such as how to express a particular idea, to solve through their own choreography.

Motivation for taking dance classes varies. Parents take youngsters to dance classes so they can develop grace and poise, acquire discipline, become physically fit, and be with peers. Dance classes tend to be the preserve of females, although jazz and hip-hop attract many males. Because males are more likely to learn sports than dance, those who have learned to dance are always in demand as partners. Students who are interested in broadening their dance experience and taking classes beyond their home studios can attend periodic convention workshops and competitions (classes are usually offered at these events), which are sponsored by over forty organizations.

Adults take dance classes to keep up with the latest steps, get exercise, gain firsthand experience in a performing art, and fantasize. As one adult student said, "Up the stairs in your business clothes. You hear the piano playing Chopin. You are beat, but begin to feel a little happier. And then the class starts. I fantasize being a princess. At the end of class I am generally always so happy. And I keep wondering what was it that made the world seem like an enchanting place" (Hanna, 1988a, p. 145).

The opportunity for human face-to-face viable contact, in an age of automated telephone responses and computer information, is a factor in drawing people to dance classes. They are a way to meet people and find fresh means of self-expression.

Many males take classes to meet females. Ballroom dance studios, often part of large national chains, attract some lonely people and, in addition to teaching students, put on regular or special event "parties" that duplicate social occasions on the outside.

Wedding preparation catalyzes crash courses in dance. A couple may spend thousands of dollars on their wedding, so they prepare for that first dance together as man and wife. Sometimes the bride's and groom's parents, relatives, and friends also take classes.

Ethnic and national groups take classes in the dances of their cultural heritage. Indian immigrants, for example, cement ties to the home country, and second-generation American-born Indians learn Indian values embedded in, and imparted through, *Kuchipudi* dance. Dancer and teacher Nilimma Devi says: "The meaning of the dance is the same as in India—and more. Parents in the U.S. see the dance as an auspicious symbol for toughness, survival, good luck, and creation. It is a link to their roots. . . . Many families dislike the Western permissiveness for females, particularly at the high school level. Indian parents hope their children can partake of the Indian values conveyed through *Kuchipudi*. A traditional message portrays the role of the ideal, beautiful, modest Indian woman" (Hanna, 1997, p. 102).

A parent, Usha Charya, explains: "Even though my daughter, Neeli, is growing up in American culture, she gets through *Kuchipudi* an appreciation for Indian customs, rituals, grace, music, skill, and mythology of India. True, she's American . . . . But at Ms. Devi's dance school, she can find a sense of identity and belonging. She won't feel she's totally different. She's a kid of the third culture—neither Indian or American" (Hanna, 1997, p. 102). Non-Indians also take ethnic and national dance classes for pleasure and to grow as dancers.

Some women take dance classes in jazz and striptease to learn to love their bodies and to get in touch with their femininity and denied sexuality. In the "The Art of Exotic Dancing for Everyday Women" class, a former exotic dancer takes students of all backgrounds and ages on a spicy journey through striptease dance. In a companion eighty-six-minute instructional video, the instructor models and breaks down the movements, and then students practice and offer tips based on what they learn. A voiceover and outline review key points. Students learn how to walk; project through body language; master stationary, revolving, squatting, and kneeling hip rolls; pose; transition from one move to another; trace lines on the body; and simulate sex. In 2002, women and men could get a sensual stripper workout at gyms from Los Angeles to New York City. The cardio striptease of bump and grind with mirrors; stripper moves, including sliding clothes back and forth between legs; and pole work offered body toning and titillation as incentive to exercise.

People flock to dance classes, from ballet to less formal styles of dance. But it should be noted that some religious groups do not sanction dancing in any format. Instruction in dancing for etiquette has diminished, although some private prep schools give their students such classes so they are versed in proper decorum.

*See also:* Dance Halls, Social Dancing, Square Dancing

## BIBLIOGRAPHY

Christensen, Anne. "Pole Cate." *New York Times Magazine* (April 28, 2002): 82–83.

Hanna, Judith Lynne. *Dance and Stress: Resistance, Reduction and Euphoria.* New York: AMS Press, 1988a.

———. "Teaching Adult Beginners." *Dance Teacher Now* 10, no. 1 (January 1988b): 26, 28–30.

———. "The Power of Dance: Health and Healing." *Journal of Alternative and Complementary Medicine* 1, no. 4 (1995): 323–327.

———. "Spotlight on Nilimma Devi: A Touch of India in America." *Dance Teacher Now* 19, no. 2 (February 1997): 97–100, 102

———. *Partnering Dance and Education: Intelligent Moves for Changing Times.* Champaign, Ill.: Human Kinetics Press, 1999.

Lopata, Helen Z., and Joseph R. Noel. "The Dance Studio—Style Without Sex." In *Games, Sport and Power.* Edited by G. P. Stone. New Brunswick, N.J.: Transaction Books, 1972.

*Judith Lynne Hanna*

# DANCE HALLS

Throughout the late nineteenth century, the traditional working-class dance was known as the "affair." These dances were typically located in rooms attached to saloons or some other multiple-purpose hall in a working-class neighborhood and were usually sponsored by mutual-aid societies, fraternal orders, and political associations, or linked to community and family events like weddings. In both cases, the dancing reaffirmed community networks and relations and ensured that the rituals of courtship were passed on to the next generation. Indeed, young women found that their parents usually accompanied them to these dances, or they found an acceptable chaperon, a practice common among emigrants from southern and eastern Europe and Mexico.

By the 1890s, working-class youth began to organize their own dances called "rackets." These dances were generally sponsored by social clubs, which typically included anywhere from a dozen to fifty or more members. Club members usually met once a week in saloons, settlement houses, rented halls, or cigar stores; or in their own hangouts, which they set up in the basements of tenement flats to entertain their dates with dances, skits, and games. Most social clubs also held a semiannual or annual dance in a neighborhood hall, using the money they raised to pay for club activities.

Over the next few decades, dancing became a veritable craze, leading to a dramatic increase in the number and types of dance halls. By the 1910s, dance palaces joined the neighborhood or saloon halls as the popularity of dancing continued to grow. The dance palace was a more elaborate and conspicuous commercialized attraction than the multiple-purpose hall and was usually larger, accommodating anywhere from 500 to 3,000 patrons. The dance palace also attracted men and women from all walks of life and nationalities, although individual dance palaces typically were segregated by class and race. The most obvious exception to this segregation was the growing craze of the 1920s among white youth to patronize clubs in African American communities, like the Cotton Club in New York City's Harlem. As a whole, dance halls appealed more to factory and office workers than to middle-class men and women who preferred the city's cabarets, which featured dancing along with dinner and a floor show.

The anonymity young couples found at dance halls encouraged the development of a peer culture. Commercial dance halls typically attracted men and women in their late teens and early twenties. Apart from their parents, they could experiment with alcohol and cigarettes and dabble in romance. Men and women were frequently seen closely embracing each other in the balcony or in the chairs and tables surrounding the dance floor. The dance hall had even earned the reputation among certain classes as a parlor because of the numbers of married couples who first met at a dance.

The new social dances from the period only reinforced the opportunity to mingle. By the late nineteenth century, pivoting, spieling, and tough dancing were beginning to replace the traditional waltz and two-step. Pivoting and spieling were a fast parody of the waltz, in which couples closely embraced each other and engaged in much twisting and twirling. With the waltz, men and women did place their hands on each other. But their shoulders were expected to be three to four inches apart, and they were not supposed to look directly into each other's eyes. The tough dances, also known as animal and rag dances, were even more out of control. Tough dances were performed from a crouched position with knees flexed and body bent. Many of these dances, like the turkey trot, bunny hug, and grizzly bear, imitated animal gestures and movements while celebrating improvisation and a sexually expressive look and feel.

Over the next few decades this form of dancing grew increasingly popular. The 1920s saw the rise of the shimmy, the black bottom, and the Charleston, while swing music was all the rage by the 1930s and young couples were dancing the lindy, also known as the jitterbug. Swing music, which came from big bands and produced an ensemble sound, began to replace the smaller jazz combos. Swing was less restrained and less ornate than its jazzy predecessors, and it was more individualistic, a sound that fit well with the lindy. Like the Charleston and other dances from the 1920s, the lindy required partners to touch hands or dance apart instead of in an exclusively face-to-face position. In particular, the lindy featured the breakaway or solo, typically reserved for the male, and the "air steps," in which dancers showed off their skill by dancing with their feet off the ground through a number of gymnastic moves.

Dance hall patrons did confront a number of problems, however. Across the country, cities and states successfully passed ordinances to restrict the use of alcohol and to prohibit certain dance moves, and patrons quickly realized that the dance hall did not always provide the intimacy and fun for which they were searching. Throughout the early twentieth century, there were almost always more men than women at dance halls. Indeed, some men claimed one had to know someone before being assured of getting a dance. The ratio was more disproportionate

**Danceland.** In April 1932 the New York City dance hall Danceland featured jazz musicians and "hostesses" who danced with men for money, which was common at that time. © *Bettmann/Corbis*

on the weekends, when there were even greater numbers of men in attendance.

Commercial leisure also cost more than men and women were able to spend. In the 1920s, women's wages averaged only 57 percent of men's, compelling many women to depend upon their male companions to help pay for commercial leisure, a practice known as "treating," in which women traded sexual favors— ranging from a simple good night kiss to more intimate sexual encounters—for access to commercial leisure. Both men and women typically found that treating failed to meet their expectations. Young men could not always afford the treats their female companions demanded, while most women feared that the system of treating ensured their dependence on men. The dilemma compelled some women to attend only chaperoned dances or to attend with a female friend to discourage any unwanted sexual advances. After World War II, the gradual move toward dances in which partners frequently lost contact gave way to freestyle dances in which the partner was optional. The rise of rock and roll in the 1950s and its use of repeated phrases and a driving beat gave rise to dances that emphasized swiveling and thrusting hips, like the jet, the locomotion, and the bop, dances that were more likely to be performed around a café jukebox than at a traditional dance hall. By 1960, the twist was all the rage and the partner had become obsolete. Popularized by Chubby Checker on *American Bandstand,* the twist was akin to toweling oneself off after a bath while grinding out a cigarette with one's toes.

Toward the end of the 1960s, rock and roll dances were beginning to fade, and there was little to replace them. Young Americans were beginning to favor heavier-sounding bands like Led Zeppelin and stars like Jimi Hendrix. Dancing was rarely seen at the concerts these bands staged. Instead, concert goers preferred to "freak out" or "trip out," often while vibrating their spines or contracting their torsos. About this same time, disco, which is simply music that is reproduced "on disk" and not performed, appeared in primarily gay and African American clubs, as disc jockeys began splicing together faster soul songs to produce a continuous dance mix. With the 1970 movie *Saturday Night Fever,* disco became a national craze, and discotheques began to replace café jukeboxes in popularity. At discotheques across the country, freestyle dance typically dominated the dance scene and even line dancing became popular.

Throughout the rest of the twentieth century, freestyle dances continued to dominate the dance scene but not without a challenge. In the 1980s and 1990s, line dancing led to a revival of country and western bars because of the ease with which dancers could pick up the steps; and raves featured trance dancing, or what can be described as dancing with an emphasis on spinal vibrations or torso and pelvic contractions reminiscent of the "tripping out" of the late 1960s. At the same time, swing dance was making a comeback. During the mid-1980s, a group of swing devotees converged on New York City to learn more about swing from the original dance masters of the 1930s and 1940s. Before long swing dance was showing up in clubs and makeshift dance floors across the country. Some dancers explained their attraction to swing because of the nostalgia of the dance, while others simply wanted to dance with their partners as opposed to dancing apart from them, a common criticism of freestyle dance. Whatever the reason, the swing revival of the mid-1980s sheds light on the extent to which social dancing has changed since the end of World War II, as well as the different meanings ascribed to dance and its importance to America's youth.

*See also:* Dance Classes, Social Dancing, Square Dancing

**BIBLIOGRAPHY**

Bailey, Beth L. *From Front Porch to Back Seat: Courtship in Twentieth-Century America.* Baltimore: John Hopkins University Press, 1988.

Buckman, Peter. *Let's Dance: Social, Ballroom & Folk Dancing.* New York: Paddington Press, 1978.

Erenberg, Lewis. *Steppin' Out: New York Nightlife and the Transformation of American Culture.* Chicago: University of Chicago Press, 1981.

Gauvreau, Mark. *If It Ain't Got That Swing: The Rebirth of Grown-Up Culture.* New York: Spence Publishing, 2000.

McBee, Randy D. *Dance Hall Days: Leisure and Intimacy Among Working-Class Immigrants in the United States.* New York: New York University Press, 2000.

Martin, Carol. *Dance Marathons: Performing American Culture of the 1920s and 1930s.* Jackson: University Press of Mississippi, 1994.

Nasaw, David. *Going Out: The Rise and Fall of Public Amusements.* New York: Basic Books, 1993.

Peiss, Kathy. *Cheap Amusements: Working Women and Leisure in Turn-of-the-Century New York.* Philadelphia: Temple University Press, 1986.

Wagner, Ann. *Adversaries of Dance: From the Puritans to the Present.* Urbana: University of Illinois Press 1997.

*Randy D. McBee*

# DANCING

**See** *Dance Classes; Dance Halls; Social Dancing; Square Dancing*

# DARTS

The game of darts is primarily a twentieth-century phenomenon, but its history goes back at least to the Middle Ages in Europe (and perhaps as far back as the Roman Empire), developing out of military training and soldiers' games. In the Middle Ages, English archers used thrown missile weapons called "dartes" during close combat. When not fighting, such weighted hand-arrows, small spears, and cut-down arrows were thrown at archery targets or cross-sections of tree trunks for competitive recreation. The naturally occurring tree rings proved perfect for scoring, and there is even evidence that the radial cracks that appeared as the wood dried eventually became the radial lines of the modern dart board. The size of the dart itself diminished as the game spread from soldiers to commoners and even to the nobility. It is believed that the Pilgrims played darts aboard the Mayflower, using the butt of a wine barrel as a target. For the rest of the dart-playing world, the game was introduced largely by soldiers of the British Empire, who threw darts in military clubs and bars set up for their recreation. However, not until 1908, during one of the most celebrated cases of "sport law," did the game gain acceptance by the general public.

## Darts in America

The vast majority of people in the United States (and around the world) play the British-style game. Notwithstanding the Pilgrims' fondness for darts, for Americans the game first became popular among U.S. military personnel stationed in England or serving in close proximity to British troops during World War II. So while there is an American-style darts game, it did not pass down through American history from the Pilgrim settlers, but in fact developed alongside, and around the same time as, the modern British game. The growth of dart throwing among military personnel stationed abroad continued during the Cold War. Veterans of the Korean War and those of the Vietnam War have stated they "learned their darts" during service in those conflicts.

However, in America itself, the British darts game remained largely the province of English and Irish expatriates in the northeast United States, especially in and around Boston. While British-style dartboards could be found in Veterans of Foreign Wars clubs and American Legion posts, it was not until the 1960s that the game began to appear in more public places, particularly bars, and especially English-style pubs. Still, by 1969, there were fewer than 1 million darts shooters in the United States. In the 1970s, though, the game's popularity would explode so that by 1976 a reported 4 million Americans were shooting darts. In 1988, the National Sporting Goods Association estimated there were 17.8 million darts shooters. In the early 2000s, millions more played in the more than 100 national and regional darts leagues and associations around the country.

## British Darts

The British-style game is played on boards of either fifteen or eighteen inches diameter. The round boards are generally made of elm, sisal-fiber, or cork. The face is split into twenty numbered and equally sized wedges. At center there are two rings known as the bull's-eye; the outer ring is worth twenty-five points and the inner, or "double bull" is worth fifty points. There are two narrow bands that circle the board, one along the edge of the gameface, the other halfway between the edge and the center, which double and triple respectively the value of the wedges they pass through. The board is hung five feet, eight inches from the floor to the bull's-eye. The shooting line, known both as the "hockey" and the "oche," is marked at either seven feet, ten inches; eight feet; eight feet, six inches; or nine feet from the wall. Most British-style games are based on beginning with a high number and shooting points until one person reaches exactly zero. Common starting scores are 1001, 501, and 301. Most competition-level games require a shooter to hit a double both before scoring can begin and in order to "zero out." As a result of the constant planning, the looking several throws ahead, and the shifting of scoring patterns, many shooters of the British game compare it to chess.

The British-style dart itself became more or less standardized as the game became a general pastime, but as shooters continue to look for the ideal combination of weight and balance, the dart itself continues to develop. Darts measure no more than six inches and weigh between nineteen and twenty-eight grams. Early darts had a four-inch wood barrel with a pointed steel tip in one end and a flight of feathers on the other. In 1898, an American patented a folded-paper flight. In the early twentieth century, flights were usually plastic and decorated with color patterns, illustrations, and designs. An all-metal barrel was patented in England in 1906; by the 1940s, copper and brass darts were standard. In the 1970s, lighter metals and alloys such as nickel, aluminum and tungsten became popular among serious shooters.

## American Darts

American-style games and boards originated around the same time as the modern British-style games and boards,

during the years following the Civil War. Nearly all forms of American-style darts games are a variation of "baseball darts." The two main variants of American-style games are based on the boards on which they are played. The Philadelphia-style board is numbered exactly as the British board, but the tripling ring is located much closer to the gameface's perimeter, near the doubling ring. Also, the numbers one through nine are generally distinguished in some way as the scoring sectors. Shooters each shoot nine rounds of three darts at the nine sectors, scoring a single, double, or triple based on the ring they hit. The highest possible score each inning is three triples (there being no home runs), and the bull's-eye being worth zero. Philadelphia darts was developed by coalminers in Pennsylvania and New Jersey, and by unskilled and blue-collar workers in and around Philadelphia itself—the center of American-style darts. The first darts equipment manufacturer, the Dart Board Equipment Company (DECO), was founded in Philadelphia, as were two other of the oldest darts companies in the United States. Founded in 1912, Apex Manufacturing continued in operation in the early 2000s, as did the Widdy Dart Board Company, which was founded in 1908, but did not begin manufacturing dartboards and darts until 1930.

The Albany-style board has only the double ring, altogether leaving out the triple ring. As with Philadelphia darts, scoring is only possible in the numbers one through nine, but in Albany darts, the scores are one point for shooting in the single band and two points for shooting in the double. Missing the numbered sector or placing a dart in the bull's-eye scores zero points. There is evidence that the Albany-style game developed from the darts games played by Irish immigrants who dug and later ran barges on the Erie Canal. Another style of American dartboard does not use wedges and rings at all, but uses a baseball field's diamond pattern, and zones for hits, scores, strikes, and outs.

American-style dartboards are usually made of blocks of soft basswood joined together. American-style darts, or "widdies," are made of wood, with a longer and sharper tip weighted with lead, and use turkey feathers for flights. Philadelphia darts measure six inches, but Albany darts games are played with Apex No. 2 darts, which measure seven and one-quarter inches and can have as many as four flights. In both variants, the board is hung five feet, three inches from the bull to the floor while the distance from the wall to the hockey is seven feet, three inches.

## 1990s to the Present

Darts became big business in the 1990s, as plastic-tipped electronic darts machines became hugely popular after computerization produced more accurate scoring systems and microprocessors enabled multiple game choices and scoring systems. By 1994, as many as 250,000 electronic darts machines were in place around the country. Backed by corporate sponsors such as Anheuser Busch, darts promoters and large darts groups such as the American Darts Organization (ADO) and the American Darters Association (ADA, founded 1991) sponsored national tournaments drawing thousands of shooters competing for cash prizes in the hundreds of thousands. Since the year 2000, however, the sport of darts declined as a money- and crowd-generating pastime. Lawsuits among the manufacturers of electronic machines hampered or cut into the efforts to maintain and grow darts leagues. Continuing efforts for acceptance of darts as an Olympic sport continued to meet no success, as questions remained as to whether darts was a true sport or more simply a pastime. Still, even in the face of such a downturn, regional and national leagues continued to draw shooters and to host events. Darts clubs existed in every branch of the U.S. military, and darts continued to be very popular in the bars and pubs where the modern game originated in the first place.

*See also:* Bars; Board Games; Computer/Video Games

**BIBLIOGRAPHY**

Carey, Chris. *The American Darts Organization Book of Darts.* New York: Lyons and Burford, 1993.

Hady, Edmund. *The American and English Dart Game, Including Tournament Rules.* Ashley, Pa.: Mayflower Grahpics, 1973.

McClintock, Jack. *The Book of Darts.* New York: Random House, 1977.

Peek, Dan William. *To the Point: The Story of Darts in America: Including a History of the Sport in Great Britain and Ireland.* Columbia, Mo.: Pebble Publishing, 2001.

Rees, Leighton. *On Darts.* New York: Atheneum, 1980.

Turner, Keith. *Darts.* New York: Harper and Row, 1980.

*Robert Arlt*

# DATING

A leisure activity related to rituals and practices of courtship and unsupervised by parents, dating developed in the twentieth century in response to changes in generational relations and gender, schooling, work, and entertainment practices. It is strongly embedded in the changes associated with the new consumer economy. Largely, though not exclusively, linked to heterosexual mores, dating came to define adolescent and young adult relations through much of the twentieth century, first in the United States and then also in other Westernized societies.

## The Evolution of Courtship Practices

In the nineteenth century, ideals of romantic love came to define courtship values aimed at choosing compatible marriage partners. As the stress on companionship between marriage partners eclipsed the earlier emphasis on patriarchy, new practices grew to replace the various forms of arranged or family-facilitated marriage that dominated marital choices among members of the middle class and the respectable working classes. Many of these were still adult-supervised and took place in social settings such as the home, churches, picnics, and other gatherings that included different generations.

At the same time, as the society industrialized and became urban, young men and women spent more time away from the watchful guidance of parents and other responsible elders. Adolescent girls spent time outside the home at work and at school. Both male and female adolescents now went regularly to schools that were expanding their age-required attendance upward into the teen years. And they went to work in impersonal factories, stores, nonfamily-based workshops, and offices. They also were frequently found in a variety of commercial amusements that proliferated in the late nineteenth- and early twentieth-century cities, such as amusement parks, dance halls, cafeterias, vaudeville houses, and movie theaters. Many of these arenas where young men and women mixed promiscuously became suspect for encouraging female immorality and challenging class boundaries. All these issues became especially acute in the context of growing immigration in the early twentieth century and the heterogeneity that threatened older limits on courtship behavior. They were also a threat to the mores of many immigrant groups, most of which were still patriarchally organized, and among whom access between young men and women was very restricted traditionally. These groups now saw their children go off to work in mixed social settings. Dating developed among young working people in response to these conditions. It was also developing simultaneously among young people at schools and colleges.

## Dating Comes of Age

Still daringly modern in the early twentieth century, dating was, by the 1920s, an established and widely recognized ritual among older adolescents and young adults. It became the means by which private and unsupervised behavior that revolved around sexuality could at once remain within respectable limits and still provide a legitimate means to experiment with the new intimacy now available for an exploration of mutual interests and sexual pleasures. Dating was not supervised directly by parents or other adults. Rather, it was an activity whose clearly defined limits on personal expression were patrolled by peer enforcement of standards that limited eligibility and datability, while establishing hierarchies of evaluation. The young often introduced new standards of attractiveness and glamour into these evaluations, by which they measured a potential dating partner by incorporating models from the popular culture. But dating still enforced class, ethnic, and racial boundaries.

Largely because of the extension of education to the majority of adolescents (including immigrants) in the 1920s and 1930s in public high schools, and to a substantial minority in colleges and universities, these new peer definitions became effective. The long hours away and shift of authority from home and work to youth-based institutions and the coeducational nature of most of these settings made peer standards in dating dominant. The school social system was based in many extracurricular activities, such as sports competitions, informal and formal social events, and fraternities and sororities. These activities and groups established the networks that regulated dating behavior. But it was the enormous expansion of popular culture media, especially the movies, popular music, and sports that provided the new sources and models for peer-defined standards of style, dress, and language around which judgments about popularity and datability revolved. The new media idols not only altered the vocabulary of acceptable and proper behavior, but as popular culture relied on overt and latent sexual themes, this helped the young to question former limits on sexual propriety in their dating behavior.

Dating rituals were fairly standardized by the 1920s, and they increasingly involved recourse to commercial recreations such as a movie, a soda shop, or a roadside restaurant. Dancing also became a part of many dates as school-sponsored dances or hops and more formal proms became common. Among wealthier young people, local hotels became favored spots for dances and dates. In places outside of large cities, dating relied on access to an automobile, and everywhere it became dependent on the outlay of significant amounts of cash to ensure that the treat for the afternoon or evening was acceptable to the dating partner. Commerce was thereby embedded into the very structure of the dating relation-

ship, which almost always meant that the male treated the female. Women, in turn, spent money on their appearance, including fashionable clothes, stylish hairdos, cosmetics, and beauty treatments. This emphasis on external criteria of success questioned former standards that highlighted inner virtues such as piety, thrift, and reliability. New consumer standards replaced these in the evaluations of possible life partners as each side made decisions about the prospective date and whether the dating would continue.

Courtship also changed in the 1920s and 1930s because exclusivity was not considered either essential to dating or its only necessary result. Some observers noted that young people had become the victims of a dating-and-rating syndrome, which sometimes overwhelmed the long-term courtship objectives of dating, as young men and women of the middle class engaged in a whirl of heterosexual social activities. Driven by considerations of status rather than companionability, it became part of a complex hierarchy of popularity and desirability. Other youth, especially those from working-class backgrounds, adopted dating for the more permanent courtship possibilities it offered as selection among dating partners narrowed earlier into committed relationships. Both dating that led to exclusive attachments and dating that was part of a busy social life included a variety of erotic practices that became standard in twentieth-century youth before the premarital sexual revolution of the late 1960s and 1970s, among them kissing, petting, and fondling.

The expenses incurred by the male dating partner have led some historians to conclude that there was an established understanding about the exchange that men expected from their female partners, as they sought some sexual compensation for expenses incurred. Whether the exchange was quite so direct and calculated or it evolved from a set of expanded possibilities for intimacy, dating did result in new and looser norms about sexual experimentation. In most cases, these activities fell short of intercourse, and it was understood that women bore the responsibility for defining limits while men would try to push those boundaries as far as possible. Among those whose dating had become exclusive in some form of official engagement, studies from the 1920s and 1930s agree that intercourse would be a likely outcome for about half of the couples. This intimacy was understood as a legitimate expression of the commitment to a loving relationship oriented to marriage.

## The Impact of World War II

World War II abruptly changed the dating routines as the national emergency left schools, colleges, factories, and offices empty of young men. The imminence of departure also encouraged more rapid sexual involvement and a rush to marriage. For the thousands of those called "Victory girls," who engaged in promiscuous relations with servicemen, the war led to short-term casual sex for unmarried and even married women, who came to value immediate over longer-term considerations. Catering to men on short-term leave, these women were targeted by the army as potential carriers of venereal disease.

During the long depression of the 1930s, most social groups delayed the time for marriage. The war radically changed this pattern, and, after the war, the trends toward early marriage continued and were soon accompanied by a dramatic baby boom that altered American family life and the preparation for marriage in significant ways. The return of the peace encouraged a return to the dating behavior established earlier, but it was now far more than in the past an active matter of adult concern and intervention. Adults manifested their concern by offering advice columns in newspapers and teen magazines, as well as in manuals for adolescents. This was usually offered by the new relationship experts who drew on the high valuation Americans placed on the science of psychology that was also involved in other aspects of child rearing.

Dating also had a shorter duration since women began to marry younger than at any time in American history. As a result, adolescents began to contemplate the road to marriage more seriously and at younger ages. In the 1950s, younger adolescents and even preteens appropriated some of the behaviors of their older brothers and sisters, and serious, "steady" relations became common in the dating process. This issue caused considerable concern to parents and experts who saw how its privacy and exclusivity created more occasions for sexual intimacy. "Going steady" was often accompanied by tokens of alliance such as pinning (wearing the fraternity or club pin of a boyfriend) or wearing a love anklet or name bracelet of a steady boyfriend.

## The Youth Culture Changes Dating

Dating as either a youth-initiated ritual or an area of adult guidance became less significant by the 1970s when the rapid changes in sexual mores that accompanied the youth culture of the 1960s removed some of the reasons for dating etiquette by legitimizing premarital sexual intercourse. This change affected young adults especially since it altered the pacing of marriage and the sequencing of premarital courtship behavior. Couples now more frequently engaged in the whole array of sexual behaviors before marriage, and they experimented with living together as couples. Monogamous lifetime partnerships were less common for those looking toward marriage, as well as for married couples, as divorce became much more common. For adolescents, too, the more open sexuality that developed during this period made dating rules far less stringent and enforceable.

After the 1970s, dating as a form of socializing and courtship continued, and it still defined many heterosexual relationships, but older sexual norms were no longer a guide to personal behavior, and all rules had become much more flexible. In a similar way, same-sex dating became a possibility as such relationships came out into the open. The effective use of birth control, the availability of abortion, even among adolescents, and the greater tolerance for personal sexual choices after the 1970s meant that the rules that had been in place for most of the century and whose objective was to maintain social standing during a life-cycle phase marked by strong sexual drive were hardly as necessary anymore. Dating was no longer the expected means for heterosexual leisure activities nor the only route that could lead to steady coupling. Other possibilities, including group activities associated with the use of intoxicants and large music "raves" have grown up as alternatives. In these new social contexts, sexual enforcement (especially toward more experimentation) is provided by overt group regulation, not through internalized rules of dating practice. In these contexts, too, sexuality is often divorced from intimacy, which had been the dominant association in dating. And as the Internet became a part of social life, courtship and marriage services that rely on the computer have become more acceptable means to facilitate marriage choices.

Dating is still a vehicle to establish relationships in the twenty-first century among adolescents and adults. While its significance appears to have declined among adolescents, dating has remained a common adult activity. For a generation of adults who take divorce for granted, dating has become a necessity as they seek to establish new partnerships. But the dominant twentieth-century restrictions on sexuality, which harshly defined what was and was not permissible, that once defined dating, have given way to a much more benign form of entertainment, an entertainment in which commerce and money are still an essential component of having a good time.

*See also:* Cyber Dating, Hook-Ups, Men's Leisure Lifestyles, Teenage Leisure Trends, Weddings, Women's Leisure Lifestyles

## BIBLIOGRAPHY

Addams, Jane. *The Spirit of Youth in the City Streets*. New York: Macmillan Company, 1909. Reprint, Urbana.: University of Illinois Press, 1972.

Bailey, Beth L. *From Front Porch to Back Seat: Courtship in Twentieth-Century America*. Baltimore: Johns Hopkins University Press, 1988.

———. *Sex in the Heartland*. Cambridge, Mass.: Harvard University Press, 1999.

Fass, Paula S. *The Damned and the Beautiful: American Youth in the 1920s*. New York: Oxford University Press, 1977.

Hine, Thomas. *The Rise and Fall of the American Teenager: A New History of the American Adolescent Experience*. New York: Avon Books, 1999.

Modell, John. *Into One's Own: From Youth to Adulthood in the United States, 1920–1975*. Berkeley: University of California Press, 1989.

Peiss, Kathy. *Cheap Amusements: Working Women and Leisure in Turn-of-the-Century New York*. Philadelphia: Temple University Press, 1987.

Rothman, Ellen K. *Hands and Hearts: A History of Courtship in America*. New York: Basic Books, 1984.

Tentler, Leslie Woodcock. *Wage-Earning Women: Industrial Work and Family Life in the United States, 1900–1930*. New York: Oxford University Press, 1979.

*Paula S. Fass*

# DINERS

The American diner, with its distinctive long counter and its reliable menu of simple but hearty fare, was a familiar feature of the urban landscape for much of the twentieth century. In addition to providing a setting for informal and inexpensive dining, it eased the entrance of affluent working-class families into mainstream, middle-income consumer culture. Ironically, the very success of diners in the post–World War II years proved to be their downfall. By introducing upwardly mobile, blue-collar families to the concept of informal commercial dining, they contributed to the popularity and proliferation of fast-food chains that offered the same service without carrying the stigma of a working-class heritage.

Diners owed their origins to the horse-drawn lunch wagons that prowled New England's manufacturing districts at night in the late nineteenth century, offering quick and cheap nourishment to industrial workers. After the turn of the century, when these lunch wagons became stationary to accommodate more elaborate cooking facilities, operators continued to place them in industrial areas.

Because of their resemblance to Pullman dining cars, they became known as "diners." In fact, some of them originated as railroad cars. Most were mass produced in factories, although some were fashioned from abandoned trolleys during the 1920s and 1930s, and others were built on-site to mimic the prefabricated variety. These diners flourished during Prohibition, when their primary source of competition—the neighborhood saloon—was eliminated. The growth of motor trucking also expanded the market for diners and accounted for their ubiquity along heavily trafficked thoroughfares. There were nearly 7,000 diners in operation on the eve of World War II.

Although primarily utilitarian in function, the workingman's diner was also a place of leisure. Patronized by regular customers, diners were gathering places where men could banter—often in salty language—in a common parlance of sports, politics, and work. The counter-and-stool arrangement also encouraged casual conversation among strangers. Because diners cultivated a constituency composed from a wide variety of ethnic backgrounds, they were sites of cultural amalgamation, places where immigrants and their children became assimilated into a more unified working-class culture through their consumer habits. Like pool halls, bowling alleys, saloons, and other working-class consumer venues of the early twentieth century, diners catered primarily to men.

After World War II, the social function of diners changed dramatically. Widespread affluence enabled blue-collar families to emulate middle-class consumer practices and consider a meal away from home as a form of recreation. Eager to tap the growing demand for leisurely dining, diner owners gravitated to suburban residential districts. They also tried to create a more refined and comfortable dining experience by installing upholstered booths for family seating, removing cooking facilities to a separate rear kitchen annex, and hiring waitresses to serve customers. If the prewar diner had functioned as an adjunct to the factory, the postwar variant would cultivate its identity as an extension of the happy suburban home. For the first time, women and children composed a significant portion of the diner's clientele.

Heightened attention to ambiance and decor was reflected in a more flamboyant architecture. With the enhanced use of stainless steel finishing, jutting pylons, and angled canopies, the structures themselves exuded modernity and the look and feel of the space age. Proprietors echoed this architectural trend in the names they chose for their businesses: Rocket Diner, Comet Diner, Flying Saucer Diner. By inference, the buildings assured upwardly mobile customers that they were as up-to-date as anyone else. At the very least, futuristic imagery created

**"Nighthawks."** Edward Hopper's (1882–1967) famous 1942 oil on canvas painting "Nighthawks." He is best known for his works of the "American scene," with this one in particular inspired by a New York City diner. © *AP/Wide World Photos*

a vast psychological distance between the suburban diners built in the 1950s and the typical workingman's lunch car of a previous generation. In response to the growing number of patrons who traveled by automobile, proprietors surrounded their buildings with huge parking lots and erected bright neon signs that could be read at high speeds. One feature that remained fairly consistent across this transition was the practice of racial discrimination. In many parts of the country, diner owners believed that the presence of African Americans would diminish the social standing of their businesses and drive away loyal white customers. During the 1960s, civil rights groups responded by staging sit-ins and pressing for new laws to ban discrimination in public accommodations.

Blending a wide variety of class and ethnic traditions, the post–World War II diner established new aesthetic and social norms for commercial dining. In so doing, it prepared the way for the fast-food empires of the 1970s. By the 1960s, a plethora of restaurant chains and independent family-style restaurants descended on the middle-income market, each operating under the same basic formula: casual atmosphere, reasonable prices, and wholesome domesticity. Most followed the example of the diner in offering customers a choice of counter seating, booth seating, and table service. Drive-ins complemented their carhop service with indoor seating. Formal full-service

restaurants abandoned rigid formalities and turned casual, perhaps even adding a counter for solitary patrons. While the chain restaurants shared many characteristics with the modern suburban diner, they remained products of very different social backgrounds. None carried the diner's burden of trying to shed an urban industrial heritage. As a result, they had an edge over the diner in attracting members of the established middle class as well as upwardly mobile working-class patrons who were intent on leaving behind their humble origins. Although some diners met this challenge successfully by employing grandiose interior decor and covering their fading steel exteriors with brick facades, many more went out of business.

Since the 1980s, diners have enjoyed a resurgence. Festooned in neon and chrome, adorned with images of Elvis Presley and Marilyn Monroe, and staffed with gum-chewing, bobby-sox wearing waitresses, the diner industry turned to nostalgia as a marketing device. In delivering a sanitized version of the 1950s, these diners embodied the national trend toward themed entertainment in consumer venues. Meanwhile, a new generation of diner aficionados energized efforts to rescue and preserve authentic diners from a bygone era.

*See also:* Coffee Houses and Café Society, Dining Out, Fast Food

**BIBLIOGRAPHY**

Gutman, Richard S. *American Diner: Then and Now.* New York: Harper Perennial, 1993.

Hurley, Andrew. *Diners, Bowling Alleys, and Trailer Parks: Chasing the American Dream in Postwar Consumer Culture.* New York: Basic Books, 2001.

Jakle, John A., and Keith A. Sculle. *Fast Food: Roadside Restaurants in the Automobile Age.* Baltimore: Johns Hopkins University Press, 1999.

Liebs, Chester H. *Main Street to Miracle Mile: American Roadside Architecture.* Baltimore: Johns Hopkins University Press, 1995.

*Andrew Hurley*

# DINING OUT

"In answer to my question of why dine out, the answers were repeatedly that it was fun, a convenience, a habit, an entertainment, a pleasure."

—Joanne Finkelstein

Few, if any, major forms of recreation in American history have changed as much as dining out. The trek from Victual Desert to Gourmet Cornucopia gained momentum as the Industrial Revolution made eating away from home a necessity for armies of workers as well as occasional travelers. But for the next 100 years, the typical restaurant aimed no higher than to emulate "home cooking." Then, in the 1960s, changing demographics, ethnic diversity, technology, and American ingenuity combined to change eating habits at a dizzying pace. By 2003, no country could match the United States in the variety of foods available nor in innovations in the preparation, service, and dining ambiance for a population that consumes 54 billion meals a year that are not prepared at home.

## The Colonial and Early American Inn and Tavern

As would be expected, opportunities for eating away from home during the colonial period were largely inherited from the British. The concept of the ordinary, at which food was included with the price of overnight lodging, the tradition of having whatever was in the pot at the tavern's fireplace, the practice of eating while standing, the acceptance of a low order of food, and a disdain for soup and all other things French, had evolved in England with little change since the fourteenth century. Though the

inns, ordinaries, and taverns were the main purveyors of food, something to eat could also be had for a price at various coffee shops, grog shops, and boardinghouses. In the taverns, men gathered to drink, to get the news, to enjoy companionship and good talk; food was secondary. In the ordinaries, a fixed menu was served at a fixed time at a fixed price. Food was plentiful enough in colonial times, but according to available accounts, most of it lacked variety, was not often enjoyed, and was devoured rather quickly. Breakfast and lunch might take ten minutes, dinner fifteen. Colonial newspapers made reference to the "bolting system" of eating that caused several to die by choking on their food. Contributing to the habit of rapid ingestion was that of serving all courses at the same time. Dining out in colonial America was most often a matter of "grab, gobble, gulp, and go."

It was not until late in the eighteenth century that some of the larger city taverns offered "fine cookery," but the farther one traveled from the cities, the plainer the food. In the more remote areas, dining out remained a matter of taking "potluck." Travelers from other countries often complained about the quality of the food, but never about the quantity unless it was too much. Dining out in colonial America was as crude a matter as public life itself.

## The Origins of the Modern Restaurant and Café

A "café" was originally defined as any place where one could enjoy coffee and spirits. Today, it is indistinguishable from "restaurant," which William Brillat-Savarin defined as a business that offers to the public a repast that is always ready and whose dishes are served in set portions on the orders of those who wish to eat them. The origin of the restaurant may be argued at length, as food shops and chophouses can be traced back to the twelfth century. Attention usually focuses, however, on the French Revolution that freed the chefs from the aristocracy, abolished the chefs' guilds, and ushered in a burgeoning middle class eager to enjoy experiences formerly restricted to the aristocracy. By the end of the eighteenth century, there were hundreds of restaurants in Paris, and these, along with the new hotels, became the "palaces of the people." The American revolution against England and the assistance of the French in that struggle engendered an affinity for and receptivity to things French. Americans who visited Paris heartily reinforced these attitudes and none more enthusiastically than Thomas Jefferson.

"Jullien's Restarator" (the word "restaurant" had not yet entered the English language) opened in Boston in

**Delmonico's Restaurant.** Patrons of Delmonico's Restaurant, the oldest restaurant in New York City (established in 1837), enjoyed a huge selection of 370 entrees when it first opened. It was founded by brothers Giovanni and Pietro Del Monico and was originally nicknamed "The Citadel." © *Corbis*

1794, the first by a French immigrant. It remained for the Delmonico family, however, to grasp the full potential of elegant dining, and its New York City restaurants, once numbering four, made millions. From the 1830s to the 1930s, Delmonico's was the last word in fine dining. But the general public was not as enamored as the notables who had visited Paris and welcomed French cuisine. Both the cuisine and the manner of serving it were matters of contention. In the colonial inns, all guests sat at long tables and ate the same food, thus promoting democracy. Delmonico's à la carte menus were considered undemocratic. More objectionable to the majority of Americans was the food itself. It was thought to be too rich, embellished with needless frills, and bad for one's health. Simple food was the overwhelming preference, and the presidential election of 1840 turned on just that issue. Martin Van Buren was associated with "fancy food," and

was defeated by William Harrison, who allegedly stood for plain food. To this day, American politicians profess to like plain food, and that is what is offered at fund-raising dinners. French cuisine would not take hold in the United States until reintroduced on television by Julia Childs in the 1960s.

Delmonico's restaurants also introduced snobbery and deference to public dining in America. It was the awe-inspiring ambience of their New York restaurants that encouraged the nouveau riche, particularly, to host elaborate dinners even though their capacity to appreciate the cuisine was woefully lacking. The influence of the restaurants founded by the Delmonicos, which lasted until Prohibition, can hardly be overestimated. Every city in the U.S. sought the distinction of having a fine restaurant in its downtown area. Delmonico's menus were copied far and wide.

**Indian restaurants.** The stretch of land on 6th St. between First and Second Avenues in East Village in New York City is dubbed "Little India." Shown here in 1995, it has many restaurants catering to traditional Indian tastes. © *Corbis*

## The Development of Restaurant Districts

The industry calls them "food clusters," planners call them "eat streets," and journalists seem to prefer "restaurant rows," but no matter the form of reference, they have become an exciting feature of many American cities. For some cities, such as Minneapolis, restaurant rows are a recent development. Earlier, as one journalist put it, that city's restaurants were scattered about like toppings on a pizza. Other cities, like Nashville, have had restaurant rows for years and have enjoyed the many advantages inherent in having restaurants in close proximity to one another. Not only the customers but smart restaurateurs as well appreciate the clustering of cafés.

Restaurant rows are desirable for the same reason the restaurants of Paris are superior to those of its suburbs. The mix of natives and visitors lends volume and vitality to the dining scene. When simple directions to easy-to-find locations solve visitors' problems as to where to eat, everyone benefits. In the "Little Italy" of one American city, there are four Italian restaurants, one of which is by far the most popular. It fills to capacity early in the evening, and latecomers not wishing to go on a waiting

list may partake of similar cuisine in the same block on the same side of the street. The lesser eateries are motivated to improve, the customer need not seek new parking, and that block of the city has a nightlife. Proximity solves many problems.

Many people go out to eat without a specific destination in mind and find it convenient to "shop" for one in a restaurant district. There, a variety of factors may influence their choice such as parking, how hungry they are, and how much they want to spend at dinner.. When all such considerations may be entertained at one general location, eating out becomes far more convenient.

Since World War II, many American cities have suffered a loss of vitality due to the middle-class "flight to the suburbs," the profusion of outlying shopping malls, and the intrusion of cold corporate towers in the best downtown locations. Efforts to revitalize cities are in vogue, and restaurant rows represent effective solutions to the problem. They create hubs of activity in the after hours reminiscent of nineteenth-century café society. Planners and city officials have come to realize the advantages of restaurant rows over convention centers, theme parks, and other

**FIGURE 1**

```
Landmarks in dining out in America

1763    Fraunces Tavern opens in New York City offering "Fine Cookery."
1815    The James cook stove replaces fireplace cooking.
1820s   Ice becomes readily available.
1831    Delmonico's introduces elegant 'sit down' dining in New
        York City.
1868    Delmonico's approves of women dining alone at luncheons.
1872    William Scott of Providence, Rhode Island, introduces the first
        horse-drawn lunch wagon.
1876    The first chain restaurant, The Harvey House, opens in Topeka,
        Kansas.
1885    The Exchange Buffet, America's first self-service restaurant,
        opens in New York City
1902    The first automat opens in Philadelphia.
1903    Hamburgers on a bun first served at the St. Louis Fair.
1904    The first cafeteria is opened in Los Angeles by Helen Mosher.
1919    Prohibition begins and within four years even the most
        prestigious restaurants go out of business.
1928    Clarence Birdseye introduces a method of quick-freezing food.
1936    Duncan Hines's Adventures in Good Eating is published and in
        three years sells more than 100,000 copies.
1940s   Railway dining cars are converted to lunch wagons.
1948    The McDonald brothers introduce the "Speedee System" which
        will soon revolutionize food service throughout the world.
1948    America's first serious cooking school opens in New Haven,
        Connecticut, later to be renamed The Culinary Institute of
        America.
1948    Kentucky Fried Chicken opens and within ten years becomes the
        largest restaurant chain in the United States.
1964    The New York Times begins reviewing restaurants.
1978    Restaurant Design is first published.
1980s   Chain restaurants begin catering to diet-restricted customers.
1982    The word "Foodie" first appears in an English magazine.
1983    The London Times calls New York City the "Eating Capital of the
        World."
```

attractions more likely to fall to competition from other cities. A city's restaurant rows fare well in good weather or bad, twelve months out of the year.

In cities where restaurant districts are not anchored by tradition and cherished landmark establishments, the question of where to locate food clusters is usually not a problem. Upscale shopping centers attract people with money, and the two activities, shopping and dining, go together as well as fish and chips. It is the large restaurant chains, far more than city officials, that decide on locations, and the major chains have always favored high traffic areas and shopping centers. There is a good bit of following the leader in locating chain restaurants, for it is well understood that when many of them share the same general location, all do better. The decision to link cities with an interstate highway system and its exits undoubtedly made the location of dining clusters easy and obvious if only for the chain operations.

## The Rise of the Chain Restaurant

In 1876, Frederick Harvey, having come to an agreement with the Atchison Topeka & Santa Fe Railway, opened the first of a chain of restaurants along the route; by 1887, there was one of his restaurants every 100 miles all the way from Kansas to California. So well managed were those train depot eateries that they continued to thrive until rail travel in the United States waned. Harvey's successful operation became the model for the many chains that would follow. As the automobile took over, drive-in restaurants sprang up where customers were usually served by carhops. By the late 1940s, however, employee salaries were consuming approximately 40 percent of gross restaurant income. At that point, Richard and Maurice McDonald took drastic steps that would eventually revolutionize food service throughout the world and not just in the realm of fast-food service. They fired the carhops, cut their menu from twenty-five items down to nine, eliminated china and flatware, and passed their savings on to their customers. Customers walked up to a service window to buy their food. Labor costs fell to 17 percent.

By the turn of the twenty-first century, trends favored chains in that middle ground between fast food and fine dining, referred to as "casual-dining" restaurants. These places offered comfortable seating, attractive decor, and ample helpings at moderate prices. A further trend, since the 1970s, was for casual-dining restaurants to limit their menus so that staff could be trained to prepare fewer dishes of better quality. Chains that once offered a large and varied menu restricted their offerings to Italian, or seafood, or barbecue, and so forth. New items were added only after careful taste testing and the elimination of any problems from procurement to service.

As in almost all areas of retailing, chains thrive to the extent that they are able to "kill off" small, local independent businesses. The chains enjoy many advantages that "mom-and-pop" establishments do not. The volume in which they purchase food and supplies gives them about a 25 percent cost advantage over small businesses, and they can afford the electronic technology that saves time and money, whereas small independents often cannot. Also strongly favoring the chains are the zoning ordinances imposed in American cities that disallow commercial establishments in residential areas. Chains depend on a high volume and fast turnover of customers and could not survive serving the small areas in which many independents once thrived. Americans desiring to eat out must drive out of the neighborhoods onto collector roads that take them to highly commercialized zones where only the chains can afford the leases. Finally, the chains benefit from the high rates of residential mobility and the high rate of automobile dependence in the United States. Whether living in a new area or traveling far from home, Americans are never far from a familiar dining logo where they know what they can expect.

278

## The Social and Economic Impact of Dining Out

Since the mid-twentieth century, the restaurant industry has nearly doubled its share of the dollars people spend on restaurant food. In the late l950s, Americans spent twenty-five cents of each food dollar dining out; by the end of the 1990s, that figure had risen to nearly fifty cents per dollar spent on food prepared in commercial kitchens. As of 2004, some 858,000 restaurants brought in over $407 billion in annual revenues. Restaurants employed 11.3 million people, more than any other private sector industry in the nation. One out of every three adults in the United States has been employed in food service at one time or another. The major reasons behind the industry's gain over home cooking are threefold. In 1960, only three wives in ten worked outside the home, but that number subsequently doubled and women are not cooking nearly as much as they once did. Secondly, free time shrunk, and eating out, which Americans have always been able to do quickly, saves time. Finally, the relative cost of dining out, as opposed to buying groceries, changed in favor of the restaurant industry. Modern technology and other innovations in food service often result in savings in both time and money for those electing to dine out.

Though the industry as a whole is thriving, operating a restaurant is a precarious business. The average life span of a million-dollar-plus restaurant in any large city is only three years. Owners thus press for profits as quickly as they can. The usual means include "pushing" high-profit-margin items such as wine and soft drinks and attempting, always, to reduce labor costs. A significant part of the labor cost is due to chronically high rates of employee attrition that, even in upscale restaurants, exceeds 80 percent. Those on hourly wages are more than twice as likely to leave as those on salary. Waiters and waitresses in the United States do not enjoy the status of their counterparts in Europe, and the conditions of their employment reflect it. Employee benefits are virtually unheard of for wait staff, and the same may be said for overtime. The industry has the highest percentage of minimum-wage employees in the nation, and some of its chains are leaders in the effort to eliminate minimum- or "fair-wage" laws by making them optional at the state level. The distinction that needs to be examined, some critics say, is that between service and servitude.

The quality of the food and the quality of service were, until the 1960s, about all with which a suitably located restaurant needed to be concerned. But vastly increased opportunities brought with them sharply increased competition. Innovations in restaurant architec-

ture exploded on the scene such that, in the early 2000s, establishments with per-person dinner checks of less than $20 spent $1,000 per seat on design and decor. Those with per-person checks exceeding $50 spent $3,000 per seat. Two-thirds of restaurant owners employed interior designers and three-quarters of them worked with architects to create enticing physical settings. Encouraged by the popular culture's emphasis on virtual reality, "theme restaurants" appeared, and though dining ambience will continue to be important, these ventures have an uncertain future. Customers all too easily become bored by the whimsical surroundings. As the French learned early in the twentieth century, features such as exotic centerpieces that distract diners from the food are usually short-lived.

As if concern over the quality of the food, service, and ambience weren't enough, restaurant owners of the early 2000s were beset with even more vexing demands. An ever-increasing number of Americans were looking for "something new, something different" when dining out. The fact that in any large city, twenty-six cuisine types were easily available (and in places like New York or Los Angeles, many more) didn't solve the problem, as evidenced by the emergence of "fusion cuisine" or the mixing of dishes from different localities. Leading the pack among those seeking new adventures in dining were the "Foodies," people who regard food as others regard paintings or drama. Once previously exotic dishes like chicken Kiev or fettuccine Alfredo become available in the frozen foods section of the supermarket, a true Foodie no longer considers them.

Satisfying an increasingly fickle diner was not only a matter of providing something new and different; by the 1980s another demand had been added. People wanted to continue to enjoy rich, tasty foods, but they didn't want as many calories. Americans were finally facing, head on, a paradox of abundance. They had become, as one observer put it, impassioned over cuisine and obsessed with dieting. The Centers for Disease Control and Prevention considers obesity to be of epidemic proportions in the United States and reports that the rate has doubled since the 1980s. Fast-food establishments get much of the blame, but it is a matter of concern for the entire industry.

Since that earlier period in the late 1940s and 1950s when dining out declined, due largely to the advent of television, it has become an integral part of the lifestyle of most Americans. The majority of adults now eat out more than six times a month and, though husbands and wives with no children are the most frequent diners, more and more households with children are dining out as parents find that "quality time" is more easily achieved in the restaurant than at home. Beyond familial "togetherness," the restaurant is now preferred over the home by seven out of ten Americans as a place to socialize with friends and better enjoy their leisure time.

The American appetite has expanded and refined considerably since those days in the 1920s and 1930s when home economists implored immigrants to abandon their "unhealthy" eating habits in favor of plain American food. We've progressed beyond the quality of dining out in the 1950s, when the main attraction, for most, was the taste of deep-fried food. Dining out in America is an ongoing revolution fueled by fierce competition and a population awakened to the pleasures now available and the promises of things yet to come. The nation's leadership in restaurant dining is not strictly culinary. In food alone, French restaurants remain to be surpassed. Where the U.S. excels is in the totality of the dining experience. The U.S. is the most innovative in restaurant architecture and design, in interior decor, in the incorporation and creation of new cuisines, and in sensitivity to the market.

Evidence of the ongoing revolution in food service is abundant. By 1990, 1,850 students were enrolled in the Culinary Institute of America, and leading chefs were earning $300,000 a year. The employment of personal chefs—about 6,000 in 2004—was expected to reach 20,000 within the next decade. Twenty-four hour a day cooking shows have emerged on cable TV, and in 2003, there were thirty-eight monthly online food magazines.

For many middle-class families, cooking at home is becoming a recreational activity while dining out has become a habit, and though the decline in home dining is lamentable in ways, few activities are as civilizing as dining out.

*See also:* Coffee Houses and Café Society; Diners; Fast Food

**BIBLIOGRAPHY**

Barr, Andrew. *Drink: A Social History of America.* New York: Carroll and Graf Publishers, 1999.

Brody, Jerome. *A Time Well Spent.* New York: Welcome Rain Publishers, 2000.

Colgan, Susan. *Restaurant Design: Ninety-five Spaces That Work.* New York: Whitney Library of Design, 1987.

Dru, Line, and Carlo Aslan. *Cafés.* New York: Princeton Architectural Press, 1988.

Finkelstein, Joanne. *Dining Out: A Sociology of Modern Manners.* New York: New York University Press, 1989.

Iggers, Jeremy. *The Garden of Eating: Food, Sex, and the Hunger for Meaning.* New York: Basic Books, 1996.

Levensten, Harvey. *Paradox of Plenty: A Social History of Eating in Modern America.* New York: Oxford University Press, 1993.

Mariani, John. *America Eats Out: An Illustrated History of Restaurants, Taverns, Coffee Shops, Speakeasies, and Other Establishments That Have Fed Us for 350 Years.* New York: William Morrow and Company, 1991.

Pillsbury, Richard. *From Boarding House to Bistro: American Restaurants Then and Now.* Cambridge, Mass.: Unwin Hyman, 1990.

Schivelbusch, Wolfgang. *Tastes of Paradise: A Social History of Spices, Stimulants, and Intoxicants.* New York: Vintage Books, 1993.

Schlosser, Eric. *Fast Food Nation: The Dark Side of the All-American Meal.* Boston: Houghton Mifflin Company, 2001.

Witt, William C. *Food and Society: A Sociological Approach.* New York: General Hall, 1995.

*Ray Oldenburg*

# DISABILITY AND LEISURE LIFESTYLES

One's leisure lifestyle consists of the day-to-day leisure engagements that are an expression of leisure preferences, awareness, and attitudes (Peterson and Sumbo, 2000). The development of one's leisure lifestyle is influenced by a myriad of factors, including one's personality, social acquaintances, work responsibilities, educational attainment, and skills and abilities, to name a few. Of the 52.6 million Americans with some level of disability, the specific impairments that they live with may, in fact, impact their leisure lifestyles. For example, an adolescent whose life revolves around basketball and who recently had a spinal cord injury may begin to play wheelchair basketball. An older adult with dementia who has a lifelong passion for gardening may need prompting to go outside and begin working in her garden.

According to the Americans with Disability Act, disability is "a physical or mental impairment that substantially limits one or more of the major life activities" (see Table 1). Typically, in order to understand an individual's experiences in a major life sphere such as leisure, one must consider the interaction between the person and the environment (see Figure 1). The characteristics of the individual encompass his or her cognitive, physical, and mental capabilities, as well as leisure-related attitudes, dispositions, likes, and dislikes. The environment, which

**TABLE 1**

**Definition of disability**

The Americans with Disabilities Act defines disability using the following criteria:

(a) a physical or mental impairment that substantially limits one or more of the major life activities

(b) a record of such an impairment

(c) being regarded as having such an impairment

may support or inhibit one's leisure lifestyle, includes activity and program opportunities, physical space, and the cultural-social context. How do people with disabilities develop and maintain a meaningful leisure lifestyle? What types of activity opportunities and physical spaces support positive leisure experiences? How may acceptance and inclusiveness within the cultural-social context promote positive leisure involvement? These questions are addressed in the following paragraphs.

## History of the Treatment of People with Disabilities

As described by Bullock and Mahon, historically the treatment of people with disabilities has been nothing short of inhumane. In ancient times, people with disabilities were considered defective, deformed, or crazy; and disability was viewed as some sort of supernatural punishment or curse. While people with less serious impairments probably survived relatively well as foragers or peasants, those with more pronounced disabilities were often used as for entertainment, if not otherwise killed. The movement to confine people with disabilities to institutions began in the twelfth and thirteenth centuries. These institutions, however, were not designed to provide care or treatment services to people with disabilities, but more simply "to get them out of circulation" (Bullock and Mahon, p. 22), to remove them from the eyes and minds of society. Colonial North America did not evolve much from this ancient approach and many early institutions were constructed. Overcrowded and prison-like, the oppressive conditions within these institutional warehouses, or asylums, as they were frequently called, continued well into the twentieth century.

According to Bullock and Mahon, "researchers have estimated that over 50,000 people with disabilities . . . were sterilized in the United States between 1925 and 1955" in efforts to prevent reproduction of those considered "manifestly unfit" (p. 25). Yet even the practice of sterilization paled in comparison to the tortures suffered

by people with disabilities as Nazi Germany practiced their killing techniques and scientific experiments. Finally, the 1950s and 1960s saw an outcropping of advocacy for people with disabilities and institutional conditions gradually began to improve with the passing of some early federal regulations. In the 1960s and 1970s, a move toward deinstitutionalization occurred, and further federal legislation strengthened the rights of individuals with disabilities.

## Legislative Influences

The Americans with Disabilities Act of 1990 has been called "one of the most important documents ever produced in the struggle for equity by people with disabilities" (Bullock and Mahon, p. 89). On 26 July 1990, President George Bush signed the Americans with Disabilities Act into law assuring the full civil rights of all people with disabilities in employment, public accommodation, transportation, state and local government services, and telecommunications. Many have referred to the Americans with Disabilities Act as "the 20th century emancipation proclamation for people with disabilities" (Bullock and Mahon, p. 83). This legislation is particularly germane to the topic of leisure lifestyle and disability as it not only prohibits discrimination, but also mandates the provision of reasonable accommodations in order to guarantee individuals full and equal participation in all state and local government services, as well as in virtually all privately owned businesses including hotels, restaurants, theaters, stores, stadiums, golf courses,

**FIGURE 1**

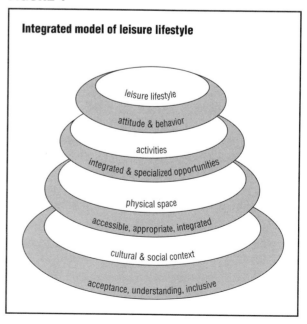

Integrated model of leisure lifestyle

theme parks, museums, libraries, and health clubs, to name a few.

Since the Americans with Disabilities Act was passed in 1990, municipal and county recreation agencies have made great strides in the movement to better accommodate, include, and involve people with disabilities in services and programs. Buildings and parks have been built or remodeled to be useable by all. Inclusive programs provide individuals with meaningful and enjoyable opportunities to build self-esteem, develop lifelong leisure skills, and make friendships. Swimming-pool lifts, sign-language interpreters, wheelchair-accessible trails, adaptive equipment, and specially trained support staff are just a few examples of how parks and recreation agencies are interpreting and implementing the guidelines of the Americans with Disabilities Act and contributing to the leisure lifestyles of individuals with disabilities in the United States.

## Descriptions of Leisure Lifestyles of Select Groups

**Individuals with Dementia: A Focus on Relationships and Rituals** More Americans are living longer. Due to this phenomenon, often referred to as "the graying of America," the prevalence of dementing illnesses, such as Alzheimer's disease, will continue to increase by epidemic proportions. Dementia is often characterized by a progressive neurological decline and loss of function related to pathological changes in the brain. Beginning with cognitive impairment, dementia may eventually impact all domains of functioning, including physical, social, and affective.

Leisure involvement plays a central role in enhancing one's quality of life. According to Marshall and Hutchinson, participation in recreational activities can arrest mental decline, generate and maintain self-esteem, reestablish dignity, provide meaningful tasks, restore roles, and enable friendships. Such activities also have benefits for the nonpharmacological management of negative behaviors associated with dementia such as increased agitation, depression, or wandering. Therefore, an important role of professional and family caregivers is to assist individuals with dementia in the continuation of a personally meaningful leisure lifestyle.

Cognitive impairment need not preclude one's ability to lead a meaningful leisure lifestyle, because so many of the activities that give life meaning are simple in nature, such as visiting with family, enjoying a home-cooked meal with friends, playing fetch with an affectionate dog, attending afternoon picnics, sipping hot chocolate, and dancing cheek to cheek. These activities do not require sequencing, problem solving, concentration, abstract thought, or other abilities typically impaired by dementia. Instead, they require social relationships, intimacy, relaxation, and appreciation.

"When I was first diagnosed, she and I were just absolutely sure that everything was over, that life was just simply going to pot. It's difficult, I think, for somebody with Alzheimer's to not just give up and say, the hell with it. I periodically do that, but then again, there are some things that I really enjoy." (Cary Smith Henderson, a man with Alzheimer's disease; Henderson, p. 77)

The leisure lifestyles of people with dementia may also be supported through the design of familiar and engaging environments that provide opportunities and cueing for self-initiated activity, foster friendships and socialization, and promote a sense of belonging or attachment. One example of this approach to meaningful leisure might include the design of a kitchen environment within a care facility, reminiscent of a farmhouse kitchen or, perhaps, something with a 1950s motif. The kitchen could provide opportunities to hand-grind coffee beans, wash dishes, knead bread dough, or ream fresh oranges. In the cupboards, one might find all of the supplies necessary in order to make a simple lunch, or perhaps a few people would simply like to share a pot of tea at the kitchen table and look through sumptuously photographed cookbooks.

There is contentment in the simple, day-to-day rituals of life. Whether residing at home or within a care facility, individuals with dementia are depending upon caregivers to afford them the moments of joy that are available through the extraordinary richness of simple tasks.

**Individuals with Spinal Cord Injuries (SCI): A Focus on Continuity and Adaptation** Impairment in physical ability may have a profound effect on an individual's leisure lifestyle, obviously changing the way in which one engages in physical activities such as volleyball, hiking, and basketball. Physical disabilities may also limit recreation involvement in less obvious ways, as voiced by Lynn, who had a spinal cord injury:

"Like one thing that I really, really miss is being able to read a book, hold a book and read it, turn pages and . . . I've been trying to learn how to do it with a mouthstick, but it's not . . . I mean a little paperback novel is very difficult to, you know, to be turning it and reading it with a mouthstick. Uh, I don't know really what I'm going to end up doing." (Kleiber, Brock, Lee, Dattilo, and Caldwell, p. 292)

Given that an SCI is an acquired disability, individuals move from a leisure lifestyle that is created based on being able-bodied to a leisure lifestyle that must accommodate changes in physical functioning. The importance of a person's lifelong leisure pursuits to his or her self-identify emerges from the voices of adults with SCI who seek continuity in their leisure and are willing to modify participation to do so. For example, Brian stated:

"I've got to be still trying to do things that I used to do but in a different way. To be a painter, artist, I've got to find a new way to either paint with my mouth . . . but I know I'm going to do something. Be able to go on. I'm not giving up, not going to quit." (Lee, Dattilo, Kleiber, and Caldwell, p. 218)

People with spinal cord injuries also experience changes in the social relationships that are central to many leisure pursuits. As discussed by Kleiber, Brock, Lee, and Dattilo (1995), an individual's lack of ability to help physically organize the food table during a family picnic, to throw a ball for a child, or to play with one's dog are all factors that shift a person's conception of leisure lifestyle as he or she deals with the adjustment to a life with an SCI.

Engagement in normative day-to-day recreation activities, such as wandering in and out of downtown stores, eating in a restaurant, and dancing to music, support the expectation that one can maintain his or her leisure lifestyle following an SCI. Many individuals, however, are challenged by this expectation as they return to the community following intensive in-patient rehabilitation. In order to address this challenge, there are a growing number of in-home programs designed to support the individual's transition to community life. Home-based programs, such as the one implemented by Loy, Broach, Kind, and Hufstetler, may involve a recreation specialist working with the individual to assess leisure needs and provide instruction on adapted leisure skills, adaptive equipment, or support for accessing community resources. Home-based programs may also pair a person who has just returned to the community with a peer who can assist with the challenges inherent in adjusting to a SCI and seeking continuity in his or her leisure lifestyle. Sable and Gravink (2002) have utilized peers to provide support and information on ways to negotiate changes in areas such as social relationships, sexuality, leisure skills, and self-advocacy.

**Moviegoers.** A young couple enjoys some popcorn while at the movies. Most theaters provide handicap-accessible seating for patrons with wheelchairs. © *Chuck Savage/Corbis*

## Community-Dwelling Individuals with Disabilities: A Focus on Inclusion

"Paul has perfect rhythm. No, he's not good at learning the actual steps but he has perfect rhythm and he is a perfect gentleman. And he is very well liked at that noon-hour country line dancing. And he went to another country line dancing class for disabled and didn't like it. . . . So that was toasted. That didn't happen. But we went to the Corral three weeks ago and did country line dancing. It was hilarious. It was fun." (Martha, a support worker to Paul; Pedlar, Haworth, Hutchinson, Taylor, and Dunn, p. 113)

Since the early 1970s, and particularly since the enactment of the Americans with Disabilities Act, increased attention has been paid to how communities afford individuals with disabilities engagement in community life. Recreation inclusion is the process by which communities empower individuals with disabilities to engage in

**TABLE 2**

---

### Inclusive recreation opportunities

**Daniel**, a young adult with a spinal cord injury, wants to go hiking in the local park with his dog. *An accessible hiking trail will allow him to do so.*

**Sarah**, a six-year-old with learning disabilities and attention deficit disorder, would like to attend the adventure camp sponsored by the local recreation center. *An extra staff member or individualized behavior plan will allow her to do so.*

**Kenny**, an eight-year-old boy who is deaf, is excited about participating in the local soccer league. *A sign language interpreter will allow him to do so.*

SOURCE: Adapted from McGovern, 1996

---

social relationships, leisure activities, and community roles that are based on their interests and aspirations. As described in Table 2, inclusion may target physical space to ensure accessibility, such as designing accessible hiking trails or installing a lift in the community center swimming pool. Inclusion may also be a result of staff support that affords an individual's full access and participation in desired activity opportunities.

Community agencies, such as school districts and leisure service agencies, may provide specialized programs that support an individual's movement towards participation in inclusive recreation. For example, Johnson, Bullock, and Ashton-Schaeffer had individuals with disabilities work with a recreation specialist to identify their leisure goals, examine options, and make decisions, as well as initiate participation in the selected inclusive recreation opportunity. Less-formalized support for involvement in activities such as lifting weights or swimming laps may come from workout buddies who are nondisabled peers. In a program run by Galambos, Lee, Rahn, and Willis, workout buddies assisted the individuals with disabilities when needed (for example, getting in and out of the pool), and both parties encouraged the other's exercise routine.

The financial impact of inclusive recreation opportunities is of growing concern. Several public recreation agencies in the Chicago area are spending more than $1 million annually on inclusive services (McGovern, 2002). Questions remain as to how communities will be able to continue to meet the growing demand for activity opportunities and physical spaces that afford people participation in the most integrated settings possible. As the demand and resulting expense of inclusion increases, communities may be forced to seek additional funding sources or face the elimination of general recreation programs for constituents with and without disabilities.

## Summary and Conclusion

A satisfying leisure lifestyle has the potential to create meaning and social connectedness in the lives of individuals with disabilities. Since the enactment of the Americans with Disabilities Act, there has been an increase in the demand for and delivery of inclusive activity opportunities, as well as in-home programs. Since the early 1990s there has also been increased emphasis placed on the design of physical environments that foster engagement in satisfying and enriching leisure activities. All of these efforts have enhanced the leisure experiences of individuals with disabilities. Continued efforts are needed to ensure that leisure-service providers are able to design effectively activity opportunities, physical space, and social environments that support the leisure lifestyles of individuals with disabilities.

*See also:* Adapted Leisure Formats

**BIBLIOGRAPHY**

Bullock, Charles, and Michael Mahon. *Introduction to Recreation Services for People with Disabilities: A Person-Centered Approach.* Champaign, Ill.: Sagamore Publishing, 2000.

Cohen-Mansfield, Jiska. "Nonpharmacologic Interventions for Inappropriate Behaviors in Dementia." *American Journal of Geriatric Psychiatry* 9 (2001): 361–381.

Galambos, L., R. Lee, P. Rahn, and B. Williams. "The ADA: Getting Beyond the Door." *Parks and Recreation* 29 (1994): 66–72.

Henderson, Cary Smith. *Partial View: An Alzheimer's Journal.* Dallas, Tex.: Southern Methodist University Press, 1998.

Johnson, Danny, Charles Bullock, and Candice Ashton-Shaeffer. "Home-Based Leisure Education for Children with Disabilities." In *In-Home Therapeutic Recreation: Successful Strategies and Services.* Edited by Barbara Wilhite, M. Jean Keller, and Linda Epps. Ashburn, Va.: National Therapeutic Recreation Society, 2002.

Kleiber, Douglas, Stephen Brock, Youngkhill Lee, John Dattilo, and Linda Caldwell. "The Relevance of Leisure in an Illness Experience: Realities of Spinal Cord Injury." *Journal of Leisure Research* 27 (1995): 283–299.

Lee, Youngkhill, John Dattilo, Douglas Kleiber, and Linda Caldwell. "Exploring the Meaning of Continuity of Recreation Activity in the Early Stages of Adjustment for People with Spinal Cord Injury." *Leisure Sciences* 18 (1996): 209–225.

Loy, David, Ellen Broach, Tammy King, and Mike Hufstetler. "'Bridging' the Gap in Today's Rehabilitation Process: An In-Home Therapeutic Recreation Service Delivery Program." In *In-Home Therapeutic Recreation: Successful Strategies and Services.* Edited by Barbara Wilhite, M. Jean Keller, and Linda Epps. Ashburn, Va.: National Therapeutic Recreation Society, 2002.

McGovern, John. "The ADA Is a Tremendous . . . Opportunity!" *Parks and Recreation* 31 (1996): 34.

———. "Special Circumstances: Is the SRA Boom of the '70s and '80s Headed for a Bust?" *Illinois Parks and Recreation* (2002): 30–35.

Marshall, Melody, and Sally Hutchinson. "A Critique of Research on the Use of Activities with Persons with Alzheimer's Disease: A Systematic Literature Review." *Journal of Advanced Nursing* 35 (2001): 488–496.

Pedlar, Alison, Larry Haworth, Peggy Hutchinson, Andrew Taylor, and Peter Dunn. *A Textured Life: Empowerment and Adults with Developmental Disabilities.* Ontario, Canada: Wilfrid Laurier University Press, 1999.

Sable, Janet, and Jill Gravink. "In-Home Therapeutic Recreation for People with Recent Spinal Cord Injury." In *In-Home Therapeutic Recreation: Successful Strategies and Services.* Edited by Barbara Wilhite, M. Jean Keller, and Linda Epps. Ashburn, Va.: National Therapeutic Recreation Society, 2002.

Stumbo, Norma, and Carol Peterson. *Therapeutic Recreation Program Design: Principles and Procedures.* San Francisco: Benjamin/Cummings, 2004.

U.S. Census Bureau. "Americans with Disabilities: Household Economic Studies." Series P70-73, 2001.

*Judith E. Voelkl and Jennifer D. Carson*

# DISNEYLAND

While the history of amusement parks and expositions in the United States stretches back into the late nineteenth century, the opening of Disneyland in Anaheim, California, on 17 July 1955, marks the beginning of a distinctive era of parks designed around fantasy "themes." All "theme parks" opened since Disneyland's debut owe their conceptualization to this initial park founded by entertainment entrepreneur Walter ("Walt") E. Disney (1901–1966), his business partner and brother, Roy Disney, and the armies of Disney employees.

## World's Fairs and Amusement Parks

The world's fairs and amusement parks in the United States doubtless contributed to Disney's conception of an amusement park for both children and adults. World's fairs, in particular, combined instruction with pleasure, while the amusement parks both small and large (for example, Coney Island) satisfied the public's interest in exotic fun. The great 1893 Columbian Exposition in Chicago, for example, combined the highest intellectual and artistic instruction with the base pleasures of the carnival-like midway. The Great Depression–era fairs—notably Chicago's Century of Progress Exposition in 1933, the New York World's Fair in 1939 to 1940, and the Golden Gate International Exposition (GGIE) in 1939—introduced other new elements later embraced by Disney. Following the rise of large, powerful corporations in the prosperous 1920s, the 1930s fairs saw the increasing presence of corporate pavilions promising a utopian future based on science and technology. Disney embraced this corporate, technology-based futurism. Walt attended the GGIE in San Francisco in 1939, where he would have seen the small-scale railroad, the Thorne Room miniatures (which later found a home in the Chicago Art Institute), the Amusement Zone, and a number of exhibits on the exposition's themes of progress in transportation and communication. Disney doubtless would have noted the fact that Treasure Island, the site of the exposition, was a completely new space created for the fair, connected to the newly completed Oakland–San Francisco Bay Bridge. In all, the GGIE provided a model for a complete, controlled space for all of the instruction and pleasure a fair could offer, along with the optimistic futurism Disney embraced.

## The Disney Empire

Walt Disney's business empire began with his cartoon enterprise, founded in the late 1920s. His signature cartoon character—Mickey Mouse—appeared first in a few silent cartoons and, finally, in the landmark cartoon film with sound, *Steamboat Willie* (1928). From there, Disney's business grew in cycles, boosted by the financial success of his first feature-length animated film, *Snow White* (1937), which won a special Oscar. Subsequent feature-length animated films—such as *Pinocchio* (1940), *Dumbo* (1941), *Bambi* (1942), *Cinderella* (1950), *Alice in Wonderland* (1951), and *Peter Pan* (1953)—provided the characters and storylines that Disney would use later in his theme park. In addition, Disney's parallel development of wildlife documentary films—such as *Seal Island* (1948), *The Living Desert* (1953), and *The Vanishing Prairie* (1954)—and big-budget fully live action films—including *Treasure Island* (1950) and *20,000 Leagues Under the Sea* (1954)—provided other characters and plots for the initial thematic design of the park.

Long before Disneyland opened, Walt Disney had learned the value of merchandising his characters, from simple plastic figures and dolls to board games and toys. Soon, copyright ownership to these characters and images became at least as valuable as Disney's rights to the films and cartoons themselves.

In the 1940s, Disney talked often about building an amusement park that would be clean and safe, a fun place for both adults and children. Initially he thought this might be a park for his employees at the newly built Disney studios, but gradually he began talking about a grander park for the public; the planning became earnest in 1952. After considering several sites, Disney settled on a 160-acre site of orange groves in Orange County, just to the south of Los Angeles.

Unlike some other producers in the film industry, Disney recognized that television could be a new important venue for his creative productions, so in 1954 he entered into a contract with the American Broadcasting Company (ABC) to produce a weekly hour-long television show *Disneyland*. The name of the show came from the park that Disney envisioned. The newly formed WED Enterprises formed a creative staff of "Imagineers" (imagination + engineers) for the park planning. For Disney, the ABC television show created a national audience of potential customers ("guests") for his new park. The television show premiered in the fall of 1954, a mere nine months or so before the park opened. ABC televised live the opening-day ceremonies at Disneyland, and both the park and television show (later picked up by NBC and renamed *The Wonderful World of Color* to reflect the television broadcasting innovation) became famously successful. In October 1955, Disney entered the after-school television market with the premiere of the *Mickey Mouse Club*, which often featured the park. Over a million people visited the park in the last half of 1955, and in 1956 the annual attendance was 3 million people.

Over the years, Disney pursued the same marketing strategy, based on the three legs of his operation—the theatrical films, the television show, and Disneyland. As new films debuted on the television program—for example, *Davy Crockett, King of the Wild Frontier* appeared first as three half-hour segments on television, then was released as a feature-length film in 1955—Disney incorporated those characters and storylines into rides at the park. Similarly, new animated feature-length films (such as 1959's *Sleeping Beauty*) and live-action films (such as 1960's *Swiss Family Robinson*) provided thematic materials for rides and costumed characters at Disneyland. Thus, visitors to the park encounter already-familiar characters, storylines, and themes.

## Disneyland Design

From the outset, Disneyland was designed carefully to maximize control over the visitors' experiences. Key to this control was the raised berm of land surrounding the park, ostensibly to carry the Disneyland Railroad in its circumnavigation of the park, but just as importantly it made Disneyland seem like a self-contained world quite isolated from everyday life. Disney wanted to be sure visitors could not see surrounding Anaheim from inside the park.

After paying for admission, visitors pass through a tunnel under the railroad berm and enter Main Street U.S.A. Main Street displays the traditional, midwestern American values of family, morality, and patriotism that small-town life represented for Disney. The storefronts are "themed" to the 1890s Gilded Age United States, and the buildings are designed with "forced perspective" (7/8 scale at the ground floor, 5/8 scale for the upper floors), a set designer's trick to make the buildings seem taller. Mainstreet is, in effect, a large movie studio set.

At the end of Mainstreet is a large, circular Plaza, where the visitor can choose to begin a visit to one of the "lands." These four "lands" match the thematic programs in the original Disneyland television program. To the visitors' left lie Adventureland and Frontierland, which are representative of America's past. To the visitors' right lies Tomorrowland, a vision of America's future, based on American science, technology, and spirit of enterprise. Straight ahead, in a line with Main Street, is Fantasyland, the world of Disney's cartoon shorts and feature-length films come to life.

Each land continues the impression that the visitor has stepped onto a movie set. Disney's collaboration with moviemakers has continued throughout the history of the park, including the Star Tours ride, based on the George Lukas films, and the Indiana Jones Adventure ride (opened in 1995), based on the Steven Spielberg films. In 2003, the Disney people turned the film/park relationship around with two films—*The Pirates of the Caribbean* and *Haunted Mansion*—based loosely on two of the park's most popular attractions.

Walt Disney announced on several occasions that Disneyland "would never be finished," and the tinkering has been constant. The park opened with twenty-six initial attractions, with another twelve completed by the end of 1955. New attractions often opened in connection with new Disney films. The Matterhorn bobsled ride opened in 1959, for example, to coincide with *The Third Man on the Mountain* (1959). New Orleans Square opened in 1963, and in 1993 the park opened its first "land" outside the railroad berm—Mickey's Toontown.

Meanwhile, Disney had learned the lesson of the depression-era fairs and sought to build mutually profitable relationships with corporations outside the film industry. Three prominent corporations—Pepsi-Cola, General Electric, and the Ford Motor Company—approached

**Disneyland.** Children dart through the entrance to Fantasyland during opening day at Disneyland in Anaheim, California on 17 July 1955. © *AP/Wide World Photos*

Disney to design their pavilions for the 1964 World's Fair in New York. When the fair closed, Disney brought these exhibits—notably Pepsi's Small World and General Electric's Carousel of Progress—back to California to incorporate into the park. The Disney parks continue developing new attractions based on corporate partnerships.

Subsequent versions of Disneyland appeared in the new parks Disney built or franchised in the 1970s and 1980s. The Magic Kingdom section of Disney World in Florida reproduces the Disneyland layout and rides, though in a larger space. Similarly, Tokyo Disneyland (opened in April 1983) and Euro Disneyland (opened in 1992 and "rebranded" Disneyland Paris in 1994) retained most of the original design of Disneyland.

A final legacy of the design of Disneyland is the creation of themed commercial spaces. Shopping centers arose in the United States in the 1950s in response to the suburbanization of the middle-class and the increasing

importance of the automobile with that suburban spread. Open-space shopping centers gave way to enclosed shopping malls in the 1960s, and it is clear from the history of malls that the designers borrowed lessons from the design of theme parks like Disneyland. By the 1980s, shopping malls increasingly looked like theme parks, incorporating amusement rides and other attractions into the enclosed spaces. At the turn of the twenty-first century, this development of public commercial space inspired by Disneyland entered a new stage when cities began creating integrated, themed "downtown" shopping districts, such a those in Brea in southern California and Emoryville in northern California. At the same time, Disney created an artificial Downtown Disney as the open mall-like commercial space separating Disneyland from Disney's California Adventure, a new park opened in 2001 and modeled more closely on the traditional amusement ride parks (such as the Los Angeles area's Magic Mountain) that have challenged Disney's leadership in theme park attendance and revenues. Disney park designs and other commercial shopping space designs continue to influence each other, recognizing that shoppers tend to linger longer and spend more money when the consumption takes place in a pleasant, safe, and familiar themed environment.

## Disneyland, Tourism, and Post-Tourism

Over the decades, culture critics of all sorts have been drawn to Disneyland as a distinctive icon of American culture. Among the critics are both detractors and fans, but even the detractors confess to taking guilty pleasure in a visit to the park. After all, Disneyland is the self-proclaimed "happiest place on earth."

A great deal of the meaning of the park lies in those values Walt quite explicitly wanted the park to represent, traditional values combining family, patriotism, a faith in science and technology, and a faith in capitalism as the guarantor of progress. The park enacts Walt's utopian hopes for cities with efficient, clean transportation systems, in stark contrast with America's cities.

The park attractions, even as they have changed over the years, enact in many ways the ideology that links commodity consumption with American democratic institutions. The Pirates of the Caribbean attraction condemns hoarding wealth and rewards consumption, according to Louis Marin's analysis, whereas the General Electric Carousel of Progress and similar attractions, usually sponsored by major corporations, reinforce the message that consumer-based, commodity capitalism is sure to deliver "the good life."

Much of this message surrounds the nuclear family (some would say the white, middle-class family) in the United States as the most important cultural institution. Disney's films celebrate the family, even though some of the films (such as *Bambi, Dumbo,* and the fairy-tale-based films) rely on an absent parent for part of their emotional appeal. Disneyland assumes that the family is the basic unit of visitors, and scholars' observations about the resemblance between religious pilgrimage and tourism helps make sense of the pilgrimage families make to Disneyland and Disney World.

Beyond these cultural themes in the park, Disneyland also attracts attention as an example of the emergence of a postmodern cultural logic or style. Despite the fact that Disneyland's faith in scientific and social progress has much in common with modernism, critics have noted that Disneyland opened in the era when modernism was giving way to postmodernism, a cultural logic or style of thinking comfortable with the blurring of the line between reality and artificiality. The postmodern sensibility enjoys the bringing together of very different design elements torn from their original contexts, for example, and enjoys the ironic reflexivity of a spectacle of images and symbols that seems to know how arbitrary are all meanings. The postmodern sensibility substitutes nostalgia for history. As a huge movie set, Disneyland seems to be the penultimate example of a postmodern tourist site.

This postmodern quality of Disneyland and of some other tourist sites has led scholars to formulate the ideas of "post-tourism" and the "post-tourist" to distinguish this newer sort of tourism from the older tourism of the nineteenth and first half of the twentieth centuries. Whereas the older sort of tourist sought an "authenticity" missing in his or her everyday life, the new post-tourist is in search of diversion. The post-tourist knows that he or she is a tourist, that the play time and space of the tourist experience is completely artificial, and that this blurring of reality and artificiality is the source of the fun.

Disneyland makes a compelling touristic site and a rich, seemingly inexhaustible site for cultural criticism because it contains so many of the themes and contradictions Americans experience in their everyday lives in the last half of the twentieth century and in the opening decade of the twenty-first. People talk increasingly about "the Disneyfication" of American culture, a sure sign of the pervasive influence of this park.

*See also:* Park Movements; Theme and Amusement Parks; Walt Disney World

### BIBLIOGRAPHY

Bryman, Alan. *Disney and His Worlds.* London: Routledge, 1995.

Disneyland. Home page at http://www.Disneyland.Disney.go.com.

Fjellman, Stephen M. *Vinyl Leaves: Walt Disney World and America.* Boulder, Colo.: Westview Press, 1992.

Mannheim, Steve. *Walt Disney and the Quest for Community.* Burlington, Vt.: Ashgate Publishing Company, 2002.

Marin, Louis. "Disneyland: A Degenerate Utopia." *Glyph, Johns Hopkins Textual Studies No. 1.* Baltimore: Johns Hopkins University Press, 1977.

Marling, Karal Ann, ed. *Designing Disney's Theme Parks: The Architecture of Reassurance.* New York: Flammorion, 1997.

Mechling, Elizabeth Walker, and Jay Mechling. "The Sale of Two Cities: A Semiotic Comparison of Disneyland with Marriott's Great America." *Journal of Popular Culture* 15 (Summer 1981): 166–179.

Orvell, Miles. "Understanding Disneyland: American Mass Culture and the European Gaze." In *After the Machine: Vi-*

*sual Arts and the Erasing of Cultural Boundaries.* Edited by Orvell Miles. Jackson: University of Mississippi Press, 1995.

Project on Disney. *Inside the Mouse: Work and Play at Disney World.* Durham, N.C.: Duke University Press, 1995.

Schickel, Richard. *The Disney Version: The Life, Times, Art and Commerce of Walt Disney.* New York: Simon and Schuster, 1968.

Smoodin, Eric, ed. *Disney Discourse: Producing the Magic Kingdom.* New York: Routledge, 1994.

Urry, J. *The Tourist Gaze: Leisure and Travel in Contemporary Societies.* London: Sage Publications, 1990.

*Jay Mechling*

# DIVING

**See** *Scuba Diving/Snorkeling*

# DOG FIGHTING

**See** *Blood Sports*

# DRAG RACING

Millions of fans watched drag racing in the early twenty-first century, and the industry generated billions of dollars. The origins of this speed-craving sport lie in the city streets of 1930s Southern California, where young men exchanged glances at stop lights and then urged their vehicles down the road in a dangerous, thrilling competition. Police began patrolling for these law-flaunting youths, and racers moved their contests to secret locations that provided the necessary flat straightaways, such as dry lake beds in stretches of desert such as Muroc in the Mojave Desert. Aficionados formed the Southern California Timing Association (SCTA) in 1937. This group organized races that focused less on rapid acceleration, as future drag races would, and more on achievable top speeds, as racers accelerated for three miles before crossing the starting line. After overuse threatened the safety of racing at the lakes, hot rodders eventually moved to airport landing strips, which conventionalized the quarter-mile course length, since that was the farthest a car could race on a landing strip while still hav-

ing enough paved ground on which to decelerate. In the early 2000s, most top racers weren't able to maintain their extremely high speeds for longer than a quarter-mile without destroying their engines.

Racing largely disappeared during World War II, but as returning GIs armed with mechanical expertise gleaned from service re-entered society, the sport returned to popularity as well. This time, it overwhelmingly featured the two-car head-to-head competition that gives the sport so much of its excitement. The first organized drag race took place at a Santa Ana airstrip in 1950, and official legitimization was not far off. In 1951, the National Hot Rod Association (NHRA) formed as an umbrella organization for the smaller racing clubs nationwide, and by 1955 it had created the National Championships. Its role has remained largely static: the NHRA oversees the main 18-race circuit of drag racing, makes and enforces the rules for the different classes of vehicles, and publishes *Hot Rod,* a periodical launched in 1948 and aimed at the enthusiast. Motorheads formed car clubs across the country in the early 1950s, and the NHRA sent its Drag Safaris or Safety Safaris across the nation to instruct these clubs in racing safety and rules.

## The Race

Drag racing began with street cars, and the first true "dragsters" were basically street cars with engines modified to produce more power and bodies modified to reduce weight. In the early 2000s there were 200 classes of vehicles grouped into twelve categories sanctioned by the NHRA, of which the two fastest and most popular were Top Fuel and Funny Cars. Top fuel cars are the fastest land racing vehicles on earth, although funny cars are not far behind. Fuel cars are light, long, and skinny, leave their rails exposed, and are seldom aerodynamically engineered. Most crucially, top fuel cars use nitromethane in their engines, a powerful, volatile concoction that also propels rockets. Fuel cars look the least like stock cars, and have varied the most in design and appearance over the years. Funny cars, also called floppers, must resemble the body design of a car manufactured within the last five years, but their bodies are made of fiberglass instead of metal and "flop" down onto the chassis of the car. The sponsors' need for product identity mandates that funny cars resemble regular cars as much as possible, by, for instance, featuring door handles even if a funny car lacks doors. They have powerful engines, but must use gasoline. Even though they are more powerful than fuel cars, and use aerodynamic styling to compensate for their

**Eddie Hill.** The first driver to achieve a burnout to heat the rear tires on his dragster in 1960, Texas-born Eddie Hill (1936– ) qualified in the top spot at the 11th Annual Autolite Nationals on 26 July 1997 at Sears Point Raceway in Sonoma, California. Top fuel dragsters, such as the one Hill is driving here, top 300 mph during the quarter-mile races. © *Ben Margot for AP/Wide World Photos*

required weight of 2,325 pounds, they consistently perform about ten miles per hour slower than fuel cars.

No matter the class, each race features two cars (or motorcycles) battling head-to-head. The loser is eliminated, and the winner moves on to face off against another racer. The NHRA awards points for several accomplishments, including elapsed time and top speed. Thus, the winner of a championship achieves victory by having accrued the most points. Since the 1980s, commercial sponsors have awarded large sums of money to the winners. Although the NHRA itself financially rewards its victors, these prizes are dwarfed by the corporate money. Building or buying a dragster is expensive in itself, but the cost of maintaining such a vehicle is prohibitive. Very few racers actually make money from the sport; most pursue it for the love of competition, the rush of speed, and the satisfaction of combining the precision engineering and innovation of the crew with the fast reaction time, hand-eye coordination, concentration, and killer instinct of the driver.

## Innovations for Speed and Safety

One of the most important parts of the drag race, the Christmas tree, debuted in 1964. A fixture of every drag race since, this tower of lights can be found at every track in America. Amber bulbs light every half-second in sequence, culminating with the green lights that signal go. The Christmas tree setup also ensures that dragsters are staged properly before the race and that they do not false-start. Known as red-lighting, a false start disqualifies the racer and immediately awards victory to the other competitor.

Other innovations, specifically safety considerations, were slow to be adopted in the 1960s. After a string of high-profile fatal top fuel crashes, Don Garlits, a highly-regarded racer, debuted a new design in 1971 that quickly caught on. Previously, the standard fuel car design, known as the slingshot, placed the engine over the rear axle and seated the driver behind it. Although this arrangement desirably centered the majority of the car's weight over the rear wheels, it left the driver exposed to extreme danger. Engine explosions were sadly common, and flying engine components or burning nitro often injured or even killed drivers. The new design, known as a mid-engine car, or middie, placed the driver in front of the engine, reducing the danger. Besides being safer, the middie was simpler to construct, lighter, more aerodynamic, and, most importantly, faster than the slingshot. The middie's success also allowed top fuel to recapture the spotlight from funny cars, which had enjoyed a vogue in the late 1960s.

Improved technology also gave drivers Nomex fireproof suits to wear, NASCAR-style fire extinguisher systems to mount in their dragsters, and improved parachutes to slow their cars. Modern parachutes can brake cars in a shorter amount of time than a race lasts. Goodyear and M&H debuted new tires in the early 1970s, which gave dragsters better traction. The NHRA eventually also sanctioned the laying of a sticky substance on the race tracks, also improving traction.

However, the NHRA does not always prize innovation, even though its official slogan is "Ingenuity in Action." In 1963, Pete Robinson returned to a technique 1950s sidewinder racers had discovered: using jacks to elevate the rear wheels above the ground, allowing them to spin before they made contact with the ground. Jacks could immediately shoot a car down the track up to five car lengths ahead of its competitor. Although such a start inhibited a car's steering capability, the gain in acceleration was tremendous. Yet the NHRA banned the use of jacks, for unclear reasons. Similarly, funny cars could eclipse records set by fuel cars if they were allowed to use canards (wings over the rear wheels that reduced air turbulence) or airfoils (similar to spoilers). However, funny cars are banned from incorporating any device that directs airflow underneath the car's body, which both these innovations do. Thus, the NHRA's very specific rules sometimes encourage and other times stifle the creativity of drivers and crews.

## Female Drag Racers and the Role of Family

Women have been top drivers at NHRA events and at other drag races, even though their numbers have been fairly low. Until the early 1960s, many women competed in the separate ladies' races until the NHRA admitted them into the regular races, recognizing that the rules did not prohibit female drivers. In the late 1960s, the NHRA cited spurious safety considerations as their reason for rescinding women's licenses. Outrage followed, and eventually the NHRA realized the need for the promotional money and fans that women drivers were

bringing in. Women finally got back their right to race in 1970. Of all the female racers, Shirley Muldowney is the most famous. In 1977, she became the first woman to win the fuel car NHRA points championship, and later became the first person, male or female, to win the same championship three times. Although women drivers faced a great deal of criticism and animosity from male drivers, standout racers such as Muldowney, Peggy Hart, Shirley Shahan, Paula Murphy, and Barbara Hamilton proved that they had just as much of a right to race as men.

Additionally, drag racing is for many a family sport, where couples, parents, and children all work together on teams and enjoy following the sport together. The Junior Drag Racing League, sponsored by the NHRA and featuring smaller dragsters and shorter distances for its youngest racers, features young boys and girls, any of whom may continue on to become a top name in racing.

## Conclusion

Drag racing is primarily a family spectator sport. Its draw is both in applauding the engineering feats that allow these specialized vehicles to soar down the track and in basking in the spectacle of the show. One of the most prominent features a spectator notices about the race is the unbelievable noise coming up from the track, especially when nitro engines ignite. The billowing smoke from the burnouts that clean each dragster's tires also functions to entertain the fans. Drag racing is an American celebration of technology, skill, nerve, and showmanship.

*See also:* Auto Racing, Drag Racing, Hot Rodding, Open Wheel Racing, Sports Car Racing, Stock Car Racing

**BIBLIOGRAPHY**

Batchelor, Dean. *The American Hot Rod.* Osceola, Wis: Motorbooks International, 1995

Moorhouse, H. F. *Driving Ambitions: An Analysis of the American Hot Rod Enthusiasm.* New York: Manchester University Press, 1991.

Post, Robert C. *High Performance: The Culture and Technology of Drag Racing 1950–1990.* Baltimore: The Johns Hopkins University Press, 1994.

Spohn, Terry, ed. *The Fast Lane: The History of NHRA Drag Racing.* New York: Regan Books, 2001.

Vincent, Peter. *Hot Rod: An American Original.* Osceola, Wis.: MBI Publishing Company, 2001.

*Elissa L. David*

# DRINKING

Americans have long had a love-hate relationship with alcohol, and per capita consumption has tended to run in long-term cycles. Men, especially white men, have always been heavy users. When the first European explorers sailed along the Atlantic Coast in the 1500s, they traded beer, wine, and hard liquor with the local inhabitants. Some Native American tribes brewed beer for ceremonial purposes, but none knew how to distill hard liquor. Prior to white contact, alcohol was used sparingly.

After the English founded Virginia in 1607 and Plymouth in 1620, they regularly imported alcoholic beverages both for the Indian trade and for their own use. During the 1600s, colonists obtained increasing quantities of West Indian rum or molasses for distillation. In general, most drinking at this time took place at home. Housewives brewed weak beer, and farmers in the northern colonies routinely pressed apples into hard cider. Alcoholic beverages were often safer than water because alcohol naturally killed dangerous bacteria commonly found in water.

By the time of the Revolution in 1776, Americans were in the midst of the first cyclical upswing in drinking. They consumed large quantities of alcohol, mostly cider and rum. Some, like John Adams, began each day with a tankard of cider. Many took a mixture of rum, sugar, and water as a beverage with every meal. Men drank far more than women. Children received watered versions of this compound. Most people believed that alcohol increased strength and improved health. The only upper limit on consumption was availability. Both farm owners and urban employers gave hired hands rum-and-water beverages with meals and during morning and afternoon work breaks.

Taverns played an important role in American life. Originally licensed primarily to serve travelers, public houses were also community centers where local men drank socially, shared news, debated politics, and even attended court sessions. Each customer was expected to buy a round, which was called "treating," and bowls of alcoholic drink were freely passed around. No one knew about germs.

## Whiskey Leads to Temperance

The Revolution brought change. When the British cut off rum and molasses imports, Americans began to distill whiskey from Indian corn using grain-distilling technology brought by recently arrived Scots-Irish immigrants.

Rum, like tea, was imported and unpatriotic, while whiskey was celebrated as the new national beverage. After 1800, Americans settled the Midwest Corn Belt, the price of corn dropped, and whiskey cost 25 cents per gallon, which was cheaper than rum, cider, beer, milk, tea, or coffee. Whiskey consumption soared, and by the 1820s, the peak of the first cycle, Americans drank about three times as much alcohol as today. The typical adult white male consumed a half pint of whiskey a day. Most liquor was taken at home as a beverage with meals rather than for recreation.

High consumption led to binge drinking, increased public drunkenness, alcohol-related crime and poverty, wife beating, and child abuse. During the 1820s, a backlash developed, as Evangelical Protestants launched the temperance movement. They denounced the "Demon Rum" and demanded that church members stop drinking. At the same time, industry flourished in the Northeast, and industrialists did not want drunken workers either to injure themselves or to wreck expensive machinery. Employers stopped providing whiskey to workers during breaks and used religious ties to hire and promote abstainers. Nonalcoholic forms of leisure emerged with the development of parks, organized sports, libraries, museums, public lectures, soda fountains, and ice-cream parlors.

By 1850, consumption had fallen by half or more, as half the population had quit. Farmers even cut down apple trees and renounced cider. In the North's rural areas and small towns, anyone who wanted respectability had to abstain, but city dwellers resisted the antiliquor campaign.

## Saloons Thrive, Immigrants Arrive

Even as drinking declined during the downswing that marked the end of the first cycle, wealthy urban men enjoyed palatial, marble-floored saloons furnished with long, carved mahogany bars, polished brass rails, impressive oil paintings (sometimes of nude women), cut-glass decanters, and boxes of expensive cigars. These establishments offered fancy mixed drinks, including the popular new cocktail, composed of whiskey, water, sugar, lemon, and bitters. Ice might be available. The gin-based martini emerged, and the first bartenders' recipe manuals were published.

After 1840, millions of Irish and German immigrants poured into America's northern cities and laid the groundwork for a later, second cycle of rising consumption. Unaffected by the temperance movement, the Irish brought a taste for whiskey, and the Germans a love of beer. The Irish quickly established saloons, which soon became the center for working-class male social life. Respectable women generally stayed away. Saloons offered friendship, entertainment, loans, information about jobs, and escape from dreary tenement apartments. They also provided the muscle and votes for city political machines. Home to many gangs, saloons often included back rooms for gambling and prostitution.

Meanwhile, immigrant Germans introduced their own style of brewing and opened suburban beer gardens where families gathered to picnic, sing, play sports, and drink beer. Immigrant drinking, including parents giving alcohol to children and serving alcohol on Sundays, angered Evangelical Protestants, who responded by trying to ban alcohol. In the 1840s, many towns and counties in the North adopted Prohibition, but local measures proved ineffective, because drinkers obtained liquor in adjacent areas. In 1851, Maine became the first state to adopt Prohibition, and while a number of states followed in the 1850s, none of these states stayed permanently "dry."

## Regional and Racial Differences

By the mid-1800s, significant regional differences in drinking could be found. The Northeast, where the Evangelical Protestant revivals had been strongest, had the highest proportion of abstainers and the lowest consumption of alcohol. The Midwest gradually adopted the same antiliquor pattern. In contrast, the West, home to many single men, had the highest consumption. Rowdy male drinking had prevailed on the frontier from the earliest days to the infamous, violence-prone saloons along the cattle trails after the Civil War. Until the very late 1800s, the West, with the exception of Mormon-dominated Utah, showed little restraint.

On the other hand, the hard-drinking South turned against alcohol after the Civil War ended in 1865. In earlier years, southern Baptists, in particular, had rarely attacked alcohol, perhaps because so many temperance leaders were Yankees who also opposed slavery. By 1900, antiliquor forces largely controlled the rural South, where they either established local option Prohibition or adopted a policy of charging high fees for liquor licenses, which limited the number of outlets. Since 1900, the South has been the region of the country both with the lowest per capita consumption of alcohol and with the highest production of moonshine (illegal, untaxed liquor).

African Americans have always been light drinkers. Slaves were legally prohibited from drinking, although planters often provided liquor for a week's merriment between Christmas and New Year's. Even after slavery ended, many blacks continued to abstain. Poverty discouraged use, and so did the black church. Today, African American consumption is low, and a high proportion of black women are abstainers. Mexican Americans and Asian Americans also have been light drinkers. Native Americans have a high proportion of both abstainers and problem drinkers.

## Women Oppose Liquor

From the beginning of the antiliquor crusade in the early 1800s, women played a major role. In 1873, women staged "pray-ins" to force saloons to close, and after 1875 the Woman's Christian Temperance Union (WCTU), an organization that eventually grew to be the nation's largest, with more than a million members, worked to ban alcohol anywhere and everywhere. In the early 1900s, Carrie Nation used an axe to smash several saloons in a direct-action campaign. Given the power of the WCTU and its allies, respectable women avoided alcohol. Schoolteachers were fired for taking a drink. Women, however, could sneak drinks at home, although female consumption overall was probably less than half that for males. Many women did use patent medicines, including Lydia Pinkham's Elixir for Female Complaints, which turned out to be highly alcoholic.

During the Civil War, the federal government imposed a high tax on distilled liquor, and after the war Americans gradually switched from expensive whiskey to cheaper beer. By 1890, beer predominated. European immigration and urbanization were accompanied by a second cycle of increasing alcohol consumption that peaked around 1900–1915. Saloons became "tied" houses; that is, brewers who provided financing dictated that a saloon could sell only one brand of beer. Working-class saloons regularly offered a "free lunch" with the purchase of a glass of beer for 5 cents. The lunch might be pickles, pretzels, and other salty foods designed to encourage drinking, or it might be more substantial fare, such as roast beef, potato salad, and raw oysters. Many poorly paid women workers ate the free lunches, although they usually entered through the rear and sat together in a back room in order to avoid scandal.

After 1870, there was also a modest increase in wine drinking. Although Thomas Jefferson and others had experimented with wine grapes in the early 1800s, few Americans drank wine at that time. By the 1840s, most Protestant churches had turned against wine, including communion wine. They argued that the wine of the Bible did not contain alcohol. Communion meant grape juice. With the acquisition of California in 1848, the United

States gained a significant wine-growing area. Italian and French immigrants established vineyards that encouraged ordinary Californians to drink wine. In the rest of the country, only the wealthy could afford expensive, imported European wine, which cost more than whiskey. Most saloons sold wine, but it was often whiskey cut with water and food coloring.

## National Prohibition Is Adopted

After 1900, antiliquor forces, led by the politically influential Anti-Saloon League, pushed for national Prohibition as a way to purge the country of alcohol. The hard-liquor industry, which had been discredited by cheating on taxes in the Whiskey Ring in 1875, was unable to mount effective opposition. Brewers, however, along with their powerful urban saloon allies, blocked Prohibition until the United States entered World War I against Germany. Then the brewers lost their influence amid anti-German hysteria. First adopted as a wartime emergency measure in 1917, Prohibition was added to the U.S. Constitution with the Eighteenth Amendment in 1920. The ban was repealed by the Twenty-first Amendment in 1933.

Prohibition ended the second cycle with a new low, as the per capita consumption of alcohol probably dropped in half. Drinking styles also changed. In many places, beer disappeared. Bootleggers preferred hard liquor because it was less bulky and easier to hide. Hard liquor was imported from Canada or Europe or distilled illegally in ways that could be dangerous. Even when not deadly, bathtub gin tasted foul. It was usually mixed with fruit juice or soft drinks. Saloons gave way to speakeasies, which paid off the police. To gain entry, customers had to know the password or sign. Patrons drank alcohol in coffee cups, so evidence could be gulped down quickly in case of a raid, and women were welcome since it reduced male rowdiness and helped camouflage the speakeasy. Americans who preferred privacy drank in hotel rooms, where bellhops provided liquor. Social drinking at home became more fashionable, too, since police rarely raided private residences.

## New Drinking Styles After Repeal

The nation's drinking habits had changed; when repeal came in 1933, the old-time saloon did not return. Many states opted for sale of hard liquor in state stores for home use only, but even in states like New York, Illinois, and California, which issued many licenses for on-premise consumption, the all-male saloon gave way to bars that catered to both men and women. State and local regula-

tion was robust. Every state imposed a minimum age for drinking; usually it was twenty-one. Most states monitored advertising, set prices, fixed hours, collected high license fees, limited the number of licenses, and controlled the kind of entertainment that took place where alcohol was sold.

During the 1930s, most traditionally dry religious groups gave up the effort to ban drinking. The alcohol industry, however, feared the antiliquor forces and purchased goodwill by funding research about drinking. Scientific interest in alcohol grew with the emergence of the concept of alcoholism as a disease. In a related development, Bill Wilson and Dr. Bob Smith founded Alcoholics Anonymous (AA) in 1935. This self-help group's Twelve Step method to gain and maintain sobriety became a model for many organizations fighting various addictions. AA also offered important fellowship to its members that substituted for saloon camaraderie.

In the 1930s, alcohol consumption remained low, partly because many Americans who came of age during the 1920s never took up drinking and partly because the poor economy during the Depression discouraged consumption. Beer remained the cheapest and most popular beverage. An increasing quantity of beer was sold in bottles or cans at grocery stores for home consumption. American whiskey had to compete with Canadian and Scotch whiskies, which were quickly available while the domestic product was being aged. Vintners took many years to replant the acres lost during Prohibition.

## Drinking Increases After World War II

A third cyclical upswing began when alcohol consumption rose during World War II, and it might have increased even more if there had not been wartime shortages caused by the use of alcohol for industrial and military purposes. After the war, veterans and their wives became a hard-drinking generation. The film *Days of Wine and Roses* (1962) portrays this era. Restaurants increasingly sought full bar licenses, and cities and states gradually loosened restrictions. The last three dry states—Kansas, Oklahoma, and Mississippi—ended Prohibition by the late 1960s, although rural counties in many states still remain "dry" as a local option.

During the 1950s, Anheuser-Busch reached men by sponsoring sports on television and became the leading brewer, but per capita beer consumption began to rise only as the baby boomers born after World War II attained drinking age in the late 1960s. Hard liquor stayed off television, and wine advertisements appeared there only in the late 1960s. Per capita wine consumption rose during the 1970s. Lightly taxed wine was cheaper than hard liquor, taking wine with meals or with marijuana gained popularity, and sweet wine coolers were introduced.

After 1945, whiskey consumption fell, and while Scotch rose at first, after the mid-1960s all darker liquors declined, while fruit-flavored vodka, gin, or light rum-based mixed drinks such as daiquiris grew in popularity. So did tequila-based margaritas, honored by Jimmy Buffett's song "Margaritaville" (1977). By the 1970s, both restaurants and home consumers favored premixed cocktails that guaranteed consistency. The 1970s brought increasing numbers of singles bars for both straights and gays, until AIDS and other diseases challenged the practice of liquor-induced easy sex. Men had long plied women with alcohol as a means to reduce female sexual inhibitions.

## Alcohol Declines After 1981

The third alcohol consumption cycle peaked in 1981. From 1981 to 1999, per capita hard-liquor sales plummeted about 40 percent, although some of this decline was due to the fact that statisticians counted lighter premixed beverages that replaced hard liquor as wine. Per capita wine consumption rose until 1986, and then declined about 20 percent by 1999. Per capita beer consumption also dropped, but only about 10 percent from the 1981 peak. In the 1990s, major beer brands lost market share to imports and microbrews, and brew pubs became popular in many cities.

The drop in alcohol consumption since 1981 has several explanations. Throughout American history, drinking has gone in cycles, and the country's most recent cycle has now entered into decline. Demographics have played a role. Both baby boomers and their parents were hard drinkers, but many boomers preferred beer and, to a lesser extent, wine to their parents' stronger mixed drinks made with hard liquor. Then, too, boomers by the 1980s were mostly in their thirties, an age when alcohol consumption begins to decline. The generation that came of age in the 1990s drank less, in part because it included fewer whites, who have been the nation's heaviest drinkers. Most recent immigrants have been from countries with light-drinking traditions, such as Mexico, the Philippines, and China.

## New Attitudes Toward Alcohol

Attitudes have also changed. By the 1970s, there was growing public concern about the role of alcohol in automobile accidents. Mothers Against Drunk Driving (MADD),

founded in 1980, successfully lobbied for tougher state and federal laws. States reduced the amount of blood alcohol that a driver could legally have from .15 to .08. For some small-bodied adults, two drinks might exceed the lower limit. Many states raised taxes on alcohol. Congress coerced the states to set the drinking age at twenty-one, and steps were taken to discourage underage drinking. Many states passed "zero tolerance" laws that imposed harsh penalties, including mandatory jail time, on underage drinkers.

In addition, colleges restricted traditional fraternity drinking parties, and date rape, often involving alcohol, became an issue. Bars were sued for allowing drunken customers to drive home, and insurers began to require bars to confiscate car keys from suspected drunks. The idea of the abstinent "designated driver" took root, and many bars in restaurants reported that alcohol sales dropped by more than half. Per capita alcohol consumption has declined the most in formerly hard-drinking states such as New York and California.

Health issues also became important. Although some studies show that a small daily amount of alcohol, especially red wine, might benefit the heart, most recent scientific investigations have focused on alcohol's negative aspects. Research in the 1980s suggested that a surprisingly small number of drinks could be harmful to a fetus, and pregnant women were advised to abstain. Bars and bottles began to carry warning labels. At the same time, the use of prescription drugs has exploded, and many drugs are incompatible with drinking.

Between the 1980s and early 2000s, schools developed major programs against tobacco, alcohol, and drugs. Smoking and drinking have declined together. Both are no longer fashionable, as can be seen from their negative portrayal in popular television shows or movies. Espresso, cell phones, and the Internet have redefined a hectic business world without three-martini lunches. At the same time, Americans have increasingly embraced leisure in more physically active ways. Jogging, active sports, fitness clubs, backpacking, and dieting have all gained in popularity. Sweating has supplanted drinking, at least for the moment.

*See also:* Bars, Coffee Houses and Café Society, Diners, Dining Out, Prohibition and Temperance

### BIBLIOGRAPHY

Barrows, Susanna, and Robin Room, eds. *Drinking: Behavior and Belief in Modern History.* Berkeley: University of California Press, 1991.

Blocker, Jack S., Jr. *American Temperance Movements: Cycles of Reform.* Boston: Twayne, 1989.

Conroy, David W. *In Public Houses: Drink and the Revolution in Authority in Colonial Massachusetts.* Chapel Hill: University of North Carolina Press, 1995.

Duis, Perry R. *The Saloon: Public Drinking in Chicago and Boston, 1880–1920.* Urbana: University of Illinois Press, 1983.

Kissin, Benjamin, and Henri Begleiter, eds. *The Biology of Alcoholism.* 7 vols. New York: Plenum Press, 1991.

MacAndrew, Craig, and Robert B. Edgerton. *Drunken Comportment: A Social Explanation.* Chicago: Aldine Publishing Company, 1969.

National Institute on Alcohol Abuse and Alcoholism, Division of Biometry and Epidemiology. Surveillance Report No. 59. *Apparent Per Capita Alcohol Consumption: National, State, and Regional Trends, 1977–99.* Available from http://www.niaaa.nih.gov.

Powers, Madelon. *Faces along the Bar: Lore and Order in the Workingman's Saloon, 1870–1920.* Chicago: University of Chicago Press, 1998.

Rorabaugh, W. J. *The Alcoholic Republic: An American Tradition.* New York: Oxford University Press, 1979.

Rosenzweig, Roy. *Eight Hours for What We Will: Workers and Leisure in an Industrial City, 1870–1920.* New York: Cambridge University Press, 1983.

Salinger, Sharon V. *Taverns and Drinking in Early America.* Baltimore: Johns Hopkins University Press, 2002.

Tyrrell, Ian R. *Woman's World/Woman's Empire: The Woman's Christian Temperance Union in International Perspective, 1880–1930.* Chapel Hill: University of North Carolina Press, 1991.

*W. J. Rorabaugh*

# DRINKING GAMES

Drinking games are defined as "an activity played for fun where the primary purpose is to drink a lot or get someone from the group drunk" (Stiefvater, p. 76A). Willy Pederson defines them as "situations in which alcohol is consumed and where the interaction is linked with definite standardized and previously agreed rules" (p. 1484). Drinking games involve a set of rules defining when and how much alcohol participants will consume. These rules ensure the consumption of large amounts of alcohol in a short time.

Drinking games are as old as games and alcohol themselves. The ancient Sumerians were accomplished brewers more than 5,500 years ago. Coincidently, the oldest known game was also found with the Sumerians. Known as the Royal Game of Ur, the game dates to 3000 B.C.. The ancient Greeks played a drinking game called *katava* in which the dregs of wine at the bottom of the drinking cup (*kylix*) were thrown against the wall in competition, after the wine had first been consumed. Early drinking games were ones of speed and endurance, and lacked complexity. Participants would gamble for the drink itself by either consuming it the quickest, (chugging), being the last member standing, or the last to relieve himself after consuming a large quantity over a period of time.

Norse mythology holds its heroes in great esteem for being able to withstand the effects of drink the longest. Washington Irving, in *Picturesque Views on the Avon*, wrote of seventeenth century village teams of topers who challenged one another to drinking contests. Drinking contests were standard fare throughout the Middle Ages and in Germany until the seventeenth century, while in the early 2000s these competitions were found in only a few social settings, such as Oktoberfest. Schivelbusch notes that drinking contests were a normal part of life in preindustrial society. In the New World, to the disdain of its Puritan founders, drinking contests were common in most taverns. In the eighteenth century, wagering and imbibing alcohol were the lubricants of most adult male leisure. Up to and through the turn of the twentieth century, "playing for drinks" was an integral part of saloon games. Two world wars and Prohibition did little to slow the play of drinking contests in the United States.

While drinking contests in America may have gotten their start in taverns and beer halls, in the early twenty-first century they were predominantly played on college campuses, where they underwent a metamorphosis in the 1940s. No longer were they simple contests of speed and endurance, or payment of a lost wager, but rather complex games with specific names of their own and rules that governed their play. The motive was simple, to consume a large amount of alcohol in short order. The first known drinking game with complex rules was invented by Yale students in the 1940s and was called "Tang." Teams of ten men and eight women would compete by lining up along opposite sides of a long table. Team members would then chug beers in rapid succession, and the first team to finish all its beers was the winner.

Studies suggest that drinking games are a popular social activity that provide a focus for social interaction. Douglas reported that 81 percent of college students had participated in drinking games at some point in their

**College Contest.** Students participate in drinking games at Manzanita Residence Hall at Arizona State University in Tempe, Arizona in 1993. © *Mark Peterson/Corbis*

lives. Crawford and Nellis conducted a study in which they found that 40 percent of students had played drinking games during the previous month.

Drinking games appear to contribute to high-risk behavior, including heavy drinking and risky sexual practices, and death due to alcohol overdose can occur. Newman et al. suggest that drinking games trivialize the dangers of heavy rapid consumption, glorify those who can "hold their liquor," reinforce peer pressures to drink heavily, generally encourage favorable attitudes toward the immoderate use of alcohol, and may lead to a diversity of negative consequences. Engs and Hanson found that college students who played drinking games had an increase in various alcohol problems (such as hangover, nausea, vomiting, driving under the influence, trouble with the law and school, job loss, lower grades, missed class and work, violence, and vandalism). Wechsler and Isaac; Williams, Kirkman-Liff, and Szivek; and McCarty and Kaye all found that increased college student alcohol use is positively related to an increase in alcohol related problems. In fact, a particularly acute problem on college campuses is binge-drinking, typically defined as drinking five or more alcoholic beverages on a single occasion. Studies generally estimate that somewhat more than 40 percent of the nation's college students can be described as binge-drinkers.

As few as three to five persons normally play a drinking game, but sometimes as many as sixteen to eighteen participate in games. Smaller groups allow for more skillful manipulation, or collusion, of the group against one member who is forced to drink larger quantities or drink more often. Whether the resultant drunkenness is a reward or a punishment in the game is generally ambiguous. Equally ambiguous is the question of competence. Whereas in conventional games the most competent player is the winner, in drinking games the least competent player (the one who has to drink the most) is often considered the winner.

Drinking games can involve physical skills (bouncing a quarter into a glass) or verbal skills (repeating tongue-twisting phrases), or drinking may occur on some agreed upon signal (for example, everybody drinks when a TV character says a name of another character). Errors are "punished" by the offender being required to take a

**FIGURE 1**

### Types of drinking games

| | |
|---|---|
| Chug-a-lugs | Competitions, usually races. |
| Consumption Games | The purpose is to consume as much alcohol without appearing drunk or "buzzed." |
| Gambling Actions | Dice or cards and some game parodies are used to determine which player must take a drink. |
| IQ Games | Involves players in intellectually challenging activities. |
| Mathematical Skills | A sequence of numbers is repeated by players who must substitute a prescribed word for multiples of particular numbers. |
| Media Interaction | A particular word or phrase from a specific text calls for all players to take a drink. |
| Motor Skill | A certain task must be performed. |
| Skill Games | A certain task must be performed. |
| Team Games | Resembling relays, these pit one group against another. |
| Unity Games | Noncompetitive games that require all to drink at certain "cues." |
| Verbal Skills | A long sequence of nonsense names or phrases must be repeated. |

SOURCE: Green and Grider, 1990; Crawford, Newman and Nellis, 1991

drink, or those who succeed may designate another player to drink.

There are a number of reasons why people play drinking games. Research has shown that 64 percent of college students played drinking games to socialize more easily with other students while 92 percent reported playing drinking games simply to get drunk. Students seem to play drinking games mainly to obtain positive reinforcement. Johnson et al. identified four primary reasons that students played drinking games: relaxation and disinhibition, fun and celebration, conformity, and sexual manipulation.

Drinking games remain a popular diversion among many Americans, particularly college students, and there is an ever-growing number of books and Web sites devoted to drinking games. While alcohol abuse and binge-drinking as a result of drinking game participation has beenshown to be a problem for many participants, drinking games appear to be firmly entrenched in American culture.

*See also:* Bars, Drinking, Teenage Leisure Trends

**BIBLIOGRAPHY**

Adams, Celeste E., and Craig T. Nagoshi. "Changes Over One Semester in Drinking Game Playing and Alcohol Use and Problems in a College Student Sample." *Substance Abuse* 20, no. 2 (1999), 97–106.

Cross, Gary S. *A Social History of Leisure since 1600.* State College, Pa.: Venture Publishing, Inc., 1990.

Douglas, P. "Bizz-Buzz, Turtles, Quarters, and One-Horse Club: The Role of Drinking Games among High School and College Students." *Alcohol, Health and Research World* 11, no. 4 (1987): 54–57.

Engs, Ruth Clifford, and David J. Hanson. "The Drinking Patterns and Problems of College Students." *Journal of Alcohol and Drug Education* 31 (1985): 65–68.

———. "Drinking Games and Problems Related to Drinking among Moderate and Heavy Drinkers." *Psychological Reports* 73, no. 1 (August 1993): 115–120.

Green, Thomas A., and Sylvia Ann Grider. "Reversal of Competence in College Drinking Games." *Play and Culture* 3, no. 2 (May 1990): 117–132.

Griscom, Andy, Ben Rand, and Scott Johnston. *The Complete Book of Drinking Games.* Memphis, Tenn.: Mustang Publishing, 2000.

*The Guinness Drinking Companion.* New York: Lyons Press, 2003.

Hintz, Martin. *Farewell John Barleycorn: Prohibition in the United States.* Minneapolis, Minn.: Lerner Publications Co., 1996.

"History of Games Timeline." Available from http://www.historicgames.com/gamestimeline.html.

Johnson, Thomas J., S. Hamilton, and V. L. Sheets. "College Students' Self-Reported Reasons for Playing Drinking Games." *Addictive Behaviors* 24, no. 2 (March–April 1999): 279–286.

McCarty, D., and M. Kaye. "Reasons for Drinking: Motivational Patterns and Alcohol Use among College Students." *Addictive Behaviors* 9, no 2 (1984): 185–188.

Newman, I. M., and J. K. Crawford. "College Drinking Games and Observed Consequences." Paper presented at the Annual Meeting of the Society for Applied Anthropology, 1991.

Newman, I. M., J. K. Crawford, and M. J. Nellis. "The Role and Function of Drinking Games in a University Community." *Journal of American College Health* 39, no. 4 (1991): 171–175.

Pedersen, Willy. "Drinking Games Adolescents Play." *British Journal of Addiction* 85 (1990): 1483–1490.

Powers, Madelon. *Faces along the Bar: Lore and Order in the Workingman's Saloon, 1870-1920.* Chicago: University of Chicago Press, 1998.

Presley, Cheryl A., Philip W. Meilman, and Jeffrey R. Cashin. "Weapon Carrying and Substance Abuse among College Students." *Journal of American College Health* 46, no. 1 (1997): 3–8.

Russell, Ruth V. *Pastimes: The Context of Contemporary Leisure.* Dubuque, Iowa: Brown and Benchmark Publishers, 1996.

Schivelbusch, Wolfgang. *Tastes of Paradise: A Social History of Spices, Stimulants, and Intoxicants.* New York: Vintage Books, 1993.

Stiefvater, Rob, S. Harper, J. Patterson, V. S. L. Williams, and M. Windle. "HBCU Student Drinking and Drinking Games." Abstract in *Alcoholism: Clinical and Experimental Research,* 26 no. 5 (2002): 76A

Wechsler, Henry, et al. "College Alcohol Use: A Full or Empty Glass?" *Journal of American College Health,* 47, no. 6 (May 1999): 247–252.

Wechsler, Henry, et al. "College Binge Drinking in the 1990s: A Continuing Problem." Results of the Harvard School of Public Health 1999 College Alcohol Survey. Available from http://www.hsph.harvard.edu/cas/.

Wilford, John Noble. "Jar in Iranian R Betrays Beer Drinkers of 3500 B.C." *New York Times.* (13 February 1994): p. A16.

Williams, F. G., Bradford Kirkman-Liff, and P. H. Szivek. "College Student Drinking Behavior Before and After Changes in State Policy." *Journal of Alcohol Education* 35 (1990): 12–15.

Wood, Mark D., Thomas J. Johnson, and K. J. Sher. "Characteristics of Frequent Drinking Game Participants in College: An Exploratory Study (Abstract)." *Alcoholism: Clinical and Experimental Research* 16 (1992): 417.

*Robert Steifvater*

# DRUG USE

**See** *Recreational Drug Use*

# EARLY NATIONAL LEISURE AND RECREATION

Historians have often characterized the early national era, or the years between the adoption of the federal Constitution in 1789 and the conclusion of Civil War in 1865, as a period of dramatic social, political, and economic change. During this time, the United States abandoned many customs, traditions, and institutions established in its colonial past, and adopted newer patterns and practices better suited to a modern nation-state. Not surprisingly, American leisure and recreation exhibited similar trends. A host of factors, including demographic change, urbanization, industrialization, the increased availability of goods and services, and the emergence of a mass audience, transformed the ways in which Americans experienced leisure and recreation. In the process, Americans retained some older forms of leisure, often adapting them to new purposes, and embraced an array of new forms of amusement and recreation.

## Preindustiral Leisure

At the end of the eighteenth century, before the Industrial Revolution had proceeded far, most Americans pursued leisure with their families, communities, or small groups of friends. Though city dwellers sometimes had a wider range of drinking establishments, theaters, and other leisure venues available to them than did country folk, both urban and rural residents amused themselves mostly with simple pleasures: reading the few books and newspapers available, or listening to them being read by others; visiting with family and friends; enjoying music and dancing at gatherings of friends; and pursuing useful pastimes such as carving, whittling, sewing, or quilting. In leisure as elsewhere, gender often determined what one did and with whom. Men hunted, fished, and visited inns, hotels, and stores to drink, socialize, and talk politics with their peers. Women found amusement and recreation in more private settings, gathering in a friend's or relative's home to sew, quilt, and exchange news. Seasonal change brought some variation to this routine, with summer permitting picnics, outings into the countryside, swimming, and other warm-weather pursuits. Winter, although it kept many Americans indoors much of the time, meant a respite from agricultural labor, conversation around the family hearth, and winter sports like skating and sleighing. Special occasions also provided opportunities for sociability and recreation: families and friends gathered to celebrate marriages and births, and the whole community turned out for speeches, parades, and barbecues on the Fourth of July.

## Leisure and Work Before Industrialization

Before industrialization transformed the American economy, leisure and recreation were intertwined with work. The patterns and rhythms of labor, in both agriculture and manufacturing, shaped the types and amount of leisure activities Americans enjoyed. Artisans and skilled craftsmen, who produced everything from shoes to coffins, integrated frequent breaks in the workday for

# Franklin Trotting Park

## NORTH CHELSEA, near Boston.

☞ **A PURSE OF $50.00**

Will be trotted for

## ON THURSDAY, SEPTEMBER 15th, 1859.

Z. G. BROWNELL names - blk. m. MIDNIGHT, of Cambridge
C. T. GREEN names - - - r. g. ROCKY MOUNTAIN, of Boston
S. EMERSON names - - - - - ch. g. SPOTTY, of Charlestown

Mile Heats, best 3 in 5 to Harness.

COACHES will leave C. C. Henry's saloon, 96 Sudbury Street, at 2 1-2 o'clock, for the Track, on the day of the Trot. Fare for the Trip, 75 Cents.

## ADMITTANCE . . . . . 50 CENTS

Trotting will commence at 4 o'clock, precisely.

**S. EMERSON, Proprietor.**

**Horse racing.** Trotting parks were popular gathering places to view sulky racing; the Franklin Trotting Park in North Chelsea, Massachusetts, drew crowds from nearby Boston for events such as these 1859 races. © *Corbis*

drinking and socializing. Each craft had its own traditions, but artisans commonly paused at midmorning for alcoholic refreshment, drank again at lunch, and broke up the afternoon with another respite. Moreover, artisans frequently set the pace of their own labor and leisure, choosing to labor slowly for the first part of the week, then working frenetically to finish their tasks before the weekend began at noon on Saturday. Having worked hard during the week, artisans and craftsmen reserved Saturday and Sunday for recreation and amusement, which often included the consumption of large quantities of alcohol. This pattern helps to account for the Anglo-American tradition of St. Monday, in which exhausted and hungover artisans worked slowly or not at all on Monday, turning it into an informal holiday.

Agricultural laborers and rural dwellers also intermixed labor and leisure. As prevailing opinion held that alcohol revived both body and mind, custom dictated that farmers provide alcoholic beverages for their workers during rests from the arduous tasks of planting and harvesting. The pattern of intense labor followed by unrestrained recreation characterized the farm as well as the workshop, especially during the fall harvest. Farm laborers, male and female, had to work unceasingly to gather crops before cold or inclement weather ruined them. At the harvest's conclusion, farmers, along with their families and hired help, joined in a celebration featuring music, dancing, and abundant food and drink. Other occasions for collective agricultural labor also combined work and play, especially when the community gathered to help with a task too big for one family to manage alone. Neighbors helped each other raise barns, butcher hogs, collect maple syrup, and shear sheep. When the day's labor was finished, all joined in a lavish dinner and party provided by the family benefiting from this shared work.

A limited number of sporting events and commercial amusements enlivened this general pattern. In all parts of the United States, horse, foot, and boat racing, as well as various forms of group hunting were popular. City residents might be able to attend the theater or circus, though some states and localities, particularly in New England, prohibited these activities as immoral. Itinerant entertainers sometimes brought exhibitions of unusual animals, dramatic readings billed as "moral lectures," musical performances, or feats of acrobatics and physical skill to even remote communities in the South and West. During the late 1820s, for instance, Raymond and Ogden's Menagerie toured rural Pennsylvania and points west, delighting spectators with tigers, elephants, ostriches, and other exotic creatures.

In areas linked to eastern manufacturing centers by good roads or rivers, commercially produced leisure goods were available: books, pamphlets, musical instruments, sheet music, and toys. At the turn of the nineteenth century, however, before the expansion of the national market and its attendant cash economy, many Americans would have been unable to purchase these goods even if they were available because of their high cost and a general lack of hard currency. Until the early decades of the nineteenth century, then, most Americans experienced leisure and recreation as their forebears had for decades, if not centuries: intermixed with work, and centered around family, friends, and small community groups.

## Regional Variation in Leisure

Regional differences added some variety to American leisure. In the Northeast, urban and manufacturing centers permitted the development of nascent leisure industries, and greater availability of commercial amusements and recreational goods. Northerners approached leisure somewhat differently than their counterparts elsewhere in the country, often opting for free-time activities that served some instrumental or useful purpose. French traveler Alexis de Tocqueville observed this tendency during his visit to the United States in the 1830s. Even the rich, who had time to spare, Tocqueville remarked in *Democracy in America,* devote their "leisure to some kind of industrial or commercial pursuit"; they would think themselves "in bad repute" if they employed their lives "solely in living," (vol. 2, p.152). By contrast, southerners rejected work as the worthiest aspect of life, adopting a leisure ethic that placed genteel amusement and repose at the pinnacle of human existence. The elegant lifestyle of the plantation elite set the tone for this ethic, and provided a model to which poorer whites aspired. White southerners seemed untroubled by the fact that involuntary labor made their leisure possible, preferring to see in African American music, dance, and communal sociability evidence of a carefree, happy black population whose love of leisure and recreation received a salutary restraint through slavery. Finally, the West exhibited patterns of leisure that combined eastern influences with a reliance on traditional pursuits imposed by necessity. Westerners partook of whatever commercial leisure they could get, but the imperatives of carving farms and towns out of undeveloped land, combined with the difficulty and expense of procuring goods and services from distant markets, often relegated western residents to simpler preindustrial amusements. In every section of the country, the experience of leisure would be changed dramatically by social and economic developments in the early decades of the nineteenth century.

## Economic Change and the Transformation of Leisure

During the first three decades of the nineteenth century, the rapidly changing U.S. economy altered the way that Americans pursued and experienced leisure and recreation. While many traditional amusements, such as barn raisings, harvest festivals, and drinking on the job, persisted throughout the nineteenth century, they began to be supplanted by new customs and practices. Changes in the nature and rhythm of work accounted for much of this transformation. In town and cities, the craft system of manufacturing, in which a master craftsman worked at home, often boarding his journeyman and apprentice employees within his household, began to break down with the emergence of industrialization and factory labor. Though factory work required less skill than the craft system, it imposed work discipline on laborers unaccustomed to the regimentation of their time and activities. Because factories required a steady, reliable workforce that would produce consistent amounts of product during the week, preindustrial patterns of work and leisure began to disappear: Employers discouraged drinking on the job, forbade socializing during work, and prohibited Monday holidays (St. Monday) to recover from the weekend's excesses. As historian Paul Faler has noted, workers responded in a variety of ways to these changes. Some adopted new standards of promptness, diligence, and temperance in an effort to gain favor and economic advancement from employers. Others rejected the new industrial discipline, clinging to older patterns of work and leisure. Preferring independence to advancement, traditionalist workers preserved drinking practices, favored periods of intense labor followed by raucous celebrations, and continued to celebrate St. Monday. Still others adopted new patterns of leisure, but not to please employers. Labor organizers who wished to limit employers' authority urged workers to be temperate and to use their leisure for reading, reflection, and intellectual improvement. Sober, literate workers, they reasoned, would be more useful in the struggle to gain concessions from employers.

## The Separation of Leisure and Work

The emerging industrial economy produced other changes in leisure as well. Leisure became increasingly separate from work, rather than intertwined with it. Employers considered the workday time that laborers should devote exclusively to the tasks at hand; recreation and amusement would have to wait until after quitting time.

In addition to separating work and leisure, industrialization also changed their venues. With the rise of factories, fewer workers labored at home. Though workers continued to recreate with their families, they also sought amusement and sociability outside of the home, in taverns, theaters, and clubs populated by other workers. A host of new leisure venues and services, ranging from ice-cream parlors and workingmen's libraries to brothels and unlicensed drinking establishments, sprang up to meet the new demands for recreation outside the home.

Women, too, felt the impact of these changes. With men away from home, child-care and family responsibilities fell more heavily on wives and mothers, curtailing, in some cases, time that might have been devoted to leisure pursuits. The new public leisure facilities often excluded women, making recreation outside the home largely a male preserve. Thus women's leisure and recreation centered more than ever on the home, and on interaction with other women. Moreover, women, especially those of the middle class, assumed responsibilities for making men's leisure time spent at home pleasant and uplifting. Women's historians have documented the importance of domesticity as a female attribute during the early national years. Social critics, clerics, and advice writers encouraged wives, mothers, and daughters to make home a cheerful, enjoyable place for men to relax and recreate with books, music, and conversation after a hard day's work. By making home a site for uplifting leisure, supporters of female domesticity argued, women could prevent men from seeking more destructive recreational alternatives such as the tavern or gambling hall.

## Market Expansion and the Transformation of Leisure

If industrialization changed the venues and rhythms of leisure, the expansion of markets transformed the number and variety of recreational options available to Americans during the first half of the nineteenth century. The creation of a national market for leisure (as well as other) goods and services proceeded from a number of factors. Urbanization provided large markets for recreation and amusement in cities. The movement of settlers westward offered new opportunities to sell manufactured goods, while population growth in eastern cities provided an industrial labor force capable of supplying them. A rapidly expanding and improving transportation network, including turnpikes and canals early in the century, and railroads during the 1830s and 1840s, made travel and the delivery of goods easier and cheaper. These developments benefited the American economy as a whole, but also had important ramifications for leisure and recreation. With expanded markets for products ranging from sporting goods to sheet music to novels, individuals, businesses, and nascent industries could make profits meeting the demand for amusement and recreation. Pianofortes manufactured in Boston or Philadelphia graced parlors in faraway Pittsburgh and Cincinnati. Catering to working-class tastes and pocketbooks, the "penny press" in New York and elsewhere churned out thousands of flimsy and lurid (though entertaining) newspapers costing only a cent. More genteel publishers put out annual "gift" books of poetry, prose, and moral exhortation, which were intended to be given as presents. Numerous individuals and stores manufactured and sold dolls, games, fireworks, and other items designed to entertain and delight children. Consequently, the number and variety of leisure options available to Americans increased dramatically in the decades before the Civil War. To some extent, this expansion of commercial leisure goods fostered traditional patterns of recreation. Mechanics banded together to buy newspapers and books and establish a workingman's library association; middle-class families purchased musical instruments and sheet music for use within their homes; the wealthy purchased elegant sideboards, decanters, china, and furniture for entertaining guests. In another sense, however, the new availability of leisure goods presaged a transformation of leisure from an activity pursued or produced by people to a commodity purchased by consumers. Nowhere was this trend more apparent than in the tremendous growth of commercial leisure services.

## The Commercialization of Leisure

Leisure services as well as goods proliferated with the expansion of national markets. Most cities and many towns had halls and auditoriums to rent for parties or lectures, and a growing number of caterers, musicians, and performers offered their services to the public. Lessons in fencing, dancing, art, and music became available for those with the money and inclination to perfect their leisure skills. Various performances, exhibitions, and shows provided spectators with a wide range of amusement and instruction. Panoramas, or large paintings, of famous battles, prominent cities, or biblical scenes proved especially popular. Baltimore's citizens, for example, thronged to a 230-square-foot painting of the Battle of North Point in 1815; in 1825, a large portrait of a manufacturing city; and in 1829, a painting depicting the doom of Sodom. Lyceums brought prominent intellectuals and public figures to urban and rural areas to give speeches and lectures. Menageries and circuses reached most of the United States, satisfying the public's desire to

see exotic animals and daring acrobats. Dramatic performances proved a consistently popular leisure activity for many Americans. By the 1820s, most major cities boasted at least one professional theater, and touring theater troupes brought tragedy, comedy, and farce to even remote parts of the United States. Sol Smith, an actor and theatrical manager, for instance, conducted an itinerant acting company through Missouri and the frontier Southwest during the 1820s and 1830s. So extensive was the demand for theater that celebrated English actors who traveled to the United States found it profitable to perform in western and southern cities like New Orleans and St. Louis, as well the theatrical centers of New York and Philadelphia. Even miners and prospectors in distant California periodically witnessed performances of Shakespeare and other dramas during the late 1840s.

With growing public appetite for commercial leisure, a mass audience for amusement and recreation took shape by the 1830s. Americans hungered for new, unique, and exciting leisure activities, and they were willing to pay for them. Increasingly, they became consumers rather than producers of leisure. A barn dance organized by friends and neighbors, for instance, paled before the elaborate and refined balls and cotillions held by clubs, societies, and dancing instructors. The novelty and variety of commercial recreation and amusement motivated many Americans to buy their leisure instead of taking an active part in creating it themselves. Here again, theater provides a case in point. Before about 1810, amateur theatricals put on by local students or other nonprofessional actors composed the bulk of dramatic performances available in many towns and cities, especially in the West. In early nineteenth-century Pittsburgh, for instance, groups of young lawyers and professionals staged farces and other entertainments on makeshift stages. Here as elsewhere, neighbors created their own theater, amusing themselves and providing entertainment for the community in the process. With the growth of commercial theater, these amateur efforts withered into insignificance. By 1850, Pittsburgh boasted no less than eleven theaters or halls suitable for professional entertainment.

## P. T. Barnum and the Commercialization of Leisure

No one understood or exploited this trend toward commercialized leisure better than did P. T. Barnum. Though best known today for his postbellum career as a circus promoter, Barnum made a fortune before the Civil War as an exhibitor of entertainers and attractions. Recognizing the public's fervent desire to be amused by the novel and unusual, Barnum searched for unique people and objects with which to satisfy it. A large part of Barnum's success lay in his ability to engage public curiosity and skepticism: He realized that people would pay to be amused, even if they suspected that they were being deceived, or "humbugged," in the process. As historian Neil Harris observed, Barnum cultivated an operational aesthetic in his audiences, encouraging them to inquire into how things worked, and how his implausible claims about his attractions could be made to seem true. In 1835, Barnum exhibited Joice Heth, an elderly African American woman whom he claimed was the 161-year-old former nurse of George Washington. Several years later, Barnum displayed the Feejee Mermaid, a grotesque, mummified monkey's body sewn to a fish tail, which he suggested was a real sea creature. Two of Barnum's most popular attractions were entertainers. Tom Thumb, a midget who sang, danced, and told jokes, made a fortune for the showman in the United States and Europe. Barnum also arranged for Jenny Lind, the celebrated Swedish soprano, to tour the United States. Though largely unknown before her arrival, Lind became wildly popular, largely due to Barnum's presentation of her as a leisure attraction that no American should miss. Barnum set the tone for future commercial leisure with his New York museum, an establishment that offered patrons a dizzying array of stage plays; animal exhibitions; and displays of curios, artifacts, and historical memorabilia. As one European visitor noted at midcentury, no trip to New York was complete without a visit to Barnum's American Museum.

## Leisure and Social Differentiation

With the expansion of opportunities for recreation and amusement, and the growth and diversification of the American population, the social function of leisure changed considerably. Though different occupational and ethnic groups had always pursued varying pastimes, leisure in the preindustrial world had to a great extent promoted a sense of community. As noted above, neighbors gathering for work, play, and celebration fostered sociability and communal solidarity: Leisure provided a common experience and identity for those participating. By the 1820s, commercialization and demographic change had altered this pattern. With new and exciting leisure options available, like those offered by P. T. Barnum, traditional forms such as husking bees, barn raisings, and country dances lost much of their luster. Unlike older recreations, new forms like popular theater, sporting events, or pleasure gardens—the precursors of modern amusement parks—did not require or necessarily promote a sense of community or neighborliness. Fre-

quently, the only trait that participants had in common was the price of admission.

Demographic change also fragmented communal leisure. Immigration, particularly from Germany and Ireland, increased markedly during the antebellum years, and these new Americans often pursued different amusements and pastimes than native-born citizens. The Irish, for instance, formed Hibernian societies, which organized social events, dinners, and celebrations of St. Patrick's Day, all in an effort to keep Irish culture and identity alive in their new home. German Americans, too, formed social clubs and fraternal organizations to provide immigrants with customary amusements. Germans frequented beer gardens for eating, drinking, singing, and socializing; established gymnasiums to provide venues for calisthenics and other sports; and formed turnvereins, organizations devoted to marching and martial exercises. Some groups founded separate leisure organizations out of necessity as much as choice. In areas with sizable free black populations, for example, African Americans who were excluded from most white organizations established their own Masonic lodges and other social clubs.

The development of party politics, which occurred during the first half of the nineteenth century, also undermined communal leisure and promoted social differentiation; political affiliation made up an important aspect of men's identities. To nourish partisan allegiance, parties established social clubs, held celebrations, and discouraged fraternization with members of other parties. During the 1830s, for instance, the Whig and Democratic Parties both held barbecues, parades, rallies, and speeches, using leisure activities to attract support and differentiate themselves from their rivals. Even ostensibly communal leisure on national holidays like the Fourth of July or Washington's birthday highlighted political differences rather than a shared patriotism. All over the United States, political celebrations used festivities to deride their opponents in parades, speeches, and after-dinner toasts. In 1840, for example, Uniontown, Pennsylvania, Democrats used their Independence Day celebration of the "Sabbath of American liberties" to denounce their political opponents, toasting the "rough sea of Whiggery, the deep dead sea of Federalism, floating with 'log cabins and hard cider' to the port of Democracy."

## Leisure and Class

Leisure fragmented along class as well as ethnic and political lines. The American class structure, like the political party system, solidified during the decades before the Civil War. As Americans strove to establish class identities, they used leisure activities to signify their position in

American society. The wealthiest Americans, especially in urban areas like New York, Charleston, Boston, and New Orleans, strove for a refined, genteel style of leisure. Upper-class pastimes included travel to visit friends and relatives; elegant, costly balls; dinners, parties, and other social occasions; fox hunting; and the enjoyment of fine art and music. The middle class, conscious of its inferiority in wealth, nonetheless considered its approach to leisure superior to what it considered the extravagance and decadence of elite amusements. Middle-class leisure emphasized respectability, morality, and edification. Lectures; religious activities; membership in charitable, intellectual, or service organizations; and decorous social gatherings were staples of middle-class recreation. Recreation at home, in the bosom of one's family, also made up an important aspect of middle-class leisure. The parlor became a center for this domestic leisure, where family members could read, converse, or listen to music played on the pianoforte or other instruments.

Rejecting both upper-class elegance and middle-class restraint, working-class leisure stressed informality and raucous enjoyment. Constrained by lack of funds, workers' leisure depended on casual drinking and socializing with friends, family, and coworkers; reading the antebellum era's many inexpensive books and newspapers; parties with singing, dancing, and eating; and patronage of inexpensive commercial amusements. Labor unions, trade and craft associations, and occupational groups also provided opportunities for recreation and amusement. A carpenters' guild might offer its members a lending library, sponsor a float and celebration during a holiday parade, or organize an entire celebration of the Fourth of July or Thanksgiving.

## Class Segregation in Leisure

Inclination and financial constraints imposed de facto class segregation on many aspects of leisure during the early national era. As commercial amusements assumed a larger role in American leisure, financial resources influenced how and with whom people spent their leisure. Upper- and middle-class Americans gravitated toward more costly pastimes and activities that separated them from what they considered the less respectable working class. Emerging leisure industries catered to the desire for class-specific recreation. In theaters, for instance, a tripartite seating arrangement separated the classes: The well-to-do occupied expensive private boxes; the middle class and prosperous artisans sat in the pit immediately in front of the stage; and apprentices, unskilled laborers and other impoverished workers filled the gallery behind the pit. In New York, whole theaters took on class char-

acters. During the 1830s and 1840s, New York's Bowery Theater furnished working-class dramatic fare, while the Park Theater attracted a more aristocratic crowd. This class division in leisure could produce unfortunate results. In 1849, a mob of workers stormed the Park Theater to protest an insult to an American actor appearing at the Bowery by an English tragedian then playing at the Park. The mob was dispersed only when a local militia fired into the crowd, killing nearly twenty people.

Class segregation also characterized other areas of leisure, such as the emerging custom of summer vacationing. In hot, crowded, and often unhealthful cities, many people sought an escape from oppressive urban summers. As in the case of theater, leisure entrepreneurs offered a variety of options. By the early decades of the century, wealthy urban dwellers traveled to elegant summer resorts, frequently located at natural springs that promised health benefits as well as recreational opportunities. In the South, the plantation gentry favored a number of Virginia springs, where they could socialize with other members of the plantation elite, and survey matrimonial prospects for their sons and daughters. For wealthy northerners, Saratoga Springs in New York served a similar function. Middle-class vacationers, who usually could not afford the cost of travel or board at elite resorts, chose from a variety of regional mineral springs. In Pennsylvania, Bedford Springs offered patrons opportunities for sociability, relaxation, and romance similar to those at elite resorts, albeit among a slightly less elevated clientele. For the working class, for whom an extended vacation at an expensive resort was not financially feasible, day trips to rural retreats or recreational facilities provide the only relief from sweltering cities and towns. In areas with access to lakes, rivers, or the seashore, steamboats or other conveyances transported working-class constituencies on outings for swimming, boating, and other outdoor activities. Around some cities, pleasure gardens offered arbors, trails, flower gardens, and other attractions to urban amusement seekers. In antebellum Pittsburgh, for example, Greenwood and Rosedale Gardens, both a short distance from the city on the Monongahela River, charged a small admission price to use facilities for picnics, walks, sports, and dancing.

## The Reform of Leisure

Many Americans welcomed the new opportunities for recreation and amusement afforded them by market expansion, demographic change, and industrial growth.

Others found new leisure practices and products disturbing, with some reformers condemning them outright as immoral and destructive. Opposition to theater had a long history in the Anglo-American world by the early nineteenth century, but it acquired a new urgency with the increase in theatrical activity. Clerics and moralists emphasized the corrupting influence of the theater and the loose morals of actors, but reserved especial opprobrium for the infamous third tier of boxes. This, the highest level of boxes in many urban theaters, provided a venue for prostitutes to solicit clients, and sometimes even to ply their trade.

Social commentators, politicians, and religious figures questioned the moral tendencies of other aspects of the new leisure as well. Novels, their critics charged, created imaginary worlds that seduced the weak-minded (by this they meant primarily women) from recognizing the demands of duty and morality. Excessive drinking, which had not been a major problem in the eighteenth century, increased dramatically during the early national period, motivating a reappraisal of alcohol's role in leisure. Gambling, which many observers linked to drinking and prostitution, also seemed to be on the rise. Indeed, a host of sexually oriented leisure activities for men, ranging from brothels to exhibitions of "model artistes," or nude women, shocked and dismayed reformers. Even nonsalacious commercial amusements such as the circus, boxing matches, and dance halls alarmed the moral establishment, especially when they remained open on Sunday, the Christian Sabbath. Some of the concern about leisure reflected nativism as much as moral qualms. Native-born white Americans disdained the amusements of German and Irish immigrants in particular. The Irish drew fire for what many considered their inordinate use of liquor, while Germans were taken to task for their use of Sundays for eating and socializing with family and friends.

## Reform Movements

Though many local efforts sprang up to deal with particular abuses, two major national reform movements emerged to address issues raised in part by new leisure practices. The temperance movement, which originated early in the century, aimed first at promoting moderation in drinking and eliminating illegal vendors of liquor. By the 1830s, however, temperance advocates became convinced that total abstinence from alcohol provided the only sure protection against drunkenness. Their tactics shifted from moral suasion, the attempt to convince individuals not to drink, to legal coercion, the effort to make states and localities pass prohibitory legislation. The campaign for coercive legislation culminated in the 1850s, when Maine passed a prohibition law in 1851, providing a model that more than ten other states followed.

Sabbatarianism, the other major reform movement aimed at reforming leisure, focused on the violation of the Christian Sabbath. Rather than pursuing religious observance and devotions, Sabbatarians charged, too many Americans spent the day in secular pursuits. Though they objected to business activities on Sunday as well, reformers expressed horror that many of their fellow citizens treated the Lord's day as a mere opportunity for leisure and amusement. A host of commercial amusements remained available on Sunday, making matters even worse. Through a combination of moral suasion and legislative coercion, Sabbatarians hoped to remedy this assault on Christian piety. Clergymen preached sermons and denounced Sunday recreation in print, while secular critics militated for the passage of "Blue Laws" (so called because the first ones enacted were printed on blue paper) that mandated the Sunday closing of a variety of businesses.

## The Impact of Civil War

By the eve of the Civil War, the pattern of leisure expansion had been set. Leisure industries, based mostly in the Northeast, supplied consumer goods as well as commercial amusements to customers all over the United States. The Civil War disrupted this system temporarily, but did little to change it. During the war, much of the North's industrial capacity shifted away from consumer goods and toward war material, though the production of leisure goods continued. Perhaps more important, southern markets became unavailable to northern manufacturers and performers, making distribution impossible. The South, which lagged behind the North in manufacturing, devoted all of its resources to the war effort, causing shortages of leisure products such as novels and books; food, dishes, and furniture for entertaining; and musical instruments and sheet music. After the war, the South's economic prostration strengthened further the predominance of the North as the center of leisure industries.

*See also:* Barn Raising, Drinking, Genre Reading, Prohibition and Temperance, Sabbatarianism, Vacations, Working-Class Leisure Lifestyles

### BIBLIOGRAPHY

Aron, Cindy S. *Working at Play: A History of Vacations in the United States.* New York: Oxford University Press, 2001.

Brown, Dona. *Inventing New England: Regional Tourism in the Nineteenth Century.* Washington, D.C.: Smithsonian Institution Press, 1995.

Butsch, Richard L., ed. *For Fun and Profit: The Transformation of Leisure into Consumption.* Philadelphia: Temple University Press, 1990.

Chambers, Thomas A. *Drinking the Waters: Creating an American Leisure Class at Nineteenth-Century Mineral Springs.* Washington, D.C.: Smithsonian Institution Press, 2002.

Click, Patricia C. *The Spirit of the Times: Amusements in Nineteenth-Century Baltimore, Norfolk, and Richmond.* Charlottesville: University of Virginia Press, 1989.

Dulles, Foster Rhea. *A History of Recreation: American Learns to Play.* Englewood Cliffs, N.J.: Prentice-Hall, 1965.

Faler, Paul. "Cultural Aspects of the Industrial Revolution: Lynn, Massachusetts, Shoemakers and Industrial Morality, 1826–1860." *Labor History* 15 (1974): 367–394.

Harris, Neil. *Humbug: The Art of P. T. Barnum.* Chicago: University of Chicago Press, 1973.

Johnson, Claudia D. "That Guilty Third Tier: Prostitution in Nineteenth-Century American Theaters." In *Victorian America.* Edited by D. W. Howe. Philadelphia: University of Pennsylvania Press, 1976.

Johnson, Susan Lee. "Bulls, Bears, and Dancing Boys: Race, Gender, and Leisure in the California Gold Rush." *Radical History Review* 60 (1994): 3–37.

Levine, Peter. "The Promise of Sport in Antebellum America." *Journal of American Culture* 2 (1980): 623–634.

Lewis, Charlene M. Boyer. *Ladies and Gentlemen on Display: Planter Society at the Virginia Springs, 1790–1860.* Charlottesville: University of Virginia Press, 2001.

Martin, Scott C. *Killing Time: Leisure and Culture in Southwestern Pennsylvania, 1800–1850.* Pittsburgh, Pa.: University of Pittsburgh Press, 1995.

Mintz, Steven. *Moralists and Modernizers: America's Pre–Civil War Reformers.* Baltimore: Johns Hopkins University Press, 1995.

Rorabaugh, W. J. *The Alcoholic Republic: An American Tradition.* New York: Oxford University Press, 1998.

Ross, Steven J. *Workers on the Edge: Work, Leisure, and Politics in Industrializing Cincinnati.* New York: Columbia University Press, 1985.

Sears, John F. *Sacred Places: American Tourist Attractions in the Nineteenth Century.* New York: Oxford University Press, 1989.

Sellers, Charles. *The Market Revolution: Jacksonian America, 1815–1846.* New York: Oxford University Press, 1991.

Stott, Richard. *Workers in the Metropolis: Class, Ethnicity and Youth in Antebellum New York City.* Ithaca: Cornell University Press, 1990.

Tocqueville, Alexis de. *Democracy in America.* 2 vols. Edited by Phillips Bradley. New York: Alfred A. Knopf, 1945.

Wilentz, Sean. "Artisan Republican Festivals and the Rise of Class Conflict in New York City, 1788–1837." In *Working Class America: Essays on Labor, Community and American Society.* Edited by Michael H. Frisch and Daniel J. Walkowitz. Urbana: University of Illinois Press, 1983.

*Scott C. Martin*

# EASTER

Although Easter represents the central celebration of the Christian faith, the United States lacks deep-rooted Easter traditions, despite Christianity's imprint. Appropriately, in a country that has led the world in commerce, the marketplace shaped Easter into a national holiday using a combination of Old World religious and folk symbols. Yet while the marketplace helped secularize the holiday, it also spread Easter's religious observance and provided Americans with new opportunities for social expression and interaction.

In antebellum America, Puritans and later evangelicals such as Baptists, Presbyterians, and Methodists suppressed Easter and other traditional festivals. For them, the Bible's failure to mention either Easter or Christmas celebrations suggested the pagan origins of both. More important, these Sabbatarians viewed the Easter season's lengthy liturgical calendar as a threat to systematic industry and piety. Nevertheless, parochial celebrations of Easter persisted among minority denominations such as Lutherans, Moravians, Episcopalians, and Roman Catholics. Not until decades after the Civil War did a nationally recognized holiday emerge from a bricolage of merchandizing, Protestant genteel culture, and localized folk customs.

Resistance to celebrating Easter gradually eroded as the expanding American marketplace catered to the genteel quest for romantic escape. Victorians dusted off and tamed traditional holidays as family-centered festivities. Even in the early development of Easter as an American holiday, the marketplace, churches, and consumers interacted to create a celebration. Ironically, churches promoted Easter's secularization and commercialization by adopting marketing techniques to boost attendance, retain membership, or meet the need for Easter celebration stimulated by the market. Churches with few liturgical Easter traditions added floral decorations in high church style, and distributed flowers, cards, candy, or novelties to parishioners and Sunday-school children.

The Easter parade provides an example of market-church symbiosis that grew into an American Easter trademark. The parade emerged in mid-nineteenth-century New York with a throng of churchgoers strolling along Fifth Avenue to view floral decorations in houses of worship. By late in the century, after merchants combined promotion of spring styles with Easter, the procession evolved into a fashion parade with spectators arriving from out of town. New York's annual event became a model for similar parades in Boston, Philadelphia, and smaller towns and cities. While for many years it served as a middle- and upper-class pageant for social display, the creation of mass markets democratized the parade by the mid-twentieth century. As portrayed by Irving Berlin's 1948 film *Easter Parade,* which depicted an Easter buying spree with a backdrop featuring a cathedral, aspiring working-class women also paraded by that time.

If churches could help promote commercialization of the holiday, commerce could spread the holiday's religious as well as secular observance. By the 1880s, store window dressers employed Christian symbols such as floral crosses or religious banners to sell Easter-related goods, and some department stores created cathedral-like shopping concourses with Christian iconography. Yet often merchants combined religious images with customs that originated elsewhere and sometimes took on a sacred aura (even the Easter lily was introduced in the 1880s from Bermuda by an enterprising florist). Within a few decades around the turn of the twentieth century, American merchandizing had transformed locally employed folk symbols of spring—including colored eggs, bunnies, chicks, and lambs—into standard emblems of American Easter by using their images for advertising, candies, cakes, toys, and knickknacks. Early German immigrants, for example, brought the tradition of coloring, hiding, and exchanging eggs as well as the legend of the egg-producing Easter bunny. Commercial promotion of egg dyes and egg-shaped candies spread the custom of children's Easter "nests," egg hunts, and later, baskets in America. Early in the twentieth century, the Easter bunny rivaled the egg as an Easter symbol through its ubiquitous appearance as a confection, toy, and as a seasonal counterpart to Santa later when toy departments featured a costumed "Easter bunny." Similarly, the White House egg roll, also based on Germanic custom, became like the Easter parade an annual event on America's festive calendar when publicized in the nationalizing culture after its inaugural in 1878.

Since more than a century ago, critics have charged that commerce not only revived pagan spring symbols at the expense of the religious, but also revived the pagan festival itself by transforming a Christian commemoration of self-sacrifice and suffering into an orgy of self-indulgence. But at the same time, merchandizing created new social opportunities by expanding the popularity of the holiday. For instance, although relegated to managing the home when Easter emerged, women shaped the holiday as consumers. Unempowering though the Easter parade may have been, it enabled women to momentarily break through gender strictures and move from the periphery to the center of public life. By buying and exchanging Easter cards and goods, they shifted the cele-

bration from church to family and friends. Activities such as coloring and hiding eggs, or filling baskets with candy and gifts, transformed Easter into a family-centered holiday. Easter offered parents harried in the modern world another opportunity to bond with children.

In the early twenty-first century, the Easter celebration reflected contemporary America's atomization and corresponding segmented markets instead of class-based or mass markets of the past. Class might have been gone, but so was the blurring between the religious and secular in national life. Religious themes disappeared from Easter in public culture, due not only to secularization but also to the decline of large denominations and the rise of independent evangelical churches. In national marketing, Easter dissolved into a spring festival where folk symbols abounded in Easter candy (such as ubiquitous yellow marshmallow "peeps"), the Easter bunny at malls, and fashions designated as "spring" rather than "Easter."

Ironically, Easter flourished at the local level as it did before the market nationalized the holiday. Many festivities suggested the segmented marketing trend toward individual self-fulfillment as well as consumer self-indulgence. New York's Easter Parade, for example, devolved into a spring frolic of costumed revelers; donating blood at Easter, a practice loaded with both Christian and pagan symbolism, became an Easter tradition for some Americans; and decorating lawns and trees with plastic eggs, an ersatz revival of a German folk custom, grew in popularity.

Among churches, community organizations, and families, customary activities such as passion plays, sunrise observances, egg hunts, and egg collecting mixed indiscriminately with commerce as they did in premodern times. Christian retailing, with outlets commonly found in local churches as well as malls, counted Easter as a "spike" in annual sales ranking in the billions. And in the 1970s, some churches began using malls for Easter sunrise services. While religiously minded critics might decry the venue, it simply represents the historical truth of Easter celebrating in America: the union of the marketplace and the resurrection, both sources of renewal, possibilities, and regeneration.

*See also:* Christmas, Mardi Gras

## BIBLIOGRAPHY

Aikman, Lonnelle. *The Living White House.* Washington, D.C.: White House Historical Association, 1987.

Lord, Priscilla Sawyer, and Daniel J. Foley. *Easter the World Over.* Philadelphia: Chilton Book Company, 1971.

Schmidt, Leigh Eric. "The Commercialization of the Calendar: American Holidays and the Culture of Consumption, 1870–1930." *Journal of American History* 78, no. 3 (December 1991): 887–916.

———. *Consumer Rites: The Buying and Selling of American Holidays.* Princeton, N.J.: Princeton University Press, 1995.

Santino, Jack. *All Around the Year: Holidays and Celebrations in American Life.* Urbana: University of Illinois Press, 1994.

Weiser, Francis X. *Handbook of Christian Feasts and Customs: The Year of the Lord in Liturgy and Folklore.* New York: Harcourt, Brace, 1958.

*James Weeks*

# EDUCATION

**See** *Adult Education (Earlier)*

# ETHICS

**See** *Leisure, Theory of; Work and Leisure Ethics*

# ETHNIC LEISURE LIFESTYLES

**See** *Asian American Leisure Lifestyles, Latinos Leisure Lifestyles, Muslim American Leisure Lifestyles*

# EXERCISE

**See** *Aerobic Exercise*

# EXPANSION OF LEISURE TIME

The movement to reduce working time lasted well over a century in the United States, involved ordinary people and how they lived their lives each day, and embodied key values of the nineteenth and early twentieth centuries, among them liberty and progress. It was one of the longest, broadest, and most important movements in American history. Indeed, the movement reached well beyond North America, occurring in most industrial nations at roughly the same periods of time.

Average work hours, days, weeks, years, and lives were steadily reduced throughout the nineteenth century. The process accelerated during the period 1900 to 1920 when working hours declined nearly 16 percent in the United States. Altogether, work time was cut by more than half before World War II.

## Working-Class Origins

Lasting over a century, the movement was also one of the few, true working-class movements. Historians agree, ordinary workers provided the movement's impetus by pressuring employers, forming unions, or "voting with their feet," moving from job to job in search of better hours. Owners and managers generally opposed each phase of the movement. Progressive reformers acted primarily as a cheering section, embroidering their own dreams and values. Politicians who passed supporting legislation usually followed in the wake of the movement, validating what workers had already achieved and using the issue to gain political support.

Historians have also made the case that workers' desire for shorter hours gave life to and sustained the labor movement. The first historians to write about the labor movement, John R. Commons and his associates, found that during the labor's earliest years, the 1820s and 1830s, the "most frequent cause complaint among the workers was the lack of leisure" (pp. 170–172, 384–385). Helen Sumner argued that workers' struggle to reduce working hours was "the cause of the awakening" of the labor movement (pp. 169–192).

Those who followed Commons and Sumner have agreed with and extended their argument, claiming that the movement was an enduring source of union strength, a powerful organizing issue, a rallying point during strikes, and a potent political issue. Working shorter hours was the dynamo of the labor movement, without which the movement has lost its momentum and cohesion, torn apart by competition for jobs and wages.

An excellent case may be made that the end of the shorter hours movement is directly related to the modern decline of the labor movement.

During its Forty-sixth Annual Meeting in 1926, actively campaigning for a five-day week and looking forward to a six-hour day, the American Federation of Labor recommitted itself and organized labor to the "progressive shortening of the hours of labor." This vision of steady, *continual* work reduction had been present from the inception of the American labor movement.

Commons concluded that "the earliest evidence of [labor] unrest" in the United States was a pamphlet circulated during the 1827 carpenters strike in Philadelphia for a ten-hour day. Written by William Heighton, "An Address to the Members of Trade Societies and to the Working-Class Generally" called for working hours to be reduced from "12 to 10, to 8, to 6, and so on" until "the development and progress of science have reduced human labor to its lowest terms."

With the coming of industrialization, the workplace became a place of alienation and exploitation. Part of the workers' battle was to regain at least some control of their work. However, a significant part of their struggle was to free themselves from bosses, time clocks, and the new industrial work discipline by reducing their work time and reclaiming their lives. Leisure and liberty share much more than a similar dictionary definition.

During the ten-hour struggle, workers defended their actions using liberty's rhetoric. Carpenters paraded in the streets of Boston, Massachusetts, under the French revolutionary banners and condemned the "despotic servitude" of the dawn-to-dusk schedule in 1825. Striking for ten hours in 1827, Philadelphia, Pennsylvania, carpenters resolved, "All men have a just right, derived from their Creator, to have sufficient time each day for the cultivation of their mind and for self-improvement." Such clear references to the revolutionary notions of natural rights were reiterated by the famous "Boston Ten-Hours Circular" of 1835, which condemned long hours as an offense against both God and against the natural rights of man: "The God of the Universe has given us time, health, and strength. We utterly deny the right of any man to dictate to us how much of it we shall sell" (Hunnicutt).

According to the historian David Roediger, the demand for work reduction "evoked . . .visionary. . .hopes for a radically reshaped society." For example, Richard Trevellick, a nineteenth-century organizer for the National Labor Union, wrote; "Add another two hours to the liberty term, and we shall increase the ratio of progress threefold. . .laboring men and women educated to a standard of physical, mental, moral and social excellence . . .will be. . .security against idleness, vice, degradation and misery" (Roediger, 1980, p. 5).

The "progressive shortening of the hours of labor" was a distinctive working-class vision of liberty because it was at odds with the dominant, laissez-faire liberalism of the nineteenth century. Propertied classes and businessmen understood liberty primarily as government protection of property rights and contracts. Workers used the same language of liberty to justify their right to sell their labor when and as they pleased, shocking the sensibilities of those who understood liberty in terms of ownership and the right to do business. Workers clung to the Declaration of Independence's "Pursuit of Happiness," attempting to realize this promise by forcing reductions in working hours. Labor's initial success with the ten-hour day was reinforcement by Martin Van Buren's ten-hour executive order in 1840. Even though it applied only to work under government contracts, the order helped establish a national standard.

## The Eight-Hour Day

After the Civil War, labor continued to pursue the "progressive shortening of the hours of labor," opening a new initiative for the eight-hour day. The short-lived National Labor Union organized to pressure Congress to pass eight-hour legislation. The Knights of Labor was more effective, making good on its original promise to be an advocate for the eight-hour day. In the 1870s and 1880s, this issue, above all others, heightened awareness of labor's struggles and won vital public support.

The eight-hour struggle lasted for fifty years and was the focus of much of labor's activities. Some of the most notable events in the history of labor involved this aspect of the shorter-hours struggle, most notably the Haymarket Massacre in Chicago in 1886.

In 1868, Congress passed an eight-hour day for government employees. After government officials reduced pay proportionally, Ulysses S. Grant issued two executive orders in 1869 and 1872, affirming the eight-hour day with the same wages, to little effect. It was not until 1892 that Congress passed an effective eight-hour day for all federal workers, with no pay cut. Subsequently, the issue was an integral part of reform politics through Franklin Delano Roosevelt's second term. Reduction of work hours featured prominently in the Populists' Omaha platform in 1892 as well as Theodore Roosevelt's 1912 Bull Moose platform and campaign, appearing again in both the Democratic and Republican platforms in 1932.

But the eight-hour day was slow in coming. Notwithstanding labor's concerted efforts, it was not until Woodrow Wilson's administration that the eight-hour day came near to being a national standard. The reasons for this eventual success were complex, including the fruition of labor's long struggle, federal railroad legislation, and state laws.

However, one of the most important was the uncharacteristic support of some businessmen and managers. "Scientific managers" such as Frederick Taylor, initiating the modern profession of business administration, labored to discover the obvious: that most workers got tired after working eight hours and were much less productive afterward. Thus, managers proclaimed, it made sound business sense to lay on another shift of fresh, productive workers after eight hours.

Following the "discovery" of fatigue, business managers throughout the nation began to institute the short schedule, particularly in continuous industries. However, the deal came with significant strings attached. Attempting to control the workplace totally, these first modern business managers offered workers a hard bargain: give up control at the workplace to "science" and rational organization in exchange for increased freedom and control represented by more time off the job.

This offer divided workers, and continues to do so. Many have been willing to make the trade, giving up on the possibility of reforming the workplace. However, most workers have resisted the deal, pressing to regain increased control at work at the same time realizing the increased freedom represented by leisure's expansion. The control of one's life represented by freedom from work has not excluded the struggle to regain freedom and control at work.

Following one of its culminating eight-hour victories, the steel strike of 1919, labor began to press for a shorter workweek during the 1920s. Inspired by the Jewish communities in the Northeast, which had initiated a movement of their own to reclaim their traditional Sabbath, labor pressed for half days off on Saturday, and then for a five-day week. Again, labor found dubious support from businesspeople such as Henry Ford, who instituted a five-day week with no pay cut in 1926, but attaching the loss of control qualification.

Flush with success with the shorter workweek, organized labor turned to the six-hour day as the remedy for unemployment when the Great Depression began. Union leaders had always argued that shorter hours were necessary to balance labor supply and demand. The Great Depression brought this traditional remedy to center stage in American politics, and labor redoubled its efforts to reduce work time "to its lowest terms."

## Good Reasons for Shorter Hours: Power, Education, and Culture

During the century of shorter hours, labor and workers gave substantial meaning to the liberty rhetoric present at the start of the movement. Through time, labor defined in detail what this new freedom was for; political participation and worker education headed the list. The struggle for shorter hours developed as a leisure move-

ment as ordinary working people filled the cultural space opening up in their lives.

From the beginning of the shorter hours process, workers identified leisure with political participation, initially asking simply for time enough to vote. However, labor soon realized the potential that expanding leisure represented for increased political involvement and power. Expanding leisure provided ordinary people with time for discussing, debating, and articulating their plight and points of view in the political arena. It provided unprecedented opportunities for political campaigning and union organization. Leisure was a new social interstice for engagement and dissent, for the construction of a working-class identity, and for its effective political expression.

Union leaders organized the first national unions to pressure state and local governments to support labor's political agenda, primarily, the progressive shortening of the hours of labor.

Arguably the most vocal and certainly the most consistent opposition to work reduction came from those who believed that "idle hands are the Devil's workshop"; that shorter hours "radicalized" ordinary people. Those in power, more than any other group, realized that workers were using their "extra" time to gain political advantage and challenge existing power structures.

Shorter hours began to give substance to Abraham Lincoln's vision of a rebirth of liberty as government for, of, and by the people. Increased leisure helped to lay the foundations of a true democracy of ordinary working people. Beginning to transform politics into a participatory activity, leisure helped to level the political playing field. Those who were spending the new coin of time to gain access to the political process began to challenge the power of wealth and position.

Part of labor's political strategy involved "worker education." Unions opened night schools, provided a host of educational resources for workers, and vigorously supported public education as ways to inform workers about public issues and give them necessary communication skills for political engagement. However, workers also embraced the new educational opportunities as ways to improve their leisure. Just as the new free time began to provide ordinary people access to politics, leisure enriched by education offered the possibility of an increased civic engagement and democratic participation in cultural activities. The focus of the early adult educational effort was of course basic literacy and vocational training. Teachers were surprised to find workers requesting courses in the liberal and even fine arts.

The night schools that flourished in the early twentieth century were, at least in part, a response to new aspirations among workers who found expanded opportunities to express and create their own culture. Just as leisure had begun to disperse political power, so, too, the new free time enabled a challenge to traditional elite forms of cultural creation and expression. Gaining a modicum of political power, workers also sought fledgling access to the finest human achievements in literature, arts, and sciences.

However, the more important kind of cultural expression and creation made available by the new leisure had to do with the daily lives of ordinary people. The quotidian—ordinary time with family, with friends at the local bar, with neighbors sitting on the front porch—was the primary beneficiary of the new leisure.

The work reduction movement, developing into a leisure movement, represented a genuinely democratic vision of progress. Founded on advances in civic arenas such as the family, community, voluntary associations, and religious institutions, this vision of human advancement was distinctive because it represented an alternative to dominant ideas of progress as extensions of national power and prestige (Manifest Destiny) and as the unlimited expansion of industrial production and accumulations of wealth.

As ordinary people began to live with the new time won from work, new kinds of leisure infrastructures—private, public, and commercial—formed. Saloons, benevolent associations, ethnic societies, vacations and vacation resorts, travel opportunities, lunchrooms, poolrooms, bowling allies, fraternal clubs, social centers, and churches and synagogues provided workers with places and new ways to express traditional cultures, create new cultural forms, and to "fashion their [own] understanding and response to the problems of industrial life" (Hunnicutt, 1988, p. 12). Serving to enrich and transform the quotidian, this leisure infrastructure also laid a foundation for expanding working-class self-awareness.

Just as important is the fact that Americans began to build up infrastructures of "social capital": networks of free associations, reservoirs of goodwill and conviviality, webs of common discourse and understanding, agreement/meaning. The political scientist Robert Putnam has argued convincingly that such "social capital" is the bedrock of democracies, without which political order and economic health are endangered. Others scholars, following Jürgen Habermas, propose that culture is formed and sustained by such systems of shared meaning—that "communicative action" taking place in the civic arena, is more im-

portant for social well-being and stability than expanding material wealth.

## Leisure's Supporters: Founders, Intellectuals, Reformers, Industrialists

Since the Revolution, some of the most articulate and influential Americans embraced versions of "humane," or "moral," progress similar to what workers were envisioning. John Adams, for example, described what he thought freedom would bring to future generations. Progress would be a movement beyond practical politics and commerce into an arena where the "pursuit of happiness" would be possible. During activities that were worthwhile in and of themselves—music and the fine arts, the life of the mind, the experience of beauty—Americans might come to realize the full promise of freedom.

Certainly his was an elite view—something he envisioned for *his* children. Nevertheless, like the liberal promises of the Declaration of Independence, the cultural promise of humane progress was democratized as it attached to the work reduction movement.

A vital part of the leisure movement in the United States was the leisure visions of intellectuals and social critics who saw work reduction as the culmination of human progress. Progress in two parts—material and "moral"—was at the heart of the Enlightenment. Enlightenment figures such as Thomas Jefferson believed that reason would free humans from the tyranny of tradition and arbitrary rule. Just as importantly, science would also free humans from poverty and need. Understanding nature, humans would create the technology necessary to free themselves from the tyranny of necessity. "Labor-saving devices" were science's original social mandate, justifying and legitimizing science and technology's growth through the nineteenth and early twentieth centuries. The Enlightenment founded the enduring expectation that reason would eventually free humans to concentrate more on how to live than on how to make a living.

Nineteenth-century economists such as John Stuart Mill made similar claims. Mill added a criticism of the irrational increase and accumulation of wealth beyond reasonable limits, proposing instead the expansion of leisure as the rational alternative. According to Mill and others who followed, such as R. H. Tawney (British economic historian and influential social critic and reformer of the early twentieth century), human material needs were finite. Once they were met, a realistic economic possibility considering the growth of science and technology, the economy should become "stationary." Difficulties would arise if the industrial nations, besotted by their success or driven by greed, turned their backs on work reduction. If progress were redefined irrationally as ever-new luxuries and preposterous accumulations of wealth, a heavy price would be paid. Not only would the exploitation of workers continue (as they were made to work longer than "necessary"), nature would be destroyed and the promise of "moral" progress lost.

Work reduction was the rational course, the only alternative to material "progress" beyond reasonable levels. In a stationary economy, "no one is poor, no one desires to be richer." Labor would be paid a fair wage. Wealth accumulations would be held in check. Humans would then make real progress, having "sufficient leisure, both physical and mental. . .to cultivate freely the graces of life."

Mill's version of rational progress was influential in the United States, popularized by one of the best-known American economists of the early twentieth century, Simon Patten. Patten agreed that "too much work" in the age of abundance would create a generation of "gluttons," who in their single-minded scramble for more, gradually lost sight of the "non-economic" pleasures and challenges life offered (Hunnicutt, 1988, p. 34).

Arguably, the most articulate advocate of "moral" progress was the economist/theologian Monsignor John Ryan. One of the most prominent American economists during the New Deal, Ryan made the same points Mill, Tawney, and Patten made; increasing leisure represented reasonable progress, but perpetual economic growth was irrational and hence unsustainable.

However, Ryan expanded this economic argument, presenting a more extensive moral defense of shorter work hours. Ryan began by making organized labor's point—that shorter hours would provide unemployment relief during the Great Depression. He went on to show that shorter hours was the most effective way to redistribute wealth automatically, guarding against growing misdistributions of wealth and power that would eventually doom democracies.

Workers demanding more leisure would make labor scarcer and hence better paid. Workers with more income would be able to demand effectively that adequate necessities be produced. Capital would be forced to follow and to abandon luxuries. Wealth, instead of pooling in large fortunes and corporations, would flow into society in the form of leisure, avoiding unreasonable accumulations that are natural parts of expanding economies based on the perpetual creation of new goods and services.

Finally, Ryan added a vision of what progress as leisure offered humanity. Following the wisdom of thousands of years of Western civilization, he concluded:

> . . .When men have produced sufficient necessaries and reasonable comforts and conveniences to supply all the population, they should spend what time is left. . .in the pursuit of the higher life. If American industries can make the requisite leisure possible, they will have provided at least the opportunity for a more rational society than any people has yet enjoyed.. . . [Authentic] human life. . .consists in thinking, knowing, communing, loving, serving, and giving, rather than in having.. . . Its supreme demand is that we should know more and love more, and that we should strive to know the best that is to be known and to love the best that is to be loved (Hunnicutt, 1988, p. 97).

Becoming aware of the 100-year-long work reduction process, economists confidently predicted that work's long-term decline would continue. John Maynard Keynes, the best-known economist of the century, wrote in the early 1930s: "When we reach the point when the world produces all the goods that it needs in two days, as it inevitably will. . .we must turn our attention to the great problem of what to do with our leisure." Indeed the time was rapidly approaching when "three hours [work] a day [will be] quite enough to satisfy the old Adam in most of us!" (p. 369).

Keynes understood the coming age of leisure more as a challenge than a sure promise. Even though leisure opened up progress in extra-economic realms of freedom, humans would still have to struggle. Realizing leisure's promise of humane freedom would be humanity's last, most profound challenge, greater even than "solving the economic problem."

Economists were not alone in their hopes for and concerns about increased leisure. For decades before and after the turn of the twentieth century, writers recognized that industrial progress was nearing the time when everyone would have "enough." Premised on "necessity's obsolescence," utopian books flooded the market after the 1888 publication of Bellamy's *Looking Backward*, many employing 'the traditional utopian theme of the four- or six-hour workday. Bellamy set the tone, imagining a twenty-first-century world blessed by technology that freed humans from work and "necessity" for the best part of their lives. The inhabitants of Bellamy's "perfect society," realizing that "it is not our labor, but the higher and larger activities. . .the intellectual and spiritual enjoyments and pursuits. . .that are. . .the main business of life," founded their society on leisure. Work was put in its proper, rational place as means to an end rather than an end in itself.

This view of progress spread even to conservative business people. Walter Gifford, president of AT&T, the largest corporation in the United States in the 1920s, was one of several business leaders who recognized that "industry. . .has gained a new and astonishing vision." The final, best achievement of business and the free market need not be perpetual economic growth and everlasting consumerism, but "a new type of civilization," in which "how to make a living becomes less important than how to live." As it had been doing for a century,

> machinery will increasingly take the load off men's shoulders. . . .Every one of us will have more chance to do what he wills, which means greater opportunity, both materially and spiritually. . . .[Steadily decreasing work hours] will give us time to cultivate the art of living, give us a better opportunity for. . .the arts, enlarge the comforts and satisfaction of the mind and spirit, as material well-being feeds the comforts of the body (Gwinn).

A few such "liberation capitalists" embraced this view, including the British soap-king Lord Leverhulm and American cereal maker W. K. Kellogg. Such a vision permeated the age, shared by people across the political spectrum. Educators began to prepare for the coming age of leisure, gearing their curricula to "education for the worthy use of leisure," one of the National Education Association's "Cardinal Objectives of Education." Academics found new, even pressing reasons to continue teaching the liberal arts, the traditional heart of higher education. A playground and recreation movement formed and began to build parks, community centers, and recreation centers to serve the new leisure. Labor leaders, fighting for five-day week and the six-hour day, employed the vision to rally their forces and popularize their cause. Politicians, seeking labor's support, employed similar rhetoric, particularly during the 1920s and Great Depression. Scientists and engineers such as Charles Proteus Steinmetz and B. F. Skinner, continuing to champion "labor-saving devices," claimed to be the guarantors of expanding leisure for "higher" human achievements.

Religious leaders, particularly Jewish leaders of the Sabbath crusade, saw in the new leisure the possibility of a regeneration of the life of the spirit and the renewed importance of religious practice. Indeed, leisure asked one of the most profound of religious questions, "What is worth doing in and for itself?" Faced with this awful question in their new freedom, humans would automatically turn to the age-old insights found only in the traditional religions. Musicians, artists, novelists and poets began to explore local folk culture, leading the way to what they envisioned would be a renaissance of democratic cultural creation and participation.

## The End of Shorter Hours

However, the work reduction movement ended after World War II. The vision of humane progress founded on leisure's expansion, and the leisure movement it engendered, faded as well (Hunnicutt, 1988, pp. 1–8).

Even though productivity rates have increased steadily since the Great Depression, Americans have chosen to express the wealth that increased productivity represents by buying more rather than working less—even to the point of "selling off" leisure to work and buy more. One of the primary reason for this dramatic historic change is the emergence of consumerism in the 1920s—a time when advertising came of age and marketing departments became more important than production departments in companies across the nation. In the 1920s, this development was called the "New Economic Gospel of Consumption," a trend Herbert Hoover's Committee on Recent Economic Changes documented in detail. Business embarked on a campaign to convince Americans that it was better to buy new, and more things than to keep reducing work hours—a campaign that shows little sign of slowing down. Periodically, when the need arose, the campaign has been reaffirmed, such as during the 1950s and 1990s.

The second reason the expansion of leisure ended may be discovered in the politics of the Great Depression. During the 1930s, Roosevelt committed government to the support of the "New Economic Gospel of Consumption," beginning the federal underwriting of "managed capitalism." Combating unemployment, Roosevelt committed government to perpetually create new work to replace the work being "lost" to increased productivity. Defining, for the first time and arbitrarily, "full-time jobs" as forty hours or better per week, Roosevelt opposed work sharing (a legislated solution to unemployment, supported by labor that would have advanced the century-long work reduction process in order to stabilize the economy). Instead, he inaugurated governmental programs and policies supporting economic expansion, liberal treasury policy, deficit spending (to "re-employ the idleness"), public works projects, expanding government payrolls, and subsidies to business.

Since the depression, government policy has been constant, to expand the economy by whatever means necessary in order to assure "full employment." The alternative political solution to unemployment, work reduction, has been virtually lost in the United States, even though the issue has reappeared in Europe.

Whereas working hours remained constant, from just after WWII until the 1970s, some observers argue persuasively that they reversed direction and expanded dramatically since the mid-1970s; that the average Joe or Jill works over a month more now. Whereas Keynes predicted that the "challenge of leisure" would emerge by the middle of the twentieth century, the public issue troubling the industrial nations at the close of the century was "overwork." The media continued into this century to be filled with stories about the damage done to communities and families, to the health of individuals and the nations, by the epidemic of longer work hours.

Scholars quibble, making much over "incremental advances" in work reductions, and looking diligently for "trends." Economists, for example, examine minute fluctuations in the average retirement age, concluding that the leisure of retirement may have increased, slightly. Slight differences in vacation time are similarly touted as significant. The facts that Europeans have four to five weeks of vacation, while vacations in the United States have averaged two weeks for over sixty years, are seen as evidence that working time may still be changing in important ways—that Europe may be "leading" the way for longer U.S. vacations.

However, just as many observers now predict later retirements, increased overtime, expanding numbers of people joining the work force, and longer hours in general as the economy sags, government debt mounts, and what the average American "needs" continually expands.

But the most significant change correlating to the historical variations in leisure's expansion and contraction; to the century-long decline in working hours, the subsequent "end of shorter hours," and the modern "overwork" phenomenon, is cultural. In the nineteenth and early twentieth centuries, workers, union leaders, politicians, intellectuals, dreamers, reformers, and industrialists understood human progress, in part, as the open-ended expansion of leisure. Work would soon become subordinate to leisure. Humans would solve, for once and for all, the "economic problem." Making a living would soon take second place to having a life.

By contrast, at the beginning of the twenty-first century, few Americans remained who looked forward to the "progressive shortening of the hours of labor." Few continued to see expanding leisure as the antidote to capital-

ism's dangerous excesses, the way to protect the environment, a strategy to relieve the exploitation of workers, or the culmination of progress and liberty. Few expected "the economy" would be less of a problem in the future than it was then. This change was the most important way to explain the "end of shorter hours."

Without labor's larger dream of "reducing human labor to its lowest terms," small fluctuations in working days, weeks, months, or years did not represent significant "trends." The century-long trend of work reduction, which saw working hours cut virtually in half, was the fruit of a vision.

Before significant new "trends" in the expansion of leisure are claimed, the opposing, now-dominant vision of the perpetual expansion of the economy and "standard of living," as well as the modern project to re-create "full-time" work for everyone forevermore, must be challenged, and the old vision of leisure as the place for human progress, or something similar, must be recovered.

*See also:* Interwar Leisure and Recreation, Rational Recreation and Self-Improvement, Shortage of Leisure, Working-Class Leisure Lifestyles

**BIBLIOGRAPHY**

Cahill, Marion Cotter. *Shorter Hours: A Study of the Movement Since the Civil War.* New York: Columbia University Press, 1932.

Commons, John Rogers, David Joseph Saposs, Helen Laura Sumner Woodbury, Edward Becker Mittelman, Henry Elmer Hoagland, John B. Andrews, Selig Perlman, Don D. Lescohier, Elizabeth Brandeis, and Philip Taft. *History of Labour in the United States.* New York: Macmillan Company, 1918.

Cross, Gary S. *Worktime and Industrialization: An International History, Labor and Social Change.* Philadelphia: Temple University Press, 1988.

———. *A Quest for Time: The Reduction of Work in Britain and France, 1840–1940.* Berkeley: University of California Press, 1989.

Gordon, Suzanne. *Prisoners of Men's Dreams: Striking Out for a New Feminine Future.* 1st ed. Boston: Little, Brown and Company 1991.

Gorz, Andreâ. *Critique of Economic Reason.* New York: Verso, 1989.

Gutenberg Internet Project. Available from http://www.ibiblio.org.

Gwinn, Sherman. "Days of Drudgery Will Soon Be Over: An Interview with Walter S. Gifford." *American Magazine* (November 1928).

Heighton, William. "An Address to the Members of Trade Societies and to the Working Classes Generally." Philadelphia, Historical Society of Pennsylvania Archives, 1827.

Hinrichs, K., William Roche, and Carmen Sirianni. *Working Time in Transition: The Political Economy of Working Hours in Industrial Nations, Labor and Social Change.* Philadelphia: Temple University Press, 1991.

Hunnicutt, Benjamin Kline. *Work Without End: Abandoning Shorter Hours for the Right to Work, Labor and Social Change.* Philadelphia: Temple University Press, 1988.

———. *Kellogg's Six-Hour Day, Labor and Social Change.* Philadelphia: Temple University Press, 1996.

Jenkins, Clive, and Barrie Sherman. *The Collapse of Work.* London: Eyre Methuen, 1979.

Jones, Ethel B. *An Investigation of the Stability of Hours of Work per Week in Manufacturing, 1947–1970.* Athens, Ga.: Division of Research, College of Business Administration, University of Georgia, 1974.

Keynes, John Maynard. *Essays in Persuasion.* London: Macmillan, 1933.

Millis, Harry Alvin, and Royal Ewert Montgomery. *Organized Labor.* 1st edition. *Labor Movement in Fiction and Non-Fiction.* New York: AMS Press, 1976.

National Bureau of Economic Research, and Edward Eyre Hunt. *Recent Economic Changes in the United States; Report of the Committee on Recent Economic Changes, of the President's Conference on Unemployment, Herbert Hoover, Chairman, Including the Reports of a Special Staff of the National Bureau of Economic Research, Inc.* 1st ed. New York: McGraw-Hill Book Company, 1929.

Owen, John D. *The Price of Leisure: An Economic Analysis of the Demand for Leisure Time.* Rotterdam, The Netherlands: Rotterdam University Press, 1969.

———. *Working Hours: An Economic Analysis.* Lexington, Mass.: Lexington Books, 1979.

President's Research Committee on Social Trends., and Wesley Clair Mitchell. *Recent Social Trends in the United States: Report of the President's Research Committee on Social Trends.* New York: McGraw-Hill Book Company, 1933.

Ranciáere, Jacques. *La Nuit des Prolâetaires, Espace du Politique.* Paris: Fayard, 1981.

Roediger, David R. "The Movement for the Shorter Working Day in the United States Before 1866." Ph.D. dissertation, Northwestern University, 1980.

Roediger, David R., and Philip Sheldon Foner. *Our Own Time: A History of American Labor and the Working Day.* New York: Greenwood Press, 1989.

Rosenzweig, Roy. *Eight Hours for What We Will: Workers and Leisure in an Industrial City, 1870–1920, Interdisciplinary Perspectives on Modern History.* New York: Cambridge University Press, 1983.

Rybczynski, Witold. *Waiting for the Weekend.* New York: Viking, 1991.

Schor, Juliet. *The Overworked American: The Unexpected Decline of Leisure.* New York: Basic Books, 1991.

*Benjamin Kline Hunnicutt*

# EXTREME SPORTS

Extreme sports, variously known as "whiz" sports, adventure sports, "panic" sports, alternative sports, "X" sports, and, in 2004 as "action" sports, describe a way of being, rather than a finite set of activities. Though ESPN (Entertainment and Sports Programming Network, based in the United States) may have first successfully coined the term "extreme sport" in alignment with their 1995-produced Extreme Games, the types of activities that compose "extreme" sports, linked somewhat to sport, have been around for many years. The key common element in extreme sports appears to be a desire by the participant for what Roger Caillois, in his book *Man, Play, and Games,* termed "vertigo" in physical activity. Secondary reasons for participating seem to include a desire to meet challenges that have never been met, akin to the challenge of natural elements as obstacles and coparticipants; a desire, at least in the late twentieth century, by participants to be in control of their own physical being, without the intrusion of adult supervision and guidance; a lived-rhetoric that is antiestablishment in its nature.

But, fundamentally, the "extreme" element of these sports is an insistence on the aspects of physical movement that may disorient, temporarily confuse, or cause a so-called "adrenaline rush" to the participant. In fact, sport psychologists are exploring the possibility that there may be a gene keyed to a need for such thrill seeking in certain individuals. However, it is clear that, as a socially constructed model, the idea of "extreme sports" resonates with a Westernized justification of personal hedonism that is becoming globalized. Certain individuals appear to seek activities that have been situated as out-of-the-ordinary, thrilling, and that involve both spatial and temporal extraordinary kinds of disorientation.

As a made-for-television activity, extreme sports has co-opted lifestyle activities such as roller blading (or in-line skating), skateboarding, snowboarding, street luge, bungee jumping, wakeboarding, and other grassroots forms of leisure and recreational activity for their broadcasts. In some cases, the co-optation has resulted in both mainstream and dominant acceptance and co-optation of the sports by larger governing bodies. In snowboarding, for example, according to Duncan Humphreys, the International Olympic Committee (IOC) co-opted the sport for the Olympics by assigning the oversight of snowboarding to the Federation Internationale du Ski (FIS). By assigning oversight to a *ski* federation, the IOC alienated many snowboarders who believed in their independence and in their outsider status in relation to mainstream sport.

While resistance to mainstream co-optation is a common ethos that runs through many of the extreme sports, such resistance can result in the sport remaining underground and underappreciated. In some cases, such as bungee jumping (which was in the Extreme Games in 1995 and 1996), resistance to normative value structures and disinterest by the media still runs high, and the activity has been largely ignored. However, summertime extreme sports include such activities as sport climbing, stunt bike riding, extreme adventure racing (much like the teams that compose the Eco-Challenge), and wakeboarding. With ESPN's advertising might, these sports have become more accepted through television exposure.

Finding the Summer Extreme Games potentially lucrative, in 1997, ESPN began the Winter X Games. The sports initially included were snowboarding, supermodified shovel racing, ice climbing, snow mountain bike racing, and crossover slope-style snowboarding. The next year, ESPN included snocross, with snowmobiles racing one another, multiple contestant free skiing, multiple contestant snowboarding, snow mountain bike racing, individual snowboarding (slope-style, big air, and half-pipe), and speed ice climbing.

## Historical Antecedents of Extreme Sports

The will to challenge the limits of human ability and to confront and surpass natural barriers has been a part of human physical endeavors for many thousands of years. Any so-called "superhuman" feat (such as the building of the Pyramids, creation of the Roman Appian Way, the design and execution of the Great Wall of China, or the erection of the Golden Gate Bridge) could categorically be classed within this grouping. However, examples of "sporting" extremism also abound.

While based in sacred elements, the ancient Mayans played ball games, including the game of *tlachtli*, in an open court, sometimes to the death. The losing captain would be decapitated, but this was considered an honor and was believed to convey him expeditiously to his afterlife. In the Middle Ages, for example, whole villages participated in village-versus-village games, occasionally resulting in death. One such game was *ponte*. In this capture the flag–like game, the citizens met on a bridge, and jabbed or knocked at one another with a *targone*, a kind of jousting stick.

But the real advent of extremelike sports came about with the growing presence of an individuated ethos within sport. Comparisons between individuals, teams, and na-

tions served as real antecedents to thrill-seeking types of sports. Many origination stories prevail for the current extreme sports landscape, but a few examples of activities throughout the ages will suffice. Since its advent in 1783, ballooning and balloon races have been a part of the extreme landscape; a form of "in-line" skating is said to have begun in the early 1700s in Holland, when someone fastened wooden spools to his shoes to simulate ice skating during the nonwinter months; ancient Polynesians were said to both body surf and surf with board planks; bullfighting began in 1133, in Vera, Logroño; some forms of spelunking and competitive caving have existed for centuries; cliff diving has been, in some forms, in existence as long as there have been courageous souls to attempt it. And the list goes on.

But there have also been, within the list of sport activities, a variety of ways of testing one's limits. Championship bare-knuckles boxing, which proliferated in the 1800s in the western world particularly, evolved into endurance contests, where one man would be left standing after dozens of rounds. Underwater swimming for distance, for time, for depth, for speed down and back up—all of these ways were fabricated in order to somehow test the limits of human endurance and fortitude. Round-the-world balloon and yacht races have flourished for years. Mechanized vehicular races—such as airplane speed or endurance races—also would fall into the category of extreme sports, and they would be antecedents to BMX races, monster truck contests, and so forth, that were in vogue in the early 2000s. All of these forms of sporting endeavor tested the concept of "extreme," for as soon as one type of activity became extreme, another would spring up to replace it.

The common element connecting most of these activities was a test of time, of space, or of both time and space. Limits in a multitude of dimensions seem to characterize whether an activity is "extreme" or merely mainstream. And the bettering of old records—records being, according to Allen Guttmann (via Max Weber), a fairly modernist concept in sports—certainly may create more interest in the sport activity.

## Proliferation of Extreme Sports

Although ESPN is clearly credited as the primary corporate source promoting extreme sports, individuals and other corporations have also had an impact on the proliferation of extreme activities in the popular imaginary, electronic media, and leisure-time pursuits. Such activities as boarding (including surfing, skateboarding, snowboarding, Snurfing, windsurfing), sailing (including sky surfing, parasailing, hang-gliding, windsurfing, sailing, wakeboarding), and motor-driven sports (such as motocross, jet-skiing, one-time motorcycle leaps, snowmobiling) all have common characteristics, which serve to drive ever-new amalgams of these activities. And while ESPN has dominated the global cable market in purveying such sport forms through broadcasts of the Winter and Summer X Games, other competitive "Olympic style" events, as well as weekly local or regional events, have blossomed. The process of such proliferation has tended to follow the historical process of the spread of sports generally.

First, there are the innovators of the sport, individuals who, with an idea like fastening roller skate wheels to the bottom of a board, experiment with combinations of things already known and those unknown. Then there is a core group of those who practice, refine, and demonstrate the new activity. Though this group tends to be small, the members seek new participants. However, truly mass participation starts fairly slowly, with a general resistance by the innovators of the new activity toward an eventual and, some practitioners say, inevitable "spoiling" of their space, time, and ethos.

But as the mass participation begins to catch on, critical mass is approached, and the sports begin to conform more to massified, mainstream types of sport activities in their use of space, alignment with corporate interests, time constraints, and mainstream acceptance of ethos, styles, and argot. As well, the mainstream acceptance seems to facilitate a lessening of the cultural impression that the activity is, indeed, "extreme" or innovative. And then the cycle, with a new amalgamated activity, begins again.

Many of the new activities are drawn eclectically or as amalgamations from other sport forms. For example, as identified in Joe Tomlinson's book *The Ultimate Encyclopedia of Extreme Sports,* there is land and ice yachting, combining water-based sailing efforts on a different surface; there is BASE jumping, or "sky-diving" from land-based implements such as buildings, antenna towers, spans, and earth; there is free diving, where an individual ocean dives for depth, the current record being over 400 feet.

While these activities and sports are not vigorously promoted by the media, the media do have an active role in the public's acceptance for such activities. Not only do extreme athletes compete in the weeklong ESPN X Games in summer and winter, but they also have a variety of venues in which to perform and, ultimately, make a living. Some of these media- and corporate-driven events include the Gravity Games, Sheshreds, Tony Hawk's Boom Boom Huckjam Tour, the Vans Triple Crown, and

a variety of other sport-specific national and international tours. Prior to the X Games, for example, there are regional competitions that stimulate interest in local and international competitions, creating greater numbers of spectators who identify with the athletes. Often, equipment or clothing companies eager to align themselves with the "authentic" extreme sports sponsor these events. The events also may consist of traveling groups of "professional" athletes, who, in a sense, are "barnstorming" through the country promoting their sport.

## Examples of Extreme Sports

Many individuals from a variety of nations have experimented with the extreme elements of sports' activities. Robert Rinehart has listed a variety of these innovative sport forms. Some of the nonmainstream sporting events that might be classified as "extreme" include (but are not limited to) the following: "hang gliding, high wire, ski flying, soaring, caving, land and ice yachting (ice sailing), mountainboarding, showshoeing, speed biking, speed skiing, steep skiing, air chair, Jet Skiing, open water swimming, powerboat racing, snorkeling, speed sailing, . . . trifoiling . . . skateboarding, whitewater kayaking . . . professional beach volleyball [and korfball]" (though these may be seen as marginalized mainstream sports). There are "ultimate fighting . . . windsurfing, surfing . . . "extreme" skiing, deep-water diving (fixed weight, variable weight, and absolute diving), paragliding, sandboarding, and the Miner's Olympics." Other activities include "para-bungee (bungee from a hot-air balloon), bungee from a helicopter, underwater hockey, canoe polo, bicycle polo, jai alai (which, similar to pelota, is a new-world form with slightly different cultural significance, rule structure, and context), scuba (self contained underwater breathing apparatus) diving (e.g., for depth, time under, etc.), BASE jumping, indoor climbing (artificial climbing wall), ultra marathoning, netball, and bicycle stunt and freestyle" (p. 506). As Peter Donnelly points out, "There is also real risk—in solo climbing, deep sea diving, ocean yacht racing, hot air balloon epics, Himalayan and other high altitude mountaineering. . . . (1997).

As in most of the extreme world, much of the tours, sports, competitions, and stars and equipment are in rapid flux, vying for space in the ever-expanding extreme universe. The "extreme-scape" is constantly changing, so that new sports, contests, tricks, success and failure rates, critical mass of participants and spectators, and corporate intervention and sponsorship are always in flux. But the constants for these activities that are considered extreme appear to be perceived high risk factor, an emphasis on vertiginous aspects of physicality, usually a stress on individuality, and a shared antimainstream ethos.

*See also:* Bicycling; Mountain Climbing; Olympics; Parachute Jumping; Rock Climbing; Scuba Diving/Snorkeling; Skateboarding; Skiing, Alpine; Snowboarding; Triathlons; Wind Surfing

## BIBLIOGRAPHY

Beal, Becky. "Disqualifying the Official: An Exploration of Social Resistance through the Subculture of Skateboarding," *Sociology of Sport Journal.* 12 (1995): 252–267.

———. "Alternative Masculinity and its Effects on Gender Relations in the Subculture of Skateboarding," *Journal of Sport Behavior.* 19 (3) (1996): 204–220.

Caillois, Roger. *Man, Play, and Games.* New York: Free Press, 1961.

Donnelly, Peter. "Re: Still More on X-Games. Sociological Aspects of Sports Discussion." Personal correspondence. 3 February 1997.

Guttmann, Allen. *From Ritual to Record: The Nature of Modern Sports.* New York: Columbia University Press, 1978.

Rinehart, Robert E., and Synthia S. Sydnor, eds. *To the Extreme: Alternative Sports, Inside and Out.* Albany, N.Y.: State University of New York Press, 2003.

Rinehart, Robert E. "Emerging Arriving Sport: Alternatives to Formal Sports." In *Handbook of Sports Studies.* Edited by Jay Coakley and Eric Dunning. London: Sage Publications, 2000.

Wheaton, Belinda. "'New Lads'? Masculinities and the 'New Sport' Participant," *Men and Masculinities 2* (2000): 434–456.

*Robert E. Rinehart*

# FADS

A distinguishing characteristic of fads is quickness of rise and fall in popularity in concert with wide-ranging distribution. The fad itself is marked by play-like, leisure, or recreation associations, linked to desire rather than goals. Fads speak to wants rather than needs, and thus fit well in the areas of fashion, style, taste, and cultural preference.

Because fads are necessarily observable and communicable, they are typically identified as artifacts, behaviors, beliefs, materials, or objects. While they may exist with substantial interest and intensity, fads may usefully be defined as being short-lived and ultimately transient in nature. Because speed is so closely associated with the distribution of fads within a social setting, it is unlikely that they existed in pre-industrial times, at least in the form known in the early 2000s.

As a result, fads act as powerful elements of culture, quickly moving through it, free of apparent utility yet responding to traditional market forces. If local area shortages exist, grey market or even black market provision may come into being, mediating the demand for supply and reflecting popular demand for the fad material. Fads are often strongly embraced by participants, while the non-participating observer fails to understand the motivation involved, or the justification for the resources consumed.

Moreover, it may be difficult to differentiate among legitimate innovation, cultural diffusion, taste evolution, technological transition, tradition, routine self-expressive action and activity, and fad. Fads may burst into promi-nence, recede greatly from public view, and then settle into a niche of longtime use, perhaps to become a tradition of sorts. For example, hoola-hoops, a great fad of the 1950s, and Frisbees (the popular brand name of flying disks), enormously popular in the late 1960s, have become amusing, traditional items for young people and teens in the early twenty-first century. Apparently, the inherent enjoyment of these objects was durable and cross-generational.

In the 1970s, the number of eight-track cassette tape systems rose rapidly and dramatically, and then fell just as precipitously when better technology was introduced. In the last three decades of the twentieth century, racquetball clubs opened all over the nation, and the sport of racquetball became enormously popular. By the 1990s, many of these businesses had failed, and racquetball became just another game on the sports scene.

The miniaturization of electronic devices—such as the Sony Walkman radio and cassette tape player—that allowed commuters to enjoy their own music in private spread widely in the general population, predictably so because such devices solved an existing problem. These small machines sold rapidly when they came out in the early 1980s and were marketed with a great deal of attention to design and style, and they also offered a practical and useful response to an environmental condition.

Such combinations of style and practicality can also be found in fashion. In Renaissance Venice, *chopine* stilt shoes elevated women above the wet ground. These shoes then became popular again in the 1960s and once again in the 1990s, illustrating an example of a fashion-based fad.

**"Pet rock."** Once an advertising executive in California, Gary Dahl gained fame from his creation of the "Pet Rock," which was even accompanied by training manuals. Originally introduced at a gift show in San Francisco during August 1975, the "pet" came in a carrying case that resembled a real pet carrier. © *Corbis*

The published history of the "pet rock" fad, which may not be entirely accurate, offers insight into the transit of the phenomena. In 1975, Gary Dahl, apocryphally following a conversation about the hardship involved in caring for living pets, invented the "pet rock." Dahl crafted a clever handbook wittily describing the tongue-in-cheek care of one's large pebble (described in written accounts as a "Rosarita beach stone"), and ensconced the new pet in shredded padding in a special little box reminiscent of a pet carrier. The promoter pitched the gimmick at the San Francisco gift fair and soon enough, media coverage bloomed. Dahl's unusual idea was the focus of a half-page article in *Newsweek,* and he was invited for two visits on *The Tonight Show*. Sales went through the roof, and the promoter "reportedly" sold millions of dollars worth of pet rocks.

### Three Elements Encourage Fads to Exist

Presuming fads are undertaken for fun, or as self-expression, they will more likely exist if alternative, traditional ways of living have changed, are in a process of change, or are undergoing a period particularly receptive to embracing the "new." Fads must be communicated through the host population—the people who follow the fad—rapidly, so communications must be expedient. In the case of goods, the objects or material must be plentiful enough to be commonly available or reasonably accessible.

Historically, two important and closely-linked events took place that set the stage for fads to become a commonplace part of contemporary life. The distribution of the nation's people changed radically with the emergence of cities as the centers of employment, and an enormous increase in goods and services was made available due to the evolution of the factory system.

For fads to flourish, the host group must be receptive, and the means of production and the means and method of consumption must be supportive. During World War II, in the United States, fads tied to manufactured goods were rare, because industrial production was turned to satisfying the needs of the war effort. Following the war, that extraordinary productive capacity existed in a time of well-resourced consumers. Predictably, fads involving manufactured goods became more common.

The phenomena of fads seems far less common, perhaps rare or even virtually nonexistent, during the preindustrial period. During that period, there was little time for something seemingly as frivolous as a fad (which often does not lead to the betterment of society). Change and innovation certainly occurred, and people did alter the way they behaved, but such changes happened slowly, and only after it was proven that there was a need for a change. For example, a new plow might be invented and adapted, but only after it was shown to be an improvement over the previous plow. The industrial revolution, however, lead to the ability, and the need, to produce nonnecessary goods, which could be cheaply introduced into the marketplace. The introduction and great expansion of wage work created the opportunity to commodify many traditional features of agricultural life. In fact, in time, virtually all features of agricultural life would be commodified: patterns of labor, entertainment, folk manufacturing, and foods and beverages (for example, the advent of pasteurization allowed the canning of fruit juice and related health benefits).

The circumstances of the industrial revolution lead to active social change that fundamentally altered—and often extinguished—competing or alternative forms of entertainment, leisure, recreation, and self-expression. Some traditional rural pastimes conflicted with the needs of the factory system, and such pastime tended to be resistant to commercialization and the control of the ever more powerful industrial-merchant class. For example, wages spent on prostitution, street corner gambling, or other ad hoc vice could not also be spent buying manufactured goods or services on the legitimate market.

Urbanization accompanying industrialization pulled rural populations toward the high-density areas; the invention of sophisticated mechanical farm machinery foreshadowed that those populations would begin to be pushed away from rural areas by dwindling labor demands. Although family relationships and interrelationships are never static, to many observers the changes taking place at that time were new and dangerous. Structural changes took place, with the working class adapting to new circumstances through a typical vocabulary of appropriation, hybridization and reconstitution, resistance, and subsumation. That is, the working class took over ideas it came into contact with, as people blended their own ways of doing things with new ways; alternately, they resisted making any change or they buried cultural habits out of sight.

As an example of this, amateur naturalism bloomed in the late 1800s as an enormous fad on the coattails of the cheap manufacture of nature and travel books. The ability to act on the impulse to become a "serious amateur" was provided by the invention of fast transportation to and from the countryside via steam rail.

Rural settings became identified with expressive leisure instead of labor, as it was for agricultural workers. Moreover, rail business bosses understood that by providing an incentive to travel, they added a new market to the existing profit-making services. Indeed, it was a powerful amalgam of agendas—influential hunters and transportation barons—that shouldered legislation into being that created the nation's astonishing treasure of parks and natural or wilderness lands. The bubble of amateur naturalism burst soon enough, but the invented industry of leisure and recreation travel is the world's second biggest business in the early 2000s.

## Fads: Means and Methods, Opportunity, and Motivation

It might be argued that fads have always existed, that they were just quieter, smaller, and restricted in geography prior to the means, methods, and opportunity for the phenomena to be expansive and broadly distributed. However, although there is no accepted etymology for the word "fad," the record seems to show that it first appears on or very shortly after 1867. In the contemporary meaning, fads are seen as having characteristics that can only exist under certain conditions, and they are closely related to leisure—done only for self-expression. Perhaps, as with hoola-hoop, pet rocks, or short-lived "celebrity diets," it is useful to consider magnitude. The more fully and powerfully the behavior, event, or item fits the defining characteristics, the higher the confidence that it may usefully be categorized as a legitimate fad.

Fads can be predicted to come into being when the ability to participate and the presence of the necessary elements co-exist with the willingness for an individual, as a member of a participant group, to take part. In industrialized settings, this is clearly seen by the production of goods or services, and by the ability of the consumer to respond. Because consumers can alter, combine, usurp, resist, and otherwise respond in ways differently from the provider's intention, fads might well involve an unusual or innovative use of a product or service. Thus, a fad can be said to be a type of leisure that has no intended goal beyond self-expression. Fads may be, at the same time, recreation. But, since the fad can conceivably increase risk or jeopardy for the participant, fads may also absolutely fail the requirement that recreation be "good for" the participant.

*See also:* Commercialization of Leisure; Contemporary Leisure Patterns; Fashions; Leisure, Theory of

**BIBLIOGRAPHY**

Bourdin, Ruth. *Women and Temperance: The Quest for Power and Liberty, 1873–1900.* New Brunswick and London: Rutgers University Press, 1990.

Clarke, John, and Chas Critcher. *The Devil Makes Work.* New Zealand: MacMillan, 1985.

Donlon, Jon G. "A Travel Model In The Runway Setting: Strip-Tease As Exotic Destination." In *Sex Tourism And Prostitution: Aspects Of Leisure, Recreation, And Work.* Edited by Martin Oppermann. Elmsford, New York; Cammeray, Australia; and Tokyo: Cognizant Communication Corporation, 1998.

Flaherty, David H. "Law and the Enforcement of Morals in Early America." *Perspectives in American History* 5 (1971): 203–253.

Gay, Peter. *Pleasure Wars: The Bourgeois Experience—Victoria to Freud.* New York: W.W. Norton and Company, 1998.

Hobson, Barbara Meil. *Uneasy Virtue: The Politics of Prostitution and the American Reform Tradition.* New York: Basic Books, Inc., 1987.

MacLeod, David I. *Building Character in the American Boy: The Boy Scouts, YMCA, and Their Forerunners 1870–1920.* Madison and London: University of Wisconsin Press, 1983.

Nielsen, Alen. *The Great Victorian Sacrilege: Preachers, Politics and the Passion, 1879–1884.* Jefferson, North Carolina, and London: McFarland and Company, 1991.

Pivar, James J. *Purity Crusade: Sexual Morality and Social Control, 1868–1900.* Westport, Conn: Greenwood Press, 1973.

Sweetman, David. *Explosive Acts: Toulouse-Lautrec, Oscar Wilde, Felix Feneon and the Art and Anarchy of the Fin De Siecle.* New York and London: Simon and Schuster, 1999.

*Jon Griffin Donlon*

# FAIRS

**See** *Carnivals, Agricultural Fairs, World Fairs*

# FANS AND FAN CLUBS

A fan is an audience member for any form of modern popular culture (including literature, sports, theater, music, film, and television) who has developed a sustained and meaningful attachment to that form or any of its elements, such as particular performers or works. The origin of the term is ambiguous, deriving either from "fanatic," a seventeenth-century derogatory English word for religious zealots, or from "fancy," a more benign nineteenth-century word for the followers of pastimes like pigeoning or boxing. Whether one views the attachment of fans to forms of popular culture as positive or negative, fandom implies a devotion or loyalty that challenges conventions of audience behavior. While most people participate in a performance by temporarily adopting a particular audience role that requires particular behaviors and fosters intense feelings of identification, fans permanently adopt the audience role, working to extend and sustain feelings of identification beyond performance and into everyday life.

Fans are always a minority at the margins of popular culture audiences, separating themselves as a group with their own fashion, knowledge, slang, and rituals. Specific fan activities include accounting, in which fans engage in detailed comparison, evaluation, and interpretation about performers and their works; collecting, in which fans bring together and display objects that enable them to either remember particular fan experiences or intensify their devotion; storytelling, in which fans tell complex narratives to one another about their own fan experiences as a way to shape a sense of shared experience; and socializing, in which fans regularly come together at meetings, parties, and conventions and work to create and maintain a group identity.

## Origins

The phenomenon of fandom first developed during the commercialization of popular culture in the nineteenth century, when the forces of industrialization transformed informal pastimes into products to be consumed. Previously, small groups of local amateurs together created, shared, and enjoyed their own cultural activities. Commercialization, however, required people to assume new, specialized roles that had less to do with close social connections than with impersonal market forces: One group of people produced culture as paid writers, composers, actors, and players, and another much larger group of people received it as paying readers, spectators, and listeners. Fan behavior appeared in the 1840 and 1850s as a way to close the distance between producers and audiences in the market system and to minimize the perceived anonymity of commercial consumption. Fans were those who refused to accept the limited and temporary participation afforded by the purchase of cultural experiences;

**Thalia.** In July 2003 Mexican singing sensation Thalia (1971– ) had fans lined up for her record store appearance in Los Angeles for the release of her self-titled album. Pop music stars tend to have some of the most vocal and avid fans in the modern era. © *Reed Saxon for AP/Wide World Photos*

they sought alternative means of participating in popular culture that involved lasting personal connection and depth of feeling.

In literary history, fans emerged with the development of mass publishing and authorship in the eighteenth century and the subsequent development of silent reading, which encouraged an individualized experience of a story. Before mass publishing, authors were members of an elite class; they would write and publish their work in limited editions to share with small circles of literate friends. Most authors were not considered as important as their works; often authors' names did not even appear on books. But mass publishing and silent reading enabled large numbers of readers to intimately experience the narrative voice of someone they had never met and to feel a strong bond with his or her characters. European readers of Jean-Jacques Rousseau were among the first to demonstrate this relationship to authors and books; they frequently sent Rousseau letters in which they talked about their attraction to his "spirit" and de-

sire to meet him. In the United States, this sort of behavior continued, with readers flocking to New York City throughout the nineteenth century in order to visit the alleged gravestone of the main character in the best-selling novel *Charlotte Temple* (1794), and with thousands of American readers attempting to meet British novelist Charles Dickens during his visit to the United States in 1842.

In American music history, the first fans were urban "music lovers" who, after 1840, focused more on hearing public concerts than making music themselves in the home. In particular, music lovers embraced the Romantic aesthetic that valued the concept of the individually authored "musical work" and eschewed the socializing common to concerts of the day; instead of talking and meeting with friends, they gave silent and intense attention to a work's unique, emotional qualities. This focused listening was facilitated by an increasing number of concert tours by virtuoso players and singers in the 1850s, including Henry Russell, Ole Bull, Henri Vieuxtemps,

Leonard De Meyer, Maria Alboni, Jenny Lind, and Maurice Gottschalk. All cultivated ecstatic and obsessive responses and created a new body of dedicated listeners, many of whom attended multiple concerts, rhapsodized in diaries about performers' character and skill, and showed keen interest in their personal lives. Jenny Lind's tour of the United States in 1850, managed by P. T. Barnum, was one of the most significant; not only did audiences fill the streets just to see and touch Lind, but Barnum effectively fed such audience interest with widespread merchandising of Jenny Lind–branded soap, boots, lamps, and hats.

New feelings of connection and loyalty exhibited by literary and music consumers in the 1830s and 1840s came more naturally to the working-class "kranks," or members of fraternal baseball clubs, in the 1850s and 1860s. Fiercely loyal to their local neighborhood, or "home," teams, kranks were known for brawling with one another and disrupting games if things were not going their way. This kind of dedication intensified when baseball became a professional league sport in the 1880s, with a roster of the best national players working under team contracts and hordes of public spectators attending games by paid admission. In fact, the term "fan" first appeared in a newspaper in 1899 as a reference to spectators for Kansas City's baseball team. By 1920, the increasing availability of public transportation for team travel, the extraordinary feats of star players like Ty Cobb, Honus Wagner, and Babe Ruth, and a successfully promoted connection between baseball and community pride created a wellspring of spectator interest and investment, and "rooting for one's team" became an important and organized part of the game itself.

One of the most significant forces in the development of modern fandom was the elaborate star system of theater and, later, film, which actively capitalized on audiences' desire for a deeper, more personal connection with performers. In the beginning of the nineteenth century, any play was always done by the local theater company in the local theater for a local audience. But after the Civil War, plays were generally staged by national traveling acting troupes, which put on plays night after night in various cities. In order to attract audiences, such troupes often touted their roster of particular and unique actors. The ploy soon took on a life of its own when people came to recognize actors regardless of their troupes. Audiences began demanding to see specific actors outside of character in "curtain speeches" and eventually developed a taste for realism on the stage in which actors did not present the heroic stereotypes of melodrama but rather what audiences thought were the actors' *own* traits and emotions.

Such individual star promotion was taken to another level in Hollywood in 1910, when film producer Carl Laemmle, in a Barnum-like stunt, floated a rumor that one of his actresses, Florence Lawrence, had died, and then arranged for her to miraculously appear in St. Louis. By the 1930s and 1940s, Hollywood had developed a process by which all actors were transformed by marketing departments into recognizable and individual "personalities" with whom audiences could identify. In particular, studios collaborated closely with the many movie magazines of the era, which often featured old, new, and up-and-coming stars in them. The magazines—including *Photoplay, Modern Screen, Screenland, Movie Stories,* and *Screen Album*—reviewed every single film released and also included recipes, advice columns, beauty and fashion tips, and product endorsements from stars, as well as opportunities for fans to write in and ask questions of their favorite players. In the 1920s, the Hollywood star system was so successful that many fans across the country adopted stars' looks and lifestyles; some even went to Hollywood hoping to become stars themselves.

## Twentieth-Century Transformations

The development of mass mediated communications in the twentieth century significantly transformed the earlier conditions that produced fan behavior. Producers and audiences continued to be separated not only by distinct roles but also by complex processes of communication in which the production of cultural products took place physically and temporally apart from an audience's reception of them. Such separation fostered greater mystery about performers and a desire to connect directly with them. At the same time, communication technologies, like the radio, phonograph, and television, enabled audiences to experience popular culture in the intimacy of their own homes and to incorporate it into their daily lives like never before. The phonograph, and subsequent recording devices like audio- and videocassette recorders also encouraged obsessive repetition and study, which further enhanced fans' feelings of connection to performers and works.

Not surprisingly, given the contradictions of separation and intimacy set up by modern communications, fan behavior in the twentieth century became far more visible and intense than it was in the nineteenth century. The first hint of the role the media would play in fandom was the 1927 funeral of silent film star Rudolph Valentino, at which an unexpected crowd of 50,000 grieving fans showed up and rioted when they were unable to view the actor's body. Such spectacles continued in the late 1930s when swing dancers, known as bobby soxers or jitterbugs, screamed and rushed the stage at the sight of big-band performers like Benny Goodman and Frank Sinatra. Music fan behavior reached its pinnacle during the rock-and-roll era with the near riotous hysteria created by mobs of young teenage fans at concerts by Elvis Presley and the Beatles in the 1950s and 1960s.

Accompanying this new fan visibility was an organized effort by fans to publicly symbolize their devotion by grouping together into regional and national clubs. Such clubs were begun by fans of particular movie stars in the 1920s and 1930s and quickly became popular; by the early 1930s, for example, the Shirley Temple Fan Club had 384 branches with nearly 4 million members (Barbas, p. 113). Later, clubs appeared in all forms of popular culture, dedicated to film styles, film stars, music groups, singers, and television personalities, genres, and shows. Each club typically featured membership dues, membership cards, regular meetings or conventions, and newsletters. Fan clubs generally operated without any help or support from entertainment corporations; in fact, clubs were known for their distrust of the executives for which stars worked and often campaigned against corporations on stars' behalf. Early movie fan clubs, for example, practiced "boosting," in which they flooded studio executives with letters of support of their favorite stars in order to help them land better roles; many clubs also responded with angry petitions and letters to any perceived slights of their stars by the studios or the press. Such activity waned with the decline of the Hollywood studio system in the 1950s, but since the 1960s, TV fan clubs—for shows like *Star Trek, Cagney & Lacey,* and *Beauty and the Beast*—have similarly organized write-in campaigns to force producers to correct undesired plot developments or reverse series cancellations.

One of the most important distinctions between fan clubs was whether one was "official," operating with a star's blessing and endorsement, or "unofficial," not known or condoned by a star. The bonus of belonging to an official fan club was often some form of direct contact with the star, usually in the form of a signed photograph or letter. Official fans club members also had the benefit of exclusive access to information about a star's personal and professional life. Some fans, however, came to see such membership as inauthentic and manufactured, especially as studios and record companies, over time, started to pay increasingly close attention to fan clubs in an effort to assess the market and tap into a steady base of paying customers. Thus arose a "do-it-yourself" ethic among some fans as a way to avoid corporate manipulation. Punk fans in the 1970s, for example, adopted many of the activities of official fan clubs, such as writing and distributing magazines and adopting distinctive fashions, but they did so

for their own purposes, many of which directly mocked or challenged the mainstream entertainment industry. For example, instead of registering with nationally organized clubs, complete with badges and stationery, punk fans congregated in local "scenes," put together by word of mouth and celebrated in homemade publications called "zines," which were passed out at shows. Science-fiction television fans in the 1970s and 1980s were especially notorious for skirting issues of copyright and circulating their own fiction and art that featured established television characters in alternative (including erotic) plots and situations never intended by producers.

All of this activity was further transformed with the development of the Internet. Before the widespread adoption of the personal computer in the early 1980s, both official and unofficial fan clubs existed thanks to publications and regular face-to-face contact at concerts or conventions (known as "cons" in the science fiction fan world). While useful in building a sense of community, such publications and events were fleeting, sporadic, and costly. But the advent of the Internet in the 1970s provided a cheap, effective alternative. In particular, the development of computer bulletin boards or discussion lists in the early 1980s provided an instant medium for fans to come together, discuss events, and trade stories, tapes, and knowledge, and fans quickly adopted it as a means to create community.

Fans who first embraced the Internet were generally established groups who used it to supplement extensive communal networks and institutions that already existed offline; Deadheads (fans of the rock group Grateful Dead), for instance, were among the earliest users of the WELL, a San Francisco–based computer network (Rheingold, p. 49). By the mid-1990s, however, with the development of the World Wide Web, online activity went from peripherally supporting fandom to becoming a central manifestation of fandom itself. Today, many fan communities have moved toward an exclusive online existence, jettisoning the fanzines and conventions that used to be part and parcel of fan culture. The most significant symbol of this transformation was the disbanding of the National Association of Fan Clubs in 2002; after twenty-five years of publishing a national directory and providing support for fan clubs across the United States, the association determined that it was impossible to compete with the immediacy of the Internet and keep up with the sheer amount of celebrity information on the World Wide Web.

## Assessing Fandom

While fandom has existed in the United States for nearly 200 years, its value and meaning remain highly disputed.

Images of fans as obsessive loners who stalk stars, for example, continue to be prevalent in fiction, movies, and music; real-life cases of celebrity stalkers lend proof to alleged connections between fandom and antisocial behavior. Indeed, several media critics have branded fandom a pathology, worrying about the psychological effects of fans' feelings of personal connection with media figures they have never actually met and the ways in which such attachments might replace meaningful relationships with real people. On the other hand, ethnographic studies of fandom have shown fans to be quite concerned with connections not simply to stars but also with other fans, something that engenders strong feelings of community and goodwill; the majority of fans seem to be well adjusted and otherwise "normal" individuals, with healthy relationships with spouses, families, and friends.

In such debates about fandom's psychological effect, issues of power and control are central. Some scholars see fans as oblivious to the market relations involved in the buying and selling of cultural expression; fans are alleged to be engaging in an unnatural and ultimately passive enthusiasm that naively supports corporate power. Others, however, see fan activities (particularly write-in campaigns and fan fiction writing) as examples of social power. Feminist critics, for example, have interpreted the screaming, shaking, seat wetting, and trancelike states exhibited by young women rock-and-roll fans in the 1960s as a kind of protofeminism, a moment in which women, unable to participate fully in a patriarchal society, could for the first time exert some form of power uncontrolled by men. Fandom clearly has a complicated relationship to the entertainment business; while fans are, in many ways, ideal consumers, devoted to the purchase of particular types of products and feeding a profit-oriented entertainment industry, their focus is entirely on maintaining their connection to performers and works. Sometimes fans spend as much time and energy subverting common business practices (through illegal trading and copying of products, setting up information networks apart from industry advertising, and developing their own means of accessing stars outside of "official" marketed venues) as they do supporting them.

In the end, fans' participation in popular culture appears more religious than anything else; like many religions, fandom involves a feeling of connection with an unattainable "other," highly ritualized devotional activities, shared moments of conversion, regular textual interpretation, and reverence for significant places and sites. Some scholars have even characterized various fan groups as modern "cults." Others, however, have emphasized that, while fandom shares a number of characteristics with practices of religious devotion, fans themselves resist literal interpretations of fandom as religion; such interpretations usually have a negative connotation and denigrate fans' own participation in traditional religious denominations. Instead, religious discourse can be seen as the only discourse available in society that adequately describes the intensity of feeling inherent in devotion. Whether it constitutes a form of religion or not, the important point is that fandom, like religion, has served as a potent source for creating identity, meaning, and community in daily life. From its beginnings in letter writing and public spectacles to its current existence online, fandom has been a valuable means for thinking about how we understand ourselves and our relationships to others in an increasingly commercialized and mediated society.

*See also:* Fads; Fashions

## BIBLIOGRAPHY

Bacon-Smith, Camille. *Enterprising Women: Television Fandom and the Creation of Popular Myth.* Philadelphia: University of Pennsylvania Press, 1992.

Barbas, Samantha. *Movie Crazy: Fans, Stars, and the Cult of Celebrity.* New York: Palgrave, 2001.

Braudy, Leo. *The Frenzy of Renown.* New York: Vintage Books, 1997.

Cavicchi, Daniel. *Tramps Like Us: Music and Meaning Among Springsteen Fans.* New York: Oxford University Press, 1998.

Doss, Erika. *Elvis Culture: Fans, Faith, and Image.* Lawrence: University of Kansas Press, 1999.

Gledhill, Christine, ed. *Stardom: Industry of Desire.* New York: Routledge, 1991.

Gorn, Elliott J., and Warren Goldstein. *A Brief History of American Sports.* New York: Hill and Wang, 1993.

Hills, Matt. *Fan Cultures.* London: Routledge, 2002.

Jenkins, Henry. *Textual Poachers: Television Fans and Participatory Culture.* New York: Routledge, 1992.

Lewis, Lisa. *The Adoring Audience: Fan Culture and Popular Media.* New York: Routledge, 1992.

Rheingold, Howard. *The Virtual Community: Homesteading on the Electronic Frontier.* Revised edition. Cambridge, Mass.: MIT Press, 2000.

Schickel, Richard. *Intimate Strangers: The Culture of Celebrity.* Garden City, New York: Doubleday, 1985.

*Daniel Cavicchi*

# FANTASY SPORTS

"Fantasy sports" originated as a baseball management simulation game commonly attributed to sportswriter and editor Daniel Okrent. In the early 1980s, Okrent and friends created and began play within the Rotisserie League Baseball at the La Rotisserie Francaise restaurant on East Fifty-Second Street between Lexington and Third Avenues in Manhattan. Through subsequent commercial publication of the league's yearly competitions, the Rotisserie baseball (roto-baseball) game system proved widely popular and spawned similar game systems based on many other real-world competitions.

The original Rotisserie baseball rules allowed the Okrent group to simulate the activities of major league baseball team owners in the evaluation, purchase, and trade of professional baseball players. Within the game, the projected season performances of major league baseball players were assigned ordinal rankings within eight performance categories; these professional players were then "purchased" by team owners using a limited supply of funds. The owner purchasing those players who scored highest in the game's performance categories at the end of the professional baseball season won the game.

The appeal of this simulation involved both the quantitative analysis of athletic performance and, more innovatively, the social play that took place within a fixed group of ten to twelve owners. Prior to 1980, many games based on the quantification of athletic performances had been available for individual and group play (e.g., Strat-O-Matic Baseball, created by Hal Richman in 1948); Okrent's system, however, was the first widely accepted method of formalizing the related social play within a small group context.

Since the 1980s, the basic mechanics of the Rotisserie baseball system have been adapted to the simulation of other sports, such as fantasy football and fantasy basketball. This related group of simulations is then characterized as "fantasy games." In all such simulations, game players adopt the fantasy role of "owning" the quantitative performances of popular media figures (professional athletes, rock stars, and others) in order to compete and interact within a community of fellow players/owners.

## Quantitative Analysis

The original Rotisserie baseball game's eight performance categories—batting average, home runs, runs batted in, stolen bases, wins, saves, earned run average, and pitching "ratio" ([hits allowed + walks allowed] / innings pitched)—spurred widespread interest in statistics and the statistical analysis of baseball. Statistical analysis had long been a part of baseball fan discussion, with well-established, fan-related organizations devoted to the topic—such as the Society for American Baseball Research (SABR), begun in 1971. However, Rotisserie base-

ball was instrumental in introducing a great variety of statistical terms and concepts to a broad audience; these terms and concepts have since become an integral part of mass media coverage of the sport.

On-base average, slugging percentage, and other statistics more meaningful and valuable to predicting player performance than the original eight used in Rotisserie baseball were first popularized and promulgated by publications catering directly to fantasy baseball players. Two of the most influential of these publications during the early development of fantasy baseball were the yearly *Bill James Baseball Abstract* (1982–1988) and the *Elias Baseball Analyst* (1985–1993); these and similar books, articles, and newsletters supplemented (and often corrected) the more whimsical analyses published annually in *Rotisserie League Baseball* (Bantam Books), which was written by members and, later, descendants of Okrent's proto-league.

## Social Play

Clearly more compelling—and innovative—than the quantitative precision of the original Rotisserie baseball rules was their dramatic intrigue. The social interactions and play among the owners within Okrent's league provided models for thousands of owners who, like the colorful cast of characters in Rotisserie League Baseball, spent more time on the art of the deal than the science of player evaluation. By reconstituting the intimacy of the relationship between mass media sports figures and their fans, fantasy games such as Rotisserie baseball benefited both producers and consumers of mass media sports-related entertainment content.

The social interactions within small groups of fantasy sports players gratified and sustained fan interests by providing a more personalized and active form of participation than any other available to fans of professional sports that were increasingly shaped by media demands, political concessions, and financial concerns. Simultaneously, fantasy sports remained dependent on those professional league competitions they simulated; and, through the use of standardized rules, fantasy sports play both maintained a mass audience and sustained a mass market for the consumption of sports-related products. Each of these outcomes benefited the sports entertainment industries, and, over time, these industries have become increasingly supportive of fantasy sports play. Even peripheral (and seemingly dysfunctional) outcomes of fantasy sports play—such as fan interest being transferred from local teams to individual athletes—are consonant with professional leagues that commonly promote and market star players and performances while reassigning and reconstituting local teams.

## Current Games

The popularity of fantasy games grew rapidly during the 1980s, creating a cottage industry of writers, editors, analysts, and statisticians—most devoted to fantasy baseball. The baseball strike of 1994 put many of the original fantasy game services out of business, and, aided by the increasing commercialization of the Internet, fantasy games have since largely migrated to online, fee-based services. Yahoo! is now the single largest provider of fantasy sports leagues, with more than 5 million registered users during the 2001 baseball season.

In several instances, the small group context so fundamental to the original Rotisserie Baseball rules has been modified by online, commercial versions of fantasy games (such as the online offerings of ESPN, CBS Sportsline, and Fox Sports) that are designed to maximize the number of players/owners participating. Some of these games, which have little or no social interaction among very large numbers of players/owners, are better classified as betting games or, more generically, as games of chance. Similarly, simulation systems that pit only two players/owners—or two player/owner teams—against each other are better classified as either strategy or war games, depending on the mechanics of the simulation involved. Fantasy games as a separate genre of play require both competition among a small group of players/owners and a set of rules guiding their social interactions within the fantasy (simulated) context.

*See also:* Computer's Impact on Leisure, Internet

### BIBLIOGRAPHY

Elias Sport Bureau. *The Elias Baseball Analyst.* New York: Collier Books. 1985–1993.

James, Bill. *The Bill James Baseball Abstract.* New York: Ballantine Books. 1982–1988.

Waggoner, Glen, ed. *Rotisserie League Baseball.* 1st edition. New York: Bantam Books. 1984.

Yahoo! Sports Fantasy Games. 2002. Available from http://fantasysports.yahoo.com.

*David Myers*

# FASHIONS

Fashions in clothing are frequently regarded as frivolous, but major changes in clothing styles are generally indicators of important shifts in social relations and in levels of social tension. Fashion as a form of popular culture can be interpreted using theories that have been developed to explain other types of popular culture, such as theories of social reproduction, semiotic analyses of meaning in cultural images and artifacts, postmodern assessments of contemporary culture, and theories concerning the production of culture in cultural industries. Analysis of meanings of clothing and how meanings of specific items of clothing change over time is necessary in order to interpret changes both in the nature of fashion and in the motivations of fashion adopters. What induces the public to adopt fashions is an important area of study that draws on sociological and social-psychological theories. Fashion is created and produced in organizations that constitute a cultural industry, which can be compared with other types of cultural industries, such as film and music. The tensions between high culture and popular culture that exist in other areas of cultural consumption are reproduced in the fashion system as designers draw on themes from popular culture but also attempt to associate themselves with the arts and to use artistic strategies similar to those of avant-gardes in the arts.

## Origins of Modern Fashion

In Europe, fashions in clothing began in the late Middle Ages when developments in dressmaking led to the production of types of clothing that fit the body closely in contrast to sacklike costumes worn in previous eras. In the close-fitting style, stylistic details could be varied continually. Until the Industrial Revolution led to some redistribution of income in the nineteenth century, fashion was confined largely to those with considerable means since material was expensive and clothing was made by hand. By the end of the nineteenth century, some clothing was manufactured, and the price of material had declined. Clothing was one of the first forms of popular culture that became available to all social classes. Its symbolic importance is suggested by the fact that in the United States, workers increased their expenditures on clothing as their incomes rose.

In the late nineteenth and early twentieth centuries, the fashion system was highly centralized. Paris was the center of fashion for women's clothes while London was the center of fashion for men's clothes. A few designers in Paris decided what would be fashionable in a large number of Western and Western-oriented countries. The most influential designer was Charles Frederick Worth, an Englishman (1825–1895) who worked in Paris and created styles that were adopted by the upper and middle classes all over Europe and America. Worth created the tradition of haute couture, clothes made to order for clients who ordered them directly from designers. For a costume to be considered elegant, every detail had to be correct. Fashion evolved in an orderly manner, following a succession of cycles based on shapes of the skirt: bell, back-fullness (the bustle), and tubular. Fashionable dresses were composed of huge quantities of fabric and trimmings. Decisions by Paris designers to use a particular type of material or accessory had enormous consequences for fashion industries in the Western world, affecting the price of textiles and sometimes the survival of entire factories. During most of the nineteenth century, fashionable dress styles restricted women's movements, impeding activities such as climbing stairs or walking in the streets. They included in different periods tightly laced corsets, wide crinolines, tight sleeves, enormous bustles, and long trains.

Fashionable clothing was a type of nonverbal communication that conveyed information about the wearer's social role, social standing, and personal character. Upper- and middle-class women devoted a great deal of time and money to creating elaborate wardrobes that presented them appropriately to members of their social milieus. Fashionable clothing exemplified the doctrine of separate spheres that was supported by other social institutions. It was entirely suitable for the subordinate and passive roles women were expected to perform.

Fashionable clothing styles created in France expressed French conceptions of how bourgeois women should dress. French designers responded slowly to changes that were taking place in the lifestyles of middle- and upper-class women. Alternative styles, more appropriate for women's new roles in the workplace and for new forms of leisure, such as sports, gradually appeared in England and in the United States in the late nineteenth and early twentieth centuries. In these countries, women's movements lobbied against fashionable styles and advocated dress reforms without much success. New styles of clothing, in the form of uniforms, emerged in schools and colleges, where women performed gymnastics and engaged in sports. Resorts, where women played actively or took up swimming, were another site for experimenting with new types of clothing. At the end of the nineteenth century, bicycling became extremely popular with both men and women but entailed the use of clothing that was very different from fashionable styles.

During and after World War I, changes in clothing styles pioneered in the late nineteenth century began to appear in fashionable clothing, particularly in styles created by French designers, such as Paul Poiret and Gabrielle Chanel. A major trend in the period between the two

**Charles Frederick Worth.** Founder of the former Maison Worth in Paris and London, Charles Frederick Worth (1825–1895) was a top designer of women's fashions and considered to be the creator of haute couture. © *Getty Images*

world wars was a movement toward physical mobility and freedom through the simplification of fashionable clothing, as seen in shorter hemlines, looser and more comfortable styles, and the use of more practical fabrics that either had been formerly reserved for working-class men's clothing or were the result of new technological developments. Hemlines rose and fell periodically, but it was not until the late 1960s that the thigh-length mini-skirt made its first appearance.

Another important trend was toward androgyny in women's clothes and in their appearance in general, as exemplified by the popularization of short hair styles and the gradual acceptance of men's pants as female attire. In the 1920s, the fashion ideal in France was a "boyish" look (*la garçonne*) that represented a desire to break with conventional behavior through "the blurring or reversal of gender roles" (Roberts, p. 66). The equivalent in the United States was the "flapper."

Although some upper-class and working-class women wore pants between the two world wars, pants were not widely accepted until the 1970s when fashion designers, such as Yves Saint Laurent, finally began to include them in their collections. Blue jeans, which were invented in the mid-nineteenth century and had originally been worn exclusively by men, became a highly fashionable item of clothing for both sexes.

The fashion system was supported and made possible by values and attitudes toward social class and personal identity that were widely accepted in industrial societies during the late nineteenth and early twentieth centuries. Identification with social class was a major factor affecting the way individuals perceived their identities and their relationships with their social environments. Conformity to strict sets of rules about how certain items of clothing should be worn (gloves, shoes, hats, hemlines, and colors) signified that the individual belonged to or aspired to belong to the middle class. Acceptance of these rules was based on fear of exclusion. Violation of these rules indicated that the individual was not aware of the correct mode of behavior. Class-based fashion involved a high level of consensus among designers and the public.

Toward the end of the 1960s, the fashion system underwent major changes. In the new fashion system, fashion ceased to be dictated entirely by class considerations and became a means for expressing nuances of individuality, based on perceptions of gender, age, and race as well as political and social values. While clothes in the workplace continued to express class distinctions, leisure clothing was more likely to be used to convey personal identity rather than social class affiliation. As Anthony Giddens has argued, developing and nurturing personal identity became a major project for many people in the late twentieth century.

Class cultures were less homogenous than before; leisure cultures based on popular culture in the form of film, music, and sports proliferated and provided resources for discovering and expressing identities. Consequently, the number of sources of fashion ideas increased greatly, providing people with alternatives to ideas disseminated by the fashion industry. Fashions proposed by the fashion industry were no longer automatically accepted. Fashion creators ceased to view the fashion consumer as a fashion victim and began to see her as an autonomous individual who created a personal style that was meaningful to herself, by incorporating elements of fashionable styles rather than adopting an exact copy of a particular style. However, many women were not interested in fashion. In the late twentieth century, the proportion of the female population that followed fashion was estimated to be between one-fifth and one-third (Gutman and Mills, Krafft).

The public's desire for fashionable clothing that expressed their personal identities undermined the highly centralized system in which French fashion had predominated. This was replaced by a more decentralized system in which successful luxury fashion industries developed in several other countries, such as the United States, Italy, Japan, Great Britain, Germany, and Belgium. Many other countries have small luxury fashion industries. In this system, France, Italy, Great Britain, and the United States are the most influential.

## Theoretical Perspectives on Fashion

The nature of and shifts in the character of fashion since the mid-nineteenth century have been examined from many different perspectives. At the beginning of the twentieth century, Georg Simmel developed the earliest theory of social change in fashion. According to Simmel's model, fashions in clothing were adopted first by the upper class, whose members sought to differentiate themselves from other social classes and to reinforce their social status. Fashions diffused next to the middle class and then to the lower class. By the time a specific fashion had been adopted by the lower classes, the upper class had already adopted newer styles since the previous style had lost its capacity to differentiate between them.

This model is useful for understanding the fashion system during the earlier period but is less useful in the contemporary period. Now some fashions originate among the lower classes and among marginal subcultures, such as the hippies, and are disseminated upward in a "bottom-up" process. In this model, dissemination upward does not occur in a systematic fashion from lower social levels to higher social levels, but may occur at any higher level where people, and particularly young people as heavy consumers of popular culture, are exposed to these trends. Dissemination occurs most rapidly when designers in the fashion industry pick up these trends, which are then disseminated downward in the social system.

What motivates people to follow fashion? Different theories have been applicable at different periods. In societies characterized by distinct class cultures, such as the late nineteenth and early twentieth centuries, Pierre Bourdieu's (1984) theory of cultural capital can be applied to fashion. Understanding the nuances of fashionable dress can be conceptualized as a form of cultural capital available to women belonging to the upper class and used as a means of attaining or reinforcing class status. Thorstein Veblen's theory of conspicuous consumption in which goods are a means of displaying personal wealth also applies to the behavior of some fashion followers, particularly those who are upwardly mobile.

In late-twentieth-century societies, where developing and nurturing personal identity have become a major project for many people, Fred Davis's symbolic interactionist theory is relevant for understanding how fashion is perceived. According to Davis, fashionable clothing is attractive to the consumer because it expresses ambivalences surrounding social identities, such as "youth versus age, masculinity versus femininity, androgyny versus singularity . . . work versus play . . . conformity versus rebellion" (pp. 17–18). Fashionable clothes redefine these tensions and embody them in new styles.

Postmodernist theory (Baudrillard) suggests that fashionable styles no longer have any inherent meanings but are made up of signifiers whose connotations are constantly changing, detached from their original cultural contexts. This theory suggests that fashion consumers are "sartorial bricoleurs," selecting clothes for their capacity to create a "look" and not for the messages they convey. Consumers' selections of styles can no longer be explained on the basis of their backgrounds or values. Instead, fashion consumers engage in style "surfing," moving quickly from one style to another without any ideological commitment. David Muggleton describes the postmodern fashion consumer for whom "the trappings of a spectacular style are their right of admission to a costume party, a masquerade, a hedonistic escape into a blitz culture fantasy, characterized by political indifference" (p. 49).

In his study of British adolescents who belonged to middle- and lower-class subcultures, Muggleton found that adolescents who engaged in style "surfing" were perceived as superficial. Styles were not adopted and rejected on superficial grounds. The British adolescents in his study selected their clothes to express their identities and believed that their clothes expressed their inner selves. However, their conceptions of their identities were constantly evolving and changing. This meant that their clothing styles also changed frequently. To an uninformed observer, their clothing selections appeared to be random, but, in fact, changes in their clothing reflected changes in how they perceived their identities.

Susan Kaiser et al. argue that postmodern culture produces a situation in which fashionable styles and the adaptations consumers create from them are highly ambiguous. Adopting a symbolic interactionist approach, they argue that consumers struggle to make sense both of fashionable styles and of one another's clothing. In the process, they create new variations on current styles that may be incorporated into styles produced by the fashion industry. The latter employs fashion forecasters to comb the globe for sites where trendy young people gather in order to identify combinations of items that may be successful in the future.

## Resistance to Fashion

The notion of what constitutes resistance to fashion is complex and has become increasingly difficult to identify. Cultural studies as developed in Britain locates resistance to the dominant culture in subcultures, usually belonging to the working class. Clothing styles are particularly suitable for expressing resistance because of the ease with which they can be altered and adapted. Alternatives to the dominant culture are composed of oppositional elements from different class and ethnic cultures. Eventually, alternative cultures are assimilated by the dominant culture in less threatening forms. Angela McRobbie (1988) shows how urban street stall markets in London constituted a focal point for the transmission of influences from street cultures to young fashion designers and art students.

When the level of tension between a subculture and the dominant culture is pronounced, alternative clothing styles are likely to be perceived as highly provocative. Throughout the nineteenth and twentieth centuries, clothes worn by African Americans were often considered inappropriate and offensive by whites. During the 1930s and 1940s, the zoot suit, worn by African Americans and Hispanics, became both an affirmation of subcultural identity and a statement of rebellion. Its most distinctive features were the peg-top pants that ballooned at the knees, the knee-length coat, its bright colors, and the flashy accessories, such as a long gold watch chain. Because it required more cloth than was permissible during wartime rationing, it became a symbol of resistance to the war and was the focus of riots between young black and Hispanic men and uniformed white soldiers.

Dick Hebdige, in a classic work using the cultural studies approach, traced the origins of the punk style to alienated youth in the British working class. Reacting against the hierarchical British class structure, working-class British youth expressed their frustrations by inventing unconventional styles of clothing that combined trends from commercial goods and elements from marginal ethnic cultures. The aim was to subvert the rules of fashionable clothing. Each choice of a garment or an accessory was seen as a creative act, as part of a practice of subversive consumption. In this environment, a young fashion designer and a musical entrepreneur who developed the first punk music group created the punk clothing style, using razor-slashed T-shirts, sewn to simulate scars, T-shirts showing the Queen of England with a safety pin through her nose and mouth, bondage chains, and hair styles in garish colors. Although its oppositional characteristics were muted, the punk style was rapidly accepted by fashion designers in Britain and elsewhere, and remains influential.

In the late twentieth and early twenty-first centuries, the creation and popularization of oppositional clothing is closely linked to popular music. Clothing worn by successful pop singers, such as Madonna, influences the clothing choices of their fans. New music groups, often African American, with distinctive clothing styles that subvert the clothing norms of the dominant culture, are constantly emerging. However, the rapidity with which successful groups are assimilated by the dominant culture through the medium of the music industry diminishes their potential for subcultural subversion.

The extent to which fashion as part of the dominant culture provides potential for resistance is limited. The images of women's roles projected by fashion tend to be ideologically conservative and often demeaning for women. Designers' cooptation of subversive elements from oppositional subcultures is more likely to be linked to a marketing strategy than to ideological commitment. Renato Poggioli argues that fashion is more concerned with the appearance of change and novelty than with bringing about any real change in the dominant culture. However, consumers may use fashion in oppositional ways. Mary Douglas argues that consumers may as often reject as accept the types of identities associated with products, and, in this sense, shopping becomes a form of social protest. Anthony Freitas et al., on the basis of a study of "least favorite" clothes, found that people tend to reject certain types of clothing that are associated with specific statuses (e.g., age, race, sexual orientation) as a way of indicating their lack of connections with specific groups. Focus groups conducted with young and middle-aged women showed that many of them rejected the images of women in fashion photographs taken from *Vogue*.

## Meanings of Clothing

Semiotics provides tools for analyzing the meanings of particular items of clothing. From this point of view, clothing can be seen as a "language," which consists of images that are meaningful in specific social contexts in which they reinforce the structure of social interaction and the system of statuses and roles. Using concepts from semiotics, clothes can be viewed as signifiers whose meanings or "signifieds" can be identified. Some clothing signifiers are stable and correspond to "closed" texts; others are unstable and resemble "open" texts. Using this type of analysis, it is possible to develop typologies of the cloth-

ing signifiers that are most widely used or most characteristic of a particular period.

For example, Nathan Joseph argues that the distinction between uniforms and quasi-uniforms as compared to nonuniforms, such as leisure clothing and costumes, is essential for understanding the significance of clothing in Western society. The uniform has four major characteristics: (1) It designates membership in a group, often a formal organization; (2) It maximizes a specific status position, membership in a particular group, and conceals other status positions; (3) It is a certificate of the legitimacy of the individual as a representative of a particular group; and (4) It suppresses individual idiosyncrasies of behavior, appearance, and sometimes physical attributes. Quasi-uniforms are worn by members of nongovernmental organizations and have less legitimacy than uniforms worn by members of governmental organizations. Standardized clothing, such as mechanics' coverall and cowboy costumes, is different from uniforms in that it denotes membership in a diffuse, unorganized group rather than in a specific organization.

Ruth Rubinstein has identified six distinct types of clothing signifiers in American society. Her analysis is based on a distinction between signs and symbols. A sign has a single meaning that is widely recognized in the society in which it is used, while a symbol may be interpreted in many different ways, depending on the social status of those who are using specific symbols and of those who are interpreting them. These categories have analogies to the distinction between closed and open texts and to Joseph's distinction between uniforms and nonuniforms. Rubinstein's six categories include clothing signs, which correspond to Joseph's conception of uniforms; clothing symbols such as designer clothes and jewelry, which can be interpreted in a variety of ways; clothing tie-signs, which identify their wearers as members of marginal subcultures (such as the Amish or Hasidic Jews); clothing tie-symbols, which are a means of representing their wearers' affiliations with political causes or social issues; personal dress, which refers to the distinctive qualities of clothing people wear in public; and contemporary fashion, which represents the style of clothing at a particular time and which is influenced by political events and economic conditions, as well as collective memory.

The significance of items of clothing changes in different types of societies. The shift from a modernist to a postmodernist culture can be seen in the changing meanings of items, such as hats and T-shirts. During the nineteenth and early twentieth centuries, the article of clothing that played the most important role for indicating social distinctions among men was the hat. Virtually every man wore a hat when outside his home, regardless of social class. Since different types of hats were identified with different social strata, hats were used to claim and to maintain social status. At times, they were used to blur class boundaries by expressing a status to which a person aspired. Because men represented their families in public space, men's hats rather than women's were used to indicate the status of the family. Women's hats represented conspicuous consumption rather than coded signals referring to social rank. Occasionally a particular hat style, such as the straw boater in the last quarter of the nineteenth century, was worn by all social classes and also by women, before disappearing entirely from use except in popular entertainment.

The short-sleeved T-shirt imprinted with letters and/or images appeared in the 1940s, and, with the development of new technologies for printing on cloth in the 1950s, it became increasingly suitable for conveying visual and verbal messages. Because it is available at all price levels, rich and poor alike wear the T-shirt. Approximately 1 billion T-shirts are purchased annually in the United States. The T-shirt performs a function formerly associated with the hat, that of identifying an individual's social location. Instead of social status, the T-shirt speaks to all shades of issues related to ideology, difference, myth, politics, race, gender, and leisure. For example, it has been used to express racism and antiracism, sexism and antisexism, conservatism and liberalism.

Using the categories of closed and open texts, hats were closed texts, garments with fixed meanings. Another type of garment with fixed meanings is the business suit, which has distinct connotations of status and elitism. Garments with fixed meanings are generally worn in class societies or, in the early 2000s, in bureaucratic organizations typical of most workplaces.

Garments with open meanings, such as T-shirts and blue jeans, are more likely to appear in societies organized around lifestyles rather than social classes because members of different lifestyles wish to express different meanings using the same type of garment. Unlike hats, whose meanings were universally understood, T-shirts speak to like-minded people. A particular T-shirt may not be meaningful to those with different views and affiliations. The blue jean can also be considered as an open text since it continually added new meanings during the course of the twentieth century and into the new millennium. Starting in the middle of the nineteenth century as a form of clothing for men performing hard work outdoors, the blue jean became identified in the mid-twentieth century with social resistance and eventually with social conformity when the fashion industry began to produce trendy versions of the blue jean for both sexes. These examples illustrate the fact that, as society changes, not only the styles of clothes change but the same types of clothes express meanings, such as social status and social identity, in different ways.

## Fashion as a Cultural Industry

During the late twentieth century, fashion as a cultural industry became increasingly similar to other culture industries, such as the film industry and the music industry. Fashion firms increased in size, formed oligopolies, and were bought by conglomerates. In the late nineteenth and early twentieth centuries, fashion was produced in small French firms whose principal activity was making made-to-order clothes for clients. Industrial companies produced cheaper clothing for the middle and lower classes. Designer firms had relatively stable clienteles composed of members of the aristocracy, the upper middle class, wealthy bohemians, and foreigners. Designers met many of their clients and understood the social milieus in which they moved.

In the postwar period, luxury designer fashion firms underwent enormous changes. Profits were obtained primarily from sales of perfume and accessories and from licensing the right to reproduce designs by other firms. Clothing styles were used to create a prestigious image to enhance the sales of other products. In order to be successful, these companies found it necessary to sell their products in many other countries. The level of investment required to start this type of business soared. Young designers were increasingly unable to start their own firms and began their careers designing clothes for existing firms. As in other culture industries, conglomerates bought the most successful firms. In keeping with predictions based on theories concerning the production of culture, which argue that market structure and the organization of businesses in culture industries affect the level of innovation, oligopolization of the fashion industry and globalization of fashion markets have created a situation in which small firms are less likely to be recognized as innovative by fashion experts while large firms are able to survive with a low level of product innovation. McRobbie (1998, p. 180) argues that small British design firms function as "transitional structures" that serve to establish their owners' skills and reputations but can seldom be transformed into more permanent structures because of the lack of venture capital needed to compete in the global marketplace.

**Ralph Lauren.** Models walk the catwalk in New York City displaying pieces from Ralph Lauren's (1939– ) 2001 fall collection. The popular designer began his entrepreneurial career in 1968 by founding Polo Fashions. © *AP/Wide World Photos*

The roles of luxury fashion designers have distinctive characteristics in different countries, depending on the history of the fashion industry, the nature of the clientele, and the relative influence of marginal subcultures. In France, the status of the fashion designer continually increased in the twentieth century. The analogies of fashion creation to the arts were made explicit with the creation of fashion museums in several cities and the development of Paris as an international fashion center, where designers from all over the world displayed their creations.

In England, until the 1960s, fashion designers were considered artisans rather than artists. The clienteles of the most successful designers were composed of royalty and other members of the upper class, whose conservative tastes inhibited the aesthetic aspects of fashion design. Beginning in the late 1960s, young fashion designers

from the working class were trained in art schools, where they were influenced by urban working-class subcultures and rebellious music and produced subversive designs. In the 1960s, an era that also generated world-famous British musicians, such as the Beatles and the Rolling Stones, a few young designers, such as Mary Quant and Biba, received a lot of publicity.

However, the British clothing industry has been largely unreceptive to the work of British designers, preferring standardized clothing for mass markets. McRobbie found that British fashion designers' training in art school encouraged them to view themselves as artists in Bourdieu's sense of the term—as an elite concerned with aesthetic issues and disdainful of practical considerations. She shows that this conception of the occupation is inappropriate for coping with the economic conditions young designers face in the marketplace after graduation. Nevertheless, McRobbie argues that the source of many new fashion trends in Europe and America lies "in the experimental funhouse of the British youth culture and club culture scene, in and around the art schools, in young graduates' studios and in the small units, shops, and stall-type outlets which they supply" (1998, pp. 183–184).

In the United States, a few designers achieved great success and notoriety creating clothes for Hollywood films in the 1930s and 1940s, but most designers worked anonymously for large clothing manufacturers, adapting Paris fashions for American customers. Beginning in the 1960s, they began to develop their own firms, which were oriented either toward the very rich, as a kind of niche market, or toward the creation of brands representing distinct lifestyles. In both cases, American designers were highly skilled at marketing their wares. The myth of the designer as artist was much less powerful.

Both British and French designers sometimes adopted strategies associated with avant-gardes but could also be identified as postmodernist. In this sense, their artistic behavior is similar to that of many creators in various forms of popular culture, such as television, film, and music video. For the avant-garde fashion designer, the major technique for communicating meaning is symbolic subversion; for the postmodernist designer, intertextuality. These two tendencies are very different from the classical approach to fashion design that reworked elements from the past to produce styles that, while related to the past, were neither copies nor pastiches. As with avant-garde creators in other forms of popular culture, avant-gardism represents a set of techniques that are generally adopted for specific purposes rather than as part of an ideological commitment. These techniques are often used at the beginning of the designer's career as a way of attracting attention and a clientele. In fashion design, the coexistence of avant-gardism and postmodernism has led to enormous variety but not to coherent messages.

## Conclusion

Fashion is a complex phenomenon that needs to be understood both on the macro and the micro levels, using "a tapestry of arguments" (McRobbie, 1998, p. 186). The characteristics of fashion and the ways in which it is transmitted vary, depending upon whether societies are more or less stratified and whether the distribution of income is more or less egalitarian. Fashion is created in clusters of formal and informal organizations whose characteristics also influence the nature of fashion in a particular time and place. Fashion creators respond to the needs and desires of their target consumers but often ignore the needs of others, particularly those who are marginal, economically or socially. Alternative fashion codes and discourses emerge from these groups and are often assimilated later by mainstream designers. In different periods, consumers have sought to express different types of meanings through clothing, including the affirmation of social status and the expression of personal identity or have simply engaged in postmodernist "style surfing." A variety of theoretical approaches, such as symbolic interactionism, postmodernism, social reproduction, cultural studies, and semiotics, have been applied to the subject of fashion, but this activity has not produced a coherent field of study, possibly because scholars who have studied the subject have come from many different disciplines.

*See also:* Beauty Culture, Fads, Fans and Fan Clubs, Men's Leisure Lifestyles, Teenage Leisure Trends, Women's Leisure Lifestyles

## BIBLIOGRAPHY

Barber, Bernard, and L. S. Lobel. "Fashion in Women's Clothes and the American Social System." *Social Forces* 31 (1952): 124–131.

Baudrillard, Jean. *Selected Writings.* Edited by Mark Poster. Cambridge, and Palo Alto, Calif.: Polity Press and Stanford University Press, 1988.

Becker, Howard. *Art Worlds.* Berkeley: University of California Press, 1982.

Blumer, H. "Fashion." *International Encyclopedia of the Social Sciences.* New York: Macmillan, 1968.

Bourdieu, Pierre. *Distinction: A Social Critique of the Judgment of Taste.* Cambridge, Mass.: Harvard University Press, 1984.

———. *The Field of Cultural Production.* Cambridge: Polity Press, 1993.

Cosgrove, S. "The Zoot Suit and Style Warfare." In *Zoot Suits and Second Hand Dresses.* Edited by Angela McRobbie. Boston: Unwin Hyman, 1988.

Crane, Diana. "Postmodernism and the Avant-Garde: Stylistic Changes in Fashion Design." *Modernism/Modernity* 4, no. 3 (1997a): 123–140.

———. "Globalization, Organizational Size, and Innovation in the French Luxury Fashion Industry: Production of Culture Theory Revisited." *Poetics* 24 (July 1997b): 393–414.

———. *Fashion and Its Social Agendas: Class, Gender, and Identity in Clothing.* Chicago: University of Chicago Press, 2000.

Davis, Fred. *Fashion, Culture, and Identity.* Chicago: University of Chicago Press, 1992.

De La Haye, Amy, and Cathie Dingwall. *Surfers Soulies Skinheads and Skaters: Subcultural Style from the Forties to the Nineties.* Woodstock, N.Y.: Overlook Press, 1996.

Douglas, Mary. *Thought Styles: Critical Essays on Good Taste.* London: Sage Publications, 1996.

Finkelstein, Joanne. "Chic Outrage and Body Politics." *European Journal of Women's Studies* 3 (1996): 231–249.

Freitas, Anthony, Susan Kaiser, Joan Chandler, Carol Hall, Jung-Won Kim, and Tania Hammidi. "Appearance Management as Border Construction: Least Favorite Clothing, Group Distancing, and Identity . . . Not!" *Sociological Inquiry* 67 (1997): 323–335.

Giddens, Anthony. *Modernity and Self-Identity.* Cambridge: Polity Press, 1991.

Gutman, Jonathan, and Michael K. Mills. "Fashion Life Style, Self-Concept, Shopping Orientation, and Store Patronage: An Integrative Analysis." *Journal of Retailing* 58 (Summer 1982): 64–86.

Hebdige, Dick. *Subculture: The Meaning of Style.* New York: Methuen, 1979.

Jones, Mablen. *Getting It On: The Clothing of Rock 'n' Roll.* New York: Abbeville Press, 1987.

Joseph, Nathan. *Uniforms and Nonuniforms: Communication Through Clothing.* Westport, Conn.: Greenwood Press, 1986.

Kaiser, Susan B. *The Social Psychology of Clothing and Personal Adornment.* New York: Macmillan, 1985.

Kaiser, Susan, Richard H. Nagasawa, and Sandra S. Hutton. "Fashion, Postmodernity and Personal Appearance: A Symbolic Interactionist Formulation." *Symbolic Interaction* 2 (1991): 165–185.

Krafft, Susan. "Discounts Drive Clothes." *American Demographics* 13 (1991):11.

McRobbie, Angela. "Second-Hand Dresses and the Role of the Ragmarket." In *Zoot Suits and Second-Hand Dresses.* Edited by Angela McRobbie. Boston: Unwin Hyman, 1988.

———. *British Fashion Design: Rag Trade or Image Industry?* London: Routledge, 1998.

Melinkoff, Ellen. *What We Wore: An Offbeat Social History of Women's Clothing, 1950–1980.* New York: William Morrow, 1984.

Muggleton, David. *Inside Subculture: The Postmodern Meaning of Style.* New York: Berg, 2000.

Poggioli, Renato. *The Theory of the Avant-Garde.* Translated by Gerald Fitzgerald. Cambridge, Mass.: Harvard University Press, 1968.

Polhemus, Ted. *Street Style: From Sidewalk to Catwalk.* London: Thames and Hudson, 1994.

Roberts, Mary Louise 1994 *Civilization Without Sexes: Reconstructing Gender in Postwar France, 1917-1927.* Chicago: University of Chicago Press, 1994.

Rubinstein, Ruth P. *Dress Codes: Meanings and Messages in American Culture.* Boulder, Colo.: Westview Press, 1995.

Simmel, Georg. "Fashion." *American Journal of Sociology* 62 (1957): 541–558. Originally appeared in 1904.

Smith, Bonnie G. *Ladies of the Leisure Class: The Bourgeoises of Northern France in the Nineteenth Century.* Princeton, N.J.: Princeton University Press, 1981.

Steele, Valerie. *Paris Fashion.* New York: Oxford University Press, 1988.

White, Shane, and Graham White. *Stylin' African American Expressive Culture from Its Beginnings to the Zoot Suit.* Ithaca, N.Y.: Cornell University Press, 1998.

Wolf, Naomi. *The Beauty Myth: How Images of Beauty Are Used Against Women.* New York: William Morrow, 1991.

Young, Agnes. *Recurring Cycles of Fashion, 1760–1937.* New York: Harper, 1937.

*Diana Crane*

# FAST FOOD

Fast food is an umbrella term, encompassing a broad category of foods, a type of restaurant delivery, and a style of eating. Fast food includes many different types of relatively inexpensive foods, ranging from pizza to hamburgers to ethnic specialties, which are sold and packaged in similar manners. Usually served freshly prepared and hot, fast foods are commonly packaged for off-site, or "to-go," consumption, either in aluminum foil, waxed paper, or a cardboard box. Customers usually purchase fast food across a counter, or through a drive-up window, though table service is occasionally available when seating space is provided for customers. Popularly called "fast food," these foods and delivery formats are known in the restaurant industry as quick-service foods. Hamburgers remain the dominant food product in this quick-service market, but a plethora of other offerings, such as chicken, fish, hot dogs, pasta, burritos, and roast beef, now compete for consumer dollars. The aggregate sales of the fast-food industry in the United States consistently represent an increasingly larger percentage of overall consumer dollars spent on food, reflecting fast food's growing role in American society.

History does not document the precise origins of modern fast food. In ancient cities, food vendors sold prepared wares on the streets to both urban residents and travelers. Though the precise food offerings varied depending on area and time period, such street foods were usually inexpensive and simple, designed for easy and immediate consumption. Immigrants arriving from Europe, Africa, and Asia carried a multitude of different foods to America, including many of these simple street foods. Reserving elaborate and labor-intensive cooking for holidays and celebrations, most of these immigrants groups favored a few simple food items for their daily fare, usually being the common "peasant" or street foods of their homelands. Mexicans still ate beans and tortillas, Italians ate pasta and flat breads, Asians ate rice-based dishes, and Germans ate dark breads and fatty sausages. Daily fare for virtually all immigrant groups was simple, inexpensive, and familiar.

Many of these immigrant favorites became the "fast foods" of the early twentieth century. Pushcart vendors sold ethnic fare such as meatballs, sausage, or stew at factory gates, catering to the needs and tastes of hungry workers. These pushcart food items proved to be popular among the male immigrant factory workers, but they never gained a popular mainstream following.

Appearing at the beginning of the twentieth century, urban diners were a transitional link between pushcart food vendors and our modern era of fast food. Diners were small neighborhood restaurants, usually offering very limited seating, and an equally limited menu, featuring items cooked and served on a "short-order" basis. Catering to primarily working-class customers, urban diners became popular by offering hearty fried meals for an inexpensive price. In addition to being known for their good food, diners were also distinctive in that they were often fabricated from old rail- or streetcars. In addition to diners, hot-dog stands became popular in New York in the 1890s, beginning in resort areas and later spreading throughout the city and beyond. Though the hot dog would consistently remain behind the hamburger in fast-food popularity, it became a mainstay of baseball parks, street cart vendors, and outdoor picnics throughout the twentieth century.

## Modern Fast Food

Modern fast food began in the early 1900s with the introduction and effective marketing of the recognizable hamburger sandwich. Prior to the twentieth century, ground meat was not mainstream fare in America, usually served only in the form of meatballs wrapped in bread by food vendors at county fairs and other summer festivals. Conflicting regional stories exist as to who exactly invented the hamburger sandwich, but its most verifiable originator was Wichita fry cook Walt Anderson, who began selling a flattened ground-beef patty on a bun in 1916. His hamburger sandwiches proved popular among hungry customers, quickly allowing Anderson to open additional hamburger stands. Partnering with Edgar "Billy" Ingram in 1921, he formed the White Castle System of Eating Houses, a restaurant chain that became the prototype for modern fast-food companies. Over the next decade, Anderson and Ingram's White Castle System spread from Wichita to most of the major cities in the midwest and on the east coast. Different from earlier short-order restaurants, White Castle offered a very streamlined menu, with only hamburgers, Coca-Cola, coffee, and pie. Throughout the company there was a standardized architecture for all its buildings, uniform food-quality rules and preparation methods, and strict guidelines for employee performance and hygiene. White Castle stressed high-quality ingredients, permanence, and meticulous cleanliness, deliberately attempting to overcome commonly held negative views about ground meat and transient, unsanitary food vendors. Anderson and Ingram encouraged customers to buy their burgers in large quantities, "by the sack," on a carry-out "to-go" basis. They were successful wherever they opened new restaurants, frequently with customers lined up for blocks waiting to buy their burgers. Other entrepreneurs observed this overnight success and rapid growth across the northeast and immediately opened their own hamburger restaurants, often closely copying White Castle's architecture, name, products, and marketing campaigns. Cities throughout the United States quickly became saturated with new hamburger chains, soon making the hamburger sandwich America's single most-consumed food. In fact, by 1930, the president of the American Restaurant Association proudly proclaimed that apple pie and the hamburger were the two truly "American foods."

Continued popularity for the hamburger during the 1930s guaranteed that it was not just a passing fad. Despite the economic hardships of the Great Depression, and the closings of countless businesses, the fast-food hamburger industry continued to grow. Most chains sold their burgers for five cents, making them still affordable for all but the most destitute. The 1930s was also an era of innovations in the fast-food industry, introducing new products and delivery strategies. On the West Coast, Bob Wian's Big Boy Restaurants featured a multilayered, two-patty hamburger sandwich, while the midwest Kewpee

Hamburger chain constructed special windows in the sides of their restaurants, designed to serve food to motorists driving by in their cars. Men remained the mainstay of fast-food restaurant labor, but some companies began hiring young women as "car-hop" waitresses. Customers seemed to appreciate these innovations, buying an ever-increasing number of hamburgers each year throughout the decade.

This growth in the fast-food industry abruptly halted with the beginning of World War II. Extreme labor shortages and food rationing devastated all types of restaurants, and hamburger chains were especially hard hit by worker and meat scarcity. Major chains, with hundreds of outlets, either shrank to a fraction of their former size or closed down entirely. The federal government diverted large amounts of needed sugar, beef, pork, and coffee to the U.S. troops overseas, leaving consumers limited, and often only rationed access to these items. With millions of men off serving in the military, hamburger companies reluctantly hired women in their remaining restaurants, but after doing so, they quickly realized that these female replacements proved to be far superior workers. By 1945, company closures caused by supply and labor problems had temporarily crippled the restaurant industry, but also created a void to be filled by new chains in the postwar years.

The American economy regained a more normal peacetime footing within a few years after the war. Sporadic food shortages remained common, largely due to the United States needing to supply starving, war-torn nations around the world. Several of the surviving, but cash-strapped leading prewar fast-food chains remained in their original urban neighborhoods, either failing to see the profit potential in the growing suburban market, or simply lacking the necessary capital to expand their operations. In fact, all types of restaurateurs were slow to enter the suburban marketplace, possibly wary about consumer buying patterns in these new and untested communities

## Fast Food in the Suburbs

By the mid-1950s, new restaurants chains began directing their marketing efforts at the burgeoning suburban areas. The McDonald's hamburger chain led the expansion into these new bedroom communities, opening hundreds of restaurants across the United States. Offering a streamlined menu of hamburgers, French fries, soda, and milk shakes, this California-based chain became an overnight success and soon was the benchmark for fast-food chains everywhere. All McDonald's restaurants served their burgers in an unerringly identical fashion; a

1.6-ounce meat patty between a soft bun, topped with catsup, mustard, onions, and a pickle. Suburban customers seemed especially attracted to this safe level of predictability: their meals were the same each time, and the same as everyone else's. Avoiding urban areas, McDonald's exclusively targeted suburbia, building their walk-up stands near busy intersections and shopping areas. Though convenient for motorists, these locations were often inaccessible to pedestrians.

Brothers Maurice and Richard McDonald founded the company in 1939, in San Bernardino, California, but salesman Ray Kroc directed its rapid growth in the 1950s. Kroc devised a plan to aggressively expand with very little capital investment. Rather than building company-owned stands, Kroc sold strictly controlled franchises to local investors. By purchasing a franchise, franchisees bought use of the trademarked McDonald's company name, license for its distinctive sloped-roofed architecture and "golden arches," food item preparation methods, and national advertising support. Kroc's successful sale of franchises enabled his chain to grow to over 1,000 units by the end of the decade, making it the largest restaurant company in the country. Suburbanites fueled this successful growth by responding to McDonald's with enthusiasm, turning virtually every new franchise into an overnight financial success.

Closely following McDonald's into the suburban marketplace was Miami-based Insta-Burger King. Founded in 1954 by Jim McLamore and David Edgerton, Insta-Burger King spread throughout Florida, then to larger southeastern cities. Shortening his company name to Burger King, McLamore sought to have a restaurant in every town in the United States by the close of the 1950s. Falling short of that goal, he succeeded in franchising over 700 units, building a chain second only to Kroc's. Direct competition between McDonald's and Burger King became fierce in many areas, with each company often building restaurants either next door or across the street from the other. Both stressed low-priced hamburgers and efficient customer service in their advertisements. McLamore made his Burger King products distinctive by "flame broiling" hamburgers to customer order, instead of McDonald's more usual method of frying. Despite McLamore's claim of better quality, suburban consumers seemed to prefer McDonald's simple and standardized fare.

The fast growth and financial success of both Burger King and McDonald's encouraged even more national competition in the fast-food hamburger market. Soon a multitude of other fast-food restaurants appeared in suburban shopping areas, vying for consumer dollars. Most new chains were regional in scope, but some became national contenders. The Burger Chef chain appeared in the late 1950s and quickly saturated the eastern half of the country with franchises by the early 1960s. Burger Chef never achieved the level of national following enjoyed by McDonald's and Burger King, even though it did license over 1,000 active franchises by 1968. Even Wendy's, a popular Columbus, Ohio–based chain begun in 1969 by entrepreneur Dave Thomas, never ventured past a third-place standing. New fast-food chains featuring other food items, such as chicken, tacos, and pizza, however, posed the greatest threat to the two fast-food giants in the late 1960s.

By the end of that decade, McDonald's and Burger King competed for customers with newcomers Kentucky Fried Chicken, Pizza Hut, and Arby's. Many fast-food consumers preferred these alternative meals, and the market continued to diversify, welcoming other new chains, such as Taco Bell, Long John Silver's, and Roy Rogers. In addition to this increased variety of food offerings, a plethora of regional hamburger chains expanded quickly in the late-1960s, further saturating the fast-food industry. By the early 1970s, however, the bubble of franchise chain expansion finally burst, resulting in the demise of the smaller fast-food chains, and a further consolidation of market share by McDonald's, Burger King, and, soon after, Wendy's. This power distribution in the fast-food industry remained constant for the remainder of the twentieth century. Several new chains appeared in the 1980s and 1990s, and several others closed down, but the industry leaders remained firmly entrenched.

The growth of the fast-food industry, especially since World War II, reflects many drastic changes in American society. As mentioned earlier, the modern fast-food industry grew up in the midst of new suburban communities. Many of these new suburbanites had grown up in urban ethnic enclaves, maintaining strong ties to their countries of origin. Once in the suburbs, a prevailing norm of conformity encouraged many to shed or downplay their ethnic identities. Portraying themselves as purely American and demonstrating economic prosperity through purchasing consumer goods became a strong focus in their lives. Fast food became these new suburbanites' culinary "common ground," allowing everyone to dine together on what they perceived to be a genuinely American food. In a sense, eating fast-food hamburgers at these new franchised chain restaurants became a rite of acceptance into nonethnic suburbia.

The success of fast food also reflects a change in American lifestyles. Though originally marketed to a walking-city customer base, fast food became inexorably linked to the automobile soon after World War II. As cars proliferated to the point of several per family, American society became increasingly automobile dependent. This enhanced transportation resulted in greater time expectations, with people cramming increasingly more activities into each day. By the 1960s, many women had entered the full-time workforce, reducing the amount of time that traditional homemakers spent preparing daily meals. Rather than cooking meals and consuming them together, many families on increasingly tight schedules opted to purchase quickly available prepared fast foods. As leisure time became scarce, fast food became more convenient to the eating habits of the average American. In fact, fast food restaurants even became the central focus of leisure time, often the congregating spots for senior citizens in the morning and groups of teenagers later in the day.

## Criticism of Fast Food

While fast food, and especially the fast-food hamburger, has become a staple of the modern American diet, may critics charge that it causes a variety of public health problems, different environmental concerns, and an excessive homogenization of both American culture and other societies throughout the world. Many medical researchers contend that fast food typically gives consumers excessive fat and little nutritional value, leading to numerous obesity-related health problems. Recent national outbreaks of *E. coli* contamination and other serious pathogens have led to public scrutiny of meat purity. Still other research questions issues such as steroid and antibiotic use in cattle production, and its potentially deleterious effects on human health. Though fast food is part of the mainstream, eaten by millions of Americans each day, healthcare professionals almost uniformly condemn its regular consumption as an unsafe dietary practice.

Second to the health-related criticisms have been the environment concerns, especially about harmful packaging and the destruction of rain forests to produce lower-cost beef. A controversy ensued in the 1980s, when environmental groups condemned the fast-food industry for its use of excessive and nonbiodegradable packaging. Chains found the petroleum-based plastic and Styrofoam packaging to be advantageous because they better retained heat and cold and were significantly more moisture resistant. Environmentalists contended that the same qualities that made these substances moisture resistance also made them virtually impossible to decay in garbage landfills. Under growing public pressure, several of the leading chains attempted to appease critics by recycling used packaging into other plastic products, but eventually they returned to using primarily paper and cardboard containers.

Perhaps the most abstract criticism of fast food is a testament to its rampant popularity. Social critics condemn the saturation of fast food in American society and its spread throughout the world as a breakdown in cultural and culinary diversity, and to a greater extent the imposition of generic American consumer culture on developing nations. "McDonaldization" has become a common term for an overwhelming homogenizing force that destroys the unique and wonderful aspects of diverse cultures. Although fast food in itself is not the sole "McDonaldizing" phenomena, nor does it seem to be an orchestrated conspiracy, it is often the most obvious symptom of a spreading American consumer culture. Golden arches appearing on a busy city intersection in the developing world often becomes the scapegoat for a much larger onslaught.

*See also:* Coffee Houses and Café Society; Diners; Dining Out

**BIBLIOGRAPHY**

Boas, Max. *Big Mac: The Unauthorized Story of McDonald's.* New York: Mentor, 1976.

Emerson, Robert. *Fast Food: The Endless Shakeout.* New York: Lebhar-Friedman Books, 1979.

Jakle, John and Keith Sculle. *Fast Food: Roadside Restaurants in the Automobile Age.* Baltimore: Johns Hopkins University Press, 1999.

Mariani, John. *America Eats Out.* New York: Morrow, 1991.

*David Gerard Hogan*

# FIELD HOCKEY

Field hockey is the oldest-known ball-and-stick game and is believed to date from the earliest civilizations. Although the exact origin of the game remains unknown, 4,000-year-old drawings found in the tomb at Beni-Hasen in the Nile Valley of Egypt depicted men playing the sport. Throughout the following centuries, variations of the game were played by a spectrum of cultures ranging from Greeks and Romans to Ethiopians and Aztecs. The Arabs, Greeks, Persians, and Romans each had their own versions of hockey. Traces of a stick game played by the Aztec Indians have also been found. Hockey can also be identified with other early games such as hurling and shinty. During the Middle Ages, a French stick game called hoquet was played, and the English word may have derived from this. The sport is referred to as field hockey to distinguish it from the sport of ice hockey.

Modern hockey was developed in the British Isles, but it was not until the first half of the nineteenth century that field hockey became well established. The first club was Blackheath, headquartered in southeast London prior to 1861. The club played on a large piece of open ground with crudely designed sticks and a "ball" that was a solid cube of black rubber. At this time, there were few offensive or defensive tactics involved in the game, and, although Blackheath was the first club, it was Teddington, another London club, that modernized and refined the game by introducing several major variations into hockey, including banning the use of hands or the lifting of sticks above the shoulder. They also began to use a sphere as the ball, instead of the rubber cube. Most important, they instituted the striking circle that was incorporated into the rules of the newly founded Hockey Association in London in 1886.

After modern field hockey had developed in the British Isles in the late nineteenth century, it spread throughout the British Empire. The British army introduced the game to India and throughout the British colonies, leading to the first international competition in 1895. Hockey first appeared on the Olympic program at the 1908 London Games and again in 1920 at Antwerp. The sport was featured on the program at Amsterdam in 1928 and has been an Olympic sport ever since. The call for more international matches led to the introduction of the World Cup (1971), and some of the other major international tournaments include the Asian Cup, Asian Games, European Cup, and Pan American Games. India is the most powerful field hockey nation in Olympic history. Between 1928 and 1956, India won six gold medals and thirty consecutive games. The streak ended in 1960 with a loss to Pakistan in the finals. Field hockey has become an integral part of national sports in both India and Pakistan. By 2003, field hockey was played all over the world by a variety of countries, and it was recognized as the second-largest team sport in the world, just behind soccer.

Although by the twentieth century field hockey was a popular women's sport, it was once considered far too dangerous for female participation. The ball, originally made from rubber, used in field hockey often travels at very high speeds, posing a risk to all players. Goalies are particularly vulnerable because they often must use their entire body to prevent the opposing team from scoring a goal. Therefore, field hockey goalies protect themselves with a shield of plastic armor. Field hockey quickly became popular with women whose previous introduction to sport included the "socially acceptable" outdoor ac-

tivities of croquette and lawn tennis. With more and more women becoming active in the sport, the liberating game of field hockey earned the dubious title as the only team sport considered proper for women. By 1887, the first women's hockey club appeared in East Mosley, England, and was quickly followed by the creation of the All England Women's Hockey Association in 1889. The sport spread across the Atlantic in 1901, when English physical education instructor Constance Applebee introduced the sport to the United States while attending a seminar at Harvard. Appalled at the parlor games passing for exercise among young American women, Applebee borrowed some sticks and a ball and staged the first hockey exhibition in the United States behind the Harvard gymnasium. The game received an enthusiastic response, and Applebee quickly spread the sport to some of the region's most prestigious women's schools.

Field hockey took its most important step forward in 1924 when the Fédération Internationale de Hockey (FIH), the world governing body for the sport, was founded in Paris under the initiative of Frenchman Paul Léautey. Léautey, who would become the first president of the FIH, was motivated to action following hockey's omission from the program of the 1924 Paris Games. To form the sport's international governing body, Léautey called together representatives from seven national federations; the seven founding members, which represented both men's and women's hockey in their countries, were Austria, Belgium, Czechoslovakia, France, Hungary, Spain, and Switzerland.

The women's game developed quickly in many countries. For example, by the early 1920s, several colleges and clubs sponsored field hockey teams for women in the United States. The U.S. women's touring field hockey team participated in its first international competition in 1920, and two years later the United States Field Hockey Association was founded for the purpose of promoting and generating enthusiasm for the sport. In 1927, the International Federation of Women's Hockey Associations (IFWHA) was formed. Its founding members were Australia, Denmark, England, Ireland, Scotland, South Africa, the United States, and Wales. The IFWHA merged with the FIH in 1982. In many ways, the FIH serves as the guardian of the sport. It works in cooperation with both the national and continental organizations to ensure consistency and unity in hockey around the world. The FIH not only regulates the sport, but also is responsible for its development and promotion so as to guarantee a secure future for the field hockey.

*See also:* Ice Hockey, Olympics, Women's Leisure Lifestyles

## BIBLIOGRAPHY

Adelson, Bruce. *Field Hockey*. Philadelphia: Chelsea House Publisher, 2000.

Anders, Elizabeth, and Sue Myers. *Field Hockey: Steps to Success*. Champaign, Ill.: Human Kinetics, 1998.

Axton, William, and Wendy Martin. *Field Hockey*. Indianapolis, Ind.: Masters Press, 1993.

Mackey, Helen. *Field Hockey, An International Team Sport*. Englewood Cliffs, N.J.: Prentice-Hall, 1963.

*Philip F. Xie*

# FIGHTING

**See** *Boxing, Recreational Fighting*

# FILM VIEWING

**See** *Movies' Impact on Popular Leisure*

# FIREWORKS

**See** *Fourth of July*

# FISHING, FRESHWATER

Fishing comes in a variety of forms. The earliest fishing was undoubtedly subsistence fishing. A person captured the fish in the most effective way possible, and then that person, his family, or his tribe consumed it. At some point, an entrepreneurial fellow came up with the bright idea of not only getting fish for oneself and family but getting enough fish to be able to barter with or sell to others. That was the birth of commercial fishing. Subsistence and commercial fishing are practiced today in virtually every modern society. On a global scale subsistence fishers far outnumber all other type of fishers. In terms of the number of fish captured, commercial fishing eclipses other forms by far.

In contrast, sport fishing is a relatively new phenomenon and is differentiated from the other types of fishing by the participants' voluntarily limiting techniques and equipment in an effort to make the activity as fair as possible. For example, fishing with underwater explosives is effective, but it is not very "sporting." In the last century, governmental agencies in North America, as well as in all other developed countries, have adopted laws to ensure a fair contest. Sport fishing can be divided into two different categories—that which takes place in the oceans (saltwater fishing) and that which takes place on lakes, ponds, and streams (freshwater fishing).

It is impossible to determine when the first person decided to fish for fun or for sport. Fishing for enjoyment by Japanese nobility in about 200 A.D. is the earliest mention of the sport. Not until nearly 1,500 years later do we find significant writing about sport fishing. Charles Waterman has surmised that sport fishing was overshadowed in development and in its documentation by hunting because fishing lacked the element of bravery ascribed to hunting. Fishing was a more pensive activity and did not lend itself to particularly heroic writings.

Most early literature about freshwater sport angling is primarily English. Izaak Walton wrote *The Compleat Angler* in 1653, and it remains the classic to this day. The English penchant for freshwater sport fishing eventually found its way to the United States; however, it did not become popular until the middle of the nineteenth century. In England fishing for fun had been reserved for aristocracy, and the frontiersmen in America, even if they had found the time to engage in the pastime, were loath to do anything even remotely similar to that of English aristocracy. Starting in the eastern states with trout fishing, moving to the southern states with black bass fishing, and then reaching the Midwest and West with fishing for nearly all species, freshwater sport fishing was finally established as one of the most popular leisure activities for Americans by the end of the nineteenth century.

## Development of Freshwater Sport Fishing

The freshwater fishing common in 2004 is largely the result of the technological advances of the past century. Early fishers used equipment that would be laughable by today's standards. All of their equipment was fashioned by the anglers themselves from the materials that were readily available. While there are hundreds of different types of equipment used by modern anglers, a review of the development of reels, rods, boats, and electrical equipment provides an overview of the evolution of the major types of freshwater fishing equipment.

Reels were an invaluable addition to early fishing. For some time line for fishing had been wrapped around a convenient-sized object and pulled off as needed. Some

**Fly fishing.** Lynn Burry stands in the Whitewater River in Brookville, Indiana, fly fishing. Fly fishing, in which the fishermen often craft their own special "flies" to use as bait, is one of the most popular forms of freshwater fishing and was featured prominently in the 1992 film *A River Runs Through It.* © *AP/Wide World Photos*

of these crude wooden spools can still be found in antique angling equipment collections. Of course this cumbersome method of storage reduced early anglers' ability to reach fish in areas other than their immediate surroundings. In England, the Nottingham reel was the epitome of reels in the 1700s. This reel was fashioned of wood, as were reels of lesser quality in other parts of the world. Around 1820, great advances were made in the construction of reels. Better raw materials and more sophisticated tools allowed for the construction of metal reels. In the United States several watchmakers made reels of brass that contained steel gears. In the early 2000s, reels were made of metal and plastic and came in a variety of designs for different types of fishing. For example, reels were designed specifically for the size of the fish pursued, for the characteristic of the species angled for, and for the anticipated climatic and geographical fishing conditions.

Fishing rods are designed to get the bait to the fish and to reduce the stress on the fragile line once a fish has taken the bait. Waterman insightfully notes that the earliest devices were "more poles than rods." They were long (up to fourteen feet) and heavy by modern standards. A variety of woods were used for the first rods. A major advance was the use of bamboo for fly fishing rods, a welcome upgrade from the heavy rods that did not allow anglers the sensitivity they sought. Since that time rods have progressed through various construction materials and designs. The most desirable qualities in fishing rods have always been durability, strength, maneuverability, and sensitivity. Fiberglass was the material of choice in the 1960s and 1970s. Graphite rods and composites of new materials were common in the early 2000s. As with reels, rods came in a variety of sizes and shapes, depending on the conditions and the methods used for fishing.

Freshwater sport fishing is almost universally predicated upon enticing a fish to "take" an object on the end of the line. The object typically contains a hook of some sort to keep the fish on the line. Such objects run the gamut from different natural baits such as worms, minnows, and insects to an even greater variety of human-made baits. Artificial flies are fashioned from fur and feathers. Lures are made from wood, metal, plastic, and rubber, and are designed to imitate natural food or to incite fish to strike the object out of the urge to protect itself.

346

Boats have been an important part of freshwater fishing for the past two centuries. Just as with the development of rods, reels, and lures, sport fishers' needs and the availability of new materials have driven the development of boats. The first fishing boats for freshwater were wooden and propelled by paddles or poles. Fiberglass and aluminum became popular boat construction materials in the middle of the twentieth century. Paddles and poles were largely replaced by outboard motors driven by gasoline or by electricity. The early bass boats of the 1950s and 1960s were fairly expensive and entailed a large commitment from the typical angler. However, at the beginning of the twenty-first century, a reliable boat could be purchased by most fishers without undue financial burden.

The most remarkable advances have come about in the use of electronic fishing equipment since the 1980s. Fish detectors are now available that allow anglers to search for fish in even the most turbulent and deepest waters. Global locating systems using Earth-orbiting satellites make it possible for fishers to return to the same spot on a body of water time after time.

The evolution of fishing equipment has contributed to the continuing popularity of freshwater fishing, but some have suggested that the increase of technology has destroyed the delicate balance that exists between fish and fisher. They claim that the fish no longer have a chance. Because the equipment has changed dramatically in ways that allow anglers to pursue their prey more effectively, laws and regulations have been established to keep the contest even. For example, many lakes and streams have numerous restrictions on the equipment and the methods that can be used to catch fish.

## Specialization of Freshwater Sport Fishing

The ongoing development of fishing equipment corresponds to the specialization of freshwater sport fishing. Whereas in previous centuries, anglers were content to catch any type of fish with any method, the anglers of the early 2000s typically had very specific goals and techniques. They specialized not only in the species of fish pursued but in the methods and the resources on which the activity took place. Hobson Bryan's classic study of the specialization of fishers laid the groundwork for research into specialization in many other areas of human activity.

## Commercialization of Freshwater Sport Fishing

Commercialism is the process by which an increasing number of tangible and intangible items are produced and marketed for the purpose of being sold. Leisure and recreation have become increasingly commercialized. Richard Butsch has noted: "In ways that are obvious even to the casual observer, leisure activities have become commercialized. Two centuries ago Americans purchased few leisure goods or services: made their own music and toys for their children and drank homemade cider. Today, most of our leisure activities depend upon some purchased commodity: a television set, a baseball, tickets to the theater" (p. 3).

Freshwater sport fishing has not been immune from claims of commercialism. Anglers no longer make their own fishing rods and reels. Instead, they purchase them from local sporting goods stores or international conglomerates. While anglers once found fishing bait by wading in streams, looking under rocks, and walking through the forests, modern anglers meander through jungles of fishing equipment at huge sporting goods outlets to find what they need. It is not uncommon for anglers to pay for the opportunity to participate in their sport. Such an act was disdainful fifty years ago. Whereas previously, fishing skills were acquired through years of observation and instruction by parents and friends, modern anglers are more likely to learn from a guide or at a special school for a fee. Based upon decades of critique of the capitalist system, historians and sociologists have argued that such commercialism has devalued the activity of sport fishing.

## Sport Fishing Tournaments

A logical result of the natural competitiveness of anglers and recent advances in marketing is the modern fishing tournament, in which participants attempt to catch the most fish and the largest fish within a prescribed time period using equipment and techniques previously determined. Prizes, ranging from thousands of dollars and fully equipped boats in the larger contests to $10 pots in the smaller contests, are awarded to the winners. Fishing tournaments are controversial for a number of reasons. Some believe that the obvious display of competition reflects badly on the sport; some believe that such an intense concentration of angling negatively impacts the resources; some believe that tournaments open the door to even more commercialization of the sport.

## Freshwater Fishing Resource Management

Successful fishing depends on healthy and productive fisheries. Before the number of anglers swelled to 2004 levels, streams and lakes in the United States and Canada were able to naturally provide fish from year to year. By the beginning of the twenty-first century, it was necessary to carefully manage natural resource areas in ways that would ensure fish populations for anglers. State and federal agencies were given the responsibility of designing and operating a system that recognized the needs of a diverse population of anglers while protecting North America's water resources. Most of the costs for the operations of the agencies and their programs were funded through the purchase of required annual fishing licenses.

## Freshwater Fishing and Tourism

Freshwater sport fishing is a multibillion-dollar business in the United States and Canada. According to the American Sportsfishing Association, in 2001, 45 million American anglers spent nearly $42 billion on fishing tackle, trips, and related services. Several times that amount is spent on fishing equipment and services. Moreover, millions of dollars are spent each year on related goods and services such as travel and lodging. Because of the potential for freshwater fishing to pump large amounts of money into local and state economies, communities and states are developing resources and programs to attract anglers.

Of course, tourism has the potential to affect communities negatively. Resource depletion, impact on the local infrastructure, and social disruption are common threats from the activity. Modern research seeks to understand the phenomenon in an effort to minimize the adverse effects of freshwater fishing tourism while increasing the potential for positive results.

*See also:* Camping; Fishing, Saltwater/Deep Sea; Hunting

## BIBLIOGRAPHY

American Sportsfishing Association. Available from http://www.asafishing.org.

Bryan, Hobson. *Conflict in the Great Outdoors: Toward an Understanding and Managing of Diverse Sportsmen Preferences.* Tuscaloosa: University of Alabama Press, 1979.

Butsch, Richard, ed. *For Fun and Profit: The Transformation of Leisure into Consumption.* Philadelphia: Temple University Press, 1990.

Cross, Gary. *A Social History of Leisure Since 1600.* State College, Pa.: Venture, 1990.

Gabrielson, Ira, ed. *The Fisherman's Encyclopedia.* Harrisburg, Pa.: Stackpole Company, 1958.

Trench, Charles Chevevix. *A History of Angling.* Chicago: Follett Publishing Company, 1974.

Waterman, Charles F. *A History of Angling.* Tulsa, Okla.: Stillwater Press, 1981.

*Daniel G. Yoder*

# FISHING, SALTWATER/ DEEP SEA

Throughout history, people have fished for many reasons. Certainly, many anglers consume the fish they catch, but sport fishers engage in this activity primarily for the challenge rather than for the practical benefit of consuming or selling that which they catch.

## History of Saltwater Fishing

Of course, humans have been taking fish from the sea for nearly as long as they've been on Earth. But taking fish for sport is a more recent phenomenon. From the scattered references to fishing in the sea, it appears that freshwater fishing for sport predated saltwater fishing as sport. Charles Waterman argues that early ocean fishing was such a dangerous and difficult economic pursuit "that it is no wonder that it was a long time before anyone seriously considered fishing in the sea for fun" (Waterman, p. 122). It was the mid- and late nineteenth century that saltwater fishing became widely recognized as sport. Interestingly enough, the English infatuation with freshwater fishing for trout and salmon may have been somewhat of an impediment to the elevation of saltwater fishing. As a result, at the end of the nineteenth century, the hotbeds for saltwater fishing were near the United States, New Zealand, and Australia.

No history of saltwater fishing would be complete without mention of the Tuna Club of Avalon, Santa Catalina, which was formed in 1899 and whose members fished primarily off the coast of Northern California. As a handful of pioneers demonstrated that large ocean fish (notably tuna and a variety of billed fish) could be hooked and brought to boat with artificial baits similar to those used by Englishmen for trout and salmon, the sport gained popularity. During these early years a few prominent anglers/authors—Frederic Aflalo from Great Britain and Zane Grey from the United States—caught the imagination of sportsmen from around the world with stories of heroic battles with various denizens of the deep. Later, Ernest Hemingway mesmerized readers with exploits of fishing the high seas. By then, saltwater fishing for sport was well established.

## Types of Saltwater Game Fish

Several hundred species are considered game fish. The most popular can be placed into three broad classes.

**Marlin fishing.** One of the most popular big game fish worldwide is the marlin. There are three main types of marlin: pacific blue, black, and striped. A saltwater fish, it is easily recognizable by its elongated, pointy snout. © *Corbis*

**Billfish** To the uninformed or to the novice fisher, deep-sea fishing is the pursuit of billfish. Billfish are to saltwater fishing as salmon are to freshwater fishing. Most people see or envision scenes of great silver billfish leaping several feet out of the deep blue water with the equally blue sky behind them. The category of billfish includes swordfish, spearfish, sailfish, and the various marlins—white, blue, black, and striped. In particular, marlins hold a very privileged position in sea angling. Peter Goadby writes of the marlins, "No fish creates more excitement than marlin; no other fish has gained more respect, is instinctively thought of for tag and release and is more important to the economy of the recreational fishing port and fishing destinations and sport fishing generally" (Goadby, p. 71). Marlins are such incredible fighters that it was not until 1903 that the first was caught on a rod and reel. The largest marlin ever caught on rod and reel weighed in at 1560 pounds.

**Tuna** All of Earth's oceans have tuna. This group of game fish ranges from the twenty-pound skipjacks to the giant bluefin tuna that can reach weights of 1,800 pounds. Frank Moss states that the tuna "are the most powerful fish that swims" (Moss, p. 3). He goes on to compare these fish to torpedoes with their ability to fold their fins into shallow depressions on their bodies. The small but incredibly powerful tail can propel these game fish up to sixty miles per hour. A 183-pound bluefin tuna that was caught off the coast of Northern California in 1898 "triggered the formation of a club and from it, the rules and ethics and the sport of offshore fishing worldwide" (Goadby, p. 115).

**Sharks** Sharks hold an interesting position for saltwater anglers. For the first fifty years of the sport, they were considered at best a nuisance and at other times a major problem. It was not unusual for a fisherman to hook and fight a game fish only to have it attacked and shredded by sharks shortly before it was brought to boat or shore. That began to change in the second half of the twentieth century when the shark showed that it could be a wonderful fighter—some making spectacular leaps and other doggedly diving to the depths of the ocean. Six species of shark—the mako, porbeagle, white, thresher, blue, and tiger—are considered game fish. The largest saltwater game fish ever caught on rod and reel is a 2,664-pound great white shark.

## Saltwater Fishing Techniques

Anglers have been incredibly innovative in their efforts to capture saltwater game fish. Most fish are caught from large, seafaring boats. Typically, the boat moves at a moderate pace, and baits, both natural and artificial, are trolled or dragged behind it. The moving bait attracts a variety of species of fish. Trolling works best for species that primarily feed near the surface of the ocean. Some species of saltwater game fish, however, rarely come to the surface of the ocean. For them, anglers usually drift baits deep in the ocean or anchor and drop baits down to where they are.

Not all saltwater fishing is undertaken from large boats. Some species such as tarpon and bonefish are found near shore or in shallow water. For these, anglers use small boats that can maneuver in just a few feet of water. Finally, a significant amount of saltwater fishing, though not deep-sea fishing, takes place not from boats of any sort but from piers, rocky outcrops, and beaches.

Some species of fish may be easily enticed to take a bait on a hook, but others require a great deal more effort and skill. Ingenious anglers who pursue species such as bluefin tuna or billfish may use kites that carry the bait and line far away from the boat and impart a particularly lively movement to the bait, attracting the fish. For sharks especially, a large amount of bait (chum) is put into the water in an effort to attract fish and cause a feeding frenzy. Chum usually consists of ground-up baitfish, and the chum areas can spread out over several hundred yards. Some anglers do not consider chumming an ethical fishing practice.

## Organizations and Tournaments

Although the majority of saltwater fishers are not members of any club or association, these small and large organizations have been a profound influence on the sport. There exist literally thousands of local clubs, hundreds of state and regional clubs, and a few national and international organizations. The first club was the Tuna Club at Avalon, Santa Catalina, founded in 1899. The largest, and arguably most important, organization today is the International Game Fishing Association (IGFA). The IGFA, as do many other clubs on a much smaller scale, encourages ethical fishing behavior, including adherence to rules and regulations, the generation and exchange of information, the projection of a positive image for the sport, and conservation for fishes and fishing-related resources.

Without fishing clubs it is unlikely that competitive tournaments could be held. The operation and supervision of a tournament is best accomplished not by a handful of unrelated anglers but by a coordinated team of volunteer club members. Although some tournaments are highly visible and offer considerable prize money, most are small local events that offer little more than fellowship and fun.

## Conservation

Worldwide, most species of game fish are in decline, primarily due to pollution, commercial fishing, and sport fishing. Not just billfish, tuna, and sharks, but red drum, bluefish, and even rockfish have fallen victim to this trend. Landings in both the Atlantic and Pacific Oceans peaked many years ago, and today they are considerably lower. Several organizations—including the Costal Conservation Association, IGFA, National Coalition for Marine Conservation, Recreational Fishing Alliance, and the Billfish Alliance—are aware of the status of many species and have initiated efforts to reverse the disturbing trends.

Freshwater fishing practices "catch and release"; saltwater fishing practices "tag and release." Not only does this practice return the fish to its natural environment—to perhaps be caught again—it is a mainstay for much current research on many saltwater species. By understanding the movement of fishes, conservationists are better prepared either to maintain current populations or to increase the numbers of game fish in the world's oceans.

*See also:* Camping; Fishing, Freshwater; Hunting

### BIBLIOGRAPHY

Dunn, Bob, and Peter Goadby. *Saltwater Game Fishes of the World: An Illustrated History.* Portland, Oreg.: Frank Amato Publishers, 2000.

Goadby, Peter. *Saltwater Gamefishing: Offshore and Onshore.* Camden, Maine: International Marine Publishing Company, 1992.

Heilner, Van Camen. *Salt Water Fishing.* 2d ed. New York: Alfred A. Knopf, 1953.

International Game Fish Association. "World Saltwater Records." Available from http://www.schooloffyflyfishing.com/resources.

Moss, Frank T. *Successful Ocean Game Fishing.* Camden, Maine: International Marine Publishing Company, 1971.

Waterman, Charles F. *A History of Angling.* Tulsa, Okla.: Winchester Press, 1981.

*Daniel G. Yoder*

# FLYING

**See** *Air Travel and Leisure*

# FOLK MUSIC

**See** *Traditional Folk Music Festivals*

# FOOD

**See** *Cooking for Fun; Diners; Dining Out; Fast Food*

# FOOTBALL

During the course of the nineteenth century, the United States faced the transition from a rural, agrarian society to an urban, industrial one. Immigrants flooded the overcrowded cities, threatening the political power of American nativists. Women threatened men as they clamored for greater independence, suffrage, education, and a semblance of equal rights. By the end of the era, the country contended with Great Britain and European nations for international power; but first Americans had to heal sectional strife after the Civil War and establish their own national identity. One of the ways in which the United States addressed these issues proved to be a new game: football.

In the years following the Civil War, rapid industrialization caused many men to lose their independence and become employees for wages, a blow to their self-esteem. The concomitant lack of a war, in which men traditionally proved their manhood, also caused them to question their waning masculinity. For middle-class and wealthy young men who didn't perform manual labor, football began to serve as a surrogate form of war to prove their bravery. Choking, tripping, and punching an oppo-

nent were all part of the early game, and flying-wedge plays and aerial attacks later associated the game with military purposes. Charges of brutality persisted for years, and big hits continue to fascinate spectators today.

## Origins of American Football

Kicking games had been played for centuries in Europe, usually among young men within a community or in opposition to nearby villages. Schoolboys adopted such games for their leisure time, and the games were transported with colonists to America. Harvard students used soccerlike games as an excuse for intramural mayhem in the 1820s. Yale students became so unruly during such affairs that school administrators banned the games in 1860, but Boston high school boys initiated play during that same decade.

Different versions of the games evolved: one in which players were allowed to kick the ball only, and another in which players were able to advance the ball by running with it. In 1869, Princeton met Rutgers in a series of the soccer-style games. The initial match on November 6 is considered the first intercollegiate football game to be held in the United States, and the game's first rivalry. Columbia joined the competition the following year, and Princeton codified ten rules in 1871. Harvard began playing by rugby rules in 1872, and Yale used as many as twenty players. The lack of uniformity led to a rules convention, which was held in New York in 1873. The meeting would eventually become an annual affair, with revisions that produced the modern game of football over the next fifty years.

In 1874, Harvard played a series of games with McGill University of Montreal. Though victorious, Harvard favored the faster-paced rugby style of its opponent and adopted the game as its own. In a further break from the British concept of amateurism, Harvard handpicked its best players in an attempt to win, judging the outcome more important than the exercise. Spectators were also charged 50 cents, thus leading to the commercialization of intercollegiate athletics.

The Harvard rivalry with Yale, which began in 1875, necessitated compromise, as both teams played by different rules. The top college teams agreed on use of the rugby rules the next year, but they disagreed on the number of players, with Harvard favoring fifteen rather than eleven.

High school boys followed the lead of their older counterparts and began organizing formal games as well. By the late 1870s, the game had spread to high schools in the Philadelphia and Chicago areas. The college players

> "... football ... embodies so many factors that are typically American ... virile, intensive, aggressive energy that makes for progress is the root which upholds and feeds American supremacy and American football."
>
> **James Knox, Harvard University, cited in John A. Blanchard, ed., *The H Book of Harvard Athletics, 1852–1922*. Harvard Varsity Club, 1923.**

introduced equipment innovations as well, adopting canvas jackets and pants for protection but also greasing them to foil tacklers. Players wore their hair long for added protection from head blows until the advent of headgear and nosepieces, the forerunners of face masks, in the 1890s.

As the intensity of rivalries grew, school and community pride fostered a need to win. American competitiveness further distinguished the nation from the British, who played for the love of the game. The American emphasis on winning led to strategic innovations as well. In 1879, Princeton introduced the rise of interference to protect the ball carrier from tacklers, as well as the onside kick to retain possession of the ball (the onside kick occurs when one team, during the kickoff, kicks the ball only a short distance in hopes that they can recover the loose ball before the other team can; it is often used late in games when one team needs to get the ball to try to score quickly). Walter Camp of Yale chaired the rules committee in 1880 and led that regulating body through significant revisions until his death in 1925. Camp initiated the scrimmage line in 1880, divorcing football from the rugby scrum and requiring separate offensive and defensive strategies.

In 1882, Camp introduced the concept of downs and yardage (originally three downs to gain five yards) to eliminate boring, plodding, ball-control offenses designed simply to keep the ball away from opponents. The emphasis still remained on the kicking game, however, as field goals counted for five points and points after touchdowns counted for four.

Debates over player eligibility ensued as teams sought the best athletes in order to win, and Camp assumed the role of coach at Yale, a transition from the previously student-directed activity. As coach, Camp organized the team along corporate lines and instituted scientific training regimens, position specialization, and alumni boosterism. Along with his rule-making responsibilities, such efforts earned him the nickname "Father of American Football."

Issues of brutality, eligibility, and impartiality led to further rule changes, including the adoption of a referee in lieu of alumni judges in 1885. Additional referees were added in subsequent years. Teamwork, the clocklike precision of plays, and the increasing specialization of player responsibilities reflected the industrial process taking place in the United States, and newspapers promoted greater interest in the sport. By the 1880s, high schools and colleges in the Midwest and South had adopted the game, and play began in California by 1886. Football surpassed baseball as the most popular sport on college campuses by 1887.

## Commercialization

The commercialization of football proceeded apace, with the championship game—usually contested between the Big Three of Harvard, Princeton, and Yale—occurring in New York to maximize spectators. The 1893 affair between Princeton and Yale drew 40,000 spectators, and countless others witnessed the four-hour parade that preceded the game; football had become a national spectacle that brought pride, prestige, and money to the team coffers. The largesse derived from such ventures eventually led school authorities to establish greater control over student-run activities and the profits that derived from them.

Star athletes became lionized on campus and received preferential treatment in separate dorms, on training tables, and in the classroom. In 1889, Walter Camp and sportswriter Caspar Whitney further acknowledged their heroic status by selecting the first of their all-American teams. All members of the original unit emanated from the Big Three institutions, further establishing the masculinity, morality, and Anglo leadership of their clientele in the face of the overwhelming immigrant hordes who populated the cities. Such pronouncements also made statements to Great Britain and other powers that the United States was developing a virile leadership as an emerging world power.

Internecine rivalries continued, however, as teams sought national and local esteem by defeating competitors. In the quest for victory, Harvard instituted spring practices in 1889, and devised shifts to gain a numerical advantage or exploit physical mismatches. Both high schools and colleges utilized tramp athletes, some of whom weren't even enrolled as students, to maximize their winning chances. Successful teams were feted with banquets, gifts, and adulation, a practice that led to the birth of professional football.

In 1892, Walter "Pudge" Heffelfinger, a Yale all-American and the dominant player of the era, began accepting "expense" money and then outright payment of $500 for his services when he appeared for the Allegheny Athletic Association against a rival Pittsburgh club. Professionalism spread throughout Pennsylvania and as far as Montana within five years. The practice took particular hold in towns and small cities in Ohio, which battled for civic pride as well as commercial and industrial rivalry. By 1920, the professional teams of the Midwest met in Canton, Ohio, to form the American Professional Football Association, which soon changed its name to the National Football League.

High schools, colleges, and pro teams all contended for local, state, and regional championships as football provided the venue for larger societal struggles. By the 1890s, the Midwest vied with the East for cultural leadership, and Chicago fully expected to supercede New York in that respect. Led by the universities of Michigan and Chicago, midwestern schools challenged their eastern counterparts, but they refused to acknowledge such defiance. Differing styles of play and separate rules committees exacerbated tensions, as eastern teams clung to conservative mass power plays to grind out low-scoring victories, while midwesterners favored speed, wide-open end runs, and fast-paced, high-scoring tactics. High school teams decided the issue in 1902 when a Brooklyn team traveled to Chicago to meet its champion and suffered a humiliating 105-0 defeat. When New Yorkers claimed that Brooklyn represented less than their best team, Chicago's new champion administered a 75-0 beating in New York the next year. At the collegiate level, Michigan's "point-a-minute" team scored 501 points while holding opponents scoreless in 1901, then beat Stanford 49-0 in the first Rose Bowl game. The 1905 showdown between midwestern powers Chicago and Michigan became the first of many so-called games of the century. Interstate and interregional play had been well under way by then and became commonplace even at the high school level.

Bowl games and championships required adequate venues if schools were to maximize the commercial potentials of such spectacles. In 1903, Harvard built the first concrete stadium, which seated 40,000. Many others soon followed, and Chicago's Soldier Field, erected in 1924, accommodated more than 100,000. Enormous arenas on college campuses symbolized football's power and its commercial appeal nationwide, and even high schools constructed edifices that far outstripped the town population and hardly rationalized massive expenses for such limited usage.

Schools paid handsomely for winning coaches as well. They especially coveted players from Yale, the most

dominant team of the nineteenth century; by 1901, Walter Camp had placed more than 100 of his former protégés around the country. One of them, Amos Alonzo Stagg, one of the original all-Americans, gained faculty status at the University of Chicago in 1890 and a salary exceeding that of many distinguished professors. In 1905, Harvard's twenty-seven-year-old coach, Bill Reid, garnered $7,000 when top professors got only $5,500. That pattern established salary structures still prevalent at collegiate and interscholastic levels.

Schools expected coaches to be male role models as well as tacticians. As girls and young women began playing tennis, golf, and basketball, and infringing on power sports like cycling and baseball, males felt threatened and their masculinity diminished. Football became a refuge for boys and young men, who had labored under the influence of their mothers and female teachers in the elementary schools. Male coaches instilled toughness, aggressive competitiveness, discipline, a strong work ethic, and teamwork, which would benefit them in the corporate world and the civic polity. Coaches enjoyed widespread popularity, and surveys between 1905 and 1907 showed that 78 percent of high schools and 432 of 555 cities fielded football teams.

The emphasis on aggressive masculinity did little to suppress the violent nature of the game. Women protested, but their voices were marginalized. Males even served as cheerleaders for years because men would not allow themselves to be led by women in the masculine arena, where females were confined to their own cheering section. In such an environment aggressiveness reigned and injuries mounted. In 1905, at least eighteen deaths and 159 serious injuries occurred. Harvard alone suffered twenty-nine fractures, twenty-nine dislocations, and nineteen concussions among its players. The death toll rose to thirty-three by 1909.

While players wore their injuries as badges of honor, faculty and administrators interceded, and some schools switched to rugby. President Theodore Roosevelt took it upon himself to save the game he deemed essential to robust masculinity by inviting coaches of the Big Three to the White House in 1905 and eliciting promises of reform. While the coaches effected little change, college authorities formed a governing body in 1906 that eventually became the National Collegiate Athletic Association. Faculty members assumed similar control at the high school level.

In their endeavors to limit the mass plays that caused so many of the injuries, they allowed for the forward pass to open up the game in 1906. An incompletion, however, resulted in a loss of the ball, and the new rules required

**Jim Thorpe.** Widely regarded as one of the greatest all-around American athletes, Jim Thorpe (1888–1953) played for the Carlisle Indian School's football team and led them to the national collegiate championship in 1912. In the Summer Olympics of that year, he won gold medals in the decathlon and pentathlon. He played professional baseball and football; in 1963 he was inducted into the National Football League's Hall of Fame as an inaugural member. © *AP/Wide World Photos*

ten yards to gain another set of downs. Opponents ganged up on the receivers as they awaited the pass, causing even more harm, until further rule revisions in 1910. Notre Dame's stunning 35-13 upset of Army by use of the pass in 1913 confirmed its effectiveness.

That game also established Notre Dame as a football power, symbolic of Catholic inclusion in mainstream American culture. Under the guidance of a Norwegian immigrant coach, Knute Rockne, Notre Dame used largely ethnic players, including Poles, Italians, and even Jews, to attain national prominence. Its famed Four Horsemen achieved legendary status as 1924 national champs. Catholic high schools copied Notre Dame's tactics and carried the religious banner against public school, ostensibly Protestant, opponents. Chicago's Prep Bowl featured Catholic and Public School League champs for the city championship at Soldier Field. The 1937 specta-

cle drew more than 120,000 fans, the most to witness a football game of any kind in the United States.

Football helped to integrate other minority groups as well. William Henry Lewis of Harvard became the first of many blacks to achieve all-American status. He went on to become an assistant attorney general. Fritz Pollard played for Brown in 1916, the first African American in the Rose Bowl and the first to quarterback and coach a pro team in the NFL.

Native Americans learned to play football at residential schools around the country, which were intended to assimilate them into white culture. The most famous of such schools, Carlisle in Pennsylvania, produced Jim Thorpe and a host of star players. Carlisle proved a perennial power and a major attraction, often employing trick plays attributed to their innovative coach, Glenn "Pop" Warner, whose name lives on in the appellation for youth football leagues. Thorpe, who played into the mid-1920s, became the NFL's biggest star and its first president.

Other ethnics found greater assimilation through football as well. George Halas, of Czech parentage, played for an industrial team, which he eventually owned as the head of the Chicago Bears. The fledgling NFL teams employed numerous ethnic and many working-class players who had no opportunities for higher education. By 1920, increasing numbers of working-class children attended high school, where they, too, enjoyed the game. One, Harold "Red" Grange, gained national celebrity as star of the University of Illinois team. His exploits as a Chicago pro attracted more than 70,000 in New York in 1925, which provided some credibility for the young and struggling NFL.

While football brought alternative groups into the mainstream culture, it also assuaged long-held sectional rifts. The American South, left behind by the northern industrial economy and still harboring a lost-cause mentality from the Civil War, found recompense in football. Georgia Tech won the national championship in 1917, and tiny Centre College of Kentucky upset Harvard, symbol of the northeastern elite, in 1921. Led by Alabama, southern teams won numerous bowl games throughout the 1920s and 1930s to resurrect southern pride and restore its honor.

Bowl games, too, brought greater attention to the region. The Sugar, Cotton, and Orange Bowls, along with a plethora of smaller events, drew recognition for southern agricultural products and highlighted southern commercial centers during the Depression of the 1930s. The Grambling College marching band originated in 1926, and its halftime exhibitions often overshadowed the game, eventually winning international acclaim for the

**Joe Namath.** Named Most Valuable Player of Super Bowl III in Miami, Florida, quarterback Joe Namath (1943– ) is best known for guaranteeing a victory in that game for his underdog New York Jets against the Baltimore Colts. Namath delivered, leading the Jets to an unlikely 16–7 win. The Hall of Famer (inducted 1985) played from 1965 to 1976 with the Jets but spent his final season in Los Angeles with the Rams. © *AP/Wide World Photos*

small Louisiana school. Its performance set the entertainment standard and established the increasing importance of the halftime show when it appeared at the first Super Bowl in 1967.

In 1935, the Downtown Athletic Club of New York decided to recognize individual achievement on the field by awarding the Heisman Trophy to the outstanding collegiate player each year. Individualism, highly prized in American culture, can still be obtained within the framework of a team, similar to the collective nationalism and patriotism shown by Americans and demonstrated before each game's rendition of the national anthem.

By the 1930s, variations of football aimed to be more inclusive, spreading its benefits to even the smallest communities. Hawaiians played a version of barefoot football on the beach, while six-man football originated in Nebraska in 1934 to allow opportunities for small-town boys. Other states adopted six-man or eight-man rules, and park districts offered Pop Warner football or similar youth programs to ever younger participants. Religious groups, such as the Catholic Youth Organization, installed football teams at the elementary level in interscholastic leagues, providing experienced players to its high school forces. The Pop Warner organization enrolled more than 300,000 participants in its programs, and offered national championships in both flag and tackle football, held at Disney World by the 1990s.

The choice of such a site, in Orlando, Florida, is indicative of football's power as an integrative force. African Americans gained entry to northern white teams at the high school, collegiate, and professional levels by virtue of their abilities, but in the South opportunities proved more limited. Segregated black schools began fielding their own teams, with the first game between African

> "... the gentlemen who compose the Yale team have cultivated a habit of losing their tempers, and mauling their antagonists with doubled fists; and though this imparted an increased interest in the game, and seemed to offer exquisite gratification to the cultured spectators, it is not without its drawbacks."
>
> **The Tufts Collegian, on the Tufts-Yale game of 1877 in the Harvard Advocate, 24:5 (16 Nov. 1877): 49.**

American schools taking place in 1892 between Biddle (now Johnson C. Smith) University and Livingstone College in North Carolina. White southern schools refused to play northern institutions that had black players. The northerners often agreed to suspend African Americans for games at southern venues. After 1934, pro football owners, too, banished blacks from the highest levels of play until 1946, when the new All-American Football Conference, a rival to the NFL, signed the best players regardless of skin color (two years before Jackie Robinson had desegregated major league baseball.) In 1947, Harvard brought a black player to Virginia, and Penn State included its African Americans in the 1948 Cotton Bowl, thus beginning the erosion of segregation practices. North Texas State integrated its team in 1959 and won a Sun Bowl berth. By the 1960s, Coach Bear Bryant at Alabama realized that the South could no longer sustain its football prestige without the assistance of black talent. His ensuing recruitment efforts signaled the end of exclusion for other southern institutions.

Football became truly national in 1951 when an Alaskan high school fielded a team, playing its first game against the servicemen at Elmendorf Air Force Base. By 1955, Anchorage High School hosted a team from Huntsville, Texas, in the first Santa Claus Bowl.

The widespread use of television in the 1950s further abetted the spread of the game and brought additional revenue to both college and professional teams. The exciting "sudden-death" overtime for the 1958 championship between the Baltimore Colts and New York Giants ensured future television audiences for the NFL. The promise of television profits spawned the American Football League (AFL), which began play in 1960 as yet another rival to the NFL. Competition for players drove salaries even higher, and the success of the AFL engendered the first Super Bowl between league champions in 1967. The rivals merged after the 1969 season, and Super Bowl III assured the growth of the annual extravaganza

and growth of the game when brash, young Joe Namath and the New York Jets gave the AFL its first win.

By the 1970s football superseded baseball as the national game, and professional coaches assumed the status of national icons, their star status often equaling that of their players. Vince Lombardi led small-town Green Bay, Wisconsin, to the top echelons of the NFL. In an urban, corporate world, Green Bay represented a vanishing lifestyle for many Americans, but one that could still triumph as a David among Goliaths in the football world. George Allen and Don Shula brought accolades to the nation's capital and Miami, respectively, while Tom Landry made the Dallas Cowboys America's team and Mike Ditka became a civic hero in Chicago.

Buoyed by television income, college programs grew by astronomical proportions as the NCAA, acting as a cartel, negotiated package deals and guaranteed widespread exposure. The adoption of two-platoon football in 1965 afforded even greater specialization into offensive and defensive units and increased scoring, much to the pleasure of fans. Newspapers, too, stimulated interest by national rankings. By the 1980s, the athletic frenzy produced sports channels that broadcast athletic events around the clock.

National rankings included high school teams, usually from football hotbeds in Florida, California, Ohio, or Pennsylvania. But in Texas, high school football paralleled the status of a secular religion. Crowds outnumbered town populations, and an Odessa team built a stadium with artificial turf to seat more than 19,000, at a cost of more than $5 million. Season tickets were contested in wills and divorce settlements. Throughout the state, more than 4 million Texans attended high school games each weekend. The Massillon, Ohio, team drew more than 120,000 spectators in one season, and it had a million-dollar budget and a live tiger for a mascot. Mascots, bonfires, pep rallies, tailgate parties, and elaborate halftime shows and television were all included as part of the game experience. High school football, like its collegiate counterpart, had become big business.

The business of football caused a fissure in the collegiate ranks as top-ranked teams reluctantly shared their television profits with other NCAA schools. In 1976, the major powers formed their own College Football Association to enhance their own income, and won concessions from the NCAA. Notre Dame eventually signed its own network contract, further accentuating the split in college ranks. The quest for football supremacy led colleges to pour increasing amounts of money into athletic budgets, facilities, and services. Recruitment scandals became commonplace, and most teams operated at a deficit, which was considered an acceptable loss in the pursuit of institutional prestige.

At the professional level the NFL conglomerate produced flourishing profits spurred by growing television packages, new and expanding stadiums, increasing marketing of team merchandise, and the globalization of the game. NFL Europe operated as a minor league for the parent organization, and Pop Warner as well as collegiate teams played in Mexico. Worldwide telecasts of football games brought American culture to the rest of the world.

Both boys and girls can begin formal football play as early as age six in community programs. Flag football accommodates both male and female players in older age groups, while others play in wheelchair and semipro leagues. That level of inclusiveness and interest is evidence of the game's long history: its evolution during the coming of age of the United States as a world power, the establishment of its national identity, its ability to foster national unity while celebrating sectional differences, the perception of football as a meritocracy accepting of disparate groups, and the community pride inherent in a winning team. Perhaps more so than any other sport, football portrays the aggressive, competitive spirit, as well as the corporate, commercial character of America.

*See also:* Football, Collegiate; Professionalization of Sport; Soccer

## BIBLIOGRAPHY

Barber, Phil, and Ray Didinger. *Football America: Celebrating Our National Passion.* Atlanta: Turner Publishing, 1996.

Bissinger, H. G. *Friday Night Lights: A Town, a Team, and a Dream.* New York: HarperCollins, 1991.

Carroll, Bob. *The Ohio League, 1910–1919.* North Huntington, Pa.: Pro Football Researchers Association, 1997.

Doyle, Andrew. "Bear Bryant: Symbol of an Embattled South." *Colby Quarterly* 32, no.1 (March 1996): 72–86.

Gems, Gerald R. *For Pride, Profit, and Patriarchy: Football and the Incorporation of American Cultural Values.* Lanham, Md.: Scarecrow Press, 2000.

Hurd, Michael. *Black College Football, 1892–1992: One Hundred Years of History, Education, and Pride.* Virginia Beach, Va.: Donning Company, 1993.

Jable, J. Thomas. "The Birth of Professional Football: Pittsburgh Athletic Clubs Ring in Professionals in 1892." *The Western Pennsylvania Historical Magazine* 62, no. 2 (April 1979): 131–147.

Lester, Robin. *Stagg's University: The Rise, Decline, and Fall of Big-Time Football at Chicago.* Urbana: University of Illinois Press, 1995.

McClellan, Keith. *The Sunday Game: At the Dawn of Professional Football.* Akron, Ohio: University of Akron Press, 1998.

Maltby, Marc S. *The Origins and Early Development of Professional Football.* New York: Garland Publishing, 1997.

Nelson, David M. *The Anatomy of a Game: Football, the Rules, and the Men Who Made the Game.* Newark: University of Delaware Press, 1994.

Oriard, Michael. *Reading Football: How the Popular Press Created an American Spectacle.* Chapel Hill: University of North Carolina Press, 1993.

————. *King Football: Sport and Spectacle in the Golden Age of Radio and Newsreels, Movies and Magazines, the Weekly and the Daily Press.* Chapel Hill: University of North Carolina Press, 2001.

Smith, Ronald A. *Big-Time Football at Harvard, 1905: The Diary of Coach Bill Reid.* Urbana: University of Illinois Press, 1994.

Sperber, Murray. *Shake Down the Thunder: The Creation of Notre Dame Football.* New York: Henry Holt and Company, 1993.

Umphlett, Wiley Lee. *Creating the Big Game: John W. Heisman and the Invention of American Football.* Westport, Conn.: Greenwood Press, 1992.

Watterson, John S. *College Football: History, Spectacle, Controversy.* Baltimore: Johns Hopkins University Press, 2000.

Whittingham, Richard. *Rites of Autumn: The Story of College Football.* New York: Free Press, 2001.

*Gerald R. Gems*

# FOOTBALL, COLLEGIATE

American football's origins can be traced back to England and the split between football players into two groups, "ruggers" (those who played a game similar to modern rugby) and "soccers" (those who played a game most closely related to modern soccer). By the mid-1800s, both forms of football had immigrated to American colleges, first with a form of association football (the game played by the "soccers") called "ballown," which was played at Princeton University, and later a hybrid form of soccer and rugby, which was played at numerous university campuses across the northeastern part of the United States. This new hybrid, which would later become modern-day American football, both in form and in structure, emanated out of the rigidity of industrial production, the urbanizing tendencies of population distribution, and the expansionary propensities of nineteenth-century American ideology.

In 1866, *Beadle's Dime Book of Cricket and Football* offered codification (albeit vague) of the first rules of the

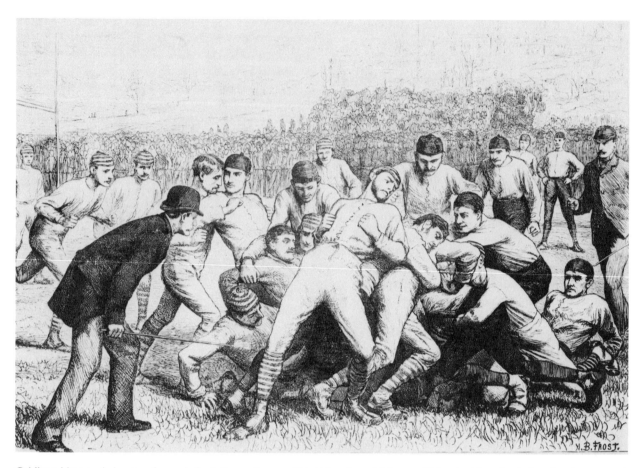

**Gridiron history.** A drawing of an early football game between Yale University and Princeton University. The schools first played against each other in 1869, making their rivalry the second-oldest in the sport. Princeton had played Rutgers University earlier in 1869 in what is regarded as the first intercollegiate game. © *Corbis*

soccer-rugby fusion that was to become American football. This publication signaled the trend toward formalization indicative of most organized sports that emanated from the latter part of the nineteenth century. College football, indeed most American and British sports in the mid-to-late 1800s, exhibited many of the rationalizing tendencies of the industrial era due to the pervasive productivist logics of the era and sport's tendency to develop in urbanized manufacturing centers. Prior to 1866, each university had its own nuanced set of rules for playing American football. However, the codification of college football found in *Beadle's* facilitated "intercollegiate" competition, as, for the first time, rival schools could compete against one another with the same conventions. Thus, in 1869, the first intercollegiate football game played in the United States took place when Princeton challenged Rutgers to a game that resulted in a 6–4 Rutgers victory. This game, and the popularity of subsequent intercollegiate contests between northeastern universities, resulted in a meeting in New York four years later where Yale, Princeton, Co-

lumbia, and Harvard developed the first set of formal rules for intercollegiate football.

With a general foundation in place, intercollegiate football in the 1870s saw continued spread in popularity across the United States. The advent of new modes of transportation, particularly the expansion of the transcontinental rail system, which was completed on 10 May 1869, enabled teams to travel to new regions, and opened new flows of people and (sport) culture to the western part of the continent. Signs of the sport's popularity were evidenced by the expansion of intercollegiate contests to the southern United States. In 1873, for example, two southern schools, Virginia Military Institute and Washington and Lee, played against each other in a well-documented contest. Only a few years later, in 1879, the first intercollegiate game to be played in the Midwest took place between the University of Michigan and Racine College. As the sport grew in recognition throughout the decade and participation expanded to the ends of the country, developments were under way back in the northeastern United States that would shape college football for the next century and beyond.

## College Football's First Rivalry: Harvard and Yale

Founded on the rules developed in 1873 and the subsequent games played under those parameters, and in response to football's growing status, Harvard and Yale formed the first Intercollegiate Football Association in 1876. Not only did the new organization serve as a governing body for the infant sport, but these measures also further positioned the two institutions at the focal point of college football up until the turn of the century. Throughout the 1880s, games between the two sides garnered a great deal of media attention from popular newspapers, and game attendance was in such demand that spectators would pay up to $60 per ticket. Indeed, most of the rules and rule makers of early intercollegiate football emanated from either the Harvard or Yale programs from that era. Despite Yale's continued success on the field during the early stages of the rivalry, both schools reaped fiscal and cultural benefits from the earliest college football spectacles. Examples of the thousands of dollars in revenues from their Harvard-Yale football games include Harvard's ability to build a 22,000 seat on-campus stadium for the football team in 1903, and Yale's propensity to charter four-car passenger trains to their away games.

The early success of college football was further enhanced by the contributions of Walter Camp to the Harvard-Yale rivalry of the late nineteenth century. Considered the "father of American football," Camp is widely thought to be the most influential person in the history of the sport. As both a player (1876–1879, 1880–1881) and coach of the Yale football team in the latter part of the nineteenth century, Camp's foresighted imagination for developing rules and strategies reshaped college football's style on the field and enhanced its popularity off the field. In 1880, and again in 1882, Camp introduced numerous changes to the rules of the game, most notably: the number of players (down to eleven per team), size of the field (similar to today's dimensions), a system of downs (three attempts to gain five yards), change of possession (previous rules allowed one team to maintain possession for an entire half), and yard lines (one horizontal line every five yards down the field). These rules created the basis for college football's break with rugby by concretizing particular aspects of play which differed significantly from traditional rugby rules.

Walter Camp's legacy is further cemented by his relationship with journalist Caspar Whitney and his men-

**FIGURE 1**

### Major rule changes in intercollegiate football

1873
- Players cannot run with the ball
- Scores can be made by kicking or butting the ball across the opponents goal line and under the cross bar
- Passes can only be made laterally and backward
- Tackling below the waist is prohibited
- Field dimensions: 140 yards x 70 yards
- Time: two 45-minute periods
- Definitive change of possession

1880
- Introduction of a line of scrimmage
- Field dimensions: 110 yards x 53 1/3 yards

1882
- System of downs instituted (5 yards in three downs)

1883
- Scoring system instituted: 5 points for a field goal; 4 points for a kick following a touchdown; 2 points for a touchdown; and 1 point for a safety

1884
- Scoring change: 4 points for a touchdown and 2 points for a free kick

1888
- Tackling below the waist is allowed

1894
- Flying wedge is outlawed
- Time: two 35-minute periods

1897
- Touchdown is worth 5 points
- Free kick after touchdown is reduced to 1point

1906
- Legalization of the forward pass
- Creation of a neutral zone at the line of scrimmage
- Raising the yardage required for a first down from 5 to 10 yards
- Time: two 30-minute halves
- Disqualification of players guilty of fighting with or kneeing an opposing player

1909
- The value of a field goal is reduced from 4 points to 3 points

1910
- Time: four 15-minute quarters
- Only backs and ends are eligible to received forward passes
- Seven players are required to be on the line of scrimmage
- Banning of interlocking blocking technique

SOURCE: Whittingham, Richard. *Rites of Autumn: The Story of College Football.* New York: Free Press, 2001.

torship of college football legends Amos Alonzo Stagg and John Heisman. In 1889, Camp and Whitney, a long-standing supporter of college football, introduced the first "All-America" team—their selections of the best players from across the country. This tradition continued, and, by 1898, the first official "All-America" team chosen by Walter Camp was published in *Collier's* magazine. Two of Camp's former players, Amos Alonzo Stagg and John Heisman, further contributed to the revolution of alignments and formations, innovative rules, and pioneering strategies that shaped football leading up to the turn of the century. As a coach, Stagg's University of Chicago teams were some

## The First Bowl Game

"... it is up to me to give them a carnival far superior to anything they have ever seen ... you would not be put to one penny of expense from the time you left your University until you returned, including entertainment while here ...."

**James R. H. Wagner, President of the 1902 Rose Bowl, in his invitation to University of Michigan to play in that game against Stanford University.**

With that invitation to the Fielding Yost's University of Michigan team, James Wagner set into motion the creation of the "Granddaddy of them All," the annual Rose Bowl college football spectacular. Before that first game was held in 1902, the centerpiece of the annual Tournament of Roses Parade in Pasadena, California, was a polo match. When organizers decided that polo wasn't drawing enough attention to their parade and festival, a tournament committee member suggested that a football game between two national powers might be a good drawing card. Wagner agreed, and the first game was set in motion.

To represent the West Coast, Wagner selected Stanford University, champions of what was then known as the "Pacific Coast Universities." To create as much interest in the game as possible, Wagner selected Michigan as Stanford's opponent. Michigan, led by coach Yost, was the talk of the nation that year. The team was unscored upon in ten games, outscoring the opposition 501–0, a remarkable accomplishment. Yost accepted Wagner's invitation, and the team traveled by rail to California, leaving Ann Arbor on December 17.

On New Year's Day, the two teams made their way to the stadium through a huge throng that had turned out for the game. Ironically, the official colors selected for that year's Tournament of Roses were blue and gold, which were almost identical to Michigan's colors of maize and blue. This infuriated the Stanford fans, who began to tear down blue and gold banners and flags as the game drew near. Before the game, Michigan actually participated in the Tournament of Roses Parade, riding on a float and waving to the crowd.

With 8,000 fans looking on, the game itself turned out to be an anticlimactic finish to an exciting day. Stanford held its ground at first, but before the first half had ended, Michigan had begun to flex its muscle and took a 17–0 lead. In the second half, Michigan simply wore down Stanford and scored almost every time it had the ball. With eight minutes left in the game and the score 49–0 Michigan, Stanford captain Ralph Fisher asked Yost if he would accept Stanford's concession; he would, and the first Rose Bowl was in the books. Michigan closed the season with an 11–0 record and outscored its opponents 550–0, a mark that will certainly never be broken in modern football.

Unfortunately for football fans, Michigan did its job *too* well. Because the game was so lopsided, Wagner and tournament committee members feared that the public would be bored by any future games, so football was dropped from the tournament schedule in 1903. And what was it replace by? Why, chariot races of course. It would be sixteen years before football was once again added to the Tournament of Roses schedule, with the Rose Bowl finally becoming a permanent part of the New Year's festivities.

---

of the most recognizable teams in early midwestern collegiate football. Heisman, the person for which college football's most celebrated trophy is named, is credited with being the first coach to suggest that the forward pass be legalized. While the end of the century was highlighted by great rivalries such as Harvard-Yale, legendary personalities such as Camp, Stagg, and Heisman, and modern rule changes that would reshape the game, a new decade awaited college football: a decade in which new challenges would threaten the existence of the adolescent sport.

## Troubled Times

The end of the Spanish-American War in 1898 ushered in unimpeded expansion across the continent. Just as

people moved westward, so too did the games they played. The increased interest in college football in the West was best exemplified by the first Rose Bowl game in Los Angeles, played on New Year's Day in 1902. However, during this period the role of college football in both sport and academic landscapes was under scrutiny due to the violent nature of the sport and the unethical practices of coaches and athletes both on and off the field. Detractors from the field of higher education such as Harvard President Charles Eliot viewed college football as a threat to the moral and academic integrity of the mission of American universities. Furthermore, religious officials within the community were quick to challenge the violent nature and perceived lack of ethics in the new sport.

Conversely, one of college football's biggest proponents, then American president Theodore Roosevelt, held fast to the rough and violent features of football. Prior to and during his presidency, Roosevelt stood by the notion that the American people had become soft, and aggressive sports such as college football were necessary to curtail the tendency toward latency.

By 1905, college football supporters and reformers were in the middle of a highly publicized battle in what would become college football's most critical season. The game was filled with problems both on and off the field, as the use of "mass plays," the "flying wedge," and other controversial strategies resulted in increased injuries, while rampant professional involvement threatened the amateur ethos of college football. A report on the state of college football published early that year profiled the violent nature of turn-of-the-century college football, proclaiming that eighteen deaths and an estimated 150 serious injuries were directly attributable to the rough play of college football. In a somewhat unprecedented move, Roosevelt intervened by inviting football insiders from the major eastern football-playing universities—Harvard, Yale, and Princeton—to the White House to discuss possible reform measures. The effects of these meetings were minimal, in part due to Harvard's reluctance to cooperate with Princeton and Yale, standing firmly behind their own codes of football conduct. Later in 1905, New York University chancellor Henry Mc-Cracken called representatives from nineteen institutions of higher education to New York for a second series of conferences aimed at reforming or, if need be, abolishing college football. While only twelve schools sent representatives to the first meeting, the decision was made to reform—rather than abolish—the sport.

The New York Conference and the second series of "big three" meetings rendered three important practical, if not philosophical, changes to intercollegiate football. First was the formation of the Inter Collegiate Athletic Association (ICAA), set to codify and govern all the football related activities of its member institutions. This governing body of college football would later become the National Collegiate Athletic Association (NCAA)—the institute now responsible for governing all contemporary intercollegiate athletics. Now empowered to reform college football, the newly formed ICAA sought to unify the detracting institutions with the newly formed governing body. Subsequently, a second outcome of the New York Conference was the inclusion of the old committee (comprised of the "big three" along with Cornell and Pennsylvania), into the newly formed ICAA. However, this was done following numerous concessions by ICAA member schools to the incoming programs. The third and most

substantial consequence of the New York meetings of 1905 and 1906 was the implementation of numerous rule changes that would forever affect the game. Based largely on the Harvard's recommendations, the ICAA elected to legalize the forward pass, create a neutral zone at the line of scrimmage, increase the yardage required for a first down from five to ten, and disqualifying players "guilty of fighting or kneeing" an opposing team's player (Whittingham, p. 40). Many of these rules were adopted to open up play, thus decreasing the risk of injury and reducing the amount of foul play.

The reform measures instituted between the 1905 and 1906 seasons temporarily silenced many of the critics of college football. Satisfied by the measures taken by the ICAA, most institutions were willing to retain their football programs despite the continuing (although declining) number of deaths resulting from participation in the sport—three in 1906, two in 1907, seven in 1908 (Watterson, 2000, pp. 108–110). Despite institutional support for the game, these deaths instantiated claims of college football's barbaric nature, thus fueling a new thread of public debates. The critical vox populi that had been quelled, or at least softened, through the rule changes in 1906 arose again to threaten the existence of college football. New York and Washington, D.C., public schools banned football, and western universities such as Stanford threatened to abolish the sport or revert back to the English version of rugby.

Responding to the second wave of public scrutiny, in 1910 the ICAA officially changed its name to the NCAA, and also ushered in broad sweeping rule changes to limit the number of "mass" or "wedge" type formations and the opportunities for violence in-between plays. The highlights of the new rules were: changing the format of play from two thirty-minute halves to four fifteen-minute quarters; banning the flying tackle; requiring seven players to line up at the line of scrimmage; prohibiting the interlocking of arms for the purposes of blocking; permitting only backs and ends to be eligible to catch a forward pass. These rule changes signified an important break in the code of play in football from the traditional rules of rugby. Furthermore, this reformed version of football embodied the social and cultural logics of industrial America, and facilitated the virtually unimpeded growth of the sport throughout the "Roaring 1920s."

## The Emergence of the College Football Spectacle

The more aesthetically pleasing game that had materialized from the reform meetings of the century's first

**Michigan Stadium.** In Ann Arbor, Michigan, the football stadium that houses the University of Michigan Wolverines is perhaps the best-known landmark on the campus. Opened in 1927 and now known as "The Big House," the stadium has a capacity of 107,501 and each week is host to the largest crowd to watch a college football game in the United States. In this photo, Michigan and Syracuse face off in the second week of the 1998 season, with Syracuse prevailing 38–28. © *Paul Warner for AP/Wide World Photos*

decade drew increasing amounts of public and media attention during the 1910s. While World War I forced fiscal contraction of large, public American universities, the refined style of play and improved levels of performance primed college football for wider consumption during the succeeding decade. Beyond the rule transformations of the preceding decade, the unparalleled growth in college football's popularity and participation between 1920 and 1950 was largely attributable to three symbiotically interrelated factors: professionalization under a chimera of amateurism, inherent hypocrisy of the university in allowing recruitment of athletes while admonishing the professional nature of college football, and the commercialization of college football, largely through its relationship with the mass media.

First, the veneer of the amateur ethos upon which collegiate athletics was founded enabled football-playing universities to develop deep-seeded ties with alumni, the media, and other supporters under the guise of the "purity" of amateur sport. Despite the illusion of authenticity, issues of amateurism and professionalism have long cast a shadow over college athletics in America. Professionalism in college athletics can be traced back to intercollegiate rowing in the 1860s and 1870s, when

northeastern colleges hired skilled rowers to compete on behalf of their schools. Schools with winning football traditions during the era—particularly Yale, Notre Dame, and Michigan—experienced large financial gains through the sport. To this end, Yale University was rumored to have a separate, rather sizable bank account with excess revenue created directly from the football team. Thus, success on the gridiron was an integral part of the formula for generating operating funds for many of these institutions, particularly in postwar times of monetary hardship. This, coupled with the NCAA's and university officials' inability to regulate participation in intercollegiate football, resulted in rampant illegal professional involvement for the sake of winning.

Second, the increased role of professional coaches and the pressures of winning resulted in intensified recruiting practices among college football programs. Particularly in the 1920s, a decade of continued growth, during which college football attendance doubled and revenues from the games tripled, most universities increased the number of full-time coaches under their employment. College football coaches at larger football-playing institutions such as Michigan, Chicago, Harvard, and Notre Dame typically earned higher salaries than full-time, tenured professors at those same universities. Some of the more notable coaches of the era included Knute Rockne from Notre Dame, Fielding Yost from Michigan, and Robert Zuppke of Illinois. New controversies began to swirl during the 1920s, as numerous coaches and staff members were implicated in scandals involving illegal recruiting and professionalism.

The third aspect of college football that contributed to its successful thrust into the American popular cultural conscience was the sport's relationship with the media. The increasing cultural popularity of film and radio in the 1920s helped to celebrate both individual and team performances in sport during the "Golden Decade". The earliest forms of this sport/media relationship nurtured public awareness of celebrities such as Jack Dempsey, Babe Ruth, the Four Horsemen of Notre Dame, and Red Grange. Just as college football depended on the news media to create celebrities and spectacularize the game and its players for the sake of promoting and growing the sport, reporters during the era built their own reputations around the sports they covered. Grantland Rice, perhaps the most famous of all college football writers, was notorious for sensationalizing athletes and their performances. For example, Rice immortalized the renowned Four Horsemen of Notre Dame in a game report published in the *New York Herald-Tribune* in 1924. The four athletes that comprised the Notre Dame backfield, despite only average statistical performances during their intercollegiate careers, are among the most heralded of all American athletes of the early twentieth century, thanks to Rice's portrayal of their achievements.

Another one of college football's most revered stars —Red Grange of the University of Illinois—was possibly the most important athlete in the development of modern college football. For example, in a well-documented performance in 1924 against a favored University of Michigan team, Grange scored six touchdowns in front of over 65,000 fans. The media rhetoric surrounding this and other games stirred public interest in Grange, and, by association, the sport, thus helping to cement college football spectacles of the early twentieth century as some of the most significant cultural forms of the era. In fact, college football, rather than its professional counterpart, was the more popular of the two during the first quarter of the twentieth century. Indeed, it was not until the 1950s and the marriage between professional football and television that the NFL moved past college football in popular cultural cache.

Just as the 1920s ushered in the concurrent growth of both college football and American cultural life, the game, as well as most aspects of American economic and social activity, suffered substantial setbacks during the 1930s. This period saw a split between those institutions dedicated to sustaining intercollegiate sport, and those who, in large part due to economic reasons, eliminated intercollegiate sport in favor of an academic focus. This was best exemplified by the creation of numerous football conferences, including the Big Ten (the Big Six Conference at the time) in 1928 and the Southeastern Conference in 1932. While most large public institutions continued to invest resources in college football, some historically successful institutions such as the University of Chicago (where Amos Alonzo Stagg coached from 1892 to 1932) abolished football during the decade in response to the growing scandals and the increasing economic demands of the sport.

## College Football in War and Prosperity

The two decades of college football succeeding the 1930s were greatly influenced by war, technological innovations, and a period of emphatic patriotism across the United States. As World War II began in 1939, and American forces were sent abroad, back in the United States, college football and television started to form an alliance that would increase the cultural significance of both in the coming years. The first televised college football game was played between Pennsylvania and Maryland on 5 October 1940. A few years later, in 1951, the NCAA approved the telecast of one intercollegiate football game each Saturday afternoon throughout the season. Notably, technological advances in college football during the era went beyond the mere introduction of television. For instance, Cecil Isbell of Purdue became the first coach to lead his team from the press box by employing new means of communication to orchestrate the on-field action.

One result of U.S. involvement in war was increased patriotic sentiment and discourse through the various burgeoning media streams. College football, marketed as a distinctly American sport form reflective of American political, technological, and cultural logics, echoed this trend in its creation of college All-Star games such as the one witnessed by 79,000 at Soldier Field in Chicago in 1934, which pitted college football's best players against the defending National Football League champions, the Chicago Bears (the game ended in a 0–0 tie). Furthermore, college bowl games like the Liberty Bowl, which began play in 1959, often strategically aligned themselves with American patriotic imagery and rhetoric through halftime pageantry, in-stadium signage and theatrics, and other strategically contrived forms of discourse.

Another important development for college football during the postwar era were the provisions of the Ser-

**"Touchdown Jesus."** On the south wall of Hesburgh Library in South Bend, Indiana, is a massive mosaic depicting Christ stretching out his arms in blessing to the church. Because it can be seen above the north end zone of Notre Dame Stadium and appears to be signaling a score, the mosaic has been dubbed "Touchdown Jesus". The mosaic didn't help Notre Dame the day this photo was taken, as it lost to Texas A&M University 24-10 on 2 September 2000. © *Tom Hauck/Getty Images*

viceman's Readjustment Act of 1944, or what is more commonly known as the G.I. Bill. The measure set aside billions of dollars in federal aid for returning servicemen and servicewomen who wished to pursue college educations. Soldiers returning from both World War II and the Korean War took advantage of the G.I. Bill, as large numbers of veterans and military personnel enrolled in colleges and universities nationwide. The influx of student population at some major universities resulted in a need for increased campus housing, classrooms, and other facilities. One result of the G.I. Bill was that, by the end of mid-1960s, more than 40 percent of all young men in the United States were enrolled in an institution of higher education. For college football, higher enrollment impacted not only the pool of potential players (the male student body) a head coach could select his team

from, but also a boost in student support for the university and its teams.

A second result of the G.I. Bill was the increased number of male student athletes at major universities. Servicemen returning from duty were recruited by the institutions to play football, which resulted in an increase in the number of "scholarship" athletes on each team. During this time period, numerous universities were indicted for providing unauthorized aid to their student athletes under the guise of the G.I. Bill. Student athletes would receive preferential treatment and extra remuneration beyond what was typically afforded recipients of the G.I. benefits. To curb such activity, and to universalize the aid given to athletes, the member institutions of the NCAA in 1951 passed a Sanity Code. After much debate, the Sanity Code was created as a compromise between liberals, who felt that student athletes deserved privileges (particularly those students who were funded through the G.I. Bill) but that such benefits should be documented and made public, and conservatives, who held fast to ideals of amateurism in intercollegiate sport. In the end, however, the Sanity Code failed to eradicate professionalism in college football and to publicize the imbursements provided to student athletes.

Another important, and indeed related, result of the G.I. Bill of 1944 was the specialization of football skills and positions at the college level. Prior to the midcentury scholarship boom, due to the low number of scholarships available, most teams would field the best players on both offensive and defensive sides of the ball. This meant that most players would play the entire game, and learn both offensive and defensive skills. However, with a bevy of players at their disposal, many of different sizes, shapes, and skill levels, coaches of the 1950s and beyond were able to create specialized roles for each player. It was during this period that separate units for offense, defense, and special teams became more commonplace in the college game. Furthermore, increase team size translated into higher cost for the university, especially in providing room and board, travel, and equipment for the larger teams.

## A New Dawn Fades

Prior to the war-ridden era of the 1940s, very few African Americans represented major public institutions in intercollegiate football contests. While northern schools demonstrated some progress in integrating their sports teams, universities in the South were often staunch defenders of segregation both on the field and in the classroom. One example of a broader, but not universal, trend among northern schools to include African Americans in intercollegiate sport came during the World War I era when two African Americans, Fritz Pollard and Paul Robeson, became high-profile football All-Americans at Brown and Rutgers. In the North, the presence of African American football players continued to grow throughout the early part of the twentieth century. However, from the period spanning Jackie Robinson's entry into major-league baseball in 1947 through to the adoption and implementation of the Twenty-fourth Amendment, which abolished segregation in 1962 to 1964, African Americans were restricted from playing on the football teams of almost every major southern school. The south, and states to the west, where southerners from previous generations had migrated, still very much held to segregationist values and the Jim Crow laws that promoted such segregationist practices. To such an end, during this era southern schools oftentimes refused to play northern schools if they had a black player on the team.

Numerous incidents of student protest and boycotting of football contests, as well as American policy changes on issues of race equality, eventually resulted in a more equal distribution of participants in college football. In 2000, for example, the NCAA reported that 43.2 percent of Division I-A football players were African American. However, only three of the 117 head coaches coaching Division 1A teams in 2003 were African American. Moreover, the commercialization of intercollegiate football led to both the symbolic and material exploitation of African American athletes, who were led to believe that college football was a means to social equality. Black athletes were (and still are) recruited to play football for large public institutions, yet more than half have never received a university degree, while their white teammates have tended to graduate at a rate almost 20 percent higher. In pursuit of revenues and renewed alumni and booster interest, the alienation of athletes in college football from their opportunities to gain an education, coupled with the fact that sport is often viewed in the African American community as a primary means of gaining social equality, has resulted in another persistent problem for the game.

The Reaganite policies of the 1980s ushered in unimpeded deregulation of the exchange of economic and cultural goods. In American intercollegiate football, such economic and political shifts translated to the expansion of their product through newly permitted television mediums, and primarily cable television. In an ever-more open, and highly competitive, market these cable channels, particularly those who devoted their content strictly to sports, were in search of more products to fill their time slots. College football, and other sports, grew in popular-

ity as a direct result of institutional alignments with these emerging media forms. While this enabled continued growth for the sport, it also created a highly lucrative industry where amateur, teenage athletes were presented to vast audiences. Division 1-A, which is comprised of 117 of the nation's largest universities, has ensured lucrative contracts with numerous media platforms, most notably is the $400 million in contractual revenues from the American Broadcasting Company (ABC) for rights to broadcast the top four college football bowl games through the 2006 season. These athletes were turned into celebrities and marketed by their universities in an effort to maximize notoriety and exposure for the institution. However, virtually none of the revenues generated for the universities trickles down to the athletes.

Other problems that have emerged during the second half of the twentieth century also relate to the commercial nature of college football and the emphasis by colleges and universities on intercollegiate athletic performance over academics. In many ways, this has always been the case, but historically bound opportunities to expand college football's commercial and cultural appeal have furthered the economic interests of these institutions and fostered growth in college football's social importance. College football is a multibillion-dollar industry, garnering vast economic revenue through sponsorship, television and other media contracts, alumni and booster support, brand licensing, and ticket sales. To this end, college football teams have become such a priority to the universities that they purportedly represent, most "big-time" programs operate under budgetary constraints separate from each university's general fund, and football-related university employees typically earn twice the salary of academic faculty. As of 2004, several college football teams spent over $100,000 per player per year on travel, equipment, room and board, and other expenditures. These issues are obviously only a few of the many that will continue to confront the game of college football as it progresses through the twenty-first century.

*See also:* Football, Professionalization of Sport, Stadiums

## BIBLIOGRAPHY

Carroll, John M. *Fritz Pollard: Pioneer in Racial Advancement.* Urbana: University of Illinois Press, 1999.

———. *Red Grange and the Rise of Modern Football.* Urbana: University of Illinois Press, 1999.

Guttmann, Allen. *From Ritual to Record: The Nature of Modern Sports.* New York: Columbia University Press, 1978.

Jencks, Christopher, and David Riesman. *The Academic Revolution.* Garden City, N.Y.: Doubleday and Company, 1968.

Leslie, W. Bruce. *Gentlemen and Scholars: College and Community in the "Age of the University"*. University Park: Pennsylvania State University Press, 1992.

Lester, Robin. *Stagg's University: The Rise, Decline, and Fall of Big-Time Football at Chicago*. Urbana: University of Illinois Press, 1995.

Lucas, Christopher J. *American Higher Education: A History*. New York: St. Martin's, 1994.

McQuilkin, Scott A., and Ronald A. Smith. "The Rise and Fall of the Flying Wedge: Football's Most Controversial Play." *Journal of Sport History* 20 (1993): 57–64.

Nelson, David. *Anatomy of a Game: Football, the Rules, and the Men Who Made the Game*. Newark, N.J.: University of Delaware Press, 1994.

Oriard, Michael. *Reading Football: How the Popular Press Created an American Spectacle*. Chapel Hill: University of North Carolina Press, 1993.

Rader, Benjamin G. *American Sports: From the Age of Folk Games to the Age of Televised Sports*. 4th edition. Upper Saddle River, N.J.: Prentice Hall, 1999.

Sears, Hal D. "The Moral Threat of Intercollegiate Sports: An 1893 Poll of Ten College Presidents, and the End of 'the Champion Football Team of the Great West.'" *Journal of Sport History* 19 (1992): 211–226.

Smith, Ronald A. *Sports and Freedom: The Rise of Big-Time College Athletics*. New York: Oxford University Press, 1988.

Sperber, Murray. *Shake Down the Thunder: The Creation of Notre Dame Football*. New York: Henry Holt, 1993.

Spivey, Donald. "'End Jim Crow in Sports': The Protest and New York University, 1940–1941." *Journal of Sport History* 15 (1988): 282–303.

Telander, Rick. *The Hundred Yard Lie: The Corruption of College Football and What We Can Do to Stop It*. New York: Fireside, 1989.

Watterson, John S. "The Football Crisis of 1909–1910: The Response from the Eastern 'Big Three.'" *Journal of Sport History* 8 (1981): 33–49.

———. *College Football: History, Spectacle, Controversy*. Baltimore: Johns Hopkins University Press, 2000.

Weyand, Alexander M. *The Saga of American Football*. New York: Macmillan, 1955.

Whittingham, Richard. *Rites of Autumn: The Story of College Football*. New York: Free Press, 2001.

Wiggins, David. "'The Future of College Athletics Is at Stake': Black Athletes and Racial Turmoil on Three Predominantly White University Campuses, 1968–1972." *Journal of Sport History* 15 (1988): 304–333.

*Joshua I. Newman*

# FOURTH OF JULY

When delegates to the Continental Congress adopted the Declaration of Independence, they created not only the

---

## John Adams's Prescription for Celebrating Independence

The Second Day of July 1776 will be the most memorable Epocha, in the History of America. I am apt to believe that it will be celebrated, by succeeding Generations, as the great anniversary Festival. It ought to be commemorated, as the Day of Deliverance by solemn Acts of Devotion to God Almighty. It ought to be solemnized with Pomp and Parade, with Shews, Games, Sports, Guns, Bells, Bonfires and Illuminations from one End of this Continent to the other from this Time forward forever more.

John Adams wrote this famous prescription for future celebrations of the American Independence Day upon the Continental Congress's adoption of the resolution for independence on 2 July 1776. Americans instead ended up celebrating the Fourth of July, when Congress approved the Declaration of Independence.

**Source: John Adams to Abigail Adams, 3 July 1776, in *Adams Family Correspondence*, ed. L. H. Butterfield, the Adams Papers, series 2. Cambridge, Mass.: Harvard University Press, Belknap Press, 1963.**

---

first modern nation but also the first modern national holiday. The first anniversary of independence was widely celebrated. Naval ships fired symbolic thirteen-gun salutes, and troops paraded and drilled. In Philadelphia, delegates to the Congress dined together while a band of captured Hessians provided music. Bonfires and fireworks lit the evening, and patriots illuminated their windows with candles and punished loyalists by breaking their unlit windows.

The Fourth of July provided a rallying point for revolutionary fervor throughout the war, and the holiday spread rapidly. The Continental Army celebrated by firing salutes, distributing extra rum, and pardoning prisoners. Town observances included bell ringing, thirteen-gun salutes, fireworks, military parades, oratory, dinners, and toasting.

## The Early Fourth

Once independence had been won, the purpose of the Fourth changed from renewing revolutionary ardor to constructing American nationalism. By the late eighteenth century, Fourth of July celebrations in towns across the United States contained four components: (1)

FOURTH OF JULY

the oration and the reading of the Declaration of Independence; (2) the military parade and drill; (3) private dinners and toasting; and (4) fireworks and illuminations. The oration was the centerpiece of the celebration and taught Americans the lessons of the Revolution. In America, orators proclaimed, power resided with the people; therefore, Americans must be both virtuous and vigilant to preserve their liberties. Speakers asserted that unity was essential to the nation's continued independence and declaimed on the genius of the Declaration of Independence and the Constitution in forging that union.

## The Battle for the Fourth: 1788 to 1865

The advocates of the Constitution held the dubious honor of being the first to use the symbolic power of the Fourth to legitimize their own cause. Federalists suggested that the Constitution was the fulfillment of the Revolution by holding ratification processions on the Fourth of July in Philadelphia and other cities. The federal processions of 1788 deliberately presented an image of unanimity regarding the Constitution that belied the fierce fights over ratification. In Albany, New York, for example, anti-Federalists countered the Federalist procession with one of their own, which ended with a ritualistic burning of the Constitution and a violent brawl with the Federalists.

Although these fights subsided after ratification, the underlying divisions over the nature of the republic continued to flare up on Independence Day. By the mid-1790s, Federalists and Republicans were holding separate celebrations in Boston, New York, and other cities, with each party proclaiming itself the true heir to the Revolution. After the War of 1812, partisan ferocity declined with the Federalist Party, but politically divisive Fourths reemerged in the 1830s with rising sectionalism.

Other divisions penetrated the Fourth in the antebellum era as well, leading to fragmentation of the holiday. Many Americans did not participate in celebrations at all, either by choice or by exclusion. The public Fourth was preeminently a white male preserve. While men celebrated with oratory, guns, and alcohol, women spent the holiday visiting female friends and relatives. Urban workers often had to work on the Fourth, as did farmers, since the holiday fell during haying season in much of the nation. Urban Fourths became dominated by the carnivalesque celebrations of the working poor, which featured noise, indulgence, mayhem, and spectacle, all fueled by alcohol and gunpowder. Vendors sold food and alcohol, and gangs of rowdy youths drank, shot guns, brawled, and threw firecrackers at the respectable sorts who ventured out on city streets. In response, the urban middle

### Frederick Douglass's 1852 Oration in Rochester, N.Y.

I am not included within the pale of this glorious anniversary! Your high independence only reveals the immeasurable distance between us. The blessings in which you this day rejoice are not enjoyed in common . . . . This Fourth of July is yours, not mine. You may rejoice, I must mourn. To drag a man in fetters into the grand illuminated temple of liberty, and call upon him to join you in joyous anthems were inhuman mockery and sacrilegious irony.

This eloquent expression of African Americans' ambivalence toward the Fourth of July is excerpted from Frederick Douglass's Fourth of July address to the Rochester Ladies' Anti-Slavery Society in 1852.

**Source: Douglass, Frederick. "What to the Slave is the Fourth of July?" Oration, 4 July 1852, Rochester, New York; reprinted in** Black Scholar **7 (July-August 1976): 33–34. (Emphasis in original.)**

class increasingly withdrew from public celebrations entirely in favor of private picnics.

African Americans were not particularly welcome at public celebrations, and faced harassment and even attack from whites on the Fourth. Some refused to observe the day at all in protest of its hypocrisy, while others organized separate exercises, at which they celebrated the progress already made toward abolition and worked for national emancipation. Black New Yorkers, for instance, annually celebrated their emancipation on the Fifth of July.

In the antebellum era a variety of reformers inaugurated celebrations of the Fourth to promote their own visions of the American nation. Newly formed journeymen's unions sponsored parades and dinners, at which they articulated an artisan republicanism that placed skilled workers at the heart of the nation. Radical workers and reformers rewrote the Declaration of Independence on the Fourth to justify their own struggles for liberation. Church groups, Sunday schools, temperance advocates, and abolitionists all linked their causes to the Revolution. Temperance advocates, for instance, called for freedom from the slavery of the bottle and claimed that the founding fathers had been teetotalers.

Abolitionists turned the holiday into a pointed attack on America's fall from the promise of 1776. Orators pointed out the incongruity of slavery in the land of lib-

Encyclopedia of **Recreation and Leisure** in America

367

**Independence Day.** Fireworks streak across the night sky on the Fourth of July in 1996 at the Washington Monument in Washington D.C. © *AP/Wide World Photos*

erty. In his famous Fourth of July address before the Rochester Ladies' Anti-Slavery Society in 1852, Frederick Douglass denounced Independence Day as a cruel joke to African Americans and asserted that they could not celebrate it until they were free. On another Fourth, abolitionist William Lloyd Garrison dramatically burned a copy of the Constitution to protest its acceptance of slavery.

As the most radical abolitionists rejected it, white southerners embraced the Constitution on the Fourth to defend their "peculiar institution." After secession, however, they returned to the Declaration of Independence to support their own revolution. Northerners in turn used the wartime Fourths to proclaim the necessity of unity and loyalty to the republic and its Constitution.

## Reforming the Fourth

After the Civil War, the antebellum fragmentation returned, broken by occasional displays of unity such as those for the widely celebrated centennial. Philadelphia staged a huge civic procession on the eve of the holiday, and its exercises included the reading of an original man-

uscript of the Declaration of Independence by Virginian Richard Henry Lee, grandson and namesake of the author of the original resolution for independence. In Boston, a descendant of John Winthrop, the first governor of the Massachusetts Bay Colony, addressed the centennial audience.

The centennial unity proved fleeting, however, and Americans continued to celebrate in groups so that they could shape American nationalism to their own purposes. Immigrants combined ethnic and American nationalism on the Fourth, asserting that the two were not incompatible. Similarly, Native Americans turned the holiday, which the government had imposed as an assimilative force, into a vehicle of cultural survival by performing prohibited dances and rituals. African Americans celebrated their freedom by recounting their contributions to American independence. They were elated when black boxer Jack Johnson defeated Jim Jeffries on 4 July 1910, but glee turned to terror as angry white mobs rampaged against them.

Urban workers, meanwhile, continued to celebrate independence in the pursuit of recreation and amusement, preferring to spend their rare holiday in pleasure rather than listening to oratory. The Fourth found them on steamboat and rail excursions and at minstrel shows, picnics, fireworks displays, circuses, baseball games, regattas, bicycle races, and rodeos.

One constant of the Fourth was fireworks. Americans had long proclaimed their patriotism noisily by expending massive amounts of gunpowder and shooting off firecrackers. In the early twentieth century a coalition of reformers, doctors, journalists, women's clubs, and educators, alarmed at the threat to persons and property, organized the Safe and Sane Fourth of July movement. Newspapers and the American Medical Association publicized the problem by publishing holiday casualty lists, and Sane Fourth Associations sought legislation restricting the sale of guns and fireworks. By 1911, dozens of cities had adopted such legislation. Reformers also created alternative celebrations, including pageants, sporting competitions, folk festivals, and processions, drawing heavily on immigrant cultural traditions. In 1914, Cleveland's Sane Fourth Committee organized a reception for the city's new citizens, and the next year more than a hundred towns celebrated the Fourth as National Americanization Day, with citizenship receptions, patriotic oratory, and pageantry.

In response to the pressure to demonstrate their patriotism during World War I, immigrant leaders, in conjunction with the Committee on Public Information, made the Fourth of July 1918 a massive demonstration of loyalty. A uniform national program of exercises included raising and saluting the flag, reading President Woodrow Wilson's holiday address and the Declaration of Independence, listening to patriotic oratory, welcoming new citizens, and singing "America."

## The Contemporary Fourth

Naturalization ceremonies remain a common feature of the contemporary Fourth, with the most symbolic at Thomas Jefferson's Monticello. The battle between reformers and noise enthusiasts still reverberates as well, as thousands of Americans cross state lines each June to purchase forbidden fireworks. Modern-day Americans celebrate the Fourth in a variety of ways. Most towns held bicentennial celebrations in 1976, and many still stage annual parades or festivals. Picnics, family reunions, and sporting events are popular holiday pastimes. Because of the significance of its date, the Fourth escaped the holiday exodus to Mondays, but it has become a popular time for summer vacations. At least one factor has remained constant. Fireworks still constitute the most universal and popular aspect of the Fourth, from elaborate municipal displays to the kids with sparklers and firecrackers.

*See also:* Frolics, Labor Day, Memorial Day, Parades, Patriotism and Leisure

### BIBLIOGRAPHY

Appelbaum, Diana Karter. *The Glorious Fourth: An American Holiday, an American History.* New York: Facts On File, 1989.

Dennis, Matthew. *Red, White, and Blue Letter Days: An American Calendar.* Ithaca, N.Y.: Cornell University Press, 2002.

Newman, Simon P. *Parades and the Politics of the Street: Festive Culture in the Early American Republic.* Philadelphia: University of Pennsylvania Press, 1997.

Smilor, Raymond W. "Creating a National Festival: The Campaign for a Safe and Sane Fourth, 1903–1916." *Journal of American Culture* 2 (Winter 1980): 611–622.

Sweet, Leonard I. "The Fourth of July and Black Americans in the Nineteenth Century: Northern Leadership Opinion within the Context of Black Experience." *Journal of Negro History* 61 (July 1976): 256–275.

Travers, Len. *Celebrating the Fourth: Independence Day and the Rites of Nationalism in the Early Republic.* Amherst: University of Massachusetts Press, 1997.

Waldstreicher, David. *In the Midst of Perpetual Fetes: The Making of American Nationalism, 1776–1820.* Chapel Hill: University of North Carolina Press for the Omohundro Institute of Early American History and Culture, 1997.

*Ellen M. Litwicki*

# FOX HUNTING
**See** *Blood Sports*

# FRISBEE
**See** *Ultimate Frisbee*

# FROLICS

A frolic is a planned party, usually in a rural setting. From the colonial period until the late nineteenth century, Americans of different races and ethnicities applied the term "frolic" to a wide array of festivities that fall into two basic categories: work frolics and holiday frolics. Both types functioned to strengthen community bonds through celebration and reciprocity.

## Work Frolics

Work frolics derived from similar European and African traditions of communal agricultural labor. An individual, family, or community confronted with a task too large to complete on its own invited neighbors to help them. In return, the host provided refreshments and revelry. Work frolics composed a vital segment of the rural economy in America until the late nineteenth century. For over 200 years, the relatively low cost of renting or owning land in America resulted in a shortage of rural wage laborers. Faced with scarce labor and high wages for the few laborers available, farmers relied on the work frolic as a means for exchanging labor. Attendance at a work frolic granted neighbors the right to call on the host when they needed help. Besides meeting economic realities, work frolics contributed to the formation of communities by tying people into local networks of obligation.

Farmers called work frolics to accomplish a range of tasks, including corn husking, house (or barn) raising, quilting, sewing, apple butter making, chopping wood, log rolling, sugar (or syrup) making, spinning, hunting, and nut cracking. These events required planning and preparation. Seasonal cycles of agriculture meant all farmers had to tap their maple trees, husk their corn, and boil their apples within the same few weeks.

To ensure farmers did not deplete their labor force by planning frolics on the same day, families collaborated to produce a frolic schedule. Hosts also finished preliminary tasks to allow visitors to focus on the large projects that the host family could not complete alone. For example, quilting bee hosts cut the pieces of cloth, carded the stuffing, and stretched the lining on the quilting frame before workers arrived. The "bee" involved only applying the stuffing and stitching the quilt's panels. Competition drove workers to accomplish their tasks quickly. Teams of participants vied to husk more ears of corn. Log-rolling teams strove to move the most wood. At sewing and spinning bees, contests measured either the quantity of work completed or the highest quality of work.

Obligatory reciprocity promised hosts that their neighbors would show up, but the party after the work served as a secondary lure. Hosts usually offered simple food such as bread and cheese, although barbecued meat and fancier cakes were not unknown. Standard fare included alcoholic beverages throughout the colonial era. Nineteenth-century temperance movements influenced some hosts to abstain from proffering alcohol. Typically, small turnouts plagued these dry work parties. Most workers felt short-changed when hosts did not meet traditional expectations of decent food and alcohol. Entertainment at the parties consisted of music and dancing.

Environment, farm size, race, and gender impacted the form and experience of work frolics. A farmer chopped enough logs for a log rolling only when he had to clear acreage, so chopping frolics and log rollings primarily took place on the frontier. On the other hand, the presence of corn on virtually every American farm made husking bees a frequent occurrence nationwide. Since the limited labor power of small family farms necessitated outside help more often than large commercial farms or southern plantations boasting sizable labor forces, families working on small farms participated in more work parties than wage laborers on commercial farms or slaves on plantations.

When southern planters did call for a work frolic, it was an event of enormous proportions. The corn harvest prompted the most common work frolic in the slave South. During the harvest season, slaves and their owners rotated around local plantations to help "shuck" the corn crop ("shucking" is the southern term for husking). Shucking frolics resembled white husking bees, replete with competition and a celebration provided at the master's expense. These frolics differed slightly from white work frolics, as the slaves' African heritage heavily influenced the party's music and dancing. Shucking frolics granted slaves from different plantations a rare opportunity to socialize. Many African American communities maintained the tradition of the corn shucking after eman-

cipation, when African Americans began working small plots of land in family units and so continued to need help at harvest time.

Quilting bees, spinning bees, and sewing frolics involved "women's work." These events shared the long hours and competitive framework of male-oriented work frolics, but they took place indoors and only women attended. In the colonial era, urban town houses as well as rural homes hosted women's work frolics because basic linen and wool cloth produced by women at home remained cheaper than commercial cloth. In rural areas, women often scheduled their work frolics on the same day as men's frolics. After both groups finished their work, they joined together for the party. Whether or not the women had a frolic of their own, they cooked and prepared for the evening party.

Not all work frolics centered on gendered tasks. At apple bees, men and women pared and sliced side by side, then took turns stirring the kettles and churning the butter. Men and women both husked corn at husking bees. Daylong mixed-gender work parties acquired a reputation as sites for courtship. The woods and orchards that hosted maple sugar frolics and apple bees allowed couples ample private space. Both whites and blacks adhered to a ritual that permitted a husker unveiling a red ear of corn to demand a kiss from someone of the opposite sex. Even when gender lines divided work at a frolic, the party and dancing afterward presented young men and women with the opportunity to mingle.

## Holiday Frolics

Like work frolics, holiday frolics were planned events that brought together a broad segment of the community. But holiday frolics were purely celebratory. Tasks limited the number of participants at a work frolic and restricted the started earlier in the day and drew more participants. Of course, smaller-scale holiday parties existed. Traditional nineteenth-century New England Thanksgiving frolics generally included only close kin or members of the household. Food, drink, music, and competitive games were characteristic components of both holiday and work frolics.

In colonial America, holiday frolics sometimes celebrated traditional ethnic or religious holidays such as Pinkster (the Dutch celebration of Pentecost). They also marked informal civic holidays like muster day (when local militia gathered to drill), court days, and trade fairs. Urban populations took to the streets on such days, but in rural areas the barbecue emerged as the most common form of holiday frolic. Barbecues were a kind of gigantic potluck. Individuals and families brought their own foods to accompany the spit-roasted pig and alcohol donated by a local gentleman. Dancing, horse racing, and games lent a competitive and festive atmosphere to the party.

The plurality and diffusion of religious and ethnic groups in America, as well as the rise of more ascetic evangelical denominations, reduced the number and frequency of large-scale religious holiday frolics in the nineteenth century. After the Revolution, the Fourth of July and Election Day emerged as the dates of the biggest holiday frolics. Political parties organized the bulk of the fetes on both these days, hoping to construct among their partisans a community loyal to the party. The traditional assortment of games, food, and liquor remained central to these patriotic events, and the rise of urban parks bequeathed a rural aesthetic to holiday frolics taking place within city limits. Eighteenth-century gentlemen had sponsored barbecues to maintain ties of patronage and deference, which kept them in power. Parades and speeches at nineteenth-century holiday frolics simply communicated the frolics' political agenda more overtly.

Other types of holiday frolics had no affiliation with any specific holiday. Starting in the 1840s, a "pic-nic" referred to a meal eaten by city dwellers on a day trip into the countryside. The small size of the excursion party rendered picnics a scaled-down version of the barbecue. Games, drinking, and a glutinous amount of food typified the experience. In the North, snow combined with the wintertime reduction of farmwork to inspire widespread "sleighing frolics" among young adults. On a planned day, they crammed into a sleigh with all their friends and rendezvoused with other sleighs full of people at a local tavern. Sleighs often raced on the way to the tavern and before returning home, by which time many drivers were fairly intoxicated. Like maple sugar frolics and apple bees, sleighing presented young adults with unsupervised time conducive to courting.

## Frolics Today

Work frolics and holiday frolics dotted the calendars of Early Americans from the seventeenth century until the late nineteenth century. Already by the 1850s, the term frolic was shedding its meaning as a reference to planned parties. Today, work frolics have virtually disappeared from the American social landscape. Rising land prices throughout the late nineteenth and twentieth centuries increased the number of agricultural wage laborers while the mechanization of farmwork reduced the need for more voluntary forms of help. Yet work frolics have not entirely disappeared. No longer meeting at house raisings or quilting bees, farm families meet at the county fair, an event of extended duration that mixes the fruits of labor with eating, drinking, socializing, and entertainment.

As work frolics have declined, holiday frolics have proliferated. Sponsored by towns or public institutions, the planned barbecue or patriotic celebration survives as the community picnic or summer concert series. The Fourth of July has become less political over the course of the twentieth century as a result of election reform and the decline of partisanship among the general population, but depoliticization has not altered the Fourth of July's place as a preeminent day for community holiday parties. As events intended to galvanize community bonds, frolics have undergone several transformations and yet continue to offer Americans a counterbalance to the heavy cultural weight of individualism.

*See also:* Barn Raising, Colonial-Era Leisure Lifestyles, Fourth of July, Plantation Entertaining, Prohibition and Temperance, Quilting Parties

## BIBLIOGRAPHY

Abrahams, Roger D. *Singing the Master: The Emergence of African-American Culture in the Plantation South.* New York: Pantheon Books, 1992.

Brandau, Rosemary. "Early Fair Foods and Barbecues." Colonial Williamsburg Foundation Research Report. Williamsburg, Va.: Colonial Williamsburg Foundation, 1985.

Dulles, Foster Rhea. *A History of Recreation: America Learns to Play.* New York: Meredith Publishing Co., 1965. The original edition was published in 1940.

Faragher, John Mack. *Sugar Creek: Life on the Illinois Prairie.* New Haven, Conn.: Yale University Press, 1986.

Hern, Mary Ellen Wisniewski. "Pic-Nic." Master's thesis, Winterthur Program in Early American Culture, 1987.

Martin, Scott C. *Killing Time: Leisure and Culture in Southwestern Pennsylvania, 1800–1850.* Pittsburgh, Pa.: University of Pittsburgh Press, 1995.

Nylander, Jane C. *Our Own Snug Fireside: Images of the New England Home, 1760–1860.* New Haven, Conn.: Yale University Press, 1994.

Struna, Nancy L. *People of Prowess: Sport, Leisure, and Labor in Early Anglo-America.* Urbana: University of Illinois Press, 1996.

Waldstreicher, David. *In the Midst of Perpetual Fetes: The Making of American Nationalism, 1776–1820.* Chapel Hill: University of North Carolina Press, 1997.

*Kenneth Cohen*

# G

## GAMBLING

Betting was and is a remarkably universal human activity. Various forms came with each immigrant group, Asian or European, who at different times joined the Native American populations in the New World. Keno, for example, which people of the twenty-first century enjoy in electronic form, originated out of a traditional gambling game brought to the American West by Chinese workers already intensely familiar with forms of wagering. Native Americans themselves from prehistoric times already were engaging in ritual contests and betting. In the Old World, not only dice but crooked dice were found in ancient Egyptian tombs. According to the Bible, when Jesus was on the cross, the soldiers cast lots for his clothing (Matthew 27:35). Traditional European justice often involved the use of lots, which suited well populations familiar over many centuries with gaming and betting. Indeed, the ancient Romans had already made a distinction between games of chance (which they forbade) and games of skill.

None of this wagering was a productive activity, but people found betting enjoyable and sometimes preoccupying to the point of serious addiction. In the classic formulation, games carried out in a repeated or ritualistic manner constituted play. Thus, some people used gambling to fill leisure time. Others considered making bets a recreation. People were well aware that gambling belonged in a category that was not work—except for the so-called professional gamblers, who appeared conspicu-

ously in the nineteenth century. Indeed, the ways in which wagering violated the work ethic provided motivations and arguments for both moralists and defiant gamblers.

Gambling appeared in two forms. Sometimes it was a form of recreation in itself. One could gamble alone, as with a machine game such as a slot machine. Or one could make gambling a social activity, as in bingo gatherings or card games. Often, however, gambling occurred in connection with other recreational and leisure activities.

Always the most widespread arena for betting was any kind of contest or sport. For those who could not participate—and often for the participants as well—making a wager on the outcome of a contest was an important activity. The history of sports is inextricably bound with the history of gambling, including all kinds of human, animal, and machine contests.

Moreover, beginning early in the Western world, gambling became associated with a whole set of additional activities, many of which were not "respectable" or were decidedly antisocial. By the nineteenth century, a social constellation of so-called minor vices was well established in the United States; people commonly thought of gambling as part of a complex of activities that included drinking, smoking, sexual naughtiness, and various other minor infractions of good order and bourgeois parsimony. By the beginning of the twentieth century, a cabaret model was in place, which included various kinds of entertainment with gambling, with an additional implication that patrons were at least a bit upscale. As tourism developed, gambling sites often attracted travelers or others who indulged in the conspicuous consumption of betting. The

**Las Vegas.** Casinos and hotels light up the night for gamblers and tourists in 1950s Las Vegas. The birth of "the Strip" in Las Vegas forever changed the face of legalized gambling in America and established a gambling Mecca that people from all walks of life could visit and enjoy. © *Corbis*

ultimate development was the "Las Vegas package" of the second half of the twentieth century, in which gambling was central to a complex of activities that included shows, eating and drinking, and even prostitution in a holiday setting in which ordinary middle-class standards of behavior—beyond the work ethic—could be set aside temporarily.

But the custom of betting had much deeper cultural roots than commercial packaging. Placing a wager for most people in America from the beginning carried powerful implications for gender. Making extravagant bets or putting one's property at hazard often fulfilled a stereotype of aggressive masculinity. Of great popular interest and appeal was still another stereotype out of the nineteenth century: the romantic gambling lady. But the laying of a wager was still overwhelmingly a masculine act—and still often conflated with sports of all

kinds. To augment a contest with a material dimension added or enhanced the risk factor typically associated with masculine stereotypes, especially young, virile masculinity in which risky behavior was an important element.

Most of the best sources for our knowledge of gambling in earlier times are the words and actions of Americans who condemned or regulated or taxed making a bet. In addition, journalists over many generations featured unusual gambling events and especially people who won big. Hence most older gambling history tended to be either antiquarian accounts of colorful personalities or narratives of moral and legal crusades. Everyday wagering outside of recorded institutions was hard to uncover. Only at the end of the twentieth century did historians, with the help of sociologists, begin to explore many of the cultural dimensions of gambling.

## Colonial Americans

Intimate knowledge of various types of gambling was part of the cultural baggage of the first generations of English colonists. As a prosperous mercantile society developed, so did gambling. To begin with, promoters of both public and private ventures used public lotteries to raise funds. Perhaps most notable was the English lottery supporting the first settlement in Virginia, between 1612 and 1624. Moreover, as part of their conspicuous consumption, English aristocrats gambled ostentatiously. They particularly bet on horse races, which had the snobbish sobriquet of "the sport of kings." But they also placed wagers on other games and contests and sports of all kinds. In many such games and contests, people of every class joined in the betting, from cards to cock fighting (which was very popular in Britain but did not carry over as much to the American colonies).

Colonists of all classes and backgrounds, therefore, brought with them customs of placing bets on games, contests, and sports. In the southern settlements, particularly, aristocrats imitated the British upper classes and tried to use ostentatious gambling as a mark of high social status. Members of the other social groups, including enslaved people, also placed bets and gambled freely. At one point, however, in Virginia, sumptuary legislation forbade nonaristocrats from actually participating in the races. But betting was endemic. In the eighteenth century, the southern colonies, especially, had a strong tradition of brutal sporting events in which competing, fighting, and betting mixed together. One colorful such contest was gander pulling, in which the participants attempted to yank the head off a live, greased gander.

Calvinists, who were particularly numerous in New England, knew the general proclivity to gamble, and they condemned card playing and similar gaming activity. They had good theological reasons. Because justice was often obtained by the drawing of lots—a device that permitted God to show His will—any trivial use of chance, as in cards, was but trifling with the Almighty. Playing cards was bad enough, but betting compounded the offense. For generations, evangelicals preached against games involving "chance" because the players trifled with Providence as well as thrift.

Yet, beyond upper-class social competition in betting, large parts of the population did indeed make bets as part of their diversions. From the beginning, of course, gambling flourished where other violations of bourgeois work and order were occurring. It was in this way that unproductive betting developed a generally recognized association with the least desirable parts of the population. Yet many residents continued to enjoy wagering in any number of ways. Gambling, then as later, generated ambivalent attitudes and divided opinions.

In the revolutionary years and after, numerous witnesses described the ways in which Americans, particularly those in male groups, placed bets. George Washington was said to have won or lost in a single evening as much as £9 playing cards. Fighting of various kinds, among both humans and animals, invariably generated not just points of honor but sums placed on the outcome of the contests. Public lotteries continued in the New World. Benjamin Franklin actually led an effort to finance the defenses of Philadelphia by means of such a special-purpose lottery.

Gambling became particularly conspicuous on the American frontier. Placing bets was an important part of many lives lived under dangerous and difficult conditions. Travelers left vivid accounts of eye gouging and other brutal contests in which large amounts of money traded hands among the cheering onlookers. And, of course, traditionally not only machismo but omnipresent hard drink encouraged men (notably) to hazard anything they owned. John M. Findlay cites a British visitor who believed inhabitants of Western towns were "generally devoted to gambling on horse races, cockfights, card games, and billiards" as well as the usual personal fights (p. 35).

## Institutionalization of Gambling in the Nineteenth Century

What was new in the nineteenth century was the way in which gambling became institutionalized and commercialized. While impromptu and informal games and contests continued, lotteries, racing, casinos, riverboats, and other gambling establishments brought betting into the realm of profit making and business. In the process, the recreational and leisure aspects of placing a bet became much more formally institutionalized. While it is true, as historians have argued, that each institutionalization had an independent history, over decades the general trend toward organization and institutionalization framed all gambling as American society generally became more commercialized.

The history of lotteries illustrates the trend, and, because public campaigns and governments were so often involved, the record is relatively accessible. During the Revolution, the Continental Congress tried to raise funds by means of a lottery, and after independence, various states authorized a wide variety of drawings for public and private purposes—public works, industrial development, and charitable institutions and causes. The lottery device flourished and grew in the early nineteenth century and was especially important in financing schools and churches as well as economic infrastructure. Twenty-four states approved lotteries for internal improvements between 1790 and 1860. But with increasing frequency, private contractors conducted the lotteries, and wholesalers and brokers delivered the tickets to consumers. Therefore an additional keen profit motive furthered the promotion of lottery gambling.

While lotteries flourished for years before the Civil War, the contract system eventually discredited those lotteries, and officially approved schemes diminished greatly, to the point of prohibition. Yet for many decades, lottery speculation flourished alongside land speculation and other schemes. It was especially the addition of contractors and brokers that opened the way for widespread swindling. Lottery managers would not pay out what they had promised, or they would simply disappear with the money. Various states from time to time banned the sale of lottery tickets, but chances were widely available from other states. By 1860, however, lotteries were generally illegal. The ultimate demise of the lottery as a public institution came after the ignominious scandals of the later Louisiana lottery, which inspired Congress in 1895 to pass a law forbidding interstate commerce in lotteries.

As the lotteries grew in the early nineteenth century, poor people who could not afford the substantial price of a ticket still found a way to bet on the drawing. For them, policy gamblers took small sums from people and paid off just as the real lottery would, except in proportionally miniscule amounts. Policy gambling was illegal, and fraud was common, but it grew and expanded. Observers at the time especially attributed policy betting to African American people, but many small-time bettors participated. They often based their wagers on dreams; dream books, which explained how to apply a dream to a bet, flourished for generations as policy evolved into common numbers games.

Some betting games were particularly widespread in the antebellum period. One was faro, a card game in which the house took only perhaps three percent—if honestly conducted, which it almost never was. Myriad confidence games operated, such as an ancestor of the shell game—where a bet was placed on which of three or more shells or cases concealed a hidden object—played with needle cases. For the upper classes attempting to imitate European aristocrats, luxurious commercial gaming houses, if not casinos, were available; other entrepreneurs opened a range of less-respectable establishments to service the less affluent.

The most colorful gambling of the early nineteenth century was, of course, that carried on aboard the Mississippi riverboats (557 boats were in operation in 1860). The so-called professional gamblers contributed substantially to institutionalizing gambling customs. They introduced various games such as twenty-one that were suited for commercialized gambling, and they Americanized poker with wild cards and bluffing and spread the game wherever gambling was a business. Roulette wheels were usually too heavy to carry on the boats, but a casino was licensed briefly in New Orleans in 1827, combining luxurious appointments and snob appeal (the European model) with American democratic openness for the clientele.

The casino model was not necessary for the riverboat gamblers, who had much background in card rooms and other traditional gambling establishments that flourished privately or outside of the law. Gambling onshore continued to take place in taverns and other such establishments, reinforcing the impression that betting was associated with marginal or criminal people. The fact that so many gamblers—typically the "card sharps" (or "sharpers")—were dishonest further reinforced the association. But gambling nevertheless functioned as a business, open to all. Notoriously in California during the gold rush, for example, the business ran day and night, but in established enterprises, "the house" depended more often on a percentage of the money bet than upon skill or cheating to guarantee a profit. Gambling establishments featured the most commercial games, with rapid resolution and turnover: roulette, dice throwing, and card games such as faro and twenty-one.

## Speculation and Prohibition

After the Civil War, state legislators became increasingly sensitive to the opponents of gambling; into the 1920s, governments made betting illegal in different ways and in different degrees across the United States, and visible gambling declined in quantity. As new immigrants and new technologies and new sites challenged the evangelicals and Progressives, betting changed dynamically. By 1907, two new states had entered the union with constitutions that banned any gambling. Yet with the rise of commercial sports, opportunities to place bets increased greatly.

It was in the period from 1868 to the early 1890s that the Louisiana lottery flourished and fell—with the corruption and scandal that removed the lottery from a viable means of raising funds for public purposes. In many areas of the country, card rooms and other places for gambling continued as before, albeit frequently under imminent danger of prosecution. For the wealthy, however, a number of casinos did spring up, including one in the Broadmoor in Colorado that operated from 1891

**Sulky racing.** This 1869 engraving shows a race between trotters Mountain Boy and Lady Thorn at Prospect Park Fair Grounds in Brooklyn, New York. A sulky is simply a single passenger vehicle; higher-wheel sulkies would later be replaced by bicycle-type models that were lighter but more stable. Stakes horse racing—in which the winning horses earned cash prizes—had come to the U.S. just five years before this race, establishing a popular new venue for gambling. © *Bettmann/Corbis*

to 1897. Richard A. Canfield, who ran gambling houses for the affluent in New York, Saratoga, and Newport, articulated the business basis of these new institutions. They had the trust of the customer because no cheating was necessary. "The percentage in favor of a gambling house is sufficient to guarantee the profits of the house. All any gambler wants is to have play enough for a long enough time and he'll get all the money any player has."

The way in which such entrepreneurs as Canfield came into the business is illustrated by a former prize fighter (who won substantial sums betting on himself), John Morrissey, who opened increasingly opulent gambling parlors until he finally settled in Saratoga Springs, where he could cater to the very wealthy. There, in 1864, he helped organize the first stakes horse racing in the United States—the first horse racing in the United States in which the winners won cash prizes—marking the beginning of serious commercialization of that gambling sport.

Horse racing, with betting at the track, was the premiere sporting activity connected with gambling. The first Kentucky Derby was run in 1870. In the 1870s, Oliver Wendell Holmes wrote,

'Twas on the famous trotting-ground

The betting men were gathered round

From far and near. . .

By 1891, New York had started regulating horse racing. By the 1920s, more than 300 racetracks were in operation, although for a time antigambling pressures reduced the numbers greatly. As racing developed, the pressure of bookmakers changed the sport. Short sprint races replaced longer contests so as to provide more opportunities for betting. State legislators, however, generally moved to suppress open gambling in connection with the tracks.

But many other sports became important to gambling in the late nineteenth century. Bare-knuckle boxing generated an enormous amount of both organized and unorganized wagering. Early in the twentieth century, Theodore Roosevelt and other leaders called for the reform of college football, which had fallen under the influence of professional gamblers, as had college boat races. Americans more and more often were betting on the emerging professional baseball teams. Team owners were active gamblers, betting on their own teams. Large groups of more humble people engaged in wagering were conspicuous in the bleachers during every game. The extent of the involvement of baseball with gambling was dramatized by the famous Black Sox scandal of 1919.

In the late nineteenth century, as historian Ann Fabian has written, speculation became a highly valued activity in American society. She points out that as commercial speculators grew in numbers and boldness, they tended to try to marginalize the more unrespectable speculation of people who bet on cards and numbers and contests. The most striking contrast was the legality of the praiseworthy speculation on the stock and commodity markets by moneyed people while the operators of bucket shops for poor people were subject to prosecution. In the bucket shops, one could bet on changes in the stock market with small change and risk being arrested for antisocial gambling. In the stock exchange, doing exactly the same thing with stocks was constructive capitalism.

Even as the prohibition of gambling was proceeding, technology brought big changes in betting, whether legal or illegal. At the end of the nineteenth century, the nickel slot machine was invented (the usual date given is 1887, the inventor Charles Fey of San Francisco). From the mid-nineteenth century on, newspapers greatly increased their circulations and became great metropolitan dailies by indulging in yellow journalism. Sports news, which notoriously included betting odds, was an important part of this transformed social institution. The telegraph further stimulated sports betting. By furnishing immediate news of the outcome in many contests, wire services opened up many new opportunities for exciting wagers. Gamblers used the telegraph directly, establishing betting parlors with direct Western Union connections to sporting events. These gambling establishments were called pool rooms. Approximately 2,000 were reported to have existed early in the twentieth century in New York City alone; such gambling centers existed alongside solo illegal bookmakers far into the twentieth century.

## Government Gets into the Business

Despite the general prohibition of gambling, governments from time to time made exceptions, and slowly, especially in the 1930s, legal gambling began to expand. Indeed, a pattern emerged: In times when state governments were hard-pressed financially, most notably in the 1930s and 1970s, more and more gambling enterprises became legal because they furnished revenue to the governments. The very legislators who could legalize benefited directly from doing so: By authorizing taxes on the betting, lawmakers were freed from having to impose other taxes; they thus appeared to get something for nothing for their constituents.

Meantime, in the 1920s, the media discovered the gangsters and syndicates who dominated illegal gambling and other activities such as prostitution and other rackets, with sidelines in bootlegging and major crimes. This discovery was, as historian Mark Haller points out, a lit-

tle late. By the 1920s, local operatives, tied into local politics, dominated illegal gambling, not the organized crime syndicates of the late nineteenth century. Indeed, perhaps 30,000 illegal bookies were then operating in urban centers. Moses Annenberg by the 1930s dominated the information necessary for racetrack betting by monopolizing the wire services and publishing the *Daily Racing Form*. He recognized how pervasive sports betting had become: "If people can wager at a racetrack why should they be deprived of the right to do so away from a track? How many people can take time off from their jobs to go to a racetrack?"

But the patrons of local entrepreneurs, people who were betting on sporting events and using other kinds of gambling for recreation, were also changing. First, the white Protestant populations, in which antigambling sentiment was strong, were diminishing as the demographic base shifted to other population groups during the rest of the twentieth century. Roman Catholics, who increased relatively as well as absolutely, did not maintain doctrinal prohibitions against gambling, although church leaders often condemned various practices on Christian social grounds. Most noticeably, however, and in the second place, the cultural changes associated with World War I, the 1920s, the Great Depression, and World War II altered the place of gambling in American life.

During World War I, a substantial segment of the young men of the country learned in the barracks that they could while away time pleasurably by surreptitious gambling. Not only card games, but especially craps, a dice game, became part of the firsthand experience of "boys" from antigambling families as well as those for whom betting was already part of supermasculine life. Similar experiences affected a much larger part of the population during World War II.

The new mass media, particularly the tabloid newspapers and the moving pictures, also spread ambivalent or favorable attitudes toward the minor vices in general. The popular writer Damon Runyon was especially important in conveying a benign image of the bookies and bettors of the big cities, as in the classic musical *Guys and Dolls*. They were often comic characters and, therefore, no longer appeared threatening, even though they operated illegally and on the margins of society. By the 1920s and 1930s, sports journalism was more sensational than ever. Boxing (legalized by New York in 1920) made a big comeback. Bookies also found themselves compelled to work with not only baseball games (and baseball pools) but college football. By the 1930s, the football pool card had joined the baseball pool card as a mass consumption item. As radio began broadcasting sports, many listeners enhanced their recreational pleasure by risking some money on the outcome. By the middle of the century, one expert estimated that $100 million was bet on college football alone, one-tenth of it on the Army–Notre Dame game.

The major new media model, however, was the cabaret, in which trendy people mixed with socially marginal people in a framework of drinking, smoking, gambling, and presumed sexual permissiveness. Of particular importance in transforming cultural attitudes was the transfer of the stylish cabaret model to the casino in the gambling ships that were notable in the early 1930s. They carried passengers outside the continental limits, where gambling (and, incidentally, during Prohibition years, drinking) could take place legally. Los Angeles was a major port for such ships, and they caught the imagination of writers of both fiction and movies, who popularized romantic versions of the floating casinos and the lifestyle that went with them. After the gambling ships shut down, southern Californians, at least, could go to a division point on the Union Pacific Railroad, Las Vegas, and find a reasonable substitute.

That is because in 1931, the government of the state of Nevada, in a desperate attempt to develop revenue without using taxes, legalized casinos. First, criminals with experience and funds moved in; corporations followed. But with the help of publicity in the mass media, Reno and Las Vegas provided a model of a new area for vacation—not only from work, but from conventional social standards.

The other area in which at least some state governments were willing to legalize gambling in the interwar period was horse racing. The parimutuel system appeared first in one state and then another, most notably Illinois in 1927, which served as a model for legislators elsewhere. In 1933, the parimutuel machine in New Hampshire became a part of the state fiscal system. By 1935, sixteen states were taxing racetrack betting directly.

While gambling appeared in the media usually in the form of casino or racetrack images, many Americans found other means of risking their money in the interwar years, particularly in urban settings. The media continued to publish odds on various sporting contests. The numbers game involved many small bettors; numbers apparently saved many members of the Detroit and Chicago African American communities during the worst years of the Great Depression by providing an income when no legitimate work was available.. Bingo, which started out primarily as a carnival game, became increasingly popular and was often played in a charity or church setting (Frederick Lewis Allen quotes the ironic announcement: "Bingo every night in the Holy Spirit Room."). Another

sanitized form of depression gambling was bank night at the movies. Those who attended the movies could win either money or a prize, such as a set of dishes, using their admission tickets as lottery tickets. Other businesses, too, used lottery methods—drawings and raffles—as promotional gimmicks (already in the nineteenth century such marketing schemes had stimulated criticism, not least because entrepreneurs often did not hold the promised drawings). Altogether, extremely large numbers of otherwise innocent citizens by the 1930s and 1940s had become used to lottery-type gambling simply by participating in normal spending activities or by supporting charitable causes. By the 1950s, politicians who attempted to curb the abuses of the bingo craze found themselves unable to act because they appeared to be opposing religion and charity.

## The Slow Shift to Legalization and Partial Acceptance

In the second half of the twentieth century, small-time socializing at bingo and bank night at the movies, along with numbers and sports betting, became transformed into very different institutions and major economic and political forces. Even social card playing for stakes became more often institutionalized in commercial card rooms (especially in California, where they had long been available by local option). Gambling became commercialized entertainment for many people while remaining an expensive ritual of risk—play—for many others. In either case, the substance and form of betting meshed with the patterns of a culture of consumption in which many activities and institutions joined gambling in violating work-ethic and other bourgeois values.

A number of writers have traced the growth of casinos, which were ultimately the victory of Las Vegas public relations. These were not the old aristocrats' casinos of Europe, but a very democratic American version in which, ultimately, entertainment mixed with vice. The Las Vegas story began with legalization in 1931 and establishment of the Strip in 1941. In 1946, gangsters definitely took over, to be succeeded by businesspeople, state regulation, and, in 1969, the entry of corporate ownership and the ultimate acceptance of gambling entertainment as just another business. Later, in the age of the globalization of business in general, the American style of casino spread all over the world. The first step, however, was to Atlantic City, New Jersey, from 1976 to 1978.

In 1978, some Florida Seminoles opened a high-stakes bingo operation that started a whole new trend of Native American casinos operating in defiance of local law and custom (confirmed legally from 1987 to 1988).

**Lottery winners.** Joe Kainz and his wife Sue hold a commemorative lotto check for winning "The Big Game" in May 2000. The Chicago-area couple shared the $363 million prize with one other winner. By 1989, state lotteries were held in 75 percent of U.S. states. © *Corbis*

In 1990, Iowa authorized some limited riverboat gambling, and in a rush a number of other states saw an opportunity to raise revenues without raising taxes by letting casinos open legally. During the 1990s, there was what one scholar has characterized as "an explosion" of casinos in the United States. By 1987, slot machines had become the most popular form of amusement in such establishments, and some states even authorized such mechanical (and taxable) devices for the diversion of patrons at racetracks, which were suffering from the competition.

Permitting businesspeople to operate gambling establishments was one matter, but, at the same time, many states were themselves going into the business of gambling. The new form was a revival of the public lottery. In 1964, New Hampshire legislators were the first to try to avoid raising taxes by operating a state lottery. New

York joined in 1967, and, in 1969, New Jersey managed a format that was so successful that it served as a model for other states. By 1974, Massachusetts had introduced the instant lottery, the success of which was widely imitated, and in 1975 New Jersey pioneered a numbers game version. Even California finally joined in 1984. By 1989, three-fourths of the U.S. population lived in states with state lotteries, and in those states, the average annual household expenditure for lotteries was $240.

The conspicuous part played by legislators indicated how powerful the political forces favoring extending gambling had become. But the economic forces were even more intimidating. Large retailers such as 7-Eleven backed lotteries because they could sell chances—and were well rewarded for it. The great national accounting firms found legal gambling accounts particularly lucrative, and those firms had links to every major power broker. Suppliers of machines and electronic equipment (including General Electric) were deeply involved in lotteries. Other groups, too, such as small operators of off-track betting (authorized by New York in 1971), aggregated into political and economic forces.

For most gamblers, the major development of the late twentieth century (although the new forms had roots in the 1930s) was sports betting. Two particular factors changed the whole landscape. One was television, which made watching sports a major American activity, dwarfing the live attendance and radio listening of previous times. The other was the point spread, which was, typically, announced from Las Vegas. The point spread meant that betting could occur even when two teams were extremely unevenly matched: one could bet that the team that would obviously lose would lose by less or more than a certain number of points; thus, all team contests, not just close games, became exciting betting subjects. Football and basketball, both collegiate and professional, took on new meaning for those with even a little money to wager—legally or illegally. Professional football's Super Bowl Sunday became a generally acknowledged national carnival, implicitly based on many ordinary citizens' money at risk.

Did legalized gambling supply the entertainment and recreation that might supplant illegal (and untaxed) betting? Sociologists generally concluded that gambling simply begat more gambling, as habit, ritual, or just attitude. Economists believed rational choice might lead clear thinkers to continue to use illegal bookies because the rake-off was less than when taxes had to be added on to the take, as in the lotteries. On the whole, there was a major change so that gambling in general became much more socially acceptable among large parts of the U.S. population in the closing decades of the twentieth century.

## A Growth Industry: Technology, Media, and Consumerism

Some scholars believed that what they were seeing was commercial forces coming in to serve people with working-class backgrounds who had a lot of money to spend. Such commentators could point out how technology was being drawn into the service of betting. Television, as numerous scholars such as Benjamin Rader, Richard O. Davies, and Richard G. Abram have pointed out, transformed sports so as to make them subservient to betting. "Jimmy the Greek" Snyder, who reported bookie odds from Las Vegas, became a television personality in the 1970s. The content of the rest of television not only built on the traditional Hollywood glamorization of casinos and betting but also contributed active

cultural content, as in the popular show *Wheel of Fortune,* launched in 1975. Video games, as they came in, were rapidly adapted to gambling, and, in 1989, South Dakota became the first state to authorize video lottery terminals. In the 1990s, a whole new realm opened up with Internet gambling, which could be done online with a credit card. What the impact of this rapidly growing activity would be was unclear, but that it would be great seemed certain to observers at the turn of the twenty-first century.

Those observers and others commented on the way in which libertarian attitudes were permitting "market forces" and "social choice" to shape not only commercial but recreational activities that involved gambling, whether by operating chance machines, by emotionally or rationally calculating odds on contests, or by indulging in social activities that were based on or involved betting. Economic considerations were replacing moral considerations and thriftiness both. Gambling was, after all, not only one of the major entertainment industries but—at $50 billion and 600,000 employees for commercial legal games alone in 1997—one of the major businesses of the United States.

Moreover, the commentators continued, gambling was well adapted to the pervasive consumer society that had succeeded a bourgeois producer society. Gamblers and high rollers had long represented an ultimate of conspicuous consumption. But in gambling, it was the act that was important, not any product. Betting was therefore the essence of imaginative consuming, perfectly suited to the culture. Now participants could enjoy their fantasies at home via television or computer. Or they could participate on the job through the compulsory office or work-crew football pool. Or they could make wagering activities part of tourism or vacations or the contrived sociability of card rooms, bingo halls, or casinos. Gambling also could involve fooling the purchaser, the con game that gave additional enjoyment to shopping and deciphering ads. In the last six or seven decades of the twentieth century, thinking about shopping and purchasing, which could include risking money in other ways, became a major if not dominant entertainment mode. Many commentators concluded that gambling was no longer a socially deviant activity in the United States.

The separate histories of lotteries, sports betting, card games, machine betting, and other risky speculations reflected the specialized and bureaucratic pattern of American society in the late nineteenth and early twentieth centuries. By the end of the twentieth century, however, gamblers were often taking on a new identity. A successful mass magazine, *Gamblers World,* described as being "for the individual who enjoys action," first appeared in

1973. Many individuals still specialized in taking risk for pleasure, but many others now identified with celebrities and peers who liked "action" of any kind—from dice games to sports betting to speculating in collectibles such as oriental rugs. Theirs was a new, classic "consumption community." Many Americans in the age of mass media and impulses conveyed electronically were cut loose from bourgeois restraints, and they found that they could identify with the macho television hero, Maverick: "Gambling was his game."

*See also:* Atlantic City, Card Games, Horse Racing, Las Vegas

**BIBLIOGRAPHY**

Abt, Vicki, James F. Smith, and Eugene Martin Christiansen. *The Business of Risk: Commercial Gambling in Mainstream America.* Lawrence: University Press of Kansas, 1985.

Barker, Thomas, and Marjie Britz. *Jokers Wild: Legalized Gambling in the Twenty-first Century.* Westport, Conn.: Praeger Publishers, 2000.

Burnham, John C. *Bad Habits: Drinking, Smoking, Taking Drugs, Gambling, Sexual Misbehavior, and Swearing in American History.* New York: New York University Press, 1993.

Clotfelter, Charles T., and Philip J. Cook. *Selling Hope: State Lotteries in America.* Cambridge, Mass.: Harvard University Press, 1989.

Davidson, D. Kirk. *Selling Sin: The Marketing of Socially Unacceptable Products.* Westport, Conn.: Quorum Books, 1996.

Davies, Richard O., and Richard G. Abram. *Betting the Line: Sports Wagering in American Life.* Columbus: Ohio State University Press, 2001.

Drzazga, John. *Wheels of Fortune.* Springfield, Ill.: Charles C. Thomas, 1963.

Ezell, John Samuel. *Fortune's Merry Wheel: The Lottery in America.* Cambridge, Mass.: Harvard University Press, 1960.

Fabian, Ann. *Card Sharps, Dream Books, and Bucket Shops: Gambling in 19th-Century America.* Ithaca, N.Y.: Cornell University Press, 1990.

Findlay, John M. *People of Chance: Gambling in American Society from Jamestown to Las Vegas.* New York: Oxford University Press, 1986.

Haller, Mark H. "Bootleggers and American Gambling, 1920–1950." In *Gambling in America.* Edited by Commission on Review of National Policy Toward Gambling. Washington, D.C.: U.S. Government Printing Office, 1976.

International Gaming Institute, University of Nevada, Las Vegas. *The Gaming Industry: Introduction and Perspectives.* New York: John Wiley and Sons, 1996.

Kallick, Maureen, Daniel Suits, Ted Dielman, and Judith Hybels. *A Survey of American Gambling Attitudes and Behav-*

*ior.* Ann Arbor: University of Michigan, Institute for Social Research, 1979.

Lears, Jackson. *Something for Nothing: Luck in America.* New York: Viking, 2003.

McMillen, Jan, ed. *Gambling Cultures: Studies in History and Interpretation.* London: Routledge, 1996.

Mirkovich, Thomas R., and Allison A. Cowgill. *Casino Gaming in the United States.* Lanham, Md.: Scarecrow Press, 1997.

The National Gambling Impact Study Commission. Final Report. Washington, D.C.: The Commission, 1999.

Nibert, David. *Hitting the Lottery Jackpot: State Governments and the Taxing of Dreams.* New York: Monthly Review Press, 2000.

Reith, Gerda. *The Age of Chance: Gambling in Western Culture.* New York: Routledge, 1999.

Thompson, William N. *Gambling in America: An Encyclopedia of History, Issues, and Society.* Santa Barbara, Calif.: ABC-Clio, 2001.

Wiggins, David K., ed. *Sport in America: From Wicked Amusement to National Obsession.* Champaign, Ill.: Human Kinetics, 1995.

*John C. Burnham*

# GAMES

**See** *Board Games; Card Games; Childhood and Play; Computer/Video Games; Gambling*

# GANGS

**See** *Recreational Fighting*

# GARAGE AND YARD SALES

Each year, Americans host an estimated 6.5 to 9 million garage sales, vending used goods out of or near their homes. Typically, one or several families hold sales to recycle household goods, make a small profit, and socialize with neighbors; buyers attend to purchase low-cost items, haggle recreationally, and discover the occasional yard sale treasure. Unlike flea markets, in which numerous dealers congregate to sell assorted wares, and auctions, in which an auctioneer markets various goods to the highest bidder, many garage sale transactions occur between the original owner of an item and a buyer. The private setting and personal nature of such transactions foster exchanges that are at once commercial and hospitable.

## History of Garage and Yard Sales

In 1950s and 1960s America, increased affluence led many consumers to accumulate household goods in excess; concurrently, increased home-ownership created the venue from which to sell these goods. Suburbia became the fertile breeding grounds of garage sales, where unwanted items found new homes at the hands of housewives. A postmodern adaptation of the mid-nineteenth-century charitable fair or bazaar, the garage sale tapped a national romanticism toward history and nostalgia for used goods. Prior to 1970, goods featured at charity fairs or rummage sales became less extraordinary and more practical; while a nineteenth-century fair may have featured a booth with souvenirs and curiosities alongside a booth with historic relics, garage sales more typically featured furniture, used clothing, and appliances. Americana and collectibles, more popular in the 1960s than at any time since the nationalistic 1920s, became specialty items among the used home goods.

It was in the years leading up to 1970 that residential sales became known as "rummage sales," a term borrowed from those sales given for charitable causes; over the course of the next decade, the sharp increase in sales operated from the garage prompted a linguistic shift to the term "garage sale." During the 1970s, garage sales exploded into mainstream consciousness, earning a permanent place in American iconography and legitimizing the concept of profiting from discarded goods.

In recent years, garage sales have continued to thrive due to the national penchant for material accumulation and widespread dearth of disposable income: many Americans seek low-cost ways to satiate avid consumerist tendencies. Bucking the early sales trend of large, costly items, today's sales derive the bulk of profits through the vending of small household goods; appliances, tools, and used sporting equipment are in especially high demand. A majority of sales take place on spring and fall Saturday mornings in suburbia and small cities; to a lesser extent, they occur in urban areas as stoop or apartment sales. Due to their relative inaccessibility, rural sales tend not to attract as many participants as do their suburban counterparts. Sale nomenclature varies by geographical location: residential sales are known as yard sales in the Midwest, porch or "gimme" sales in the South, tag sales in the East, and garage or g-sales in the West.

## Typical Garage Salers: Characteristics of Buyers and Sellers

Garage sale vendors range from single adults, families, and children to multiple families, local and charitable organizations, collectibles dealers, entire communities, and even celebrities. Typically, however, sellers are thirty to forty year-old amateurs who host sales to clear out attics and basements; parents and the elderly are common participants. A smaller population of low-income vendors operates regular sales in order to supplement income; these sellers often buy goods at other sales to resell for profit at their own. Garage sale shoppers primarily consist of twenty to forty year-olds seeking to outfit children and homes at low cost. As a rule, participants reside in middle- or working class America, with yearly incomes of buyers slightly exceeding those of sellers. Although some sales take place between relatives and friends, transactions most often occur between slight acquaintances and strangers.

The typical garage sale participant is also female: two-thirds of all garage salers are women. Since many sales-associated tasks are directly related to housekeeping, women traditionally have been the primary participants. Especially during the early years of garage sales, sellers' roles reflected the sexual division of labor: female vendors completed tasks such as housecleaning and item arranging, while their husbands performed the physical tasks of putting up signs, moving heavy items, and disassembling goods after the sale. Even in the early 2000s, men often assume only a peripheral role in sales events, with women serving as sales managers and price-setters. Female shoppers out-attend male buyers, as well. With the rise of profit-oriented and online garage sales, however, sales participation has become slightly less stratified by gender.

## Recreational and Social Impacts of Garage Sales

Although participants may have financial motivations for hosting or attending garage sales, most also consider them recreational events. Yard sales invite buyers to socialize with hosts and other participants, providing opportunities to rekindle old acquaintances and meet new neighbors. Some buyers come purely for recreational purposes, appreciating the mystery of a used item's past and the excitement of haggling for a deal or discovering a rare item. Sellers value the environmental and emotional rewards associated with giving used possessions new life; as a result, they frequently de-emphasize the financial gains from transactions, giving away items or offering very low prices to personable or needy customers. Many hosts also enjoy the chance to temporarily own and operate a small business; in the garage sale setting, they are empowered to make business decisions regarding pricing and selling. The inclusive nature of sales often serves as a social equalizer, for they create a rare setting in which participants of all socioeconomic backgrounds can interact.

Due to the personal and social setting of garage sales, a certain etiquette exists that is absent from most other commercial settings. Buyers who violate this ethos risk having their offers rejected by offended hosts; sellers risk hosting an unsuccessful sale. Common buyer faux pas include arriving overly early to sales, paying with large bills, scoffing at sales items or otherwise disrespecting sellers' property, and haggling over-aggressively. Garage sale hosts are considered bad-mannered when they sell to early birds, over-price items or do not clearly mark prices, and fail to take down signs and items from their yards following the event.

## Commercial Impacts of Garage Sales

In spite of the recreational aspects of sales, garage sales are at base commercial transactions, each year generating between 1.5 and 2 billion dollars in revenue nationwide. Profits often go unreported for tax collection, although many city governments benefit by requiring hosts to pay sale permit fees. The average sale generates from $100 to $200 in profits, with prices marked at around 20 percent of items' original value. Although in the past sellers held events more to clean house than to profit, in recent years sales have become increasingly profit-driven, a trend primarily due to the emergence of online markets for used goods. The success of the online auction site Ebay has encouraged a rash of online garage sales to spring up, allowing individual buyers and sellers to interact in a virtual environment. Some of these websites charge commission for items sold on site, while others profit entirely through advertisements. Another common profit-making tactic is for garage salers to resell their purchases online.

Although online sales have increased garage sale profit potential, traditional sales in the early 2000s are often viewed with bemusement: they are portrayed as an uniquely American oddity attracting participants who are at once eccentric and outdated. One sale even has become a national tourist attraction: the World's Longest Yard Sale, which extends 450 miles from Alabama to Kentucky, draws approximately 5,000 vendors and 50,000 gawking buyers over a four-day period each year. As diverse as their featured wares, garage sales reinvent suburban families as hagglers and entrepreneurs, old junk as prized possessions, and lazy Saturday mornings as exciting recreational opportunities.

*See also:* Auctions, Collecting; Hobbies and Crafts

### BIBLIOGRAPHY

Atkin, Ross. "One Woman's Mission—Getting Books to Needy Kids." *Christian Science Monitor* 92, no. 239 (1 Nov. 2000): 16.

Bryan, Carol. "The (Knick) Knack of Great Yard and Flea Sales." *Library Imagination Paper* 22, no. 4 (Fall 2000): 4.

Burnside, Scott. "Yard Sale Game Is Here." *Kentucky New Era* 6 (Sept. 2003). Available from http://www.kentuckynew-era.com/.

Caplin, Joan. "Sharon Wolford." *Money* 32, no. 2 (Feb. 2003): 31.

"The Dark Side of Selling." *Maclean's* 114, no. 28 (9 July 2001): 10.

Doughton, K. J. "Review of *G-Sale.*" *Film Threat* 27 June 2003. Available from http://www.filmthreat.com.

Evarts, Eric C. "Spring Clearance." *Christian Science Monitor* 92, no. 126 (22 May 2000): 11.

Gardner, Marilyn. "Domestic Downsizing: The Fine Art of Unloading 'Stuff.'" *Christian Science Monitor* 87, no. 194 (31 Aug. 1995): 13.

———. "When Packrats Confront their 'Surfeit of Stuff." *Christian Science Monitor* 91, no. 169 (28 July 1999): 19.

———. "A Seasonal Yearning—One More Fresh Start." *Christian Science Monitor* 93, no. 95 (11 Apr. 2001): 15.

Herrmann, Gretchen M. "His and Hers: Gender and Garage Sales." *Journal of Popular Culture* 29. no. 1 (Summer 1995): 127–145.

———. "Gift or Commodity: What Changes Hands in the U.S. Garage Sale?" *American Ethnologist* 24, no. 1 (Feb. 1997): 910–930.

———. "Negotiating Culture: Conflict and Consensus in U.S. Garage-Sale Bargaining." *Ethnology* 42, no. 3 (Summer 2003): 237–252.

Herrmann, Gretchen M. and Stephen Soiffer. "For Fun and Profit: An Analysis of the American Garage Sale." *Urban Life* 12, no. 4 (Jan. 1984): 397–421.

———. "Visions of Power: Ideology and Practice in the American Garage Sale." *Sociological Review* 35, no. 1 (Feb. 1987): 48–83.

Hevesi, Dennis. "If There's a Stoop, Look for a Sale." *New York Times.* (9 June 1994): B1.

"Junkapalooza." *People* 58, no. 10 (2 Sept. 2002): 108–109.

Kennedy, Nathaniel. "But Can You Get it Wholesale?" *Kiplinger's Personal Finance Magazine* 52, no. 7 (July 1998): 115–117.

Knight, Dana Bodnar. "The Rabid Gardeners' Yard Sale." *Horticulture* 73, no. 4 (Apr. 1995): 20–24.

LaFleche, Heidi. "Time to Recycle." *Yahoo! Internet Life* 8, no. 6 (June 2002): 84.

LePelley, Richard. "One Man's Trash Is Another Man's Yard Sale." *Christian Science Monitor* 92. no. 167 (20 July 2000): 19.

Levine, Beth. "Not for Sale." *Good Housekeeping* 233, no. 2 (Aug. 2001): 177–179.

Morris, Nomi. "Craig Kielburger." *Maclean's* 109, no. 52 (23 Dec. 1996): 46–47.

Oberman, Sheldon. "Garage Sale Tour Is a Good Way to See the City." Available from http://www.sheldonoberman .com/garage.htm.

"127 Corridor Sale." 127 Sale: Summary, 2003. Available from http://www.127sale.com/#summary.

Poniewozik, James. "The Great American Garage Sale." *Salon.com* (1 June 1999). Available from http://www.salon .com/.

Razzi, Elisabeth. "A Profitable Way to Ditch Your Junque." *Kiplinger's Personal Finance Magazine* 50, no. 6 (June 1996): 100–101.

Schmeltz, L. R. *The Backyard Money Machine: How to Organize and Operate a Successful Garage Sale.* Bettendorf, Iowa: Silver Streak Publications, 1993.

Stillinger, Elizabeth. *The Antiquers.* New York: Alfred A. Knopf, 1980.

Tutelian, Louise. "Parent to Parent." *Family Life* (Aug. 2000): 49.

Twigg, Nancy. "Yard Sale Etiquette." Mommysavers.com. Available from http://www.mommysavers.com/.

Walsh, Jim. "The Toaster Formerly Known as His." *Rolling Stone* 822 (10 Sept. 1999): 22.

Webster, Harriet, and Jonathan Webster. *The Underground Marketplace: A Guide to New England and the Middle Atlantic States.* New York: Universe Books, 1981.

Williams, Michael, and Pam Williams. *Garage Sale Magic! How to Turn Your 'Trash' into Cash!* Buffalo Grove, Ill.: Freedom Publishing, 1994.

Wolcott, Jennifer. "Treasure Hunt." *Christian Science Monitor* 91, no. 101 (21 Apr. 1999): 13.

*Abby L. Schlatter*

# GARDENING AND LAWN CARE

The nineteenth century was a period of immense gardening enthusiasm in the United States as a growing middle class of leisured women, and men working in office jobs, looked to horticulture as a moral and physical outlet. Victorian women were urged to provide a floral retreat from the world for their families as an antidote to increasing urbanization. Women moving westward took with them seeds, cuttings, and bulbs to domesticate their strange new homes. The nineteenth century was a period of enthusiasm for "botanizing" (collecting and learning about plants). Many people joined the new garden and horticultural societies, and participated in garden shows. Hundreds of new plants were introduced from Asia, Africa, and Central and South America, and many amateurs worked to hybridize fruit trees, vegetables, roses, and other plants to produce prize-winning fruits and flowers. Beginning in the 1830s, nurseries, mail-order catalogs, and horticulture periodicals provided seeds, plants, tools, and information for the new gardening enthusiasts.

The formal English, French, Italian, and Japanese garden styles adapted by wealthy Americans were paralleled by informally planted gardens of hardy old-fashioned flowers that could be maintained by one person, tucked into the small lots of the new middle-class suburbs.

## The Origin of Lawns and Park Suburbs

The lawn as a garden feature appeared in many different landscape modes. In the United States, the aesthetic of the lawn as a part of the home grounds came from the parks of English country estates designed in the eighteenth century. Terraced or geometric lawns came from the French and Italian garden traditions. The English parks contained meadows cropped by cattle, sheep, or deer. In smaller domestic spaces, grass was cut by scythes, and skilled workers were difficult to find and expensive to hire. Until the late nineteenth century, lawns were found at the houses of the political and cultural elite who had the money and time to devote to the grounds of their estates. The first U.S. patent for a lawn mower was awarded in 1869, making it possible for an ordinary individual to keep grass mowed at an even height without the expense of skilled labor or the inconveniences of grazing animals. Other inventions soon followed, including rubber hoses, sprinklers, lawn rollers, rakes, and edgers, to help the new upwardly mobile middle class achieve proper lawns and affirm their new status.

Nineteenth-century upper-class suburbs outside cities such as Boston, New York, and Chicago were modeled on the country-estate aesthetic of placing houses in a park-like setting. One of the earliest was Llewelyn Park in Orange, New Jersey, laid out in 1853. Hedges and fences around individual properties were eliminated so that the community would look like a park. In most neighborhoods, this was not possible until the 1880s when fence laws required the owners of cattle and pigs to keep them confined rather than let them roam the streets.

In addition to lawn mowers and other tools, the new suburban residents found that they needed appropriate types of grass to grow and maintain lawns in different regions of the United States. Cool-weather grasses

## Experimental Grass Gardens

The USDA established experimental turf gardens to grow foreign grasses. One of these was in Arlington, Virginia, where the Pentagon is today. The garden was moved to Beltsville, Maryland in the 1940s. After the war, a uniform nursery testing system to compare grasses under widely diverse conditions eventually included sixty-six nurseries in forty-one states.

imported from Europe (such as Kentucky blue grass) would not grow in arid or hot regions of the country. As communities grew across the continent, and national magazines promoted the front-lawn aesthetic, increasing demand for the necessary equipment and plants spurred the growth of what became a multibillion-dollar industry.

The game of golf was introduced into the United States from Scotland in the 1880s and was played on the lawns of wealthy individuals' estates, and in cow pastures. As golf clubs and associations were organized and began developing dedicated golf courses, a need arose for grasses that would stand up to frequent cutting and use. Several members of these early golf associations employed by the U.S. Department of Agriculture (USDA) were able to interest their colleagues in this problem. The USDA began sending agents around the world in the nineteenth century to find better forage and hay grasses for farmers. In the early twentieth century, these agents also began looking for turf grasses that could be used for golf courses and, by extension, lawns. Demand for large quantities of weed-free grass seed for golf courses spurred the growth of companies such as O. M. Scott and Sons. Recognizing the growing interest in lawns, Scott targeted golf-club members in their marketing campaigns for lawn seed and equipment. Its successful advertising and promotional literature urged homeowners to emulate golf course fairways and putting greens in their own yards.

In the 1920s, the first communities surrounding golf courses were built for wealthy suburbanites, and homeowners were encouraged to keep their home lawns to the standard of the golf course so that it would look as if the course continued to flow around the houses. This aesthetic was revived in the 1950s after World War II, with the democratization of golf, and continues into the 2000s with countless retirement communities built around golf courses throughout the country.

## Growth of the Suburbs and the City Beautiful Movement

The early park suburbs were soon followed by suburban communities on railroad and streetcar lines that made it possible for middle-class men to commute into the city every day. The ideal was a single-family house in its own grounds that would be a haven for the wife and children from the increasing pollution and crowding of the cities. Horticulture magazines and advertising showed well-kept lawns adorned with trees and shrubbery as the mark of prosperous and tasteful households. New homeowners were advised to keep the front yard simple, should they not have the time or money to keep up a more elaborate garden, and to concentrate on maintaining a lawn, a few trees, and shrubs to mask the foundations of the house.

Backyards became less utilitarian, with the outhouse replaced by indoor plumbing, the barn replaced by the garage, woodsheds replaced by coal furnaces and gas stoves, and smaller lots that made henhouses and home orchards obsolete. Automobile suburbs began appearing in the 1920s in areas previously unreachable by public transportation. The automobile forced people to move from the front porch into the backyard to escape the procession of glaring headlights at night, the dust, and the new smell of exhaust. This private space at the back of the house gradually became the family gathering place, children's playground, and private garden.

The City Beautiful movement began at the 1893 Chicago World's Fair. Visitors impressed by the white buildings and landscaped grounds returned home with new ideas about the organization of urban and suburban spaces. New concepts of zoning and land use included setback regulations that required houses to be set back from the streets in new housing developments. Grass was the cheapest and quickest ground cover, a way to mask the scars of a new development, especially on land that had once been farm fields.

The front lawn aesthetic was adopted enthusiastically by the women of the Garden Clubs of America who initiated community fix-up and clean-up campaigns with prizes for the best lawns and gardens. Some clubs targeted black and immigrant neighborhoods in their efforts to make the community look "nicer," and gardening classes in public schools were seen as important tools of assimilation.

Community beautification projects lasted into the 1930s as towns and cities competed with each other during the Great Depression to attract businesses and jobs. However, general interest in lawns and gardening declined as few new homes were built during the 1930s, and many people were unable to afford the costs of garden hobbies. As the economy improved at the end of the

**Yard work.** Modern-day lawn care was greatly improved by the 1899 patent of John Albert Burr. He created an improved version of the original lawn mower by including traction wheels and a rotary blade. Today's mowers—like this one—continue to build on Burr's original design. © *Field Mark Publications*

1930s, articles in newspapers and popular magazines once again gave Americans encouragement, instruction, and advice on lawn care and gardening. Government agencies, private foundations, businesses, schools, magazines, and seed companies worked together to provide land, instruction, public-service booklets on the basics of gardening, and seeds for individual and community gardens. In the 1940s, the call to plant a victory garden was answered by nearly 20 million Americans who produced up to 40 percent of all that was consumed. Despite the exhortations of the lawn-care industry, few Americans had the time during the war years to "boost morale at home" by keeping up their lawns.

## The Quest for Lawn Perfection

Over time the definition of a good lawn changed from a mown pasture to a green velvety carpet. Early lawns were

like Persian carpets with a variety of grasses and wildflowers growing in them. Gradually the aesthetic changed and nurseries promoted weed-free grass seed for a lawn of a uniform color and texture. Such uniformity has always been difficult to attain, but many homeowners in the period before World War II tried using liquids such as kerosene and turpentine to kill weeds in their yards as well as digging them out by hand. DDT, hailed as a miracle pesticide during World War II, was used for eradicating everything from body lice to mosquitoes to lawn and garden pests. After the war, new chemical fertilizers, herbicides, and pesticides became available for home use and were marketed by the lawn-care industry as the answer to all lawn and garden problems. Lawn-care advertising exhorted men to use the tools of war (chemicals and power machinery) to beat Mother Nature to a standstill in the yard. Power mowers became status symbols in the new suburban developments that mushroomed around American cities in the 1950s. Riding mowers were marketed as "little cars" to new homeowners with more money and leisure than their parents had.

The number of articles on lawn care and gardening published in popular magazines exploded after World War II with the expansion of suburbia and home ownership. Garden centers and nurseries proliferated, offering seeds, plants, tools, the new chemical fertilizers, and pesticides and herbicides, as well as classes on growing and maintaining gardens and lawns. Turf farms took the place of traditional farms on the outskirts of growing cities to provide instant lawns for the new suburban houses. As housing developments spread during the 1950s and 1960s, lawn and turf grasses covered the country. Americans drained swamps, irrigated deserts, and felled forests, changing the ecological makeup of America by creating millions of acres of savanna. Grass spread around homes, and covered parks, playing fields, and the medians and sides of the new interstate highway system.

After Rachel Carson published *Silent Spring* in 1962, warning of the dangers of DDT, Americans turned to other chemicals such as chlordane to maintain weed- and pest-free lawns and gardens. Home owners concerned about using potentially hazardous chemicals hired lawn-care companies, a practice that that soon became a nationwide status symbol.

## Alternatives to Lawns

In the late twentieth century, a backlash began to develop to the millions of acres of artificially green and uniform lawns in the United States. A growing interest in native plants, water shortages, and concerns about the overuse and abuse of chemicals and the environment drew some homeowners to consider alternative landscapes. Wildflower meadows in the Northeast, home prairies in the Midwest, and desert gardens in the Southwest replaced the regimentation of monoculture lawns. These new landscape styles have challenged zoning regulations and been the occasion for lawsuits from outraged neighbors. Interest in xeriscaping—the use of native plants that do not require watering—is growing and being encouraged by municipalities concerned about water use throughout the country. The new large houses on small lots leave owners with less lawn to mow. Many people are happy to give up lawn care to professional services when they move into town house and retirement communities. The aesthetic of the green velvety carpet, or of the golf course around a home, is under attack, but it may yet survive as scientists work to hybridize dwarf grasses that need little mowing or watering. The herbaceous border, a mixture

of annual and perennial plants around a grassy lawn popularized by horticulture writers in the 1880s, has remained the ideal of many American gardens into the twenty-first century.

*See also:* Hobbies and Crafts, Home Decoration, Home Improvement, Men's Leisure Lifestyles, Suburbanization of Leisure, Women't Leisure Lifestyles

**BIBLIOGRAPHY**

Fogle, David P., Catherine Mahan, and Christopher Weeks. *Clues to American Gardens.* Washington, D.C.: Starrhill Press, 1987.

Handlin, David P. *The American Home: Architecture and Society, 1815–1915.* Boston: Little, Brown and Company, 1979.

Hill, May Brawley. *Grandmother's Garden: The Old-Fashioned American Garden, 1865–1915.* New York: Harry N. Abrams, 1995.

Hunt, John Dixon, and Joachim Wolschke-Bulmahn, eds. *The Vernacular Garden.* Washington, D.C.: Dumbarton Oaks Research Library and Collection, 1993.

Jenkins, Virginia Scott. *The Lawn: A History of an American Obsession.* Washington, D.C.: The Smithsonian Institution Press, 1994.

Kolodny, Annette. *The Land Before Her: Fantasy and Experience of the American Frontier 1630–1860.* Chapel Hill: University of North Carolina Press, 1984.

Schroeder, Fred E. H. *Front Yard America: The Evolution and Meanings of a Vernacular Domestic Landscape.* Bowling Green, Ohio: Bowling Green State University Popular Press, 1993.

Stilgoe, John R. *Borderland: Origins of the American Suburb, 1820–1939.* New Haven, Conn.: Yale University Press, 1988.

Teyssot, Georges, ed., *The American Lawn.* New York: Princeton Architectural Press, 1999.

*Virginia Scott Jenkins*

# GAY MEN'S LEISURE LIFESTYLES.

The importance of leisure to the development of gay male identities and networks throughout the past century cannot be overstated. Men have come together in parks, bars, bathhouses, and bookstores to have sex, make friends, and build communities. Leisure, manhood, and homosexuality have coalesced through intersections with capitalism, urbanization, technology, and law.

## Capitalism: Production, Reproduction, and "Excessive" Recreation

In "Capitalism and Gay Identity," John D'Emilio observes that the rise of wage labor and commodity production made possible the emergence of modern homosexual identity. Wage labor disassociated an individual's income from its dependency on the family. The growth of commodity-based economies shifted production from households to the market, and consumption from families to individuals. In the late nineteenth and early twentieth centuries, men found new opportunities for expressions of homosexuality, and gender transgression as production and reproduction became less strictly intertwined.

On the other hand, American capitalism largely developed within a moral system of male-centered, family-oriented property ownership. The need for financial security that familial dependency places on the breadwinner(s) assists capitalism by ensuring a degree of workforce stability. D'Emilio suggests this contradiction of capitalism—both destabilizing the family and insisting on its centrality—fuels hostility toward gay men, who appear to live on the spoils of production without embracing the societal duties of marriage and reproduction. Moreover, during the late nineteenth and early twentieth centuries, medical-juridical professions and popular culture came to view male homosexuality and gender inversion, in part, as excesses of leisure and metropolitan modernity.

Modern male homosexuality as it developed throughout the first half of the twentieth century might be understood as a disruption of the supposedly natural binding of production to reproduction. Instead of the duties of procreation, gay men seemed to be chiefly concerned with what American capitalism relegated to recreation

## Urbanization: Commercialized Leisure, Public Space, and Private Parties

Through urbanization, the recreational sites of the city became the terrain of what George Chauncey calls the "gay world." In the first half of the twentieth century, this world was largely one of leisure, accessed through commercialized, public, and private spaces.

The development of commercialized urban leisure shaped gay male culture in venues devoted to entertainment, health, and socializing. Entertainment spaces, such as vaudeville theaters, burlesque halls, and cabarets provided female impersonators with performance venues that, in turn, attracted audiences of gay men. Huge drag balls were the biggest gay events in the early twentieth century, attracting hundreds of participants and onlook-

ers. The back rows of darkened movie houses provided cover for anonymous sex between men. Moreover, the movies themselves, like opera, theater, and dance, were a source of archetypal models for shared queer camp sensibilities of gender subversion and irony.

The health movement, intending to uplift men by building muscular and moral fiber, provided other sites. The Young Men's Christian Association (YMCA) provided an ideal space for men to gather for sex and socializing. As John Gustav-Wrathall explains, these male-only spaces had little supervision and, because of their Christian mission, were mostly free from police surveillance. Bathhouses also provided health-oriented commercial spaces for male sex and camaraderie. Particularly as the popularity of bathhouses decreased among the general population in the 1930s and 1940s, owners cultivated gay clientele. Regular visits helped gay men build social networks they may not have been free to embrace outside the baths.

Commercialized leisure venues geared mostly toward socializing—namely, bars and cafeterias—gained prominence in the gay world by the second third of the twentieth century. Before World War II, gay bars existed in large cities. War migration of young, single men to cities brought many into gay subcultures. Gay bars opened in midsize towns such as Denver, Cleveland, and Kansas City. By the mid-1960s, many cities began to have gay bars that appealed to specific crowds, from the well-groomed and understated sweater set to the rougher, more masculine, motorcycle club-inspired leather men, to the commercialized sex trade of hustlers and johns. In some cafeterias, particularly after the dinner crowd had gone home, managers tolerated flamboyant behavior among the young and low-income gay men who found such establishments the cheapest, friendliest place to socialize.

Public spaces also allowed men the freedom to explore same-sex erotic opportunities as a component of their leisure. As Chauncey describes, streets, parks, and public toilets in New York City in the early twentieth century were locations for both furtive encounters and a self-conscious gay subculture. Public spaces gave men living with families or in cramped quarters a place to meet openly. Such public space and cruising culture became a means through which many men who came for the sex ended up socialized into the gay world.

Once in that world, men enjoyed private parties held at houses and apartments. In Harlem throughout the 1920s, for example, African American men and women hosted rent parties where same-sex coupling and socializing occurred alongside heterosexual affairs. In well-to-do white enclaves, parties might be subdued affairs or decadent bacchanalias. Private parties sustained gay men through good times and bad and, to some extent, sheltered them from the surveillance and regulation in more visible leisure venues.

## Technology: Mechanics of Mobility, Circuits of Community

In urban and nonurban environments, technological innovations served gay male leisure. Mass production of the automobile facilitated both the migration of men into existing urban gay subcultures (as either tourists or transplants) and queer circulation throughout rural and suburban regions. Both the car and the roadside rest stop were, by the mid-twentieth century, well-established sites for gay male connections. As printing technologies became more accessible and inexpensive from the 1940s onward, newsletters, fliers, bar guides, maps, and physique magazines became increasingly commonplace means of publicizing gay leisure in a more structured circuit of activities and locations. Sound recording brought artists popular with gay men to gay bar jukeboxes and lip-synching drag queens. Recordings by queer performers such as female impersonator Ray Bourbon inspired listening parties and a shared sense of camp among men in towns of all sizes. Much later, the Internet would revolutionize the ways that gay men could connect both locally and globally.

## Law: Policing and Contested Leisure

Although relegated to "leisure" in the American capitalist system, gay men in the midcentury were, as William Eskridge notes, "smothered by law" in everything from employment to family to recreation. Sodomy laws, disorderly conduct and solicitation regulations, policies that revoked the liquor licenses of bars serving homosexuals or allowing cross-dressing, and police surveillance and brutality were only the most formal mechanisms to prevent gay men from having fun together. The development of collective gay identity and community has always been built through "contested leisure," in which men struggled for free association and pursuits of pleasure within social, legal, political, and economic constraints that sought to contain or eradicate such men and their leisure.

Contested leisure suggests two interrelated meanings. First, because the leisure lifestyles and locations of gay men are contested by society, they require constant nurturing and risk taking in order to flourish. Second, such leisure contests the meaning of leisure itself in a way that reworks the categories of work and family. Especially

in the second half of the twentieth century, as gay men increasingly owned and worked in sites of gay leisure, work and leisure distinctions became fuzzy. Moreover, gay men created alternative families through networks of friends. In so doing they subverted the singular definition of "normal" family, asserting that leisure created family, rather than being somehow apart from it.

In addition, gay men, along with transgender people and lesbians, used their sites of contested leisure to demand greater access to supposedly universal rights of assembly and the pursuit of happiness. In *Reilly v. Stouman* (1951), the California Supreme Court ruled San Francisco's Black Cat Café could not lose its liquor license just for having a homosexual customer base. At the same bar, drag performer José Sarria performed satirical operettas criticizing police abuses to mostly gay audiences. At the end of the show, he had the audience join hands and sing "God Save Us Nelly Queens." On 28 June 1969, patrons of the Stonewall Inn, a gay bar in Greenwich Village, fought back against the latest round of police harassment, helping to spark Gay Liberation.

## The Gay Liberation Leisure Boom

Since the 1960s, gay leisure has exploded as relative freedom of association and expression has coupled with commercialization and social organizing. As Martin Levine suggests, as gay people dramatically reduced criminal, psychiatric, and social antihomosexual stigma, they removed barriers to the gay worlds' growth, particularly in cities. As police harassment of bars decreased, for example, such bars proliferated. Since the 1970s, gay bar patrons have danced, expressed physical intimacy, and used drugs with little fear of public scandal or arrest. In growing gay neighborhoods, gay-owned retail venues emerged, selling everything from cookies to sex toys. Gay bookstores became cultural gathering spots. In the 1970s and 1980s, gay theater sprang up, as did other cultural events and organizations, such as film festivals, choruses, and marching bands. Health-related gay male leisure expanded to include athletic teams, leagues, and gyms. Gay travel agents arranged gay-themed domestic and international vacation packages.

Spending leisure time and discretionary income in these venues could feel like an act of self-affirmation and solidarity. Coming out, socializing, and participating in recreational sex took on the symbolic weight of personal liberation, community building, and social transformation. In addition, gay men, along with lesbians, bisexuals, and transgendered people, began to occupy public space in more spectacular ways. Most notable have been the pride parades and festivals that began the year after

Stonewall. While these more visible modes of publicity transformed earlier models of gay leisure and public space, they did not supplant it. Men, some identified as gay, others not, still cruised streets, parks, and public rest rooms for sex.

The onset of AIDS in the early 1980s profoundly changed the "spare time" activities of many gay men. Caretaking, health maintenance, spiritual exploration, political activism, and grieving took precedence for many. Still, older institutions survived, including bars and cultural events. Even public sex and bathhouses persisted, although in more modest forms as both government and gay people grappled with ways to cultivate a culture of "safe sex." In some places, such as San Francisco, local officials closed the baths amid heated debates within the gay community as to whether such measures deterred unsafe sex or just encouraged it to take place in unregulated settings.

## Contemporary Gay Rights and Recreation

Leisure continues to define gay male identity and community. Yet "being gay" has, ironically, become less about leisure than about securing access to more traditional realms of political representation, economic equity, social services, and family law. As more gay men conceptualize their families as approximations of the traditional model of married parents and possibly children; define their homosexuality as an issue of civil rights; or occupy, as openly gay men, nongay-specific commercialized, public, and private leisure sites, the distinction between gay leisure and mainstream leisure becomes more difficult to discern. Blurring lines even further has been the corporate discovery of the "gay market," in which gay men have become a target demographic for the same leisure-related services and products consumed by everyone else.

This process is far from complete. Antigay military policies, violence against gays, compartmentalization within corporate-produced popular culture, and exclusions from such basic institutions as marriage and adoption continue to make gay men's leisure contested. Moreover, sites and participants of gay male leisure that do not conform with the processes of civil integration find themselves increasingly marginalized in public discourse. Public sex is now policed and pathologized from both traditional institutional forces and prominent segments of the gay community. Gay relationships and definitions of family that do not fit into the civic and workplace discourses of "domestic partnership" and "family leave" find their appeals for time off from work to spend leisure time with chosen families of gay friends taken less seriously than the requests from gay men in couples and with children.

Despite being more widespread than ever, leisure holds a diminished place within gay identity and community in comparison to the gay world prior to a rights discourse. Still, it is a critical means through which gay men experience collective joy, passion, camaraderie, and belonging. Gay leisure has been and will hopefully always be a site of contestation, a means of both fitting into and disrupting the hegemony of American heterosexual capitalism.

*See also:* Lesbian Leisure Lifestyles; Men's Leisure Lifestyles

### BIBLIOGRAPHY

Altman, Dennis. *The Homosexualization of America: The Americanization of the Homosexual.* New York: St. Martin's Press, 1982.

Chauncey, George. *Gay New York: Gender, Urban Culture, and the Making of the Gay Male World, 1890–1940.* New York: Basic Books, 1994.

Clarke, Eric O. *Virtuous Vice: Homoeroticism and the Public Sphere.* Durham, N.C.: Duke University Press, 2000.

D'Emilio, John. "Capitalism and Gay Identity." In *Powers of Desire: The Politics of Sexuality.* Edited by Ann Snitow, Christine Stansell, and Sharon Thompson. New York: Monthly Review Press, 1983.

Eskridge, William N. *Gaylaw: Challenging the Apartheid of the Closet.* Cambridge, Mass.: Harvard University Press, 1999.

Gustav-Wrathall, John. *Take the Young Stranger by the Hand: Same-Sex Relations and the YMCA.* Chicago: University of Chicago Press, 1998.

Hennessey, Rosemary. *Profit and Pleasure: Sexual Identities in Late Capitalism.* New York: Routledge, 2000.

Levine, Martin P. "The Life and Death of Gay Clones." In *Gay Culture in America: Essays from the Field.* Edited by Gilbert Herdt. Boston: Beacon Press, 1992.

Somerville, Siobhan B. *Queering the Color Line: Race and the Invention of Homosexuality in America.* Durham, N.C.: Duke University Press, 2000.

*Don Romesburg*

# GENRE READING

A genre is a category of literature that producers and audiences self-consciously recognize as marked by a distinctive style, form, or content. In contemporary usage, genre reading usually refers to genres that developed historically from pulp magazines in the early twentieth century—mysteries, Westerns, romances, and science fiction (sometimes including fantasy and horror). Genre fiction emerged because it made the business of publishing much more predictable and profitable; it made books into commodities that could be marketed much like soap or cornflakes to a specific audience of known size. Because genre fiction was always profit-driven and emerged from the pages of cheap magazines and paperbacks, it is frequently seen as lacking aesthetic or literary value.

## A History of Cheap Publishing in America

From the 1840s to the 1890s, dime novel entrepreneurs like Beadle & Adams and Street & Smith pioneered the sale of cheap, mass-produced sensation fiction to the urban, working classes. Sold for five to ten cents, they featured tales of adventure on the frontier, accounts of great strikes, stories about crime in the cities, and narratives of honest working girls who marry millionaires. This blatantly commercial fiction was largely written by unknown authors who were paid by the word, and representatives of genteel culture disapproved of the whole enterprise. Public libraries did not carry dime novels; "respectable" magazines condemned them as sensational; and aristocratic societies for the prevention of vice prosecuted their publishers.

In an attempt to better market their cheap fiction, dime novels were often organized into series featuring a common setting (the West, the city), a central character (Buffalo Bill, Nick Carter, Old Sleuth), or a theme (war, love). Dime novel fiction was thoroughly commodified, and the various characters and series functioned like a brand name for consumers who wanted to buy the same set of narrative pleasures month after month. Michael Denning cautions, however, that genres in the dime novel overlapped and were very much in flux.

Modern notions of romances, Westerns, science fiction, and mystery arose in the pages of the dime novel's heirs, pulp magazines. When changes in postal rates in the 1890s made it prohibitively expensive to distribute dime novels through the mail, many of the largest publishers simply repackaged their cheap fiction as pulp magazines, selling the same kinds of stories at the newsstand instead. Named for the cheap, wood-pulp paper on which they were published, pulp magazines were unambiguously "trash." Pulp writer Erle Stanley Gardner described himself not as an author, but as a "fiction factory." Most studies maintained that pulp audiences were socially and economically marginal—young, working class, poorly educated, and often immigrant. Librarians, social workers, and middle-class reformers lamented that the "proletariat" read little else besides pulp magazines.

At first, most pulps were general-fiction magazines, but specialization for niche markets began soon after. For example, the aptly named *All-Story* had been replaced by *Love Story, Detective Story,* and *Western Story* by 1930. Between the world wars there were about 200 highly specialized pulp titles dedicated to detective fiction, pirates, boxing, war, football, Westerns, aviation, science fiction, and romance. The readerships were clearly gendered. The endless variety of action/adventure pulps were for men; the romances, for women.

The pulp magazine market folded in the early 1950s from competition with comic books, television, and their descendants—mass-market paperbacks. Spurred by new technological innovations—the much faster magazine rotary press and quick-drying, synthetic glue—the paperback appeared on the scene in 1939 when Pocket Books launched a series of twenty-five-cent books to be sold and distributed like magazines at newsstands, drugstores, train stations, and bus depots instead of trade bookshops. The men who had learned how to sell cheap fiction in the pulp magazine business are the ones who started many of the paperback publishing houses, and paperbacks shared the pulps' low literary reputation and less-than-elite audience.

## Genre Fiction and the Business of Publishing

Genre fiction took the guess work out of the business of publishing. Books are notoriously difficult to market and advertise, because each book is considered to be unique. As a consequence, publishing has never been a particularly predictable or profitable business. However, genre fiction offers publishers a way of selling similar books to the same audience again and again. It has a unique form of literary production that Robert Escarpit calls "semi-programmed issue." Programmed issue (publication by subscription) offers a publisher a formal count of buyers to determine the size of the print run. Semiprogrammed issue uses some informal means (usually subscription lists from newsletters or magazines on a similar topic) to get an approximate count of the number of buyers for a particular kind of book. A publisher can estimate how big the audience for a new mystery is from the number of subscribers to *Ellery Queen's Mystery Magazine,* and can advertise the novel to interested parties in that periodical.

In *The Political Unconscious* Fredric Jameson explains, "Genres are essentially literary institutions, or social contracts between a writer and a specific public, whose function is to specify the proper use of a particular cultural artifact" (p. 106). That is to say that the genre label is both a promise to readers that it will meet a certain set of conventional expectations and an implicit set of instructions for the ways of reading the book will reward. Each genre meets specific needs for its particular audience.

## Mysteries

Mysteries were the first mass-market category of fiction in the United States. Their audience came to book publishers already constituted from detective fiction pulps in the 1920s. Mystery readers make a distinction between "classical" mysteries written by authors like Agatha Christie and Dorothy Sayers and hard-boiled detective stories written by authors like Dashiell Hammett and Raymond Chandler. A classical mystery, often called a "cozy," frequently involves a closed community—a family, a small town. These books are intellectual puzzles in which a detective uses rational means to explain a crime, identify the single individual responsible for it, and ultimately restore social order by expelling that individual from the larger community. These stories allow readers to engage latent feelings of hostility and violence generated by the repressiveness of families or other institutions at the same time as they offer reassurance that we live in a just, rational society in which evil is the result of single individuals rather than corrupt social institutions (Cawelti, p. 105).

Hard-boiled stories, which originated in *Black Mask* and other pulps in the 1920s, were initially targeted to white, working-class men in America. These tough-guy detective stories addressed the deskilling of manual work, the rise of consumer culture, the changing role of women, and the links between class, language, and culture. Hard-boiled heroes rely as much on brawn and tough talk as on their brains, and the worlds they inhabit are often overrun by systemic crime. Hard-boiled writers saw their fiction as a manly, American, "realistic" reaction against the silly, aristocratic English-country-house fiction written by women that dominated the literary marketplace between the world wars.

Fredric Jameson argues that detective stories are thoroughly commodified, that the ending or solution is what readers care about, so that the rest of the story is degraded to a means to that end (1979, p. 132). Studies of real readers reveal a variety of different ways of reading, many of which have nothing to do with the ending and a great deal to do with characters, language, setting, and other aspects that resonate with readers' everyday lives. Genre reading, then, is a good deal more complex, contradictory, and deeply enmeshed with readers' social and institutional positions than critics' models of reading would predict.

**Agatha Christie.** Best-selling author Agatha Christie (1890–1976) became one of the most acclaimed mystery writers in history. The English novelist wrote more than seventy detective books, many of which included her most popular characters Hercule Poirot and Miss Jane Marple. © *AP/Wide World Photos*

## Romances

Street & Smith's pulp magazine *Love Story*, edited during its heyday by New Woman and former dress model Daisy Bacon, achieved the largest circulation of any pulp magazine when it peaked at 600,000 in the 1930s. Mass-market romance novels appeared on the scene in the late 1950s, when sales of mysteries began to decline and publishers—impressed by the sales of a number of gothic romances—began placing romances at grocery stores, drugstores, and (later) chain bookstores in malls. Harlequin Enterprises, a Canadian publisher, conducted unprecedented market research with women readers in the early 1970s in order to tailor their regular, monthly releases exactly to readers' specifications. Their substantial success inspired copycat lines from a number of other publishers.

Janice Radway's study of romance readers concludes that romances are a compensatory literature that makes the exhausting work of loving and nurturing a family bearable by giving a woman time and space for herself (time spent reading) and the fantasy of being loved and cared for by a man (the romance hero) as she loves and cares for her family. At the same time, the best-loved romances were lessons in patriarchy. In them, the distant, angry, or hostile hero is transformed by the heroine's love into a demonstrative, loving husband, suggesting that women should "read" coldness and anger as (misunderstood) signs of the depth of a man's affection.

## Westerns

Writers such as Zane Grey, Owen Wister, Louis L'Amour, and others from the 1890s through the 1950s nostalgically re-created an idealized American frontier for male readers. As the United States became increasingly urban and industrial, the labor process was deskilled, class and ethnic tensions often erupted into violence, and cities became overcrowded. Westerns offered men the fantasy of a class-free world full of open spaces in which a rugged, manly hero could single-handedly enforce justice, changing the world through the force of his individual will. Militarism excited by the war with Spain made the gun-toting cowboy the quintessential American hero.

Jane Tompkins argues that the Western was also an attempt to wrest control of the literary marketplace and the larger culture for men and their embattled concerns from the women who had dominated it since the mid-nineteenth century. The most popular fiction of the nineteenth century was sentimental fiction written by, for, and about women. After the Civil War, women also increasingly overran the (once all-male) public sphere as Progressive reformers, seeking to make the world a safer place through temperance, social settlements, and prison reform; founding kindergartens, playgrounds, libraries, and hospitals for the insane; and agitating for pure food and drugs, better municipal sanitation, and woman suffrage. The Western was a world without such women (and the kitchens, churches, and children associated with them), a world that placed men and manhood at the center of American life (pp. 43–44).

## Science Fiction

Although a long tradition of narratives about the supernatural and space travel can be traced from ancient times, science fiction as a self-conscious body of narratives arose from pulp magazines in the 1920s. Hugo Gernsback, a Luxembourg emigrant, inventor, and electronics expert, founded *Amazing Stories* in 1926 after the success of a number of stories he ran as filler in his technology journal, *Modern Electronics*. The success of *Amazing Stories* spawned imitators—most notably Gernsback's own *Wonder Stories* as well as *Astounding Stories,* edited in its heyday by Jack Campbell. Until after World War II, science

fiction existed almost exclusively in the pulps, introducing audiences to now well-known writers such as Isaac Asimov, Robert Heinlein, Theodore Sturgeon, Arthur C. Clarke, and Ray Bradbury.

From the beginning, there was a close relationship between readers and writers of science fiction. *Amazing Stories* had always printed the full names and addresses of fans who wrote letters to the editor, facilitating the finding of pen pals and the founding of fan organizations. Often prominent fans in their late teens or early twenties were hired to edit the most important pulp titles. Initially, fans were almost exclusively white, male, and young. Self-professed nerds, many were well educated in science and technology, and the early promoters of the genre prided themselves on the "good science" in the fiction.

Early science fiction was marked by the privileged, masculine bias of its readers and writers. It shared an often-unquestioning faith in technology to solve the problems of modern society. It looked at the earth, undersea, outer space, other planets, nature, and (often) women and people of other races/species as so much territory to be colonized and subdued with the superior technology controlled by (white, male) heroes.

However, science fiction is above all about the encounter with difference, and its readers and writers certainly perceived themselves as alienated. Science fiction presents readers with a world that is profoundly different from the one in which they live, but it brings them into confrontation with the real world by denaturalizing some of its most common assumptions. What does it mean to encounter other worlds? People not like us? Nations or cultures living by different principles? What is the place of gender or race or nation in organizing our world and others? Science fiction is often a thought experiment about alternative ways to organize the world and the place of science and technology in it. After all, alien abduction is not so different from being kidnapped into slavery; interspecies contact is easily read as interracial or intercultural exchange; and conquering space ("the final frontier") can be a figure for colonizing less-developed nations.

The 1960s and 1970s revolutionized science fiction, appropriating it as a space to think about difference and diversity in alternative ways. African American and feminist writers such as Samuel Delany, Octavia Butler, Marion Zimmer Bradley, Ursula Le Guin, Marge Piercy, and Joanna Russ transformed the genre by imagining worlds without or beyond gender and race, worlds in which people's relationships to one another, to other living things, and to nature were imagined along different lines. Contemporary cyberpunk narratives such as William Gibson's *Neuromancer* (1984) increasingly raised questions about how new computer and communications technology transform people's identities for the postmodern world.

*See also:* Books and Manuscripts, Comic Book Reading, Comic Magazines, Literary Societies and Middle-Brow Reading

## BIBLIOGRAPHY

Cawelti, John G. *Adventure, Mystery, and Romance: Formula Stories as Art and Popular Culture.* Chicago: University of Chicago Press, 1976.

Denning, Michael. *Mechanic Accents: Dime Novels and Working-Class Culture in America.* Revised edition. New York: Verso Publishing Company, 1998. The original edition was published in 1987.

Escarpit, Robert. *The Book Revolution.* London: George G. Harrap and Company, 1966.

Jameson, Fredric. "Reification and Utopia in Mass Culture." *Social Text* 1 (Winter 1979): 130–148.

———. *The Political Unconscious: Narrative as a Socially Symbolic Act.* Ithaca, N.Y.: Cornell University Press, 1981.

Radway, *Janice. Reading the Romance: Women, Patriarchy and Popular Literature.* Chapel Hill: University of North Carolina Press, 1991. The original edition was published in 1984.

Roberts, Adam. *Science Fiction.* New York: Routledge, 2000.

Smith, Erin A. *Hard-Boiled: Working-Class Readers and Pulp Magazines.* Philadelphia: Temple University Press, 2000.

———. "'Both a Woman and a Complete Professional': Women Readers and Women's Hard-Boiled Detective Fiction." In *Reading Sites.* Edited by Elizabeth Flynn and Patrocinio Schweickart. New York: Modern Language Association Press, 2004.

Tompkins, Jane. *West of Everything: The Inner Life of Westerns.* New York: Oxford University Press, 1992.

*Erin A. Smith*

# GILDED AGE LEISURE AND RECREATION

During the Gilded Age, Victorian values clashed with a brash new order of commercial entertainment and leisure venues. "Daring" stage entertainments and their denunciation became common features of the social landscape, as commercialism liberalized social codes. Changes in leisure and recreation from 1865 to 1890 reflected the era's rapid transformations, which stemmed from improvements in rail and communication networks and innovations in printing, manufacture, and marketing. The new amusements also reflected the age's disparities in wealth, as well as the corruption and social injustices that prompted Mark Twain and Charles Dudley Warner to nickname the era "The Gilded Age." The period's amusements and leisure patterns also reflected a cultural shift, as the working class, the emerging middle class, and elites of the Gilded Age found new ways, at home and in public, to pursue happiness in a world increasingly brave and new.

## Gilded Parlors

The Gilded Age's industrial abundance prompted the commercialization of parlor culture. To house an emerging middle class, in the late nineteenth century the first suburbs developed in Brooklyn and in similar neighborhoods outside Philadelphia and Boston. In these new bedroom communities the nineteenth-century cult of domesticity reblossomed. This ideology dictated that the father would enter the perilous public sphere to earn a living, while the mother would stay at home to provide her family with moral nurture. The parlor, at the center of the middle-class woman's sphere, was the family's moral refuge. To furnish the parlor to an appropriate standard of comfort and status, the family of the period could turn to the era's new chain stores, department stores, and catalog houses.

Numerous department stores appeared in this period —for example, Macy's in 1860 and Bloomingdale's in 1872 (the same year that the Montgomery Ward mail-order business began). As historian William Leach argued in *Land of Desire: Merchants, Power, and the Rise of a New American Culture,* the Gilded Age department store was an incubator of consumer culture. Its luxurious architecture, opulent displays and trimmings, pageants and concerts, and offers of free delivery and lax return policies weaned the public from the Protestant values of thriftiness and austerity and nurtured a new desire for exotic luxuries. The department store also provided a respectable public space to which women could safely venture.

Such shopping venues and the social values they encouraged opened the middle-class parlor to a flood of gadgets, toys, and new media. From stores or catalogs parents could purchase magic lanterns along with prepared slides of microscopic organisms or exotic landscapes. Apparatus for viewing stereographic slides also were common in parlors. Families would purchase sets of such three-dimensional slides to gaze at natural vistas, foreign cities, and photographs of recent or past news events; for example, in the 1880s, the firm of Taylor and Huntington began to market slides of Matthew Brady's Civil War battlefield photographs.

Following the assumptions of the cult of domesticity, gender roles were inscribed into the playthings in the homes of the wealthy and middling class. Soldiers, miniature printing presses, storefronts, and steam engines were appropriate for boys, while dolls, dollhouses, and their furnishings were standard for girls. In *Made to Play House: Dolls and the Commercialization of American Girlhood*, Miriam Formanek-Brunell described the "doll culture" that introduced consumerist desires into girls in this era. Prior to the 1880s, girls would be expected to sew costumes for dolls and so employ their domestic skills. By the 1880s, ready-made doll costumes became standard; these might include mourning clothes so that girls could stage doll funerals, or visiting cards, so that girls could more realistically stage tea parties and social events. By the 1890s, memoirs such as *Dolly's Experience: Told by Herself* as well as magazines such as the *Doll's Dressmaker* further reinforced girls' interest in domesticity and consumption.

## Reading and Urbanization

The Gilded Age, with its compulsory education laws and high literacy rates—in 1870 about 88 percent for white Americans and 20 percent for black Americans—saw a large growth in available reading for all, whether women's parlor magazines such as *Ladies' Home Journal*, genteel magazines for men and women such as *Harper's Weekly* and *Scribner's*, or dime novels by authors such as Ned Buntline, available at train station kiosks for working-class readers.

The most common of publications, and one of the binding forces of the new urban landscape, was the newspaper. From 1870 to 1900, 1,500 new daily newspapers appeared in America. Enormous increases in urban populations in the late nineteenth century encouraged foreign-language newspapers in Yiddish and German as well as the return of a more populist style of news reporting. Charles A. Dana, publisher of the *New York Sun*, which had a circulation of 130,000 in 1876, wrote that his newspaper would offer "a daily photograph of the whole world's doings in the most luminous and lively manner." While Dana's reference to photography followed the era's high regard for "realism" and quasi-scientific approach to all endeavors, the "lively manner" of the *Sun* also pointed to the fact that its publisher was not above offering sentiment and color in reporting.

More clearly at the center of the era's New Journalism, which mixed activism with sentiment, was Joseph Pulitzer, who reigned first at the *St. Louis Post and Dispatch* and later at the *New York World*. While at the *Dispatch*, Pulitzer announced that his paper "will serve no party but the people . . . will oppose all frauds and shams wherever and whatever they are." In both of his newspapers, Pulitzer mixed sensational stories and gossip with reform crusades and investigations of political corruption. Appealing to New York's large immigrant population, the *World* pushed for tenement and sweatshop reforms, relying on emotionally charged headlines such as "How Babies Are Baked" to report on deaths in tenements after a heat wave in the summer of 1883.

The new formula for journalism also transformed reporters into celebrities. Nellie Bly, born Elizabeth Jane Cochrane, one of the era's best-known reporters, developed a style that mixed crusading with sensationalism. At the *Pittsburgh Dispatch* and later at Pulitzer's *World*, Bly cultivated an undercover reporting style to show, for example, what it was like to be committed to one of the era's insane asylums in "Ten Days in a Madhouse" (1888), or to observe child labor in factories and housing conditions for the poor. In another "undercover" effort, she encouraged the attention of mashers in order to skewer them in print. Bly's greatest fame came, however, when she traveled around the world for the *New York World* in less than Jules Verne's prescribed eighty days. Reflecting the era's high commercial style, Bly began to be marketed as a character in Victorian trade card sets, in a board game that the *World* developed, and in a popular song "Globe Trotting Nellie Bly."

## Working-Class Heroes

While newspapers offered a daily photograph of the whole world's doings, other media catered to the public's taste for escape. A fascination with past "golden ages" and the authority that these ages implied led, for example, to the elitist Gothic revival style in architecture and to the immense popularity of the novel *Ben Hur* (1880), set in ancient days and bearing Christian values; meanwhile, dime novels, the most abundant form of literature in the late nineteenth century, offered working-class and immigrant men and women tales of rugged individualism and survival. Wilderness tales for urban readers could feature pirates, soldiers, outlaws, Indian fighters, frontiersmen, and gunfighters, as well as rough-and-tumble women dressed as men who took their place among the adventurers. In contrast, dime novels with urban settings often set their heroes in the midst of the harsh urban environment and the labor difficulties of this period.

The dime novel's origins were in the numerous antebellum story papers, which sold for 20 cents a copy, had circulations as high as 100,000, and offered serialized adventure stories. Beginning in the 1860s, dime-novel publishers such as Street and Smith and Beadle and Adams applied a factory system to the story paper formula to create entire novels for 10 cents. These publishers often farmed out plot sketches and characters to authors, the more adept of whom could write two 40,000-word stories a week; the resulting dime novels were then distributed to newsstands in first runs of about 50,000 copies.

Publishers such as Beadle and Adams also enforced moral standards and insisted authors not offend "good taste." Nevertheless, predictably, the sensationalism in dime novels drew the ire of reformers. Anthony Comstock, with the support of Protestant elites, targeted dime novels along with pornography in his 1873 Committee for Suppression of Vice in New York, which lobbied successfully to make mailing pornography illegal. While the dime novels were often violent, nationalistic, and racist, those with urban settings made heroes of the working-man and reflected a moral outlook. Horatio Alger's often-derided "rags-to-riches" stories exposed some of the harsh realities of New York City street life while extolling the importance of a moral outlook and wise economic practices for youths to survive the streets. Historian Michael Denning, in *Mechanic Accents: Dime Novels and Working-Class Culture in America*, described the many dime novels featuring a worker or "mechanic" that added a more pronounced socialist subtext to the Horatio Alger success formula and stressed the dignity of labor in an era when workers were often regarded as disposable goods.

## Leg Shows and Burlesque

The reform-minded members of society viewed Gilded Age theater in much the same way that Anthony Comstock viewed the dime novel. While stages retained the earlier nineteenth-century mix of Shakespeare productions, minstrel shows, and countless versions of Harriet Beecher Stowe's *Uncle Tom's Cabin*, the Gilded Age added "leg shows," variety theater, spectacular restagings of events such as the destruction of Pompeii, and extravaganzas such as circuses and Wild West shows. Historian Lawrence Levine, in *Highbrow/Lowbrow: The Emergence of Cultural Hierarchy in America*, established that, as these popular venues developed, elite audiences began to sacralize art forms such as opera, ballet, orchestral music, and Shakespeare dramas to create elite performance halls removed from rowdy venues.

The liberalized social codes that later would appear in everyday life surfaced early on in theater. In 1866, *The*

*Black Crook*, the first modern musical, played at Niblo's Theater in Manhattan. It was notorious for including a chorus line of female dancers, in this case, a group of stranded French ballet dancers. Two year later, in 1868, Lydia Thompson and Her British Blondes, a female troupe, came to the United States and mounted a comic version of a Greek tragedy, playing both men's and women's roles, broadly caricaturizing both sexes. Their comedy also featured skimpy costumes.

As early as 1869, a suffragette decried this trend. In "About Nudity in the Theaters" Olive Logan complained of the era's numerous "leg shows" that showcased attractive but generally untalented woman. Logan insisted that for a young woman to pass an audition in 1869, she need only to have her hair dyed yellow; a body symmetrically formed; a willingness to bare her legs; and an ability to sing brassy songs, dance the can-can, wink at men, and attract wealthy admirers.

Robert C. Allen, in *Horrible Prettiness: Burlesque and American Culture*, depicted burlesque performers in these first shows as feisty women contesting the gender assumptions of the era. Allen further argued that this early burlesque later declined into the "kootch" dances of the 1890s and the striptease born in 1917 at Minsky Brothers'. While some of the performers who suffragette Logan described may have been "feisty" women braving the public sphere, her critique establishes that sexuality as a selling point entered American popular culture early on and that the kootch dancer of the 1890s had her precursor in the can-can dancer of the 1860s.

## Identity Theft and Minstrelsy

While burlesque troupes such as Lydia Thomson and her British Blondes explored gender roles on stage, minstrelsy, the most popular theatrical form in mid-nineteenth-century America, parodied racial identities. The minstrel show involved white performers, generally from working-class immigrant backgrounds, who "blacked up" by smearing burnt cork on their faces. Playbills often included illustrations of the troupe both in respectable poses as "white" men and in their outrageous costumes and makeup as "black" minstrels. As in any carnival setting, the donning of a mask gave the performer license to perform in an uninhibited manner. A performance would include songs and ballads, dances, skits, burlesque operas, parodies of popular plays, and comic speeches, relying on dialect and gestures meant to reflect African American folkways. In the process the minstrel performers created and promulgated stereotypes of African Americans as childlike and nonthreatening plantation hands or as egotistical urban dandies.

The racism in such shows was uncloaked. In 1848, when the minstrel show was at the height of its popularity, Frederick Douglass, in the antislavery weekly *Northstar,* denounced minstrel performers as "the filthy scum of white society, who have stolen from us a complexion denied by nature, in which to make money, and pander to the corrupt taste of their white fellow citizens." Later scholars such as Robert C. Toll in *Blacking Up: The Minstrel Show in Nineteenth-Century America* and Eric Lott in *Love and Theft: Blackface Minstrelsy and the American Working Class* argued that, while the minstrel show abetted derisive stereotypes, it also provided some interchange between African American and white American cultural forms and created a transgressive space in which to explore class and racial politics.

## Rise of Vaudeville

By the 1870s, with the end of Reconstruction, variety theater and its grab-bag approach to entertainment became a greater draw than minstrelsy. Early variety had taken place in the lowbrow concert saloon, where drunken male audiences mixed with prostitutes while acrobats, jugglers, singers, and dancing girls performed. By the late nineteenth century, the concert saloon tradition had blended with burlesque to offer kootch dancers and off-color comedy to male audiences, while a cleaned-up variety theater became codified on vaudeville circuits.

Tony Pastor is generally credited for pioneering the "wholesome" approach to variety. In the string of theaters he owned around New York City, he prohibited alcohol and banned low humor. Following Pastor's lead, beginning in the 1880s, vaudeville theater operators B. F. Keith and Edward F. Albee created an East Coast vaudeville empire, while Martin Beck developed the Orpheum Circuit in the West. Their central offices arranged booking and pay scales for the entire circuit. The theaters were often grandiose in décor. Along with the elegant settings, and the banning of alcohol and low humor, vaudeville circuit bookers attempted to domesticate a diverse audience by varying the ten acts of a typical bill to include spectacles, comedy, and such highbrow acts as snippets of Shakespeare's plays, or renditions of opera or classical music. By developing a standardized and sanitized entertainment formula, vaudeville paved the way for the mass entertainment later offered by Hollywood.

## Entertainment as Medicine

Humbler in scope than rivals such as vaudeville and circus, the Gilded Age's medicine shows were early "infomercials" that intermixed free variety entertainments with product sales pitches. Prior to the Civil War, patent medicine peddling had been a booming business—many "penny-press" newspapers relied heavily on advertisements for wonder medicines such as Dr. Wheeler's Balsam, Parr's Life Pills, or Lydia E. Pinkham's Vegetable Compound. By the 1850s, over 1,500 patent medicines were marketed in America, with larger companies spending as much as $100,000 a year in advertising.

In the 1870s, patent medicine firms begin to send medicine shows on tours that might include as many as fifty performers. The medicine show functioned as a small-scale circus traveling to those towns that circuses would ignore, offering parades and several days of free performances. Bills changed nightly during visits, and might offer exhibitions of trick shooting, minstrelsy, banjo, songs, hypnotism, dances, Punch and Judy shows, menageries, and countless pitches for Hamlin Company's "Wizard Oil" or the many compounds of the Kickapoo Indian Medicine Company of New Haven.

## Jumbo Tent Shows

If the medicine show sprang forth from the medium of print advertising, the American circus was nurtured by railroads, both as the preferred transportation method and as the medium that created many of the new towns the circus would visit. Prior to the Civil War, the expenses and difficulties of rail travel meant that wagon-drawn shows could mount larger productions at lower costs. After the Civil War the development of a standard-gauge rail network shifted the balance.

Showman P. T. Barnum, whose American Museum in New York City closed after repeated fires in the 1860s, soon turned to the commercial possibilities of the circus. Rather than rent cars owned by railroads, in 1872 the circus of Barnum, Coup and Castello bought and built their own train cars to carry performers, workers, circus animals, and equipment. Their circus, larger than that of any rival wagon show, was a financial success in its first year. Barnum, who had presented "human oddities" at his American Museum for decades, also made the "freak show" or sideshow a common element of the circus.

Barnum's growing circus reflected the economic trends of the late nineteenth century; while companies grew and devoured competitors, and a gluttonous financier like Diamond Jim Brady became a folk hero, Barnum and his partners expanded the circus to two rings with simultaneous attractions. Barnum's later partnership with James Bailey led to ballyhoo about their elephant "Jumbo" and the creation of the three-ring circus in 1881, a distinctly American cultural form that guaranteed frenzy and spectacle. In 1902, William Dean Howells complained of circus performances that "glutted rather than fed."

## The Scout of the Plains

Developing alongside the American circus, the Wild West show offered a portable nationalistic spectacle rooted in the West of dime novels. Author Ned Buntline had made Buffalo Bill Cody, a former Pony Express rider, buffalo hunter, and Army scout, the hero of many dime novels. In 1872, Cody debuted on the stage in a production of Buntline's "Scout of the Plains." Cody, who published dime novels about his own exploits as well as an autobiography in 1879, in 1883 organized "Buffalo Bill's Wild West," bringing the dime novel to life as a theatrical extravaganza.

The show offered a heroic version of the conquest of the American West that ignored economics and focused on the bravery and tribulations of white frontiersmen and the treachery and nobility of savage Indians. The troupe's 1887 European tour was a crowd pleaser that included sharpshooter Annie Oakley, Sitting Bull, and numerous other Native American performers. Buffalo Bill's Wild West featured reenactments of Indian raids, prairie fires, cyclones, military drills, and bison hunts. Cody's success spurred several rival shows, including "Pawnee Bill's Historic Wild West," which opened in 1888. Although Cody continued to appear with his troupe, the close logistical and theatrical ties between the circus and Wild West surfaced in 1894, when circus magnate James Bailey purchased and took over management of the Buffalo Bill Wild West Show.

## Elite Sports

Alongside the circus and Wild West show, the Gilded Age saw the transformation into mass spectacles of many participatory sports first nurtured in elite settings. In this era, social elites took to tennis, rowing, yachting, golf, football, and horse racing. Football began in this period as an offshoot of rugby played at eastern colleges. Largely through the guidance of Yale coach Walter Camp, it developed into the modern game. Historian Michael Oriard, in *Reading Football: How the Popular Press Created an American Spectacle*, argued that football grew in popularity because, unlike the meandering "plotless" format of a soccer or rugby match with its nonstop flow, football as Camp fashioned it lent itself to dramatic narrative form—newspaper reporters responded and their coverage engendered mass interest.

Horse racing, too, became a large spectator sport via elite sponsorship in the Gilded Age. Retired Tammany Hall politician and boxing champion John Morrisey opened a racetrack in 1863 at Saratoga Springs, a health spa and resort for the wealthy in upstate New York. Morrisey persuaded wealthy partners to join him in the venture, and they created an extensive August racing season, replacing the one- or two-day races common elsewhere. By 1875, the Kentucky Derby, at Churchill Down, in Louisville, Kentucky, joined the Preakness Stakes at Pimlico Park, in Baltimore, Maryland, and the Belmont Stakes held at Jerome Park in Westchester County, New York, to create American racing's Triple Crown. By 1890, over 300 tracks were operating across the country.

## The National Pastime

In Mark Twain's *A Connecticut Yankee in King Arthur's Court* (1889), the nineteenth-century innovations that mechanic Hank Morgan brings to early England include electricity, the stock market, and a lineup for two baseball teams of knights dubbed the "Bessemers" and the "Ulsters." By the time Twain wrote *A Connecticut Yankee,* baseball was already the nation's premier spectator sport. It emerged from variations on the English games of cricket and rounders in the 1840s, when a group of clerks, storekeepers, and professionals formed the New York Knickerbocker Baseball Club and developed some of the modern game's rules. By the 1850s, as America edged toward a sectional conflict, enthusiasts were promoting baseball as the American "national pastime," seeing it as a medium for creating unity. The dime-novel publishing house of Irwin P. Beadle offered the game's first guidebook, *Beadle's Dime Baseball Player,* in 1860, offering "elementary instructions of this American game of ball," along with rules, regulations, names of teams, and essays arguing the game's physical and moral benefits. Civil War soldiers, who learned to play baseball in pickup games, further disseminated the game after the war's conclusion. Numerous amateur teams and leagues developed; entrepreneurs who built stadiums and charged admission and salaried players soon followed.

All-professional teams became common in the 1870s, and, by 1875, the Boston Red Stockings drew 70,000 fans to their stadium. The following year, the new owner-controlled National League of Professional Baseball Clubs barred liquor sales, gamblers, and Sunday games; the season after that, professional baseball had its first large gambling scandal when four members of the Louisville Grays, charged with throwing games during the last weeks of the pennant race, were banned from life from the National League.

By the mid-1880s interleague play began between the National League and the American Association, a new rival that had permitted liquor sales at stadiums as well as Sunday games. In the 1889 season, 2 million fans attended major league play. With a solid tradition of gambling scandals, drunken fans, carousing players, and guidebooks and magazines that encouraged the statistical analysis of teams and players, baseball was well enshrined as the first major spectator sport in late nineteenth-century America.

## Protestant Entertainment

Debates about the morality of working-class sports venues such as bare-knuckle boxing, as well as efforts to ban liquor and Sunday games in baseball, suggest how entertainment mirrored the tensions then common between America's elites and the working class; these tensions had erupted into violence during the widespread railroad strikes of 1877, as well as at the Haymarket Riot of 1884 and the subsequent trial that led to the hangings of four of Chicago's labor leaders. Throughout this period, social elites searched for methods to impose order and unity on civic society and on entertainment and leisure venues as well. The emergence of the Women's Christian Temperance Union, Dwight Moody's revivals, and the creation of the Chautauqua Institute all point to the Protestant elite's efforts to find substitutes for liberalized secular culture. These movements also reveal a Protestant leadership willing to accept and appropriate some of the terms of the new commercial venues.

In 1873, Dwight Moody, formerly a successful shoe salesman, leader of a popular Sunday School in Chicago, and president of Chicago's YMCA, teamed up with gospel singer Ira Sankey and began a series of urban revivals that attracted huge audiences. During an early tour in England, he drew crowds of 20,000 or more. His subsequent revivals in the United States also drew crowds larger than 10,000. Moody would advertise in newspaper amusement sections, hire choirs of 500 singers, and rely on his own considerable storytelling and preaching skills to gain converts and to build an evangelical empire that included the Moody Bible Institute, the Northfield School in Massachusetts, and the Moody Press.

In 1873, the same year that Moody began preaching, members of the Women's Temperance Crusade marched on saloons in twenty-three states where they held impromptu prayer meetings, sang hymns, and asked the saloon owners to stop the sale of alcohol. The following year, leaders of this movement met at the Chautauqua Institute in upstate New York and the Women's Christian Temperance Union (WCTU) was formed. The WCTU sought to end the domestic violence and disruptions its members connected to the lively saloon culture of the era. Under the WCTU's second president, Francis Willard, suffrage became a club goal as she transformed the union into an international political movement; learning from Moody, she also made WCTU meetings and rallies entertaining, offering not only speeches and prayers but also performances that included, for example, 300-voice choirs. While condemning public amusements and frivolous entertainment, the WCTU offered its members community, a large circulation newspaper, and moral entertainments.

## Backwoods Uplift

Protestant "uplift" and reform blended with tourism in the turn-of-the-century's Chautauqua movement, which also tapped into the earlier American cultural forms of the camp meeting and the lyceum. The camp meeting was a country revival in which a temporary tent and shed city was established and people from the surrounding country converged to hear preaching, find God, and socialize. The lyceum movement of the antebellum, dedicated to public education, created 3,000 institutes in the United States that sponsored lectures, built libraries, and educated the public.

In 1869, farm manufacturer and revivalist Lewis Miller and Methodist Episcopal bishop John H. Vincent adopted the lyceum approach to attract summer vacationers to a rural New York retreat that they had begun as a training post for Sunday school teachers. Accessible by railroad, their Chautauqua Institute offered clean, rural living and inspirational speakers. In two-week visits, families could attend workshops, sermons, and devotional meetings, while also enjoying concerts, bonfires, humorous lectures, concerts, and fireworks. Tennis and golf were also available. Members of the Chautauqua's "Literary and Scientific Circle" took home-correspondence courses, read numerous books, and were honored at a "Recognition Day" ceremony in a structure decorated with busts of Plato, Socrates, Homer, Virgil, Goethe, and Shakespeare.

Vincent's Chautauqua Institute inspired numerous imitators at vacation areas throughout the country. By the 1890s, 10,000 reading circles based on Chautauqua principles had emerged throughout the country. Yet the movement can be characterized as a cultural format in retreat: just as elite audiences had retreated to opera houses, the Chautauqua provided uplift on nature preserves far from the cities. In the movement, Protestant leadership appropriated features of commercialized entertainment forms and continued the trend of packaging religion as a consumer product.

## Democracy and Commercialism

While true mass culture entertainment would not arrive in the United States until the advent of movies, radio, and television in the twentieth century, the basic recipe was concocted in the Gilded Age. The then-"massing" culture developed standardized packages of the "exotic" such as the three-ring circus, the dime novel, the vaudeville palace, and the department store that helped shape the consumer society to come. When Victorian values and older ideals of "uplift" clashed with the new commercial order, the outcome was either short-lived reform efforts or the birth of hybrid forms reflected in the Chautauqua Institute, the National League's decision to ban Sunday games and alcohol, or Dwight Moody's revivals.

The rise of commercialized leisure also transformed American values and democratic practices. Media as diverse as baseball and Pulitzer's *New York World* helped to unify a divided populace and to promote democracy and a sense of community. Department stores and vaudeville houses with their palatial architecture championed a version of populist "equality," but they also encouraged consumerist passivity. Commercial culture liberalized social behavior norms, yet the era's theater and literature frequently promoted sexual, racial, and ethnic stereotypes. Although the era's commercialism could contribute to reform, at the same time it could reinforce existing social inequities; this paradox was rooted in the era's conflicting visions of freedom—embodied in the figure of the earnest suffragette and her commercialized alter ego, the brash dancing girl.

*See also:* Baseball Crowds; Baseball, Amateur; Early National Leisure and Recreation; Football; Football, Collegiate; Genre Reading; Impresarios of Leisure, Rise of; Media, Technology, and Leisure; Progressive-Era Leisure and Recreation; Prohibition and Temperance; Railroads and Leisure; Summer Resorts; Tourism; Wild West Shows

**BIBLIOGRAPHY**

Allen, Robert C. *Horrible Prettiness: Burlesque and American Culture.* Chapel Hill: University of North Carolina Press, 1991.

Blumin, Stuart M. *The Emergence of the Middle Class: Social Experience in the American City, 1760–1900.* New York: Cambridge University Press, 1989.

Cross, Gary. *Kids' Stuff: Toys and the Changing World of American Childhood.* Cambridge, Mass.: Harvard University Press, 1997.

Davis, Janet M. *The Circus Age: Culture & Society Under the American Big Top.* Chapel Hill: University of North Carolina Press, 2002.

Denning, Michael. *Mechanic Accents: Dime Novels and Working-Class Culture in America.* New York: Verso, 1987.

Emery, Michael, and Edwin Emery. *The Press and America: An Interpretive History of the Mass Media.* 7th Ed. Englewood Cliffs, N.J.: Prentice-Hall, 1992.

Formanek-Brunell, Miriam. *Made to Play House: Dolls and the Commercialization of American Girlhood.* Baltimore: Johns Hopkins Press, 1993.

Kasson, John F. *Amusing the Million: Coney Island at the Turn of the Century.* New York: Hill and Wang, 1978.

Kibler, M. Alison. *Rank Ladies: Gender and Cultural Hierarchy in American Vaudeville.* Chapel Hill: University of North Carolina Press, 1999.

Leach, William. *Land of Desire: Merchants, Power, and the Rise of a New American Culture.* New York: Pantheon Books, 1993.

Levine, Lawrence W. *Highbrow/Lowbrow: The Emergence of Cultural Hierarchy in America.* Cambridge, Mass.: Harvard University Press, 1988.

Logan, Olive. "About Nudity in the Theaters." In *Democratic Vistas: 1860–1880.* Edited by Alan Trachtenberg. New York: George Braziller, 1970.

Lott, Eric. *Love and Theft: Blackface Minstrelsy and the American Working Class.* New York: Oxford University Press, 1993.

McNamara, Brooks. *Step Right Up.* Jackson: University Press of Mississippi, 1975.

Moore, R. Laurence. *Selling God: American Religion in the Marketplace of Culture.* New York: Oxford University Press, 1994.

Oriard, Michael. *Reading Football: How the Popular Press Created an American Spectacle.* Chapel Hill: University of North Carolina Press, 1993.

Rader, Benjamin G. *Baseball: A History of America's Game.* Urbana: University of Illinois Press, 1992.

Rydell, Robert W. *All the World's a Fair: Visions of Empire at American International Expositions, 1876–1916.* Chicago: University of Chicago Press, 1984.

Rydell, Robert W., John E. Findling, and Kimberly D. Pelle. *Fair America: World's Fairs in the United States.* Washington, D.C.: Smithsonian Institution Press, 2000.

Snyder, Robert W. *The Voice of the City: Vaudeville and Popular Culture in New York.* New York: Oxford University Press, 1989.

Toll, Robert C. *Blacking Up: The Minstrel Show in Nineteenth-Century America.* New York: Oxford University Press, 1974.

Trachtenberg, Alan. *The Incorporation of America: Culture and Society in the Gilded Age.* New York: Hill and Wang, 1982.

*Fred R. Nadis*

# GIRL SCOUTS

**See** *Scouting Movements*

# GLOBALIZATION OF AMERICAN LEISURE

The logos of McDonald's, Starbucks, Nike, and Disney have become so common abroad that it often seems U.S. leisure activities are global. While American leisure products do dominate their markets, others have failed or have been copied, if not pirated, by foreign entrepreneurs. As eye-catching as the brands of U.S. companies are, their spread owes to financial and organization features, technical prowess, and help from the American government.

The first leisure product exported from the American colonies was tobacco, reaching 102 million pounds by 1775. Britain so taxed the colonies' exports that export taxes were prohibited in the U.S. Constitution, and "free trade" became an article of faith. But for the next century, aside from fur for top hats, Americans exported few leisure goods; their agricultural products they traded internally, developing transportation systems and logistical talents that proved useful later on.

## Export of Film

Film was the first modern American leisure product to be exported successfully, and it is a model of how an export can achieve global dominance. In 1905, the world film market was still open. The French firm Pathé controlled 50–70 percent of new releases in the United States in 1906, while U.S. filmmakers battled over the rest of the domestic market, seeking advantage by suing one another over patent and license infringements. In 1908, as a result of suits by Thomas Edison and a succession of licensing agreements by distributors, two quasi-cartels arose: one mostly American, the MPPC (Motion Pictures Patents Company); the other mostly foreign, the Sales Corp. They established uniform licensing fees, admissions, and import quotas. American films were already being exported, with Britain as the largest market—London alone had 300 movie theaters in 1911 (Thompson).

Exports were important to film early, because 99 percent of the product's cost (actors, equipment, sets) went into making the first print. The "second print" was almost free, and any income it made was profit. Thus Vita-

graph, the third-largest U.S. company in 1912, produced more prints by 1912 at its Paris plant than at its U.S. plant.

World War I disrupted the powerful French, German, and Italian film industries, but left the U.S. producers and the large Anglo-American market relatively unscathed. The United States began producing narrative-driven film spectacles, such as D. W. Griffith's *Birth of a Nation* (1915), whose popularity drove up production costs by 1,000 percent between 1915 and 1925. Stars such as Douglas Fairbanks and Mary Pickford pioneered on- and off-screen lifestyles that emphasized personal freedom and consumption. The advertising of products in or with films, which began in 1916, grew dramatically as ad agencies saw that movie chains offered a national audience. By the early 1920s their large domestic audience, the high cost of filmmaking, and the "aura" of American freedom and wealth had already created something like a brand, which gave U.S. filmmakers advantages as exporters of film.

Many European countries owed large debts to the United States after the war, and importing film was one form of payment. American banks, which opened abroad to handle reparations and reconstruction, were positioned to finance the export of U.S. film. Given the low cost of the "second print," American firms could sell in Europe at prices lower than even healthy European producers could have met. As a result, U.S. film quickly dominated countries in Scandinavia and the Baltics. The war also shifted the center of world film distribution to New York. America's late entry into World War I meant that U.S. ships served Latin American, Asian, and even European markets without peril. By 1919, U.S. filmmakers had systems of international finance and channels of distribution that gave them worldwide scope. Exports of U.S. film rose from 36 million feet in 1915 to 235 million feet in 1925. Meanwhile imports of foreign film to the United States declined from 16 million feet in 1913 to only 7 million feet in 1925 (Izod, pp. 62–63).

A high level of technical innovation has spurred the export of many U.S. leisure goods, from film and carbonated soft drinks to fiberglass golf clubs. The introduction of sound film in 1927 was an early example of the opportunities and problems of high-tech leisure exports. There were also German and British sound film systems, but Warner Brothers went deep into debt to solve sound's production problems and to retool its theaters for audio. When audiences flocked to *The Jazz Singer* in 1927 to hear Al Jolson, Warner Brothers began to make large profits, and other U.S. competitors had to mortgage themselves similarly. Moviemaking became so expensive that the number of U.S.-produced films fell by 30 percent between 1927 and 1930 (Izod, p. 79). Attendance soared, however, and exports rose dramatically by 1931. These huge investments paid off nicely in the mid-1930s. But sound film also posed a problem—the language barrier. Although Louis B. Mayer in 1928 naïvely declared that sound film would lead to the universal use of English, foreign audiences began to lose interest. It became clear that sound film created language markets, with the largest—English, French, German, and Spanish—possessing intrinsic economies of scale. Here there were no extra "second-print" costs. But for smaller language markets, distributors set up dubbing and subtitling services. These added to "second-print" costs, but not enough to level the playing field for native producers, because the cost of entry to sound film was so high by 1930 that only internationally capitalized and distributed film companies could compete. By 1932, U.S. films captured 95 percent of the British, 75 percent of the French, and 68 percent of the Italian markets (Guback, p. 8).

The advent of the Technicolor musical (*The Gold Diggers of Broadway,* 1930) upped the ante again and led U.S. producers into the music business. Fierce domestic competition for viewers during the Great Depression fueled more innovations: crime films, sound effects, and deep-focus lenses. Foreign film government recognized film's importance. One by one, European nations set up quotas on the number of U.S. films that could be imported. Germany established a 1:1 ratio, while France created a complex 1:7 ratio exchange of import permits. The United States retaliated, but ultimately the "quota wars" were futile because, to ensure their foreign distribution, the U.S. firms opened foreign subsidiaries. Paramount and MGM went so far as to loan Germany's UFA film group the money it needed to survive. In return, they gained a guaranteed distribution outlet in the joint subsidiary Parufamet (Thompson, pp. 110, 119).

## Exporting Film: 1930 to Post–World War II

Like other new industries, film next went through a period of product differentiation. Each studio created a house look, leading to the "classic Hollywood style." MGM had brilliant, plush interiors and a high key lighting style. Warner became known for urban realism and "noir" styling. Disney pioneered cartoons. This differentiation was necessary in their home market, where the Depression had introduced fierce competition, but it also overwhelmed competitors overseas. There was also new financial oversight. The banks that supplied their production loans reviewed the domestic and foreign potential of the films that studios made; these banks included not only American but European firms, such as Deutsche

Bank and Credit Lyonais. Hollywood studios also collaborated on a Production Code Administration (PCA) seal, without which no film could be distributed in major U.S. theater chains. This practice blocked some foreign producers. Meanwhile, the U.S. government tacitly accepted Hollywood's vertical integration, block-booking, and blind-bidding practices, in effect creating a film cartel. With its huge domestic audience secured, the U.S. film industry arrived at the formula of its modern success— pay for production costs at home and make profit abroad.

When Axis powers invaded nation after nation in the late 1930s, however, U.S. film not only lost these advantages but was also shut out of Europe. By 1940, it was distributed only in Switzerland, Sweden, and Portugal. But the domestic market remained strong, as did exports to Latin America and Asia. Close cooperation between Hollywood and the government led producers to begin shipping newsreels to these markets to counter Axis propaganda. By 1943, the cooperation turned to collaboration, as pro-American war films proliferated.

After the war the Motion Picture Export Association (MPEA) worked closely with the government in overseas screening and distribution. In some countries film imports were part of aid under the Marshall Plan. No censorship was necessary, because Hollywood scoured its films of material offensive to foreign markets and even added foreign scenes. There was a hunger for Hollywood film in markets that had become addicted, such as Austria (see Wagnleitner). Having built up a huge export backlog during the war, the studios finagled until they could give Europeans what they wanted. They inundated France and Germany, offering films so cheaply that local producers could not compete. Italy received an average of 570 new American films each of the four years after the war (Izod, p. 118). Britain reacted first, imposing quotas on U.S. film, followed in 1948 by France and Germany. But these quotas failed much as the 1920s quotas had. Not only did foreign audiences want the U.S. product, but the U.S. studios set up foreign production companies, which took advantage of cheaper locations and labor. They became "multinationals" before the word was invented.

## The Modern Era: Platforms and Sequels

Before World War II, eight out of ten U.S. films recouped their costs at home. Afterward, only one in ten could do so. By the mid-1950s, some 40 percent of ticket revenue for U.S. film was already coming from overseas, a figure that increased to 53 percent by the early 1960s, with Europeans paying 80 percent of that figure (Izod, p. 161). Japan was also becoming a lucrative market. Thus, the studios hired commissars of "foreign correctness" and began to look for international appeal. Where it was possible to insert a foreign scene, they did. Biblical epics, musicals, and comedies of sexual innuendo proved popular overseas. In order to evade foreign import quotas and limits on repatriation of profit, U.S. producers began "runaway production," shooting their films overseas. In 1949, U.S. studios produced only 19 films abroad, but by 1969 that number had reached 183 (Izod, p. 159).

In the early 1950s, Disney began to create a new kind of studio. With its iconic characters and focus on the family audience, it already presented an internationally flavored "brand" of "American life." It cross-promoted its animation films, theme parks, and toys; it streamlined distribution; and it pioneered television rentals. This matrix of rebroadcast possibilities, product tie-ins, and presold distribution is now called a "platform." The efficacy of a platform was such that the one-time television rental of a Disney film, which cost $10,000 in 1955, rose to $2 million by 1965.

Other studios caught on. The internationally flavored *The Sound of Music*, which cost $10 million, eventually made $100 million in rentals for 20th Century Fox. *The Godfather* demonstrated that once a studio built a platform, sequels could extend its life (Paramount, 1972, 1974, 1990). The most lucrative example was the series of *Star Wars* movies (20th Century Fox, 1977, 1980, 1983, 1999, 2002, 2005). In the 1970s, videotape rentals of films became a major source of profit; both *Jaws* and *Star Wars* earned $100 million in videotape rentals, and some films that failed in theaters made profits in rental stores. DVDs joined the picture in the 1990s.

As this business pattern proved spectacularly profitable, it attracted foreign investment, ranging from Australia's News Corporation (Fox) to Japan's Sony (MGM) and France's Vivendi (Universal). The cross-media marketing of these corporations tied films into their music and television offerings, fast-food promotions, toys, theme parks, beverages, and even autos. Disney and McDonald's struck up a notable partnership.

By 1973, the overseas sales of U.S. filmmakers reached $415 million, exceeding their domestic sales. Governments from France to Japan (which had quietly become the single biggest importer of U.S. films) set up national film boards to direct their own production of not only domestic features (to exemplify national culture) but also international films on the American model. The mecca of funds, given its highly developed production, distribution alliances, and tax breaks, was "Hollywood," which by 2000 included not only U.S. film studios, but German, French, and Japanese banks, as well as individ-

ual financiers, and even oil sheiks. These investors used complex tax shelters to produce major "American" films for worldwide distribution. To repatriate their profits and hedge against currency fluctuations, they also sought out promising foreign films to show in the growing "art" markets of the United States. In 1963, there were already eighty distributors releasing over 800 foreign films a year to 500 art cinemas in the States (Izod, p. 147).

By 2000, the typical U.S. blockbuster film was *X-Men*, based on an American comic book. It starred an Australian (Hugh Jackman), a couple of Britons (Ian McKellen, Patrick Stewart), and some exotic Americans (Halle Berry, Rebecca Romijn-Stamos), and was filmed in Canada. Seven production companies were involved, four of them American. There were eleven distributors, nine of them subsidiaries of Australia's Fox empire that dealt with the French-, Spanish-, Japanese-, German-, Italian-, and Portuguese-language markets. Fifteen U.S. special effects companies were employed, and they outsourced some work to Taiwan, Spain, Mexico, and the Philippines.

The flip side of this hit was *Bend It like Beckham* (2002), which Fox imported because of these same tax laws, quotas, and repatriation rules. Five British firms, four German firms, and one U.S. firm produced this soccer film. Indian/British director Gurinder Chadha had met no major success until Fox put her film on 555 American screens. By May 2003, her $6 million film had grossed over $100 million, not counting resales, video rentals, or the DVDs (in three languages) and audiotapes of the music (available at Amazon.com) by various Sikh and Punjabi artists, who also received royalties.

## Television

As in film, a large native-language market, technical innovation, and innovative financing spurred the export of U.S. television programs. By 1955, there were 36 million sets in the United States and 4.5 million in Britain, but only 300,000 elsewhere in Europe, with a sprinkling in the rest of the world, mainly Japan. When U.S. equipment makers agreed on the NTSC broadcast standard, and the Ampex Corporation in 1956 demonstrated the magnetic tape recording of video and audio, the export of programming became possible. But the initial export market was in equipment, where U.S. executives warned against the Soviet Union "getting a jump" during the Cold War. Equipment manufacturers undertook promotional tours of Mexico, Cuba, and Brazil in the early 1950s, hooking up with local radio and advertising moguls who were politically connected. These nations' television systems developed on the U.S. model of unrestricted advertising. In Mexico City, radio magnate Emilio Azcarraga and publisher Romulo O'Farrill opened a $3 million production facility in the 1950s when there were only 30,000 sets in the country (Smith, p. 58).

Only when foreigners had sets could they watch programming. CBS was first to establish a foreign distribution subsidiary, followed by ABC and NBC. They learned from the film industry's experience, not making series or even pilots themselves. Rather, they licensed programs from independent producers, which they then syndicated at home and abroad. By 1961, CBS Films was selling about 1,500 half-hour episodes in fifty-five countries (Smith, p. 60). *The Lone Ranger* showed in twenty-four countries, and *Lassie* made $4 million in foreign revenue by 1958. Five of the top ten shows in Japan in 1958 were U.S. series or clones. But what happened next in that country was significant. Riding their own technical innovation, such as a superior Toshiba recording system, the Japanese made TV their own. They passed from copying shows to creating their own unique music, cooking, and comedy formats. Although Japan continued to import popular U.S. dramas such as *Dallas* and *Dynasty* (and later *Ally McBeal*), it used the 1964 Tokyo Olympics as a technological springboard, and by the 1970s, Japan exported cartoon *anime* and the "funniest home video" genre to the United States.

The introduction of UHF channels in the 1960s and cable in the 1970s multiplied the outlets for programming, and soon they were on the air at all hours, creating an insatiable demand for shows. The large English-language base of the United States meant that successful programs could easily be syndicated and sold in Britain, Canada, and Australia. If popular, they could be dubbed and sold in other language markets. But as Japan showed, the best bet was drama, preferably with high production values and stars. U.S. producers saw that a sporting event or a music show might sell for rebroadcast once, but that no one rented it in the growing marketplace for TV videos.

Meanwhile public television systems, subsidized by foreign governments, attempted to keep quality high. The BBC in Britain, CBC in Canada, ORTF in France, and ARD and ZDF in Germany continued to produce the kind of programming that had no secondary market. But these public television systems still had to attract advertisers via ratings, and ratings showed that viewers watched foreign drama. For example, the U.S. miniseries *Roots* (1977) and *Holocaust* (1978) were very successful in Europe. The BBC responded with its own drama series, such as *Upstairs, Downstairs,* that competed in the U.S. public market but not the commercial one.

Rogue television stations broadcasting from Monte Carlo or the English Channel also drew viewers from public systems by showing U.S. and other syndicated programs. When cable and satellite TV joined the rogues in the 1980s, the national systems partially capitulated in order to retain some control over their markets. France privatized the first channel (TF1) in 1987, and created a regional network (France3), a cable system (CanalPlus), and a private network (La Cinq, 40 percent owned by Italian Silvio Berlusconi). By 1990, the number of worldwide TV broadcasters had so expanded that the demand for programming was voracious. Televisions flickered in villages of the Andes and Mekong, while Japanese and Mexican homes kept on TVs in the kitchen from dawn until midnight. U.S. companies still controlled the most lucrative sector of worldwide syndication, but Indian musicals, Egyptian soap operas, Mexican *telenovelas,* and English Primier League soccer were also exported.

By 2002, the advent of high-quality, inexpensive videotape cameras and editing equipment, and satellite or UHF broadcasting systems, meant that a primitive TV station could be started in an underdeveloped nation for $500,000. Most African nations had their own broadcasting systems and produced some of their own programs. In Jamaica the most popular drama was the domestically produced *Claffy,* in Zimbabwe *The Mukadota Family,* in Nigeria *Mirror in the Sun.* Even war-ravaged Cambodia had three domestic channels and was producing a popular soap opera in Khmer.

This preference for cultural specificity and the multiplicity of channels posed a problem for U.S. television exporters during the recession of 2000–2003, when the Fox network introduced "reality" programming, a genre that was not highly exportable. In France, Germany, Japan, and elsewhere, domestic "star search" and "roommate" programs trounced imports. In most European nations, native-language programming dominated prime time, but in earlier and later periods syndicated shows of U.S. origin—from *The Muppets* and *The Simpsons* to *Buffy the Vampire Slayer* and *NYPD Blue*—supplied 20–50 percent of content. Culturally specific U.S. hits such as *Seinfeld* did not export as well. After 2000 Latin America used as much Mexican and Spanish programming as American, and Asian and African outlets mixed British and French shows with U.S. imports. Indian, Egyptian, and Mexican soap operas undercut the price of U.S. syndications and exploited a growing diasporic language market. China was a hot new market, with Fox, AOL Time Warner, and other content providers vying to establish footholds; however, the Mandarin/Cantonese language division and licenses restricting the broadcasts to southern development zones near Hong Kong and

**McDonald's in China.** The first McDonald's restaurant opened in Beijing, China, in 1991. There were 500 McDonald's in China by 2002. © *Corbis*

diplomatic enclaves around northern cities limited the access of non-Chinese broadcasters.

## Fast Food and the Franchise System

The United States did not invent fast food. From Britain's fish and chips to Vienna's *kartoflen,* from Mexican tacos to Japanese sushi and *taco-yaki,* fast food has existed for centuries. What McDonald's founder Ray Kroc did was to apply the principles of "Fordism" to fast food. He developed a procedure for every work action, specifying exact times for frying, grilling, and toasting, and he demanded absolutely consistent ingredients, dictating even the amount of water in French fries. As even critics admit, McDonald's lowered the cost and increased the speed, consistency, sanitation, and friendliness of eating fast.

The export of U.S. fast food dates to 1967, when McDonald's opened a franchise in Canada on the U.S. drive-in model. A few years later, a similar franchise failed in Holland, where people did not drive to dine. When Kroc opened a McDonald's in Tokyo in 1971, he created an urban walk-in model so successful that, by 1995, McDonald's had 1,482 franchises in Japan (Watson, p. 3). By 2001, only half of the company's 30,000 stores were in the United States, and more than 50 percent of McDonald's $15 billion revenues and $1.64 billion profits came from overseas.

As striking as the systematization of eating was, the franchise and management systems accompanying it were more important. Franchising was a relatively new idea in the 1960s. By 2003, local franchisees owned 70 percent of McDonald's restaurants worldwide, including thousands of foreign locations. The parent company's revenues derive not so much from hamburgers as from its leasing arrangements and myriad internal taxes on ingredients, promotions, advertising, and sales, and from its huge real estate operations. These practices have been copied, sometimes by foreigners schooled at McDonald's own "Hamburger University," and today such brands as KFC, Pizza Hut, and Taco Bell—all owned by YUM! Brands Inc.—operate similarly. British-owned Burger King (11,330 shops in fifty-eight nations) even runs its own Hamburger University in Kuala Lumpur, Malaysia.

By 2000, McDonald's faced native franchise competition in each of the 121 countries where it operated, including Flunch in France, Yoshinoya in Japan, and Russkoye Bistro in Russia. In response, McDonald's became more locally oriented, serving beer in Germany, pickled dishes in Latvia, vegetable McNuggets in India, espresso and cold pasta in Italy, and teriyaki burgers throughout Asia. It sponsored soccer teams, had music nights, and hosted religious groups. These adaptations, plus its child and family orientation (Playlands, birthday parties, Ronald McDonald), its reliable product, and sanitation, secured McDonald's reputation. Despite a long-running libel case in Britain, anti-globalization protests in France, and Muslim concerns in Asia, it was still at the top of the over twenty multinational fast-food franchisers. In 2002, however, McDonald's lost money for the first time, and the 2,000 shops in Japan were spun off as an autonomous Japanese corporation.

Other U.S. food franchisers copied McDonald's methods. In the 1990s, Starbucks, capitalizing on Americans' discovery of European coffee (its founder admitted deriving his model from Milanese cafés), followed the formula, even to starting its initial overseas coffee shops in Japan. By 2000, smaller American franchisers, from Big Boy to Dairy Queen and Schlotzky's Delicatessen, also franchised overseas. Thus, U.S. logos proliferated, perhaps deceptively. Mister Donut and 7-Eleven in Japan were actually Japanese companies. Many Holiday Inns abroad were British-owned, as were KFC, Pizza Hut, and Taco Bell.

While McDonald's and Starbucks succeeded, other fast-food franchisers failed overseas. Taco Bell bombed in Mexico, Wendy's stumbled in Japan, and bagel shops never got off the ground. The U.S. domestic market had splintered, becoming hypercompetitive and oriented to exotic tastes and novelty. "Foreign" logos, from Au Bon Pain to Yoshinoya, began to appear in the States. McDonald's had to close some shops and diversified into Aroma Café, Boston Market, Chipotle Mexican Grill, Donato's Pizza, and Prêt a Manger. As these names suggest, the "globalization" of fast foods and their franchising had become an American import, as well as an export, by 2003. As in television, the largest players in the world market set their sights on China. McDonald's had 500 shops there at the end of 2002, with plans to open 100 more each year—and, in many locations, Tricon was opening KFCs right across the street from each other—but both faced competition from much cheaper Chinese imitators.

## Leisure Air Travel

Since the 1930s, when they bought rides in open-cockpit biplanes, Americans have flown for fun. Air travel developed into a leisure activity by 1940, long before it was a business necessity. The large domestic market gave U.S. aircraft makers economies of scale, while the government subsidized the passenger and cargo business with airmail contracts. Outside the United States, most airlines were government-owned; these national carriers were slow to recognize that travel to resorts, both at home and abroad, could be as important as capital-to-capital and diplomatic routes. Air France maintained unprofitable routes to Dakar and Abidjan, while American airlines packed planes to Disney World and Universal Studios. Eventually Frenchmen discovered that for the price of a French ticket they could fly to Disney World and then to Martinique on U.S. carriers. The U.S. travel industry offered low fares by seeking bids from multiple suppliers of everything, leasing airplanes through subsidiaries, convincing ambitious cities to build convenient airports, and grouping hotel rooms and rental cars in "packages," often with free theme park admissions.

Through their control of landing rights, however, European nations kept U.S. airlines largely out of their leisure travel markets until the 1960s. Then, as in television, "rogue" operators arose. Icelandic Air, with landing rights in Luxembourg, undercut most established transatlantic fares. First Europeans, then Asians, traveling in the States discovered how much cheaper airfares were, and they looked for similar savings at home. Meanwhile, some European entrepreneurs began to copy the

U.S. "package vacation," often substituting a beach for a theme park. Lauda Air of Austria specialized in vacation charters to Mediterranean beaches. Hong Kong and Bangkok became centers of Asian package tours. In the 1980s, Britain broke from the European Economic Union to negotiate binationally with the United States on landing rights. In the 1990s, Virgin Atlantic (which also marketed music) and Ryan Air established themselves in the British/Irish market as low-cost carriers. After the terrorist attacks on the United States in 2001 and the SARS outbreaks in 2003, international air travel fell off considerably, but domestic leisure travel held up. In the tight market several airlines went bankrupt, but ticket prices stayed low, and several other European nations appeared ready to follow Britain in binational negotiations with the States.

## Theme Parks

Like Starbucks, Disneyland had a European model. Walt Disney always said his inspiration for Disneyland (1955) was Copenhagen's Tivoli Gardens. To the fantasy of his films he added, like Ray Kroc, systematization, cleanliness, and a child/family atmosphere. Disney was slower than Starbucks or McDonald's to expand overseas, but when he did he followed a known path: first Japan (Tokyo Disneyland, 1983), then Europe (Euro-Disney, 1992). As scholars have noted, both foreign parks respond more to foreign conceptions of the United States rather than to Disney's vision. Other theme park companies followed Disney abroad, but less successfully. Roller-coaster-oriented Magic Mountain (1971), part of the Six Flags chain, has six smaller parks overseas. Universal Studios, which first offered back-lot tram tours of its Hollywood sets (1964), expanded to Orlando, Florida (1990), then to Barcelona, Spain (1994), Peking, China (1998), and Japan (2001). Its foreign parks have had mixed success, as the company passed from U.S. management to Japanese (Matsushita) and then French (Vivendi). Like Universal, Warner Brothers opened a theme park in Madrid in 2002 with rides based on its movies.

Foreign competition is stiff in the theme park business. In cultural cousin Britain, the largest parks are Blackpool Pleasure Beach, which offers free admission, and Alton Towers. Fuji Film runs the most successful chain (Fuji-Q High Land) in Japan, where the most popular new parks are urban *onsen*, blending the traditional countryside hot springs experience with shopping, massage, restaurants, and perhaps a ride or two. Meanwhile one foreign company has exported its theme parks to the States: Denmark's Lego opened Legolands in Orlando and California, as well as in Canada and Germany.

**Hideo Nomo.** Fans stopped work and withstood the rain outside of Tokyo's Shibuya station to catch a glimpse of the Los Angeles Dodgers' rookie pitcher Hideo Nomo who became the first Japanese national to appear in the All-Star Game. Played at the Ballpark in Arlington, Texas on Tuesday, 11 July 1995 the live broadcast was seen on Wednesday morning in Japanese time. © *Katsumi Kasahara for AP/Wide World Photos*

## Sports

Even though golf dates to the 1400s, the U.S. Golf Association was not formed until 1895. But golf caught on so quickly that by 1900 New York and Massachusetts each had over 150 clubs. By 1970, golf was a multimillion-dollar-a-year U.S. business, with franchises, celebrity tournaments, TV coverage, clothing and fast-food tie-ins, and auto sponsors. American designers exported "Nicklaus" and "Palmer" branded golf courses to France,

Germany, and Spain, as well as the Far East, where the Japanese embraced the sport with zeal. Before World War II there were only 23 courses in Japan, but by 2000 there were over 2,000 golf courses, with another 1,000 planned. Japanese investors, with considerable attention, bought the famed Pebble Beach course in the United States in 1990.

Japan also embraced baseball, introduced by American missionaries around 1900. However, the Japanese game developed slightly different rules and an entirely different ethos, which focused on teamwork. Baseball also became popular in Mexico and the Caribbean, which had become major sources of professional players for U.S. teams by 2000. The most globalized of American sports, however, was basketball, which the United States allowed its pros to play at the Los Angeles Olympics (1984). This decision stimulated nascent professional leagues from France, China, and Argentina, though basketball remained a minor sport in Europe when compared with soccer, skiing, and auto racing, and in Asia when compared with ping-pong, badminton, and cricket. U.S. football, despite a costly development league in Europe, remained a niche sport, whose failure demonstrates that sports are just as deeply local in nature as other cultural practices.

## Discussion

Englishman William Cobbett, visiting the United States in 1818, described the main male pastimes as drinking and hunting. "You cannot go into hardly [sic] any man's house, without being asked to drink wine, or spirits, even in the morning," he wrote (Cobbett, p. 197). Alexis de Tocqueville (1835–1940) explained that, since democracy tended to have a leveling effect, Americans would probably have to import leisure activities, especially literature.

Only after Victorian prosperity enabled Americans to lavish money on their free time did a critique of U.S. leisure values develop. Thorstein Veblen's *The Theory of the Leisure Class* (1899) focused a Marxian lens on Americans' leisure use of time and goods. Theodore Adorno and the Frankfort Group (1930–1955) were disturbed by the growth of U.S. popular "culture industries," which they said stirred up dissatisfaction and "false needs" for capitalism to supply. Adorno believed that film in particular "dehumanized" viewers and that the "cultural industry" aimed at creating an all-encompassing "social delusion" (Adorno, pp. 63, 271). In his *Prison Notebooks: 1929–37*, Antonio Gramsci added to the Marxian critique a theory of cultural "hegemony." In the 1960s, Herbert Marcuse (*One Dimensional Man*) gave a more libidinally inflected leftist reading of American leisure.

In the 1970s, the term "multinational corporation" became common. Levinson and Barnett/Müller argued that new, large companies such as IBM were more powerful and different than those preceding them. Edward Said's *Orientalism* then gave structure to a theory of postcolonialism that, although it concerned high cultural representations of the Middle East, was widely construed as a demonstration of a broader U.S. "cultural imperialism." Emily Rosenberg argued that this imperialism had rolled on the rails of military and diplomatic power during the two world wars. Wagnleitner seconded Rosenberg's views, using archival data on the U.S. Marshall Plan in Austria, especially pertaining to film and music.

A turning point in the discussion came when John Tomlinson pointed out that the "hegemony" and "false consciousness" arguments of neo-Marxism ignored individual agency and amounted to "paternalist socialism" (Tomlinson). Nonetheless, black-and-white analyses held the stage into the mid-1990s, such as Benjamin Barber's *Jihad vs. McWorld* and George Ritzer's *Expressing America*. Anti-globalization foes rallied around Frederic Jameson and Duke University Press. In 1997, Richard Pells returned to Tomlinson's point and Wagnleitner's methodology, arguing not only that Europeans had never been colonized by U.S. popular culture, but that they had drastically transformed the parts of it they adopted.

Subsequent discussions were more nuanced. James L. Watson's collection on McDonald's in Asia generally showed that fast food had to be adapted before it was adopted. Phillip and Roger Bell's study of *Americanization and Australia* included several positive analyses of U.S. cultural exports. There was even a positive assessment of U.S. film's impact on German cinema (Gemunden). Journalist Thomas L. Friedman took a pro-globalism view, arguing that underdeveloped nations needed the "software" of American institutions as well as the "hardware" of investment. After violent anti-globalization protests in Seattle and Genoa aimed largely at the United States, World Bank, and IMF, Antonio Negri and Michael Hardt presented an abstruse extension of Gramsci's hegemony thesis in *Empire*. Yet to be explored were the reception of U.S. leisure products and activities abroad and "failure studies" (why foreigners will not buy U.S. autos and appliances, or why football has never caught on). Nor have there been studies of the effect of piracy and copyright violation, which are widespread, in undermining the market for U.S. products, or of how U.S. tax shelters and trade laws aided the growth of leisure exports.

*See also:* Commercialization of Children's Play, Commercialization of Leisure, Fast Food, Movies' Impact on Popular Leisure, Tourism, Professionalization of Sport

## BIBLIOGRAPHY

Adams, Judith A. *The American Amusement Park Industry: A History of Technology and Thrills.* Boston: Twayne Publishers, 1991.

Adorno, Theodor W. *The Culture Industry: Selected Essays on Mass Culture.* London: Routledge, 1991.

Balio, Tino. *The American Film Industry*. Madison: University of Wisconsin Press, 1976.

Barber, Benjamin. *Jihad vs. McWorld: How Globalism and Tribalism Are Reshaping the World*. New York: Times Books, 1995.

Barnett, Richard, and Herbert Müller. *Global Reach: The Power of the Multinational Corporations*. New York: Simon and Schuster, 1974.

Bordwell, David, Janet Staiger, and Kristin Thompson. *The Classic Hollywood Cinema*. London: Routledge, 1985.

Cobbett, William. *A Year's Residence in the United States of America*. New York: Clayton and Kingsland, 1818. Reprint, Carbondale: Southern Illinois University Press, 1964.

Friedman, Thomas. *The Lexus and the Olive Tree: Understanding Globalization*. New York: Farrar, Straus, and Giroux, 1999.

Gemunden, Gerd. *Framed Visions: Popular Culture, Americanization, and the Contemporary German and Austrian Imagination*. Ann Arbor: University of Michigan Press, 1998.

Gramsci, Antonio. *Selections from the Prison Notebooks*. London: Lawrence and Wishart, 1971.

Guback, Thomas H. *The International Film Industry*. Bloomington: Indiana University Press, 1969.

Hendry, Joy. *The Orient Strikes Back: A Global View of Cultural Display*. New York: Berg, 2000.

Huntington, Samuel P. *The Clash of Civilizations and the Remaking of World Order*. New York: Simon and Schuster, 1996.

Izod, John. *Hollywood and the Box Office, 1895–1986*. London: Macmillan, 1988.

Jameson, Fredric. "Postmodernism, or the Cultural Logic of Late Capitalism." *New Left Review* 146 (1984): 53–93.

Jameson, Fredric, and Masao Miyoshi, eds. *The Cultures of Globalization*. Durham, N.C.: Duke University Press, 1998.

MacCannell, Dean. *The Tourist: A New Theory of the Leisure Class*. Berkeley: University of California Press, 1999.

Marling, Karal Ann. *Designing Disney's Theme Parks: The Architecture of Reassurance*. New York: Flammarion, 1997.

Negri, Toni, and Michael Hardt. *Empire*. Cambridge, Mass.: Harvard University Press, 2001.

Pells, Richard. *Not like Us: How Europeans Have Loved, Hated, and Transformed American Culture Since World War II*. New York: Basic Books, 1998.

Raz, Aviad E. *Riding the Black Ship: Japan and Tokyo Disneyland*. Cambridge, Mass.: Harvard University Press, 1999.

Ritzer, George. *Expressing America: A Critique of the Global Credit Card Society*. Thousand Oaks, Calif.: Pine Forge Press, 1995.

Rosenberg, Emily. *Spreading the American Dream: American Economic and Cultural Expansion, 1890–1945*. New York: Hill and Wang, 1982.

Said, Edward. *Orientalism*. New York: Random House, 1978.

Sklar, Robert. *Movie-Made America*. London: Chappell, 1978.

Smith, Anthony. *Television: An International History*. London: Oxford University Press, 1995.

Thompson, Kristin. *Exporting Entertainment*. London: British Film Institute, 1985.

Tocqueville, Alexis de. *Democracy in America*. 1835. Reprint, Garden City, N.Y.: Doubleday and Company, 1969. Translated by George Lawrence.

Tomlinson, John. *Cultural Imperialism*. Baltimore: Johns Hopkins University Press, 1991.

Wagnleitner, Reinhold. *Coca-Colonization and the Cold War*. Translated by Diana M. Wolf. Chapel Hill: University of North Carolina Press, 1994.

Watson, James, ed. *Golden Arches East: McDonald's in East Asia*. Stanford, Calif.: Stanford University Press, 1997.

Watts, Steven. *The Magic Kingdom: Walt Disney and the American Way of Life*. New York: Houghton Mifflin, 1997.

Wilson, Ron, and Wimal Dissanayake, eds. *Global/Local*. Durham, N.C.: Duke University Press, 1996.

*William Marling*

# GOLF

Golf is one of the most popular outdoor sports in the world. It can be enjoyed from childhood to old age by both genders, and offers every kind of competition, in individual or team format: against other golfers, against personal or external records or standards—especially the standard score of "par" for each hole—and even against the elements, as weather can often affect performance. The handicap system of scoring allows players of differing abilities to enjoy more equitable competition, also. The sport is played in aesthetic, parklike surroundings that can accommodate large numbers of spectators, and is a healthy pastime around which a social etiquette involving a high degree of expected sportsmanship has evolved. Given the propensity of Americans to embrace sport, it is not surprising that the United States has attained a unique status in this challenging activity.

## Origins and Early History

The origins of golf have been traced back to ancient Egypt, Imperial Rome, and later medieval European games such as *jeu de mail* and *kolven*, among others. However, the Scots deserve credit for the invention of modern golf, through the formation of the first clubs, codification, and export to other lands, during the eighteenth and nineteenth centuries. The Royal and Ancient Golf Club of St. Andrews, established in 1754, was the sole arbiter of the sport, until this responsibility was later shared with the United States Golf Association (USGA). In most countries where golf took root, emigrant Scots planted the seeds, and the United States was no exception.

## American Origins

The origins of golf on the North American continent are obscure, with perhaps the earliest participation being "in days lang syne" at distant posts of the Hudson's Bay Company (chartered in 1670) in British North America (now Canada). A notice in the *Charleston City Gazette* (13 October 1795) provides definite evidence of a South Carolina Golf Club in existence there before 1800; other references indicate golf clubs in Georgia, also, between 1811 and 1818, although apparently none survived. American golf began its permanent existence with John Reid, "the Scotsman who re-introduced golf to the United States," in 1888, when Reid and some friends formed the St. Andrews Golf Club of Yonkers, New York, using a six-hole layout. Other enthusiasts founded the Shinnecock Golf Club on Long Island, the first incorporated club in the United States. Charles Blair Macdonald, educated in Scotland, designed and built the first eighteen-hole course in the United States for the Chicago Golf Club, formed in 1893. These founders represented a wealthy elite, with plenty of leisure time—reflected in the memberships by the inclusion of financial and industrial leaders and the professional classes. They were pioneers of the country club, an institution that later became even more significant in the development of American golf.

By 1894, several clubs existed, but delegates from only five clubs formed the USGA in December of that year. The USGA held its first amateur championship in 1895 at Newport, Rhode Island, and its first open championship on the same course the following day. For teaching purposes, golf and country clubs employed professionals, who could compete with amateurs in open tournaments and were heavily favored. Such championships "contributed mightily to the spread of golfing fever" (Betts, p .197), which soon gripped the American public. Illustrating the remarkable early popularity and progress of the American golf range, there were between 472 and 743 clubs by 1917, apparently one-fifth of them daily-fee courses. By then the United States had become a major golfing nation of nearly 2 million golfers, and women were a significant part of the development.

## The Female Pioneers

At a time when Victorian taboos restricted female participation in most sports, golf's relatively genteel character and conservative dress allowed women to compete at any early stage, although they were grudgingly extended

**Mildred "Babe" Didrikson Zaharias.** Voted the most outstanding woman athlete of the century by the Associated Press in 1950, "Babe" Didrikson Zaharias (1914–1956) won eighty-two tournaments including the British Ladies Amateur Championship in 1947. She also competed in the PGA's 1945 Los Angeles Open and won three track and field gold medals in the 1932 Summer Olympics. © *AP/Wide World Photos*

the privilege at certain times only. The first national tournament for American women was also held in 1895, although only thirteen ladies took part. Teenager Beatrix Hoyt set a high standard by winning three years running from 1896, an example followed by other consistent winners. Dorothy Campbell, between 1909 and 1911, won national championships in both Britain and the United States, demonstrating that golf competition had become an international event for all by this time. These pioneers paved the way for other female champions during the first half of the century, such as Patty Berg (1918– ), Betty Jameson, Louise Suggs (1923– ), and Olympic athlete and all-round sportswoman Mildred ("Babe") Didrikson Zaharias (1914–1956). When the Ladies Professional Golf Association (LPGA) was incorporated in 1950, these four players were the first ones to be inducted into its Hall of Fame a year later.

## The Ouimet Factor

One individual who influenced early American golf in a unique way was Francis Ouimet. In 1913, this twenty-year-old defeated two of Britain's greatest golfers, Harry Vardon and Ted Ray, in a playoff at the U.S. Open, at Brookline, Massachusetts. It was the first such victory by an American and the first time an amateur had won this prestigious event. A former caddy from a modest background, Ouimet was "golf's version of the Horatio Alger success story" (Rader, p. 227). His victory was a turning point, and the balance now shifted toward American dominance of the sport for most of the remaining century. Ouimet went on to captain the U.S. team six times in the Walker Cup, a contest between American and British amateur golfers begun in 1922, in which the United States won twenty-nine of the first thirty-one matches. Vardon was one of "the "Great Triumvirate" (the others being British golfers J. Braid and J. H. Taylor), and soon after Ouimet's triumph, three American golfers could claim to be their immediate successors.

### An American Triumvirate: Walter, Bobby, and Gene

The winner of the 1914 U.S. Open was an American professional, the flamboyant Walter Hagen (1892–1969), who did much to break down social barriers in golf with his unconventional behavior. Among other victories, this showman went on to win four British Opens, two U.S. Opens, and five U.S. Professional Golfers' Association (USPGA) championships (begun in 1916). Hagen's greatest rival was the intellectual amateur Bobby Jones (1902–1971), who, in a brief eight-year career, also enjoyed great success. In 1930, Jones achieved the "grand slam," winning the U.S. Amateur and Open titles alongside the two British equivalents in the same year, a feat never duplicated. (Four professional tournaments—"majors"—now constitute the modern grand slam: the U.S. and British Opens, the U.S. PGA championship, and the Masters tournament, which is always held at Augusta National and was founded by Jones himself in 1934.) Gene Sarazen (1902–1999) won seven majors; he is remembered also for his invention of the sand wedge, the club that revolutionized the technique of playing bunker shots.

### Innovations in Equipment

Sarazen's invention was part of the constant quest for superior performance through better equipment. Thus, steel shafts replaced wooden ones early in the twentieth century, later joined by graphite and other composite materials. Wooden or iron clubheads also gave way to steel, until the more recent use of larger titanium versions, and other products of technological wizardry. The unreliable feathery golf ball, made with boiled feathers stuffed inside a leather casing, was replaced in the middle of the nineteenth century by the much cheaper gutta-percha ball. The introduction of a rubber-cored ball around the turn of the century was the invention of an American dentist, Dr. Coburn Haskell, and "brought about an even greater interest in the game" (Pinner, p. 26). Since then the modern game has been inundated by the manufacture of differently constructed balls made of various materials, all of them promising to increase accuracy and/or distance for millions of golfers worldwide, as companies attempt to cater to an almost insatiable demand for golf paraphernalia.

### The Second American Triumvirate

Better equipment contributed to lower scores in the tournaments of the 1930s, when the number of golf and country clubs became lower, too, as about one-third of them folded due to the Great Depression. Still, this period saw the emergence of three American golfers who arguably would appear on any short list of the greatest of all time: Ben Hogan (1913–1997), Byron Nelson (1912– ), and Sam Snead (1912–2002).

### Golf for All: Country Clubs and Public Links

Cheaper equipment and American heroes of both genders, together with "automobility," suburbanization, and the Gospel of Relaxation (Cross, pp. 184–196), served toward making golf one of the most popular outdoor recreations to date, but no innovation accomplished this more than the simultaneous evolution of the country club and the municipal golf course.

The first country club was founded at Brookline in 1882, but its activities did not include golf until 1893, following the example set by Reid and others elsewhere. Such clubs soon became the rage, with golf their most popular offering. The club movement received further impetus from Ouimet's triumph at Brookline, and carried these social institutions "into new regions and dotted the land with fairways and putting greens from Puget Sound to Palm Beach" (Krout, p. 295). By 1929, the number of country clubs was estimated at 4,500, the highest ever attained, until the Depression and World War II caused a significant decrease. They recovered during the 1950s and were estimated to be around 3,300 by 1962, with a membership of 1.7 million. Golf was apparently the main reason for joining, others being given as status and business contacts. By this time, too, country clubs generally fell into one of six categories—top status, middle class, minority, community, proprietary, and industrial—making membership widely available.

For urban-dwelling prospective golfers who did not wish to join "the country club set," an alternative arose in the form of "public links," beginning in 1895 when a group of New York golfers asked the Parks Commission to provide links in Van Cortland Park, which became the first municipal course in the country. (In 1895, also, the first American golf book, *Golf in America: A Practical Manual,* by James P. Lee, was published in New York.) Other public courses soon followed in Boston, Buffalo, Chicago, Indianapolis, and elsewhere, including Toledo, where the first municipal links championships were held in 1922, and President Harding presented a cup for intercity competitions a year later. By 1929, there were over 300 municipal courses in the United States.

Although the number of country clubs dropped drastically during the Depression—some becoming bankrupt, others adapting as daily-fee courses to survive—the number of municipal courses actually increased to about 700, many of them provided under Public Works programs. Of about 5,200 golf courses nationwide in 1941, some 2,000 were either municipal or privately owned daily-fee courses. By the dawn of the television age, then, Americans from all walks of life enjoyed more opportunities for golf as a popular recreation than ever before.

## The Media and the Messengers

Initially, modern sporting exploits were broadcast by radio and depicted in black-and-white film, but the attractions of golf became manifest through the advent of television in the 1950s. Americans viewed President Eisenhower's enthusiastic participation in golf, accompanied by a host of celebrities (comedian Bob Hope was one famous example) and joined by large commercial concerns in the sponsorship of new tournaments. Reception was later enhanced by the use of color and satellite technology so that fans could enjoy viewing sports events in their homes from virtually anywhere.

The new medium was complemented in particular by one charismatic American golfer whose heyday coincided with its arrival: Arnold Palmer (1929– ). Aside from winning seven majors, Palmer's swashbuckling style of play won him a legion of followers, soon dubbed "Arnie's Army." Palmer's greatest rival was fellow American Jack Nicklaus (1940– ), who had an unsurpassed record of winning eighteen professional majors and was honored by *Golf* magazine (September 1988) as the "Player of the Century." The depth of American talent during the first three decades of the television age also included such champions as Nancy Lopez (1957– ), Lee Trevino (1939– ), Tom Watson (1949– ), and Kathy Whitworth (1939– ). However, the first triumvirate of television, broadcast as the "Big Three of Golf," consisted of Palmer, Nicklaus, and South African Gary Player (1935– ), the last providing the best individual example of the rising foreign challenge to American golfing supremacy.

## Global Golf

As the United States had challenged British supremacy at the beginning of the twentieth century, so, too, has the rest of the world challenged American dominance in golf in the late nineteenth and early twenty-first centuries. Prior to 1978, Player was the only foreigner to win the Masters; by 2003, it had been won thirteen times by eight other non-Americans. Their names, and others, also appeared regularly in the World's Top Ten players' ranking. International players played on the most lucrative American tours, including the Champions Tour (launched in 1981 as the "Senior Tour" and renamed in 2002), while American golfers can be found competing on the European Tour, and others.

The most prestigious and now fiercely contested team competition is the Ryder Cup, a biennial match begun in 1927 and initially between professional golfers of the United States and Great Britain and Northern Ireland. However, the contests became so one-sided in the Americans' favor that in 1977 it was decided to include European players; since 1979, each side has claimed six victories. A similar event begun in 1994 is the President's Cup, between the U.S. PGA Tour and an international team named the Rest of the World (except Europe). Here the United States won three of the first five matches, against a loss and a controversial tie in 2003. Close competition ensues in other team competitions as well, such as the aforementioned Walker Cup, and in the Solheim Cup (the women's equivalent to the Ryder Cup, begun in 1990).

## Eldrick "Tiger" Woods

In men's golf, in the early 2000s, American Tiger Woods threatened to reign supreme in the number-one spot for a record span of time and had the potential to eclipse Nicklaus's records and justify "the greatest golfer ever" label that many were already using to describe him. Woods inspired an international generation of young and fearless long-hitting challengers, and, as a black American role model, Woods was credited with encouraging more participation in golf by disadvantaged youth from minority ethnic backgrounds (see sidebar).

## From Sport to Lifestyle

American golf is not immune to problems. Diplomacy is constantly necessary in relations between tours, players,

## A Grand (Tiger) Slam

Until the 1930s, amateur golf still produced players capable of challenging the professionals. At that time, the four championships that were regarded as the "majors" were the U.S. Open, the British Open, the U.S. Amateur, and the British Amateur. In 1930, the legendary Bobby Jones completed what became known as the "Grand Slam" when he won all four of those tournaments in the same year-the first man to do so.

With the introduction of The Masters tournament at Augusta National Golf Club in 1934, the four tournaments that made up the majors-and hence, the Grand Slam-changed. In place of the two national amateur championships, The Masters and the PGA Championship became part of the four tournaments that comprised the slam. In the years that followed, the golfing world waited and wondered if any golfer would ever equal Jones's feat and complete a modern Grand Slam. As of 2004, no one had been equal to the task.

In fact, only five golfers (four of them American, along with South African Gary Player) even completed what is known as the "career Grand Slam"-winning all four major tournaments over the course of their golfing career. Ben Hogan, Jack Nicklaus, Gary Player, Gene Sarazen, and Tiger Woods all won the four modern majors at some point in their careers-but never in the same calendar year. Other golfers came close to the career slam but came up one short, among them Arnold Palmer and Tom Watson.

Before Tiger Woods began to rewrite the record books, Ben Hogan came the closest to winning the Slam. In fact, he was actually treated to a victory parade in New York after he won the British Open in 1953, which followed on the heels of his victories in the U.S. Open and The Masters ear-

lier in that year. However, injuries from a 1949 car accident kept Hogan from competing in the PGA Championship, so he never had the chance to complete the slam.

That leaves Woods. The wildly popular international star had already won seven majors by 2004. Woods won his first major, The Masters, in 1997 in a manner that proclaimed his potential for greatness. His four-round total of 270 broke the Augusta record, as did his margin of victory (twelve strokes). At the age of twenty-one, he was the youngest Masters champion ever. With wins in six more majors between 1998 and 2002 (including two more Masters) there was little doubt that he was the golfer with the best chance to pull off a Grand Slam Besides, Woods has already completed a Grand Slam of sorts-or at least he completed what has since become known as "the Tiger Slam."

The "Tiger Slam" unfolded in 2000 and 2001. In 2000, Woods won the U.S. Open, the British Open, and the PGA Championship, which were the final three majors of the year. Only a loss in The Masters in April kept him from the true slam. However, in 2001, Woods took care of that oversight when he opened the season with his second Masters title. With that win, he became the first man to hold all four majors titles at the same time. While purists were right to say that this wasn't a true Grand Slam, since all four wins were not in the same calendar year, Woods's feat was nonetheless a remarkable accomplishment.

For only the second time in his career, Wood failed to win a major in 2003 (although he was Player of the Year for the fifth straight year), and critics claimed his best golf was behind him. His supporters quickly dismissed such talk as ludicrous and in fact, many golf analysts did feel that Woods was still the golfer with the best chance to one day complete a true Grand Slam.

and sponsors, especially where huge sums of money are involved (much of which is impressively donated to charities). The rules of golf elicit constant monitoring in a time of rapid technological change, and environmental concerns have subjected golf course maintenance and design to increasing scrutiny and legislation. Women's concerns revolve mainly around seeking more equitable purses for LPGA tournaments and ending discrimination by golf clubs with only male memberships (such as Augusta National). Yet the overall picture is one of optimism

and progress. More than 27 million Americans are embracing golf as never before. Golf retail shops can be found at nearly every major airport. It is a staple of weekend television, and even has a cable channel devoted to it twenty-four hours a day: "Golf is a leitmotif for our 50 States, the de facto language of business, the second sport of professional athletes, and the preferred pastime of celebrities" (Yun, pp. 106–120).

Golf courses—most of them lined with homes— were being built faster than Americans could use them,

**Tiger Woods.** Caught up in the excitement of competing in his first tournament as a professional in 1996, Tiger Woods flashes an exuberant smile. Woods only finished sixtieth in the Greater Milwaukee Open, but within a year, he had become the best player in the game and a huge marketing draw. © *AP/Wide World Photos*

and there was a $75 billion boom in golf developments after the early 1990s. Perhaps the comprehensive status of American golf can best be summed up in a nutshell by the significant statement that golf "crossed the line from sport to lifestyle" (McCallen, p. 147).

*See also:* Professionalization of Sport, Suburbanization of Leisure, Tourism

**BIBLIOGRAPHY**

Alliss, Peter, ed. *Golf, a Way of Life: An Illustrated History of Golf.* London: Cresset Press, 1989.

Arlott, John, ed. *The Oxford Companion to Sports and Games.* London: Oxford University Press, 1975.

Baker, William J. *Sports in the Western World.* Totowa, N.J.: Rowman and Littlefield, 1982.

Betts, John Rickards. *America's Sporting Heritage, 1850–1950.* Reading, Mass.: Addison-Wesley Publishing Company, 1974.

Boyle, Robert H. *Sport: Mirror of American Life.* Boston: Little, Brown and Company, 1963.

Campbell, Malcolm. *The New Encyclopedia of Golf.* London: Dorling Kindersley, 2001.

Cross. Gary. *A Social History of Leisure since 1600.* State College, Pa.: Venture Publishing, 1990.

Henderson, Robert W. *Ball, Bat, and Bishop.* New York: Rockport Press, 1947.

Krout, John Allen. *Annals of American Sport.* New York: United States Publishers Association, 1929.

McCallen, Brian. "Second Home Living." *Golf* (November 2002): 146–157.

Morrison, Ian. *The Hamlyn Encyclopedia of Golf.* Twickenham, Eng.: Hamlyn Publishing, 1986.

Pinner, John. *The History of Golf.* New York: Gallery Books, 1988.

"Player of the Century." *Golf* (September 1988): 44–78.

Rader, Benjamin G. *American Sports: From the Age of Folk Games to the Age of Spectators.* Englewood Cliffs, N.J.: Prentice Hall, 1983.

Stirk, David. *Golf: The History of an Obsession.* Oxford: Phaidon Press Limited, 1987.

Williams, Michael. *The Official History of The Ryder Cup, 1927–1989.* London: Stanley Paul, 1989.

Yun, Hunki. "Who You Are: Report on the American Golfer." *Golf* (September 2002): 106–120.

*Gerald Redmond*

# GRANGE MOVEMENT

**See** *Agricultural Fairs*

# GRAPHIC ARTS

Graphic arts is a subcategory of visual arts and includes traditional arts mediums such as drawing, painting, and printmaking, as well as innovative mediums such as photography and computer generated art. Graphic arts work requires creativity and is meant to be visually pleasing. In order to produce interesting work, one must use imagination and have an understanding of quality design. From a professional perspective, graphics and photographic images are used to replace written text in advertisements so that readers and viewers will find the work more interesting and inspiring.

People engage in the production and consumption of graphic arts in a variety of ways. In the early 1960s, Polaroid developed an instant color film camera, while Kodak released the Instamatic camera. These innovative cameras allowed many people to enjoy recreational photography as a hobby without a major investment. The Boys and Girls Clubs of America used these types of cameras to begin their National Photography Program for children. In the early twenty-first century, many colleges and universities offered advanced instruction in graphic arts, and most people are typically exposed to graphic arts in educational settings from kindergarten to high school. In 1997, the National Endowment of the Arts (NEA) suggested that a strong correlation exists between children who received arts education and those who engaged in art creation as adults.

Typically, a strong economy can increase the value of art within a society. For example, in the mid-1990s the economy helped to restore the importance of visual arts in educational settings. Typically philanthropic efforts provide more incentives and grant opportunities when the economy is strong. By the late 1990s, however, a slumping economy had reduced the amount of national and state funding for educational instruction. In the late 1980s and the early 1990s more than 15 percent of all elementary schools offered no visual art classes and 24 percent of the schools that did offer them employed teachers who had no formal training or education in the arts. Therefore, almost 40 percent of students nationally received inadequate art instruction.

## Graphic Arts Supporters

Most communities provide various methods to support graphic art activities. Private companies provide printed media, financial support, and instruction for many graphic art endeavors. This support allows entire communities to view art and to acquire a taste for numerous art mediums. Some private art supply and equipment stores have expanded their services to include workshops and skill classes to increase their overall profits while attracting well-known instructors to teach. Nonprofit organizations and governmental recreation departments offer educational instruction, workshop opportunities, art festivals, and performance opportunities.

Many graphic art activities are very equipment-intensive or media-specific. To offset cost in these activities, some nonprofit art cooperatives and art guilds have begun purchasing costly equipment and providing studio space for artists who are financially constrained. This strategy has provided more opportunities for graphic artists while at the same time increasing the number of art participants. Courses, workshops, or seminars in the visual arts are taught by various skilled instructors, including educators, professional artists, and laypeople. Some workshops last only one day, and some courses can be extended over a six-month period. Cost for the various visual art activities depends on the skill level of both the instructors and the participants, the type of facility being used, and the art medium employed.

## Graphic Arts Participants

According to the NEA1997 Survey of Public Participation in the Arts report, the highest rates of personal participation in graphic arts were for the activities of photography (17 percent) and painting or drawing (16 percent).

The 2002 Annual Craft and Hobby report suggests the typical graphic arts participant is more likely to be a female who is married with children, has more education, and earns a higher income than non-art participants. These women range from ages thirty-five to fifty-five and are employed on a part-time basis. Three categories exist to describe their various annual art expenditures: heavy users who spend more than $500, medium users who spend $70 to $500, and light users who spend less than $70. Heavy users who spend more than $1,200 annually, and make up almost 25 percent of the art participants, account for almost 77 percent of retail sales. Medium users account for 21 percent, and light users account for 2 percent of retail sales.

Graphic art participation levels range from beginner to advanced. Getting started in an art class or workshop can be intimidating, especially if a person lacks skills or access to an art facility. Each level requires different motivations, skills, and equipment. For example, amateur photographers may be interested in increasing their understanding of photography, enhancing their ability to operate a camera, and learning where to rent camera equipment. Advanced photographers, however, may be motivated by a specific photography technique, such as film development. Because of their involvement, they may have invested thousands of dollars worth of supplies, including camera lenses, lighting equipment, and dark room materials. Though skill levels differ for both types of photographers, the outcome or motivation may be the same increased skill level and improved outcome or personal satisfaction.

### Impacts on Visual Art Participants

Art programs benefit a wide range of age groups, from children to senior citizens. Recreational art program research suggests that regardless of how a person participates in graphic arts, he or she benefits from the experience. For example, some benefits for the participants mat be enhanced creativity, self-confidence, aesthetic appreciation, socialization, and personal enjoyment, all the while reducing stress and tension. When a person enjoys an art experience, it enhances one's emotional and mental development and expands one's thoughts about culture. In short, it makes individuals more socially conscious of who one is in society, which positively affects the community by enriching one's purpose in life.

Artistic expression programs also instill ownership and empowerment for contemporary society's youth by allowing them to voice their personal beliefs. At the same, these programs may also enhance their communication and socialization skills, opening up a variety of opportunities for them in other aspects of life. Art activities demonstrate that the challenge of representing or reflecting life through art is a rewarding and valuable experience that is unmatched by other media.

*See also:* Leisure Education; Photography; Woodworking

### BIBLIOGRAPHY

Bergonzi, L., and J. Smith. "Effects of Arts Education on Participant in the Arts. (Research Division Report No. 36)." Santa Ana, Calif.: Seven Locks Press, 1997.

Boys and Girls Club of America. "Programs: The Arts." Available from http://www.bgca.org

Carey, N., M. Sikes, R. Foy, J. Carpenter. *Arts Education in Public and Secondary Schools.* National Center for Educational Statistics, NCES 95–082. Washington, D.C.: Department of Education, 1995.

Chambers, Karen S. *Artist's Resource: The Watson-Guptill Guide to Academic Programs, Artists' Colonies and Artist-in-Residence Programs, Conferences, Workshops.* New York: Watson-Guptill Publications, 2000.

Hesemann, T. *National Craft and Hobby Consumer Usage and Purchase Study, Executive Summary.* Elmwood, N. J.: Hobby Industry Association, 2002.

Photo.net. Home page at from http://www.photo.net/

Randall, P. *Art Works: Prevention Programs for Youth and Communities.* National Endowment of the Arts. Washington, D.C., 1997.

Riley, K. "Research Update: Recreational Art Programming." *Parks and Recreation* 6 (2000): 26–33.

"What Every Young American Should Know and Be Able to Do in the Arts." *The National Standards for Arts Education.* Available from http://www.menc.org/publication/

*Kevin Riley*

# GRAPHIC NOVELS

**See** *Comic Book Reading; Comic Magazines*

# GYMNASTICS

German immigrants to the United States in the middle years of the nineteenth century brought their systems of physical training with them. The German system was based on the development by Frederich Jahn of apparatus upon which skills of strength and agility were performed, often in a competitive setting. These apparatus have developed, with remarkably little change, into the modern events of present Olympic gymnastics as floor exercise, pommel horse, rings, vaulting, parallel bars, and horizontal bar. Together they were thought to compose a program of physical training that strengthens and conditions the total body.

Scandinavian immigrants, on the other hand, utilized group calisthenics, tumbling, vaulting, and some specialized suspended beams. Their program was much less strength oriented and emphasized agility and flexibility in a cooperative rather than a competitive setting.

Ethnic immigrants practicing both systems established social clubs in the new country in which many aspects of the mother culture could be practiced, preserved, and passed on to the next generation. Their physical culture was thus preserved along with artistic, expressive, and social activities. The Germans called these social clubs "turnvereins," but they went by different names depending on the importing ethnic group.

## The Hegemony of German "Artistic Gymnastics"

In the late 1800s, educators in the United States began to see the value of including physical activities in the school educational program. Given the lack of trained physical training specialists among American educators, they turned to those who had been involved in the training of physical activities. The German turners met this need. They had established, early in their presence in this country, training schools for the development of gymnastic leaders in their turnvereins. These early physical educators brought with them the primary activity of the turner system—gymnastics—and thereby gymnastics got an early foothold in the schools. Some schools, perceiving an inappropriateness of heavy apparatus for girls, sought to institute the Scandinavian system into their programs for females.

## Gymnastics in the Schools (1875–1910)

Gymnastics was the prevailing mode of physical education in secondary schools during the last quarter of the nineteenth century. However, it was not popular with many students because of its heavy emphasis on discipline and obedience, and it was subject to criticism by many educators who sought a more "natural" form of physical activity. In 1891, James Naismith, at the International YMCA Training School (now Springfield College), introduced a game activity designed to appeal to

students. This game—basketball—caught on rapidly and was spread through the schools and YMCAs in which graduates of the school were employed. Between 1900 and 1910, the growing "games movement" essentially displaced gymnastics as the primary activity of physical education.

## The Amateur Athletic Union and the Olympic Games

Outside the schools, competitive physical activities were catching on in a wide array of sports and games. Clubs sponsoring these activities competed against one another and soon began bringing in skilled performers to ensure victory and the resulting prestige. The Amateur Athletic Union (AAU) was formed to cope with this problem. They registered all known "amateur" athletes and limited competitions to people on that list. People who had played for money or who were not known in the area were excluded. The AAU became a national force as they authorized state affiliates.

Concurrently, the Olympic movement was generating in Europe. Its philosophy called for sport to be a developmental activity for male youth, and, consequently, older or "professionalized" persons were to be excluded. The AAU became instrumental in certifying to the Olympic organizers the "amateur" status of American athletes and thereby became recognized as the "governing body" for gymnastics and many other American sports in the eyes of the International Olympic Committee and the international sports federations.

## Regression to the Clubs (1914–1945)

World War I (1914–1918) led to a rejection of things not seen as "American." This rejection, added to the setback from the "games movement," sounded the death knell for gymnastics until after the World War II (1941–1945). Gymnastics did not actually die, but it retreated into the turnvereins and other ethnic clubs that kept many of their activities quiet inside the walls of the club. However, except for the actual war years, they continued to conduct national championships for their members.

## The "Athletics Expansion" and the "Fitness Movement"

After World War II, many veterans went to colleges and became teachers, many of whom were physical educators. Their military experiences had instilled in them a high value for sports for fitness and personal growth. Many of them endorsed the expansion of athletics programs beyond the traditional sports of football, basketball, and baseball. In the early 1950s, concern rose about the lack of physical fitness among American youth as a result of the report by H. Kraus and R. Hirschland that showed that American boys were less "fit" than their European counterparts. A strong emphasis on physical fitness was added to sports skill training in physical education and athletics programs were further expanded toward an ideal of "a sport for every boy." Gymnastics prospered from this movement. It was added as part of many physical education programs and boys' gymnastics competitive teams were established in many areas across the country followed rapidly by the proliferation of college men's teams.

## Conflict Between the Bureaucracies

While many gymnasts got their start in clubs and high schools, they experienced their growth to maturity as athletes on college teams. Many, if not most, Olympic gymnasts during the 1950s and 1960s were members of college teams whose competition was regulated by the National Collegiate Athletic Association (NCAA). This recognized status of the NCAA promoted tension between the college coaches and the administrators of the AAU. The AAU was reluctant to share decision making with the college coaches and even more so to share positions as coaches and managers of the Olympic teams. College coaches banded together with others who were dissatisfied with the tight hold of the AAU and formed the United States Gymnastic Federation (USGF), which then conducted its own national championships. When the USGF athletes sought to compete in the Olympic qualifying meet, AAU officials informed them that they were not eligible for consideration for the Olympic team. Threats of lawsuits and mutual boycotts followed as the leaders fought for control. In the end, the International Gymnastics Federation (FIG)—the international governing body—resolved the issue by shifting its recognition from the AAU to the USGF.

## Title IX and the Expansion of Women's Sports

In the late 1950s and early 1960s, gymnastics for girls changed rapidly. Heretofore, girls, when they did compete, participated on the same or slightly modified apparatus as boys and experienced little public recognition. Dance and tumbling began to dominate floor exercise, springboards added excitement to vaulting, and, most of all, the uneven bars were widened and stabilized so that side swinging was possible, thus enabling girls to perform

**Mary Lou Retton.** At the 1984 Summer Olympics in Los Angeles, Mary Lou Retton (1968- ) captured five medals while on Team USA including gold for the all-round gymnastics competition. © *AP/Wide World Photos*

movements of great skill and agility, much like men on the horizontal bar. Female gymnasts had arrived as athletes.

In the 1960s, pressure mounted to provide greater opportunities for girls in sport. The performances of American women, seen in the Olympic Games for the first time on television, were poor in comparison to women from other countries. Supporters of women's sport began to press for greater opportunity for girls and women. The newly formed Association for Intercollegiate Athletics for Women (AIAW) made efforts to overcome the philosophical opposition by women's physical education groups to adopting the "male model" of sport. Slowly women's teams were established in many sports (including gymnastics) at both high school and college level.

In 1972, Congress passed and the president signed Title IX of the Educational Amendments Act. This act stated that individuals could not be denied any educational opportunity on the basis of their sex. The act put great pressure on schools and colleges to provide equal opportunity in sport. Women's teams were "adopted" or established by athletic departments, and the NCAA began to sponsor championships, which drew women away from the existing AIAW championships because the NCAA sponsored the meets on the same day as the AIAW meets and subsidized the teams' expenses. Naturally, the NCAA soon became the dominant administrative group for women's college athletics.

## The Development of Private Gymnastics Clubs

By the late 1970s, gymnastics was thriving at both the high school and the college level. However, success had its problems. The high school limitation on the length of the training season and the lack of technical expertise on the part of many high school coaches led to the formation of many private gymnastics clubs led by experienced college gymnasts who could not find teaching positions or who chose not to join high school programs. These clubs offered the opportunity for year-round training under the guidance of an experienced coach. As the most committed athletes chose the private clubs, the clubs became the preferred recruiting ground for college coaches, and high school gymnastics became teams for the second level of talent.

## The "Economic Crunch" and the Constriction of School Gymnastics

From the beginning, the expansion of athletics programs for both men and women was fraught with financial problems. At first, added teams ran on a shoestring. Hand-me-down uniforms and transportation in private cars were the norm. In colleges, junior varsity and freshman teams in the traditional men's sports were frequently discontinued to shift funds to the new programs. Through it all, athletics administrators resisted attempts to cut back on the costs of the traditional high-visibility teams. For those few schools that had considerable income from "cash cow" sports, women's and men's nonrevenue sports flourished. However, those schools were the exception. For most schools, as the costs of achieving success in high-visibility sports rose, as the law demanded equal expenditures for women's sports, and as nonrevenue sports sought to emulate the "sport style" of the major sports, the numbers did not add up. Administrators were unable to meet the expanding athletics budgets without diverting monies from academic programs. Protests from faculties grew, and athletic directors responded by reducing the scope of the programs. Since they saw too much at stake in high-visibility men's sports to cut those, and since they were

under legal mandate to provide equity for women, they saw few cost-cutting options other than the elimination of men's and, in some cases women's, nonrevenue sports, gymnastics among them.

As more and more schools cut the smaller men's nonrevenue sports, many of those sports no longer had enough participating schools with which to stage national championships. NCAA rules mandated the minimum number of schools that had to participate in a sport in order to hold a championship event in that sport, and more and more sports were falling below the cutoff line. If it had not been for a concerted effort to preserve collegiate championships for the "Olympic sports" for which college athletics was the gateway, championships in those sports would have been eliminated. By the turn of the twenty-first century, only about twenty colleges and universities still sponsored men's varsity gymnastics teams. High schools also followed this pattern, resulting in many fewer high school teams.

## The Future of Gymnastics in the United States

While gymnastics in the early years of the twenty-first century was experiencing hard times in the schools and colleges, it continued to have wide appeal to young people. Its inherent self-testing character and its presentation on television every Olympiad as a glamorous activity for young people gave the sport continued adherents and enthusiasts. Those young people will determine the direction for the future of the sport. During the high school years, many parents will subsidize their children's enthusiasm by paying for club memberships. But where will gymnasts be able to practice their sport after leaving high school? Lacking opportunities for college scholarships and opportunities to practice their sport as members of college teams, all but the best will have to turn to other activities in which their training background is applicable. Typically gymnasts are energetic, goal-oriented, and self-disciplined; they will, consequently, find other activities in which to utilize these attributes.

*See also:* Basketball, "Muscular Christianity" and the YM(W)CA Movements, Olympics

## BIBLIOGRAPHY

Clement, Annie. *Law in Sport and Physical Activity.* Indianapolis, Ind.: Benchmark Press, 1988.

Eisen, George, and D. K. Wiggins. *Ethnicity and Sport in North American History and Culture.* Westport, Conn.: Greenwood Press, 1994.

Flath, Arnold W. A. "A History of Relations Between the National Collegiate Athletic Association and the Amateur Athletic Union of the United States." Ph.D. diss., University of Michigan, 1964.

Guttman, Allen. *The Olympics: A History of the Modern Olympic Games.* Champaign: University of Illinois Press, 2002.

Korsgaard, Robert. "A History of the Amateur Athletic Union of the United States." Ed.D. diss., Teachers College, Columbia University, 1952.

Kraus, H., and R. Hirschland. "Minimum Muscular Fitness Tests in School Children." *Research Quarterly* 25 (1954): 178.

Laptad, Richard E. "The Origin, Development and Function of the United States Gymnastics Federation. Ed.D. diss., University of Oregon, 1971.

Suggs, W. "A Federal Commission Wrestles with Gender Equity in Sports." *Chronicle of Higher Education* (3 January 2003): A41.

———. "Budget Problems and Title IX Spur Sports Cutbacks at 3 Colleges." *Chronicle of Higher Education* (10 January 2003): A33.

Wallechinsky, D. *The Complete Book of the Olympics.* New York: Viking Press, 1984.

Wong, G. *Essentials of Amateur Sports Law.* Westport Conn.: Greenwood Press, 1994.

Zeigler, E. *A History of Physical Education and Sport in the United States and Canada.* Champaign Ill.: Stipes Publishing Company, 1975.

*Erik K. M. Kjeldsen*

# HALLOWEEN

Halloween is thought to have derived from a pre-Christian festival known as Samhain (pronounced "Sah-wen") celebrated among the Celtic peoples. The various peoples whom we now refer to as "Celts" once lived across Europe, but in time they came to inhabit the areas known today as Ireland, Scotland, Wales, Brittany, and Cornwall. Today's Irish, Welsh, and Scots peoples are the descendants of these peoples, as are their Gaelic languages.

## Halloween in the Old World and the New

Samhain was the principal feast day of the year; it was New Year's Day of a year that began on 1 November. Traditionally, bonfires were lit as part of the celebration. It was believed that the spirits of those who had died during the previous twelve months were granted access into the Otherworld during Samhain. Thus, spirits were said to be traveling on that evening, as the Celtic day was counted from sundown to sundown.

Scholars know little about the actual practices and beliefs associated with Samhain. Most accounts were not written down until centuries after the conversion of Ireland to Christianity circa 300 A.D., and then by Christian monks recording ancient sagas. From the evidence, we know that Samhain was a focal point of the yearly cycle, and that traditions of leaving out offerings of food and drink to comfort the wandering spirits had joined the bonfire custom. Also, the tradition of mumming—

dressing in disguise and performing from home to home in exchange for food or drink, as well as pranking, perhaps in imitation of the wandering spirits, or simply as a customary activity known to accompany periods of liminality and transition throughout Europe—had become part of the occasion. With the acceptance of Christianity, the times of the pre-Christian festivals were used as occasions for church feast and holy days. In the sixth century, 1 November became the Feast of All Saints, or All Hallows. Many of the folk traditions surrounding this occasion continued, and the Eve of All Hallows, Hallow Evening, has become conflated into the word "Halloween." In the ninth century, 2 November was assigned the Feast of All Souls, a day set aside for prayers for all the faithful departed who had died during the year previous.

Halloween was brought to North America with Irish and British colonists, although it was not widely observed until the large influx of European immigrants in the nineteenth century, especially the Irish fleeing the potato famine in the 1840s and thereafter. Into the nineteenth century in New England, one was more likely to encounter some version of Guy Fawkes Day, known also as Bonfire Night and Pope Day (because of its antipapist nature). The day commemorated the apprehension of Guido Fawkes on 5 November 1605 in a plot to blow up the Houses of Parliament in London. He was hung, drawn, and quartered. Effigies called "guys" were immolated on bonfires in British New England, and this tradition continued into the twenty-first century in Great Britain and parts of Canada. In the United States,

Halloween, celebrated on 31 October, is a time for parties and pranking. As a festival of autumn, the fruits, vegetables, and foods associated with it are those of the harvest. Games were and are still played with apples, and the primary symbol of Halloween is the jack-o'-lantern, the great carved pumpkin. Likewise, both apple pie and pumpkin pie are commonly served.

In Ireland, however, Halloween is much more a harvest festival than it is in the United States, where Thanksgiving has become the official day of thanks for abundance. As Samhain, November Eve was one of the four great quarter days of the year, each one marking the beginning of a new season. Samhain also marked the start of a new year. Halloween commands a place of honor in Ireland today greater than in the United States. And, in fact, it functions much like the American Thanksgiving does. Family meals and a gathering of relatives are common. There is pranking throughout the season, and Halloween rhyming, in which young people go from door to door for weeks in advance of 31 October, and present a rhyme or perform a song of some sort in return for nuts, apples, or money. The money is spent on fireworks. Also well in advance of the actual day, lanterns are carved out of large turnips, called "swedes," or rutabagas in the United States. These are given a face and a handle, and are carried about or set on walls to create a spooky atmosphere. When the old tradition of the turnip lantern was brought to the New World, settlers found the already hollow pumpkin to be preferable to the hard turnip, and so the pumpkin replaced the turnip in the United States. But the pumpkin is a fruit introduced to Europeans by Native Americans and is not native to Ireland, Great Britain, or the rest of Europe.

By carving a face on a turnip or a pumpkin, one transforms the organic item into a cultural one. The jack-o'-lantern is the wandering spirit of a man who was refused entry into either heaven or hell in the afterlife. He is condemned to wander this earth, carrying a lantern to guide his way. He is a trickster; he will lead hapless souls who follow his light to no good. The turnip lantern is said to represent the spirits of the dead—ghosts. The organic items are made to reference the supernatural. Also, they are turned into another kind of cultural item: food. Pumpkin pies and mashed turnips are foods of the season, and they represent domestic aspects of Halloween. The wild, unpredictable outside and the safe, nuturing inside are two poles of this festival. Halloween combines danger and safety, as when trick-or-treaters in the United States are invited in for cider and doughnuts. In Ireland, the inversive elements usually precede the day itself, which is given over to parties, special meals, and tradi-

tional games. These games are often played with the seasonal foods, such as dunking for apples, but they are also used in a playful way as divination games. For instance, Halloween in Ireland is also known as Nut Crack Night, because a common game is to place two nuts together near the hearth, name them for an adolescent or courting couple, then see what the effect of the heat is on the nuts. If they explode and pop away from each other, their relationship is doomed.

## Foods and Games of the Holiday

Divination and Halloween food come together in the apple tarts (pies) and the cakes known as barm brack. "Barm brack" means speckled bread. It is a corn loaf, and it is baked with tokens inside, usually a ring, but also a thimble or a button. To get the ring means you will be married; the button suggests bachelorhood for a man, and the thimble suggests spinsterhood for a woman. There may be other tokens as well. The apple tart is also baked with charms, usually a coin (preferably silver.) This means good luck for the recipient. These food customs are widespread in Ireland—one sees the bake shops advertising their apple tarts and barm bracks "with rings and mottoes." Likewise, in the supermarkets, quantities of apples, hazelnuts, peanuts in the shell (called "monkeynuts"), and even coconuts are displayed alongside soft drinks and false faces.

Many are the divination games and rites of Halloween. It is said, for instance, that one should peel an apple continuously, so that the peel is in one long piece, then toss it over one's left shoulder. As it lands, the peel will form the initial of one's future love. Typically, these games are played by girls, to whom the indoor, domestic, nurturing realm is given, while the adolescent boys collect bonfire materials and engage in games of macho daring with firecrackers. Halloween is in these ways very gendered.

According to some accounts, the Halloween supper has featured roast fowl or even meat, but as the day before a holy day of obligation in the Catholic Church, Halloween has traditionally been a day of abstinence from meat. The dishes most associated with Halloween in Ireland, colcannon, champ, and boxty, are all made from root vegetables and those earthy harvests such as potatoes and cabbage. Champ is mashed potatoes, frequently with leeks, and served with a pool of melted butter in the top. Colcannon is potatoes and cabbage. Boxty is mashed potatoes mixed with grated raw potatoes, onion, and cabbage. The ingredients are mixed together, boiled, then cut into portions and fried.

These traditional foods are emblematic of Halloween for many in Ireland. Sometimes, portions were left out for the fairies. In an article published in 1958, K. M. Harris quotes a man who recalls his mother putting salt on the head of each child to prevent him or her from being taken away by the "wee people" on Halloween. He also recounts her placing a thimble-full of salt on each plate. If the salt fell down, that person would die in the next twelve months. We see in these beliefs the continued association of food with the supernatural, and perhaps also an echo of the old new year's day of Samhain in the idea that what happens on this night affects the next twelve months.

## Celebrating Halloween in the Twentieth Century and Beyond

Periods of transition and seasonal change frequently are felt to be times when the barriers between the natural and the supernatural—between our world and the otherworld—are opened. During such times, spirits and other worldly creatures such as fairies are especially active. They are dangerous and must be appeased; thus, the offerings of food. But they are also tricksters and can be imitated, therefore lending an air of inversion to Halloween. In the United States, 31 October has become a major celebration that appeals to adults as well as children, as shown by the elaborate homemade and store-bought decorations people use to decorate their homes, and also by the adult street festivals, masquerades, and parties found all over the United States. Commercially, Halloween has become second only to Christmas in the amount of revenue it generates.

Ironically, by the mid-twentieth century, Halloween in the United States had become almost exclusively a children's event. The custom of trick-or-treating (the American version of Halloween rhyming) seems to have been introduced in the 1930s as an alternative to the children's pranking activities—sometimes dangerous, such as logs in the road. Trick-or-treating became a widespread activity after World War II. While treats could include apples and homemade sweets, the favored treat was commercially produced candy. In the United States, then, Halloween has always reflected the commercial culture of capitalism. In recent decades, stories known as "urban legends" have circulated, describing poisoned treats and apples with razor blades hidden in them. While there has been no substantial verification of the stories, the belief is widespread. The result is that homemade treats and natural fruits are looked at suspiciously—many communities offer Halloween treat X-raying services—so now more than ever, the commercially produced sweet is preferred.

By the late twentieth century, as the generation that had enjoyed Halloween as children became adults, the holiday returned to being one in which different age groups engaged. College students hosted large costume parties. Cities such as New York, Boston, Washington, D.C., and San Francisco had major street festivals. As a day of public costuming and inversion, a time when people confronted images of the taboo—representations of death, evil, and chaos—Halloween had long been used by the gay population as a "safe" time to parade in drag, to publicly display an identity that they felt they had to keep hidden the rest of the year. By the end of the century, the rest of the population joined them to create a kind on national Mardi Gras. Unlike the actual Fat Tuesday, however, this carnival is in the autumn, and it combines seasonal images of the harvest with images of human death (ghosts and skeletons) as well as other unspeakables. All of this is done as the nights grow longer and winter approaches, and it is done with a sense of humor. Halloween is a time when it is safe to play with our fears, to allow our demons to come out from under the bed and take center stage once a year.

*See also:* Commecialization of Children's Play, Commercialization of Leisure

### BIBLIOGRAPHY

Ellis, Bill. "'Safe' Spooks: New Halloween Traditions in Response to Sadism Legends." In *Halloween and Other Festivals of Death and Life.* Edited by Jack Santino. Knoxville: University of Tennessee Press, 1994.

Harris, K. M. "Extracts from the Committee's Collection." *Ulster Folklife* 4 (1958): 37–49.

Rogers, Nicholas. *Halloween: From Pagan Ritual to Party Night.* New York: Oxford University Press, 2002.

Santino, Jack, ed. *All Around the Year: Holidays and Celebrations in American Life.* Urbana: University of Illinois Press, 1994.

———. *Halloween and Other Festivals of Death and Life.* Knoxville: University of Tennessee Press, 1994.

———. *The Hallowed Eve: Dimensions of Culture in a Calendar Festival in Northern Ireland.* Lexington: University Press of Kentucky, 1998.

Tuleja, Tad. "Trick or Treat: Pre-Texts and Contexts." In *Halloween and Other Festivals of Death and Life.* Edited by Jack Santino. Knoxville: University of Tennessee Press, 1994.

*Jack Santino*

# HAM RADIO

**See** *Amateur Radio*

# HANDBALL

Striking a ball with the hand has an ancient ancestry, dating at least as far back as 2000 B.C. in Egypt. Most accounts place the introduction of hardball handball to America in the early 1800s, though some records indicate a primitive form arriving around the mid-1700s. In 1860, Abraham Lincoln, while awaiting word of his nomination, "remained at Springfield—joining in a game of hand ball—favorite pastime of the professional men of the town" (Yukic, 1972, p. 3). Handball today is played in a variety of ways with a small rubber, or soft, ball, on one-wall, three-wall, and four-wall courts, including singles, doubles, and threes ("cutthroat").

## From Game to National Sport: Urban One-Wall to Championship Four-Wall

Handball in America arose as the product of a changing environment. As urbanization and Irish immigration increased throughout the latter half of the nineteenth century, so did the popularity of handball, especially the one-wall game. This version could be improvised on most buildings, even those in congested neighborhoods. Starting around 1910, New York City beaches began building specifically designed one-wall courts for bathers. Thousands of municipal and YMCA one-wall courts in the East and Midwest soon followed the success of these courts on the East Coast. Jewish Community Centers, universities, and private athletic clubs also constructed and promoted mostly four-wall play.

Though the first four-wall courts could be found in 1856 (Milwaukee) and 1873 (San Francisco), a more formal, organized game was introduced to the United States in the late 1800s by Irish immigrants. Handball officially arrived in 1886 with the first four-wall championship court built in Brooklyn, New York. It was there in 1886 that American Phil Casey, considered by many to be the father of modern handball in America, won the first World Handball Title and $1,000. Most of the top players were Irish immigrants, like Casey, who built their own courts ("Casey's Court" in Brooklyn). Professional players and cash prizes dominated the sport at this time, featuring matches as long as the best-out-of-fifteen games

to twenty-one points. Championships required the completion of a "rubber," meaning a match had to be played in both the United States and Ireland before determining a winner. With travel difficulties, a rubber could easily take a year to complete. The first widely sanctioned rules were also published in 1886.

The status of handball players, contrary to most sports, evolved from professional to amateur status. U.S.-Irish prize matches soon became too argumentative, hostile, and difficult to stage, mostly due to difficulty of travel; differences in courts, rules, and balls; and interference by backers and promoters. Such matches ceased between 1909 and the advent of the World Championships in 1964. The Amateur Athletic Union (AAU) sponsored its first hardball handball tournament in 1897. In 1915, the Detroit Athletic Club began the first major promotion of four-wall indoor courts, widely publicizing their construction and the ensuing four national invitational tournaments. In 1919, at the Los Angeles Athletic Club, the AAU began sponsorship of a four-wall softball handball championship that would last for almost six decades. This period marked the beginning of four-wall amateur handball as the dominant version of the game, capturing the attention of the nation's media and spectators.

Soon, with thousands of players and fans, top amateurs riveted attention where professionals once laid claim. In the early 2000s, four-wall handball dominated the sport, except in New York City, where racquetball usage and one-wall tournaments were widely sanctioned. Four-wall typically offered more advanced tactics and skills, requiring endurance and innovative play off the back wall, side walls, and ceiling. Matches were best of three or best of five, greatly shortened from the era of two-day contests, and the rules no longer allowed kicking the ball.

## Trends Over Time: Organization, Equipment, and Women

The direction and growth of handball have been influenced by numerous organizations, which struggled at various junctures to gain administrative control of the sport. Besides the AAU and the National Jewish Welfare Board, the YMCA played a major part in the growth of the game. The national Y sanctioned its own national four-wall handball tournament in 1925 and, via their handball committee, assembled the rules that evolved into the Unified Handball Rules in 1959. In 1951, as a result of a feud between Avery Brundage, president of the AAU, and Chicago businessman Bob Kendler, the United States

**YMCA in New York City.** Three students from the Bronx High School of Science play one-wall handball at the Bronx YMCA in New York City in 1954. The game was very popular at YMCAs across the country. © *Hulton Archive/Getty Images*

Handball Association (USHA) was formed under Kendler's exclusive control. With the support of the major players, the USHA was able to focus wider attention on handball by sanctioning national and regional tournaments, providing player accident insurance, promoting junior play, and establishing its own magazine, *Ace*. The USHA sponsored the first intercollegiate tournament in 1954. Kendler also successfully applied this model of sports promotion to racquetball.

Courts and equipment have changed considerably over time. While courts originally were much larger, around sixty feet by thirty feet, with walls thirty feet or higher, today's indoor courts measure forty feet long by twenty feet wide by twenty feet high. While pine and other woods are still the predominant choice for flooring, the walls have evolved from thick brick and mortar to lightweight composite materials. Partial glass walls began appearing around 1940 in order to increase spectatorship. Kendler is credited with building the first glass-walled court for use in televising the sport in 1950. Glass wall courts are now constructed on all four sides.

Initially, the ball was similar to a small baseball, though hardball handball is virtually extinct today. Standardization of a soft ball began in the late 1800s (about the size of a tennis ball at the time), with the rubber version used in the early twenty-first century ending up just larger than a golf ball. At advanced levels, the ball travels up to eighty miles per hour. Though the game was played for years with little protection for the hand, padded gloves became standard issue for most players.

While men have comprised most of the participants over time, women began recreational play around the turn of twentieth century. A 1904 photograph from Teachers College, Columbia University, depicts four female students playing four-wall handball as part of their physical education class. Women's professional involvement in the sport did not begin until the 1970s.

Professional handball returned in the winter of 1973 to 1974 with a five-stop tour sanctioned by the National Handball Club under Kendler. While not an Olympic sport, a Neilsen Survey estimated a stable base of about 1 million players playing in more than 2,000 private and

1,000 public facilities across the country in the early twenty-first century. Players from the U.S., Canada, and Mexico have dominated the pro and open ranks, with players from Ireland challenging for the national and world championships in the early 2000s. The USHA and the World Handball Council organize and promote the World Championships of Handball every three years. The 2003 championship was held in Ireland.

*See also:* Racquetball

**BIBLIOGRAPHY**

McElligott, Tom. *The Story of Handball: The Game, the Players, the History.* Dublin: Wolfhound Press, 1984.

O'Connor, Tom. "History of Handball." Available from http://ushandball.org.

Phillips, B. E. *Handball: Its Play and Management.* New York: Ronald Press Company, 1957.

Yukic, Thomas S. *Handball.* Philadelphia: W. B. Saunders, 1972.

*James A. Therrell*

# HANDICAPPED LEISURE

**See** *Adapted Leisure Formats; Disability and Leisure Lifestyles*

# HERITAGE SITES

In terms of international tourism, "heritage" refers to conserving and transmitting cultural or natural resources that are important to a country's identity. Included under this broad meaning of heritage are segments of the tourist market such as ecotourism, "adventure" vacations, and visiting sites of historic or cultural significance. But in the West, particularly the United States and Britain, heritage has assumed a narrower meaning associated with nostalgia. During the past quarter century, an enthusiasm for the past has been manifested in a marketplace of collecting, preserving, restoring, presenting, and reenacting. Part of this vogue is represented in touring heritage sites, environments that plunge visitors into historical scenarios. Travel to heritage sites composes a significant and increasing segment of the domestic tourist

industry, according to the Travel Industry Association of America.

## Travel to Historic Places

Heritage sites have their origin in travel to places of historic significance. In the United States, touring before the Civil War chiefly consisted of travel to scenic places promoted by railroads, landscape artists, and writers. A "grand tour" analogous to the European Grand Tour featured a mix of natural wonders and technological marvels, such as the Catskills and Niagara Falls via railroads and canals. Scenery and evidence of progress aided self-definition for the young nation's genteel middle class. Although tourists visited a few historic sites such as Bunker Hill or Mount Vernon, influential Americans lamented the landscape's general lack of historic associations akin to those found in Europe.

By the final decades of the nineteenth century, the pace of change and the nation's centennial encouraged reflection on America's past. History infused a new civil religion that served as an anodyne to change and compensation for religious doubt raised by science. A new commercial culture prompted by more money and leisure time exploited American historical themes through the era's great fairs, cycloramas, department store displays, and stage spectacles. Railroads in need of passengers became vehicles in the service of patriotism by sponsoring excursions and package tours to historic sites. Cultural leaders, uneasy about new immigrant masses, promoted pilgrimages to historically significant places for working-class denizens who now enjoyed enough time and money for day travel. Historic touring helped disseminate a narrative of national triumph and destiny for a diverse people.

Aging Civil War veterans created national shrines through lavish monumentation of battlefields they frequented in large numbers. Erected from 1870 to 1910 during the nation's most active monument-building period, Civil War monuments reflected the more popular taste of new tourists with a style of action statuary that replaced earlier symbolic monuments of the genteel. The trend affected Revolutionary War–era sites sacralized by time and associations with national birth. Beyond monuments, historic sites also generally featured private museums of memorabilia and relics, and sometimes guides who laced their tours with human-interest stories. Combined with picnics and other recreation, touring historic sites for both the middle and working class could offer entertainment under the guise of inspiration and enhanced national loyalty.

**Greenfield Village.** Workers in period costumes can be seen from a Model T automobile on the ninety-acre grounds of Greenfield Village in Dearborn, Michigan. They are part of a parade to celebrate the village's reopening on 10 June 2003 after a nine-month, $60 million renovation. Founded in 1933 by Henry Ford (1863–1947) and named a National Historic Landmark in 1981, it provides an educational experience in America's past for its 1 million annual visitors. © *Carlos Osorio for AP/Wide World Photos*

The automobile's primacy over railroads in the twentieth century transformed nineteenth-century shrines. Touring changed from a communal experience of rail travel and hotels into a private activity shared with family members. Tourists took to the roads with different expectations. The car—along with movies, radio, television, mass magazines, newspapers, advertising, and highways—blended working-class and genteel culture into mass culture. In the new environment, monuments and museums stuffed with antiquities no longer adequately transmitted historic meaning. Americans exposed to this visual culture needed more representation and less symbolism than their predecessors when they visited historic places. They also expected spaces free of factories, utility polls, highways, billboards, and other modern clutter. Moreover, the shock of two world wars interspaced by depression lengthened the distance between past and present, adding to the difficulty of retrieving national memory.

Beginning in the 1920s, historic sites that met the new criteria were fashioned by government and automotive-related industries, ironically two organizations responsible for producing the landscape that tourists sought to escape. Henry Ford assembled Greenfield Village in Michigan (1929) and John D. Rockefeller Jr. restored Colonial Williamsburg (1932), both historic environments re-created for tourists. Ford, who once referred to textual history as "bunk," hoped Americans could appreciate the American past through the objects that shaped it. Both projects were followed by similar ventures at sites such as Old Sturbridge Village, Massachusetts (1936), and Mystic Seaport, Connecticut (1930). (American restoration projects lagged behind similar ventures in Europe, the first of which was Skansen, a village featuring traditional Swedish buildings and crafts, established near Stockholm in 1897.)

Government launched similar initiatives when the U.S. Department of the Interior's National Park Service (NPS) absorbed hundreds of historic sites from other cabinet departments during the New Deal. The first director of the NPS historical division hoped to "breathe the breath of life into American history for those to whom it has been a dull recitation of facts" by re-creating "the color, pageantry, and dignity of our national past" (Verne

Chatelain, quoted in Unrau and Willis, p. 22). To produce historic-looking scenes, the NPS began removing modern appurtenances from landscapes, adding period fencing, and restoring buildings to their original appearance. Interpretive maps, illustrations, and recorded narration placed along park roads for drive-by touring also were added.

NPS planned for a deluge of postwar tourists through Mission 66, which added visitors' centers, programs, new sites, and sometimes facilities for food and housing. Postwar families largely accounted for the flood of tourists that paralleled the nation's suburban growth. Reminders of the American past in popular entertainment, interior design, and advertising helped reassure settlers on the new "crabgrass frontier." Family vacations to historic places offered more than a sense of rootedness and an opportunity to restore family bonds detached by frenetic suburban life. Responsible parents also intended to teach children patriotic lessons as an antidote to godless communism. Still, conditioned by the cultural nationalism of media images as well as dazzling fantasies such as Disneyland's "Frontier Land" and "Main Street," families on vacation expected to "see" history like the entertainment they viewed in the family room.

## The Heritage Boom

National convulsions of the 1960s and 1970s again transformed both historic places and tourists. Vietnam, Watergate, civil unrest, economic spasms, and resulting exhaustion shattered established notions about national destiny and America's divine mission. Families went out of fashion, their decline aided by the women's movement and marketing trends encouraging individual fulfillment rather than family-centered consumption. Devices intended to facilitate communications further isolated individuals while ratcheting up the tempo of life. Terms used to describe the present, such as "poststructural" or "post-postmodern," suggest an age adrift. The shift from the Cold War's remote threat to terrorism's hot war, where everyone is perpetually in the war zone, added further insecurity.

Fragmented Americans grasped at mooring offered by the stability of the past, but it was a past selectively used and severed from the national narrative. Heritage met psychic needs with both identity enhancement and a surrogate "narrative of triumph" (Engelhardt, p. 3). Relief from doubts about national purpose following the nation's defeat in Vietnam could be found in an ersatz past. It joined a variety of packaged commercial venues, ranging from "adventure" vacations to Disney World, which

paradoxically sold ersatz authenticity as escape from unreality. More demanding work schedules also forced greater intensity into available vacation time. Heritage traded history's flow for a capacity to situate consumers in a past of their choosing.

Heritage obviously differs from memory prompted by monuments, but it also diverges significantly from earlier "living" museums. For one reason, with a site's connections to history swept away, heritage relies more heavily on sensory experience to evoke emotion and subjective experience. Authentic sounds, sights, and often smells confront tourists who touch as well as gaze. For another, attention to authentic detail is much keener. Earlier, public and private developers of historic sites added features to the landscape that simply presented the appearance of age without concern for historic accuracy. And while in the past anachronisms on the landscape were often tolerated, heritage demands that nothing pollutes what is labeled with the neologism "viewshed"—a term that refers to a visually-pure landscape unsullied by features not from the represented historic period. Paradoxically, purity extends only as far as the consumer image of the authentic rather than its reality.

Unlike the unifying force of earlier American shrines, heritage sites tend to fragment society. The vogue among hyphenated Americans (i.e., Americans of mixed or diverse backgrounds) for "roots" in the late twentieth century spawned attractions that attempted to resuscitate "authentic" racial and ethnic legacies. White males, diminished from fewer social outlets and the women's movement, responded with their own heritage activities, such as restoring locomotives and wargaming. Marketing techniques that used the late twentieth century's diffusion of media outlets to exploit divisions in American society further fragmented society by producing consumer groups of heritage enthusiasts. They created another difference between old and new historic attractions by serving as producers as well as consumers of heritage sites. Constituent support groups, including aficionados ("buffs") or reenactors, for example, shape heritage sites through development projects and public exhibitions of history "being made."

Although touring historic sites always has been part of the marketplace, heritage blurs previously discrete distinctions between market and memory. Whereas on the one hand heritage popularizes the past, it also transforms it into a market decision by relying on the consumer's experience to shape the product. Gift shops stuffed with collectible kitsch that dwarf souvenir selections of previous generations cater to individual consumer taste much like the central attraction sells subjective experiences. Critics have not failed to note the similarities between heritage sites and malls, which have grown more heritage-like in creating a shopping "experience" fulfilling individual desires. Furthermore, the visual and tangible focus of heritage owes a debt to images produced by the entertainment industry that whet the public's narrative imagination. Surround sound, high-definition television, and giant screens provide "authentic" experiences that legitimate historic sites. Films and television programs such as *Gettysburg, The Patriot,* and Ken Burns's *The Civil War* can prompt a flood of tourists to validate the images depicted on-screen by visiting the site and entering the narrative.

## Heritage Sites

The proliferation of heritage sites in a number of forms during the late twentieth century reflected the public vogue for a past that entertains and titillates. Many sprouted out of the ground like mushrooms. For example, the Pequot Museum in Mashantucket, Connecticut, built by the tribe with casino proceeds, mists and chills visitors as they descend into a darkened Ice Age tunnel complete with tableaux that can be touched. At the Pamplin Park Civil War Museum near Petersburg, Virginia, floors rumble and jets of air simulate whistling bullets. Pamplin Park represents one of several Civil War museums that opened in the 1990s within driving range of Gettysburg, creating a Civil War tourist vortex out of the southern Pennsylvania-Virginia corridor. At the National Civil War Museum in Harrisburg, Pennsylvania, a bricolage of expensive relics, hi-tech displays, and, according to the museum's promotional brochure, "life-size dioramas. . .help elevate the typical museum experience by touching visitors' emotions" about the Civil War. Among many new outdoor museums, such as coal mines and farms, tourists not only watch how people labored in the past, but sometimes even can join in the work.

In addition to the new heritage sites, established historical tourist attractions have embraced heritage. At Colonial Williamsburg, for example, visitors now are feted with "living history" mob scenes, slave patrols, or "tea with Martha Washington." Tourists to Gettysburg, where reenacting once was considered profaning, can mingle with reenactors who stage "authentic" camps on the battlefield and fire Civil War weapons. Gettysburg visitors now commonly replicate Pickett's Charge during a mile-long walk "into the Union guns" that includes graphic narration. A Civil War show at the Western Reserve Historical Society in Cleveland invites visitors to handle weapons and crawl inside an authentic Union tent,

while tourists can "dress up like Indians" at the annual reenactment of the Battle of the Little Bighorn in Hardin, Montana. Scenarios of questionable accuracy abound, such as the authentic slave cabins in Charleston, South Carolina, which have been refurbished for lodging with air-conditioning and English hunting prints.

Both the new and the older heritage sites often host festival days to boost attendance and publicize continuously. Some might be ethnic festivals, while others are designed to attract heritage enthusiasts such as collectors or reenactors. At "Looking for Lincoln" days in Springfield, Illinois, visitors "relax, enjoy free cider and popcorn," "encounter some of Lincoln's old friends," and "enjoy the same kinds of entertainment available in Lincoln's Springfield." Some heritage attractions are permanent festivals using authentic settings that more overtly demonstrate the bond between heritage and the marketplace. In the final decades of the twentieth century, developers cashed in on the economic potential of heritage—what one pundit called "the successful packaging of authenticity." Old buildings, and in some cases monumental architecture, were converted to shopping malls. Evoking the past in malls such as South Seaport in New York City, Faneuil Hall in Boston, or Union Station in Washington, D.C., upgrades shopping not only by boosting the value of goods on display, but also providing shoppers with a comforting environment that encourages spending. Because only the ambiance of authenticity matters, developers also designed new malls with an antique look. The transformation of historic places into malls could be reversed so that malls could be turned into historic places.

## Consumers

Sanitizing the past has earned heritage sites a reputation as enjoyable and relaxing family places. Gone are disease, hunger, desperation, horror, unpleasant hygiene, and ugly "inhabitants." Unlike Cold War parents, however, modern parents are part of a specialized market of heritage consumers who join children in suspending belief and pretending staged attractions are authentic. Teaching patriotism has been displaced by participating in the "memory bath" along with the kids. The baby boom generation includes many who failed to define maturity the same way as their parents, who were confronted in their formative years by depression and war.

While heritage tourists participate in the scene rather than exclusively watch, other patrons help manufacture the site through contributions, volunteer work, or acting out historical scenarios. These enthusiasts find community in an isolating society by sharing their interest electronically through Internet chat rooms and listservs. As with other heritage patrons, historical meaning is insignificant for these "buffs" who try to recapture childhood through play or hobbies. Railroad buffs restore coaches and engines with the zeal of young model builders; volunteers erect fencing on battlefields as if moving pieces on a play set; reenactors engage in "make believe" to sense the intensity of combat, if only for an instant. Heritage sites serve as personal fantasies for baby boomers not only by allowing them to slip into an earlier time, but through the sense of control they attain over historic events.

## Criticism of Heritage

What makes heritage attractive to these specialized consumers is what critics decry. Scholars such as David Lowenthal and Robert Hewison point out that heritage is ahistorical, that "hands-on" experience in manufactured scenarios is no substitute for the knotty issues debated by history. History flows into the present; heritage, on the other hand, is fractured from the present, cleansed, and enjoyed at a distance. Unlike history, critics charge, heritage reveals truth determined by the widest audience of consumers. Advocates promote the seeing, doing, and feeling of heritage as an antidote to boredom induced by history lectures and texts. At a 1999 Civil War reenactment, for example, history teachers were encouraged to bring their classes "so their students' dry and dusty history textbooks may come alive." If heritage is so popular and superior to history, critics ask, then why is the public more ignorant of basic historical information than ever before? History may teach how to make relevant judgments and discriminate, but many have noted the undiscriminating nature of heritage. The marketplace tends to flatten the historical importance of sites so that Cleveland's Rock and Roll Hall of Fame or Graceland, for example, become the equivalents of Independence National Park.

Just as consumer culture in the twentieth century has enticed Americans away from politics and community life, heritage as part of that culture is pulling Americans away from history. What may be most troubling about heritage is its assurances of truth without asking questions. It is likely that global homogenization will increase the number and popularity of heritage sites as people search for identity in groups smaller than nations. The market will aid this process by segmenting potential buyers and herding them into "tribes" of heritage consumers. And the cultural populism of the entertainment industry, with authority vested in gate receipts, will likely continue. Critics hope that heritage will, as its advocates claim, lead consumers to further explore the past through history.

*See also:* Disneyland, Historical Reenactment Societies, National Parks, Niagara Falls, Shopping Malls, State Parks

### BIBLIOGRAPHY

Cross, Gary. *An All-Consuming Century: Why Commercialism Won in Modern America.* New York: Columbia University Press, 2000.

Engelhardt, Tom. *The End of Victory Culture: Cold War America and the Disillusioning of a Generation.* New York: Basic Books, 1995.

Hewison, Robert. *The Heritage Industry: Britain in a Climate of Decline.* London: Methuen Publishing, 1987.

Kammen, Michael. *Mystic Chords of Memory: The Transformation of Tradition in American Culture.* New York: Alfred A. Knopf, 1991.

Lowenthal, David. *The Past Is a Foreign Country.* Cambridge, U.K.: Cambridge University Press, 1985.

———. *Possessed by the Past: The Heritage Crusade and the Spoils of History.* New York: Free Press, 1996.

MacCannell, Dean. *The Tourist: A New Theory of the Leisure Class.* New York: Schocken Books, 1976; reprint, Berkeley, Calif.: University of California Press, 1999.

Prentice, Richard. *Tourism and Heritage Attractions.* New York: Routledge, 1993.

Travel Industry Association of America. *The Historic/Cultural Traveler.* 2001 Edition. Washington, D.C.: Research Department, Travel Industry Association of America, 2001.

Unrau, Harlan, And G. Frank Willis. "To Preserve the Nation's Past: The Growth of Historic Preservation in the National Park Service During the 1930s." *Public Historian* (Spring 1987).

Urry, John. *Consuming Places.* New York: Routledge, 1995.

Weeks, Jim. *Gettysburg: Memory, Market, and an American Shrine.* Princeton, N.J.: Princeton University Press, 2003.

*Jim Weeks*

# HIKING
**See** *Backpacking and Hiking*

# HIP-HOP MUSIC
**See** *Rap Music Audiences*

# HISTORICAL REENACTMENT SOCIETIES

The area of historical reenactment has taken on many different forms since its beginnings in northern Europe in the 1890s. Historical reenactment, also known as living history, can be defined as the use of the fives senses as well as intellect and emotion to animate and provide an "historical experience" to the learner (Boardman, p. 1). The interest in historical reenactment and the degree of authenticity to which it is practiced appears to follow the public's interest in the anniversaries of historical events as well as the evolution of educational approaches through the history of the twentieth century. Historical reenactment provides the individual with a myriad of opportunities to explore his or her own sociocultural history, identity, and the experiences of one's ancestors along with many other personal benefits.

## Development of Living History Organizations

The development of living history organizations in the United States can be traced to the promotion of hands-on learning by such people as Henry Ford with the founding of Greenfield Village, Michigan, in 1929, and the founders of the Witter Agricultural Museum at the New York State Fair in 1933. After World War II, these factors, coupled with the model provided by the northern European folk parks, led to the creation of new open-air museums in the United States such as Colonial Williamsburg in Virginia, Old Sturbridge Village in Massachusetts, and the Farmers Museum in Cooperstown, New York.

Often, when people think of living history organizations, they tend to think about those organizations that attempt to re-create military organizations of the past such as those who re-create units of the American War for Independence and the American Civil War. However, there is also a significant portion of "living historians" who eschew the grandiosity of many of the military battles to focus on the everyday experience of the common civilian throughout our history. One such organization that follows this philosophy is the Association for Living History, Farm, and Agricultural Museums (ALHFAM). ALHFAM was founded in 1970 at Old Sturbridge Village as an outgrowth of the conversation and experimentation of the 1960s that suggested a need to organize a cooperative environment in which museums could communicate more effectively with people in disciplines such as education, history, agriculture, archaeology, and others,

that had the potential to contribute to the living history process. ALHFAM has continued to develop and serve the public through the 1990s and early 2000s as an "organization of people who work to bring history to life" (Boardman, p. 2).

Military reenactment groups have followed a path of development similar to that of open-air museums. In the interests of safety, educational standards, and historic authenticity, military reenactment units typically are associated with umbrella organization such as the North-South Skirmish Association (NSSA). The NSSA was founded in 1950 to "commemorate the heroism of the men, of both sides, who fought in the American Civil War (1861–1865)," as well as to provide opportunities for its members to compete in the shooting of Civil War–era weapons. Coincidentally, this surge in popularity was associated with the upcoming centennial of the American Civil War and the popular interest in re-creating battles and events of this period.

The formation of the NSSA was an outgrowth of the resurgence in interest in the preservation of the craftsmanship and artistry of traditional muzzle-loading firearms, which resulted in the formation of the National Muzzle Loading Rifle Association (NMLRA) in 1933. Another umbrella organization that provides standards for military reenactment units is the Brigade of the American Revolution (BAR). This national-level organization, founded in 1962, is an international organization dedicated to re-creating the life and times of the common soldiers of the American War for Independence. The BAR represents organizations and individuals that portray soldiers of all armies involved in the conflict, as well as civilian men, women, and children from all walks of life. The BAR has grown to include over 3,000 members enrolled in over 130 separate units.

Units, clubs, or groups that are affiliated with these umbrella organizations are held to the highest standards for authenticity related to their time period. An example of a typical BAR unit is the Second New York (re-created). Two New York families interested in American history founded the Second New York in late 1971. These two families started a living history association formed under the umbrella of the Brigade of the American Revolution and stated as their goal an organization "dedicated to educating its members and the public in the period of our War for Independence by portraying the life and times of the New York soldier during that cause." Organizations such as the Second New York often have very exacting standards for the authenticity of materials used by their members. The standards often dictate the types of cloth that can be used for clothing, the number

## Genesee Country Village and Museum

It is a cool summer morning in a typical Upstate New York village. The old Toll House sits quietly awaiting another day of traffic. A small gentleman dressed in light blue knickers, a sweater vest and a golf cap quickly wheels by on a high-wheeled bicycle. This scene, not out of the ordinary in 1892, is actually occurring 100 years later at the Genesee Country Village and Museum in Mumford, New York.

A visitor at the Toll House called out to ask him how he gets off the bike. The rider immediately stopped the bike and skillfully stepped down and, after only a moment, he was up and peddling away.

Douglas Redmond, a grey-haired, handsome gentleman, takes pride in educating visitors on the particulars of his 1892 bicycle. During the weekdays, Doug works in the research and development department of a Buffalo, New York company. As Doug engaged the visitor in conversation about his love for bicycling back into history, he handed the visitor a brochure for a bicycle museum that he was endorsing. His interest in bicycles of the nineteenth century led him to peo-ple with similar interests. A couple with whom he had become friends started a small, but unique, pedaling history museum. This couple, like others he has come to know, also shares his love and interest in bicycles.

Why does Doug commute over an hour each way to ride his bicycle around the museum's village for five hours twice on a weekend? According to Doug, he loves blending into the landscape of this nineteenth century village. He can safely ride this classic bike in a quiet setting free from the sidewalks and traffic of today's busy neighborhood streets. As Doug pedals by, visitors stop in their tracks and point and look in amazement.

How does the museum compensate him? Doug says they offer him as many free tickets as he would like to return to the village. However, he says that he only takes two, for himself and his wife. He says that compensation is not the primary factor that brings him and others like him to historical settings. What Doug says is the most important factor to him, and others like him, is the camaraderie and the sense of place. Doug transports himself to a place where time has stood still. Here he is an active participant in a simpler time. A time where the pace was slow, hard work was the norm, and leisure time was treasured.

---

of stitches that can be used per inch in their hand-sewn-only clothing, and the type of accoutrements and weapon that can be used.

An example of a nonmilitary living history club is La Compagnie des Hivernants de la Rivière Saint Pierre (The Company of the Winterers of the St. Peter's River). This club, also known as HSP, is a social and educational organization that was formed in 1978 to share information, knowledge, and experiences of the fur-trade era, by sponsoring events and activities that interpret and dramatize this period. HSP, as a club, strives to represent an accurate depiction of the French Canadian, British, and American employees of the fur-trading companies that once traveled the current boundaries between the United States and Canada. These depictions include engages—or indentured servants, clerks, and managers—as well as the families of these employees. While not military in nature, the standards set by this club are as high as any regimental military unit. The club expects that clothing and equipment, even food, be accurate to the time period that is being depicted at any one of the varieties of sites where they actively interpret.

Another organization that has a relatively long history in the United States, as well as internationally, is the Society for Creative Anachronism (SCA). This organization, founded in 1966, attempts to re-create medieval Europe and the days of chivalry through careful research into the customs and dress of the time. However, the SCA differs from other organizations that are tied more closely to American history in that the members of the SCA have literally "created" what they consider the "known world" as a basis for their current activities. The SCA participates heavily in the popular "Renaissance fairs" of today, as well as hosting events and mock battles that are open only to members.

The time periods represented in living history are multitude. Time periods represented depend largely on individual interests, but as a rule are generally tied to the history of a geographic region. There is nothing to limit an interested individual in the continental United States from portraying a Roman soldier or classical Greek persona, but the opportunities for some of the benefits to the individual are more limited than the portrayal of a character that has a history closely tied to the geographic region.

**Gettysburg reenactment.** On 4 July 1998 the 135th Annual Gettysburg Civil War Battle Reenactment drew about 20,000 participants to the event in Gettysburg, Pennsylvania. © *Jon Adams for AP/Wide World Photos*

## Why Do People Do It?

There are many reasons reported regarding the motivations of individuals to participate in living history activities. Jay Anderson in the *Living History Sourcebook* proposes that many people are motivated by, surprisingly, fear to get involved with living history. In essence, when as children they visited historical sites, these static places—which appear to have been frozen in time—provoked in them fear; that fear can be a very alluring emotion. Another primary interest in living history is that of personal enjoyment resulting from the highly social atmosphere of the hobby. The camaraderie and inherent interdependence of many historical social settings remind us of a more simple time. As modern life becomes more complex, the popularity of experiencing it in terms that are more concrete provides allure to many living historians. A desire for familial closeness leads many families to engage in this activity together; in many cases, men, women, and children can equally contribute to the historical experience.

Another motivating factor in the decision to engage in living history as a hobby is a particular interest in one's family history or genealogy. Living history provides par-

ticipants with exciting opportunities to delve into the experience of one's ancestors and to attempt to see the world through their eyes. By participating in living history, one can enhance the sense of place and time, which makes the oftentimes-dry family history come alive with all the senses. This "feeling" of history creates a connectedness with the past and engenders a deeper understanding as to possibly why we behave and do things the way we do.

Another allure of engagement in living history activity is the furthering of personal educational interests. An interest in a particular aspect of a time may lead individuals to portray characters to which that particular aspect applies. As an example, a person with an interest in primitive shooting sports may acquire a muzzle-loading musket and, as he or she pursues the sport, may develop an interest in how the weapon was used as a tool for defense or to provide food. This may lead the individual to seek out people with similar interests and become involved with a club that focuses on portraying the lives of people who would have used these tools in their daily lives. Then, rather than just shooting a muzzle-loading firearm at a paper target, the act of shooting becomes an action that

tory activities during time away from school as a means of achieving personal enjoyment as well as a means of honing skills that can be used in the classroom.

## What Does Participation in Living History Entail?

Participation in living history activities involves various degrees of personal commitment depending on the motivations of the participant. At the most basic level, individuals join groups that focus more on the social aspect of the experience with a moderate to low level of focus on the actual authenticity of the portrayal. At the other end of the extreme, living history can become, for some, a way of life in which the participant never totally disengages from the hobby. Financial aspects of the involvement in living history are generally reflected by the level at which the participant engages. In the case of military-based living history, such as those involving re-created units of the American War for Independence or the American Civil War, the initial costs can be quite significant. The cost of obtaining uniforms, weapons, and accoutrements can run into the thousands of dollars. As an example, a generic Civil War reenactor without ties to a specific unit (which may have special requirements for equipment) may expect to pay approximately $800 to $1,000 for a musket, approximately $400 for a uniform, plus the costs of period correct shoes, accoutrements (belts, cartridge box, bayonet, headwear, canteen, etc.), cooking implements, and a shelter.

That is not to say that the interested individual must have significant financial resources in order to be involved in living history. Those who have an interest in the everyday lives of our ancestors can be involved in re-creating civilian aspects of daily life. This area of interest can be much more affordable for the interested individual, especially if the individual has some of the skills necessary to create his or her own clothing and accoutrements. With adequate research, most of the clothing that one would need could be obtained for no more than the cost of needles and thread, appropriate cloth, and a pattern. In this case, the significant costs would be for headwear and correct shoes, and a "kit" could be put together for less than $300.

Aside from the monetary commitment, the greatest resource demand on the individual is time. Much time must be devoted to research and interaction with others, as well as to traveling to and attending events. Many reenactors (with and without ties to a particular site) spend a great deal of time traveling from event to event. As an example, the 135th annual reenactment of the battle of Gettysburg, in July 1998, drew over 20,000 reenactors from California to Maine. Participating in living history can

has context and provides the individual with a deeper understanding of the historical importance of gun care, safety, efficiency, and so forth. The same example could be used for any number of historical implements from spinning wheels to canoes. The object becomes more than a dusty artifact with a label. It becomes a small part of a much larger picture and life.

Personal education is merely one aspect of the motivations for individuals to participate in living history activities. Another motivating factor is the desire to share with others one's knowledge and experience related to a particular historical time, place, or experience. This motivating factor often leads teachers to practice living his-

produce many benefits for the individual, and provide a host of opportunities for leisure experiences. Living history participation can be a lifelong leisure pursuit, is not limited by age or infirmity, and can be individually tailored to the skill and interest levels of the individual.

*See also:* Heritage Sites; Memorial Day; Wild West Shows

**BIBLIOGRAPHY**

Alderson, William T., and Shirley Payne Low. *Interpretation of Historic Sites.* 2d edition. Nashville, Tenn.: Association for State and Local History, 1985.

Anderson, Jay. *The Living History Sourcebook.* Nashville, Tenn.: Association for State and Local History, 1985.

Association for Living Historical Farms and Agricultural Museums. "Living History Help." Available from http://www.alhfam.org.

Boardman, Kathryn. "Revisiting Living History: A Business, an Art, a Pleasure, an Education." Summary of panel discussion presented at the 1997 annual conference of the National Council on Public History. Available from http://www.alhfam.org.

Grinder, Alison L., and E. Sue McCoy. *The Good Guide: A Sourcebook for Interpreters, Docents, and Tour Guides.* Scottsdale, Ariz.: Ironwood Press, 1985.

Knudson, Douglas M., Ted T. Cable, and Larry Beck. *Interpretation of Cultural and Natural Resources.* State College, Pa.: Venture Publishing, 1995.

Lowenthal, David. *The Past Is a Foreign Country.* New York: Cambridge University Press, 1985.

Reid, D. "Research and Living History: Facing Challenges." Available from http://www.alhfam.org.

Roth, Stacy F. "Past into Present: Effective Techniques for First-Person Historical Interpretation." Association for Living Historical Farms and Agricultural Museums. Available from http://www.users.voicenet.com/.

Second Battalion of Foot, New York Provincial Forces (1775). "Living History Since 1972." Available from http://members.aol.com/SecondNewYork.

Tilden, Freeman. *Interpreting Our Heritage.* 3d edition. Chapel Hill: University of North Carolina Press, 1977.

*James A. Newman*

# HOBBIES AND CRAFTS

Hobbies constitute one of three basic types of serious leisure. A hobby is a systematic, enduring pursuit of a reasonably evolved and specialized free-time activity having no professional counterpart. Such leisure leads to acquisition of substantial skill, knowledge, or experience, or a combination of these. Although hobbyists differ from amateurs (another type of serious leisure) in that they lack a professional reference point, they sometimes have commercial equivalents and often have small publics who take an interest in what they do.

Hobbies and hobbyists can be classified as follows: 1) collectors; 2) makers and tinkerers; 3) activity participants; 4) competitors in sports, games, and contests; and 5) enthusiasts in liberal arts fields. Collectors abound; some are well known, like stamp and coin collectors, some more obscure like collectors of leaves and jukeboxes. Next are the making (building, raising) and tinkering hobbies, which result in such craft products as quilts and furniture, in mature flora and fauna (such as plants, dogs, fish), or in completed do-it-yourself projects when done for fun, for example, tinkering with a car or repairing a household gadget. Activity participants find leisure in noncompetitive, rule-based pursuits, including fishing, kayaking, and barbershop singing. By contrast, competitors in games, sports, and contests thrive on competition in, for instance, orienteering, long-distance running, and competitive swimming. The rules guiding rule-based pursuits are, for the most part, either subcultural (informal) or regulatory (formal). Thus, seasoned hikers in the Rocky Mountains know they should stay on established trails, pack out all garbage, be prepared for changes in weather, and make noise to scare off bears and cougars.

Liberal arts hobbyists are enamored of acquiring knowledge for its own sake. Many accomplish this feat by reading voraciously in an art, sport, cuisine, or language. Others develop a passion for a culture (for example, ancient Greek, Native American) or a history (military, European); or they study a science, philosophy, or literature (for instance, French poetry, nineteenth-century Russian novels). Some go beyond reading to expand their knowledge further through cultural travel or documentary videos.

Hobbies sometimes evolve into professions, in the process transforming the hobbyists into amateurs. This transition was made at different points in history by all contemporary amateur-professional fields in art, science, sport, and entertainment. Nevertheless, commercial equivalents of hobbies, like making and selling furniture or trout flies, dealing in antiques or paintings, and offering fishing or ballooning trips, are, at bottom, businesses, not professions.

Research on hobbies has been uneven. Jeff Bishop and Paul Hoggett conducted the classic study centered on a variety of amateur and hobbyist groups in two communities in England. Apart from attractiveness of the hobby itself, they identified three further reasons for widespread participation in these groups: the presence of an appealing leisure subculture, the possibility for individual members to make their own contributions, and the effectiveness with which member diversity is handled. Research on collectors and liberal arts hobbyists is rare, while research on making and tinkering is more common. Activity participation (the leisure of activity participants defined earlier) and competitive sports and games have drawn the greatest scholarly attention.

## Hobbyism: Past and Present

With *Hobbies: Leisure and the Culture of Work in America,* Steven Gelber has written the definitive history of hobbies. The broad trends he observed, based on examination of British and American sources, apply more generally to industrialized capitalist Europe and North America from mid-nineteenth century to the end of the 1950s, the point at which he terminated his analysis.

Gelber holds that "industrialism quarantined work from leisure in a way that made employment more worklike and nonwork more problematic. Isolated from each other's moderating influences, work and leisure became increasingly oppositional as they competed for finite hours" (p. 1). Americans, he says, responded in two ways to the threat posed by leisure as potential mischief caused by idle hands. Reformers tried to eliminate or at least restrict access to inappropriate activity, while encouraging people to seek socially approved free-time outlets. Hobbies and other serious leisure pursuits were high on the list of such outlets. In short, "the ideology of the workplace infiltrated the home in the form of productive leisure" (p. 2).

Hobbies were particularly valued because they bridged especially well the worlds of work and home and both sexes found hobbies appealing, albeit mostly not the same ones. Some hobbies allowed homebound women to practice, and therefore understand, worklike activities, whereas other hobbies allowed men to create, in the female-dominated house, their own businesslike space—the shop in the basement or the garage. Among the various hobbies, two stood out as almost universally approved in these terms: collecting and handicrafts. Still, before approximately 1880, when hobbies came to be seen as productive use of free time, these two types of hobbies, as well as others, were considered "dangerous obsessions."

Gelber notes that, although the forms of collecting and craftwork have changed somewhat during the past 150

years, their meaning has remained the same. Hobbies have, all along, been "a way to confirm the verities of work and the free market inside the home so long as remunerative employment has remained elsewhere" (pp. 3–4).

As for social class both craftwork and collecting appear to be more inclusive of white-collar workers and blue-collar producers than they are exclusive of them. Nonetheless, socioeconomic data for these hobbies are presently thin and even thinner back in time, so definitive statements on this question must wait. Meanwhile, Gelber is convinced that hobbies have always transcended class much more readily than they have transcended gender, which squares with Robert Stebbins's observations on this question for all serious leisure.

Gary Cross observes that, during much of the nineteenth century, employers and upwardly mobile employees looked on "idleness" as threatening industrial development and social stability. The reformers in their midst sought to eliminate this "menace" by, among other approaches, attempting to build bridges to the "dangerous classes" in the new cities and, by this means, to transform them in the image of the middle class (p. 130). This plan led to efforts to impose (largely rural) middle-class values on this group, while trying to instill a desire to engage in rational recreation—in modern terms, serious leisure—and consequently to undertake less casual leisure.

## Popularity of Hobbies

The amateur activities are the most restrictive of the three types of serious leisure. Executing them at a satisfying level requires routine training and practice in art, sport, or entertainment, while science requires extensive development of knowledge and, in some instances, technique. This restrictiveness is one of the reasons why Stebbins estimates that no more than 20 percent of North Americans pursue an amateur career of some sort (p. 49). His experience in serious leisure research suggests, however, that the proportion of hobbyists is significantly larger.

Still, no one can say with precision how much larger the proportion is, for no one has studied the distribution of serious leisure participants in a Western society, the type of society where, as of 2004, it appeared to have reached its richest expression. Stebbins's hunch that there are proportionately more hobbyists than amateurs follows from his observation that many hobbies are reasonably accessible. Notwithstanding certain exceptions, most of them are learned informally, commonly by reading books or articles, listening to or watching tapes, and talking with other hobbyists. Acquiring knowledge in this manner is relatively inexpensive, and easily molded around the enthusiast's work, leisure, and family schedules. Furthermore, many hobbies can be pursued within the participant's own timetable; the participant need not wait for a scheduled meeting, practice, rehearsal, or public match or performance.

Although it may be relatively inexpensive to launch a hobby, it may be costly to continue with it. Some items make expensive collectibles; some equipment used for constructing or repairing things is costly. Some hobbyist fly fishers, cross-country skiers, and animal breeders sink large sums of money into their pastimes, not unlike the amateurs who run up sizable family debts buying a good violin, telescope, or set of golf clubs. In this sense, then, certain hobbies are no more accessible than many amateur activities.

Two additional points remain to be made about hobbies. First, when compared with the other durable benefits of a hobby, its monetary return is secondary. Studies of hobbyists support this claim, in that remuneration is rarely mentioned as a reason for engaging in this kind of serious leisure. In other words, neither hobbies nor amateur pursuits are viewed primarily as supplements to the practitioner's main income; they are not "second jobs." In fact, a certain devotion animates pursuit of these forms of serious leisure, leading many hobbyists to take them up despite possible, if not real, financial loss. Indeed, even if they did earn a substantial amount of money in the pursuit, this would be but one reward of many and, according to evidence at hand, one of the least significant. Thus "sideline" businesses, including some so-called "hobby farms," are logically excluded from consideration as true hobbies.

Second, some hobbyists fit more than one category, as do builders of motorized model airplanes who, as competitors, fly their constructions in local contests. Classification of individual hobbyists also depends partly on the circumstances in which they undertake their activities. For example, swimmer number one is termed a player because he competes in swimming meets. Swimmer number two is termed an activity participant because she swims for the satisfaction gained from developing and maintaining her skill, as well as for the exercise it provides.

## Collecting

Collecting and craftwork number among the most popular types of hobbies. Russell Belk offers the following definition of collecting: "Collecting is the process of ac-

tively, selectively, and passionately acquiring and possessing things removed from ordinary use and perceived as part of a set of non-identical objects or experiences" (p. 67). Accumulation of possessions differs from collecting in that it lacks selectivity, may be simply a refusal to dispose of things, and is no cause for pride. Hoarding is selective and active, but focuses on utilitarian items that may be needed in the future. Moreover, the items hoarded are identical. The distinction drawn here between collecting, accumulating, and hoarding is widely accepted among scholars in this field. Robert Overs, Sharon Taylor, and Catherine Adkins classified collecting into nine categories: autographs, photographs, and posters; coin, currency, and medals; stamps; natural objects (including fossils and butterflies); models (such as airplanes, trains); dolls; art objects (such as violins, paintings); antiques; and miscellaneous crafts (for example, comics, sports cards).

Allan Olmsted, in a literature review, observed that most children collect things long before adolescence. Later, especially among females, collecting decreases noticeably as they enter adulthood. Men, who dominate the world of serious collectors, renew their interest in collecting during middle age. Adult collectors of both sexes quickly become involved in complex social worlds centered on their objects of interest, as found in shows, auctions, catalogs, dealers' shops, flea markets, and garage sales. Some research in the area, says Olmsted, supports the proposition that collecting is leisure (a hobby), whereas other research gives weight to the idea that it is obsessive consumer behavior.

Finally, there are collectors who acquire objects for extrinsic speculation and profit, even though they, like pure collectors, also genuinely appreciate various intrinsic qualities of those objects. But these motives clash, causing personal tension when such collectors face the opportunity to sell at significant profit items integral to their collections. It follows that full-time dealers in collectables are businesspeople, not hobbyist collectors.

## Craftwork

In the field of leisure and recreation, "craft" refers to a pursuit requiring manual dexterity or application of artistic skill and sometimes both. Howard Becker holds that craft products are designed as useful objects, though they may also be beautiful (artistic). Overs, Taylor, and Adkins list eight types of crafts along with a miscellaneous category: cooking, baking, and candy making; beverage crafts; decorating activities; interlacing, interlocking, and knot making; toy, model, and kit assembly; paper crafts;

**Comic-Con.** The San Diego Convention Center houses the largest comics and popular arts convention in the United States. In 2003 Comic-Con International held its thirty-fourth annual event and among the industry professionals who participated was *Lord of the Rings*, special effects artist Richard Taylor, representing the company he co-founded in 1994, Weta Workshop Ltd. His team won five Academy Awards for its work in the trilogy which included creating the eerie Gollum, the creature pictured in the foreground. © *Mike Blake for Reuters NewMedia Inc./Corbis*

leather and textile crafts; and wood- and metalworking. Among the miscellaneous crafts are making candles, creating mosaics, and cutting and polishing stones. Not found in this list are the ceramic crafts, an unfortunate omission since they were among the most popular in the early twenty-first century. Do-it-yourself activities, which may combine several crafts, constitute a hobby only if approached as leisure. Moreover, some do-it-yourself activities involve not so much creating something new—not a craft—as repairing or tinkering with something old, as in fixing a car or washing machine.

Many crafts, for fullest satisfaction, depend on developing substantial, specialized skills, as seen in using a knife to whittle, a needle to sew, or a plane to make furniture. Other crafts, when pursued at the most rewarding levels, require considerable background knowledge. Cooking, do-it-yourself repairs, and the beverage crafts exemplify well this prerequisite. Furthermore, hobbyists who assemble toys, models, and other objects from kits,

like those who sew from patterns and cook from recipes, must have a propensity for following often complicated instructions and paying attention to detail. Those in woodworking and metalworking, along with some do-it-yourselfers, must also develop a capacity for creating their own plans and designs. Lastly, some of these activities can be highly artistic, as evident in working with rocks, making mosaics, and decorating various objects.

Stebbins observed that hobbies with developmental requirements usually offer leisure careers, which unfold along lines of improvement in skill, knowledge, artistry, attention to detail, or a combination of these. In this sense, careers in the making and tinkering hobbies resemble those in the amateur fields. Still, certain construction hobbies have comparatively light developmental requirements; they revolve primarily around amassing completed projects. This often happens in the paper crafts, miscellaneous crafts, and interlacing and interlocking activities.

Notwithstanding these occasional specialized requirements, the making and tinkering activities, on the whole, have always been a highly democratic form of serious leisure, open to a vast range of humankind in many different societies. Culturally learned preferences aside, none of these hobbies is limited to one sex, while all can appeal to the entire age range of adults possessing the physical and mental capacities to carry them out with significant satisfaction. It is quite possible that a properly conducted international survey would find more people engaging in these hobbies than in any of the other four types.

## Professionalizing Hobbies

Some hobbies appeaed, in the early 2000s, to be in the process of professionalizing in that, for more and more participants, they offered possible full-time employment. This tendency was evident in chess, darts, shuffleboard, and bicycle racing where, if the trend continued, it would dramatically transform the performance standards guiding all participants, including the hobbyists. Moreover, as a parallel development, the professionals would expand and enrich the social worlds of those activities in proportion to their presence and influence. In consequence, leisure participants in those fields would be transformed into amateurs.

*See also:* Coin Collecting, Collecting, Rational Recreation and Self-Improvement, Stamp Collecting

### BIBLIOGRAPHY

Becker, Howard S. *Art Worlds.* Chicago: University of Chicago Press, 1982.

Belk, R. W. *Collecting in a Consumer Society.* New York: Routledge, 1995.

Belk, R. W., M. Wallendorf, J. F. Sherry, and M. B. Holbrook. "Collecting in a Consumer Culture." In *Highways and Buyways: Naturalistic Research from the Consumer Odyssey.* Edited by R. W. Belk and M. Wallendorf. Provo, Utah: Association for Consumer Research, 1991.

Bishop, Jeff, and Paul Hoggett. *Organizing Around Enthusiasms: Mutual Aid in Leisure.* London: Comedia Publishing Group, 1986.

Cross, Gary. *A Social History of Leisure Since 1600.* State College, Pa.: Venture Publishing, 1990.

Gelber, Steven M. *Hobbies: Leisure and the Culture of Work in America.* New York: Columbia University Press, 1999.

Olmsted, Allan D. "Collecting: Leisure Investment or Obsession?" *Journal of Social Behavior and Personality* 6 (1991): 287–306.

Overs, Robert P., Sharon Taylor, and Catherine Adkins. *Avocational Counseling Manual: A Complete Guide to Leisure Guidance.* Washington, D.C.: Hawkins and Associates, 1977.

Stebbins, Robert A. *After Work: The Search for an Optimal Leisure Lifestyle.* Calgary, Alberta: Detselig, 1998.

———. *New Directions in the Theory and Research of Serious Leisure.* Mellen Studies in Sociology, vol. 28. Lewiston, N.Y.: Edwin Mellen Press, 2001.

*Robert A. Stebbins*

# HOCKEY

**See** *Field Hockey; Ice Hockey*

# HOLIDAYS

**See** *Christmas; Easter; Fourth of July; Halloween; Labor Day; Mardi Gras; Memorial Day; New Year's; Thanksgiving*

# HOME BREWING

In 1979, President Jimmy Carter signed a bill into law legalizing the home brewing of beer. This act, however, did not mark the beginning of home brewing. Beer has been speculated to be the oldest alcoholic beverage known to civilization. Wherever cereal grains could be grown, beer could be made. Ancient peoples all made a rough form of beer. Six-thousand-year-old Babylonian clay tablets give detailed recipes and show the brewing of beer. Third century B.C. Egyptian recipes describe the making of a strong beer flavored with fruit and spices.

Throughout the centuries, the art and craft of brewing beer developed. Saint Gall, a monk from Ireland, is credited with being the first modern brewer for bringing methods from the Celts to medieval Europe. Charlemagne (742?–814 A.D.) assigned Saint Gall to manage the craft for the Holy Roman Empire and positioned monks to control brewing. Consequently, brewing became a recognized trade. The Royal Family in Belgium recognized brewing in the thirteenth century and a guild was formed.

By the late fifteenth century, Germans established standards for brewers, and in 1516 William VI, elector of Bavaria, established the most famous beer purity law. This law, known as Reinheitsgebot, permitted only four ingredients in the production of beer: water, malted barley, malted wheat, and hops.

### Colonial America

The first beer brewed in America was in the Roanoke, Virginia, colony in 1587. In the colonies, beer was a major dietary staple, consumed by everyone, young and old. Beer was important because good drinking water was in short supply. Those who drank beer rather than impure water generally avoided getting sick. This was well known before the connection was made between boiling water for brewing beer and sanitation.

During the early colonial years most brewing and drinking was done in the home. Home brewing had an impact on early colonial architecture because many colonists added small brew rooms to their homes. One notable home brewer during this time was George Washington, who had a brew house at Mount Vernon. His handwritten recipe for beer, dated 1757, is preserved and can be seen at the New York Public Library. Thomas Jefferson, another home brewer, collected books on brewing that are part of his extensive library at Monticello.

Alehouses or taverns were established in towns and villages where the brewers had businesses. Residents socialized, discussed politics, and shared news with the community. These early colonial breweries found it hard to come by the traditional raw ingredients for beer because they had to be imported from England, so brewers often replaced the ingredients with what was readily available. Maize, molasses, bran, persimmons, potatoes, birch bark, ginger, and allspice are examples of the creative alternatives brewers used in producing beer. By the late-eighteenth century, as farmers cultivated locally available grains, the production quality of beer improved. Commercial breweries developed throughout the land. In 1840, there were about 140 breweries operating in the United States, with at least one in each of the original thirteen colonies.

### Prohibition

By 1919, thousands of breweries existed. They were large and small, supplying beer with distinctive styles to their respective regions. The Volstead Act, the Eighteenth Amendment to the Constitution, ushered in Prohibition and completely shut down the brewing industry for thir-

teen years (18 January 1920, to 5 December 1933). While the manufacture and sale of alcohol was illegal, the ingredients to produce them were not. Malt syrup, an essential ingredient for making beer, was produced in huge quantities by many former breweries (ostensibly for baking purposes) to avoid bankruptcy. Home brew, or *heimgemacht*, as the Germans called it, flourished during Prohibition. Millions of Americans made home-brewed beer. Quality was not important, nor was taste as long as it contained alcohol. Home-brewed beers were characterized as thick and mud brown in appearance, with a yeasty aroma and a soapy taste. By 1929, the Prohibition Bureau, using sales figures for hops, malt, and other ingredients, estimated that Americans brewed 700 million gallons of beer at home. In some cities so much was being made that sewer systems were backed up by spent hops.

When Prohibition ended in 1933, the commercial production of beer was legalized. Homemade wine was legalized also, but home-brewed beer was not because of a stenographer's omission of the words "and/or beer" in the Federal Register. Home brewing was abandoned in favor of the lightly hopped beers professional brewers produced. The stigma attached to home brew as a muddy, distasteful, and amateurish libation was so great that forty years passed before Americans once again became interested in making their own beer.

### Modern Times

Home brewing was legalized in Great Britain in 1963. Manufacturers there took an interest and produced state-of-the-art home-brewing ingredients, kits, and malt extracts. There was money to make and spend on home-brew products, and the United States was a recipient of the best technology Great Britain had to offer.

These events fueled an already growing resurgence in American home brewing that began before California senator Alan Cranston introduced legislation to legalize it in 1978. Home brewers were making beer again because domestic beer lacked the rich, malty taste they liked. They also shared a creative desire to brew a beer to their own personal taste. Congress passed Cranston's bill to repeal federal restrictions on home brewing, and President Carter signed it into law in February 1979. An adult twenty-one years or older is permitted to brew up to 100 gallons of beer a year for personal use. Selling it is illegal, but it can be removed from the brewery for organized tastings.

In Boulder, Colorado, Charlie Papazian began brewing and teaching classes in home brewing in the early

1970s. His first book, *The Joy of Brewing*, was written in 1976. In 1978, he formed the American Homebrewer's Association and began publishing *Zymurgy* magazine. In 1984, Avon Books published his work *The Complete Joy of Home Brewing*, which is considered the definitive text on home brewing for beginners and intermediates. Its sequel, *The New Complete Joy of Home Brewing*, was published in 1991.

Papazian considers home brewing to be a hobby in which time, money, and thought are invested, and from which there is an end product that meets a person's creative needs. Most home brewers do it for fun and pleasure. They enjoy making beer; enjoy tasting the beer they make; are enthusiastic about the history, technology, and science of brewing; and like meeting others with the same interests. Membership in the American Homebrewer's Association is over 25,000. The organization estimates there are over 1.5 million home brewers in the United States representing every demographic segment of society.

*Brew Your Own*, established in 1995, is the largest circulation magazine for people interested in making their own beer, reaching over 116,000 readers with each issue. Their audience is 96 percent male, who are, on average, forty-three years of age with a mean household income of $80,676. Each spends an average of $506 a year on home-brewing supplies and equipment and brews an average of 8.3 batches a year. Seventy-nine percent of readers rely on *Brew Your Own* as their only beer-related publication.

## Clubs and Competition

In addition to brewing beer for fun and pleasure, brewers are often involved in home-brew clubs and participate in home-brew competitions. Clubs form for various combinations of social interactions and activities focused on home brewing: education about beer, brewing techniques, and knowledge; promotion of the hobby; and enjoyment of home brewing.

Home-brew competitions are organized and/or sponsored by many different organizations. For example, the American Homebrewer's Association runs the National Homebrew Competition. Home-brew clubs, brew pubs, home-brew shops, and other beer-related organizations also sponsor competitions. Brewers enter competitions for several reasons. If the goal is to perfect a recipe within the guidelines of a specific style, it is a great way to get feedback on one's beer; home brewers entering a competition get objective feedback on their beer from people who are trained to evaluate it. And entering a com-

petition is fun. It allows brewers to compare their product against other people's beer.

## Brewing Beer

Home brewing beer can be simple when using malt extract in a recipe or with a ready-made brew kit. It can also be quite complicated when using all-grain brewing techniques that require knowledge of brewing chemistry and specialized equipment for the brewing process. At the most basic level, beer can be made by mixing together malted barley extract, water, and hops and boiling to make what is called "wort." The wort is cooled and placed in a fermenter, and yeast is added. Fermentation then occurs, converting sugars in the wort to carbon dioxide and alcohol. When fermentation is finished, the new beer is mixed with a small amount of primer (corn sugar) and placed in sealed bottles or kegs. Primer initiates additional fermentation to carbonate the beer. When the beer is aged, it is ready to drink. Aging time depends on beer style and can range from two weeks to one year.

## Equipment

There are specialty shops that sell ingredients and equipment for brewing beer. Many do mail-order business and/or are on the Internet and feature online ordering. Basic equipment includes a five-gallon pot for boiling the wort, a fermentation vessel (food-grade plastic bucket or a glass carboy), a priming tank (bucket or carboy), a plastic siphon hose, airlocks and rubber stoppers, a hydrometer to measure specific gravity and a jar for it, a floating thermometer, a bottle brush, sanitizing solution, about sixty non-screw-top bottles, a bottle capper, and caps. Many shops sell starter kits that include this essential equipment, along with an instruction book and ingredients for brewing quality beer at home.

*See also:* Drinking, Prohibition and Temperance, Wine Tasting

**BIBLIOGRAPHY**

About *Brew Your Own*. Available from http://www.byo.com/ aboutus/.

CNN Interactive. "Charlie Papazian Biography." Available from http://www.cnn.com/FOOD/resources/.

Eckhardt, Fred. "History of Homebrew, Part II." Available from http://celebrator.com/200002/homebrew1.html.

Emma, Sal. "United We Brew: Cool Homebrew Clubs." *Brew Your Own*. Available from http://www.byo.com/feature/ 496.html.

Jabloner, Amy. "Homebrewing During Prohibition." *Brew Your Own* (December 1997): 30–38.

Miller, Carl H. "We Want Beer: Prohibition and the Will to Imbibe, Part 1." Available from http://www.beerhistory.com/library/.

Miller, Dave. *Brewing the World's Great Beers: A Step-By-Step Process.* Pownal, Vt.: Storey Communications, 1992.

Moore, William Home. *Beermaking: The Complete Beginner's Guidebook.* 3d ed. San Leandro, Calif.: Ferment Press, 1991.

Nachel, Marty, and Steve Ettlinger. *Beer for Dummies.* Foster City, Calif.: IDG Books Worldwide, 1996.

The North State Brewer's Cooperative. "Lesson 2: History and Basic Equipment/Ingredients/Process." Available from http://www.northstatebrewers.org/.

Papazian, Charlie. *The New Complete Joy of Home Brewing.* New York: Avon Books, 1991.

———. *The Home Brewer's Companion.* New York: Avon Books, 1994.

Russell, Scott. "How to Win at Homebrew Competitions." *Brew Your Own* (August 1998): 32–41.

Smith, Gregg. "Brewing in Colonial America, Part 1." Available from http://www.beerhistory.com/.

———. *The Beer Enthusiast's Guide: Tasting & Judging Brews from Around the World.* Pownal, Vt.: Storey Communications, 1994.

"Starting and Running a Homebrew Club." Available from http://www.beertown.org/homebrewing/.

Ward, Philip. *Home Brew: Techniques and Recipes for the Home Brewer.* New York: Lyons and Burford Publishers, 1995.

*Stephen Jay Langsner*

# HOME DECORATION

Do-it-yourself home decoration was a hot topic in the early twenty-first century. Cable television programs taught decorative painting and the basics of furniture arrangement; mail-order companies offered high-style accessories and ready-made draperies and slipcovers; there was even a home-decorating book club. The leisure-time home decorator was graced with an abundance of information and purchasing options, from cable television programs to in-store crafts classes. Home "improvement"—remodeling the architecture of a house—was an activity that men and women shared. Home decoration, however, remained primarily a woman's game.

In the eighteenth century, a handful of wealthy Americans furnished the rooms of their new Georgian-style mansions to reflect their status and membership in a transatlantic elite. The restored interiors of Mount Ver-non, George Washington's plantation, reflect the "good taste" of the time, a taste that produced elegant and rather impersonal public rooms. Women from well-to-do families sometimes made needlework chair covers or pictures, but the abundance of accessories, houseplants, framed pictures, and textiles that characterized the home-decorated room of 100 years later were not in evidence in the mansion houses of the time. Because self-conscious interior decoration was rare, it must have seemed particularly impressive to ordinary folk who lived in tiny houses of two, three, or four rooms—not much room for useless ornaments of any kind, even assuming that the hardworking women dwelling there had time to make them, or the money to purchase them.

Before factory production of the sewing machine began in the 1850s, women who did their own housework and sewing had little or no time to devote to embellishing their physical surroundings; they were too busy hemming bed sheets and sewing straight seams by hand. Curtained beds, which tended to be the single most expensive item in household inventories through the 1820s, were small islands of decorative splendor in sparsely furnished rooms that almost never had either carpets or curtains.

Once women were able to devote less time to basic home sewing, many of them turned those hours of labor toward adorning their households. Do-it-yourself home decoration became a truly popular activity, thanks also to the declining prices of attractive, factory-woven fabrics by the mid-century. Several chronological surveys of interior decoration document the trend toward visual complexity and material abundance in American rooms. Elizabeth Donaghy Garrett's *At Home: The American Family 1750–1870* is a well-illustrated survey of décor and housekeeping practices organized by room. Jane C. Nylander's *Our Own Snug Fireside: Images of the New England Home 1760–1860* offers a detailed account of decorating practices, including information on the burdens of sewing. William Searle's *The Tasteful Interlude: American Interiors Through the Camera's Eye, 1860–1917* is still the most comprehensive collection of photographs documenting the period of greatest elaboration in American décor, the Victorian era. Its limitation is the absence of color; the parlors, dining rooms, and halls of Victorian houses were usually decorated in deep shades of red, green, sienna brown, golden yellow, and dark blue. Even so, the careful planning evident in even the most modest interiors suggests just how important home decoration was to the women who lived their lives within these rooms.

Until the 1870s, the *beau ideal* (or ideal of beauty) for home decoration can be expressed simply: everything should match, having been purchased in sets, and the upholstery (the draperies and fabric covers for beds and seating furniture) in well-decorated rooms should be of a single color. The décor of these rooms should appear to be clearly planned, orderly, and symmetrical, rather than a randomly placed, simple accumulation of goods. People who could afford rooms that met this ideal—and there were very few of them—demonstrated that they had the means to do all their buying at once. (Purchasing a new set of bedroom or living-room furniture continued to suggest the same in the early twenty-first century). A few Americans could afford to use skilled upholsterers, the interior decorators of the time, but even well-to-do women were often accomplished seamstresses. They were able to make patterns for, and sew bed "furnishings," draperies, slipcovers, and other decorative textile objects for their houses. One of the best overviews of the complexities of home sewing before the sewing machine, including for interior decoration, is a period source, *The Workwoman's Guide*, written by "A Lady."

During the first half of the nineteenth century, a new American middle class coalesced, one that had more money to spend and was preoccupied with appropriate forums for displaying respectable identity. The cultural ideal of domesticity, the belief that the private home should be a haven for family life and that its operation was solely the province of women, gave new impetus to do-it-yourself home decoration. Their houses were larger, with distinct public spaces intended for company, but the stakes were now higher than a simple display of means. By the mid-nineteenth century, advice writers like Harriet Beecher Stowe and Catherine E. Beecher argued that home decoration had a moral influence on family life: the "aesthetic element. . . holds a place of great significance among the influences which make home happy and attractive, which give it a constant and wholesome power over the young, and contributes much to the education of the entire household in refinement, intellectual development, and moral sensibility" (p. 84). In other words, happy family life was not dependent on regular meals and basic physical comfort alone; it was now a component of interior decoration.

The sisters addressed their chapter "Home Decoration" to an aspiring woman, who had to economize and plan carefully—and do everything herself. If she wanted a parlor, the most important room of the Victorian household, she had to hang the wallpaper, sew the curtains, upholster a homemade wooden "lounge" (the futon sofa of its day) and "ottomans," turn a "broken-down arm-chair" into an "easy-chair," and cover an unattractive center table with 30 yards of the same fabric, a "green chintz."

The Beecher sisters also included a few suggestions for homemade ornaments, including "rustic" picture frames made from twigs and a hanging planter made from a coconut shell. These kinds of projects, including wax flower arrangements, needlework lamp mats, calling-card receivers, and other small items, were a mainstay of the women's magazines of the time, particularly *Godey's* and *Peterson's*, whose editors provided pictures and instructions every month. The materials came from "fancy goods" stores, the forerunner of crafts shops of the twenty-first century. For women without drawing talent, these shops even sold canvas for Berlin needlework with the patterns already painted as a guide. These were the forerunner of the modern craft kit.

In 1868, a British curator, Charles Locke Eastlake, published a book called *Hints on Household Taste*. Eastlake's book appeared in an American edition in 1872, and became arguably the first bestseller devoted entirely to household interior decoration. His success set off a flurry of publishing do-it-yourself decoration books, which, at the time, were called "household art" books. Their authors encouraged women to express themselves by making their rooms "artistic." The old ideal of rigidly matching décor went out the window, which suited many do-it-yourselfers since they could not afford it in the first place. Books were directed both to wealthy women, like Clarence Cook's *The House Beautiful*, and to women who lived with tight budgets, as in the case of *Our Homes: How to Beautify Them*, which was published for rural and small-town women. Authors of decorating advice encouraged women to take up decorative needlework and other crafts, including indoor gardening and painting on china and fabric. They also encouraged women to use unconventional and less expensive materials, such as burlap, old wool blankets, and muslin, to create tasteful embellishments for their houses.

The household art craze resulted in rooms that were riots of pattern and color, epitomized by the crazy quilt, an innovation of the 1880s. Patchworks made from silks and velvets, embroidered with flowers, insects, and other motifs, crazy quilts were intended for use as parlor throws rather than as bedcovers. Like Berlin work (or what is now called needlepoint), they are often early examples of the use of craft kits; many women purchased bags of fancy fabric scraps to make them. The household art movement also expanded the range of women's decorating activities into areas like wood working and successive crazes for new crafts such as decalomania (decoupage, or decorating with paper cutouts) and pyromania (decorative wood-burning). The point to all this activity was that rooms now embodied the creativity of women, rather than simply being containers for displaying possessions.

By the early twentieth century, a backlash against this exuberant do-it-yourself decoration appeared in such women's magazines as *Ladies' Home Journal* and the *Modern Priscilla*. Both the arts and crafts movement and the colonial revival encouraged women to continue as decorating do-it-yourselfers, but they promoted simpler décor. The authors of this advice were often products of the new departments of home economics in land grant colleges (colleges specializing in agriculture and manufacturing programs). They attempted to train their readers, and the students in their classes, in the "domestic science" of their homemaking, including their efforts at interior decoration. For example, the *Modern Priscilla Home Furnishing Book* encouraged women to study the science of color harmony and to apply geometry to arranging small accessories. It also invited women to tackle home decorating tasks that would once have been unthinkable, including stripping and painting old furniture white and reweaving cane-seat chairs. Some old techniques, particularly making hooked or braided rag rugs, survived as "colonial" crafts. All advice on home decorating, however, still assumed that its female readers could sew with some skill, even if they no longer made most, or any, of their family's clothing. Movies also helped to shape women's taste by providing close-up examples of attractive interiors in use.

The 1950s and 1960s saw home decorators see-sawing in an era of prosperity between "modern" interiors and versions of "colonial" décor that also encompassed other styles. Women's magazines and books continued to be important sources of ideas for do-it-yourself decorators. Reflecting the status anxiety of the 1950s, the authors of *Revive Your Rooms and Furniture* encouraged homemakers to "look at each room in your home with impersonal eyes, as a stranger would," before tackling the "tired and out-of-date" rooms that women had tolerated during the Great Depression and war years (p. 7). The new medium of television also began to offer information and decorating advice in the home. The first home-decorating program to air on television is undocumented, but "how-to" programs were not the only places that women gathered information on how to furnish. Soap operas, dramatic series, and even situation comedies displayed the array of goods that postwar capitalism supplied, and showed how to put them together. Additionally, the craft kit continued to expand in popularity, including the paint-by-number craze and the use of new plastics like Styrofoam to create decorations. The first do-it-yourself decorative painting techniques

were introduced to home decorators, particularly "antiquing," where gilt paint, brushed and rubbed on, highlighted painted furniture surfaces of cream, gold, or avocado green paint.

In the last quarter of the twentieth century, the single most important trend for do-it-yourself decorating was the "American Country" look. To some extent, American Country expanded upon the earlier colonial revival's interest in American vernacular or "folk" art. Mary Emmerling's *American Country: A Style and Source Book* was the pioneering text of this decorating approach. With its emphasis on vernacular, homemade and improvised objects, including an aesthetic that embraced the appearance of wear and use, Emmerling's text invited American women to embrace décor that was overtly anti-modern. While women could make some elements of country décor themselves, much of the aesthetic consisted of artful assemblage of goods purchased in flea markets and garage sales to make cozy, homey rooms.

American Country soon split into two distinctive approaches to home décor. One, based on the classic Emmerling style, included sophisticated preferences for rooms that were deliberately anachronistic and even dilapidated, with dramatically faded textiles and worn objects. Some country decorators went to extraordinary lengths to hide modern amenities inside period cabinetry; hence the origin of the television "armoire." The other, more popular, approach to country décor used objects representing a softer, quaint vision of farm life—quilts, statuary geese wearing decorative bows, baskets of dried herbs and flowers, mottoes with humorous or inspirational texts, and stenciling that recalled nineteenth-century "theorum" painting of flower baskets and fruit. Martha Stewart, whose catering business begat how-to books on holidays and weddings, followed by books on decorating and a lifestyle magazine *Martha Stewart Living* in 1990, had used some country motifs, but her style represented an upper-middle-class alternative to the busyness of home-made American Country rooms. In fact, the signature Martha Stewart look was clean, orderly, and serene, with echoes of the classic living spaces of the 1920s through the 1950s. It demanded a level of organization that many busy women found difficult to attain.

For busy American women, holiday decorating became the most important form of do-it-yourself home decoration. There Martha Stewart was an important voice for the re-creation of family holiday traditions, including special decorations that had a homemade, nostalgic quality. Christmas décor expanded dramatically in the 1990s and early 2000s, and it was supplemented by whole new constellations of objects designed to mark the passage of Halloween, Valentine's Day, Easter, and the Fourth of July. Holiday decorating was typically laid over the existing foundation of home décor, and it allowed a greater expression of play and whimsy, precisely because it was temporary.

Hobby decorators in the early twenty-first century were awash in information and products intended to make their dwellings more attractive. The difficulty, then, was finding the time to sift through that abundance at a time when employment, an increased number of social activities outside the home, and increasingly important and complex high-tech media equipment made it very difficult to practice what lifestyle-trends guru Faith Popcorn once christened "cocooning," (which Popcorn defined as "the need to protect oneself from the harsh, unpredictable realities of the outside world" at her Web site).

Magazines such as *Martha Stewart Living*, as well as other forms of media, recognized how valuable women's time had become as they tried to balance the pressures of modern life against the desire to cocoon and did whatever they could to make home decoration easier. Issues of Stewart's magazine from the early 2000s featured party favors and accessories utilizing patterns that could be scanned and printed with a color inkjet printer. For more ambitious decorators, the projects themselves were different, as skilled sewing played a very small part in many home decorating projects. Other mass media devoted to home décor, including the programming on Home and Garden Television, pushed constant innovation, such as fantasy-themed décor for such settings as young professionals' apartments and children's bedrooms. The *Complete Idiot* series of advice books even included a decorating guide. Craft kits allowed women to try their hands at making faux stained glass, artificial wreaths for every season, no-sew valences, and painted stenciling on walls. The treasure hunt that goes into selecting appropriate consumer goods to be recombined as home décor is now the single most important home-decorating practice.

*See also:* Antiques, Collecting, Home Improvement, Quilting Parties, Women's Leisure Lifestyles

**BIBLIOGRAPHY**

Beecher, Catherine E. and Harriet Beecher Stowe. *American Woman's Home or, Principles of Domestic Science.* 1869. Reprint, Hartford, Conn.; The Stowe-Day Foundation, 1987.

Brostrom, Ethel and Louise Sloane. *Revive your Rooms and Furniture.* New York: Viking Press, 1959.

Cook, Clarence. *The House Beautiful.* New York: Scribner, Armstrong and Company, 1878. Reprint, New York: Dover Publications, 1995.

Eastlake, Charles Locke. *Hints on Household Taste in Furniture, Upholstery, and Other Details.* 1st American ed., Boston: J.R. Osgood and Company, 1872. Reprint, New York: B. Blom., 1971.

Emmerling, Mary Ellisor. *American Country: A Style and Source Book.* New York: Clarkson Potter, 1980.

Garrett, Elizabeth Donaghy. *At Home: The American Family 1750–1870.* New York: Harry N. Abrams, 1990.

Grier, Katherine C. *Culture and Comfort: Parlor Making and Middle Class Identity, 1850–1930.* Washington, D.C.: Smithsonian Institution Press, 1997.

Leavitt, Sarah Abigail. *From Catherine Beecher to Martha Stewart: A Cultural History of Domestic Advice.* Chapel Hill: University of North Carolina Press, 2002.

Martin, George A. *Our Homes: How to Beautify Them.* New York: Orange Judd Company, 1888.

*Modern Priscilla Home Decorating Book.* New York: Modern Priscilla Company, 1925.

Nylander, Jane C. *Our Own Snug Fireside: Images of the New England Home 1760–1860.* Reprint, New York: Knopf: Distributed by Random House, 1993.

Searle, William. *The Tasteful Interlude: American Interiors Through the Camera's Eye, 1860–1917,* 2d. ed., Nashville, Tenn.: American Association for State and Local History, 1981.

*The Workwoman's Guide by A Lady: A Guide to 19th Century Decorative Arts, Fashion and Practical Crafts.* 1838. Reprint, Guilford, Conn.: Opus Publications, Inc., 1986.

Young, Mary Ann and David Nussbaum. *The Complete Idiot's Guide to Decorating Your Home.* Indianapolis, Ind.: Alpha Books, 2000.

*Katherine C. Grier*

# HOME IMPROVEMENT

While home improvement, or "do-it-yourself" (DIY) has been a part of most American households since the erection of the first dwelling in what became the United States, the idea of constructing home additions, finishing basements, and engaging in many forms of refurbishing living spaces as a leisure time pursuit dates only from the end of the nineteenth century.

Historian Steven Gelber notes how a new craftsmanship emerged on weekends in the 1890s among affluent suburban American men who formerly would have hired a handyman, gardener, or carpenter. The appeal was often a nostalgic quest for rural or craft competencies, as expressed predominantly by the middle-class male. The DIY movement was also a creative compensation for unrewarding work, as middle-class men increasingly abandoned entrepreneurship and became white-collar employees. DIY was leisure, a desirable activity with little direct economic advantage, but it was also consistent with a still-powerful work ethic. In addition, it often had practical benefits for the family and could be justified as an investment and as cost saving. It gave men a role, and even a place, in the new suburban home, even while they spent most of their waking hours in the office or commuting. Men renewed their relationship with the home by shifting from work to leisure activities in gardening and minor carpentry.

The boundary between home improvement as work and leisure was certainly porous for most men of relatively modest means and without servants. Since the 1840s, with the development of balloon-frame housing (with walls constructed of nailed precut 2'x 4' strips of lumber), amateur home construction has been a possibility given the low skills required, especially when house plans were available to the ordinary would-be home owner eager to save money. By 1900, however, DIY was embraced even by the wealthy, who had no economic reason to engage in it. At this time, as the old bourgeois ideal of the masculine library separate from the feminine parlor gave way to the gender neutral living room, even men who had no need to do their own repairs or home improvements found a new refuge from wives and children in basements or backyard work rooms. Finally, home improvement activities had the virtue of being a leisure built around traditional male tools—saws, hammers, screwdrivers, wrenches, and the like—that reinforced male identity.

New technologies and consumer goods also contributed to the home improvement movement. Handicraft magazines abounded in the interwar years. *Popular Mechanics* (founded in 1902) mixed reports on the latest advances in science and gadgetry with practical instructions on everything from window repair and toymaking, to the construction of basement workshops and even houses. This magazine offered men domestic leisure while affirming their desire to be part of a wider world of technological competency. These predominately weekend activities made for a "masculine domesticity" in the early twentieth century, according to Margaret Marsh, and were encouraged by wives in the hopes of making husbands "companions," not merely breadwinners. Masculine domesticity represented a moderate compromise with feminism by integrating men into a domestic sphere

largely controlled by women. Magazines and toolmakers promoted home improvement projects for the sake of recreating male bonds, presumably lost when fathers no longer passed on job skills to their offspring, making, as an ad for Stanley Tools stated, "father and son partners!"(*Better Homes and Gardens,* September 1926, p.3).

After World War II, returning veterans embraced the home improvement movement as a way of building family "togetherness" around the security of the home. Government mortgage insurance programs for veterans encouraged home buying and highway construction, and promoted the construction of private houses in the suburbs. Since the later 1930s, the federal guarantees also made home-improvement loans that would allow for the exterior and interior modernization of existing homes through renovations such as exterior finishing, insulation, roofing, heating and cooling systems, easily available. Large builders such as Levitt and Sons accounted for two-thirds of housing construction by 1949, leading to a nearly 20 percent increase in suburban housing between 1950 and 1956 alone. Despite the fact that these tract houses looked alike, wage-earning suburbanites often individualized the appearance of these houses. Thus, contrary to the expectations of many critiques, the "Levittowns" in New York and Pennsylvania, with their hundreds of "cracker box" houses, did not become suburban slums. Remodeling made them into middle-class homes, even though their owners might have remained working-class. Owners converted unfinished attics into bedrooms. They remodeled to eliminate what they saw as wasted floor space, and finished basements into "rec rooms" when children demanded play areas. Even in more substantial homes, by building pine-paneled recreation rooms and creating vine-covered trellises in the backyard, men proved to themselves that they still could do something creative by themselves, and for themselves, apart from the modern world of machines or the corporate office.

Home improvement has emerged as an independent industry since the postwar period. Commercial hobby kits eased tasks for the layman, and magazines provided guidance in giving men a sense of competency in a craft. The advent of the power drill and saw, marketed after World War II, greatly eased home repairs and expanded the DIY cult. These tools of male domesticity helped to comprise a $12 billion per year industry by 1960. Hardware retailers and cooperative chains such as True Value and Ace Hardware began to advertise themselves as suppliers for amateur remodelers. By the 1970s, the neighborhood hardware store increasingly gave way to large, suburban home centers. In further shifting their focus from contractors to DIY customers, home-center chains such as Home Depot and Lowe's greatly expanded their sales volume and, in effect, the home improvement market.

Television home improvement shows, as well, have contributed to the expansion of the industry and the culture of DIY. In 1979, Bob Vila's *This Old House* debuted on public television. The show followed the step-by-step renovation of a Victorian era house and became a long-running success. As historian Carolyn Goldstein points out, the fascination with the "old" has been of growing importance in home improvement since the 1960s. Nostalgia, and a rising interest in craftsmanship among homeowners, contributed to a popular interest in old-looking homes with modern amenities such as central heating. Manufacturers and retailers responded to the desire of consumers to uniquely historicize their suburban homes by marketing cheap imitation molding or columns and other Victorian-style elements.

By the late 1990s, highly successful home improvement programs (often sponsored by big retail outlets) had begun to blur the distinction between the traditionally male dominated realm of home improvement (carpentry work, for example) and the largely "feminine" sphere of interior decorating and design. During the 1980s, advertisers, such as those for power tools, began to acknowledge the increasing role of women in DIY activity. No longer solely a male refuge, home improvement projects, as portrayed in cable television's immensely popular *Trading Spaces* (debuted in 2000), became a leisure activity for couples or for the entire family.

*See also:* Gardening and Lawn Care, Hobbies and Crafts, Home Decoration, Interwar Leisure and Recreation, Men's Leisure Lifestyles, Postwar to 1980 Leisure and Recreation, Women's Leisure Lifestyles, Woodworking

**BIBLIOGRAPHY**

Gelber, Steven. "Do-It-Yourself: Construction, Repairing, and Maintaining Domestic Masculinity," *American Quarterly* 49, no. 1 (March 1997): 89–112.

———. *Hobbies: Leisure and the Culture of Work in America.* New York: Columbia University Press, 1999.

Goldstein, Carolyn M. *Do It Yourself: Home Improvement in 20th-Century America.* New York: Princeton Architectural Press, 1998.

Marcus, Bernie, and Arthur Blank (with Bob Andelman). *Built From Scratch: How a Couple of Regular Guys Grew the Home Depot from Nothing into $30 Billion.* New York: Crown Business, 1999.

Marling, Karal Ann. *As Seen on TV: The Visual Culture of Everyday Life in the 1950s.* Cambridge, Mass.: Harvard University Press, 1994.

Marsh, Margaret. *Suburban Lives.* New Brunswick, N.J.: Rutgers University Press, 1990.

Vila, Bob, with Jane Davidson. *This Old House: Restoring, Rehabilitating, and Renovating an Older House.* Boston and Toronto: Little, Brown and Company, 1980.

*Gary Cross and Jan Logemann*

# HOME MOVIES

The history of home moviemaking can be traced back to 1923 and Eastman Kodak's introduction of the 16mm Ciné-Kodak system. Though the production of home movies had been technically possible for several decades prior to the 1920s, this new equipment and the narrow-gauge, direct-reversal film it utilized was more affordable, safer, and less cumbersome than previous apparatus. The introduction of 8mm film in 1932 again cut the cost of home moviemaking, opening up this activity to those on even modest budgets. In 1935, the Eastman Kodak Company further revolutionized amateur moviemaking with the development of Kodachrome film, thereby allowing full-color movies to be taken.

The year 1965 saw two major, though divergent, developments in home moviemaking technology. While Kodak marketed its new Super 8 format, offering substantial improvements on standard 8mm film, Sony announced what can be considered the first amateur-use videotape recorder. The displacement of traditional film by video in the 1980s was rapid—by 1981, sales of Super 8 cameras had dropped to 200,000 units per year, from 600,000 just four years earlier. Meanwhile, video camera sales rose from 200,000 in 1981 to over 1 million by the mid-1980s. As the average price of a camcorder plummeted from $1,534 in 1985 to $401 in 2002, so the percentage of households owning such an item grew swiftly, from 1 percent in 1985 to 43 percent in 2002. Those figures included digital units, which continued to supplant what had become the dominant video format, VHS (see Table 1).

Beyond the tremendous technological advances demonstrated by the development of home moviemaking equipment, home movies also serve a vital role as historical social documents. These audiovisual recordings of events and people range from the most mundane and

**TABLE 1**

### Sales and ownership of camcorders, 1985–2000

| Year | Units Sold (thousands) | Dollar Value (millions) | Average Price | Proportion Households Owning (%) |
|------|------------------------|-------------------------|---------------|----------------------------------|
| 1985 | 517 | $793 | $1,533.85 | 1 |
| 1990 | 2,962 | $2,260 | $763.00 | 11 |
| 1995 | 3,560 | $2,130 | $598.31 | 22 |
| 2000 | 5,848 | $2,838 | $485.29 | 40 |

SOURCE: eBrain Market Research, 2003

intimate happenings of family life, to family events and vacations, to one of the most infamous amateur movies ever, Abraham Zapruder's footage of the 1963 assassination of President John F. Kennedy.

The examination of home movies as cultural artifacts, of their representation of everyday life and their reflection of contemporaneous leisure patterns, is gaining increasing popularity among anthropologists and film historians. Patricia Zimmermann provides a useful history of amateur film from a Foucaultian perspective, in which the home movie is viewed as a socially and politically constructed discourse, embedded in specific economic, social, and political processes. From the glorification of family togetherness and the ideal of the nuclear family unit in the 1950s, to more recent use of amateur film technology to portray marginalized elements of society including AIDS sufferers and victims of police brutality, home movies continue to offer a relatively accessible means of communication and personal expression.

As with most amateur pastimes, home moviemaking has spawned a variety of related activities, from books and periodicals to clubs, contests, and festivals. The success of ABC's primetime show *America's Funniest Home Videos* indicates the continuing popularity of home moviemaking and watching. First aired in 1990, the show was one of several reality-based offerings to debut in that era, precursors to the nation's obsession with this genre in the 2000s.

*See also:* Media, Technology, and Leisure, Movies' Impact on Popular Leisure

### BIBLIOGRAPHY

Chalfen, Richard. "Cinéma Naïveté: A Study of Home Moviemaking as Visual Communication." *Studies in the Anthropology of Visual Communication* 2 (1975): 87–103.

Goldsmith, Arthur. "Photons and Electrons." *Popular Photography* 91, no. 9 (September 1984): 47.

Kattelle, Alan D. *Home Movies: A History of the American Industry, 1897–1979.* Nashua, N.H.: Transition Publishing, 2000.

Zimmermann, Patricia R. *Reel Families: A Social History of Amateur Film.* Bloomington, Ind.: Indiana University Press, 1995.

*Sarah Nicholls*

# HONEYMOONING

Honeymoons have become an integral part of marriage rituals, often exceeding wedding ceremonies in cost and duration. The term *honeymoon* dates to the 1500s and once referred to newlyweds' emotional state: "Married persons ... love well at first, and decline in affection afterwards: It is honey now, but will change as the moon" (Thomas Blount, *Glossographia,* quoted in Bulcroft, p. xiii). Prior to the nineteenth century, weddings in America and Europe were commonly raucous, communal affairs that afforded the couple little privacy. Wedding guests accompanied the bride and groom to the bedroom, playing pranks and departing only when the curtains on the bed were drawn. Wealthy couples often traveled after their weddings, accompanied by family and friends, to visit relatives unable to attend the ceremony. These trips were thought to strengthen the newlyweds' ties to their extended family and community, rather than to each other. Some upper-class American couples embarked on "bridal tours" of Europe, accompanied by family members, in the 1840s and 1850s.

Greater availability and affordability of transportation enabled middle-class newlyweds to travel beginning in the 1860s. The post-wedding trip changed from communal bridal tour to private honeymoon as Victorian society placed increased importance on the couple as an autonomous unit and mandated smaller, more modest weddings. The honeymoon, often taken in a secluded location, was thought to provide newlyweds a reprieve from prying family members and well-wishers as well as enable them to express their sexuality privately and discreetly.

Newlyweds in the early 1900s were presented with a range of honeymoon options; the groom typically selected the location and paid for the trip. While some couples stayed at a seaside resort, others camped, canoed, or took bicycle tours. Gradually the meaning of the honeymoon became connected to the destination itself: natural wonders such as Niagara Falls were believed to mirror and enhance the intensity of the couple's romance. Niagara Falls remained a popular honeymoon destination from the 1930s through the 1950s, both for its natural beauty and the anonymity it provided to bashful couples who could blend in among other honeymooners.

The 1950s witnessed a revival of large communal weddings, and the honeymoon became a means for middle-class couples to display their prosperity. Brides began to take the primary role in planning honeymoons, as middle-class women defined themselves in terms of marriage and family. However, postwar honeymooners contended with a new set of anxieties: honeymooning was seen as a critical sexual rite of passage, and experts warned that wedding night incompatibilities could ruin a marriage.

Honeymoon destinations changed with the growth of the tourist industry. Starting in the 1960s, more couples opted for travel packages to exotic destinations such as Hawaii and the Caribbean. As travel expenses increased, one cost-saving trend of the early 2000s was the "destination wedding," in which couples invited close family and friends to a small ceremony in a tropical locale that doubled as their honeymoon destination.

Honeymoons remain a popular custom despite significant changes in marriage trends. As the average age of first marriage increases and remarriages become more common, both bride and groom have greater autonomy and financial resources to devote to a honeymoon. Given couples' high rates of premarital sex and cohabitation, honeymoons may no longer serve as a sexual rite of passage, but they still enable newlyweds to develop emotional bonds in a space apart from family and domestic life.

*See also:* Niagara Falls, Tourism, Vacations, Weddings

**BIBLIOGRAPHY**

Bulcroft, Kris, Linda Smeins, and Richard Bulcroft. *Romancing the Honeymoon: Consummating Marriage in Modern Society.* Thousand Oaks, Calif.: Sage Publications, 1999.

Dubinsky, Karen. *The Second Greatest Disappointment: Honeymooners, Heterosexuality, and the Tourist Industry at Niagara Falls.* New Brunswick, N.J.: Rutgers University Press, 1999.

Freeman, Elizabeth. *The Wedding Complex: Forms of Belonging in Modern American Culture.* Durham, N.C.: Duke University Press, 2002.

Geller, Jaclyn. *Here Comes the Bride: Women, Weddings and the Marriage Mystique.* New York: Four Walls Eight Windows, 2001.

Gillis, John. *For Better, For Worse: British Marriages, 1600 to the Present.* New York: Oxford University Press, 1985.

Ingraham, Chrys. *White Weddings: Romancing Heterosexuality in Popular Culture.* New York: Routledge, 1999.

Otnes, Cele C., and Elizabeth H. Pleck. *Cinderella Dreams: The Allure of the Lavish Wedding.* Berkeley: University of California Press, 2003.

Rothman, Ellen. *Hands and Hearts: A History of Courtship in America.* New York: Basic Books, 1984.

*Katherine Lehman*

# HOOK-UPS

Instead of conventional dates, many college students engage in "hook-ups," or casual sexual encounters with friends or strangers. The term "hook-up" covers a range of practices, from kissing to sexual intercourse, and the appeal of the term may well lie in its ambiguity: Students can boast they "hooked up" without necessarily implying they had sex.

A study by the conservative Institute for American Values (IAV) brought national media attention to collegiate hook-up culture. Based on a nationwide survey of single, heterosexual college women, the 2001 study reported that many women reached their junior and senior years having barely dated; the few dates that did occur centered around organized fraternity or sorority events. Rather, college women chose to hang out with mixed-sex groups of friends, or engaged in a series of hook-ups with men they met at parties. Commonly, women and men within a social group hooked up, becoming "friends with benefits" rather than a romantic couple.

Some women interviewed for the study reported feeling vulnerable after a hook-up, as it was often their partner who determined whether the encounter would lead to a relationship. While the IAV contended that a pervasive hook-up culture thwarted women's desires to develop emotional attachments to men and eventually marry, some college women reported feeling empowered by their ability to express sexuality without commitment, and to focus on their studies and career goals rather than romance.

Several significant shifts in college life may have contributed to the rise of hook-up culture. Women have outnumbered men on college campuses since 1980—the national ratio in 1997 was 79 men for every 100 women—perhaps encouraging students to seek multiple partners rather than pairing up. Coed dormitories have become the norm at many universities: Students' daily encounters with the opposite sex both facilitate hook-ups and lessen the need for couples to socialize on dates. Marriage is a less immediate goal for students in the early twenty-first century than in generations past: Couples often marry in their late twenties or thirties, and are statistically less likely to have met in college. The increased mobility of students after college further lessens the incentive for developing long-term relationships.

Hooking up may fill students' emotional and social needs as well. From high school through college, couples are more likely to meet in groups than in pairs, as group support reduces awkwardness and the risk of rejection inherent in dating. Many college students say they prefer hook-ups and "friends with benefits" to the other romantic extreme on campus: "joined at the hip" couples who quickly commit to an exclusive, daily relationship.

The hook-up trend has led some to call for the return of courtship rules and the renewed role of colleges and universities in regulating sexual behavior. To counter what the media labeled a "post-dating" or "undating" culture, conservative groups such as the Independent Women's Forum advertised in college newspapers, urging students to "take back the date" by buying someone dinner or flowers. Dating in college, however, was not entirely obsolete in 2004: African American students at Howard University reported that "hook-up" had a dual meaning, referring either to a sexual encounter or a romantic dinner date.

*See also:* Cruising, Dating, Men's Leisure Lifestyles, Teenage Leisure Trends, Women's Leisure Lifestyles

**BIBLIOGRPAHY**

Beckett, Whitney. "What Lies Between the Hookup and the Marriage?" *Duke University Chronicle* (5 Sept. 2003).

Dunn, Lillian. "Hooking Up a Definition." *Swarthmore (Pa.) Phoenix* (29 Jan. 2004).

English, Bella. "Dinner and a Movie? No Thanks." *The Boston Globe* (11 Dec. 2003): B17.

Fletcher, Michael A. "Campus Romance, Unrequited." *The Washington Post.* (26 July 2001).

Marquardt, Elizabeth, and Norval Glenn. 2001. *Hooking Up, Hanging Out and Hoping for Mr. Right: College Women on Dating and Mating Today.* Institute for American Values. Available from http://www.americanvalues.org/.

McKnight, Ashley. "Out of Date." *The Columbus Dispatch.* (20 Nov. 2003): 1G.

*Katherine Lehman*

# HORSE RACING

Horse racing is a sport in which horses compete to determine which is fastest—and for purse money; races are divided into those in which a rider sits on the horse's back and those in which the horse pulls a small buggy (harness racing). Horses with riders are usually thoroughbreds, while those in harness racing are called standardbreds. Thoroughbred racing includes both flat and jump races; while flat races are held on dirt and grass courses, steeplechase and hurdle races are run on grass courses, and horses jump over a number of barriers set up on the course. Racing in Europe, Japan, Australia, and New Zealand is exclusively on grass courses, while racing in North and South America is on both dirt and grass courses.

## History

The early history of horse racing is sketchy, with most attention devoted to England, beginning in the 1600s. Records indicate that chariot racing and mounted races were a part of the ancient Olympic Games (700 B.C. to 394 A.D.) and were used as public entertainment in the Roman Empire. Racing was popular in the Middle East and North Africa; Europeans became familiar with these races during the Crusades (eleventh to thirteenth centuries) and brought many horses back to Europe. Charles II, who reigned from 1660 to 1685, was known for his interest in racing and is credited with starting the King Plates, writing the rules for the races, and making Newmarket the center of English racing.

The settlers brought horses with them when they came to America; they had brought at least seven by 1610 and continued their interest in racing, usually match races between two horses over several four-mile heats. Racing was more popular in the South, and Virginia became the horse center in America. As Edward Hotaling noted: "Like flies to molasses, the whole South took to 'the races.' . . . They seemed an extension of the establishment's favorite fantasy, that life was a chivalric pageant out of medieval England, the obverse of the North's delusional, anti-English Puritanism" (p. 22). By 1840, the South had sixty-three racetracks; the Northeast had only six. While most racing was local or regional, the Union Course on Long Island, New York, promoted the popular North-South races. The first North-South race was held in 1823; American Eclipse, the northern horse, beat Sir Henry in three four-mile heats. Other North-South races were held in 1832, 1840, and 1845.

The Civil War devastated the horse business in the South; after 1865, the racing world centered on New York. Saratoga was opened in 1863, followed by Jerome Park in New York City in 1866. The Kentucky Derby was started in 1875, the Preakness in 1873, and the Belmont in 1867. These three races were linked to form the Triple Crown series in 1930. Winning all three races at their varying distances—a mile and a quarter (Derby), a mile and three-sixteenths (Preakness), and a mile and one-half (Belmont)—within five weeks has been extremely difficult. As of 2004, only eleven horses had won all three races in a single year, none since 1978. The Breeders' Cup was started in 1984 and was marketed as the World Championship of horse racing.

## Breeding

Historians trace all thoroughbreds to three stallions: the Darley Arabian, the Godolphin Barb, and the Byerly Turk, which were brought to England between 1690 and 1730 and bred to a number of English mares to replenish the declining English stock. Stallions such as Medley (1783), Shark (1788), Messenger (1788), and Diomed (1798) brought the thoroughbred line to America. The offspring of matings between the stallions and mares were recorded (Stud Book) to ensure the standard of the breeding and the quality of the horses. The first General Stud Book was published in England in 1791; the Jockey Club took over the registry of horses in North America in 1896. At the same time, while some acknowledge the presence of mixed breeds, doubting the claim of the "pure" thoroughbred, the Jockey Club controls what horses can run in American races: Only those registered with the Jockey Club as thoroughbreds are eligible.

The rule for breeding has been "to breed the best with the best and hope for the best." It follows that well-bred horses should win the most races and the richest races, and pedigree is often used to evaluate the performances of horses. When a well-bred horse wins, his pedigree is responsible, but when a lesser-bred horse is successful, it is often attributed to luck. Moreover, when the decision is made to have the horse become a sire or broodmare, a horse's success on the track is often overlooked in favor of his breeding. For example, Sunday Silence won two of the three Triple Crown races (the Kentucky Derby and the Preakness) and the Breeders' Cup Classic in 1989, defeating Easy Goer in all three races, yet his breeding was considered lesser than that of Easy Goer. Sunday Silence was then sold to Japanese owners, and he later became the leading sire in Japan. Easy Goer was kept in the United States. Moreover, Secretariat, whom many believe to be

> ## African Americans in Racing
>
> Thirteen of the fifteen riders in the first Kentucky Derby were African Americans, and African American jockeys won fifteen of the first twenty-eight Derbies. Moreover, the winning trainers in the first three Derbies—1875, 1876 and 1877—were African Americans, as were the winning trainers in 1884, 1885, and 1891, the last year an African American schooled the winning horse. The situation was different in the twentieth century, however; when Marion St. Julien rode Curule in the Kentucky Derby in 2000, he was the first African American jockey to ride in the Derby in seventy-nine years. Since 1930 the presence of African American trainers has been spotty; there were two in 1932 and one each in 1934, 1944, 1951, and 1989, the last year in which an African American trained a Derby horse (as of 2004). Eight African American owners have entered horses in the 128 runnings of the Derby; the first and only winning owner was Dudley Allen, who entered Kingman in 1891; the most recent African American owned entry was in 1994.

among the greatest American horses, winning the Triple Crown in 1973, had an undistinguished career as a sire.

Another concern with breeding is the hardiness of the horse. Many believe that the emphasis on breeding for speed rather than stamina, coupled with the increasing use of medications to "help" horses to perform on the track, has contributed to less sturdy stock. There is no national standard for drug use; each state has its own rules, and many suspect that the rules are too lax, contributing to abuse for the horses and to uncertainty among bettors. Instead of breeding the best (strongest) to the best (strongest), horses going to the breeding shed are often those who were kept on the racetrack by medicine. Horses no longer run as many races, they have longer rests between races, and they run shorter distances than their progenitors. By 2004, most races ranged between three-fourths of a mile (six furlongs) and a mile and one-sixteenth; races of a mile and a quarter were considered problematical for most horses. Also relevant to the hardiness is the age at which horses begin racing. Historically, horses were at least five years old before racing; in England; the Kings Plates races were for six-year-olds. However, horses now begin racing at two and often are no longer racing at six. The stress of racing is not beneficial to young horses, but the economics of the sport

## Racing

Races are organized by racing secretaries employed by race tracks to attract owners to enter their horses. While the public pays most attention to stakes races like the Kentucky Derby, the Arlington Million, and the Breeders' Cup, most races are claiming and allowance races. Claiming races are the lowest level of racing and range from a low of about $5,000 to $80,000 or more; horses entered in a claiming race are "up for bid" and any authorized owner can bid for a horse prior to the race. Following the race the person who bid for the horse becomes the new owner and must pay the claiming price set for that race. Allowance races are those with certain conditions for eligibility, such as the number of wins a horse has or the amount of money it has won in its lifetime or within a certain time period; horses in allowance races cannot be claimed. Young horses usually proceed through allowance conditions before entering stakes races. On an average nine-race program there would be five claiming races, two allowance races, and two maiden races—races for horses who had never won a race. Maiden Special Weight races are for better horses, while Maiden Claiming races are for those unsuccessful at the higher level. Other races include handicap races, in which racing secretaries assign horses to carry varying amounts of weight in an effort to attract more horses and to make the race more competitive. For example, while all horses carry the same weight in the Kentucky Derby and the Breeders' Cup races, the Melbourne Cup, the most popular race in Australia, is a handicap race. Good horses will often not be entered in handicap races if the owner or trainer feels that the weights assigned to their horse will make it too difficult for it to win.

make two-year racing a necessity. In other words, horses need to "earn their keep." The Triple Crown races are for three-year-olds only. Historically, the rationale for racing was the "improvement of the breed," but many now question that outcome. In fact, some in the American Jockey Club acknowledge that their control of the Stud Book is more for integrity than for the improvement of the breed (Case, p. 45).

## Structure of Horse Racing

The horse business is composed of the owners, for both breeding and racing; the trainers, who prepare the horses for racing; the jockeys, who ride the horses; the tracks, which organize and hold the races; and the fans, who wager on the races. Added to the mix are state governments, which tax the money bet on each race. Often, the motivations of each group are different, and these differences are one of the problems facing racing. Owners—and trainers—hope to win money by racing, but they also want to protect the reputation of their better horses for breeding; they usually pick and choose which races to enter, often avoiding any competition with rival horses until meeting in prestigious races such as the Kentucky Derby or the Breeders' Cup. It is also common for a horse that wins the Kentucky Derby to be retired soon afterward, a way to protect the reputation of the horse for breeding. The tracks prosper by offering races with large purses for owners that will also attract spectators and bettors.

Bettors prefer competitive races with many horses, that is, more betting options. Fans want to watch competitive races between horses they recognize or with whom they can identify. Racing on dirt in North America is necessary because racing is a year-round sport; owners know that their horses need to work (race) to defray the costs of their upkeep. Daily racing on grass is not possible; racing in Europe and Australia, for example, moves from track to track, and a particular track may have only forty to fifty race days per year. While racetracks in North America also have meets, and racing may move from track to track during the year, a meet will last for sixty to ninety consecutive days. Moreover, most racing is regulated by state organizations, which act independently and for their own interests; there is often little cooperation across state boundaries. In an attempt to provide some structure or consensus among horse-racing interests, the National Thoroughbred Racing Association (NTRA) was formed in 1997; however, the NTRA has little power to regulate racing and so far has only been a marketing group. As of 2004, certain groups were vying for control over racing by buying race tracks in several states. For example, Churchill Downs Inc. owned Churchill Downs in Kentucky and purchased Ellis Park in Kentucky, Calder in Florida, Hollywood Park in California, Arlington Park in California, and Hoosier Park in Indiana. Magna Corporation owned Santa Anita in California, Gulfstream Park in Florida, and Laurel and Pimlico tracks in Maryland. The other major player was the New York Racing Association (NYRA), which controled racing at three tracks: Aqueduct, Belmont, and Saratoga.

## Social Aspects

Horse racing is known as the "sport of kings," a phrase coined in England around the time of Charles II and used

**Secretariat.** Jockey Ron Turcotte rides the famed Triple Crown winner Secretariat in 1973 at Belmont Park in New York. Secretariat is considered to be one of the greatest American horses ever. It rekindled interest in the sport of horse racing when it won the Triple Crown, taking the Belmont Stakes by a record thirty-one lengths. © *AP/Wide World Photos*

to refer to those who have the means to own and race horses. Case's *The Right Blood* and Hotaling's *They're Off: Horseracing at Saratoga* describe the aristocratic aspect of racing. At the same time, racing is often described as similar to boxing in that the sport brings all classes of people together. For example, in the 1800s, the typical relationship was composed of the plantation master, who owned the horses; the African American slaves, who were the early jockeys and trainers; and the fans, who came from all classes. There were over 100 African American jockeys in the late 1800s, and Isaac Murphy was the best, winning three Kentucky Derbies (1884, 1890, 1891) and 44 percent of his races. By the 1930s, however, there were no African Americans jockeys. Fewer than ten African American jockeys were riding in thoroughbred races in 1975. Marlon St. Julien rode Curule in the Kentucky Derby in 2000, becoming the first African American jockey in the Derby since 1921 (see sidebar). Diversity came later for women and Hispanics. On 7 February 1969, Diane Crump became the first woman to ride in a

pari-mutuel race, and two weeks later Barbara Jo Rubin became the first woman to win a pari-mutuel race. Julie Krone was the first female jockey to win a Triple Crown race, winning the Belmont in 1993.

## Wagering

Gambling and horse racing have always been linked. Even when gambling was not legal, it was often carried on privately. The owners of the horses in the early match races bet on their own horses and often had a third person handle the bets. Soon the third person arranged for all bets and kept a "book" of the wagers, hence, the term "bookie." Bookmaking began around 1788 in England; the first American bookmaking business was organized in Philadelphia in 1866. Bookies were eventually allowed to pay for the right to accept bets at the racetracks; all bookies were placed in a separate area, the "betting ring," and race goers could shop for the most favorable odds. If the money waged on a single horse would cause a bookie to lose money if that horse won, he would "lay

## Women in Racing

Mrs. Laska Durnell was the first female owner to enter a horse in the Kentucky Derby; her horse Elwood won in 1904. In 1942, seven of the eight top finishers in the Derby were owned by women, and female owners were commonplace in 2004. Penny Chenery owned Secretariat, perhaps the most celebrated horse in the latter half of the twentieth century. Ten female trainers have started horses in the Derby, with Shelley Riley coming the closest to a Derby win with Casual Lies, who was second in 1992. Jenine Sahadi was the first woman to train a Breeders' Cup Winner in 1996 and she won again in 1997. In 2002, Laura de Seroux trained Azeri to a Breeders' Cup win and the horse was later voted Horse of the Year. Diane Crump, Patricia Cooksey, Andrea Seefeldt, and Julie Krone (twice) have ridden in the Kentucky Derby. Krone was the first woman to ride in the Breeders' Cup. While the number of female jockeys has increased, it was still a struggle for them to find mounts in the early 2000s.

off" the wagers by placing win bets on that horse with other bookies.

The pari-mutuel betting system, developed in France, is the most common form of betting in American racing. With the pari-mutuel system, customers bet against the other bettors; all the money is included within a single pool, and the odds are determined by the interest of the bettors. If the odds go down on one horse, they will increase on the other horses in the race. In short, there is no need for a bookie and the house (the racetrack) usually has sufficient money in the pool to pay the winning bettors. The track could still lose money, however, because rules require that all payouts must be at least ten cents on a two-dollar bet. Another significant aspect of pari-mutuel betting is that the state and/or whoever operates the wagering can take money from the pool before the payouts are made. Approximately 20 percent of all money wagered is not returned to the bettors but is shared by the state, the track, the horsemen, and others. The size of the takeout varies by state and is often a sensitive issue for horseplayers.

## Popularity

Thoroughbred racing was the number one spectator sport for most of the twentieth century, with yearly attendance of 40,377,000 (1965) and 48,824,000 (1974) compared to 23,437,000 (1965) and 30,630,000 (1974), respectively, for major league baseball, which was second in attendance. In 1979, the *Daily Racing Form* reported that horse racing was still the number one spectator sport even though attendance dropped over one million that year (Rudy, p. 339). While it was common for tracks to have crowds between 20,000 and 50,000 in the 1940s, attendance had declined by the early 2000s, except for special events such as the Triple Crown races and the Breeders' Cup. The all-time record for thoroughbred racing is 163,628 for the 1974 Kentucky Derby; 100,311 attended the 1999 Preakness. The Breeders' Cup races attracted 80,452 fans in 1998; on-track attendance at the 2003 Breeders' Cup at Santa Anita was 51,648. At the same time, the average daily on-site attendance at race tracks has declined. Attendance at Belmont Park, for example, has steadily declined from 23,006 in 1973 to 5,930 in 2003. (*American Racing Manual*, 2001; *Daily Racing Form*, 2003).

Moreover, while horse racing was among the top five spectator sports after World War II, interest had waned so that only 1 to 2 percent listed horse racing as their favorite sport in 2000 (McDaniel and Vander Velden). Racing is also plagued by poor demographics; the image of the typical track patron is an old, retired, blue-collar male. While there was a marketing effort to bring horse racing back into mainstream America, many point to mistakes that horse racing made following the war. Racing leaders did not get in on the rise of television, deciding to protect the on-track attendance by not embracing television. However, by 2004 it had to compete with the major professional and collegiate team sports for attention. Promoting the Triple Crown and the Breeders' Cup is highlighted, and television ratings increase when there is a possibility of a Triple Crown winner. As a way to generate "team spirit" interest as opposed to interest in a single horse, the inaugural Sunshine Millions was run in January 2003 and featured races between horses bred in California and those from Florida. It is difficult to become a fan of a favorite horse when its racing career is so short and its handlers avoid competition with rivals; rivalries between Swaps and Nashua (1955), Alydar and Affirmed (1978), and Sunday Silence and Easy Goer (1989) captured the imagination of fans and the NTRA would like to develop more of them.

While large crowds at racetracks were once the norm and the benchmark for racing interest, they are no longer useful measures. Outside of races like the Kentucky Derby, Preakness, Belmont, and Breeders' Cup, track attendance is down. "Handle," the amount of money wagered, is now the benchmark, and more money is now wagered from bettors not at the track. Obviously, larger audiences mean more betting, but patrons can now bet on races at tracks all over the world; videos of races are simulcast to other racetracks and beamed to betting places (off-track) with no live racing. Moreover, in many states it is possible to bet online. Thus, when a racetrack reports the amount of money bet, it is broken down into "on-track," within state, and out-of-state subtotals. The "out-of-state" handle is usually the largest.

With the money wagered at a track the measure of success, and with most bettors not on-site, competition for the gambling dollar has increased. The tracks with the best racing attract the most wagers and the best horses will race at the tracks with the largest purses. To increase the quality of racing several states (Delaware, West Virginia, Louisiana) have legalized slot machines at racetracks and have used the slot money to increase the purses for horse racing. States without slot machines are at a disadvantage, which has prompted many of them (Maryland, New Jersey, New York, Pennsylvania, and others) to consider legalizing slot machines or video poker machines at racetracks to support horse racing

*See also:* Colonial-Era Leisure and Recreation, Southern America Leisure Lifestyle

## BIBLIOGRAPHY

"African-Americans." Available from http://www.kentuckyderby .com/2002/.

*American Racing Manual.* New York: Daily Racing Form Press, 2001 edition.

Bowen, Edward. *The Jockey Club's Illustrated History of Thoroughbred Racing in America.* Boston: Bullfinch Press, 1994.

Case, Carole. *The Right Blood: America's Aristocrats in Thoroughbred Racing.* New Brunswick, N.J.: Rutgers University Press, 2001.

*The Daily Racing Form,* 5 November 2003.

Davidson, Scooter Toby, and Anthony, Valerie, eds. *Sport of Kings: America's Top Women Jockeys Tell Their Stories,* Syracuse, N.Y.: Syracuse University Press, 1999.

Hillenbrand, Laura. *Seabiscuit: An American Legend.* New York: Random House, 2001.

"The History of the Thoroughbred in America." Available from http://www.racingmuseum.org.

"Horseracing." *Encyclopedia Britannica Deluxe Edition,* CD Version, 2003.

Hotaling, Edward. *They're Off! Horseracing at Saratoga.* Syracuse, N.Y.: Syracuse University Press, 1995.

———. *The Great Black Jockeys: The Lives and Times of the Men Who Dominated America's First National Sport.* Rocklin, Calif.: Forum, 1999.

Kay, Joyce, and Vamplew, Wray. *Encyclopedia of English Horseracing.* London: Frank Cass and Company, 2003.

Law, Tom, and Michele MacDonald. "Stars Out in Full Force." *Thoroughbred Times* 19, no. 5 (2003): 26–27.

McDaniel, Steve, and Lee Vander Velden. "Profile of Those Expressing Interest in Thoroughbred Horseracing." Unpublished study, University of Maryland, 1998.

Rudy, William. *Racing in America, 1960–1979.* New York: The Stinehour Press, 1980.

Simon, Mary, and Mark Simon. *Racing Through the Century: The Story of Thoroughbred Racing in America.* Mission Viejo, Calif.: Bowtie Press, 2003. See the Afterword.

"Women in the Derby." Available from http://www .kentuckyderby.com/2002/.

*Lee Vander Velden*

# HOT RODDING

Hot rods, cars modified to increase primarily their performance and secondarily their aesthetics, first appeared in Southern California in the 1920s and 1930s. Popular early models were Ford roadsters such as the Model-T, Model-A, or 1932 Ford, better known as the Deuce. Roadsters are open cars that seat only two or three passengers, and for many years they were the only cars that buffs modified or souped up. Some historians assert that the term "hot rod" derives from the phrase "hot roadster," while others explain that rods are key engine parts that heat up when pushed to achieve the extreme speeds hot rodding entails. Either way, the term entered the American lexicon in 1945, at the end of World War II. Before that, enthusiasts tinkered with cars on their own, without the benefit of how-to magazines or speed shops. These early motorheads often got their parts on the cheap, by scavenging junkyards or even stealing them from parked cars.

As thousands of GI's returned home following World War II, they applied their increased technical know-how to the hobby many of them had put on hold for the duration of the war. As gas and tire rationing plans were lifted, car enthusiasts flocked to the ranks of two different auto hobbies. Some pursued European sports cars, and thus emphasized handling, while others gravitated towards hot rodding, which focused on American cars and engineering them to go as fast as possible. Many of these ex-servicemen experimented with fuel additives that had been used in military aircraft, which caused plenty of repercussions throughout the hobby. The popularity of the postwar do-it-yourself movement meshed perfectly with hot

**Hot rods.** Bob Miller watches Jim "Mil-Strup" Wenstrup as he works on a hot rod car in Philadelphia in 1953. Hot rods were a big part of the cruising lifestyle popular in the 1950s. © *AP/Wide World Photos*

rodding, which valued constant tinkering. The postwar affluence allowed both the older, seasoned servicemen and a new crowd of showy teenagers to participate in the hobby, as wealthier families moved beyond the one-car-per-household rule that had been *de rigeur* before the war.

This divide between more responsible purists and dramatic, aggressive youngsters greatly affected the growth of hot rodding. Police forces, parents, and the press expressed concern about the growing number of young drivers speeding brazenly down the public streets, with no regard for their own safety or that of others. By 1948, some car club umbrella groups had decided to take a stand, and developed *Hot Rod* magazine out of their newsletters and bulletins. The magazine promoted safety precautions and responsible driving, and strove to distinguish between the maniacal teenagers and the safety-oriented, civic-minded car buffs who constituted what they considered the real population of hot rodders. *Hot Rod* was instrumental in institutionalizing the quarter-mile drag race as what real hot rodders did with their souped-up vehicles. Wally Parks, who took over as the magazine's editor in 1949, believed that by channeling rowdy youths off the streets, where they were a public menace, and into the organized, orderly world of drag racing, he could repair hot rodding's

tarnished image and protect the sport from being banned or strictly regulated by outside forces. Parks encouraged a wholesome ethic for hot rodders, suggesting that readers visit their local police to establish good ties, always stop to help stranded motorists, and refrain from using frightening or dangerous-sounding club names. One of the other main results of Parks's leadership, the establishment of the quarter-mile race, changed the nature of hot rodding, since this race valued rapid acceleration—and thus shortest elapsed time—instead of the previously sought highest achieved speed. The tension between these two goals continues to exist in the hot rodding culture. Drag races still measure both statistics for each race, although race winners are those with the lowest elapsed time, not necessarily the highest speed.

## Style

While hot rodding has always been associated with drag racing, the aesthetic aspect of the sport, primarily in terms of the modification of stock to "custom" cars, has been equally important. Although any car could be converted into a hot rod or custom car, until 1955, hot rodders favored Ford bodies, engines, and other parts. Ford made parts that were cheap, easy to find, and easy to interchange among model years. In 1955 there was the debut of the small-block (265-cubic-inch displacement) V-8 engine, which combined small size and a favorable power-to-weight ratio. It soon displaced the famous "flathead" Ford V-8 as the favorite "mill" among hot rodders. Whichever type of car a hot rodder worked on, they all had to have I-beam or tubular front axles, which was a tradition in the community. In the late 1940s to mid 1950s, a dropped or "Dago" axle became an integral part of the hot rod. The West Coast made popular the "raked" look, in which the back of a car's body was elevated by the use of "big-n-littles"—taller tires in the rear, smaller ones in the front. This gave the car a pleasing, aggressive stance. As the 1940s ended, closed cars began to surpass open-wheel roadsters in popularity. A hot rod is a hot rod because of its general aesthetic or overall look. No specifications exist that can include or disqualify a vehicle from hot rod status.

## Later Years

Most hot rodders feel that the golden years of their hobby were 1945 to 1960. These were the years before major sponsorships commercialized the industry and political dissent and a changing U.S. culture questioned the values hot rodders espoused. Although many hot rodders attributed changes in their hobby to these issues, experts date some problems that arose within hot rodding to as early as 1955. Cheating ran rampant, and professionalism threatened the amateur code that had previously characterized hot rodding due to the influx of large corporate sponsorships and prize money outlays. In the late 1950s, worries that drag racing was not removing the danger from public streets resurfaced. In these years, most strips fell under commercial ownership. As airports saw more business, they had little room for racers, who were forced to race on the commercial strips, pushing amateur racers out. *Hot Rod* magazine also changed direction, increasing coverage of more general automotive issues, which angered and isolated old-fashioned enthusiasts.

By the early 1970s, a different aesthetic had taken over. Hot rods featured bubble paint, cartoon-like designs, and chassis designs that elevated the body and left the wheels sticking out of cars. These changes reflected how far hot rodding was moving from its roots, and many enthusiasts disliked the new look. The 1970s also saw corresponding changes in the drag racing industry. As the National Hot Rod Association (NHRA) consolidated programs, amateurs had even less opportunity to participate. States legislated against the environmental damage hot rods and drag races caused, including noise and other pollution. Moreover, the increasing professionalization of the sport was at odds with the civic-mindedness that had long been an important part of hot rodding.

## Resurgence

Hot rodders are almost exclusively male, although there is some evidence that the hobby is attracting more women. In the old days, enthusiasts might have been family men holding down jobs who tinkered with cars in their spare time, or they could have been young men souping up their parents' cars or ones they had saved for and bought on their own. The hot rodder considered himself—and still did in the early 2000s—an individual, a free thinker, someone who lived a different lifestyle, outside the mainstream. Many hot rodders are men in their 50s, who developed a love for the cars of the old days in their youth, and who can finally afford to maintain one of these high-maintenance cars. One of the most important parts of the hot rod lifestyle is the camaraderie and friendship that develops among enthusiasts. Friendly rivalries exist, between Ford and Chevy owners, for instance, or between different car clubs, but most hot rodders identify as part of a larger community as well.

## Street Rods and Custom Cars

Some of these nostalgia-seekers are happier owning street rods, which are period cars that have newer parts inside them, making them much more reliable. While alterations to hot rods focus on performance and aesthetics, owners customize street rods to be comfortable, including such luxuries as electric windows and air conditioning, both unthinkable in a hot rod. Since street rods do not demand an owner's constant attention, true hot rodders sometimes look down on them as showpieces barely distinguishable from custom cars. Custom cars are modified versions of stock vehicles. "Show cars" are the most highly modified of custom cars, often built from the gound up and one of a kind. They are meant to be seen, not to be driven. Custom cars do not get dirty, since their owners do not race them. They are expensive to create, and involve a high degree of artistic vision. One of the most important rules of thumb for customizing is that newer parts can go on older cars, but never vice versa. Customizers often mix parts—putting Buick fenders on a Ford body, for instance—in attempts to maximize the most impressive, best-looking parts of a car to create a uniquely attractive vehicle. The basic goal is to make any car look lower, longer, and wider. No matter what type of car they are working on, modern hot rodders often refer to old magazine pictures and try to recreate what they see there. Period touches are much prized.

## Cultural Influences of Hot Rodding

Hot rodding has had a significant effect on American culture beyond racing and the cars themselves. The 1950s and 1960s saw the development of hot rod music, largely out of Southern California. Groups such as the Beach Boys, Jan and Dean, and Commander Cody & the Lost Planet Airmen had numerous hit songs including "Little Deuce Coupe," "409," "Drag City," and "Hot Rod Lincoln," the latter being in the "rockabilly" genre. The hot rod, immortalized in music and as depicted in B movies such as *Teenage Thunder* (1958) and fine films such as *American Grafitti* (1973), symbolized freedom, creativity, and rebelliousness among America's youth.

## Conclusion

Hot rodding celebrates hands-on, creative engineering, combined with an eye for aesthetics. It celebrates America's heritage as a car-producing and car-loving nation, as well as the balance between the individual and the larger community. Hot rodding maintained its popularity in the early twenty-first century because it did not indulge in pure nostalgia, but allowed innovation and creativity. Most importantly, enthusiasts in 2004 were just as anxious to put their cars to the test and see what they had under that smartly painted hood.

*See also:* Auto Racing, Drag Racing, Open Wheel Racing, Sports Car Racing, Stock Car Racing

## BIBLIOGRAPHY

Batchelor, Dean. *The American Hot Rod.* Osceola, Wis.: Motorbooks International, 1995.

Moorhouse, H. F. *Driving Ambitions: An Analysis of the American Hot Rod Enthusiasm.* New York: Manchester University Press, 1991.

Post, Robert C. *High Performance: The Culture and Technology of Drag Racing 1950–2000.* Baltimore: The Johns Hopkins University Press, 2001.

Spohn, Terry, ed. *The Fast Lane: The History of NHRA Drag Racing.* New York: Regan Books, 2001.

Vincent, Peter. *Hot Rod: An American Original.* Osceola, Wis.: MBI Publishing Company, 2001

*Elissa L. David*

# HUMOR

**See** *Joking*

# HUNTING

From the moment their feet touched land, early seventeenth-century European immigrants to America hunted wild game out of necessity for their survival. However, the motives, means, and opportunities to engage in recreational hunting in America only emerged in the early nineteenth-century. Why this delay in the birth of an activity ardently pursued by millions of Americans?

## Colonial Hunting and Its Economic and Social Meanings

European colonists stepped ashore in a wildlife wonderland, teeming with seemingly limitless numbers of edible creatures and no laws restricting access, unprecedented in the homelands they left behind. In contrast, the wildlife in their lands of origin existed solely for the sporting pleasures of the sociopolitical elites. Europe's feudal system denied the agricultural masses the right to weapons, hunting dogs, and other tools useful in bringing wild protein to the tables of peasants. As late as the nineteenth century, only .01 percent of Englishmen were legally eligible to hunt. Not until 1880 did the right to hunt even rab-

bits arrive at the doorsteps of English commoners (Herman, pp. 247–248).

America's European colonists eagerly added wild flora and fauna to their resource base and survived their precarious toehold on the North American continent because of those food sources. They hunted at first while establishing their farms, but reduced their dependence on hunting as soon as possible as a marker of achieving agricultural self-sufficiency. A colonist who continued to devote much time to hunting risked descending to the status of social pariah.

Some colonists opted to become commercial hunters, pursuing the lucrative trade in deerskins and other pelts and furs. Demand for such asset stripping seemed insatiable. For example, in the two decades before the American Revolution, the port of Savannah, Georgia, alone shipped 600,000 deer hides (Koller, p.18). The American farmer, however, achieved status by overcoming and controlling nature by making her agriculturally fruitful. Hunters lived off the land and did not aid in conquest of the wilderness. They rose to top ranks of social personages only when they used their hunting skills while answering the call to arms in defense of the nation.

## The Development of Elite Hunting

The frontier riflemen who rallied to fight the British during the Revolution attained national heroic status after participating in celebrated battles, such as King's Mountain. Daniel Boone, while contributing only modest military service in the Revolution, demonstrated a heroic capacity to enter the wilderness on successful hunts and expand the nation's geographic knowledge as a spin-off of his wanderings. The national image of wilderness hunters began to turn the corner in the early nineteenth century, as exploration and natural history study became expressions of the quest for progress.

The Lewis and Clark expedition to explore the Louisiana Purchase and document its natural history generated a national cast of heroic hunter-naturalists. James Audubon expanded the hunter-naturalist role, creating a fashion of natural history study by recreational hunters who justified their trophy rooms as displays of scientific knowledge. Hunting and taxidermy walked hand in hand, and private and public museums flourished, transforming recreational hunting into productive leisure. Because the nascent industrialism of the United States in the early nineteenth century deprived urban males of extensive contact with wilderness, the newly formed legitimacy of recreational hunting led them to seek respite from the toils of commerce by traveling to rural environs with guns, dogs, and fishing rods.

American recreational hunters gained a voice through the writings of Henry William Herbert (Frank Forester), who articulated the gentleman's sporting code of the English upper classes. For two decades his magazine articles and books fostered the infancy of outdoor journalism in America. Herbert conveyed the English elite's version of true sportsmanship: self-restraint in the hunting field, skilled use of arms to ensure humane kills, thorough knowledge of and respect for the game animals one attempted to harvest, and harvesting no more than could be put to immediate use.

The American recreational hunter constructed his self-image from an amalgam of English elite sporting values, along with the evolving image of the American hunter-hero as naturalist and self-reliant individualist who successfully entered the wilderness and mastered its animal resources. The best of two worlds resulted: reproducing the status-enhancing activities of the British elite and achieving personal renewal through submersion in the wilderness as a self-renewal experience.

By 1850, middle-class urban hunters began forming hunting clubs, staging dinners, and lobbying legislatures to establish and enforce game laws that controlled numbers harvested, open seasons, and methods of hunting. A form of class warfare emerged between middle-class recreational hunters and lower- and working-class subsistence and market hunters.

Market hunting became increasingly lucrative as westward-moving railroads provided rapid transport to eastern urban game markets. Throughout the remainder of the nineteenth century, the middle-class recreational hunters never relented in their campaign to save game for current and future generations of recreational hunters. Teddy Roosevelt stands out among those raising their voices in sporting journals and in legislative halls, warning of game species' declines because of unrestricted market hunting.

The turn of the century witnessed a triumph of recreational hunting interests when the federal Lacey Act passed, sounding the death knell of market hunting by ending the interstate shipment of wild game that was harvested in violation of state laws. During his presidency, Teddy Roosevelt continued to create game land refuges, first initiated with the founding of Yellowstone National Park in 1872.

The year 1900 also marked the trough of decline in game animal numbers in America, especially the white-tail deer. International treaties with Mexico and Canada in the twentieth century established critical protections for migrating waterfowl in the form of refuges for nesting and migration pathways. Wise wildlife-management practices throughout the twentieth century restored many American wildlife species to presettlement numbers. A little-contested claim insists that whitetail deer are more numerous in 2004 than when the Pilgrims stepped ashore on Plymouth Rock. In sum, America's political leaders saved recreational hunting for the common man as well as the well-heeled elite sportsman.

While recreational hunting flourished among the middle-class elite during the nineteenth century because of hunting's dual associations with the English social elites and American frontier hunter heroes, the twentieth century witnessed a dramatic surge of hunting's popularity among the rural and working classes. The burgeoning popularity resulted from significant price declines in sporting arms, automobile transportation, and highway construction that provided access to productive game lands. The urban industrial labor force in states such as Michigan negotiated labor contracts with flexible vacation times and other clauses that recognized the importance of hunting and fishing seasons to factory workers.

## Perpetuation of Hunting Traditions in Rural and Small-Town America

Hunting traditions grow out of group experiences, which gratify group members and motivate them to intentionally replicate those experiences in the future. In the mid-nineteenth century, middle-class elite recreational hunters formed hunting clubs and bought or leased private hunting grounds for exclusive use of members, thus providing themselves access to desirable hunting environments. Most of those organizations no longer survive. On the other hand, rural and small-town America often exists in the midst of wildlife habitats found in farm-field edge rows and woodlots in which all interested community members are welcome to hunt.

Hunting seasons generally open after the harvest, when crop stubble and residues provide prime hunting for quail, pheasants, deer, and other game animals. Opening of the season for locally abundant species generates school closings as well as attenuated hours for some businesses. Some churches offer up prayers for divine protection of hunters in the forests and fields during the season. In deer-hunting areas, some towns erect "meat poles," where each day's harvest can be publicly displayed. Communities still stage "game dinners" as fund-raisers for local church and school projects.

The economic impact matters in communities where the hunting seasons lure hunting tourists to avail themselves of local guides, hotels, restaurants, and sporting goods stores. Small towns offering nearby access to deer, ducks, geese, pheasants, quail, elk, or other popular species are specially blessed financially. In short, hunting traditions flourish, whether for local consumption or external exploitation, in towns or rural areas with abundant hunting opportunities, past and present.

## The Culture of the Vacation Hunting Trip

Courier and Ives' sporting prints of the mid-nineteenth century portrayed middle-class recreational hunters afield, in forests, on lakes and streams, harvesting nature's wild bounty under the watchful, approving eyes of their wilderness guides. Hunting and fishing in the nineteenth century became the most popular participatory outdoor sports; vacations from urban occupations provided the necessary venue. Nineteenth-century hunting "vacations," as described in William Faulkner's *The Bear,* involved a small army of friends, relatives, hired camp cooks, and other miscellaneous helpers invading a hunting area and inhabiting the camp for the duration. A weekend, a week, two weeks, a month could be dedicated to pursuing the yearly hunting experience.

In the twentieth century, factors such as industrial paid vacations and plants closed for maintenance, repairs, or inventory reduction contributed to America's creation of a vacation mentality. Industrial working-class males often split vacations between a week with the family at the lake during the summer and a week with the boys in the deer woods in the fall. While the numbers of women joining men in the hunting field slowly inch up, recreational hunting remains overwhelmingly an adult male interest.

## The Mostly Male Rituals of the Hunting Season

Rituals of the hunt occur everywhere recreational hunting exists. European hunting rituals include carefully organized group hunts with ancient hunting horn signals choreographing the stages of the pursuit from open to close. Post-hunt rituals focus on proper respect shown slain game by means of artful display of the bag and group moments of silence while the hunting horn announces appreciation to St. Hubertus, patron saint of hunters.

American hunters have not reproduced those rituals left behind on long-ago European shores. American hunting rituals, most commonly found in the behaviors of those pursuing America's most important game animal, the whitetail deer, include such hunting folkways as preferences for trophies of larger and older male deer to earn hunter bragging rights. The mostly male hunting rituals are legendary, humorous at times, scandalous by repute, and contribute many of the fondest memories retained by their practitioners. One ritual is equality: sharing the hunt harvest with members of the groups on a roughly equal basis. Members of the hunting camp/community adopt equalitarian roles, leaving behind their civilian statuses. Tasks in a hunting camp are assigned by age and experience. If the members are roughly equal in age and experience, they distribute camp chores in random rotation, unless unusually able specialists negotiate access to tasks at which they clearly excel.

In group hunts, the group leader randomly rotates posts or stands so that all have chances at the more productive stands, as well as those offering lesser probabilities of success. Missed shots often provide occasions for hilarity in the form of shirttails being pruned or some other mild degradation ceremony. Young and first-time hunters who succeed in harvesting their quarry may receive congratulations in the form of blood from the downed animal being smeared on their faces during the cleaning stage. Every experienced hunter likely remembers his own moment of being "blooded."

Trophy displays of antlered heads of deer or bearskin rugs also qualify as a mostly male ritual, with trophy rooms often being relegated to basements, attics, or garage workshops. Among the more disreputable rituals are hunting camps devoid of razors and regular bathing, the promiscuous consumption of alcohol and tobacco products, and meals fit only for carnivores requiring the constant attendance of antacids. Men sitting about playing card games, overeating, and engaging in a generally politically incorrect atmosphere of conversation and conduct compose the image of hunting camps envisioned by those not present.

## Opposition to Hunting

As early as the Renaissance and Enlightenment periods some voices insisted hunting for sport exacerbated the development of cruelty in men's characters. The cruelty theme motivated much of the subsequent opposition to recreational hunting, from the formation of the Society for the Prevention of Cruelty to Animals in England (1824) to its American counterpart (1866). The tremendous popularity of recreational hunting in the nineteenth century overpowered these voices. During the last quarter of the twentieth century, the animal rights movement dramatically turned up the volume of protest against

**Bird hunting.** Hunters come back from a successful hunting trip. In bird hunting, the dogs are used to retrieve the downed birds from the water. © *Corbis*

hunting for sport. Organizations such at PETA (People for the Ethical Treatment of Animals) and CASH (Committee to Abolish Sport Hunting) insist such activities must be extinguished. Animals have rights, the anti-hunters proclaim, and interfering in the natural life courses of animals is immoral. Walt Disney's classic animated film *Bambi* illustrates the ease with which sport hunting can be put on the defensive.

Hunting opponents also argue that wildlife agencies serve as a tool for hunters to ensure them adequate wildlife targets. Therefore the agencies refuse to enact adequate measures to control wildlife populations without having to resort to hunting as a management tool. In fact, antihunting voices advance the counterintuitive argument that removing deer from a herd actually stimulates multiple births and net gains in herd numbers. Opponents also support more restrictive firearms controls, asserting that hunters manifest masculinity anxieties, that is, they claim that hunters use firearms to prove their capacities to dominate other beings with the use of deadly force. These strategies, as well as other public relations tactics, all add up to a vigorous culture war delineating

apparently irreconcilable differences. Human population growth and real estate development unwittingly reduce habitat essential for wildlife. Game species such as deer and geese readily adapt to close contact with humans and compete for space. Hunters and hunting opponents clash about appropriate control measures.

## Political and Cultural Power of the Hunting Lobby and Culture

Recreational hunting topped the list of most popular participatory outdoor pastimes in the nineteenth century. This popularity continued into the twentieth century, perhaps reaching its zenith in 1945 when 25 percent of all adult American males engaged in recreational hunting (Herman, p. 271). Recreational hunters strongly supported the 1937 enactment of the Pittman-Robertson Act, which collects excise taxes on new sales of hunting equipment. As of 2003, this law contributed roughly $155 million per year to wildlife management services. Those monies, plus $420 million per year from license sales, funded three-quarters of the budgets of most state wildlife agencies.

On the other hand, percentages and numbers of recreational hunters sagged in the last half of the twentieth century. In 2001, 13 to 14 million Americans sixteen years and older, roughly 6 percent of this age cohort, participated in recreational hunting. This total represents a dramatic decline from the roughly 19 million licensed hunters after World War II. Between 1991 and 2001, the number of all hunters declined by 7 percent. Such reductions, in both absolute numbers and percentages, may be due to challenges facing the carrying capacity of recreational hunting: population growth and loss of wildlife habitat. Perhaps a more powerful explanation for decreased participation in recreational hunting resides with the increasingly dominant urban lifestyles and worldviews, which exist across a cultural divide from the rural and small town culture, which still nourish recreational hunting.

Opposition to hunting has energized the hunting community to successfully seek passage of "anti-hunter-harassment" laws in all fifty states. Thousands of chapters of wildlife species-specific organizations promote habitat protection, restoration, and acquisition for ducks, deer, quail, wild turkey, elk, and various game fishes. SCI (Safari Club International) promotes a positive image of recreational hunting with its "Sportsmen Against Hunger" program that recruits hunter donations of thousands of pounds of game meat to charitable organizations. Hunter safety programs required of new hunters claim to have steadily reduced hunting season accidents to record low levels. In sum, the hunting community recognizes its controversial public face and strives continuously to massage its image.

Will recreational hunting survive in the twenty-first century? Hunting opponents trumpet the message that their constituency is ever younger while hunters grow ever older. Hunters face an uphill battle to recruit the next generation of hunting enthusiasts. The culture war will continue.

*See also:* Blood Sports; Colonial-Era Leisure and Recreation; Fishing, Freshwater; Fishing, Saltwater/Deep Sea; Men's Leisure Lifestyles; Southern America Leisure Lifestyles; Target Shooting

**BIBLIOGRAPHY**

Aron, Cindy S. *Working at Play: A History of Vacations in the United States.* New York: Oxford University Press, 1999.

*Back Then: A Pictorial History of Americans Afield.* Wautoma, Wis.: Willow Creek Press, 1989.

Herman, David Justin. *Hunting and the American Imagination.* Washington, D.C.: Smithsonian Institution Press, 2001.

Hummel, Richard L. *Hunting and Fishing for Sport: Commerce, Controversy, Popular Culture.* Bowling Green, Ohio: Bowling Green State University Popular Press, 1994.

Koller, Larry. *The Treasury of Hunting.* New York: Odyssey Press, 1965.

Lamar, May, and Rich Donnell. *Hunting: The Southern Tradition.* Dallas: Taylor Publishing Company, 1987.

McClane, A. J. *McClane's Great Fishing and Hunting Lodges of North America.* New York: Holt, Rinehart and Winston, 1984.

Marks, Stuart A. *Southern Hunting in Black and White: Nature, History, and Ritual in a Carolina Community.* Princeton, N.J.: Princeton University Press, 1991.

Miller, John M. *Deer Camp: Last Light in the Northeast Kingdom.* Cambridge, Mass.: MIT Press, 1992.

Posewitz, Jim. *Inherit the Hunt: A Journey into the Heart of American Hunting.* Helena, Mont.: Falcon Publishing, 1999.

Regan, Tom. *The Case for Animal Rights.* Berkeley: University of California Press, 1983.

Reiger, John. *American Sportsmen and the Origins of Conservation.* New York: Winchester Press, 1975.

Samuel, David E. *Know Hunting: Truths, Lies, and Myths.* Cheat Lake, W.V.: Know Nothing Publications, 1999.

Sheehan, Laurence, Carol Sama Sheehan, and Kathryn George. *The Sporting Life: A Passion for Hunting and Fishing.* New York: Clarkson Potter Publishers, 1992.

Swan, James A. *In Defense of Hunting.* San Francisco: HarperCollins, 1995.

Waterman, Charles F. *Hunting in America.* New York: Holt, Rinehart and Winston, 1973.

———. *The Hunter's World.* New York: Random House, 1976.

Wegner, Robert. *Legendary Deer Camps.* Iola, Wis.: Krause Publications, 2001.

Williams, Marjorie. *The Bucks Camp Log: 1916–1928.* Wautoma, Wis.: Willow Creek Press, 1974.

*Richard Hummel*

# ICE HOCKEY

As for most sports, the origins of ice hockey have long been the subject of debate. Some contend the game was borne of the transposition of imported, and already existing, sports such as hurley or field hockey onto the frozen lakes and ponds of North America during the early 1800s. Others suggest this was preceded by a form of the game played by the indigenous populations of Canada and the northern United States. Then again, some argue, pointing to paintings from seventeenth-century Europe, that even these versions of ice hockey had their antecedents.

Regardless of the contentious nature of its inception, however, ice hockey, as it is now known undoubtedly evolved in the Dominion of Canada. Indeed, ice hockey's governing body, the International Ice Hockey Federation (IIHF), has officially recognized the Victoria Skating Rink in Montreal, Canada, as the birthplace of the organized version of the game. Moreover, no other country is more closely associated with the sport, in either historical or contemporary terms. And it is in Canada that the game was formalized, rationalized, and later professionalized.

As the IIHF has suggested, the earliest recorded game of organized ice hockey took place in Montreal's Victoria Skating Rink on 3 March 1875. With skates and sticks, the nine-man sides took to an ice surface of 80 by 204 feet, scoring goals not with the then customary rubber ball, but a flat circular piece of wood—the precursor of the modern puck. Eight years later, the city would also play host to hockey's first championship series when teams from Montreal and Quebec City gathered at the 1883 Montreal Winter Carnival. From there, the game would grow steadily, owing much to the sponsorship of Canadian governor general Sir Frederick Arthur Stanley, who was instrumental in developing hockey in Ontario, and who would donate the Stanley Cup to be awarded annually to the amateur champions of Canada—the trophy today remains ice hockey's most prestigious prize.

Much of this early growth was also fostered by touring exhibition squads, with a number of Canadian teams touring the United States in the 1890s and early part of the 1900s. The era also saw the beginnings of professionalism, when, by the middle of the 1890s, it was widely rumored that members of these teams were accepting payments to play. At the time, the game was considered to be strictly amateur—a gentleman's sport—and the supposed payment of players became the subject of controversy and debate across Canada. However, while the leagues they played in were still officially deemed to be "amateur," it was becoming increasingly clear that players were receiving regular payments at the time. It was hardly a surprise, therefore, when the sport's first officially professional league, the International Hockey League, was established only a few years later, in 1904. Throughout the first decade of the 1900s, Canada had to face the growing reality of professionalism. And, by the 1908 to 1909 season, professionalism had taken over the highest levels of Canadian hockey.

Initially, professionalism saw the advent of a series of competing regional leagues, dominated by the National

**Miracle on Ice.** At the 1980 Winter Olympics the United States hockey team celebrates its victory against the heavily favored Soviet team in the semifinal match, a stunning upset that has since become known as the "Miracle on Ice." The U.S. went on to defeat Finland in the final game to capture the gold medal. © *AP/Wide World Photos*

Hockey Association (which, in 1917, would become the National Hockey League, or NHL) in the East, and the Pacific Coast Hockey League and Western Canada Hockey League in the West. However, from 1904 to the 1920s, a number of leagues and teams came and went—with many in the West, in particular, floundering—and, by 1926, the NHL all but stood alone as the dominant professional ice hockey league in North America. Yet even the NHL itself would struggle through much of the 1930s, with the Great Depression fiscally wounding several clubs, and the outbreak of the war in 1939 further depleting rosters. And, while the league continued to play throughout the duration of hostilities, the NHL would eventually be left with only six teams by the end of the 1940s.

Though interest in hockey would grow across the continent during the next decade, and while the newly consolidated NHL became relatively well established during this time, the 1950s were nonetheless marked by

plunging attendance. Much of this was owed to the advent of television, which saw many fans choosing to stay at home in favor of alternative forms of entertainment. Yet while a number of teams came close to folding (in particular, Boston and Chicago), the league survived, and later thrived into the 1960s, a decade marked by the league's expansion into Philadelphia, Pittsburgh, Minnesota, Oakland, Los Angeles, and St. Louis. Expansion was so successful, that in 1970, the league added two more teams, the Buffalo Sabres and the Vancouver Canucks.

The prosperity of the sport in the 1960s and 1970s saw ice hockey, and the NHL, more specifically, become an attractive option for financial investment. Entrepreneurs seeking to profit from hockey's success soon courted expansion franchises. In 1972, one group of investors, disgruntled at the slow pace at which the league was willing to grant these franchises, formed the rival World Hockey Association (WHA), signing NHL players (most notably, Chicago Blackhawks star Bobby Hull) to large contracts with the new league. The battle between the NHL and WHA would be a feature of professional ice hockey throughout the 1970s. However, arguably because more established NHL fans saw it as an inferior or secondary league, the WHA began to struggle, and, by decade's end, the leagues would merge. In decades since, the NHL has continued to expand, and while its viewership may be proportionately low in comparison to football or basketball, ice hockey has become one of America's preeminent professional sports.

Ice hockey's appeal at the collegiate level, however, is perhaps a more regionalized affair in the United States. Teams from either the Midwest or Northeast have dominated the National Collegiate Athletic Association (NCAA) national tournament (now known as the "Frozen Four") since its inception in 1948—with the University of Michigan's record nine titles topping the list. The sport's roots in U.S. colleges date back at least as far as the first documented college hockey game in 1896 between Johns Hopkins and Yale Universities. In the time since, and even though the college game is perhaps more prominent in the Midwest and the Northeast, NCAA Division One ice hockey has grown to encompass six conferences spanning much of the United States: the Eastern College Athletic Conference, the Hockey East Association, the Central Collegiate Hockey Association, College Hockey America, the Metro Atlantic Athletic Conference, and the Western Collegiate Hockey Association.

Traditionally, though the vast majority of players in the NHL are acquired from Canada's professional "major junior" leagues, a number of top Americans playing in the NHL come from the collegiate ranks, including Chris Chelios (who played at the University of Wisconsin), Brian Leetch (Boston College), and Chris Drury (who won an NCAA Championship with Boston University in 1995). Further, U.S. Olympic hockey teams have historically been largely composed of either current or former collegiate players. Undoubtedly, the most famous moment in U.S. hockey is the 1980 "Miracle on Ice," when a U.S. team made up almost entirely of collegians beat the highly favored (and, for all intents and purposes, fully professional) Soviet team enroute to the gold medal.

Interestingly, despite its purported overall dominance of the sport, the Salt Lake Games was Canada's first Olympic gold in ice hockey since 1952. Indeed, while Canadian teams may have ruled the early years of Olympic ice hockey (beginning with its introduction as a demonstration sport at the 1920 Antwerp Summer Games), since the mid-1950s the Olympics have been dominated by the Soviet Union: between 1956 in Cortina d'Ampezzo and

1992 in Albertville, the Soviets never failed to win a medal. Rationalizing their lack of Olympic success, many Canadians put the Soviet's accomplishments down to the fact that Canada's best players were in the professional NHL. Such arguments were, however, called into question during the now-famous 1972 "Summit Series," when the Soviets only narrowly lost to a Canadian team overflowing with NHL All-Stars. In many ways, the Summit Series helped to regalvanize the centrality of hockey to Canadian nationalism, with Paul Henderson's series-winning goal ranking as one of the most memorable, and oft-immortalized, moments in Canadian history.

Some have speculated that Canada's declining superiority in the sport of ice hockey, particularly at what has traditionally been perceived as the highest level of amateur competition, was a contributing factor in the NHL allowing its best players to represent their various countries at the Olympics for the first time in Nagano, Japan, in 1998 (which necessitated the NHL to suspend its regular season for three weeks). Notably, despite sending a team laden with NHL All-Stars, the Canadians failed even to win a medal at Nagano. Though being cause for concern for many Canadians, their failure to capture a medal was recognition of the growing internationalization of the sport of ice hockey. Indeed, although the NHL has expanded to thirty teams throughout North America, only six are based in Canada (the cause of much ire for many Canadian nationalists). Moreover, the league's composition is increasingly international: once almost exclusively the domain of Canadians, the NHL now also boasts players from not only the United States, but also more distant places such as Russia, Sweden, Finland, and the Czech Republic. And, with the NHL's U.S. television rights now owned by ESPN and ABC, subsidiaries of the Disney global media conglomerate, it would seem that that such internationalization of the game is set to continue in coming decades.

*See also:* Field Hockey, Olympics, Professionalization of Sport

## BIBLIOGRAPHY

Dryden, Ken. *The Game.* Toronto: Macmillan, 1985.

Dryden, Ken, and Roy MacGregor. *Home Game: Hockey and Life in Canada.* Toronto: McClelland and Stewart, 1989.

Goyens, Chrys, and Frank Orr. *Blades on Ice: A Century of Professional Hockey,* Markham, Canada: TPE Publications, 2000.

Gruneau, Richard, and David Whitson. *Hockey Night in Canada: Sport, Identities, and Cultural Politics.* Toronto: Garamond Press, 1993.

Stewart, Mark. *Hockey: A History of the Fastest Game on Ice.* New York: Franklin Watts, 1998.

Young, Scott. *War on Ice: Canada in International Hockey.* Toronto: McClelland And Stewart, 1976.

*Andrew Grainger*

# IMPRESARIOS OF LEISURE, RISE OF

A great leisure impresario's brilliance lies ultimately in extraordinary promotional energies, especially the ability to advertise and orchestrate existing elements within the popular amusement culture, to find profitable new ways to cater to the public's thirst for novelty and sensation. Master showman, obsessive gambler, and compulsive womanizer Florenz Ziegfeld Jr. (1867–1932) had a business card that read "Impresario Extraordinaire," and with good reason; he was compelled by a dream of "demolishing all the current methods of staging shows" (Ziegfeld, p. 12). No credible account of those who shaped the emergence of a distinctly American form of mass entertainment can, though, exclude Massachusetts-born showman Phineas Taylor Barnum (1810–1891), who first used extensive advertising, large-scale investment, and mass ticket sales to promote popular amusement forms. Yet according to Neil Harris in *Humbug,* "deception, hoaxing, humbugging, cheating, these were some of the words Americans commonly associated with Barnum, during his lifetime and ever since" (p. 57). Such pejorative language offers only a partial insight into why Barnum became, and in popular memory has remained, such an exemplary American impresario.

## P. T. Barnum

Barnum's celebrity as an impresario during his own lifetime was indeed extraordinary. Variety, animal exhibits, circus acts, and especially "freak shows" owe much of their subsequent momentum to his popularization of these amusement forms. Starting out in the 1830s as a hoaxer, or "confidence man," who exhibited Joice Heth (supposedly George Washington's 161-year old nurse) and the Feejee Mermaid (a shrunken composite of monkey and fishtail), he successfully reinvented himself from the 1840s onward as a flamboyant entertainer, a circus promoter, and, finally, a respected international showman who would pay almost any price for an attraction. Yet for all his reputation today as a "circus man," Bar-

num was always first and foremost a "museum man." The first American Museum (1841–1865) under his management in lower Manhattan—a cornucopia of freaks and magicians, dioramas and panoramas, aquariums, waxworks and menageries, obscure relics and stuffed animals—merits recognition as a pivotal institution in the development of the nineteenth-century "culture of exhibition." The gulf between today's more grand museums and the fairground "freak show" has never been as wide as the former would have us believe.

Barnum was the central figure in recognizing that Americans would pay for popular entertainment to fill their leisure time. The great impresario was able to expand his businesses commercially because, from the American Museum and associated lecture room stage onward, he stayed carefully within the pale of middle-class respectability and thereby guaranteed a large family attendance at his various amusements. Despite his reputation as the "prince of humbugs" for his supposed hypocrisy and hucksterism, Barnum's legitimate show exhibits, such as the midget Tom Thumb, Jumbo the elephant, the Nova Scotia Giantess, or Chan and Eng (the Siamese Twins), far outrivaled his hoaxes. "He would introduce to America the modern public museum, the popular concert, and the three-ring circus, all forerunners of vaudeville, motion pictures, and television," claimed novelist Irving Wallace in his 1959 biography of Barnum (p. 9).

Barnum, we now know, instigated none of the preceding but instead took over, publicized, and energized preexisting forms, like the dime museum, the public concert, the menagerie, the "freak show," and the three-ring circus. If not the founding father of commercial amusements he is so often considered to be, Barnum was vital to the cultural formation of both the show business ethos and the American sense of national identity. A characteristic Yankee, the irrepressible Barnum believed in the tireless improvement both of himself and of new modes of public entertainment. Twitchell supplies an apt metaphor: "Barnum's American Museum, his hoaxes, his big-top circus, his sideshows, first shifted the economic engines of modern show business into gear" (p. 61).

## The Barnum and Bailey Circus

A century and more after Barnum's death, this vigorous entrepreneur and master of the art of self-promotion retains his self-appointed title as the World's Greatest Showman largely because, in the 1880s, he became proprietor of the famous Barnum & Bailey circus, sideshows, and menagerie that featured Jumbo the elephant. Yet Barnum was over seventy years old in 1881 when he merged with James Anthony Bailey (1847–1906) to create "The Greatest Show on Earth." And he was in semi-retirement, his name already before the American public for thirty years, when, late in 1870, he entered into promoting the circus business that was to occupy so much of his attention over the remaining twenty or so years of his life. Barnum's future associate Bailey (born McGinness) had started out by delivering circus handbills, but before he was thirty he had taken the Cooper & Bailey Circus to Australia, New Zealand, and South America. Then he purchased Seth. B. Howes's superb "Great London Circus" and made Cooper & Bailey into a serious competitor with P. T. Barnum.

A baby elephant brought Bailey into partnership with Barnum because, when Cooper & Bailey's "Hebe" pachyderm gave birth, Barnum telegraphed a $100,000 offer for the new arrival. Bailey cleverly reproduced the telegram in his extensive advertising with the comment: "This is what Barnum thinks of Cooper & Bailey's baby elephant." Outsmarted, Barnum sued for peace with "a foeman worthy of my steel," and the two circuses combined (May, p. 121). After the amalgamation, James E. Cooper opted out and James L. Hutchinson became the third partner, having made a profit from selling Barnum's oft-revised autobiography on commission. "Barnum & Bailey's The Greatest Show on Earth" first opened in New York on 18 March 1881 in the new Madison Square Garden and was preceded by a huge torchlight parade that attracted 500,000 spectators.

The Barnum, Bailey, and Hutchinson circus partnership had one of its greatest coups the following year with Barnum's £2,000 purchase of "Jumbo," the largest elephant in captivity, from the London Zoo. Hutchinson soon withdrew from the partnership, and, from 1885 to 1887, "Chilly Billy" Cole and Bailey's old partner James E. Cooper replaced Bailey as managers. When the famous Barnum and Bailey partnership of the "Greatest Show on Earth" was revived, the slight, nervous, much younger (by thirty-seven years), and full-bearded Bailey became the dominant figure in its management and direction. Barnum usually liked to take the complete credit for everything he was involved with, but in practice he had little to do with the day-to-day operations of the Barnum & Bailey big top; the old man had lost interest in the daily routine of running such a large and synchronized operation. He gained most satisfaction from being, as Les Harding remarks, "the showman *par excellence,* the master of self-publicity, of flash and notoriety" (p. 85). Yet even Barnum had to admit that Bailey's hard work, energy, and supervision of the smallest details on site was as great an asset to the circus as his own notoriety. Al-

though their relationship was often strained, the famous partnership lasted until Barnum's death.

## Impresarios of Vaudeville

**Tony Pastor** Only twelve years old and billed as an "infant prodigy," Brooklyn-born Italian American Tony Pastor (1834–1908), the "father of vaudeville," obtained his first job as a New York entertainer late in 1846, engaged by P. T. Barnum to appear in blackface on the American Museum's lecture room stage as a minstrel troupe "endman," playing the tambourine, joking, and singing. He soon left Barnum to perform under the big top for the next thirteen years, touring the country as a circus acrobat, ringmaster, and singing clown. Subsequently, having outgrown circuses, Pastor worked during the 1860s and 1870s as a comic and ballad and minstrel singer in variety theaters, which he also managed, on the Bowery and on Lower Broadway, before moving in 1881 to his final and acclaimed theatrical destination on New York's Fourteenth Street, near Union Square. Pastor's career as both performer and impresario best exemplifies the transition from variety to vaudeville in New York, even if he continued to call his entertainment "variety" in a desire not to alienate those audience members accustomed to the more liberated style of the popular genre.

"Variety" was associated with beer gardens, loose morals, and the Bowery working class, while "vaudeville" had snobbish uptown French associations that suggested refinement and good taste. Some historians of vaudeville have made a case for earlier attempts at assuring respectability by Pastor's predecessors, such as Moses Kimball in Boston and Barnum in New York, who from the 1840s onward offered safely decent "lecture room" or variety theater performances as an extension of their "museums." These early showmen also maintained an image of morality by censoring plays to please even the most fastidious, excluding prostitutes, and prohibiting the sale of alcohol, while advertising their museum exhibits as educational and morally uplifting. Yet the transformation of the sometimes dubious variety acts found in New York's honky-tonks, beer gardens, free-and-easies, and concert saloons into the new and "respectable" vaudeville owed more, ultimately, to performer-manager Tony Pastor and his much-advertised cleanup campaign, begun even before the watershed years of the early 1880s.

**B. F. Keith and E. F. Albee** Despite Pastor's earlier innovations in the primary theatrical location of New York City, vaudeville as an embryonic form of mass entertainment really only emerged out of impresario Benjamin Franklin Keith's "New York" or Gaiety Dime Museum in

Boston from 1883, with its second-floor lecture theater showing variety performances to improve a faltering "freak show" business. Keith (1846–1910) had entered the show business through the two-bit candy concession at a circus. Within two years he had begun his association with another "grifter" (another word for a confidence man), former circus "outside" ticket man and "fixer" (legal adjuster) Edward Franklin Albee (1857–1930). From 1885, the two partners ran continuous variety programs in the dime museum's theater, rather than several shows a day of eight to ten acts, allowing audiences to come and go at their own convenience. This adjustment made the shows more attractive to women who were out shopping nearby.

The two impresarios also moved away from the rather sleazy "freak show" atmosphere of the dime museum by staging an abridged one-hour version of Gilbert and Sullivan's *Mikado,* a current success in a major Boston theater. Together Keith-Albee built the opulent Colonial Theatre, opened in 1893, mostly with money borrowed from the wealthy Catholic Diocese of Boston. Moving into New York's Union Square Theatre in that same year and with Keith's theaters in Philadelphia, otherwise known as the "Sunday School" circuit, the Keith-Albee management banned smoking, hat wearing, whistling, stamping, spitting on the floor, and crunching peanuts. Other managers followed Pastor and Keith-Albee's lead in the move away from bawdy and male-orientated variety, restricting drinking to intermissions or removing bars from the premises entirely and thereby making vaudeville safe for women and the "respectable" lower-middle and then middle classes to attend.

## Impresario of the Follies

The guarantee that a vaudeville entertainer had finally reached the apex of the profession from the 1910s into the 1920s, after years of dragging his or her act around booking circuits like Keith-Albee and performing before unappreciative audiences, was an appearance in the *Ziegfeld Follies,* the most prestigious Broadway showcase for rising performers. Thus, future movie comedian W. C. Fields (1880–1947), after twenty years in vaudeville as an "eccentric juggler," first achieved celebrity status in the *Follies* during World War I, appearing alongside such luminaries as Eddie Cantor, Will Rogers, and Fanny Brice. Theatrical producer and impresario Florenz, or "Flo," Ziegfeld Jr., whose German-Jewish immigrant father ran the Chicago Musical College, grew up in an atmosphere of relative comfort, austere Lutheran morals, and classical music. Yet the teenage Flo supposedly ran away for a few weeks with Buffalo Bill's Wild West show when it

came to town and also participated in small-time vaudeville enterprises.

At age twenty-six, the budding impresario used his promotional skills in lavishly advertising muscular strongman "the Great [Eugen] Sandow," who, in August 1893, during the Chicago World's Fair, opened at the family-owned Trocadero nightclub and became an immediate sensation. After an extended two-year vaudeville tour with Sandow, ambitious showman Ziegfeld moved to Broadway and produced a successful hit comedy, *A Parlour Match,* with vaudeville comedians Charles Evans and William Hoey. He then took the show to London, where Florenz met a sensational new music hall singer from Paris, the Polish-French Anna Held (1873–1918). Ziegfeld was smitten and wooed the petite Held away from both her *Folies Bergère* contract and her Spanish gambler husband with promises of Broadway wealth and fame. In 1897, his new client was unveiled in New York. Then, like Barnum at midcentury with Swedish soprano Jenny Lind, Ziegfeld successfully marketed Held to an adoring public, by inventing, for example, her custom of bathing in milk every day at the Savoy Hotel and by producing a run of musical comedies in which she appeared.

As a showman cut from the Barnum mold, Ziegfeld strove to replace the popular, multiethnic but often crude appeal of vaudeville with a sophisticated, romantic entertainment that would flaunt a changing lineup of glamorous chorus girls yet still maintain respectability. In 1906, he lost 2.5 million francs in one session gambling at the Casino in Biarritz, but a new contract with theater owner Lee Shubert came to the rescue. Ziegfeld made a further deal in 1907 with prominent "Syndicate" theatrical bookers Marc Klaw and Abe Erlanger to produce a revue-style *Follies,* based on the *Folies Bergère* of Anna Held's fame but set on the rooftop garden of the New York Theatre. This show, which featured the "Anna Held Girls" both as drummer boys and in a bathing-pool act, was not an instant success with sophisticated Broadway audiences. On tour it picked up more appreciative reviews and, back in New York, Ziegfeld engaged star vaudeville singer Nora Bayes to provide additional support. For the subsequent *Follies* of 1908 a new beauty, Lillian Lorraine, was engaged and massively promoted; recognizing that she had become superfluous, Anna Held departed temporarily for Europe. For close to twenty-five years, the self-indulgent, promiscuous, and rich Ziegfeld (who married Billie Burke in 1914) had a series of affairs with beautiful and susceptible *Follies* showgirls.

Ziegfeld may not have rated comedians like Fields, Cantor, and Rogers too highly, but he knew that comedy interludes were essential between the parades of beautiful women, at times in dance scenes "glorifying the American girl," for his kind of lavish, racy, and escapist revue entertainment to work properly. The famous "Ziegfeld Look" of the *Follies* at the New Amsterdam Theatre, on the corner of Forty-second Street and Seventh Avenue, was exemplified from 1915 onward by the brilliant Viennese designer Joseph Urban and the costumier Lady Duff-Gordon. Ziegfeld also continued to produce full-length musical comedies and innovative popular musicals like *Showboat* (1927) on Broadway, but he lost his entire fortune in the 1929 Wall Street crash. Impresario Billy Rose (1895–1966), a highly successful producer in the 1930s and 1940s of expensive musicals and aquatic showcases, was the most Barnumesque and flamboyant of Ziegfeld's Broadway successors. Ultimately, the label "Produced Under the Personal Direction of Florenz Ziegfeld" was to define an era, not only on the American stage but also in American popular culture.

The impresario or showman of an earlier time has now become an iconic American figure and since Barnum has been constantly replicated. Society would be greatly the loser for the disappearance of the larger-than-life promoter, creating huge hits and pushing big flops, earning millions then losing the lot, but always brimming with new schemes, some of them successful, others disastrous.

*See also:* Carnivals, Circuses, Commercialization of Leisure, Gilded Age Leisure and Recreation, Progressive-Era Leisure and Recreation, Urbanization and Leisure

## BIBLIOGRAPHY

Allen, Robert C. "B. F. Keith and the Origins of American Vaudeville." *Theatre Survey* 21, no. 2 (November 1980): 105–115.

Butsch, Richard. *The Making of American Audiences: From Stage to Television, 1750–1990.* Cambridge, U.K.: Cambridge University Press, 2000.

Cook, James W. *The Arts of Deception: Playing with Fraud in the Age of Barnum.* Cambridge, Mass.: Harvard University Press, 2001.

Davis, Lee. *Scandals and Follies: The Rise and Fall of the Great Broadway Revue.* New York: Limelight Editions, 2000.

Fretz, Eric. "P. T. Barnum's Theatrical Selfhood and the Nineteenth-Century Culture of Exhibition." In *Freakery: Cultural Spectacles of the Extraordinary Body.* Edited by Rosemarie Garland Thomson. New York: New York University Press, 1997.

Harding, Les. *Elephant Story: Jumbo and P. T. Barnum Under the Big Top.* Jefferson, N.C.: McFarland and Company, 2000.

Harris, Neil. *Humbug: The Art of P. T. Barnum.* Chicago: University of Chicago Press, 1973.

Matlaw, Myron. "Tony the Trouper: Pastor's Early Years." *The Theatre Annual* 24 (1968): 70–90.

May, Earl Chapin. *The Circus from Rome to Ringling.* New York: Dover Publications, 1963.

Saxon, A. H. *P. T. Barnum: The Legend and the Man.* New York: Columbia University Press, 1989.

Snyder, Robert W. *The Voice of the City: Vaudeville and Popular Culture in New York.* Chicago: Ivan R. Dee, 2000.

Toll, Robert C. *On with the Show! The First Century of Show Business in the United States.* New York: Oxford University Press, 1976.

Twitchell, James B. *Carnival Culture: The Trashing of Taste in America.* New York: Columbia University Press, 1992.

Wallace, Irving. *The Fabulous Showman: The Life and Times of P. T. Barnum.* New York: The New American Library, 1959.

Ziegfeld, Richard, and Paulette Ziegfeld. *The Ziegfeld Touch: The Life and Times of Florenz Ziegfeld, Jr.* New York: Harry N. Abrams, 1993.

*John Springhall*

# IMPROVISATIONAL THEATER
**See** *Amateur Theatrics*

# INITIATIONS
**See** *Rites of Passage*

# INTERNET

The technical accomplishments leading to the construction and prevalence of the Internet are well documented. Much of this documentation is available over the Internet itself, including those resources published by administrative groups responsible for Internet standards and practices.

## A Brief History of the Internet

In brief, the Internet originated with the conceptualization and realization of a robust packet-switched network. The first packet-switched network designs came from Paul Baran's research at RAND Corporation in the 1960s

**World Wide Web pioneer.** Tim Berners-Lee sits in his office at the Massachusetts Institute of Technology in 1998. Nearly a decade earlier, in 1989, Lee invented the portion of the Internet known as the World Wide Web, which has since revolutionized international communications, business, and leisure. © *AP/Wide World Photos*

and, independently, from Donald Davies and his colleagues at the U.K. National Physics Laboratories. Shortly thereafter, Leonard Kleinrock and UCLA's Network Management Center used packet-switching techniques to develop and refine the ARPANET, the immediate precursor to the Internet. The first ARPANET connection was successfully completed in 1969.

Packet-switching—a method of communicating data from one computer to another—allowed the construction of a single network capable of linking together a large number and variety of interior hardware and software configurations. Packet-switching technologies were standardized and put into widespread use as the Transmission Control Protocol/Internet Protocol (TCP/IP) in 1983. The implementation of TCP/IP led to exponential growth in the capacity and use of the Internet: Internet backbone speeds increased from roughly 56 kilobits per

second to over 2 gigabits per second by 2002; hosts grew from about 500 in 1983 to close to 150 million by the early 2000s.

Two major events since 1983 drastically changed the appearance and use of the Internet, making the fledgling network both more accessible to mass audiences and more adaptable to recreational and leisure-time use. The first was the commercialization of the Internet in 1991; the second was the 1993 public release (through the Mosaic browser) of Tim Berners-Lee's earlier software innovation, the World Wide Web (WWW).

Commercialization radically changed the content available over the Internet, and the World Wide Web provided a new method—based on a simplified visual interface and command structure embedded with hyperlinks—for transferring files. Both these changes were instrumental in the rapid global diffusion, acceptance, and use of today's Internet.

## Popular Uses of the Internet

Though the Internet does not yet have the volume or history of research dedicated to other popular media (e.g., television and film), Internet studies are, in general, more timely and accessible than those devoted to older media. In addition to a growing number of studies using conventional research methods—widely available within online archives—Internet research benefits from the constant monitoring and updating of data that measure the technical components of network use.

Though Internet use continued to grow dramatically, in 2004 it had yet to achieve the widespread penetration of television. Prior to the last decade, Internet use had been confined to a relatively younger, more affluent, and much more highly educated segment of the world's population than the television-viewing audience. However, many of these differences were shrinking as the Internet user population grew—most particularly in developed countries. For instance, the average age of the Internet user in the United States was approaching forty in 2004, and the percentage of women using the Internet at home had grown over the previous five years to be roughly equal that of men.

E-mail is clearly the most common use of the Internet for the 60 million Americans who go online every day. Sending and receiving messages over the Internet is most often accomplished asynchronously, though synchronous communications software—for example, "Instant Messaging" services—is increasingly popular among the Internet's younger users.

The most popular functions of the Internet for mass audiences (other than e-mail) are associated with information receiving rather than information sending. Most often, the information sought is intended for recreational and leisure-time use. For instance, searching for news and weather information has not rated as highly in user surveys as has searching for "hobby" information.

Although there is some evidence that the Internet has partially displaced television viewing as a leisure-time activity, there is less evidence of similar displacements of newspaper reading, radio listening, or other media-related activities. In comparison to other media use, then, the Internet is best regarded as a time-enhancing rather than time-displacing technology.

Research is less clear concerning the impact of the Internet on socializing with friends, family interactions, and the psychological well-being of its heaviest users. Some researchers have found social relationships formed during Internet use are less intimate and less fulfilling than those formed in more conventional contexts, resulting in an increased likelihood of depression and loneliness; others—including some of the Internet's heaviest and most accomplished users—have emphasized the more positive aspects of those relationships established and sustained through computer-mediated communications and the Internet.

## Communications Play on the Internet

**E-mail** Electronic mail was implemented on the ARPANET by Ray Tomlinson in 1971—a couple of years after that network became functional. Not part of the original network design, the first electronic mail protocols were intended to aid technical resource sharing and scientific information exchange over the ARPANET. However, stripped of the formal mediation between sender and receiver that dominated telex and telegram transmissions, e-mail messages came to be used in more spontaneous, intimate, and expressive ways. Almost immediately after becoming publicly available, e-mails—and similar, related forms of computer-mediated communications (CMC)—were transformed into personalized contexts for play.

The personal nature of e-mail encouraged its rapid growth through the late 1970s, when proprietary systems of dial-up message exchange services (e.g., MCI Mail, CompuServe) were developed and marketed for use with home computers. The personal computer revolution also proved a catalyst for the development of private bulletin board systems (BBS); personal computer owners and enthusiasts installed and widely used these systems in the late 1970s and early 1980s as free e-mail storage and forwarding systems within local telephone exchanges. Early BBS functions and capabilities were eventually absorbed into the Internet, which was able to connect larger audiences over much broader geographical areas at less cost. However, many of the most unique and most playful characteristics of e-mail first appeared during the early promulgation of personal bulletin board systems; representative examples of these include "emoticons," "flaming," and the now ubiquitous "spamming."

Initial studies of Internet communications emphasized the faceless nature of the medium and its corresponding lack of "social presence." However, e-mail users were quick to find methods of communicating emotional content that were analogous to the facial expressions, verbal tones, and body language of offline communications—though often quite different in form.

Emoticons are the most obvious examples of the personalization of e-mail texts. Playful creations of early e-mail users, these text-based symbols are created by using the visual characteristics of keyboard characters (for example :-) indicates a smiley face). Emoticons, related forms of ASCII art—any use of the visual appearance of the ASCII (American Standard Code for Information Interchange) characters—and the numerous shorthand acronyms of listservs had a similar function: to create a communications context unbound by the limitations and technical requirements of the medium. Sometimes, these new forms of play have been extreme.

Flaming, for instance, was a common and largely unexpected phenomenon of early communications play on home bulletin board systems: a barrage of critical messages sent in reply to previous messages. These criticisms were commonly lengthy, colorful, and even lurid—motivating further flaming in reply. Many bulletin board systems were entirely devoted to flaming activities, with groups of BBS users creating flaming clubs to hurl verbal barbs at one another—for no purpose other than play.

Spamming—sending unsolicited or junk e-mail (or spam) to often unwilling recipients—likewise represents an extreme form of systemic play within CMC, with both positive and negative impact. The ease with which mass-mailing lists could be compiled and employed within CMC contexts led to the widespread distribution of spam that, like the distribution of flames, was more often a form of play for senders than receivers—at least it was initially. By 2004, spam for tens of thousands of dubious commercial products and offers had become such a serious problem that the U.S. Congress had passed laws trying to limit its spread.

Software cracks, viruses, and Web site assaults (such as denial of service attacks) are similar forms of dysfunctional play within prevailing economic and social contexts. While initially these too might have been nothing more than personal expressions of identity within a mass-mediated communications environment otherwise governed by technical rules and limitations, by 2004 these attacks had also become much more harmful.

**Chat** E-mail is an asynchronous form of communication. By the late 1980s network software began to appear allowing synchronous—or real-time—message exchanges analogous to those of verbal conversations. Communications play over the Internet now commonly includes these synchronous forms, well represented by Internet Relay Chat (IRC), which was developed in 1988, and its many descendants, such as AOL's Instant Messenger.

Synchronous, online group communications software for recreational use originated as a MUD (multiuser dungeon) in 1979 when Roy Trubshaw and Richard Bartle at Essex University in the United Kingdom collaborated on the first online multiplayer adventure game: MUD1. MUD1 was a multiplayer adaptation of Will Crowther's ADVENT, or The Colossal Cave (1975), which eventually spawned an entire genre of single-player computer adventure games. MUD1—and MUDs in general—allowed a number of players to interact with one another (chat) in real time within a text-based virtual landscape (or "dungeon") using a rudimentary parser—a computer program that interprets the syntactic structure of a series of symbols or commands—and simple subject-verb commands ("use key," "open door"). Later versions of the software were labeled Multi-User Domains (or Dimension) to divorce their use from dedicated adventure game play.

MOOs—object oriented MUDs—were a subsequent refinement of the MUD software that allowed a more interactive virtual environment and user modifications of that environment. Both MUDs and MOOs have been adopted for a variety of educational and professional uses, but are most commonly used as a form of recreational communications and role-play over the Internet. Along with the evolution of graphics displays, the virtual environment for these role-playing activities has moved from a text-based screen to a more visual—and increasingly three-dimensional—context.

MUD1 was licensed to CompuServe as British Legends and discontinued as a commercial service in 1999. Other versions of the MUD software have since been used to develop more commercially viable MMORPGs, or massively multiplayer online role-playing games. The first widely played MMORPG was Ultima Online (1997), a multiplayer adaptation of Origin Systems' Ultima, a long-lived single-player computer role-playing-game series.

Everquest, a rather conventional role-playing game in the Dungeons and Dragons tradition with an innovative three-dimensional interface, came to dominate the MMORPG market soon after its release by Verant Interactive in 1999. The game, acquired by Sony Online Entertainment in 2000, had grown to over 250,000 subscribers by 2004 and created a strong secondary market of related web sites, offline information resources, and character equipment and item barter and exchange.

MMORPGs provide an imaginative and mutable context for play and are associated with large and active online—and offline—communities of players, which extend and reinforce that play. Further evolution and refinement of MMORPGs are likely as the form proves increasingly profitable.

In 2004, synchronous communications play over the Internet—including use of generic network chat applications—was much less common than e-mail and World Wide Web use. Internet Relay Chat, for instance, had changed little in form, function, or primary use since its inception in Finland in 1988. While e-mail has proven a popular alternative to conventional postal services, IRC and its derivatives have not been as widely used as substitutes for offline social interactions. Synchronous communications play over the Internet remained restricted to a relatively younger, more affluent, and more technically inclined group than users of the Internet as a whole—and there were questions as to whether the most active users of role-playing games benefit from their play or were perhaps even harmed by it.

## Social Impact of Internet Play

The recreational use of the Internet can be applied to such a broad class of CMC-related activities that there is little fundamental distinction between recreational and non-recreational use of the medium. Databases, educational programs, and business web sites—among many other online forms—engage users with graphics displays, software interfaces, and client-server hardware that parallel those used (and often first developed) to facilitate games and play.

One of the most critical issues left undecided concerning the recreational use of the Internet as of 2004 was whether online communications functions negatively inhibited or more positively supplemented and sustained offline social relationships. This was an issue raised most pointedly regarding Internet-based role-playing activities in MUD and MOO environments. Survey research presented evidence documenting both positive and negative outcomes—including contrary results published by the same research teams.

Research has found evidence of online communications activities that enhanced and substituted for (in some diminished capacity) offline interactions, but there was little similar evidence indicating that face-to-face social interactions were wholly eliminated in favor of their online facsimiles. Aside from those studies citing Internet "addiction" (an affliction most often compared to gambling addiction) among a small percentage of the user population, the most recent studies and analyses as of 2004 displayed a growing reluctance to accept those theoretical models that explained and predicted Internet use and effects based solely on the unique technological characteristics of computer-mediated communications.

To a great extent, controversies over the impact of Internet use for recreation and leisure appear similar to those controversies concerning the impact of play with other media and within other contexts. Perhaps it is only because the Internet has spread so widely and so quickly that these controversies have had little chance to be resolved with any significant measure of accuracy or satisfaction. However, it is also likely that Internet entertainment and play are more distinctive in form than in function from their offline counterparts. If so—if indeed the debate over Internet use and its outcomes is rooted in yet controversial characteristics of human behavior rather than in some more definitive and objective characteristics of networked digital media—then there is little assurance that resolutions will be soon forthcoming.

Play on the Internet, like play in many other contexts, continues to have variable and often unpredictable effects. Internet play raises issues of privacy, censorship, and security that are undetermined—and perhaps undeterminable—by existing social policies, legal precedents, or cultural values. Internet research, while topical and timely, has yet to establish clear and detailed trends of Internet use and effects within a stable communications environment.

As Internet content and functions continue to evolve rapidly, it is likely much about the future use of the Internet will confound contemporary media theory. However, many aspects of the recreational use of the Internet appear determined by those characteristics of human communicators that persist across media and cultures. Human play is one of the most fundamental of those characteristics.

*See also:* Computer/Video Games, Computer's Impact on Leisure

### BIBLIOGRAPHY

Bartle, Robert. "Early MUD History." 1990. Available from http://www.ludd.luth.se/mud.

Kraut, Robert, Michael Patterson, Vicki Lundmark, Sarah Kiesler, Tridas Mukhopadhyay, and William Scherlis. "Internet Paradox: A Social Technology that Reduces Social Involvement and Psychological Well-Being?" *American Psychologist* 53 (1998): 1017–1031.

Kraut, Robert, Sara Kiesler, Bonka Boneva, Jonathon Cummings, Vicki Helgeson, and Anne Crawford. "Internet Paradox Revisited." *Journal of Social Issues* 58 (2002): 49–74.

Nie, Norman H., and Lutz Erbring. "Internet and Society: A Preliminary Report." Stanford Institute for the Quantitative Study of Society (SIQSS). Available from http://www.stanford.edu/group/siqss.

Oikarinen, Jarkko. "IRC History." Available from http://www.the-project.org/history.html.

Pew Research Center. "Pew Internet & American Life." Available from http://www.pewinternet.org/reports.

Rheingold, Howard. *The Virtual Community: Homesteading on the Electronic Frontier.* Reading, Mass.: Addison-Wesley Publishing Company, 1993.

Short, John, Ederyn Williams, and Bruce Christie. *The Social Psychology of Telecommunications.* London: Wiley, 1976.

Smith, Jennifer, and Andrew Cowan. "Frequently Asked Questions: Basic Information about MUDs and MUDding." Available from http://www.mudconnect.com/.

Toth, Viktor. "Welcome to the Home of MUD1—British Legends!" Available from http://www.british-legends.com/.

Yamauchi, Yutaka, and Jean-Francois Coget. "Untangling the Social Impact of the Internet: A Large-Scale Survey." Information Systems Working Paper 1-02. The Anderson School at UCLA. 2002. Available from http://www.anderson.ucla.edu.

*David Myers*

# INTERWAR LEISURE AND RECREATION

The decades between the two world wars were arguably the most important years for leisure and recreation in the history of the United States. Public recreation facilities, parks, playgrounds, and community centers expanded at unprecedented rates. National park and recreation organizations flourished. Amusements and commercial recreation grew as never before. Fads and fashions, once the dalliances of the rich, swept the nation. Technology improved; radio and the movies came into their own. The automobile opened new vistas to a newly mobile public.

## Debate Over Increased Leisure

But more importantly, the 1920s and 1930s saw the culmination of the century-long work-reduction movement as labor turned to the five-day week and then the six-hour day, the next steps in its campaign for the "progressive shortening of the hours of labor." Not only had working hours been continually getting shorter for 100 years, the process seemed to be accelerating. Working hours were getting shorter faster, as evidenced by the 16 percent reduction of working hours that had occurred during the two decades before the end of World War I. Labor's new initiatives presaged reductions that were to be even more rapid. Leisure and recreation became public and political issues, discussed and debated as never before, or since.

As the 1920s began, few expected that the trend would end. On the contrary, hundreds of books and articles were written predicting that work would soon become a subordinate part of life, and rightly so. For example, speaking before the Young Men's Hebrew Association in New York, Julian Huxley called the two-day workweek "inevitable" for the simple reason that "the human being can consume so much and no more. . . ." John Maynard Keynes, George Bernard Shaw, prominent business leaders, and even historians predicted the dawning of a new age of leisure.

A leisure movement and vision had gained prominence. Increasing productivity made it inevitable that more and more people would eventually get "enough" simply because human needs that could be expressed in the marketplace were finite. As more efficient work led to the increased satisfaction of economic "necessity," the economy would begin to stabilize (or "mature"). An age of "abundance" was at hand. Having "enough," humans would be able to progress beyond work and the marketplace, spending more of their lives "outside" in those regions of human existence that were "free" and worthwhile in and for themselves. Beginning with the family and moving outward toward community and the state, people would gain increasing access to political participation, cultural expression, and creation. Advancing even further beyond the confines of utility, the average individual might even approach the realms of mind and spirit previously reserved mainly for the elite, directly experiencing nature, history, art, literature, and the life of the mind—enjoying those "given" parts of humanity that were, in their essence, free. This did not seem to be so much a distant dream as an emerging reality in the 1920s, a reality made manifest through the advent of shorter working hours.

However, such great expectations were not greeted with universal enthusiasm. Businesspeople, academics, and social critics were worried that ordinary humans would be corrupted by too much time on their hands. Some, such as Keynes, were simply concerned that leisure would become a problem, challenging humans to live up to their freedom. Many more feared that mass leisure would lead to social chaos. American industrialists and managers identified shorter hours with union "radicalism," predicting the spread of communist revolutions to American shores if the eight-hour day or five-day week became a reality.

At the start of the 1920s, most businesspeople, industrialists, and their supporters were more concerned with their immediate future than with the effect of leisure on the human condition. The decade began with a postwar depression that appeared to be different from previous economic downturns. Observers speculated that it was distinctive because too much rather than too little was being produced.

Businesspeople and journalists feared that the then current overproduction was more than a temporary economic dislocation. Perhaps overproduction was now a signal that industrial production was exceeding what people wanted to buy and were willing to give up their lives to work for. What John Stuart Mill and other economists had predicted seemed to be about to come true. Once humans got enough, they would naturally turn from work to spend time in the freer parts of their lives. Businesspeople and their supporters recognized "abundance" as a threat, a threat embodied by steadily increasing leisure.

The "threat of leisure" was clear. As people turned from work to pursue happiness in "higher," better, and freer activities, the business of America would cease to be business. The economy and work would take secondary places in American society, assuming the role of servants to a new social and cultural center.

## Commercialization of Leisure

However, by mid-decade, a new buoyant business philosophy began to dispel these fears. Abandoning their worries about "abundance," and facing the "threat of leisure" head-on, the American business community discovered and then embraced a "New Economic Gospel of Consumption." Led by economists, American business leaders began to believe that human needs for industrial products were not limited to a "natural" set of goods and services—that humans would never get "enough" and necessarily turn from work to increasing leisure (Hunnicutt, pp. 37-44).

Countering the leisure vision, a new work-expansion vision gained prominence. A new utopian hope was born: that industry could manufacture new "needs" as efficiently as it had been producing goods and services. Human needs for industrial products and services could be expanded eternally. Only improved advertising, marketing, and product development were necessary. With the help of advertising, Americans would always find new reasons to continue working "full-time." As each new luxury became an everyday necessity, a process would be set in motion that would ensure perpetual economic growth. "Abundance" would cease to threaten the nation with further erosions of work.

During the 1920s, advertising came into its own in the United States. Within companies, marketing departments gained prominence over production departments for the first time. Mass media, funded by the new marketing imperative, expanded as never before. Radio, for

example, began the 1920s with one Pittsburgh, Pennsylvania, station, but entered the 1930s with two national networks, the Columbia Broadcasting System and the National Broadcasting Company, which together had over 400 local affiliates. In 1920, a radio was a novelty. By 1930, over 40 percent of American families had one.

Herbert Hoover's Committee on Recent Economic Changes investigated these developments extensively, reporting in 1929 that

> . . . as a people we have become steadily less concerned about the primary needs—food, clothing and shelter—and we now demand a broad list of goods and services which come under the category of "optional purchases." . . . The conclusion is that economically we have a *boundless field* before us; that there are new wants which will make way endlessly for newer wants, as fast as they are satisfied . . . (Emphasis added; *Report of the Committee on Recent Economic Changes*, p. xv).

Moreover, leisure, held at bay by a standard forty-hour-or-more work week, was being turned into an economic advantage. Hoover's committee documented this development as well, concluding

> It was during the period covered by the survey [the 1920s] that the conception of leisure as "consumable" began to be realized upon in business in a practical way and on a broad scale. . . .[The] leisure that results from increasing man-hour productivity helps to create new needs and new broader markets . . . (*Report of the Committee on Recent Economic Changes*, p. xvi).

The great discoveries made during the decade, according to Hoover and his committee, discoveries comparable to the "boundless fields" of America's original frontier, were that all human values and goods could be expressed through the marketplace and all "higher" activities performed as work. There were no nonpecuniary, or "free," activities that necessarily transcended work and the economy. Leisure had no privileged position, no special claims to liberty or the "realm of freedom."

Some of the most vital areas of economic growth involved commodification of the new leisure, and the transfiguration of free activities into jobs. Amusements, storytelling and conversation (radio), sports, the automobile and other transportation, recreational equipment, new fads such as mahjongg and Ping-Pong, and sheet music and records gave new employment to millions and sorely needed investment opportunities to a nation embarrassed by the "oversaving" of its wealthy.

**TABLE 1**

| | | |
|---|---|---|
| 1. Government Expenditures | | |
|    a. Municipalities | $ | 147,179 |
|    b. Counties | | 8,600 |
|    c. States | | 28,331 |
|    d. Federal | | 9,300 |
| **Total** | **$** | **193,410** |
| 2. Travel and mobility | | |
|    a. Vacation Travel in the USA | | |
|       i. Automobile touring | | 3,200,000 |
|       ii. Travel by Rail | | 750,000 |
|       iii. By air and water | | 25,000 |
|    b. Vacation Travel Abroad | | |
|       i. To Canada | | 266,283 |
|       ii. To Mexico | | 55,642 |
|       iii. Travel Overseas | | 391,470 |
|       iv. Miscellaneous | | 77,326 |
|    c. Pleasure use of cars, boars, etc | | |
|       i. Autos (except touring) | | 1,246,000 |
|       ii. Motor Boats | | 460,000 |
|       iii. Motorcycles | | 10,796 |
|       iv. Bicycles | | 9,634 |
| **Total** | **$** | **6,492,151** |
| 3. Commercial Amusements | | |
|    a. Moving Pictures | | 1,500,000 |
|    b. Other Admissions | | 166,000 |
|    c. Cabarets and Night Clubs | | 23,725 |
|    d. Radios and Radio Broadcasting | | 525,000 |
| **Total** | **$** | **2,214,725** |
| 4. Leisure Time Associations | | |
|    a. Social and Athletic Clubs | | 125,000 |
|    b. Luncheon Clubs | | 7,500 |
|    c. Lodges | | 175,000 |
|    d. Youth Service | | 75,000 |
| **Total** | **$** | **383,500** |
| 5. Games, Sports, Outdoor Life, Etc. | | |
|    a. Toys, Games, Playground Equipment | | 113,800 |
|    b. Pool, Billiards, Bowling Equipment | | 12,000 |
|    c. Playing Cards | | 20,000 |
|    d. Sports and Athletic Goods | | 500,000 |
|    e. Hunting and Fishing Licenses | | 12,000 |
|    f. Resort Hotels | | 75,000 |
|    g. College Football | | 21,500 |
|    h. Camps | | 47,000 |
|    i. Fireworks | | 6,771 |
|    j. Phonographs and Records | | 75,000 |
| **Total** | **$** | **883,071** |
| **Total annual cost of recreation (figures from 1928–30, in thousands of dollars)** | **$** | **10,165,857** |

SOURCE: Recent Social Trends p.949

More than ever before, investors bought "growth stock" in companies that served the new leisure market, or provided products specifically designed for people to use during their free time. Existing commercial recreation expanded as never before. Vaudeville, burlesque shows, cabarets and nightclubs, dance halls, pool halls, and amusement parks were among the growth "industries." Entrepreneurs developed and expanded many of the forms of entertainment and leisure products that have become familiar. Commercial parks such as Coney Island, hotels, and excursion packages, sales of phonographs and records, sports equipment, board and parlor games, and bicycles flourished.

Motion-picture attendance more than doubled during the 1920s. By 1930, over 100 million people were going to the movies each week. "Talkies" were not introduced until 1926. Still, by 1932, nearly two-thirds of the nation's movie houses were wired for sound. When the Great Depression began, Americans were spending over $1.5 billion annually on the movies.

Motion-picture production, distribution, and exhibition became a national industry. Observers estimated that by the end of the decade, Americans had invested more than $2 billion. A third of a million people found employment in the industry. Building from its humble base in a few nickelodeons in the 1910s, the movie industry boasted over 22,731 theaters nationwide by 1930.

Hollywood perfected its organization, adopting the "studio system" and creating a tight web of distributors and exhibitors, ensuring vertical and horizontal control of the industry. The "star" system came into its own. Actors such as Charlie Chaplin, Buster Keaton, Douglas Fairbanks, and Mary Pickford amassed fortunes. The industry also introduced, and then perfected by mass production, the film genres, or formulas, that it continues to use: slapstick, romantic comedy, western, adventure, horror, and so forth.

The decade also witnessed a dramatic growth of spectator sports. College football led the way. Attendance at college football games more than doubled. Receipts grew over 200 percent from $2.5 million to $8.3 million. Colleges and universities embarked on major construction projects, expanding stadia capacity nearly 150 percent, from just under 1 million to over 2.3 million seats.

Baseball revenues grew as well, but somewhat slower than football. Major league receipts increased 10 percent, class "AA" 20 percent. However, radio reached many millions more, who sat to listen instead of watch. Night games were introduced in 1935 so that people could go to the ballpark without having to miss work or school. Boxing reached something of a historical peak during the 1920s with champions such as Jack Dempsey and Gene Tunney making national headlines (*Report of the President's Research Committee on Social Trends*; *Report of the Committee on Recent Economic Changes*).

Sports came into their own as true "professions." Not only had sports emerged as serious moneymaking concerns, they were afforded increasing historical significance. Sportswriters began to keep careful, more extensive records from season to season, defining champions as record breakers.

The modern practice of taking sports events seriously as history-making occurrences spread during the decade to include all major sports. Record breakers attracted fans. There could be only a limited number of team championships per season. However, a Babe Ruth hitting home runs at a record-shattering pace, or a football player passing or rushing more than anyone had done previously, drew fans to watch even a losing team. Records multiplied; in baseball, careful attention was paid to batting averages, "runs batted in," home-runs, "earned run averages," and so forth, on to dozens of categories.

During the interwar period, organizers and promoters designed new national prizes and awards, reinforcing the historical significance of what were once simple playing and local games. For example, the American League created an early version of the modern Most Valuable Player award in 1922 (the National League following suit in 1923) and the Downtown Athletic Club of New York City introduced the Heisman Trophy for college football in 1936.

Hoover's Committee estimated that Americans were spending nearly $10.25 billion on "leisure and recreation," nearly 13 percent of the nation's total budget, by the end of the 1920s. Historians and economists still agree that recreational spending increased rapidly during the 1920s. The economist John Owen suggests such spending increased 47 percent from 1909 to 1930, constituting the most rapid increase in the nation's history (Hunnicutt, 1988, p. 23). However, later observers saw the totals differently, estimating that recreational spending was no more than 4.7 percent of the nation's total budget by 1930. (See Table 1)

The difference may be explained by the Hoover Committee's inclusion of automobile expenses as part of recreational spending. The committee understood that the rise of automobile manufacture was proof that Americans were buying new things to use in their new leisure. J. F. Steiner, the author of the committee's report on recreation, claimed that when automobiles were used for vacations, such expenses (amounting to well over $3 billion annually by 1930) should naturally be included as part of the nation's recreational budget. Moreover, using national traffic surveys of *daily* automobile use, Steiner concluded that "at least one-fourth of the use of passenger cars is for recreation," assigning an additional recreational spending figure of $1.246 billion (*Report of the President's Research Committee on Social Trends*, p. 948).

One of the most impressive examples of what Hoover's Committee predicted coming true was that "optional spending" for recreation and leisure would become necessities, continually opening the way for new spending. After the Great Depression, statisticians separated automobile expenses from recreational spending altogether and began to view automobiles as one of the most important sectors of the nation's total budget in its own right.

However, for some, such figures were more the occasion for alarm than for rejoicing about healthy economic growth. For example, Jay Nash criticized the rapid growth of professional sports and commercial recreation, pointing out that Americans were becoming passive in their free time, consuming rather than creating their amusements. He warned that that a new malady, "spectatoritis," infected the nation. Critics also feared that people were also becoming passive in more significant parts of their lives. Family life suffered and the community weakened, as previously free kinds of convivial and discussional activities were made into work, produced and sold, and distributed by mass media cut off from local roots (Hunnicutt, 1988, p. 137).

For such critics, a more promising national growth occurred in the public sector devoted to leisure service. The National Recreation Association, critical of the expansion of commercial recreation and the growth of passive recreation and amusement, labored to enlarge free and public places for healthier kinds of recreation. Local politicians, club members, and "recreation professionals" joined together to resist the advance of consumerism and mass culture, struggling to find ways to protect local culture and culture making. They sought to preserve and encourage free local group activities and associations: clubs, storytelling, choirs, community bands and orchestras, community drama and festivals, local sports, voluntary and charitable organizations. Such individuals sought to serve the new leisure in new, public ways that would resist the commodification of local culture.

Hoover's Committee on Recent Social Trends investigated the growth of participatory sports and recreations during the 1920s, noting that the rise of active sports somewhat counterbalanced the expansion of passive watching. Steiner wrote, "The two most important trends in recreation in this country have been . . . commercial recreation . . . for passive amusements, and the rapid growth of private and public facilities for the participation in . . . recreational activities (*Report of the President's Research Committee on Social Trends*, p. 954).

To meet the new demand, the nation built nearly 4,000 new golf courses between 1923 and 1930, more than a 200 percent increase. Tennis playing and tennis courts expanded nearly as rapidly. Clubs devoted to active sports and games doubled their membership dues between 1921 and 1930.

Public infrastructure providing for the new leisure expanded as well. Municipal park acreage increased by 238 percent between 1907 and 1930—a period of very rapid growth occurring between 1925 and 1930 when municipal park acreage expanded from 201,445 to 279,257 acres. During the decade, National Parks and Forests expanded rapidly and saw record numbers of visitors. A newly mobile public headed for the out-of-doors, ballooning National Park attendance by 202 percent and visits to National Forests by 560 percent (*Report of the President's Research Committee on Social Trends,* pp. 912-957).

The interwar years was a period of remarkable increases in local voluntary associations. Club membership grew rapidly. Local businesspeople performed yeoman community service, founding luncheon clubs such as Rotary International, Kiwanis, and Lions. Membership in luncheon clubs expanded over 700 percent between 1917 and 1929. Hoover's Committee found in the early 1930s that "fraternal societies . . . are reaching the peak of their development"; the nine leading fraternal organizations having increased their memberships 100 percent between 1905 and 1926. During the 1920s, municipal community centers more than doubled as well. Local schools were given double duty as the community schools movement successfully transformed hundreds of local schools into after-hours "community clubs" (*Report of the President's Research Committee on Social Trends,* pp. 937–937).

Women's clubs expanded as well. Following the ratification of the Nineteenth Amendment in August 1920, women's groups such as the League of Women Voters (LWV) and the National Women's Party (NWP) reformed to promote equal rights and, in the case of the NWP, promote an Equal Rights Amendment to the Constitution.

Women's groups were particularly interested in shorter work hours as a strategy to allow more women access to the workforce. Women, more than any other group, had difficulties finding jobs that allowed time enough to meet traditional demands made on them by their homes. They were among the strongest supporters of the six-hour day for just this reason.

For rural women, few organizations competed with home-demonstration agents and the clubs they founded for building "social capital" among women largely isolated on their farms. In 1920, the Farm Bureau Federation formed, establishing and offering educational and support services to 210,560 groups of women by 1922, building to 403,602 groups by 1929. Other women's clubs, such as the Junior Leagues of America, followed suit, providing unprecedented opportunities for women for social engagement outside both the home and the job. Women also increased their participation in sports and recreation, expanding their horizons and their freedom as they rode bicycles, played tennis and golf, and swam in record numbers (Gordon).

Historians have demonstrated that the times spent working have offered workers few opportunities for self-expression and for the formation of working-class identities. The same might be said of working women, who found purpose and the identity of their movement in that portion of their lives lived beyond the workplace, in the new "leisure" they won from both their jobs and their traditional social roles.

## Impact of the Great Depression

With the onset of the Great Depression, the new social and economic projects of the 1920s to commodify leisure, expand work into previously free activities, and perpetually expand economic need appeared to many to have reached dead ends. The massive unemployment of the 1930s demonstrated to people such as William Green, president of the American Federation of Labor, that "free time will come, the only choice is unemployment or leisure" (Hunnicutt, 1988, pp. 77, 103).

Just as they had done in the early 1920s, observers concluded that the economic dislocation that was the Great Depression resulted from overproduction—from industry producing more than people were willing to work for and buy. The New Economic Gospel of Consumption appeared to be a false testament. Industrial progress naturally entailed increasing freedom from work. There was no way around more free time. Inexorably it would come, either in the healthy form of leisure or the disastrous form of massive unemployment.

The depression hit the new forms of commodified leisure hard. For example, attendance at baseball games and movies sagged alarmingly. The movie industry overextended its capital investment, trying to retain its customer base with new theaters and the new "talkies" technology, more than tripling its debt. Still, during the first years of the depression, movie attendance and revenues fell more than 40 percent. The industry faced bankruptcy. More than a third of the nation's theaters closed. Struggling to keep their customers, theaters slashed ticket prices, offered double features, give-away gimmicks, and lottery schemes. Baseball followed suit, offering more entertainment (doubleheaders, night games) at lower prices. As commodified forms of leisure failed, public leisure services thrived: noncommercial activities and nonprofit organizations expanded. Unable to afford the new and expensive, "goods-intensive" (a spending ratio requiring more goods and less free time) recreation, Americans began to turn to "time-intensive" (fewer goods to more time) leisure activities. Attending public facilities, visiting parks, reading, engaging in conversations, playing games at home, participating in community activities (dances, sports, band concerts, etc.) began replacing seeing movies, going to restaurants, motoring, and so forth.

The movement away from leisure spending, and toward less expensive forms of recreation is hard to document. Few records exist that note such changes nationally. One hard historical fact is clear, however: recreation spending lagged far behind leisure's increase during the 1930s.

By far the best and most informative historical studies of changing leisure patterns are local. Extensive interviews have been done with the Kellogg workers in Battle Creek, Michigan, who lived through the Great Depression, and who had the benefit of working a six-hour day because of W. K. Kellogg's (the company owner) desire to combat unemployment in the city.

Public recreation expanded substantially in Battle Creek. Library use doubled, visits to city parks grew. Moreover, workers, particularly working women, reported spending much more of their time than before with their families, "doing things around the house," "reading to the children," "visiting," and so forth. They also consistently reported spending more time (than before or since) in participating in community organizations, going to church, singing in choirs, helping out in the neighborhood, volunteering at schools and churches, attending clubs, fraternities, etc. Men shared these recollections. The 1930s media confirmed these memories. (In 1932, agents from the Women's Bureau of the Department of Labor interviewed nearly all of the women who worked at Kellogg's. Local and national media reported extensively on Kellogg's six-hour day and workers' opinions about the experiment.)

Kellogg workers talked frequently about increased use of "public space," for which there is no historical record apart from their memory. They spoke of time spent together on front porches and in living rooms; of backyards and sidewalks regularly filled with people visiting, telling stories, and debating issues. The women interviewed in the 1990s were young during the depression, and frequently they recalled the sports activities of their youth. Community team sports thrived, according to their reports. Businesses in town regularly sponsored teams. Local enthusiasm for games such as ping-pong and roller skating flared briefly during the 1930s.

Such local developments may represent the most important trend in recreation of the Great Depression.

Without reformers offering them "guidance," residents of Battle Creek began on their own to explore the new interstice of time between work and "home duties" opening for them. Many reported finding active, community-based alternatives to passively watching others do things, or using leisure to consume goods and services. The 1930s may well have been a time when "spectatoritis" and commodified leisure were in retreat, and a more community-based, active, engaged recreation began to emerge.

The "extra two hours" provided by Kellogg's six-hour day was something of a testing time, a laboratory of sorts for experimentation with new kinds of social forms and cultural ways. Several of the Kellogg managers and workers feared the new time as a place for dangerous experimentation, repeating to interviewers the old adage about idle hands, devils, and workshops. One wrote: "The six hr. shift was the reason for much hanky-panky going on in both sexes!" (Hunnicutt, 1996, p. 185).

During the 1930s, the federal government expanded its support of public leisure services, instituting a number of public works projects designed to help expand a leisure-support infrastructure, vital for the coming new leisure. Agencies such as the Federal Emergency Relief Administration, the Civil Works Administration, the Civilian Conservation Corps, and the National Youth Administration spent nearly $1.5 billion on the construction of parks, swimming pools, camps, and trails, employing recreation leaders in record numbers. The Works Progress Administration funded millions of dollars of construction at dozens of zoos, providing for inexpensive recreation during the depression and World War II.

## The Response of America to Joblessness and to the Challenge to the Centrality of Work

More importantly, the work reduction movement gained unparalleled national support, emerging as a central political issue during the Great Depression. The nation, with nowhere else to turn, responded to mass unemployment (25 percent or more of the workforce) by initiating a share-the-work movement, attempting to provide more jobs by reducing the hours of those who were still employed.

Expanding leisure as social and political issues gained unprecedented prominence, appearing as never before or since to be the unavoidable national destiny. With the politicization of work reduction, the leisure movement reached its historical high-water mark. Debate about the value of leisure, apart from its economic importance, filled the nation's presses and airways. Never before or since has increasing leisure seemed so inevitable, so likely to become soon the dominant social reality, presenting the nation with unparalleled challenges and opportunities.

An abundance of free time had inundated the nation. The task ahead was to redistribute the freedom from work represented by unemployment in healthy forms of shorter work hours. The challenge of the future would be to train humans in "the wise use of leisure" and to build public-sector infrastructures (parks, libraries, community centers) to support and serve the new freedom.

However, paying heed to his advisors such as Rexford Tugwell, and feeling the pressure from the business community, Franklin Delano Roosevelt retreated from his initial support of the Black-Connery Bill (the "work-sharing" bill that would have mandated a thirty-hour week). Many observers, particularly businesspeople, felt that a six-hour day would "tip the balance," refocusing the nation's attention from business and work to life beyond the marketplace. Commerce and its disciples would take second place.

By 1935, FDR and his advisors had developed a new, coherent economic strategy to counter work-hours reduction and to deal with the nation's unemployment crisis. Relying on new economic "counter-cyclical" spending theories developed in the 1920s, the administration introduced a bold new vision of government's role in society and the economy. Redefining work sharing and increasing leisure as "sharing the poverty," and for the first time defining a "full-time" job as a forty-hour or more work week, FDR began deliberately to create new work to replace work historically "lost" to machines.

After 1934, the New Deal's primary legislative achievements put this new philosophy into operation. Key administration figures such as Rexford Tugwell directly attacked the leisure movement/vision while crafting the work-creation alternative to work sharing. Tugwell wrote that the time had arrived to "seize on the prospect of the final release from labor and put it for a time at the center of our thinking." However, Tugwell condemned the prospect. Leisure would never provide humans with a sense of purpose and direction. Leisure could never be the source of meaning and identity. Only work could provide these things. Human progress must be redirected from "abundance" to the perpetual creation of new work. If business and industry were unable to provide people with "full-time" work, government must step in (Hunnicutt, 1996, p. 251ff).

Roosevelt committed the federal government to underwriting the New Economic Gospel of Consumption. He began marshaling the resources of government to support perpetual economic growth in order to protect the newly defined public good, "full-time" jobs for all. With FDR's support of work creation though government expansion and economic growth, the progressive shortening of the hours faded as a public issue. The leisure movement and vision receded as well, replaced by a new social ideal and political vision of "full-time" work for everyone, in perpetuity.

## The Eclipse of the Leisure Movement

Roosevelt and his administration concluded that it was not vacant "free time" or vapid leisure that humans needed and longed for; it was worthwhile jobs. For the New Deal and the generations that followed, progress lay on the frontiers of new work, not the backwaters of mass leisure/idleness.

The advent of government-supported work creation was arguably the watershed of twentieth-century domestic politics, setting the tone for politicians across the political spectrum who have followed, who have consistently campaigned on the slogan JOBS, JOBS, JOBS.

The brief account here may offer a few pertinent historical insights into work's modern ascendancy, which eclipsed the leisure movement and brought progressive shortening of the hours of labor to an end.

*See also:* Automobiles and Leisure; Baseball, Crowds; Basketball; Football; Impresarios of Leisure, Rise of; Postwar to 1980 Leisure and Recreation; Prohibition and Temperance; Progressive-Era Leisure and Recreation; Railroads and Leisure; Tourism; Working-Class Leisure Lifestyles

### BIBLIOGRAPHY

Bernstein, Irving. *The Lean Years: A History of the American Worker, 1920–1933*. Boston: Houghton Mifflin, 1960.

Burns, Cecil Delisle. *Leisure in the Modern World*. New York: Century Company, 1932.

Cross, Gary S. *Worktime and Industrialization: An International History, Labor and Social Change*. Philadelphia: Temple University Press, 1988.

———. *A Quest for Time: The Reduction of Work in Britain and France, 1840–1940*. Berkeley: University of California Press, 1989.

Cutten, George Barton. *The Threat of Leisure*. New Haven, Conn.: Yale University Press, 1926.

Gordon, Suzanne. *Prisoners of Men's Dreams: Striking Out for a New Feminine Future*. 1st ed. Boston: Little, Brown and Company, 1991.

Hinrichs, K., William Roche, and Carmen Sirianni. *Working Time in Transition: The Political Economy of Working Hours* in *Industrial Nations, Labor and Social Change*. Philadelphia: Temple University Press, 1991.

Hunnicutt, Benjamin Kline. *Work Without End: Abandoning Shorter Hours for the Right to Work*. Philadelphia: Temple University Press, 1988.

———. *Kellogg's Six-Hour Day, Labor and Social Change*. Philadelphia: Temple University Press, 1996.

Huxley, Julian. "Professor Huxley Predicts 2-Day Working-Week." *New York Times,* 17 November 1930.

Jacks, L. P. *The Education of the Whole Man.* New York: Harper and Brothers, 1931.

Jacks, L. P., and National Recreation Association. *Education Through Recreation.* New York: Harper and Brothers, 1932.

Lundberg, George Andrew, Mirra Komarovsky, and Mary Alice McInerny. *Leisure: A Suburban Study.* New York: Columbia University Press, 1934.

Lynd, Robert Staughton, and Helen Merrell Lynd. *Middletown, a Study in Contemporary American Culture.* New York: Harcourt Brace and Company, 1929.

———. *Middletown in Transition: A Study in Cultural Conflicts.* New York: Harcourt Brace and Company, 1937.

National Bureau of Economic Research, and Edward Eyre Hunt. *Recent Economic Changes in the United States: Report of the Committee on Recent Economic Changes, of the President's Conference on Unemployment, Herbert Hoover, Chairman, Including the Reports of a Special Staff of the National Bureau of Economic Research, Inc.* 1st ed. New York: McGraw-Hill Book Company, 1929.

Overstreet, H. A. *A Guide to Civilized Loafing.* 1st ed. New York: W. W. Norton and Company, 1934.

Owen, John D. *The Price of Leisure: An Economic Analysis of the Demand for Leisure Time.* Rotterdam: Rotterdam University Press, 1969.

———. *Working Hours: An Economic Analysis.* Lexington, Mass.: Lexington Books, 1979.

President's Research Committee on Social Trends, and Wesley Clair Mitchell. *Recent Social Trends in the United States: Report of the President's Research Committee on Social Trends.* New York: McGraw-Hill Book Company, 1933.

Roediger, David R., and Philip Sheldon Foner. *Our Own Time: A History of American Labor and the Working Day.* New York: Greenwood Press, 1989.

Russell, Bertrand. *In Praise of Idleness and Other Essays.* New York: W. W. Norton and Company, 1935.

*Benjamin Kline Hunnicutt*

# JEWISH AMERICAN LEISURE LIFESTYLES

In 1934, Jews across America turned their eyes toward the Detroit Tigers' race to wrest the pennant from the New York Yankees. Baseball, the national pastime, had been a favorite sport among Jews for many years. The year the Tigers battled against the Yankees, however, Hank Greenberg, a Jewish player for Detroit, gained Jewish and national attention not simply for his batting record, but also for his public religious observance. In a famous rabbinical decision, Greenberg was advised that he could play in the game that coincided with Rosh Hashanah, but not the one that fell on the Jewish holiday Yom Kippur. American leisure culture made room for an all-star slugger who trotted off the field to the call of Jewish observance. Jews recall his decision not to play on Yom Kippur often just as vividly as they recall his crucial role in the Tigers' pennant victory.

Jews have participated in and created American leisure culture by infusing American space and time with Jewish culture and traditions, while they have also refashioned their own practices according to American leisure patterns. Since Jewish arrival in the United States, dated to the late seventeenth century, Jews have adapted to American opportunities and expectations, at the same time that they have created their own uniquely American culture. As the population of Jews grew in the middle of the nineteenth century, particularly with the entrance of German-Jewish immigrants, Jewish Americans created new realms of leisure practice that ran parallel to American leisure culture. When Eastern European Jewish immigrants entered the United States, German Jews along with other progressive reformers, attempted to Americanize these new immigrants by, in part, introducing them to American culture and leisure practices. In the twentieth century, Jews continued to expand the scope of their leisure activities and found more and more opportunities to join with mainstream America in leisure pursuits. At the same time, Jewish holiday observance and ethnic institutions grew, widening the realm of Jewish cultural activity, yet also replicating American consumer patterns.

## Nineteenth-Century Leisure Culture

Historians estimate that between 150,000 and 200,000 Jews arrived in the United States between 1820 and 1880. The majority came from Germany and Central Europe looking for economic opportunity and hoping to flee the increasing anti-Semitism in Western and Central Europe. Although many of these Jews settled in cities, some sought opportunities in small towns and frontier settlements. Synagogues were erected in large cities and small towns alike, and slowly European-trained rabbis made their way over to the United States to tend to the new settlement of Jews. Jewish communities were established that not only provided for the religious needs of their inhabitants, but also created social and leisure space that often echoed American patterns.

In 1843, a handful of German Jewish men founded B'nai B'rith. B'nai B'rith, literally the "sons of the

485

covenant," was modeled on American fraternal societies and provided its members with social and recreational activities similar to the popular Masonic organizations. The Jewish fraternity paralleled American institutions and offered Jews the opportunity to participate in leisure and cultural activities from which they were otherwise excluded. Aside from providing the equivalent of health and life insurance, B'nai B'rith sponsored lectures, concerts, and other secular activities. Jewish women quickly formed a women's auxiliary to B'nai B'rith.

American industrialization in the late nineteenth century benefited many German Jewish immigrants, who entered the ranks of the middle class, founding banks and department stores (including Bloomingdale's and Macy's). At the same time, however, new global demographic trends shifted the contours of the Jewish American population as immigrants from Eastern Europe flooded onto American shores.

## Eastern European Immigrants and Early-Twentieth-Century Consumption and Leisure

Eastern European Jewish immigrants, like their German Jewish counterparts, came to the United States in search of economic betterment, but they came in far larger numbers and settled more exclusively in urban environments. The United States these immigrants encountered was far different than it had been just decades prior. Urban economies revolved around new trends in industrialization and particularly the demand for cheaply produced consumer goods. Eastern European Jews predominately manned the factories and shops that produced ready-made clothing. Before they could even afford to enjoy the fruits of American industrialization, Eastern European Jews were creating the products of modern life.

The abundance of the New World stood in sharp contrast to the impoverished lives that many Jews in the United States continued to live. Often making their homes in dirty and crowded tenement apartments, each member of the family was expected to earn money and help with the task of daily survival. City-dwelling, middle-class German Jews, initially cool to the un-American and foreign new immigrants, set up charities and benevolent associations for them and also encouraged Eastern European Jews to educate themselves and their children. Indisputably, part of Americanizing was participating in American consumer and leisure culture. Progressive reformers hoped to rid foreigners of their presumed backwardness by offering them opportunities to engage in American recreational and cultural activities. Children, in particular, were the focus of reform activities.

In the summer of 1902, two German Jewish women arranged for a group of Jewish immigrant children with their mothers to take streetcars to Detroit's Belle Isle. The group spent the day frolicking on the island park and learning the value of outdoor play and relaxation. In New York City, as well as in most other major U.S. cities of the time, similar activities were planned for new immigrants. The immigrants themselves also created realms of leisure space, often pausing to read Yiddish newspapers or to observe Jewish holidays.

The public school system, which grew in the nineteenth century and by the twentieth century accommodated many new immigrant children, provided a space not simply for education but for socializing with peers. For the children of immigrants, the public school system offered a pathway toward middle-class professions and American respectability. Jewish children also met non-Jews through their schooling and learned new vocabulary, games, and ideas from them. In New York City, some Jewish boys continued their education at City College, which by the 1920s had a thriving Jewish student body.

Even with meager salaries, as Jews acclimated to American life, they often managed to save money to move from the crowded tenement districts to cleaner and roomier urban neighborhoods. Urban life educated them in American styles, and many Jews attempted to outfit themselves and their apartments in the latest American fashions—from placing pianos in their parlors to wearing shirtwaist dresses (a style of dress whose tailored details are copied from men's shirts). Jewish women, in particular, were characterized, often in disdainful terms, as aspiring consumers. Many toiled to create homes that echoed American styles and offered a space of relaxation and comfort.

## The Life of the Soul

Jewish holidays were the focal point of Jewish leisure culture. Although critics over the years have accused Jews of leaving their religious observance behind in the Old World, it is clear that religion melded with American leisure patterns and did not simply become replaced by them. The Jewish Sabbath, celebrated on Friday night and Saturday, was historically the centerpiece of Jewish life. In the United States, Saturday was often a day of work, like any other day, and many Jewish immigrants had to violate Sabbath rules to keep their jobs. The Friday night meal, however, became a focus of Jewish activity and was paradigmatic of Jewish holiday observance with its emphasis on family togetherness and food.

Holiday observance, tracked through the first half of the twentieth century, reveals the rapid pace through which Jews attained middle-class status. Jewish festivals became connected to consumer goods and elaborate celebrations, prepared almost exclusively by women. As early as 1900, New York City department stores created "Passover Departments" to ease the preparations for the spring holiday and to introduce women to an array of new products. At the same time, the stores shifted the very practice of the holiday by passing out instruction guides about how to conduct a proper Passover Seder. Bringing family together, eating special foods, and marking a connection to Jewish history permeated holiday celebrations, even if Jewish law and Orthodox observance were often muted or ignored.

The Jewish holiday Hanukkah, traditionally one of the minor festivals, attained a new place of prominence following World War II and rivaled Christmas with its gift giving and focus on children. Christmas, which appeared more like an American holiday than a Christian holiday, had attracted Jews, and some had started to experiment with Christmas observance. Jewish leaders shunned such practices, and Hanukkah was gradually remodeled as a Jewish alternative to Christmas. Consumer desires were closely tied to the new holiday; by the 1940s, one advertiser proclaimed, "Every home should own at least one [Hanukkah menorah]" (Joselit, p. 237).

Religious space, and not simply religious holidays, coincided with leisure starting in the early twentieth century. Synagogue centers, far from simply providing venues for religious services, served as sports clubs, reception halls, and meeting spaces. Activities for children and families dominated the agendas of the new synagogue centers. The Brooklyn Jewish Center, erected in the 1920s, served Jewish families who had moved out of the Lower East Side to find more spacious and middle-class housing. The center, in addition to holding Sabbath and holiday services, also housed a Hebrew school, a sisterhood, youth group meetings, and Friday evening lectures and musical services. Dances and parties were held frequently at the Center, and the basement held a pool.

Although Jewish religious practice and belief were modified as Jews entered the American middle class and sought more leisure outlets, Jewish culture remained at the center of Jewish leisure activities. Additionally, Jews tended to spend their leisure time with other Jews, a function, on one hand, of the predominately Jewish neighborhoods in which Jews lived, and, on the other, of exclusion from non-Jewish leisure and social activities.

## Jews on the Move: Suburbanization, Hollywood, and Israel

In the aftermath of World War II, Jews joined other Americans in a mass exodus from urban neighborhoods. For Jews, the movement toward more comfortable, economically viable lives was a story as old as their immigration to America. Education, professional-level jobs, and access to cars and America's growing highway system enabled Jews, along with other middle-class Americans, to relocate to suburbs. Jews dotted the suburban landscape with new synagogues, which tended to be affiliated with the Conservative denomination, not Orthodoxy. Critics often complained that the suburb encouraged conformity. From the identical homes outfitted with the same appliances to the way that individuals practiced religion, some people worried that the suburbs bred a culture of similarity and conformity, while others praised suburban culture for its tolerance of various American ethnic groups.

The spread of mass culture—including radio, film, and television—starting in the 1920s had already created a common cultural ground in which Jews and non-Jews participated. American radio programs, movies, and, later, television shows attracted Jews and educated them in American culture. Yet, as with other forms of leisure culture, Jews did not simply receive American media; instead, they participated in sculpting it.

Jewish movie moguls—including Samuel Goldwyn, Carl Laemmle, Marcus Loew, Louis B. Mayer, and Harry and Jack Warner—were pioneers in the growing American film industry, located by the end of World War I in Hollywood. The nearly exclusively Jewish character of Hollywood alarmed some Americans, like Henry Ford, who believed that Jewish control of the American entertainment industry was part of a worldwide Jewish conspiracy. Few of the films produced by these men touched on Jewish themes, but Jews and Jewish subjects did occasionally appear in film. *The Jazz Singer,* starring Al Jolson, a Jewish immigrant, examined the tension between an Orthodox father and a secularizing son.

Starting in the decade after World War II, more and more Jews left their homes on the East Coast or in the Midwest and relocated to southern California. Los Angeles, in particular, was rapidly expanding and offered economic opportunities for newcomers. California also enticed Jews because of its newness and the seeming flexibility of its social structure. Although Jews built synagogues throughout the Los Angeles area and established Jewish social clubs, they also believed that in their new sunny homes, they could choose their Jewish activities and identification more freely than they had been able to when living close to their extended families and near historically Jewish centers of life.

Whether Jews moved to suburbs or to southern California, by the 1950s, Jewish identity had changed in many ways. Jews were enrolling in colleges and universities at rates disproportionately higher to other American groups, and Jews had experienced and were continuing to experience upward mobility unlike most other immigrant groups. With increasing wealth, more and more Jews were able to participate in leisure activities—like skiing, boating, and vacationing—that had earlier been reserved for only the elite among them. Again, however, Jewish culture was intertwined in many of these activities.

The establishment of Jewish overnight summer camps in the 1950s and 1960s enabled Jewish children to play outdoors, while also participating in Jewish activities—such as observing the Sabbath, speaking Hebrew, or learning about Israel. Parents could simultaneously indulge in their own leisure activities, bereft of children. Travel also became part of Jewish youth culture with the advent of the teen tour to Israel. On these tours, sponsored by Zionist, religious, and communal organizations, children were introduced to the joy of travel at the same time that they learned about their heritage, hiking through the desert, swimming in the Red Sea, and visiting kibbutz farms.

## Conclusion

By the end of the twentieth century, Jews were consumers of American mass and leisure culture in many ways that were indistinguishable from other Americans. Aside from very religious communities, most American Jews watched the same television programs, listened to the same songs, went to the same movies, and played the same games and sports as their non-Jewish neighbors. Yet, leisure culture continued to intersect with Jewish culture and ethnic practices in distinctive ways.

As Jews entered the middle class, their leisure practices shifted or Americanized to echo American styles of leisure culture. Jews shared with other middle-class Americans an increase in consumer spending, a greater emphasis on child-centered activities, and the desire to separate the realm of work from the realm of leisure. The pairing, however, of Jewish observances and cultural practices, including Jewish holidays, Jewish support for Israel, Jewish education, and Jewish cuisine, with leisure sculpted certain uniquely Jewish leisure practices.

The Sabbath, for the Jews, is traditionally called a day of rest. Leisure, then, or at least a break from work-a-day life, is built into the Jewish time cycle. When Jews immigrated to the United States from Europe, rabbis and traditionalists worried that there would be no Sabbath in the United States. Their worries were justified to an extent; keeping the Jewish Sabbath in the States was economically and socially a difficult task. Yet, the importance of rest and the importance of pairing it with a consciousness of Jewishness—whether Jewish family, community, observance, or history—remained vital for Jewish Americans.

*See also:* Movies' Impact on Popular Leisure, Urbanization of Leisure

### BIBLIOGRAPHY

Brumberg, Stephan. *Going to America, Going to School: The Jewish Immigrant Public School Encounter in Turn-of-the-Century New York City.* New York: Praeger Publishers, 1986.

Diner, Hasia R. *A Time for Gathering: The Second Migration, 1820–1880.* Baltimore: Johns Hopkins University Press, 1992.

Heinze, Andrew. *Adapting to Abundance: Jewish Immigrants, Mass Consumption, and the Search for American Identity.* New York: Columbia University Press, 1990.

Hoberman, J., and Jeffrey Shandler. *Entertaining America: Jews, Movies, and Broadcasting.* Princeton, N.J.: Princeton University Press, 2003.

Joselit, Jenna Weissman. *The Wonders of America: Reinventing Jewish Culture, 1880–1950.* New York: Hill and Wang, 1994.

Kaufman, David. *Shul with a Pool: The "Synagogue-Center" in American Jewish History.* Hanover, N.H.: University Press of New England, 1999.

Moore, Deborah Dash. *B'nai B'rith and the Challenge of Ethnic Leadership.* Albany, N.Y.: State University of New York Press, 1981.

———. *To the Golden Cities: Pursuing the American Jewish Dream in Miami and L.A.* Cambridge: Harvard University Press, 1994.

Prell, Riv-Ellen. *Fighting to Become Americans: Jews, Gender and the Anxiety of Assimilation.* Boston: Beacon Press, 1999.

Shapiro, Edward. *A Time for Healing: American Jewry Since World War II.* Baltimore: Johns Hopkins Press, 1992.

*Lila Corwin Berman*

# JOGGING

**See** *Marathons; Running and Jogging; Triathlons*

# JOKING

Joking extends well beyond telling "jokes" and sharing "joke genres" to include a *joie-de-vivre* so often more characteristic of leisure. Like leisure, joking is a form of humor consistent with a type of play. If joking, like play and leisure, represents the world of the possible, then the potential for joking to be of benefit to all individuals becomes possible.

There are many reasons to tell jokes. According to Paul McGhee, people joke to enjoy physical sensations. Physical incongruities lead to important serotonin infusions, and are experienced physiologically as pleasurable. One jokes to make sense out of nonsense, for the mastery and competency that can be achieved in creativity. People joke to keep themselves from hurting, so that they do not feel so bad in a difficult or unpleasant situation. Consequently, joking can function to protect a fragile ego from a bruising by taunts or malicious comments. One also can joke to hurt others; put-downs can be a means of maintaining a superior position in a socially vertical hierarchy. Or, by contrast, joking in the form of "comic social relief" can be used to defuse awkward social situations and distress. Humor has as its benefit the ability to facilitate social connections and interactions.

Thinking about joking on an international level is evocative. Interactive incongruity humor, which Ann Marie Guilmette suggests is the state of being consciously aware of alternatives, is helpful in understanding joking between nations. Like Arthur Koestler's concept of bisociation, Henri Louis Bergson's concept of incongruity humor, and Brian Sutton-Smith's "ambiguity of play," that allow for antisocial characters, "marginalized" yet diverse identities, and "imaginal" self-creating and sustaining persona would be featured in many such intercultural exchanges. Joking between different social groups is better explained in a social-normative context. Rather than "put-downs" and negative comparisons, the basis for much of the joking among ethnic group participants is reliant on understanding the values and beliefs that can be tolerated if safely and nonthreateningly violated. In comparing cultures, the simple depictions of acceptable colors in a social situation can be illuminating. For instance, the color white is used by various cultures to evoke sometimes very different meanings in comparison.

According to McGhee, "put-down humor," especially targeted at ethnic groups, was very popular in the 1970s and 1980s. As the country became more sensitized to ethnic, racial, and gender differences, the offensive quality of such humor received more attention. While this "political correction" of humor led to a sharp reduction in these types of jokes, many individuals continued to disparage and victimize individuals and groups that they did not care for or understand, or who threatened to become more powerful than the dominant culture in the society.

The unique features of early American humor are centered in the diversity of styles and multiplicity of functions that joking has served since the first visitors arrived on the North American shores. As the radical, disgruntled and persecuted groups fled Europe to escape the tyranny of the hierarchical political and religious nobility, they likely brought a "superiority humor" style of joking with them. While these groups may once have joked about the government that they felt harmed them, away from its influence, people may then have turned to humor about groups they deemed below themselves. This so-called "ethnic" humor does persist especially during conflict over scarce resources, but it has been curtailed in the name of equity seeking in contemporary society.

In contrast to the court jesters and clowning imported to North America, the early settlers perhaps shifted away from this superiority style to a reliance on "physical incongruity humor" (the equivalent of slapstick comedy) as the basis for their joke genres. Much of the storytelling would have been directed against the self, and the initial feelings of inadequacy and incompetence, especially in trying to eke out an existence on formidable wilderness lands. The depiction of such incompetence in narratives, theatrics, and role-playing mimicry would have produced much enjoyment and embarrassed relief. According to Don L. F. Nilsen, writers and storytellers created "larger-than-life" frontier heroes in an effort to confirm that mere mortals could not have tamed the "Wild West." The lives and deaths of characters such as Wild Bill Hickok, Pie-Biter Jim Baker, Paul Bunyan, Black Nell, Calamity Jane, John Henry, and Pecos Bill are featured in many a tale. The epitaph on the tombstone of Pecos Bill reads "Here lies Pecos Bill, He always lied, and always will. He once lied loud; he now lies still" (Nilsen, *Humor Scholarship: A Research Bibliography,* p. 136). Another example of frontier humor is the story of a "sod-buster" who staggers into the barbershop (where a frontier doctor could be found if available) complaining of back pain. Thinking that the cowboy has hurt his back wrangling cattle and wild horses or toting heavy sacks of grain and feed, the doctor tells the fellow that it will be a few minutes before he can see him. The fellow loudly announces that he is heading to the saloon until the doctor is ready for him, and as he turns to leave the barbershop, he amazes everyone with the large knife wedged into his back.

The "ambiguity" of the English language readily creates joking opportunities. The word "trunk," with a multiplicity of semantic meanings, may be the most interesting from which humor could abound. And the most classic leisure experience of "fishing" is used for symbolic and metaphoric extensions in educational and business contexts. Some examples such as "casting the net widely," "landing the big one," "fishing for ideas," "feeding you a line," "fell for my ideas hook, line, and sinker," "hoping you'll feel prepared to 'tackle' these difficult issues," "hoping to "lure" you into classes," "the deal sounds "'fishy'" to me," require linguistic sophistication.

Joking has always been, and will continue to be, a barometer of emerging issues in any society. People joke for their own amusement and entertainment, serving an important intellectual function. When the world of the possible is realized, one experiences a profound sense of mastery and resulting satisfaction as in the purest form of leisure (daydreaming).

As well, joking (especially in communications) is a two-edged sword. The same joke in a relevant context may be amusing for a variety of interpretations and types of humor. Lawrence La Fave's notion of an "identification class" allows "attitude switching" to account for much enjoyment. For example, "What's the difference between a man and a carp?" "One is a scum-sucking bottom-feeder, and the other is a fish!" may be offensive to males, and hence may not be amusing. However, if part of the joke is varied to "What's the difference between an Enron Executive and a carp?," with the same response, and even presuming that the executive is a male, it may now possibly be transformed to amusement rather than an offense for many males.

Throughout North American history, language play enjoyed the same progressive development as did earlier styles. Joking in the form of language play, early in the history of ostracized black adolescent males, pertained to "sounding." Sounding was utilized most frequently as a form of verbal assault (which started as something such as "Yo mama is. . ."). Puns (clever "turns of phrase") followed thereafter as cognitive capacity building. Eventually, irony in the form of left-handed insults and compliments (as circumstances dictated) emerged. Each of these forms of language play represented the verbal repartee, discourse, and dialogue necessary in communicating social status and relationships.

With the advent of schools and the return to societal contemplation as the basis for leisure, language play again emerged to join the other prevailing styles. Alleen Pace Nilsen and Don. L. F. Nilsen, in their *Encyclopedia of 20th Century American Humor,* focus on the patterns, trends, and connections in the humor used by Americans during the second half of the twentieth century. Many of their more than 100 entries describe a diversity of linguistic forms of humor such as caricature, exaggeration, irony, paradox, satire, slapstick, understatement, and wordplay. Performance humor is described through entries on

stand-up comedy, radio humor, movies, drama, late-night television, sit-coms, and programs for children. Visual humor is treated in entries on public art, architecture, cartoons, comic books, and animation. The functions of these literary forms of humor are discussed as tools of persuasion, ways to attract attention, establish superiority, gain status, test limits, and save face.

Essentially the physical, physiological, emotional, intellectual, cognitive, and social basis for most experiences can be realized through joking. Superiority humor communicates messages of conflict and competition between individuals and groups, while also being powerful in radicalizing the social order. Arousal humor can be cruel and insensitive to the pains and sufferings of one's fellow human beings, while at the same time leading to repression, denial, and guilt, so that human angst can permit individuals to dwell on and recover from their own personal sorrows and debilities. Physical, cognitive, and verbal incongruities in humor alone, when essentially safe and nonthreatening violations of expectancy, allows one to rise above all of the human messes into Henri Louis Bergson's world of sublime wonder. Only when physical, intellectual, and cognitive forms of joking surpass and outperform the other, more negative types based in emotions and on social relations does joking fulfill a humane and just function and existence.

Joking serves as expressive communication, as a reminder not to focus on what one cannot do in one's life, but rather to look for the world of possibilities and alternatives suggested by lifestyles that may be more leisurely and positively enlivened!

*See also:* Racial Diversity and Leisure Lifestyles

## BIBLIOGRAPHY

Bergson, Henri Louis. *Laughter: An Essay on the Meaning of the Comic.* New York: MacMillan, 1911.

Brenneis, D. "Fighting Words." In *Not Work Alone.* Edited by Jeremy Cherfas and Roger Lewin. London: Temple Smith, 1980.

Guilmette, Ann Marie. *Psychophysical and Psychosocial Humour Judgements as a Function of Interactive Incongruity Humour.* Unpublished doctoral dissertation. Windsor, Ontario: University of Windsor, 1980.

Hobbes, Thomas. *Leviathan, or, The Matter, Forme, & Power of a Common-wealth Ecclesiasticall and Ccivill.* London: Printed for Andrew Ckooke [i.e. Crooke], at the Green Dragon in St. Pauls Church-yard, 1651.

Koestler, Arthur. *The Act of Creation.* New York: Macmillan, 1964.

La Fave, Lawrence. *Humor Judgments as a Function of Reference Groups: An Experimental Study.* Unpublished doctoral dissertation. Norman: University of Oklahoma, 1961.

McGhee, Paul E. *Health, Healing, and the Amuse System: Humor as Survival Training.* Dubuque, Iowa: Kendall Hunt Publishing Company, 1999.

Nilsen, Alleen Pace, and Don L. F. Nilsen. *Encyclopedia of 20th Century American Humor.* New York: Oryx Press, 2002.

Nilsen, Don L. F. *Humor Scholarship: A Research Bibliography.* Westport, Conn.: Greenwood Press, 1993.

Sutton-Smith, Brian. *The Ambiguity of Play.* Cambridge, Mass.: Harvard University Press, 1997.

*Ann Marie Guilmette*

# JUDO

**See** *Martial Arts*

# KARATE

**See** *Martial Arts*

# KITE FLYING

The exact date and origin of the kite is not known, but historians believe that kites were flown in China more than 2,000 years ago. One legend suggests that the first kite was born when a Chinese farmer tied a string to his hat to keep it from blowing away in a strong wind. The earliest written account of kite flying was about 200 B.C., when the Chinese general Han Hsin of the Han dynasty flew a kite over the walls of a city he was attacking to measure how far his army would have to tunnel to reach past the defenses. By knowing this distance, his troops reached the inside of the city, surprised their enemy, and emerged victorious. Eventually, traders spread kite flying from China to Korea, and across Asia to India. Each area developed a distinctive style of kite, as well as a specific cultural purpose for flying them.

During the Silla dynasty of Korea, around the year 600, General Gim Yu-sin was ordered to subdue a revolt. However, his troops refused to fight because they had seen a large shooting star fall from the sky and believed it to be a bad omen. To regain control, the general used a large kite to carry a fireball into the sky. The soldiers, seeing the star return to heaven, rallied and defeated the rebels. In Korea, therefore, people viewed the kite as a miracle weapon to overcome an enemy invasion, or as a useful pastime play for friendship. Linda Park, in her book *Kite Fighter,* described a famous story in Korea that dates back to 1473. This book is about two Korean brothers named Kee-sup and Young-sup, who both loved to fly kites, but only Young-sup could launch a kite successfully alone. One day when both brothers were at the hillside flying their kites, they met the king (who was their same age) face-to-face and formed a special friendship. Kite flying was an important recreational activity and provided a socializing opportunity in Korea.

Buddhist monks brought kites to Japan about the seventh century. They were used to avert evil spirits and to ensure rich harvests. Kite flying became very popular in Japan during the Edo period. For the first time, Japanese below the samurai class were allowed to fly kites. The Edo (now Tokyo) government tried unsuccessfully to discourage this pastime as "too many people became unmindful of their work" (Moulton, p. 16). According to one Japanese story, about 300 years ago, a thief was said to use a large kite to carry himself to the top of Nagoya Castle in order to steal a golden statue from the roof. All he was able to remove were a few small pieces. Later, he was captured and punished severely when he bragged of his exploits.

The earliest evidence of Indian kite flying comes from miniature paintings from the Mogul period, around 1500. A favorite theme was of a young man skillfully using his kite to drop messages to a lover who was being held in strict seclusion from him and the rest of the world. There are many stories about how the people of Micronesia used leaf kites to carry bait far out over the water where the garfish fed. The Polynesians have myths about two brother gods introducing kites to man when they had a kite duel. The winning brother flew his kite the highest. There are still contests in the islands where the highest flying kite is dedicated to the gods. Marco Polo carried stories of kites to Europe around the end of the thirteenth century. Illustrations of the period show nonflying dragon kites on military banners. Sailors also brought kites back from Japan and Malaysia in the sixteenth and seventeenth centuries. Kites were regarded as curiosities at first and had little impact on European culture. In the eighteenth and nineteenth centuries, kites were used as vehicles and tools for scientific research.

Benjamin Franklin and Alexander Wilson used their knowledge of kite flying to learn more about the wind and weather. Sir George Caley, Samuel Langley, Lawrence Hargrave, Alexander Graham Bell, and the Wright brothers all experimented with kites and contributed to development of the airplane. During World War I, the British, French, Italian, and Russian armies all used kites for enemy observation and signaling. The introduction of airplanes quickly made these units obsolete. The German navy continued to use man-lifting box kites to increase the viewing range of surface-cruising submarines. In World War II, the U.S. Navy found several uses for kites. Harry Saul's Barrage Kite prevented airplanes from flying too low over targets. Pilots lost at sea raised the Gibson-Girl Box Kite so they could be found. And Paul Garber's Target Kite, a large steerable diamond shape, was used for target practice and aircraft recognition at sea. As the airplane became firmly established, the kite was used less for military purposes or scientific research and more for recreational flying.

The last fifty years has seen renewed interest in kiting. New materials like ripstop nylon, fiberglass, and carbon graphite have made kites stronger, lighter, more colorful, and more durable. Important inventions like Francis Rogallo's flexi-wing and Domina Jalbert's parafoil kites helped develop modern hang gliders and sport parachutes. In 1972, Peter Powell introduced a toy dual-line stunter, and the public began to fly kites not only for fun, but also for sport. Enthusiasts experimented with new designs that could fly precise maneuvers, go faster, or perform intricate tricks. Larger and more powerful kites were designed, and in the 1980s, Peter Lynn of New Zealand introduced a stainless-steel kite-powered buggy. In the 1990s, kite traction on wheels, over water, and on ice became increasingly popular (for example, using kite power to pull sleds in wintry regions). Computer-aided kite design was created in Asia and kite flying has become a combination of modern technology and traditional recreational activity.

*See also:* Hobbies and Crafts

## BIBLIOGRAPHY

Eden, Maxwell. *The Magnificent Book of Kites*. Pittsburgh, Pa.: Sterling House, 2002.

Kent, Sarah. *The Creative Book of Kites*. New York: Smithmark Publishing, 1996.

Moulton, Ron. *Kites*. London: Pelham Books, 1979.

Park, Linda. *The Kite Fighters*. New York: Clarion Books, 2002.

Pelham, David. *Kites*. New York: Overlook Press, 2000.

Wang, Hongxun. *Chinese Kites: Traditional Chinese Arts and Culture*. Chicago: Foreign Language Press, 1989.

*Philip F. Xie*

# LABOR DAY

Labor Day originated in the organizing efforts of labor unions after the Civil War, and became a battleground in the struggle between pragmatic unionists, who accepted capitalism, and radical unionists, who opposed it. On 5 September 1882, New York's Central Labor Union (CLU), a socialist-leaning federation, sponsored a labor festival to coincide with the Knights of Labor's annual conference in New York City. Among the main organizers were machinist Mathew Maguire, tailor Robert Blissert, and carpenter Peter J. McGuire. Their goals included recruiting unaffiliated workers, legitimizing unions, and demonstrating to employers, politicians, and the public the importance and power of industrial labor.

The first Labor Day featured a procession of ten to twenty thousand union members, many wearing the uniforms of their trades, such as the leather aprons and work clothes of the machinists. Socialists sported red badges or ribbons to denote their politics. Some unions demonstrated their crafts; for example, cigar makers rolled cigars. Marchers carried banners expressing support for the eight-hour movement and labor candidates, opposing child labor, and proclaiming the power of unions. Knights of Labor officers, including national leader Terence Powderly, reviewed the parade. Afterward, workers heard oratory by union leaders and sympathetic journalists, picnicked with their families, drank German beer, watched fireworks, and danced to union bands.

## Spread

The CLU repeated the festival in 1883, and, in 1884, it decided to make the event an annual holiday, setting the date as the first Monday in September, which gave workers a rare two-day weekend (few had Saturdays off at that time). The Knights of Labor and the Federation of Organized Trades and Labor Assemblies (predecessor of the American Federation of Labor) both endorsed the CLU's holiday in 1884, and more than 400 cities celebrated Labor Day by 1889. Despite the hostile climate toward organized labor, the holiday won rapid government approval. Oregon recognized Labor Day in 1887, and thirty other states had done so by the time Congress made it a federal holiday in 1894. By legalizing Labor Day, the government acknowledged the essential role of industrial labor (and the power of the labor vote), but the legislation did not force private employers to grant their workers a paid holiday. As the *Chicago Daily Socialist* noted in 1909, "All admit that when a man knocks off work on Labor Day his time is also knocked off the time sheet."

By the end of the century local and state politicians were actively courting the labor vote on Labor Day. Even national politicians put in appearances. In 1900, both Republican vice presidential candidate Theodore Roosevelt and Democratic presidential candidate William Jennings Bryan reviewed Chicago's Labor Day parade and spoke at the picnic that followed.

**International Ladies Garment Workers Union.** Members of the International Ladies Garment Workers Union (ILGWU) participate in a Labor Day parade in New York City in 1909. Created in 1900 the group fought for workers rights. The parade of union workers was designed to demonstrate the power of organized labor and was the centerpiece of early Labor Day festivities. © *Corbis*

## The Meaning of Labor Day

From the start, Labor Day reflected the desires of both union leaders and the rank and file by combining ideology and recreation. The centerpiece was the parade of union workers. The massed workers visually demonstrated labor's strength and solidarity. So important did they consider the procession that many unions fined members for not marching. After the parade, labor leaders declaimed on union concerns. Finally, food, dancing, and recreational activities catered to workers' craving for entertainment.

The tensions between pragmatic and radical unions also shaped early Labor Day celebrations. Socialists asserted that legalization of the holiday had undermined its effectiveness as a demonstration of class solidarity, while pragmatic unionists downplayed class rhetoric in favor of patriotism. Unions affiliated with the pragmatic American Federation of Labor (AFL) dominated Labor Day exercises by the 1890s. Their celebrations proclaimed labor's partnership with capital and the Americanism of union members. They featured profuse displays of the Ameri-

can flag and banned both foreign and red flags. Some radical unions withdrew from AFL exercises to protest this message. Socialists in Chicago, for instance, held alternative exercises on the Sunday before Labor Day.

## Changing Practices and Meaning

Whether pragmatists or socialists, union leaders fought to keep Labor Day focused on the concerns of organized labor, but they increasingly ran up against their members' preferences for recreation. Businesses fed these desires, offering holiday excursions, sporting events, and movies. Many unions responded by shifting the Labor Day balance more toward amusement, dispensing with oratory and even dropping the procession, replacing them with baseball games, bicycle races, boxing matches, and other games.

Because of its connection to organized labor, Labor Day waxed and waned with union fortunes in the twentieth century. During strikes and major organizing drives, unions rallied the troops for parades and celebrations.

Unions and Labor Day declined in the reactionary 1920s but revived during the Great Depression. Under the organizing efforts of the left-leaning Committee on Industrial Organization (later Congress of Industrial Organizations [CIO]) and abetted by the Wagner Act, which finally lent government support to unions, union membership soared, and Labor Day gained increased prominence. Celebrations in the war years showcased labor's Americanism and support for the war, but in the repressive Cold War climate, labor militancy and Labor Day declined again. The normalization of the five-day workweek had made the holiday a three-day weekend, and the very successes of organized labor allowed prosperous working-class families to take holiday trips rather than attend union festivities. The long decline of organized labor, set in motion by the industrial crises of the 1970s, sealed Labor Day's ultimate transformation into the unofficial end of summer vacation, marked by holiday trips and back-to-school sales.

In 2004, Labor Day was celebrated in all fifty states and Puerto Rico. It lacked the stature of other national holidays, however, largely because it was deeply entwined with organized labor, and Americans were historically ambivalent, when not downright hostile, toward unions. Nevertheless, Labor Day retained the power to rally union members. In 1982, unions in New York commemorated the holiday's centennial in the spirit of the original festival by protesting President Ronald Reagan's labor policies. And in the early twenty-first century, union strongholds in areas such as Buffalo, New York, revived Labor Day parades, but they faced an uphill battle in the antiunion climate of the time.

*See also:* Fourth of July, Memorial Day, Patriotism and Leisure, Thanksgiving

**BIBLIOGRAPHY**

Dennis, Matthew. *Red, White, and Blue Letter Days: An American Calendar.* Ithaca, N.Y.: Cornell University Press, 2002.

Grossman, Jonathan. "Who Is the Father of Labor Day?" *Labor History* 14 (Fall 1973): 612–623.

Kazin, Michael, and Steven J. Ross. "America's Labor Day: The Dilemma of a Workers' Celebration." *Journal of American History* 78 (March 1992): 1294–1323.

Litwicki, Ellen M. *America's Public Holidays, 1865–1920.* Washington, D.C.: Smithsonian Institution Press, 2000.

Watts, Theodore F. *The First Labor Day Parade, Tuesday, September 5, 1882: Media Mirrors to Labor's Icons.* Silver Spring, Md.: Phoenix Rising, 1983.

*Ellen M. Litwicki*

# LAS VEGAS

Las Vegas is so saturated with the aura of myth that it is difficult to separate fantasy from reality, even for people who are frequent visitors. Decades of hype and boosterism have created associations linked to our most deeply embedded American dreams: get-rich-quick schemes, the "Wild West," gangsters, Hollywood glitz, glamorous romance, hot entertainment, and twenty-four/seven action. Never mind that these associations work principally through slight-of-hand illusions, Americans have made Las Vegas the premier tourist destination since the 1960s, only to be surpassed recently by Orlando, Florida. At the turn of the twentieth century, over 30 million visitors came to the region a year, with about half of them flying into McCarran International Airport, the tenth busiest in the nation. Always prone to cycles in the nation's economy, tourism was down somewhat after the year 2000, but it remained healthy enough to support the relentless construction of newer and bigger gambling resort-casinos. Gross gambling revenues were more than $6 billion at the turn of the twentieth century, and eager visitors to the area spent an additional $20 billion on hotel, food, entertainment, and other expenses. This is not at all bad for a place that is located in one of the most forbidding deserts on our planet, with daily summer temperatures well into the hundreds. Every drop of water, each piece of produce and meat or fish, and all the other "necessities" of life, except for oxygen itself, must be shipped in from places outside the region.

Despite the desert surroundings, Las Vegas has always been a stopping-off point for travelers; its name means "the meadows" in Spanish. Natural springs bubbling water from underground aquifers created an oasis in a hostile climate. Antonio Armijo, a Spanish trader, found the verdant site in 1829 while searching for a direct route to California from New Mexico. Gold strikes during the 1860s in the area drew the first horde of "get-rich-quick" schemers to the area only to witness the towns they built go bust a few years later when the easy pickings ran out. Yet Las Vegas itself hung on. Banking on its reliable supply of fresh water, the town was converted into a provisioning place with lodging and a general store that prospered. By the 1900s, when the immense infrastructure project that was the transcontinental railroad came west, an entrepreneur by the name of William Clark established a railroad that linked up with the Union Pacific's main line out of Salt Lake City, Utah, and the tracks at San Pedro, California, outside Los Angeles. The Las Vegas site owned by Clark and his associates became a rest stop along the way to Salt Lake City. Lodging and provisioning remained its economic base, as in a sense it continues to do so today, along with the spectacular addition of casino gambling.

There have been many phases of growth and change in the region since that time. Tourism preceded the exploitation of casino gambling as an attraction. Las Vegas would have always remained a small town except for the construction in the late 1920s of the largest dam in the United States across Boulder Canyon just southeast of Las Vegas on the Colorado River. This project, later named for President Herbert Hoover, injected millions of government dollars into the region, creating thousands of jobs at a time when the rest of the country was suffering from an economic catastrophe. Because of government spending, Las Vegas became a boomtown in the 1930s, and it has remained so. With thousands of workers pouring into the site, Las Vegas businesspeople expanded their hotel and gambling operations. Later, during World War II, the federal government helped out again by subsidizing munitions plants in the area and by building one of the largest air force bases in the country, Nellis AFB.

## The Birth of Modern Las Vegas

Popular myth, reinforced by Hollywood films, attributes to mobster Benjamin "Bugsy" Siegel the vision that created modern-day Las Vegas. This story is incorrect. In the 1940s, the real estate entrepreneur Thomas Hull introduced the concept of the "resort" hotel to the area, following his success at developing similar places in southern California. Architect Wayne McAllister helped create a unique, Southwest style of resort—with rooms wrapping around an open court and pool area—that influenced resort hotel development across the country. Later, during the Christmas season of 1941, Siegel opened the luxurious Flamingo Hotel, also designed by McAllister. Initially a famous flop, the Flamingo prospered in the 1950s and helped induce more venture capital to expand the gambling resort-casino base of the area. Significantly, the Flamingo Hotel, as well as many others built after the 1940s, was located *outside* the city limits of Las Vegas on what is now known as the Strip, aka, Las Vegas Boulevard. Since that time, it has technically been Clark County, then, with its famous Strip casinos, that has eclipsed the city of Las Vegas itself as the gambling mecca of the nation.

From these beginnings, the Las Vegas region has undergone a series of transformations always resulting in an expansion of its draw as a tourist and leisure haven. During the 1960s classic Las Vegas emerged by realizing Bugsy Siegel's particular vision—the merging of Hollywood and show business glitz with casino gambling. At the Sands Hotel, Frank Sinatra's "rat pack"—consisting of Dean Martin, Sammy Davis Jr., Peter Lawford, and Joey Bishop—defined Las Vegas–style entertainment. However, it was really at the Sahara Hotel, just up the Strip to the north, where Louie Prima and Kelly Smith (along with their gifted saxophonist Sam Butera) created the "lounge act," that singular form of free, late-night Vegas entertainment that was practically extinct by 2004; that "act" helped colonize nighttime as a common period of activity. Downtown, in the city center, the venerable "Wild West" casinos such as Binion's Horseshoe and the Fremont drew in capacity crowds of gamblers because of their friendly house odds at table games. The no-frills, "tiny," 300-room Binion's still hosts the increasingly popular World Series of Poker every year.

By the 1970s, Las Vegas was the premier tourist destination in the United States. Well-known casinos such as Caesars Palace, the Sahara, the Alladin, the Stardust, and the Frontier, along with the Flamingo and the Sands (many of which were located on the Strip in Clark County), packed people in at capacity. The Desert Inn innovated first-class eighteen-hole golf in Las Vegas and became an unparalleled luxury resort. Yet, all of these hotel casinos were of modest size compared to the giant resorts that were to come, although the range of up to 2,000 rooms was the envy of tourist resorts around the world.

## The Mega-Resorts Take Over

During the 1980s a new player, Steve Wynn, entered the scene. His vision involved pushing the limits of extravagance and capacity, and he built the first of Las Vegas's "mega-resorts." His Mirage hotel casino, completed in 1989, boasted 3,000 rooms set on 100 acres with an eighteen-hole golf course, tennis courts, and many dining alternatives. Along with changing the scale of Las Vegas tourist destinations forever, Wynn also solidified the essential relationship between the mega-resorts and the role of theming embedded in architectural forms as a means of attracting visitors. His Mirage amplified the always popular "tropical paradise" resort motif with a white tiger display in the lobby, a $14 million dolphin pool habitat on the grounds, and, directly outside, a simulated tropical island and lagoon with a faux exploding volcano that erupted nightly every fifteen minutes. Passersby walking on the Strip could not avoid being attracted by the spectacle of flames, sound, and light that did more than anything else to announce a new elaboration of the always excessive, ultra-hyped Las Vegas style.

The New York-New York mega-resort, which opened on 3 January 1997, features a re-creation of the skyline of New York City that includes replicas of twelve famous skyscrapers and this 150-foot replica of the Statue of Liberty. © *Richard Cummins/Corbis*

By the twenty-first century, Las Vegas reigned supreme as the hotel capital of the world, in addition to being its premier casino gambling mecca. The MGM Grand, Las Vegas's first billion-dollar casino, boasted the Earth's largest capacity with over 5,000 rooms, and new resorts rivaling it, such as Mandalay Bay, Treasure Island, and the new Aladdin, were also constructed on the Strip. To make room for the mega-resorts, many of the old-school Vegas casinos were torn down—the land they sat on was far more valuable than the buildings themselves. Las Vegas also saw other billion-dollar-plus buildings constructed by rivals Steve Wynn, who built the luxurious Bellagio, and Sheldon Adelson, who constructed the spectacularly themed Venetian almost directly across the street from the Bellagio. Theming, too, became the principal means of distinguishing one prodigious project from another: New York–New York simulated Manhattan; the Paris Hotel and Casino simulated Paris; the Venetian reproduced a Hollywood set simulation of Venice, Italy, that included a version of its famous canals; the Luxor simulated a Hollywood version of ancient Egypt; the Excalibur simulated King Arthur's England.

The Las Vegas region is a pastiche of tourist attractions that operate seven days a week, twenty-four hours a day. Destinations continually reinvent themselves according to shifting market needs. During the economic slump in the early 1990s, for example, some casinos countered the "Sin City" image by transforming themselves into family-oriented destinations. Circus-Circus, always a family place, added a five-acre, $90 million amusement park in 1993. Soon after, the MGM Grand opened with a thirty-three-acre theme park featuring amusement rides and Universal Studios—style Hollywood back-lot attractions. As the economy picked up and the dot.com frenzy hit the United States at the turn of the twentieth century, family emphasis disappeared and casino resorts aimed for both young adults and established middle-agers with money. So-called "fine dining," dance clubs, even art exhibits such as the multimillion-dollar collection once viewable at Steve Wynn's Bellagio were added to the mix. The old Sahara Hotel was renovated to include a NASCAR theme to attract auto racing enthusiasts, and top entertainers from around the world, such as Celine Dion, were ensconced in showrooms that catered to the "after-hours" crowds, while golfing remained as popular as ever and available on several new PGA-approved courses.

**The Dark Side of Las Vegas**

There is, of course, a downside to the Las Vegas experience. Family assets are lost at the gambling tables. Chil-

dren are told to hang out at video arcades by neglectful parents intent on spending hours gambling; in the late 1990s, at least one such child was murdered in a horrific case that drew national headlines. Despite over a decade of living under the specter of AIDS, prostitution and the sex trade in general flourish in and around the city. Las Vegas has the highest suicide rate in the country and the highest high school dropout rate. Its environmental concerns include waste from nuclear explosions in nearby Yucca Flats, poor air quality due to automobile smog, extensive pesticide and fertilizer use that threatens the quality of the water supply, cigarette smoke hazards in the casinos, and the general encouragement by resort operators of excessive eating, drinking, and gambling. Despite these problems, Las Vegas remains, after Orlando, Florida, the most successful tourist destination in the United States. Furthermore, unlike other places, it stands apart as a cultural experience that does not mirror our mundane, everyday tastes in fantasy forms, such as Disneyworld, but, instead, celebrates what we know is usually forbidden—especially the risk taking and often reckless activity of legalized gambling.

*See also:* Atlantic City, Card Games, Commercialization of Leisure, Gambling.

**BIBLIOGRAPHY**

Bowers, Michael Wayne. *The Sagebrush State: Nevada's History, Government, and Politics.* Las Vegas: University of Nevada Press, 1996.

Castleman, Deke. *Las Vegas.* Oakland, Calif.: Fodors Travel Guides, 1996.

Goodman, Robert. *The Luck Business: The Devastating Consequences and Broken Promises of America's Gambling Explosion.* New York: The Free Press, 1995.

Gottdiener, Mark, et al. *Las Vegas: The Social Production of an All-American City.* Oxford: Blackwell Publishers, 1999.

Hess, Alan. *Viva Las Vegas: After-hours Architecture.* San Francisco: Chronicle Books, 1993.

Moehring, Eugene P. *Resort City in the Sunbelt: Las Vegas 1930- 1970.* Las Vegas: University of Nevada Press, 1989.

*Mark Gottdiener*

# LATINO LEISURE LIFESTYLES

The year 2000 marked a milestone for Latinos in the United States. For the first time in U.S. history, the U.S.

Census recorded Latinos, with a population of 35 million, as the largest ethnic group. According to the 2000 U.S. Census, the three largest ethnic groups were Latinos (12.5 percent), African Americans (12.3 percent), and Asian Americans (3.7 percent). By 2050, the U.S. population will be more culturally diverse, with less than 53 percent of the population categorized as Anglo/European American; 15 percent African American; more than 24 percent Latino; nearly 9 percent Asian American, and about 1 percent Native American. People of Mexican descent constitute 58.5 percent of all U.S. Latinos. People of Puerto Rican origin embody nearly 9.6 percent of all Latinos, while people of Cuban descent (3.5 percent) and "other" Latinos (28.4 percent) account for the remainder of the Latino population in the United States. Latinos are geographically located in the "corners" of the country: northeastern United States is predominantly Puerto Rican and Dominican; southeastern Florida is predominantly Cuban; and the Southwest is predominantly Mexican and Central American. The majority of Latinos live in and around urban centers such as Los Angeles, New York, Miami, Dallas, and Chicago.

However, the 2000 census revealed that several of those Latino capitals were changing due to shifts in the nationalities of Latino immigrants. For example, Puerto Ricans once dominated the Latino culture of New York City. Puerto Ricans declined by 12 percent from 1990 to 2000, while Mexicans (the fastest growing Latino group in the U.S.) increased by 208 percent over the same time period (Miller). Chicago followed an analogous situation, with the majority of Latinos switching from Puerto Rican to Mexican due to emigration from Los Angeles and Texas. Similarly, Miami was once dominated by Cubans. Puerto Ricans increased by 9 percent from 1990 to 2000, while Cubans represented less than 45 percent of the Latino population, and the remainder was comprised of multiple Latino nationalities. The general immigration patterns of Latinos indicated two phenomena: (1) Latinos were continuing to locate in traditional Latino strongholds, however, the Latino market was more diversified with respect to national origin, and (2) Latinos were becoming more mobile, and beginning to venture outside of the traditional areas.

In areas where Latinos represented a strong majority, very little adaptation to American leisure patterns was noted, and there was a general resistance towards mainstream assimilation. Rather, a reinforcement of Latino cultural homogeneity was often realized. For example, the huge growth of the Mexican population in Chicago (75 percent of Chicago's Latinos) was "reflected in cultural developments like the Chicago Mexican Fine Arts Center Museum, located in the Pilsen/Little Village neighborhood, the largest Mexican community in the Midwest" (Miller, p. 34B).

Unlike assimilation and immigration patterns and behaviors of previous decades, Latino immigrants of the early twenty-first century were maintaining their ties to their cultural origins. Puerto Ricans were indicative of this general pattern. For example, from 1900 to 1945, Puerto Ricans primarily settled in New York City, and maintained strong cultural ties to the island. Puerto Ricans began expanding into neighboring states around New York City and as far as Chicago between 1946 and 1964. After 1965, Puerto Ricans began a "revolving door" migration pattern, where there was continuous back and forth migration from the island to the mainland. Although other Latino immigrants did not follow the exact pattern of migration because Puerto Rico is part of the United States, many cultural ties were maintained through affordable flights to the country of origin, thereby reinforcing and maintaining cultural ties.

As a result of demographic changes, recreation and leisure providers in the United States will have tremendous challenges ahead in terms of service delivery, policy-making, and identifying participation patterns and Latino recreation styles and lifestyles. The purpose of this entry is to identify recreation characteristics, patterns, and general leisure lifestyles of Latinos. More specifically, this entry focuses on the Latino events/holidays, sports, dance/music, and outdoor recreation. The intent is not to be comprehensive, but rather to illustrate unique features of the Latino recreational lifestyle. Because the Latino ethnic group is very broad, this commentary will center on the two largest Latino groups (Mexicans and Puerto Ricans), but will include other Latino groups when necessary.

## Latino Events and Holidays

Leisure and recreation for Latinos tend to be very social. In general, Latinos participate in recreational activities in larger groups than other Americans, and these groups are composed of family members, extended family members, and close friends. Many formal leisure occasions revolve around family or religious matters.

An example of a unique family leisure occasion in the Latino culture is the *quinceañera*. The quinceañera is a girl's fifteenth birthday party. In the Latino culture, the quinceañera is the girl's "coming of age," and it designates her entry into womanhood. After a wedding, it is the single most important formal event in a girl's life. It is also a communal event—family and close community friends are invited, and there is often a blessing from a priest at the

***Quinceañera.*** A Cuban girl celebrates her *quinceañera* with family and friends in Miami, Florida, in 1996. The Mexican tradition acknowledges a young girl's passage into womanhood on her fifteenth birthday. © *Patrick Ward/Corbis*

event. It is not uncommon to have more than 300 persons invited to this event. Although the quinceañera varies by Latino group, a typical quinceañera might have the following: a court of men and women representing different ages up to age fifteen; a consort for the fifteen-year-old girl; the first pair of high heels that the "new woman" will walk in (the father walks her in the heels, presenting her to the community); and the traditional song called "La Quinceañera."

A religious event found in Mexico and celebrated in the United States is *El Día de los Muertos* (The Day of the Dead). The roots of this celebration date back to the Aztecs, and were transformed by the influence of the Catholic Church during Spanish colonialism. El Día de los Muertos is celebrated in the first two days of November. Families visit the graves of their ancestors and decorate them with bright flowers and religious artifacts. Traditionally, the family has a picnic around the gravesite and dedicates the meal in memory of their loved ones, while telling stories of the ancestor's accomplishments or antics. This celebration has a very enjoyable feel to it, and it reminds the Mexicans of the human cycle of life.

Another special time of year for Mexican Americans is the month of May: 1 May is Mexico's Labor Day; Mexico's biggest spring holiday is *Cinco de Mayo* (the Fifth of May), and it is one of the most celebrated festivals throughout the southwestern United States; Mother's Day (in the United States it is the second Sunday in May) is a big holiday because Latino mothers are highly adored; and 15 May is both the Feast of San Isidro Labrador, the patron saint of farmers (Waldrop), and Teacher's Day, which is celebrated in Mexico.

A communal event found in the Puerto Rican population is the Christmas season, which begins in early December and continues through mid-January. The most prominent characteristic of this communal time is the *parrandas* (family/friends partying and singing *aguinaldos,* the typical/traditional songs of Puerto Rico). The parranda begins in the late evening hours (when people are sleeping) and lasts until daybreak. Typically, people will not be advised prior to a parranda's arrival. It begins with a few people that honor family/friends with the parranda, and they are rewarded with food and drink. They eat, sing, and dance, and then some members from the family receiving the parranda join the *trulla* (group of performers) and go on to another house. This pattern continues into the night, and the highest honor is bestowed upon the last house of the night, which may have easily more than fifty people to host.

In addition to *parrandiando* (parranda-ing), the Christmas season includes: *aguinaldo* masses, nine days prior to Christmas; *La Misa del Gallo* (Midnight Mass); *Navidad* (Christmas); *La Despedida del Año* (New Year's Eve/Day); *and Día de los Reyes* (Three Kings' Day, the Feast of the Epiphany). Dia de los Reyes (6 January) celebrates the visit to the baby Jesus by the three Magi kings. Children leave grass in a small box under the Christmas tree for the kings' camels, and are rewarded with presents. Because of the tremendous cultural impact that this season (and its myriad of leisure activities) has on Puerto Ricans, it affects seasonal visitation and tourism patterns to the island. December is a heavily traveled month in Puerto Rico, with corresponding higher airfares.

Similar to Puerto Rico's December celebrations, Mexico has the *posadas*. Typically, a village priest chants the story of *Las Posadas,* of how Mary and Joseph tried to find a room at an inn and were turned away from that shelter and others, again and again. The house(s) selected as the "inn" is blessed by the priest, and a series of celebrations and festivities follow where relatives, friends, and neighbors congregate. The tradition of the piñatas in Mexico is said to have begun during the posadas, and the first piñatas were white stars representing the star of Bethlehem. These celebrations are repeated nine nights in a row, with the final night being Christmas Eve.

## Latinos and Sports

Latinos in the United States favor some sports over others. Latinos of Mexican, South, and Central American ancestry tend to favor *fútbol* (soccer). Latinos from the Spanish-speaking Caribbean favor the sports of *pelota* (baseball), *boxeo* (boxing), and *baloncesto* (basketball), and the game of dominoes is their favorite pastime. These sports are commonly played and well-known in the United States. However, some other sports, also played in the United States, are not given much publicity.

A sport rarely played sport in the United States is jai-alai. This sport has its traditions in the Basque area of Spain and France. During Spain's colonial era, the Basques brought jai-alai to the new world, most notably to Mexico and Cuba. In the United States, jai-alai is mostly concentrated in southeast Florida (Miami), and most jai-alai enthusiasts are Cuban. Jai-alai achieved in-ternational recognition at the 1992 Olympic Games in Barcelona, Spain.

There are certain sports that are not common throughout America, but are particular to certain countries. For example, cock fighting is prevalent in Puerto Rico (which is part of the United States), Cuba, the Dominican Republic, Argentina, and Venezuela. And, although illegal in most states, it is still practiced in areas that have large concentrations of Latinos from these five areas of Latin America. Another sporting event that is not found in the United States, but is watched on television by many Latinos (especially Mexicans), is bullfighting. Neither of these sports prosper in the United States due to animal rights advocacy.

## Latinos and Entertainment

The majority of Latino entertainment involves dance and music. Although there are no specific Latino leisure zones, per se, most bar districts in urban areas with a sizeable Latino population have Latino night clubs (or section of a club) and/or Latin dance nights. Unlike the general aversion to dance shared by most men in the United States, Latino men are expected to learn to dance. An integral part of Latino cultural expression, dancing ranges from the traditional to the modern. Traditional Mexican dances are numerous and vary according to region and influence (European, Aboriginal, or African). Several of these dances can be seen in the U.S. Southwest during Mexican American festivals and celebrations.

Latinos from the Spanish-speaking Caribbean have traditional dances/music (*danzas* and *boleros* ), and more modern dances/music (*merengue, salsa,* and *bachata* ) that have been imported. Of particular importance is salsa music, which has traditionally contained politically oriented messages. In the 1960s, salsa grew out of a musical movement generated by New York Latinos, mostly Puerto Ricans. Salsa is to Latinos what blues music is to African Americans and rock music is to Anglo Americans. Salsa quickly grew internationally as a symbol of Latino solidarity and a cultural resistance to Americanization. The music commented on Latino urban life in the *barrios* (neighborhoods) of the United States, and the affirmation of Latino identity, pride, and unity in the face of socioeconomic marginalization. The Latin musical culture in the United States is heavily influenced by music from Mexico, Puerto Rico, Cuba, and the Dominican Republic. The majority of informal musical gatherings for social (such as birthdays, quinceañera, and graduations) or religious (baptisms, communions, confirmations) events are held in rented clubs or halls due to the generally large number of extended family members.

## Latinos and the Outdoors

Latinos, in general, have a very different view of the outdoors compared to other Americans. Most of the literature on Latinos in outdoor recreation has been on Mexican Americans in the U.S. Southwest. Mexican Americans differ significantly from Anglo Americans: Mexican American recreationists tend to be younger in age; they participate in recreation activities in larger groups; and they like to be concentrated together versus being dispersed throughout the recreation site. Additionally, Mexican Americans prefer to have developed areas in the outdoors versus more pristine or wilderness areas. In character with their socialization and sense of communalism, Mexican Americans mostly enjoy picnicking, relaxing, and other forms of passive behaviors in the outdoors.

Puerto Ricans in New York City have a different approach to outdoor recreation—they construct vegetable gardens on empty lots and rooftops in South Bronx and other Latino neighborhoods. Puerto Ricans have had gardens since the 1930s, and trace their yearning for a garden to their *jibaro* (independent peasant from hills of Puerto Rico) roots. In addition to gardening, fishing (a favorite pastime) offers Puerto Ricans therapeutic, social, and psychological value.

## Latinos and Leisure Presence

The Latino population in the United States is extremely varied. Latinos come from several countries, and as their numbers increase, they will continue to influence leisure patterns, behaviors, and lifestyles in their adopted country. This is evident with the increase of radio and television stations, such as Telemundo, Galavisión, and Univisión, which have catered to Latinos since the 1970s. Additionally, Latino music stars such as Selena, Gloria Estefan, Jennifer Lopez, Ricky Martin, Enrique Iglesias, and Marc Anthony have bridged Spanish and English music markets. Latinos, such as Jose Canseco (Cuban), Roberto Clemente (Puerto Rican, member of Baseball Hall of Fame), Pedro Martinez (Dominican), and Sammy Sosa (Dominican) are making inroads into Major League Baseball in the United States. As the United States becomes more demographically varied, and the Latino population increases, the nature of recreation and leisure in America will change to accommodate diverse users of recreation and leisure resources. For example, parades (such as Cinco de Mayo in various urban areas, Puerto Rican Parade in New York City and Boston) and commercial events (for example Miami's Calle Ocho dances and parades) are catering to the growing Latino population.

*See also:* Racial Diversity and Leisure Lifestyles

**BIBLIOGRAPHY**

Chavez, Deborah J. "Hispanic Recreationist in the Wildland-Urban Interface." *Trends* 29 (1992): 23–25.

Comas-Díaz, Lillian. "Hispanics, Latinos, or Americanos: The Evolution of Identity." *Cultural Diversity and Ethnic Minority Psychology* 7, no. 2 (May 2001): 115–120.

Lynch, Barbara D. "The Garden and the Sea: U.S. Latino Environmental Discourse and Mainstream Environmentalism." *Social Problems* 40, no. 1 (February 1993): 108–124.

Manuel, Peter. "The Soul of the Barrio: 30 years of Salsa." *NACLA Report on the Americas* 28, no. 2 (September/October 1994): 22–29.

Miller, M. U.S. "Latino Capitals in Flux: Immigration Patterns Are Changing the Culture of Some of the Largest Hispanic Markets." 2002 Hispanic Market Report: Urban Markets. *Multichannel News,* 23 (2002), 34B.

U.S. Bureau of the Census. *Census 2000: Summary File 1.* (October 2001). Available from http://www.census.gov/.

U.S. Bureau of the Census. *Profiles of General Demographic Characteristics: 2000.* (May 2001). Available from http://www.census.gov/.

Waldrop, Judith. "The Mexican May." *American Demographics* 14, no. 5 (May 1992): 4.

*Edwin Gómez*

# LEISURE AND CIVIL SOCIETY

The concept of civil society refers to social affiliations located between the state, on one hand, and individuals, families, and other loosely structured collectives, such as neighborhoods, on the other. Individuals affiliate with a variety of such interstitial organizations voluntarily in order to protect or further shared interests and values within the larger society. Religious institutions, professional associations, associations based on sport, leisure, and recreation, various nongovernment organizations (NGOs), and a variety of advocacy groups are examples of these affiliations.

The roots of civil society can be traced most directly to the reforms of Pericles (c. 490–429 B.C.), statesman of Athens, who consolidated Ephialtes's (d. 461 B.C.) goal of providing citizens with active roles in government. This development in Athenian democracy was based on the even earlier reforms of Solon (c. 630–590 B.C.) and others. Pericles also increased the aesthetic awareness of common folk in Athens by making drama and music accessible, but his major innovation was the introduction of payment for state service by citizens from the public treasury.

During the late 1900s, there was a renewed interest in the construction and organization of civil society. Indeed, public discourse about civil society had become globalized. For example, Internet searches of the key word "civil society" were likely to produce such matching sites as Committee of Government Representatives on the Participation of Civil Society, Voices from Serbian Civil Society, Middle East Civil Society Working Group, Philosophy and Civil Society, Postmodern Civic Culture, CIVITAS: The Institute for the Study of Civil Society, and CIVICUS: World Alliance for Citizen Participation.

Another indication of the globalization of discourse about civil society is the fact that the United Nations has its own civil society Web site (http://www.un.org/partners.civil_society/home.html) showing how the organization works with NGOs and other civil society agencies on issues of global concern. These examples of the globalization of public discourse about civil society support Don Eberly's assertion: "The most important development at the dawn of the twenty-first century may be the rediscovery of the nongovernmental sector of society, or as some call it the voluntary or social sector" (p. 3).

## The Origins of Civil Society

The classical understanding of civil society derives from political thought associated with early Hellenic city-states. Aristotle, Pericles, and Plato all had something to say about civil society, and their written works reflect the first efforts to develop systematic political theory. With the fall of the Roman Empire, classical conceptions of civil society were discarded for Christian conceptions of civil society, as perhaps best revealed in the writings of St. Augustine. In turn, Christian conceptions of civil society greatly influenced the first modern notions of civil society associated with the writings of the moral philosophers of the Scottish enlightenment, including those of David Hume, John Locke, Adam Smith, and Adam Ferguson, who published *An Essay on the History of Civil Society* in 1767.

## What Is Civil Society?

Given the many different historical periods in which civil society has been examined, the diverse cultural contexts in which civil society has been established, and the difficulties of translating a largely Western concept into Asian languages, it is not surprising that there is no consensus as to what civil society is. However, a number of working definitions provide a reasonable description of the basic features of civil society.

Joan Cohen and Andrew Arato define civil society "as a sphere of social interaction between economy and state, composed above all of the intimate sphere (especially the family), the sphere of associations (especially voluntary associations), social movements, and forms of public communication" (p. ix). In a slightly different vein, Janet Harris states: "*Civil society* refers broadly to processes of collective decision-making and action that entail (a) active, uncoerced involvement; (b) trust of one's fellow citizens; (c) responsibility and care for the well-being of others; and (d) social networks featuring many horizontal relationships—interactions among people with relatively equal status and power" (p. 138). These two sets of working definitions in combination reinforce Jamie Swift's observation: "Civil society hints at voluntarism, charity, community organizing, grassroots activity" (p. 5).

## The Appeal of Civil Society

The concept of civil society is appealing for political, popular, and professional reasons. From a political perspective, proponents of the idea of civil society can be found among communitarians, libertarians, and traditionalists. In short, the idea of civil society holds appeal for political theorists and politicians positioned left, right, and center on the political spectrum.

All political theorists and politicians recognize, in Anthony Giddens's terms, that: "The democratizing of democracy . . . depends upon the fostering of a strong civic culture" (p. 77); and that: "Civil society is the arena in which democratic attitudes, including tolerance, have to be developed" (p. 78). Giddens links the global with the local in his notion of democratizing democracy. On the one hand, he recognizes that democracy must be transnational (p. 75); while, on the other hand, he recognizes that "the democratization of democracy will take different forms in different countries, depending on their background" (p. 76). Moreover, he acknowledges that even the most mature democracies can become more democratized.

Laypeople are also attracted to the idea of a civil society. As Swift notes, people often believe that "they are merely passive spectators at a global game dominated by powerful international corporations," and thus "the idea of a civil society, the proverbial dense network of associations and small groups in which people actually do something effective, is attractive" (p. 88).

Last but not least, the concept of civil society appeals to professional educators, social workers, and social scientists, because they commonly address such key questions as: "By what process does the individual acquire democratic habits, skills and values; and how is moral conscience, so vital for a civil and human society formed?" (Eberly, p. 15). The idea of civil society is most appealing to sociologists. Indeed, several famous theorists in the sociological tradition have made substantial contributions to debates about the civil society, including Emile Durkheim, Karl Marx, Ferdinand Toennies, Alexis de Tocqueville, Antonio Gramsci, Jurgen Habermas, and Talcott Parsons.

The most direct and substantial contributions to the scholarly discourse about civil society have been by such contemporary humanistic sociologists as Robert Bellah, Peter Berger, Amitai Etzioni, and Robert Nisbet. The theory and research of these sociologists indicate the main attributes and dimensions of a strong and healthy civil society.

## The Attributes and Dimensions of a Strong and Healthy Civil Society

There appears to be consensus among theorists of civil society that the most distinguishable feature of a viable civil society "is a well-informed and active citizenry participating in public life through associations they voluntarily form" (Naidoo and Tandon, p. 7). In turn, voluntary association and associative autonomy require an enabling environment, that is, legally guaranteed and enforced rights to freely act independently of the state and marketplace.

Enabling environments for voluntary association and associational autonomy are provided by what Peter Berger and Richard Neuhaus call "mediating structures." These structures are composed of secondary or communal institutions such as the church, family, and neighborhood that stand between individuals in their private lives and their primary institutions of public life related to the state and marketplace. With respect to the theme of "democratizing democracy," Berger and Neuhaus state three relevant propositions. First, "public policy should protect and foster mediating structures" (p. 161). Second, "mediating structures are essential for a vital democratic society" (pp. 162–163). Third, "wherever possible, public policy should utilize mediating structures for the realization of social purposes" (p. 163).

Relative to big government (the state) and big business (the marketplace), communal institutions, or mediating structures, have three major distinguishing features.

First, their characteristics include voluntary membership, uncoerced civic engagement, acts of altruistic responsibility, and networks of horizontal relationships ensuring mutual interactions in terms of relatively equal power and status. The greater the density and diversity of networks of voluntary associations, the greater the degree of institutional pluralism that is important for democratizing democracy. It gives citizens greater choices of activities as well as more channels to express their interests in public life. It also "provides citizens with overlapping membership based on their varied interests, and, thus, cuts across a range of societal cleavages (e.g., race, class, ethnicity, region) that have tended to divide rather than unite people" (Naidoo and Tandon, p. 10).

Second, interactions among members of communal institutions are largely based on the classic "gift mode of exchange." As famously formulated by Marcel Mauss, individuals are morally obligated to give, to receive, and to repay. With reference to mediating structures, Jacques Godbout, in his modern account of *The World of the Gift*, contends "that families would disintegrate instantly if disavowing the demands of gift and counter-gift," and asserts that "the same holds true for friendship, comradeship, and neighbourliness" (p. 12). In short, the gift mode of social exchange fosters the nurturing and nourishing of intimate social relationships within the relatively private spheres of mediating structures.

Third, relative to primary institutions representative of the state and marketplace, the communal institutions and networks of voluntary associations constituting civil society are most responsible for promoting civic virtue and generating what Robert Putnam and others have referred to as "social capital," that is, the "connections among individuals—social net works and the norms of reciprocity and trustworthiness that arise from them" (Putman, p. 19).

More specifically, there are, according to Putman, two specific kinds of social capital called "bridging" and "bonding," respectively. Bridging social capital is "inclusive," whereas bonding social capital is "exclusive." In short, "bridging social capital can generate broader identities and reciprocity, whereas bonding social capital bolsters our narrower selves" (p. 23).

An example of bonding social capital is elite country clubs such as the Augusta National Golf Club, where the professional Masters golf tournament is played annually. Bonding social capital is often associated with "the dark side of civil society," in that "by creating strong in-group loyalty, may also create strong out-group antagonism" (p. 23). But Putman takes care to point out that social organizations cannot be neatly classified as representative of bonding or bridging social capital formations. Using the church as an example, one can note the importance of local churches with African American members for furthering civil rights in the United States during the 1960s, while also noting the detrimental social consequences of strict fundamentalism associated with particular religious sects.

## Positive Potentials of Civil Society and Social Capital

Voluntary association and the generation of social capital underpinning the foundations of civil society indicate that first and foremost "civil society represents a search for life on a more humane scale" (Eberly, p. 17). A review of related research literature offers three broad sets of generalizations regarding the positive potentials of civil society in terms of voluntary association, leisure participation, and the generation of social capital that aid in the creation of life on a more humane scale.

First, there is ample empirical evidence supporting the fact that civic engagement and the generation of social capital does in fact enhance the quality of life for participatory citizens. As Janet Harris reports: "Data from hundreds of studies in many different academic disciplines indicate that civically engaged communities have more success in education, health, government, economics, and programs addressing crime, drug abuse, and urban poverty" (p. 139). There are many mechanisms related to these positive effects. But with respect to social capital per se, Robert Putman highlights the following five features: (a) "social capital allows citizens to resolve collective problems more easily;" (b) "social capital greases the wheels that allow communities to advance smoothly;" (c) "social capital improves our lot . . . by widening our awareness of the many ways in which our fates are linked;" (d) "the networks that constitute social capital serve as conduits for the flow of helpful information that facilitates achieving our goals;" and (e) "social capital also operates through psychological and biological processes to improve individual lives" (pp. 288–289).

Second, given the significance of leisure and recreation in communities throughout the world, a case can be made that voluntary sport clubs and recreational activities are an essential feature of the communal order of civil society. Recreational sports and mass participation in all forms of physical recreation increase social capital and help to enhance the quality of life for those civically engaged. North American studies provide consistent findings that participation in leisure activities offer ben-

efits in such areas as academic achievement, development of citizenship, fostering leadership skills, and maintaining lifelong health.

Third, relative to the public, primary institutions of the state and the marketplace, secondary or communal institutions have historically been private and often the central domain of women. Moreover, they have traditionally been the most concerned with the disadvantaged, disabled, oppressed, marginalized, and poor members of society. Thus, in a reciprocal fashion, the mediating structures of civil society have the potential to provide enabling leisure and sport environments endorsing an ethic of inclusiveness and diversity.

## Leisure Participation, Voluntarism, and Social Action

Civic engagement and social action are at the core of civil society. In turn, volunteering is at the heart of social action in society in general, and leisure in particular. From a societal perspective, forces of voluntarism have been effective in social movements for positive changes related to indigenous cultures, grassroots democracy in peasant societies, trade union efforts at national political change, and women's liberation efforts worldwide. A notable example of global voluntarism focused on improving the local is the past and present worldwide efforts of the American Peace Corps. Founded under the Kennedy administration in 1961, the Peace Corps remains one of the world's preeminent volunteer associations. Since its inception, more than 168,000 people have joined to serve in 136 countries.

From a leisure perspective, volunteer efforts worldwide are associated with both representational and recreational sport. Major marathons throughout the world, "grand slam" events in professional golf and tennis, international student games, and even the Olympic Games themselves are dependent upon the volunteer efforts of thousands of individuals. As a result, the number of volunteers in the civil sector serving as coaches, organizers, medical advisers, and sponsors are in the millions worldwide.

Given the global nature of voluntarism, it is significant that the United Nations General Assembly proclaimed 2001 as the International Year of Volunteers. But is it also significant that the notions of voluntary association and voluntarism are especially American. As Alexis de Tocqueville famously observed in his tour of America in 1833: "Americans of all ages, all conditions, and all dispositions, constantly form associations" (p. 198).

The collective values of Americans observed by de Tocqueville almost surely reflected, in part, the agricultural foundation of early America. In particular, agricultural fairs, derived from European ancestors that date to ancient Greek and Roman times, contributed to early American public welfare through the exposition of new farming practices imported from Europe by major landholders, including George Washington, Thomas Jefferson, and John Randolph. Large landholders led early agricultural societies in America, and these groups often resembled academic societies, with member reading learned papers at meetings. While such societies held little interest for the great majority of farmers, their gradual democratization and expansion encouraged the participation of working farmers. Early agricultural fairs involved livestock and produce exhibitions and competitions, but, more important, they provided demonstrations of the latest in agricultural techniques.

Agricultural societies spread from New England to the southern United States and the Midwest in the early part of the nineteenth century. In the second half of the nineteenth century, although interrupted by the Civil War, both the federal and state governments in the United States fostered the redevelopment of agricultural societies due to the need for food in the growing cities but also because of the great potential for the export of agricultural products to international markets. The Grange, so named in 1867 from the Latin *granea*, meaning granary or barn, continued to organize agricultural fairs across America as of 2004. The popularity of agricultural fairs waxed and waned over time, but modern fairs became more family-oriented and involved larger numbers of urban dwellers.

Examples of contemporary voluntarism as the American way are reflected in such national voluntary organizations as Volunteers of America founded in 1896, the AmeriCorps, the Senior Corps, and the U.S.A. Freedom Corps established in 2002. To encourage the recognition of volunteer service and civic participation, President George W. Bush created by executive order in January 2003 the President's Council on Service and Civic Participation.

While voluntarism shares the idea of freedom of choice with the concept of leisure, some newer forms make the connection direct and explicit. The "volunteer vacation," for example, is a relatively recent and interesting form of voluntarism that "links science, conservation, and public involvement" (Schueller, p. 1; see also McMillon, Cutchins, and Gissinger). Examples of Audubon Volunteer Vacations include assisting in the study of the

Amazon River dolphin, surveying life-forms on the coral reefs of Fiji, recording chimpanzee behavior in Uganda, helping wetland conservation in Hong Kong, and monitoring whales off the coast of Maui. Numerous other groups in the United States sponsor volunteer vacations, as well. Amizade, a global volunteer association with headquarters in Pittsburgh, Pennsylvania, offers programs that involve community service along with educational opportunities and recreational activities in many areas of both the United States and the rest of the world. The initial goal of Amizade, named after the Portuguese word for "friendship," was to help the peoples of Amazonia save the rain forest. It has since expanded to provide volunteer service vacations in areas such as Nepal, Australia, the Navajo Nation, and the Greater Yellowstone region in Wyoming and Montana. Volunteer vacations are offered by numerous other organizations, including the American Hiking Society (which assists with footpath and shelter construction and rebuilding, often in conjunction with the U.S. Bureau of Land Management), Cross-Cultural Solutions, Earthwatch Institute, Habitat for Humanity, the Sierra Club, and the Student Conservation Association. Volunteer vacations range in price from lows of $80 for American Hiking Society trips to several thousands of dollars for events such as those associated with the Jane Goodall Institute in Uganda. These fees generally do not include travel expenses to vacation sites, but, in many cases, part of vacation fees is used to support research and conservation efforts.

The degree and kind of volunteering in the United States is clearly revealed in a report released by the Bureau of Labor Statistics in December 2002. Drawing upon a survey of Americans over the age of sixteen for the period from September 2001 to September 2002, about 59 million people, or more than one in four Americans, did some volunteer work during that twelve-month period. The degree of volunteering varied by communal institution, with the majority of volunteers involved with religious organizations (33.9 percent) or youth-development agencies (27.2 percent). Another 12.1 percent performed volunteer work for community or social-service organizations, and 8.6 percent voluntarily worked in hospitals or other health organizations. On average, volunteers spent a median of 52 hours doing volunteer activities, but more than 28 percent reported spending 100 to 499 hours doing volunteer work. A variety of volunteer activities were reported, but teaching or coaching accounted for 24.4 percent of volunteer work. In sum, volunteer activities are a major type of leisure pursuit and involve a substantial number of American citizens.

## Private Lives and Public Life

As a socially significant American phenomenon, voluntarism is often viewed in idealistic or nostalgic terms like apple pie and motherhood. But the forces of voluntarism and the generation of social capital are fraught with many private problems and public issues, only a few of which are outlined below.

**Qualified personnel** Social organizations that are dependent upon volunteers often cannot afford to be too selective. Yet volunteer effort is only as good as the quality that goes into it. For example, with respect to the area of leisure participation, millions of American children participate in sport programs coached by more than 2.5 million volunteers, 90 percent of whom lack any formal training or preparation for their coaching roles (Poinsett).

**Hybrid and hyphenated social identities** Related to the issue of recruiting qualified volunteers for varied activities and organizations is ensuring that volunteers are qualified to work with diverse cultural groups. In particular, volunteers must be capable of dealing with individuals having hyphenated social identities resulting from marked increases in the process of hybridization or hybridity in American society. For example, "during the 1980s, more immigrants came to America than any other decade in [its] history" (Wishard, p. 66). From 1980 to 1990, the number of Spanish speakers increased by 50 percent, Chinese speakers by 98 percent, and Korean speakers by 127 percent (Wallraff, p. 54).

More significant is the fact that "when today's babies enter their retirement years, white, Anglo-Saxon Americans will be a minority, while Asian-Americans, African-Americans, and Hispanic-Americans will be the majority" (Wishard, p. 66). Thus, as America emerges as a fully blown multicultural society, hybrid and hyphenated identities will become the norm and will greatly impact upon civil society in terms of civic engagement and mass participation in leisure activities.

A key question is, what impact does recent immigration and hybridization have on the generation of social capital and the democratization of democracy? The immediate answer seems to be that there is both good news and bad news. The good news is that in terms of bridging social capital, immigrants are adding a new spirit and vitality to civic society and helping to restore major cities and urban centers. The bad news is that in terms of bonding social capital, immigrants often reside in ethnic/religious ghettos.

**Inequality in social capital** Research reveals that, in general, members of minority groups—be they based on gender, race, or ethnicity—typically possess less social capital. Nan Lin suggests that principles of structural differentiation and homophily largely account for inequalities in social capital. The first principle proposes social groups differentially occupy socioeconomic positions in society, and, as a result of historical developments and institutional constraints, selected groups are disadvantaged in having unequal opportunities to acquire social capital. The second principle proposes a general tendency for "birds of a feather to flock together," that is, "a general tendency for individuals to interact and share sentiment with others with similar characteristics" (p. 787). Thus "members of a certain group, clustering around relatively inferior socioeconomic standings and interacting with others in similar social groupings, would be embedded in social networks poorer in resources as well—poorer in social capital" (p. 787).

Although Americans typically accept inequality of outcomes, be it wealth or social capital, they should not have to accept inequality of opportunity. Voluntary associations, especially those related to leisure and recreational participation, have the potential to reduce inequality of opportunity by removing structural social constraints and offering systems of social networking that cut across class, ethnic, gender, and racial lines. However, notwithstanding the potential of secondary institutions of civic society to reduce the disadvantages bestowed by the primary institutions of the state and marketplace, recent research suggests that there are emerging trends of social decapitalization.

**Social decapitalization** In a provocative article titled "Bowling Alone: America's Declining Social Capital," Robert Putman documents trends of what he calls social decapitalization in the United States. And in a recent book, also titled *Bowling Alone,* he examines patterns of civic, political, and religious participation as well as informal connections and connections in the workplace for evidence to support his thesis of declining social capital in American society. The supposed stimulus for his analysis of social decapitalization was his finding that although more Americans are bowling today than ever before, "bowling in organized leagues has plummeted in the last decade or so" ("Bowling Alone," p. 70).

Putman's thesis generated a fair amount of critical reaction. A number of social scientists, for example, disagree that social capital is in fact declining, some suggesting that social capital has not so much declined but changed to conform to new structural conditions and new forms of civic engagement. However, whatever the merits of the arguments pro and con for American society in general, it is worthwhile to seriously consider Putman's specific contention: "There is reason to believe that deep-seated technological trends are radically 'privatizing' or 'individualizing' our use of leisure time and thus disrupting many opportunities for social-capital formation" ("Bowling Alone," p. 75). Certainly the technological transformation of leisure by television, computers, video games, and other electronic technology may be generating a gap between individual and collective interests within the voluntary sector of society.

**Problems of social control and service delivery** National crises often bring out the best in people. And certainly there are highly notable cases of volunteering across age, class, ethnic, gender, and racial lines associated with responses to the terrorist attack on the World Trade Center on 11 September 2001. Volunteering as a form of national service has become a major theme of the Bush administration as evidenced by the president's creation of the USA Freedom Corps and call for Americans to volunteer for civil defense efforts in a variety of capacities. But national calls for volunteering have the inherent risk of being ideological, paternalistic, and moralistic in nature.

**Organizational issues** Traditionally, the day-to-day operations of voluntary leisure organizations have been handled in ways ranging from group consensus to volunteer boards of directors. In more recent years, authority structures have become more businesslike, sometimes with day-to-day operations operated by professional staff. However, efforts to change authority structures have sometimes met with resistance. Because such organizations have traditionally valued autonomy from government, self-help, informal operations, and control of decision making by volunteers, adopting a business model has been difficult for many organization as it conflicts with traditional voluntary culture. One problem that confronts voluntary leisure organizations is the need for funding. Since, in recent years, such groups have increasingly solicited corporate as well as government support, more rational organizing principles are needed. In this process, some volunteers have seen their roles marginalized.

Ideally, acts of volunteering should come from "a pro-active model of behavior borne out of the experience of empowerment, rather than a reactive model resulting from the notion of service delivery" (Bell, p. 27). Again, ideally, within the communal institutions of civil society, leisure organizations and recreational agencies provide the best social environments for pro-active models of volunteer behavior.

*See also:* Civic Clubs, Men; Civic Clubs, Women

**BIBLIOGRAPHY**

Bell, Margaret. "Volunteering: Underpinning Social Action in Civil Society for the New Millennium." In *Civil Society at the Millennium.* Edited by CIVICUS. Hartford, Conn.: Kumarian Press, 1999.

Berger, Peter L., and Richard John Neuhaus. *To Empower People—From State to Civil Society.* 2d ed. Washington, D.C.: AEI Press, 1996.

Cohen, Joan L., and Andrew Arato. *Civil Society and Political Theory.* Cambridge, Mass.: MIT Press, 1994.

de Tocqueville, Alexis. *Democracy in America.* Edited by Richard D. Heffner. London: Saunders and Otley, 1835. Reprint, New York: New American Library, 1956.

Eberly, Don E., ed. *The Essential Civil Society Reader.* Lanham, Md.: Rowman and Littlefield, 2000.

Giddens, Anthony. *Runaway World: How Globalization Is Reshaping Our Lives.* London: Profile Books, 1999.

Godbout, Jacques T. *The World of the Gift.* Montreal: Mcgill-Queen's University Press, 2000.

Harris, Janet. "Civil Society, Physical Activity, and the Involvement of Sport Sociologists in the Preparation of Physical Activity Professionals." *Sociology of Sport Journal* 15, no. 2 (1998): 138–153.

Kyle, Gerard T. "An Examination of Enduring Leisure Involvement." Ph.D. dissertation, Pennsylvania State University, 2001.

Lin, Nan. "Inequality in Social Capital." *Contemporary Sociology* 29, no. 6 (2000): 785–795.

Mauss, Marcel. *The Gift: Forms and Functions of Social Exchange in Archaic Societies.* New York: W. W. Norton and Company, 1967.

McMillon, Bill, Doug Cutchins, and Anne Gissinger. *Volunteer Vacations.* 8th ed. Chicago: Chicago Review Press, 2003.

Matthews, R. K. *The Radical Politics of Thomas Jefferson: A Revisionist View.* Lawrence: University of Kansas Press, 1984.

Naidoo, Kumi, and Rajesh Tandon. "The Promise of Civil Society." In *Civil Society at the Millennium.* Edited by CIVICUS. Hartford, Conn.: Kumarian Press, 1999.

Poinsett, Alex. *The Role of Sports in Youth Development.* New York: Carnegie Corporation, 1993.

Putman, Robert D. "Bowling Alone: America's Declining Social Capital." *Journal of Democracy* 6, no. 1 (1995): 65–78.

———. *Bowling Alone—the Collapse and Revival of American Community.* New York: Simon and Schuster, 2000.

Schueller, Gretel. H. "Volunteer Vacations." Available from http://magazine.audubon.org.

Swift, Jamie. *Civil Society in Question.* Toronto: Between the Lines, 1999.

Wallraff, Barbara. "What Global Language?" *Atlantic Monthly* (November 2000): 52–56, 58–61, 66.

Wishard, William Van Dusen. "Global Trends Reshaping Civil Society." In *The Essential Civil Society Reader.* Edited by Don E. Eberly. Lanham, Md.: Rowman and Littlefield, 2000.

*John W. Loy and Garry Chick*

# LEISURE CLASS

Thorstein Veblen originated the concept of the leisure class in his first and most famous book, *The Theory of the Leisure Class,* published in 1899. In this economic study of social institutions he also invented the related concepts of *pecuniary emulation, conspicuous leisure,* and *conspicuous consumption,* which shifted significantly the emphasis of social analysis from the economics of production to the economics of consumption. While Karl Marx is the classic social theorist of labor, work, production, and practical activities, Thorstein Veblen is the classic social theorist of leisure, consumption, expressive, and honorific activities.

## The Theory of the Leisure Class

As Albert W. Levi points out, the underlying thesis of Veblen's theory of the leisure class is simultaneously simple and revolutionary; namely, that elite members of society show their "superiority not by their capacity to lead, administer or create, but by their conspicuous wastefulness: by an expenditure of effort, time, and money which is intrinsically reputable in a class-conscious world" (p. 239). Members of the leisure class display their status by their expressed disdain for all forms of productive work, especially any type of manual labor. They seek self-respect from immediate peers in competition for honor through the reputable possession of wealth. They are motivated by pecuniary emulation, and this motivation is clearly reflected in their patterns of conspicuous leisure and conspicuous consumption.

Veblen notes that the common element of conspicuous leisure and conspicuous consumption is "waste." Conspicuous leisure represents a waste of time and effort, whereas conspicuous consumption represents a waste of goods. "Both are methods of demonstrating the possession of wealth, and the two are conventionally accepted as equivalents. The choice between them is a question of advertising expediency. . ." (Veblen, p. 71).

Veblen's ideas about conspicuous consumption presage sociological analysis of the contemporary consumer society and the longstanding American tradition of "keeping up with the Joneses." However, notwithstanding Veblen's several original ideas and observations, his theory of the leisure class has a number of weaknesses. Perhaps the major weakness of Veblen's theory is that he does not precisely define the leisure class, often intermixing its membership in terms of the upper classes, aristocracy, bourgeoisie, and nouveau riche.

As C. Wright Mills critically observes in the introduction to *The Theory of the Leisure Class,* Veblen does not develop *the* theory of the leisure class, but rather "*a* theory of a particular element of the upper classes in one period of history of one nation" (p. xiv). Mills further notes: "what he wrote about was mainly Local Society and its Last Resorts, and especially women of these worlds" (1953, p. xiv).

## Newport, Rhode Island, in the Gilded Age

The glamour and glitter of the summer social scenes of Newport, Rhode Island, during America's Gilded Age, from the end of the Civil War until the beginning of World War I, highlight Mills's observations and illustrate Veblen's concepts of pecuniary emulation, conspicuous leisure, and conspicuous consumption.

Perhaps the most overt and ostentatious display of wealth by members of the leisure class during the Gilded Age were the large mansions that served as the summer homes of the ultra-wealthy in Newport. These grand villas were called "cottages" in remembrance of the modest houses of the early nineteenth century! The most famous of these opulent Newport palaces include Chateau-sur-Mer, The Breakers, The Elms, Marble House, and Rosecliff, which are all maintained by the Preservation Society of Newport County and opened to the public for guided tours. These tours demonstrate the lavish lifestyles the members of the leisure class led during the Gilded Age. "Cultural advisors supplied Newport cottagers with the best international taste money could buy, filling European period-piece mansions with historical bric-a-brac and devising gardens with Japanese teahouses and Ottoman kiosks" (Sterngass, p. 221).

The cottages of the Astors, Belmonts, and Vanderbilts were privatized sites for summer dinner parties, dances, and balls for the rich and famous. Guests at a dinner party might number more than 200, and a single ball might cost in excess of $200,000 in the 1890s. Of course many servants were required to maintain the cottages and to oversee the summer activities of patrons and their guests. As Jon Sterngress records: "The Belmonts hired sixteen house servants and ten yardmen for their mansion; the Marble House trumped them with nine French chefs, while the Breakers had accommodations for at least a dozen grooms" (p. 223).

The summer parties in general and the resources of the cottages in particular were controlled by women who managed household budgets of hundreds of thousands of dollars, supervised dozens of servants, and contested with one another for social supremacy. The acknowledged "First Queen of Newport" was "the" Mrs. Astor (Mrs. William Backhouse Astor Jr., nee Caroline Webster Schermerhorn). C. W. de Lyon Nichols published a book in 1904 titled *The Ultra-Fashionable Peerage of America.* In his census of the 400 most ultra-fashionable people in America at the beginning of the twentieth century, he lists Mrs. Astor as number one, and stated: "Newport, not the White House, is the supreme court of social appeals in the United States; Mrs. Astor, and not the wife of the President of the United States, is the first lady of the land, in the realm of fashion" (p. 23).

Several "grand duchesses" vied to replace Mrs. Astor as the dominant social leader of the Newport summer scene. But it was "the great triumvirate" of Alva Vanderbilt Belmont, Mamie Fish, and Tessie Oelrichs who rose to the top of Newport's leisure-class hierarchy (O'Connor, pp. 175–215). This trio of highly willful women sponsored dramatic displays of conspicuous consumption. "Their absurd prodigality became a staple of mass circulation newspapers, such as Newport's "dog dinner," at which the guests' canine companions dined on pâté and chicken, or another dinner in which a fish-filled stream flowed languorously down the center of the table" (Sterngrass, p. 226).

While women of the ultra-smart set strived for social domination, ultra-smart men strived to become outstanding sportsmen. As Richard O'Connor wrote: "Their yachts, polo ponies and racks of English-made rifles and shotguns were more than expensive toys; they were investments in prestige, certificates of acceptance by their peers, as ennobling as a seat on the stock exchange and a decent rating in Dun & Bradstreet" (p. 132).

In large measure Newport was the birthplace of exclusive sports in America, including such imported elite English pastimes as cricket, croquet, fox hunting, golf, polo, tennis, and yachting. Most notably the first United States National Lawn Tennis Championship was held at the Newport Casino (built by James Gordon Bennett) in 1881. And in the early 2000s, the International Tennis Hall of Fame was located at the site of the old Newport Casino. The United States Golf Association, founded in 1894, held its first amateur championship in Newport in October 1895, and, on the following day, Horace Rawlins received $150 for winning the first U.S. Open on the same course.

During the Gilded Age, Newport became the yachting capitol of the world. The New York Yacht Club's annual regatta started in Newport in 1883, and Newport Harbor in the 1890s served as the home for the boats built to defend America's Cup.

Yet another elite pastime of the rich and famous was polo. The first international polo match in America was held in Newport in 1886. Mrs. John King Van Rensselaer in her 1905 account of *Newport Our Social Capital* observed: "It is at the Polo Grounds that the smart set love to gather, and there is no more brilliant sight than the ranks of handsomely appointed equipages, the gaily dressed women mixed with the bright uniforms of the players, who deem knocking about the little polo balls the greatest sport in the world" (p. 356).

In sum, the early sporting scene in Newport reflected the desire of individuals to achieve status in the sphere of leisure by large investments of capital and time in exclusive, nonproductive pastimes.

## The New Gilded Age

Since the publication of Veblen's *The Theory of the Leisure Class* a century ago, America has become an ever more consumer-oriented society, and the spheres of sport and leisure have become increasingly important for displaying social status. These historical trends are clearly evident in the patterns of conspicuous consumption and conspicuous leisure displayed by the many emergent forms of nouveau riche social formations such as business tycoons of the 1920s, Texas millionaires in the 1940s and 1950s, music and media celebrities in the l960s and 1970s, and the computer and Internet magnates of the 1980s and 1990s.

Social status involves leisure practices and pastimes that emphasize and publicly display distinctions and differences of lifestyles. It seems, however, that the major means of status signaling in the sphere of leisure have remained much the same for the past century.

Max Kaplan, for example, has identified seven distinctive ways of advertising one's wealth and social status in leisure practices that have served equally well in different historical periods. First, individuals can signal their wealth and status using *special equipment*. Such equipment may range from a $75 million yacht, to a $320,000 Rolls-Royce Phantom, to a $500 Great Big Bertha II driver from Callaway Golf.

Second, social status can be signaled by *cost of participation*. For example, the sailboat racing syndicates of billionaires Larry Ellison of the United States and Ernesto Bertarelli of Switzerland are likely to spend upward of $100 million each in competing for the America's Cup in 2007. More modest costs of participation are reflected in golf membership in private clubs. "For instance, the initiation fee at Trump International Golf Club in West Palm Beach, Fla., site of the LPGA's ADT Championship, is $350,000 with yearly dues of $13,000" (Lieber, p. 3C).

Third, prestige can be bestowed through the *cost of watching*. It is one thing to watch a professional football game from a million-dollar box seat and another to view the game from the bleachers. Even leisurely watching can serve as a status symbol as evidenced by the $250 to $1,000 daily rates to rent a cabana on the beach next to a luxury hotel.

Fourth, social status can be conspicuously displayed in terms of *time of participation*. The professional doctor, dentist, or lawyer can play golf at midday at midweek, whereas a blue-collar worker does well to play on a Saturday or Sunday afternoon. Similarly, the parvenu plutocrat can take several vacations throughout the year, whereas the average worker does well to get two weeks of annual leave.

Fifth, the social elite may set themselves apart by means of *special dress*. An expensive tennis dress, equestrian outfit, or ski apparel readily distinguishes the rich from the poor. And, of course, expensive accessories such as watches, rings, and necklaces clearly distinguish the rich from the poor. An individual wearing a $14,000 Patek Philippe classic men's gold watch readily sets himself apart from a person sporting a $25 Timex watch.

Sixth, prestige can be clearly indicated in terms of *travel costs*. The nouveau riche can travel to Paris or Monte Carlo for a leisure outing, whereas lower-status individuals stay and play at home. Similarly, the ultra-wealthy can go hunting on an African safari, while very poor go hunting in their local swamp.

Seventh, social status can be denoted by amount of *expendable assets*. The modest spend a few dollars on bingo or a friendly game of poker, whereas the wealthy can gamble for millions in reserved settings at Las Vegas casinos.

Significant symbols of affluence include living in an exclusive neighborhood, having at least a second or vacation home, and sending one's children to expensive and exclusive secondary schools, colleges, and universities. And if an individual wants to be especially conspicuous in their display of consumption, they can order white truffles at $2,500 per pound, or pay $738 for a box of twenty-five Cigars, Aniversario No. 1, Dominican Republic from Davidoff's.

In addition to Kaplan's seven status distinctions, individuals can advertise their place in the status hierarchy of society by appearance and manner, that is, *style of involvement*. For example, "the dominant classes engage in leisure pursuits that stress manners, deportment, disinterestedness, refinement, self-control, and social distance" (Booth and Loy, p. 10).

As Douglas Dowd concludes in his summary account of Veblen's *Theory of the Leisure Class*: "We do not consume in order to satisfy our basic needs for comfort and survival . . . but in order to create a decorous appearance. And the appearance sought for is the appearance of membership in the leisure class" (p.13).

*See also:* Gilded Age Leisure and Recreation

**BIBLIOGRAPHY**

Booth, Douglas, and John Loy. "Sport, Status, and Style," *Sport History Review* 30 (May 1999): 1–26.

Dowd, Douglas. *Thorstein Veblen*. New York: Washington Square Press, 1964.

Kaplan, Max. *Leisure in America*. New York: John Wiley and Sons, 1960.

Lieber, Jill. "Few Can Afford Membership in Private Club." *USA Today* (10 April 2003): 3C.

Levi, Albert W. *Philosophy and the Modern World*. Bloomington: Indiana University Press, 1959.

Nichols, C. W. de Lyon. *The Ultra-Fashionable Peerage of America*. New York: George Harjes, 1904.

O'Connor, Richard. *The Golden Summers: An Antic History of Newport*. New York: G. P. Putnam's Sons, 1974.

Sterngrass, Jon. *First Resorts: Pursuing Pleasure at Saratoga Springs, Newport, and Coney Island*. Baltimore: Johns Hopkins University Press, 2001.

Van Rensselaer, May King. *Newport, Our Social Capital*. Philadelphia: J. P. Lippincott, 1905; reprint, New York: Arno Press, 1975.

Veblen, Thorstein. *The Theory of the Leisure Class*. New York: Macmillan Company, 1899; reprint, New York: New American Library, 1953.

*John W. Loy*

# LEISURE EDUCATION

Leisure education refers to organized instruction about leisure and leisure opportunities. Such instruction has been provided to children, adolescents, adults, and members of special populations by a variety of sources for more than a century in the United States. Students studying recreation will be educated about leisure so that they can implement effective recreation and leisure programs upon graduation. Children attending summer camp will likely participate in a number of fun activities that have an educational purpose. Older adults may need some assistance identifying activities for participation. Because of the wide variety of possibilities of leisure education, the following sections will attempt to break these factors down and a clear definition of leisure education will then be provided in the conclusion of this article.

## Leisure Education in the United States

The idea that leisure education should be incorporated into schools and universities has a long-standing history. As early as the 1890s, urban school boards introduced leisure education as a concept in the form of after-school programs. These efforts were supported by the National Education Association, through the recommendation for the use of public buildings for community recreation and social opportunities. In 1918, the Commission on the Reorganization of Secondary School Education of the National Educational Association issued the *Cardinal Principles of Secondary Education,* which set forth seven objectives of education, including the "worthy use of leisure." At this time, leisure was typically seen as inferior to other aspects of life. However, in 1966, Charles Brightbill suggested that the most important responsibility of education is to ensure adequate provision of recreative leisure for health purposes as well as for the sake of its psychological and social benefits.

In 1972, the Society of Park and Recreation Educators (SPRE), a branch of the National Recreation and Park Association (NRPA), developed a national policy regarding the role of higher education in educating students about the personal and social implications of leisure. As a result of the support of SPRE and NRPA, the first leisure education conference was held in Tallahassee, Florida, in 1975. At the same time, the Lilly Endowment also supported the need to educate for the use of discretionary time, by providing a grant to NRPA to develop leisure education within existing curricula. This project was entitled the Leisure Education Advancement Project (LEAP). In

the 1980s, the American Alliance for Leisure and Recreation (AALR), also supported the importance of leisure.

Once again, more recently, there is evidence of the continuing need to understand the role of leisure education within school curricula. In March 2002, a number of recreation and leisure scholars were involved in a taskforce on leisure education in schools and presented a position statement to AALR. Therefore, it is likely that this area will continue to develop in a wide range of recreation settings, including the outdoors, schools, and clinical settings.

## Who?

There are two relevant questions when examining leisure education: (1) who provides leisure education, and (2) who benefits from leisure education? First, trained recreation and leisure professionals provide leisure education both formally and informally. In many college and university recreation and leisure studies departments, leisure education is an ongoing element in all recreation courses, directly or indirectly. Without training in this area, it is impossible to provide effective recreation programs because the professional cannot articulate to those individuals they are serving the value of leisure. In answering the second question, there are two groups that can benefit: those providing leisure services, and all other human beings. As noted previously, leisure professionals need to have the skills to educate others about leisure, so they will only benefit from leisure education themselves. And given the benefits of leisure, all other persons can benefit from leisure education. At times, specific groups are studied in relation to the influence of leisure education such as youth at risk, older adults, retirees, and many others. However, because of the many health, societal, and economic benefits that have been linked directly to leisure, it can be argued that all individuals will gain from leisure education. It is only when people are educated about these and other benefits that they can begin to understand the importance of leisure in their own lives.

## What?

There are two ways of viewing leisure education—education *for* leisure and education *through* leisure. When people talk about education for leisure, they are talking more specifically about the process of recreation and leisure professionals educating the general public of leisure involvement. As educators, recreation professionals are interested in providing information so people can participate in leisure opportunities. This is a necessity, because individuals require knowledge about skills, programs, and resources to be able to participate in leisure.

In addition to this specific knowledge, individuals must be given the opportunity to increase self-awareness in relation to leisure. This enables the individual to have a deeper understanding of the relationship between him- or herself and leisure, as well as the relationship between leisure and society. It is important that leisure educators help people clearly define what leisure means to them.

On the other hand, examining what is meant by education through leisure is also important. Leisure can also provide an excellent medium for education, both about leisure and a number of other topics. Again, the role of the leisure educator is to provide individuals with opportunities to utilize the skills and knowledge they have gained from previous education. It is crucial that individuals be encouraged to gain experience in leisure activities in order to improve skills and knowledge. In addition, such opportunities enable individuals to learn skills that can be transferred to other life domains. For example, consider the adolescent who participates in an obstacle course with a group of peers. Although this may be a fun activity, the adolescent can learn a number of valuable lessons from participation, including how to work in a group, how to make decisions, and how to solve problems. Through participation in this activity, the adolescent may begin to learn how to transfer these skills to life outside of this recreational opportunity. In this case, the adolescent is being educated through the use of leisure as a medium.

## When?

Leisure education is a developmental process, so it should be ongoing over the course of the lifespan. For leisure service providers, education should be an important element of their work. One way of ensuring this is by having a professional organization that requires continuing education units to maintain certification. So while some formal education is necessary, leisure educators must remain aware of leisure in their own lives as well. For some outside the leisure profession, leisure education may take the form of participation in a formal class, whereas for others, it will consist of self-education of the skills, resources, and availability of leisure opportunities. While formal education may not continue, some form of reflection and evaluation of one's own participation in leisure should be happening on a regular basis.

## Where?

Again, it is somewhat challenging to identify a specific "where" in relation to leisure education. However, a number of places have been developed to meet the requirements of leisure education, including in hospitals,

> "The popular assumption is that no skills are involved in enjoying free time, and that anybody can do it. Yet the evidence suggests the opposite: free time is more difficult to enjoy than work. Having leisure at one's disposal does not improve the quality of life unless one knows how to use it effectively, and it is by no means something one learns automatically . . . . All of this evidence points to the fact that the average person is ill equipped to be idle"
>
> Csikszentmihalyi, Mihalyi. *Finding Flow: The Psychology of Engagement with Everyday Life.* New York: HarperCollins Publishers, 1997, p. 65.

schools, adventure-based camps, community centers, and universities, to name a few. Leisure education is often a crucial factor in therapeutic recreation. In fact, leisure education is one of the primary components of the most commonly used therapeutic recreation service delivery model. Without some form of education, individuals with special needs cannot begin to experience independent leisure participation. Leisure is often used in schools to provide opportunities for children and youth to learn skills that will transfer to other aspects of their daily lives. Adventure-based camps such as Outward Bound rely on the principles of experiential education to teach a number of different groups various life skills. Similar activities have also been implemented as part of a wellness program offered by some larger corporations to increase employee satisfaction and productivity. Leisure education can occur anywhere a need is identified. Again, as noted above, some of these settings may have been developed for leisure education, while others may be a little subtler, depending on the needs of the persons involved.

## Why?

Leisure ideas have been traced back to the beginning of time, with notions of leisure evident in the work of Greek philosophers Aristotle and Plato. Leisure was viewed as a method of personal growth and social advancement. Although this perspective changed drastically in the 1500s with the introduction of the Protestant work ethic, in which leisure was viewed as sinful, we have also seen the pendulum swing again the other way, where leisure participation is viewed as an important part of a balanced lifestyle. In addition to the historical roots of leisure, it is also important to consider the health and economic benefits associated with leisure. Studies have shown that leisure is associated with psychological health and that leisure helps reduce the consequences of stress. Some specific examples of these health benefits include improved mood, increased self-esteem, increased life-satisfaction, and decreased depression, anxiety, and loneliness. With such benefits possible from leisure participation, it is evident that leisure education is a valuable tool to all individuals who hope to improve their overall quality of life.

## How?

How is leisure education implemented? Again, it is important to consider both the formal and informal aspects of leisure education. Students in leisure studies departments are educated formally so they can provide leisure opportunities for others. Part of this education consists of how to develop, implement, and evaluate programs, while another part of this education involves the assessment of personal values, attitudes, and beliefs of leisure as well as personal involvement in leisure. Teaching another individual something that does not have some personal meaning to the teacher is impossible. For example, an individual cannot teach another person how to drive a car if that individual has not driven one. An understanding of *how* to drive a car, without the personal experience of actually *driving*, is not enough when teaching another individual. The same can be said of leisure. If a leisure-service provider does not understand and practice involvement in leisure, how can such a person be expected to guide another person to participate? With almost all types of leisure, the service provider is offering some kind of leisure education. Whether by educating a group on how to play basketball or providing the opportunity for that group to play so that skills may be enhanced, leisure education is happening.

## Defining Leisure Education

Based on those elements discussed above, leisure education carries diverse connotations. To some, it means teaching sports, while to others it means providing information about leisure in the education system. Leisure education has been viewed in two main ways: as the process of teaching knowledge and skills about a number of activities, or as the process of educating people of the importance of leisure by providing opportunities for participation. The most common understanding of leisure education, however, has been that of teaching others how to best use their free time. Leisure education then should be viewed in terms of process rather than content. It is viewed as a process though which individuals develop "an understanding of leisure, of self in relation to leisure, and of the relationship among leisure, their own lifestyle, and

society" (Mundy, p. 5). The primary goal then of leisure education is to enable individuals to enhance the quality of their lives through leisure.

## Domains of Leisure Education

Although there are a number of different models of leisure education, there are some commonalities among the domains to be addressed in such a model. In this section, these domains will be discussed in a general manner; however, more detailed treatments of any of the specific models are available as well (such as, Bullock and Mahon; Dattilo, Leisure Education Program Planning; Mundy). Typically, leisure education models will include leisure awareness, self-awareness, social skills, leisure skills, and leisure resources.

Leisure awareness focuses on helping an individual understand the concept of leisure. One way of addressing this is by exposing the individual to a variety of leisure pursuits. Self-awareness helps the person individualize his or her understanding of leisure. A primary goal of this element is to assist the individual to identify preferred leisure opportunities. Social skills are those that are needed to interact with other people. These skills are often crucial for inclusion in leisure opportunities, as many pursuits tend to involve others. Leisure skills include two types of skills, those that are required to participate in a specific opportunity such as playing badminton, and more indirect skills, such as decision making, planning, and problem solving. Individuals require both types of skills, sometimes referred to as traditional and nontraditional, to participate in a variety of leisure pursuits. Finally, the individual has to gain an understanding of leisure resources available to him or her. These may include people, places, and equipment, but unless an individual can access leisure, he/she will be unable to participate.

Leisure-service providers must be aware of each of these components and include them in some manner when providing leisure education. Without addressing each factor, an important element of the experience may be lost. Providers do not need to develop their own model for practice; they need only look to those who have already created such models. In selecting a model that fits the needs of a client group, leisure-service providers will find some models that are more appropriate for client-centered clinical settings, while others are more general and can be used in almost any setting.

## Conclusion

In many ways, leisure education has become a significant component of leisure-service delivery in almost all settings, including treatment centers, schools, community centers, and corporations. Consequently, leisure-service providers must develop a solid understanding of leisure education and how to provide such education in a wide array of contexts. To ensure this happens, those training future professionals must provide necessary training and encourage others to seek out educational opportunities to ensure the best practice possible for clients.

*See also:* Adapted Leisure Formats, Adult Education (Earlier), Disability and Leisure Lifestyles

## BIBLIOGRAPHY

American Association for Leisure and Recreation. *Leisure Education in the Public Schools.* Reston, Va.: AAHPERD, 1986.

Brightbill, Charles, C. *Educating for Leisure-Centered Living.* Harrisburg, Pa.: Stackpole Books, 1966.

Bullock, Charles, C., and Michael J. Mahon. *Introduction to Recreation Services for People with Disabilities: A Person Centered Approach.* Champaign, Ill.: Sagamore Publishing, 1997.

Caldwell, Linda, L., E. A. Smith, and Ellen Weissinger. "The Relationship of Leisure Activities and Perceived Health of College Students." *Society and Leisure* 15 (1992): 545–556.

Coleman, David. "Leisure Based Social Support, Leisure Dispositions, and Health." *Journal of Leisure Research* 25 (1993): 350–361.

Csikszentmihalyi, Mihalyi. *Finding Flow: The Psychology of Engagement with Everyday Life.* New York: HarperCollins Publishers, 1997.

Dattilo, John. *Leisure Education Program Planning: A Systematic Approach.* 2d ed. State College, Pa.: Venture Publishing, 1999.

Dattilo, John, and William, D. Murphy. *Leisure Education Program Planning: A Systematic Approach.* State College, Pa.: Venture Publishing, 1991.

Iso-Ahola, Seppo E. "Leisure Lifestyle and Health." In *Leisure and Mental Health.* Edited by David M. Compton and Seppo E. Iso-Ahola. Park City, Utah: Family Developmental Resources, 1994.

Kelly, John R. *Leisure.* 3d ed. Needham Heights, Mass.: Allyn and Bacon, 1996.

Kelly, John R., and Geoffrey Godbey. *The Sociology of Leisure.* Champaign, Ill.: Sagamore Publishing, 1992.

Mundy, Jean. *Leisure Education: Theory and Practice.* 2d ed. Champaign, Ill.: Sagamore Publishing, 1998.

Pesavento, Lisa C., ed. "Leisure Education in the Schools." A position statement presented to the American Association for Leisure and Recreation, 2002.

Peterson, Carol Ann, and Scout Lee Gunn. *Therapeutic Recreation Program and Design: Principles and Procedures.* 2d ed. Englewood Cliffs, N.J.: Prentice-Hall, 1984.

*Anne-Marie Sullivan*

# LEISURE, THEORY OF

The study of leisure presents interesting theoretical challenges. The first challenge exists because leisure has both an empirical and a normative dimension, each present at the same time. Borrowing from ethical theory, leisure contains both an *is* and an *ought:* One can observe leisure as it is in the world and one can also say what leisure ought to be. The leisure one observes exists in specific activities; leisure as ought to be exists in norms and ideals. People experience something of this in their own lives as a contrast between the leisure they have and the leisure they wish to have, or between how they actually use their leisure and how it should be used. Leisure is something people both have and aspire to have. The extent to which leisure's empirical and normative dimensions are congruent—the fit between what people do in their leisure and what they should do, the leisure they have and the leisure they aspire to have—is always an open question, but there can be little doubt that these dimensions are closely intertwined. One task for theories of leisure is to articulate leisure's empirical and normative dimensions, examine their congruence (or lack of it), and explore the implications this has for us as individuals and as a society.

A second theoretical challenge exists because leisure is never merely abstract. People are familiar with leisure in ways they are not familiar with quarks, fractals, or the time shift continuum. They have first-hand experience of leisure as participants and observers, because leisure is part of their daily lives. Yet precisely this familiarity raises barriers to a fuller understanding of leisure. When people are familiar with something, they often take it for granted, regarding it as given or unproblematic. In the case of leisure, this tendency is reinforced by sociocultural influences, which have been particularly strong in the United States, that reduce leisure to a supposedly marginal element of people's lives, making it less likely that leisure's complexities and importance will be recognized. Somewhat paradoxically, then, a second task for theories of leisure is to rescue leisure not from obscurity, but rather from the consequences of its very familiarity.

A third theoretical challenge arises because despite being part of daily life, people often experience or think about leisure in very different ways. This point has not always been fully appreciated. Modern social science, of which leisure research is a part, was built on the twin convictions that (a) human behavior has common denominators (b) which it is the purpose of social science to uncover. These convictions were especially strong in the United States from about the mid-1950s to the mid-1980s.

## Theories of Leisure: A Quick Survey

With this background in hand, it is possible to survey some of the theories of leisure that have been influential. This survey cannot do justice to the complexities some of these theories involve, but it can suggest the range of such theories along with the characteristic questions they address.

A good deal of the most influential research on leisure has been primarily descriptive and organized around definitions of leisure. This has an important consequence, namely, it increases the difficulty of evaluating any propositions derived from these definitions without also challenging the descriptions on which they are based. This has created a tendency to accumulate successive descriptive accounts of leisure rather than developing these accounts into theoretically refined statements. Descriptions of leisure commonly include references to the presence of choice or, alternatively, the absence of compulsion; the presence of intrinsic rather than extrinsic motivations, and the absence of internal or external constraints on carrying individual preferences into action. These elements are in turn often bundled together under the broad and therefore imprecise label of freedom. Most research of this sort in the U. S. has, however, concentrated on individual choices and preferences, and has thus neglected important historical, socio-cultural influences affecting the structure and content of individual action, not least during leisure. These issues will recur throughout the following survey, which begins with a look at two individuals whose theories of leisure are most widely recognized.

**Weber: The Protestant Ethic** Max Weber, one of the towering figures in modern sociology, made foundational contributions in numerous fields of sociological analysis. Among them was the study of religion's influences on social norms and individual action. This is the context within which Weber's classic study *The Protestant Ethic and the Spirit of Capitalism* (1904-1905/1930) took shape. Weber understood modern capitalism as an ongoing quest for gain in itself. Profits are accrued not so they may be spent but so they may be reinvested to accrue still further profits. The continuous process of systematic labor, gain, and reinvestment distinguishes modern capitalism from all other economic and social systems. Yet Weber also believed such sustained labor and self-denial run against human nature, making some incentive necessary to overcome this hitherto limiting barrier. Weber observed that although capitalism appeared in various forms and places earlier in history, it developed most thoroughly, both economically and socially, only in those parts of Western Europe and North America that were dominated by Protestantism. Why?

Weber's answer was the Protestant ethic, a distinctive set of social norms that evolved from changes in religious doctrine during the Reformation (roughly 1500 to 1650). Weber argued that the Protestant ethic encouraged the asceticism and provided the incentives necessary for capitalism to overcome the constraints of tradition. Asceticism—defined as stringent self-discipline, austerity, abstinence—was essential to reinvesting rather than spending profits, a key element in modern capitalism. The incentives for such future-oriented self-denial were originally religious, eternal salvation and the glorification of God through diligent work. When the religious doctrines underlying these incentives weakened, as they did in the U. S. beginning no later than the mid-eighteenth century, the ascetic character traits encouraged by the Protestant ethic were becoming secular social norms. The incentives were also becoming secularized. Diligent work earned the individual a reputation for having an upright character, for being self-supporting and reliable. Considerable importance was attached to personal reputation, in business and in society, so there remained strong incentives for conforming to the Protestant ethic in its secularized form. If it was no longer associated with eternal salvation, the Protestant ethic did point the way to earthly success.

The Protestant ethic did not exclude leisure, but it did insist on leisure of a very particular sort. Leisure was not to obstruct fulfilling the duties of one's calling or diligent work. Idleness or mere amusement was not to be tolerated. Leisure was for rejuvenating the mind and body, not enjoyment for its own sake. Not only did excess or indulgence threaten diligence, they revealed a weak character. Proper leisure, according to the Puritan minister Benjamin Colman (1707), is properly "grave, serious, and devout, all of which it may be and yet free and cheerful" (p. 1). Such leisure is "sober mirth" that both knows and keeps it bounds.

Weber's theory has two significant weaknesses. The first of these is that he misread the history of capitalism and perhaps also misunderstood Catholic doctrine. The second is his failure to provide an adequate explanation of the Protestant ethic's transition from a body of religious doctrine to secular social norms. Nonetheless, Weber's *The Protestant Ethic and the Spirit of Capitalism* is undoubtedly the most widely known and discussed theory of leisure, one whose influence must be reckoned with to this day.

**Veblen: Conspicuous Consumption** Thorstein Veblen's *The Theory of the Leisure Class* (1988/1931) may be the only serious rival to Weber's *The Protestant Ethic* as the most widely known theory of leisure. The two theories take quite different approaches. Weber believed the emergence of modern capitalist society depended on the special circumstances created by the Protestant ethic. Veblen regarded modern capitalist society as the result of universal economic processes that are the basis of all human culture.

In Veblen's theory, two distinctions are fundamental to human social organization. The first distinction is between two forms of labor, industry and exploit; the second is between those who labor and those who do not. The structure of any society, however simple or complex, is derived from these basic distinctions. *Industry* is the making of something new, from scratch, giving raw materials form and purpose. *Exploit* is the turning to one's own ends something made by someone else, the results of someone else's industry. (Note how Veblen has loaded the dice by his choice of terms here.) Class distinctions began as differences between those engaged in industry and those engaged in exploit. Since industry was regarded as ignoble and exploit as honorable, exploit soon became associated with higher social standing. Eventually it became a mark of social distinction that one did not need to work at all in order to satisfy the everyday needs of life.

The origins of the leisure class lie in the transition from class distinctions based on type of labor to class distinctions based on ownership of goods and property. Economic growth accelerates this transition by enabling more and more people to acquire goods beyond a bare minimum. The usual assumption is that people acquire goods in order to use them in some fashion, but according to Veblen this assumption holds only so long as conditions of scarcity apply. Veblen argued instead that *emulation* is the real reason people acquire goods. Emulation is a natural process by through which people guide their behavior by making social comparisons between themselves and others. Ownership of goods and property lends itself especially well to such comparisons. It allows an "invidious distinction" (p. 26) to be drawn with precision among members of society according to their relative "pecuniary strength" (p. 86), that is, their ability to acquire and to display goods and property. Leisure is thus doubly valuable. It signifies that an individual need not work while providing an opportunity to display pecuniary strength. For the leisure class, this is a way of life.

Veblen was critical of the leisure class as it existed in the United States. Yet his theory is misunderstood if treated only as an expression of his disapproval of the leisure class's profligacy and disdain for productive labor. The true social significance of the leisure class lies in its role as the target of emulation by members of other classes. People want what remains just beyond their grasp, not

what is beyond the range of possibility. Their reference is the standard of acquisition and display prevailing at the next level above them in society. Through an ongoing process of "invidious comparison" (p. 103) between people at one level with those at the next, the standards of acquisition and display among the leisure class trickle down from one level to the next. All standards of acquisition and display, argues Veblen, may be "traced back by insensible gradations to the usages and thought of the highest social and pecuniary class—the wealthy leisure class" (p. 104).

Perhaps the greatest weakness in Veblen's theory is his assumption of a unified leisure class, whose members share similar backgrounds and outlooks. Studies of the wealthy indicate this assumption does not hold, particularly when the distinction between earned wealth and inherited wealth is made. Veblen's theory also does not account for the power of marketing or the mass media to shape standards of popular taste and consumption.

**Sociological Theory** A considerable amount of sociological research on leisure was conducted during the second half of the twentieth century, most of it within one of three macro theoretic frameworks. Recall that a macro theory addresses society as a whole, its process and formation. Researchers work within macro theoretic frameworks to investigate more specific but possibly still quite broad questions.

The three frameworks will be addressed in roughly chronological order. The first of them is functionalism, which focuses on the integration of the different elements in a society into a cohesive whole. There are certain universal functions that must be performed for this to happen in any society, for example, status allocation, conflict reduction, or legitimation of authority. Although these functions must be performed in every society, they are not necessarily performed in the same ways or by the same structures. Functionalist leisure researchers ask what contributions leisure makes to performing these functions and thus contributing to societal integration and cohesion. A number of answers were offered, among them leisure as reward for work, as a "pressure valve" for release of individual and group tensions, and as a distraction from possible economic or social inequities.

The second macro theoretic framework is structuralism, which emphasizes the organization of a society into structured patterns of interaction. Families, friendship networks, race, social class, and formal organizations are examples of such structures. People occupy social roles within or because of these structures. A relatively fixed set of expectations is attached to each social role independently of the occupants in that role, and no matter what each occupant's skills might be, that occupant is expected to comply with the role. Structuralist leisure research, therefore, examines the influence of social structures on leisure; among the most frequently examined structures have been occupation, socio-economic class, gender, race, and age.

The third macro theoretic framework is post-structuralism, whose influence became more pronounced during the century's last thirty years or so. Post-structuralism recognizes and works with many of the same categories as structuralism, but it denies that those categoreies aer permanent, Instead, it treats them as more fluid, more ambiguous, and contingent, and therefore less fixed or permanent. Social roles are the consequences of boundary negotiations that are rather fixed according to location within a specific structure. Another difference is post-structuralism's recognition that individuals can fill multiple social roles simultaneously; structuralism, on the other hand, tends to restrict analysis to one social role at a time. Above all, post-structuralism rejects the universalism in functionalism and some forms of structuralism.

The existence of several theoretical frameworks, plus a wide range of questions addressed and methods applied, makes it difficult to summarize sociological theories of leisure (for evidence, see the leading textbook by Kelly & Godbey, 1992). As a result, two examples must suffice here.

The British sociologist Stanley Parker contributed significantly to analyzing the relationship between leisure and work. He regarded modern leisure as a reaction to modern work, fueled by increasing individual freedom in industrial society and the growth of social institutions specifically associated with leisure. Parker also thought modern leisure might develop sufficiently to become "an alternative source of ethical values" (1976, p. 29) challenging the primacy of work-based values. Yet Parker also argued that the distinction people make between leisure and work in their daily lives must not be overestimated. He challenged the value of conventional definitions of leisure as freely chosen activity. Though activities can be arranged on a continuum from compulsory to freely chosen, people may freely chose work as well as leisure.

Parker mixed structuralism with functionalism, which was not uncommon. The most powerful influences on leisure were, according to Parker, occupation, sex, and social class. Leisure has micro level and macro level functions: for individuals, it provides "relaxation, entertainment and personal development"; for society, it contributes to "maintaining the social system and achieving collective ends" (1983, pp. 33, 41). The most important factor in fulfilling these functions is the relationship between leisure and work.

Parker identified three dimensions in that relationship: involvement, activities, and attitudes. That is: the extent of one's work involvement may affect the extent of one's leisure involvement; one's work activities may influence one's choice of leisure activities; one's attitudes toward work may shape one's attitudes toward leisure. Each dimension of the leisure-work relationship can take three forms, which Parker labeled identity, contrast, and separateness. At the individual level, the identity relationship would mean that one's leisure and work activities are similar, that one is roughly equally involved in both, or that one has the same attitudes toward both. The contrast relationship reverses the pattern: One's leisure and work activities, involvement, or attitudes are different. Parker notes that these differences are deliberate and often quite sharp. The separateness relationship entails differences between leisure and work activities, involvement, or attitudes, but these differences are *not* deliberate. The individual distinguishes between leisure and work, but does not define them in terms of each other.

Parker drew several conclusions based on the then-existing research. He was noncommittal about the effects of work involvement on leisure involvement, but believed evidence suggested that work activities affected leisure activities. The clearest case was the contrast relationship between physically demanding work and physically inactive leisure. Occupation also had a distinct effect on the relationship between work and leisure attitudes. Managers and professionals reported that work was their central life interest, an identity relationship; industrial workers located their central life interests outside work, a contrast or separateness relationship.

Joffre Dumazedier, a French sociologist, contributed a number of early empirical studies that formed the basis of his subsequent speculations on the future and meanings of leisure in industrial society. Like Parker, Dumazedier was interested in the leisure-work relationship, but unlike Parker, Dumazedier had post-structural tendencies. Finally, again like Parker, Dumazedier believed modern leisure was decisively shaped by modern work, but Dumazedier also thought that the modern leisure-work relationship was changing in ways making its continuation unlikely. He thought a new leisure ethic of self-fulfillment was likely to replace it.

Dumazedier (1974) characterized leisure as "a periodical release from employment" (p. 15). He insisted that leisure was created by the structure of modern work and is a phenomenon "born of the industrial revolution" (p. 13). Two features of modern work were essential in the creation of leisure. First, work had to become free-standing, independent of traditional social statuses and the obligations attached to them. Second, *paid* work had to become the dominant form, creating the distinction between paid work time and nonwork time. The roots of modern leisure as "a periodical release from employment," something done after one's paid work obligations are fulfilled, lie in this distinction. For Dumazedier, leisure's subsequent development was an extension of its origins in the changing social structure of work.

Dumazedier conceptualized leisure in strongly individualist terms. Leisure is something the individual pursues of one's "own free will" for purposes separate from one's work, family, or social duties (1960, p. 527). In his view, modern leisure reflects the continued weakening of "a whole series of mediating [social] institutions" (1974, p. 39), leaving individuals steadily more dependent on themselves but also increasing their available time with no obligations and their control over it. Time previously allocated to fulfilling the obligations of traditional social statuses or to "rest and recuperation" for work could now be devoted to "the self-fulfillment of the individual" (p. 40). Dumazedier did not doubt that free time available for leisure would continue to increase, or that as people became more and more independent of social institutions and the obligations they imposed, people would use their leisure for the "creation and re-creation" of their individual personalities (p. 41). This was his "central hypothesis" (p. 43), that out of this process a new leisure ethic would develop, no longer oriented around workplace, family, or society, but instead around individual self-fulfillment and self-expression simultaneously.

## Social Psychological Theories of Leisure

During the 1970s, partly in response to the fragmentation of sociological leisure research, there was an increasingly strong interest in the social psychological analysis of leisure. This became the dominant approach during much of the next thirty years. Social psychology had several attractions for leisure researchers, foremost among them a seemingly powerful conceptualization of leisure entailing three propositions: 1) Leisure consists of freely chosen activities, 2) participation in these activities is intrinsically motivated, that is, these activities are chosen for their own sakes, and 3) the individual has a sense of control over their outcome. The ease with which these propositions could be operationalized for use in empirical research was a further attraction.

The most influential social psychological theory of leisure was John Neulinger's (1981). Neulinger argued that the "one and only one essential criterion" for explaining leisure is the "condition of perceived freedom" (p. 16), which he defined as a state in which one "feels that what he/she is doing is done by choice and because one wants to do it" (p. 15). Significantly, Neulinger insisted that "*any* activity" meeting this criterion "may be associated with the experience of leisure" (emphasis added; p. 16). Asserting that "everyone knows the difference" between choosing to participate and being forced to participate in an activity, Neulinger blithely dismissed any need to explore the complexities of defining freedom. Going still further, he dismissed the distinction between "true freedom" and the "illusion" of freedom as "irrelevant" (p. 15). What matters, he believed, is the perception of freedom, not its reality. "Perceived freedom," which Neulinger readily admitted might be illusory, became the core criterion of his theory. It remains one of the most frequently used terms in leisure research.

A second social psychological theory of leisure was developed by Seppo Iso-Ahola (1980) using the concept of optimal arousal. Arousal is a response to stimulation; psychological arousal is one such response. Levels of psychological arousal are affected by such factors as the familiarity or novelty of the stimulation, its intensity, the presence or absence of threat, and an individual's perceived competence. Whenever psychological arousal levels are too high or too low, the result in an uncomfortable psychological state. Thresholds vary among individuals, but when the elements of stimulation are balanced—neither too high nor too low—they create a blend of challenge and competence experienced by the individual as an optimal level of arousal. According to Iso-Ahola, the presence of optimal arousal explains leisure. In theory people will select both leisure activities and leisure environments in search of this optimal arousal experience.

The third and final social psychological theory to be mentioned here is Mihalyi Csikszentmihalyi's theory of flow. Csikszentmihalyi (1975 and expanded in 1990) described flow in four case studies of people engaged in intensely absorbing types of work and play. He reported that, at some point, these people became so deeply engrossed in their activities that they ceased to be aware of effort, the passage of time, or anything more than their immediate surroundings. They focused solely on the immediate experience and the satisfaction of meeting the challenges intrinsic to the activities in which they were engaged. These activities had become *autotelic,* that is, self-directing and self-justifying. Borrowing the term from a rock climber who described "flowing up the rock,"

Csikszentmihalyi labeled this the "flow experience." Flow requires that an individual's commitment and competence match the challenges of an activity in a specific environment. During the flow experience, people become so totally engaged that individual, activity, and environment seemingly merge.

Social psychological theories have been attractive in part because of the apparent clarity with which they define leisure, but therein also lies their fundamental weakness. They lack what may be called adequate discriminant power. Recall the earlier discussion of theory, in which it was stated that a theory must allow people to discriminate between what is leisure and what is *not* leisure. None of the social psychological theories discussed here meets this test. Csikszentmihalyi's flow theory applies to work as well as leisure, so this is less of a problem than it is for Neulinger's and Iso-Ahola's theories. Their weakness stems from the inadequacy of conceptualizing leisure solely as a psychological experience. None of the three experiences proposed as the core criterion for leisure—perceived freedom, optimal arousal, and flow—is found exclusively during leisure. Each also occurs during other activities, such as paid and unpaid work, study, fulfilling family and social responsibilities, and even personal care. Csikszentmihalyi recognizes this, but again, his is not a theory of leisure per se. Not only do Neulinger's and Iso-Ahola's theories fail to acknowledge that perceived freedom and optimal arousal occur outside leisure. They also omit such vital factors as sociocultural definitions of what count as leisure activities. These theories reduce individuals to vessels for perception or arousal, isolated from the contexts in which they act and which give their actions their full human richness. This is particularly troubling in Neulinger's theory. Given his cavalier disregard for any difference between actual freedom and the illusion of freedom, Neulinger's inattention to contextual factors affecting the scope of individual action trivializes the efforts people must make to meet the challenges posed by their social and material circumstances.

**Prescriptive Theory** One theme has appeared throughout this survey: freedom. From the ancient Greeks to the present, leisure has consistently been associated with freedom. Assumptions about the form and content of freedom in leisure have varied considerably, however. In most sociological and social-psychological theories, freedom is conceived as some form of choice—for example, the ability to chose in which activities to participate. Choice is not a very strict criterion for freedom, however. All that matters in most theories of leisure is that one choose an activity. Within broad limits, one's reasons for

choosing that activity are immaterial. Note that a motivation is not the same as a reason. It is not adequate in itself to stipulate that a choice must be both noncompulsory and intrinsically motivated, that an activity must be worth doing for its own sake. People still require reasons why the activity is worth doing for its own sake. This is the task of prescriptive theories of leisure.

The conceptions of freedom in prescriptive theories tend to be very different than those encountered in sociological or social psychological theories. Freedom does not exist in choosing or even in the social and material conditions necessary to act on one's choice, but rather in having the character necessary to make the *right* choice according to a higher standard of ethical conduct. Rather than being understood as doing what one chooses, then, freedom in leisure may be understood as doing what one is called to do, fulfilling the requirements of moral and social duty, or responding to the demands of humanity's higher natures. Such leisure is not simply an abstract ideal. One sees it regularly manifested in public service, charitable volunteering, lifetime education, and spiritual or religious activity.

Aristotle developed the earliest, most influential, and perhaps still the most fully articulated prescriptive theory of leisure. To understand it requires some quick background. For Aristotle, each human activity aimed at a characteristic good in which it naturally culminated. Differences among those characteristic goods at which they aimed formed the basis for a hierarchy of activities according to their excellence, from least to most. Any activity pursued for its own sake had greater excellence than one whose good served only as a means to fulfill some other good. Greater excellence was associated with activities whose goods required those capacities that are uniquely human, such as the ability to reason and the desire for knowledge. Several criteria determined the excellence of such activities: the required type of reason, the purpose to which reason was applied, and how far the *actual* activity incorporated its *ideal* qualities. The ideal was both a standard against which the actual could be assessed and the "final cause" toward which the actual developed naturally if uncorrupted or unimpeded. This close linkage of the ideal, the actual, and action was characteristic of Aristotle's moral and political thought.

The highest good at which human action aims is *eudaimonia,* which means felicity or true happiness. Aristotle believed *eudaimonia* was achieved only through a life devoted to the right use of leisure, but he fell into something of a contradiction on that point. He described two ways leisure could be rightly used: first, through active participation in the civic and political life of the community; second, through a life of philosophical contemplation. In Book X of the *Nichomachean Ethics* Aristotle wrote that philosophy—the study of first principles, metaphysics, and logic—was the highest form of human reason and thus the best use of leisure. Yet in opening the *Nichomachean Ethics* he proclaimed politics the "master science" (p. 1084a). It concerned the *polis*, or city-state, the best form of human association with the highest purpose, creating citizens who were "good and capable of noble acts" (p. 1099b). Leisure was required both for learning about and doing good and noble acts. Scholars have argued for centuries over which was Aristotle's "true" position, but fortunately, the answer to that question does not matter in this essay. What matters is that Aristotle regarded leisure as the arena in which the highest human capacities were best used. Leisure, then, was for Aristotle an essential aspect of being human that people are led by their very nature to use well, for it is the "first principle of all action" (*Politics*, p. 1337b).

A second influential prescriptive theory of leisure was outlined by the theologian Josef Pieper in his *Leisure, the Basis of Culture* (1948/1963). Pieper's theory is a blend of Aristotelian contemplative leisure and Christianity. He believes that *Acedia*, that is, idleness or sloth, is one of the deadly sins and that it poses a threat to, and must be distinguished from, leisure. Pieper began by noting that leisure requires being at one with oneself, accepting who one is. Both idleness and what Pieper called "incapacity for leisure" interfere with achieving this state (all quotations are from pp. 40-41). He attributed the source of this incapacity to a ceaseless search for activity masquerading as taking charge of life. Thus neither free time nor free choice result in leisure, but simply allow the search for activity to be extended further. Leisure is "utterly contrary" to any work or work-like activity aimed at acquisition or control. It is instead a "form of silence," a "contemplative state," a "condition of the soul" creating "an inward calm" through which one rises above mundane concerns in order to "steep oneself in the whole of creation." Similar ideas are found in Francis Bregha's (1991) essay on leisure and freedom, in which he argues that although people now have greater freedom than ever before when making leisure choices, these seldom bring satisfaction in the absence of the moral guidance formerly provided by religious teachings.

Before closing this section, it should be noted that there is a prescriptive element, often unacknowledged, in a great deal of contemporary leisure research. Research intended to inform public policy making, for example, must by its nature address the desirability and feasibility of policy goals, including the use of scarce public resources to achieve them. Promotional campaigns like the so-called leisure benefits movement draw on research findings to bolster claims about the importance of leisure. Less obvious is the prescriptive element in researchers' decisions when selecting which leisure activities to analyze. Researchers tend to concentrate on a subset of leisure activities that Rojek (1999, p. 81) called "normal leisure," among them outdoor pursuits, sports, tourism, organized camping, hobbies, fitness, and socializing. Less desirable activities—variously termed "blue," "dark," or "deviant"—are seldom if ever studied as leisure. When they are studied, it is most likely with regard to their remediation or elimination. Leisure research thus displays a certain normative imbalance that leaves a considerable range of potentially leisure activity unexamined.

## Conclusion

What are the current prospects for leisure theory in 2004? They are best described as guarded. The influence of social psychological theory continues, though there have been few recent significant refinements (for an exception, see Kleiber, 1999). Although social psychological concepts are well established in leisure research, it remains to be seen whether they will yield new insights. Economic theories being applied in tourism research and related subfields are directed more at consumer behavior than at leisure behavior. Stockdale (1989) complained that much of leisure research consists of "information gathering" with little concern for theory development; this continued to hold true in 2004. Nonetheless, several developments hold promise, including the following three items.

First there is the continuing strength of the cultural studies approach to leisure research. Investigators working within this approach point out that conventional meanings of leisure are socially conditioned and value-laden, which renders "conventional associations of 'freedom,' 'choice,' and 'self-determination with leisure" questionable (Rojek, 1995, p. 1). The meanings of these and other key terms—choice, satisfaction, preference, and leisure itself—are not fixed or neutral. They are instead the result of interactions among individual action, sociocultural influences, historical tradition, and material circumstances. These interactions are not random, so they yield distinct patterns of leisure activities, attitudes, meanings, and values. Two consequences of the cultural studies approach are particularly worth mentioning: the growing attention to so-called marginalized or excluded groups, such as racial and ethnic minorities and a more nuanced appreciation of popular culture's significance for leisure.

The maturation of feminist leisure research is a second development holding promise for continuing theoretical promise. The presence in leisure research of many different types of feminism has stimulated conceptual and methodological debates whose beneficial effects have fortunately spilled over into other subfields. Among other contributions, feminist researchers have pointed to gender-based differences in the process of identity formation during leisure. They have also analyzed the influence of gender-based social roles and stereotypes on women's participation in leisure activities. Perhaps most importantly, feminist researchers have been the most consistent challengers of the "universalizing" assumptions found in sociological and social psychological theory.

Finally, there is renewed interest in the significance of formal and informal social structures for leisure. Some time ago, Kelly (1978) pointed out that social role constraints exist during leisure in ways inconsistent with conventional definitions of leisure. More recently, Shaw and Dawson (2001) made a related point regarding the effects of role obligations attached to parenting on the motivational basis of family leisure. Rather than being freely chosen or intrinsically motivated, family leisure is often purpose-driven. Shaw and Dawson proposed the concept of purposive leisure to account for these social role effects. Further attention to the significance of social roles for leisure may encourage more nuanced theory-building. Other evidence of renewed interest in social structures is Hemingway's (1999, 2001) discussion of social networks and social capital generation in leisure, which suggested that leisure may contribute to the growth of community and participatory citizenship. The importance of administrative structures was demonstrated by Glover (2004), who applied citizenship theory in an analysis of different community centers and the resulting senses of belonging and involvement among the people who used them. Stebbins (2001) provided a more general statement regarding the significance of social organization for leisure. These efforts suggest there may be a growing awareness of the need for leisure theory to concern itself again with leisure's structural and institutional dimensions.

Each in its own way, these general developments—cultural studies, feminism, and renewed interest in social structure—address the theoretical challenges outlined at the start of this discussion. Whether they do so satisfactorily, and whether they will overcome the prevailing theoretical inertia in leisure research generally, remains to be seen. At the very least, however, the body of work surveyed here can leave no doubt that leisure is indeed a far more complex and important phenomenon than commonly assumed.

*See also:* Contemporary Leisure Patterns, Leisure and Civil Society, Leisure Class

## BIBLIOGRAPHY

Aristotle. "Nichomachean Ethics." Translated by W. D. Ross and J. O. Urmson. In *The Complete Works of Aristotle.* Edited by Jonathan Barnes. Princeton, N.J.: Princeton University Press, 1984.

———. "Politics." Translated by B. Jowett. In *The Complete Works of Aristotle.* Edited by Jonathan Barnes. Princeton, N.J.: Princeton University Press, 1984.

Bregha, F. "Leisure and Freedom Re-Examined." In *Recreation and Leisure: Issues in an Era of Change.* Edited by T. Goodale & P. Witt, 3rd ed. State College, Pa: Venture Publishing, 1991.

Colman, Benjamin. *The Government and Improvement of Mirth, According to the Laws of Christianity, in Three Sermons.* Boston: B. Green, 1707.

Cross, Gary. *Kids' Stuff: Toys and the Changing World of American Childhood.* Cambridge, Mass.: Harvard University Press, 1997.

Csikszentmihalyi, Mihaly. *Beyond Boredom and Anxiety: The Experience of Play in Work and Games.* San Francisco: Jossey-Bass, 1975, 2000.

———. *Flow: The Psychology of Optimal Experience.* New York: Harper and Row, 1990.

Dumazedier, Joffre. "Current Problems of the Sociology of Leisure." *International Social Science Journal,* 4 (1960): pp. 522–531.

———. *Sociology of Leisure.* Translated by Marea A. McKenzie. New York: Elsevier Scientific Publishing Company, 1974.

Glover, T. D. "The 'Community' Center and the Social Construction of Citizenship." *Leisure Sciences* 26 (2004): pp. 63–83.

Hemingway, J. L. "Leisure, Social Capital, and Democratic Citizenship." *Journal of Leisure Research* 31 (1999): pp. 150–165.

———. "What Goes Around Comes Around: Teaching for and about Social and Human Capital in Leisure Studies." *Schole* 16 (2001): pp. 1–13.

Hunnicutt, Benjamin Kline. *Kellogg's Six Hour Day.* Philadelphia: Temple University Press, 1996.

Iso-Ahola, Seppo E. *The Social Psychology of Leisure and Recreation.* Dubuque, Iowa: Wm. C. Brown, 1980.

Kelly, John R. "Situational and Social Factors in Leisure Decisions." *Pacific Sociological Review* 21 (1978): pp. 313–330.

Kelly, John R. and Geoffrey Godbey. *The Sociology of Leisure.* State College, Pa.: Venture Publishing, 1992.

Kleiber, Douglas A. *Leisure Experience and Human Development.* New York: Basic Books, 1999.

Linder, Staffan Burenstam. *The Harried Leisure Class.* New York: Columbia University Press, 1970.

Neulinger, John. *The Psychology of Leisure.* 2d ed. Springfield, Ill.: Charles C. Thomas, 1981.

Parker, Stanley. *The Sociology of Leisure*. London: Allen and Unwin, 1976.

———. *Leisure and Work*. London: Allen and Unwin, 1983.

Pieper, J. *Leisure: The Basis of Culture*. Translated by A. Dru. New York: New American Library, 1963. (Original work published 1948.)

Riesman, David. *The Lonely Crowd: A Study of the Changing American Character*. Abridged ed. New Haven, Conn.: Yale University Press, 1961. The original edition was published in 1950.

Rojek, C. *Decentering Leisure: Rethinking Leisure Theory*. Thousand Oaks, Calif.: Sage Publications, 1995.

———. "Deviant Leisure: The Dark Side of Free-Time Activity." In *Leisure Studies: Prospects for the Twenty-First Century*. Edited by E. L. Jackson and T. L. Burtonz. State College, Pa: Venture Publishing, 1999.

Shaw, S. M. and D. Dawson. "Purposive Leisure: Examining Parental Discourses on Family Activities." *Leisure Sciences* 23 (2001): pp. 217–231.

Stebbins, R. A. *The Organizational Basis of Leisure Participation: A Motivational Exploration*. State College, Pa: Venture Publishing, 2002.

Stockdale, J. "Concepts and Measures of Leisure Participation and Preference." In *Understanding Leisure and Recreation: Mapping the Past, Charting the Future*. Edited by E. Jackson and T. Burton. State College, Pa: Venture Publishing, 1989.

Veblen, Thorstein B. *The Theory of the Leisure Class: An Economic Study of Institutions*. New York: The Modern Library, 1934. The original edition was published in 1899.

Weber, M. *The Protestant ethic and the spirit of capitalism*. Translated by Talcott Parsons. London: Allen andUnwin, Ltd., 1930. The original edition was published in 1904–1905.

Wilson, John. *Politics and Leisure*. Boston: Unwin Hyman, 1988.

*John L. Hemingway*

# LESBIAN LEISURE LIFESTYLES

Lesbian leisure lifestyles are as diverse as the leisure lifestyles of any other segment of American society, and in many ways reflect the same behavioral choices and experiences found among heterosexual women. Lesbian women's leisure, like other people's leisure, is influenced by age, ethnicity, past experiences, personality, and a myriad of other factors, as much as it is by sexual orientation. Because sexual orientation can remain hidden, lesbians are not always distinguishable from nonlesbian women. These factors make it impossible to offer a general description of lesbian leisure lifestyles.

One factor shared by all lesbians, however, is their awareness that American culture views homosexuality as deviant. As such, lesbians (and all nonheterosexual individuals) live in a society that marginalizes and stigmatizes them through social processes that award or withhold privilege based on sexual orientation. This process also privileges men over women, whites over blacks, the young over the old, and so forth. Thus, although lesbians and gay men share an experience of discrimination because of sexual orientation, lesbians face added marginalization due to their gender, and lesbians who are black or old are marginalized even further. Any discussion of lesbian leisure lifestyles must therefore examine the ways in which lesbians have been affected by, and respond to, those unique discriminatory discourses that label them as deviant.

## The Significance of Leisure

The relevance of leisure stems from the ways that leisure links to identity and community. Unlike many other facets of one's daily life, leisure is unique in the degree to which it promotes self-expression and facilitates selective interaction with others. For many people, leisure offers social validation and a sense of community that no longer comes through family, church, or neighborhood connections. This understanding of leisure has been premised upon studies of normative heterosexual individuals, leading researchers to posit a multitude of beneficial outcomes associated with leisure. Until recently, researchers overlooked people such as lesbians, whose leisure experiences might be replete with messages that marginalize, stigmatize, and devalue their identities. For those individuals, social validation is often scarce, and unguarded self-expression could be dangerous. This makes leisure a much more complex phenomenon for lesbians than what is represented in the leisure literature.

## Historical Foundations

Prior to the mid-twentieth century, the label "lesbian" was relatively unknown. Same-sex desire has existed throughout the centuries (the lesbian poetry of Sappho dates back to 630 BC), but homosexuality referred to sexual activity and was not subsumed as a category of identity. The difficulty in exploring the historical foundations of lesbians' leisure is therefore compounded by a lack of visible record about who those early lesbian women were. One indirect link between leisure and lesbian identity can be found in discussions in the early twentieth century that warned women to limit their participation in sport lest they were perceived as "mannish" and become unattractive marriage partners for men. American culture still uses this threat to restrict girls and women from participating in sports. In a more positive light, the early

**Gardening.** A lesbian couple shops for plants for their home garden. As societal norms changed in the late twentieth century, it became more common for lesbian couples to experience leisure activities together. © *Steve Prezant/Corbis*

twentieth century also produced many women in the arts who had open relationships with other women (such as author Gertrude Stein, poet Emily Dickensen, or musician Bessie Smith). Their visibility undoubtedly bolstered the courage of countless other women who sought validation for their own lesbian lifestyles. Thus, heterosexual discourse has been intertwined with, and challenged by, leisure venues for a long time.

Historians often refer to the Stonewall Riots of 1969 as the beginning of the modern gay and lesbian movement. Gay bars had long been a cornerstone in the lives of urban gays and lesbians, representing one of the few public places where they could openly assemble. The Stonewall Inn in New York City was a gay bar, and the riots ensued when patrons fought back during a police raid (raids were common at that time to deter the "immoral" lifestyles of homosexuals). That the patrons rose up in defense of a bar reveals the cultural significance that this leisure setting had within the gay community.

Also influential during this period was the passage of Title IX, federal legislation that opened up sports and related programs for girls. Because access was legally man-

dated, the stigma of sports as "mannish" began to erode. Ironically, by providing an expanding array of sport opportunities for girls and women, Title IX also increased the visibility of lesbian athletes. Prominent figures such as Billy Jean King, a lesbian tennis professional, became visible role models for lesbian girls, and sports and physical recreation began to offer forms of social validation that had previously been denied.

Lesbians also benefited from the larger women's movement that resulted in new freedoms for women in general. As societal norms changed, it became more common for women to visit parks, attend movies, eat out, and engage in other public activities without a male escort. These changes opened many leisure venues for lesbians, offering an increased opportunity to engage in public leisure with less danger of revealing their sexual identities. Unfortunately, the necessity of passing as heterosexual maintained the stigma associated with being lesbian.

One other significant event from this era was the emergence of women's music festivals. Much more than a concert, these events would last for days while concertgoers camped out in nearby fields. These concerts promoted a feminist agenda in an all-women environment, creating a culture of acceptance that lesbians found freeing and invigorating. The social validation and affirmation provided by those events was influential in building a sense of community among young lesbians nationwide.

## Stigma and Discrimination

One way to highlight the unique elements of lesbians' leisure is to examine the effects of stigma and discrimination at different points in their lives. Starting with adolescence, a period defined by sexual questioning and insecurity, leisure is a powerful arena that reaffirms the hetero-normative expectations of society. Sex-segregated activities such as girls-only organizations reinforce the cultural uniqueness of girls as girls while promoting an expectation that girls' emerging sexual awareness would be aimed at boys. In a similar fashion, sex-mixed activities such as dances and dates are also entrenched in the expectation of heterosexual attraction. While offering opportunity for heterosexual girls to examine and become comfortable with their emerging sexual identities, these leisure events provide some of the earliest stigmatizing messages to lesbian adolescents that their own sexual feelings are wrong. Lesbian girls learn that it is dangerous to openly reveal their attraction to other girls, and leisure contexts are often less-than-hospitable environments.

Lesbian adolescents learn the importance of passing as heterosexual, a survival strategy that carries over into adulthood, where the dangers of homophobic aggression are increased. In addition to homophobia, lesbians also face the broader forms of sexism and violence aimed at women in general. All women are vulnerable to sexual harassment in public, but a form of symbolic protection occurs when women are with men. Because lesbians are less likely to be in the company of men, they are at increased risk for this type of harassment. Even gay bars, the symbolic core of gay solidarity, cater more frequently to the interests of gay men, and the male clientele sometimes resent the intrusion of lesbians into "their" space.

Passing as heterosexual becomes more problematic when lesbians move out of anonymous public space and into leisure settings where they are likely to be recognized. Lesbian teachers, for example, often face a threat of losing their jobs if their sexual orientation were to become known. For those women, public leisure engagements are characterized by a dynamic tension between the comfortable validation of shared leisure and the concurrent need to hide the nature of their relationships. Common events such as parties and community gatherings carry an expectation of bringing, or at least talking about, a

male partner—which adds to the complexity of a simple conversation. Lesbians have been known to "borrow" male friends, who pose as dates, in order to make these events more tolerable.

It is not unusual for women to come out as lesbian well into their adult years, after having had a traditional marriage and raising children. For these women, long time leisure patterns are often destroyed. They might be excluded from holidays and family gatherings unless family members are accepting of their new partners; likewise, social invitations that had been common during marriage often disappear when a woman takes on a lesbian partner.

An added burden for older lesbians is their consequent rejection by the younger lesbian community. Ageism is as salient among lesbians as it is in other segments of society. Leisure venues within the lesbian community are often developed with younger interests in mind, and older lesbians find themselves marginalized by the very community they initially worked to establish.

## Proactive Leisure Responses

For most lesbians, leisure choices are relatively indistinguishable from those of heterosexual women. They go to movies, dine out, shop, hike, and attend public events. They also sit at home, read books, watch TV, and at times get lonely or bored. In these ways, lesbian leisure lifestyles mimic the leisure routinely seen in other segments of the population. Since social validation might be lacking and self expression is often guarded in public leisure venues, however, lesbians have created a rich network of alternative leisure opportunities including, most importantly, the common dinners and informal get-togethers that occur in their own homes. In addition, sites such as feminist coffee shops and bookstores facilitate lectures, concerts, and other events that promote a sense of community among lesbians. In many large metropolitan areas, local groups have established gay and lesbian sports leagues. There is a broader national response as well. An underground network of lesbian-owned campgrounds has existed for years. More recently, a profitable tourism industry has emerged, promoted by books and websites that list gay-friendly lodging, restaurants, and tour operators (such as the International Gay and Lesbian Travel Association at www.iglta.org).

By establishing leisure alternatives away from the public gaze, lesbians have found ways to facilitate self expression and social validation that is denied them in more public leisure contexts. The essential characteristic of these sites is an absence of stigma, replaced instead by an atmosphere of acceptance and affirmation. Because of the pervasive discourse that marginalizes lesbians in other aspects of their lives, these private leisure contexts provide an important place to build identity and community.

*See also:* Gay Men's Leisure Lifestyles, Women's Leisure Lifestyles

**BIBLIOGRAPHY**

Beemyn, B., ed. *Creating a Place for Ourselves: Lesbian, Gay, And Bisexual Community Histories.* New York: Routledge, 1997.

Cahn, S. K. "From 'Muscle Moll' to the 'Butch' Ballplayer: Mannishness, Lesbianism, and Homophobia in U.S. Women's Sport." *Feminist Studies* (1993): 343.

Jacobson, S. and Samdahl, D. M. "Leisure in The Lives of Old Lesbians: Experiences with and Responses to Discrimination." *Journal of Leisure Research* 30 (1999): 233–255.

Jacobson S. & Grossman, A. H. "Older Lesbians and Gay Men: Old Myths, New Images, and Future Directions. In *The Lives of Lesbians, Gays, and Bisexuals: Children to Adults.* Edited by R. Savin-Williams and K. Cohen Fort Worth, Tx: Harcourt Brace, 1996.

Johnson, C. W. *Gone Country: Negotiating Masculinity in a Country Western Gay Bar.* Unpublished dissertation, University of Georgia, 2002.

Kennedy, E. L. and Davis, M. D. *Boots of Leather, Slippers of Gold: The History of a Lesbian Community.* New York: Routledge, 1991.

Kivel, B. D. and Kleiber, D. A. "Leisure in the Identity Formation of Lesbian/Gay Youth: Personal, But Not Social." *Leisure Sciences* 22 (2000): 215–232.

McLemee, S. "A Queer Notion of History." *Chronicle of Higher Education* 50, no. 3 (2003): A14.

Ruby, J. "Women-Only and Feminist Spaces: Important Alternatives to Partriarchy. *off our backs* 33, no. 5 and 6 (2003): 13.

Samdahl, D. M. "A Symbolic Interactionist Model of Leisure: Theory and Empirical Support." *Leisure Sciences* 10 (1988): 27–39.

Zimmerman, B., ed. *Lesbian Histories and Cultures: An Encyclopedia.* New York: Garland Publishers, 2000.

*Diane M. Samdahl*

# LITERARY SOCIETIES AND MIDDLEBROW READING

Literary societies, or book groups, are among the most contradictory leisure activities in the United States. They appear democratic and open to any reader, and yet they are frequently exclusive, maintaining barriers of class and race. While these groups often support reading that encourages readers to "lose" themselves in the emotional pleasures of a book, they also present reading as "work" that must be done properly. These groups take reading, which seems a solitary activity, and turn it into a social event. Finally, the members of these societies hope to gain the status and prestige of serious process of reading, yet their critics dismiss them, using the label "middlebrow," because they do not work hard enough.

## Gaining Status Through Books

In the eighteenth-century American colonies, gentlemen were the only people with the leisure and money to pursue literary study. Thus, reading became a status activity associated with wealth and prestige. Even before the American Revolution, both college-educated professionals and artisans who lacked access to colonial colleges appropriated the status value of literature by forming groups to discuss and debate literature. Early literary societies formed at colleges and after college; alumni in urban areas reconstructed these societies in clubs with names such as the Belles-Lettres Club. Alongside those groups, less elite groups organized study clubs to gain the cultural authority of more gentlemanly professionals. Perhaps the most well known is Benjamin Franklin's Junto. Founded in 1727 to investigate virtue through reading and discussion, the club's members were largely young tradesmen. For Franklin, at least, this group provided both an opportunity to discuss philosophical issues and a way to demonstrate his interest in books—an interest that eventually gave him entry to the world of colonial gentlemen.

Throughout the early nineteenth century, literary self-improvement societies for men flourished. These societies often modeled themselves on those formed by New York literary and cultural elites. However, their influence and ideas expanded to include working- and middle-class men who were ambitious to develop their minds and follow Franklin's example. Clerks and tradesmen founded the Detroit Young Men's Society (DYMS) in 1832 to promote literary discussion and debate. Membership grew throughout the years before the Civil War as the DYMS provided tradesmen and mechanics access to the education and networks their elite peers formed in college. However, by the 1880s, male participation in literary societies declined, and the DYMS held its last meeting in 1881.

## Gender and Nineteenth-Century Literary Societies

DYMS declined just as women's literary societies, like the Shakespearians in Osage, Iowa, boomed. In fact, the reasons for the decline in men's groups made reading groups increasingly attractive for women. The women who joined the Shakespearians were the upper crust of Osage society, wives and daughters of the bankers, lawyers, and most successful tradesmen. The Shakespearians solidified these women's social status; no Catholic or working-class women belonged. Nonetheless, the membership was open to daughters of the town's most prominent Jewish merchants. The Shakespearians demonstrate the difficulty of making broad generalizations about such diverse organizations.

The same gender roles that prohibited these women from work assigned culture to their sphere. For men, literary study appeared both effeminate and no longer an effective way to advance. Those men who remained interested in literature focused their literary activities on the craftsmanship of rare books, seemingly a manlier topic. At the same time, the expansion of higher education in the United States increased the number of people, most often men, who could go to college. Women also had more opportunities to attend college, but many remained anxious about leaving their assigned role in the home. Thus, by 1906, the General Federation of Women's Clubs included some 5,000 literary and study groups. Historians have estimated that this number represents only 10 percent of the total numbers of women's literary societies of the time.

Many women's literary societies grew out of Bible study groups and maintained the air of worship and solemnity toward the other works they read. Dues varied from $1 to $25 per year. Some such as the Fortnightly Club of Hot Springs, Arkansas, described themselves as balancing "mental cultivation and social intercourse." Others, such as the Fortnightly's sister club in Fort Smith, Arkansas, called themselves "a study club of high order, with a university standard" (Croley, p. 223). Clubs' descriptions focused on their members' efforts to develop and expand their minds through the study of classic, already respected authors. Shakespeare's works were a staple, but clubs also covered a wide range of other genteel authors, from Whittier to Browning and from Dante to Dickens. Many of these same clubs also read less culturally sanctioned novels such as Sarah Grand's *Heavenly Twins* (1898), which dealt with marriage-induced depression and sexually transmitted diseases. Meetings usually consisted of one member presenting a paper on the author under discussion and other members responding

> "One club, which exerts considerable effort to keep 'mental and social culture' as its sole aim by requiring attendance at all meetings and serving no refreshments, is nevertheless the most socially exclusive of all clubs. It has a strictly limited membership, meets during only seven months of the year at the conspicuously leisurely hours of nine to eleven in the morning, and allows no written papers, its purpose being 'to revive the lost art of conversation.'"
>
> **Lynd, Robert S. and Helen M. Lynd, *Middletown*, p.296**

to her paper. Most clubs also had social events to which men were invited or where members dressed up as their favorite (often male) authors.

## Race, Class, Politics, and Literary Societies in the Nineteenth Century

Rather than allowing working-class women to join their groups, some women's literary societies formed working-class auxiliaries as part of their philanthropic activities. Those working-class women who did join frequently criticized their sisters for their snobbery. However, working women, too, had long formed their own literary societies, beginning with the literary societies formed by operatives at the Lowell Mills in the 1820s. Not surprisingly, these reading and writing groups were often connected to labor organizations. Even outside of union activates, members of these working-class groups encouraged new thinking about working class and national identity, attempting to revise ideas about cultural inclusiveness.

Historians debate the value of women's study clubs. Some believe these clubs served a conservative function by diverting women from the political realities of their lives, while others believe the club movement provided women with an important first step toward political independence. Whatever their value to causes such as gaining the vote or labor organization, women in these clubs self-consciously worked to read and study "serious" works so that they could legitimate the time they spent away from their homes and family. Many may have joined clubs as a way to fill their leisure time, but their studies were hardly leisurely.

While women's literary societies grew in the late nineteenth and early twentieth centuries, so did African American literary societies. African American reading groups grew out of the mutual improvement societies that free blacks formed in the 1770s. Throughout the early nineteenth century, these groups met to discuss literature and politics. Unlike other literary societies, these groups turned "reading" into community events by having the works for discussion read out loud so that even people who were illiterate could join discussion. Some African American societies were exclusively male or restricted to upper-class members. By the late nineteenth century, however, African American reading groups such as the Bethel Historical and Literary Association in Washington, D.C., and the Boston Literary and Historical Association had hundreds of people attending their meetings. Like women's literary societies, these groups focused on reading the established great authors. Nonetheless, they had a much more self-consciously political aim, including African American authors alongside Shakespeare and Scott and linking their reading practices to ideas about political and social inclusion. Members found that asserting their own sense of literary value developed their sense of social value.

## The Critics and Middlebrow Reading

Although members of these literary societies devoted themselves to "the best" reading as genteel standards defined it, critics had little sympathy with their efforts to make themselves more cultured. Edward Bok, editor of the *Ladies Home Journal,* dismissed women's literary societies because the "undigested superficial knowledge" women gained was "worse than no knowledge at all." While Bok did not use the word, he was accusing these literary societies of what would come to be called middlebrow reading.

Middlebrow initially indicated what Van Wyck Brooks called the "genial middle ground" between highbrow and lowbrow, in other words, between serious art and mass-produced junk. However, critics of middlebrow condemned both its middleness and its geniality, seeing middlebrow culture as an attack on the boundaries between highbrow and lowbrow culture. In the eyes of its critics, middlebrow championed shortcuts, promised that literary culture would provide access to cocktail party conversations, and valued superficial emotional identification with characters above the tough-minded truths highbrow modernists presented. Even worse, the purveyors of the middlebrow sold prepackaged culture, removing individual choice by relying on genteel experts. Its critics feared that middlebrow literature would ultimately standardize culture. These qualities, however, made middlebrow literature more available and more appealing to many readers.

While critics of middlebrow believed it marked the end of serious, noncommercial culture, the most important change that new, commercial middlebrow institutions such as the Book-of-the-Month-Club (BOMC) created was the shift from clubs that met for self-improvement toward clubs that never met. In the late nineteenth century, those literary societies that felt somewhat insecure about their own tastes could invest in a number of different commercially available programs. In 1878, for example, after successfully starting the Chautauqua movement, John Heyl Vincent created a set of readers and guides for study groups in the Chautauqua Literary and Scientific Circle (CLSC). These guides were available by mail and encouraged recipients to read and study together. The BOMC, founded in 1926, on the other hand, sent books directly to subscribers' homes. Earlier literary societies formed libraries and reading rooms. The BOMC provided readers with their own private library. The social aspects of nineteenth-century literary societies became more diffuse, although there still appeared to be social advantages to subscribing to the BOMC. People who subscribed to the BOMC, or other book clubs such as Dr. Eliot's Five-Foot Shelf and the Literary Guild, responded to advertisements that promised social and career success as result of reading the books sent to their homes. BOMC advertisements also appealed to readers by asking "Why do you disappoint yourself?," promising buyers that they would achieve a sense of mastery and personal satisfaction from their reading.

During the 1940s and 1950s, while the BOMC continued to send recent good books to people's homes, the Great Books program returned people to study groups devoted to timeless classics. The great books program attempted to get people to read the classic works of Western Civilization as a way to develop their minds and better understand their lives. Mortimer Adler, who appropriated the idea from John Erskine, created several community seminars in the 1930s. In 1943, he launched his most successful effort, a Great Books seminar for business executives and their wives. The so-called "Fat Man's Great Books Class" allowed the university to demonstrate its value to businessmen and businessmen to demonstrate their allegiance to unchanging virtues amid the flux of the war and troubled postwar period. Eventually, the "Fat Man's" class expanded beyond Chicago and beyond wealthy businesspeople to professional and middle-class businesspeople. Throughout the 1940s, Adler combined the Great Books seminar with a publishing program, a series called *The Great Books of the Western World,* allowing people to acquire culture in their homes in much the same way the BOMC did.

> "Winfrey's aesthetic system thus reflects neither the values and assumptions of a high culture aesthetic, nor a more popular aesthetic. Instead, she combines something we might call a "celebrity aesthetic," one that celebrates the good taste of the rich and famous, with an "aesthetic intimacy," one based upon trust in the recommendations of a close friend. Furthermore, Winfrey's success suggests that, if followed, her recommendations may make one similarly successful."

> Hall, R. Mark "The 'Oprahfication' of Literacy: Reading 'Oprah's Book Club,'" p. 653.

## Late-Twentieth-Century Revival of Literary Societies

In the twentieth century, sociologists and scholars have traced a decline in group-oriented activities in the United States. However, despite dire predictions, Great Books seminars, women's and African American's literary societies and the BOMC continue. In the later twentieth century, established literary societies took on new roles and new formats. Studies of these groups showed that they no longer stood in the place of a college education; in fact, many were college alumni associations. Members relied on these groups to maintain social distinctions and cultural capital developed in college but only occasionally used literary societies for career or social advancement. In addition, even as literary societies continued to read "the best" literature, members felt more power to criticize those taste judgments. Still for both men and women, literary societies appeared to be a way to expand what they saw as the narrow focus of their lives and come to a clearer understanding of themselves and their world.

The very changes in bookselling and technology that many feared would decrease reading actually increased the number of book clubs throughout the country. Although many feared the World Wide Web would focus reading away from traditional print books, the Web has also provided a location for readers to meet and interact. There are groups for readers of any kind of text, from groups devoted to discussion of the Bible and other sacred texts to groups devoted to Stephen King and Danielle Steel. Readers of highbrow texts, from William Blake to Thomas Pynchon, who are scattered across the world have created extremely active lists and through e-mail re-create communities that readers had in the nineteenth century. Chain stores, too, have provided new forums for book discussions. Many, especially Barnes and Noble, have a corporate policy of encouraging societies, providing members with books and places to meet. While getting people in the stores for groups and selling them the books is profitable, these stores also create clubs that cannot be restrictive in their membership.

Finally, specialty stores have provided meeting places for readers of genre fiction, particularly romances and mysteries. While traditional groups tend to focus on one text, these groups' discussions range across their favorite genre. Often members come to meetings with bags full of books to trade and share. Beyond their unusual discussion activities, these groups often read books in ways that revise the texts' apparent meanings. Despite what many highbrow readers think, Janice Radway, Elizabeth Long, and Erin Smith have shown romance reading and mystery reading may reveal a certain, tentative resistance to the apparent social messages of their texts and a reassessment of hierarchical taste judgments that devalue genre fiction.

Perhaps the most surprising new type of book club is Oprah Winfrey's Book Club, a "club" started in 1994 by talk show host Winfrey to promote reading through her television show and celebrity status. While some readers may have simply tuned into Winfrey's show to hear the book discussion, other readers participated in the club in more elaborate ways. Some readers discussed on Winfrey's Web site; others actually met one another and formed literary societies around Winfrey's choices. Despite initial selections such as Toni Morrison's *Song of Solomon*, Winfrey faced the same charges of superficiality, commercialization, and standardization that the BOMC faced. Winfrey has argued that she is democratizing literary culture by providing Americans with a new arbiter of culture, one who values the voices of women and African Americans. In April 2002, Oprah put her book club on hiatus and then in the summer of 2003 reconvened the book club with a new focus on literary classics.

Attitudes toward literary societies in the early twenty-first century remained similar to those of the eighteenth century. As a leisure activity, they reinforce American ideas that leisure should be "well spent." Literary societies offer social interaction, mental development, and cultural status.

*See also:* Books and Manuscripts, Genre Reading, Men's Magazines, Rational Recreation and Self-Improvement, Women's Magazines

**BIBLIOGRAPHY**

Allen, James Sloan. *The Romance of Commerce and Culture: Capitalism, Modernism, and the Chicago-Aspen Crusade for Cultural Reform.* Chicago: University of Chicago Press, 1983.

Croly, J. C. "Jennie June." *The History of the Woman's Club Movement in America.* New York: Henry G. Allen and Company, 1898.

Gere, Ann Ruggles. *Intimate Practices: Literacy and Cultural Work in U.S. Women's Clubs, 1880-1920.* Urbana: University of Illinois Press, 1997.

Kett, Joseph F. *The Pursuit of Knowledge Under Difficulties: From Self-Improvement to Adult Education in America, 1750–1990.* Stanford, Calif.: Stanford University Press, 1994.

Long, Elizabeth. *Book Clubs: Women and the Uses of Reading in Everyday Life.* Chicago: University of Chicago Press, 2003.

McHenry, Elizabeth. *Forgotten Readers: Recovering the Lost History of African American Literary Societies.* Durham, N.C.: Duke University Press, 2002.

Pawley, Christine. *Reading on the Middle Border: The Culture of Print in Late 19th Century Osage, Iowa.* Amherst, Mass.: University of Massachusetts Press, 2001.

Radway, Janice. *Reading the Romance: Women, Patriarchy, and Popular Literature.* Chapel Hill: University of North Carolina Press, 1984.

———. *A Feeling for Books: The Book-of-the-Month Club, Literary Taste, and Middle-Class Desire.* Chapel Hill: University of North Carolina Press, 1997.

Rubin, Joan Shelley. *The Making of Middlebrow Culture.* Chapel Hill: University of North Carolina Press, 1992.

*Catherine Turner*

# LITTLE LEAGUE

The idea for Little League Baseball was conceived by Carl E. Stotz, of Williamsport, Pennsylvania, in August of 1938. Originally, Stotz's plan was to create a youth league for his two nephews and their friends that was a miniature version of major league baseball, and as such each player was outfitted with a team uniform and each game started with a brand new baseball. To make the game competitive and fun for the children between the ages of nine and twelve, Stotz made changes to the size of the regulation major league baseball field.

Through trial and error, Stotz determined that the distance between bases should be sixty feet and the distance between home plate and the pitchers mound would be thirty-eight feet from home plate. Later, in 1943, a home run fence was added to the field, which was 175 feet down the left and right field line and 188 feet to centerfield. Over the ensuing years, changes were made to the field dimensions, and as of 2003, the pitchers mound was forty-six feet from home plate, while the four-foot-tall home run fence stood 205 feet from home plate to left, center, and right field. Comparatively, a standard Little League baseball field is roughly two-thirds the distance of a Major League baseball field.

In further effort to make the game of Little League baseball an enjoyable experience for all children, Stotz instituted rules that encouraged more participation by the kids playing the game, and less participation from the adult coaches. Some notable rules are that each child on a team must have at least one at-bat or one inning in the field during the game, and that at least one base coach must be a player from the team.

## Expansion

The first Little League consisting of three teams started in the spring of 1939 amidst much local fanfare, but the onset of World War II curtailed any large growth during the organization's formative years. However, soon after the war ended, curiosity about Stotz's youth league started to rise. New Jersey became the second state to charter a Little League team in 1947, and a season-ending eight-team, single-elimination tournament for eleven- and twelve-year-olds was held in Williamsport, Pennsylvania, in August. The 1948 tournament was sponsored nationally by U.S. Rubber and largely contributed to the growth of Little League, so much so that by 1951 there were 776 leagues, including one from outside the United States in British Columbia, Canada.

Worldwide expansion of Little League became a continuing effort of the organization, and in 1957 the first international champion at the Little League World Series hailed from Monterrey, Mexico. Starting in 1959, the World Series tournament moved from Max M. Brown Memorial Park located on the west side of Williamsport to Lamade Stadium in South Williamsport, where the tournament has been played ever since. Taiwan entered the international tournament in 1969, and they would go on to win the World Series title seventeen times between 1969 and 1997, at which time they revoked their membership in Little League due to an inability to conform to zoning eligibility rules (twelve leagues from Taiwan reentered Little League competition in 2003).

Between 1971 and 1991, the structure of the Little League World Series remained the same: four teams from

**2003 Little League World Series.** R. J. Neal (left) led his Boynton Beach, Florida, team to a 9–2 victory with a two-run homer that helped defeat the team from Saugus, Massachusetts, in the U.S. Finals of the Little League World Series on 23 August 2003. The event is held annually in South Williamsport, Pennsylvania, and culminates with the U.S. champion playing the international champion for the world title. Boynton Beach went on to lose the next day to Tokyo, 10–1. © *Gene J. Puskar for AP/Wide World Photos*

international regions and four teams from U.S. regions would play in a single-elimination tournament format resulting in a final pairing of one team from the international division and one from the United States. Two important changes in 1992 brought about the first major expansion in the Little League World Series. The first was that the Series changed from a single-elimination tournament to an eight-team Olympic-style pool-play tournament, where everyone in the International pool and National pool played each other once. The top two teams in each pool then advanced to play each other in the International and National championship games, and the winner from that round would play for the World Series championship, for a total of fifteen games. The second change was the addition of lights to Lamade

Field in order to accommodate the additional time necessary to play the games.

Nine years later, in 2001, Volunteer Stadium was erected 100 feet from Lamade Stadium so that the World Series could accommodate a sixteen-team, thirty-two-game tournament (eight International, eight National, split into four, four-team pools) that took ten days to complete.

## Sponsorship

Since its inception, Little League Baseball has run solely on the sponsorship money donated from local companies and corporations. The first local sponsor of Little League, Lundy's Lumber, continued to sponsor many youth sports in Williamsport, including Little League, as of the early 2000s. As mentioned previously, the first national sponsor for Little League was U.S. Rubber, which owned the Keds shoe company. After a successful run sponsoring the international tournament, U.S. Rubber ended its relationship with Little League in 1956. Since that time many high profile companies like Pizza Hut and Mongoose Bikes have been a part of the event as corporate sponsors. In 2003 Honda, Bubbalicious, Oxi-Clean, Russell Athletic and New Era, Musco Sports Lighting, Active Team Sports, CNA Insurance, Choice Hotels International, RC Cola, Wilson Sporting Goods, MasterfoodsUSA, Snickers and Stouffer's were all corporate sponsors of Little League.

## Media Coverage

Much like sponsorship, media coverage has been a part of Little League since its first game, with the inaugural game's box score appearing in the *Williamsport Sun*. Local coverage of the series continued to grow as Williamsport's local radio station, WRAK, covered the first championship game in 1948, and highlights of the game appeared on CBS television. Media coverage of the World Series intensified as Little League continued to grow. ABC's *Wide World of Sports* started airing the tape-delayed final on television in 1960, and further helped the proliferation of Little League. ABC started airing the final game live in 1985, and their sister channels, ESPN and ESPN2, began airing early round games in 1997. Little League programming was so popular that all three channels expanded their coverage of Little League as the tournament expanded. In 2003 ABC, ESPN, and ESPN2 aired twenty-seven of the thirty-two games during the tournament, and the final game garnered a higher rating than game seven of the NHL Stanley Cup finals.

## Participation

From 1939 to 1972, only boys were permitted to participate in Little League Baseball. However, with the advent of Title IX, in 1972, Little League was forced to allow girls to play. In 1983, Victoria Roche, a participant on the European team from Belgium, was the first female to reach the World Series. The influx of girls in Little League caused participation numbers to rise to new heights. As of 2003, 2.3 million children ages nine to twelve, in 104 countries and all fifty states, competed in Little League Baseball. Of those children, only those between the ages of eleven and twelve can compete on tournament teams with the hope of reaching the Little League World Series in Williamsport.

*See also:* Baseball, Amateur; Baseball Crowds

**BIBLIOGRAPHY**

Frommer, Harvey. *Growing Up at Bat: 50 Years of Little League Baseball.* New York: Pharos Books, 1989.

*Little League World Series Media Guide.* Williamsport, Pa., 2003.

*Little League World Series Souvenir Program.* Lexington, Ky.: Host Communications, 2003.

Sundeen, J. T. "A Kid's Game?: Little League Baseball and National Identity in Taiwan." *Journal of Sport & Social Issues* 25 (2001):251–265.

*2003 Tee Ball, Minor League, Little League Baseball, Junior League, Senior League, Big League Baseball: Official Regulations and Playing Rules For all Divisions of Little League Baseball With Tournament Rules and Guidelines.* N.p., 2003.

Van Auken, Lance and Robin. *Play Ball!: The Story of Little League Baseball.* University Park, Pa.: The Penn State University Press, 2001.

*Ryan E. White*